1,523 ACT®

Practice Questions

7th Edition

By the Staff of The Princeton Review

PrincetonReview.com

Penguin Random House

The Princeton Review
110 East 42nd Street, 7th Floor
New York, NY 10017
E-mail: editorialsupport@review.com

Published in the United States by Penguin Random House LLC, New York, and in Canada by Random House of Canada, a division of Penguin Random House Ltd., Toronto.

ISBN: 978-0-525-57031-8
ISSN: 1943-4847

Editor: Meave Shelton
Production Editors: Emma Parker and Sarah Litt
Production Artist: Jason Ullmeyer

Printed in the United States of America.

10 9 8 7 6 5 4 3 2

Seventh Edition

Editorial
Rob Franek, Editor-in-Chief
David Soto, Director of Content Development
Stephen Koch, Student Survey Manager
Deborah Weber, Director of Production
Gabriel Berlin, Production Design Manager
Selena Coppock, Director of Editorial
Aaron Riccio, Senior Editor
Meave Shelton, Senior Editor
Chris Chimera, Editor
Anna Goodlett, Editor
Eleanor Green, Editor
Orion McBean, Editor
Patricia Murphy, Editorial Assistant

Penguin Random House Publishing Team
Tom Russell, VP, Publisher
Alison Stoltzfus, Publishing Director
Ellen Reed, Production Manager
Amanda Yee, Associate Managing Editor
Suzanne Lee, Designer

Acknowledgments

The Princeton Review would like to extend very special thanks to our contributing authors: Alice Swan, Amy Minster, Cat Healey, Cynthia Ward, Gabby Budzon, Jomil London, Scott O'Neal, Jimmy Williams, Lori DesRochers, Steve Ronkowski, Jenine Faulkner, Jess Thomas, Anne Goldberg-Baldwin, Dave MacKenzie, Sarah Guo, Christina Torturo, Nicole Cosme, Sara Kuperstein, Susan Swinford, Elizabeth Owens, Simón Weffer, Chris Chimera, Stacey Cowap, Grace Cannon, and Spencer LeDoux.

We are also grateful to the Production team for their careful attention to every page: Jason Ullmeyer, Emma Parker, Sarah Litt, and Deborah Weber.

Finally, special thanks to Adam Robinson, who conceived of and perfected the Joe Bloggs approach to standardized tests, and many of the other successful techniques used by The Princeton Review.

Contents

Get More (Free) Content viii
Introduction 1
How to Approach the ACT Online Test 5
Test 1 21
- English 22
- Math 36
- Reading 54
- Science 62
- Writing 74
- ACT Bubble Sheet 77
- ACT Essay Paper 81

Test 1 Answers and Explanations 85
Scoring Your Practice Exam 88
Test 1 English Answers and Explanations 90
Test 1 Math Answers and Explanations 103
Test 1 Reading Answers and Explanations 116
Test 1 Science Answers and Explanations 125
Test 1 Essay Checklist 134
Mini Practice Drills 135
Mini Practice Drills Answer Key and Explanations 177
English Practice Section 1 213
English Practice Section 1 Answers and Explanations 227
English Practice Section 2 243
English Practice Section 2 Answers and Explanations 257
English Practice Section 3 273
English Practice Section 3 Answers and Explanations 287
Math Practice Section 1 303
Math Practice Section 1 Answers and Explanations 325
Math Practice Section 2 339
Math Practice Section 2 Answers and Explanations 363
Math Practice Section 3 381
Math Practice Section 3 Answers and Explanations 401
Reading Practice Section 1 415
Reading Practice Section 1 Answers and Explanations 425
Reading Practice Section 2 437
Reading Practice Section 2 Answers and Explanations 447
Reading Practice Section 3 461
Reading Practice Section 3 Answers and Explanations 471
Science Practice Section 1 485

Science Practice Section 1 Answers and Explanations 499
Science Practice Section 2 511
Science Practice Section 2 Answers and Explanations 525
Science Practice Section 3 535
Science Practice Section 3 Answers and Explanations 549
Writing Practice Section 1 559
ACT Essay Paper 562
Writing Practice Section 2 567
ACT Essay Paper 570
Writing Practice Section 3 575
ACT Essay Paper 578
Writing Test—Essay Checklist 582
Test 2 583
- English 584
- Math 598
- Reading 618
- Science 626
- Writing 638
- ACT Bubble Sheet 641
- ACT Essay Paper 645

Test 2 Answers and Explanations 649
Scoring Your Practice Exam 652
Test 2 English Answers and Explanations 654
Test 2 Math Answers and Explanations 669
Test 2 Reading Answers and Explanations 682
Test 2 Science Answers and Explanations 693
Test 2 Essay Checklist 700
Test 3 701
- English 702
- Math 716
- Reading 736
- Science 744
- Writing 756
- ACT Bubble Sheet 759
- ACT Essay Paper 763

Test 3 Answers and Explanations 767
Scoring Your Practice Exam 770
Test 3 English Answers and Explanations 772
Test 3 Math Answers and Explanations 787
Test 3 Reading Answers and Explanations 799
Test 3 Science Answers and Explanations 811
Test 3 Essay Checklist 821

Get More (Free) Content

at PrincetonReview.com/prep

As easy as 1•2•3

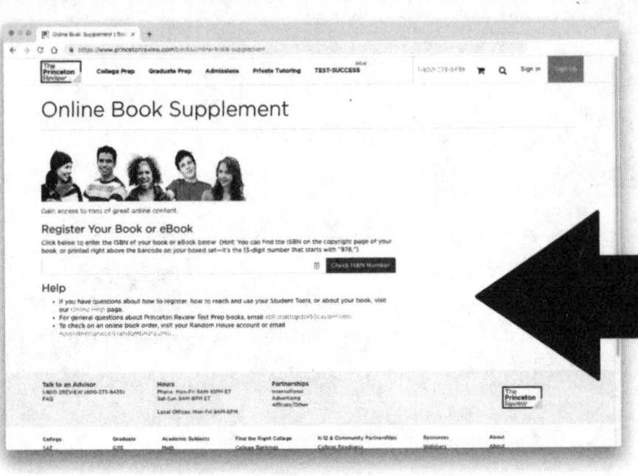

1 Go to PrincetonReview.com/prep and enter the following ISBN for your book:

9780525570318

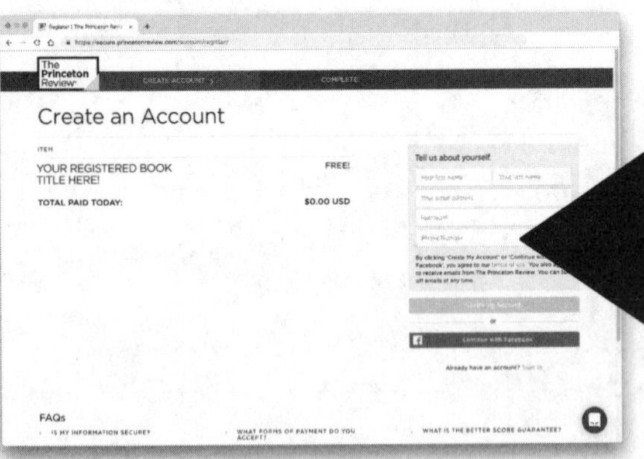

2 Answer a few simple questions to set up an exclusive Princeton Review account. *(If you already have one, you can just log in.)*

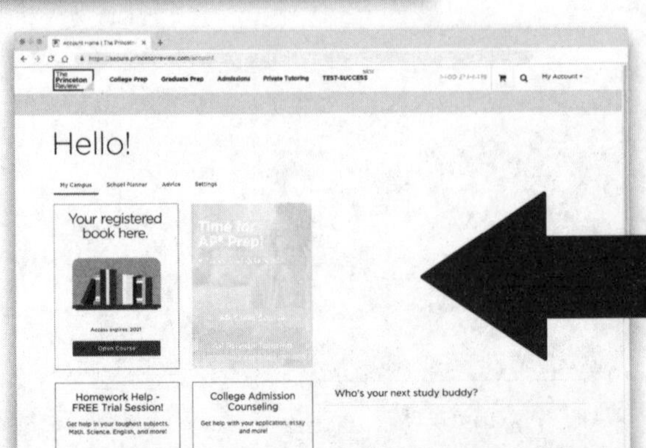

3 Enjoy access to your **FREE** content!

Once you've registered, you can...

- Get our take on any recent or pending updates to the ACT
- Take a full-length practice ACT
- Use our online proctor to correctly time your practice sections or full tests
- Enter your answers in our online bubble sheet to get an approximate scaled score with question categories and explanations.
- Get valuable advice about the college application process, including tips for writing a great essay and where to apply for financial aid
- If you're still choosing between colleges, use our searchable rankings of *The Best 387 Colleges* to find out more information about your dream school.
- Check to see if there have been any corrections or updates to this edition

Need to report a potential **content** issue?

Contact **EditorialSupport@review.com** and include:

- full title of the book
- ISBN
- page number

Need to report a **technical** issue?

Contact **TPRStudentTech@review.com** and provide:

- your full name
- email address used to register the book
- full book title and ISBN
- Operating system (Mac/PC) and browser (Firefox, Safari, etc.)

Introduction

So you think you need more practice? Well, we have tons of practice right here for you. We have accumulated the equivalent of six full ACTs to help you get your best possible score on this beastly test! After all, the harder you practice, the better you'll be on test day.

Since you probably know the basics of how the test is conducted, we'll spare you that information. What we will give you here is a breakdown of the "tests" on the ACT.

1. English Test (45 minutes—75 questions)
In this section, you will see five essays on the left side of the page. Some words or phrases will be underlined. On the right side of the page, you will be asked whether the underlined portion is correct as written or if one of the three alternatives listed would be better. The English test covers topics in grammar, punctuation, sentence structure, and rhetorical skills.

2. Math Test (60 minutes—60 questions)
These are the regular, multiple-choice math questions you've been doing all your life. The easier questions tend to come in the beginning and the difficult ones in the end, but the folks at the ACT try to mix in easy, medium, and difficult problems throughout the math test. A good third of the test covers pre-algebra and elementary algebra. Slightly less than a third covers intermediate algebra and coordinate geometry (graphing). Regular geometry accounts for less than a quarter of the questions, and there are four questions that cover trigonometry.

3. Reading Test (35 minutes—40 questions)
In this section, there will be four reading passages of about 800 words each—the average length of a *People* magazine article but maybe not as interesting. There is always one prose fiction passage, one social science passage, one humanities passage, and one natural science passage, and they are always in that order. One of the passages is made up of two shorter pieces on a similar topic instead of one long article. After reading each passage, you have to answer 10 questions.

4. Science Test (35 minutes—40 questions)
No specific scientific knowledge is necessary for the science test. You won't need to know the chemical makeup of hydrochloric acid or any formulas. Instead, you will see 6 or 7 passages depending on the make-up of that particular test. In 5 or 6 of those, you will be asked to understand scientific information presented in graphs, charts, tables, and research summaries. In addition, you will have to make sense of one disagreement between two or three scientists. (Occasionally, there are more than three scientists.)

5. Experimental Section
All students who take the ACT without accommodations will have a 20-minute experimental section after the Science Test. This section contains multiple-choice questions and it could cover any subject. *This section has no effect on your score,* so don't worry about it. Yes, you have to sit through it, but you don't even have to answer the questions if you don't want to.

6. Optional Writing Test (40 minutes)
The ACT contains an "optional" writing test featuring a single essay. Not many schools require the "ACT Plus Writing" version of the test anymore. You should obviously take it if you're applying to one of the schools that does require it, and if you're unsure where you're going to apply, it's probably a good idea to take it in case you end up needing it. You will be asked to write an essay stating your position on a given prompt that the test writers deem "relevant" to high school students. Your essay will be read by two different readers. Each will give your essay a

score between 1 and 6 in each of four domains (leading to four different subscores from 2–12). Your writing score is then calculated by averaging the four 2–12 subscores and rounding to the nearest whole point for a total score of 2–12.

If you are unsure about any of the sections or if you want more strategies for conquering these kinds of questions, you can find more information at PrincetonReview.com or you can review our comprehensive guide, *ACT Prep*.

What you should also know is that the key to raising your ACT score does not lie in memorizing dozens of math theorems, the periodic table of elements, or obscure rules of English grammar. There's more to mastering this test than just improving math, verbal, and science skills. At its root, the ACT measures academic achievement. It doesn't pretend to measure your analytic ability or your intelligence. The people at ACT admit that you can increase your score by preparing for the test, and by spending just a little extra time preparing for the ACT, you can substantially change your score on the ACT (and the way colleges look at your applications). After all, out of all the elements in your application "package," your ACT score is the easiest to change.

That being said, we have included in this book three complete practice ACT exams and more than three exams' worth of drill questions. Rest assured that these tests and questions are modeled closely on actual ACT exams and questions, with the proper balance of questions reflective of what the ACT actually tests.

At the beginning of this book, you'll find one complete ACT practice test. After you've taken that test, score it to learn your strengths and weaknesses. Next in the book, you will find mini-practice drills that are designed to reinforce some of the basic and common English, Math, and Science skills that will serve you throughout the rest of the ACT. After that, you will see three full-length drills for each subject type. The questions are compiled in the same arrangement as you would see on a real test, so you can keep track of your timing and your progress. These drills can help you get outstanding scores on the subjects you already do well in and better scores on the subjects you might be struggling with. After the drills, you'll find two more complete ACT practice tests. We suggest you use these to gauge your full testing capacity by taking them in an environment as close to the real conditions as possible. After the drills, you shouldn't be worried about your scores, and these two final practice exams will not only give you more practice, but will also give you some assurance that all that practice will pay off in the end.

A final thought before you begin: the ACT does not predict your ultimate success or failure as a human being. No matter how high or how low you score on this test initially, and no matter how much you may increase your score through preparation, you should never consider the score you receive on this or any other test a final judgment of your abilities. When it's all said and done, we know you'll get into a great school and that you'll have an incredible experience there.

We wish you the best of luck, even though you won't need it after all this practicing!

The Princeton Review

How to Approach the ACT Online Test

In this chapter, you'll learn what to expect on the ACT Online Test, including how to apply its computer-based features and our strategies to the question types in each section—English, Math, Reading, Science, and Writing.

At the time of this book's printing, the option to take the ACT online at a testing center was postponed. ACT also plans to offer at-home online testing, although an exact rollout date has not yet been announced. For up-to-date news on both options, check the ACT website..

WHAT IS THE ACT ONLINE TEST?

The ACT Online Test is the ACT that you take on a computer, rather than with a pencil and paper. Despite the name, you can't take the ACT from the comfort of your own home; instead, you'll have to go to a testing center (possibly your high school) and take the test on one of the center's computers.

The ACT Online Test has the same overall structure, timing, and number of questions as the pencil-and-paper ACT. The scoring, score range, and scoring method are also the same. If the ACT Online Test is basically the same as the pencil-and-paper ACT, who would take the ACT Online Test?

WHO TAKES THE ACT ONLINE TEST?

ACT has been offering versions of the ACT on computer since about 2016. The first students to take the ACT on the computer were students taking the test at school. Schools and school districts decided whether to give the test on the computer.

As of September 2018, all students taking the ACT outside of the United States take the test on a computer (except for those students with accommodations requiring the use of a traditional pencil-and-paper test).

Starting sometime in 2021, students in the United States will have the option of taking the ACT Online Test instead of the traditional pencil-and-paper version. Students choosing this option will get their scores in about two to three business days (e.g., take the test on Saturday, have your score the next Wednesday). In addition, any students taking advantage of the Single-Section Retesting must do so on the computer.

Single-Section Retesting is an incredible option for students. However, colleges still have the option to accept or not accept these new scores. Research your target schools early so you know your options!

Single-Section Retesting

If you are happy with the score you receive from a single test administration, you will still have the option to send just that score to colleges. If your score in one section is not as high as you'd like, you now have a chance to correct that. Students who have already taken the full ACT may choose to take one, two, or three sections again using Single-Section Retesting. ACT will then produce a "superscore" consisting of your best results in all tests (English, Math, Reading, Science, and Writing (if you took it)). Note that not all colleges accept a superscored ACT, so do your research before taking advantage of this option.

ACT ONLINE TEST FEATURES

So, besides the obvious fact that it's taken on a computer, what are the differences between taking the ACT on the computer and taking it on paper? Let's start with what you can't do on the ACT Online Test. You can't "write" on the screen in a freehand way. You're limited in how you're able to mark the answer choices, and each question appears on its own screen (so you can't see multiple questions at one glance). You will also be given a small "whiteboard" and dry erase pen with which to make notes and do work.

So, what features does the ACT Online Test have?

- Timer
  - You can hide the timer by clicking on it.
  - There is a 5-minute warning toward the end of each test. There is no audible signal at the 5-minute warning, only a small indicator in the upper-right corner of the screen.
- Nav tool
  - You can use this tool to navigate directly to any question in the section.
  - The Nav tool blocks the current question when opened.
  - It also shows what questions you have flagged and/or left blank.
  - You can flag questions in this menu.
- Question numbers at the bottom of the screen
  - You can click on these numbers to navigate directly to any question in the section.
  - These numbers also indicate whether a question has been flagged and/or left blank.
- Flag tool
  - You can flag a question on the question screen itself or by using the Nav tool.
  - Flagging a question has no effect besides marking the question for your own purposes.
- Answer Eliminator
  - Answer choices can be "crossed-off" on-screen.
  - An answer choice that's been eliminated cannot be chosen and must be "un-crossed-off" first by clicking the answer choice.
- Magnifier
  - You can use this to magnify specific parts of the screen.
- Line Mask
  - This tool covers part of the screen. There is an adjustable window you can use to limit what you can see.
  - This is an excellent tool if you need an aid to help you focus on specific parts of the text or figure.
  - However, not everyone will find this tool useful, so do not feel obligated to use it!
  - Note that you cannot highlight the text in the window of the Line Mask.
- Answer Mask
  - This tool hides the answer choices of a question.
  - Answers can be revealed one at a time.
- Screen Zoom
  - This tool changes the zoom of the entire screen (as opposed to the magnifier, which magnifies only one part of the screen).
  - Your screen zoom setting will remain the same from question to question.
- Highlighter
  - You can use this tool to highlight parts of passage text, question text, or answer text.
  - You cannot highlight within figures.
  - If you highlight in a passage with multiple questions, your highlights will only show up on that question. (In other words, if you highlight, for example, question 1 of a Reading passage, questions 2–10 of that same passage will not show those highlights.)
  - Turning off the highlighter tool removes your highlights.

- Shortcuts:

Keybind	Function	Keybind	Function
Ctrl + H	Toggle Help	Ctrl + Enter	Answer Question
Ctrl + F	Flag Item	Alt + M	Toggle Magnifier
Ctrl + I	Item Navigation	Alt + H	Toggle Highlighter
Alt + P	Previous Question	Alt + E	Toggle Answer Eliminator
Alt + N	Next Question	Alt + A	Toggle Answer Masking
A-E or 1-5	Select Alternative	Alt + L	Toggle Line Masking

- The Writing test is typed, rather than written by hand.

You will also be given a small "whiteboard" and dry erase pen with which to make notes and do work.

HOW TO APPROACH THE ACT ONLINE TEST

The strategies mentioned in this chapter are thoroughly discussed in our comprehensive guide, *ACT Prep*, so be sure to pick up a copy of that book if you have not already done so. These approaches were created in reference to the pencil-and-paper format, but they still apply to the ACT Online Test with some adjustments. This chapter assumes your familiarity with these strategies and will show you how to make the best use of them given the tools available in the computer-based format.

You will also want to incorporate some computer-based practice into your prep plan. ACT's website has practice sections for each of the four multiple-choice parts of the test and for the essay. We recommend that you do those sections toward the end of your preparation (and close to your test date) to give yourself an opportunity to practice what you've learned on a platform similar to the one you'll be using on the day of the test.

Remember!
Your goal is to get the best possible score on the ACT. ACT's goal is to assign a number to you that (supposedly) means something to colleges. Focus on your goal!

If you are planning to take the ACT online, you should practice as if you're doing all your work on the computer, even when you're working in a physical book. Use a highlighter, but don't use the highlighter on any figures (as the ACT Online Test won't let you do so). Use your pencil to eliminate answer choices and have a separate sheet of paper or a whiteboard to do any work you need to do, instead of writing on the problem itself.

Also, remember that our approaches work. Don't get misled by ACT's instructions on the day of the test—their way of approaching the test won't give you the best results!

Overall

Your Personal Order of Difficulty (POOD) and Pacing goals will be the same on the ACT Online Test as on the pencil-and-paper version. Because it is easy to change your answers, put in your Letter of the Day (LOTD) when skipping a Later or Never question. Use the Flag tool on the Later questions so you can jump back easily (using either the navigation bar at the bottom of the screen or the Nav tool).

Process of Elimination (POE) is still a vital approach. On both the paper-and-pencil ACT and the ACT Online test, there are more wrong answers than correct ones. Eliminating one you know are wrong helps you to save time, avoid trap answers, and make a better guess if you have to. On the ACT Online Test, you cannot write on the test, but you can use the Highlighter tool. Turn on these tools (and the Line Mask, if desired) at the beginning of the English section and use them throughout.

ENGLISH

The Basic Approaches to both Proofreader and Editor questions are the same on the computerized and the paper versions of the ACT. When you decide to skip a question to come back to it Later (for example, a question asking for the introduction to the topic of the passage before you've read any part of the passage), flag the question so you can easily jump back to it before moving on to the next passage. When you have five minutes remaining, flag your current question and use the Nav tool to make sure you've put in your LOTD for any questions that you haven't done, then return to your spot and work until time runs out.

For a comprehensive review of all sections of the ACT and the strategies mentioned throughout this chapter, check out our book, *ACT Prep*.

When you work Proofreader questions, you can use the Highlighter tool to help you focus on the key parts of the text. Let's see an example:

Use the tools available to help you focus on the key portions of the text. Practice with a highlighter when you're working on paper (instead of underlining with your pencil).

Sneaking down the corridor, the agent, taking care not to alert the guards, spotting the locked door.

A. NO CHANGE
B. spot
C. are spotting
D. spots

Here's How to Crack It

Verbs are changing in the answer choices, so the question is testing subject/verb agreement. The verb must be consistent with the subject. *The agent* is the subject; highlight it:

Sneaking down the corridor, the agent, taking care not to alert the guards, spotting the locked door.

A. NO CHANGE
B. spot
C. are spotting
D. spots

The agent is singular, so the verb must be singular. Eliminate (B) and (C), as both are plural. *Spotting* cannot be the main verb of a sentence, so eliminate (A). The correct answer is (D).

Similarly, the Highlighter tool is helpful on Editor questions. Use the tool on both the passage and the question to help you focus on the relevant parts of each.

As it's name suggests, the Indian fantail is not native to North America. In fact, its establishment here was quite accidental. In 1926, the San Diego Zoo acquired four pythons from India for its reptile exhibit. The long trip from India required, that, the pythons be provided with food for the journey, and a group of unfortunate fantails was shipped for just that purpose. Two lucky fantails survived, and their beautiful appearance caused the San Diego Zoo to keep and breed them for the public to see. Eventually, some of the animals escaped captivity and developed populations in the wild, all thanks to those two birds!

Given that all the choices are true, which one provides the most relevant and specific information at this point in the essay?

- A. NO CHANGE
- B. and they have quite an appetite.
- C. because no one wanted them to starve.
- D. and they are quite picky in what they'll eat.

Here's How to Crack It

The question asks for the *most relevant and specific information.* Highlight those words in the question. The first sentence of the paragraph focuses on the *Indian fantail,* and the sentence after the underlined portion discusses *(t)wo lucky fantails.* The final sentence discusses *the animals* that escaped. Highlight these words in the paragraph.

Your screen should look like this:

As it's name suggests, the Indian fantail is not native to North America. In fact, its establishment here was quite accidental. In 1926, the San Diego Zoo acquired four pythons from India for its reptile exhibit. The long trip from India required, that, the pythons be provided with food for the journey, and a group of unfortunate fantails was shipped for just that purpose. Two lucky fantails survived, and their beautiful appearance caused the San Diego Zoo to keep and breed them for the public to see. Eventually, some of the animals escaped captivity and developed populations in the wild, all thanks to those two birds!

Given that all the choices are true, which one provides the most relevant and specific information at this point in the essay?

- A. NO CHANGE
- B. and they have quite an appetite.
- C. because no one wanted them to starve.
- D. and they are quite picky in what they'll eat.

Use POE, focusing on whether the choice is consistent with the highlights in the passage. The sentence as written discusses *a group of unfortunate fantails*; keep (A). Choices (B), (C), and (D) do not talk about the Indian fantail; instead, they focus on the pythons. This is inconsistent with the goal of the sentence and the content of the paragraph; eliminate those answers. The correct answer is (A).

Finally, you can't write in the passage, so you'll need to approach the Vertical Line Test slightly differently. On the paper-and-pencil ACT, you would use this strategy for questions about punctuation, drawing a vertical line where the punctuation breaks up the ideas in the text. On the computerized ACT, you should use the whiteboard to handle these questions.

I'm not searching for a ghost or yeti, my phantom is the Indian fantail. These beautiful creatures are members of the pigeon family, but you could not tell that by looking at them.

- **A.** NO CHANGE
- **B.** yeti: my phantom
- **C.** yeti my phantom
- **D.** yeti, since this

Here's How to Crack It

Punctuation is changing in the answer choices, so the question is testing STOP and GO punctuation. There is Half-Stop punctuation in (B), so use the Vertical Line Test. You cannot draw a line in the text, so draw a "t" on your whiteboard, with "yeti" in the bottom-left and "my" in the bottom-right:

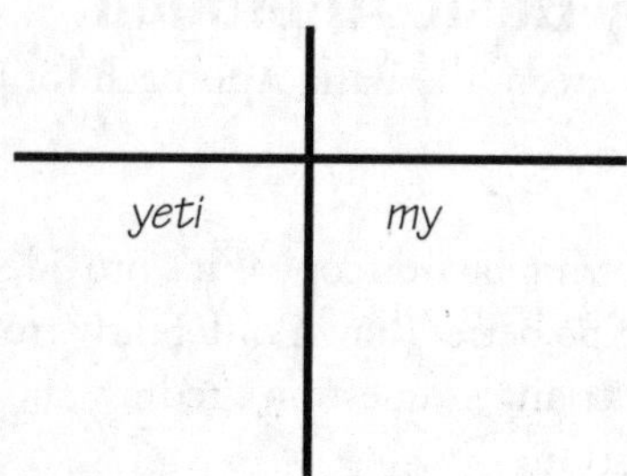

Read each part of the sentence and determine whether it is complete or incomplete. *I'm not searching for a ghost or yeti* is a complete idea; write "C" in the upper-left of the "t." *My phantom is the Indian fantail* is also a complete idea; write "C" (for "complete") in the upper-right of the "t." Your board should look like this:

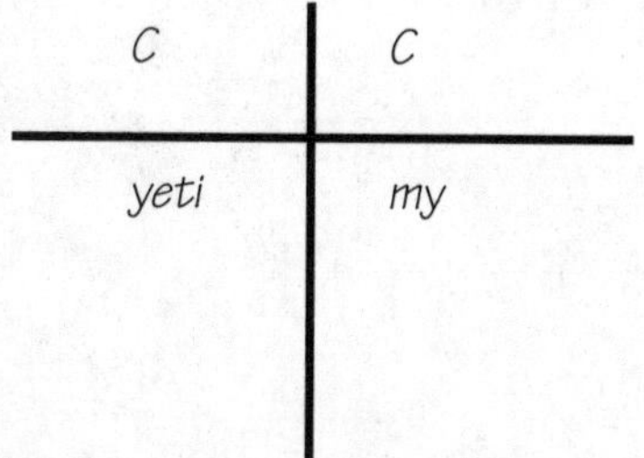

Eliminate any answer that cannot link two complete ideas. Both (A) and (C) use GO punctuation, which cannot link complete ideas; eliminate (A) and (C). Choice (D) adds *since*, which makes the idea to the right of the line incomplete. However, *since* is used to show time or causation, which does not work in the context of the sentence. Eliminate (D). The correct answer is (B).

MATH

First off, you'll still need to bring your calculator to the ACT Online Test—which is a good thing! You're already comfortable with your personal calculator, so there will be one less thing to worry about on the day of the test.

Write it down!
It is tempting to do all your work in your head. Don't fall into this trap! It's easier to make mistakes when you're not writing down your work, and you'll often have to "go back" if you don't have something written down. Use your whiteboard!

When choosing questions to do Later, flag the question so you can easily navigate back to it after doing your Now questions. Do put in your LOTD when doing so; you don't want to accidently leave a question blank! When you get the five-minute warning, finish the question you're working on, flag it (so you can find your spot easily), then put in your LOTD for every unanswered question. Then you can go back to working until time runs out.

Use the Highlighter tool to highlight what the question is actually asking, especially in Word Problems. Of course, you'll want to use your whiteboard when working the steps of a math problem (don't do the work in your head!).

ACT Online Geometry Basic Approach

Because you can't write on the screen, the Basic Approach for Geometry questions needs a few slight tweaks:

1. Draw the figure on your whiteboard (copy if it's provided; draw it yourself otherwise). If the figure would be better drawn differently from the way ACT has drawn it (for instance, a similar triangles question), redraw the figure in a way that will help you answer the question.

2. Label the figure you drew on your whiteboard with the information from both ACT's figure and the question.

3. Write down any formulas you need and fill in the information you know.

Let's see how that works on a question.

In the figure below, triangle ABC is similar to triangle DEF. What is the length of EF ?

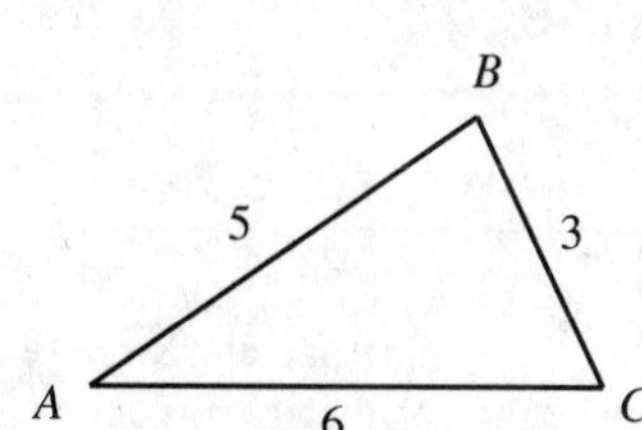

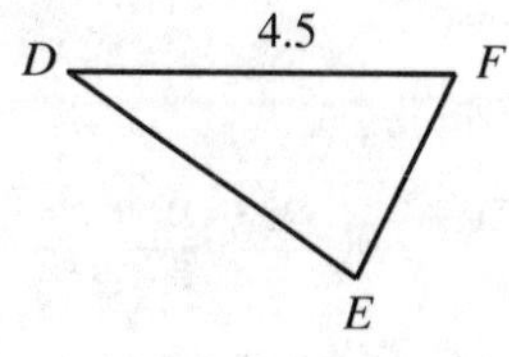

- **A.** 1.5
- **B.** 2.25
- **C.** 3
- **D.** 4
- **E.** 4.5

Here's How to Crack It

The question asks for the length of EF, so highlight that in the question. Follow the Geometry Basic Approach. Start by drawing the figure on your whiteboard. Because the triangles are similar, redraw triangle DEF to be oriented the same way as ABC. Label your figure with the given information.

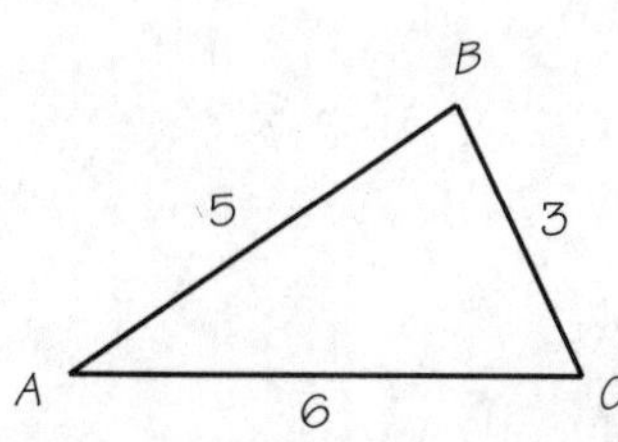

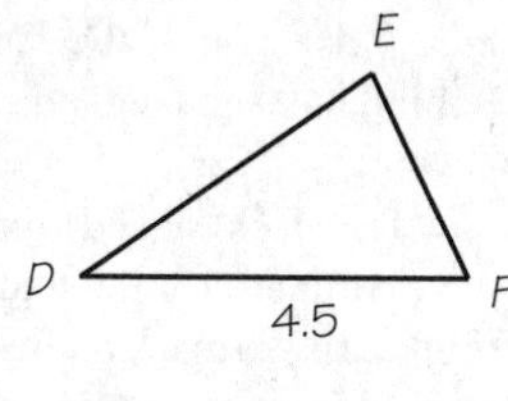

Write down the equation you need and fill in the necessary information. AC corresponds to DF, and BC corresponds to EF. Set up a proportion: $\frac{AC}{DF} = \frac{BC}{EF}$. Fill in the information from your figure: $\frac{6}{4.5} = \frac{3}{x}$, where x is equal to EF. Cross-multiply to get $6x = 3(4.5)$, or $6x = 13.5$. Divide both sides by 6 to get $x = 2.25$. The correct answer is (B).

READING

First off, there are a few differences between the pencil-and-paper ACT and the ACT Online Test. In the ACT Online Test, there are no line references; rather, the relevant part of the text is highlighted. The passage will also "jump" to the highlighted text if it's off the screen when you go to that question. This may disorient you at first: be prepared for this to happen.

Let's see an example.

...protested every step. We could still run, but, Hook worried, for how long? In a cross-country race, only a team's top five runners score, and we weren't those five. Our job was to finish ahead of as many of our rival teams' top fives as we could.

Leah was a senior that year, my freshman year. All season, she'd been counting down to this last race, praying her body wouldn't say *No*. She and I joked that we needed to go to the Knee Store and pick out new knees, ones that wouldn't crack and pop and burn all the time. It was hard to watch a teammate in that much pain, but Leah was a trooper, never slacking from workouts, never stopping to walk, never losing sight of the next person in front of her to catch.

The crack of the starter's pistol sent us surging out of that little crop of trees and onto the race course. I hollered, "See you at the Knee Store!" Behind me, she laughed.

The pack stayed tight through the first quarter-mile, and I was surrounded by so many bodies I couldn't think. I just ran, putting one foot in front of the other, trying not to fall. Trying to look beyond the jostling mass surrounding me, I could barely...

Reading on a computer screen can be disorienting. Practice by reading articles or other passages on the computer when possible.

The narrator's references to the Knee Store primarily serve to suggest that:

- **A.** Leah wishes to buy better knee supports.
- **B.** the narrator and Leah use humor to cope with their pain.
- **C.** the narrator desires to learn more about her injury.
- **D.** Leah's injuries, unlike the narrator's, have become unbearable.

Here's How to Crack It

The question asks what the *references to the Knee Store...suggest.* The references to the *Knee Store* are highlighted in the text. Note that the text has shifted down to the highlighted portions. The window indicates that Leah and the narrator *joked that we needed to go to the Knee Store.* Leah *laughed* after the narrator referred to the Knee Store. Therefore, the answer should be consistent with joking and laughing. Choice (A) takes the reference too literally; eliminate (A). "Humor" is consistent with the text's references to *joked* and *laughed*; keep (B). There's no indication of the narrator's goal to *learn more about her injury,* nor does the text support the idea that Leah's injuries *have become unbearable,* eliminate (C) and (D). The correct answer is (B).

When you have five minutes remaining, flag your current question and use the Nav tool to make sure you've put in your LOTD for any questions that you haven't done. Then return to your spot and work until time runs out. If you've just started or finished a passage, click through the questions to look for Easy to Find questions in the remaining time, and don't forget to put in your LOTD for any question you don't answer!

The biggest difference between the ACT Online Test and the paper-and-pencil ACT is that you can only see one question on the screen at a time. Rather than looking over the questions at a glance, you must click from question to question. This feature means that the Reading Basic Approach (covered below) needs to be modified in order to be as time efficient as possible.

ACT Online Reading Basic Approach

1. **Preview**
   Read only the blurb—do not go through and map the questions. Instead, write the question numbers on your whiteboard to prepare to Work the Passage.

2. **Work the Passage**
   This step is *even more* optional on the ACT Online Test than on the pencil-and-paper ACT. You haven't mapped the questions, and your highlights only show up on one question. If you do decide to Work the Passage, ensure that you're getting through the passage in 2–3 minutes. More likely, you'll find it best to just skip this step and move on to the questions after reading the blurb and setting up your whiteboard.

You don't get points for reading—only for answering questions correctly. Determine whether Working the Passage helps you answer questions correctly and quickly.

3. **Select and Understand a Question**
   When Selecting a Question, if a question is Easy to Find (a portion of the text is highlighted or you Worked the Passage and know where in the passage the content you need is), do it Now. Understand the question, then move on to Step 4.
   If the question is not Easy to Find (in other words, you don't immediately know where in the passage to go), write down the question's lead words on your whiteboard next to the question number. Include EXCEPT/LEAST/NOT if the question includes those words. If there are no lead words, flag the question.

   After you do all the questions with highlights, then Work the Passage, scanning actively for your lead words. Once you find a lead word, do the corresponding question. After answering the questions with lead words, finish with the flagged questions.

4. **Read What You Need**
   Find the 5–10 lines you need to answer the question. Remember that only the quotation will be highlighted—the answer is not necessarily highlighted. You must read the lines before and after the highlighted portion to ensure that you find the correct answer to the question. If you find the Line Mask tool helpful, use it to frame your window.

5. **Predict the Correct Answer**
As you read, look for evidence for the answer to the question in your window and highlight it using the highlighter tool. (You can highlight text that ACT has already highlighted—the color will change to "your" highlighting color.) As always, base your prediction on the words in the passage as much as possible.

6. **Use POE**
Use the Answer Eliminator tool to narrow the answer choices down to one answer. If the question is an EXCEPT/LEAST/NOT question, instead write ABCD on your whiteboard and mark each answer T or F for True or False (or Y or N for Yes or No) and choose the odd one out.

Dual Reading Approach

The questions for Dual Reading passages are grouped with the questions about Passage A, then those about Passage B, then those about both passages. Each question should be labeled with an indicator for the passage the question refers to. Work each passage separately, answering all the Passage A questions you plan to answer before moving onto the Passage B questions.

You should also write down the Golden Thread of each passage on your whiteboard—either after Working the Passage or after finishing the questions on that passage. That will aid you in answering the questions about both passages.

SCIENCE

The overall approach to the Science test is the same on the ACT Online Test as it is on the traditional pencil-and-paper version. There are a few small adjustments to make, but the overall strategy remains the same.

The Flag tool is very important when identifying Later passages and questions. On a Later passage, flag the first question, then put your LOTD for every question on the passage. Make a note on your whiteboard of the first question in the passage so you can easily jump back to the passage.

When working a Now passage, you may still encounter a Later question. For these stand-alone Later questions, flag the question but don't put in your LOTD. When you get to the end of a passage, check the bar at the bottom of the screen to make sure you have answered every question up to that point.

Science Basic Approach

There are a few small changes to the Science approach when taking the ACT Online Test.

1. **Work the Figures**
You can't highlight the figures. Experiment with taking quick notes about the variables, units, and trends on your whiteboard and determine whether it helps you find the needed information quickly.

2. **Work the Questions**
   Highlight the words and phrases from the figures in the question to help guide you to the relevant information.

3. **Work the Answers**
   Use the Answer Eliminator tool to work POE on answer choices with multiple parts.

Let's look at an example.

A block is placed on a frictionless horizontal surface at point Q. The block is pushed with a plunger and given initial velocity v along the horizontal surface. At point R, the block slides up a ramp with coefficient of friction f to a maximum distance L along the ramp. The distance between points Q and R is 1.0 m.

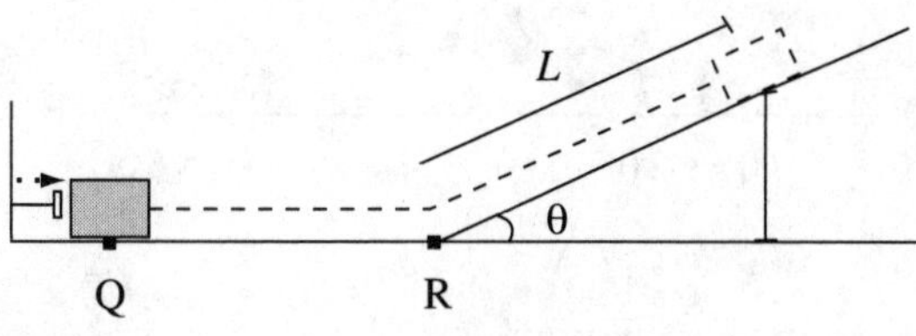

Figure 1

Figure 2, below, shows how L varies with v for different f on a ramp with $\theta = 20°$. Figure 3 (on the following page) shows how L varies with v for different θ on a ramp with $f = 0.1$.

Scrolling Passages
Most passages in Science will require scrolling down to see all the figures. Look for a scroll bar for every passage!

Key	
Marker	f
□	0.15
○	0.30
△	0.60
×	0.90

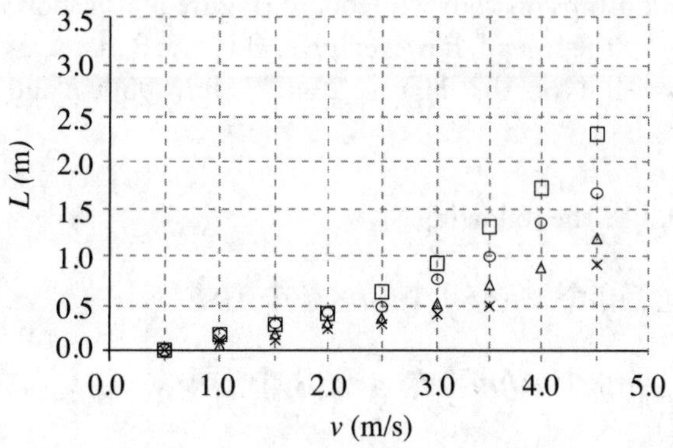

Figure 2

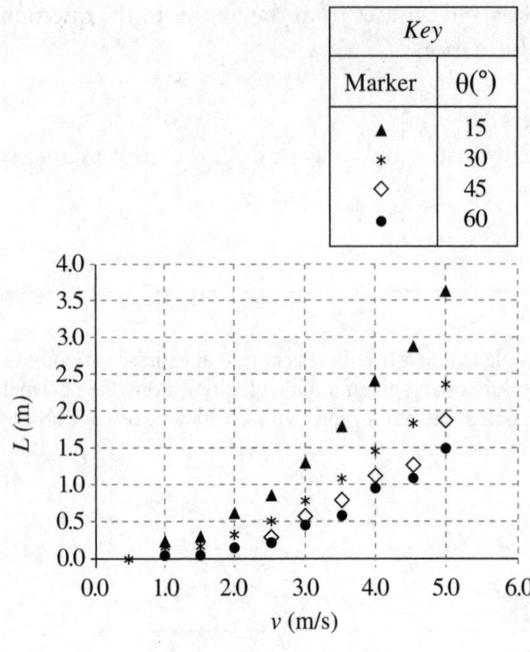

Figure 3

If $f = 0.90$ for the sliding block and $v = 5.5$ m/s, L will most likely be closest to which of the following?

- **A.** 0.3 m
- **B.** 0.7 m
- **C.** 1.5 m
- **D.** 3.0 m

Here's How to Crack It

Start by Working the Figures. Figure 1 shows the points Q and R and variables L and θ, but there are no numbers or trends. Figure 2 shows a direct relationship between L (m) and v (m/s); mark this on your whiteboard. Furthermore, the legend gives values of f; as f increases, L decreases. Mark these relationships on your whiteboard. Figure 3 also shows a direct relationship between L (m) and v (m/s); the legend, however, gives θ (°). As θ increases, L decreases. Put these on your whiteboard as well. Note that Figures 2 and 3 show both L and v; Figure 2 has f, whereas Figure 3 has θ.

Your whiteboard should look like the following:

Figure 2: L (m) ↑ v (m/s) ↑ and f ↑ L ↓

Figure 3: L (m) ↑ v (m/s) ↑ and θ ↑ L ↓

The question refers to the variables f, v, and L; highlight those variables. Figure 2 has all three variables. The highest value of v given in the figure is 4.5, so start there and use the trend to make a prediction about a v of 5.5. At $v = 4.5$ and $f = 0.90$, L is approximately 0.9. The trend is increasing, so a v of 5.5 must result in an L value of greater than 0.9; eliminate (A) and (B).

An L value of 3.0 would be higher than any value already in Figure 2, and extending the trend for the line created by the $f = 0.90$ marks would not result in L increasing to 3.0 by the time v reaches 5.5; eliminate (D). Although you can't physically extend the line because it's on a computer screen, it may be a good idea to use your finger to trace where you would draw on the screen. The correct answer is (C).

You'll still approach the passage that's all or mostly text as if it is a Reading passage. Unlike in Reading, you will want to Map the Questions during the Preview step, as there will not be a group of questions about each passage like there is in the Dual Reading passage. Instead, the questions will not be asked in any particular order, so use your whiteboard to map out which scientist(s) or experiment(s) each question refers to. As with the other sections, at the five-minute warning, flag your question, put in your LOTD on any unanswered question, then keep working until time runs out.

WRITING

As you have probably guessed, you'll be typing the Writing test on the ACT Online Test. But before we get to writing the essay, there are a few minor points to note about the format of this test on the computer.

First, you won't be able to highlight when Working the Prompt or Perspectives, so be sure to write notes on your whiteboard. Second, ACT has given the prompt and perspectives on one screen, then repeated them on the screen that contains a text box. Feel free to do your work on the screen within the text box. If you're used to making your essay outlines on a computer, you can use the text box to do so here, as long as you remember to delete any notes before the section comes to an end.

When writing the essay, all the same points apply to both the pencil-and-paper and online tests (have a clear thesis, make and organize your arguments in a way that is easy to follow, etc.). When you have 5 minutes left, quickly type up a conclusion paragraph (if you haven't already), then go back and finish up your body paragraph ideas. It's more important to have a conclusion than it is to have perfect body paragraphs. Finally, spend a minute or two at the end to quickly fix any obvious typos or grammatical issues.

When you practice the Writing test at home, type your essay in a word processing program instead of writing it by hand. Be sure to turn off spell check, as the ACT does not provide it, so you don't want to rely on it.

That's it! Everything you've learned for the pencil-and-paper ACT can be applied to the ACT Online Test with a few small tweaks. You've got this!

Test 1

Please turn to page 77 to find the bubble sheet for this test.

ENGLISH TEST

45 Minutes—75 Questions

DIRECTIONS: In the five passages that follow, certain words and phrases are underlined and numbered. In the right-hand column, you will find alternatives for each underlined part. In most cases, you are to choose the one that best expresses the idea, makes the statement appropriate for standard written English, or is worded most consistently with the style and tone of the passage as a whole. If you think the original version is best, choose "NO CHANGE." In some cases, you will find in the right-hand column a question about the underlined part. You are to choose the best answer to the question.

You will also find questions about a section of the passage or the passage as a whole. These questions do not refer to an underlined portion of the passage but rather are identified by a number or numbers in a box.

For each question, choose the alternative you consider best and blacken the corresponding oval on your answer document. Read each passage through once before you begin to answer the questions that accompany it. For many of the questions, you must read several sentences beyond the question to determine the answer. Be sure that you have read far enough ahead each time you choose an alternative.

Passage I

The Record

The moment I had been anticipating finally came on a seemingly routine Monday. I arrived home to find a flat package; left by the delivery man[1] casually leaning against the front screen door. Reading the words *Caution! Do not bend!* scrawled on[2] the top of the box, I immediately recognized my uncle's sloppy handwriting. I quickly ushered the box inside, and[3] my heart skipping a beat (or two). I knew what the box contained but still felt as anxious as a child on Christmas morning. Could this *really* be the old vinyl record?

My hands trembled as I opened the box, of which[4] I was thrilled to see that it did indeed contain the record I had been seeking for years. To an outsider, this dusty disc with its faded hand-written label would seem inconsequential. To others, on the other hand, it was worth something far greater.[5] The record was a compilation from the greatest musician I had ever known—my grandfather.

1. A. NO CHANGE
   B. package, left by the delivery man
   C. package; left by the delivery man,
   D. package, left by the delivery man,

2. F. NO CHANGE
   G. were scrawled on
   H. scrawl on
   J. scrawled

3. A. NO CHANGE
   B. inside,
   C. inside and
   D. inside, when

4. F. NO CHANGE
   G. box that
   H. box, and
   J. box

5. Given that all the choices are true, which one would most effectively illustrate the difference between outsiders' perception of the record and its actual significance to the writer's family?
   A. NO CHANGE
   B. In fact, the recording was not heard by many people outside my family.
   C. To my family, however, it was a precious heirloom.
   D. The disc would be in better condition had my uncle stored it in a sleeve.

GO ON TO THE NEXT PAGE.

Several years before he married my grandmother, Papa would make[6] his living as a folk singer in a band. Performing[7] in music halls and local festivals. He recorded a single album produced by Great Sounds Records[8] before giving up his professional music career to pursue business. This record was all that remained of his life's passion—in fact,[9] there had been[10] only one surviving copy since Papa's death 10 years earlier. It took many years of begging and pleading[11] to convince my uncle to pass the record down to me.

I brought out my old record player from the attic and gently placed the disc on the turntable. As soft, twanging notes filled the room, I was transported to my grandfather's cabin, located at the foot of the mountains.[12] My cousins and I would gather around the campfire every night to roast marshmallows, cook hotdogs, and listen to my grandfather's old stories. Of the many familiar favorites, Papa would pick up his guitar and play all of our familiar tunes.[13]

When the record started playing one of my favorite songs, I struggled to hold back my tears. It was a bittersweet reminder of

6. F. NO CHANGE
G. would have made
H. would have been making
J. had made

7. A. NO CHANGE
B. band; performing
C. band, which he had performed
D. band, performing

8. F. NO CHANGE
G. album, produced by Great Sounds Records,
H. Great Sounds Records album
J. album

9. A. NO CHANGE
B. even so,
C. since,
D. for example,

10. F. NO CHANGE
G. had been about
H. is
J. was to be

11. A. NO CHANGE
B. begging
C. pleadingly begging
D. begging the plea

12. At this point in the essay, the writer wants to suggest the significance of his grandfather's cabin to the writer's upbringing. Given that all the choices are true, which one would best accomplish that purpose?
F. NO CHANGE
G. where I had spent many childhood summers.
H. which I still remembered well.
J. a family property for many generations.

13. A. NO CHANGE
B. Playing all of our favorite songs, the many familiar tunes and guitar would be picked up by Papa.
C. Papa would also pick up his guitar and strum familiar tunes, playing all of our favorite songs, of which there were many.
D. Picking up his guitar, Papa would also play strumming familiar tunes all of our favorite, of which there were many, songs.

GO ON TO THE NEXT PAGE.

the man I loved and missed,[14] Papa's gentle voice on the record,

14. F. NO CHANGE
 G. missed for
 H. missed.
 J. missed

however, assured me,[15] that he was still with me, both in spirit and in song.

15. A. NO CHANGE
 B. me
 C. me—
 D. me;

Passage II

Road Trips Back Home

During my junior year of college, it became a kind of ritual for a group of us to hop in a car and "discover" a new suburb every month. At first, we all agreed, we had come to college in this major city to escape what we thought were our boring lives in our various places of origin, but after a time, we realized that it would be impossible for us to turn our backs on our old lives[16] completely. I grew up in Pennsylvania, many parts of which look like the ones we drove to.[17]

16. F. NO CHANGE
 G. lives,
 H. live's
 J. lives'

17. Given that all the choices are true, which one best supports the point that the narrator and his friends all shared a common background?
 A. NO CHANGE
 B. Many suburbs have become as populous as the cities they surround.
 C. The first major migration of families from the city to the suburbs occurred in the late 1940s and early 1950s.
 D. Our hometowns were all over the map, but they all shared a palpable likeness.

The first stop was typically some old diner, which reminded each of us of one from our various hometowns. There we'd usually sit, chat with the restaurant's owners[18] drink a cup of coffee, and figure out which new and exciting place we'd be driving to next. Even now I can remember one diner in Maryland, whose sign we could see flickering from the highway as we turned off looking forward to it in anticipation.[19] Although we had all agreed that it had to be a new town each time, we

18. F. NO CHANGE
 G. owners;
 H. owners'
 J. owners,

19. A. NO CHANGE
 B. in anticipation.
 C. excited and looking forward to it.
 D. in anticipation and expectation.

GO ON TO THE NEXT PAGE.

tacitly agreed a few times to break the rules and come back to this place. [20]

After we had taken nourishment (usually a grilled cheese sandwich, a patty melt, or something similarly nutritious that could be ordered from [21] the menu) for our "big night out," we would then drive on. We got to know the lay of the land so well that we could usually just follow our noses to the kinds of places we liked to visit in these towns, typically stopping by the biggest retailer we could find. There we'd buy industrial-sized packs from childhood [22] of instant noodles, huge packs of soda, and other types of foods we all remembered but which we were either too embarrassed to buy in front of other people at the University market, or which were too expensive in the city, where there is a lot more variety. [23]

Going [24] to as many places like this as we could, we were always sure to happen upon something strangely familiar to us. The place—whether it was one of a million grocery stores, movie theaters, or fast-food restaurants—were [25] unimportant; it seemed that everywhere had something special for at least one of us,

20. At this point, the writer is considering adding the following true statement:

> Many diners have been forced to shut down to make way for larger, national chain restaurants.

Should the writer make the addition here?

- **F.** Yes, because it provides important contextual information relevant to the passage.
- **G.** Yes, because it helps readers to see why the narrator was drawn to this particular diner.
- **H.** No, because it interrupts the flow of the paragraph, which is primarily a personal reflection.
- **J.** No, because it alters the focus of the paragraph from a discussion of driving to a discussion of specific places.

21.
- **A.** NO CHANGE
- **B.** whom could be ordered from
- **C.** whom could order
- **D.** that were ordering

22. The best placement for the underlined phrase would be:
- **F.** where it is now.
- **G.** after the word *noodles.*
- **H.** after the word *soda.*
- **J.** after the word *remembered.*

23. Which choice most effectively supports and elaborates on the description in an earlier part of this sentence?
- **A.** NO CHANGE
- **B.** where prices for such basic foods were steep.
- **C.** where we didn't like to drive the car.
- **D.** where most of us had only small refrigerators.

24. Which of the following alternatives to the underlined portion would NOT be acceptable?
- **F.** As we went
- **G.** While going
- **H.** While we went
- **J.** We went

25.
- **A.** NO CHANGE
- **B.** was
- **C.** have been
- **D.** are

GO ON TO THE NEXT PAGE.

and even now, many years on, I still think of these trips fondly. 26

Looking back, I'm still not sure why we took these trips.

Nevertheless, I have been living in an urban environment 27 now for almost eight years, and should I ever have to move back to the suburbs, I will certainly go reluctantly. Sometimes, though, even now that I live in a different city, I'll still sneak out to those kinds of places once in a while and just drive about the town. 28 I guess, in a way, many of those early memories are like that diner sign we could see from the highway; most people would never notice that old sign, but to those of us who cherish it in our hearts, 29 we all harbored a great hope that it would still be burning the same as we remembered every time we drove by or came back. 30

26. Given that all the choices are true, which one most effectively signals the shift in focus that occurs when moving from this paragraph to the next?
F. NO CHANGE
G. we all remained friends until we graduated.
H. I regret not having spent more time in the city when I had the chance.
J. I haven't been back to any of those places since I graduated.

27. A. NO CHANGE
B. Therefore,
C. Nonetheless,
D. DELETE the underlined portion.

28. Which of the following alternatives to the underlined portion would NOT be acceptable?
F. among the town.
G. about.
H. around.
J. around the town.

29. A. NO CHANGE
B. have a great fondness for it
C. have strong feelings of adoration for it
D. cherish it

30. F. NO CHANGE
G. we were coming back.
H. were returning.
J. there was a return by us.

GO ON TO THE NEXT PAGE.

Passage III

The following paragraphs may or may not be in the most logical order. Each paragraph is numbered in brackets, and question 45 will ask you to choose where Paragraph 3 should most logically be placed.

The Palio of Siena

[1]

Siena is an old, picturesque city located in the hills of Tuscany. Even though[31] its inhabitants live modern lives, many historical markers from as far back as medieval Italy still remain throughout the city. [32] Another remnant from Siena's rich history that still plays a very prominent role today is the tradition of *Il Palio*.

[2]

Il Palio di Siena is a biannual horse race that is held twice a year,[33] once in July and once in August. A field of ten bareback horses races three laps around a dangerously steep track circling the city's central plaza, the *Piazza del Campo*, each with two dreaded right-angle turns.[34] Even though *Il Palio*

31. Which of the following alternatives to the underlined portion would be LEAST acceptable?
    A. Although
    B. While
    C. Though
    D. When

32. Which of the following true statements, if inserted here, would best connect the first part of Paragraph 1 with the last part while illustrating the main idea of this paragraph?
    F. Like most Italian cities, Siena is very serious about soccer, a modern sport codified in England in the 1800s.
    G. Cobblestone streets and Gothic architecture are blended with modern sidewalk cafes and trendy designer stores.
    H. The city of Siena is certainly a mixture of ancient and contemporary practices.
    J. Siena is a major cultural center that offers numerous examples of art and architecture by Renaissance masters.

33. A. NO CHANGE
    B. a biannual race that is held two times a year,
    C. a horse race that is held twice a year,
    D. a biannual horse race, held

34. Assuming that a period will always be placed at the end of the sentence, the best placement for the underlined phrase would be:
    F. where it is now.
    G. after the words *horses races* (setting the phrase off with commas).
    H. after the word *laps* (setting the phrase off with commas).
    J. after the word *plaza* (setting the phrase off with commas).

GO ON TO THE NEXT PAGE.

lasted[35] only about 90 seconds, its importance in Siena goes far beyond the race itself.

35. A. NO CHANGE
B. will last
C. lasts
D. had lasted

[3]

Members are fiercely committed emotionally, socially, and financially to their own *contrada*. Because the members[36] voluntarily tax themselves to support their own *contrada* and to invest in a good horse and jockey for the biannual race. Jockey salaries for a single race often exceed 250,000 euros! This is, however,[37] a small price to pay to achieve victory at *Il Palio*. Seeing the colors and arms of their *contrada* in the winner's circle is the most glorious event—even more so than getting married for[38] many Sienese citizens. Old men weep openly out of sheer joy, and elated adults and children parade. Throughout[39] the city with their newly won silk banner, also called the *palio*.

36. F. NO CHANGE
G. Though they
H. In addition, they
J. They

37. A. NO CHANGE
B. moreover,
C. for instance,
D. therefore,

38. F. NO CHANGE
G. married—for
H. married, for
J. married; for

39. A. NO CHANGE
B. parade; throughout
C. parade throughout
D. parade throughout,

[4]

The brief race is a spectacular culmination of an entire way of life in Siena. Every citizen belongs to one of seventeen city districts, collectively known as the *Contrade*.[40] *Contrada* is the term for a single district that has its own color and arms, such as the *Aquila* (the eagle) or *Bruco* (the caterpillar). A *contrada* is the source of so much local patriotism that every important event; from[41] baptisms to food festivals, is celebrated only within one's own *contrada* and fellow members, who[42] become more like family.

40. F. NO CHANGE
G. *Contrade*
H. *Contrade*,
J. *Contrade* yet

41. A. NO CHANGE
B. event, from
C. event: from
D. event—from

42. F. NO CHANGE
G. for whose
H. whose
J. whom

[5]

After the actual race day, the *Palio* festivities continue for a minimum of two weeks. Thousands of visitors from around the

GO ON TO THE NEXT PAGE.

world travel to Siena during the summer; not only to witness [43] the exciting race but also to attend the after-parties were thrown [44] by the locals. While the *Palio* is not as important to outsiders who do not live in Siena as it is to the Sienese, the race and the festivities that follow are a spectacular experience.

43. A. NO CHANGE
B. summer. Not
C. summer not
D. summer, not

44. F. NO CHANGE
G. thrown
H. were threw
J. threw

Question 45 asks about the preceding passage as a whole.

45. For the sake of the logic and coherence of this essay, the best placement for Paragraph 3 would be:
A. where it is now.
B. before Paragraph 1.
C. before Paragraph 2.
D. before Paragraph 5.

Passage IV

The following paragraphs may or may not be in the most logical order. Each paragraph is numbered in brackets, and question 59 will ask you to choose where Paragraph 2 should most logically be placed.

Sherwood Anderson the Pioneer

[1]

Sherwood Anderson saw his first novel, *Windy McPherson's Son*, published in 1916, but it was not until 1919 with the publication of his masterpiece *Winesburg, Ohio* that Anderson was pushed to the forefront of it [46] in American literature. The latter book, something between a short story collection and a novel, helping [47] to inaugurate an age of a truly homespun American Modernism.

46. F. NO CHANGE
G. this
H. a new movement
J. a thing

47. A. NO CHANGE
B. which helped
C. helped
D. was helped

GO ON TO THE NEXT PAGE.

[2]

As other writers began to supplant him in the popular imagination, Anderson <u>tireless</u> [48] continued his literary experimentation until his death in 1941. In the contemporary popular imagination, Anderson's influence often <u>appears to be</u> [49] diminishing. But it takes only a few pages of *Winesburg, Ohio* or many of his other short stories, articles, and novels to see that Anderson is still very much with us today and that much of what we understand about ourselves as Americans was made clear to us only by the pen of the advertising man from Ohio.

[3]

Sherwood Anderson would be seen by a new generation of American writers as the first author to take a real step <u>until</u> [50] creating a type of literature that was in tune with something previously only associated with Europe. Anderson was able to <u>fuse</u> [51] his sense of the passing of the Industrial Age in America with a type of uniquely American expression that sought to replace previous literary conventions with more local expressions of fragmentation and alienation.

[4]

With *Winesburg, Ohio*, Anderson <u>inspired</u> [52] a younger group of writers, among whose ranks were Ernest Hemingway and William Faulkner, to embrace their American experiences and to express them in ways separate from those being expressed by European writers or American <u>expatriates, as American writers living abroad were known.</u> [53] When *Winesburg, Ohio* finally

48. The best placement for the underlined word would be:
- **F.** where it is now.
- **G.** before the word *death.*
- **H.** after the word *experimentation.*
- **J.** before the word *literary.*

49. Which of the following alternatives to the underlined portion would NOT be acceptable?
- **A.** can seem to be
- **B.** appeared to be
- **C.** seems to be
- **D.** can appear to be

50.
- **F.** NO CHANGE
- **G.** at
- **H.** toward
- **J.** DELETE the underlined portion.

51.
- **A.** NO CHANGE
- **B.** fuse;
- **C.** fuse:
- **D.** fuse,

52. Which of the following alternatives to the underlined portion would be LEAST acceptable?
- **F.** encouraged
- **G.** motivated
- **H.** forced
- **J.** emboldened

53.
- **A.** NO CHANGE
- **B.** expatriates, as American writers living abroad, were known.
- **C.** expatriates as American writers living abroad were known.
- **D.** expatriates as American writers living abroad, were known.

GO ON TO THE NEXT PAGE.

appeared in 1919, its general reception was positive, but limited [54] to those who were able to find copies of the book. Anderson's later books, such as *Dark Laughter*, would go on to sell many more copies. [55]

[5]

In the 1920s, Anderson wrote some direct responses to the more explicit examples of literary Modernism in Europe. In the 1930s, Anderson wrote *Beyond Desire.* [56] But Anderson's most important contributions in the 1920s and 1930s are best felt indirectly through the works of the various writers [57] he inspired. Anderson was among the first to explore the troubled relationship between the city and the rural town, the direct style to which we so often apply the name, "American," [58] and the idea that deeply intellectual concerns can be relevant to everyday people as much as they can to academics. Even today, Anderson's initial treatment of these themes remains an important starting point for anyone interested in American culture.

54. F. NO CHANGE
G. positive but limited,
H. positive; but limited
J. positive but limited

55. Given that all the choices are true, which one best supports the point that although Anderson's book was difficult to find, those who read it were very impressed?
A. NO CHANGE
B. Many critics still preferred the older European models of writing.
C. *Winesburg, Ohio* remains one of Anderson's best-loved books.
D. Those who did secure a copy of *Winesburg, Ohio* felt that it inaugurated a new age in American literature.

56. Given that all the following are true, which one, if added here, would provide the clearest and most effective indication that Anderson was doing things that had not been done before in American literature?
F. This book addressed social questions that previously only social scientists and propagandists had dared to touch.
G. This later book was heavily influenced by the literature of the Southern Populist movement.
H. Many literary critics have hailed *Beyond Desire* as the highlight of Anderson's later work.
J. This book was not as widely revered as *Winesburg, Ohio.*

57. The best placement for the underlined phrase would be:
A. where it is now.
B. after the word *contributions.*
C. after the word *1930s.*
D. after the word *inspired* (ending the sentence with a period).

58. F. NO CHANGE
G. name "American,"
H. name "American"
J. name, "American"

GO ON TO THE NEXT PAGE.

Questions 59 and 60 ask about the preceding passage as a whole.

59. For the sake of the logic and coherence of this essay, Paragraph 2 should be placed:

A. where it is now.
B. after Paragraph 3.
C. after Paragraph 4.
D. after Paragraph 5.

60. Suppose the writer's goal was to draft an essay that would show the influence of one American author on the work of future authors. Does this essay successfully accomplish this goal?

F. Yes, because it describes an interesting group of authors and focuses on the literature of a particular country.
G. Yes, because it gives a brief description of Sherwood Anderson's writing career and discusses his influence on writers whom his work inspired.
H. No, because it limits the focus to the contrasts between American writing and European writing.
J. No, because it refers only to events that took place in the twenties and thirties.

Passage V

Women at Work

World War II offered numerous employment opportunities for women in the United States. As the men headed to the war front, the work force retracted and diminished[61] on the home front, and women begun[62] to take over responsibilities traditionally assigned to men. These[63] responsibilities included work previously deemed inappropriate for women.

The government realized that participation in the war but[64] required the use of all national resources. American industrial facilities were turned into war production factories, and the government targeted the female population as an essential source of labor. Women worked in factories and shipyards

61. **A.** NO CHANGE
B. retracted diminishingly
C. diminished
D. DELETE the underlined portion.

62. **F.** NO CHANGE
G. has began
H. would of begun
J. began

63. **A.** NO CHANGE
B. The traditionally male
C. Which
D. That

64. **F.** NO CHANGE
G. and it
H. although it
J. DELETE the underlined portion.

GO ON TO THE NEXT PAGE.

as riveters, welders, and machinists making everything from uniforms to munitions to airplanes, they directly contributed to the war effort. The number of women in the workforce increased from 12 million in 1940 to 18 million in 1944. By 1945, 36% of the laborers were women.

The increased presence of women in wartime workforces were not limited to factories and shipyards. [68] Thousands moved to Washington D.C. to fill government jobs exclusively held by men before the war. Some women engaged in farm labor, and others joined the military as field nurses. The shortage of men also led to openings in non-traditional fields, such as day-care. Since many players had been drafted into the armed services, Major League Baseball parks around the country were on the verge of collapse when a group of Midwestern businessmen devised a brilliant solution to the player shortage.

The All-American Girls Professional Baseball League was created in 1943 and offered a unique blend of baseball and softball suitable for female players. Founder, Philip K. Wrigley and League president, Ken Sells promoted the new league with aggressive advertising campaigns that promoted the physical attractiveness of female athletes. Photographs displayed women

65. **A.** NO CHANGE
B. machinists, making
C. machinists. Making
D. machinists, who made

66. **F.** NO CHANGE
G. workforce, for example in factories and shipyards,
H. workforce, such as factories and shipyards,
J. factory and shipyard workforce

67. **A.** NO CHANGE
B. are
C. was
D. have been

68. At this point, the writer is considering adding the following true statement:

> The marriage rate increased significantly during the war, as did the rate of babies born to unmarried women.

Should the writer add this sentence here?
F. No, because it does not echo the style and tone that has already been established in the essay.
G. No, because it is not relevant to the essay's focus on the changing roles of women during World War II.
H. Yes, because it contributes to the essay's focus on women's roles in the home during World War II.
J. Yes, because it provides a contrast between women in the home and women in the workplace.

69. Given that all the choices are true, which one provides the most logical transition to the information presented in the rest of this essay?
A. NO CHANGE
B. the most notable of which was baseball.
C. which many women had to give up after the war.
D. shaking American society to the core.

70. **F.** NO CHANGE
G. Founder Philip K. Wrigley and League president
H. Founder Philip K. Wrigley, and, League president
J. Founder, Philip K. Wrigley, and League president,

GO ON TO THE NEXT PAGE.

players with bright smiles on their faces and baseball mitts in their hands.[71] Their silk shorts, fashionable knee-high socks, red lipstick, having[72] flowing hair directly contrasted with the competitive, masculine nature of the game. [73] These photographs are indicative of the delicate balance between feminine appeal and masculine labor that was expected of all women throughout World War II. Although its'[74] success lasted only a decade, the All-American Girls Professional Baseball League's role in expanding opportunities for women during World War II and thereafter is everlasting. [75]

71. Given that all the choices are true, which one most effectively helps the writer's purpose of helping readers visualize the players in the photographs?
   A. NO CHANGE
   B. at the plate during a live game.
   C. clearly focused on playing well.
   D. showing close camaraderie.

72. F. NO CHANGE
   G. their
   H. with
   J. and

73. If the writer were to delete the words *silk*, *fashionable*, and *red* from the preceding sentence, it would primarily lose:
   A. details that have already been presented in the vivid imagery of the previous sentence.
   B. a digression from the focus of this paragraph on the athletic talent of the players.
   C. description of what was written in the captions accompanying the photographs.
   D. details that highlight the femininity of the players in contrast to the masculinity of the game.

74. F. NO CHANGE
   G. it's
   H. their
   J. its

Question 75 asks about the preceding passage as a whole.

75. Suppose the writer's goal was to write an essay that would illustrate the range of non-traditional activities women pursued during wartime. Does this essay achieve that goal?
   A. Yes, because it explains the impact of the All-American Girls Professional Baseball Team on public perception of women.
   B. Yes, because it gives several examples of women performing jobs during World War II that were typically filled by men.
   C. No, because it limits its focus to the type of work women engaged in during World War II.
   D. No, because it explains that women's importance in the workforce, especially in baseball, lasted only several years.

END OF TEST 1
STOP! DO NOT TURN THE PAGE UNTIL TOLD TO DO SO.

NO TEST MATERIAL ON THIS PAGE.

GO ON TO THE NEXT PAGE.

MATHEMATICS TEST

60 Minutes—60 Questions

DIRECTIONS: Solve each problem, choose the correct answer, and then darken the corresponding oval on your answer document.

Do not linger over problems that take too much time. Solve as many as you can; then return to the others in the time you have left for this test.

You are permitted to use a calculator on this test. You may use your calculator for any problems you choose, but some of the problems may best be done without using a calculator.

Note: Unless otherwise stated, all of the following should be assumed:

1. Illustrative figures are NOT necessarily drawn to scale.
2. Geometric figures lie in a plane.
3. The word *line* indicates a straight line.
4. The word *average* indicates arithmetic mean.

DO YOUR FIGURING HERE.

1. In the hiking trail shown below, X marks the trail's halfway point. If $\overline{YZ}$ measures 24 kilometers and is $\frac{1}{3}$ the length of $\overline{XZ}$, what is the total length, in kilometers, of the trail?

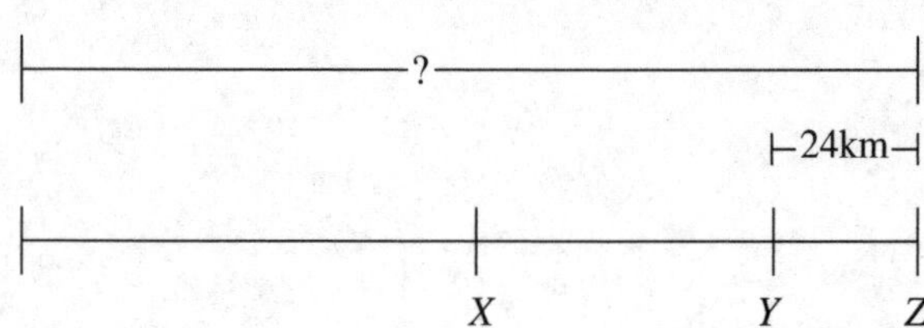

A. 144
B. 104
C. 96
D. 72
E. 48

2. What is the value of x when $\frac{4x}{5}+7=6$?

F. $\frac{5}{4}$
G. $-\frac{4}{5}$
H. -1
J. $-\frac{5}{4}$
K. -5

GO ON TO THE NEXT PAGE.

DO YOUR FIGURING HERE.

3. Cyclist *A* averages 80 pedal revolutions per minute, and Cyclist *B* averages 61 pedal revolutions per minute. At these rates, how many more minutes does Cyclist *B* need than Cyclist *A* to make 9,760 pedal revolutions?

A. 19
B. 38
C. 122
D. 141
E. 160

4. The perimeter of a square is 36 inches. What is the area of the square, in square inches?

F. 6
G. 9
H. 18
J. 36
K. 81

5. For the rectangle shown in the standard (x,y) coordinate plane below, what are the coordinates of the unlabeled vertex?

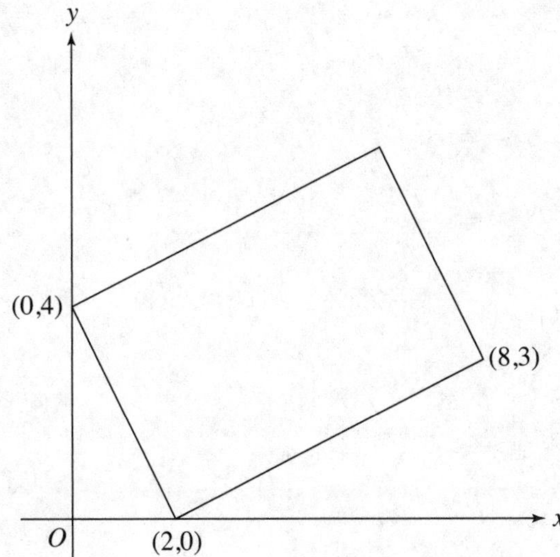

A. (4,5)

B. (4,7)

C. $\left(5,\frac{7}{2}\right)$

D. (6,7)

E. (10,4)

GO ON TO THE NEXT PAGE.

6. Carla has 5 times as many notebooks as her brother does. If they have 42 notebooks between them, how many notebooks does Carla have?

F. 30
G. 33
H. 35
J. 37
K. 47

DO YOUR FIGURING HERE.

7. If G is in the interior of right angle $\angle DEF$, then which of the following could be the measure of $\angle GEF$?

A. 85°
B. 95°
C. 105°
D. 115°
E. 125°

8. Susie has three T-shirts: one red, one blue, and one black. She also has three pairs of shorts: one red, one blue, and one black. How many different combinations are there for Susie to wear exactly one T-shirt and one pair of shorts?

F. 3
G. 6
H. 8
J. 9
K. 27

9. 20% of 20 is equal to 50% of what number?

A. 2
B. 4
C. 8
D. 10
E. 200

10. There are 45 musicians in an orchestra, and all play two instruments. Of these musicians, 36 play the piano, and 22 play the violin. What is the maximum possible number of orchestra members who play both the piano and the violin?

F. 9
G. 13
H. 22
J. 23
K. 36

GO ON TO THE NEXT PAGE.

DO YOUR FIGURING HERE.

11. What is the largest value of m for which there exists a real value of n such that $m^2 = 196 - n^2$?

A. 14
B. 98
C. 182
D. 196
E. 392

12. Phil earned \$800 at his summer job and saved all of his earnings. He wants to buy a deluxe drum kit that is regularly priced at \$925 but is on sale for $\frac{1}{5}$ off. The drum kit is subject to 5% sales tax after all discounts are applied. If Phil buys the kit on sale and gives the sales clerk his entire summer earnings, how much change should he receive?

F. \$23
G. \$37
H. \$40
J. \$77
K. None; Phil still owes \$171.25.

13. Which of the following numbers is an imaginary number?

A. $\sqrt{64}$

B. $\sqrt{11}$

C. $-\frac{4}{\sqrt{3}}$

D. $-\sqrt{-64}$

E. $-\sqrt{64}$

14. Which of the following correctly factors the expression $25x^4 - 16y^8$?

F. $(25 - 16)(x^2 - y^4)(x^2 + y^4)$
G. $(5x^2 - 4y^4)(5x^2 + 4y^4)$
H. $(25x^2 - y^4)(x^2 + 16y^4)$
J. $(5x^4 - 4y^8)(5x^4 + 4y^8)$
K. $(5x^4 - 8y^8)(5x^4 + 2y^8)$

GO ON TO THE NEXT PAGE.

15. The figure below shows a portion of a tile floor from which the shaded polygon will be cut in order to make a repair. Each square tile has sides that measure 1 foot. Every vertex of the shaded polygon is at the intersection of 2 tiles. What is the area, in square feet, of the shaded polygon?

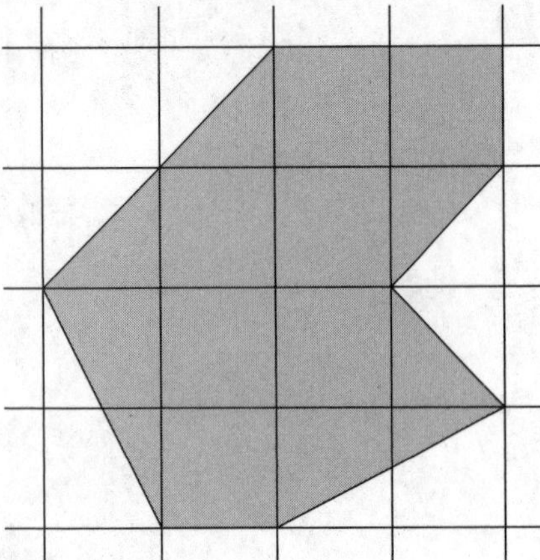

A. 9.5
B. 10.0
C. 10.5
D. 11.0
E. 11.5

16. The percent P of a population that has completed 4 years of college is given by the function $P(t) = -0.001t^2 + 0.4t$, where t represents time, in years. What percent of the population has completed four years of college after 20 years, to the nearest tenth?

F. 0.1
G. 7.6
H. 8.0
J. 8.4
K. 160.0

17. At Fatima's Fruits, a bag of eight grapefruits costs $4.40. At Ernie's Edibles, a bag of three grapefruits costs $1.86. How much cheaper, per grapefruit, is the cost at Fatima's Fruits than at Ernie's Edibles?

A. $0.07
B. $0.35
C. $0.59
D. $1.17
E. $2.54

18. Which of the following is equivalent to $(x^4 - 4)(x^4 + 4)$?

F. $2x^4$
G. $x^8 - 16$
H. $x^8 + 16$
J. $x^{16} - 16$
K. $x^8 - 8x^4 - 16$

DO YOUR FIGURING HERE.

GO ON TO THE NEXT PAGE.

DO YOUR FIGURING HERE.

19. Wade is making a tile mosaic. He begins the project by laying tile at a speed of 50 pieces per hour for 3.5 hours. He is then interrupted from his work for 60 minutes. He resumes working and lays tile at a speed of 35 pieces per hour, until he has laid 280 pieces of tile total. How many hours did Wade spend working on the mosaic after he started working again?

A. 2.5
B. 3
C. 3.5
D. 4
E. 4.5

20. Point *C* (1,2) and point *D* (7,–10) lie in the standard coordinate plane. What are the coordinates of the midpoint of $\overline{CD}$?

F. (1, 8)
G. (3,–6)
H. (4,–4)
J. (4,–6)
K. (7,–4)

21. Michael is planning to put fencing along the edge of his rectangular backyard, which is 22 yards by 16 yards. One long side of the backyard is along his house, so he will need to fence only 3 sides. How many yards of fencing will Michael need?

A. 38
B. 54
C. 60
D. 76
E. 352

22. What is the *y*-intercept of the line given by the equation $7x - 3y = 21$?

F. -7

G. $-\frac{7}{3}$

H. $\frac{7}{3}$

J. 7

K. 21

GO ON TO THE NEXT PAGE.

DO YOUR FIGURING HERE.

23. On April 8th, a flower at Blooming Acres Florist was 15.0 centimeters tall. On April 16th, the flower was 17.4 centimeters tall. If the flower grew at a constant rate, on what day was the flower 16.5 centimeters tall?

A. April 11th
B. April 12th
C. April 13th
D. April 14th
E. April 15th

24. Which of the following expressions is equivalent to the expression given below?

$$(2x^3 - x - 1) - 3(x^4 + 2x^3 - 2x^2 - x + 3)$$

F. $x^{14} - 3$
G. $-3x^{14}$
H. $-3x^4 + 8x^3 - 6x^2 - 4x + 8$
J. $-3x^4 + 4x^3 - 2x^2 - 2x - 3$
K. $-3x^4 - 4x^3 + 6x^2 + 2x - 10$

25. The playground equipment shown below has a ladder that is 6 feet tall and a diagonal slide that is 7 feet long. If the ladder makes a right angle with the ground, approximately how many feet is the base of the slide from the base of the ladder?

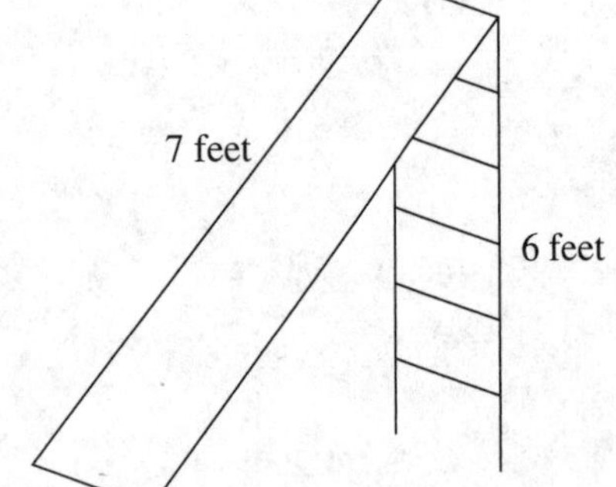

A. 2
B. 4
C. 6
D. 8
E. 10

26. In a data set of 5 points, the mean, median, and mode are each equal to 8. Which of the following could be the data set?

F. {5, 7, 8, 8, 12}
G. {7, 7, 8, 8, 12}
H. {7, 8, 8, 8, 12}
J. {7, 8, 8, 10, 12}
K. {7, 8, 8, 12, 12}

GO ON TO THE NEXT PAGE.

DO YOUR FIGURING HERE.

27. In a certain sequence of numbers, each term after the 1st term is the result of adding 2 to the previous term and multiplying that sum by 3. If the 4th term in the sequence is 186, what is the 2nd term?

A. 2
B. 4
C. 18
D. 60
E. 174

28. Which of the following values of x does NOT satisfy the inequality $|x - 3| \geq 12$?

F. –15
G. –12
H. –9
J. 9
K. 15

29. For all real numbers s, t, u, and v, such that $s + t + u = 29$ and $s < v$, which of the following statements is true?

A. $s + t + v < 29$
B. $t + u + v > 29$
C. $s + t + v = 29$
D. $s + u + v = 29$
E. $s + t + v > 29$

30. In the figure below, rectangle $ABCD$ shares $\overline{CD}$ with ΔCDE, diagonal $\overline{BD}$ of the rectangle extends in a straight line beyond D to E to create $\overline{DE}$, and the measure of $\angle CDE$ is 155°. What is the measure of $\angle CBD$?

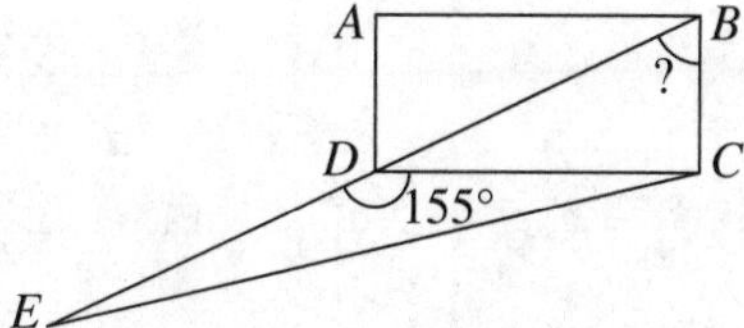

F. 25
G. 55
H. 65
J. 90
K. 155

31. If a, b, and c are positive prime numbers, in the equation $a - b = c$, either b or c must represent which number?

A. 13
B. 11
C. 7
D. 5
E. 2

GO ON TO THE NEXT PAGE.

DO YOUR FIGURING HERE.

32. Pierre competes in a triathlon, along a course as shown in the figure below. He begins swimming at starting point *S* and swims straight across the lake, gets on his bicycle at station *A*, bikes to station *B*, and then runs to finishing line *F*. The judges use a stopwatch to record his elapsed times of t_A, t_B, and t_F hours from point *S* to points *A*, *B*, and *F*, respectively. If the distance, in miles, between points *S* and *A* along the racecourse is denoted by *SA*, then what is Pierre's average speed for this race, in miles per hour?

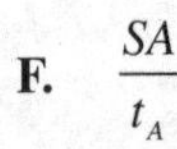

F. $\frac{SA}{t_A}$

G. $\frac{SB}{t_B}$

H. $\frac{SF}{t_F}$

J. $\frac{SA}{t_F}$

K. $\frac{SF}{t_A}$

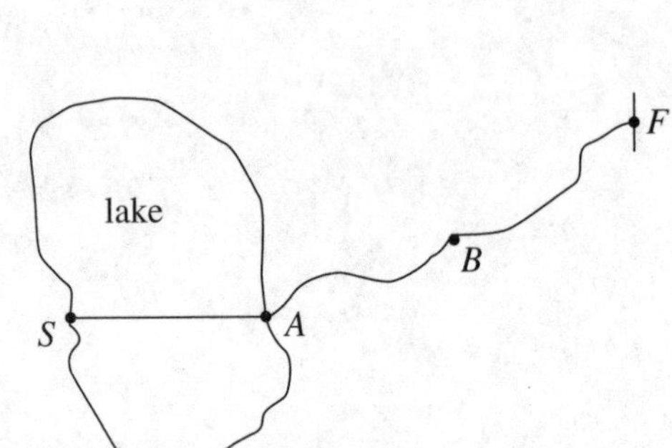

33. The triangle shown below has a hypotenuse with a length of 13 feet. The measure of $\angle A$ is 20° and the measure of $\angle B$ is 70°. Which of the following is closest to the length, in feet, of $\overline{BC}$?

(Note: $\sin 70° \approx 0.9397$
$\cos 70° \approx 0.3420$
$\tan 70° \approx 2.747$)

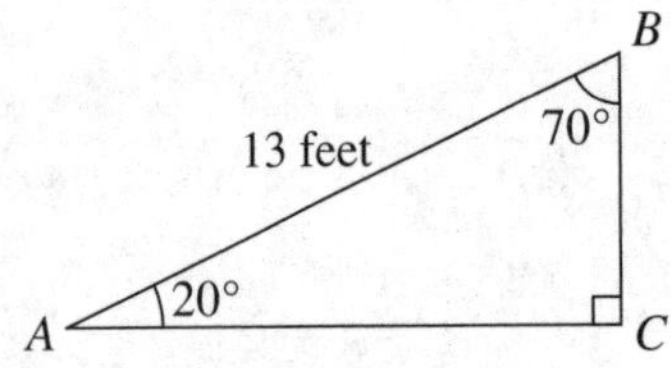

A. 4.4
B. 5.0
C. 12.0
D. 12.2
E. 35.7

34. What is the value of $\frac{8}{y^2} - \frac{x^2}{y}$ when $x = -3$ and $y = -4$?

F. $-\frac{11}{4}$

G. $-\frac{7}{4}$

H. $\frac{7}{4}$

J. $\frac{11}{4}$

K. $\frac{56}{9}$

GO ON TO THE NEXT PAGE.

35. As shown in the figure below, with angles as marked, a ramp is being designed that will have a vertical height of 4 feet. Which of the following is closest to the horizontal length of the ramp, in feet?

DO YOUR FIGURING HERE.

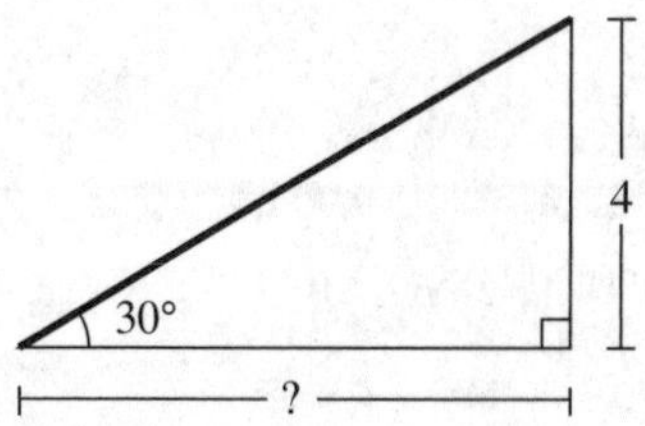

A. 5
B. 6
C. 7
D. 8
E. 9

36. In the diagram below, ΔABC is isosceles and ΔBCD is equilateral. $\overline{AB} = \overline{BC}$ and the measure of $\angle ABC$ is half the measure of $\angle BAC$. What is the measure of $\angle ABD$?

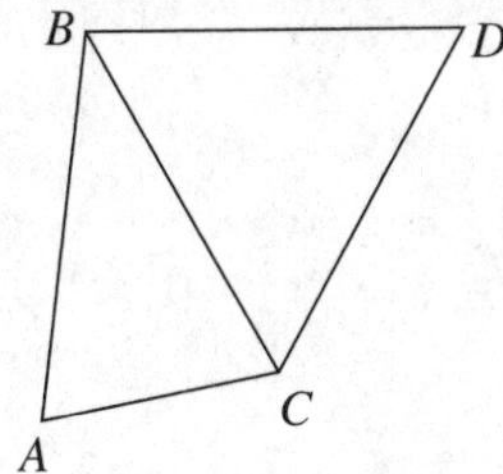

F. 36°
G. 60°
H. 72°
J. 96°
K. 150°

GO ON TO THE NEXT PAGE.

DO YOUR FIGURING HERE.

Use the following information to answer questions 37–39.

The coordinates of the vertices of ΔMON are shown in the standard (x,y) coordinate plane below. Rectangle $MPQR$ is shown shaded. Point P lies on $\overline{MO}$, point Q lies on $\overline{ON}$, and point R lies on $\overline{MN}$.

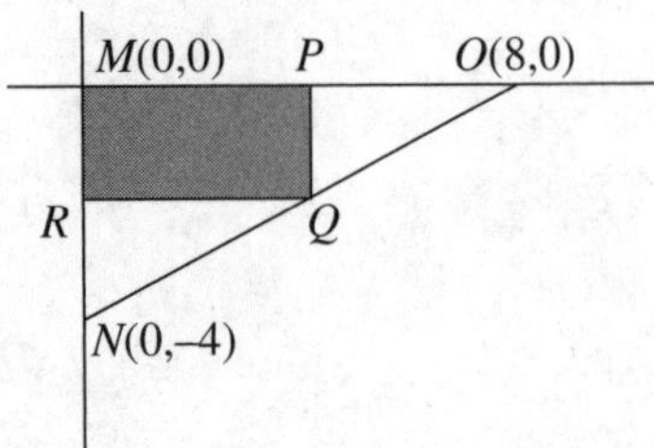

37. What is the slope of $\overline{ON}$?

A. -2

B. $-\frac{1}{2}$

C. 0

D. $\frac{1}{2}$

E. 2

38. Which of the following is closest to the perimeter, in coordinate units, of ΔMON ?

F. 12.0
G. 16.9
H. 18.0
J. 20.9
K. 92.0

39. What is the value of $\cos(\angle MNO)$?

A. $\frac{4}{\sqrt{80}}$

B. $\frac{8}{\sqrt{80}}$

C. $\frac{1}{2}$

D. 2

E. $\frac{\sqrt{80}}{8}$

GO ON TO THE NEXT PAGE.

40. In a Spanish class there are m students, of which n did NOT pass the last exam. Which of the following is a general expression for the fraction of the class that did receive a passing grade?

DO YOUR FIGURING HERE.

F. $\frac{m-n}{m}$

G. $\frac{m}{n}$

H. $\frac{m-n}{n}$

J. $\frac{n-m}{n}$

K. $\frac{n-m}{m}$

41. The solution set of $5x + 9 \geq 2(3x + 4) + 7$ is shown by which of the following number line graphs?

A. 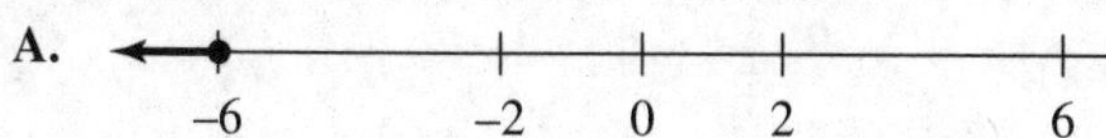

B. –6 –2 0 2 6

C. –6 –2 0 2 6

D. –6 –2 0 2 6

E. –6 –2 0 2 6

42. An artist wants to cover the entire outside of a rectangular box with mosaic tiles. The dimensions of the box shown below are given in centimeters. If each tile is exactly one square centimeter, and the artist lays the tiles with no space between them, how many tiles will he need?

F. 75
G. 96
H. 108
J. 126
K. 150

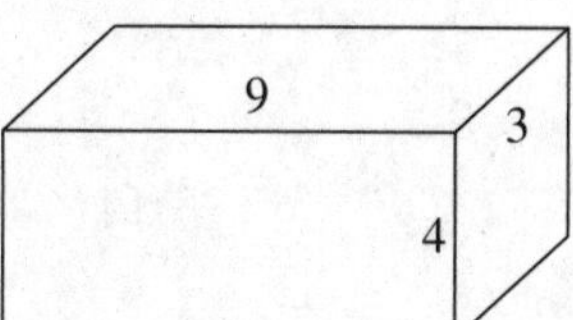

GO ON TO THE NEXT PAGE.

DO YOUR FIGURING HERE.

43. In the figure shown below, $\overline{BC}$ and $\overline{EF}$ are parallel and $\overline{AE} = \overline{FD}$. If $\angle ABC$ is 130° and $\angle BAE$ is 22°, what is the measure of $\angle AEF$?

A. 50°
B. 118°
C. 152°
D. 158°
E. 164°

44. Given the figure below, what is the area of the trapezoid, in square inches?

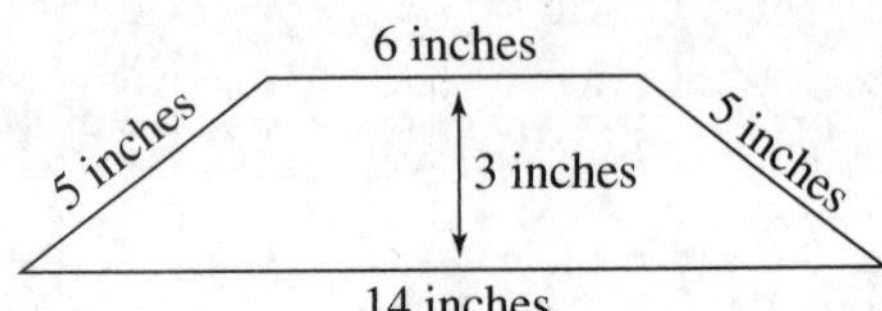

F. 18
G. 30
H. 42
J. 50
K. 52

45. What is the solution set of $\sqrt[5]{x^2 + 4x} = 2$?

A. {4}
B. {8}
C. {–4, 8}
D. {–8, 4}
E. $\{-2, \pm 2\sqrt{2}\}$

GO ON TO THE NEXT PAGE.

DO YOUR FIGURING HERE.

46. As shown in the figure below, a skateboard ramp leading from the top of a boulder is 10 feet long and forms a 32° angle with the level ground. Which of the following expressions represents the height, in feet, of the boulder?

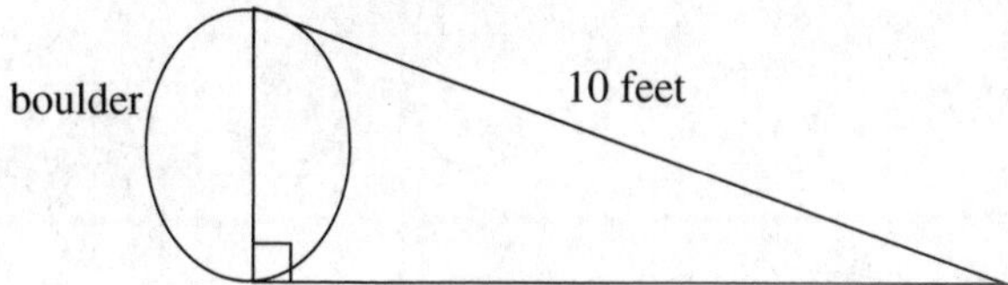

F. $10 \tan 32°$

G. $\dfrac{\sin 32°}{10}$

H. $\dfrac{10}{\cos 32°}$

J. $10 \sin 32°$

K. $10 \cos 32°$

47. The 4 integers j, j, k, and n have an average of 0. Which of the following equations *must* be true?

A. $k = n$
B. $k = -j$
C. $k + n = -2j$
D. $k + n = 0$
E. $k + n = j$

48. If $f(x) = \sqrt{x}$ and the composite function $f(g(x)) = \sqrt{4x^2 - 5}$, which of the following could be $g(x)$?

F. $\sqrt{4x^4 - 5}$

G. $\sqrt{16x^4 - 25}$

H. $2x^2 - 25$

J. $4x^2 - 5$

K. $16x^4 - 5$

GO ON TO THE NEXT PAGE.

DO YOUR FIGURING HERE.

Use the following information to answer questions 49–51.

In the qualifying rounds for a race, Rusty and Dale drive their cars around a 6,000-foot oval track. Rusty and Dale each drive 8 laps in the qualifying rounds in lanes of identical length.

49. On day one of the qualifying rounds, Rusty and Dale start from the same point, but their cars are reversed and each drives opposite ways. Rusty drives at a constant speed that is 8 feet per second faster than Dale's constant speed. Rusty passes Dale for the first time in 150 seconds. Rusty drives at a constant rate of how many feet per second?

A. 16
B. 20
C. 24
D. 32
E. 40

50. On the second day of the qualifying rounds, Rusty averages 180 seconds per lap until he begins the last lap. He then goes into a lower gear. He averages 190 seconds per lap for this qualifying round. How many seconds does Rusty take to drive the final lap?

F. 155
G. 160
H. 185
J. 200
K. 260

51. Dale drives 6 laps in 90 minutes. At what average rate, in feet per hour, does Dale drive these 6 laps?

A. 400
B. 5,400
C. 10,000
D. 24,000
E. 48,000

---

52. Circle *A* has its center at point (–5,2) with a radius of 2, and circle *B* is represented by the equation $(x + 4)^2 + (y - 2)^2 = 9$. Where is point (–2,2) located?

F. Inside circle *A* only
G. Inside circle *B* only
H. Inside both circle *A* and circle *B*
J. Outside both circle *A* and circle *B*
K. Cannot be determined from given information

GO ON TO THE NEXT PAGE.

53. A heart-shaped ornament is made from a square and two semicircles, each of whose diameter is a side of the square. The ornament is shown in the standard (x,y) coordinate plane below, where 1 coordinate unit represents 1 inch. The coordinates of six points on the border of the ornament are given. What is the perimeter, in inches, of the ornament?

DO YOUR FIGURING HERE.

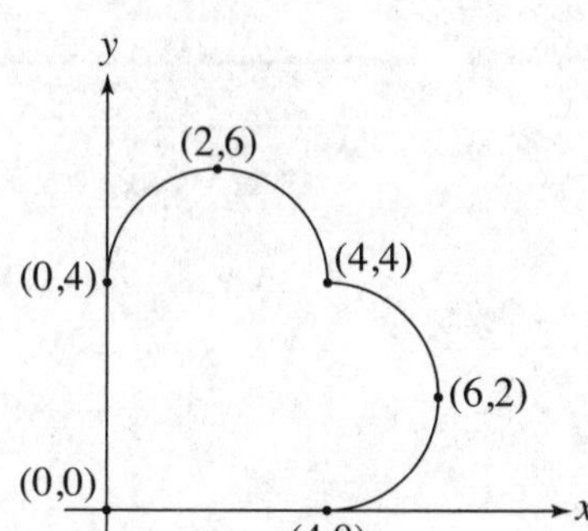

A. $4 + 2\pi$
B. $8 + 4\pi$
C. $8 + 8\pi$
D. $16 + 4\pi$
E. $16 + 8\pi$

54. A function $f(x)$ is defined as even if and only if $f(x) = f(-x)$ for all real values of x. Which one of the following graphs represents an even function $f(x)$?

F.

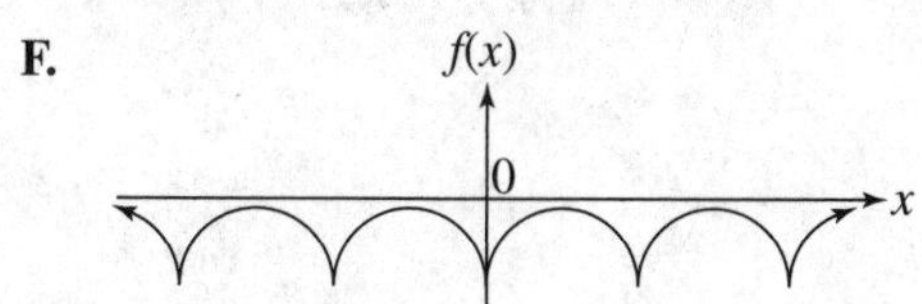

G.

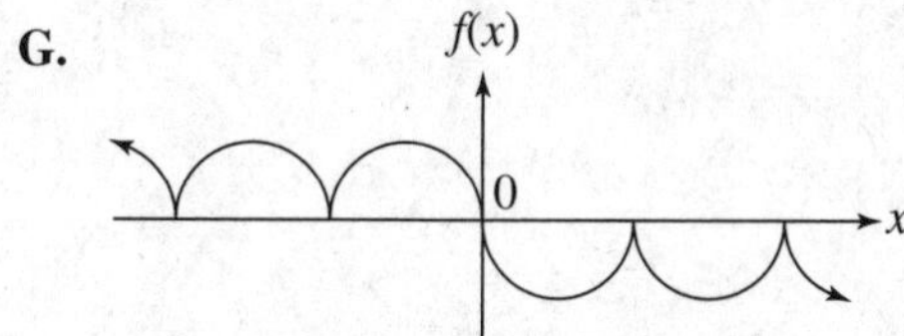

H.

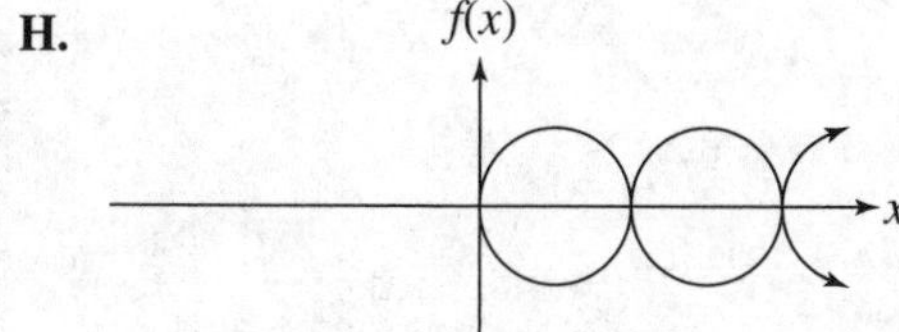

J.

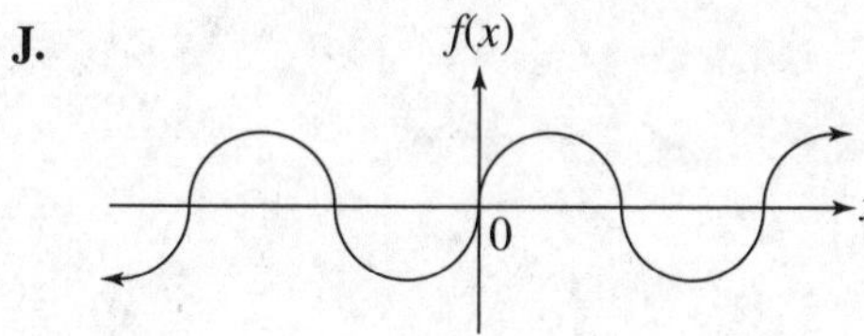

K.

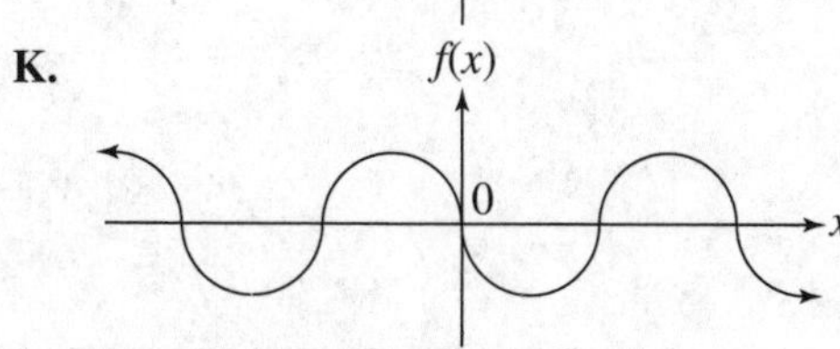

GO ON TO THE NEXT PAGE.

DO YOUR FIGURING HERE.

55. In the standard (x,y) coordinate plane, point A is located at $(w,w + 5)$ and point B is located at $(4w,w - 5)$. In coordinate units, what is the distance between A and B ?

A. 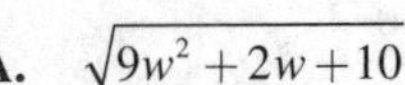 $\sqrt{9w^2+2w+10}$

B. $\sqrt{9w^2+100}$

C. $9w^2+100$

D. $|w|\sqrt{11}$

E. $|w|$

56. RST is a right triangle with side lengths of r, s, and t, as shown below. What is the value of $\cos^2 S + \cos^2 R$?

F. 1

G. $\sqrt{2}$

H. $\sqrt{3}$

J. $\frac{\sqrt{2}}{2}$

K. $\frac{1+\sqrt{2}}{3}$

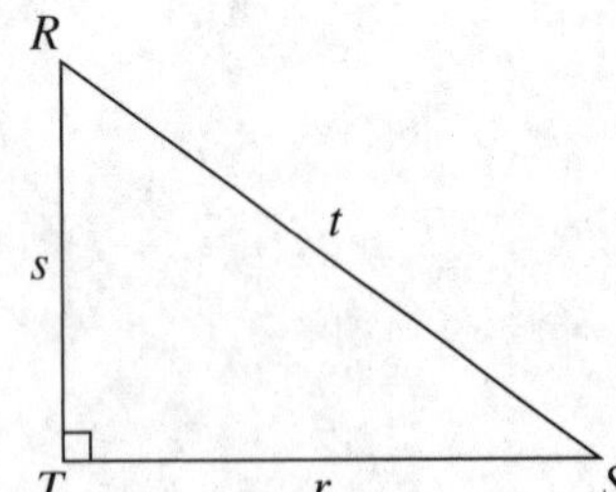

57. In isosceles triangle ABC below, the measures of $\angle BAC$ and $\angle BCA$ are equal and $\overline{DE} \parallel \overline{AC}$. The diagonals of trapezoid $DECA$ intersect at F. The lengths of $\overline{DF}$ and $\overline{EF}$ are 6 centimeters, the length of $\overline{DE}$ is 9 centimeters, and the length of $\overline{AC}$ is 27 centimeters. What is the length, in centimeters, of $\overline{FC}$?

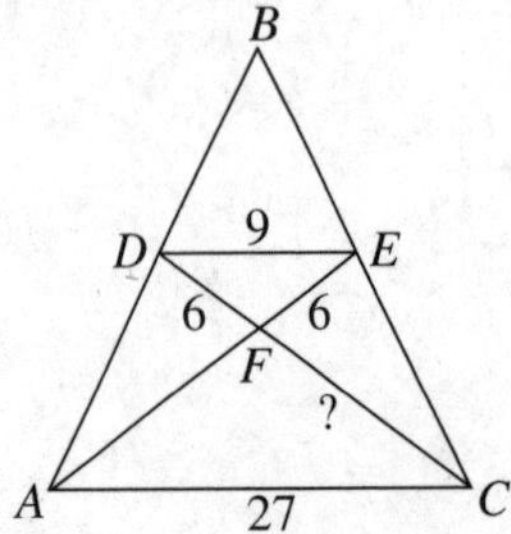

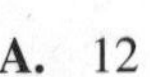

A. 12
B. 15
C. 18
D. 33
E. 36

GO ON TO THE NEXT PAGE.

58. Which of the following represents the product of the matrices below?

DO YOUR FIGURING HERE.

$$\begin{bmatrix} 4 & -2 \\ 3 & -6 \end{bmatrix} \times \begin{bmatrix} 0 \\ 2 \end{bmatrix}$$

F. $\begin{bmatrix} -4 \\ -12 \end{bmatrix}$

G. $\begin{bmatrix} -12 \\ 0 \end{bmatrix}$

H. $\begin{bmatrix} -6 \end{bmatrix}$

J. $\begin{bmatrix} 6 & -12 \end{bmatrix}$

K. $\begin{bmatrix} -4 & -12 \end{bmatrix}$

59. If $\dfrac{(n+1)!}{(n-1)!} = 20$, then $n! = ?$

A. 6
B. 10
C. 12
D. 24
E. 120

60. What is the ratio of a circle's radius to its circumference?

F. $2\pi{:}1$
G. 2:1
H. $\pi{:}1$
J. $1{:}\pi$
K. $1{:}2\pi$

END OF TEST 2
STOP! DO NOT TURN THE PAGE UNTIL TOLD TO DO SO.
DO NOT RETURN TO THE PREVIOUS TEST.

READING TEST

35 Minutes—40 Questions

DIRECTIONS: There are four passages in this test. Each passage is followed by several questions. After reading each passage, choose the best answer to each question and blacken the corresponding oval on your answer document. You may refer to the passages as often as necessary.

Passage I

PROSE FICTION: This passage is adapted from the short story "Ruby" by Tristan Ivory (©2007 by Tristan Ivory).

Ruby's Downhome Diner was an institution. If you only spent one night in Franklin, Texas, someone would inevitably direct you right off Highway 79 and Pink Oak Road to Ruby's Downhome Diner, Ruby's, or The Downhome; whatever name the locals gave you, there was always something there that you would enjoy.

Ruby's was named after Ruby Sanders, my grandmother. She had opened the diner with money she saved from cleaning houses and with personal loans from friends. By the time I was born, Ruby's did enough business to pay off all debts and obligations. It didn't take long before my grandmother was a person of considerable stature in and around Robertson County, just like the restaurant that bore her name.

Ever since I was knee-high, I spent each sweltering summer with my grandmother. This, truth be told, meant that for all practical purposes I lived at Ruby's Downhome. Time familiarized me with all nuances within the diner: there were five steps and four ingredients that separated peach preserves from peach cobbler filling; Deputy Sheriff Walter Mayes preferred his eggs, always cooked over-easy, to finish cooking on the top of his ham before it was transferred to his plate; Mr. Arnold delivered the milk and the buttermilk on Mondays, Thursdays, and Saturdays; and there were days when I would need to go to the general store to pick up whatever was in short supply. By the time I entered high school, I could have run the diner from open to close if my Grandmother were absent, but she never was.

Perhaps the single greatest contributing factor to the success of Ruby's Diner was the omnipresent personality of its namesake. Even the most hopelessly spun-around visitor who happened inside those doors would know who Ms. Ruby was. There were no sick days, vacations, or holidays. Between 5 A.M. and 9 P.M., you knew where Ruby Sanders could be found. If the diner were a sort of cell, then my grandmother was its nucleus; without the nucleus, the cell would surely perish.

The people who worked at Ruby's were as dedicated as Ruby herself. There were the regulars: Del (short for Delmont) did double duty as a short-order cook and janitor, while Marlene and Deborah waited tables. Extra help would be hired from time to time depending on the season and individual need. No matter how long those extra helpers stayed, they and everyone else who worked at the Downhome were family, and no one ever fell out of touch.

Ruby's did the things you'd expect a diner to do, as well as the things you wouldn't. You could stop in and get yourself a nice cool drink for the road. Or you could pull up a stool at the counter and grab a steaming hot bowl of red pepper chili with a slice of corn pone or a dish of chilled and creamy homemade ice cream. Or better still, you could grab a booth and try any number of full-plate entrees made to order. But you could also order a wedding cake a week in advance, take a weekend course in food preparation, or, when the time came, have your wake catered with dignity and grace.

When I was very young, I would spend most of my time exploring every inch of Ruby's until the entire layout was printed indelibly in my mind. I could walk blindfolded from the basement where the dry goods were kept, up to the kitchen with the walk-in refrigerator filled with perishables, over to the main restaurant with row after row of booths and counter and stools, well-worn but always cleaned after each patron had finished, and finally to the front porch, with its old wooden swing. I can see my grandmother moving from her station near the door to the kitchen, over to the counter and tables, and then back to the front again. Even now, I can see Del speedily making a double order of hash, Deborah picking up a generous tip, and Marlene topping off a customer's sweet tea. Every summer sunset from that porch seemed to be more magnificent than the last.

As I got older, I took on more responsibility. There were fewer sunsets to watch and more work to be done. It was hard but never dull work. The company kept me coming back despite the increasing allure of summer football leagues and idle moments with friends or girls. After all, the woman who built Ruby's was strong enough to make me forget those things, if only for the summer. I didn't know that I would never return after my sophomore year of college, and for that, I am glad—I could not have asked for a better end to my long history at Ruby's. It warms my heart when I think of the last memory of Ruby Sanders: tying her silver hair into a tight bun, hands vigorously wiping down tables with a rag, enjoying a story and a laugh as we closed for the night.

GO ON TO THE NEXT PAGE.

1. The narrator's point of view can most correctly be described as that of an adult:

A. remembering the events that brought a particular place into existence.
B. analyzing how different his current life is from how things were when he was younger.
C. thinking about the qualities of his grandmother and her restaurant that made her well-respected in the community.
D. curious as to how many people's lives were positively impacted by his grandmother and her diner.

2. One of the main purposes of the first part of the passage (lines 1–27) is to:

F. explain how Ruby got the money to pay for the diner and her eventual success in paying off her debts.
G. state that the diner had taken its name from the narrator's grandmother although many of the locals called it by different names.
H. explain how Ruby was able to become the most important person in Franklin and that her restaurant was the best place for visitors to the city.
J. introduce the primary setting of the story and to describe a central character.

3. Based on the narrator's characterization, Ruby Sanders would best be described as:

A. always at the diner, though she often preferred to be absent.
B. the main force holding the diner and its employees together.
C. carefree, particularly when it came to hearing humorous stories.
D. the only woman the narrator had ever respected.

4. Information in the last paragraph most strongly suggests that the narrator felt his last summer at the diner to be:

F. disappointing because he didn't know it would be his last.
G. something he was forced to do when he would rather have been playing football.
H. pleasant although he did not know it would be his last.
J. exhausting because of all his new responsibilities.

5. According to the narrator, working at Ruby's Diner was:

A. easy but tedious.
B. difficult but enjoyable.
C. hard and monotonous.
D. unpredictable and overwhelming.

6. According to the narrator, his grandmother was like the diner in that she had:

F. a position of high standing within the community at large.
G. a desire to make all people feel comfortable no matter who they were.
H. an ability to make money within the community.
J. a refusal to settle for anything but the best.

7. The statement in lines 44–45 most strongly suggests that the Downhome Diner:

A. served the community in ways beyond simple dining.
B. was the most significant place within Robertson County.
C. gave the people who worked there great importance in Robertson County.
D. was a place where the waiting times were often unpredictable.

8. The narrator describes Ruby's Downhome Diner as providing all of the following EXCEPT:

F. cooking classes.
G. football leagues.
H. wedding cakes.
J. corn pone.

9. The passage indicates that one of the ways in which the narrator was familiar with Ruby's Downhome Diner was shown by his:

A. ability to teach the cooking classes held on the premises.
B. awareness of the habits of visitors to Robertson County.
C. detailed memory of the layout of the kitchen and the restaurant.
D. unwillingness to leave at the end of each summer before his return to school.

10. According to the narrator, which of the following most accurately represents the reason he was able to forget the summer activities outside while working at his grandmother's restaurant?

F. His tips and wages helped to contribute to his college tuition.
G. His grandmother's restaurant was chronically understaffed.
H. It helped him to gain stature in and around the community.
J. He admired his grandmother's strength.

GO ON TO THE NEXT PAGE.

Passage II

SOCIAL SCIENCE: This passage is adapted from the entry "Happiness" from The Psychologist's Scientific Encyclopedia (© 2004 by The Scientific Press of Illinois).

Lee D. Ross, a psychologist at Stanford University, has a friend who lost both her parents in the Holocaust. According to the woman, the awful events of the Holocaust taught her that it was inappropriate to be upset about trivial things in life and important to enjoy human relationships. Even though the circumstances of her life were tragic, the woman was extremely happy, perhaps due to an innate sense of well-being.

According to psychologists, most of our self-reported level of happiness, a measure researchers call "subjective well-being," seems to be genetically predetermined, rather than caused by experience. A study carried out by Auke Tellegen and David Lykken of the University of Minnesota compared the subjective well-being scores of both fraternal and identical twins, some of whom were raised together and some of whom were separated and raised in different families. By comparing the scores of the twins, Tellegen and Lykken determined that most of the differences in people's levels of happiness are determined by differences in genetic makeup.

A genetic predisposition toward a certain level of happiness means that regardless of what happens in a person's life, he or she will eventually adjust to the new circumstances and report the same level of subjective well-being as before. The tendency for people to maintain a consistent level of happiness despite their circumstances, known as "hedonic adaptation," benefits those whose life-experiences are beset by adverse conditions, such as permanent disability or sudden loss of income. Because they return to a "genetic set point," they eventually feel just as happy as they did before the unfortunate event.

However, hedonic adaptation also affects the happiness of people who experience positive changes in their lives. For example, in one study conducted in the 1970s among lottery winners, it was found that a year after the winners received their money, they were no happier than non-winners.

Despite the quantity of research that supports hedonic adaptation, there is still some debate within the scientific community over how much people can change their baseline happiness. Kennon M. Sheldon, a psychologist at the University of Missouri-Columbia, explains that many research psychologists hypothesized that certain behaviors, such as choosing particular goals in life, could affect long-term happiness. However, scientific literature suggests that these behaviors provide only a temporary increase in subjective well-being.

Sheldon worked alongside Sonja Lyubomirsky of the University of California at Riverside and David A. Schkade of the University of California at San Diego to determine exactly what is known about the science of happiness. They compiled the findings of existing scientific studies in the field of happiness and determined that 50 percent of subjective well-being is predetermined by the genetic set point, while only about 10 percent is influenced by circumstances.

However, people are not completely at the mercy of their genes. Lyubomirsky notes that 40 percent of what contributes to people's happiness is still unexplained, and she believes that much of this may be attributable to what she calls "intentional activity," which includes mental attitudes and behaviors that people can modify and improve. Conscious choices such as demonstrating kindness, fostering optimism, and expressing gratitude may work to influence subjective well-being in much the same way that diet and exercise can affect a person's inherited predisposition toward heart disease. Lyubomirsky hopes to learn the specific mechanisms by which these conscious strategies counteract genetic forces. She and Sheldon are currently expanding their study of subjective well-being to large groups of subjects to be observed over extended periods of time. Using these longitudinal studies, the researchers hope to discover the inner workings of the correlations between behaviors and mood.

Lyubomirsky and Sheldon's studies have found that simply choosing "happy" activities may not be the most effective way to increase happiness. Lyubomirsky says that other factors, such as variation and timing of intentional activities, are crucial in influencing happiness. For example, one study has shown that subjects who varied their acts of kindness from one day to the next experienced greater happiness than those who repeated the same kind act many times. Another study demonstrated that writing a list of things to be grateful for only once a week was more effective in improving levels of happiness than keeping a gratitude journal every day.

The study of happiness is still a relatively new area of psychological research. Traditionally, much more psychological research focused on depression and other disorders associated with destructive mental health, leading some psychologists to suspect that overall levels of subjective well-being are low. But now that more studies are focused on positive psychology, there is evidence to the contrary. Researchers have discovered not only that personal choices improve subjective well-being from a genetic set point, but also that this level is higher than traditionally expected. According to surveys conducted by the University of Chicago, only about one in ten people claim to be "not too happy." Most Americans describe themselves as "pretty happy," and 30 percent as "very happy," even without using intentional activities specifically to improve their well-being.

GO ON TO THE NEXT PAGE.

11. The passage's focus is primarily on the:

A. search for the specific genes known to cause hedonic adaptation.
B. scientific studies investigating various influences on happiness.
C. attempts by experimental psychologists to develop cures for depression.
D. conflicting opinions of psychologists regarding the influence of genes on happiness.

12. Based on the passage, the subjects in the studies by Tellegen and Lykken and the subjects in studies by Lyubomirsky and Sheldon were similar in that both groups were:

F. part of large groups studied over an extended time.
G. intentionally engaged in acts of kindness.
H. asked to describe their own subjective well-being.
J. either identical or fraternal twins.

13. Which of the following questions is NOT answered by the passage?

A. To what extent is a person's level of happiness determined by his or her circumstances?
B. According to Lyubomirsky and Sheldon's studies, what are some specific things people can do to improve their subjective well-being?
C. Does the choice of specific life goals affect happiness over a lifetime?
D. According to Tellegen and Lykken, were twins who were raised together happier than twins who were raised apart?

14. The passage most strongly suggests that the primary goal of Lyubomirsky and Sheldon's research is to:

F. discover the specific mechanisms that may help people overcome the level of happiness determined by their genetic set point.
G. contradict Tellegen and Lykken's findings that genes are the primary determinant in a person's overall level of happiness.
H. find out whether keeping a gratitude journal or engaging in kind acts is more effective at improving happiness.
J. determine which behaviors most completely eliminate hedonic adaptation.

15. Which of the following statements best summarizes the findings of the University of Chicago surveys on happiness?

A. Earlier psychologists were mistaken to believe people are generally depressed and experience low levels of happiness.
B. Depression and other destructive mood disorders are uncommon in America.
C. People are happier if they do not try to improve their subjective well-being by writing in a gratitude journal.
D. Most people report a level of happiness higher than was traditionally expected by psychologists and researchers.

16. According to the passage, all of the following are true of the Lykken and Tellegen study EXCEPT:

F. The subjects were paired groups of twins.
G. Subjects rated their happiness.
H. The twins studied were all raised together.
J. The study found happiness is genetic.

17. According to the passage, "hedonic adaptation" (lines 24–25) is a useful trait because it can help people to:

A. restore levels of happiness that have been interrupted or altered by tragic events.
B. forget that they have suffered a permanent disability or loss of income.
C. adjust quickly to positive circumstances like winning the lottery and become happier.
D. identify with immediate family members who share their genes and choose those who are more inclined to be happy.

18. If the author were to delete the first paragraph, the passage would primarily lose:

F. the idea that events people experience are not the least important factor influencing their subjective well-being.
G. a useful illustration of the idea that there may be little relationship between a person's circumstances and his or her level of happiness.
H. a clear and complete articulation of the essay's main point regarding hedonic adaptation.
J. all examples of adverse conditions people may overcome because of their genetic predisposition to happiness.

19. The main purpose of the final paragraph is to:

A. conclude that psychological researchers make many errors and tend to focus on the negative.
B. disprove the idea suggested by Ross's anecdote by showing that Americans are also happy.
C. cite a specific study that gives a positive view of people's overall levels of happiness.
D. undermine Lyubomirsky and Sheldon's studies indicating that people need to apply effort in order to become happier.

20. According to the passage, which of the following researchers have an ongoing collaboration?

F. Tellegen and Lykken
G. Sheldon and Schkade
H. Sheldon and Lyubomirsky
J. Schkade and Lykken

GO ON TO THE NEXT PAGE.

Passage III

HUMANITIES: Passage A is adapted from "Living Between Worlds: Searching for Identity" by Kenora Crowfeather (© 1998 by Birch Bark Press). Passage B is adapted from *American Indian Stories* by Zitkala-Sa (Gertrude Simmons Bonnin).

Passage A by Kenora Crowfeather

As I gaze at the picture of Zitkala-Sa that confronts me from the cover of her collected writings, *American Indian Stories*, I see a beautifully proud Sioux woman. Long, glossy black braids frame her serious and unflinching face, hang like heavy silken cords in front of her traditional dress, and end somewhere out of the bottom of the frame, past her waist I imagine. It is hard to make myself believe that the woman in this picture was named Gertrude Simmons Bonnin; Zitkala-Sa (Red Bird) was her pen name.

Zitkala-Sa's life-long struggle with the clash between Native American culture and white men has intrigued me for the better part of two decades since I first began reading her essays. Returning home after a long trip and feeling unsettled is not unique to her experience, but the clash between Native Americans and the "pale-faces" who misunderstood and exploited them adds fire to Zitkala-Sa's chronicles of her school years, which might otherwise have been written by any angst-filled teenager.

The daughter of a white man and a Sioux woman, Zitkala-Sa spent the first years of her life firmly ensconced in Native American life with her mother on the Pine Ridge Reservation in South Dakota. She chose to leave home at age eight to go to a missionary school in Indiana. Her memoirs describe her unhappiness at school: her dismay at having her hair cut and her moccasins taken away and her rage at the unjust rules and willful neglect on the part of the teachers. Yet when she returned home, she remained unsatisfied. She was able to wear her beloved moccasins again, but she felt friendless and misunderstood. She had discarded her school clothes and so was ill-equipped to socialize with the young people on the reservation who had adopted that style of dress.

Her return to school and the white man's world for a time confused me, despite my understanding of her urge to leave. How could she have gone to work at an institution so like her first, hated school? How could she have abandoned her mother and her heritage?

In the midst of my indignation, I forgot that Gertrude Bonnin was the daughter of a white man. Her mother, though she never learned English, married three different white men over the course of her life. The clash between the two cultures began deep within Gertrude before she was even born. She was destined to feel like an outsider anywhere, and leaving home allowed her to embrace her Sioux identity. Pursuing education among white men was not, in the end, abandoning her culture, but rather a step in her journey towards becoming an advocate for Native American rights.

Passage B by Zitkala-Sa (Gertrude Simmons Bonnin)

After my first three years of school, I roamed again in the Western country through four strange summers.

During this time I seemed to hang in the heart of chaos, beyond the touch or voice of human aid. My brother, being almost ten years my senior, did not quite understand my feelings. My mother had never gone inside of a schoolhouse, and so she was not capable of comforting her daughter who could read and write. Even nature seemed to have no place for me. I was neither a wee girl nor a tall one; neither a wild Indian nor a tame one. This deplorable situation was the effect of my brief course in the East, and the unsatisfactory "teenth" in a girl's years.

It was under these trying conditions that, one bright afternoon, as I sat restless and unhappy in my mother's cabin, I caught the sound of the spirited step of my brother's pony on the road which passed by our dwelling.

I met him there with a hurried greeting, and, as I passed by, he looked a quiet "What?" into my eyes.

"No, my baby sister, I cannot take you with me to the party to-night," he replied. Though I was not far from fifteen, and I felt that before long I should enjoy all the privileges of my tall cousin, Dawée persisted in calling me his baby sister.

That moonlight night, I cried in my mother's presence when I heard the jolly young people pass by our cottage. They were no more young braves in blankets and eagle plumes, nor Indian maids with prettily painted cheeks. They had gone three years to school in the East, and had become civilized. The young men wore the white man's coat and trousers, with bright neckties. The girls wore tight muslin dresses, with ribbons at neck and waist. At these gatherings they talked English. I could speak English almost as well as my brother, but I was not properly dressed to be taken along. I had no hat, no ribbons, and no close-fitting gown. Since my return from school I had thrown away my shoes, and wore again the soft moccasins.

While Dawée was busily preparing to go I controlled my tears. But when I heard him bounding away on his pony, I buried my face in my arms and cried hot tears.

GO ON TO THE NEXT PAGE.

Questions 21–23 ask about Passage A.

21. The author's attitude towards Zitkala-Sa can best be described as:

A. impatient because Zitkala-Sa's writings reveal her as a spoiled teenager.
B. admiring because Zitkala-Sa established herself as an advocate for Native Americans.
C. disapproving because Zitkala-Sa abandoned her mother and her culture.
D. confused because of Zitkala-Sa's difficulty choosing between conflicting cultures.

22. The author describes the clash of Native American and white cultures as:

F. the reason that Zitkala-Sa eventually abandoned her mother and adapted to a white lifestyle.
G. extra detail that is ultimately unimportant in Zitkala-Sa's chronicles of her school years.
H. the cause of Zitkala's unhappiness at school.
J. the dramatic material that makes Zitkala-Sa's writing compelling.

23. When Crowfeather claims "It is hard to make myself believe that the woman in this picture was named Gertrude Simmons Bonnin" (lines 7–8) she is most nearly referring to:

A. the apparent incongruity between a picture of a Sioux woman and a white woman's name.
B. the confusion created by Bonnin's use of a pen name.
C. her belief that the picture had been incorrectly identified and was not of Bonnin.
D. her preference for Bonnin's traditional Sioux name.

Questions 24–27 ask about Passage B.

24. The author "cried hot tears" (line 84) because:

F. her brother refused to take her to the party.
G. she missed the Indian maids who had gone away to school.
H. her mother was incapable of comforting her.
J. she wished she had a muslin dress with ribbons.

25. The passage most strongly suggests that when she returned home from school, Zitkala-Sa was:

A. content to be back home where she could wear moccasins again.
B. distraught to find that she wasn't happy at home.
C. eager to teach her mother to read and write.
D. upset that her brother still thought of her as a baby.

26. The narrator's statement in lines 55–56 most nearly describes:

F. her average height.
G. the awkwardness of her teenage years.
H. her sense of not belonging.
J. the rejection she felt from her family.

27. In line 73, the word "civilized" is used to describe:

A. the good manners the young people used at the party.
B. the change of living quarters on the reservation from teepees to houses.
C. the education the young people had received while away at school.
D. the young people's adoption of aspects of white culture.

Questions 28–30 ask about both passages.

28. Both passages emphasize Zitkala-Sa's:

F. refusal to fit in on the reservation after she returned home from school.
G. desire to become an advocate for sending Native Americans to school.
H. difficulty getting along with her mother as a teenager.
J. sense of not belonging either at home or in the world of white men.

29. In both passages, moccasins function as a symbol of:

A. the oppression of Native Americans by white men.
B. Zitkala-Sa's frustration at being caught between two cultures.
C. Native American culture.
D. comfortable and practical footwear.

30. The author of Passage A would most likely view the events described in Passage B as:

F. a struggle that ultimately led Zitkala-Sa to have a strong sense of identity.
G. an emotional outburst by Zitkala-Sa typical of a teenage girl.
H. a time when Zitkala-Sa came to fully appreciate Sioux culture.
J. a period of conflict between Zitkala-Sa and her mother and brother.

GO ON TO THE NEXT PAGE.

Passage IV

NATURAL SCIENCE: This passage is adapted from the article "A Tree Frog Grows Up in Hawaii" by Ashley C. Tulliver (© 2005 by Ashley Tulliver).

As night falls on Hawaii's Big Island, a low, jarring sound begins. It is a faint murmur at first, but as the darkness deepens, the sound grows louder, rending the stillness of the evening. These deep cries, from male *E. coquí* frogs, are met with lower, guttural croaks from their prospective mates; during this time, the sound for which the coquí is named (ko-KEE) fills the air. This sound has become the theme song of a growing environmental problem: invasive species' threat to ecological biodiversity.

Native to Puerto Rico, the small tree frogs—measuring about five millimeters long—probably arrived in Hawaii as passengers aboard potted plants imported from the Caribbean. Once coquíes explored their new environment, they found an abundance of food, including insects, tiny spiders, and mites. In addition, they faced little ecological competition, as there are no other amphibians native to the islands, nor are there the snakes, tarantulas, or other Caribbean hunters that usually serve to keep the coquí population in check.

The way the coquí hatch also gives the coquí an advantage in Hawaii's ecosystem. Frogs usually hatch into tadpoles, which require a consistent and substantial amount of water to survive. By contrast, the coquí emerges from the egg as a tiny but fully formed frog, which allows it to thrive in saturated moss, the dampened plastic that importers wrap around plants, or even a drop of water on a plant leaf. Moreover, young coquíes don't begin to emit their signature calls until they are about a year old; consequently, avian predators are unable to locate the tiny frogs by sound.

Perhaps the coquí's most noteworthy feature is its extremely loud calling song. To a listener one to two feet away, a single coquí can produce a mating call up to 100 decibels. The unusual volume of the frog's call is compounded by two other factors. First, coquíes congregate closely on relatively small parcels of land; one recent survey found 400 adult frogs in one 20-by-20-meter plot. This degree of concentration amplifies the sound the frogs make. Second, coquíes tend to overlap their calls, with a single coquí seeking to fill gaps in other frogs' songs with its own effort to attract a mate. As a result, coquíes create a "wall of sound" that is even more pronounced because Hawaii boasts few other night-calling species. For these reasons, human residents of Hawaii tend to regard coquíes as nuisances, polluting the air with their incessant noise.

Conservationists worry about other ramifications of the coquí's invasion of the Hawaiian ecosystem. One problem is that while the coquí receives the bulk of residents' attention because of its nocturnal serenades, another, quieter genus of the frog—the greenhouse frog—represents an equal threat to the biodiversity of the island. As voracious insectivores, coquíes and greenhouse frogs are threatening the survival of arthropods (invertebrate animals with jointed legs, including insects, scorpions, crustaceans, and spiders), whose populations are already close to extirpation due to other foreign predators. Ornithologists fear that depleting the insect population could result in serious consequences for Hawaii's food web, especially considering that the birds native to the islands are also insectivores.

Symbiotic interactions between the coquí and other invasive species pose another ecological threat. The presence of coquíes could permit the flourishing of other so-called "dissonant" species, such as non-native snakes that prey upon the frogs. Herpetologists have speculated that nematodes and other types of vertebrate parasites can be transported with coquíes and can infect indigenous fauna. Furthermore, many ecologists believe the proliferation of these frogs will further homogenize the island's biota.

Debate persists about how best to reduce or even eradicate the population of coquíes and their cousins in Hawaii. Hand-capturing the tiny frogs is probably the most environmentally sensitive way to remove them from their habitat, but their sheer number renders this approach inefficient. The maximum concentration of pesticides that would not damage fauna or flora has not been potent enough to kill the frogs. Seeking a more creative solution, scientists have had some success treating the frogs with caffeine citrate, a drug typically prescribed to treat breathing and metabolic abnormalities in humans. Caffeine citrate can penetrate the coquí's moist skin, and the drug's high acidity essentially poisons the animal and inactivates its nervous systems. From a biodiversity standpoint, this technique has the added benefit of posing almost no danger to plants, which lack a nervous system, or to insects, which have an impenetrable, hard exoskeleton.

Even if new techniques finally exterminate the coquí, experts are skeptical that the invader's current effects on the 1,000 acres of Hawaii's ecosystem can be reversed. This patch of land is not expansive in comparison to Hawaii's total 4.1 million acres, yet it is an indication of potential widespread disaster: since the habitat and its native residents have thus far been able to adjust to the presence of coquíes, eliminating the frogs could yield unintended and far-reaching consequences to the biodiversity of the habitat beyond arthropods. For now, scientists are likely to continue the delicate balancing act of limiting the coquí's population growth while preventing further damage to Hawaii's ecosystem.

GO ON TO THE NEXT PAGE.

31. Which of the following questions is NOT answered by this passage?

A. On an annual basis, how often do coquí frogs mate and produce offspring?
B. Which predators native to Puerto Rico are absent in the Hawaiian islands?
C. What behavioral factors influence the volume of the coquí's calls?
D. How could the coquí potentially disrupt the food chain on the islands it inhabits?

32. It is most reasonable to infer from the passage that the lack of amphibian life in Hawaii:

F. benefits coquíes, which don't have to compete for food and space.
G. provides little opportunity for coquíes to form symbiotic relationships.
H. forces coquíes to build their own nests in order to mate and breed.
J. is a result of invasive species' attacks on the biodiversity of the islands.

33. Which of the following statements about the noise levels produced by the coquí is supported by the passage?

A. The coquí males have lower, guttural croaks than do females of the species.
B. Calls are louder when coquíes are defending their territory than when they are mating.
C. The calls of coquí sound particularly loud because there are no gaps of silence.
D. Coquí are noisier at dawn and dusk than at other times of day.

34. The primary purpose of the third paragraph (lines 19–28) is to:

F. describe wet weather conditions in Hawaii necessary for the coquí to breed.
G. provide a physical description of the coquí's habitat in Hawaii compared to that in Puerto Rico.
H. explain the ecological and behavioral advantages that permit the coquí to thrive in Hawaii.
J. give an overview of the amphibian life cycle, from the tadpole to frog stage.

35. Compared to the language of the first paragraph, the language of the sixth paragraph (lines 58–66) is more:

A. opinionated.
B. scientific.
C. optimistic.
D. casual.

36. As it is used in line 53, the word *extirpation* most nearly means:

F. competition.
G. extinction.
H. overpopulation.
J. pursuit.

37. Which of the following ideas is presented in the passage as theory and not fact?

A. Coquí frogs cluster together in high concentrations, amplifying the sound they make.
B. Store-bought poisons, in permissible doses, are not strong enough to kill the frogs.
C. The exoskeleton of insects is a better defense against caffeine citrate than the skin of amphibians.
D. A decrease in Hawaii's insect population causes a decrease in bird populations.

38. The passage states that coquíes often carry parasites called:

F. nematodes.
G. arthropods.
H. scorpions.
J. arachnids.

39. Which of the following statements best reflects the information provided in the passage about the relevance of the greenhouse frog to the discussion of the coquí?

A. The greenhouse frog lives primarily indoors, whereas the coquí lives primarily in island rain forests.
B. The greenhouse frog is less prominent than the coquí but can be equally damaging to the Hawaiian ecosystem.
C. The greenhouse frog does not pose as dangerous a threat to the Hawaiian ecosystem as the coquí does.
D. It is easier to locate and eliminate the coquí because the greenhouse frog does not produce loud mating calls.

40. The phrase "1,000 acres" (line 85) refers to which type of land in Hawaii?

F. Caribbean ecosystem
G. Bird sanctuary
H. Rain forest
J. Coquí habitat

END OF TEST 3.
STOP! DO NOT TURN THE PAGE UNTIL TOLD TO DO SO.
DO NOT RETURN TO A PREVIOUS TEST.

SCIENCE TEST

35 Minutes—40 Questions

DIRECTIONS: There are six passages in the following section. Each passage is followed by several questions. After reading a passage, choose the best answer to each question and blacken the corresponding oval on your answer sheet. You may refer to the passages as often as necessary.

You are NOT permitted to use a calculator on this test.

Passage I

A group of students studied the frictional forces involved on stationary objects.

In a series of experiments, the students used rectangular shaped objects of various materials that all had identical masses. One end of a plastic board coated with a polymer film was fastened to a table surface by a hinge so the angle θ between the board and table could be changed, as shown in Figure 1.

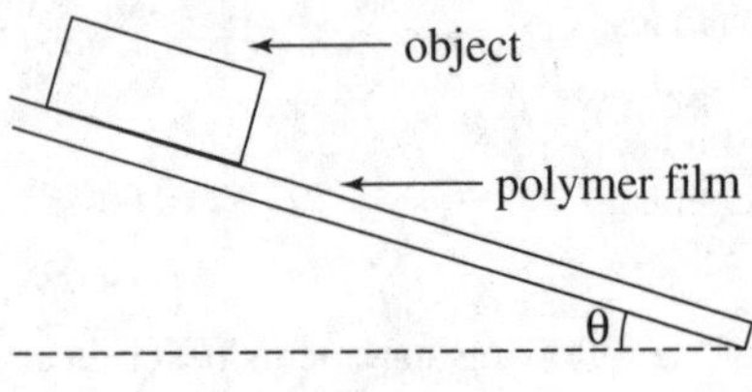

Figure 1

Objects were placed on the opposite end of the board, and the angle θ at which the object started to slide was recorded. The tangent of this angle represents the coefficient of static friction between the object and the polymer surface. This coefficient is proportional to the force required to move a stationary object. Higher coefficients mean that greater forces of friction must be overcome to initiate movement.

The dimensions of the objects gave them 3 distinct *faces* of unequal area as shown in Figure 2. Unless otherwise stated, the objects were placed on the ramp with Face A down.

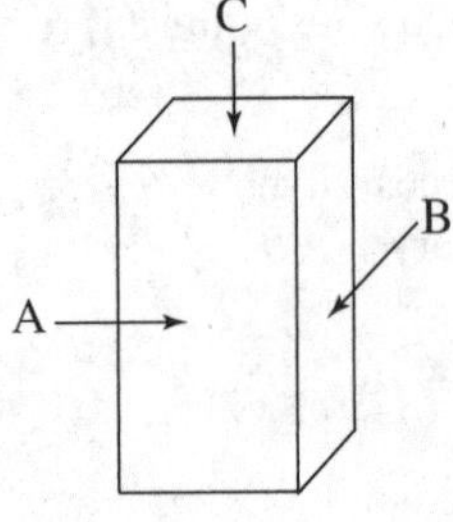

Figure 2

Experiment 1

Four objects made of different materials were placed on the ramp at a temperature of 25°C. The ramp was gradually raised and as soon as the object started to move, the angle θ of the ramp was recorded in Table 1.

Table 1

Object material	θ (degrees)
Granite	12.1
Copper	16.8
Wood	22.0
Brick	31.1

Experiment 2

The procedure for Experiment 1 was repeated with the wooden object, varying which face was placed down on the ramp. Results were recorded in Table 2.

Table 2

Face	θ (degrees)
A	22.0
B	22.0
C	22.0

Experiment 3

The procedure for Experiment 1 was repeated with the wooden object, varying the temperature of the polymer ramp. Results for 5 temperatures were recorded in Table 3.

Table 3

Temperature (°C)	θ (degrees)
0	18.5
25	22.0
50	25.4
75	29.0
100	32.5

GO ON TO THE NEXT PAGE.

Experiment 4

The procedure for Experiment 1 was repeated with multiple wooden objects. For each trial, the objects were stacked on top of each other before raising the ramp. The angle θ where the stack started to slide was recorded in Table 4.

Table 4

Number of objects	θ (degrees)
2	22.0
3	22.0
4	22.0

1. If the procedure used in Experiment 3 had been repeated at a temperature of 62.5°C, the angle required for the object to start moving down the ramp most likely would have been closest to which of the following?

A. 27.2 degrees
B. 29.2 degrees
C. 30.3 degrees
D. 31.4 degrees

2. Suppose the students had placed the 4 objects used in Experiment 1 on the ramp when it was flat and pushed each of the objects, such that the amount of force applied to each object gradually increased until it moved. Based on the results of Experiment 1, the object made of which material would most likely have taken the *greatest* amount of force to start moving?

F. Brick
G. Wood
H. Copper
J. Granite

3. Based on the results of Experiments 1 and 4, what was the effect, if any, of the weight of the object on the coefficient of static friction?

A. The coefficient of static friction always increased as the object's weight increased.
B. The coefficient of static friction always decreased as the object's weight increased.
C. The coefficient of static friction increased and then decreased as the object's weight increased.
D. The coefficient of static friction was not affected by the weight of the object.

4. In Experiment 1, the reason the students used objects made of different materials was most likely to vary the amount of frictional force between the:

F. plastic board and the polymer surface.
G. various objects and the polymer surface.
H. objects made of different materials when brought into contact with each other.
J. stacked objects, so that the objects would not fall over when the angle of the ramp was raised high enough to cause motion.

5. Which of the following ranks the different types of objects used, in order, from the material that presented the greatest resistance to movement to the material that presented the least resistance to movement?

A. Granite, copper, wood, brick
B. Copper, wood, granite, brick
C. Granite, wood, brick, copper
D. Brick, wood, copper, granite

6. The main purpose of Experiment 3 was to determine the effects of temperature on which of the following variables?

F. Coefficient of static friction between wood and wood
G. Coefficient of static friction between wood and polymer
H. Mass of the wooden object
J. Total frictional force of the polymer on all objects placed on the ramp

7. Suppose the procedure in Experiment 1 were repeated in a new trial with the granite block placed with Face C against the polymer surface of the ramp. Based on the results in Tables 1 and 2, the force required to move the stationary block in the new trial would be:

A. less than the force required to move the block in Experiment 1 because the force is directly proportional to the surface area.
B. the same as the force required to move the block in Experiment 1 because the force is directly proportional to the surface area.
C. less than the force required to move the block in Experiment 1 because the force is directly proportional to the coefficient of static friction.
D. the same as the force required to move the block in Experiment 1 because the force is directly proportional to the coefficient of static friction.

GO ON TO THE NEXT PAGE.

Passage II

Despite a global campaign since 1988 to eradicate *poliomyelitis* (polio), the virus that causes this disease continues to be endemic in four countries. This polio virus, which can exist as Type 1, Type 2, or Type 3, is most often transmitted through water that is contaminated by human waste. People can be immunized from this virus with a highly effective vaccine, which can be administered orally or by injection. Recent analyses of polio virus transmission have focused on the four polio-endemic countries: India, Pakistan, Afghanistan, and Nigeria.

Study 1

In 2004, a temporary ban on polio vaccines was instituted in Nigeria in response to concerns that they were contaminated. Researchers reviewed World Health Organization (WHO) records to determine the number of Type 1 polio virus infections that were reported in Nigeria in 2004 and tallied their findings by month (see Figure 1). The World Health Organization has noted that in polio-endemic countries, official records underestimate the number of people actually infected, because numerous infected individuals do not report their symptoms to clinics or rely on local therapists who are not surveyed. In a polio-endemic country, for every person who has reported an infection, as many as ten people may actually be infected in the local population.

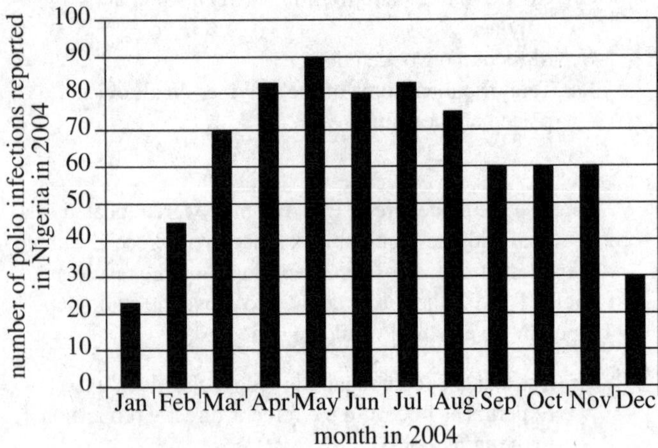

Figure 1

Study 2

Although polio eradication efforts have been most consistent in the urban areas of polio-endemic countries, these areas also have a high risk for a reemergence of polio, especially when the large urban populations are exposed to water contaminated with wastes that harbor the polio virus. In 2007, researchers analyzed the number of people who reported infections with Type 3 polio virus in the five largest cities in India. These cities were Mumbai in western India, New Delhi and Kolkata in northern India, and Chennai and Hyderabad in southern India. The analysis was undertaken in the months of June and August. June 2007 was chosen as a representative month for the dry summer season in India, during which there was minimal rainfall. August 2007 was chosen as a representative month for the wet monsoon season in India, during which there was daily rainfall. The results of the findings are shown in Figure 2.

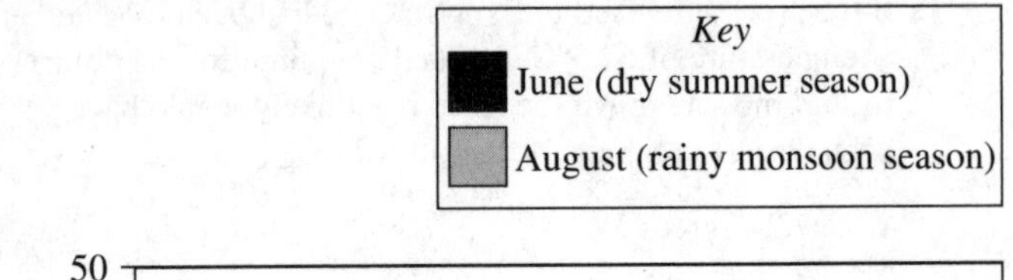

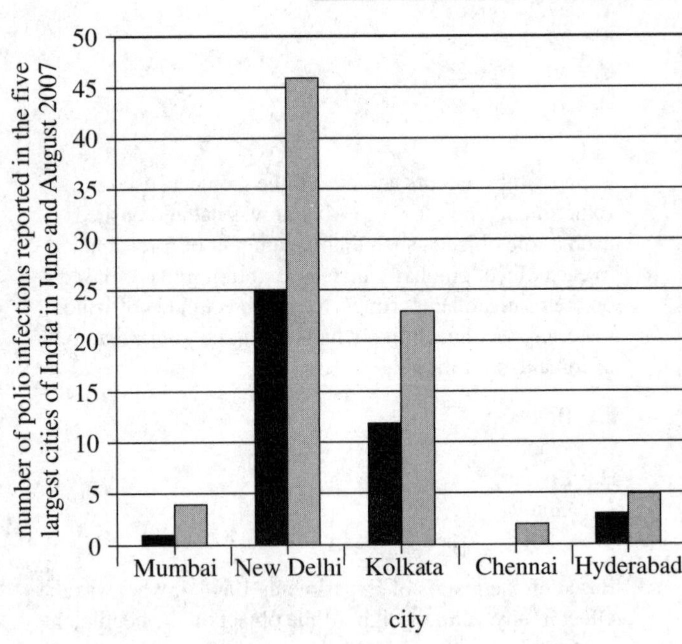

Figure 2

GO ON TO THE NEXT PAGE.

8. Based on Figure 1, which of the following is closest to the average number of polio cases reported per month in Nigeria in 2004 ?

F. 35
G. 55
H. 65
J. 75

9. According to Figure 1, the greatest increase in the number of reported polio infections in Nigeria occurred between which two months?

A. February and March
B. March to April
C. April to May
D. November and December

10. It is estimated that for every person infected with the polio virus in an endemic country, there are 200 people at risk for contracting the virus. Given the results of Study 1, how many people would have been at risk for becoming infected with the polio virus in Nigeria in June 2004 ?

F. 80
G. 200
H. 800
J. 16,000

11. Given the information in Figure 2, which of the following might explain the difference in reported cases of polio in major Indian cities between June and August of 2007 ?

A. Water is more likely to become contaminated with polio-infected human waste in periods of high rainfall.
B. Water is less likely to become contaminated with polio-infected human waste in periods of high rainfall.
C. The polio virus infects more people in India during the summer and monsoon seasons than during the autumn and winter seasons.
D. Those diagnosed with the polio virus in June are able to recover by August.

12. Which of the following hypotheses was most likely tested in Study 2 ?

F. The number of reported cases of polio infections varies significantly between Nigeria and India.
G. Most cases of polio infections are not reported to medical authorities in India.
H. Polio infections affect more people in certain regions in India than in other regions.
J. The number of reported cases of polio infections in India is greatest during the summer and least during the winter.

13. Polio-endemic countries are located in warm climates that harbor many mosquitoes. Would the presence of mosquitoes directly affect the transmission of the polio virus?

A. Yes, because the polio virus is primarily transmitted through mosquitoes.
B. Yes, because the polio virus is primarily transmitted through human waste.
C. No, because the polio virus is primarily transmitted through mosquitoes.
D. No, because the polio virus is primarily transmitted through human waste.

14. The comparison of reported polio infections in India in 2007, as shown in Figure 2, indicates that relative to the number of people in Kolkata infected with polio in June, the number of people infected with polio in Kolkata in August was approximately:

F. half as much.
G. the same.
H. twice as much.
J. ten times as much.

GO ON TO THE NEXT PAGE.

Passage III

Soil salinity is the concentration of potentially harmful salts dissolved in the groundwater that fills soil pores. Salinity is determined by measuring a soil's *electrical conductivity (EC)* and *exchangeable sodium percentage (ESP)*. High EC indicates a high concentration of dissolved salt particles; ESP indicates the proportion of electrical conductivity that is due to dissolved sodium ions.

Soil samples were collected from five different distances west of a particular river. Figure 1 shows the electrical conductivity of the soil samples (in milli-Siemens per centimeter, mS/cm) at four different depth ranges measured.

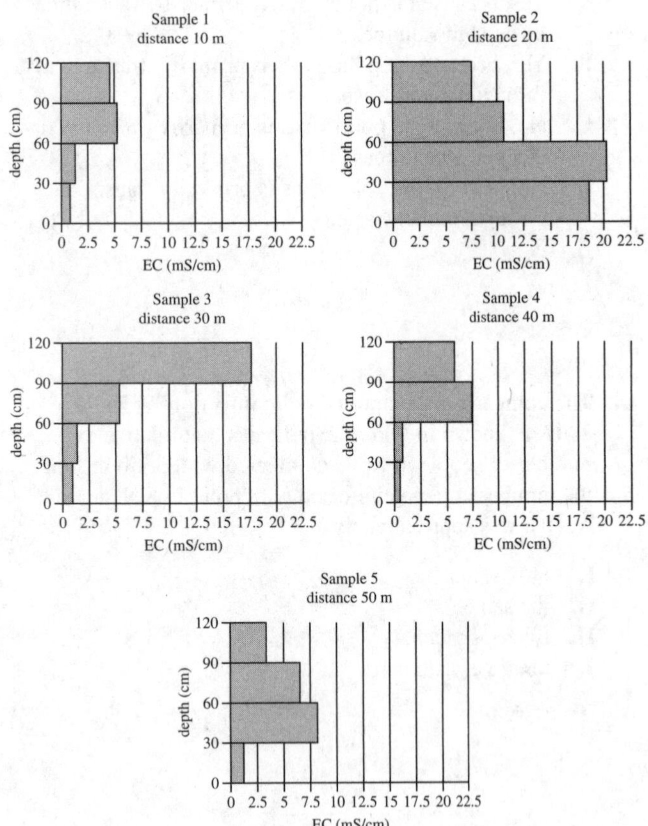

Figure 1

Figure 2 shows the exchangeable sodium percentage of the five sites at different depths.

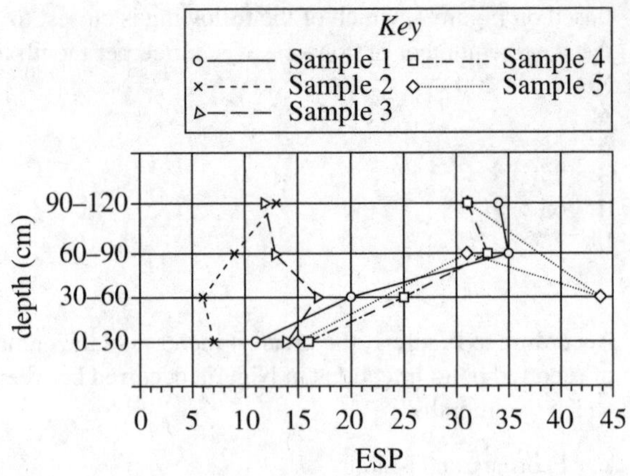

Figure 2

15. In Sample 2, as the EC increases from its lowest value to its highest value, the ESP:

    A. increases only.
    B. decreases only.
    C. increases and then decreases.
    D. decreases and then increases.

16. Figure 2 indicates that, compared with the soil tested in Sample 1, the soil tested in Sample 4 contains:

    F. a higher percentage of sodium ions throughout.
    G. a lower percentage of sodium ions throughout.
    H. a higher percentage of sodium ions at shallower depths only.
    J. a lower percentage of sodium ions at shallower depths only.

17. According to Figure 2, in the soil collected in Sample 3 at a depth of 30–60 cm, approximately what percent of the soil conductivity is due to sodium ions?

    A. 14%
    B. 17%
    C. 24%
    D. 44%

18. Based on Figures 1 and 2, the electrical conductivity due to sodium ions in the sample collected 40 m west of the river was:

    F. greatest at a depth of 90–120 cm.
    G. greatest at a depth of 0–30 cm.
    H. least at a depth of 30–60 cm.
    J. least at a depth of 0–30 cm.

GO ON TO THE NEXT PAGE.

19. Based on Figure 2, which of the following figures best represents the exchangeable sodium percentage for the five soil samples collected at a depth of 90–120 cm ?

A.

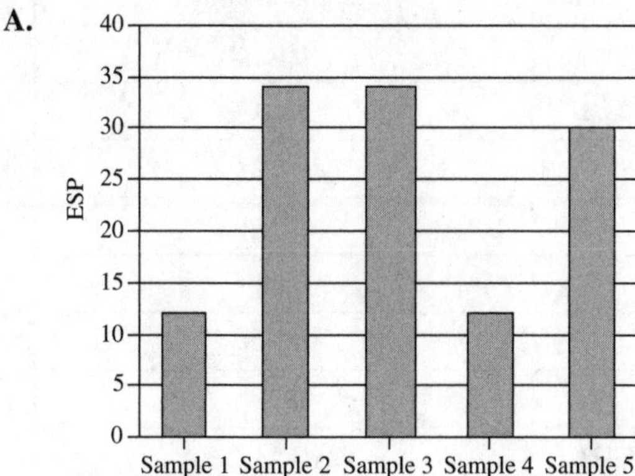

B.

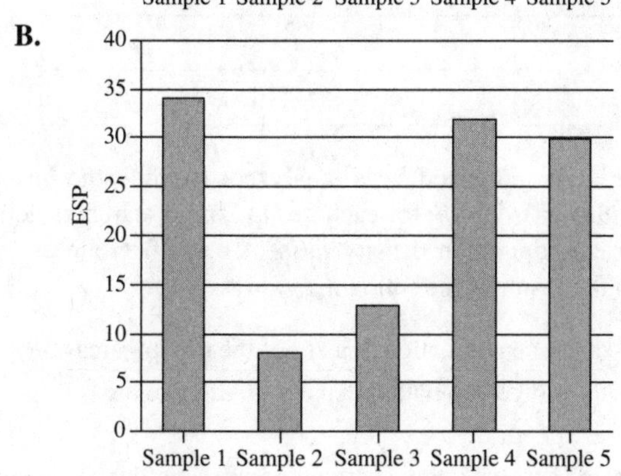

C.

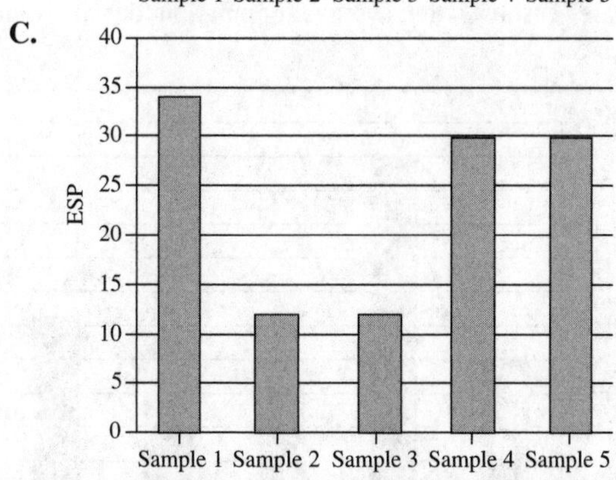

D.

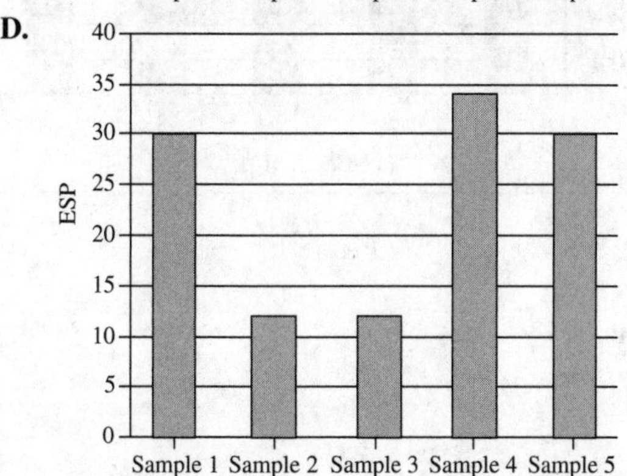

20. A student claimed that as soil moves away from a major water source, such as a river, the salinity of the soil increases. Is this claim supported by Figures 1 and 2 ?

F. No; the electrical conductivity and exchangeable sodium percentage both decreased from Sample 1 to Sample 5.

G. No; there was no consistent trend for electrical conductivity and exchangeable sodium percentage.

H. Yes; the electrical conductivity and exchangeable sodium percentage both increased from Sample 1 to Sample 5.

J. Yes; the electrical conductivity increased and exchangeable sodium percentage decreased from Sample 1 to Sample 5.

GO ON TO THE NEXT PAGE.

Passage IV

A group of researchers performed the following study in order to investigate declines in primarily carnivorous polar bear populations in the Arctic over a 10-year period.

Study

The researchers obtained previously collected data from several areas previously identified as polar bear habitats. From this data, the researchers selected sixty 5 km × 5 km blocks that do not overlap with one another. The blocks were selected to fall into six groups, each with a different set of conditions selected in order to conform to criteria for listing animals as threatened species. Previous research has indicated that Arctic sea ice and available food are among the factors which may affect polar bear populations.

Table 1 identifies each of the groups utilized in the study. Conditions other than the ones listed were considered to be normal.

Table 1

Group	Conditions
1	These areas had significantly decreased populations of marine mammals consumed by polar bears.
2	These areas had significantly increased populations of seaweed commonly consumed by marine mammals.
3	These areas had been subject to excess thawing of Arctic sea ice.
4	These areas were subject to the same conditions as Groups 1 and 3.
5	These areas were subject to the same conditions as Groups 2 and 3.
6	These areas represent unaffected polar bear habitat.

Data for each of the plots was collected, and the population density of polar bears was calculated in terms of adult polar bears/km^2. Table 2 shows the population density of the blocks in Group 6.

Table 2

Area label	Population density of Group 6 areas (polar bears/km^2)
A	0.93
B	2.10
C	0.21
D	0.72
E	0.88
F	0.72
G	0.91
H	0.53
I	1.12
J	0.74

The data collected was analyzed to find the *average population density ratio* for each group. The researchers defined the average population density ratio of a given group as being equal to the result of the following expression:

$$\frac{\text{average population density of the group's areas}}{\text{average population density of Group 6 areas}}$$

Figure 1 shows the average population density ratio of Groups 1–5.

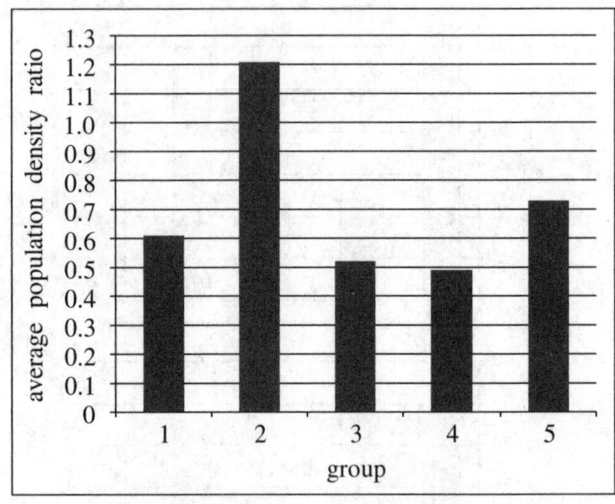

Figure 1

GO ON TO THE NEXT PAGE.

21. Which of the following statements provides the best explanation for why the researchers collected data for Group 6 in their study?

A. Group 6 provided data indicating the types of predators that most threaten polar bears in their natural habitat.
B. Group 6 provided a standard by which the other groups could be compared in order to determine how each set of conditions affected polar bear populations.
C. Group 6 provided a means by which the researchers could carefully identify and select the conditions for the remaining five groups.
D. Group 6 provided a means of determining the greatest number of polar bears that would be likely to survive in an area of 25 km^2.

22. Which one of the following is a question that most likely explains why Group 2 areas were included in the study?

F. Does an increase in the food source of their prey affect the population density of polar bears?
G. If additional masses of seaweed were to be introduced to the Arctic, would polar bears be increasingly omnivorous?
H. If additional masses of seaweed were to be introduced to the Arctic, would prey population density increase?
J. Does an increase in the number of prey animals living in the same area as polar bears affect the amount of Arctic ice?

23. Which of the following correctly ranks Groups 1–5 from the group where the conditions are *most* conducive to polar bear population density in the study to the group where the conditions are *least* conducive?

A. Group 1, Group 2, Group 3, Group 4, Group 5
B. Group 4, Group 3, Group 1, Group 5, Group 2
C. Group 2, Group 5, Group 1, Group 3, Group 4
D. Group 2, Group 1, Group 5, Group 3, Group 4

24. Which of the following is most likely an organism that the researchers identified as exhibiting a significantly decreased population when defining Group 1 ?

F. Snowy owl
G. Seal
H. Salmon
J. Polar bear

25. *Synergy* between two effects is said to exist when their combined effect is greater than the sum of each effect considered separately. The study appears to be designed such that the researchers can investigate possible synergy in which of the following two groups?

A. Groups 1 and 2
B. Groups 1 and 4
C. Groups 4 and 5
D. Groups 1 and 3

26. Before performing their analysis of the data, the researchers developed four different hypotheses. Each one of the four hypotheses below is supported by the results of the study EXCEPT:

F. Declining prey populations have had some effect on polar bear populations.
G. The melting of Arctic sea ice has a greater effect on polar bear populations than declining prey populations.
H. Declining prey populations have a greater effect on polar bear populations than the melting of Arctic sea ice.
J. The melting of Arctic sea ice has had some effect on polar bear populations.

27. According to the information in the passage and Table 2, which of the following is closest to the total number of polar bears found in all ten areas of Group 6 ?

A. 10
B. 45
C. 90
D. 225

GO ON TO THE NEXT PAGE.

Passage V

Methane (CH_4) is an important energy source and a powerful greenhouse gas. CH_4 levels in the atmosphere are increasing, largely as a result of increasing livestock populations and energy emissions. Two scientists debate possible consequences of rising levels of atmospheric methane.

Scientist 1

Increasing CH_4 levels are a serious concern because, in the atmosphere, CH_4 can be converted into *formaldehyde* (H_2CO). H_2CO is a dangerous chemical, banned in some countries and used as an embalming fluid in others.

When *ozone* (O_3) is struck by solar radiation (light) in the presence of water, *hydroxyl radicals* (·OH) are created (Reaction 1):

(1) $$\text{light} + O_3 + H_2O \rightarrow 2{\cdot}OH + O_2$$

When ·OH comes into contact with CH_4, another radical, $\cdot CH_3$, is formed (Reaction 2):

(2) $$\cdot OH + CH_4 \rightarrow \cdot CH_3 + H_2O$$

In the presence of oxygen (O_2) and nitric oxide (NO), the highly reactive $\cdot CH_3$ is converted into H_2CO (Reaction 3):

(3) $$\cdot CH_3 + NO + 2O_2 \rightarrow H_2CO + NO_2 + HO_2$$

The product HO_2 is unstable and reacts with NO, yielding more ·OH (Reaction 4):

(4) $$HO_2 + NO \rightarrow NO_2 + \cdot OH$$

Together, Reactions 2–4 are called a *chain reaction* because the ·OH formed in Reaction 4 can react with another CH_4 molecule in Reaction 2:

(2) $$\cdot OH + CH_4 \rightarrow \cdot CH_3 + H_2O$$

(3) $$\cdot CH_3 + NO + 2O_2 \rightarrow H_2CO + NO_2 + HO_2$$

(4) $$HO_2 + NO \rightarrow NO_2 + \cdot OH$$

As a result, one ·OH can convert a great deal of CH_4. At current CH_4 levels, this chain reaction is the primary fate of atmospheric ·OH, making the formation of H_2CO an urgent concern.

Scientist 2

H_2CO is a dangerous chemical, but atmospheric formaldehyde levels will not increase dramatically due to methane emissions. *Carbon monoxide* (CO) generation may be the greater concern. Hydroxyl radicals can break down methane, leading to the formation of H_2CO and nitric oxide, as in Reactions 1–4; in the presence of light, however, H_2CO quickly decomposes to CO and *hydrogen*, H_2 (Reaction 5):

(5) $$H_2CO \rightarrow H_2 + CO$$

Furthermore, the ·OH generated by Reactions 1 and 4 will react rapidly with any H_2CO in the atmosphere to produce CO and water (Reaction 6):

(6) $$H_2CO + 2{\cdot}OH \rightarrow CO + 2H_2O$$

In addition to reducing the amount of H_2CO by breaking down the H_2CO molecule, this reaction removes OH from the atmosphere, inhibiting the chain reaction of Reactions 2–4.

28. Further investigation has shown that Reaction 6 occurs on a large scale. Which of the following statements explains how the new evidence *most weakens* the argument of Scientist 1 ?

F. The ·OH produced in Reaction 4 reacts with CH_4.
G. The ·OH produced in Reaction 4 reacts with H_2CO.
H. The H_2O produced in Reaction 6 reacts with light and O_3.
J. The ·OH produced in Reaction 6 reacts with H_2CO.

29. Which of the following substances do the two scientists agree must be present in order for $\cdot CH_3$ to be generated by atmospheric methane?

A. H_3O^+
B. NO_2
C. HNO_3
D. O_3

GO ON TO THE NEXT PAGE.

30. Which of the following graphs reflects Scientist 1's hypothesis of how levels of H_2CO in the atmosphere will change as more CH_4 is released into the atmosphere?

F.

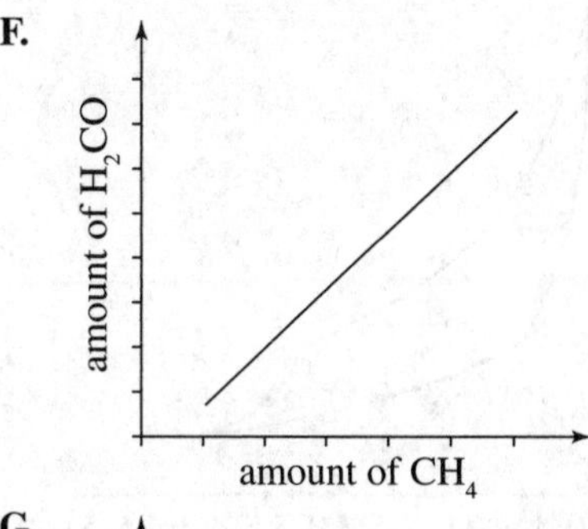

G.

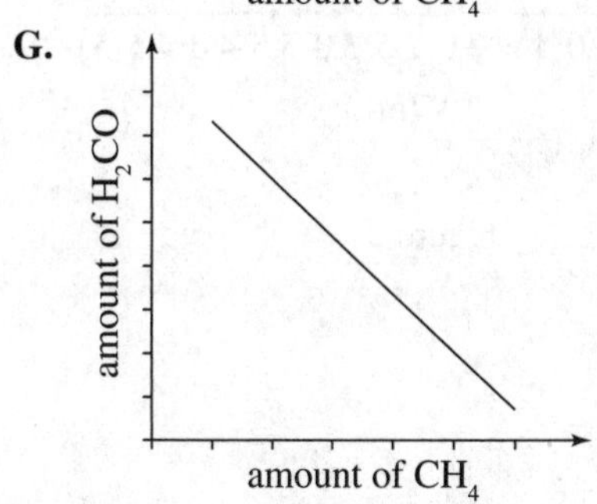

H.

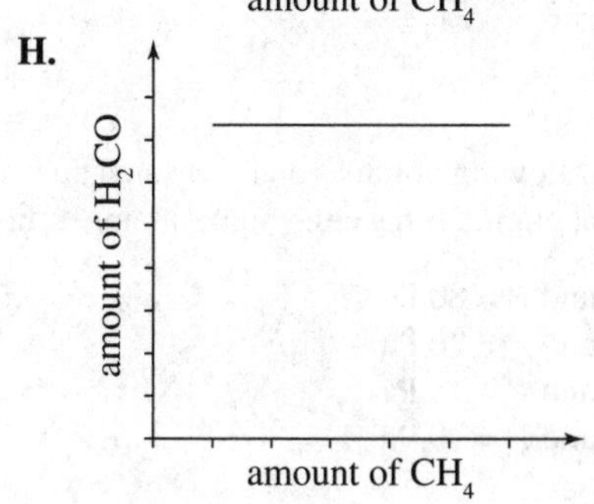

J.

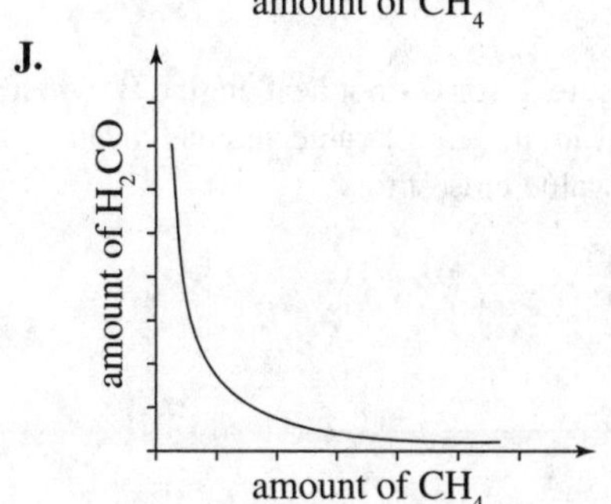

31. A student suggested that the molecular mass of either product in Reaction 5 would be greater than the molecular mass of the reactant in Reaction 5. Is he correct?

A. No; H_2CO is composed not of molecules, but of atoms.
B. Yes; the mass of a molecule of H_2CO is greater than the mass of either reactant.
C. No; the mass of a molecule of H_2CO is greater than the mass of either product.
D. Yes; the mass of a molecule of CO is greater than the mass of a molecule of H_2.

32. In certain parts of the atmosphere, the amount of O_3 is decreasing. As O_3 levels decrease, which of the following would Scientist 1 *most strongly agree with* regarding the levels of $\cdot CH_3$ and H_2CO in the atmosphere?

F. The amount of $\cdot CH_3$ would increase and the amount of H_2CO would decrease.
G. The amount of $\cdot CH_3$ would decrease and the level of H_2CO would remain constant.
H. The amounts of $\cdot CH_3$ and H_2CO would both decrease.
J. The amounts of $\cdot CH_3$ and H_2CO would both increase.

33. Of the following statements, with which would Scientist 2 *most strongly disagree*?

A. O_3 is involved in the generation of H_2CO in the atmosphere.
B. $\cdot OH$ is contributing to the formation of carbon monoxide in the atmosphere.
C. Solar radiation contributes to the breakdown of CH_4.
D. As CH_4 emissions increase, levels of H_2CO will rise dramatically.

34. After examining Scientist 1's hypothesis, Scientist 2 claimed that Reaction 3 would lead to increased levels of carbon monoxide. By which of the following explanations would Scientist 2 most likely support this argument?

F. Reaction 3 reduces the amount of NO present, inhibiting Reaction 4.
G. Reaction 3 produces H_2CO, which can react in Reaction 5 and Reaction 6.
H. Reaction 3 produces HO_2, which can react with H_2CO to produce CO.
J. Reaction 3 reduces the amount of O_2 present, making it more difficult for CO to form.

GO ON TO THE NEXT PAGE.

Passage VI

A *Carnot heat engine* is an engine which runs by compressing and expanding a gas and transferring heat.

Figures 1 and 2 show the changes in pressure, *P*, and volume, *V*, that occur as two Carnot heat engines, A and B, run. For every gas, $PV = \Omega T$, where Ω is a constant and *T* represents the temperature.

The cycle begins as the gas is at its highest temperature and pressure. First, the gas expands, so volume increases while pressure decreases. As the gas expands, it can do work, such as pushing a piston. After the gas has run out of thermal energy and can no longer do work, it is at its lowest temperature and pressure. At this point, the gas begins to be compressed. As the gas is compressed, pressure increases while volume decreases. Once the pressure and volume reach a certain point, the temperature begins to rise again. In every Carnot heat engine, the gas ends at the same pressure, temperature, and volume as it began, thus completing a cycle.

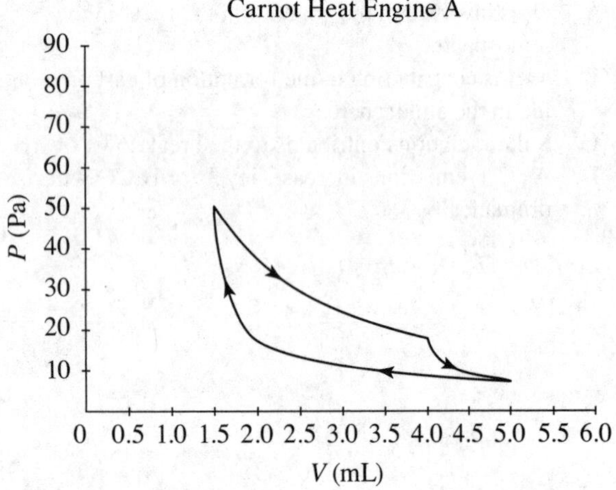

Figure 1

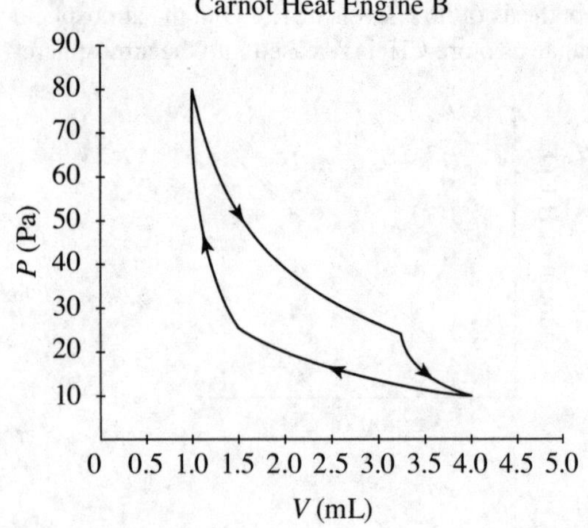

Figure 2

35. At which of the following volumes and pressures does the gas in Carnot heat engine B have the highest temperature?

A. $V = 1.0$ mL and $P = 80$ Pa
B. $V = 2.0$ mL and $P = 20$ Pa
C. $V = 3.5$ mL and $P = 15$ Pa
D. $V = 4.0$ mL and $P = 10$ Pa

36. According to Figure 2, for Carnot heat engine B, when *V* was decreasing from its largest value and had a value of 2.0 mL, *P* had a value closest to:

F. 10 Pa.
G. 20 Pa.
H. 40 Pa.
J. 70 Pa.

GO ON TO THE NEXT PAGE.

37. For a new Carnot heat engine, F, a partial graph of V versus P is obtained.

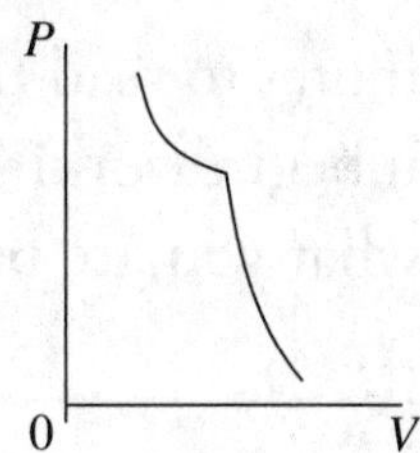

If Carnot heat engine F behaves like Carnot heat engines A and B, the remainder of the graph of V versus P for Carnot heat engine F will look most like which of the following?

A. P, 0, V

B. P, 0, V

C. P, 0, V

D. P, 0, V

38. For Carnot heat engine A, the minimum value of P was obtained at a V closest to:

F. 0.5 mL.
G. 2.0 mL.
H. 4.0 mL.
J. 5.0 mL.

39. Consider the largest value of V and the smallest value of V in Figure 2. How are these values related?

A. The smallest value of V is –4 times the largest value of V.
B. The smallest value of V is $\frac{1}{8}$ times the largest value of V.
C. The smallest value of V is $\frac{1}{4}$ times the largest value of V.
D. The smallest value of V is 4 times the largest value of V.

40. The *reversible isothermal expansion* step of a Carnot heat engine cycle takes place when P is decreased from its highest value and V is increased from its lowest value. According to Figure 1, the *reversible isothermal expansion* step for Carnot heat engine A begins when V is closest to:

F. 1.5 mL.
G. 2.25 mL.
H. 3.0 mL.
J. 3.5 mL.

END OF TEST 4
STOP! DO NOT RETURN TO ANY OTHER TEST.

Directions

This is a test of your writing skills. You will have forty (40) minutes to read the prompt, plan your response, and write an essay in English. Before you begin working, read all material in this test booklet carefully to understand exactly what you are being asked to do.

You will write your answer on the lined pages in the answer document provided. Your writing on those pages will be scored. You may use the unlined pages in this test booklet to plan your essay. Your work on these pages will not be scored.

Your essay will be evaluated based on the evidence it provides of your ability to:

- clearly state your own perspective on a complex issue and analyze the relationship between your perspective and at least one other perspective
- develop and support your ideas with reasoning and examples
- organize your ideas clearly and logically
- communicate your ideas effectively in standard written English

Lay your pencil down immediately when time is called.

DO NOT OPEN THIS BOOK UNTIL YOU ARE TOLD TO DO SO.

Composition paper for the essay can be found beginning on page 81.

Cell Phones While Driving

In only a short time, the use of cell phones, or "smartphones," has significantly increased. In direct relation, problems with their use at certain times have also risen. While driving, people use the smartphone for various activities such as texting, searching the Internet, or mapping a route with GPS. Certain studies suggest that operating a vehicle while using a cell phone is almost as severe, if not the same, as driving while intoxicated. Certain parts of the world have banned talking on the phone while driving, whereas regulations in the United States currently vary from state to state.

Read and carefully consider these perspectives. Each suggests a particular way of thinking about the conflict between driving with a cell phone and both public and personal safety.

Perspective One

Teenage drivers are more likely to use phones in cars. Teens are already the highest-risk drivers, so a cell-phone ban would decrease reckless driving at a proportionately higher rate among the most dangerous group.

Perspective Two

There will always be distractions. Anything—other passengers, commotion outside, news interruptions on the radio—might distract a driver. Rather than ban cell phones, spend time teaching drivers how to better handle interferences.

Perspective Three

Holding a cell phone while driving is dangerous. One hand is not on the steering wheel, which can significantly hinder the reaction time one needs to deal with an occurrence. In the case of an emergency, having one hand unavailable will slow the driver's reaction time and increase the chance of an accident.

Essay Task

Write a unified, coherent essay in which you evaluate multiple perspectives on the usage of cell phones while driving. In your essay, be sure to:

- clearly state your own perspective on the issue and analyze the relationship between your perspective and at least one other perspective
- develop and support your ideas with reasoning and examples
- organize your ideas clearly and logically
- communicate your ideas effectively in standard written English

Your perspective may be in full agreement with any of the others, in partial agreement, or wholly different. Whatever the case, support your ideas with logical reasoning and detailed, persuasive examples.

ACT Diagnostic Test Form

USE A SOFT LEAD NO. 2 PENCIL ONLY. (Do NOT use a mechanical pencil, ink, ballpoint, correction fluid, or felt-tip pen.)

E-MAIL: ______________________

PHONE NO.: ______________________
(Print)

SCHOOL: ______________________

CLASS OF: ______________________

IMPORTANT: Please fill in these boxes exactly as shown on the back cover of your tests book.

2. TEST FORM

3. TEST CODE

0 1 2 3 4 5 6 7 8 9

ALL examinees must complete Blocks A, B, C, and D – please print.

A NAME, MAILING ADDRESS, AND TELEPHONE
(Please print.)

Last Name | First Name | MI (Middle Initial)

House Number & Street (Apt. No.); or PO Box & No.; or RR & No.

City | State/Province | ZIP/Postal Code

Area Code / Number | Country

B MATCH NAME
(First 5 letters of last name)

A B C D E F G H I J K L M N O P Q R S T U V W X Y Z

C MATCH NUMBER

1 2 3 4 5 6 7 8 9 0

D DATE OF BIRTH

Month | Day | Year

January
February
March
April
May
June
July
August
September
October
November
December

Marking Directions: Mark only **one** oval for each question. Fill in response completely. Erase errors cleanly without smudging.

Correct mark:

Do NOT use these *incorrect* or *bad* marks.

Incorrect marks:
Overlapping mark:
Cross-out mark:
Smudged erasure:
Mark is too light:

BOOKLET NUMBER

1 2 3 4 5 6 7 8 9 0

FORM

Print your 3-character **Test Form** in the boxes above and fill in the corresponding oval at the right.

BE SURE TO FILL IN THE CORRECT FORM OVAL.

PRE

THIS PAGE INTENTIONALLY LEFT BLANK

The Princeton Review Diagnostic ACT Form

USE A SOFT LEAD NO. 2 PENCIL ONLY. (Do NOT use a mechanical pencil, ink, ballpoint, correction fluid, or felt-tip pen.)

TEST 1: ENGLISH

1 Ⓐ Ⓑ Ⓒ Ⓓ	14 Ⓕ Ⓖ Ⓗ Ⓙ	27 Ⓐ Ⓑ Ⓒ Ⓓ	40 Ⓕ Ⓖ Ⓗ Ⓙ	53 Ⓐ Ⓑ Ⓒ Ⓓ	66 Ⓕ Ⓖ Ⓗ Ⓙ
2 Ⓕ Ⓖ Ⓗ Ⓙ	15 Ⓐ Ⓑ Ⓒ Ⓓ	28 Ⓕ Ⓖ Ⓗ Ⓙ	41 Ⓐ Ⓑ Ⓒ Ⓓ	54 Ⓕ Ⓖ Ⓗ Ⓙ	67 Ⓐ Ⓑ Ⓒ Ⓓ
3 Ⓐ Ⓑ Ⓒ Ⓓ	16 Ⓕ Ⓖ Ⓗ Ⓙ	29 Ⓐ Ⓑ Ⓒ Ⓓ	42 Ⓕ Ⓖ Ⓗ Ⓙ	55 Ⓐ Ⓑ Ⓒ Ⓓ	68 Ⓕ Ⓖ Ⓗ Ⓙ
4 Ⓕ Ⓖ Ⓗ Ⓙ	17 Ⓐ Ⓑ Ⓒ Ⓓ	30 Ⓕ Ⓖ Ⓗ Ⓙ	43 Ⓐ Ⓑ Ⓒ Ⓓ	56 Ⓕ Ⓖ Ⓗ Ⓙ	69 Ⓐ Ⓑ Ⓒ Ⓓ
5 Ⓐ Ⓑ Ⓒ Ⓓ	18 Ⓕ Ⓖ Ⓗ Ⓙ	31 Ⓐ Ⓑ Ⓒ Ⓓ	44 Ⓕ Ⓖ Ⓗ Ⓙ	57 Ⓐ Ⓑ Ⓒ Ⓓ	70 Ⓕ Ⓖ Ⓗ Ⓙ
6 Ⓕ Ⓖ Ⓗ Ⓙ	19 Ⓐ Ⓑ Ⓒ Ⓓ	32 Ⓕ Ⓖ Ⓗ Ⓙ	45 Ⓐ Ⓑ Ⓒ Ⓓ	58 Ⓕ Ⓖ Ⓗ Ⓙ	71 Ⓐ Ⓑ Ⓒ Ⓓ
7 Ⓐ Ⓑ Ⓒ Ⓓ	20 Ⓕ Ⓖ Ⓗ Ⓙ	33 Ⓐ Ⓑ Ⓒ Ⓓ	46 Ⓕ Ⓖ Ⓗ Ⓙ	59 Ⓐ Ⓑ Ⓒ Ⓓ	72 Ⓕ Ⓖ Ⓗ Ⓙ
8 Ⓕ Ⓖ Ⓗ Ⓙ	21 Ⓐ Ⓑ Ⓒ Ⓓ	34 Ⓕ Ⓖ Ⓗ Ⓙ	47 Ⓐ Ⓑ Ⓒ Ⓓ	60 Ⓕ Ⓖ Ⓗ Ⓙ	73 Ⓐ Ⓑ Ⓒ Ⓓ
9 Ⓐ Ⓑ Ⓒ Ⓓ	22 Ⓕ Ⓖ Ⓗ Ⓙ	35 Ⓐ Ⓑ Ⓒ Ⓓ	48 Ⓕ Ⓖ Ⓗ Ⓙ	61 Ⓐ Ⓑ Ⓒ Ⓓ	74 Ⓕ Ⓖ Ⓗ Ⓙ
10 Ⓕ Ⓖ Ⓗ Ⓙ	23 Ⓐ Ⓑ Ⓒ Ⓓ	36 Ⓕ Ⓖ Ⓗ Ⓙ	49 Ⓐ Ⓑ Ⓒ Ⓓ	62 Ⓕ Ⓖ Ⓗ Ⓙ	75 Ⓐ Ⓑ Ⓒ Ⓓ
11 Ⓐ Ⓑ Ⓒ Ⓓ	24 Ⓕ Ⓖ Ⓗ Ⓙ	37 Ⓐ Ⓑ Ⓒ Ⓓ	50 Ⓕ Ⓖ Ⓗ Ⓙ	63 Ⓐ Ⓑ Ⓒ Ⓓ	
12 Ⓕ Ⓖ Ⓗ Ⓙ	25 Ⓐ Ⓑ Ⓒ Ⓓ	38 Ⓕ Ⓖ Ⓗ Ⓙ	51 Ⓐ Ⓑ Ⓒ Ⓓ	64 Ⓕ Ⓖ Ⓗ Ⓙ	
13 Ⓐ Ⓑ Ⓒ Ⓓ	26 Ⓕ Ⓖ Ⓗ Ⓙ	39 Ⓐ Ⓑ Ⓒ Ⓓ	52 Ⓕ Ⓖ Ⓗ Ⓙ	65 Ⓐ Ⓑ Ⓒ Ⓓ	

TEST 2: MATHEMATICS

1 Ⓐ Ⓑ Ⓒ Ⓓ Ⓔ	11 Ⓐ Ⓑ Ⓒ Ⓓ Ⓔ	21 Ⓐ Ⓑ Ⓒ Ⓓ Ⓔ	31 Ⓐ Ⓑ Ⓒ Ⓓ Ⓔ	41 Ⓐ Ⓑ Ⓒ Ⓓ Ⓔ	51 Ⓐ Ⓑ Ⓒ Ⓓ Ⓔ
2 Ⓕ Ⓖ Ⓗ Ⓙ Ⓚ	12 Ⓕ Ⓖ Ⓗ Ⓙ Ⓚ	22 Ⓕ Ⓖ Ⓗ Ⓙ Ⓚ	32 Ⓕ Ⓖ Ⓗ Ⓙ Ⓚ	42 Ⓕ Ⓖ Ⓗ Ⓙ Ⓚ	52 Ⓕ Ⓖ Ⓗ Ⓙ Ⓚ
3 Ⓐ Ⓑ Ⓒ Ⓓ Ⓔ	13 Ⓐ Ⓑ Ⓒ Ⓓ Ⓔ	23 Ⓐ Ⓑ Ⓒ Ⓓ Ⓔ	33 Ⓐ Ⓑ Ⓒ Ⓓ Ⓔ	43 Ⓐ Ⓑ Ⓒ Ⓓ Ⓔ	53 Ⓐ Ⓑ Ⓒ Ⓓ Ⓔ
4 Ⓕ Ⓖ Ⓗ Ⓙ Ⓚ	14 Ⓕ Ⓖ Ⓗ Ⓙ Ⓚ	24 Ⓕ Ⓖ Ⓗ Ⓙ Ⓚ	34 Ⓕ Ⓖ Ⓗ Ⓙ Ⓚ	44 Ⓕ Ⓖ Ⓗ Ⓙ Ⓚ	54 Ⓕ Ⓖ Ⓗ Ⓙ Ⓚ
5 Ⓐ Ⓑ Ⓒ Ⓓ Ⓔ	15 Ⓐ Ⓑ Ⓒ Ⓓ Ⓔ	25 Ⓐ Ⓑ Ⓒ Ⓓ Ⓔ	35 Ⓐ Ⓑ Ⓒ Ⓓ Ⓔ	45 Ⓐ Ⓑ Ⓒ Ⓓ Ⓔ	55 Ⓐ Ⓑ Ⓒ Ⓓ Ⓔ
6 Ⓕ Ⓖ Ⓗ Ⓙ Ⓚ	16 Ⓕ Ⓖ Ⓗ Ⓙ Ⓚ	26 Ⓕ Ⓖ Ⓗ Ⓙ Ⓚ	36 Ⓕ Ⓖ Ⓗ Ⓙ Ⓚ	46 Ⓕ Ⓖ Ⓗ Ⓙ Ⓚ	56 Ⓕ Ⓖ Ⓗ Ⓙ Ⓚ
7 Ⓐ Ⓑ Ⓒ Ⓓ Ⓔ	17 Ⓐ Ⓑ Ⓒ Ⓓ Ⓔ	27 Ⓐ Ⓑ Ⓒ Ⓓ Ⓔ	37 Ⓐ Ⓑ Ⓒ Ⓓ Ⓔ	47 Ⓐ Ⓑ Ⓒ Ⓓ Ⓔ	57 Ⓐ Ⓑ Ⓒ Ⓓ Ⓔ
8 Ⓕ Ⓖ Ⓗ Ⓙ Ⓚ	18 Ⓕ Ⓖ Ⓗ Ⓙ Ⓚ	28 Ⓕ Ⓖ Ⓗ Ⓙ Ⓚ	38 Ⓕ Ⓖ Ⓗ Ⓙ Ⓚ	48 Ⓕ Ⓖ Ⓗ Ⓙ Ⓚ	58 Ⓕ Ⓖ Ⓗ Ⓙ Ⓚ
9 Ⓐ Ⓑ Ⓒ Ⓓ Ⓔ	19 Ⓐ Ⓑ Ⓒ Ⓓ Ⓔ	29 Ⓐ Ⓑ Ⓒ Ⓓ Ⓔ	39 Ⓐ Ⓑ Ⓒ Ⓓ Ⓔ	49 Ⓐ Ⓑ Ⓒ Ⓓ Ⓔ	59 Ⓐ Ⓑ Ⓒ Ⓓ Ⓔ
10 Ⓕ Ⓖ Ⓗ Ⓙ Ⓚ	20 Ⓕ Ⓖ Ⓗ Ⓙ Ⓚ	30 Ⓕ Ⓖ Ⓗ Ⓙ Ⓚ	40 Ⓕ Ⓖ Ⓗ Ⓙ Ⓚ	50 Ⓕ Ⓖ Ⓗ Ⓙ Ⓚ	60 Ⓕ Ⓖ Ⓗ Ⓙ Ⓚ

The Princeton Review Diagnostic ACT Form

USE A SOFT LEAD NO. 2 PENCIL ONLY. (Do NOT use a mechanical pencil, ink, ballpoint, correction fluid, or felt-tip pen.)

TEST 3: READING

1 Ⓐ Ⓑ Ⓒ Ⓓ	8 Ⓕ Ⓖ Ⓗ Ⓙ	15 Ⓐ Ⓑ Ⓒ Ⓓ	22 Ⓕ Ⓖ Ⓗ Ⓙ	29 Ⓐ Ⓑ Ⓒ Ⓓ	36 Ⓕ Ⓖ Ⓗ Ⓙ
2 Ⓕ Ⓖ Ⓗ Ⓙ	9 Ⓐ Ⓑ Ⓒ Ⓓ	16 Ⓕ Ⓖ Ⓗ Ⓙ	23 Ⓐ Ⓑ Ⓒ Ⓓ	30 Ⓕ Ⓖ Ⓗ Ⓙ	37 Ⓐ Ⓑ Ⓒ Ⓓ
3 Ⓐ Ⓑ Ⓒ Ⓓ	10 Ⓕ Ⓖ Ⓗ Ⓙ	17 Ⓐ Ⓑ Ⓒ Ⓓ	24 Ⓕ Ⓖ Ⓗ Ⓙ	31 Ⓐ Ⓑ Ⓒ Ⓓ	38 Ⓕ Ⓖ Ⓗ Ⓙ
4 Ⓕ Ⓖ Ⓗ Ⓙ	11 Ⓐ Ⓑ Ⓒ Ⓓ	18 Ⓕ Ⓖ Ⓗ Ⓙ	25 Ⓐ Ⓑ Ⓒ Ⓓ	32 Ⓕ Ⓖ Ⓗ Ⓙ	39 Ⓐ Ⓑ Ⓒ Ⓓ
5 Ⓐ Ⓑ Ⓒ Ⓓ	12 Ⓕ Ⓖ Ⓗ Ⓙ	19 Ⓐ Ⓑ Ⓒ Ⓓ	26 Ⓕ Ⓖ Ⓗ Ⓙ	33 Ⓐ Ⓑ Ⓒ Ⓓ	40 Ⓕ Ⓖ Ⓗ Ⓙ
6 Ⓕ Ⓖ Ⓗ Ⓙ	13 Ⓐ Ⓑ Ⓒ Ⓓ	20 Ⓕ Ⓖ Ⓗ Ⓙ	27 Ⓐ Ⓑ Ⓒ Ⓓ	34 Ⓕ Ⓖ Ⓗ Ⓙ	
7 Ⓐ Ⓑ Ⓒ Ⓓ	14 Ⓕ Ⓖ Ⓗ Ⓙ	21 Ⓐ Ⓑ Ⓒ Ⓓ	28 Ⓕ Ⓖ Ⓗ Ⓙ	35 Ⓐ Ⓑ Ⓒ Ⓓ	

TEST 4: SCIENCE

1 Ⓐ Ⓑ Ⓒ Ⓓ	8 Ⓕ Ⓖ Ⓗ Ⓙ	15 Ⓐ Ⓑ Ⓒ Ⓓ	22 Ⓕ Ⓖ Ⓗ Ⓙ	29 Ⓐ Ⓑ Ⓒ Ⓓ	36 Ⓕ Ⓖ Ⓗ Ⓙ
2 Ⓕ Ⓖ Ⓗ Ⓙ	9 Ⓐ Ⓑ Ⓒ Ⓓ	16 Ⓕ Ⓖ Ⓗ Ⓙ	23 Ⓐ Ⓑ Ⓒ Ⓓ	30 Ⓕ Ⓖ Ⓗ Ⓙ	37 Ⓐ Ⓑ Ⓒ Ⓓ
3 Ⓐ Ⓑ Ⓒ Ⓓ	10 Ⓕ Ⓖ Ⓗ Ⓙ	17 Ⓐ Ⓑ Ⓒ Ⓓ	24 Ⓕ Ⓖ Ⓗ Ⓙ	31 Ⓐ Ⓑ Ⓒ Ⓓ	38 Ⓕ Ⓖ Ⓗ Ⓙ
4 Ⓕ Ⓖ Ⓗ Ⓙ	11 Ⓐ Ⓑ Ⓒ Ⓓ	18 Ⓕ Ⓖ Ⓗ Ⓙ	25 Ⓐ Ⓑ Ⓒ Ⓓ	32 Ⓕ Ⓖ Ⓗ Ⓙ	39 Ⓐ Ⓑ Ⓒ Ⓓ
5 Ⓐ Ⓑ Ⓒ Ⓓ	12 Ⓕ Ⓖ Ⓗ Ⓙ	19 Ⓐ Ⓑ Ⓒ Ⓓ	26 Ⓕ Ⓖ Ⓗ Ⓙ	33 Ⓐ Ⓑ Ⓒ Ⓓ	40 Ⓕ Ⓖ Ⓗ Ⓙ
6 Ⓕ Ⓖ Ⓗ Ⓙ	13 Ⓐ Ⓑ Ⓒ Ⓓ	20 Ⓕ Ⓖ Ⓗ Ⓙ	27 Ⓐ Ⓑ Ⓒ Ⓓ	34 Ⓕ Ⓖ Ⓗ Ⓙ	
7 Ⓐ Ⓑ Ⓒ Ⓓ	14 Ⓕ Ⓖ Ⓗ Ⓙ	21 Ⓐ Ⓑ Ⓒ Ⓓ	28 Ⓕ Ⓖ Ⓗ Ⓙ	35 Ⓐ Ⓑ Ⓒ Ⓓ	

I hereby certify that I have truthfully identified myself on this form. I accept the consequences of falsifying my identity.

____
Your signature

____
Today's date

The Princeton Review
Diagnostic ACT Form

ESSAY

Begin your essay on this side. If necessary, continue on the opposite side.

Continue on the opposite side if necessary.

The Princeton Review
Diagnostic ACT Form

Continued from previous page.

PLEASE PRINT YOUR INITIALS

First	Middle	Last

The Princeton Review
Diagnostic ACT Form

Continued from previous page.

PLEASE PRINT YOUR INITIALS

First	Middle	Last

The Princeton Review
Diagnostic ACT Form

Continued from previous page.

PLEASE PRINT YOUR INITIALS

First	Middle	Last

Test 1
Answers and Explanations

TEST 1 ENGLISH ANSWERS

1. D
2. F
3. B
4. H
5. C
6. J
7. D
8. J
9. A
10. F
11. B
12. G
13. C
14. H
15. B
16. F
17. D
18. J
19. B
20. H
21. A
22. J
23. B
24. J
25. B
26. F
27. D
28. F
29. D
30. F
31. D
32. G
33. D
34. H
35. C
36. J
37. A
38. G
39. C
40. F
41. B
42. F
43. D
44. G
45. D
46. H
47. C
48. J
49. B
50. H
51. A
52. H
53. A
54. J
55. D
56. F
57. A
58. G
59. D
60. G
61. C
62. J
63. A
64. J
65. C
66. F
67. C
68. G
69. B
70. G
71. A
72. J
73. D
74. J
75. B

TEST 1 MATH ANSWERS

1. A
2. J
3. B
4. K
5. D
6. H
7. A
8. J
9. C
10. H
11. A
12. F
13. D
14. G
15. D
16. G
17. A
18. G
19. B
20. H
21. B
22. F
23. C
24. K
25. B
26. F
27. C
28. J
29. B
30. H
31. E
32. H
33. A
34. J
35. C
36. J
37. D
38. J
39. A
40. F
41. A
42. K
43. C
44. G
45. D
46. J
47. C
48. J
49. C
50. K
51. D
52. G
53. B
54. F
55. B
56. F
57. C
58. F
59. D
60. K

TEST 1 READING ANSWERS

1. C
2. J
3. B
4. H
5. B
6. F
7. A
8. G
9. C
10. J
11. B
12. H
13. D
14. F
15. D
16. H
17. A
18. G
19. C
20. H
21. B
22. J
23. A
24. F
25. B
26. H
27. D
28. J
29. C
30. F
31. A
32. F
33. C
34. H
35. B
36. G
37. D
38. F
39. B
40. J

TEST 1 SCIENCE ANSWERS

1. A
2. F
3. D
4. G
5. D
6. G
7. D
8. H
9. A
10. J
11. A
12. H
13. D
14. H
15. B
16. H
17. B
18. J
19. C
20. G
21. B
22. F
23. C
24. G
25. D
26. H
27. D
28. G
29. D
30. F
31. C
32. H
33. D
34. G
35. A
36. G
37. C
38. J
39. C
40. F

SCORING YOUR PRACTICE EXAM

Step A

Count the number of correct answers for each section and record the number in the space provided for your raw score on the Score Conversion Worksheet below.

Step B

Using the Score Conversion Chart on the next page, convert your raw scores on each section to scaled scores. Then compute your composite ACT score by averaging the four subject scores. Add them up and divide by four. Don't worry about the essay score; it is not included in your composite score.

Score Conversion Worksheet		
Section	**Raw Score**	**Scaled Score**
1	______/75	______
2	______/60	______
3	______/40	______
4	______/40	______

Scale Score	English	Math	Reading	Science	Scale Score
36	75	60	40	40	**36**
35	73–74	59	39	39	**35**
34	72	58	38	38	**34**
33	71	57	37	37	**33**
32	70	56	36	—	**32**
31	69	54–55	34–35	36	**31**
30	68	53	33	35	**30**
29	67	51–52	32	34	**29**
28	65–66	49–50	30–31	33	**28**
27	64	46–48	29	32	**27**
26	62–63	44–45	28	30–31	**26**
25	60–61	41–43	27	28–29	**25**
24	58–59	39–40	26	27	**24**
23	55–57	37–38	24–25	25–26	**23**
22	53–54	35–36	23	23–24	**22**
21	50–52	33–34	22	21–22	**21**
20	47–49	31–32	21	19–20	**20**
19	44–46	28–30	19–20	17–18	**19**
18	42–43	25–27	18	15–16	**18**
17	40–41	22–24	17	14	**17**
16	37–39	18–21	16	13	**16**
15	34–36	15–17	15	12	**15**
14	31–33	11–14	13–14	11	**14**
13	29–30	9–10	12	10	**13**
12	27–28	7–8	10–11	9	**12**
11	25–26	6	8-9	8	**11**
10	23–24	5	7	7	**10**
9	21–22	4	6	6	**9**
8	18–20	3	5	5	**8**
7	15–17	—	—	4	**7**
6	12–14	2	4	3	**6**
5	9–11	—	3	2	**5**
4	7–8	1	2	—	**4**
3	5–6	—	—	1	**3**
2	3–4	—	1	—	**2**
1	0–2	0	0	0	**1**

TEST 1 ENGLISH ANSWERS AND EXPLANATIONS

Passage I

1. **D** Punctuation changes in the answer choices, so this question tests how to connect ideas with the appropriate punctuation. The phrase in the second part of the sentence, *left by the delivery man casually leaning against the front screen door,* is not an independent clause. A semicolon can only come between two independent clauses, so eliminate (A) and (C). The difference between (B) and (D) is the comma after *man*. The comma is necessary because the phrase *left by the delivery man* is unnecessary information that could be removed from the sentence without changing its main meaning. Eliminate (A). The correct answer is (D).

2. **F** Verb forms change in the answer choices. In this sentence, all the answer choices are consistent with the subject, *words,* so this question tests which form is most clear. The sentence uses *scrawled* as an adjective to describe *the words,* not as a verb, so eliminate (G). Eliminate (H) also because it's missing the necessary *-ed* ending. Choice (J) is missing the word *on* to make the sentence idiomatically correct, so eliminate it as well. The correct answer is (F).

3. **B** Commas and transition words change in the answer choices, so this question tests how to connect ideas with the appropriate punctuation. The phrase in the second part of the sentence, *my heart skipping a beat (or two),* is not an independent clause. A comma followed by *and* can only come between two independent clauses, so eliminate (A). Neither the word *and* nor the word *when* is necessary to make the meaning of the sentence clear, so eliminate (C) and (D). The correct answer is (B).

4. **H** Commas and transition words change in the answer choices, so this question tests how to connect ideas with the appropriate punctuation. The first part of the sentence, *My hands trembled as I opened the box,* is an independent clause. The second part of the sentence (after the transition), *I was thrilled to see that it did indeed contain the record I had been seeking for years,* is also an independent clause. Two independent clauses must be separated by some type of punctuation other than a comma, so eliminate (J). Since the second part of the sentence already contains the pronoun *it* that refers to *the box,* it is not necessary to add either of the relative pronouns *that* or *which;* eliminate (F) and (G). Choice (H) correctly links the two independent clauses with a comma followed by the coordinating conjunction *and.* The correct answer is (H).

5. **C** Note the question! The question asks for the answer that *most effectively illustrates the difference between outsiders' perception of the record and its actual significance to the writer's family,* so it tests consistency. Eliminate answers that are inconsistent with the purpose stated in the question. Choices (A) and (B) both address how people outside the family might feel about the record, but they do not say anything about the writer's family; eliminate (A) and (B). The way in which the record was stored is not relevant to the purpose stated in the question, so eliminate (D). Only (C)

addresses the *significance* of the record *to the writer's family,* by calling it a *precious heirloom*. The correct answer is (C).

6. **J** Verbs change in the answer choices, so this question tests consistency of verbs. A verb must be consistent in tense with the rest of the sentence. The non-underlined words *Several years before* indicate that the tense of the underlined verb should be past perfect. Eliminate (F), (G), and (H) because they all include the word *would,* which unnecessarily makes the verb conditional. Choice (J) correctly uses the past perfect tense. The correct answer is (J).

7. **D** Punctuation changes in the answer choices, so this question tests how to connect ideas with the appropriate punctuation. The phrase in the second part of the sentence, *performing in music halls and local festivals,* is not an independent clause. Both periods and semicolons can only be used between two independent clauses, so eliminate (A) and (B). Adding *which* to the sentence makes it sound like Papa "had performed the band" instead of the "band performing." Eliminate (C). The correct answer is (D).

8. **J** The length of the phrase around the word *album* changes in the answer choices, so this question tests concision. The information about who produced the record is not relevant to the main idea of the sentence, so eliminate (F), (G), and (H). Choice (J) is concise and makes the meaning of the sentence clear. The correct answer is (J).

9. **A** Transitions change in the answer choices, so this question tests consistency of ideas. A transition must be consistent with the relationship between the ideas it connects. The phrase that is introduced by the underlined transition, *there had been only one surviving copy…,* supports the idea in the first part of the sentence: *This record was all that remained of his life's passion*. Eliminate (B) because *even so* indicates a contrast between ideas. The second idea is neither a cause nor an example of the first idea, so eliminate (C) and (D). The correct answer is (A).

10. **F** Verbs change in the answer choices, so this question tests consistency of verbs. A verb must be consistent in tense with the rest of the sentence. The sentence is in past tense, so the underlined verb should also be in past tense. Eliminate (H) because *is* is present tense. Although *was* in (J) is past tense, the addition of *to be* indicates something that had not yet happened in the past, which is not the case here. Eliminate (J). There is no reason to add the word *about,* so eliminate (G). The correct answer is (F).

11. **B** The length of the phrase around the word *begging* changes in the answer choices, so this question tests concision. *Begging* and *pleading* mean the same thing in this context, so there is no reason to use both words; eliminate (A), (C), and (D). Choice (B) is concise and makes the meaning of the sentence clear. The correct answer is (B).

12. **G** Note the question! The question asks for the answer that describes *the significance of his grandfather's cabin to the writer's upbringing,* so it tests consistency. Eliminate answers that are inconsistent with the purpose stated in the question. The *location* of the cabin is not relevant, so eliminate (F). Neither how well the writer *remembered* the cabin nor how many *generations* it had been in

the family is relevant to *the writer's upbringing,* so eliminate (H) and (J). Choice (G) refers to the writer's *childhood,* which is consistent with the idea of *upbringing* in the question. The correct answer is (G).

13. **C** The order of words changes in the answer choices, so this question tests misplaced modifiers. Eliminate answers that have an unclear word order. The opening phrase of (A), *Of the many familiar favorites,* describes *Papa* instead of *tunes,* so eliminate (A). Choice (B) also contains a misplaced modifier: it sounds as though *the many familiar tunes* are *playing all our favorite songs.* Eliminate (B). The word *strumming* in (D) is incorrectly used to describe *familiar tunes;* eliminate (D). Choice (C) makes the meaning of the sentence clear. The correct answer is (C).

14. **H** Punctuation changes in the answer choices, so this question tests how to connect ideas with the appropriate punctuation. The sentence as written contains two independent clauses: *It was a bittersweet reminder of the man I loved and missed* and *Papa's gentle voice on the record, however, assured me that he was still with me, both in spirit and in song.* Placing either a comma or no punctuation at all between two independent clauses creates a run-on sentence, so eliminate (F) and (J). The word *for,* which indicates the two clauses agree with each other, is inappropriate here since the word *however,* which indicates a contrast, appears in the second clause. Eliminate (G). Choice (H) correctly uses a period to separate the two independent clauses. The correct answer is (H).

15. **B** Punctuation changes in the answer choices, so this question tests how to connect ideas with the appropriate punctuation. The phrase after the underlined portion, *that he was still with me, both in spirit and in song,* is a continuation of the idea just before it, *Papa's gentle voice...assured me;* it is neither an independent clause nor a separate idea. That means there is no reason to put punctuation between *me* and *that.* Eliminate (A), (C), and (D). The correct answer is (B).

Passage II

16. **F** Apostrophes change in the answer choices, so this question tests apostrophe usage. A noun with an apostrophe shows possession; since nothing belongs to *lives,* no apostrophe is needed. Eliminate (H) and (J). There is no reason to include a comma after *lives,* so eliminate (G). The correct answer is (F).

17. **D** Note the question! The question asks for the answer that indicates that *the narrator and his friends all shared a common background,* so it tests consistency. Eliminate answers that are inconsistent with the purpose stated in the question. Eliminate (A) because it discusses only the narrator, not the friends. Eliminate (B) and (C) because they discuss neither the narrator nor his friends. Choice (D) uses the word *our* to refer to the narrator and his friends, and it indicates that their hometowns *shared* something. The correct answer is (D).

18. **J** Apostrophes change in the answer choices, so this question tests apostrophe usage. A noun with an apostrophe shows possession; since nothing belongs to *owners,* no apostrophe is needed. Eliminate

(H). Punctuation also changes in the answer choices, so the question also tests how to connect ideas with the appropriate punctuation. The phrase *drink a cup of coffee, and figure out which new and exciting place we'd be driving to next* is not an independent clause. A semicolon can only come between two independent clauses, so eliminate (G). The phrase *chat with the restaurant's owners* is one item in a list of activities that the narrator and his friends would engage in. A comma is necessary to separate the items in the list of three or more items, so eliminate (F). The correct answer is (J).

19. **B** The length of the phrase around the word *anticipation* changes in the answer choices, so this question tests concision. *Looking forward to* means the same thing as *anticipation,* so there is no need to use both terms; eliminate (A). *Excited* and *expectation* are similarly redundant, so eliminate (C) and (D). Choice (B) is concise and makes the meaning of the sentence clear. The correct answer is (B).

20. **H** Note the question! The question asks whether a sentence should be added to the end of the paragraph so it tests consistency. A sentence should be added only if it is consistent with the focus of the paragraph. This paragraph is focused on a particular diner that the narrator and his friends visited, and the new sentence is about *Many diners.* It is thus not consistent, so eliminate (F) and (G). The paragraph is not about *driving,* nor is the new sentence about *specific places,* so eliminate (J). Choice (H) gives an accurate reason why the sentence should not be included. The correct answer is (H).

21. **A** Pronouns change in the answer choices, so this question tests consistency of pronouns. A pronoun must be consistent with the noun it refers to. The word *whom* can only be used to refer to people. In this case the pronoun refers to food, so eliminate (B) and (C). Choice (D) changes the sentence to mean that food items *were ordering,* rather than that they *could be ordered.* Eliminate (D). The correct answer is (A).

22. **J** Note the question! The question asks for the best placement for the underlined portion, so it tests consistency. The underlined portion must be consistent with the word or phrase it is next to. The narrator is not buying either *industrial-sized packs, noodles,* or *soda from childhood,* so eliminate (F), (G). and (H). The phrase *from childhood* accurately describes what the narrator and his friends *remembered.* The correct answer is (J).

23. **B** Note the question! The question asks for the answer that best *supports and elaborates on the description in an earlier part of this sentence,* so it tests consistency. Eliminate answers that are inconsistent with the purpose stated in the question. The phrase just before the underlined portion mentions that some foods were *too expensive in the city.* This has nothing to do with *variety,* whether or not anyone *likes to drive,* or the size of *refrigerators,* so eliminate (A), (C), and (D). The statement in (B) that *prices for...basic foods were steep* is consistent with the idea: *expensive.* The correct answer is (B).

24. **J** Note the question! When a question asks which answer would *NOT* be acceptable, eliminate answers that **are** acceptable. The answer choices have the option of either including or omitting a conjunction, so this question tests complete sentences. As written, the sentence starts with the phrase *Going to as many places as we could,* which is followed by a comma and then the independent clause

we were always sure to happen upon something strangely familiar to us. Replacing the underlined portion with *While going* retains this correct sentence structure, so eliminate (G). Choices (F) and (H) both add the subject *we* to the opening phrase, but they also both add conjunctions (*as* and *while,* respectively) that turn the opening part of the sentence into a dependent clause. The non-underlined comma works to separate a dependent clause from an independent clause, so eliminate (F) and (H) because they are both acceptable. Choice (J) turns the opening phrase of the sentence into an independent clause. A comma cannot be used to separate two independent clauses, so (J) is NOT acceptable. The correct answer is (J).

25. **B** Verbs change in the answer choices, so this question tests consistency of verbs. A verb must be consistent in number with its subject. The subject of the underlined verb is *place,* which is singular, so the verb should also be singular. The phrase between dashes in the sentence is extra descriptive information and cannot be the subject of the verb. Eliminate (A), (C), and (D) because they all contain plural verbs. The correct answer is (B).

26. **F** Note the question! The question asks which answer best *signals the shift in focus…when moving from this paragraph to the next,* so it tests consistency. Eliminate answers that are inconsistent with the purpose stated in the question. This paragraph describes some of the things the narrator and his friends did on their road trips, and the next paragraph focuses on the writer's present-day life. Neither paragraph discusses how long the friendship lasted, so eliminate (G). The next paragraph indicates that the narrator still lives in the city, so eliminate (H) because it indicates that the writer does not live in the city. The idea of whether the writer has *been back* to any of the places he visited is not relevant to either paragraph, so eliminate (J). Choice (F) effectively transitions between the past and the present. The correct answer is (F).

27. **D** Transitions change in the answer choices, so this question tests consistency of ideas. There is also the option to DELETE; consider this choice carefully as it's often the correct answer. A transition must be consistent with the relationship between the ideas it connects. The sentence before the underlined portion states that the writer is *not sure why we took these trips.* The sentence introduced by the transition describes where the narrator lives. These ideas do not contrast with each other, so eliminate (A) and (C). The second sentence is not a conclusion based on the idea in the first sentence, so eliminate (B). The correct answer is (D).

28. **F** Note the question! When a question asks which answer would *NOT* be acceptable, eliminate answers that **are** acceptable. Prepositions change in the answer choices, so the question tests idioms. The underlined phrase uses a preposition to describe where the narrator drives. *About* and *around* (with or without *the town*) are both acceptable prepositions to use in this context, so eliminate (G), (H), and (J). The word *among* is not generally used to describe where one drives, and it also can be used only with a plural noun. Choice (F) incorrectly uses the singular noun *town* after *among.* Choice (F) is the correct answer.

29. **D** The length of the phrase changes in the answer choices, so this question tests concision. To *cherish* something, to *have a great fondness for it,* and to *have strong feelings of adoration for it* all mean the same thing. Choice (D) is concise and makes the meaning of the sentence clear. The correct answer is (D).

30. **F** Verbs change in the answer choices, so this question tests consistency of verbs. A verb must be consistent in tense and form with other verbs in the sentence. The underlined phrase is the second in a list of two things; the first is *we drove by.* When there is a list of activities in a sentence, the verbs should all be in the same form. Because *drove* is in the simple past tense, the correct answer should also be in the simple past tense. Eliminate (G) and (H) because they both contain *-ing* forms of a verb. Eliminate (J) because it is in passive voice and is not concise. The correct answer is (F).

Passage III

31. **D** Note the question! When a question asks which answer would *NOT* be acceptable, eliminate answers that **are** acceptable. Transitions change in the answer choices, so this question tests consistency of ideas. A transition must be consistent with the relationship between the ideas it connects. The beginning of the sentence mentions *modern times,* while the second part describes the presence of *historical markers from as far back as medieval Italy.* Choices (A), (B), and (C) all contain contrasting transition words that appropriately connect these ideas. Eliminate (A), (B), and (C). Choice (D) indicates that the two parts of the sentence are similar, which is not the case. The correct answer is (D).

32. **G** Note the question! The question asks for the answer that best connects the two parts of the paragraph *while illustrating the main idea,* so it tests consistency. Eliminate answers that are inconsistent with the purpose stated in the question. The first part of the paragraph mentions the contrast between *modern times* and *historical markers* in Siena, and the second part introduces *another remnant from Siena's rich history.* Because of the word *another,* the best answer should introduce a *remnant from…history. Soccer* is not a remnant from history, so eliminate (F). Choices (H) and (J) both refer to history, but in a general way. Choice (G) gives the specific examples of *cobblestone streets and Gothic architecture,* which are historical remnants. The correct answer is (G).

33. **D** The length of the phrase describing the *horse race* changes in the answer choices, so this question tests concision. The word *biannual* means *twice a year,* so there is no need to include both terms. Eliminate (A) and (B). Choices (C) and (D) both express the same idea, but (D) is more concise. The correct answer is (D).

34. **H** Note the question! The question asks for the best placement for the underlined portion, so it tests consistency. The underlined portion must be consistent with the word or phrase it is next to. The underlined phrase is a descriptive phrase that must refer to a plural noun, since *each* indicates more than one. Eliminate (F) and (J) because the nouns *Piazza del Campo* and *plaza* are both singular.

The word *races* functions as a verb in the sentence, not as a noun, so the underlined portion cannot describe *races*. Eliminate (G). The underlined portion can be used to describe *laps* since it is a plural noun. The correct answer is (H).

35. **C** Verbs change in the answer choices, so this question tests consistency of verbs. A verb must be consistent in tense with the rest of the sentence. The sentence is in present tense, so the underlined verb should also be in present tense. Eliminate (A) and (D) because they are in past tense. Eliminate (B) because it is in future tense. The correct answer is (C).

36. **J** The answer choices have the option of either including or omitting a conjunction, so this question tests complete sentences. The presence of the conjunction *because* at the beginning of the sentence makes it an incomplete sentence, so eliminate (F). Choice (G) has the same problem because of the word *though;* eliminate (G). Choices (H) and (J) both contain complete sentences. The phrase *In addition* does not make the meaning of the sentence clearer, so eliminate (H). The correct answer is (J).

37. **A** Transitions change in the answer choices, so this question tests consistency of ideas. A transition must be consistent with the relationship between the ideas it connects. The previous sentence describes the large sums of money that jockeys receive: *salaries for a single race often exceed 250,000 euros.* The sentence with the underlined transition says that *this is…a small price to pay.* These ideas contrast with each other, so eliminate (B), (C), and (D), which all contain transitions that do not indicate a contrast. The correct answer is (A).

38. **G** Punctuation changes in the answer choices, so this question tests how to connect ideas with the appropriate punctuation. The phrase at the end of the sentence, *for many Sienese citizens,* is not an independent clause. A semicolon can only come between two independent clauses, so eliminate (J). Note the non-underlined dash earlier in the sentence: two dashes can be used to separate an unnecessary phrase from the rest of the sentence. The phrase *even more so than getting married* is extra description, but is not necessary to the main meaning of the sentence, so it should be set off with commas or dashes on both sides. Because there is a non-underlined dash at the beginning, there also needs to be a dash at the end. Eliminate (F) and (H). The correct answer is (G).

39. **C** Punctuation changes in the answer choices, so this question tests how to connect ideas with the appropriate punctuation. The phrase at the end of the sentence, *throughout the city with their newly won silk banner, also called the palio,* is not an independent clause. Both periods and semicolons can only be used between two independent clauses, so eliminate (A) and (B). There is no reason to put a comma after *throughout,* so eliminate (D). The correct answer is (C).

40. **F** Punctuation changes in the answer choices, so this question tests how to connect ideas with the appropriate punctuation. As the sentence is written, *Every citizen belongs to one of the seventeen city districts, collectively known as the Contrade,* it is an independent clause. The following sentence, *Contrada is the term for a single district that has its own color and arms, such as the Aquila (the eagle) or Bruco (the caterpillar),* is also an independent clause. Two independent clauses must be connected by some

type of punctuation other than a comma. Eliminate (G) and (H). Although a comma followed by the coordinating conjunction *yet* could come between two independent clauses, there is no contrast between the two sentences as the word *yet* implies. Eliminate (J). The correct answer is (F).

41. **B** Punctuation changes in the answer choices, so this question tests how to connect ideas with the appropriate punctuation. The phrase at the beginning of the sentence, *A* contrada *is the source of so much local patriotism that every important event,* is not an independent clause. A semicolon can only be used between two independent clauses, so eliminate (A). Both a colon or a long dash can only be used after an independent clause, so eliminate (C) and (D). The comma in (B) serves to offset the phrase *from baptisms to food festivals,* which is not necessary to the main meaning of the sentence. The correct answer is (B).

42. **F** Pronouns change in the answer choices, so this question tests consistency of pronouns. A pronoun must be consistent with its role in the sentence. The word *whose* is a possessive pronoun, but there is no need for a possessive in the sentence, so eliminate (G) and (H). To decide between *who* and *whom,* substitute *they* or *them* into the sentence. The *-m* words go together, so if *them* works, chose *whom.* In this case, the phrase would be *they become more like family,* so *who* is the appropriate choice. Eliminate (J). The correct answer is (F).

43. **D** Punctuation changes in the answer choices, so this question tests how to connect ideas with the appropriate punctuation. The phrase at the end of the sentence, *not only to witness the exciting race but also to attend the after-parties thrown by the locals,* is not an independent clause. Both periods and semicolons can only be used between two independent clauses, so eliminate (A) and (B). Because the two parts of the sentence express separate ideas, a comma is necessary to separate them; eliminate (C). The correct answer is (D).

44. **G** Verb forms change in the answer choices. In this sentence, all the answer choices are consistent with the subject, *after-parties,* so this question tests which form is most clear. The sentence uses *thrown* as an adjective to describe *the after-parties,* not as a verb, so eliminate (F). Choice (G) appropriately uses the past participle *thrown* as an adjective. Eliminate (H) and (J) because *threw* is the simple past tense, which cannot be used as an adjective. The correct answer is (G).

45. **D** Note the question! The question asks for the best placement for Paragraph 3, so it tests consistency of ideas. Paragraph 3 must be consistent in focus with the paragraphs before and after it. Paragraph 3 begins with a discussion of *members.* This idea is not consistent with the end of Paragraph 2, which talks about *the race itself.* Eliminate (A). The ideas of the *contrade* and their *members* are introduced in Paragraph 4. Paragraph 3 ends with a discussion of celebrations, and that idea continues in Paragraph 5. Therefore, Paragraph 3 logically belongs between Paragraphs 4 and 5. The correct answer is (D).

Passage IV

46. **H** Pronouns and nouns change in the answer choices, so this question tests the idea of clear. A pronoun can only be used when it is clear what it refers to. It is not clear what the pronoun *it* refers to, so eliminate (F). Choices (G) and (J) are similarly unclear, so eliminate those answers as well. Choice (H) fixes the problem by replacing the pronoun *it* with a specific noun. The correct answer is (H).

47. **C** Verbs change in the answer choices, so this question tests consistency of verbs. Verbs must be consistent in tense with other verbs in the paragraph. The paragraph is in past tense, so the underlined verb must also be in past tense. *Helping* is present tense, so eliminate (A). Adding the word *which* to the sentence makes it incomplete, so eliminate (B). Choice (C) appropriately uses past tense, so keep (C). Adding the word *was* changes the meaning of the sentence in an unclear way, so eliminate (D). The correct answer is (C).

48. **J** Note the question! The question asks for the best placement for the underlined portion, so it tests consistency. The underlined portion must be consistent with the word or phrase it is next to. The word *tireless* is an adjective, which can only be used to describe a noun, so it cannot describe the verb *continued;* eliminate (F). It does not make sense to describe *death* as *tireless,* so eliminate (G). *Tireless* can describe *literary experimentation,* but it would not come between those two words, so eliminate (H). The correct answer is (J).

49. **B** Note the question! When a question asks which answer would *NOT* be acceptable, eliminate answers that **are** acceptable. Verbs change in the answer choices, so this question tests consistency of verbs. A verb must be consistent in tense with the rest of the sentence. The phrase *In the contemporary popular imagination* indicates that the sentence is in present tense. Choices (A), (C), and (D) all contain present tense verbs, so they are all acceptable and can be eliminated. Choice (B) is not acceptable because it contains a past tense verb. The correct answer is (B).

50. **H** Prepositions change in the answer choices, so the question tests idioms. There is also the option to DELETE; consider this choice carefully as it's often the correct answer. The sentence requires a preposition between *step* and *creating,* so eliminate (J). Neither *until* nor *at* is the idiomatically correct preposition to use with the phrase *take a step,* so eliminate (F) and (G). The correct idiom is *take a step toward.* The correct answer is (H).

51. **A** Punctuation changes in the answer choices, so this question tests how to connect ideas with the appropriate punctuation. The opening phrase of the sentence, *Anderson was able to fuse,* is not an independent clause. A semicolon can only be used between two independent clauses, so eliminate (B). A colon can only be used after an independent clause, so eliminate (C). There is no need to break up ideas in the sentence with a comma, so eliminate (D). The correct answer is (A).

52. **H** Note the question! When a question asks which answer would *NOT* be acceptable, eliminate answers that **are** acceptable. Vocabulary changes in the answer choices, so this question tests which words give the clearest meaning. Both *encouraged* and *motivated* mean something very similar

to *inspired,* as the sentence is written, and are therefore both acceptable. Eliminate (F) and (G). *Emboldened* means *gave courage,* which is also acceptable in this context; eliminate (J). *Forced* does not retain the same meaning, so (H) is not acceptable. The correct answer is (H).

53. **A** Commas change in the answer choices, so this question tests comma usage. The phrase *as American writers living abroad were known* is a descriptive phrase that is not necessary to the main meaning of the sentence, so it should be separated from the rest of the sentence with a comma. Eliminate (C) and (D) because they do not include a comma before the phrase. Choice (B) includes an unnecessary comma after *abroad,* so eliminate it. The correct answer is (A).

54. **J** Punctuation changes in the answer choices, so this question tests how to connect ideas with the appropriate punctuation. The phrase *limited to those who were able to find copies of the book* is not an independent clause. A comma followed by *but* can only be used between two independent clauses, so eliminate (F). A semicolon can also only come between two independent clauses, so eliminate (H). There is no reason to put a comma after *limited,* so eliminate (G). The correct answer is (J).

55. **D** Note the question! The question asks for the answer that *best supports the point that although Anderson's book was difficult to find, those who read it were very impressed,* so it tests consistency. Eliminate answers that are inconsistent with the purpose stated in the question. *Anderson's later books* are not relevant, so eliminate (A). Eliminate (B) because it doesn't mention Anderson or his readers at all. Choice (C) doesn't address the idea that the book was *difficult to find,* so eliminate it. Choice (D) is consistent with the idea in the question. The correct answer is (D).

56. **F** Note the question! The question asks for the answer that best indicates *that Anderson was doing things that had not been done before in American literature,* so it tests consistency. Eliminate answers that are inconsistent with the purpose stated in the question. The *literature of the Southern Populist movement* is not relevant, so eliminate (G). The opinions of neither critics nor readers address whether Anderson was doing something new, so eliminate (H) and (J). Choice (F) describes something that had not previously been done in a novel. The correct answer is (F).

57. **A** Note the question! The question asks for the best placement for the underlined portion, so it tests consistency. The underlined portion must be consistent with the word or phrase it is next to. *Contributions* refers to Anderson, so it does not make sense to add the phrase *of the various writers* after that word; eliminate (B). The underlined phrase cannot properly describe *the 1930s,* so eliminate (C). The phrase also cannot describe the verb *inspired,* so eliminate (D). The phrase does logically describe *works.* The correct answer is (A).

58. **G** Commas change in the answer choices, so this question tests comma usage. The phrase *the direct style to which we often apply the name "American"* is a descriptive phrase that is not necessary to the main meaning of the sentence, and it should therefore be set off from the rest of the sentence with commas. Eliminate (H) and (J) because neither includes a comma after *"American."* Eliminate (F) because there's no reason to include a comma after *name.* The correct answer is (G).

59. **D** Note the question! The question asks for the best placement for Paragraph 2, so it tests consistency of ideas. Paragraph 2 must be consistent in focus with the paragraphs before and after it. Paragraph 2 discusses Anderson's death in *1941* and his influence *today.* It should be placed in logical sequence with other dates in the passage. Paragraph 5 discusses *the 1920s and 1930s,* so Paragraph 2 should follow Paragraph 5. The correct answer is (D).

60. **G** Note the question! The question asks whether the essay describes the *influence of one American author on the work of future writers,* so it tests consistency. Determine whether the essay is consistent with this idea. The essay is consistent with this idea, as it discusses the influence of Sherwood Anderson, so eliminate (H) and (J). The essay focuses only on Anderson, not on a *group of authors,* so eliminate (F). The correct answer is (G).

Passage V

61. **C** The length of the phrase describing what the *workforce* did changes in the answer choices, so this question tests concision. There is also the option to DELETE; consider this choice carefully as it's often the correct answer. The sentence needs a verb, so eliminate (D). The words *retracted* and *diminished* mean the same thing in this context, so there is no reason to use both terms. Eliminate (A) and (B). The correct answer is (C).

62. **J** Verbs change in the answer choices, so this question tests consistency of verbs. A verb must be consistent in number with its subject. The subject of the verb is *women,* which is plural, so the underlined verb should also be plural. Eliminate (G) because *has begun* is singular. A verb must also be consistent in tense with the rest of the sentence. The other verbs in the sentence, *headed* and *diminished,* are in simple past tense, so the underlined verb should also be in simple past tense. Eliminate (H) because *would of begun* is an incorrect verb construction: correctly written, the phrase would be *would have begun.* Eliminate (F) because it contains the past participle *begun. Began* is simple past tense. The correct answer is (J).

63. **A** Pronouns change in the answer choices, so this question tests consistency of pronouns. A pronoun must be consistent in number with the noun it refers to. The underlined portion refers to *responsibilities,* which is plural, so the pronoun must also be plural. Eliminate (D) because *that* is singular. Eliminate (C) because the word *which* makes the sentence into a fragment. The previous sentence says that the responsibilities were *traditionally assigned to men,* so there is no need to repeat that idea; eliminate (B). The correct answer is (A).

64. **J** The answer choices have the option of either including or omitting a conjunction, so this question tests complete sentences. There is also the option to DELETE; consider this choice carefully as it's often the correct answer. The word *that* in the non-underlined portion of the sentence connects the statement that the *government realized* something to the thing it realized (what was *required* for *participation in the war*), so there is no need to use another conjunction. Eliminate (F), (G), and (H). The correct answer is (J).

65. **C** Punctuation changes in the answer choices, so this question tests how to connect ideas with the appropriate punctuation. The beginning part of the sentence, *Women worked in factories and shipyards as riveters, welders, and machinists,* is an independent clause. The second part, *making everything from uniforms to munitions to airplanes, they directly contributed to the war effort,* is also an independent clause. Two independent clauses need to be separated by some kind of punctuation other than a comma, so eliminate (A) and (B). There is no need to add the word *who,* so eliminate (D). The correct answer is (C).

66. **F** The length of the phrase describing *workforce* changes in the answer choices, so this question tests concision. The previous sentence states that *women worked in factories and shipyards,* so there is no need to repeat that idea. Eliminate (G), (H), and (J). The correct answer is (F).

67. **C** Verbs change in the answer choices, so this question tests consistency of verbs. A verb must be consistent in number with its subject. The subject of the underlined verb is *presence* (the phrase *of women in wartime workforces* is a prepositional phrase that modifies *presence* and cannot be the subject of the verb). *Presence* is singular, so the underlined verb should also be singular. Eliminate (A), (B), and (D) because they all contain plural verbs. The correct answer is (C).

68. **G** Note the question! The question asks whether a sentence should be added to the end of the paragraph, so it tests consistency. A sentence should be added only if it is consistent with the focus of the paragraph. The paragraph is focused on women in *wartime workforces,* but the new sentence discusses *marriage* and *babies born to unmarried women.* The new sentence is not consistent with the focus of the passage, so eliminate (H) and (J). The *style and tone* of the new sentence are consistent with the passage, so eliminate (F). Choice (G) correctly states that the subject of the new sentence is not consistent with the paragraph. The correct answer is (G).

69. **B** Note the question! The question asks for *the most logical transition* between ideas in the passage, so it tests consistency. A transition must be consistent with the ideas it connects. The following sentence begins to discuss *Major League Baseball,* and (B) is the only answer that mentions *baseball.* Eliminate (A), (C), and (D) because they focus on ideas that are unrelated to the sentence that follows. The correct answer is (B).

70. **G** Commas change in the answer choices, so this question tests comma usage. The name *Philip K. Wrigley* is necessary to clarify who the *founder* is and should therefore not be set off by commas; eliminate (J). Similarly, the phrase *Philip K. Wrigley and League president* is necessary to the sentence, so eliminate (F). There is no need for a comma either before or after the word *and,* so eliminate (H). The correct answer is (G).

71. **A** Note the question! The question asks for the answer that best helps *readers visualize the players in the photographs,* so it tests consistency. Eliminate answers that are inconsistent with the purpose stated in the question. Choice (A) includes the visual details *bright smiles on their faces and baseball mitts in their hands,* so it is consistent with the purpose stated in the question. Eliminate (B), (C), and (D) because they lack any such visual details. The correct answer is (A).

72. **J** The word in front of *flowing hair* is changing, so this question tests consistency. The sentence contains a list, so the underlined word should keep *flowing hair* consistent with the other items in the list. The word *and* is necessary to complete the end of the list. Choices (F), (G), and (H) all make *flowing hair* not consistent with the other items in the list *(silk shorts, fashionable knee-high socks, red lipstick),* so eliminate them. The correct answer is (J).

73. **D** Note the question! The question asks what would be lost if some words were deleted, so it tests consistency. Eliminate answer choices that are not consistent with the role of the words. The words in question are all adjectives describing items in the list. Those details do not appear in the *previous sentence,* so eliminate (A). The paragraph is not focused on *athletic talent,* so eliminate (B). The list describes what is in the photographs, not the *captions accompanying the photographs,* so eliminate (C). Choice (D) correctly describes that the adjectives serve to *highlight the femininity of the players,* so it is consistent with the role of those words. The correct answer is (D).

74. **J** Pronouns and apostrophes change in the answer choices, so this question tests pronoun consistency and apostrophe usage. A pronoun must be consistent in number with the noun it refers to. The underlined pronoun refers to *the All-American Girls Professional Baseball League,* which is singular, so the pronoun should also be singular. Eliminate (H) because *their* is always plural on the ACT. The word *its'* never occurs in English, so eliminate (F). *It's* is a contraction of *it is,* which is not necessary here, so eliminate (G). Choice (J) appropriately uses the singular possessive pronoun *its.* The correct answer is (J).

75. **B** Note the question! The question asks whether the essay illustrates *the range of non-traditional activities women pursued during wartime,* so it tests consistency. Determine whether the essay is consistent with this idea. The essay does discuss a variety of roles women took on during the war, so eliminate (C) and (D). The passage was about more than just the *All-American Girls Professional Baseball League,* so eliminate (A). Choice (B) is consistent with the focus of the passage. The correct answer is (B).

TEST 1 MATH ANSWERS AND EXPLANATIONS

1. **A** The question asks for the total length of the trail. Since $\overline{YZ}$ is $\frac{1}{3}$ the length of $\overline{XZ}$, $\overline{XZ}$ is $3 \times 24 = 72$ kilometers. Since X is the halfway point of the trail, the trail's entire length is twice $\overline{XZ}$, or $72 \times 2 = 144$ kilometers. The correct answer is (A).

2. **J** The question asks for the value of x, so isolate the variable. First subtract 7 from both sides to get $\frac{4x}{5} = -1$. Next, multiply both sides by 5 to get $4x = -5$. Finally, divide both sides by 4 to get $x = -\frac{5}{4}$. Choice (F) neglects the negative sign. Choice (G) is the reciprocal of the correct answer. Choices (H) and (K) are partial answers. The correct answer is (J).

3. **B** The question asks for the difference in the time the two cyclists take to complete 9,760 pedal revolutions. Determine how many minutes it takes each cyclist to make 9,760 pedal revolutions. Cyclist A takes 9,760 rev ÷ 80 rev/min = 122 minutes. Cyclist B takes 9,760 rev ÷ 61 rev/min = 160 minutes. So, Cyclist B takes 160 – 122 = 38 more minutes than Cyclist A. Notice that (C) and (E) are partial answers. Choice (D) is the sum of each cyclist's rate, and (A) is the difference of their rates. The correct answer is (B).

4. **K** The question asks for the area of a square. The formula for the area of a square is $A = s^2$, so first find the length of a side, based on the perimeter given. The formula for the perimeter of a square is $P = 4s$. That means that $36 = 4s$; divide both sides of the equation by 4 to get $s = 9$. Use the side length in the area formula to get $A = 9^2 = 81$. The correct answer is (K).

5. **D** The question asks for the coordinates of the unlabeled vertex of the rectangle. Use Process of Elimination. Because the unlabeled point is higher up on the graph than the point on the y-axis, the y-coordinate must be larger than 4; eliminate (C). The unlabeled point is to the left of the point (8,3), so the x-coordinate must be less than 8; eliminate (E). The unlabeled point is not in the center of the rectangle horizontally (i.e., halfway between 0 and 8 on the x-axis), so eliminate (A) and (B). Alternatively, since the figure is a rectangle, opposite sides must be equal in length and parallel, meaning they have the same slope. The slope of the side between the points (2,0) and (8,3) is 6 units right and 3 units up. The side between the point (0,4) and the unlabeled point will have the same length and slope, so the coordinates of the unlabeled point are (0 + 6,4 + 3) = (6,7). The correct answer is (D).

6. **H** The question asks for the number of notebooks Carla has. Set up an equation. If Carla's brother has x notebooks, Carla has $5x$ notebooks, and $5x + x = 42$. To find x, first add like terms to get $6x = 42$; then divide both sides by 6 to get $x = 7$. That means that Carla has 5(7) = 35 notebooks. Alternatively, use the answer choices to solve this problem: since the answers represent the number of notebooks Carla has, divide the answers by 5 to determine how many notebooks her brother

has. Then add that number to the original answer and choose the one that totals 42. A calculation error of $x = 6$ leads to (F). Choices (J) and (K) add and subtract numbers from the problem without answering the question. The correct answer is (H).

7. **A** The question asks for a possible value for the measure of $\angle GEF$. A right angle has a measure of 90°; therefore, any angle contained within a right angle must be smaller than 90°. The correct answer is (A).

8. **J** The question asks for the number of combinations of two things. Susie has 3 options for her T-shirt and 3 options for her pair of shorts. Susie can combine any of the T-shirts with any of the pairs of shorts, so there are 3×3, or 9, combinations. Choices (F) and (G) do not account for all possible combinations. Choice (H) is 2^3 rather than 3^2. The correct answer is (J).

9. **C** The question asks for the value of a series of percents. Use the words in the problem to create an equation: *percent* means "divide by 100," *of* means "multiply," and *what number* means "use a variable." The resulting equation is $\frac{20}{100} \times 20 = \frac{50}{100} \times y$. Do the multiplication to find $4 = 0.5y$; then divide both sides by 0.5 to get $y = 8$. Be careful of (B), which is 20% of 20, and (D), which is 50% of 20. The correct answer is (C).

10. **H** The question asks for the maximum number of orchestra members who play both instruments. Use Process of Elimination. The number of piano players exceeds the number of violin players; thus, the number of musicians who play both instruments cannot exceed the number who play violin, eliminating (J) and (K). Since all 22 musicians who play the violin could also play the piano, (H) gives the maximum possible number. The correct answer is (H).

11. **A** The question asks for the largest value of m for which n is a real number. In order to make m^2 (and therefore m) as large as possible, make n^2 as small as possible. The square of any real number can't be negative, so the smallest that n^2 can be is 0. This makes $m^2 = 196$, so m equals either –14 or 14. Alternatively, try the answer choices. Plugging in 14 for m yields $142 = 196 - n^2$. Solve for n: the equation becomes $196 = 196 - n^2$. Subtract 196 from both sides to get $0 = -n^2$, so $n^2 = 0$, and $n = 0$. All other choices will end up with a negative value for n^2, which means n would not be a real number. Choices (B), (C), (D), and (E) are based on multiplication, division, or subtraction, not on taking a square root. The correct answer is (A).

12. **F** The question asks how much change Phil receives. Work through the problem one step at a time. First, find the sale price of the drum kit. To solve this problem, break it down into manageable pieces. $\frac{1}{5} \times \$925 = \$185$, so the sale price of the drum kit is $925 – $185 = $740. Since the sales tax is $0.05 \times \$740 = \$37$, the total owed is $740 + $37 = $777. Phil receives back the amount he gave the sales clerk minus the amount he owes: $800 – $777 = $23. Choice (G) is the amount of tax paid.

Choices (H) and (J) resemble numbers from steps within the problem, and (K) calculates the taxed price without applying the sale discount. The correct answer is (F).

13. **D** The question asks for an imaginary number. Taking the square root of a negative number yields an imaginary number. Choice (C) is tricky—this number is not *rationalized* (that is, it has a square root in the denominator), but that does not mean it is not a *real number*. The correct answer is (D).

14. **G** The question asks for the factored form of the expression in the question. The general quadratic expression $a^2 - b^2$ equals $(a - b)(a + b)$. In this question, take the square root of $25x^4$ and the square root of $16y^8$; thus $a = 5x^2$ and $b = 4y^4$. The correctly factored form is $(5x^2 - 4y^4)(5x^2 + 4y^4)$. Alternatively, try using FOIL (First, Outer, Inner, Last) on the answer choices. Choice (G) becomes $25x^4 - 20x^2y^4 + 20x^2y^4 - 16y^8 = 25x^4 - 16y^8$. Choice (F) correctly factors the variables but not the coefficients, introducing an incorrect factor of the coefficients. Choices (H) and (K) incorrectly factor the coefficients. Choice (J) incorrectly factors the variables. The correct answer is (G).

15. **D** The question asks for the area of the unshaded region. Use the formula *Shaded Area* = *Total Area* – *Unshaded Area*. In this case, the *Total Area* is the area of the square, which is $4^2 = 16$. To find the *Unshaded Area*, add up the areas of the 4 unshaded triangles. Starting at the lower left of the figure and going clockwise, those areas are $\frac{1}{2}(1\times2)+\frac{1}{2}(2\times2)+\frac{1}{2}(2\times1)+\frac{1}{2}(1\times2)=5$. Therefore, the *Shaded Area* = 16 – 5 = 11. The correct answer is (D).

16. **G** The question asks for the value of the given function after a certain amount of time. To find the percent, *P*, substitute 20 for *t* to calculate $-0.001(20)^2 + 0.4(20) = 7.6$. Choice (F) is the rounded value of 0.076%, which is not equivalent to 7.6%. Choices (H) and (J) may be the result of not paying attention to the order of operations (PEMDAS) or distribution of the negative sign. Choice (K) results if t^2 and t are switched. The correct answer is (G).

17. **A** The question asks for the difference in the prices of grapefruits at the two stores. Work through the problem one step at a time. Find the cost per grapefruit at each store by dividing the cost of each bag by the number of grapefruits in each bag. The cost per grapefruit at Fatima's is \$4.40 ÷ 8 = \$0.55, while the cost per grapefruit at Ernie's is \$1.86 ÷ 3 = \$0.62. Find the difference: \$0.62 – \$0.55 = \$0.07. Choice (B) comes from multiplying \$0.07 by the difference in the number of grapefruits (8 – 3 = 5). Choice (C) comes from averaging \$0.55 and \$0.62. Choice (D) comes from adding \$0.55 and \$0.62. Choice (E) is the difference in costs of the two bags. The correct answer is (A).

18. **G** The question asks for the answer that is equivalent to the expression given in the question. In order to multiply factors, use FOIL (First, Outer, Inner, Last). Remember to *add* exponents when multiplying numbers with the same base and watch the signs carefully. The expression becomes $x^8 + 4x^4 - 4x^4 - 16 = x^8 - 16$. Choice (F) adds rather than multiplies the factors. Choice (J) multiplies the exponents instead of adding them. Choices (H) and (K) confuse the signs. The correct answer is (G).

19. **B** The question asks how much time it took to finish the mosaic after the interruption. Work through the problem one step at a time. First, calculate the number of tile pieces laid in the first period of work: $\frac{50 \text{ pieces}}{1 \text{ hour}} \times 3.5 \text{ hours} = 175$ pieces. Next, figure out how many tile pieces still need to be laid down. Subtract 280 pieces – 175 pieces = 105 pieces. Calculate the number of hours he spends in the second work session by dividing $\frac{105 \text{ pieces}}{35 \text{ pieces per hour}} = 3$ hours. Choice (D) incorrectly adds the 60 minutes during which Wade was interrupted to the time it took to complete the mosaic. The correct answer is (B).

20. **H** The question asks for the coordinates of the midpoint. To find the midpoint of a line, take the average of the *x*-coordinates $\left(\frac{x_1 + x_2}{2}\right)$ and the average of the *y*-coordinates $\left(\frac{y_1 + y_2}{2}\right)$ of the endpoints. The midpoint here is $\left(\frac{1+7}{2}, \frac{2+(-10)}{2}\right) = (4,-4)$. Choices (F), (G), and (K) incorrectly average the *x*-coordinates. Choice (J) incorrectly averages the *y*-coordinates. The correct answer is (H).

21. **B** The question asks for the required amount of fencing. Draw a picture and label it with the information provided in the question.

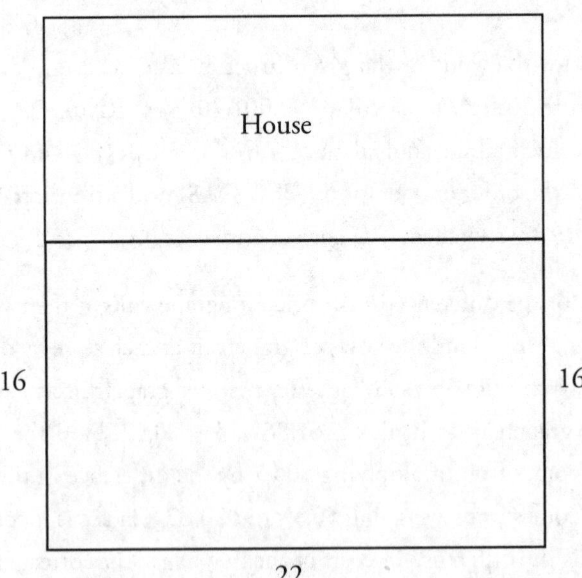

Add the lengths of the two short sides of the backyard and one long side: 16 + 16 + 22 = 54. Choice (C) is the sum of two long sides and one short side. Choice (D) is the perimeter of the backyard, but the problem says the fencing is needed only on 3 sides. Choice (E) is the area of the backyard. The correct answer is (B).

22. **F** The question asks for the y-intercept of the given line. One way to solve this problem is to rewrite the equation in the slope-intercept form, $y = mx + b$. First, subtract $7x$ from both sides of the equation to get $-3y = -7x + 21$. Then divide both sides by –3 to get $y = \frac{7}{3}x - 7$. In this equation, –7 is the value of b, the y-intercept. Alternatively, plug $x = 0$ into the equation as-is, since the y-intercept occurs at $x = 0$. The equation becomes $7(0) - 3y = 21$. Solve for y: the equation becomes $-3y = 21$ and dividing both sides by –3 results in $y = -7$. Choice (H) is the slope of the line, and the other choices do not modify the equation correctly. The correct answer is (F).

23. **C** The question asks for the day on which the flower reached a certain height. Work through the problem one step at a time. Find the flower's growth rate by dividing the total growth by the number of days: $\frac{17.4-15.0}{16-8} = \frac{2.4}{8} = 0.3$ cm per day. To find when the flower was 16.5 cm tall, first determine how much it has grown since April 8: $16.5 - 15 = 1.5$ cm. Then find how many days it took to grow that much by dividing the growth by the rate to get $\frac{1.5 \text{ cm}}{0.3 \text{ cm/day}} = 5 \text{ days}$. The day that is 5 days after April 8 is April 13. The correct answer is (C).

24. **K** The question asks for the expression equivalent to the one given. First distribute –3 to each term in the second parentheses. The result is $2x^3 - x - 1 - 3x^4 - 6x^3 + 6x^2 + 3x - 9$. Combine like terms to get $-3x^4 - 4x^3 + 6x^2 + 2x - 10$. Choices (H) and (J) incorrectly distribute the –3. Choices (F) and (G) incorrectly combine terms and exponents. The correct answer is (K).

25. **B** The question asks for the distance between the end of the slide and the ladder. Draw a line along the bottom of the figure to indicate this distance, and label it x. The question indicates that the ladder is at a right angle with the ground, so use the Pythagorean Theorem ($a^2 + b^2 = c^2$) to solve $6^2 + x^2 = 7^2$, which becomes $36 + x^2 = 49$. Subtract 36 from both sides of the equation to get $x^2 = 13$; then take the square root of both sides to get $\sqrt{13}$, which rounds to 4. The correct answer is (B).

26. **F** The question asks for the data set that fits certain requirements—the mean (average), median (middle value), and mode (number that appears most often) all equal 8. Start with the easiest terms to calculate and use Process of Elimination. All five answer choices have a median of 8, but (G) and (K) can be eliminated because their modes are not 8. Calculate the mean of the remaining answer choices by adding the numbers and dividing by the number of terms. The mean of (F) is $\frac{5+7+8+8+12}{5} = \frac{40}{5} = 8$. The means of (H) and (J) are 8.6 and 9, respectively. The correct answer is (F).

27. **C** The question asks for the second term in the sequence. Try the answer choices to see which one matches the information in the question. For (C), if the 2nd term is 18, then the 3rd term is (18 + 2) × 3 = 60, and the 4th term is (60 + 2) × 3 = 186. Alternatively, work backward: if the 4th term is 186, then the 3rd term is (186 ÷ 3) – 2 = 60, and the 2nd term is (60 ÷ 3) – 2 = 18. Choices (B) and (D) are the 1st and 3rd terms of the sequence, respectively. The correct answer is (C).

28. **J** The question asks for the value that does *NOT* satisfy the given inequality, so eliminate answers that **do** satisfy it. One approach to this problem is to test all the answer choices. When 9 is put in as the value of x, the result is $|9 - 3| \geq 12$, which becomes $6 \geq 12$. This is false. Alternatively, solve algebraically. The inequality becomes two expressions: $x - 3 \geq 12$ or $x - 3 \leq -12$. Solve by adding 3 to both sides of both inequalities to get $x \geq 15$ or $x \leq -9$. Only (J) does not fit these ranges. The other choices either place the inequality signs in the wrong direction or confuse the positive/negative values within the absolute value. The correct answer is (J).

29. **B** The question asks which statement is true based on the given information. Use Process of Elimination. Given that v is larger than s, then $t + u + v$ must be larger than $s + t + u$, since $t + u$ is equal in both expressions. Because $s + t + u = 29$, $t + u + v$ must be larger than 29. Choices (A), (C), (D), and (E) are not necessarily true, because no information is given about the relationships of t, u, and v. Another way to approach this question is to try out numbers for the variables: for example, let $s = 20$, $t = 5$, $u = 4$, and $v = 21$. Using these numbers, (A), (C), and (D) are false. Now try different numbers: $s = 5$, $t = 4$, $u = 20$, and $v = 6$. Choice (B) is still true (30 > 29), but (E) is now false (15 > 29). The correct answer is (B).

30. **H** The question asks for the measure of $\angle CBD$. Start with Process of Elimination. Eliminate (J) and (K) immediately, as $\angle CBD$ is clearly less than 90° in the figure. Because $ABCD$ is a rectangle, $\angle DCB = 90°$. A triangle has 180°, so find $\angle CBD$ by adding $\angle BDC$ and $\angle DCB$ and subtracting from 180. To find $\angle BDC$, use the fact that there are 180° in a line, so $\angle BDC = 180 - \angle CDE = 180 - 155 = 25$. Use this to find $\angle CBD$ as $180° - (25° + 90°) = 180° - 115° = 65°$. Choices (F), (J), and (K) are all angles within the figure, but do not answer the question. The correct answer is (H).

31. **E** The question asks for the number that must be part of the given equation. Test the prime numbers from the answer choices in the equation. Since all the numbers in the equation $a - b = c$ must be positive prime numbers, the only possible result for c can be 2 (for example, 13 – 11 = 2, and 7 – 5 = 2). The only exceptions to $c = 2$ are 5 – 2 = 3, 13 – 2 = 11, and 7 – 2 = 5. Even so, the only number common to all of these equations is 2. The correct answer is (E).

32. **H** The question asks for Pierre's average speed, or rate, for the entire race. Use the formula *distance* = *rate* × *time*. The total number of miles he covers is the distance from starting point S to finish line F, which is SF. Eliminate (F), (G), and (J) because they don't include the entire length of the racecourse. The total elapsed time from point S to point F is t_F. Eliminate (K) because it doesn't use the elapsed time clocked at the end of the race. The correct answer is (H).

33. **A** The question asks for the length of one leg of a right triangle. Given the length of one side and the measure of an angle of the triangle, use SOHCAHTOA. The length of the hypotenuse is provided, and $\overline{BC}$ is adjacent to the 70° angle, so use $\cos 70° = \frac{\text{adjacent}}{\text{hypotenuse}} = \frac{\overline{BC}}{13}$. Use the given decimal value for cos 70° to get $0.3420 = \frac{\overline{BC}}{13}$; then multiply both sides of the equation by 13 to get $\overline{BC}$ = 13(0.3420) ≈ 4.4. Choices (D) and (E) are the result of using either the sine or the tangent functions. Choices (B) and (C) may be the result of assuming that the figure is a 5:12:13 right triangle. The correct answer is (A).

34. **J** The question asks for the value of the given expression with specific numbers for x and y. Plug –3 into the expression for x and –4 for y to get $\frac{8}{(-4)^2} - \frac{(-3)^2}{(-4)} = \frac{8}{16} - \frac{9}{(-4)} = \frac{2}{4} + \frac{9}{4} = \frac{11}{4}$. Choices (F) and (G) confuse the signs. Choice (K) switches x and y. The correct answer is (J).

35. **C** The question asks for the horizontal length of the ramp, which is the longer leg of the right triangle as shown in the figure. The ramp forms a 30°-60°-90° triangle with side lengths in a ratio of $1{:}\sqrt{3}{:}2$. Since the shortest leg measures 4, the other leg of the triangle will be $\sqrt{3}$ times the short side: $4\sqrt{3} = 6.92 \approx 7$. Choice (D) gives the length of the ramp itself, not the horizontal length. The correct answer is (C).

36. **J** The question asks for the measure of an angle. First, label the figure with information from the question. ΔBCD is equilateral, so $\angle CBD$ is 60°. $\angle ABD$ must be larger than 60°, eliminating (F) and (G). To find $\angle ABC$, make it equal to x. Both $\angle BAC$ and $\angle BCA$ are then $2x$. Since a triangle has 180°, $x + 2x + 2x = 180°$. Combine like terms to get $5x = 180°$; then divide both sides by 5 to get $x = 36°$. Since x is the measure of $\angle ABC$, that means that $\angle ABD = 36° + 60° = 96°$. Choice (K) mistakenly calculates $\angle ABC$ to be twice, rather than half, the measure of $\angle BAC$. The correct answer is (J).

37. **D** The question asks for the slope of a line. Use the standard slope formula with points (8,0) and (0,–4) to get $m = \frac{y_2 - y_1}{x_2 - x_1} = \frac{(-4)-(0)}{(0)-(8)} = \frac{-4}{-8} = \frac{1}{2}$. Choice (E) mistakenly flips the x and y. Choice (B) is the result of missing a negative sign. The correct answer is (D).

38. **J** The question asks for the perimeter of a triangle. The perimeter is the sum of the sides, so start by finding the lengths of the sides. The leg of the triangle along the x-axis has a length of 8, and the leg along the y-axis has a length of 4. Since this is a right triangle, use Pythagorean Theorem ($a^2 + b^2 = c^2$) to find the hypotenuse. With the values given in the figure, this becomes $(8)^2 + (4)^2 = c^2$, and $c^2 = 64 + 16 = 80$, so $c = \sqrt{80} \approx 8.9$. To find the perimeter, add these sides together to get 20.9. The correct answer is (J).

39. **A** The question asks for the cosine of an angle. Use SOHCAHTOA. The definition of cosine is $\cos\theta = \frac{\text{adjacent}}{\text{hypotenuse}}$. The side adjacent to $\angle MNO$ is 4, and the hypotenuse (the value of which was calculated in question 38) is $\sqrt{80}$. Accordingly, the cosine of $\angle MNO$ is $\frac{4}{\sqrt{80}}$. Choices (D) and (E) could be eliminated because the cosine of any angle is always less than 1. Choice (B) gives the sine of $\angle MNO$, and (D) gives the tangent. The correct answer is (A).

40. **F** The question asks for a fraction of the students. A fraction is a part/whole relationship, so this fraction is equal to $\frac{\text{\# of students who passed}}{\text{total \# of students}}$. If there are m students in the class, m must be the denominator, so eliminate (G), (H), and (J). The number of students who received a passing grade is calculated by subtracting the number who didn't pass the last exam, n, from the total number of students, m. Choice (K) would give a negative fraction, which is not possible. The correct answer is (F).

41. **A** The question asks for the graph of an inequality on a number line. First, solve the inequality. Distribute the 2 on the right side of the inequality to get $5x + 9 \geq 6x + 8 + 7$. Add like terms to get $5x + 9 \geq 6x + 15$. Isolate the x by subtracting $6x$ and 9 from both sides to get $-x \geq 6$; then divide both sides by -1 to get $x \leq -6$. Remember to flip the sign when dividing by a negative number. Next, compare the simplified inequality to the graphs in the answer choices. The graph of this inequality should have a bold line to the left of -6; eliminate (B) and (E). There should be a closed dot at -6, so eliminate (C) and (D). Choice (B) results from forgetting to flip the sign. Choice (E) results from missing a negative. The correct answer is (A).

42. **K** The question asks for the number of tiles needed to cover the surface of the box. Work through the question one step at a time. The tiles must equal the surface area of the box, which is the sum of the areas of all 6 faces. There are three sets of faces: front/back, top/bottom, and the two sides. The sum of the areas of the faces is $2(4 \times 9) + 2(3 \times 9) + 2(3 \times 4) = 72 + 54 + 24 = 150$. Because each tile covers 1 cm^2, the artist must have 150 cm^2 ÷ 1 cm^2 = 150, (K). Choice (F) finds the area of only three faces, and (G) and (J) account for only two of the three pairs of faces. Choice (H) finds the volume of the box. The correct answer is (K).

43. **C** The question asks for the measure of an angle. The figure is an odd shape, but the question mentions parallel lines, so look for angles made with a line intersecting the parallel lines. Draw in $\overline{AD}$, which is parallel to both $\overline{BC}$ and $\overline{EF}$, to find $\angle BAD$. The interior angles of two parallel lines add up to 180°, so subtract $\angle ABC$ (130°) from 180° to yield $\angle BAD = 50°$. Subtract $\angle BAE$ from the larger angle $\angle BAD$ to get $\angle EAD = 50° - 22° = 28°$. Since $\angle AEF$ and $\angle EAD$ are also interior angles of two parallel lines, subtract: $180° - \angle EAD = 180° - 28° = 152° = \angle AEF$. Alternatively, extend $\overline{AE}$ to $\overline{BC}$ and find the third angle of the triangle. The same rule applies—the third angle of this triangle is the opposite interior angle of $\angle AEF$. The correct answer is (C).

44. **G** The question asks for the area of the trapezoid. To find the area of a trapezoid, multiply the height by the average of the bases. The bases are 6 and 14, so their average is $\frac{6+14}{2} = 10$. Therefore, the area of the trapezoid is (10)h = 10(3) = 30. Alternatively, break the trapezoid up into a rectangle and two right triangles, find the area of each of those shapes, and add them together. Choice (J) is the result of using the length of one of the slanted sides instead of the height. Choices (F) and (H) are the result of multiplying the height by the length of only one base. The correct answer is (G).

45. **D** The question asks for the solution set to the given equation. To isolate x, first raise both sides of the equation to the fifth power to get rid of the fifth root: $\left(\sqrt[5]{x^2+4x}\right)^5 = 2^5$ becomes $x^2 + 4x = 32$. Then, subtract 32 from both sides to get a standard quadratic form: $x^2 + 4x - 32 = 0$. Factor the quadratic to get $(x + 8)(x - 4) = 0$. Set each factor equal to 0 and solve to find that $x = -8$ or $x = 4$. Alternatively, try the answers in the equation to determine all those that work. Choice (A) gives only one of the possible values for x. Choice (C) reverses the signs. Choice (E) is the result of taking away the radical but squaring the 2, rather than raising it to the fifth power, and then using the quadratic formula. The correct answer is (D).

46. **J** The question asks for the height of the boulder, which is the same as a short leg of a right triangle. Use SOHCAHTOA. The length of the ramp is the hypotenuse of the triangle, and the height of the boulder is the side opposite the angle of 32°. Use sine with these two sides to get $\sin 32\infty = \frac{\text{opposite}}{\text{hypotenuse}} = \frac{h}{10}$. Multiply both side by 10 to get $h = 10 \sin 32°$. The correct answer is (J).

47. **C** The question asks which statement *must* be true based on the given information. Use Process of Elimination. Since average is $\frac{\text{sum}}{\text{\# of terms}}$, the sum of $j + j + k + n$ must equal 0 to make the average equal 0. Combine like terms to get $2j + k + n = 0$; then subtract $2j$ from both sides of the equation to get $k + n = -2j$. Alternatively, plug in numbers. For example, make $j = 2$; then the sum of k and n must be –4. If $k = -3$ and $n = -1$, all choices except (C) are wrong. Choices (A) and (B) are not necessarily true (for example, if $j = -3$, k could equal 4 and n could equal 2). Choices (D) and (E) are true only when j is equal to 0. The correct answer is (C).

48. **J** The question asks for the definition of a function. In function notation, the number inside the parentheses is the *x*-value that goes into the function, and the value that comes out of the function is the *y*-value. In this case, *g*(*x*) is the input for *f*(*x*). Since *f*(*x*) is defined as $\sqrt{x}$, try the answer choices. Put each one under a square root and choose the one that matches $\sqrt{4x^2 - 5}$. Only (J) works. Taking the square root of the expressions in any of the other answer choices does not result in the correct expression. The correct answer is (J).

49. **C** The question asks for Rusty's rate in the given situation. Work through the problem one step at a time. The time when Rusty and Dale meet is 150 seconds, and the total distance they have driven when their cars meet is 6,000 feet (see diagram).

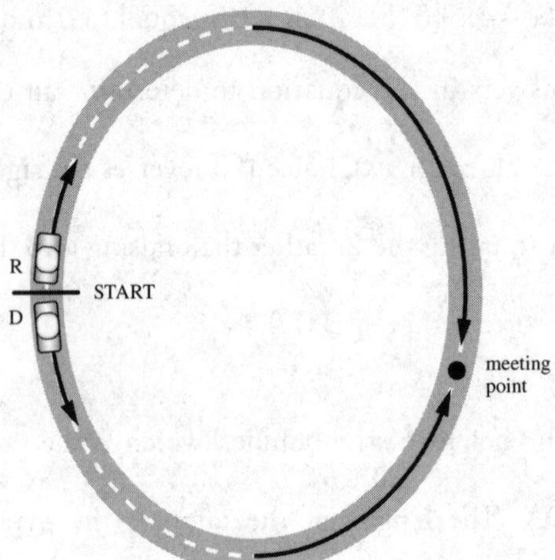

Use the distance formula, *distance* = *rate* × *time,* to get 6000 ft = *r*(150 sec). That means their combined rate is $\frac{6{,}000 \text{ ft}}{150 \text{ s}} = 40$ ft/s. The combined rate can be expressed as $r_R + r_D = 40$ ft/s. Because Rusty drives 8 ft/s faster than Dale does, their rates can be expressed as follows: $r_R - 8 = r_D$. Use substitution to get $r_R + r_R - 8 = 40$ ft/s, or $2r_R - 8 = 40$ ft/s. To solve for r_R, first add 8 to both sides to get $2r_R = 48$ ft/s; then divide both sides by 2 to get $r_R = 24$ ft/s. Choice (A) gives Dale's rate, (B) is what their rates would be if they were traveling at the same speed, and (E) is the combined rate. The correct answer is (C).

50. **K** The question asks for the time it takes Rusty to drive the final lap. Since Rusty drives the first 7 laps at an average time of 180 seconds, multiply these values together to find that he drives the first 7 laps in a total time of 1,260 seconds. Complete the same operation for the second set of numbers: since Rusty drives 8 laps at an average time of 190 s, multiply these values together to find that he drives all 8 laps in a total time of 1,520 seconds. Now take these two totals and find the difference between them for the time of the last lap: 1,520 seconds – 1,260 seconds = 260 seconds. Choice (H) is the result of averaging 180 and 190 without taking into account the 7 laps that were driven at an average of 180 seconds each. The correct answer is (K).

51. **D** The question asks for a rate and gives different units. First, find the total distance. Dale drives 6 laps, each of which is 6,000 feet, for a total of 36,000 ft in 90 minutes. The question asks for this value in feet per hour, so convert the 90 minutes to 1.5 hours. The rate is 36,000 ft ÷ 1.5 hrs = 24,000 ft/hr. Choice (A) is feet/minute. The correct answer is (D).

52. **G** The question asks for the location of a point in relation to two circles. Draw the two circles on the coordinate plane and plot the point (–2,2). The equation of a circle is $(x - h)^2 + (y - k)^2 = r^2$, where (h, k) is the center of the circle and r is the radius. Thus, circle B has its center at (–4,2) with a radius of 3. A drawing of this will show that the point lies outside circle A and inside circle B.

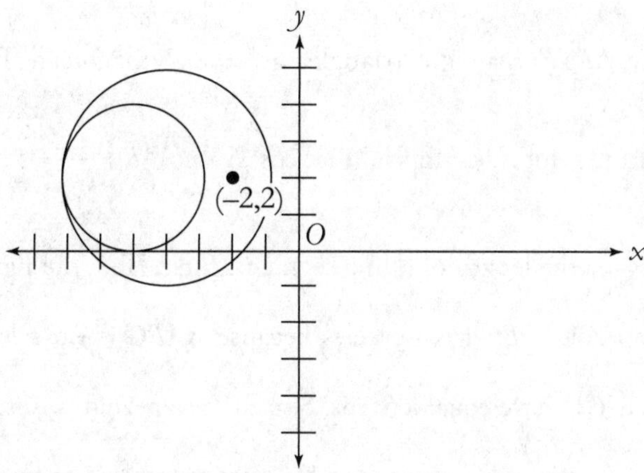

The correct answer is (G).

53. **B** The question asks for the perimeter of a figure. The perimeter is the distance around the shape's outline. There are two straight lines: from (0,0) to (0,4) and from (0,0) to (4,0), each with a length of 4. The straight lines total 8, eliminating (A), (D), and (E). The curved parts are two semicircles and two semicircles make one complete circle, so find the circumference of one circle with radius 2: $C = 2\pi r = 2\pi(2) = 4\pi$. The entire perimeter is thus $8 + 4\pi$. Choice (D) gives the area of the ornament. The correct answer is (B).

54. **F** The question asks which graph represents an even function. An even function is defined in the question as a function for which the value of $f(x) = f(-x)$. This means that $f(x)$ has the same value for both x and $-x$. If the graph of an even function is folded along the y-axis, the two sides of the graph will be mirror reflections of each other. Choices (G), (J), and (K) are odd functions, in which $f(-x) = -f(x)$ for all values of x. Odd functions rotate 180° about the point (0,0). Choice (H) is not a function, because it does not pass the Vertical Line Test; the same x value yields two values for $f(x)$. The correct answer is (F).

55. **B** The question asks for the distance between two points. Use the distance formula: $d = \sqrt{(x_2 - x_1)^2 + (y_2 - y_1)^2}$. Plug in the values of the points given in the question to get $d = \sqrt{(4w - w)^2 + (w - 5 - (w + 5))^2} = \sqrt{(3w)^2 + (-10)^2} = \sqrt{9w^2 + 100}$. The correct answer is (B).

56. **F** The question asks for the value of an expression involving cosine. The definition of cosine is $\cos\theta = \frac{\text{adjacent}}{\text{hypotenuse}}$. In this triangle, $\cos S = \frac{r}{t}$ and $\cos R = \frac{s}{t}$. Therefore, $\cos^2 S + \cos^2 R = \frac{r^2}{t^2} + \frac{s^2}{t^2}$, or $\frac{r^2 + s^2}{t^2}$. Since ΔRST is a right triangle, use the Pythagorean Theorem to determine that $r^2 + s^2 = t^2$. Substitute t^2 for $r^2 + s^2$ to find that $\cos^2 S + \cos^2 R = \frac{t^2}{t^2} = 1$. The correct answer is (F).

57. **C** The question asks for the length of a line segment. First, label the figure with information from the question. Trapezoid $DECA$ is isosceles because ΔABC is isosceles and, since $\overline{DE} \parallel \overline{AC}$, line segments $\overline{AD}$ and $\overline{CE}$ have equal lengths. Since the trapezoid is isosceles, the diagonals are congruent. Thus, ΔDFE and ΔAFC are similar. Set up a proportion to find the missing side: $\frac{9}{6} = \frac{27}{\overline{FC}}$. Cross-multiply to get $9\overline{FC} = 162$; then divide both sides of the equation by 9 to find that $\overline{FC} = 18$. Choice (A) is the short side of ΔDFE multiplied by 2. Choice (B) is 9 + 6. Choice (D) is 27 + 6 and (E) is 27 + 9. The correct answer is (C).

58. **F** The question asks for the product of two matrices. The dimensions of a matrix product are determined by the number of rows in the first matrix and the number of columns in the second matrix, in this case 2 × 1. Thus, (H), (J), and (K) have the wrong dimensions. To find the product value,

multiply rows by columns and add the products of one row-column: $(4 \times 0) + (-2 \times 2) = -4$ and $(3 \times 0) + (-6 \times 2) = -12$. Thus, the matrix is $\begin{bmatrix} -4 \\ -12 \end{bmatrix}$. The correct answer is (F).

59. **D** The question asks for the value of $n!$. The symbol ! denotes a factorial, which is the product of decreasing consecutive integers starting from the integer in front of the ! sign. (For example, $5! = 5 \times 4 \times 3 \times 2 \times 1 = 120$.) Simplify this expression by separating the two largest factors in the numerator: $\frac{(n+1)(n)[(n-1)!]}{(n-1)!} = 20$. The $(n - 1)!$ expression in the numerator and denominator cancels out, leaving $(n + 1)(n) = 20$, which means that $n + 1 = 5$, and $n = 4$. The question asks for $n!$, so $4! = 4 \times 3 \times 2 \times 1 = 24$. Alternatively, try out some values for n. If $n = 4$, $n! = 4 \times 3 \times 2 \times 1 = 24$. The value of $(n + 1)! = (4 + 1)! = (5)! = 120$, and the value of $(n - 1)! = (4 - 1)! = (3)! = 3 \times 2 \times 1 = 6$. The value of $\frac{(n+1)!}{(n-1)!} = \frac{120}{6} = 20$. This matches the information in the question, so $n = 4$ and $n! = 24$. Choice (A) is 3. Choice (B) is half of 20. Choice (C) is half of 24. Choice (E) is 5. The correct answer is (D).

60. **K** The question asks for a ratio between two measurements of a circle without giving any specific measurements. To simplify this abstract problem, substitute a value for the circle's radius. If the radius is 3, the circumference is $2\pi r = 2(\pi)(3) = 6\pi$. The ratio can be expressed as $\frac{\text{radius}}{\text{circumference}} = \frac{3}{6\pi} = \frac{1}{2\pi}$. Choice (F) gives the ratio of the circumference to the radius. Choices (H) and (J) work with the diameter instead of the radius, and (G) finds the ratio of the diameter to the radius. The correct answer is (K).

TEST 1 READING ANSWERS AND EXPLANATIONS

Passage I

1. **C** The question asks for the narrator's point of view. Because this is a general question, it should be done after all the specific questions. The passage focuses on Ruby and her diner, so the answer to this general question should mention both of them. Eliminate (A) because it refers only to *a particular place* and does not mention Ruby. Eliminate (B) because it mentions neither Ruby nor the diner. Choices (C) and (D) both mention Ruby and her diner, but (D) brings in the unrelated idea of *how many people's lives were positively impacted* by them. Eliminate (D). The correct answer is (C).

2. **J** The question asks for the main idea of lines 1–27, so read those lines. The lines introduce Ruby and her diner, and the third paragraph describes how much time the narrator spent at the diner. Although the second paragraph describes *how Ruby got the money to pay for the diner and her eventual success in paying off her debts,* that describes only a small part of lines 1–27, not their main purpose; eliminate (F). The first paragraph mentions that *the locals called [the diner] by different names,* but this is also a detail; eliminate (G). Lines 11–13 say that *my grandmother was a person of considerable stature in and around Robertson County, just like the restaurant that bore her name,* but the idea in (H) that she is *the most important person in Franklin* is not directly supported; eliminate (H). Choice (J) accurately describes lines 1–27. The correct answer is (J).

3. **B** The question asks how best to describe Ruby Sanders. Because this is a general question, it should be done after all the specific questions. The fourth paragraph describes how Ruby was *omnipresent* at the diner, but there is no indication that she *preferred to be absent;* eliminate (A). Lines 34–35 use the metaphor of a cell to describe Ruby's importance to the diner: *without the nucleus* (that is, Ruby), *the cell* (the diner) *would surely perish.* This supports the idea in (B). Lines 79–80 describe Ruby *enjoying a story and a laugh,* but this is one small detail, not the main characterization of her; eliminate (C). The passage does not discuss any women other than Ruby at any length, so it is not possible to say whether Ruby was *the only woman the narrator had ever respected;* eliminate (D). The correct answer is (B).

4. **H** The question asks how the narrator felt about his last summer at the diner based on the last paragraph. Read the last paragraph. Lines 74–76 state that the narrator *didn't know that [he] would never return,* and that *[he] could not have asked for a better end.* There is no indication that it was *disappointing,* so eliminate (F). There is also no indication that he was *forced* to do anything, so eliminate (G). Choice (H) is supported by lines 74–76. Line 68 says that the narrator *took on more responsibility,* but there is no indication of that responsibility being *exhausting;* eliminate (J). The correct answer is (H).

5. **B** The question asks what working at Ruby's Diner was like. Look for the word *work* to find the answer to the question. Lines 69–70 say *It was hard but never dull work.* Choice (A) is the opposite of

this idea, so eliminate it. Choice (B) matches lines 69–70. *Monotonous* is also contradicted by *never dull,* so eliminate (C). There is no indication of either *unpredictable* or *overwhelming,* so eliminate (D). The correct answer is (B).

6. **F** The question asks for a comparison that the narrator makes between his grandmother and the diner. Look for comparative language in the passage. In lines 11–13, the narrator says that Ruby *was a person of considerable stature in and around Robertson County, just like the restaurant that bore her name,* which matches (F). Eliminate (G) because it describes Ruby, but not the diner. Eliminate (J) for the same reason; it could describe Ruby, but not the diner. Choice (H) is the opposite; it could describe the diner, but not Ruby. Eliminate (H). The correct answer is (F).

7. **A** The question asks what is suggested about the Downhome Diner by lines 44–45, so read a window around those lines. The sixth paragraph, which starts on line 44, describes the wide array of services the diner offered, which supports (A). No other places in Robertson County are discussed, so eliminate (B). The only person whose stature in Robertson County is discussed is Ruby, and that discussion is in lines 11–13, not lines 44–45; eliminate (C). There is no discussion of *waiting times,* so eliminate (D). The correct answer is (A).

8. **G** The question asks what Ruby's Downhome Diner does not provide. When a question asks which answer is **not** in the passage, eliminate answers that **are** in the passage. Use words from the answer choices to locate the relevant portions of the passage. The sixth paragraph describes *cooking classes, wedding cakes,* and *corn pone* as things that Ruby's Diner offers, so eliminate (F), (H), and (J). *Football leagues* are mentioned in the last paragraph, but they are not something offered at the diner. The correct answer is (G).

9. **C** The question asks how the passage indicates the narrator's familiarity with the diner. Lines 55–56 state that *the entire layout [of the diner] was imprinted indelibly in [the narrator's] mind. Cooking classes* are mentioned in the sixth paragraph, but there is no indication that the narrator taught them; eliminate (A). *Visitors to Robertson County* are mentioned in the first and fourth paragraphs, but their *habits* are not described, so eliminate (B). Choice (C) is supported by lines 55–56. The last paragraph talks about a *summer before [the narrator's] return to school,* but there is no indication of *unwillingness to leave,* so eliminate (D). The correct answer is (C).

10. **J** The question asks what allows the narrator to forget the summer activities outside while working at his grandmother's restaurant. Look for the words *summer* and *work,* which appear in the last paragraph. Lines 70–74 say that *The company kept [the narrator] coming back,* and that *the woman who built Ruby's was strong enough to make [him] forget* summer activities. There is no discussion of *tips and wages,* so eliminate (F). There is no indication the diner was *understaffed,* so eliminate (G). There is no discussion of the narrator's *stature in…the community,* so eliminate (H). The paragraph does discuss *his grandmother's strength.* The correct answer is (J).

Passage II

11. **B** The question asks for the primary focus of the passage. Because this is a general question, it should be done after all the specific questions. The passage describes a variety of studies on the question of happiness. There is no mention of a *specific gene,* and *hedonic adaptation* is only part of the focus of the passage, so eliminate (A). Choice (B) accurately summarizes the passage. The passage discusses possible ways to increase happiness, but not *cures for depression,* so eliminate (C). None of the psychologists disagree on *the influence of genes on happiness,* so eliminate (D). The correct answer is (B).

12. **H** The question asks for a similarity in the subjects of the studies by two pairs of researchers. Look for the words *Tellegen and Lykken* and *Lyubomirsky and Sheldon* in the passage. Tellegen and Lykken's study is described in the second paragraph, which states that their study *compared the subjective well-being scores of both fraternal and identical twins.* Lyubomirsky and Sheldon's study is described in the sixth through eighth paragraphs. Lines 65–67 mention their subjects, when it says the researchers are *expanding their study of subjective well-being to large groups of subjects to be observed over extended periods of time.* Eliminate (F) and (J) as each of those choices describes only one of the pairs of researchers. The eighth paragraph describes one of Lyubomirsky and Sheldon's studies in which participants *intentionally engaged in acts of kindness,* but again, this is just one pair of researchers. Eliminate (G). Both pairs of researchers depended on *subjective well-being,* so the correct answer is (H).

13. **D** The question asks which question is *NOT* answered by the passage. When a question asks which answer is **not** in the passage, eliminate answers that **are** in the passage. Use words from the answer choices to locate the relevant portions of the passage. Line 52 states that *about 10 percent [of subjective well-being] is influenced by circumstances,* which effectively answers the question in (A); eliminate (A). Lines 72–74 state that *Lyubomirsky says that...variation and timing of intentional activities, are crucial in influencing happiness,* which effectively answers the question in (B); eliminate (B). Lines 41–44 mention that *choosing particular goals in life* is one of several things that *provide only a temporary increase in subjective well-being,* which effectively answers the question in (C); eliminate (C). The passage does not provide details about the question posed in (D). The correct answer is (D).

14. **F** The question asks for the primary goal of Lyubomirsky and Sheldon's research. Look for the words *Lyubomirsky* and *Sheldon* in the passage: their research is described in the sixth through eighth paragraphs. Lines 63–64 say that *Lyubomirsky hopes to learn the specific mechanisms by which these conscious strategies counteract genetic forces,* which supports (F). Lines 50–51 state that Lyubomirsky and Sheldon *determined that 50 percent of subjective well-being is predetermined by the genetic set point,* which agrees with, rather than contradicts, Tellegen and Lykken's findings; eliminate (G). *Keeping a gratitude journal* and *engaging in kind acts* are both examples given in the eighth paragraph of activities that subjects in Lyubomirsky and Sheldon's studies engaged in, but they did not study the relative effects of the two activities, so eliminate (H). The studies aimed to *counteract genetic forces,* not to *completely eliminate* them, so eliminate (J). The correct answer is (F).

15. **D** The question asks for a summary of the University of Chicago surveys on happiness. Look for the words *University of Chicago* in the passage. Lines 90–95 describe the surveys, and lines 89–90 indicate that the results were unexpected, in that the genetic set point of well-being *is higher than traditionally expected.* Although the survey results were unexpected, the surveys themselves did not reference *earlier psychologists,* so eliminate (A). There is no indication of the rates of *depression and other destructive mood disorders...in America,* so eliminate (B). The survey results indicate that people are generally happy *even without using intentional activities specifically to improve their well-being,* but it does not compare those who engage in activities such as *writing in a gratitude journal* to those who do not, so eliminate (C). Choice (D) is supported by lines 89–90. The correct answer is (D).

16. **H** The question asks what is not true of Lykken and Tellegen's study. When a question asks which answer is **not** in the passage, eliminate answers that **are** in the passage. Look for the words *Lykken* and *Tellegen* in the passage; their study is described in the second paragraph. Lines 13–14 indicate that they studied twins, so eliminate (F). Line 13 indicates that the study used *subjective well-being,* which in lines 8–9 is defined as *self-reported levels of happiness,* so eliminate (G). Lines 14–15 states that *some of [the twins] were raised together and some...were separated and raised in different families,* which contradicts (H). Lines 17–18 say that the researchers *determined that most of the difference in people's levels of happiness are determined by differences in genetic makeup,* so eliminate (J). The correct answer is (H).

17. **A** The question asks why hedonic adaptation is helpful. Read a window around the given lines. Lines 25–29 describe how hedonic adaptation *benefits those whose life-experiences are beset by adverse conditions* because it allows them to *return to a "genetic set point"* of happiness, which means that *they eventually feel just as happy as they did before the unfortunate event.* This explanation supports (A). There is no indication that people regain happiness because they *forget that they have suffered,* so eliminate (B). Choice (C) can be eliminated because, while *winning the lottery* is discussed in lines 32–34, the passage says that *a year after the winners received their money, they were no happier than non-winners,* which contradicts (C). The discussion of hedonic adaptation makes no mention of *family members who share...genes,* so eliminate (D). The correct answer is (A).

18. **G** The question asks what would be lost if the first paragraph were deleted. Read the first paragraph. The first paragraph describes a Holocaust survivor who, *even though the circumstances of her life were tragic,...was extremely happy, perhaps due to an innate sense of well-being.* The story may suggest that events are unimportant in determining a person's well-being, which contradicts (F), so eliminate (F). The story supports the idea in (G). The paragraph does not discuss *hedonic adaptation,* so eliminate (H). The paragraph gives only one example of one person overcoming *adverse conditions,* so eliminate (J). The correct answer is (G).

19. **C** The question asks for the main purpose of the final paragraph, so read the final paragraph. That paragraph compares traditional views of happiness within psychology with new findings based on *surveys conducted by the University of Chicago.* The paragraph focuses only on *the study of happiness*

within *psychological research,* not on *psychological researchers* in general or their error rates, so eliminate (A). The paragraph does not contradict that idea presented by Ross's anecdote in the first paragraph, so eliminate (B). The results of the University of Chicago surveys did give *a positive view of people's overall levels of happiness,* so keep (C). Although the surveys showed that *most Americans described themselves as "pretty happy"...even without using intentional activities...to improve their well-being,* it does not address the question of whether effort can make people happier, so eliminate (D). The correct answer is (C).

20. **H** The question asks which pair of researchers has an ongoing collaboration. Use the names in the answer choices to find the relevant portions of the passage. *Tellegen* and *Lykken's* study is described in the past tense in the second paragraph, so eliminate (F). *Sheldon* is paired with *Lyubomirsky,* not with *Schkade,* so eliminate (G). Lines 64–65 say that *[Lyubomirsky] and Sheldon are currently expanding their study,* which supports (H). *Lykken* is paired with *Tellegen,* not with *Schkade,* so eliminate (J). The correct answer is (H).

Passage III

21. **B** The question asks for the author's attitude towards Zitkala-Sa. Because this is a general question, it should be done after the specific questions for Passage A. There is no indication that the author believes Zitkala-Sa was *a spoiled teenager,* so eliminate (A). Lines 45–46 describe Zitkala-Sa *becoming an advocate for Native American rights,* so keep (B). Although the fourth paragraph describes the author's *indignation* at Zitkala-Sa's return to school, the final paragraph indicates that the author eventually understands that *leaving home allowed her to embrace her Sioux identity,* so eliminate (C). Choice (D) can be eliminated for the same reason: the author was initially *confused,* but came to understand Zitkala-Sa's choices. The correct answer is (B).

22. **J** The question asks for the author's description of the clash between Native American and white cultures. Look for the word *clash* in the passage. Lines 14–17 say that *the clash between Native Americans and the "pale faces" who misunderstood and exploited them adds fire to Zitkala-Sa's chronicles of her school years."* Eliminate (F) because Zitakala-Sa eventually *embraced her Sioux identity;* she did not adopt a *white lifestyle.* Lines 14–17 indicate that the clash between cultures was important, so eliminate (G). Zitkala-Sa's *unhappiness at school* is described in the third paragraph. Although *her dismay at having her hair cut and her moccasins taken away* could be interpreted as a clash between cultures, there are other factors mentioned: *her rage at the unjust rules and the willful neglect on the part of the teachers.* Eliminate (H). Choice (J) is directly supported by lines 14–17. The correct answer is (J).

23. **A** The question asks what the quoted lines refer to. Read a window in the passage around the given lines. Before the statement in lines 3–5, the author describes a picture of *a beautifully proud Sioux woman,* including details of her *long, glossy black braids* and *traditional dress.* The author then says *it was hard to make myself believe that the woman in this picture was named Gertrude Simmons Bonnin.* The contrast between the appearance of the Sioux woman and her name supports (A). There is

no indication that the pen name caused *confusion,* so eliminate (B). There is also no indication that the author believes *that the picture had been misidentified,* so eliminate (C). The author mentions Bonnin's Sioux name, but never expresses a *preference* for it, so eliminate (D). The correct answer is (A).

24. **F** The question asks why the author *cried hot tears.* Read a window in the passage around the given line. Line 83 says that the tears came *when I heard him bounding away on his pony.* Lines 65–66 indicate that this refers to the author's brother going to a party: *"No, my baby sister, I cannot take you with me to the party to-night."* This supports (F). *Indian maids* are mentioned in line 72, but there is no indication that the author *missed* them; eliminate (G). Although line 53 says that the author's mother *was not capable of comforting her daughter,* that statement refers to the author's general unhappiness, not the specific tears in line 84; eliminate (H). Lines 75–76 mention *muslin dresses, with ribbons,* but that is a description of the girls going to the party, not the reason for the author's tears. Eliminate (J). The correct answer is (F).

25. **B** The question asks about Zitkala-Sa's feelings when she returned home from school. Lines 49–50 say that Zitkala-Sa was *beyond the touch or voice of human aid* during her summers home. Although lines 80–81 say that she had *thrown away [her] shoes, and wore again the soft moccasins,* there is no indication that she was *content;* eliminate (A). The second paragraph supports the idea that she was *distraught,* so keep (B). Line 52 says that Zitkala-Sa's mother *had never gone inside of a schoolhouse,* but there is no indication that Zitkala-Sa wanted to *teach her to read and write;* eliminate (C). Line 68 says that *Dawée persisted in calling me his baby sister,* but there is no specific support for the idea that this, in particular, caused the author to be *upset.* Eliminate (D). The correct answer is (B).

26. **H** The question asks what the given lines describe. Read a window in the passage around lines 55–56. Lines 49–55 describes how the author was *beyond the touch or voice of human aid,* and that *even nature seemed to have no place for [her].* Although height is mentioned *(I was neither a wee girl nor a tall one),* it is one example of her feelings, not the main idea described; eliminate (F). Similarly, teenage years are mentioned in lines 57–58, but are only a part of a larger problem; eliminate (G). Choice (H) is supported by the entire second paragraph, so keep it. Although lines 50–53 say that the narrator's *brother…did not quite understand my feelings* and that her mother *was not capable of comforting her daughter,* that does not mean that they *rejected* her, so eliminate (J). The correct answer is (H).

27. **D** The question asks what the word *civilized* is used to describe. Read a window in the passage around the given lines. The previous sentence says that the young people who had gone to school in the East *were no more young braves in blankets and eagle plumes, nor Indian maids with prettily painted cheeks,* and the following sentence describes how they now wore *the white man's coat and trousers,* and *tight muslin dresses.* There is no mention of *manners,* so eliminate (A). There is also no mention of *living quarters,* so eliminate (B). Although school is mentioned, the description has more to do with clothing than with *education,* so eliminate (C). Clothing is an *aspect of white culture,* so keep (D). The correct answer is (D).

28. **J** The question asks what both passages emphasize about Zitkala-Sa. Eliminate any answer choices that misrepresent either passage. Both passages discuss her difficulties fitting in when she returned from school, but neither passage indicates that there was a *refusal* to do so; eliminate (F). Although Passage A says that Zitkala-Sa went *to work at an institution…like her first…school,* there is no indication that she became *an advocate for sending Native Americans to school;* eliminate (G). Passage B says that Zitkala-Sa's mother *was not capable of comforting her,* but that is not the same as *difficulty getting along with her mother;* eliminate (H). Lines 41–42 in Passage A say that Zitkala-Sa *was destined to feel like an outsider anywhere,* and line 54 says that *Even nature had no place for [her],* both of which support the idea of *not belonging* in (J). The correct answer is (J).

29. **C** The question asks what moccasins are a symbol of in both passages. Look for the word *moccasins* in both passages. In Passage A, lines 23–26 describe Zitkala-Sa's *unhappiness at school,* and that fact that *her moccasins [were] taken away* is an example of what made her unhappy. When she returned home, *she was able to wear her beloved moccasins again.* Passage B also describes her wearing moccasins at home, in lines 79–81: *Since my return from school I had thrown away my shoes, and wore again the soft moccasins.* While the taking away of moccasins might symbolize oppression, the moccasins themselves cannot symbolize oppression since they are described as *beloved* and *soft;* eliminate (A). Similarly, the moccasins do not symbolize *frustration,* so eliminate (B). The moccasins are mentioned in both passages in the context of Zitkala-Sa not being dressed like the other young people who wore their school clothes, so they could be a symbol of Native American culture; keep (C). The moccasins are described as *soft,* which could support the idea of *comfortable,* but they **are** comfortable footwear, not a *symbol* of it, so eliminate (D). The correct answer is (C).

30. **F** The question asks how the author of Passage A would view the events in Passage B. Eliminate any answer choices that don't agree with the main idea of Passage A. Passage A continually refers to the *clash between Native American culture and white men,* and lines 42–43 state that *leaving home allowed [Zitkala-Sa] to embrace her Sioux identity.* This supports the ideas of a *struggle* and a *strong sense of identity* in (F). Lines 16–18 say that the clash of culture *adds fire to Zitkala-Sa's chronicles… which might otherwise have been written by any angst-filled teenager;* in other words, the author is saying she is **not** a typical teenager, so eliminate (G). Lines 43–46 say that *Pursuing her education… was…a step in her journey towards becoming an advocate for Native American rights.* Thus, her school years were only the beginning of her appreciation of Sioux culture, so eliminate (H). Passage A makes no mention of Zitkala-Sa's relationships with her mother and brother, so eliminate (J). The correct answer is (F).

Passage IV

31. **A** The question asks which question is *NOT* answered by the passage. When a question asks which answer is **not** in the passage, eliminate answers that **are** in the passage. Use words from the answer choices to locate the relevant portions of the passage. The third paragraph discusses how coquí frogs hatch, but there is no discussion of how they *mate* or *produce offspring,* so keep (A). The

second paragraph notes that coquí frogs are native to Puerto Rico, and lines 16–18 state that in Hawaii the frogs don't face danger from *the snakes, tarantulas, or other Caribbean hungers that usually serve to keep the coquí population in check.* This effectively answers the question in (B), so eliminate (B). Lines 36–38 describe how *coquíes tend to overlap their calls,* which results in louder sound than individual calls would. This effectively answers the question in (C), so eliminate (C). Lines 50–55 state that *coquíes...are threatening the survival of...insects,* and that *ornithologists fear that depleting the insect population could result in serious consequences for Hawaii's food web.* This effectively answers the question in (D), so eliminate (D). The correct answer is (A).

32. **F** The question asks what can be inferred about the lack of amphibian life in Hawaii. Look for the words *amphibian* and *Hawaii* in the passage. Lines 15–16 say that coquíes *faced little competition [in Hawaii], as there are no other amphibians native to the islands.* This supports (F). *Symbiotic relationships* are discussed in the sixth paragraph, but there is nothing there about the lack of amphibian life in Hawaii; eliminate (G). There is no discussion of coquíes building nests, so eliminate (H). Lines 15–16 say that amphibians are not native to Hawaii, so their lack cannot be due to *invasive species' attacks;* eliminate (J). The correct answer is (F).

33. **C** The question asks what the passage says about the noise level produced by the coqui. Look for the word *noise* in the passage. The fourth paragraph discusses the coquíes' *extremely loud calling song.* Lines 36–39 state that *coquíes tend to overlap their calls* and that, as a result, they *create a "wall of sound."* Lines 4–5 indicate that female coquíes have the *lower, guttural croaks,* so eliminate (A). The passage does not discuss coquíes *defending their territory,* so eliminate (B). Choice (C) is supported by lines 36–39. Lines 1–3 say that *as night falls..., the sound grows louder,* but there is no mention of what happens at dawn; eliminate (D). The correct answer is (C).

34. **H** The question asks for the primary purpose of the third paragraph, so read the third paragraph. The paragraph says that *the way the coquí hatch also gives the coquí an advantage in Hawaii's ecosystem,* and that *young coquíes don't begin to emit their signature calls until they are about a year old; consequently, avian predators are unable to locate the tiny frogs by sound.* Lines 23–25 emphasize the small amount of water coquíes need to survive: *saturated moss, the dampened plastic that importers wrap around plants, or even a drop of water on a plant leaf.* This contradicts (F), so eliminate (F). Puerto Rico is mentioned in the second paragraph, not the third, so eliminate (G). Choice (H) is supported, so keep it. The paragraph discusses coquíes (which do not have a tadpole stage) in particular, not amphibians in general, so eliminate (J). The correct answer is (H).

35. **B** The question asks for the difference in the language used in the sixth paragraph as compared to the first paragraph. Read both paragraphs. The first paragraph uses descriptive language to evoke the sense of the coquí's call: *a low, jarring sound begins...the sound grows louder, rending the stillness of the evening.* The sixth paragraph uses words like *symbiotic, "dissonant" species, herpetologists, vertebrate parasites, indigenous fauna,* and *biota.* These words are not *opinionated,* so eliminate (A). They are *scientific,* so keep (B). The paragraph discusses *another ecological threat,* so it is not *optimistic;* eliminate (C). The words used are formal, not *casual,* so eliminate (D). The correct answer is (B).

36. **G** This question asks what the word *extirpation* means in line 53. Go back to the text, find the word *extirpation,* and mark it out. Carefully read the surrounding text to determine another word that would fit in the blank based on the context of the passage. Lines 50–51 say that *coquíes...are threatening the survival of arthropods.* The phrase *already close to* indicates that *extirpation* is similar to *threatening the survival,* so *extirpation* could be replaced with "dying out." *Competition* means "rivalry," which does not match "dying out," so eliminate (F). *Extinction* means "dying out," so keep (G). *Overpopulation* is the opposite of "dying out," so eliminate (H). *Pursuit* means "following," which does not match "dying out," so eliminate (J). The correct answer is (G).

37. **D** The question asks which idea is presented as theory rather than fact. Use words from the answer choices to locate the relevant portions of the passage. Lines 32–41 describe *two...factors* that influence *the unusual volume of the frog's call.* The first is that *coquíes congregate closely on relatively small parcels of land,* and the second is that *coquíes tend to overlap their calls,* which creates *a "wall of sound."* This supports (A), so eliminate (A). Lines 71–73 say that *The maximum concentration of pesticides that would not damage fauna or flora has not been potent enough to kill the frogs,* which supports (B). Eliminate (B). Lines 76–82 discuss the use of *caffeine citrate* to kill the frogs. The passage states that caffeine citrate has the *benefit of posing almost no danger to...insects, which have an impenetrable, hard exoskeleton.* This supports (C), so eliminate (C). Lines 54–57 say that *Ornithologists fear that depleting the insect population could result in serious consequences for Hawaii's food web, especially considering that the birds native to the islands are also insectivores.* The phrase *fear that* indicates that this idea is theory, rather than established fact. The correct answer is (D).

38. **F** The question asks what the parasites the coquíes carry are called. Look for the word *parasites* in the passage. Lines 62–64 say that *Herpetologists have speculated that nematodes and other types of vertebrate parasites can be transported with coquíes.* This matches (F). *Arthropods, scorpions,* and *arachnids* are all mentioned in the fifth paragraph, which does not discuss *parasites,* so eliminate (G), (H), and (J). The correct answer is (F).

39. **B** The question asks what the relevance of the greenhouse frog is to the discussion of the coquí. Look for the phrase *greenhouse frog* in the passage. Lines 47–49 state that *another, quieter genus of the frog—the greenhouse frog—represents an equal threat to the biodiversity of the island.* There is no discussion of where the greenhouse frogs live, so eliminate (A). Choice (B) is supported by lines 47–49. Choice (C) says the opposite of lines 48–49, so eliminate it. Although the passage says the greenhouse frogs are *quieter* than coquíes are, there is no discussion of which is *easier to locate and eliminate,* so eliminate (D). The correct answer is (B).

40. **J** The question asks what the term *1,000 acres* refers to in line 85. Read a window in the passage around the given line. Line 85 indicates that the *1,000 acres* are part of *Hawaii's ecosystem,* not the *Caribbean ecosystem,* so eliminate (F). There is no mention of either a *bird sanctuary* or the *rain forest* in this context, so eliminate (G) and (H). Lines 84–85 discuss *the invader's* (that is, the coquí's) *effects on the 1,000 acres of Hawaii.* Therefore, the *1,000 acres* must be *coquí habitat.* The correct answer is (J).

TEST 1 SCIENCE ANSWERS AND EXPLANATIONS

Passage I

1. **A** The question asks for the angle of the ramp if Experiment 3 had been repeated at a temperature of 62.5°C. Look at Table 3 and find where 62.5°C would fit in with the existing data. As temperature increases in Table 3, the angle also increases. A temperature of 62.5°C would fall between 50°C and 75°C, so the angle for 62.5°C would fall between 25.4 and 29.0. Eliminate (B), (C), and (D). The correct answer is (A).

2. **F** The question asks which material would have taken the *greatest amount of force to start moving,* based on the results of Experiment 1. Look at the results of Experiment 1. Table 1 lists the different materials in order of increasing angle. The object made of brick required the largest ramp angle before any movement took place, which means it is most resistant to movement. Therefore, the brick object would also require the greatest amount of force to start moving on a flat surface. Eliminate (G), (H), and (J). The correct answer is (F).

3. **D** The question asks for the effect of the weight of the object on the *coefficient of static friction,* based on the results of Experiments 1 and 4. Look at the results of Experiments 1 and 4. Table 1 lists the different materials in order of increasing ramp angle. Table 4 lists the number of objects and the ramp angle. Experiment 4 used only wooden objects, so compare the angle for wood in Table 1 with the results in Table 4. In all cases, the angle is 22.0. Because adding more objects does not change the results, choose the answer that indicates no change. Eliminate (A), (B), and (C). The correct answer is (D).

4. **G** The question asks why the students used objects of different materials in Experiment 1. Look at the description of Experiment 1, and eliminate any answer choices that do not accurately describe it. In Experiment 1, the objects were placed on the ramp. According to Figure 1, the ramp was covered in a *polymer film*. The objects of different materials were what moved against the surface of the ramp, not the *plastic board* that made the ramp, so eliminate (F). Choice (G) accurately describes the experiment, so keep it. Eliminate (H) because only one object was tested at a time. No objects were *stacked* in Experiment 1, so eliminate (J). The correct answer is (G).

5. **D** The question asks for a list of different materials, from *greatest resistance to movement to least resistance to movement.* Find the experiment that varies the materials and look at the results. Table 1 lists the different materials in order of increasing ramp angle. An increased angle indicates greater resistance to movement, so brick, which has the greatest angle, has the most resistance to movement. Eliminate (A), (B), and (C). Note that (A) has the materials listed in order from least resistance to greatest resistance, the opposite of what the question asks. The correct answer is (D).

6. **G** The question asks about the purpose of varying the temperature in Experiment 3. Look at the results of Experiment 3. Table 3 lists the ramp angle required for the wooden object to move at a

variety of temperatures. Eliminate any answer choices that do not accurately describe Experiment 3. According to Figure 1, the ramp was covered in a *polymer film*. Eliminate (F) because the ramp was not *wood*. Keep (G) because it accurately describes Experiment 3. Eliminate (H) because there is no mention of *mass* anywhere in the experiment. Eliminate (J) because Experiment 3 tested only the wooden object, not *all objects*. The correct answer is (G).

7. **D** The question asks about the force required to move the stationary block if *Experiment 1 were repeated with the granite block placed with Face C against the surface of the ramp*. Look at Tables 1 and 2. According to Table 2, the angle at which the object started to slide was identical, no matter which face of the block was placed down on the ramp. This means that if Experiment 1 were repeated with the granite block on Face C, the force required to move the block would be the same as if it were on Face A. Eliminate (A) and (C). Since the blocks start to slide at the same angle regardless of what face of the block is placed down on the ramp, the surface area of the block is not important in determining the force required for movement. Eliminate (B). The true determinant of the force is the coefficient of friction. The correct answer is (D).

Passage II

8. **H** The question asks which of the following is closest to the *average number of polio cases reported per month in Nigeria in 2004*. Refer to Figure 1, which displays the total number of polio cases for each month in Nigeria in 2004. Eliminate (F) because only 2 months had fewer than 35 cases reported, and most months had 60 or more cases, so this is far too low to be the average. Eliminate (J) because most of the months had far fewer than 75 cases, so this is way too high. To choose between (G) and (H), draw a horizontal line at 60 cases per month. Notice that half of the values are well above this line and four of those months (April through July) are at least 20 cases above this line. On the other hand, only 3 values fall below this line. Therefore, the average is greater than 60. Eliminate (G). The correct answer is (H).

9. **A** The question asks when the *greatest increase in the number of reported polio infections in Nigeria occurred*, according to Figure 1. Use the answer choices to find the greatest increase in Figure 1. Between February and March, the number of cases went from about 45 to 70, an increase of about 25. From March to April, the number of cases went from 70 to about 82, an increase of about 12. Eliminate (B) since this is a smaller increase than February to March. From April to May, the number of cases went from about 82 to 90, an increase of about 8. Eliminate (C) since this is also less than the increase in (A). There was a decrease in cases reported from November to December, so eliminate (D). The correct answer is (A).

10. **J** The question asks how many people were *at risk for becoming infected with the polio virus in Nigeria in June 2004*, according to the results of Study 1. Look at Figure 1. In June 2004, there were 80 *polio infections reported in Nigeria*. Eliminate (F) because it gives the number of infections reported rather than the number of people at risk. The question says that *for every person infected with the*

polio virus…there are 200 people at risk, so multiply 80 × 200 to find that 16,000 people were *at risk.* The correct answer is (J).

11. **A** The question asks for the reason for the *difference in reported cases of polio in major Indian cities between June and August of 2007,* according to Figure 2. Look at Figure 2. The data shows the number of reported polio infections in five cities during the months of June and August 2007. The dark bars indicate the number of infections in June, and the light bars indicate the number of infections in August. The key indicates that June is *dry summer season* and August is *rainy monsoon season.* Eliminate any answer choices that do not accurately describe the data in the figure. Choice (A) is consistent with the data. There are both more cases of polio and more water in August, so eliminate (B). There is no data for *autumn and winter seasons,* so eliminate (C). Eliminate (D) because it is inconsistent with the increase in infections in August. The correct answer is (A).

12. **H** The question asks for the hypothesis tested in Study 2. Look at the results of Study 2. Figure 2 shows the number of reported polio infections in five cities during the months of June and August 2007. The dark bars indicate the number of infections in June, and the light bars indicate the number of infections in August. The key indicates that June is *dry summer season* and August is *rainy monsoon season.* Eliminate any answers choices that do not accurately describe the data in the figure. Figure 2 does not show any data for *Nigeria,* so eliminate (F). The figure shows only infections that were reported; it does not present any data about infections that are *not reported to medical authorities,* so eliminate (G). The figure shows more cases in New Delhi and Kolkata than in the other cities, which is consistent with (H). There is no data about *winter* in the figure, so eliminate (J). The correct answer is (H).

13. **D** The question asks whether *the presence of mosquitoes* is related to *the transmission of the polio virus.* Since there is no information about *mosquitoes* in the figures, look for the key word *mosquitoes* in the text of the passage. The text of the passage doesn't say anything about *mosquitoes,* so eliminate (A) and (C). Choices (B) and (D) both refer to *human waste,* so look for that term in the text of the passage. The first paragraph states that the *polio virus…is most often transmitted through water that is contaminated by human waste.* Thus, *mosquitoes* would not affect the *transmission of the…virus,* so eliminate (B). The correct answer is (D).

14. **H** The question asks about the relationship between the *number of people in Kolkata infected with polio in June* and *the number of people infected with polio in Kolkata in August,* according to Figure 2. Look at Figure 2. The key indicates that the dark bar represents June; the dark bar above Kolkata is about 12. The light bar represents August; the light bar above Kolkata is about 24. Eliminate (F) because it gives the opposite of the relationship the question asks for (i.e., June to August instead of August to June). Eliminate (G) because the numbers for the two months are not *the same.* Choice (H) accurately represents the data. The correct answer is (H).

Passage III

15. **B** The question asks what happens to the ESP as the EC increases from its lowest to its highest value in Sample 2. Refer to Sample 2 in Figure 1 and look at the trend for EC at the four different depth ranges. EC is the lowest at a depth of 90–120 cm. The next highest EC is at a depth of 60–90 cm, then 0–30 cm. The highest EC is at a depth of 30–60 cm. Now examine what happens to the ESP at these depths in Sample 2 of Figure 2. At a depth of 90–120 cm, when the EC is the lowest, the ESP is about 13. At a depth of 60–90 cm, the ESP is 9 and at a depth of 0–30 cm, the ESP is 7. When the EC is the highest, at a depth of 30–60 cm, the ESP is the lowest, at 6. Since the ESP continually decreases as the EC increases, the correct answer is (B).

16. **H** The question asks about the soil in Sample 4, as compared to the soil in Sample 1, according to Figure 2. Look at Figure 2, which shows depth and ESP for five different samples. Look for the key term *ESP* in the passage; the first paragraph says that *ESP* is *exchangeable sodium percentage,* which *indicates the proportion of electrical conductivity that is due to dissolved sodium ions,* so compare the ESP for Samples 1 and 4. The key indicates that Sample 1 is represented by the solid line with circles, and Sample 4 is represented by the alternating dash and dot line with squares. At depths of 0–30 cm and 30–60 cm, the ESP for Sample 1 is lower than that for Sample 4. At depths of 60–90 cm and 90–120 cm, the ESP for Sample 1 is higher than that for Sample 4. Eliminate (F) and (G) because the relationship between the two samples is not consistent at all depths. Choice (H) is consistent with the data, and (J) gives the opposite relationship. The correct answer is (H).

17. **B** The question asks for the percent of soil conductivity *due to sodium ions* for Sample 3 at a particular depth, according to Figure 2. Look at Figure 2. Figure 2 shows depth and ESP for five different samples. Look for the key term *ESP* in the passage; the first paragraph says that *ESP* is *exchangeable sodium percentage,* which *indicates the proportion of electrical conductivity that is due to dissolved sodium ions.* The key for Figure 2 indicates that Sample 3 is represented by the long-dashed line with triangles. At a depth of 30–60 cm, the ESP for Sample 3 is 17. The correct answer is (B).

18. **J** The question asks for the *electrical conductivity due to sodium ions* in a particular sample, according to Figures 1 and 2. Look at both figures. Only Figure 1 has any information about *distance;* Sample 4 was located at 40 m. Figure 2 shows depth and ESP for five different samples. Look for the key term *ESP* in the passage; the first paragraph says that *ESP* is *exchangeable sodium percentage,* which *indicates the proportion of electrical conductivity that is due to dissolved sodium ions.* The key for Figure 2 indicates that Sample 4 is represented by the alternating dash and dot line with squares. The greatest ESP for Sample 4 occurs at 60–90 cm, so eliminate (F) and (G). The lowest ESP for Sample 4 occurs at 0–30 cm; eliminate (H). The correct answer is (J).

19. **C** The question asks for the best representation of *exchangeable sodium percentage* of the five samples at a particular depth, in bar graph form. Look for the key term *exchangeable sodium percentage* in the passage; the first paragraph says that *ESP* is an abbreviation for *exchangeable sodium percentage.* Figure 2 shows depth and ESP for the five different samples, so look at Figure 2. At a depth of 90–120 cm, Samples 2 and 3 both have ESPs between 10 and 15. Eliminate (A) and (B) because

they give the wrong value for one or both of those samples. Figure 2 shows that Sample 1 has the highest ESP at a depth of 90–120 cm, so eliminate (D). The correct answer is (C).

20. **G** The question asks whether the proposed claim that the salinity of soil increases as the soil moves away from a major water source is supported by Figures 1 and 2. Eliminate any answer choices that do not accurately describe both figures. Neither Figure 1 nor Figure 2 shows a consistent decrease from Sample 1 to Sample 5, so eliminate (F) and (J). Neither figure shows a consistent increase either, so eliminate (H). Choice (G) is consistent with the data because there is no consistent trend from Sample 1 to Sample 5 in either figure. The correct answer is (G).

Passage IV

21. **B** The question asks why the researchers collected data for Group 6. Look at the information given for each group in Table 1. Group 6 is described as *Unaffected polar bear habitat.* There is no information about *predators that most threaten polar bears,* so eliminate (A). A *standard by which the other groups could be compared* could describe Group 6, because there were no unusual factors in the Group 6 habitat; keep (B). Because the Group 6 habitat had no unusual factors, it could not have helped the researchers *identify and select the conditions for the remaining five groups;* eliminate (C). Figure 1 shows that Group 2 had a higher population density than Group 6 did, so Group 6 does not show *the greatest number of polar bears that would be likely to survive in an area of 25 km^2*. Eliminate (D). The correct answer is (B).

22. **F** The question asks why Group 2 was included in the study. Look at the information given for Group 2 in Table 1. Group 2 was in areas that *had significantly increased populations of seaweed commonly consumed by marine mammals.* The other figures in the passage give data about population density of polar bears for the different groups, so population density of the polar bears is what the study was measuring. Eliminate (G), (H), and (J) because none of them addresses the population density of polar bears. The correct answer is (F).

23. **C** The question asks for a list of Groups 1–5 in order from *most conducive to polar bear population density* to *least conducive*. Figure 1 gives data about population density for Groups 1–5, so eliminate any answers that don't match the data in Figure 1. Group 2 has the highest population density ratio, so it should be first on the list; eliminate (A) and (B). Group 5 has the second highest population density, so eliminate (D). Note that (B) has the groups listed in order from *least* to *greatest*, the opposite of what the question asks. The correct answer is (C).

24. **G** The question asks for the organism with a decreased population in Group 1. Look at the information given for Group 1 in Table 1. Group 1 was in areas that *had significantly decreased populations of marine mammals consumed by polar bears.* Eliminate (F) and (H) because neither the *snowy owl* nor *salmon* is a mammal. Polar bears do not eat polar bears, so eliminate (J). The correct answer is (G).

25. **D** The question asks for the groups that the study tested *synergy* between, according to the given definition. Look at the information given for each group in Table 1. No group combined the conditions in Groups 1 and 2, so eliminate (A). Group 4 included the conditions for Group 1, but there was no combination of Groups 1 and 4, so eliminate (B). Both Groups 4 and 5 included the conditions for Group 3, but there was no combination of Groups 4 and 5, so eliminate (C). Group 4 included the conditions for both Groups 1 and 3, so Group 4 was meant to study the combined effects of the conditions from Groups 1 and 3. The correct answer is (D).

26. **H** The question asks which hypothesis is not supported by the results of the study. When a question asks which answer is **not** in the passage, eliminate answers that **are** in the passage. Group 1 had *declining prey populations* as described in (F), and Figure 1 indicates that Group 1 had lower than average population density: the formula above Figure 1 shows that the *population density ratio* in Figure 1 is calculated by dividing each group's average population density by the average population density of Group 6, the unaffected habitat. A population density ratio of less than 1 shows a decline in population, while a ratio of greater than 1 shows an increase. Group 1 thus effectively answers the question in (F); eliminate (F). Group 3 had *melting Arctic sea ice* as described in (G), and the population density ratio in Figure 1 is lower for Group 3 than it is for Group 1, which had *declining prey populations.* The question in (G) is answered, so eliminate (G). Choice (H) presents the opposite hypothesis of the one in (G); since (G) is correct, (H) must be incorrect. Keep (H). Group 3's population density ratio is less than 1, which effectively answers the question in (J), so eliminate (J). The correct answer is (H).

27. **D** The question asks *which of the following is closest to the total number of polar bears found in all ten areas of Group 6.* Table 2 shows the population density for all 10 blocks in Group 6. The population density in Table 2 is expressed as the number of polar bears per km^2, but according to the passage, each block measured in the study represents a 5 km by 5 km area, or 25 km^2. Start by examining Area A in Table 2, which has a population density of 0.93. This can be rounded to about 1 polar bear per km^2. However, since each block is actually 25 km^2, there are approximately 25 polar bears in Area A. Repeat this logic with Area B, which has a population density of about 2 polar bears per km^2, to find that there are about 50 polar bears in Area B. So far, there are 75 total polar bears in Areas A and B alone. Eliminate (A) and (B). There are still 8 more areas to be calculated, so there must be many more polar bears than 90. Eliminate (C). The correct answer is (D).

Passage V

28. **G** The question asks which choice *most weakens* the argument of Scientist 1, based on the new information about Reaction 6. Look at the description of Reaction 6. Scientist 2 says that *the •OH generated by Reactions 1 and 4 will react rapidly with any H_2CO in the atmosphere to produce CO and water.* Eliminate (F) because •OH reacts with CH_4 in Reaction 2, which has nothing to do with Reaction 6. Choice (G) accurately describes both Reaction 4 and Reaction 6, so keep it. Choice (H) accurately describes Reaction 1, but it does not *weaken* the argument of Scientist 1: if Reaction 1

happens as a result of Reaction 6, it would then set up the chain of Reactions 2–4 that Scientist 1 describes. Eliminate (H). Eliminate (J) because Reaction 6 does not produce •OH. Choice (G) weakens the argument of Scientist 1 because it gives an alternate explanation for what happens to the •OH produced in Reaction 4 that is not going back to the beginning of the chain reaction that Scientist 1 describes. The correct answer is (G).

29. **D** The question asks which substances both scientists agree must be present for *•CH_3 to be generated by atmospheric methane.* Look at each scientist's explanation one at a time, and use Process of Elimination. The generation of •CH_3 is described by Scientist 1 in Reaction 2, and one of the important components of Reaction 2, •OH, is generated in Reaction 1. Neither Reaction 1 nor Reaction 2 includes H_3O^+, NO_2, or HNO_3, so eliminate (A), (B), and (C). O_3 is one of the reactants of Reaction 1, so keep (D). Scientist 2 does not explicitly discuss the generation of •CH_3 but does say that *the •OH generated by Reactions 1 and 4 will react rapidly with any H_2CO in the atmosphere,* which means Scientist 2 believes that those reactions occur. The correct answer is (D).

30. **F** The question asks which graph shows Scientist 1's idea of the relationship between H_2CO and CH_4. Look for the key terms *H_2CO* and *CH_4* in Scientist 1's hypothesis. Reactions 2 and 3 show that CH_4 starts a chain of reactions that increases H_2CO. Thus, if CH_4 levels rise, H_2CO levels will also rise. Keep (F) because it accurately describes this relationship. Eliminate (G) and (J) because they both show H_2CO decreasing as CH_4 rises. Eliminate (H) because it shows H_2CO levels remaining constant. The correct answer is (F).

31. **C** The question asks whether the student's suggestion is correct. The suggestion is that *the molecular mass of either product in Reaction 5 would be greater than the molecular mass of the reactant in Reaction 5.* Look at Reaction 5. Because both sides of the reaction contain the same atoms, the reactant (that is, the left side) is heavier than either product (the right side) because the reactant contains all the atoms in the reaction, while each product contains only a portion of them. Thus, the student's suggestion is wrong; eliminate (B) and (D). Although the reason in (A) is true (H_2CO is a molecule that is made up of atoms), it does not describe why the student is incorrect. Eliminate (A). Choice (C) accurately describes why the student is incorrect. The correct answer is (C).

32. **H** The question asks which statement Scientist 1 would *most strongly agree* with, based on decreasing O_3. Look for the key terms *O_3*, *•CH_3*, and *H_2CO* in Scientist 1's hypothesis. O_3 appears in Reaction 1, the beginning of a series of reactions that increase first •CH_3 and then H_2CO. Thus, there is a direct relationship between O_3 and •CH_3 and H_2CO, so if O_3 *decreases,* the other two will also decrease. Eliminate (F) and (G) because O_3 does not have different effects on •CH_3 and H_2CO. Eliminate (J) because •CH_3 and H_2CO would not *increase.* The correct answer is (H).

33. **D** The question asks which statement Scientist 2 would *most strongly disagree* with. Look at Scientist 2's hypothesis. Scientist 2 states that *atmospheric formaldehyde levels will not increase dramatically due to methane emissions.* O_3 is described in Reaction 1, and Scientist 2 indicates that Reaction 1 does occur, so eliminate (A). Scientist 2 states that *•OH generated by Reactions 1 and 4 will react rapidly*

with any H_2CO in the atmosphere to produce CO, which supports (B). Eliminate (B). *Solar radiation* and CH_4 are described in Reactions 1 and 2, and Scientist 2 believes Reaction 1 happens and never specifically mentions Reaction 2; eliminate (C). Choice (D) is directly contradicted by Scientist 2. The correct answer is (D).

34. **G** The question asks how Scientist 2 would support the new claim that Reaction 3 leads to increased levels of carbon monoxide. Look at Scientist 2's hypothesis and at Reaction 3. Scientist 2 never discusses NO, so eliminate (F). Choice (G) accurately describes Reactions 3, 5, and 6, so keep (G). Choice (H) accurately describes Reaction 3, but Scientist 2 never discusses HO_2, so eliminate (H). Choice (J) also accurately describes Reaction 3, but Scientist 2 never discusses O_2, so eliminate (J). The correct answer is (G).

Passage VI

35. **A** The question asks at which volume and pressure the gas in Carnot heat engine B will have the highest temperature. According to the first sentence of Paragraph 3 of the passage, the cycle begins when the gas is *at its highest temperature and pressure.* Refer to Figure 2 to study Carnot heat engine B. The highest pressure point on this graph is at 80 Pa when the volume is at 1.0 mL. This point, therefore, also represents the point of the highest temperature. The correct answer is (A).

36. **G** The question asks for the value of *P* under certain conditions according to Figure 2. Read the question carefully and look up the given values on Figure 2. The question specifies *when V was decreasing from its largest value. V* is on the *x*-axis of Figure 2, and its largest value is at 4.0. Look at the arrows on the lines on the graph to determine when *V* was *decreasing.* The left, or lower, part of the graph has arrows pointing to the left, which gives decreasing values for *V,* so look at the lower line on the graph. The question asks for the value of *P* when *V* is 2.0, so find 2.0 on the *x*-axis. Draw a line up to the lower part of the graph; then draw a horizontal line to the *y*-axis to find the value of *P,* which is about 20. The correct answer is (G).

37. **C** The question asks for the other part of the partial graph shown in the question. Look for the answer that will give a graph most consistent with those shown for engines A and B. Both Figure 1 and Figure 2 have two parts to the graphs that slope down to the right. Eliminate (A) because it has a line that slopes up to the right. Eliminate (D) because its shape would not complete the graph. Notice that the shape of the partial graph given in the question more closely resembles the line with arrows pointing from the upper left to the lower right of both figures. Therefore, the correct answer should have a similar shape to the line with arrows pointing from the lower right to the upper left on both figures. Eliminate (B). The correct answer is (C).

38. **J** The question asks for the value of *V* when *P* was at its minimum for engine A. Engine A is shown in Figure 1, so look at Figure 1. First, determine the minimum value of *P*. *P* is on the *y*-axis, and its minimum is about 7.5 Pa. Draw a vertical line from this lowest point to the *x*-axis to determine the value of *V,* which is about 5.0. The correct answer is (J).

39. **C** The question asks for the relationship between the largest and smallest values of V in Figure 2. Look at Figure 2. V is on the x-axis; its minimum value is 1.0 mL, and its maximum value is 4.0 mL. Eliminate (A) because the minimum value is not negative. Eliminate (B) because $\frac{1}{8}$ of 4.0 is 0.5. Eliminate (D) because it says the smallest value is larger than the largest value. The correct answer is (C).

40. **F** The question asks for the value of V when the *reversible isothermic expansion* begins for engine A. The question defines the *reversible isothermic expansion* as the time *when P is decreased from its highest value and V is increased from its lowest value.* Engine A is shown in Figure 1, so look at Figure 1. The *highest value* for P and the *lowest value* for V both occur at the same point, at the upper left of the graph. Draw a vertical line from that point to the x-axis to determine the value of V at that point. V is 1.5 mL. The correct answer is (F).

WRITING TEST

Essay Checklist

- ❒ Clearly state your own perspective.
- ❒ Reference the ideas of all 3 perspectives.
- ❒ Use examples to explain your point of view.
- ❒ Have 2–3 body paragraphs with 5–7 sentences each.
- ❒ Have an introduction and a conclusion paragraph.
- ❒ Write neatly.
- ❒ Use a formal tone and a mature level of vocabulary.
- ❒ Avoid spelling and grammar errors.

Mini Practice Drills

When preparing for the ACT, taking full practice sections or tests will help you to refine your pacing and work on all the various question types on the test. Sometimes, though, you just want to work on one particular topic. The following drills focus on one topic at a time and include some of the more basic skills needed to do well on the test, along with a few trickier Math concepts. Only try the drills on Vectors, Matrices, and Statistics after you have mastered the other topics.

SUPPLY THE PRONOUN DRILLS SET 1

Directions: Fill in the correct pronoun. Choose from the following list: *I, me, you, he, him, she, her, it, we, us, they, them, who, whom.*

1. I liked birthday parties when I was younger, but now that I'm a teenager, I'm kind of tired of ______.
2. Bob and I were hoping to get theater tickets, but ______ got there too late.
3. It's hard for me to imagine giving up chocolate-chip cookies, nor do _____ intend to try.
4. My landline hasn't rung for five years, so I don't know ______ is calling.
5. When I was in the beauty pageant, the judges had a tough time choosing between Sally and ______.
6. Fred claimed he'd left me very clear directions, but the location of the secret entrance remains a mystery to ______.
7. Honestly, ________ do you think you're fooling?
8. Almost all Americans are literate, but that doesn't mean _____ read.
9. The professor's argument was important even if _____ was kind of obvious.
10. After college, Joe and Miranda could have lived wherever _____ wanted.

SUPPLY THE PRONOUN DRILLS SET 2

Directions: Fill in the correct pronoun. Choose from the following list: *I, me, you, he, him, she, her, it, we, us, they, them, who, whom.*

1. I will follow _______, follow ______ wherever he may go.
2. I'm supposed to do my homework, but _____ would rather not.
3. You can't have ice cream *and* cake: just pick one of ______.
4. Linda told me ______ would bring a dessert, but ______ must have forgotten our conversation because she brought roasted turnips.
5. The map isn't very helpful, so we're hoping someone will just give _____ directions.
6. You want $500? But I don't even know ______ you are.
7. Eugene is a smart guy, but _____ can't use pronouns correctly.
8. Alice was already a great teacher, so the class wasn't much of a challenge for _____.

9. Evan, with _______ I went to summer camp, is now a lawyer.

10. If this is your first time at the ballet, _______ are in for a treat.

FIX THE COMMA DRILLS SET 1

Directions: For each question, choose the option that uses commas correctly.

1. **A.** After the storm however, it was a lot cooler.

B. After the storm, however, it was a lot cooler.

2. **F.** The driving or uptempo beat is the backbone of "Single Ladies."

G. The driving, or uptempo, beat is the backbone of "Single Ladies."

3. **A.** My favorite TV show on the FX channel is *Atlanta.*

B. My favorite TV show, on the FX channel, is *Atlanta.*

4. **F.** John Oliver famous from *The Daily Show* has a really funny podcast called *The Bugle.*

G. John Oliver, famous from *The Daily Show*, has a really funny podcast called *The Bugle.*

5. **A.** The three Rs—reading, writing, and 'rithmetic—are the fundamentals of any education.

B. The three Rs—reading, writing and 'rithmetic—are the fundamentals of any education.

6. **F.** The stunning, often breathtaking, views from the New Jersey palisades are unrivaled.

G. The stunning often breathtaking views from the New Jersey palisades are unrivaled.

7. **A.** Hurriedly, I ran to class after oversleeping.

B. Hurriedly I ran to class after oversleeping.

8. **F.** A racquetball player, with a new racquet, has an advantage.

G. A racquetball player with a new racquet has an advantage.

FIX THE COMMA DRILLS SET 2

Directions: For each question, choose the option that uses commas correctly.

1. **A.** He walked, rather than sprinted to the doorbuster sale.

B. He walked, rather than sprinted, to the doorbuster sale.

2. **F.** All things considered, therefore, you should probably stay away from that place.

G. All things considered therefore you should probably stay away from that place.

3. **A.** To get uptown, you can take a train, a bus or a taxi.

B. To get uptown, you can take a train, a bus, or a taxi.

4. **F.** Honestly, I thought the play was pretty boring.

G. Honestly I thought the play was pretty boring.

5. **A.** Ideally you should write your paper a few days in advance and let it sit.

B. Ideally, you should write your paper a few days in advance and let it sit.

6. **F.** Carefully, she lifted the soufflé out of the oven so as not to ruin it.

G. Carefully she lifted the soufflé out of the oven so as not to ruin it.

7. **A.** Actor, George Clooney, is very interested in political issues.

B. Actor George Clooney is very interested in political issues.

8. **F.** One of my friends had a job selling knives, which is a terrible job.

G. One of my friends had a job selling knives which is a terrible job.

FIX THE APOSTROPHE DRILLS SET 1

Directions: In each of the following sentences, one word is used incorrectly. Find the incorrect word and rewrite the correct word above it.

1. My guitars totally out of tune.

2. I know apples are better for you, but I prefer orange's.

3. I buy cherry's only when they're on sale.

4. This one belongs to the adults, but this one is the childrens.

5. Someone is calling me, but I have no idea who's number it is.

6. Toni Morrison has written a lot of books, but my favorite of her's is *Jazz*.

7. The painters masterpiece hangs in the National Gallery in Washington.

8. How a county votes can be predicted by each political parties representation there.

9. Each families holiday traditions are slightly modified.

10. Who'se next to present?

FIX THE APOSTROPHE DRILLS SET 2

Directions: In each of the following sentences, one word is used incorrectly. Find the incorrect word and rewrite the correct word above it.

1. His sights' were set on the sundae bar.

2. The girl's went to soccer practice.

3. If you mess up "there" and "they're," your not much of a grammarian.

4. I sometimes worry that I'm addicted to chocolate-chip cookie's.

5. I wanted to go see a movie, but now its too late.

6. Even if you don't know any Beatles lyrics, the melody's are probably familiar.

7. The band members instruments were stolen along with the van.

8. I have no idea what my neighbors do for work: I think they're Soviet spies'.

9. There are so many good baseball player's in the world, it's amazing some guys ever make it to the big leagues.

10. Students' performance on the reading comprehension portion of the test has a lot to do with their vocabulary's.

FIX THE SUBJECT-VERB AGREEMENT DRILLS SET 1

Directions: Fix the subject-verb agreement. Identify the incorrect verb, and rewrite the correct verb above it as your answer.

1. Every one of us have gone on an ice-cream binge at some point.

2. Each corner of each state of the United States contain something interesting.

3. His sordid descriptions and love of shock distracts readers from the more important qualities of his work.

4. The mastery of logic and logic games are essential to success on the LSAT.

5. Common sense and confidence is essential to success on the ACT.

6. Whichever major you choose, both physics and math requires a ton of calculus.

7. Reading all the classics are the best part of being an English major.

8. Although not as visibly fit as the other Olympians, each of the skeet shooters have to go through rigorous training.

9. The doctors in the pediatrics ward has to be pretty tough not to be moved by some of the cases they see.

10. Each of the teams play with a distinct style.

FIX THE SUBJECT-VERB AGREEMENT DRILLS SET 2

Directions: Fix the subject-verb agreement. Identify the incorrect verb, and rewrite the correct verb above it as your answer.

1. The collection of old radio programs are available online.
2. Winning tournaments were all in a day's work for the tennis champ.
3. A dog owner who lives in one of the major cities have more pet-owning fun than one who lives in the suburbs.
4. One of those guys hate me, and I have no idea why.
5. There don't have to be a reason to do something nice for someone else.
6. The sand on South Florida's beaches seem to be almost white.
7. Are anybody else watching this great documentary about bee stings?
8. The faculty, with all its brilliant professors, are very well respected.
9. There isn't too many people left on Friendster.
10. The colors she uses for nail polish says a lot about her personality.

VERB CONSISTENCY DRILL

Directions: Fix the verb consistency errors in the following sentence by underlining the incorrect verb and writing the correct form above it. Circle the contextual clues within the sentence that help you to identify the error.

1. In her earliest daydreams, she imagines becoming the world's greatest tennis player.
2. If Annie knew the temperature was going to drop so abruptly, she would have brought a jacket.

3. I had not yet began to eat the dessert when the phone rang.

4. At the time when his coach was demanding an even greater commitment, Fabian recognizes that he could not balance academics and athletics effectively any longer.

5. The more experimental Modernist novels emphasize the constructed nature of narrative and prompting the reader to consider the arbitrary designations of *beginning* and *end.*

6. Once smart phones became commonplace, people could make spontaneous recordings of events in a way that simply will not occur before that.

7. Anticipating the film's impact, the critic suggested that the audience's expectations are forever shifted by the ending.

8. Cats seem not so much to crave human company as to tolerate it, while dogs, with tails wagging and bodies aquiver with excitement, joyously seeking out human companionship.

9. Last summer, while I was just dreaming of grand adventures, she has started checking off the items on her bucket list.

10. Yet most people's experience of pumpkin as an ingredient is extending only as far as the pumpkin pie they eat on Thanksgiving.

QUESTIONS DRILL

Directions: The following questions contain clues within the questions themselves that point to the correct answer, even without having a passage to reference. Underline the key words within the question and select the answer that those clues point you towards.

1. Which choice most effectively emphasizes the puzzling nature of the scene the author encountered?

A. dazzled
B. confounded
C. startled
D. intrigued

2. Given that all of the choices are true, which one best uses a comparison to illuminate a characteristic of cats that potential cat owners need to be aware of?

   F. A surprising finding of the study was that cats are not particularly good at catching rats.
   G. While numbers vary some by country, purebreds make up only about 10% of the domestic cat population.
   H. Unlike dogs, cats cannot survive on a vegetarian diet.
   J. As any cat owner knows, cats are indifferent to praise, but they can nevertheless be trained relatively easily.

3. Which of the following true statements best introduces an irony the author identifies in Aretha Franklin's career?

   A. Thus President Obama remarked of her, "American history wells up when Aretha sings."
   B. It is only fitting, then, that Franklin was the first woman inducted into the Rock and Roll Hall of Fame.
   C. Her voice itself was so extraordinary that her immense talents as a pianist and arranger are often overlooked.
   D. Aretha's sisters Erma and Carolyn were also singers and songwriters.

4. Which of the following best expresses the uncomfortable conditions in the room in which the experiment took place?

   F. stifling
   G. warm
   H. unfurnished
   J. sterile

5. Which of the following would most clearly and effectively express the tension between the participants?

   A. harmonious
   B. charged
   C. noteworthy
   D. unusual

6. Which of the following details most effectively furthers the author's aim of helping the reader to visualize the forest path?

   F. like ones I'd explored often as a child
   G. often used by deer in the winter
   H. littered with red, orange, and yellow leaves
   J. damp and smelling of leaf mold

7. Which choice best emphasizes the extremely challenging nature of the task being undertaken?

   A. arduous
   B. grimy
   C. unpleasant
   D. superficial

8. Which of the following true statements about Death Valley, if added here, would best illustrate how extreme its climate is?

F. The Badwater Basin salt flats are among the largest protected salt flats in the world.
G. The valley was given its English name after 13 pioneers in one wagon train died while trying to cross it.
H. Over 80 species of birds have been spotted in the area around Darwin Falls.
J. On July 15, 1972, the highest ground surface temperature ever recorded on Earth, 201°F, was recorded at Furnace Creek.

9. Which choice provides the most specific description of the window panels?

A. priceless
B. bright
C. gorgeous
D. jewel-toned

10. Which choice best emphasizes the dramatic nature of the manager's words?

F. announcement
G. bombshell
H. farewell
J. conclusion

ANGLE DRILLS SET 1

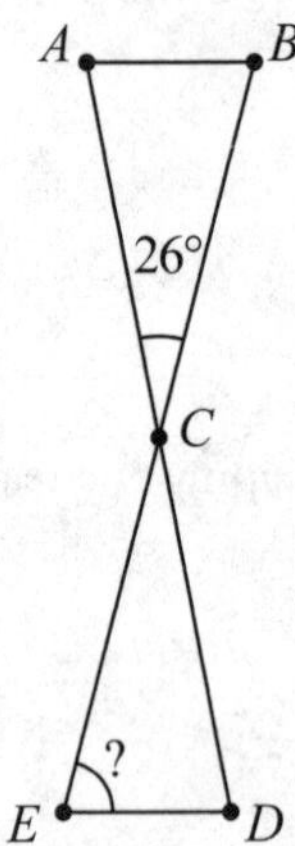

1. In isosceles triangle EDC, what is the measure of $\angle CED$?

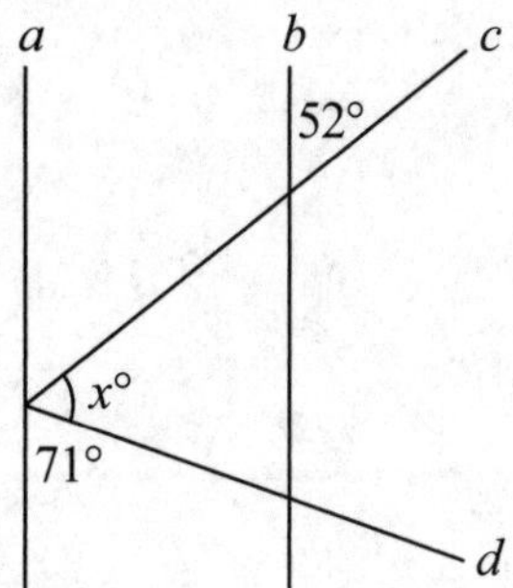

2. Lines *a* and *b* are parallel. What is the value of *x* ?

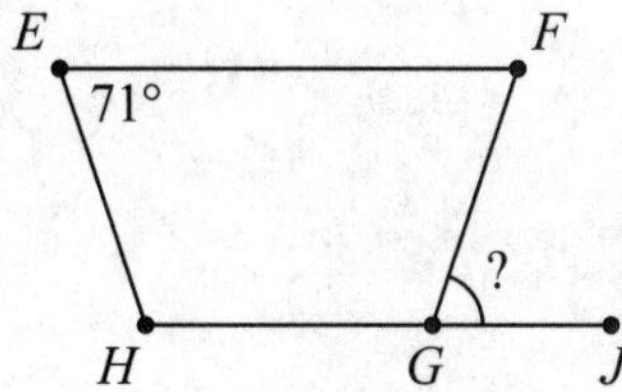

3. *EFGH* is an isosceles trapezoid. What is the measure of $\angle FGJ$?

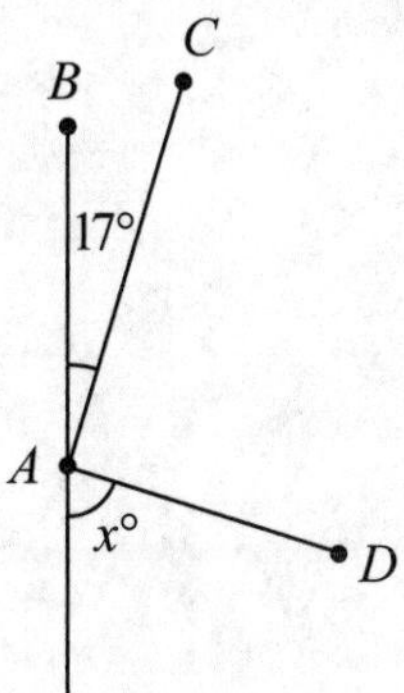

4. Lines $\overline{CA}$ and $\overline{AD}$ are perpendicular. What is the value of *x* ?

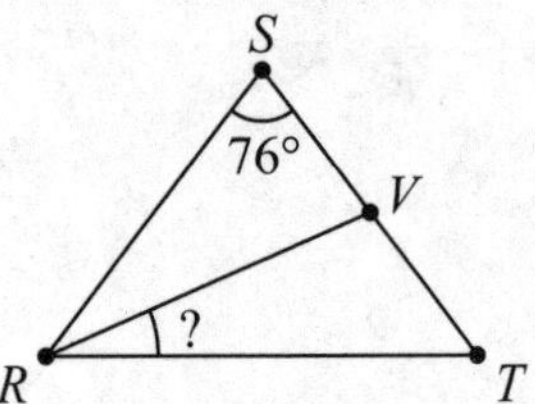

5. $\overline{RT} \cong \overline{ST}$, and $\overline{RV}$ bisects $\angle SRT$. What is the measure of $\angle VRT$?

6. In square *ABCD,* not shown, diagonals $\overline{AC}$ and $\overline{BD}$ meet at point *E.* What is the measure of $\angle AEB$?

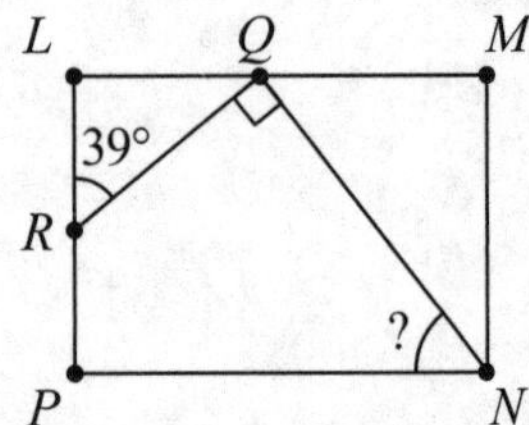

7. *LMNP* is a rectangle and $\angle RQN$ is a right angle. What is the value of $\angle PNQ$?

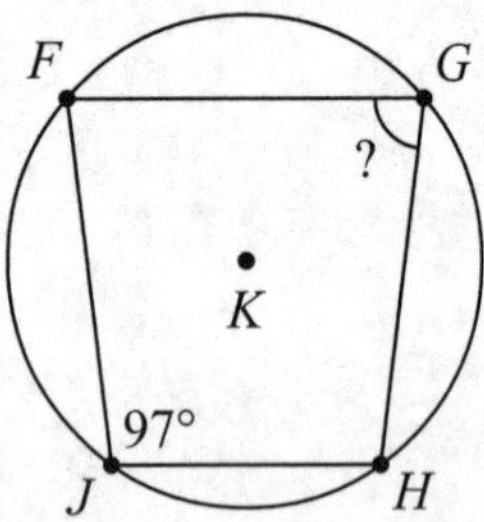

8. In circle *K,* chords $\overline{FJ}$ and $\overline{GH}$ are equal. What is the measure of $\angle FGH$?

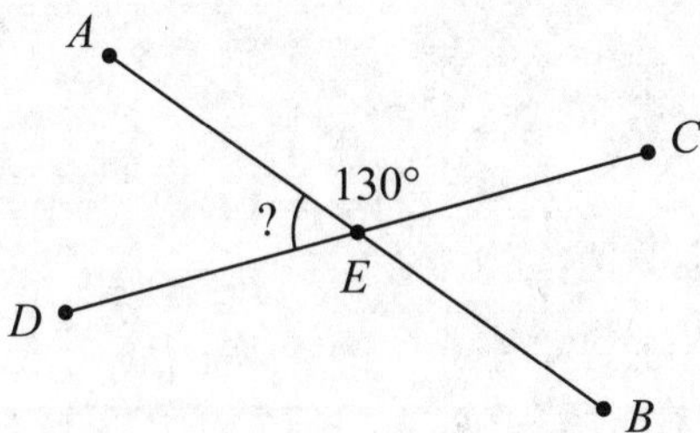

9. Lines $\overline{AB}$ and $\overline{CD}$ intersect at point E. If $\angle AEC = 130°$, what is the measure of $\angle AED$?

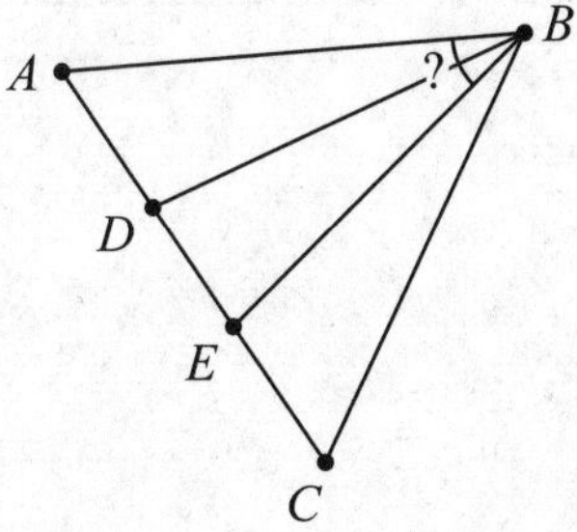

10. In equilateral triangle ABC, $\overline{DB}$ and $\overline{EB}$ divide $\angle CBA$ into three equal angles. What is the measure of $\angle ABE$?

ANGLE DRILLS SET 2

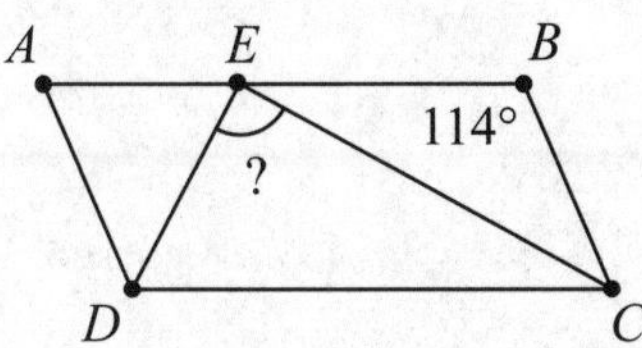

1. In parallelogram $ABCD$, $\overline{DE}$ bisects $\angle ADC$, and $\overline{EC}$ bisects $\angle DCB$. What is the measure of $\angle DEC$?

2. In ΔABC, not shown, $\angle ABC = 40°$, and $\frac{4}{3}\angle BAC = \angle BCA$. What is the measure of $\angle BCA$?

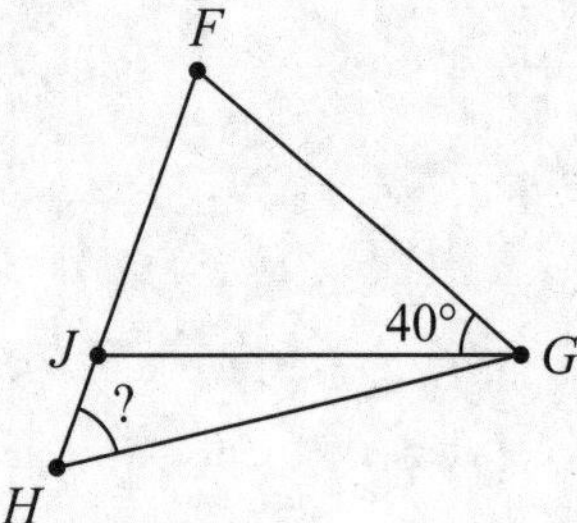

3. The measure of $\angle HGF$ is 53°, and $\overline{JG} \cong \overline{FG}$. What is the measure of $\angle JHG$?

4. $\angle DEF$ and $\angle GEF$, not shown, are complementary. If $\angle DEF = 29°$, what is the measure of $\angle GEF$?

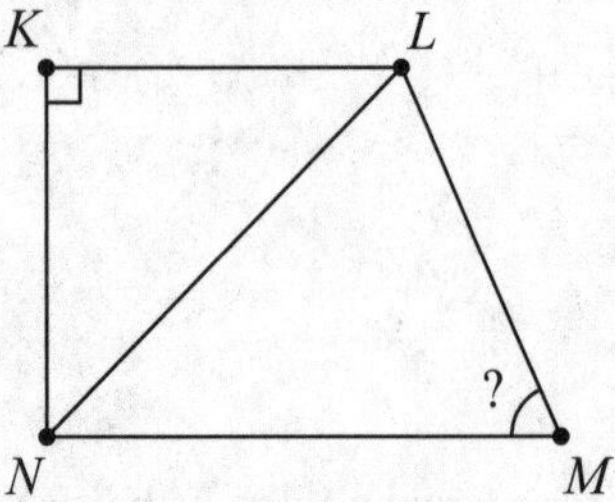

5. $\angle NKL = 90°$, $\overline{MN}$ is perpendicular to $\overline{KN}$, $\angle KNL \cong \angle KLN$, and $\angle NLM \cong \angle NML$. What is the measure of $\angle NML$?

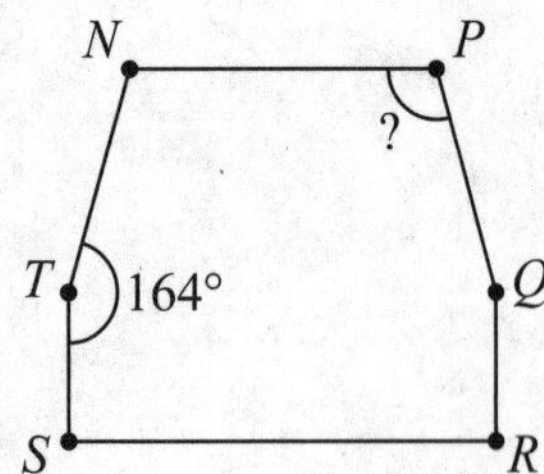

6. $\overline{ST} \cong \overline{QR}$, $\overline{TN} \cong \overline{PQ}$ and $\angle STN = 164°$. If $\overline{ST}$ and $\overline{QR}$ are both perpendicular to $\overline{SR}$, what is the measure of $\angle NPQ$?

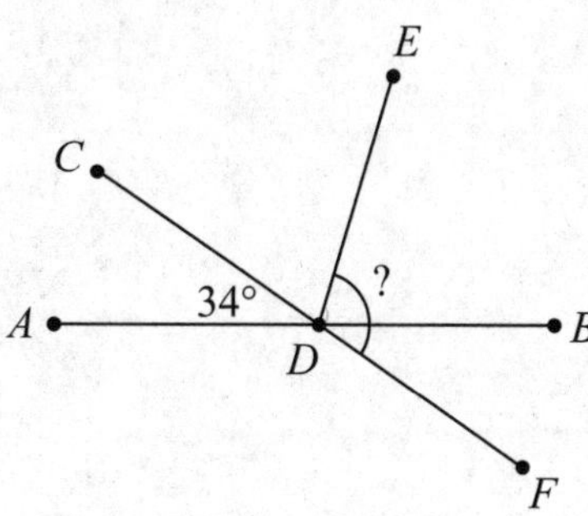

7. $\overline{DE}$ bisects $\angle CDB$. $\overline{ADB}$ and $\overline{CDF}$ are line segments. What is the measure of $\angle EDF$?

8. $\angle HJK$ and $\angle KJL$, not shown, are supplementary. If $\angle HJK = 2x$ and $\angle KJL = 7x$, what is the measure of $\angle KJL$?

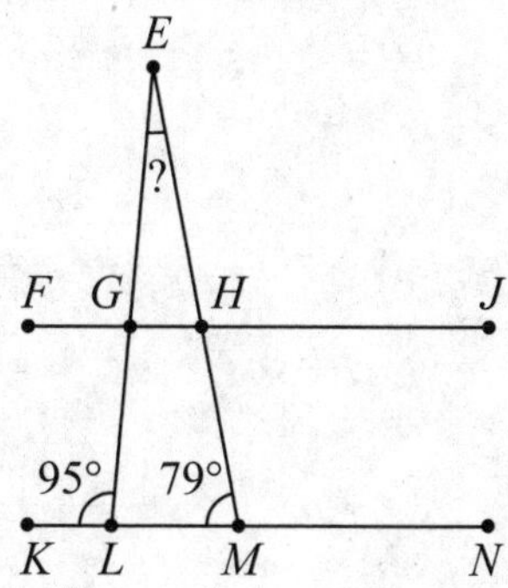

9. $\overline{FJ}$ is parallel to $\overline{KN}$, $\angle KLG = 95°$, and $\angle LMH = 79°$. What is the measure of $\angle GEH$?

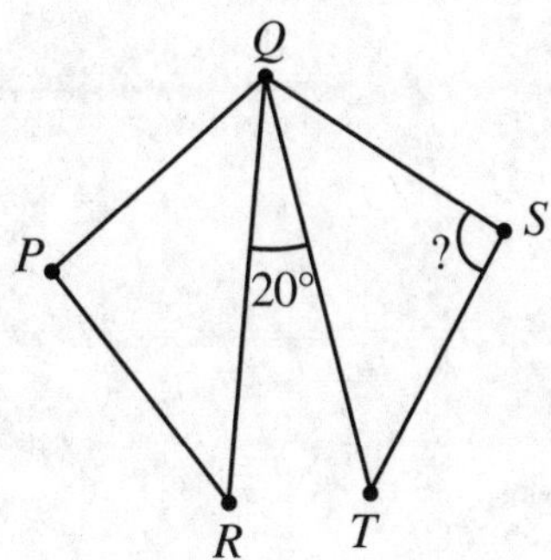

10. $\overline{PQ} \cong \overline{PR}$, ΔPQR is similar to ΔSQT, and $\angle PQS = 106°$. What is the measure of $\angle QST$?

AREA AND PERIMETER DRILLS SET 1

Use the following illustration for questions 1 and 2.

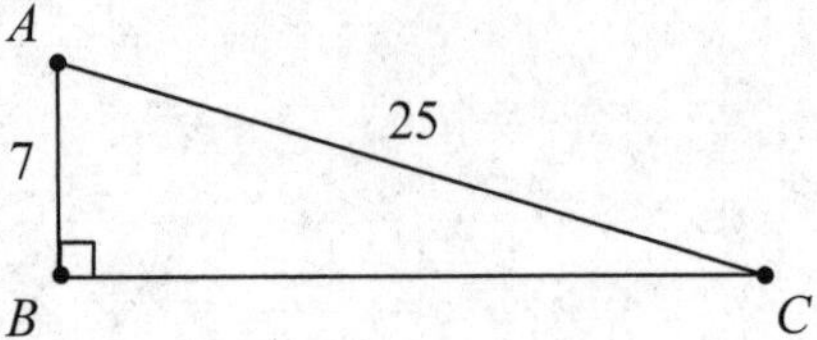

1. What is the area of ΔABC?

2. What is the perimeter of ΔABC?

Use the following illustration for questions 3 and 4.

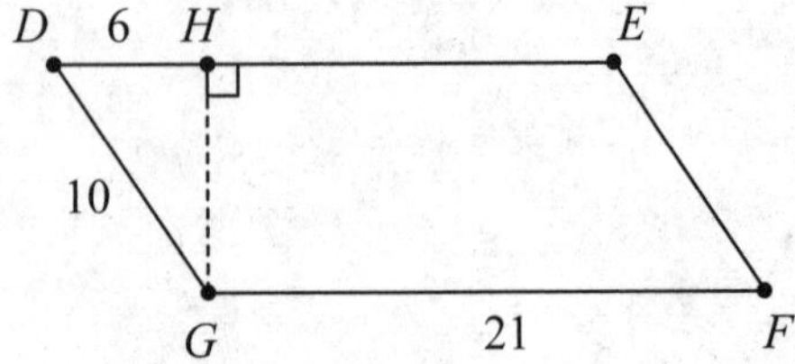

3. What is the perimeter of parallelogram $DEFG$?

4. What is the area of parallelogram $DEFG$?

Use the following illustration for questions 5 and 6.

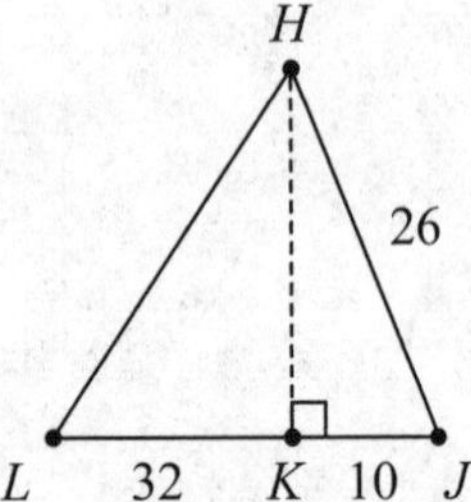

5. What is the perimeter of ΔHJL?

6. What is the area of ΔHJL?

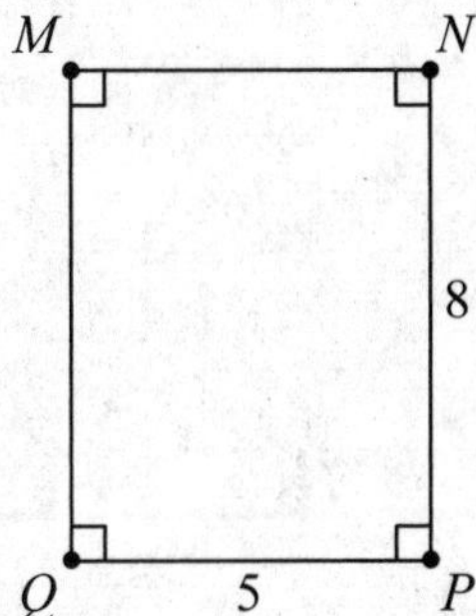

7. What is the area of rectangle *MNPQ* ?

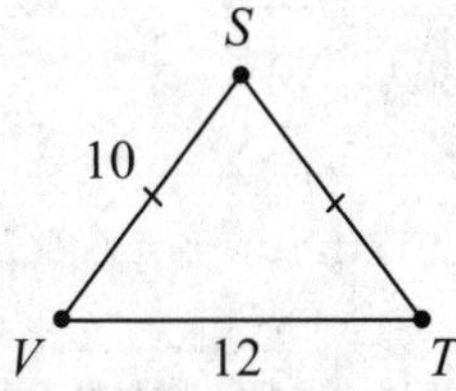

8. In ΔSTV, $\overline{SV} \cong \overline{ST}$. What is the area of ΔSTV?

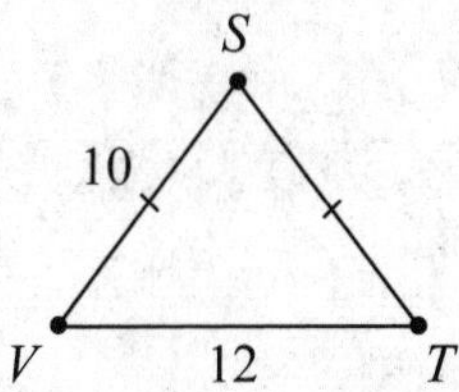

9. In ΔSTV, $\overline{SV} \cong \overline{ST}$. What is the perimeter of ΔSTV?

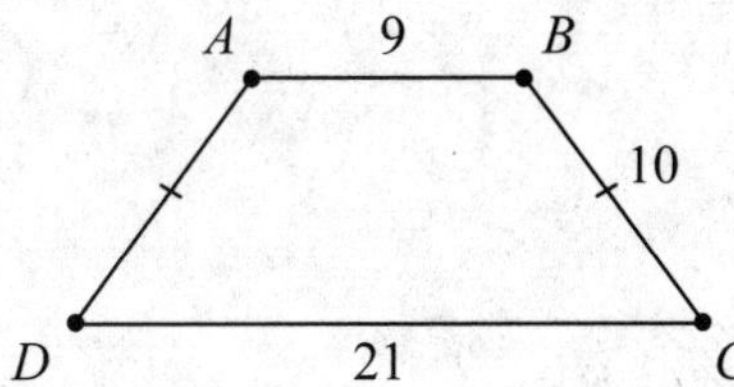

10. In trapezoid *ABCD*, $\overline{AD} \cong \overline{BC}$. What is the area of trapezoid *ABCD* ?

AREA AND PERIMETER DRILLS SET 2

Use the following illustration for questions 1 and 2.

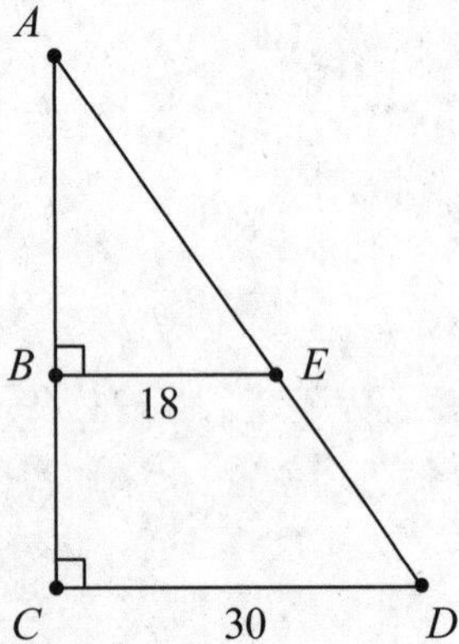

1. Right triangles *ABE* and *ACD* are shown above, and $\overline{AE} \cong \overline{CD}$. What is the area of ΔACD?

2. Right triangles *ABE* and *ACD* are shown above, and $\overline{AE} \cong \overline{CD}$. What is the perimeter of ΔABE?

Use the following illustration for questions 3 and 4.

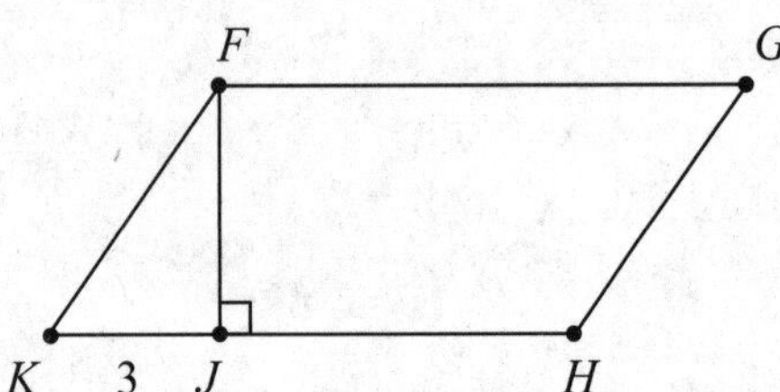

3. In parallelogram *FGHK*, $\overline{JK} \cong \overline{FJ}$, and $\overline{FK} \cong \overline{JH}$. What is the area of parallelogram *FGHK*?

4. In parallelogram *FGHK*, $\overline{JK} \cong \overline{FJ}$, and $\overline{FK} \cong \overline{JH}$. What is the perimeter of parallelogram *FGHK*?

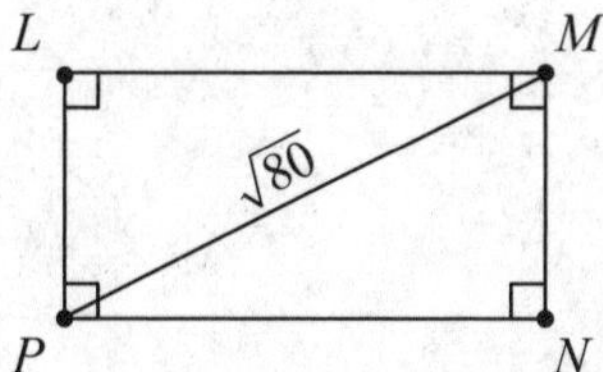

5. In rectangle *LMNP*, $\overline{LM}$ is twice as long as $\overline{LP}$. What is the area of rectangle *LMNP*?

Use the following illustration for questions 6 and 7.

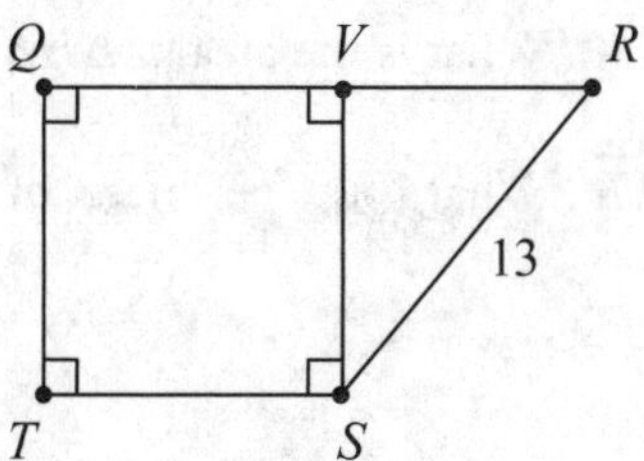

6. Square *QVST* has an area of 144. What is the area of trapezoid *QRST*?

7. Square *QVST* has an area of 144. What is the perimeter of trapezoid *QRST*?

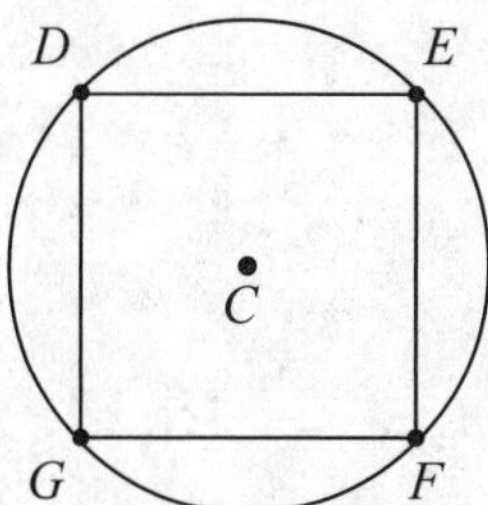

8. Square *DEFG* is inscribed in the circle with center *C* and a radius of $4\sqrt{2}$. What is the area of square *DEFG*?

Use the following illustration for questions 9 and 10.

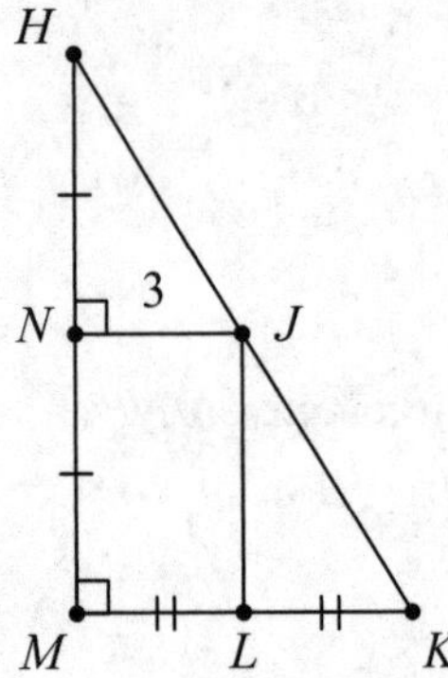

9. The area of rectangle $NJLM$ is 21, $\overline{HN} \cong \overline{NM}$, and $\overline{ML} \cong \overline{LK}$. What is the area of ΔHKM?

10. The area of rectangle $NJLM$ is 21, $\overline{HN} \cong \overline{NM}$, and $\overline{ML} \cong \overline{LK}$. What is the perimeter of ΔHKM?

CIRCLE DRILLS SET 1

Use the following figure for questions 1–3.

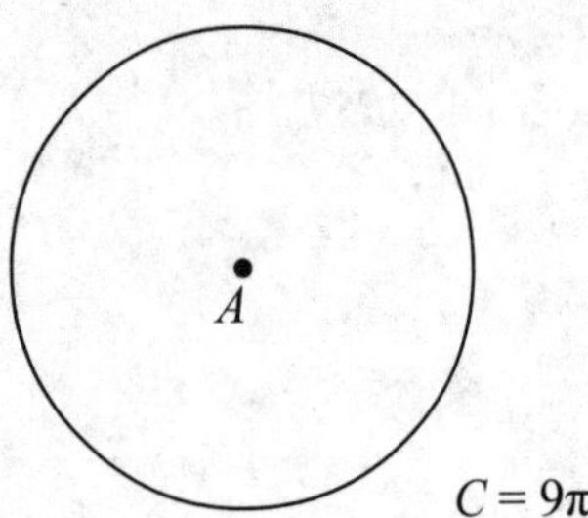

1. What is the area of the circle with center A?

2. What is the radius of the circle with center A?

3. What is the diameter of the circle with center A?

Use the following figure for questions 4–6.

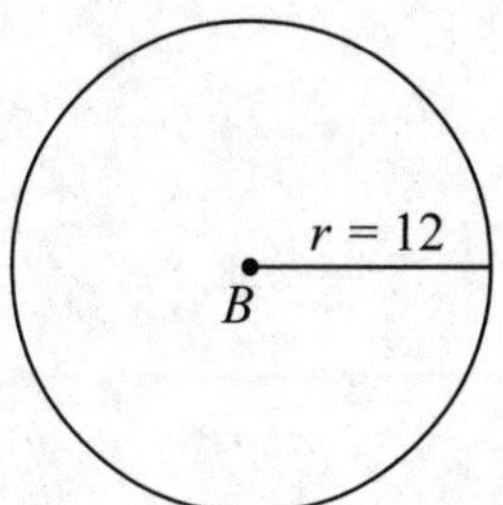

4. What is the circumference of the circle with center B?

5. What is the area of the circle with center B?

6. What is the diameter of the circle with center B?

Use the following figure for questions 7–9.

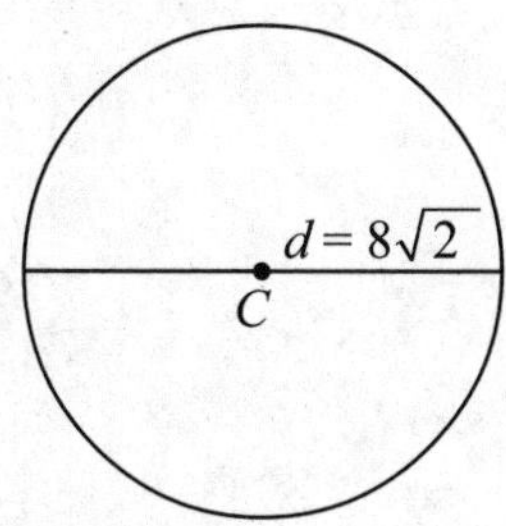

7. What is the circumference of the circle with center C?

8. What is the area of the circle with center C?

9. What is the radius of the circle with center C?

Use the following figure for questions 10–12.

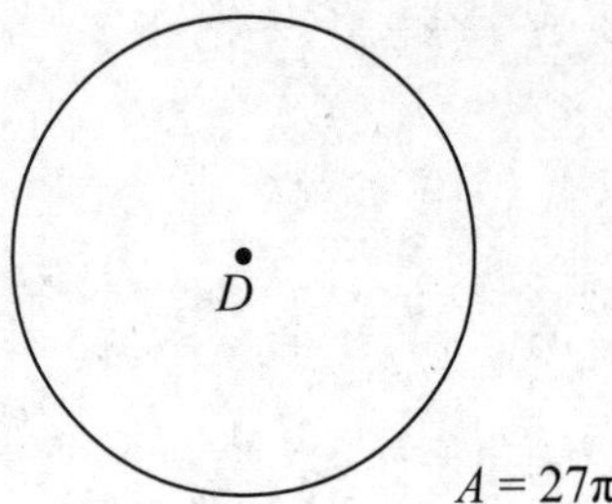

10. What is the circumference of the circle with center D?

11. What is the radius of the circle with center D?

12. What is the diameter of the circle with center D?

CIRCLE DRILLS SET 2

Use the following figure for questions 1–3.

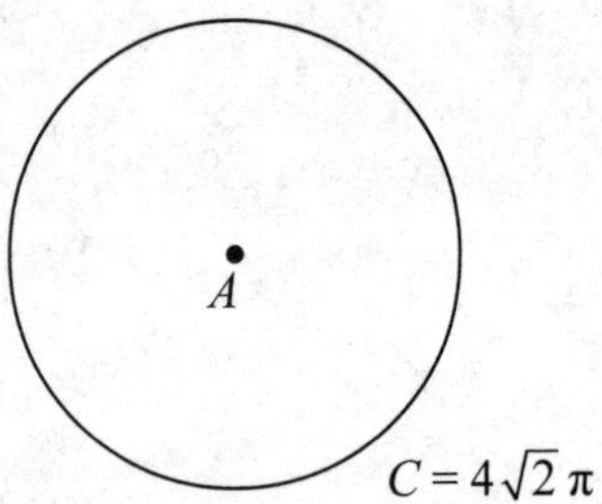

1. What is the area of the circle with center A?

2. What is the radius of the circle with center A?

3. What is the diameter of the circle with center A?

Use the following figure for questions 4–6.

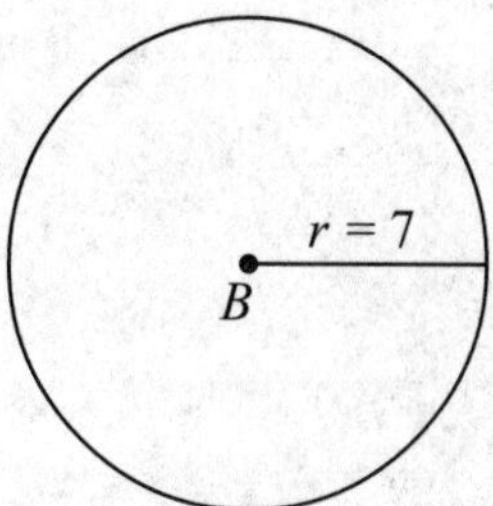

4. What is the circumference of the circle with center B?

5. What is the area of the circle with center B?

6. What is the diameter of the circle with center B?

Use the following figure for questions 7–9.

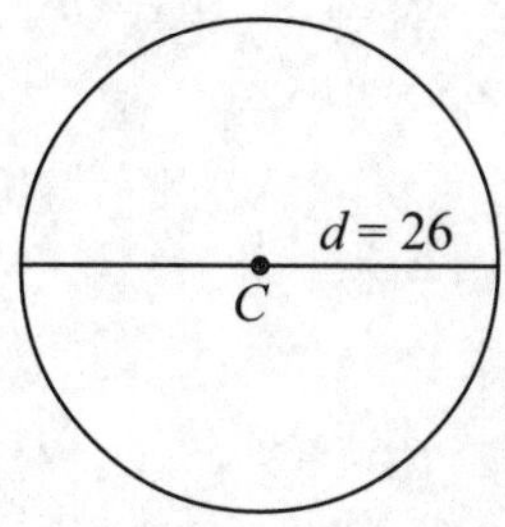

7. What is the circumference of the circle with center C?

8. What is the area of the circle with center C?

9. What is the radius of the circle with center C?

Use the following figure for questions 10–12.

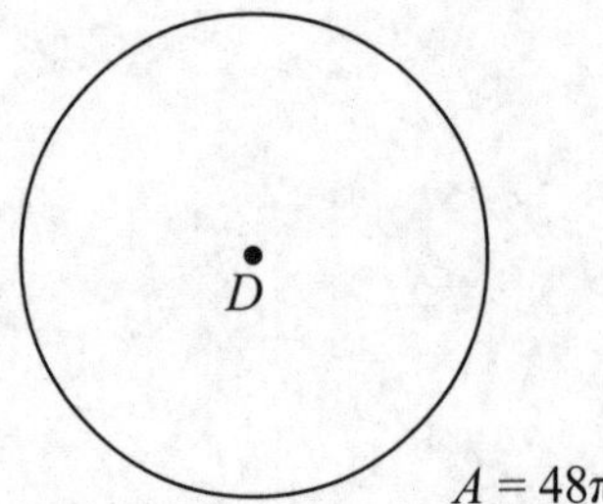

10. What is the circumference of the circle with center D?

11. What is the radius of the circle with center D?

12. What is the diameter of the circle with center D?

MANIPULATING EQUATIONS DRILLS SET 1

Solve for x in each of the following equations.

1. $3(x - 2) = 6$

2. $\frac{2x+2}{2} = 3$

3. $\frac{3-x}{2} = 5$

4. $3 - 4x = -x$

5. $-3(4 - x) = x$

6. $\frac{-2}{2-x} = \frac{6}{x}$

7. $\sqrt{x-4} = 3$

8. $\sqrt{\dfrac{x+2}{4}} = 1$

9. $3x + 2 = \dfrac{3x^2 + 2}{x}$

10. $\dfrac{x(4x-2)}{2} = 2 + 2x^2$

MANIPULATING EQUATIONS DRILLS SET 2

Solve for x in each of the following equations.

1. $\dfrac{(x+4)}{2} = 5$

2. $5(x - 2) = 15$

3. $2(4 - x) = 8$

4. $\dfrac{8-2x}{3} = -2x$

5. $-(1 - x) = 2x$

6. $\sqrt{12-x} = 2$

7. $\sqrt{5(9-x)} = 5$

8. $\dfrac{1}{2x} = \dfrac{-2}{x+5}$

9. $\dfrac{6x(x-2)}{3} = 2x^2 - 4$

10. $2 - 3x = \dfrac{-9x^2 - 12}{3x}$

STATISTICS DRILL

1. A box contains 20 letter tiles of the same size: 5 As, 8 Ds, 4 Es and 3 Bs. Which of the following expressions gives the probability of selecting, at random and without replacement, the letters for the word "DAD" in that order?

A. $\left(\frac{8}{20}\right)\left(\frac{5}{19}\right)\left(\frac{3}{18}\right)$

B. $\left(\frac{8}{20}\right)\left(\frac{5}{19}\right)\left(\frac{7}{18}\right)$

C. $\left(\frac{8}{20}\right)\left(\frac{5}{19}\right)\left(\frac{8}{18}\right)$

D. $\left(\frac{8}{20}\right)\left(\frac{5}{20}\right)\left(\frac{7}{20}\right)$

E. $\left(\frac{8}{20}\right)\left(\frac{5}{20}\right)\left(\frac{8}{20}\right)$

2. A math teacher recorded the amount of time, in minutes, that her students spent on homework on Tuesday night. The time each student spent on homework that night is represented in the stem-and-leaf plot below.

Stem	Leaf
1	2 3 9
2	1 2 7 8 9
3	2 5 6
4	3 8

Key 2 | 7 = 27 minutes

What is the probability that a student chosen at random from the class will have spent *fewer than* 35 minutes on homework on Tuesday?

F. $\frac{4}{17}$

G. $\frac{9}{17}$

H. $\frac{4}{13}$

J. $\frac{9}{13}$

K. $\frac{10}{13}$

3. A standardized testing company reviewed each of 10 students' test scores in Math to determine if students were scoring as predicted. The table below summarizes the 10 Math test scores.

Score	Number of Testers
18	1
23	3
29	4
31	1
35	1

Which of the following values is the mean of the 10 test scores?

A. 13.6
B. 26.9
C. 29.0
D. 31.5
E. 35.4

4. At a fundraiser, participants can trade tickets for a chance to spin a wheel that has 9 equal sections. One of the sections is labeled \$9.00, three of the sections are labeled \$3.00, and the remaining five sections are labeled \$0.00. The participant will win the amount of money indicated by the section on which the wheel lands. To the closest penny, what is the expected value a participant will win by spinning the wheel one time?

F. \$0.00
G. \$0.33
H. \$1.33
J. \$2.00
K. \$4.00

5. A six-sided die marked with only the odd integers from one to eleven is thrown 19 times. The dot plot below shows the frequency of the result of each of the 19 rolls. Which of the following statements about the mean, median, and mode of this set is true?

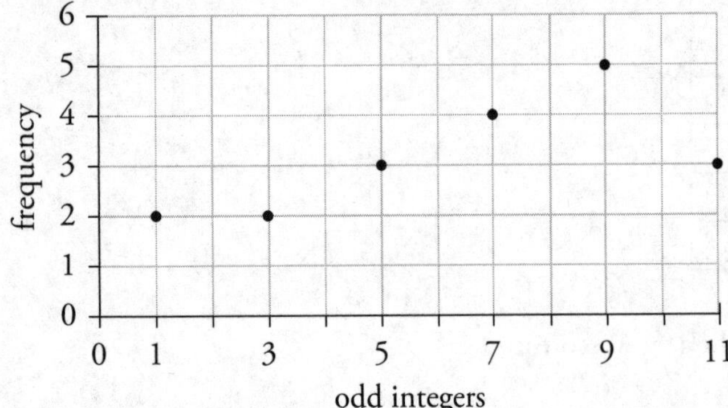

A. The mean is equal to the median, and the median is equal to the mode.
B. The mode is greater than the mean, and the mean is equal to the median.
C. The mean is greater than the median, and the median is greater than the mode.
D. The mean is equal to the mode, and the median is greater than the mean.
E. The mode is greater than the median, and the median is greater than the mean.

6. The probablities that each of three independent events will occur are given in the table below.

Event	Probability
A	0.3
B	0.8
C	0.6

What is the probablility that both Event C and Event A will occur?
Note: probability of both Events C and A occurring is P(C and A).

F. 0.90
G. 0.48
H. 0.45
J. 0.30
K. 0.18

7. George and Aubrie plan to meet for a photo shoot in Port Jervis. George will need to take a 15-minute stretch break during his trip. He will begin his trip 840 km from Port Jervis and drive at a constant speed of 120 km/hr for 4 hours. After the break, he will drive the remaining distance to Port Jervis at a constant speed of 45 km/hr. Aubrie begins her trip 525 km from Port Jervis and will drive at a constant speed of 105 km/hr, stopping once for 45 minutes for lunch. To the nearest 0.1 hour, Aubrie must leave how much later than George in order for them to arrive at the photo shoot at the same time?

A. 5.8
B. 6.5
C. 7.3
D. 8.0
E. 12.3

8. The odds in favor of an event are defined as the ratio of the probability that an event will occur to the probability that the event will NOT occur. In a Korean language club, the probabilty of Ranela being chosen to speak last is $\frac{2}{7}$. What are the odds in favor of Ranela being chosen to speak last?

F. $\frac{2}{8}$
G. $\frac{2}{7}$
H. $\frac{2}{5}$
J. $\frac{5}{2}$
K. $\frac{7}{2}$

9. The table below lists statistics for the Green Valley soccer team regarding the number of points the team scored in its first 4 games.

Statistics	Points
Minimum	7
Medium	9
Mode	9
Range	18

What is the mean number of points the team earned in the first 4 games, if it can be determined?

A. 7.0
B. 9.0
C. 12.5
D. 13.5
E. Cannot be determined from the given information

10. To award discount tickets to a Renaissance Festival, the ticket window staff will run a promotion using a total of 7 different pictures of items with discounts marked on the backs. The bodice, vest, pauldron, and boot pictures give 10% off, the shield and wooden sword pictures give 15% off, and the leather armor picture gives 70% off. Each patron will select one picture at random to determine the discount they will receive on their tickets. Given that the tickets to the Faire cost $40 each, what is the average discount amount, in dollars, that the ticket booth can expect to give each patron during this promotion?

F. $ 8.00
G. $20.00
H. $28.00
J. $32.00
K. $36.00

11. A standard normal probability distrubution function is represented in the standard (x,y) coordinate plane below, where $\mu = 10$ and $\sigma = 2.73$. Which of the following percentages is closest to the percent of data points that are within 3 standard deviations from the mean in a normal distribution.

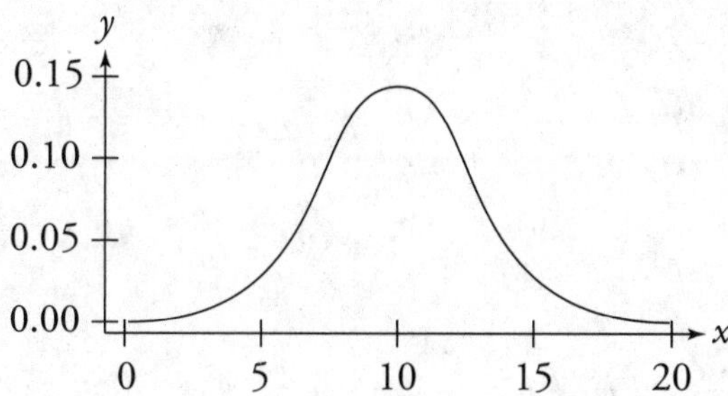

A. 66%
B. 68%
C. 95%
D. 97%
E. 99%

12. The bar graph below shows the distribution of ages, in years, of 14 students.

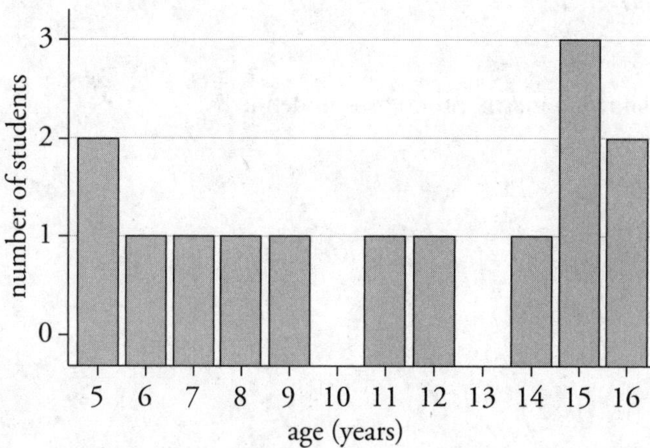

Using the data from the bar graph, what is the positive difference of the median and the mean of this distribution?

F. 0.0
G. 0.5
H. 3.5
J. 15.0
K. 22.5

VECTOR MATRIX DRILL

1. Which of the following matrices is equal to the matrix product $\begin{bmatrix} -6 & 3 \\ 1 & -2 \end{bmatrix} \cdot \begin{bmatrix} -1 \\ 3 \end{bmatrix}$?

A. $\begin{bmatrix} -3 \\ 5 \end{bmatrix}$

B. $\begin{bmatrix} 15 \\ -7 \end{bmatrix}$

C. $\begin{bmatrix} 6 & -3 \\ 3 & -6 \end{bmatrix}$

D. $\begin{bmatrix} -6 & 1 \\ 6 & -1 \end{bmatrix}$

E. $\begin{bmatrix} 6 & 9 \\ -1 & -6 \end{bmatrix}$

2. $A = \begin{bmatrix} 3 \\ 2 \end{bmatrix}$ $\quad B = \begin{bmatrix} 1 & 8 \\ 7 & 3 \end{bmatrix}$ $\quad C = \begin{bmatrix} 4 & 8 \\ 1 & 7 \end{bmatrix}$ $\quad D = \begin{bmatrix} 5 & 6 \\ 1 & 9 \\ 8 & 3 \end{bmatrix}$

Four matrices are given above. Which of the following matrix products is undefined?

F. BA

G. BC

H. BD

J. CB

K. DA

3. The Wittenberg Boating Club sponsors a 2-day sailing excursion. A group of 35 members and 15 nonmembers attend both days of the excursion. For the first day, members are charged \$25 and nonmembers are charged \$35. For the second day, members are charged \$15 and nonmembers are charged \$25. Which of the following product matrices represents the total charges each day made to the 35 members and 15 nonmembers who attended both days of the excursion?

A. $\begin{bmatrix} 35 & 35 \\ 15 & 15 \end{bmatrix}\begin{bmatrix} 25 & 15 \\ 35 & 25 \end{bmatrix}$

B. $\begin{bmatrix} 35 & 15 \\ 35 & 15 \end{bmatrix}\begin{bmatrix} 25 & 15 \\ 35 & 25 \end{bmatrix}$

C. $\begin{bmatrix} 15 & 35 \end{bmatrix}\begin{bmatrix} 25 & 15 \\ 35 & 25 \end{bmatrix}$

D. $\begin{bmatrix} 35 & 15 \end{bmatrix}\begin{bmatrix} 25 & 35 \\ 15 & 25 \end{bmatrix}$

E. $\begin{bmatrix} 35 & 15 \end{bmatrix}\begin{bmatrix} 25 & 15 \\ 35 & 25 \end{bmatrix}$

4. What is the matrix product $\begin{bmatrix} -1 & 0 & 1 \end{bmatrix}\begin{bmatrix} x \\ y \\ z \end{bmatrix}$?

F. $\begin{bmatrix} -x & 0 & x \\ -y & 0 & y \\ -z & 0 & z \end{bmatrix}$

G. $\begin{bmatrix} x & 0 & -x \\ y & 0 & -y \\ z & 0 & -z \end{bmatrix}$

H. $\begin{bmatrix} -x & -y & -z \\ 0 & 0 & 0 \\ x & y & z \end{bmatrix}$

J. $\begin{bmatrix} -xz \end{bmatrix}$

K. $\begin{bmatrix} z-x \end{bmatrix}$

5. Vectors $\overrightarrow{WX}$ and $\overrightarrow{YZ}$ are shown in the standard (x,y) coordinate plane below. Which of the following is the unit vector notation of the vector $\overrightarrow{WX} + \overrightarrow{YZ}$?

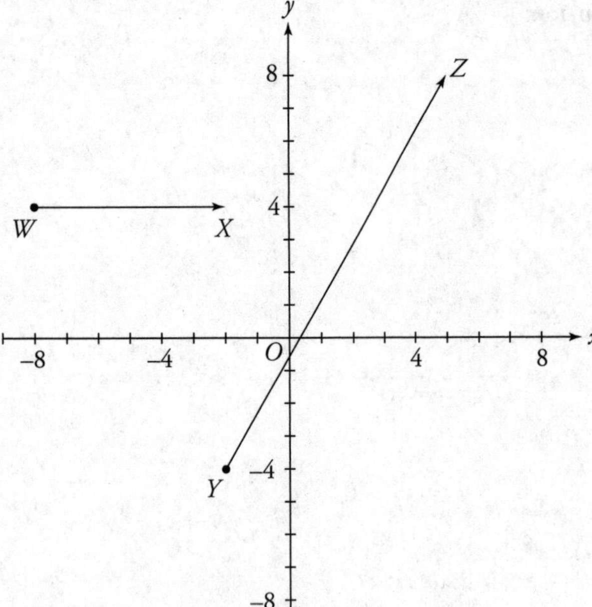

A. -8**i** + 8**j**

B. -1**i** + 8**j**

C. 5**i** + 12**j**

D. 13**i** + 12**j**

E. 13**i** + 18**j**

6. What is the matrix product $\begin{bmatrix} 0 \\ 1 \\ -1 \end{bmatrix}\begin{bmatrix} 3x & 2x & x \end{bmatrix}$?

F. $\begin{bmatrix} x \end{bmatrix}$

G. $\begin{bmatrix} 3x & 2x & x \end{bmatrix}$

H. $\begin{bmatrix} 0 \\ 6x \\ -6x \end{bmatrix}$

J. $\begin{bmatrix} 0 & 0 & 0 \\ 3x & 2x & x \\ -3x & -2x & -x \end{bmatrix}$

K. $\begin{bmatrix} 0 & 3x & -3x \\ 0 & 2x & -2x \\ 0 & x & -x \end{bmatrix}$

7. The component forms of vectors **a** and **b** are given by $\mathbf{a} = \langle -3,8 \rangle$ and $\mathbf{b} = \langle 4,6 \rangle$. If $(-2\mathbf{a}) + 3\mathbf{b} + \mathbf{c} = 0$, what is the component form of **c** ?

A. $\langle -18,-2 \rangle$

B. $\langle -6,-34 \rangle$

C. $\langle 7,-2 \rangle$

D. $\langle 6,34 \rangle$

E. $\langle 18,2 \rangle$

8. The unit vector notation of vector v is $4\mathbf{i} + 3\mathbf{j}$. Which of the following vectors in the (x,y) coordinate plane could be vector $\mathbf{v}$?

F. 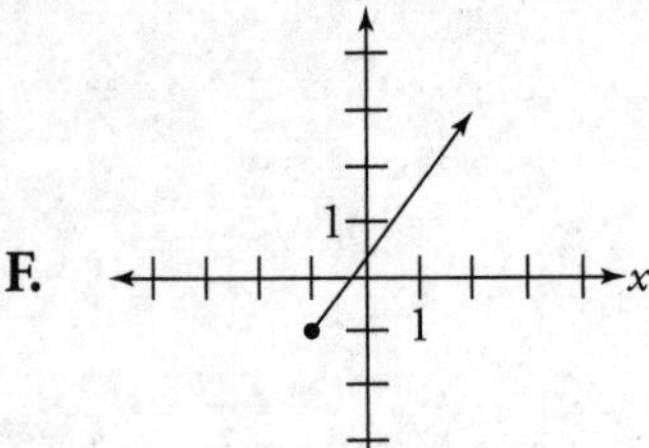

G. 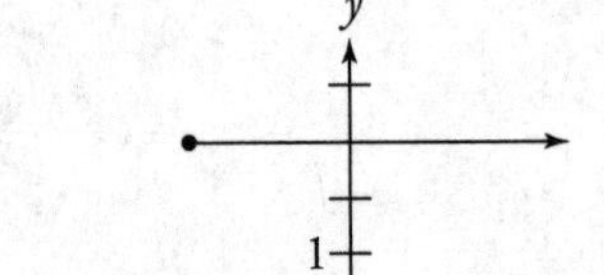
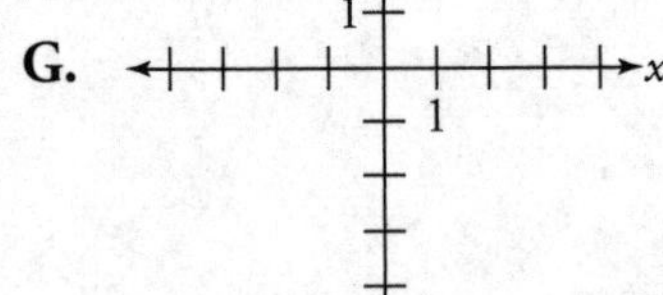

H. 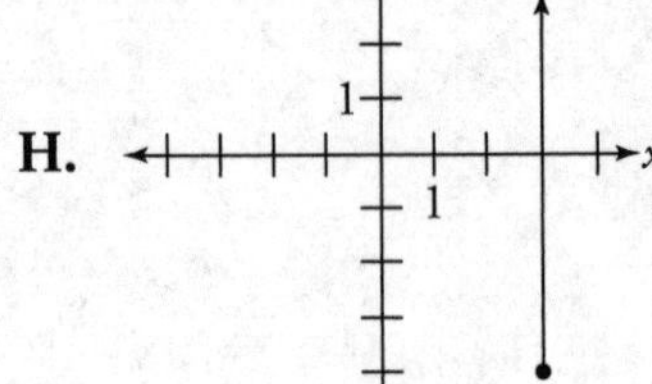

J. 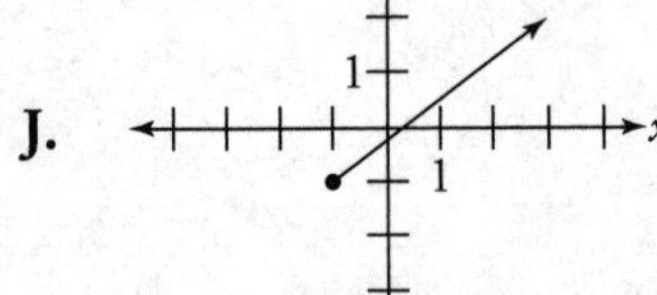

K. 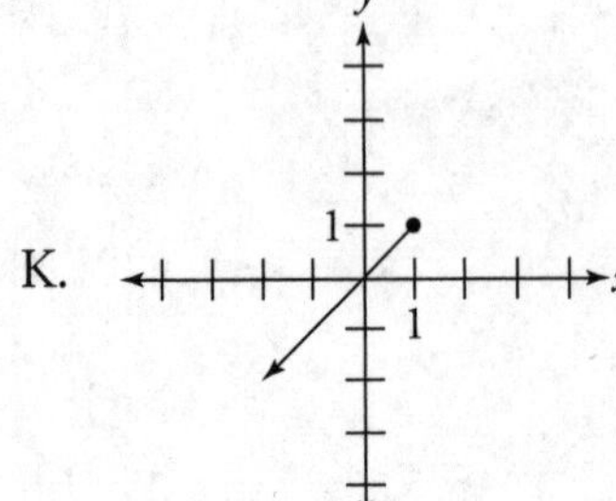

9. Which of the following matrix products is defined?

A. $\begin{bmatrix} 2 & -1 \\ 3 & 0 \end{bmatrix}\begin{bmatrix} 5 & -3 \end{bmatrix}$

B. $\begin{bmatrix} 5 & -3 \end{bmatrix}\begin{bmatrix} 5 & -3 \end{bmatrix}$

C. $\begin{bmatrix} 7 \\ 6 \end{bmatrix}\begin{bmatrix} 7 \\ 6 \end{bmatrix}$

D. $\begin{bmatrix} 7 \\ 6 \end{bmatrix}\begin{bmatrix} 5 & 3 \end{bmatrix}$

E. $\begin{bmatrix} 7 \\ 6 \end{bmatrix}\begin{bmatrix} 2 & -1 \\ 3 & 0 \end{bmatrix}$

10. Which of the following matrix products is equal to the matrix $\begin{bmatrix} 0 \\ 0 \end{bmatrix}$?

F. $\begin{bmatrix} 4 & -6 \\ -2 & 3 \end{bmatrix}\begin{bmatrix} 3 \\ 2 \end{bmatrix}$

G. $\begin{bmatrix} 3 & 2 \end{bmatrix}\begin{bmatrix} 4 & -2 \\ -6 & 3 \end{bmatrix}$

H. $\begin{bmatrix} 0 & 0 \end{bmatrix}\begin{bmatrix} 0 \\ 0 \end{bmatrix}$

J. $\begin{bmatrix} 3 & 2 \end{bmatrix}\begin{bmatrix} 4 & 2 \\ 6 & 3 \end{bmatrix}$

K. $\begin{bmatrix} 4 & 6 \\ 2 & 3 \end{bmatrix}\begin{bmatrix} 3 \\ 2 \end{bmatrix}$

11. The component forms of vectors **x** and **y** are $\mathbf{x} = \langle 5,-12 \rangle$ and $\mathbf{y} = \langle 7,10 \rangle$. If $\mathbf{z} = \mathbf{y} - \mathbf{x}$, then what are the components of **z**?

A. $\langle -12,2 \rangle$

B. $\langle -2,-22 \rangle$

C. $\langle 2,-2 \rangle$

D. $\langle 2,22 \rangle$

E. $\langle 12,2 \rangle$

GRAPH-READING DRILLS SET 1

Reading various types of charts and graphs is a fundamental skill for ACT Science. Practice your skills with the following questions.

Use the following table and illustration for questions 1–4.

Table 1	
Substance	van 't Hoff factor *
Sucrose	1.0
NaCl	1.9
$MgCl_2$	2.7
$FeCl_3$	3.4
*Values at 300 K	

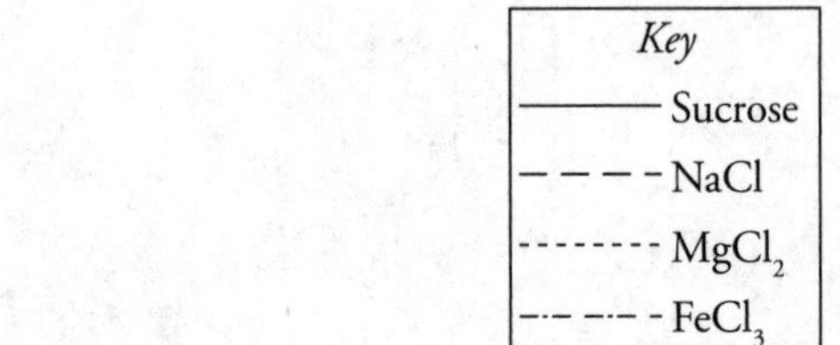

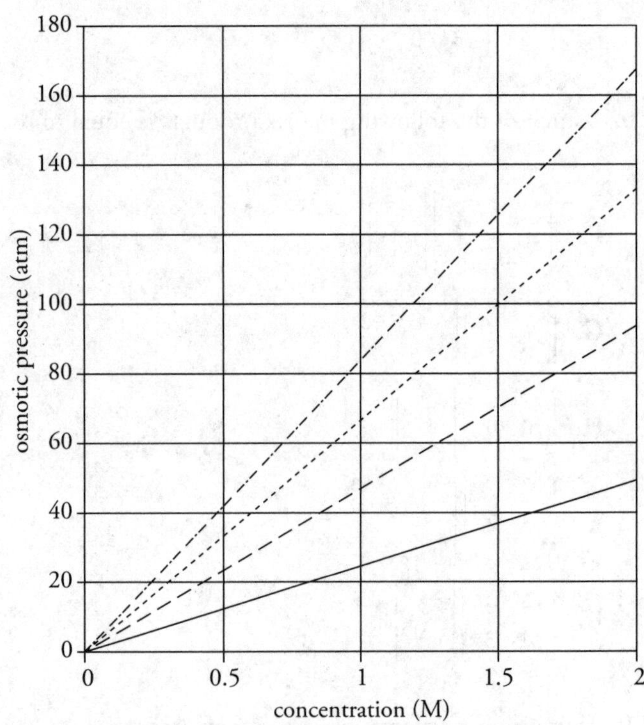

Figure 1

1. What do the different lines on Figure 1 show?

2. What is the relationship between concentration and osmotic pressure?

3. What do Table 1 and Figure 1 have in common?

4. What is the relationship between van 't Hoff factor and osmotic pressure at concentration of 1 *M*?

Use the following table and illustration for questions 5–8.

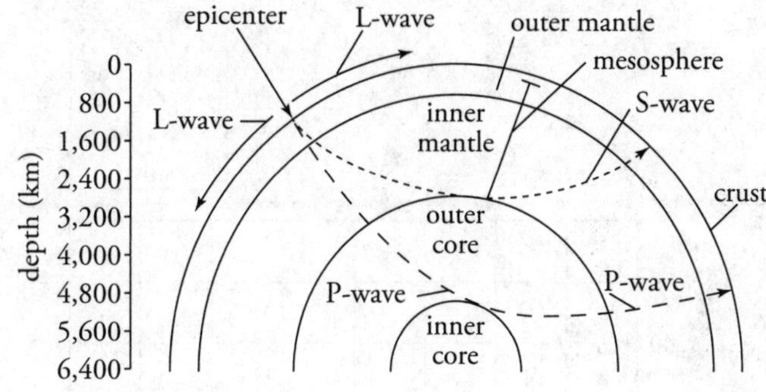

Figure 2

Table 2		
Seismic wave	Depth range (km)	Crust velocity (m/s)
L-wave	0–10	2.0–4.5
S-wave	0–2,921	3.0–4.0
P-wave	0–5,180	5.0–7.0

5. What does Figure 2 show?

6. What do Figure 2 and Table 2 have in common?

7. Which types of waves could occur in the outer mantle?

8. Which types of waves could occur in the inner core?

Use the following illustrations for questions 9–12.

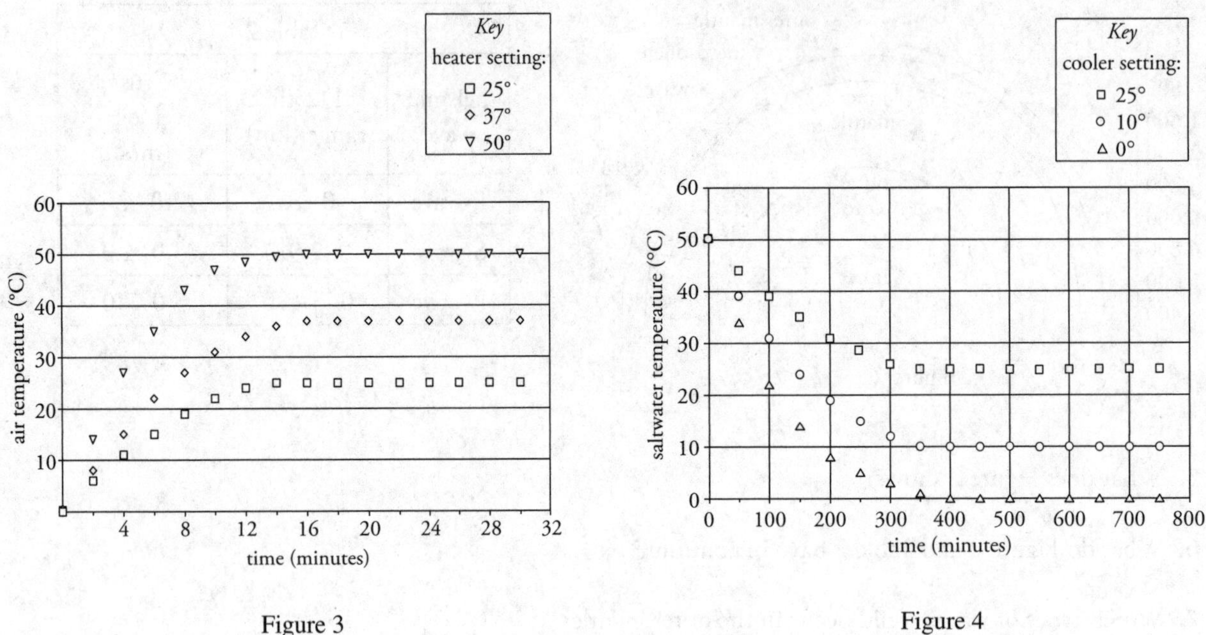

Figure 3

Figure 4

9. What do the different symbols in Figures 3 and 4 represent?

10. What do Figures 3 and 4 have in common?

11. Do both Figures 3 and 4 have the same relationship between temperature and time?

12. Does increasing the heater or cooler setting have the same effect on air temperature and saltwater temperature over time?

GRAPH-READING DRILLS SET 2

Use the following table and illustrations for questions 1–6.

Table 1	
Color	Wavelength (nm)
Violet	380–430
Blue	430–500
Green	500–565
Yellow	565–585
Orange	585–630
Red	630–750

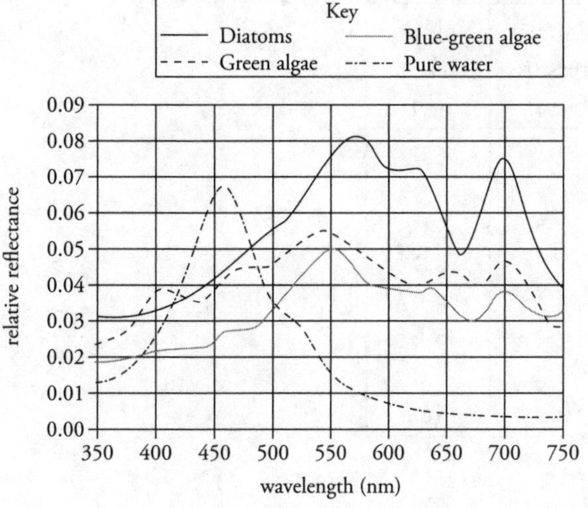

Figure 1

Figure 2

1. What do Figures 1 and 2 have in common?

2. Which line in Figure 1 is the line in Figure 2 closest to?

3. What does Table 1 have in common with Figures 1 and 2?

4. Which line has the highest reflectance at a wavelength of 400?

5. Which color has the highest reflectance in blue-green algae?

6. Which line or lines have peaks of reflectance in the blue spectrum?

Use the following tables for questions 7–12.

Table 2

300°C	Initial pressure (atm)	Final pressure (atm)	Volume change (L)
Oxygen	1	2	–5.00
Oxygen	2	4	–5.00
Oxygen	3	6	–5.00
Argon	2	4	–5.00
Argon	4	5	–2.00
Carbon dioxide	1	5	–8.00
Carbon dioxide	3	6	–5.00
Carbon dioxide	4	10	–6.00

Table 3

25°C	Initial pressure (atm)	Final pressure (atm)	Volume change (L)
Methane	1	2	–5.00
Methane	2	4	–5.00
Helium	1	2	–5.00
Helium	1	5	–8.00
Helium	2	5	–6.00
Nitrogen	1	5	–8.00
Nitrogen	2	4	–5.00
Nitrogen	4	5	–2.00

Table 4

–200°C	Initial pressure (atm)	Final pressure (atm)	Volume change (L)
Neon	1	2	–5.02
Neon	2	4	–5.03
Neon	4	8	–5.06
Helium	1	2	–4.98
Helium	2	4	–4.97
Hydrogen	1	2	–5.01
Hydrogen	1	5	–8.02
Hydrogen	1	10	–9.03

7. What do Tables 2–4 have in common?

8. What does it mean that all the numbers in the volume change column are negative?

9. Do the numbers in the columns for initial pressure or final pressure show any consistent trends?

10. In Table 3, what generally happened to volume with a greater increase in pressure?

11. In Table 2, what is a possible reason that the volume change for all three trials of oxygen was the same, while the volume change for different trials of argon and carbon dioxide were different?

12. What is the difference between the results for helium in Table 3 versus the results for helium in Table 4?

Mini Practice Drills Answer Key and Explanations

SUPPLY THE PRONOUN DRILLS SET 1

1. them
2. we
3. I
4. who
5. me
6. me
7. whom
8. they
9. it
10. they

SUPPLY THE PRONOUN DRILLS SET 2

1. him, him
2. I
3. them
4. she, she
5. us
6. who
7. he
8. her
9. whom
10. you

FIX THE COMMA DRILLS SET 1

1. B
2. G
3. A
4. G
5. A
6. F
7. A
8. G

FIX THE COMMA DRILLS SET 2

1. B
2. F
3. B
4. F
5. B
6. F
7. B
8. F

FIX THE APOSTROPHE DRILLS SET 1

1. guitar's
2. oranges
3. cherries
4. children's
5. whose
6. hers
7. painter's
8. party's
9. family's
10. who's

FIX THE APOSTROPHE DRILLS SET 2

1. sights
2. girls
3. you're
4. cookies
5. it's
6. melodies
7. members'
8. spies
9. players
10. vocabularies

FIX THE SUBJECT-VERB AGREEMENT DRILLS SET 1

1. has
2. contains
3. distract
4. is
5. are
6. require
7. is
8. has
9. have
10. plays

FIX THE SUBJECT-VERB AGREEMENT DRILLS SET 2

1. is
2. was
3. has
4. hates
5. doesn't
6. seems
7. is
8. is
9. aren't
10. say

VERB CONSISTENCY DRILL

1. imagined
2. had known
3. begun
4. recognized
5. prompt
6. did
7. would be
8. seek
9. started *or* had started
10. extends

QUESTIONS DRILL

1. B
2. H
3. C
4. F
5. B
6. H
7. A
8. J
9. D
10. G

ANGLE DRILLS SET 1

1. 77°
2. 57
3. 71°
4. 73
5. 38°
6. 90°
7. 39°
8. 83°
9. 50°
10. 40°

ANGLE DRILLS SET 2

1. 90°
2. 80°
3. 57°
4. 61°
5. 67.5°
6. 106°
7. 107°
8. 140°
9. 16°
10. 94°

AREA AND PERIMETER DRILLS SET 1

1. 84
2. 56
3. 62
4. 168
5. 108
6. 504
7. 40
8. 48
9. 32
10. 120

AREA AND PERIMETER DRILLS SET 2

1. 600
2. 72
3. $9 + 9\sqrt{2}$
4. $6 + 12\sqrt{2}$
5. 32
6. 174
7. 54
8. 64
9. 42
10. $20 + \sqrt{232}$

CIRCLE DRILLS SET 1

1. $\frac{81}{4}\pi$
2. 4.5 or $\frac{9}{2}$
3. 9
4. 24π
5. 144π
6. 24
7. $8\sqrt{2}\pi$
8. 32π
9. $4\sqrt{2}$
10. $6\sqrt{3}\pi$
11. $3\sqrt{3}$
12. $6\sqrt{3}$

CIRCLE DRILLS SET 2

1. 8π
2. $2\sqrt{2}$
3. $4\sqrt{2}$
4. 14π
5. 49π
6. 14
7. 26π
8. 169π
9. 13
10. $8\sqrt{3}\pi$
11. $4\sqrt{3}$
12. $8\sqrt{3}$

MANIPULATING EQUATIONS DRILLS SET 1

1. 4
2. 2
3. –7
4. 1
5. 6
6. 3
7. 13
8. 2
9. 1
10. –2

MANIPULATING EQUATIONS DRILLS SET 2

1. 6
2. 5
3. 0
4. –2
5. –1
6. 8
7. 4
8. –1
9. 1
10. –2

STATISTICS DRILL

1. B
2. J
3. B
4. J
5. E
6. K
7. B
8. H
9. C
10. F
11. E
12. G

GRAPH-READING DRILLS SET 1

1. Different substances
2. Direct
3. Substances
4. As van 't Hoff factor increases, osmotic pressure increases
5. A cross-section of a planet
6. Depth and waves
7. S and P
8. None
9. Different heater and cooler settings
10. Time
11. No
12. Yes

VECTOR MATRIX DRILL

1. B
2. H
3. E
4. K
5. D
6. J
7. A
8. J
9. D
10. F
11. D

GRAPH-READING DRILLS SET 2

1. Relative reflectance and wavelength
2. Diatoms
3. Wavelength
4. Green algae
5. Green
6. Pure water
7. Initial pressure, final pressure, and volume change
8. Decrease in volume
9. No
10. Greater decrease in volume
11. Different relationship between initial and final pressure
12. Less change in volume

SUPPLY THE PRONOUN DRILLS SET 1

1. **them** A pronoun must be consistent in number with the noun it refers to and must be the correct case. The blank refers to *parties,* which is plural, and it is also the object of the preposition *of.* The correct pronoun, *them,* is a plural object pronoun.

2. **we** A pronoun must be consistent in number with the noun it refers to and must be the correct case. The blank refers to *Bob and I,* which is plural, and it is the subject of the verb *got.* The correct pronoun, *we,* is a plural subject pronoun.

3. **I** A pronoun must be consistent in number with the noun or pronoun it refers to and must be the correct case. The blank refers to *me,* which is first-person singular, and it is the subject of the verb *intend.* The correct pronoun, *I,* is a singular subject pronoun.

4. **who** A pronoun must be consistent in case with the noun it refers to. The blank refers to an unknown person, and it is the subject of the verb *is calling.* The correct pronoun, *who,* is a relative subject pronoun.

5. **me** A pronoun must be consistent in case with the noun it refers to. The blank refers to the speaker of the sentence, *I,* and it is one of two objects of the preposition *between,* so the object case is needed. The correct pronoun, *me,* is a first-person object pronoun.

6. **me** A pronoun must be consistent in number with the noun or pronoun it refers to and must be the correct case. The blank refers to *me,* which is first-person singular, and it is the object of the preposition *to.* The correct pronoun, *me,* is a singular object pronoun.

7. **whom** A pronoun must be consistent in case with the noun it refers to. The blank refers to an unknown person, and it is the object of the verb *fooling.* The correct pronoun, *whom,* is a relative object pronoun.

8. **they** A pronoun must be consistent in number with the noun it refers to and must be the correct case. The blank refers to *Almost all Americans,* which is plural, and it is also the subject of the verb *read.* The correct pronoun, *they,* is a plural subject pronoun.

9. **it** A pronoun must be consistent in number with the noun it refers to and must be the correct case. The blank refers to *argument,* which is singular, and it is also the subject of the verb *was.* The correct pronoun, *it,* is a singular subject pronoun.

10. **they** A pronoun must be consistent in number with the noun it refers to and must be the correct case. The blank refers to *Joe and Miranda,* which is plural, and it is also the subject of the verb *wanted.* The correct pronoun, *they,* is a plural subject pronoun.

SUPPLY THE PRONOUN DRILLS SET 2

1. **him, him**

   A pronoun must be consistent with the pronouns that appear elsewhere in the sentence and must be the correct case. The blanks refer to the pronoun *he,* which is a third-person singular noun, and both blanks are the object of the verb *follow.* The correct pronoun for both blanks, *him,* is a third-person object pronoun.

2. **I** A pronoun must be consistent with the pronouns that appear elsewhere in the sentence. The blank refers to the pronoun *I,* and it is the subject of the verb *would.* The correct pronoun, *I,* is a subject pronoun.

3. **them**

   A pronoun must be consistent in number with the noun it refers to and must be the correct case. The blank refers to *ice cream* and *cake,* which is plural, and it is also the object of the preposition *of.* The correct pronoun, *them,* is a plural object pronoun.

4. **she, she**

   A pronoun must be consistent in number with the noun it refers to and must be the correct case. The blanks refer to *Linda,* as does the *she* in *she brought roasted turnips,* and *Linda* is third person singular. The first blank is the subject of the verb *would bring,* and the second blank is the subject of the verb *must have forgotten,* so the correct pronoun for both blanks is the singular subject pronoun *she.*

5. **us** A pronoun must be consistent with the pronouns that appear elsewhere in the sentence and must be the correct case. The blank refers to the pronoun *we,* which is first-person plural, and it is also the object of the verb *give.* The correct pronoun, *us,* is the first-person plural object pronoun.

6. **who** A pronoun must be the correct case for its context. The word that goes in the blank needs to be a pronoun that refers to the *you* addressed in the previous sentence, and it is also the subject of the verb *are.* The correct pronoun, *who,* maintains the correct case.

7. **he** A pronoun must be consistent in number with the noun it refers to and must be the correct case. The blank refers to *Eugene,* which is singular, and it is also the subject of the verb *can't use.* The correct pronoun, *he,* is a singular subject pronoun.

8. **her** A pronoun must be consistent in number with the noun it refers to and must be the correct case. The blank refers to *Alice,* which is singular, and it is also the object of the preposition *for.* The correct pronoun, *her,* is a singular object pronoun.

9. **whom**

   A pronoun must be the correct case for its context. The blank refers to *Evan* and is the object of the preposition *with.* The correct pronoun, *whom,* is a relative object pronoun.

10. **you** A pronoun must be consistent with the pronouns that appear elsewhere in the sentence. The blank refers to the pronoun *your* and is also the subject of the verb *are.* The correct pronoun is *you,* which is the second-person subject pronoun.

FIX THE COMMA DRILLS SET 1

1. **B** The word *however* can be removed from the sentence without changing the sentence's meaning, so the word should be set off from the rest of the sentence with commas. Choice (A) is missing the comma before *however.* Choice (B) correctly places commas on both sides of *however.*

2. **G** The phrase *or uptempo* can be removed from the sentence without changing the sentence's meaning, so the phrase should be set off from the rest of the sentence with commas. Choice (F) is missing the comma before *or* and after *uptempo.* Choice (G) correctly places commas on both sides of *or uptempo.*

3. **A** The phrase *on the FX channel* cannot be removed from the sentence without changing the sentence's meaning, so the phrase should not be set off from the rest of the sentence with commas. Choice (A) correctly omits commas around the phrase.

4. **G** The phrase *famous from* The Daily Show can be removed from the sentence without changing the sentence's meaning, so the phrase should be set off from the rest of the sentence with commas. Choice (F) is missing the comma before *famous* and after *Show.* Choice (G) correctly places commas on both sides of the phrase.

5. **A** Commas should be used to separate items in a list of three or more items, so there should be a comma after *reading* and another after *writing.* Choice (A) correctly includes both commas. Choice (B) omits the comma after *writing.*

6. **F** The phrase *often breathtaking* can be removed from the sentence without changing the sentence's meaning, so the phrase should be set off from the rest of the sentence with commas. Choice (F) correctly places commas on both sides of the phrase.

7. **A** The word *hurriedly* can be removed from the sentence without changing the sentence's meaning, so the word should be set off from the rest of the sentence with a comma. Choice (A) correctly places a comma after *hurriedly.*

8. **G** The phrase *with a new racquet* cannot be removed from the sentence without changing the sentence's meaning, so the phrase should not be set off from the rest of the sentence with commas. Choice (F) places commas on both sides of the phrase. Choice (G) correctly omits commas around the phrase.

FIX THE COMMA DRILLS SET 2

1. **B** The phrase *rather than sprinted* can be removed from the sentence without changing the sentence's meaning, so the phrase should be set off from the rest of the sentence with commas. Choice (A) omits the comma after *sprinted.* Choice (B) correctly includes commas before and after the phrase.

2. **F** The word *therefore* can be removed from the sentence without changing the sentence's meaning, so the word should be set off from the rest of the sentence with commas. Choice (F) correctly places commas on both sides of *therefore.*

3. **B** Commas should be used to separate items in a list of three or more items, so there should be a comma after *a train* and after *a bus.* Choice (A) omits the comma after *a bus.* Choice (B) correctly includes commas after each item in the list of transportation options.

4. **F** The word *honestly* can be removed from the sentence without changing the sentence's meaning, so the word should be set off from the rest of the sentence with a comma. Choice (F) correctly places a comma after *honestly.*

5. **B** The word *ideally* can be removed from the sentence without changing the sentence's meaning, so the word should be set off from the rest of the sentence with a comma. Choice (A) omits the comma after *ideally.* Choice (B) correctly places a comma after *ideally.*

6. **F** The word *carefully* can be removed from the sentence without changing the sentence's meaning, so the word should be set off from the rest of the sentence with a comma. Choice (F) correctly places a comma after *carefully.*

7. **B** The name *George Clooney* cannot be removed from the sentence without changing the sentence's meaning, so the phrase should not be set off from the rest of the sentence with commas. Choice (A) places commas on both sides of the name. Choice (B) correctly omits commas around the name.

8. **F** The phrase *which is a terrible job* can be removed from the sentence without changing the sentence's meaning, so the phrase should be set off from the rest of the sentence with a comma. Choice (F) correctly places a comma after *knives.*

FIX THE APOSTROPHE DRILLS SET 1

1. **guitar's**

   An apostrophe is used when a verb has been contracted. In this sentence, the phrase *guitar is* has been contracted, so the word *guitars* should be written as *guitar's.*

2. **oranges**

   An apostrophe is only used to indicate possession or contraction, not to indicate that a noun is plural. The word *orange's* should be written as *oranges.*

3. **cherries**

An apostrophe is only used to indicate possession or contraction, not to indicate that a noun is plural. The word *cherry's* should be written as *cherries.*

4. **children's**

An apostrophe is used to indicate possession. In this sentence, the word *childrens* refers to the people who possess the *one* mentioned earlier, so it should be written as *children's.*

5. **whose**

The correct possessive case of the pronoun *who* is *whose:* the word *who's* indicates that the phrase *who is* has been contracted. In this sentence, the word *who's* refers to the person possessing the phone number, so it should be written as *whose.*

6. **hers**

The correct possessive case of the pronoun *her* is *hers:* the word *her's* incorrectly suggests a contracted verb. The word *her's* should be written as *hers.*

7. **painter's**

An apostrophe is used to indicate possession. In this sentence, the word *painters* refers to the person whose *masterpiece* is on display, so it should be written as *painter's.*

8. **party's**

An apostrophe is used to indicate possession. In this sentence, the phrase *each political parties* refers to the entity possessing *representation,* so the word *parties* should be written as *party's.*

9. **family's**

An apostrophe is used to indicate possession. In this sentence, the phrase *each families* refers to the singular entity possessing *traditions;* the word *families* should be written as *family's.*

10. **who's**

An apostrophe is used when a verb has been contracted. In this sentence, the phrase *who is* has been contracted, so the word *Who'se* should be written as *Who's.*

FIX THE APOSTROPHE DRILLS SET 2

1. **sights**

   An apostrophe is only used to indicate possession or contraction. Nothing belongs to *sights* here—it is the subject of the verb *were set*—so no apostrophe is necessary. The word *sights'* should be written as *sights.*

2. **girls**

   An apostrophe is only used to indicate possession or contraction. The word *girl's* operates as the subject of the verb *went,* not as the entity possessing anything, so the word should be written as *girls.*

3. **you're**

   Don't be distracted by "there" and "they're" here—the error isn't either of those, but after them. The word *your* is the possessive form of the pronoun *you.* In this sentence, *your* should be written as *you're,* which is the contraction of *you are,* in order to provide a subject and a verb to the second half of the sentence.

4. **cookies**

   An apostrophe is only used to indicate possession or contraction, not to indicate that a noun is plural. The word *cookie's* should be written as *cookies.*

5. **it's**

   The word *its* is the possessive form of the pronoun *it.* In this sentence, *its* should be written as *it's,* which is the contraction of *it is,* in order to provide a subject and a verb to the second half of the sentence.

6. **melodies**

   An apostrophe is only used to indicate possession or contraction, not to indicate that a noun is plural. The word *melody's* should be written as *melodies.*

7. **members'**

   An apostrophe is used to indicate possession. In this sentence, the phrase *band members* refers to the people possessing *instruments,* so the word *members* should be written as *members'.* Because the possessing noun is plural, the apostrophe goes after the *s,* not before it.

8. **spies**

   An apostrophe is only used to indicate possession or contraction, not to indicate that a noun is plural. The word *spies'* should be written as *spies.*

9. **players**

An apostrophe is only used to indicate possession or contraction, not to indicate that a noun is plural. The word *player's* should be written as *players.*

10. **vocabularies**

An apostrophe is only used to indicate possession or contraction, not to indicate that a noun is plural. The word *vocabulary's* should be written as *vocabularies.*

FIX THE SUBJECT-VERB AGREEMENT DRILLS SET 1

1. **has** The subject of this sentence is *Every one,* which is singular. The verb *have* is plural, so it does not agree with its subject: it should be rewritten as *has.*

2. **contains**

The subject of this sentence is *Each corner,* which is singular. The verb *contain* is plural, so it does not agree with its subject: it should be rewritten as *contains.*

3. **distract**

The subject of this sentence is *descriptions and love,* which is plural. The verb *distracts* is singular, so it does not agree with its subject: it should be rewritten as *distract.*

4. **is** The subject of this sentence is *mastery,* which is singular. The verb *are* is plural, so it does not agree with its subject: it should be rewritten as *is.*

5. **are** The subject of this sentence is *Common sense and confidence,* which is plural. The verb *is* is singular, so it does not agree with its subject: it should be rewritten as *are.*

6. **require**

The subject of this sentence is *physics and math,* which is plural. The verb *requires* is singular, so it does not agree with its subject: it should be rewritten as *require.*

7. **is** The subject of this sentence is *Reading,* which is singular. The verb *are* is plural, so it does not agree with its subject: it should be rewritten as *is.*

8. **has** The subject of this sentence is *each,* which is singular. The verb *have* is plural, so it does not agree with its subject: it should be rewritten as *has.*

9. **have** The subject of this sentence is *doctors,* which is plural. The verb *has* is singular, so it does not agree with its subject: it should be rewritten as *have.*

10. **plays** The subject of this sentence is *Each,* which is singular. The verb *play* is plural, so it does not agree with its subject: it should be rewritten as *plays.*

FIX THE SUBJECT-VERB AGREEMENT DRILLS SET 2

1. **is** The subject of this sentence is *collection,* which is singular. The verb *are* is plural, so it does not agree with its subject: it should be rewritten as *is.*

2. **was** The subject of this sentence is *Winning,* which is singular. The verb *were* is plural, so it does not agree with its subject: it should be rewritten as *was.*

3. **has** The subject of this sentence is *A dog owner,* which is singular. The verb *have* is plural, so it does not agree with its subject: it should be rewritten as *has.*

4. **hates** The subject of this sentence is *One,* which is singular. The verb *hate* is plural, so it does not agree with its subject: it should be rewritten as *hates.*

5. **doesn't** This is an inverted sentence structure: its subject is *a reason,* which is singular. The verb *don't* is plural, so it does not agree with its subject: it should be rewritten as *doesn't.*

6. **seems** The subject of this sentence is *sand,* which is singular. The verb *seem* is plural, so it does not agree with its subject: it should be rewritten as *seems.*

7. **is** The subject of this sentence is *anybody,* which is singular. The verb *are* is plural, so it does not agree with its subject: it should be rewritten as *is.*

8. **is** The subject of this sentence is *faculty,* which is a collective noun; it refers to a group of people, but it is singular. The verb *are* is plural, so it does not agree with its subject: it should be rewritten as *is.*

9. **aren't** This is an inverted sentence structure: its subject is *people,* which is plural. The verb *isn't* is plural, so it does not agree with its subject: it should be rewritten as *aren't.*

10. **say** The subject of this sentence is *colors,* which is plural. The verb *says* is singular, so it does not agree with its subject: it should be rewritten as *say.*

VERB CONSISTENCY DRILL EXPLANATIONS

1. **imagined**

   The phrase *in her earliest daydreams* suggests that her imagining happened in the past. The verb *imagines* should be underlined and rewritten in its past tense form, *imagined.*

2. **had known**

   The word *if* indicates that the first clause is one that identifies a hypothetical circumstance; *she would have brought* tells what she would have done if the hypothetical circumstance had happened. The verb *knew* should be underlined and rewritten in its past perfect form (to indicate the hypothetical situation), *had known.*

3. **begun**

The phrase *when the phone rang* indicates that the events in the sentence occurred in the past. The word *had* in *had not yet* is used to form a past perfect verb. The verb *began,* which is the simple past tense form of the verb *begin,* should be underlined. The simple past tense cannot be used with the helping verb *had,* so the verb *began* should be rewritten as its past participle, *begun.*

4. **recognized**

The phrase *when his coach was demanding* indicates that Fabian's action of recognition happened in the past, and the phrase *could not balance* also indicates that the past tense is needed. The present tense verb *recognizes* should be underlined and rewritten in its past-tense form, *recognized.*

5. **prompt**

The sentence indicates that the *more experimental Modernist novels* do two things: *emphasize the constructed nature of narrative* and encourage a reader to *consider the arbitrary designations.* The verbs used to introduce both the actions should be in the same form, so *prompting* should be underlined and rewritten as *prompt,* which is present tense and is consistent with *emphasize* and *consider.*

6. **did**

The phrase *once smart phones became* indicates that the event being described in the main part of the sentence happened in the past. The helping verb *will* creates a future tense verb and should be underlined and rewritten as *did* to create the past-tense *did not occur.*

7. **would be**

The phrase *anticipating the film's impact* suggests that the critic imagined a shift in audience expectations that had not yet occurred but that the critic thinks will happen after people see the movie. The present tense verb *are* should be underlined and rewritten as *would be* to indicate that the critic was predicting that the shift would happen.

8. **seek**

The parallel phrases *cats seem* and *while dogs* indicate that the verb describing the dogs' actions should be consistent in form with the verb describing the cats' behavior. The verb *seeking* should be underlined and rewritten in its plural present-tense form, *seek.*

9. **started *or* had started**

The phrases *last summer* and *while I was just dreaming* indicate that the other person's actions happened in the past, not in the present. The verb *has started* would be used to indicate events that are ongoing and should be underlined. Since the context indicates that the other person's actions began and finished in the past, *has started* could be changed to either *started* or *had started.*

10. **extends**

The phrase *the pumpkin pie they eat on Thanksgiving* signals that *most people's experience of pumpkin* is based on a regularly occurring or habitual event. The simple present tense is used in such cases, as it is in the phrase *they eat on Thanksgiving.* The verb *is extending* should be underlined and rewritten in the simple present tense, *extends.*

QUESTIONS DRILL EXPLANATIONS

1. **B** Key words to underline within the question are *emphasizes the puzzling nature of the scene,* so the correct answer should be consistent with describing a confusing situation. *Dazzled* means amazed, *confounded* means confused, *startled* means surprised, and *intrigued* means curious. The correct answer is (B).

2. **H** Key words to underline within the question are *best uses a comparison, illuminate a characteristic of cats,* and *potential cat owners need to be aware of,* so the correct answer should be a comparison that would be relevant for anyone who might be taking care of a cat. Only (H) uses a comparison—to dogs—in order to differentiate care for cats from care for other pets, so the correct answer is (H).

3. **C** Key words to underline within the question are *best introduces an irony* and *Aretha Franklin's career,* so the correct answer should be an ironic fact about Franklin's work. Choices (A) and (B) use words like *thus* and *fitting* to introduce their statements, so they are not clearly ironic, and (D) introduces information about Franklin's sisters' careers, not her own. The correct answer is (C), which explains that Franklin's *extraordinary* voice often overshadowed her other *immense talents*—she was so talented, in fact, that some of her talents weren't even really noticed.

4. **F** Key words to underline within the question are *best expresses the uncomfortable conditions in the room,* so the correct answer should be consistent with describing an unpleasant environment. *Stifling* means suffocating or smothering, *warm* means moderately heated, *unfurnished* means lacking furniture, and *sterile* means clean or disinfected. The correct answer is (F).

5. **B** Key words to underline within the question are *express the tension between the participants,* so the correct answer should mean something like *polarized* or *uncomfortable. Harmonious* means in agreement, *charged* means polarized, *noteworthy* means remarkable, and *unusual* means out of the ordinary. The correct answer is (B).

6. **H** Key words to underline within the question are *furthers the author's aim of helping the reader to visualize the forest path,* so the correct answer should include visual details about a wooded setting. Choices (F) and (G) do not mention details specific to that path, while (J) mentions olfactory details instead of visual details. Choice (H) includes details about the color and distribution of leaves, so (H) is the correct answer.

7. **A** Key words to underline within the question are *emphasizes the extremely challenging nature of the task,* so the correct answer must mean something like *difficult* or *requiring massive effort. Arduous* means of extraordinary difficulty, *grimy* means unclean or filmy, *unpleasant* means distasteful, and *superficial* means shallow. The correct answer is (A).

8. **J** Key words to underline within the question are *Death Valley* and *illustrate how extreme its climate is,* so the correct answer will focus on the climate conditions in the area. Choices (F), (G), and (H) provide information about the size, history, and wildlife of certain areas in the valley, but not the climate. Choice (J) describes the measurement in Death Valley of *the highest ground surface temperature ever recorded on Earth,* so the correct answer is (J).

9. **D** Key words to underline within the question are *most specific description of the window panels,* so the correct answer should provide specific information about the panels. *Priceless, bright,* and *gorgeous* do not provide specific information about the appearance of the window panels, while *jewel-toned* names a specific attribute of the glass. The correct answer is (D).

10. **G** Key words to underline within the question are *the dramatic nature* and *manager's words,* so the correct answer must be consistent with a surprising or theatrically delivered speech. *Announcement, farewell,* and *conclusion* describe types of statement, but none is necessarily a dramatic statement, while *bombshell* suggests that the manager's words had an effect like the dropping of a bomb. The correct answer is (G).

ANGLE DRILLS SET 1 EXPLANATIONS

1. **77°** Angles $\angle ACB$ and $\angle ECD$ are vertical angles, so $\angle ECD$ must also measure 26°. Since triangle *ECD* is isosceles, the two unknown angles must be equal to one another. Subtract the known angle from 180° to find how many degrees are left to be divided between the two unknown angles: 180° – 26° = 154°. Divide 154° by 2 to find that $\angle CED = 77°$.

2. **57** Whenever you are given two parallel lines with a transversal crossing over both of them, label every angle as a "big" or a "small." Any big angle plus any small angle will always equal 180°, but in this case, the big angle is made up of two angles, 71° and $x°$. Solve $x° + 71° + 52° = 180°$ to find that $x = 57$.

3. **71°** In an isosceles trapezoid, the angles of each base will be equal. Since $\angle E = 71°$, $\angle F$ will also measure 71°. Subtract these two measures from the 360° inside any quadrilateral to find the sum of the base angles: 360° – 71° – 71° = 218°. Since $\angle H$ is equal to $\angle HGF$ because of the properties of an isosceles trapezoid, divide 218° by 2 to find the value of $\angle HGF$ is 109°. Angles $\angle HGF$ and $\angle FGJ$ are supplements, so their measures must add up to 180°: therefore, $109° + \angle FGJ = 180°$ can be solved to find that $\angle FGJ$ is 71°.

4. **73** Since $\overline{CA}$ and $\overline{AD}$ are perpendicular to one another, $\angle CAD$ must measure 90°. The sum of all the angles forming straight line $\overline{AB}$ must be 180°, so subtract the two known angles to find x: $180° – 90° – 17° = x°$; $x = 73$.

5. 38° Since $\overline{RT} \cong \overline{ST}$, ΔRST is an isosceles triangle. The angles opposite congruent sides in an isosceles triangle are equal, so $\angle SRT = 76°$. To *bisect* means to divide into two equal parts. Since $\overline{RV}$ bisects $\angle SRT$, $\angle SRV = \angle VRT$, and $\angle SRV + \angle VRT = 2(\angle VRT) = 76°$. That means that $\angle VRT = \frac{76\infty}{2} = 38°$.

6. 90° You should always draw a picture when none is provided. Your picture should show a square with two diagonals that go from opposite corners of the square and meet in the middle. Since diagonals in a square are also angle bisectors, the eight angles at the corners all equal $\frac{90\infty}{2} = 45°$. Subtract the two known angles in triangle *AEB* from 180° to find the measure of $\angle AEB$: $180° – 45° – 45° = 90°$.

7. 39° Angles $\angle QRP$ and $\angle LRQ$ form a straight line, so $\angle QRP = 180° – 39° = 141°$. The four angles in any quadrilateral always add up to equal 360°, so subtract the three known angles to find $\angle PNQ$: $360° – 141° – 90° – 90° = 39°$.

8. 83° Since $\overline{FJ} = \overline{GH}$, quadrilateral *FJHG* is an isosceles trapezoid. In an isosceles trapezoid, the angles of each base are equal to one another, making $\angle JHG = 97°$. To find $\angle FGH$, start with the 360° that make up any quadrilateral and subtract the two known angles: $360° – 97° – 97° = 166°$. Since the two unknown angles are equal to one another, divide this result by 2 to get the final answer: $\frac{166\propto}{2} = 83°$.

9. 50° The two angles that form line $\overline{DC}$ will add up to 180°. Solve $130° + \angle AED = 180°$ to find that $\angle AED = 50°$.

10. 40° In an equilateral triangle, all three angles are equal. Since the three angles of a triangle must add up to 180°, divide 180° by 3 to find that each angle will measure 60°. Lines $\overline{DB}$ and $\overline{EB}$ divide $\angle ABC$ into three equal angles, so each angle will measure $\frac{60\infty}{3} = 20°$. Angle $\angle ABE$ is made by combining two of these 20° angles, so it must measure $20° + 20° = 40°$.

ANGLE DRILLS SET 2 EXPLANATIONS

1. 90° Find $\angle DEC$ by using the properties of ΔDEC. Opposite angles in a parallelogram are equal, so $\angle ADC = 114°$. $\angle ADC$ is bisected by $\overline{DE}$, so $\angle EDC$ is $\frac{114\propto}{2} = 57°$. Adjacent angles in a parallelogram always add up to 180°, so $\angle BCD = 180° – 114° = 66°$. Angle $\angle BDC$ is bisected by $\overline{EC}$, so $\angle ECD = \frac{66\infty}{2} = 33°$. Now that you know two angles in ΔDEC, subtract them both from 180° to find the missing angle: $180° – 33° – 57° = 90°$.

2. 80° When no diagram is provided, you should always draw a picture and fill in what you know. Looking at your picture, you can see that $180° – 40° = 140°$, which is what remains to be split between the two unknown angles. Set $\angle BCA = x$ and use the relationship $\frac{4}{3}\angle BAC = \angle BCA$ to find that $\angle BAC = \frac{3}{4}x$. Since these two angles will total up to 140°, solve the equation $x + \frac{3}{4}x = 140°$ to find that $x = 80°$.

3. 57° $\overline{JG} \cong \overline{FG}$, so triangle *JGF* is isosceles. The two base angles of an isosceles triangle are equal to one another, so subtract the known angle and divide by 2 to find the measure of the bases: $\frac{(180° - 40°)}{2} = 70°$. Angles $\angle FJG$ and $\angle HJG$ form a straight line; therefore, $\angle HJG = 180° - 70° = 110°$. Since $\angle HGF = 53°$, $\angle JGH$ is $53° - 40° = 13°$. With two of the angles in triangle *JGH* now known, subtract these values from 180° to find $\angle JHG$: $180° - 13° - 110° = 57°$.

4. 61° Complementary angles add up to 90°, so solve $29° + \angle GEF = 90°$ to find that $\angle GEF$ is 61°.

5. 67.5° Start with ΔKNL. Because $\angle KNL \cong \angle KLN$, ΔKNL is isosceles and will have congruent base angles. Subtract the known angle from 180° and then divide the result by two to find the measure of $\angle KNL$: $\frac{(180° - 90°)}{2} = 45°$. $\overline{MN}$ is perpendicular to $\overline{KN}$, so $KNM = 90°$. Subtract the known portion off of $\angle KNM$ to find that $\angle LNM$ is $90° - 45° = 45°$. Triangle ΔNLM is isosceles because it has two equal angles, so repeat the steps from above to find $\angle NML$: $\frac{(180° - 45°)}{2} = 67.5°$.

6. 106° Start with the given angle measure. Since $\overline{ST}$ and $\overline{QR}$ are both perpendicular to $\overline{SR}$, *STQR* must be a rectangle and $\angle STQ = 90°$. $\angle STN = \angle STQ + \angle NTQ$, so $\angle NTQ = 164° - 90° = 74°$. Now consider trapezoid *TNPQ*. $\overline{TN} \cong \overline{PQ}$, so *TNPQ* must be an isosceles trapezoid with two pairs of congruent base angles. Because of this, $\angle TQP = 74°$. The angles in any quadrilateral always add up to 360°, so subtract the two known angles from 360° and then divide the result by 2 to find $\angle NPQ$: $\frac{(360° - 74° - 74°)}{2} = 106°$.

7. 107° Since any two angles that form a straight line add up to 180°, $\angle CDB = 180° - 34° = 146°$. Line $\overline{DE}$ bisects $\angle CDB$, so $\angle CDE$ and $\angle EDB$ each equal $\frac{146\propto}{2} = 73°$. This gives you part of angle $\angle EDF$. The other portion of $\angle EDF$, $\angle FDB$, is a vertical angle to $\angle ADC$, so it also equals 34°. Add these two parts together to get the final answer: $34° + 73° = 107°$.

8. 140° Supplementary angles always add up to 180°, so $2x + 7x = 180°$ can be solved to find that $x = 20°$. Plug this value for x into the measure of $\angle KJL$ to find the answer: $7(20) = 140°$.

9. **16°** Any time a line crosses two parallel lines, label each angle as a "big" or a "small." Take it one line at a time to find the measures of the angles inside of ΔGEH. $\angle FGE$ and $\angle KLG$ are both bigs, so $\angle FGE = 95°$. $\angle FGE$ is supplementary to $\angle HGE$, so $\angle HGE = 180° - 95° = 85°$. Look at the other transversal, $\overline{EM}$. $\angle LMH$ and $\angle FHE$ are both smalls, so $\angle FHE = 79°$. Subtract the two known angles inside triangle ΔGEH to find $\angle GEH$: $180° - 79° - 85° = 16°$.

10. **94°** Since ΔPQR is similar to ΔSQT, angles $\angle PQR$ and $\angle SQT$ are congruent. These two angles plus $\angle RQT = 106°$, so subtract the known portion of the total angle and divide the result by 2 to find the measure of $\angle SQT$: $\frac{(106° - 20°)}{2} = 43°$. Because $\overline{PQ} \cong \overline{PR}$, ΔPQR is isosceles, and because this triangle is similar to ΔSQT, ΔSQT is also isosceles. In this isosceles triangle, angle $\angle SQT$ is congruent to $\angle QTS$, so $\angle QTS = 43°$. Subtract the two known angles from 180° to find $\angle QST$: $180° - 43° - 43° = 94°$.

AREA AND PERIMETER DRILLS SET 1 EXPLANATIONS

1. **84** The area formula for a triangle is $A = \frac{1}{2}bh$. Find the base by using the Pythagorean Theorem: $7^2 + b^2 = 25^2$; $49 + b^2 = 625$; $b^2 = 576$; $b = 24$. This makes the triangle a 7-24-25 Pythagorean triple. Apply the area formula: $A = \frac{1}{2}(7)(24) = \frac{1}{2}(168) = 84$.

2. **56** You know two of the side lengths, so find the missing side by using the Pythagorean Theorem: $7^2 + b^2 = 25^2$; $49 + b^2 = 625$; $b^2 = 576$; $b = 24$. This makes the triangle a 7-24-25 Pythagorean triple. To find the perimeter, add the three side lengths: $7 + 24 + 25 = 56$.

3. **62** In a parallelogram, opposite sides have equal lengths. To find the perimeter, add the side lengths: $21 + 10 + 21 + 10 = 62$.

4. **168** The area formula for a parallelogram is $A = bh$. Find the height by using the Pythagorean Theorem: $6^2 + b^2 = 10^2$; $36 + b^2 = 100$; $b^2 = 64$; $b = 8$. This makes the triangle a multiple of the 3-4-5 Pythagorean triple. To find the area, apply the parallelogram area formula: $A = (8)(21) = 168$.

5. **108** First, find $\overline{HK}$ using the Pythagorean Theorem: $10^2 + b^2 = 26^2$; $100 + b^2 = 676$; $b^2 = 576$; $b = 24$. Triangle ΔHJK is a multiple of the 5-12-13 Pythagorean triple. Now that you know two sides of ΔHLK, use the Pythagorean Theorem again to find $\overline{LH}$: $24^2 + 32^2 = c^2$; $1600 = c^2$; $c = 40$. This makes ΔHLK a multiple of another Pythagorean triple, the 3-4-5. With all outer sides known, add the three lengths together: $26 + 42 + 40 = 108$.

6. **504** The area formula for a triangle is $A = \frac{1}{2}bh$. Find height $\overline{HK}$ by the Pythagorean Theorem, $a^2 + b^2 = c^2$: $10^2 + b^2 = 26^2$; $100 + b^2 = 676$; $b^2 = 576$; $b = 24$. Triangle ΔHJK is a multiple of the 5-12-13 Pythagorean triple. With the height now known, use the area formula: $A = \frac{1}{2}(42)(24) = \frac{1}{2}(1{,}008) = 504$.

7. **40** The area formula for a rectangle is $A = lw$. $A = (8)(5) = 40$.

8. **48** Create a height for the triangle by drawing a line from S that is perpendicular to $\overline{VT}$. This line makes two right triangles with bases of $\frac{12}{2} = 6$ and hypotenuses of 10. Use the Pythagorean Theorem to find the height: $6^2 + b^2 = 10^2$; $b^2 = 64$; $b = 8$. This triangle is a multiple of the 3-4-5 Pythagorean triple. Plug in a height of 8 and the full base into the triangle area formula: $A = \frac{1}{2}bh = \frac{1}{2}(8)(12) = \frac{1}{2}(96) = 48$.

9. **32** Since $\overline{SV} = \overline{ST}$, $\overline{ST} = 10$. Add the lengths of the sides together: $10 + 12 + 10 = 32$.

10. **120** The area formula for a trapezoid is $A = \frac{1}{2}(b_1 + b_2)h$. Find the height by drawing lines from points A and B that are perpendicular to $\overline{DC}$. These lines create two triangles with bases of 6, because $\frac{(21-9)}{2} = 6$. Each of these triangles is a 6-8-10 triple, so the height is 8. Apply the formula: $A = \frac{1}{2}(b_1 + b_2)h = \frac{1}{2}(9 + 21)(8) = \frac{1}{2}(30)(8) = \frac{1}{2}(240) = 120$.

AREA AND PERIMETER DRILLS SET 2 EXPLANATIONS

1. **600** Since you need to find the height of ΔACD to find its area, use similar triangles ΔABE and ΔACD to find $\overline{AC}$. Start with what is given. $\overline{CD} = \overline{AE}$, so $\overline{AE} = 30$. Find $\overline{AB}$ by using the Pythagorean Theorem: $18^2 + b^2 = 30^2$; $324 + b^2 = 900$; $b^2 = 576$; $b = 24$. Triangle ΔABE is a multiple of the 3-4-5 Pythagorean triple. With $\overline{AB} = 24$, use a proportion to find height $\overline{AC}$: $\frac{18}{30} = \frac{24}{x}$ can be solved to find $\overline{AC} = 40$. Plug this height and the base into the triangle area formula: $A = \frac{1}{2}bh = \frac{1}{2}(30)(40) = \frac{1}{2}(1{,}200) = 600$.

2. **72** To find perimeter, add up all three side lengths. The question says that $\overline{AE} \cong \overline{CD}$, so $\overline{AE} = 30$. To find the length of $\overline{AB}$, use the Pythagorean Theorem: $\overline{AB}^2 + 18^2 = 30^2$, which means that $\overline{AB}^2 + 324 = 900$. Subtract 324 from both sides to get $\overline{AB}^2 = 576$; then take the square root of both sides to get $\overline{AB} = 24$. Alternatively, use the 3-4-5 right triangle ratio multiplied by 6. Since $\overline{AE} = 5 \times 6 = 30$ and $\overline{BE} = 3 \times 6 = 18$, then $\overline{AB}$ must be equal to $4 \times 6 = 24$. To find the perimeter, add up the three sides: $18 + 24 + 30 = 72$.

3. $\mathbf{9 + 9\sqrt{2}}$

The area formula for a parallelogram is $A = bh$. The height is 3, since $\overline{KJ} = 3$ and $\overline{KJ} = \overline{FJ}$. To find the length of the base, find $\overline{KF}$, which is the hypotenuse of right triangle ΔKJF. Use the Pythagorean Theorem: $3^2 + 3^2 = c^2$; $18 = c^2$; $c = 3\sqrt{2}$. This $x : x : x\sqrt{2}$ ratio is the pattern for every isosceles right triangle. Since $\overline{KF} = 3\sqrt{2}$ and $\overline{KF} = \overline{JH}$, the base of the parallelogram is $3 + 3\sqrt{2}$. Use the parallelogram area formula: $A = bh = (3)(3 + 2\sqrt{2}) = (3)(3) + (3)(3\sqrt{2}) = 9 + 9\sqrt{2}$.

4. **$6 + 12\sqrt{2}$**

You must find the lengths of sides $\overline{KF}$ and $\overline{KH}$ to find the perimeter. $\overline{KF}$ is the hypotenuse of right triangle ΔKJF, so use the Pythagorean Theorem: $3^2 + 3^2 = c^2$; $9 + 9 = c^2$; $c^2 = 18$; $c = 3\sqrt{2}$. This $x : x : x\sqrt{2}$ side ratio is true for every isosceles right triangle. Since $\overline{KF} = 3\sqrt{2}$ and $\overline{KF} = \overline{JH}$, add together $\overline{JH}$ and $\overline{KJ}$ to find that the base of the parallelogram is $3 + 3\sqrt{2}$. Opposite sides of a parallelogram have equal lengths, so you now know every side length. Add them all together to find the perimeter: $3\sqrt{2} + (3 + 3\sqrt{2}) + 3\sqrt{2} + (3 + 3\sqrt{2}) = 6 + 12\sqrt{2}$.

5. **32** Use the information given and the Pythagorean Theorem to find the lengths of the two sides. Since $\overline{LM}$ is twice as long as $\overline{LP}$, you should plug in sets of doubles until a pair fits into right triangle ΔLMP. Triangle ΔLMP has a hypotenuse of $\sqrt{80}$, so test your side lengths with the Pythagorean Theorem. 4 and 8 work: $4^2 + 8^2 = c^2$; $80 = c^2$; $c = \sqrt{80}$. Plug these side lengths into the area formula: $A = lw = (4)(8) = 32$.

6. **174** The area of trapezoid $QRST$ is the sum of the areas of square $QVST$ and ΔVRS. The square's area is given, but you'll have to find both the base and height of ΔVRS to use the area formula for a triangle, $A = \frac{1}{2}bh$. Work backward from what is given. Since the area of the square is 144, use the area formula for a square, $A = s^2$, to find the length of its sides: $144 = s^2$, so $s = 12$. Plug $\overline{VS} = 12$ into the triangle, and use the Pythagorean Theorem to find that $\overline{VR} = 5$. ΔVRS is a 5-12-13 Pythagorean triple. Plug the base and height into the triangle area formula: $\frac{1}{2}(12)(5) = \frac{1}{2}(60) = 30$. Add this area to the area of the square to get the final answer: $30 + 144 = 174$.

7. **54** To find the perimeter of this trapezoid, find the lengths of every side. Work backward from what is given. Since the area of the square is 144, use the area formula for a square, $A = s^2$, to find the length of its sides: $144 = s^2$, so $s = 12$. This gives you the lengths of $\overline{TS}$ and $\overline{QT}$, but you'll need to find the length of $\overline{VR}$ to get the length of $\overline{QR}$. Use the Pythagorean Theorem to find $\overline{VR}$, the base of ΔVRS: $12^2 + b^2 = 13^2$ finds that $b^2 = 25$ and $b = 5$. Since $\overline{QR}$ is $\overline{QV} + \overline{VR}$, it must be $12 + 5 = 17$. Add together all of the side lengths to get the final answer: $17 + 13 + 12 + 12 = 54$.

8. **64** Since the area formula for a square is $A = s^2$, find the length of one of the square's sides. Start with what is given. The radius of circle C is $4\sqrt{2}$. This makes $\overline{DF}$, which is both a diameter to the circle and a diagonal to the square, equal to $8\sqrt{2}$. Line $\overline{DF}$ created two right triangles. Since all sides of a square are equal, plug in side length numbers into the Pythagorean Theorem. 8 works as a side length: $8^2 + 8^2 = c^2$; $128 = c^2$; $c = 8\sqrt{2}$. Plug the side length into the area formula: $8^2 = 64$.

9. **42** The area formula for a triangle is $A = \frac{1}{2}bh$, so find the lengths of $\overline{HM}$ and $\overline{MK}$. Line $\overline{MK}$ is equal to $\overline{ML} + \overline{LK}$, and since $\overline{ML}$ must be 3, $\overline{MK}$ is $3 + 3 = 6$. To find $\overline{HM}$, work backward from what is given. The area of rectangle $NJLM$ is 21, so plug that and the length of $\overline{NJ}$ into the rectangle area

formula: $A = lw$; $21 = 3w$; $w = 7$. Since $\overline{NM}$ is 7 and $\overline{NM} = \overline{HN}$, $\overline{HM}$ is 7 + 7, or 14. Plug the base and height into the area formula: $\frac{1}{2}(6)(14) = \frac{1}{2}(84) = 42$.

10. **$20 + \sqrt{232}$**

You need to add together the lengths of every side of the triangle to find its perimeter, so start with what is given. Opposite sides of a rectangle have equal lengths, so $\overline{ML} = 3$. Since $\overline{ML} = \overline{LK}$, side $\overline{MK} = 3 + 3 = 6$. The area of rectangle *NJLM* is 21, so plug that and the length of $\overline{NJ}$ into the rectangle area formula: $A = lw$; $21 = 3w$; $w = 7$. Since $\overline{NM}$ is 7 and $\overline{NM} = \overline{HN}$, $\overline{HM} = 7 + 7 = 14$. Now that you know the lengths of two sides, use the Pythagorean Theorem to find the missing hypotenuse: $6^2 + 14^2 = c^2$; $232 = c^2$; $c = \sqrt{232}$. Add together all the side lengths to find the perimeter: $14 + 6 + \sqrt{232} = 20 + \sqrt{232}$.

CIRCLE DRILLS SET 1 EXPLANATIONS

1. **$\frac{81}{4}\pi$** Plug the circumference 9π into the circumference formula $C = \pi d$ to find the diameter: $9\pi = \pi d$; $d = 9$. Divide the diameter in half to find that the radius is $\frac{9}{2}$. Plug $r = \frac{9}{2}$ into the area formula $A = \pi r^2$: $A = \pi\left(\frac{9}{2}\right)^2 = \frac{9^2}{2^2}\pi = \frac{81}{4}\pi$.

2. **4.5 or $\frac{9}{2}$**

Plug the circumference 9π into the circumference formula $C = \pi d$ to find the diameter: $9\pi = \pi d$; $d = 9$. Divide the diameter in half to find that the radius is 4.5, or $\frac{9}{2}$.

3. **9** Plug the circumference 9π into the circumference formula $C = \pi d$ to find the diameter: $9\pi = \pi d$; $d = 9$.

4. **24π** The formula for circumference is $C = \pi d$. Double the radius of 12 to find that the diameter is 24. Plug $d = 24$ into the circumference formula: $C = 24\pi$.

5. **144π**

The formula for area of a circle is $A = \pi r^2$. Plug in $r = 12$ to find the area: $A = \pi(12)^2 = 144\pi$.

6. **24** Double the radius of 12 to find the diameter: $12(2) = 24$.

7. **$8\sqrt{2}\pi$**

The formula for circumference is $C = \pi d$. Plug $d = 8\sqrt{2}\pi$ into the circumference formula: $C = 8\sqrt{2}\pi$.

8. **32π** The formula for area of a circle is $A = \pi r^2$. Find the radius by dividing the diameter in half: $\frac{8\sqrt{2}}{2} = 4\sqrt{2}$. Plug $r = 4\sqrt{2}$ into the area formula: $A = \pi(4\sqrt{2})^2 = (4^2)(\sqrt{2^2}) = \pi(16)(2) = 32\pi$.

9. **$4\sqrt{2}$** Find the radius by dividing the diameter in half: $\frac{8\sqrt{2}}{2} = 4\sqrt{2}$.

10. **$6\sqrt{3}\pi$** Find the radius by plugging $A = 27\pi$ into the area formula: $27\pi = \pi r^2$; $27 = r^2$; $r = \sqrt{27}$. Since $\sqrt{27} = (\sqrt{9})(\sqrt{3})$, reduce it to find that $r = 3\sqrt{3}$. Double the radius to find that $d = 6\sqrt{3}$; then plug this value into the circumference formula: $C = \pi d = 6\sqrt{3}\pi$.

11. **$3\sqrt{3}$** Find the radius by plugging $A = 27\pi$ into the area formula: $27\pi = \pi r^2$; $27 = r^2$; $r = \sqrt{27}$. Since $\sqrt{27} = (\sqrt{9})(\sqrt{3})$, reduce it to find that $r = 3\sqrt{3}$.

12. **$6\sqrt{3}$** Find the radius by plugging $A = 27\pi$ into the area formula: $27\pi = \pi r^2$; $27 = r^2$; $r = \sqrt{27}$. Since $\sqrt{27} = (\sqrt{9})(\sqrt{3})$, reduce it to find that $r = 3\sqrt{3}$. Double the radius to find that $d = 6\sqrt{3}$.

CIRCLE DRILLS SET 2 EXPLANATIONS

1. **8π** Plug the circumference $4\sqrt{2}\pi$ into the circumference formula, $C = \pi d$, to find the diameter: $4\sqrt{2}\pi = \pi d$; $d = 4\sqrt{2}$. Divide the diameter in half to find that the radius is $2\sqrt{2}$. Plug $r = 2\sqrt{2}$ into the area formula: $A = \pi r^2 = \pi(2\sqrt{2})^2 = 8\pi$.

2. **$2\sqrt{2}$** Plug the circumference $4\sqrt{2}\pi$ into the circumference formula, $C = \pi d$, to find the diameter: $4\sqrt{2}\pi = \pi d$; $d = 4\sqrt{2}$. Divide the diameter in half to find that the radius is $2\sqrt{2}$.

3. **$4\sqrt{2}$** Plug the circumference $4\sqrt{2}\pi$ into the circumference formula, $C = \pi d$, to find the diameter: $4\sqrt{2}\pi = \pi d$; $d = 4\sqrt{2}$.

4. **14π** Double the radius of 7 to find that the diameter is 14; then plug $d = 14$ into the circumference formula: $C = \pi d = 14\pi$.

5. **49π** Plug $r = 7$ into the area formula: $A = \pi r^2 = \pi(7^2) = 49\pi$.

6. **14** Double the radius of 7 to find that the diameter is 14.

7. **26π** Plug $d = 26$ into the circumference formula: $C = \pi d = 26\pi$.

8. **169π** Divide the diameter in half to find that the radius is 13. Plug $r = 13$ into the area formula: $A = \pi r^2 = \pi(13^2) = 169\pi$.

9. **13** Divide diameter $d = 26$ in half to find that the radius is 13.

10. **$8\sqrt{3}\pi$** Find the radius by plugging $A = 48\pi$ into the area formula: $48\pi = \pi r^2$; $48 = r^2$; $r = \sqrt{48}$. Since $\sqrt{48} = (\sqrt{16})(\sqrt{3})$, reduce it to $4\sqrt{3}$. Double the radius to find that the diameter is $8\sqrt{3}$. Plug $d = 8\sqrt{3}$ into the circumference formula: $C = \pi d = 8\sqrt{3}\pi$.

11. **$4\sqrt{3}$** Find the radius by plugging $A = 48\pi$ into the area formula: $48\pi = \pi r^2$; $48 = r^2$; $r = \sqrt{48}$. Since $\sqrt{48} = (\sqrt{16})(\sqrt{3})$, reduce it to $4\sqrt{3}$.

12. **$8\sqrt{3}$** Find the radius by plugging $A = 48\pi$ into the area formula: $48\pi = \pi r^2$; $48 = r^2$; $r = \sqrt{48}$. Since $\sqrt{48} = (\sqrt{16})(\sqrt{3})$, reduce it to $4\sqrt{3}$. Double the radius to find that the diameter is $8\sqrt{3}$.

MANIPULATING EQUATIONS DRILLS SET 1 EXPLANATIONS

1. **4** Divide both sides of the equation by 3: $\frac{3(x-2)}{3} = \frac{6}{3}$, which simplifies to $x - 2 = 2$. Now add 2 to both sides: $x - 2 + 2 = 2 + 2$, which simplifies to $x = 4$.

2. **2** Multiply both sides of the equation by 2: $\frac{2x+2}{2} \times 2 = 3 \times 2$, which simplifies to $2x + 2 = 6$. Now subtract 2 from both sides: $2x + 2 - 2 = 6 - 2$, which simplifies to $2x = 4$. Last, divide both sides of the equation by 2: $\frac{2x}{2} = \frac{4}{2}$, which simplifies to $x = 2$.

3. **–7** Multiply both sides of the equation by 2: $\frac{3-x}{2} \times 2 = 5 \times 2$, which simplifies to $3 - x = 10$. Now subtract 3 from both sides: $3 - x - 3 = 10 - 3$, which simplifies to $-x = 7$. Last, divide both sides of the equation by –1: $\frac{-x}{-1} = \frac{7}{-1}$, which simplifies to $x = -7$.

4. **1** Add $4x$ to both sides of the equation: $3 - 4x + 4x = -x + 4x$, which simplifies to $3 = 3x$. Now divide both sides by 3: $\frac{3}{3} = \frac{3x}{3}$, which simplifies to $1 = x$.

5. **6** First, distribute –3 to everything in the parentheses: $(-3 \times 4) - (-3 \times x) = x$, which simplifies to $-12 + 3x = x$. Now subtract $3x$ from both sides: $-12 + 3x - 3x = x - 3x$, which simplifies to $-12 = -2x$. Last, divide both sides of the equation by –2: $\frac{-12}{-2} = \frac{-2x}{-2}$, which simplifies to $6 = x$.

6. **3** Cross-multiply: $-2x = 6(2 - x)$. Now distribute the 6 to everything in the parentheses: $-2x = (6 \times 2) - (6 \times x)$, which simplifies to $-2x = 12 - 6x$. Next, add $6x$ to each side of the equation: $-2x + 6x = 12 - 6x + 6x$, which simplifies to $4x = 12$. Last, divide both sides by 4: $\frac{4x}{4} = \frac{12}{4}$, which simplifies to $x = 3$.

7. **13** Square both sides of the equation: $(\sqrt{x-4})^2 = 3^2$, which simplifies to $x - 4 = 9$. Now add 4 to each side: $x - 4 + 4 = 9 + 4$, which simplifies to $x = 13$.

8. **2** Square both sides of the equation: $\left(\sqrt{\frac{x+2}{4}}\right)^2 = 1^2$, which simplifies to $\frac{x+2}{4} = 1$. Now multiply both sides by 4: $\left(\frac{x+2}{4}\right) \times 4 = 1 \times 4$, which simplifies to $x + 2 = 4$. Last, subtract 2 from both sides of the equation: $x + 2 - 2 = 4 - 2$, which simplifies to $x = 2$.

9. **1** Multiply both sides of the equation by x: $(3x + 2) \times x = \left(\frac{3x^2 + 2}{x}\right) \times x$, which simplifies to $x(3x + 2) = 3x^2 + 2$. Now distribute the x to everything in the parentheses: $(3x \times x) + (2 \times x) = 3x^2 + 2$, which simplifies to $3x^2 + 2x = 3x^2 + 2$. Next, subtract $3x^2$ from both sides of the equation: $3x^2 + 2x - 3x^2 = 3x^2 + 2 - 3x^2$, which simplifies to $2x = 2$. Last, divide both sides by 2: $\frac{2x}{2} = \frac{2}{2}$, which simplifies to $x = 1$.

10. **–2** Multiply both sides of the equation by 2: $\left[\frac{x(4x-2)}{2}\right] \times 2 = (2 + 2x^2) \times 2$, which simplifies to $x(4x-2) = 2(2 + 2x^2)$. Now, distribute the x and the 2 to everything in the parentheses: $(4x \times x) - (2 \times x) = (2 \times 2) + (2x^2 \times 2)$, which simplifies to $4x^2 - 2x = 4 + 4x^2$. Next, subtract $4x^2$ from both sides of the equation: $4x^2 - 2x - 4x^2 = 4 + 4x^2 - 4x^2$, which simplifies to $-2x = 4$. Last, divide both sides by –2: $\frac{-2x}{-2} = \frac{4}{-2}$, which simplifies to $x = -2$.

MANIPULATING EQUATIONS DRILLS SET 2 EXPLANATIONS

1. **6** Multiply both sides of the equation by 2: $\frac{(x+4)}{2} \times 2 = 5 \times 2$, which simplifies to $x + 4 = 10$. Now subtract 4 from both sides: $x + 4 - 4 = 10 - 4$, which simplifies to $x = 6$.

2. **5** Divide both sides of the equation by 5: $\frac{5(x-2)}{5} = \frac{15}{5}$, which simplifies to $x - 2 = 3$. Now add 2 to both sides: $x - 2 + 2 = 3 + 2$, which simplifies to $x = 5$.

3. **0** Divide both sides of the equation by 2: $\frac{2(4-x)}{2} = \frac{8}{2}$, which simplifies to $4 - x = 4$. Subtract 4 from both sides: $4 - x - 4 = 4 - 4$, which simplifies to $-x = 0$. Last, divide by –1: $\frac{-x}{-1} = \frac{0}{-1}$, which simplifies to $x = 0$.

4. **–2** Multiply both sides of the equation by 3: $\left(\frac{8-2x}{3}\right) \times 3 = (-2x) \times 3$, which simplifies to $8 - 2x = -6x$. Now add $2x$ to both sides: $8 - 2x + 2x = -6x + 2x$, which simplifies to $8 = -4x$. Last, divide both sides by –4: $\frac{8}{-4} = \frac{-4x}{-4}$, which simplifies to $-2 = x$.

5. **–1** Divide both sides of the equation by –1: $\frac{-(1-x)}{-1} = \frac{2x}{-1}$, which simplifies to $1 - x = -2x$. Now add x to both sides: $1 - x + x = -2x + x$, which simplifies to $1 = -x$. Last, divide by –1: $\frac{1}{-1} = \frac{-x}{-1}$, which simplifies to $-1 = x$.

6. **8** Square both sides of the equation: $\left(\sqrt{12-x}\right)^2 = 2^2$, which simplifies to $12 - x = 4$. Now subtract 12 from both sides: $12 - x - 12 = 4 - 12$, which simplifies to $-x = -8$. Last, divide by -1: $\frac{-x}{-1} = \frac{-8}{-1}$, which simplifies to $x = 8$.

7. **4** Square both sides of the equation: $\left(\sqrt{5(9-x)}\right)^2 = 5^2$, which simplifies to $5(9 - x) = 25$. Now divide both sides by 5: $\frac{5(9-x)}{5} = \frac{25}{5}$, which simplifies to $9 - x = 5$. Next, subtract 9 from both sides: $9 - x - 9 = 5 - 9$, which simplifies to $-x = -4$. Last, divide both sides by -1: $\frac{-x}{-1} = \frac{-4}{-1}$, which simplifies to $x = 4$.

8. **–1** Cross-multiply: $1 \times (x + 5) = -2 \times (2x)$, which simplifies to $x + 5 = -4x$. Now subtract x from both sides: $x + 5 - x = -4x - x$, which simplifies to $5 = -5x$. Last, divide by -5: $\frac{5}{-5} = \frac{-5x}{-5}$, which simplifies to $-1 = x$.

9. **1** Multiply both sides of the equation by 3: $\left[\frac{6x(x-2)}{3}\right] \times 3 = (2x^2 - 4) \times 3$, which simplifies to $6x(x - 2) = (2x^2 - 4) \times 3$. Now, distribute the $6x$ and the 3 to everything in the parentheses: $(x \times 6x) - (2 \times 6x) = (2x^2 - 4) \times 3$, which simplifies to $6x^2 - 12x = 6x^2 - 12$. Next, subtract $6x^2$ from both sides: $6x^2 - 12x - 6x^2 = 6x^2 - 12x - 6x^2$, which simplifies to $-12x = -12$. Last, divide by -12: $\frac{-12x}{-12} = \frac{-12}{-12}$, which simplifies to $x = 1$.

10. **–2** Multiply both sides of the equation by $3x$: $(2 - 3x) \times 3x = \left(\frac{-9x^2 - 12}{3x}\right) \times 3x$, which simplifies to $3x(2 - 3x) = -9x^2 - 12$. Now distribute the $3x$ to everything in the parentheses: $(2 \times 3x) - (3x \times 3x) = -9x^2 - 12$, which simplifies to $6x - 9x^2 = -9x^2 - 12$. Next, add $9x^2$ to both sides: $6x - 9x^2 + 9x^2 = -9x^2 - 12 + 9x^2$, which simplifies to $6x = -12$. Last, divide by 6: $\frac{6x}{6} = \frac{-12}{6}$, which simplifies to $x = -2$

STATISTICS DRILL EXPLANATIONS

1. **B** The question asks for the probability of a certain outcome when letter tiles are selected without replacement. Since it is asking for the probability of "D" and "A" and "D" in that order, calculate the probability of each individual event and multiply. Probability is defined as $\frac{\text{number of desired outcomes}}{\text{number of total outcomes}}$. There are currently 8 "D" tiles available, so that is the *number of de-*

sired outcomes. There are 20 total tiles in the box, so that is the *number of total outcomes.* The probability that "D" will be selected on the first selection is $\frac{8}{20}$. The "D" tile remains out of the box, so there are now 19 tiles to choose from and 5 of those are "A" tiles. The probability that "A" will be selected on the second selection is $\frac{5}{19}$. Eliminate (D) and (E) because they do not include this fraction. There are now a total of 18 tiles remaining, of which 7 are "D" tiles. The probability that "D" will be selected on the third selection is $\frac{7}{18}$. Multiply the probabilities to get $\left(\frac{8}{20}\right)\left(\frac{5}{19}\right)\left(\frac{7}{18}\right)$. The correct answer is (B).

2. **J** The question asks for a probability, which is defined as $\frac{\text{number of desired outcomes}}{\text{number of total outcomes}}$. In this question, the numbers need to be determined from the stem-and-leaf plot provided. On the left side of the line on the stem-and-leaf plot is the stem, or leading value: in this instance, the tens digit of the number. On the right side of the line are the units digits of the numbers. If needed, rewrite the list of numbers as follows: 12, 13, 19, 21, 22, 27, 28, 29, 32, 35, 36, 43, 48. There are 13 total numbers to select from, so this is the *number of total outcomes.* Eliminate (F) and (G) since they do not have 13 in the denominator. Now count to see that 9 students spent *fewer than* 35 minutes on homework, which is the *number of desired outcomes.* The probability is $\frac{9}{13}$. The correct answer is (J).

3. **B** The question asks for the mean of the test scores reported in the table. The mean, or average, is defined by the equation $T = AN$, in which T is the *total*, A is the *average*, and N is the *number of things.* In this question, the number of things is 10. Read the table carefully to get the numbers to make the total, as some scores were earned by more than one tester. The total is $T = 18 + 23 + 23 + 23 + 29 + 29 + 29 + 29 + 31 + 35 = 269$. Put these numbers into the average equation to get $269 = (A)(10)$. Divide both sides of the equation by 10 to get $A = \frac{269}{10} = 26.9$. The correct answer is (B).

4. **J** The question asks for the expected value of an outcome. The expected value is found by taking the product of each value and the probability of its occurrence, then adding those results. There are 9 equal spaces on the wheel, which means that the probability of landing on any single space is 1 in 9. There is one space labeled \$9.00, three labeled \$3.00, and five labeled \$0.00. Therefore, the probability of landing on \$9.00 is $\frac{1}{9}$, the probability of landing on \$3.00 is $\frac{3}{9}$, and the probability of landing on \$0.00 is $\frac{5}{9}$. Therefore, the expected value is $\frac{1}{9}(\$9.00)+\frac{3}{9}(\$3.00)+\frac{5}{9}(\$0.00) = \$1.00 + \$1.00 + \$0.00 = \$2.00$. The correct answer is (J).

5. **E** The question asks about the mean, median, and mode of a set of data regarding the roll of a die. Since there is more than one calculation needed, break the problem into bite-sized pieces and start with the easiest calculation first. The mode is the number that appears most often in a list. According to the graph, 9 appears 5 times, and nothing else appears more than 5 times; 9 is the mode. The median is the number in the middle of a list of numbers that are in order. Write out the set of outcomes to find that the number in the middle, the median, is 7. The mode, 9, is greater than the median, 7, so eliminate (A), (C), and (D). Next, determine the mean, or average, using $T = AN$, in which T is the *total*, A is the *average*, and N is the *number of things*. The total is the sum of all the numbers in the set: $T = 1 + 1 + 3 + 3 + 5 + 5 + 5 + 7 + 7 + 7 + 7 + 9 + 9 + 9 + 9 + 9 + 11 + 11 + 11 = 129$. The number of things is 19. Therefore, the average formula becomes $129 = (A)(19)$. Divide both sides of the equation by 19 to get that $A \approx 6.79$. The mean is not equal to the median, so eliminate (B). The correct answer is (E).

6. **K** The question asks for the probability of one event AND another occurring together. This is defined as the probability of the first event times the probability of the second event. In this question, the first event, Event C, has a probability of 0.6, and the second event, Event A, has a probability of 0.3. Multiply these probabilities to get $(0.3)(0.6) = 0.18$. The correct answer is (K).

7. **B** This question asks for the difference in starting times for two individuals. Since there is a large amount of information in this word problem, use bite-sized pieces to solve for one piece of information at a time. Start with the easiest information first. Since Aubrie only travels at one speed, start with her. She travels 525 km at 105 km/hr. Use $D = RT$ *(distance = rate × time)* to find her total driving time. This becomes $525 = 105(T)$. Divide both sides of the equation by 105 to get $T = \frac{525}{105} = 5$ hours. She also takes a break for 45 minutes. To convert minutes into hours, divide the number of minutes by 60 to get $\frac{45}{60} = 0.75$ hours. Now add these numbers together to get the total amount of time it takes Aubrie to travel to Port Jervis: $5 + 0.75 = 5.75$ hours. Next, calculate the total time George travels. The question states that he travels for 4 hours at a speed of 120 km/hr. This means that he has traveled $D = (4)(120) = 480$ km in that time. After his break, he has 840 km – 480 km = 360 km left to travel. He travels those 360 km at a speed of 45 km/hr. Therefore, $360 = 45(T)$ for this part of George's trip. Divide both sides by 45 to get the amount of time he travels during the second part of the trip: $T = \frac{360}{45} = 8$ hours. George's break lasts 15 minutes, which is $\frac{15}{60} = 0.25$ hours. Therefore, the total amount of time George travels including the break is 4 hours + 0.25 hours + 8 hours = 12.25 hours. Finally take the difference of George's and Aubrie's travel times to get $12.25 - 5.75 = 6.5$ hours. The correct answer is (B).

8. **H** The question asks for the odds in favor are defined as of an event. The odds in favor are defined as $\frac{\text{probability of an event occuring}}{\text{probability of an event NOT occuring}}$. In this question, the probablity of Ranela speaking last is $\frac{2}{7}$. The probabilty of an event occurring and the probability of that event NOT occuring must add up to 1. Therefore, the probablity of her NOT speaking last is $1-\frac{2}{7}=\frac{7}{7}-\frac{2}{7}=\frac{7-2}{7}=\frac{5}{7}$. Therefore, the odds in favor of Ranela speaking last are $\frac{\frac{2}{7}}{\frac{5}{7}}=\frac{2}{7}\left(\frac{7}{5}\right)=\frac{2}{5}$. The correct answer is (H).

9. **C** The question asks for the mean, or average, of the scores of the first 4 games a team played. Use the data provided in the table to determine the scores in this data set. The minimum is given as 7, so that is the first number in the set. The mode is the number that appears on the list most often. The mode is given as 9, so there are at least two 9s in the data set. Finally, the range is the difference between the greatest number and the least number. The least number is known, and the range is given as 18, so add that to the minimum of 7 to get 25. Since there are only four numbers in the data set, the four scores are {7, 9, 9, 25}. Use the formula $T = AN$ to calculate the mean of the data set, in which T is the *total*, A is the *average*, and N is the *number of things*. The total is $T = 7 + 9 + 9 + 25 = 50$, and $N = 4$, the number of scores in the set. The formula becomes $50 = (A)(4)$, so divide both sides by 4 to get $A=\frac{50}{4}=12.5$. The correct answer is (C).

10. **F** The question asks for the expected average value of the discount amount in dollars to be given on tickets. The expected value is found by taking the product of each value and the probability of its occurrence, then adding those results. In this question, the discount percentage is given, so start by calculating the expected discount percentage. There are 7 total outcomes. Four of those outcomes result in a 10% discount, so the probability of a 10% discount is 4 in 7 or $\frac{4}{7}$. There are two possible 15% discounts and one possible 70% discount, so the probabilities of those outcomes are $\frac{2}{7}$ and $\frac{1}{7}$, respectively. To find the expected value, multiply each percent discount expressed as a decimal by its associated probability and add them to get $(0.10)\left(\frac{4}{7}\right)+(0.15)\left(\frac{2}{7}\right)+(0.70)\left(\frac{1}{7}\right)$ = $\frac{0.4}{7}+\frac{0.3}{7}+\frac{0.7}{7}$ = $\frac{0.4+0.3+0.7}{7}=\frac{1.4}{7}=0.20$. The expected value of the discount percentage is 0.20, or 20%. Since the question asks for the dollar amount of the discount, multiply the cost of the ticket, \$40, by 20% to determine the expected discount amount in dollars: (40)(0.20) = \$8.00. The correct answer is (F).

11. **E** The question asks for the percent of data points within 3 standard deviations of the mean in the graph of data with a normal distribution. The empirical rule states that 68% of data falls within one standard deviation of the mean, 95% of data falls within two standard deviations of the mean, and 99% of data falls within three standard deviations of the mean. The correct answer is (E).

12. **G** The question asks for the difference of the median and the mean of a given data set. Start by determining the easier of the two statistics, which is the median. The median is the average of the middle two numbers in a data set of an even number of ordered items. List out the numbers from the bar graph to make it easier to find this information: 5, 5, 6, 7, 8, 9, 11, 12, 14, 15, 15, 15, 16, 16. The middle numbers are 11 and 12, so the median of this list is $\frac{11+12}{2}=\frac{23}{2}=11.5$. The mean, or average, is calculated using $T = AN$, in which T is the *total*, A is the *average*, and N is the *number of things*. The total is $T = 5 + 5 + 6 + 7 + 8 + 9 + 11 + 12 + 14 + 15 + 15 + 15 + 16 + 16 = 154$, and $N = 14$. The formula becomes $154 = (A)(14)$. Divide both sides of the equation by 14 to get $A=\frac{154}{14}=11$. Finally, subtract the mean from the median to get $11.5 - 11 = 0.5$. The correct answer is (G).

VECTOR MATRIX DRILL EXPLANATIONS

The best approach to most matrix operations is going to be to input the data into a graphing calculator and allow it to do the hard work, and you should take advantage of this, as you are allowed a calculator on the ACT. That said, we believe you should understand how to solve these problems without electronic aid, so the following explanations will focus on how to solve by hand.

1. **B** Start by determining the dimensions of the product matrix, which are expressed as the number of rows by the number of columns. The dimensions of the first matrix are 2×2, and the dimensions of the second matrix are 2×1. The product matrix will have the same number of rows as the first matrix (2), and the same number of columns as the second matrix (1). Therefore, the product matrix must be 2×1. Eliminate (C), (D), and (E) because they are all 2×2 matrices. Next, find the dot product of the first row of the first matrix and the first column of the second matrix. The dot product is the sum of the products of the positions. In this case, multiply the first number in the first row of the first matrix (–6) by the first number in the first column of the second matrix (–1) and add that to the product of the second number in the first row of the first matrix (3) and the second number of the first column of the second matrix (3). This gives $(-6)(-1) + (3)(3)$, which simplifies to $6 + 9$. This equals 15, so the first row, first column of the product matrix must equal 15. Because this is only an option in (B), that is the correct answer.

2. **H** An undefined matrix product is the result of attempting to multiply two matrices with incompatible dimensions. In order to multiply matrices, the number of columns in the first matrix must equal the number of rows in the second matrix. Because the dimensions are given as rows by columns (A is 2 × 1, B and C are both 2 × 2, and D is 3 × 2), the trick is that the middle numbers of the matrices must be the same. For (F), matrix B is 2 × 2, and matrix A is 2 × 1, so multiplying these together is (2 × 2)(2 × 1). The middle numbers are the same, so this multiplication is possible. Eliminate (F) because the question asks for the product that's not possible. Choice (G) is (2 × 2)(2 × 2). The middle numbers are both 2, so this is also possible; eliminate (G). Choice (H) is (2 × 2)(3 × 2). The middle numbers do not match, so this product is undefined. The correct answer is (H).

3. **E** The product matrix should multiply the number of members by the prices charged for members and the number of nonmembers by the prices charged to nonmembers, giving a total for each day. Because there should be a total for each day, there should be only two numbers in the resulting product matrix. Choices (A) and (B) multiply a 2 × 2 by a 2 × 2. The product matrix will have the same number of rows as the first matrix (2), and the same number of columns as the second matrix (2), resulting in a 2 × 2 matrix. These matrices will have four numbers, not two, so eliminate (A) and (B). For (C), the row $\begin{bmatrix} 15 & 35 \end{bmatrix}$ would be multiplied by the first column $\begin{bmatrix} 25 \\ 35 \end{bmatrix}$. This multiplies the number of nonmembers (15) by the price that the members paid (25) and the number of members (35) by the price the nonmembers paid (35). This is incorrect, so eliminate (C). Choice (D) multiplies the row $\begin{bmatrix} 35 & 15 \end{bmatrix}$ by the column $\begin{bmatrix} 25 \\ 15 \end{bmatrix}$. The number of members (35) is multiplied by a price members paid one of the days (25), but the number of nonmembers (15) is multiplied by the other price members paid (15). This is incorrect; eliminate (D). The answer is (E).

4. **K** Start by determining the size of the product matrix. The first matrix has dimensions 1 × 3, and the second matrix has dimensions 3 × 1. The product matrix will have the same number of rows as the first matrix and the same number of columns as the second matrix. In other words, the product matrix will have the outside values of the two dimensions. Therefore, the product matrix will have dimensions 1 × 1; eliminate (F), (G), and (H). To multiply the matrices, find the dot product. Multiply each element in the row of the first matrix by its corresponding element in the column of the second matrix; then add the products. Therefore, the dot product is $(-1 \times x) + (0 \times y) + (1 \times z)$, which is $-x + 0 + z$, or $z - x$. The correct answer is (K).

5. **D** Unit vector notation is another way of describing the components of a vector. In two dimensions, **i** is the unit vector for the vector with components (1,0), and **j** is the unit vector for the vector with components (0,1). When measuring the components of a vector in the (x,y) coordinate plane, measure the displacement from the beginning of the vector to the end. Vector $\overrightarrow{WX}$ has components going 6 units directly to the right from point W to point X, so its components are (6,0). Vector $\overrightarrow{YZ}$ goes 7 units right and 12 units up, so its components are (7,12). Therefore, vector $\overrightarrow{WX} + \overrightarrow{YZ}$ will have components (6 + 7,0 + 12), or (13,12). In unit vector notation, the x-component becomes the coefficient on **i**, and the y-component becomes the coefficient on **j**. Therefore, the unit vector notation of $\overrightarrow{WX} + \overrightarrow{YZ}$ is 13**i** + 12**j**. The correct answer is (D).

6. **J** Start by determining the dimensions of the product matrix. The first matrix is 3 × 1 and the second matrix is 1 × 3. The product matrix will have the same number of rows as the first matrix and columns as the second matrix. In other words, the outside numbers of the dimensions of the two matrices being multiplied will be the dimensions of the product matrix. Therefore, the product matrix is 3 × 3. Eliminate (F), (G), and (H), as they are not the correct dimensions. Both of the remaining answers have 0 in the first row, first column position, so do not solve for that position. Instead, determine the first row, second column position. This will be the dot product of the first row of the first matrix by the second column of the second matrix: $0 \times 2x = 0$. Therefore, the first row, second column of the product matrix should be 0. The correct answer is (J).

7. **A** Work in bite-sized pieces. Both the x-components and the y-components of the three vectors in the equation must sum to 0 for the sum of the three vectors to be 0. Start by determining the x-component of **c**. The x-component of **a** is –3, and the x-component of **b** is 4. If the x-component of **c** is x, then $-2(-3) + 3(4) + x = 0$. Solve for x by first multiplying: $6 + 12 + x = 0$. Next, combine like terms: $18 + x = 0$. Subtract 18 from both sides to find that $x = -18$. Therefore, the x-component of **c** must be –18, and only one answer has this. The correct answer is (A).

8. **J** In unit vector notation, **i** represents the component (1,0), or a displacement of 1 unit to the right, and **j** represents the component (0,1), or a displacement of 1 unit up. Therefore, a vector that is represented in unit vector notation as 4**i** + 3**j** has components (4,3) and goes 4 units to the right and 3 units up. Eliminate (G) because it goes only right and (H) because it goes only up. Choice (K) moves in a negative direction in both the x and y directions, so it can be eliminated as well. Choice (F) starts at (–1,–1) and goes to (2,3). This is a move 3 to the right and 4 up, but vector **v** goes 4 right and 3 up. Eliminate (F). The correct answer is (J).

9. **D** In order for a matrix product to be defined, the number of columns in the first matrix must match the number of rows in the second matrix. In (A), the first matrix has two columns, and the second matrix has one row. This does not match; eliminate (A). In (B), both matrices have one row and two columns, so the number of columns in the first matrix is not the same as the number of rows in the second matrix; eliminate (B). In (C), both matrices have two rows and one column, so the number of columns in the first matrix is not the same as the number of rows in the second matrix. In (D), the first matrix has one column, and the second matrix has one row. The number of columns in the first matrix matches the number of rows in the second matrix, so this product will be defined. The correct answer is (D).

10. **F** Determine which matrix products result in a matrix of the correct dimensions. The matrix in the question has two rows and one column. A matrix product will have the same number of rows as the first matrix and the same number of columns as the second matrix. Choice (F) has two rows in the first matrix and one column in the second matrix; this will result in the correct dimension in the product matrix, so keep it and (K), which has the same dimensions. Choice (G) has one row in the first matrix and two columns in the second matrix. This will result in a 1×2 product matrix, not a 2×1 matrix. Eliminate (G), and also (J), which has matrices with the same dimensions. Choice (H) has one row in the first matrix and two columns in the second matrix, also resulting in a 1×2 matrix; eliminate it. Now find the dot product of one of the remaining choices: in (F), the dot product of the first row of the first matrix by the first column of the second matrix is $(4 \times 3) + (-6 \times 2)$. Multiplying results in $12 + (-12)$, which equals 0. The dot product of the second row of the first matrix by the first column of the second matrix is $(-2 \times 3) + (3 \times 2)$. Multiplying results in $-6 + 6$, which equals 0. Therefore, the correct answer is (F).

11. **D** To find the components of **z**, subtract the corresponding components of **x** from **y**. Start with the x-components. The x-component of **y** is 7, and the x-component of **x** is 5, so the x-component of **z** is $7 - 5 = 2$. Eliminate (A), (B), and (E) because they don't have the correct x-component. Next, find the y-component the same way. Vector **y** has a y-component of 10, and **x** has a y-component of -12, so **z** has a y-component of $10 - (-12) = 22$. The correct answer is (D).

GRAPH-READING DRILLS SET 1 EXPLANATIONS

1. **Difference substances**

Use the key above Figure 1 to see what the lines represent. According to the key, they are sucrose, NaCl, $MgCl_2$, and $FeCl_3$, which are different substances.

2. **Direct**

A direct relationship is one in which both variables follow the same trend—as one increases, the other also increases, or vice versa. As concentration increases, osmotic pressure also increases, since the lines are all headed upward to the right. Thus, this is a direct relationship.

3. **Substances**

The key in Figure 1 shows that the figure has the same substances that appear in the left column of Table 1.

4. **As van 't Hoff factor increases, osmotic pressure increases**

Compare the van 't Hoff factors of the substances. Sucrose has the lowest van 't Hoff factor, and the line for sucrose is the lowest line on Figure 1 at a concentration of 1 *M*. NaCl has the next lowest van 't Hoff factor, and it is the next lowest line. The other two lines continue in the same fashion, so a substance with a higher van 't Hoff factor has a higher osmotic pressure at a given concentration.

5. **A cross-section of a planet**

While this information would be provided in the text, common sense or outside knowledge can also reveal what this figure shows. The figure displays areas that can be recognized as components of a planet, such as inner core, outer core, crust, and mantle.

6. **Depth and waves**

Figure 2 shows depth in kilometers on the vertical axis, and this is also provided in the second column of Table 2. The seismic waves shown in the first column of Table 2 are also labeled on Figure 2. Crust velocity, the third column of Table 2, does not appear in the figure, nor do any of the other features from the figure appear in the table.

7. **S and P**

Find the outer mantle, which is the outermost section on Figure 2. L-waves appear to be outside the outer mantle, so they would not be included as an answer. The curve with the short dashes labeled as S-wave does pass through the outer mantle. The same is true for the P-wave curve made of long dashes.

8. **None** None of the lines for the three waves pass through the inner core, which is the innermost section of the figure, so the answer is none.

9. **Different heater and cooler settings**

Check the key that appears above each figure. For Figure 3, the symbols refer to heater settings, and for Figure 4, the symbols refer to cooler settings, all of which are in degrees.

10. **Time** Both figures show time in minutes on the horizontal axis, though the amounts of time shown are quite different. While both show some sort of temperature, one is air temperature and the other is saltwater temperature, so those are not the same thing. The symbols represent degrees in both cases, but one is heater settings and the other is cooler settings.

11. **No** This question asks about the trends shown in the figures. In Figure 3, all three lines increase and then are approximately constant, while in Figure 4, all three lines decrease and then are approximately constant. Thus, the relationships are not the same.

12. **Yes** Note the connections between the figures. At any given time on Figure 3, such as 20 minutes, the shape for the lowest heater setting, 25°, is closer to the bottom of the graph where the lower air temperatures are, and the shape for the highest heater setting, 50°, is near the top of the graph where the higher air temperatures are. This trend also holds true for Figure 4, which shows the shapes for the lowest cooler setting near the bottom of the graph and the highest cooler setting near the top of the graph. Therefore, the effect of the heater/cooler settings is the same on both figures.

GRAPH-READING DRILLS SET 2 EXPLANATIONS

1. **Relative reflectance and wavelength**

   The figures have the same variables on their horizontal axes, wavelength, and the same variable on their vertical axes, relative reflectance.

2. **Diatoms**

   The key for Figure 1 shows four different things. In Figure 2, only one is shown. Compare the line in Figure 2 to the four lines in Figure 1. The closest one is Diatoms because it also peaks between 550 and 600 nm and overall follows a similar trend.

3. **Wavelength**

   Table 1 shows color and wavelength. The figures don't show color, but they do show wavelength on the horizontal axes.

4. **Green algae**

   Look at the figures and find 400 nm on the bottom axis. In Figure 1, the highest one is the dashed line, which represents green algae, at about 0.038 relative reflectance. In Figure 2, the line is close to a relative reflectance of 0.035 at a wavelength of 400 nm, so the value for green algae is higher.

5. **Green**

   Find blue-green algae in Figure 1, represented by the lighter solid line. The question asks for the highest reflectance. The blue-green algae line is highest at a wavelength of 550 nm. Use Table 1 to determine the color, since that is the only chart that mentions color. According to Table 1, a wavelength of 550 nm corresponds with the color green.

6. **Pure water**

   Find blue in Table 1. Its wavelength is 430–500 nm. Then find those numbers on Figures 1 and 2. The question asks about peaks of reflectance. The only line that has a real peak in this range is the one for pure water, the dashed and dotted line, which peaks at a wavelength of about 460 nm.

7. **Initial pressure, final pressure, and volume change**

   The first column in the charts differs, but the other three are the same for all three tables.

8. **Decrease in volume**

   Since the column heading is *volume change,* this suggests that a negative number represents a negative change, or a decrease in volume.

9. **No**

The numbers for initial pressure do not show any trend as they increase at times, decrease at times, and stay constant at times, not following any pattern. The same is true for final pressure.

10. **Greater decrease in volume**

When the pressure increased by only 1 atm (the difference between initial and final pressure), the volume change was smaller—such as –5.00 when the pressure went from 1 atm to 2 atm for helium on Table 3. When the pressure increased more, such as going from 1 atm to 5 atm for helium, the volume change was greater at –8.00. Since the numbers are negative, this represents a greater decrease in the volume.

11. **Different relationship between initial and final pressure**

Notice that the relationship between initial and final pressure for oxygen was always the same: 1 to 2 is double the pressure, 2 to 4 is double the pressure, and 3 to 6 is double the pressure. This always resulted in a volume change of –5.00. For argon, when it doubled from 2 to 4, the result was the same, but when it didn't double, the volume change was different. The same is true for carbon dioxide. When it doubled from 3 to 6, the volume change was –5.00 as well, but for other relationships between initial and final pressure, the results were different.

12. **Less change in volume**

Both tables show a change in pressure from 1 to 2 atm, with the results of –5.00 in Table 3 and –4.98 in Table 4. This means the volume decreased a little bit less in Table 4, where the temperature is lower. The other numbers aren't exactly the same, but 2 to 5 in Table 3 is –6.00, and 2 to 4 in Table 4 is –4.97, so this seems to be consistent with the idea that the change in volume is a little bit less.

English Practice Section 1

ENGLISH TEST

45 Minutes—75 Questions

DIRECTIONS: In the five passages that follow, certain words and phrases are underlined and numbered. In the right-hand column, you will find alternatives for each underlined part. In most cases, you are to choose the one that best expresses the idea, makes the statement appropriate for standard written English, or is worded most consistently with the style and tone of the passage as a whole. If you think the original version is best, choose "NO CHANGE." In some cases, you will find in the right-hand column a question about the underlined part. You are to choose the best answer to the question.

You will also find questions about a section of the passage or the passage as a whole. These questions do not refer to an underlined portion of the passage but rather are identified by a number or numbers in a box.

For each question, choose the alternative you consider best and blacken the corresponding oval on your answer document. Read each passage through once before you begin to answer the questions that accompany it. For many of the questions, you must read several sentences beyond the question to determine the answer. Be sure that you have read far enough ahead each time you choose an alternative.

Passage I

Hats: On My Head, On My Mind

I do not remember how I came to like wearing a hat. Friends view it as an odd habit of mine, since so few people wear hats today. I think my fondness for hats comes down to the desire to proclaim[1] what type of person I am. Telling the world what kind of person resides directly below its brim is one of the principal jobs of any hat worth the name.

Even if we are not supposed to judge a book by its cover, we very often judge a person by his or her hat. [2] In a narrow sense, a top hat indicates to all that you are a magician, just as a mortarboard and tassel tells the world you just graduated. More generally,[3] a cowboy hat may say you are the strong, silent type, while a beret suggests, you are artistic and creative.[4] We even use hats as a kind of code for moral character, letting "white hats" and "black hats" serve as metaphors for "good

1. Which of the following alternatives to the underlined word would NOT be acceptable?
   A. announce
   B. declare
   C. compare
   D. advertise

2. The writer is considering deleting the preceding sentence from the essay. Should the sentence be kept or deleted?
   F. Kept, because it establishes the theme of this paragraph, the ways in which hats symbolize things about people and their actions.
   G. Kept, because it establishes the narrator's love of hats.
   H. Deleted, because the information it contains is contradicted in the previous sentence.
   J. Deleted, because the narrative is more interesting if readers are left to draw their own conclusions about the ways in which they personally interpret hats.

3. A. NO CHANGE
   B. (Do NOT begin new paragraph) Thus, as a general rule
   C. (Begin new paragraph) Generally,
   D. (Begin new paragraph) For example,

4. F. NO CHANGE
   G. suggests you are artistic, and creative.
   H. suggests, you are artistic, and creative.
   J. suggests you are artistic and creative.

guys" and "bad guys." Hats show way up in our figures of speech as well. Home is where you hang your hat, while declaring your desire to win a position is throwing your hat into the ring. How could anyone not want to wear a hat, especially because it makes your hair messy?

5. A. NO CHANGE
B. up
C. features
D. DELETE the underlined portion.

6. Given that all the choices are true, which one most strongly reinforces the author's attitude toward hats as it has been conveyed up to this point in the essay?
F. NO CHANGE
G. when it may cost a substantial amount?
H. although you may forget one in a restaurant?
J. when it can do so much?

A hat can do even more in everyday life. Deserving congratulations, I say that my hat is off to them—and then I can literally do exactly that. When someone has exciting news for me, he can tell me to hold on to my hat, if the news has to be kept secret, I can promise to keep it under my hat. He could even tell me to remain calm and not be a mad hatter. [9]

7. A. NO CHANGE
B. As they are deserving
C. When people deserve
D. To deserve

8. F. NO CHANGE
G. my hat, although the event
H. my hat. If the news
J. my hat, especially when it

9. At this point, the writer is considering adding the following true statement:

> "Mad hatter" properly refers to the many nineteenth-century hat makers who suffered extensive neurological damage after they were exposed to the toxic mercury fumes then utilized in hat construction.

Should the writer make this addition here?
A. Yes, because it helps support the idea that the author has affection for hats.
B. Yes, because it provides a striking parallel between the author's interest in hats and Lewis Carroll's.
C. No, because many individuals in the nineteenth century besides hat-makers were exposed to poisonous fumes.
D. No, because its historical explanation of the scientific origins of the image of mad hatters does not fit with the essay to this point.

Maybe the real reason I like wearing a hat, however, has to do with getting away from everyday life. What I find so interesting is the possibility of using a hat, to make myself more like someone very different from my everyday self. A fedora helps me to think of me as more of a street-smart tough-guy private eye. Another hat, appropriately battered, helps me feel

10. F. NO CHANGE
G. possibility of using a hat
H. possibility, of using a hat
J. possibility, of using a hat,

11. A. NO CHANGE
B. myself
C. my own self
D. I

like a daring adventurer his [12] search for fabulous treasures will succeed against all odds.

On my last birthday, my family that [13] gave me a Napoleon hat. I wonder, what are they trying to tell me? [14]

12. F. NO CHANGE
G. whose
H. pursuing a
J. making a

13. A. NO CHANGE
B. are those who
C. were among who
D. DELETE the underlined portion.

14. The writer is considering concluding the essay with the following statement:

Ultimately, a hat on your head guarantees a song in your heart.

Should the writer end the essay with this statement?

F. Yes, because it restates the central idea of the essay in a memorable way.
G. Yes, because hats have many uses.
H. No, because the preceding sentence expressed the same idea using different words.
J. No, because it does not have a meaningful connection to the central theme of this essay.

Question 15 asks about the preceding passage as a whole.

15. Suppose one of the writer's goals had been to indicate that items of clothing can be used to communicate things, literally and figuratively, about their wearers. Would this essay have fulfilled that goal?

A. Yes, because the essay reveals that the narrator uses hats to express his feelings and present himself as different kinds of people.
B. Yes, because the essay reveals that hats have been symbols of royalty and power for centuries.
C. No, because the essay indicates that the narrator prefers to wear hats from popular culture instead of history.
D. No, because the essay establishes that the narrator's attitude toward hats may not be shared by his family and friends.

Passage II

A Diamond in the Rough

Beginning around 1963, when cassette recorders with built-in microphones first became available for purchase, amateur songwriters were able to record songs that had been formerly [16] undocumented. One guitarist and saxophonist, Bruce Diamond, recorded nearly a hundred songs from his home in Lexington, Kentucky. Recently, hundreds of these rough recordings have been re-mastered. They have captured the attention of musicologists for a number of reasons.

16. F. NO CHANGE
    G. have been formerly
    H. are now being
    J. are formerly

First, it is seemingly apparent that Diamond's songs were [17] influenced by many different popular artists of the day. One song sounds very similar to a complicated jazz song by Charlie Parker. However, another song is the opposite of the song sounds [18] like the straightforward rock of Buddy Holly. The lyrics are very similar as well, and one is led to wonder what inspired them. [19] One music critic observed that Diamond found it completely effortless [20] to switch back and forth between very different musical genres.

17. Which of the following choices provides the most stylistically effective and concise wording here?
    A. NO CHANGE
    B. there is the impression given by Diamond's songs that he was
    C. Diamond's songs suggest that he was
    D. it is the impression Diamond's songs give that he was

18. F. NO CHANGE
    G. opposite of the song is sounding
    H. opposite; the song sounds
    J. opposite the song sounds

19. Given that all the choices are true, which of the following would best provide further detail about the lyrical subject matter?
    A. NO CHANGE
    B. dealing mostly with dating and automobiles.
    C. and he mostly uses rhymed couplets and alliteration.
    D. which are easy to understand because of Diamond's enunciation.

20. F. NO CHANGE
    G. without any strain or effort
    H. relatively simple and free of struggle
    J. totally free of complication

Diamond's recordings are noteworthy for their unique artistic voice—an interesting combination of jazz, bluegrass, and gospel styles. In one piece, Diamond starts with a long soulful intro leading into an upbeat verse. The verse's [21] tempo and tone provide an interesting contrast to the mournful opening. The chorus combines elements of both in an unexpected but balanced way. Diamond seems to express in

21. A. NO CHANGE
    B. verse,
    C. verses'
    D. verses

this song that he has overcome some emotional wounds but that <u>one remains conflicted.</u> [22] [23]

22. F. NO CHANGE
G. he remains conflicted.
H. they were conflicted.
J. he is conflicting.

23. At this point, the writer is thinking of adding the following sentence:

> We have all experienced sad events and know very well what it is like to feel conflicted.

Should the writer make this addition here?

A. Yes, because it shows the writer's compassionate feelings toward Diamond's difficult situation.
B. Yes, because it adds extra emphasis to the subject matter of one of Diamond's most well-known songs.
C. No, because it strays from the paragraph's main focus on Diamond's unique songwriting voice.
D. No, because it encourages readers to think about sad events in their own lives.

<u>While</u> [24] sources of music from major music towns like New Orleans, Detroit, and Nashville are abundant, little is known about Lexington's music scene because the town lacked a real recording studio. Therefore, <u>since they were recorded on two-inch tape,</u> [25] Diamond's songs <u>in a city like Lexington</u> [26] offer music historians a rare taste of the musical culture in the 1960s.

24. Which of the following choices would NOT be an acceptable alternative to the underlined portion?
F. Despite the fact that
G. Although
H. Since
J. Whereas

25. A. NO CHANGE
B. because a built-in microphone recorded them,
C. being that he played the songs into the recorder,
D. DELETE the underlined portion.

26. The best place for the underlined portion would be:
F. where it is now.
G. after the word *historians*.
H. after the word *taste*.
J. after the word *culture*.

No one knows how much Diamond was <u>effected by</u> [27] other musicians in Lexington, but he did perform regularly at a local blues bar and less frequently <u>at a jazz dance hall.</u> [28]

27. A. NO CHANGE
B. affected by
C. affected with
D. effected with

28. F. NO CHANGE
G. at a dance hall where jazz was played.
H. as a musician at a jazz dance hall.
J. playing jazz music at a dance hall.

One thing, though, is for sure: he records [29] an interesting portfolio of songs, and he may soon be a famous saxophonist. [30]

29. A. NO CHANGE
    B. recorded
    C. is recording
    D. has recorded

30. Given that all the choices are true, which of the following would provide the best conclusion to this essay in relation to one of its main points?
    F. NO CHANGE
    G. and now Diamond's work provides scholars with an example of Lexington's music.
    H. and he probably never had to buy another cassette recorder.
    J. and he may have performed in other cities besides Lexington.

Passage III

Going Underground

[1] When I left my home in rural Missouri to attend college in New York City, I didn't consider myself a veteran subway rider. [31] [2] Luckily, I was able to overcome this fear by having my first trip by subway guided by a neighbor, named [32] Sasha. [3] He had grown up in Manhattan, so he was familiar with the dense, intricacy [33] subway routes. [4] During his childhood, he had taken [34] the subway almost every day as a child with his family, and so I was encouraged to set off with him to learn the ins and outs of the New York subways. [5] Because of my family's warnings, [35] I was afraid to

31. A. NO CHANGE
    B. a person who knew the ins and outs of public underground trains.
    C. a master of all the skills necessary to travel by public transport.
    D. a veteran rider.

32. F. NO CHANGE
    G. neighbor; named
    H. neighbor named
    J. neighbor named,

33. A. NO CHANGE
    B. dense, intricate
    C. intricately, dense
    D. dense intricacy

34. F. NO CHANGE
    G. He had been starting to take
    H. His childhood was spent taking
    J. He had taken

35. A. NO CHANGE
    B. my familys' warnings,
    C. my families' warnings
    D. my families warnings,

take the subway at first. [36]

Sasha showed me to the stop nearest our building and led me down the steps from the busy street, steering me skillfully through the fast-moving crowd. I couldn't decide whether to buy my token from the imposing-looking woman on the left or from the imposing-looking woman on the right, but Sasha confidently tugged me right up to <u>them.</u> [37] I managed to squeak out, "Canal Street, please," and the woman silently scooped up my change and slipped a token through the slot in the window.

I couldn't tell to which platform to <u>descend, if</u> [38] I had always used landmarks to find my way around my hometown. After a little <u>searching, though,</u> [39] I saw the sign that read "Canal St." suspended above the escalator, so Sasha and I climbed aboard and rode down to our platform.

<u>I felt very conspicuous standing on the platform, waiting for our train to arrive.</u> [40] Sasha distracted me by pointing out a performer across the tracks on the other platform. At first, I was <u>confused like a whirlwind in my mind</u> [41] about what the man was doing. Then I saw that he was juggling all kinds of objects: milk crates, thick books, and even bowling balls. I wondered if he <u>would of been</u> [42] there when we returned.

When we were seated on the train, Sasha looked at me with

36. For the sake of the logic and coherence of this paragraph, Sentence 5 should be placed:

F. where it is now.
G. after Sentence 1.
H. before Sentence 3.
J. before Sentence 4.

37. **A.** NO CHANGE
B. the one on the left.
C. her.
D. the women.

38. **F.** NO CHANGE
G. descend, which
H. descend;
J. descend, even though,

39. **A.** NO CHANGE
B. searching though:
C. searching, though
D. searching, though:

40. Given that all of the choices are true, which one most effectively introduces the action in this paragraph while suggesting the narrator's discomfort in her new surroundings?

F. NO CHANGE
G. Sasha's stylish boots clicked on the floor as he walked ahead of me.
H. Although it wasn't rush hour yet, quite a few people stood waiting on the platform.
J. Sasha explained that the first subway line in New York City opened in 1904.

41. **A.** NO CHANGE
B. confused with uncertainty and curiosity
C. confused by the initial lack of understanding
D. confused

42. **F.** NO CHANGE
G. would be
H. should be
J. could of been

a pleased expression, I suppose, [43] he was proud of how well he had served as a guide. "You look like you belong here in the big city," he said, nudging me playfully in the side, which I [44] shrugged and elbowed him back. I gazed at my reflection in the window and wondered if I had already changed.

We arrived at the Canal Street station, and we rode up the escalator toward the street, taking care to stand well to one side to let more impatient passengers by. I might just as well have been exploring an undiscovered continent and was emerging, with treasures and new wonders, from fantastic caverns. [45] I'll always remember my first subway ride, when "going underground" took on an entirely new meaning.

43. A. NO CHANGE
    B. expression I suppose
    C. expression. I suppose
    D. expression, however, I suppose

44. F. NO CHANGE
    G. side, which he
    H. side. I
    J. side, where I

45. A. NO CHANGE
    B. I might just as well have been exploring fantastic caverns filled with the treasures and new wonders of an undiscovered continent.
    C. I might, filled with treasures and new wonders emerging from fantastic caverns, just as well have been exploring an undiscovered continent.
    D. Emerging from fantastic caverns, I might just as well, filled with treasures and new wonders, have been exploring a new continent.

Passage IV

Black Holes—Astronomy's Great Mystery

Black holes are likely and possibly [46] the most fascinating topic facing contemporary astronomy. The concept of a black hole—a region of space with such intense gravitational pull that nothing can escape—is truly the stuff of science fiction. That is what Albert Einstein believed, at least. His general theory of relativity predicted their existence, but he thought [47] of his prediction as an error to be corrected, not a predictor of one of the strangest astronomical phenomena yet discovered.

Because [48] Einstein didn't live to see it, the universe proved the accuracy of his calculations in 1970, when Cygnus X-1 was discovered about 7,000 light-years from Earth. It is about 8.7 times as massive as our sun yet has a small [49] diameter of only about 50 km. When you consider that the diameter of the sun could accommodate over 100 Earths, it becomes clear that

46. F. NO CHANGE
    G. very probably to be
    H. possibly
    J. a possible likeness of being

47. A. NO CHANGE
    B. thinks
    C. have thought
    D. has thought

48. F. NO CHANGE
    G. Although
    H. Since
    J. DELETE the underlined portion.

49. A. NO CHANGE
    B. less
    C. fewer
    D. too little

fitting a mass almost nine times greater than that into a space of about 31 miles is truly remarkable. [50]

How do these singularities come into existence? [51] There are [52] several theories to explain the process. The most popular hypothesis suggests that black holes are fairly common and involving [53] the disintegration of a massive star near [54] the end of its lifecycle. At that stage, the star has nearly exhausted its hydrogen supply, consequently [55] losing its ability to burn at a sufficiently high temperature to prevent its collapse. The stars exterior, [56] layers are blown away in a supernova, while the interior layers collapse into a highly dense core, which ultimately becomes the black hole.

Other theorists suggesting [57] that black holes are the result of a galactic game of bumper cars. The universe is teeming with neutron stars. These are highly compact, very hot stars formed

50. If the writer were to delete the preceding sentence, the paragraph would primarily lose:

F. a description that explains the purpose of studying black holes.
G. information that helps the reader grasp the size of black holes by presenting it in understandable terms.
H. a reference that explains how the black hole is compressed into such a small size.
J. an unnecessary detail, because this information is repeated later in the passage.

51. Which choice provides the most effective transition from the previous paragraph to the new paragraph?

A. NO CHANGE
B. Why should we study black holes at all?
C. Is the sun going to collapse and become a black hole?
D. What are the effects of such massive gravitational pull?

52. F. NO CHANGE
G. Their are
H. Their is
J. They're are

53. A. NO CHANGE
B. is involving
C. will involve
D. involve

54. Which of the following alternatives to the underlined portion would NOT be acceptable?

F. close to
G. close
H. toward
J. around

55. A. NO CHANGE
B. supply; consequently
C. supply, and consequently
D. supply. Consequently

56. F. NO CHANGE
G. stars exterior
H. star's exterior
J. star's exterior,

57. A. NO CHANGE
B. has been suggesting
C. will suggest
D. suggest

during the supernova of smaller stars that are not sufficiently massive to create black holes. Likewise, [58] on occasion these stars will actually collide with each other and together become massive enough to form a black hole.

58. F. NO CHANGE
G. Similarly,
H. However,
J. In addition,

Perhaps the most bizarre observation made about these phenomena involves the existence of "micro" or "mini" black holes. These peculiar items are very small, astronomically speaking. They have a mass far less than that of our Sun, and, frankly, the scientific community cannot explain and articulate fully [59] how stars with so little mass could have formed black holes at all. That is a question for future generations of scientists to explore.

59. A. NO CHANGE
B. cannot explain or describe in any detail
C. cannot explain
D. not only cannot explain but also can't describe

Question 60 asks about the preceding passage as a whole.

60. Suppose the writer's goal had been to write a brief essay about how Einstein's skepticism stopped scientific inquiry into the existence of black holes. Would this essay successfully fulfill that goal?

F. Yes, because black holes were not discovered until after Einstein's death.
G. Yes, because no other scientists were mentioned by name as doing research into the subject.
H. No, because Einstein later decided that black holes did exist and encouraged the scientific community to search for them.
J. No, because no discussion is made of how Einstein's doubt affected the inquiries of other scientists.

Passage V

An Argument for E-Waste Recycling

Drive through any suburb in the United States today, and it's hard to miss the bins, that have become companions [61] to America's trashcans. Recycling has become [62] commonplace, as people recognize the need to care for the environment.

61. A. NO CHANGE
B. bins that have become companions,
C. bins, which have become companions,
D. bins that have become companions

62. F. NO CHANGE
G. became
H. becoming
J. becomes

Yet most people's recycling consciousness is extending only as far as paper, bottles, and cans. People seldom find themselves confronted with the growing phenomenon of e-waste.

E-waste proliferates as the techno-fashionable constantly upgrade to the most cutting-edge devices, which the majority of them end up in landfills. Activists who track such waste estimate that users discarded nearly 2 million tons of TVs, VCRs, computers, cell phones, and other electronics in 2005. Unless we can find a safe alternative, this e-waste may leak into the ground and poison the water with dangerous toxins. [67] Burning the waste also dangerous contaminates the air.

Consequently, e-waste often contains reusable silver, gold, and other electrical conductors. Recycling these materials

63. A. NO CHANGE
B. extended
C. had extended
D. extends

64. Which choice would most effectively begin this sentence so that it emphasizes a lack of awareness of this problem?
F. NO CHANGE
G. Many in our communities simply don't realize the dangers of
H. A majority of local governments are assiduously studying
J. Little attention is paid by the people in our neighborhoods to

65. A. NO CHANGE
B. devices that
C. devices, and
D. devices after

66. F NO CHANGE
G. Activists who track such waste,
H. Activists which track such waste
J. Activists, who track such waste,

67. At this point, the writer is considering adding the following phrase to the end of the preceding sentence:

such as lead, mercury, and arsenic

Should the writer add the phrase here?

A. Yes, because it adds specific details clarifying which toxins are leaking.
B. Yes, because it supports the idea that landfills have too much waste.
C. No, because it doesn't specify how dangerous these toxins are.
D. No, because it would be redundant in a paragraph that has already mentioned which toxins e-waste contains.

68. F. NO CHANGE
G. more dangerous
H. most dangerous
J. dangerously

69. A. NO CHANGE
B. Particularly,
C. Moreover,
D. However,

reduces environmental impact by reducing both landfill waste and the need to mine such metals, which can destroy ecosystems.

A growing number of states have adopted laws to prohibit dumping e-waste. Still, less than a quarter of this refuse will reach legitimate recycling programs. [72] Some companies advertising safe disposal in fact merely ship the waste to third-world countries, where it still ends up in landfills. [73]

Nevertheless, the small but growing number of cities and corporations that do handle e-waste responsibly represent progress and a real step forward toward making the world a cleaner, better place for us all. [75]

70. **F.** NO CHANGE
G. impact;
H. impact so,
J. impact of

71. **A.** NO CHANGE
B. Adoptions are growing in state
C. States have growingly adopted
D. Growing states have adopted numbers

72. The writer is considering deleting the preceding sentence from this paragraph. Should the sentence be kept or deleted?

F. Kept, because it provides a logical transition between the first and last sentences of the paragraph.
G. Kept, because it provides meaningful statistics.
H. Deleted, because it adds no new information to the paragraph.
J. Deleted, because it would be redundant, given that the next sentence explains that some companies don't recycle.

73. At this point, the author is considering adding the following sentence:

> These organizations hamper progress by unsafely disposing of waste in an out-of-sight, out-of-mind location.

Would this be a relevant addition to make here?

A. Yes, because it completes the idea expressed in the preceding sentence.
B. Yes, because it paints such organizations in a negative light.
C. No, because it contradicts the following sentence.
D. No, because it introduces a tangential point.

74. **F.** NO CHANGE
G. a real step forward in the progress moving
H. progress
J. real forward-stepping progress

75. At this point, the writer is considering adding the following sentence:

> Today, pollution is one of the most dangerous forces threatening our environment, and the government must work to regulate its effects.

Should the writer add this sentence here?

A. Yes, because it adds important details that suggest recycling is not the only concern of environmentalists.
B. Yes, because it provides additional information discussing the impact of recycling programs in urban areas.
C. No, because it digresses from the article's main point about e-waste and related recycling issues.
D. No, because government regulation is a complicated and controversial topic addressed elsewhere in the passage.

English Practice Section 1 Answers and Explanations

ENGLISH PRACTICE SECTION 1 ANSWERS

1. C
2. F
3. A
4. J
5. B
6. J
7. C
8. H
9. D
10. G
11. B
12. G
13. D
14. J
15. A
16. F
17. C
18. H
19. B
20. F
21. A
22. G
23. C
24. H
25. D
26. J
27. B
28. F
29. B
30. G
31. A
32. H
33. B
34. J
35. A
36. G
37. B
38. H
39. A
40. F
41. D
42. G
43. C
44. H
45. B
46. H
47. A
48. G
49. A
50. G
51. A
52. F
53. D
54. G
55. A
56. H
57. D
58. H
59. C
60. J
61. D
62. F
63. D
64. G
65. C
66. F
67. A
68. J
69. D
70. F
71. A
72. F
73. A
74. H
75. C

ENGLISH PRACTICE SECTION 1 EXPLANATIONS

Passage I

1. **C** Note the question! When a question asks which answer would *NOT* be acceptable, eliminate answers that **are** acceptable. Vocabulary changes in the answer choices, so this question tests which words give the clearest meaning. Both *announce* and *declare* mean something very similar to *proclaim* in the context of the sentence and are therefore both acceptable alternatives. Eliminate (A) and (B). *Advertise* means *make known,* which is also an acceptable alternative; eliminate (D). *Compare* does not retain the same meaning, so (C) is not acceptable. The correct answer is (C).

2. **F** Note the question! The question asks whether a sentence should be deleted from the essay, so it tests the ideas of consistent and clear. If the sentence is consistent with the subject of the paragraph and makes the meaning of the paragraph clearer, it should be kept. The paragraph gives examples of how a hat visually expresses something about its wearer, so the sentence is consistent; eliminate (H) and (J). The sentence does not discuss *the narrator's love of hats,* so eliminate (G). The sentence does, as (F) says, *establish the theme of this paragraph.* The correct answer is (F).

3. **A** The answer choices contain options to start a new paragraph or not, so this question tests consistency of ideas. A new paragraph should begin when a new idea is introduced, so read the sentences before and after the proposed break to determine whether a new idea is introduced. The previous sentence gives examples of particular hats that communicate something about their wearers, and the sentence that begins with the underlined portion gives more examples of the same thing. Both sentences discuss the same topic, so there is no need to begin a new paragraph; eliminate (C) and (D). The examples given in this sentence are *more general* than the ones in the previous sentence, so keep (A). There is not a conclusion in this sentence as the transition word *thus* would indicate, so eliminate (B). The correct answer is (A).

4. **J** Commas change in the answer choices, so this question tests comma usage. There is no need for a comma after *artistic,* as the list of adjectives *(artistic and creative)* includes only two items. A comma is needed before the *and* in a list only if there are three or more items in the list. Eliminate (G) and (H). There is no need to break up the clause *a beret suggests you are artistic and creative* with a comma, so eliminate (F). The correct answer is (J).

5. **B** The number of words changes in the answer choices, so this question tests concision. There is also the option to DELETE; consider this choice carefully as it's often the correct answer. The phrase *hats show in our figures of speech* does not make sense without the underlined portion, so eliminate (D). The correct idiom is *show up,* so eliminate (C). There is no reason to add the word *way,* so eliminate (A). Choice (B) is both concise and idiomatically correct. The correct answer is (B).

6. **J** Note the question! The question asks which choice best *reinforces the author's attitude toward hats as it has been conveyed up to this point,* so it tests consistency. Eliminate answers that are inconsistent with the purpose stated in the question. There is no discussion of whether a hat *makes your hair*

messy, so eliminate (F). There is also no discussion of the *cost* of hats, so eliminate (G). The author does not mention the potential to *forget [a hat] in a restaurant,* so eliminate (H). The essay up to this point discusses the many different things a hat can communicate about a person, so keep (J). The correct answer is (J).

7. **C** The length of the phrase around the word *deserve* changes in the answer choices, so this question could test concision. The shortest answer choice, (A), makes a descriptive phrase at the beginning of the sentence: *Deserving congratulations.* This phrase describes the subject of the sentence, which is *I,* but the narrator is not the one *deserving congratulations.* Eliminate (A). Choice (D) has the same problem and can also be eliminated. It is not clear what the pronoun *they* in (B) refers to, so eliminate (B). Choice (C) has a clear meaning. The correct answer is (C).

8. **H** Punctuation changes in the answer choices, so this question tests how to connect ideas with the appropriate punctuation. The first part of the sentence, *When someone has exciting news for me, he can tell me to hold on to my hat,* is an independent clause. The second part of the sentence, *if the news has to be kept secret, I can promise to keep it under my hat,* is also an independent clause. A comma cannot be used between two independent clauses, so eliminate (F). Adding *although* to the second part of the sentence makes it a dependent clause, but there is no contrast between the two ideas as *although* would indicate, so eliminate (G). A period can be used between two independent clauses so keep (H). In (J), the second part of the sentence, *especially when it has to be kept secret, I can promise to keep it under my hat,* is an independent clause. A comma cannot be used between two independent clauses, so eliminate (J). The correct answer is (H).

9. **D** Note the question! The question asks whether a sentence should be added to the end of the paragraph, so it tests consistency. A sentence should be added only if it is consistent with the focus of the paragraph. The paragraph focuses on the meanings of different expressions that include references to hats. The new sentence gives a history of one of these phrases but is not consistent with the overall paragraph, so it should not be added. Eliminate (A) and (B). The number of *individuals in the nineteenth century* who *were exposed to poisonous fumes* is not relevant to the paragraph, so eliminate (C). Choice (D) correctly states that the new sentence *does not fit with the essay.* The correct answer is (D).

10. **G** Commas change in the answer choices, so this question tests comma usage. The phrase *of using a hat* is necessary to the main meaning of the sentence, so it should not be set off by commas; eliminate (J). There is no reason to put a comma after either *possibility* or *hat,* as neither of these places separates distinct ideas in the sentence; eliminate (F) and (H). The correct answer is (G).

11. **B** Pronouns change in the answer choices, so this question tests consistency of pronouns. All the pronouns are first-person singular, so choose the answer that has the appropriate case. The underlined pronoun is not just a subject, so eliminate the subject pronoun *I* in (D). It is also not just an object, so eliminate the object pronoun *me* in (A). A reflexive pronoun is needed here as the narrator is both the subject and the object of the verb *think.* Both (B) and (C) are reflexive, but (B) is more concise. Eliminate (C). The correct answer is (B).

12. **G** Pronouns and verbs change in the answer choices, so this question tests the idea of clear. Choices (H) and (J) can be eliminated, as neither makes sense in the context of the sentence; the second part of the sentence already contains the verb *will succeed,* so there is no need for an additional verb in the underlined portion. The subject pronoun *his* makes the second part of the sentence, *his search for fabulous treasures will succeed against all odds,* an independent clause. The first part of the sentence, *Another hat, appropriately battered, helps me feel like a daring adventurer,* is also an independent clause. Two independent clauses must be separated by punctuation, so eliminate (F), which does not contain punctuation. The relative pronoun *whose* makes the second part of the sentence into a dependent clause, so (G) works. The correct answer is (G).

13. **D** The length of the phrase changes in the answer choices, so this question tests concision. There is also the option to DELETE; consider this choice carefully as it's often the correct answer. The sentence is complete and clear without the underlined portion, so keep (D). Choice (A) makes the sentence incomplete, so eliminate (A). Eliminate (B) because the present tense verb *are* is inconsistent with the phrase *on my last birthday,* which indicates the past. Eliminate (C) because it makes the sentence incomplete. The correct answer is (D).

14. **J** Note the question! The question asks whether a sentence should be added to the end of the passage, so it tests consistency. A sentence should be added only if it is consistent with the focus of the passage. The passage focuses on the many different messages a hat can send, but it never discusses anything related to having *a song in your heart,* so the sentence should not be added; eliminate (F) and (G). It is not true that *the preceding sentence expressed the same idea,* so eliminate (H). Choice (J) correctly states that the new sentence *does not have a meaningful connection to the central theme of this essay.* The correct answer is (J).

15. **A** Note the question! The question asks whether the essay discusses *items of clothing* that *can be used to communicate things, literally and figuratively, about their wearers,* so it tests consistency. Determine whether the essay is consistent with this idea. This essay discusses both the literal and figurative messages hats can send, so it is consistent with this idea; eliminate (C) and (D). The narrator of the essay does discuss how he *uses hats to express his feelings and present himself as different kinds of people,* so keep (A). The essay never discusses that *hats have been symbols of royalty and power,* so eliminate (B). The correct answer is (A).

Passage II

16. **F** Verbs change in the answer choices, so this question tests consistency of verbs. A verb must be consistent in tense with the rest of the sentence. The other verb in the sentence, *were,* is in past tense, so the underlined verb must also be past tense. Eliminate (H) and (J) because they are in present tense. The word *formerly* indicates that the underlined verb should be in past perfect tense, so eliminate (G) because it is in present perfect tense. Choice (F) uses the appropriate tense to indicate that *songs* were *undocumented* only before cassette recorders. The correct answer is (F).

17. **C** Note the question! The question asks for the answer that *provides the most stylistically effective and concise wording,* so it tests consistency. Eliminate answers that are inconsistent with the purpose stated in the question. The words *seemingly* and *apparent* in (A) mean the same thing, so there is no need to use both. Eliminate (A). Choices (B), (C), and (D) all have the same meaning, but (C) is most concise. Eliminate (B) and (D). The correct answer is (C).

18. **H** Punctuation changes in the answer choices, so this question tests how to connect ideas with the appropriate punctuation. The word *of* in (F) and (G) is not necessary in the sentence; eliminate (F) and (G). The first part of the sentence, *However, another song is the opposite,* is an independent clause. The second part of the sentence, *the song sounds like the straightforward rock of Buddy Holly,* is also an independent clause. Two independent clauses must be separated by some type of punctuation other than a comma, so eliminate (J). Choice (H) appropriately uses a semicolon to separate the two independent clauses. The correct answer is (H).

19. **B** Note the question! The question asks for the answer that provides *detail about the lyrical subject matter,* so it tests consistency. Eliminate answers that are inconsistent with the purpose stated in the question. *What inspired* the lyrics does not say anything about the *subject,* so eliminate (A). *Dating and automobiles* does give more information about *subject matter,* so keep (B). Neither *rhymed couplets and alliteration* nor *Diamond's enunciation* gives detail about *subject matter,* so eliminate (C) and (D). The correct answer is (B).

20. **F** The length of the phrase changes in the answer choices, so this question tests concision. *Strain* and *effort* mean the same thing here, so there is no need to use both words; eliminate (G). *Relatively simple* and *free of struggle* also mean the same thing in this context, so eliminate (H). Choices (F) and (J) express the same idea, but (F) is more concise. Eliminate (J). The correct answer is (F).

21. **A** Apostrophes change in the answer choices, so this question tests apostrophe usage. A noun with an apostrophe shows possession. Since the *tempo* belongs to the *verse,* an apostrophe is needed; eliminate (B) and (D). The difference between (A) and (C) is singular versus plural possessive. The preceding sentence specifies *an upbeat verse,* so the singular possessive is appropriate here. Eliminate the plural possessive in (C). The correct answer is (A).

22. **G** Pronouns change in the answer choices, so this question tests consistency of pronouns. A pronoun must be consistent with the noun it refers to in both gender and number. The underlined pronoun refers to *Diamond,* who is male and singular. Eliminate (F) because it contains the gender-neutral pronoun *one.* Eliminate (H) because it contains the plural pronoun *they.* Eliminate (J) because Diamond is not *conflicting.* Choice (G) appropriately states that *he remains conflicted.* The correct answer is (G).

23. **C** Note the question! The question asks whether a sentence should be added to the end of the paragraph, so it tests consistency. A sentence should be added only if it is consistent with the focus of the paragraph. The paragraph focuses on Diamond's *unique artistic voice.* The new sentence discusses what *we have all experienced,* so it is not consistent. Eliminate (A) and (B). Keep (C) because

it correctly states that the new sentence *strays from the paragraph's main focus.* The new sentence may *encourage readers to think about events in their own lives,* but that is not consistent with the paragraph; eliminate (D). The correct answer is (C).

24. **H** Note the question! When a question asks which answer would *NOT* be acceptable, eliminate answers that **are** acceptable. Transitions change in the answer choices, so this question tests consistency of ideas. A transition must be consistent with the relationship between the ideas it connects. The first part of the sentence says that *sources of music from major music towns...are abundant,* and the second part says that *little is known about Lexington's music scene.* These ideas contrast with each other, so the contrasting transitions in (F), (G), and (J) are all acceptable alternatives. Eliminate (F), (G), and (J). *Since* indicates that ideas agree with each other, so (H) is not acceptable. The correct answer is (H).

25. **D** The wording of the phrase describing *Diamond's songs* changes in the answer choices. There is also the option to DELETE; consider this choice carefully as it's often the correct answer in this type of question. The beginning of the passage already makes it clear that Diamond recorded his songs on a cassette recorder with a built-in microphone, so there is no need to repeat that information. Eliminate (A), (B), and (C). The sentence is clear and concise without the underlined portion. The correct answer is (D).

26. **J** Note the question! The question asks for the best placement for the underlined portion, so it tests consistency. The underlined portion must be consistent with the word or phrase it is next to. The underlined phrase specifies a physical location (Lexington), so it must come next to something that can be tied to location. *Diamond's songs* may have been recorded in Lexington, but they don't have to be listened to in a specific place, so eliminate (F). *Historians* likewise don't have to physically be in Lexington, so eliminate (G). *Taste* also does not have to be tied to Lexington, so eliminate (H). It is logical to describe the *musical culture* as specific to Lexington, so keep (J). The correct answer is (J).

27. **B** The words *affected* and *effected* change in the answer choices, so this question tests frequently confused words. Eliminate answer choices with the incorrect meaning. *Effected* means "brought about," as in: the phrase "effected change." That is not the meaning of the word in this sentence, so eliminate (A) and (D). *Affected* means "influenced," which is the appropriate meaning here. The difference between (B) and (C) is the preposition *by* versus *with,* so the question also tests idioms. The appropriate idiom is *affected by;* eliminate (C). The correct answer is (B).

28. **F** The length of the phrase surrounding *jazz dance hall* changes in the answer choices, so this question tests concision. The non-underlined portion of the sentence specifies that Diamond *did perform;* there is no need to repeat the idea that he *played* or that the performance was *as a musician;* eliminate (G), (H), and (J). Choice (F) is concise and makes the meaning of the sentence clear. The correct answer is (F).

29. **B** Verbs change in the answer choices, so this question tests consistency of verbs. Verbs must be consistent in tense with other verbs in the sentence or paragraph. The paragraph is in the past tense, so the underlined verb should also be in past tense. Eliminate (A) and (C) because they are both in present tense. The past perfect tense in (D) would indicate that Diamond's recording activities were interrupted at some point in the past; there is no indication that this was the case, so eliminate (D). The correct answer is (B).

30. **G** Note the question! The question asks for the answer that provides *the best conclusion to this essay,* so it tests consistency. Eliminate answers that are inconsistent with the main theme of the essay. The essay focuses on the past, so eliminate (F) because it discusses the future. Keep (G) because it is consistent with the essay's focus on how Diamond's recordings provide information about the music scene in Lexington. Whether Diamond ever *had to buy another cassette recorder* is not relevant to the passage, so eliminate (H). The passage focuses on only Lexington, not *other cities,* so eliminate (J). The correct answer is (G).

Passage III

31. **A** The length of the phrase changes in the answer choices, so this question tests concision. Choice (D) is the shortest answer, but it is not as clear as the other choices because it does not specify the type of *rider.* Eliminate (D). Choices (A), (B), and (C) all express the same idea, but (A) is the most concise of these three. Eliminate (B) and (C). The correct answer is (A).

32. **H** Punctuation changes in the answer choices, so this question tests how to connect ideas with the appropriate punctuation. The beginning of the sentence, *Luckily, I was able to overcome this fear by having my first trip by subway guided by a neighbor,* is an independent clause. The end of the sentence, *named Sasha,* is not an independent clause. A semicolon can only be used between two independent clauses, so eliminate (G). There is no reason to break up the phrase *a neighbor named Sasha* with a comma either after *neighbor* or after *named,* so eliminate (F) and (J). The correct answer is (H).

33. **B** The forms of the words change in the answer choices, so this question tests the idea of clear. Look for the answer that gives the clearest meaning to the sentence. The words *dense* and *intricate* are used to describe *subway routes* in the sentence, so they must be adjectives or adverbs. The word *intricacy* is a noun, and it cannot be used to describe another noun; eliminate (A) and (D). The word *intricately* in (C) is an adverb, and could be used to describe the adjective *dense,* but there is no need to separate those two words with a comma; eliminate (C). Choice (B) appropriately uses a comma between two adjectives that both describe the same noun. The correct answer is (B).

34. **J** The length of the phrase changes in the answer choices, so this question tests concision. The non-underlined portion of the sentence specifies that the action in the underlined portion happened when Sasha was *a child,* so there is no need to repeat that idea. Eliminate (F) and (H). There is no need for the word *starting* in the underlined portion, so eliminate (G). Choice (J) is concise and makes the meaning of the sentence clear. The correct answer is (J).

35. **A** Apostrophes change in the answer choices, so this question tests apostrophe usage. A noun with an apostrophe shows possession. Since the *warnings* belong to the *family,* an apostrophe is needed in this sentence; eliminate (D). Choice (B) is an incorrect version of the plural possessive, so eliminate (B). The difference between (A) and (C) is singular versus plural possessive. Since the narrator has just one *family,* eliminate the plural possessive in (C). The correct answer is (A).

36. **G** Note the question! The question asks for the best placement for Sentence 5, so it tests consistency of ideas. The sentence must be consistent with the ideas that come both before and after it. Sentence 5 mentions the *family's warnings* and that the narrator *was afraid to take the subway.* Sentence 4 is about Sasha, the neighbor who taught the narrator to ride the subway, which is not consistent with the *family's warnings* at the beginning of Sentence 5; eliminate (F). Sentence 2 says that the narrator *was able to overcome this fear.* The phrase *this fear* must refer back to something, and the narrator's being *afraid* at the end of Sentence 5 provides that reference. Choice (G) accurately places Sentence 5 before Sentence 2. The correct answer is (G).

37. **B** Pronouns and nouns change in the answer choices, so this question tests the idea of clear. A pronoun can be used only if it is clear what it refers to. The pronoun *them* would indicate that the narrator walked up to both women, but since the women were on opposite sides, this doesn't make sense. Eliminate (A) and (D), which contains a similar error. Choice (B) makes it clear which woman the narrator approached, so keep (B). Eliminate (C) since it is not clear which woman *her* refers to. The correct answer is (B).

38. **H** Transitions change in the answer choices, so this question tests consistency of ideas. A transition must be consistent with the relationship between the ideas it connects. The first part of the sentence describes the narrator's confusion *(I couldn't tell to which platform to descend),* and the second part gives a reason for that confusion *(I had always used landmarks to find my way around my hometown).* The word *if* does not make sense in the sentence, as neither part of the sentence is dependent on the other; eliminate (F). The word *which* also does not make sense in the sentence, as it does not clearly refer back to anything. Eliminate (G). Choice (H) does not contain a transition word, but the semicolon indicates that the two parts of the sentence agree with each other. Both parts of the sentence are independent clauses, so the semicolon is appropriate punctuation; keep (H). There is not a contrast between the two parts of the sentence, so eliminate the contrasting transition *even though* in (J). The correct answer is (H).

39. **A** Punctuation changes in the answer choices, so this question tests how to connect ideas with the appropriate punctuation. The first part of the sentence, *After a little searching, though,* is not an independent clause. A colon can only be used after an independent clause, so eliminate (B) and (D). The word *though* is not necessary to the main meaning of the sentence and should be set off from the sentence with commas both before and after. Eliminate (C) because it has a comma only before *though.* The correct answer is (A).

40. **F** Note the question! The question asks for the answer that *most effectively introduces the action in this paragraph while suggesting the narrator's discomfort in her new surroundings,* so it tests consistency. Eliminate answers that are inconsistent with the purpose stated in the question. Choice (F) states that the narrator *felt very conspicuous,* which is consistent with the idea of *discomfort,* so keep (F). Both (G) and (J) focus on *Sasha,* rather than on *the narrator's discomfort,* so eliminate (G) and (J). Eliminate (H) because it focuses on *people…on the platform* and not on *the narrator's discomfort.* The correct answer is (F).

41. **D** The length of the phrase around the word *confused* changes in the answer choices, so this question tests concision. Both *uncertainty* and *lack of understanding* mean the same thing as *confused,* so there is no need to repeat those ideas. Eliminate (B) and (C). The phrase *like a whirlwind in my mind* does not make the meaning of the sentence clearer, so eliminate (A). Choice (D) is concise and makes the meaning of the sentence clear. The correct answer is (D).

42. **G** Vocabulary changes in the answer choices, so this question tests which words give the clearest meaning. The phrases *could of* and *would of* are incorrect spellings of the contractions *could've* (could have) or *would've* (would have) and are therefore both wrong. Eliminate (F) and (J). *Should* means "ought to," and *would* expresses the possibility of something happening. *Would* is the appropriate word in this context. Eliminate (H). The correct answer is (G).

43. **C** Punctuation changes in the answer choices, so this question tests how to connect ideas with the appropriate punctuation. The first part of the sentence, *When we were seated on the train, Sasha looked at me with a pleased expression,* is an independent clause. The second part of the sentence, *I suppose he was proud of how well he had served as a guide,* is also an independent clause. Two independent clauses must be separated by some type of punctuation other than a comma, so eliminate (A) and (B). Keep (C) because it separates the two independent clauses with a semicolon. There is no contrast between the two parts of the sentence, so eliminate (D) because it contains the contrasting transition *however.* The correct answer is (C).

44. **H** The number of words changes in the answer choices, so this question tests concision. Choice (H) is the most concise, and appropriately uses a period to separate an independent clause at the beginning of the sentence *("You look like you belong here in the big city," he said, nudging me playfully in the side)* from an independent clause at the end *(I shrugged and elbowed him back).* The word *which* does not make sense in the sentence, as it does not clearly refer back to anything. Eliminate (F) and (G). The word *where* also does not make sense in the sentence, as there is no location that it could refer to; eliminate (J). The correct answer is (H).

45. **B** The order of words changes in the answer choices, so this question tests misplaced modifiers. Eliminate answers that have an unclear word order. The phrase *with treasures and new wonders* should describe *caverns* rather than the narrator. Eliminate (A), (C), and (D) because they all make it sound as if the narrator is *filled with treasures and new wonders.* Choice (B) makes the meaning of the sentence clear. The correct answer is (B).

Passage IV

46. **H** The length of the phrase changes in the answer choices, so this question tests concision. The words *likely,* and *possibly* mean the same thing in this context, so there is no need to use both; eliminate (F) and (J). Choices (G) and (H) both express the same idea, but (H) is more concise. Eliminate (G). The correct answer is (H).

47. **A** Verbs change in the answer choices, so this question tests consistency of verbs. A verb must be consistent in tense with other verbs in the sentence. The other verb in the sentence, *predicted,* is in the simple past tense, so the underlined verb should also be in simple past tense. Choice (A) is in simple past tense, so keep (A). Eliminate (B) because it is in present tense. Eliminate (C) and (D) because they are both in present perfect tense. The correct answer is (A).

48. **G** The answer choices have the option of either including or omitting a conjunction, so this question tests complete sentences. There is also the option to DELETE; consider this choice carefully as it's often the correct answer. As written, the first part of the sentence, *Because Einstein didn't live to see it,* is not an independent clause. The second part of the sentence, *the universe proved the accuracy of his calculations in 1970, when Cygnus X-1 was discovered about 7,000 light years from Earth,* is an independent clause. The two parts of the sentence are correctly connected with a comma. If the underlined conjunction is removed, the first part of the sentence becomes an independent clause. Two independent clauses cannot be connected with a comma, so a conjunction is necessary; eliminate (J). The correct conjunction must be consistent with the ideas it connects. The first part of the sentence is not the cause of the second part, so eliminate (F) and (H), which both indicate a causal relationship. The two parts of the sentence contrast with one another, and *although* indicates a contrast. The correct answer is (G).

49. **A** Vocabulary changes in the answer choices, so this question tests which words give the clearest meaning. Both *less* and *fewer* can only be used in a comparison before the word *than,* which is not present in this sentence; eliminate (B) and (C). There is no indication that the diameter is *too little,* so eliminate (D). Choice (A) makes the meaning of the sentence clear. The correct answer is (A).

50. **G** Note the question! The question asks what would be lost if the previous sentence were deleted, so it tests consistency. Eliminate answer choices that are not consistent with the previous sentence. The sentence describes the mass and size of a black hole in terms of the sizes of Earth and the Sun. There is no mention of the *purpose of studying black holes,* so eliminate (F). Choice (G) accurately describes the sentence, so keep (G). The sentence says that a black hole is compressed into a small space, but it does not explain *how* it's compressed, so eliminate (H). The information is not *repeated later in the passage,* so eliminate (J). The correct answer is (G).

51. **A** Note the question! The question asks for *the most logical transition* between paragraphs, so it tests consistency. A transition must be consistent with the ideas it connects. The previous paragraph discusses the discovery of a specific black hole and describes the *remarkable* nature of black holes in general. The new paragraph describes a theory of how black holes are formed. Choice (A) is

consistent with both paragraphs. Neither paragraph discusses *why* black holes should be studied, so eliminate (B). Neither paragraph discusses the possibility of *the Sun* becoming *a black hole,* so eliminate (C). Neither paragraph discusses *the effects of such massive gravitational pull,* so eliminate (D). The correct answer is (A).

52. **F** Different forms of *their/there/they're* change in the answer choices, so this question tests frequently confused words. *They're* is the same as *they are,* which is not necessary in this sentence, so eliminate (J). *Their* is a possessive pronoun, but there is nothing in the sentence that belongs to anything, so eliminate (G) and (H). The phrase *there are* is used to indicate the presence of something, which works in this context. Choice (F) makes the meaning of the sentence clear. The correct answer is (F).

53. **D** Verbs change in the answer choices, so this question tests consistency of verbs. A verb must be consistent in tense with other verbs in the sentence. The other verbs in the sentence, *suggests* and *are,* are in simple present tense, so the underlined verb should also be in simple present tense. Eliminate (A) and (B) because there is no need for an *-ing* ending on the verb. Eliminate (C) because it is in future tense. Choice (D) is in simple present tense. The correct answer is (D).

54. **G** Note the question! When a question asks which answer would *NOT* be acceptable, eliminate answers that **are** acceptable. Vocabulary changes in the answer choices, so this question tests which words give the clearest meaning. Both *close to* and *toward* mean something very similar to *near,* as the sentence is written, and are therefore both acceptable. Eliminate (F) and (H). *Around* could also mean *near* in this context, so (J) is acceptable; eliminate (J). The word *close* by itself (i.e., not followed by *to*) does not work in the context, so (G) is not acceptable. The correct answer is (G).

55. **A** Punctuation changes in the answer choices, so this question tests how to connect ideas with the appropriate punctuation. The first part of the sentence, *At that stage, the star has nearly exhausted its hydrogen supply,* is an independent clause. The second part of the sentence, *consequently losing its ability to burn at a sufficiently high temperature to prevent its collapse,* is not an independent clause. Choice (A) correctly uses a comma to connect the two parts of the sentence. Only periods and semicolons can only be used between two independent clauses, so eliminate (B) and (D). A comma followed by *and* can also only be used between two independent clauses, so eliminate (C). The correct answer is (A).

56. **H** Apostrophes change in the answer choices, so this question tests apostrophe usage. A noun with an apostrophe shows possession. Since the *exterior* belongs to the *star,* an apostrophe is needed; eliminate (F) and (G). There is no need to break up the phrase *the star's exterior layers* with a comma, so eliminate (J). The correct answer is (H).

57. **D** Verbs change in the answer choices, so this question tests consistency of verbs. A verb must be consistent in tense with other verbs in the sentence. The other verb in the sentence, *are,* is in simple present tense, so the underlined verb should also be in simple present tense. Eliminate (A) because there is no need for an *-ing* ending on the verb. Eliminate (B) because it is in past tense. Eliminate (C) because it is in future tense. Choice (D) is in simple present tense. The correct answer is (D).

58. **H** Transitions change in the answer choices, so this question tests consistency of ideas. A transition must be consistent with the relationship between the ideas it connects. The sentence before the transition discusses *the supernova of smaller stars that are not sufficiently massive to create black holes.* The sentence that starts with the transition says that *on occasion these stars will...collide...and together become massive enough to form a black hole.* These ideas contrast with each other. Eliminate (F), (G), and (J) because they all contain transitions that indicate agreement. Choice (H) contains a contrasting transition. The correct answer is (H).

59. **C** The length of the phrase around the word *explain* changes in the answer choices, so this question tests concision. *Articulate* and *describe* mean the same thing as *explain* in this context, so there is no need to use more than one of these words; eliminate (A), (B), and (D). Choice (C) is concise and makes the meaning of the sentence clear. The correct answer is (C).

60. **J** Note the question! The question asks whether the essay describes *how Einstein's skepticism stopped scientific inquiry into the existence of black holes,* so it tests consistency. Determine whether the essay is consistent with this idea. Although the essay mentions at the beginning that Einstein did not believe in black holes, most of the essay is about current knowledge and theories of black holes, so it is not consistent with the purpose stated in the question. Eliminate (F) and (G). There is no indication in the essay that *Einstein later decided that black holes did exist,* so eliminate (H). Choice (J) accurately describes the essay. The correct answer is (J).

Passage V

61. **D** Commas change in the answer choices, so this question tests comma usage. Although phrases that start with *which* are often unnecessary, the phrase that indicates that the bins *have become companions* is necessary to the main meaning of the sentence, so it should not be set off with commas. Eliminate (C). The other answer choices correctly use the word *that* instead of *which* for a necessary phrase. Because the phrase is necessary to the sentence there is no reason to include a comma at either end of the phrase, so eliminate (A) and (B). The correct answer is (D).

62. **F** Verbs change in the answer choices, so this question tests consistency of verbs. A verb must be consistent with the rest of the sentence. The underlined verb is preceded by the helping verb *has,* which means the underlined verb must be the past participle to correctly complete the verb phrase. Eliminate (G) because it is the simple past tense of the verb, not the past participle. Eliminate (H) and (J) because they are both present tenses of the verb. Choice (F) is the past participle. The correct answer is (F).

63. **D** Verbs change in the answer choices, so this question tests consistency of verbs. A verb must be consistent in tense with other verbs in the same part of the passage. The paragraph is in present tense, so the underlined verb should also be in present tense. Eliminate (B) and (C) because they are both in past tense. Choices (A) and (D) are both in the present tense, but (D) is more concise. Eliminate (A). The correct answer is (D).

64. **G** Note the question! The question asks for the answer that *emphasizes a lack of awareness of this problem* (that is, the problem of e-waste), so it tests consistency. Eliminate answers that are inconsistent with the purpose stated in the question. *Assiduously studying* means "paying a lot of attention," so eliminate (H). It's possible that the fact that *people seldom find themselves confronted with* the problem (as (F) says) or that *little attention is paid by the people* (as (J) says) could mean they *lack awareness*, but the idea in (G), that people *don't realize the dangers,* more directly matches the idea of *a lack of awareness.* Eliminate (F) and (J). The correct answer is (G).

65. **C** Commas and transition words change in the answer choices, so this question tests how to connect ideas with the appropriate punctuation. The first part of the sentence, *E-waste proliferates as the techno-fashionable constantly upgrade to the most cutting-edge devices,* is an independent clause. The second part of the sentence, *the majority of them end up in landfills,* is also an independent clause. Adding either of the relative pronouns *that* or *which* is unnecessary because the second part of the sentence already contains the pronoun *them* that refers to *devices* in the first part of the sentence. Eliminate (A) and (B). Choice (C) correctly connects the two independent clauses with a comma followed by *and.* There is no sequence of time between the two parts of the sentence, so there is no need for the word *after;* eliminate (D). The correct answer is (C).

66. **F** Commas change in the answer choices, so this question tests comma usage. The phrase *who track such waste* is necessary to the main meaning of the sentence, so it should not be set off by commas. Eliminate (J). There is no reason to include a single comma after *waste,* so eliminate (G). The difference between (F) and (H) is *who* versus *which. Activists* are people, so they must be referred to by the pronoun *who.* Eliminate (H). The correct answer is (F).

67. **A** Note the question! The question asks whether a phrase should be added to the end of the sentence, so it tests consistency. The phrase should be added only if it is consistent with the focus of the sentence. The sentence talks about the *dangerous toxins* that e-waste produces, and the new phrase gives examples of those toxins. The new phrase is consistent with the sentence, so eliminate (C) and (D). Choice (A) accurately states that the new phrase *adds specific details.* There is no indication that *landfills have too much waste,* so eliminate (B). The correct answer is (A).

68. **J** The form of the word *dangerous* changes in the answer choices, so this question tests the idea of clear. There is no comparison in the sentence, so there is no need for either *more* or *most* in front of *dangerous;* eliminate (G) and (H). The underlined word modifies the verb *contaminates* in this sentence, so it should be an adverb. Eliminate (F) because the adjective *dangerous* can only be used to modify a noun. Choice (J) contains the adverb *dangerously,* which can modify a verb. The correct answer is (J).

69. **D** Transitions change in the answer choices, so this question tests consistency of ideas. A transition must be consistent with the relationship between the ideas it connects. The end of the previous paragraph discusses the dangers of e-waste. The new paragraph discusses the reusable materials that e-waste contains. There is a contrast between these two ideas, so eliminate (A), (B), and (C), which would all indicate that the ideas agree. Choice (D) contains a contrasting transition. The correct answer is (D).

70. **F** Punctuation and transition words change in the answer choices, so this question tests how to connect ideas with the appropriate punctuation. The first part of the sentence, *Recycling these materials reduces environmental impact,* is an independent clause. The second part of the sentence, *reducing both landfill waste and the need to mine such metals, which can destroy ecosystems,* is not an independent clause. A semicolon can only be used between two independent clauses, so eliminate (G). The word *by* effectively indicates that the second part of the sentence is the way in which *environmental impact* is reduced; keep (F). The word *so* would indicate a cause-effect relationship between the two parts of the sentence, but there is no such relationship in the sentence; eliminate (H). The word *of* reverses the relationship between the two parts of the sentence, so eliminate (J). The correct answer is (F).

71. **A** The order of words changes in the answer choices, so this question tests misplaced modifiers. Eliminate answers that have an unclear word order. Choice (A) makes it clear that the *number of states that have adopted laws* is *growing,* so keep (A). It is not *adoptions* that are *growing,* so eliminate (B). The word *growing* is not meant to describe the verb *adopted* as it does in (C); eliminate (C). It is the *number of states* that is growing rather than the *states* themselves, so eliminate (D). The correct answer is (A).

72. **F** Note the question! The question asks whether a sentence should be deleted from the essay, so it tests the ideas of consistent and clear. If the sentence is consistent with the subject of the paragraph and makes the meaning clearer, it should be kept. The paragraph focuses on how little e-waste is recycled, and the sentence gives more information on that topic. It should not be deleted, so eliminate (H) and (J). The sentence does *provide a logical transition between the first and last sentences of the paragraph,* so keep (F). The sentence does provide a *statistic,* but it is more important as a transition between the idea of increasing *laws to prohibit dumping e-waste* in the first sentence and the idea that *some companies…merely ship the waste to third-world countries, where it still ends up in landfills* in the last sentence. Eliminate (G). The correct answer is (F).

73. **A** Note the question! The question asks whether a sentence should be added to the end of the paragraph, so it tests consistency. A sentence should be added only if it is consistent with the focus of the paragraph. The paragraph focuses on how little e-waste is recycled, and the new sentence gives further details about the companies described in the last sentence. It is therefore consistent with the paragraph and should be added; eliminate (C) and (D). Keep (A), because it accurately describes the new sentence. The paragraph already *paints such organizations in a negative light,* so that is not a good reason to add the new sentence. Eliminate (B). The correct answer is (A).

74. **H** The length of the phrase surrounding *progress* changes in the answer choices, so this question tests concision. The phrase *step forward* means the same thing as *progress* in this context, so there is no need to use both terms. Eliminate (F), (G), and (J). Choice (H) is concise and makes the meaning of the sentence clear. The correct answer is (H).

75. **C** Note the question! The question asks whether a sentence should be added to the end of the passage, so it tests consistency. A sentence should be added only if it is consistent with the focus of the passage. The passage focuses on e-waste, while the subject of the new sentence is *pollution*. It is therefore not consistent and should not be added; eliminate (A) and (B). Choice (C) accurately states that the new sentence *digresses from the article's main point;* keep (C). The passage does not discuss *government regulation,* so eliminate (D). The correct answer is (C).

English Practice Section 2

ACT ENGLISH TEST

45 Minutes—75 Questions

DIRECTIONS: In the five passages that follow, certain words and phrases are underlined and numbered. In the right-hand column, you will find alternatives for each underlined part. In most cases, you are to choose the one that best expresses the idea, makes the statement appropriate for standard written English, or is worded most consistently with the style and tone of the passage as a whole. If you think the original version is best, choose "NO CHANGE." In some cases, you will find in the right-hand column a question about the underlined part. You are to choose the best answer to the question.

You will also find questions about a section of the passage or the passage as a whole. These questions do not refer to an underlined portion of the passage but rather are identified by a number or numbers in a box.

For each question, choose the alternative you consider best and blacken the corresponding oval on your answer document. Read each passage through once before you begin to answer the questions that accompany it. For many of the questions, you must read several sentences beyond the question to determine the answer. Be sure that you have read far enough ahead each time you choose an alternative.

Passage I

Building a Beauty Empire

In 1867, on an unassuming farm in tiny Delta, Louisiana, a daughter was born to [1] former slaves Minerva and Owen Breedlove. Little did anyone realize that Sarah Breedlove, orphaned at age six when her parents died, [2] would grow up to become one of the most successful African-American entrepreneurs in history. [3]

At twenty, Sarah Breedlove found herself widowed with an infant daughter, A'Lelia. Sarah packed up her few belongings

1. A. NO CHANGE
   B. by
   C. under
   D. for

2. F. NO CHANGE
   G. who became an orphan as a child at the age of six years old when her parents died,
   H. whose parents died when she was just age six leaving her to be an orphan as a young child,
   J. tragically when her parents died becoming an orphan at the young age of six years old,

3. At this point, the writer is considering adding the following true statement:

   > Also born in Louisiana, Louis Armstrong went on to exert a similarly powerful influence on 1920s American culture as a jazz trumpeter.

   Should the writer add this sentence here?

   A. Yes, because it's important to know that other influential people were born in Louisiana besides the woman portrayed in this essay.
   B. Yes, because this reference shows that music was important during this period.
   C. No, because the role Louis Armstrong played in 1920s culture is irrelevant to the main topic of this essay.
   D. No, because the 1920s were not significant years in American history.

and moved to St. Louis, hoping to take advantage of its' more numerous opportunities.
4

She supported herself as a laundress there for the next eighteen years. In 1905, she came up with an idea that would revolutionize the cosmetics industry. By ten years, she would not only oversee a vast financial empire but also become one of the best-known women in the United States.
5

Sarah invented a scalp conditioning and healing formula, in part because she had suffered from a disease that resulted in hair loss. Sarah undertook countless journeys to sell her formula door-to-door. As well as in churches and lodges. She dubbed herself Madame C. J. Walker, taking the name of
6

her second husband, Charles J. Walker, who worked in the newspaper publishing business and who also lived in St. Louis. She claimed that the secret formula for Madame Walker's Wonderful Hair Grower had come to her in a dream.
7

At this time, there were relatively few beauty parlors, so many women received beauty treatments at home. Sarah taught her methods to other women, they focused on sales and became
8

known as the "Walker Agents." Below Sarah's supervision, these agents became familiar sights in their white shirts and black skirts. Sarah called them "scalp specialists" and hair
9

and beauty "culturists" using these terms to emphasize the professional nature of the treatments.
10

4. F. NO CHANGE
   G. it's
   H. their
   J. its

5. A. NO CHANGE
   B. Up to
   C. Within
   D. Before

6. F. NO CHANGE
   G. door-to-door; as
   H. door-to-door, as
   J. door-to-door: as

7. A. NO CHANGE
   B. a man who lived in St. Louis and who worked in newspaper publishing.
   C. a St. Louis newspaper executive.
   D. a newspaper publishing businessman who was very well known in the St. Louis area.

8. F. NO CHANGE
   G. women, who
   H. women, with whom
   J. women those

9. A. NO CHANGE
   B. Above
   C. As
   D. Under

10. F. NO CHANGE
    G. "culturists"; using
    H. "culturists": using
    J. "culturists," using

[1] In 1913, she traveled to the Caribbean and to Central America, but before that Sarah concentrated on improving and developing the manufacture of her products. [2] One of the first of these charitable acts was her generous $1,000 donation to the city's YMCA. [3] In 1910, she established the Walker Company headquarters—which featured a factory in addition to salons and a training school—in Indianapolis. [4] Chosen because it was then the largest inland manufacturing city in the country, Indianapolis became both Sarah's home and the first beneficiary of her social activism and dedication to charitable causes. [13]

Social efforts dominated the latter years of Sarah's life. She contributed the largest donation to the effort to save Frederick Douglass's home, maintaining, the building as a historical museum. In 1913, she organized her agent-operators into "Walker Clubs," promoting these groups' philanthropic work by offering cash prizes to those doing the most good in their communities. Upon her death in 1919, "Madame Walker"—now often regarded as the richest self-made woman in the United States during her lifetime—donated two-thirds of her company's net profit to charitable causes.

11. Given that all the choices are true, which one provides the most effective transition from the preceding paragraph to this new one?

A. NO CHANGE
B. After her daughter A'Lelia built a magnificent townhome in an exclusive Manhattan neighborhood,
C. Aside from training a small "army" of agent-operators,
D. When Sarah had designed a special Walker Method treatment for celebrated dancer Josephine Baker,

12. **F.** NO CHANGE
G. Chose
H. Choosed
J. Choosing

13. For the sake of the logic and coherence of this paragraph, Sentence 2 should be placed:

A. where it is now.
B. before Sentence 1.
C. after Sentence 3.
D. after Sentence 4.

14. **F.** NO CHANGE
G. home, maintaining
H. home; maintaining
J. home maintaining,

Question 15 asks about the preceding passage as a whole.

15. Suppose the writer's goal had been to write a brief essay focusing on the development of the beauty industry in the early part of the twentieth century. Would this essay successfully accomplish this goal?

A. Yes, because the essay focuses on the beauty industry of the 1920s, during which Madame C. J. Walker became wealthy.
B. Yes, because the essay describes how Sarah invented a new formula to facilitate hair growth and treat scalp problems.
C. No, because the essay focuses mainly on Sarah Breedlove Walker and her place in the history of American business and culture.
D. No, because the essay describes other events taking place during this time that were more significant.

Passage II

A Tale of Two Uncles

[1] As my uncle and I finished our dinners, [16] we were hardly saying a word. [2] For the most part, it was a very ordinary birthday celebration. [17] [3] After we had my favorite meal, lamb chops, my uncle made me his famous banana split sundae for dessert. [4] Banana splits are best with two scoops of chocolate ice cream, in my opinion. [5] Normally, my uncle would get very excited watching me eat dessert and have me make wishes for the coming year. [6] However, as our spoons clinked around mounds of ice cream and banana, his mood turned sad and soft-spoken. [7] I knew the source of our tension: today was my eighteenth birthday and next month I'd be at boot camp. [18]

He said that joining the army [19] he had some strong reservations about me rather than going to college. I told him that I believed my father, who was killed serving in the Polish army, would have been proud of my decision. [20] My uncle responded that my father would have felt even better about me staying out of harm's way. In fact, my uncle continued, the reason that we moved to the United States was so that I would be more protected than I was in Poland. I think my uncle also found it surprising that I would want to join the U.S. army. He often asked me— [21] why I would risk my life for a country that was not my homeland. I told him that I considered America my new homeland. He was shocked.

16. Which of the following alternatives to the underlined portion would NOT be acceptable?
    - F. While my uncle and I finished dinner,
    - G. My uncle and I were almost finished eating, but
    - H. My uncle and I finished our dinners, however,
    - J. As my uncle and I were finishing our dinners,

17.
    - A. NO CHANGE
    - B. celebration, just like always.
    - C. celebration with nothing abnormal.
    - D. celebration and traditional.

18. Which of the following sentences is LEAST relevant to the theme of the passage and could therefore be deleted?
    - F. Sentence 2
    - G. Sentence 3
    - H. Sentence 4
    - J. Sentence 6

19. The best place for the underlined portion would be:
    - A. where it is now.
    - B. after the word *reservations*.
    - C. after the word *me*.
    - D. after the word *than*.

20. If the writer were to delete the phrase "who was killed serving in the Polish army" (and the surrounding commas) from the preceding sentence, the paragraph would primarily lose:
    - F. nothing, since this information is mentioned elsewhere in the paragraph.
    - G. evidence that the narrator's father was considered a brave man.
    - H. a necessary detail that supports the logical flow of ideas in the paragraph.
    - J. an explanation of why the narrator is unwilling to join the Polish army.

21.
    - A. NO CHANGE
    - B. me,
    - C. me
    - D. me:

[1] He began reminding me of my Polish upbringing. [2] My uncle has as many stories about my childhood <u>than I do.</u>[22]

22. F. NO CHANGE
    G. as I do
    H. then I do
    J. DELETE the underlined portion.

[3] He would take me to the local carnival in July. [23]

23. At this point, the writer is thinking of adding the following sentence:

    Different cities in Poland host carnivals during different months of the year.

    Should the writer make this addition here?

    A. Yes, because it relates to the essay's topic of celebration rituals in different cultures.
    B. Yes, because it gives the reader crucial background information about the narrator's cultural upbringing.
    C. No, because it offers information that does not help to preserve the focus of this paragraph.
    D. No, because it reiterates a detail that is mentioned elsewhere in the passage.

[4] <u>One</u>[24] would buy ourselves hotcakes and ride the Ferris wheel. [5] When the strawberries came into bloom, we would go hiking in the Tatras mountains. [6] He and I would row canoes and have swimming races from our dock out to a big rock formation and back. [7] At night, we would lie on the porch in the sleeping <u>bags,</u>[25] my grandmother had bought, <u>drink cocoa, and listen</u>[26] to the chorus of crickets. [8] My uncle <u>tells</u>[27] me ghost stories under the starlit sky. [28]

24. F. NO CHANGE
    G. You
    H. We
    J. They

25. A. NO CHANGE
    B. bags
    C. bags;
    D. bags, that

26. F. NO CHANGE
    G. drank cocoa, and listen
    H. drank cocoa, and listened
    J. drink cocoa, and listening

27. A. NO CHANGE
    B. has told
    C. would tell
    D. was telling

28. Upon reviewing this paragraph and noticing that some information has been omitted, the author composes the following sentence, using that information:

    Sometimes, in the warm months of the fall, my uncle rented a rustic vacation home on Lake Drawsko.

    For the sake of the logic of this paragraph, this sentence should be placed after Sentence:

    F. 4.
    G. 5.
    H. 6.
    J. 7.

When my uncle finished reminiscing, I assured him that I still love Poland and will never lose sight of it's [29] influence on who I am today. However, America gave my uncle an opportunity when an engineering firm in Pittsburgh offered him a job seven years ago. After we immigrated to America, [30] I became exposed to the cultural attitudes, social customs, and economic possibilities of growing up as an American child. My time in America has given me a deep love for it and loyalty to it. As we finished our dessert, I asked my uncle to make peace with my decision to defend Uncle Sam.

29. **A.** NO CHANGE
B. its'
C. its
D. their

30. Given that all of the choices are accurate, which one provides the most effective and logical transition from the preceding sentence to this one?

F. NO CHANGE
G. Pittsburgh being the biggest city in Pennsylvania,
H. He is a very well-respected engineer, and
J. Although I have visited Philadelphia, Pittsburgh is where

Passage III

Not the Same Old Song and Dance

After graduating from college, I decided to test my International Studies degree by living and working in China. I had studied [31] only a year of Mandarin Chinese at university, so I struggled with adaptation early on. I poured myself into work at first, finding that enduring the same 12-hour workdays as several of my Chinese coworkers was just as difficult as to adapt [32] to Chinese culture. All the while, at the same time, [33] I slowly taught myself more Chinese with a language CD and forced myself to interact at local places like restaurants and markets. The easiest way to adapt, however, had been right under my nose [34] the entire time.

All I had to do was spend time with my coworkers outside of work. My project team had already taken a quickly liking of [35] me, and I had been invited to several functions. I hadn't accepted yet out of fear of being unable to communicate, but my feelings of guilt at having turned down so many kind

31. **A.** NO CHANGE
B. study
C. studying
D. have studied

32. **F.** NO CHANGE
G. when adapting
H. as having adapted
J. as adapting

33. **A.** NO CHANGE
B. All the while,
C. All while at the same time,
D. While all the time was the same,

34. Which choice would most clearly and effectively express the obviousness of the best method of adaptation?

F. NO CHANGE
G. noticeable
H. doubtful
J. obscure

35. **A.** NO CHANGE
B. quick liking of
C. quick liking to
D. quickly liking to

invitations eventually outweighed that fear. When disappointed in myself, [36] I acquiesced one night, knowing this would be an important step in learning the Chinese way of life. The ensuing night would prove to be quite memorable and unforgettable. [37]

36. F. NO CHANGE
G. (Do NOT begin new paragraph) Disappointed in myself,
H. (Begin new paragraph) When disappointed in myself,
J. (Begin new paragraph) Disappointed in myself,

37. A. NO CHANGE
B. memorable and hard to forget.
C. as memorable as can be.
D. memorable.

We began the evening with dinner. I proudly requested to order since I had learned quite a lot of food vocabulary. Everyone seemed surprised, [38] and impressed by the variety of dishes I could order. Our post-dinner destination was a karaoke house (KTV), a very popular form of entertainment in China. [39] The karaoke took place in a private room with just our group. The experience was accompanied by embarrassment as [40] karaoke often provides, but mine did not come from singing.

38. F. NO CHANGE
G. seemed surprised
H. seemed, surprised
J. seemed; surprised

39. At this point, the writer is considering adding the following true statement:

Karaoke did not originate in China.

Should the writer add this sentence here?

A. Yes, because it supports that fact that karaoke is very popular despite being an import.
B. Yes, because it adds to the international flavor of the essay.
C. No, because it simply repeats a detail stated earlier in the essay.
D. No, because it doesn't add to the focus of this paragraph.

40. F. NO CHANGE
G. embarrassment as,
H. embarrassment, as
J. embarrassment, as,

When one girl refused to sing a song I had chosen, I decided to playfully chant to her the songs number [41] on the screen. The number was thirty-eight, but I chanted only three and eight, something which can be understood easily in English but is not common in Chinese. What I failed to realize was that the Chinese words for *three* and *eight*, when used as slang, can also mean *crazy*. Since my Chinese friends were not accustomed to number shortening, they could only assume I had just unreasonably insulted our female coworker. [42] After much confusion and a difficult explanation on my part, the matter was resolved, and everyone had a good laugh over it.

41. A. NO CHANGE
B. songs' number
C. song's number
D. songs's number

42. If the preceding sentence were deleted, the essay would primarily lose:

F. a repetition of the main point of the essay.
G. another example of slang errors between languages.
H. a contrast with the paragraph's opening sentence.
J. a detail of how the rest of the party reacted to the author's mistake.

A valuable lesson was certainly learned by me about differences in slang. [44] My experience with my co-workers was the first of many cultural lessons I would learn by simply being social in a foreign environment.

43. A. NO CHANGE
B. I certainly learned a valuable lesson
C. A lesson learned was certainly valuable
D. Certainly learning a valuable lesson

44. If the writer wanted to emphasize the benefit of learning slang expressions in a new language, which of the following true statements should be added at this point?
F. Slang differences are difficult to understand.
G. Slang is a popular way to communicate.
H. Learning about other slang differences can help to avoid cultural misunderstandings.
J. Daily conversation among peers often includes slang.

45. Which choice would best summarize the main point of the essay as illustrated by the narrator's miscommunication experience?
A. NO CHANGE
B. intentionally insulting a local person in a foreign country.
C. enjoying nightlife in a foreign country.
D. studying a foreign language in an isolated environment.

Passage IV

Life in the Bike Lane

[1]

When I was growing up, I used to ride my bike all the time. Even though I spent most of my childhood around the daunting, Pennsylvania, hills and mountains, I still loved to ride wherever and whenever I could. I suppose for someone who was too young to drive, the bicycle provided a certain amount of freedom.

[2]

Along came my sixteenth year and a driver's license, and that was it for the bike. When I finally got my driver's license, I felt that I had turned a page in my life, and that its old bike was part of a previous chapter. There it sat for my last two years of

46. F. NO CHANGE
G. daunting Pennsylvania hills
H. daunting Pennsylvania hills,
J. daunting, Pennsylvania, hills,

47. Which of the following alternatives to the underlined portion would NOT be acceptable?
A. Then
B. Next
C. Subsequently
D. In following

48. F. NO CHANGE
G. one's
H. your
J. my

high school and all four years of college while I gleefully drove back and forth even the <u>distances smallest in length,</u> [49] through the worst traffic and weather conditions, and amid the mounting prices of gas.

[3]

Then I moved <u>out</u> [50] on my own and found that I had moved to a place where the car had a lot less allure. Fresh out of college, I didn't have bundles of money to throw around, and in my new environs, bundles of money <u>was exactly</u> [51] what I needed to use the car with any regularity. Gas cost at least fifty cents more per gallon than I was used to, and what would've been a quick 30-minute drive where I grew up easily became a two-hour drive because of all the traffic in this new place! [52]

[4]

After I couldn't take any more, I <u>resolved and decided</u> [53] that the next time I visited my parents, I would bring the bike out of retirement. As if uncovering a lost volume of an ancient work, I entered the attic with a flashlight, <u>even if I fought</u> [54] off fear and cobwebs in equal measure. It seemed hopeless, I thought. Even if I could find my bike in this above-house cavern, it wouldn't be the same as it was before. I was so much older now, had known the pleasures of the automobile, and was out of shape from all the highway snacking and sitting. Then, there it was, and I felt the surge that the <u>gold-rushers'</u> [55] must have felt in California in the 1800s when they struck gold.

49. **A.** NO CHANGE
B. shortest and smallest distances,
C. distances that were short, not long,
D. shortest distances,

50. **F.** NO CHANGE
G. myself out
H. myself in
J. in

51. **A.** NO CHANGE
B. weren't exacting
C. was exact
D. were exactly

52. If the writer were to delete the phrase "in this new place" (placing an exclamation point after the word *traffic*), this sentence would primarily lose:
F. a contrast to the phrase "where I grew up" in the same sentence.
G. factual information regarding the purpose of the author's move.
H. a contrast to the phrase "a quick 30-minute drive" in the same sentence.
J. a logical connection to the place mentioned in Paragraph 1.

53. **A.** NO CHANGE
B. resolution in my deciding
C. resolved
D. decidedly resolved

54. **F.** NO CHANGE
G. fighting
H. because I fought
J. and had fought

55. **A.** NO CHANGE
B. gold-rusher's
C. gold-rushers
D. gold-rushers,

[5]

Needless to say, my joy at having rediscovered this long lost friend was overwhelming, but it was amplified when I had returned to my own place and began <u>by riding</u> [56] the bike around town. I had been freed from four-dollar-a-gallon gas, traffic jams, and <u>having been freed from the</u> [57] interminable wait at the bus stop!

[6]

I realized then that I had regained that freedom I had enjoyed so much when I was <u>younger, in</u> [58] my first apartment, this freedom had taken on a different character: <u>it wasn't just freedom of movement anymore.</u> [59] Now it was freedom from constraints that prevented me from doing what I wanted to do in the city, that had me sitting in traffic or spending all my hard-earned cash on gas. I had moved out of the fast lane and into the bike lane, and I was finally able to get the most out of my new life.

56. **F.** NO CHANGE
G. to riding
H. to ride
J. with riding

57. **A.** NO CHANGE
B. freed from the
C. the
D. from the freeing of the

58. **F.** NO CHANGE
G. younger, furthermore, in
H. younger. In
J. younger in

59. Given that all of the following are true, which one would provide the most effective transition to the following sentence?

A. NO CHANGE
B. not a character as in a play, but more in the sense of a "type."
C. I had resolved to ride my bike any distance shorter than ten miles.
D. I had to get the brakes fixed before I could use it a lot.

Question 60 asks about the preceding passage as a whole.

60. Suppose the writer had intended to write a brief essay detailing the transportation options for visitors to a major city. Would this essay successfully fulfill the writer's goal?

F. Yes, because the writer discusses biking, driving, and taking the bus in detail.
G. Yes, because this essay deals with the ways in which the city would have fewer traffic jams if more people rode bikes.
H. No, because the essay focuses instead on the writer's personal feelings about biking and driving in the city.
J. No, because the essay deals primarily with the convenience of driving and its superiority over other forms of transportation.

Passage V

Man's Best Friend

[1]

More and more, people are treating their pets like royalty. Though once it was considered extravagant to put a sweater or a pair of shoes on a <u>dog that</u> (61) it is almost to the point now that it is considered an abuse *not* to dress your dog for cold weather!

Large pet stores are not the only ones <u>that benefit</u> (62) from people's interest in dogs—raising pets has become an industry all its own, with significant representation in the clothing, publishing, and entertainment industries, to name a few. How did we ever get this way?

[2]

Archaeologists have found cultural and skeletal evidence of domesticated dogs as far back as 6500 BCE in Mesopotamia and as far back as 8300 BCE in what is now North America. [A] Put simply, dogs have been around as domesticated animals for a long time and in all different parts of the world. Some historians suggest that dogs as a species evolved into something close to their current form as many as 100,000 years ago, and many historians estimate that dogs were first domesticated as many as 15,000 years ago. <u>There are over 800 different breeds of dogs, and many more that cannot be classified into a single breed.</u> (63)

[3]

<u>Although</u> (64) dogs have been bred and domesticated for many reasons throughout history, the primary reason for their breeding in ancient times was their usefulness as hunting

61. **A.** NO CHANGE
B. dog, and
C. dog and
D. dog,

62. Which of the following alternatives to the underlined portion would NOT be acceptable?
F. that are benefiting
G. that have benefited
H. benefiting
J. that having benefited

63. Given that all of the choices are true, which one would most effectively conclude this paragraph while leading into the main focus of the next paragraph?
A. NO CHANGE
B. Even since these early times, people have recognized the importance of keeping domesticated dogs.
C. Many argue that the dog has been as important to the unfolding of human history as has the horse.
D. The dog is a major subspecies of the wolf, and many features of its biological makeup are still similar to those of the wolf.

64. **F.** NO CHANGE
G. Unless
H. Because
J. Whether

companions. Dogs' agility and sense of smell still, to this day, help hunters to capture their prey. Dogs were also often used as protectors; <u>whose</u>[65] primary responsibility was to sit in front of a residence or place of gathering and scare away would-be robbers and evildoers. [B]

[4]

[1] Since the eighteenth century, <u>by way of example,</u>[66] dogs have been seen more as companions and family members than in such impersonal <u>roles</u>[67] as hunters or guardsmen. [2] From this date forward, the dog has increasingly filled the role of domesticated pet, and according to the American Pet Products Manufacturers Association, 39% of Americans currently own at least one dog, and there are no <u>fewer then</u>[68] 74 million owned dogs in the United States. [3] Inspired by the ideas of the Enlightenment, a social philosophy evolved that began to treat all individuals as social equals, and people's attitudes toward dogs <u>begins</u>[69] to take on a more personal character. [70] [4] Dogs came to be prized for their loyalty and sacrifice, and as early as 1855, many have suggested, the American English phrase "man's best friend" was already commonplace in the language. [71]

65. **A.** NO CHANGE
B. his
C. their
D. who

66. **F.** NO CHANGE
G. as a consequence,
H. by contrast,
J. moreover,

67. **A.** NO CHANGE
B. roles,
C. roles:
D. roles;

68. **F.** NO CHANGE
G. less then
H. lesser than
J. fewer than

69. **A.** NO CHANGE
B. is beginning
C. began
D. had began

70. If the writer were to delete the phrase "take on a more personal character" from the preceding sentence and replace it with the word "change," the essay would primarily lose:

F. an important description of a dog-breeding technique.
G. a detail that indicates how attitudes toward dogs have changed.
H. information that emphasizes the historical importance of dogs.
J. nothing, since this detail is the topic of the preceding paragraph.

71. For the sake of logic and coherence, Sentence 2 should be placed:

A. where it is now.
B. before Sentence 1.
C. after Sentence 3.
D. after Sentence 4.

[5]

It should be no surprise, then, given this long and progressive history of dog ownership, that people come to think of their dogs more and more as near-human members of their families. [C] Think about all the indispensable, yet underappreciated roles (72) that dogs play in our lives—they are not just our pets and "best friends"; they are also necessary to law enforcement, firefighters, and the visually impaired, to name just a few. [D] Although it may seem at first that dogs are just lazy pets, on the one hand (73) they are really much more than that.

Have a look (74) around and you'll find that dogs are an essential part of our modern society. So what if they've got their own hotels and day spas these days—don't you think they've earned them?

72. **F.** NO CHANGE
G. indispensable yet underappreciated
H. indispensable; yet underappreciated
J. indispensable yet underappreciated,

73. **A.** NO CHANGE
B. for example
C. in actuality
D. more often than not

74. **F.** NO CHANGE
G. Having a look
H. To look
J. Looking

Question 75 asks about the preceding passage as a whole.

75. Upon reviewing notes for this essay, the writer comes across some information and composes the following sentence, incorporating that information:

> Furthermore, many ancient civilizations, Greek and Egyptian among them, used trained war dogs to aid them in battle.

For the sake of logic and coherence of the essay, this sentence should be placed at:

A. Point A in Paragraph 2.
B. Point B in Paragraph 3.
C. Point C in Paragraph 5.
D. Point D in Paragraph 5.

English Practice Section 2
Answers and Explanations

ENGLISH PRACTICE SECTION 2 ANSWERS

1. A
2. F
3. C
4. J
5. C
6. H
7. C
8. G
9. D
10. J
11. C
12. F
13. D
14. G
15. C
16. H
17. A
18. H
19. C
20. H
21. C
22. G
23. C
24. H
25. B
26. F
27. C
28. G
29. C
30. F
31. A
32. J
33. B
34. F
35. C
36. G
37. D
38. G
39. D
40. H
41. C
42. J
43. B
44. H
45. A
46. G
47. D
48. J
49. D
50. F
51. D
52. F
53. C
54. G
55. C
56. H
57. C
58. H
59. A
60. H
61. D
62. J
63. B
64. F
65. C
66. H
67. A
68. J
69. C
70. G
71. D
72. G
73. C
74. F
75. B

ENGLISH PRACTICE SECTION 2 EXPLANATIONS

Passage I

1. **A** Prepositions change in the answer choices, so the question tests idioms. The phrase *born to former slaves* makes it clear that *Minerva and Owen Breedlove* were the parents, so keep (A). Both *born by* and *born under* would indicate location, which is not what this sentence discusses; eliminate (B) and (C). *Born for* would indicate a purpose, which is not what this sentence discusses; eliminate (D). The correct answer is (A).

2. **F** The length of the phrase describing *Sarah Breedlove* changes in the answer choices, so this question tests concision. An *age of six* indicates a *child,* so there is no need to use both terms. Eliminate (G) and (H). *Six years old* is both *young* and an *age,* so there is no need to repeat those ideas; eliminate (J). Choice (F) is concise and makes the meaning of the sentence clear. The correct answer is (F).

3. **C** Note the question! The question asks whether a sentence should be added to the end of the paragraph, so it tests consistency. A sentence should be added only if it is consistent with the focus of the paragraph. The paragraph introduces *Sarah Breedlove,* who is the main subject of the passage. *Louis Armstrong* is not consistent with this focus, so the sentence should not be added. Eliminate (A) and (B). Choice (C) accurately states that *the role Louis Armstrong played in 1920s culture is irrelevant to the main topic of this essay.* The question of whether *the 1920s* were *significant* is not relevant to this essay, so eliminate (D). The correct answer is (C).

4. **J** Pronouns and apostrophes change in the answer choices, so this question tests consistency of pronouns and apostrophe usage. A pronoun must be consistent in number with the noun it refers to. The underlined pronoun refers to *St. Louis,* which is singular, so the pronoun should also be singular. Eliminate (H) because *their* is always plural on the ACT. Eliminate (F) because the word *its'* never occurs in English. *It's* is a contraction of "it is," which does not work in this context; eliminate (G). Choice (J) appropriately uses the possessive pronoun *its.* The correct answer is (J).

5. **C** Prepositions change in the answer choices, so the question tests idioms. Eliminate (A), (B), and (D), as none of them contains the correct idiomatic expression. Choice (C) makes it clear that the achievements described later in the sentence happened in the space of 10 years. The correct answer is (C).

6. **H** Punctuation changes in the answer choices, so this question tests how to connect ideas with the appropriate punctuation. The first part of the sentence, *Sarah undertook countless journeys to sell her formula door-to-door,* is an independent clause. The second part of the sentence, *as well as in churches and lodges,* is not an independent clause. Both periods and semicolons can only be used between two independent clauses, so eliminate (F) and (G). Choice (H) correctly uses a comma to separate the two parts of the sentence. A colon is used between an independent clause and a related list, definition, or explanation. The second part of the sentence is a continuation of the first part rather than a related explanation, so eliminate (J). The correct answer is (H).

7. **C** The length of the phrase describing Walker changes in the answer choices, so this question tests concision. All four answer choices express the same idea, but (C) is most concise. The correct answer is (C).

8. **G** Pronouns change in the answer choices, so this question could test consistency of pronouns. All the answer choices contain pronouns that are consistent with *women,* the noun that the underlined pronoun refers to. The first part of the sentence, *Sarah taught her methods to other women,* is an independent clause. As written, the second part of the sentence, *they focused on sales and became known as the "Walker Agents,"* is also an independent clause. Two independent clauses must be separated by some type of punctuation other than a comma, so eliminate (F). Choice (J) has the same problem, so eliminate (J) also. Changing the pronoun from *they* or *those* to *who* or *whom* changes the second part of the sentence. Changing the pronoun, as in both (G) and (H), makes the second part of the sentence no longer an independent clause. There is no need for the word *with* in the sentence, so eliminate (H). The correct answer is (G).

9. **D** Prepositions change in the answer choices, so the question tests idioms. Eliminate (A), (B), and (C), as none of them contains the correct idiomatic expression. Choice (D) makes it clear that Sarah provided guidance to the agents. The correct answer is (D).

10. **J** Punctuation changes in the answer choices, so this question tests how to connect ideas with the appropriate punctuation. The first part of the sentence, *Sarah called them "scalp specialists" and hair and beauty "culturists,"* is an independent clause. The second part of the sentence, *using these terms to emphasize the professional nature of the treatments,* is not an independent clause. A semicolon can only be used between two independent clauses, so eliminate (G). A colon is used between an independent clause and a related list, definition, or explanation. The second part of the sentence is a continuation of the first part rather than a related explanation, so eliminate (H). The second part of the sentence is descriptive information that is not necessary to the main meaning of the sentence, so it should be separated from the first part with a comma. Eliminate (F). The correct answer is (J).

11. **C** Note the question! The question asks for the answer that *provides the most effective transition from the preceding paragraph to this new one,* so it tests consistency. A transition must be consistent with the relationship between the ideas it connects. The previous paragraph discusses the *"Walker Agents,"* and the new paragraph describes the establishment of the Walker Company's headquarters in Indianapolis. Sarah's travel to *the Caribbean and to Central America* is not consistent with either paragraph, so eliminate (A). Sarah's *daughter A'Lelia* is also not relevant to either paragraph, so eliminate (B). Choice (C) provides an effective transition between the agents and other achievements of the Walker Company. *Josephine Baker* is not consistent with either paragraph, so eliminate (D). The correct answer is (C).

12. **F** Verbs change in the answer choices, so this question could test consistency of verbs. Eliminate (H) because *choosed* is an incorrect form of the verb "to choose." All the remaining answer choices are consistent with the subject, *Indianapolis,* so this question tests which form is most clear. The sentence uses *chosen* as an adjective to describe *Indianapolis,* not as a verb, so eliminate (G). Choice (F)

makes clear that the city was selected. Choice (J) makes it sound as if Indianapolis was making the decision, so eliminate (J). The correct answer is (F).

13. **D** Note the question! The question asks for the best placement for Sentence 2, so it tests consistency of ideas. The sentence must be consistent with the ideas that come both before and after it. Sentence 2 refers to *these charitable acts,* so it must come after a sentence that introduces the idea of *charitable acts.* Sentence 4 describes Sarah's *dedication to charitable causes,* so Sentence 2 must come after Sentence 4. The correct answer is (D).

14. **G** Punctuation changes in the answer choices, so this question tests how to connect ideas with the appropriate punctuation. The first part of the sentence, *She contributed the largest donation to the effort to save Frederick Douglass's home,* is an independent clause. The second part of the sentence, *maintaining the building as a historical museum,* is not an independent clause. A semicolon can only be used between two independent clauses, so eliminate (H). The word *maintaining* is necessary to the main meaning of the sentence and should not be set off by commas, so eliminate (F). Choice (G) appropriately uses a comma to separate the two parts of the sentence. There is no need for a comma after *maintaining,* so eliminate (J). The correct answer is (G).

15. **C** Note the question! The question asks whether the essay describes *the development of the beauty industry in the early part of the twentieth century,* so it tests consistency. Determine whether the essay is consistent with this idea. The essay focuses on one beauty company, not on the entire *industry,* so it is not consistent with the idea in the question. Eliminate (A) and (B). Choice (C) accurately describes the essay. The passage does not *describe other events taking place during this time,* so eliminate (D). The correct answer is (C).

Passage II

16. **H** Note the question! When a question asks which answer would *NOT* be acceptable, eliminate answers that **are** acceptable. Types of transitions change in the answer choices, so this question tests complete sentences. As written, the first (underlined) part of the sentence, *As my uncle and I finished our dinners,* is not an independent clause. The second (non-underlined) part of the sentence, *we were hardly saying a word,* is an independent clause. These two parts of the sentence are separated by a comma. Choices (F) and (J) retain this structure: the first part of the sentence starts with a conjunction (*while* or *as*), which makes it dependent on the second part of the sentence. Eliminate (F) and (J) because they are both acceptable alternatives. Choices (G) and (H) both remove the conjunction from the beginning of the sentence, which makes the first part, *My uncle and I finished our dinners* (or *...were almost finished eating*) an independent clause. A comma followed by *but* can be used to separate two independent clauses, so (G) is acceptable. Eliminate (G). Commas and the word *however* cannot be used to separate two independent clauses, so (H) is not acceptable. The correct answer is (H).

17. **A** The length of the phrase surrounding *celebration* changes in the answer choices, so this question tests concision. Choice (A) is concise and makes the meaning of the sentence clear. The phrase *just like always* means the same thing as *ordinary,* which is in the non-underlined portion of the sentence. There is no need to repeat this idea, so eliminate (B). The phrases *with nothing abnormal* and *traditional* also mean the same thing as *ordinary* in this context, so eliminate (C) and (D). The correct answer is (A).

18. **H** Note the question! The question asks for the sentence that is *LEAST* relevant to the passage, so it tests consistency. Eliminate the answer choices that **are** relevant to the passage. The paragraph describes the *ordinary birthday celebration* that the narrator had with his uncle just before he left for boot camp. Sentence 2 introduces the idea that the dinner mentioned in the first sentence was for a *birthday,* and the phrase *for the most part* sets up the idea that there is something slightly unusual about this dinner. Sentence 2 is relevant to the passage, so eliminate (F). Sentence 3 gives details about what the narrator and his uncle ate for dinner, and introduces the *dessert,* which is the turning point in the uncle's mood. Sentence 3 is relevant to the passage, so eliminate (G). Sentence 4 gives a general opinion about *banana splits* that is not relevant to the particular dinner described in the paragraph, so keep (H). Sentence 6 describes the shift in mood that was set up by the phrase *for the most part* in sentence 1. Sentence 6 is relevant, so eliminate (J). The correct answer is (H).

19. **C** Note the question! The question asks for the best placement for the underlined portion, so it tests consistency. The underlined portion must be consistent with the word or phrase it is next to. Where it is now, the underlined phrase describes the uncle, but it is the narrator who is *joining the army,* so eliminate (A). Choice (B) makes the same error, so eliminate (B) as well. Choice (C) appropriately places the phrase after the word *me,* to make it clear that it is the narrator who is *joining the army.* Choice (D) makes the comparison, indicated by *rather than* between *me* (that is, the narrator) and *joining the army.* These two things are not similar to each other and therefore cannot be compared. Eliminate (D). The correct answer is (C).

20. **H** Note the question! The question asks what would be lost if a phrase were deleted, so it tests consistency. Eliminate answer choices that are not consistent with the role of the phrase. The phrase is a descriptive phrase that gives more information about the narrator's *father.* The information is not *mentioned elsewhere in the paragraph,* so eliminate (F). The phrase does not state that the father was *considered a brave man,* so eliminate (G). The phrase provides a detail about the father that makes clear both why the narrator thinks his father *would have been proud* and why the uncle thinks that the father *would have felt even better about [the narrator] staying out of harm's way,* so (H) gives an accurate description of the phrase. There is no discussion of the narrator joining *the Polish army,* so eliminate (J). The correct answer is (H).

21. **C** Punctuation changes in the answer choices, so this question tests how to connect ideas with the appropriate punctuation. In this instance, the first part of the sentence, *He often asked me,* is not an independent clause. Both colons and dashes can only be used after an independent clause, so eliminate (A) and (D). There is no need to break up the sentence with a comma, so eliminate (B). The correct answer is (C).

22. **G** Comparison words change in the answer choices, so this question tests consistency. There is also the option to DELETE; consider this choice carefully as it's often the correct answer. The beginning of the sentence sets up a comparison, *My uncle has as many stories,* that is left incomplete if the underlined portion is deleted. Eliminate (J). The second part of the comparison must be consistent with the first part. Because the comparison starts with *as,* it must also end with *as.* Eliminate (F) and (H). The correct answer is (G).

23. **C** Note the question! The question asks whether a sentence should be added, so it tests consistency. A sentence should be added only if it is consistent with the focus of the paragraph. The paragraph describes the narrator's experience attending the carnival with his uncle. The new sentence makes a general statement about carnivals in Poland, so it is not consistent and should not be added. Eliminate (A) and (B). Choice (C) accurately states that the new sentence *does not help preserve the focus of this paragraph.* Eliminate (D) because the new sentence does not include *a detail that is mentioned elsewhere in the passage.* The correct answer is (C).

24. **H** Pronouns change in the answer choices, so this question tests consistency of pronouns. A pronoun must be consistent with other pronouns in the sentence. The non-underlined portion includes the first-person plural pronoun *ourselves,* so the underlined pronoun should also be first-person plural. Eliminate (F) because *One* is singular. Eliminate (G) because *You* is second person. Keep (H) because *We* is consistent with *ourselves.* Eliminate (J) because *They* is third person. The correct answer is (H).

25. **B** Punctuation changes in the answer choices, so this question tests how to connect ideas with the appropriate punctuation. The first part of the sentence, *At night, we would lie on the porch in the sleeping bags,* is an independent clause. The second part of the sentence, *my grandmother had bought, drink cocoa, and listen to the chorus of crickets,* is not an independent clause. A semicolon can only be used between two independent clauses, so eliminate (C). The phrase *my grandmother had bought* describes the *sleeping bags,* and should not be separated by a comma after *bags.* Eliminate (A) and (D). The correct answer is (B).

26. **F** Verbs change in the answer choices, so this question tests consistency of verbs. Verbs must be consistent in tense and form with other verbs in the sentence. The non-underlined verb *lie* is in present tense, so the underlined verbs should also be in present tense. Choice (F) has both verbs in present tense. Eliminate (G) and (H) because *drank* is past tense. Eliminate (J) because there is no need for the *-ing* ending on *listen.* The correct answer is (F).

27. **C** Verbs change in the answer choices, so this question tests consistency of verbs. A verb must be consistent in tense with other verbs in the paragraph. The previous sentence contains a list of verbs that begins with *would lie,* so the underlined verb should also contain *would* followed by a present tense verb. Eliminate (A), (B), and (D) because none of them contain *would.* The correct answer is (C).

28. **G** Note the question! The question asks for the best placement for a new sentence, so it tests consistency of ideas. The sentence must be consistent with the ideas that come both before and after it.

The new sentence introduces the idea of a *vacation home on Lake Drawsko.* Sentence 6 discusses *canoes and swimming races,* so the lake should be introduced before the water activities are discussed. The correct answer is (G).

29. **C** Pronouns and apostrophes change in the answer choices, so this question tests pronoun consistency and apostrophe usage. A pronoun must be consistent in number with the noun it refers to. The underlined pronoun refers to *Poland,* which is singular, so the underlined pronoun should also be singular. Eliminate (D) because *their* is always plural on the ACT. The word *its'* never occurs in English, so eliminate (B). *It's* is a contraction of *it is,* which is not necessary here, so eliminate (A). Choice (C) is the possessive form of *it,* which is what the sentence requires. The correct answer is (C).

30. **F** Note the question! The question asks for *the most logical transition* between sentences, so it tests consistency. A transition must be consistent with the ideas it connects. The previous sentence says that *America gave my uncle an opportunity,* and the sentence with the transition lists the things the narrator was *exposed to…as an American child.* Choice (F) maintains the focus of both sentences on *America,* so keep (F). *Pittsburgh* is mentioned only in the first sentence, so eliminate (G) and (J). The uncle's job is also mentioned only in the first sentence, so eliminate (H). The correct answer is (F).

Passage III

31. **A** Verbs change in the answer choices, so this question tests consistency of verbs. A verb must be consistent in tense with the rest of the sentence. The other verb in the sentence, *struggled,* is in past tense, so the underlined verb should also be in past tense. Eliminate (B) and (C) because they are both in present tense. The difference between (A) and (D) is past perfect versus present perfect tense. Present perfect tense is used to describe an action that started in the past and continues to the present, while past perfect is used to describe an action that started in the past and then stopped. The underlined verb is an action that took place before the narrator went to China, so the action ended in the past. Choice (A) has the appropriate tense. Eliminate (D) because *have studied* is present perfect. The correct answer is (A).

32. **J** Verbs change in the answer choices, so this question tests consistency of verbs. A verb must be consistent in tense with other verbs in the sentence. The underlined portion is the second part of a comparison. The verb in the first part of the comparison is *enduring,* so the underlined verb should also have an *-ing* ending. Eliminate (F) because it does not have an *-ing* ending. Eliminate (H) because there is no need for the extra word *having.* The difference between (G) and (J) is *when* versus *as. As* makes the comparison consistent with the non-underlined phrase *just as difficult,* so eliminate (G). The correct answer is (J).

33. **B** The length of the phrase changes in the answer choices, so this question tests concision. *All the while* and *at the same time* mean the same thing, so there is no need to use both terms. Eliminate (A) and (C). The additional words in (D) do not make the meaning of the sentence clearer, so eliminate (D). Choice (B) is concise and makes the meaning of the sentence clear. The correct answer is (B).

34. **F** Note the question! The question asks for the answer that *would most clearly and effectively express the obviousness of the best method of adaptation,* so it tests consistency. Eliminate answers that are inconsistent with the purpose stated in the question. Neither *doubtful* nor *obscure* is consistent with the idea of *obvious,* so eliminate (H) and (J). *Noticeable* could mean *obvious,* but *right under my nose* is a stronger statement of *obviousness.* Eliminate (G). The correct answer is (F).

35. **C** Prepositions change in the answer choices, so this question tests idioms. The correct idiom is *taken a…liking to,* not *taken a…liking of,* so eliminate (A) and (B). The difference between (C) and (D) is the adjective *quick* versus the adverb *quickly.* The word is used to describe the noun *a liking.* Adjectives are used to describe nouns, so eliminate (D). The correct answer is (C).

36. **G** The answer choices contain options to start a new paragraph or not, so this question tests consistency of ideas. A new paragraph should begin when a new idea is introduced, so read the sentences before and after the proposed break to determine whether a new idea is introduced. The previous sentence says that the narrator *hadn't accepted* her co-workers' invitations *out of fear of being unable to communicate,* and that her *feelings of guilt at having turned down so many kind invitations eventually outweighed that fear.* The sentence that begins with the underlined portion says that she *acquiesced one night.* Both sentences focus on the narrator finally accepting an invitation, so there is no need for a new paragraph. Eliminate (H) and (J). There is no need to include the word *when,* so eliminate (F). The correct answer is (G).

37. **D** The length of the phrase surrounding *memorable* changes in the answer choices, so this question tests concision. *Memorable* and *unforgettable* or *hard to forget* mean the same thing in this context, so there is no need to use both terms. Eliminate (A) and (B). The additional words in (C) do not make the meaning of the sentence clearer, so eliminate (C). Choice (D) is concise and makes the meaning of the sentence clear. The correct answer is (D).

38. **G** Punctuation changes in the answer choices, so this question tests how to connect ideas with the appropriate punctuation. The first part of the sentence, *Everyone seemed surprised,* is an independent clause. The second part of the sentence, *impressed by the variety of dishes I could order,* is not an independent clause. A semicolon can only be used between two independent clauses, so eliminate (J). A comma followed by the coordinating conjunction *and* can also only be used between two independent clauses, so eliminate (F). There is no need for a comma after *seemed,* as the second part of the sentence continues the idea begun in the first part. Eliminate (H). The correct answer is (G).

39. **D** The question asks whether a sentence should be added to the paragraph, so it tests consistency. A sentence should be added only if it is consistent with the focus of the paragraph. The paragraph discusses what the narrator and her friends did on the night she first went out with them. Although they went to a *karaoke house,* the origins of karaoke are not relevant to the paragraph. Eliminate (A) and (B). The new sentence does not *repeat a detail stated earlier,* so eliminate (C). Choice (D) accurately states that the new sentence *doesn't add to the focus of this paragraph.* The correct answer is (D).

40. **H** Commas change in the answer choices, so this question tests comma usage. The word *as* cannot be removed from the sentence on its own, so it should not be set off by commas; eliminate (J). The entire phrase *as karaoke often provides* is not necessary to the main meaning of the sentence, so it should be set off from the rest of the sentence with commas. Eliminate (F) and (G) because neither has a comma before *as*. The correct answer is (H).

41. **C** Apostrophes change in the answer choices, so this question tests apostrophe usage. A noun with an apostrophe shows possession. Since the *number* belongs to the *song,* an apostrophe is needed; eliminate (A). Choice (D) is an incorrect version of the plural possessive, so eliminate (D). The difference between (B) and (C) is singular versus plural possessive. The sentence specifies that the narrator had chosen *a song,* so the singular possessive is needed. Eliminate (B) because *songs'* is plural. The correct answer is (C).

42. **J** Note the question! The question asks what would be lost if a sentence were deleted, so it tests consistency. Eliminate answer choices that are not consistent with the sentence. The sentence says that the narrator's friends *could only assume that I had just unreasonably insulted our female coworker.* This is not *a repetition of the main theme of the essay,* so eliminate (F). Eliminate (G) because the sentence describes the friends' reaction to the narrator's error, it does not give *another example of slang errors.* Eliminate (H) because there is no *contrast* between this sentence and *the paragraph's opening sentence.* Choice (J) accurately states that the sentence describes *how the rest of the party reacted to the author's mistake.* The correct answer is (J).

43. **B** The length of the phrase changes in the answer choices, so this question tests concision. Choice (D) is the shortest option, but it removes the subject of the sentence, which makes the sentence incomplete. Eliminate (D). Choice (C) does not make clear that it was the narrator who *learned a valuable lesson,* so eliminate (C). Choices (A) and (B) both make the meaning of the sentence clear, but (B) is more concise. Eliminate (A). The correct answer is (B).

44. **H** Note the question! The question asks for the answer that emphasizes *the benefit of learning slang expressions in a new language,* so it tests consistency. Eliminate answers that are inconsistent with the purpose stated in the question. Choice (F) says that slang is *difficult to understand,* which is not a *benefit,* so eliminate (F). Choices (G) and (J) both discuss how frequently slang is used, which could be understood as a *benefit.* Choice (H) states that understanding slang *can help to avoid cultural misunderstandings,* which is a direct statement of a *benefit.* Eliminate (G) and (J) because (H) more directly matches the purpose stated in the question. The correct answer is (H).

45. **A** Note the question! The question asks for the answer that best *summarizes the main point of the essay as illustrated by the narrator's miscommunication experience,* so it tests consistency. Eliminate answers that are inconsistent with the purpose stated in the question. The narrator was *being social* when the mishap took place, so keep (A). The narrator did not *intentionally insult* anyone, so eliminate (B). It may have been at night that the mishap took place, but the focus of the passage was more on the narrator interacting with her friends than on the time of day; eliminate (C). The narrator was not *in an isolated environment,* so eliminate (D). The correct answer is (A).

Passage IV

46. **G** Commas change in the answer choices, so this question tests comma usage. The word *Pennsylvania* is necessary to the main meaning of the sentence, so it should not be set off by commas. Eliminate (F) and (J). Although *Pennsylvania hills* is in a list, there are only two items in the list. A comma is used before the *and* at the end of a list only if there are three or more items in the list; eliminate (H). The correct answer is (G).

47. **D** Note the question! When a question asks which answer would *NOT* be acceptable, eliminate answers that **are** acceptable. Transitions change in the answer choices, so this question could test consistency of ideas. All of the answer choices express the same idea, that there was a sequence of events in time. Choices (A), (B), and (C) are all acceptable alternatives, so eliminate (A), (B), and (C). Choice (D), *In following,* is idiomatically incorrect, so it is not an acceptable alternative. The correct answer is (D).

48. **J** Pronouns change in the answer choices, so this question tests consistency of pronouns. A pronoun must be consistent with other pronouns in the sentence. The sentence contains the first-person singular pronoun *I,* so the underlined pronoun should also be first-person singular. Eliminate (F), (G), and (H) because none of them contains a first-person pronoun. Choice (J) contains the first-person pronoun *my.* The correct answer is (J).

49. **D** The length of the phrase surrounding *distances* changes in the answer choices, so this question tests concision. *Shortest* and *smallest* express the same idea, so there is no need to use both words; eliminate (B). *Not long* means the same thing as *shortest,* so there is no need to use both those terms; eliminate (C). Including the phrase *in length* does not make the meaning of the sentence clearer, so eliminate (A). Choice (D) is concise and makes the meaning of the sentence clear. The correct answer is (D).

50. **F** Prepositions change in the answer choices, so the question tests idioms. The correct idiom is to *move out on my own,* not to *move in on my own,* so eliminate (H) and (J). The reflexive pronoun *myself* should be used only if *I* is both the subject and object of the verb. In this sentence, *I* is the subject of *moved out,* but there is no object. There is no reason to use *myself,* so eliminate (G). The correct answer is (F).

51. **D** Verbs change in the answer choices, so this question tests consistency of verbs. A verb must be consistent in number with its subject. The subject of the underlined verb is *bundles of money,* which is plural, so the underlined verb should also be plural. Eliminate (A) and (C) because they both contain the singular verb *was.* Choice (B) changes the meaning of the phrase in a way that makes the sentence unclear; eliminate (B). Choice (D) contains the appropriate verb and makes the meaning of the sentence clear. The correct answer is (D).

52. **F** Note the question! The question asks what would be lost if a phrase were deleted, so it tests consistency. Eliminate answer choices that are not consistent with the role of the phrase. The phrase refers to a specific *place.* Choice (F) accurately describes the role of the phrase; the first part of the sentence describes a *quick...drive where I grew up,* which is contrasted to *a two-hour drive...in this new place.* The phrase does not describe *the purpose of the author's move,* so eliminate (G). The phrase *two-hour drive* contrasts with *a quick 30-minute drive,* but the phrase in question is not about time; eliminate (H). *The place mentioned in Paragraph 1* is where the author grew up, not *this new place;* eliminate (J). The correct answer is (F).

53. **C** The length of the phrase surrounding *resolved* changes in the answer choices, so this question tests concision. *Resolved* and *decided* mean the same thing in this context, so there is no need to use both words. Eliminate (A), (B), and (D). Choice (C) is concise and makes the meaning of the sentence clear. The correct answer is (C).

54. **G** Transitions change in the answer choices, so this question tests consistency of ideas. A transition must be consistent with the relationship between the ideas it connects. The first part of the sentence says that the narrator *entered the attic with a flashlight,* and the second part describes her fighting *fear and cobwebs.* There is no contrast between the two parts of the sentence, so eliminate (F), which contains the contrasting transition *even if.* There is also no causal relationship between the two parts of the sentence so eliminate *because* in (H). The verb tense in (J) is not consistent with the simple past tense verb *entered* in the non-underlined portion of the sentence; eliminate (J). Choice (G) uses *fighting* to make it clear that the second part of the sentence describes what the narrator did when she *entered the attic.* The correct answer is (G).

55. **C** Apostrophes change in the answer choices, so this question tests apostrophe usage. A noun with an apostrophe shows possession. Since nothing belongs to the *gold-rushers,* there is no need for an apostrophe. Eliminate (A) and (B). There is no need to include a comma after *gold-rushers,* so eliminate (D). The correct answer is (C).

56. **H** Prepositions change in the answer choices, so the question tests idioms. The correct idiom is *began to* do something, so eliminate (F) and (J). The phrase *began to riding* is idiomatically incorrect, so eliminate (G). Choice (H) is idiomatically correct and makes the meaning of the sentence clear. The correct answer is (H).

57. **C** The length of the phrase changes in the answer choices, so this question tests concision. The sentence contains a list of things the narrator *had been freed from.* The items in the list are *four-dollar-a-gallon gas, traffic jams,* and *the interminable wait at the bus stop.* The phrase *freed from* at the beginning of the list refers to all three things, so there is no need to repeat it. Eliminate (A), (B), and (D). Choice (C) is concise and makes the items in the list consistent with one another. The correct answer is (C).

58. **H** Punctuation changes in the answer choices, so this question tests how to connect ideas with the appropriate punctuation. The first part of the sentence, *I realized then that I had regained that freedom I had enjoyed so much when I was younger,* is an independent clause. The second part of the sentence, *in my first apartment, this freedom had taken on a different character,* is also an independent clause. Two independent clauses must be separated by some kind of punctuation other than a comma; eliminate (F) and (J). There is no need to add the word *furthermore* to the sentence; eliminate (G). Choice (H) correctly uses a period to separate the two independent clauses. The correct answer is (H).

59. **A** Note the question! The question asks for *the most effective transition* between sentences, so it tests consistency. A transition must be consistent with the ideas it connects. The sentence with the underlined transition introduces the idea of *freedom* with a *different character.* The following sentence describes the new character of the freedom. Choice (A) describes what the freedom had been previously, so it is consistent with both sentences. Choice (B) describes what the narrator means by *character,* which is not relevant to the second sentence; eliminate (B). Choices (C) and (D) both refer to the narrator's bike but do not mention anything about *freedom.* Eliminate (C) and (D). The correct answer is (A).

60. **H** Note the question! The question asks whether the essay describes *the transportation options for visitors to a major city,* so it tests consistency. Determine whether the essay is consistent with this idea. The essay focuses on the narrator's transportation options, not on *visitors to a major city,* so it is not consistent with the idea in the question. Eliminate (F) and (G). Choice (H) accurately describes the essay. The passage does not discuss the *superiority* of *driving,* so eliminate (J). The correct answer is (H).

Passage V

61. **D** Types of transitions change in the answer choices, so this question tests complete sentences. The first part of the sentence, *Though once it was considered extravagant to put a sweater or a pair of shoes on a dog,* is not an independent clause. The second part of the sentence as written, *that it is almost to the point now that it is considered an abuse not to dress your dog for cold weather,* is also not an independent clause. These two clauses together do not make a complete sentence, so eliminate (A). Removing the word *that* from the beginning of the second part of the sentence turns it into an independent clause, but a comma followed by *and* can only be used between two independent clauses, so eliminate (B). There is no reason to include the word *and,* so eliminate (C). Choice (D) appropriately separates the two parts of the sentence with a comma. The correct answer is (D).

62. **J** Note the question! When a question asks which answer would *NOT* be acceptable, eliminate answers that **are** acceptable. Verbs change in the answer choices, so this question tests consistency of verbs. Verbs must be consistent in tense and form with other verbs in the sentence. The other verb in the first part of the sentence, *are,* is in present tense. (F) and (H) are both in present tense and

are therefore acceptable; eliminate (F) and (H). Although (G) is in the present perfect tense, it is also an acceptable alternative because present perfect describes an action that began in the past but continues in the present. Eliminate (G). Choice (J) makes the sentence incomplete, so it is not acceptable. The correct answer is (J).

63. **B** Note the question! The question asks for the answer that *most effectively concludes this paragraph while leading into the main focus of the next paragraph,* so it tests consistency. A transition must be consistent with the relationship between the ideas it connects. This paragraph discusses archaeological and historical evidence about dogs, and the next paragraph discusses the reasons that dogs *have been bred and domesticated.* The number of different breeds is not consistent with these ideas, so eliminate (A). *Early times* is consistent with this paragraph, while *the importance of keeping domesticated dogs* leads into the next paragraph, so keep (B). *The horse* is not relevant to either paragraph, so eliminate (C). The *biological makeup* of the dog and its similarity to that of *the wolf* is not relevant to either paragraph, so eliminate (D). The correct answer is (B).

64. **F** Transitions change in the answer choices, so this question tests consistency of ideas. A transition must be consistent with the relationship between the ideas it connects. The first part of the sentence says that there are *many reasons* that *dogs have been bred and domesticated,* and the second part says what the *primary reason* is. There is a contrast between the two ideas, so keep (F). Neither statement is untrue, as *unless* would indicate, so eliminate (G). There is not a cause/effect relationship between the ideas, as *because* would indicate, so eliminate (H). There is not a choice between two things, as *whether* would indicate, so eliminate (J). The correct answer is (F).

65. **C** Pronouns change in the answer choices, so this question tests consistency of pronouns. A pronoun must be consistent with the noun it refers to. The underlined pronoun refers to *dogs,* which is plural, so the underlined pronoun should also be plural. The words *who* and *whose* can only be used to refer to people, so eliminate (A) and (D). *His* is singular, so eliminate (B). The correct answer is (C).

66. **H** Transitions change in the answer choices, so this question tests consistency of ideas. A transition must be consistent with the relationship between the ideas it connects. The previous sentence discusses dogs' roles as *protectors.* The sentence with the transition says that they were *seen more as companions and family members.* There is a contrast between these two ideas, so eliminate (F), (G), and (J), which all contain transitions that indicate agreement between ideas. Choice (H) appropriately indicates a *contrast.* The correct answer is (H).

67. **A** Punctuation changes in the answer choices, so this question tests how to connect ideas with the appropriate punctuation. The first part of the sentence, *Since the eighteenth century, by contrast, dogs have been seen more as companions and family members than in such impersonal roles,* is an independent clause. The second part of the sentence, *as hunters or guardsmen,* is not an independent clause. A semicolon can only be used between two independent clauses, so eliminate (D). The second part of the sentence is a continuation of *such impersonal roles* in the first part, so there is no need to separate the two parts with any punctuation; eliminate (B) and (C). The correct answer is (A).

68. **J** The words *then* and *than* change in the answer choices, so this question tests frequently confused words. Eliminate answer choices with the incorrect meaning. *Then* is used to indicate time, while *than* is used in a comparison. There is a comparison in this sentence, so *than* is the appropriate word. Eliminate (F) and (G). The difference between (H) and (J) is *lesser* versus *fewer. Fewer* is the idiomatically correct word in this context, so eliminate (H). The correct answer is (J).

69. **C** Verbs change in the answer choices, so this question tests consistency of verbs. A verb must be consistent in number with its subject. The subject of the underlined verb is *attitudes,* which is plural, so the underlined verb should also be plural. Eliminate (A) and (B) because they both contain singular verbs. Choice (C) appropriately contains a plural verb. Eliminate (D) because *had began* is an incorrect form of the past perfect tense. The correct answer is (C).

70. **G** Note the question! The question asks what would be lost if a phrase were deleted, so it tests consistency. Eliminate answer choices that are not consistent with the role of the phrase. The phrase gives more details about how *people's attitudes towards dogs* changed. Eliminate (F) because there is nothing about *dog breeding* in the phrase. Choice (G) accurately describes the phrase. The phrase does not discuss the *historical importance* of dogs, so eliminate (H). The phrase does not repeat *the topic of the preceding paragraph,* so eliminate (J). The correct answer is (G).

71. **D** Note the question! The question asks for the best placement for Sentence 2, so it tests consistency of ideas. The sentence must be consistent with the ideas that come both before and after it. Sentence 2 refers to a date (*from this date forward*), so it must come after some mention of a specific date. In this paragraph, only Sentence 4 includes a date (*1855*), so Sentence 2 must come after Sentence 4. The correct answer is (D).

72. **G** Punctuation changes in the answer choices, so this question tests how to connect ideas with the appropriate punctuation. The first part of the sentence, *Think about all the indispensable,* is not an independent clause. The second part of the sentence (up to the dash), *yet underappreciated roles that dogs play in our lives,* is an independent clause. A semicolon can only be used between two independent clauses, so eliminate (H). The word *underappreciated* describes *roles,* which comes immediately after it, so there is no reason to put a comma between them; eliminate (J). There is no reason to include only one comma in the sentence after *underappreciated,* so eliminate (F). The correct answer is (G).

73. **C** Transitions change in the answer choices, so this question tests consistency of ideas. A transition must be consistent with the relationship between the ideas it connects. The first part of the sentence says *Although it may seem…that dogs are just lazy pets,* and the second part says *they are really much more than that.* The word *Although* at the beginning of the sentence indicates a contrast between the two parts. *On the one hand* is used to introduce the first part of a contrast, but the underlined portion introduces the second part; eliminate (A). *For example* indicates that ideas agree, so eliminate (B). *In actuality* provides a contrast to *it may seem* in the first part of the sentence, so keep (C). There is no indication that the idea in the second part of the sentence is true only some of the time, as *more often than not* would indicate, so eliminate (D). The correct answer is (C).

74. **F** Verbs change in the answer choices, so this question tests consistency of verbs. A verb must be consistent in tense and form with other verbs in the paragraph. The paragraph is in present tense, and all the answer choices are also in present tense. Changing the verb to an *-ing* form, however, makes the sentence incomplete; eliminate (G) and (J). Choice (H) also makes the sentence incomplete; eliminate (H). Choice (F) makes the sentence complete. The correct answer is (F).

75. **B** Note the question! The question asks for the best placement for the new sentence, so it tests consistency of ideas. The sentence must be consistent with the ideas that come both before and after it. The new sentence says that *ancient civilizations…used trained war dogs to aid them in battle.* Paragraph 2 discusses archaeological and historical evidence of dogs, but not their roles, so eliminate (A). Paragraph 3 discusses the roles of dogs, and in particular their roles as *hunting companions* and *protectors.* The new sentence is consistent with these ideas, so keep (B). Paragraph 5 discusses dogs' part in *modern society,* so eliminate (C) and (D). The correct answer is (B).

English Practice Section 3

ENGLISH TEST

45 Minutes—75 Questions

DIRECTIONS: In the five passages that follow, certain words and phrases are underlined and numbered. In the right-hand column, you will find alternatives for each underlined part. In most cases, you are to choose the one that best expresses the idea, makes the statement appropriate for standard written English, or is worded most consistently with the style and tone of the passage as a whole. If you think the original version is best, choose "NO CHANGE." In some cases, you will find in the right-hand column a question about the underlined part. You are to choose the best answer to the question.

You will also find questions about a section of the passage or the passage as a whole. These questions do not refer to an underlined portion of the passage but rather are identified by a number or numbers in a box.

For each question, choose the alternative you consider best and blacken the corresponding oval on your answer document. Read each passage through once before you begin to answer the questions that accompany it. For many of the questions, you must read several sentences beyond the question to determine the answer. Be sure that you have read far enough ahead each time you choose an alternative.

Passage I

André Bazin's Nouvelle Vague

André Bazin died on November 11, 1958 after over 15 years of pioneering work in film criticism. His magazine, *Cahiers du Cinéma* (Cinema Notebooks), had been issued regularly since its founding in 1951, and it had become the premier journal in French for the serious discussion of films. Bazin, working and living in Paris, had become one of the cities [1] premier intellectuals. Despite all of the achievements of Bazin's lifetime, the true fruit of his labor did not begin to become truly apparent until the year following Bazin's death. It was in 1959 in Paris [2] that the *nouvelle vague* (new wave) in French cinema exploded [3] onto the international film scene.

Bazin published his first piece of film criticism in 1943 and pioneered a new way of writing about film, he [4] championed the idea that cinema was the "seventh art," every bit as deserving

1. **A.** NO CHANGE
   B. citys
   C. cities'
   D. city's

2. **F.** NO CHANGE
   G. in 1959 in Paris,
   H. in 1959, in Paris
   J. in, 1959 in Paris,

3. Which of the following alternatives to the underlined portion is LEAST acceptable?
   A. emerged
   B. released
   C. erupted
   D. burst

4. **F.** NO CHANGE
   G. film. He
   H. film he
   J. film. Although he

as the more respected arts of: architecture, [5] poetry, dance, music, painting, and sculpture. Many before Bazin's time thought of the cinema as a simple extension of another art form: theatre. In fact, in many early writings about film, it is not uncommon to hear the authors speak of film. [6] Bazin, though, sought to show that the cinema had every bit as much creative vitality and craftsmanship as any of the other six arts. From this fundamental belief came what was possibly Bazin's greatest contribution to film criticism: *auteur* theory. [7]

Auteur is the French word for *author*, and the suggestion contained in both the word and Bazin's theory is that every film is "authored" by a single mind just as a novel or poem is the work of a single author. For Bazin, and the increasingly influential group of critics working with him at the *Cahiers du Cinéma*, the author of any film is its director, and to discern a director's true style, perspective, or his sense of voice, [8] the critic has merely to watch a group of the director's films with an eye to similarities between them. Accordingly, Bazin and the *Cahiers* group were truly the first to discuss films and the practice of cinema in general as the masterwork of directors, rather than screenwriters or actors. With *auteur* theory, nonetheless, [9] Bazin created a new way of looking at

5. **A.** NO CHANGE
   B. of, architecture,
   C. of architecture,
   D. of, architecture

6. The writer is considering adding the following phrase to the end of the preceding sentence (deleting the period after the word *film*):

   as a second-class substitute for the "legitimate theatre."

   Should the writer make this addition there?

   F. Yes, because it clarifies the sentence to show more specifically how critics talked about film.
   G. Yes, because it helps the reader to understand more clearly the subjects of Bazin's writing.
   H. No, because it fails to maintain this paragraph's focus on the *Cahiers du Cinéma.*
   J. No, because it speaks disparagingly about the practice of filmmaking.

7. At this point the writer is considering adding the following true statement:

   Bazin's work is available in a text commonly read in Film Studies classes, the collection *What Is Cinema?*

   Should the writer make this addition here?

   A. Yes, because it maintains the essay's focus on an important figure in French film criticism.
   B. Yes, because it gives a good sense of the type of reading students can expect in Film Studies classes.
   C. No, because it interrupts the discussion of a specific theory of Bazin's.
   D. No, because other information in the essay suggests that this statement is untrue.

8. **F.** NO CHANGE
   G. the director's voice,
   H. his voice,
   J. voice,

9. **A.** NO CHANGE
   B. meanwhile,
   C. still,
   D. DELETE the underlined portion.

films, and his early works on[10] such influential directors as Orson Welles, Vittorio de Sica, and Jean Renoir—remain, to this day, pioneering works of film criticism that are studied and emulated by film critics today. [11]

Bazin's greatest achievement was the strong impression he left on a young generation of French filmmakers and critics who came on to the international scene all over the world[12] just a year after Bazin's death. In 1959, two films changed the landscape of international filmmaking:[13] François Truffaut's *The 400 Blows* and Jean-Luc Godard's *Breathless*. In each film, the director has taken Bazin's emphasis on *auteur* filmmaking to heart, and in every frame, the viewer is reminded of the director's presence by the overwhelming stylistic personality of shots and scenes. Throughout the 1960s and 1970s, independent and avant-garde filmmakers in places as disparate as France, the United States, Italy, and Japan were beginning to exercise the new cinematic freedom that Bazin had charted for them. At that time,[14] whenever a national film industry completely reinvents itself, it is carried along by a group of *auteur* directors who refer to their films as part of a *new wave*. Now there are legions of filmmakers, Mohsen Makhmalbaf and Abbas Kiarostami in Iran or Alfonso Cuaron and Guillermo del Toro in Mexico, for example, whose inspiration can in some way be traced back to Bazin and his humble work as editor of the *Cahiers du Cinéma* in France way back in the 1950s.

10. **F.** NO CHANGE
G. works, on
H. works: on
J. works—on

11. Which of the following sentences, if added here, would effectively conclude this paragraph and introduce the topic of the next?
A. Bazin himself never made any films, but he always preferred the Italian Neorealist style.
B. While Bazin's magazine was the place to read about classic films, Henri Langlois's *Cinematheque* was the place to see them.
C. Despite these great written achievements in the *Cahiers du Cinéma*, Bazin's true and lasting influence lay elsewhere.
D. Many film critics working in the later part of the twentieth century, such as Christian Metz and Gilles Deleuze, are clearly indebted to Bazin.

12. **F.** NO CHANGE
G. in all parts of the world
H. in every nation and country
J. DELETE the underlined portion.

13. Which choice would most effectively guide readers to understand the great importance of the two films discussed?
A. NO CHANGE
B. came out around the same time:
C. joined the long list of films shot primarily in Paris:
D. were created by directors who knew Bazin personally:

14. **F.** NO CHANGE
G. Back then,
H. Even now,
J. In the end,

Question 15 asks about the preceding passage as a whole.

15. Suppose the author intended to write an essay that illustrates how the writings of one film critic have had an influence beyond the realm of film criticism. Would this essay successfully fulfill that goal?

A. Yes, because the essay describes Bazin's influence on the six arts of architecture, poetry, dance, music, painting, and sculpture.
B. Yes, because the essay describes Bazin's influence on both film criticism and filmmaking.
C. No, because the essay discusses *auteur* theory and French films in general.
D. No, because the essay states that Bazin's greatest achievements were as a filmmaker.

Passage II

Preventing Biblioemergencies

Before I move next week, I will unwillingly return the books that I have checked out from the library. Sadly, I never even opened a couple of them, and the return of [16] them will be painfully abrupt. [17]

16. F. NO CHANGE
G. returning
H. to have returned
J. returned

17. If the writer were to delete the words *unwillingly, sadly,* and *painfully* from this paragraph, the paragraph would primarily lose:

A. evidence undermining the author's later assertion that she loves to read.
B. the sense that the author is unhappy about her move.
C. an explanation of the motive behind the writer's intended actions.
D. its emphasis on the writer's reluctance to lose any books.

I know that I have plenty [18] of other books to read. There are at least ten unread books of my own at home and ten more that I'm expecting in the mail. Still, whenever I return a book, I get that feeling of "*what if*": What if I run out of books?

18. Which of the following alternatives to the underlined portion would NOT be acceptable?

F. a lot
G. a number
H. numerous
J. a bunch

Some friends of mine recently coined the phrase *biblioemergency* to describe just such a situation. A *biblioemergency* is when an avid reader, such as myself, discovers that she has nothing left to read, which I know that to some people that's no big deal, but to me its a disaster.

Ever since childhood, I've made it a point to carry at least one extra book sometimes two or more. People ask me why I can't just make do with an extra book in my bag. But, I always point out, what if I finish them? What would I do then?

I think this all comes from a habit developed at an early age, due to my parents' use of books as pacifiers. Whenever my mother took me to a store or to an appointment, she brought along books. As soon as I got fidgety, she'd supply me with a new book to keep me entertained, hopefully until she had finished her business. [25] Now as an adult, I nevertheless find it nearly impossible to wait patiently unless I have reading material.

19 A. NO CHANGE
B. read.
C. read that
D. read,

20. F. NO CHANGE
G. theirs
H. they're
J. it's

21. A. NO CHANGE
B. book,
C. book:
D. book;

22. F. NO CHANGE
G. the book I'm reading
H. it
J. those

23. A. NO CHANGE
B. parents
C. parents's
D. parent

24. F. NO CHANGE
G. I got fidgety
H. After fidgeting,
J. Getting fidgety,

25. At this point, the author is considering adding the following sentence.

The best ones were the ones that had both pictures and words.

If the information is taken to be true, should the author make this addition here?

A. Yes, because it gives more information that is relevant to the previous comment.
B. Yes, because it adds a detail that explains the main idea of the paragraph.
C. No, because it contradicts information given in an earlier paragraph.
D. No, because it is offensive and irrelevant to the passage as a whole.

26. F. NO CHANGE
G. yet
H. conversely
J. consequently

[1] When I've run out of books in the past, finding myself reading the backs of cereal boxes or the labels on my clothes. [2] Even though I will have to return my books to the library, I plan to packing at least four or five in my carry-on luggage, as I do every time I travel. [3] That, my friend, is an experience I never need to repeat. [4] If that sounds like a hassle, imagine the alternative. [29]

27. A. NO CHANGE
B. being that I've found
C. I've found
D. having found

28. F. NO CHANGE
G. have been packing
H. pack
J. be packing

29. Which of the following sequences of sentences makes this paragraph the most logical?
A. NO CHANGE
B. 2, 4, 1, 3
C. 3, 1, 2, 4
D. 4, 1, 2, 3

Question 30 asks about the preceding passage as a whole.

30. Upon reviewing the essay, the writer is considering removing the final paragraph. Should that paragraph be kept or deleted?
F. Kept, because it returns to the opening idea and provides a conclusion.
G. Kept, because it reveals the writer's true motivation for refusing to return the books.
H. Deleted, because it distracts from the focus of the passage.
J. Deleted, because it repeats information already given without adding any new elements.

Passage III

The Space Race

[1]

Writer and political commentator Robert Heinlein, writing about politics, stated that mankind needs to venture out into space as a matter of necessity: "The Earth is just too small and fragile a basket for the human race to keep all its eggs in." In the 1960s, the Russians and the Americans were in a fierce political competition with one another, and this competition was

31. A. NO CHANGE
B. Heinlein
C. Heinlein who was writing about politics
D. Heinlein—writing about politics—

the backdrop for the explosive race to the moon. [32] However, this was only the first step from <u>our world</u> (33) on Earth toward outer space. A longer-lasting, and some say more important, achievement has been the development of the *International Space Station.*

[2]

However, the *International Space Station* was not created overnight. It can trace <u>it's</u> (34) lineage back to <u>*Salyut 1*, the</u> (35) very first space station launched in 1971 by the Russians. In most respects, *Salyut 1* was actually a failure. For example, before <u>plummeting, to Earth, it orbited</u> (36) the planet for less than six months and was plagued by mechanical problems that ultimately resulted in the deaths of three cosmonauts. [37] Yet, the *Salyut* experiment proved that extraterrestrial habitation was possible and allowed the Russians to develop other, more technically successful space stations in the years that followed,

32. The writer is considering adding the following clause to the end of the preceding sentence (replacing the period after *moon* with a comma):

> because both the Russians and the Americans wanted to reach the moon first.

Should the writer add this phrase here?

F. Yes, because it specifies that both groups were competing.
G. Yes, because it emphasizes to the reader the ultimate goal of the race.
H. No, because it is clear from earlier in the sentence that both groups were competing to reach the moon.
J. No, because it provides additional information that distracts the reader from the primary focus of the passage.

33. **A.** NO CHANGE
B. the innermost places
C. within our planet
D. the interior

34. **F.** NO CHANGE
G. its'
H. its
J. their

35. **A.** NO CHANGE
B. *Salyut 1* the
C. *Salyut 1;* the
D. *Salyut 1*. The

36. **F.** NO CHANGE
G. plummeting to Earth, it orbited
H. plummeting to Earth. It orbited
J. plummeting to Earth; it orbited

37. The writer is considering adding the following clause to the end of the preceding sentence (replacing the period after the word *cosmonauts* with a comma):

> who were honored as heroes at their funerals.

Should the writer add this clause here?

A. Yes, because it was not the cosmonauts' fault that they were killed.
B. Yes, because it provides information that is not mentioned elsewhere in the passage.
C. No, because it distracts the reader from the main focus of the paragraph.
D. No, because no description of the funeral is provided.

the most famous of which was called *Mir*. [38]

38. Which of the following true statements, if added here, would best point out how successful *Mir* was?
   - **F.** *Mir* orbited Earth for 14 years and hosted more than two dozen long-duration crews.
   - **G.** The name *Mir* actually means *peace* in Russian.
   - **H.** Unfortunately, Russian cosmonauts would stay on *Mir* for so long that they were unable to walk when they returned to Earth.
   - **J.** *Mir* fell to Earth in 2001 and ended in a way reminiscent of *Salyut* thirty years earlier.

[3]

Not to be outdone, the Americans looked to the mixed success the Russians enjoyed with *Salyut 1* and launched their own space station in 1973 called *Skylab*. Like the Russian space station, however, *Skylab* too had operational difficulties. Hit by debris, <u>severe damage was suffered by it</u> [39] during the launch and was inoperable until astronauts repaired it during numerous spacewalks. Once it was repaired, however, astronauts focused on conducting <u>mainly</u> [40] scientific experiments, and three separate crews successfully docked there throughout 1973 <u>and 1974. Though</u> [41] additional missions were planned, none were ever launched, and *Skylab* fell back to Earth in 1979 after about six years in orbit.

39. **A.** NO CHANGE
   - **B.** it suffered severe damage
   - **C.** severely damaged it suffered
   - **D.** it was suffering from severe damage

40. The best placement for the underlined portion would be:
   - **F.** where it is now.
   - **G.** after the word *Once*.
   - **H.** after the word *focused*.
   - **J.** after the word *three*.

41. **A.** NO CHANGE
   - **B.** and 1974 though
   - **C.** and 1974, though
   - **D.** and 1974 though,

[4]

[1] This space station was <u>successful and</u> [42] launched in 2000 and has hosted more than 17 crews from numerous countries since then. [2] In the 1990s, the end of the Cold War allowed the two <u>nations</u> [43] to work together on the goal of achieving a sustainable habitat in outer space. [3] The Russian stations *Salyut* and *Mir* and the American *Skylab* laid the groundwork for the *International Space Station*. [44]

42. **F.** NO CHANGE
   - **G.** successfully
   - **H.** successfully and
   - **J.** successful

43. Which of the following alternatives to the underlined portion would be LEAST acceptable?
   - **A.** countries
   - **B.** states
   - **C.** lands
   - **D.** cities

44. Which of the following sequences of sentences will make Paragraph 4 most logical?
   - **F.** NO CHANGE
   - **G.** 1, 3, 2
   - **H.** 2, 1, 3
   - **J.** 2, 3, 1

Question 45 asks about the preceding passage as a whole.

45. Suppose the writer had intended to write a brief essay about Robert Heinlein's contributions to space exploration. Would this essay fulfill that purpose?

A. Yes, because the essay quotes Heinlein on the importance of space exploration.
B. Yes, because the essay describes the development of space stations.
C. No, because the essay is about *Mir,* which Heinlein did not explicitly discuss.
D. No, because the essay offers a broader focus on the development of space stations.

Passage IV

Inventions That Break Barriers

At the turn of the 20th century, Mary Anderson was a real-estate developer, rancher, and winemaker. We don't know her name today for any of these reasons, however. Instead, Anderson made history <u>for</u>[46] inventing automobile windshield wipers—a feat she accomplished in 1903, five years before Henry Ford even created the Model T. In 1902, while riding a trolley in New York City, she couldn't help noticing that the driver had to continually stop in order <u>to wipe</u>[47] snow and ice from the windshield. Anderson thought <u>that there had to be a better way.</u>[48]

<u>However, she</u>[49] devised a swinging arm with a rubber blade that swung back and forth, swishing rain and snow from the

46. F. NO CHANGE
G. by
H. to
J. as

47. A. NO CHANGE
B. to wiping
C. for wiping
D. and wiped

48. Which of the following alternatives to the underlined portion would NOT be acceptable?
F. she could devise a better way.
G. that there must be a better way.
H. in which there had to be a better way.
J. that a better way could be found.

49. A. NO CHANGE
B. Instead, she
C. On the contrary, she
D. She

windshield surface. Anderson's model was different from todays models, [50] though, because it was hand-activated by a lever from

50. F. NO CHANGE
G. today's models,
H. todays' models
J. today's models

inside the car. Similar devices had been attempted and tried, [51] but Anderson's was the first to work and the first to be successfully patented. Interestingly, she could not sell the rights to her invention. A Canadian company told her that drivers

51. A. NO CHANGE
B. attempted,
C. attempted, and later, tried,
D. attempted, that is, tried,

would find the movement of the arm [52] too distracting. So even though Anderson's windshield wipers became standard in cars

52. F. NO CHANGE
G. would, find the movement of the arm
H. would find the movement, of the arm,
J. would find the movement of the arm,

after 1915, her [53] invention did not make her much money.

53. A. NO CHANGE
B. its
C. it's
D. their

Today, it is difficult for us to imagine driving without windshield wipers. [54] In fact, women have been responsible for many practical inventions. Josephine Cochran, for example, declared, "If nobody else is going to invent a dishwashing machine, I will." She presented her working dishwasher at the

54. Given that all the choices are true, which one would best introduce the new subject of this paragraph?
F. NO CHANGE
G. Today, we are the lucky recipients of Anderson's invention.
H. Mary Anderson believed that driving could be made safer.
J. Anderson was not the only female innovator of her time.

1886 World's Fair. At first not a huge success; the [55] machine was used only by hotels and large restaurants. Household dishwashers did not become popular until the 1950s.

55. A. NO CHANGE
B. success. The
C. success, the
D. success: the

Historically, women have held a minority of patents. In early U.S. history, social and legal barriers often discouraged [56] women from patenting inventions. In Anderson and Cochran's time, women lacked the same legal rights as men, which

56. Which of the following alternatives to the underlined portion would be LEAST acceptable?
F. prevented
G. disturbed
H. dissuaded
J. stopped

compelled many women patented [57] their inventions under their husbands' or fathers' names. Although the true number of

57. A. NO CHANGE
B. to patent
C. patenting
D. patent

women inventors in history may not ever be known, it is evident that women like Mary Anderson and Josephine Cochran saw problems[58] and devised simple and imaginative solutions. It is unfortunate that the genius behind each of these innovations have not always been[59] rewarded or recognized, because these women helped to create the efficient world we take for granted today.

58. F. NO CHANGE
G. problems demanding solutions
H. dilemmas that could be solved
J. ways to fix problems

59. A. NO CHANGE
B. were not always
C. was not always
D. are not always

Question 60 asks about the preceding passage as a whole.

60. Suppose the writer's goal had been to write a brief essay documenting key innovations in the automobile industry. Would this essay successfully fulfill that goal?
F. Yes, because it highlights an important invention that changed the way cars are driven.
G. Yes, because it tells readers how and when a key innovation in automobiles was introduced.
H. No, because it does not include information about when the windshield wipers changed from hand-activated to automatic devices.
J. No, because it addresses only one automobile invention.

Passage V

Do Blue Bags Make a Green City?

In 1995, Chicago implemented its Blue Bag recycling program. This program was different from virtually any other throughout the world, particularly for a city of Chicago's size. Muncie, Indiana instituted a similar program, but it is a much smaller city than Chicago.[61] Chicago's idea was that you could

61. Given that all the choices are true, which one provides the most specific support for the statement in the preceding sentence?
A. NO CHANGE
B. Almost all other major cities ask their residents to sort recycling at centers or into specific receptacles.
C. Nearly every major city in the United States has an aggressive plan for recycling, but they're not all successful.
D. Chicago implemented many garbage collecting advances in the 1980s to cope with rodent problems.

throw your recycling away with your garbage as part of a program that was new to the city. All you'd have to do is make sure that when you threw your recycling into the dumpster or put it out on the street, it was in a blue garbage bag rather than a standard white or black bag. Many embraced the program because they felt it wouldn't inconvenience residents and the process would be similar to the normal garbage collection residents were used to; collecting all the recyclable waste into a bag, remembering the day for pickup, and then leaving the bag on the curb or in a dumpster. These bags would be picked up by the normal garbage collectors, and eventually, the blue bags would be removed from the garbage and rerouted to various recycling facilities.

This program hummed along, and was still going strong when I moved to Chicago. The city's goal was to improve its 13–19% recycling rate to the point where, of all the waste collected, 25% of it would be recycled. In 2005, according to a report by city officials, they had reached that goal, and many believed that Chicago was becoming a truly "green" city. Unfortunately, independent researchers told a much different tale. According to their estimates, as little as 9% of the city's waste was being recycled and the rates of recycling among residents were still around the levels they had been in the 1980s. In other words, you could say that not much changes.

[1] So what was wrong for this program? [2] The Chicago area is not overwhelmed by landfill issues as are some other major cities, so many people who live in the city didn't think recycling or diverting waste was all that important. [3] Then

62. Given that all choices are true, which description of Chicago's recycling process best supports the city's logic in its choice of program, as described in this paragraph?
   F. NO CHANGE
   G. which the garbage collectors would pick up every Wednesday.
   H. without the hassle of driving to a recycling center.
   J. instead of the old-fashioned way of throwing things away.

63. A. NO CHANGE
   B. to
   C. to,
   D. to:

64. F. NO CHANGE
   G. officials they
   H. officials. They
   J. officials; they

65. Which of the following alternatives to the underlined portion would NOT be acceptable?
   A. 1980s, so in
   B. 1980s; in
   C. 1980s: in
   D. 1980s, in

66. F. NO CHANGE
   G. had changed.
   H. would have changed.
   J. was to have changed.

67. A. NO CHANGE
   B. to
   C. with
   D. from

there were the actual mechanics of running[68] the program. [4] The biggest problem was probably the residents' lack of interest. [5] These turned out to be much more complicated than either the city or its various contractors ever expected. [6] Imagine, for example, the magnitude of manpower and financial investment with such a requiring[69] to pull these select bags out of the more than 5 million tons of garbage Chicagoans dump every year! [7] What happens to all the bags that[70] rip in transit, with all those recyclables then mixed in with all the other garbage? [71]

In May 2008, the city decided to discontinue its Blue Bag program and replace[72] it with a new one. The cloud had a silver lining, though: the controversy surrounding the Blue Bag program, which was getting press alongside larger mounting concerns about global warming and other environmental issues, made the city's residents and business owners more aware of the importance of recycling. Even during the Blue Bag program, a trip to one of the city's public recycling centers were[73] proof that Chicagoans were interested in recycling. Many times I'd go and, because the centers were so lacking in[74] recyclables, I'd have to take my recyclables to another center that was not so full. Now, to replace the Blue Bag program, the city has begun to institute the Blue *Bin* program, and there are many of us whose[75] hope that this program can right the wrongs of the last program and make Chicago the truly green city we know it can be.

68. Which of the following alternatives to the underlined portion would be LEAST acceptable?
- **F.** maintaining
- **G.** operating
- **H.** sustaining
- **J.** hiring

69.
- **A.** NO CHANGE
- **B.** of which much was required
- **C.** that were requiring much of
- **D.** that was required

70.
- **F.** NO CHANGE
- **G.** still that they
- **H.** as they
- **J.** seeing as they

71. For the sake of the logic and coherence of this paragraph, Sentence 4 should be placed:
- **A.** where it is now.
- **B.** after Sentence 1.
- **C.** after Sentence 5.
- **D.** after Sentence 7.

72. Which of the following alternatives to the underlined portion would NOT be acceptable?
- **F.** program and to replace
- **G.** program they've replaced
- **H.** program, replacing
- **J.** program and decided to replace

73.
- **A.** NO CHANGE
- **B.** was
- **C.** is
- **D.** have been

74. Which choice presents this description in a way most consistent with the writer's description of the recycling centers?
- **F.** NO CHANGE
- **G.** undersupplied with
- **H.** neglected of
- **J.** overwhelmed by

75.
- **A.** NO CHANGE
- **B.** whom
- **C.** who
- **D.** that

English Practice Section 3 Answers and Explanations

ENGLISH PRACTICE SECTION 3 ANSWERS

1. D
2. F
3. B
4. G
5. C
6. F
7. C
8. J
9. D
10. J
11. C
12. J
13. A
14. H
15. B
16. G
17. D
18. H
19. B
20. J
21. B
22. G
23. A
24. F
25. A
26. J
27. C
28. H
29. B
30. F
31. B
32. H
33. A
34. H
35. A
36. G
37. C
38. F
39. B
40. H
41. A
42. G
43. D
44. J
45. D
46. G
47. A
48. H
49. D
50. G
51. B
52. F
53. A
54. J
55. C
56. G
57. B
58. F
59. C
60. J
61. B
62. H
63. D
64. F
65. D
66. G
67. C
68. J
69. D
70. F
71. B
72. G
73. B
74. J
75. C

ENGLISH PRACTICE SECTION 3 EXPLANATIONS

Passage I

1. **D** Apostrophes change in the answer choices, so this question tests apostrophe usage. A noun with an apostrophe shows possession. *One of the...premier intellectuals* belongs to the *city,* so an apostrophe is needed; eliminate (A) and (B). The difference between (C) and (D) is the singular versus plural possessive. The *city* referred to is *Paris,* which is singular, so the singular possessive is needed in this sentence. Eliminate (C) because *cities'* is plural. The correct answer is (D).

2. **F** Commas change in the answer choices, so this question tests comma usage. The phrase *1959 in Paris* is necessary to the sentence, so it should not be set off by commas; eliminate (J). The sentence contains only one idea, so there is no need to include a comma after either *1959* or *Paris,* as neither place separates distinct ideas. Eliminate (G) and (H). The correct answer is (F).

3. **B** Note the question! When a question asks which answer would be *LEAST* acceptable, eliminate answers that **are** acceptable. Vocabulary changes in the answer choices, so this question tests which words give the clearest meaning. *Emerged, erupted,* and *burst* all mean something similar to *exploded,* as the sentence is written, so they are all acceptable. Eliminate (A), (C), and (D). The verb *released* requires an object; the new wave could have "released something," but it can't *released.* Choice (B) is not acceptable. The correct answer is (B).

4. **G** Punctuation changes in the answer choices, so this question tests how to connect ideas with the appropriate punctuation. The first part of the sentence, *Bazin published his first piece of film criticism in 1943 and pioneered a new way of writing about film,* is an independent clause. The second part of the sentence, *he championed the idea that cinema was the "seventh art," every bit as deserving as the more respected arts of architecture, poetry, dance, music, painting, and sculpture,* is also an independent clause. Two independent clauses must be separated by some type of punctuation other than a comma, so eliminate (F) and (H). Choice (G) appropriately uses a period to separate two independent clauses. Adding the word *although* to the beginning of the second part of the sentence makes it into a dependent clause. A period can only be used between two independent clauses, so eliminate (J). The correct answer is (G).

5. **C** Punctuation changes in the answer choices, so this question tests how to connect ideas with the appropriate punctuation. The first part of the sentence, *He championed the idea that cinema was the "seventh art," every bit as deserving as the more respected arts of,* is not an independent clause. A colon can only be used after an independent clause, so eliminate (A). There is no need to use a comma after *of,* so eliminate (B) and (D). Choice (C) appropriately uses a comma after *architecture* because it is the first item in a list. The correct answer is (C).

6. **F** Note the question! The question asks whether a phrase should be added to the end of the sentence, so it tests consistency. A phrase should be added only if it is consistent with the focus of the sentence. The sentence discusses how *the authors speak of film* in *early writings about film.* The new

phrase gives more detail about the way in which *the authors speak of film,* so it should be added; eliminate (H) and (J). Choice (F) accurately describes the phrase. The phrase does not mention *the subjects of Bazin's writings,* so eliminate (G). The correct answer is (F).

7. **C** Note the question! The question asks whether a sentence should be added to the end of the paragraph, so it tests consistency. A sentence should be added only if it is consistent with the focus of the paragraph. The paragraph discusses the important ideas in Bazin's *film criticism.* The new sentence names the book in which Bazin's writings are published. The name of the book is not relevant to what the important ideas in the writings are, so the sentence should not be added. Eliminate (A) and (B). Choice (C) accurately states that the new sentence *interrupts the discussion of a specific theory of Bazin's.* There is no indication that *this statement is untrue,* so eliminate (D). The correct answer is (C).

8. **J** The length of the phrase surrounding *voice* changes in the answer choices, so this question tests concision. *Voice* is the last item in a list of things that belong to a director: *style, perspective, or voice.* The phrase *a director's true* at the beginning of the list refers to all three items, so there is no need to repeat *his* or *the director's.* Eliminate (F), (G), and (H). Choice (J) is concise and makes the meaning of the sentence clear. The correct answer is (J).

9. **D** Transitions change in the answer choices, so this question tests consistency of ideas. There is also the option to DELETE; consider this choice carefully as it's often the correct answer. A transition must be consistent with the relationship between the ideas it connects. The previous sentence states that Bazin and others were *the first* to do something, and this sentence states that *Bazin created a new way of looking at films.* There is no contrast between these ideas, so eliminate (A), (B), and (C) because they all contain contrasting transitions. No transition is necessary. Choice (D) is concise and makes the meaning of the sentence clear. The correct answer is (D).

10. **J** Punctuation changes in the answer choices, so this question tests how to connect ideas with the appropriate punctuation. When there is a dash in the answer choices, look at the non-underlined portion of the sentence to see whether there is another dash in the sentence. There is a dash in the non-underlined portion, after *Jean Renoir.* The phrase *on such influential directors as Orson Welles, Vittorio de Sica, and Jean Renoir* contains a list of names that is not necessary to the main meaning of the sentence. It should therefore be set off from the sentence by either commas or dashes both before and after the phrase. Since the non-underlined dash cannot be changed, the beginning punctuation must also be a dash. Eliminate (F), (G), and (H). The correct answer is (J).

11. **C** Note the question! The question asks which answer *would effectively conclude this paragraph and introduce the topic of the next,* so it tests consistency. A transition must be consistent with the relationship between the ideas it connects. This paragraph states that Bazin's early writings are *pioneering works of film criticism that are studied and emulated by film critics today.* The following paragraph says that *Bazin's greatest achievement was the strong impression he left on a young generation of French filmmakers and critics.* Neither paragraph discusses *the Italian Neorealist style,* so eliminate (A). Neither paragraph mentions *Henri Langlois's Cinematheque* either, so eliminate (B). Choice (C) men-

tions both Bazin's *great written achievements* and his *true and lasting influence,* so it is consistent with both paragraphs. Choice (D) mentions some *film critics* who were influenced by Bazin, which is consistent with this paragraph but not with the next one. Eliminate (D). The correct answer is (C).

12. **J** The length of the phrase changes in the answer choices, so this question tests concision. There is also the option to DELETE; consider this choice carefully as it's often the correct answer. The underlined portion describes *the international scene. International* means *all over the world* or *in every nation and country,* so there is no need to repeat that idea. Eliminate (F), (G), and (H). Choice (J) is concise and makes the meaning of the sentence clear. The correct answer is (J).

13. **A** Note the question! The question asks for the answer that *would most effectively guide readers to understand the great importance of the two films discussed,* so it tests consistency. Eliminate answers that are inconsistent with the purpose stated in the question. The phrase *changed the landscape of international filmmaking* indicates that the films were of *great importance,* so keep (A). When the films *came out* has nothing to do with their *importance,* so eliminate (B). Where the films were *shot* also is unrelated to their importance, so eliminate (C). Whether the directors *knew Bazin personally* similarly has nothing to do with the films' *importance;* eliminate (D). The correct answer is (A).

14. **H** Transitions change in the answer choices, so this question tests consistency of ideas. A transition must be consistent with the relationship between the ideas it connects. The sentence before the transition discusses *filmmakers* who *were beginning to exercise the new cinematic freedom* at a particular time, *throughout the 1960s and 1970s.* The sentence beginning with the transition switches to the present tense; it discusses what happens when *a national film industry completely reinvents itself.* Neither *At that time* nor *Back then* makes the correct transition from *the 1960s and 1970s* to the present, so eliminate (F) and (G). Choice (H) appropriately introduces the present. There is no indication that the present is *the end* of filmmaking, so eliminate (J). The correct answer is (H).

15. **B** Note the question! The question asks whether the essay *illustrates how the writings of one film critic have had an influence beyond the realm of film criticism,* so it tests consistency. Determine whether the essay is consistent with this idea. The essay discusses the writings of Bazin and his influence on both film critics and directors, so it is consistent with this idea. Eliminate (C) and (D). The passage does not discuss *Bazin's influence on the six arts,* so eliminate (A). Choice (B) accurately describes the passage. The correct answer is (B).

Passage II

16. **G** Verbs change in the answer choices, so this question tests consistency of verbs. A verb must be consistent in tense and form with the rest of the paragraph. The paragraph is in future tense *(I will... return the books).* Eliminate (H) and (J) because they are both past tense. In this sentence, the underlined portion functions as a noun—the act of returning books—rather than a verb. Choices (F) and (G) both contain noun forms of *return,* but (G) is more concise. Eliminate (F). The correct answer is (G).

17. **D** Note the question! The question asks what would be lost if some words were deleted, so it tests consistency. Eliminate answer choices that are not consistent with the role of the words. The words in question are all adverbs that describe how the narrator feels about the prospect of returning her books. The words do not *undermine the author's...assertion that she loves to read,* so eliminate (A). They do not express feelings about the narrator's *move,* so eliminate (B). The words describe what the author is going to do, but they do not give her *motive,* so eliminate (C). Choice (D) accurately states that the words convey *the writer's reluctance to lose any books.* The correct answer is (D).

18. **H** Note the question! When a question asks which answer would *NOT* be acceptable, eliminate answers that **are** acceptable. Vocabulary changes in the answer choices, so this question tests which words give the clearest meaning. Note the non-underlined word *of* immediately following the underlined portion. All four answer choices convey the same meaning, but *numerous* cannot be used with *of;* (H) is therefore unacceptable. *A lot, a number,* and *a bunch* can all be used with the word *of,* so they are all acceptable. Eliminate (F), (G), and (J). The correct answer is (H).

19. **B** Punctuation and transition words change in the answer choices, so this question tests how to connect ideas with the appropriate punctuation. The sentence contains the relative pronoun *that's* in the non-underlined portion of the sentence, so there is no need for either *which* or *that* in the underlined portion; eliminate (A) and (C). The first part of the sentence, *A biblioemergency is when an avid reader, such as myself, discovers that she has nothing left to read,* is an independent clause. The second part of the sentence, *I know that to some people that's no big deal, but to me it's a disaster,* is also an independent clause. Two independent clauses must be separated by some type of punctuation other than a comma, so eliminate (D). Choice (B) appropriately uses a period to separate two independent clauses. The correct answer is (B).

20. **J** Pronouns and apostrophes change in the answer choices, so this question tests pronoun consistency and apostrophe usage. A pronoun must be consistent in number with the noun it refers to. The underlined pronoun refers to *a biblioemergency,* which is singular, so the underlined pronoun should also be singular. Eliminate (G) and (H) because *theirs* and *they're* are both plural. *It's* is equal to *it is,* which works in this sentence, so an apostrophe is needed. Eliminate (F). The correct answer is (J).

21. **B** Punctuation changes in the answer choices, so this question tests how to connect ideas with the appropriate punctuation. The first part of the sentence, *Ever since childhood, I've made it a point to carry at least one extra book,* is an independent clause. The second part of the sentence, *sometimes two or more,* is not an independent clause. A semicolon can only be used between two independent clauses, so eliminate (D). A colon is used between an independent clause and a related list, definition, or explanation. The second part of the sentence is a continuation of the first part rather than a related explanation, so eliminate (C). The second part of the sentence is not necessary to the main meaning of the sentence, so it should be separated from the first part with a comma. Eliminate (A) because it doesn't contain a comma. The correct answer is (B).

22. **G** Pronouns and nouns change in the answer choices, so this question tests the idea of clear. A pronoun can be used only if it's clear what it refers to. A pronoun must also be consistent with the noun it refers to. There is no plural noun that the underlined pronoun could refer to, so eliminate (F) and (J) because *them* and *those* are both plural. *It* could refer to *an extra book,* but *the book I'm reading* gives a clearer idea of the narrator's meaning. Eliminate (H). The correct answer is (G).

23. **A** Apostrophes change in the answer choices, so this question tests apostrophe usage. A noun with an apostrophe shows possession. The *use of books as pacifiers* belongs to the *parents,* so an apostrophe is necessary; eliminate (B) and (D). *Parents's* is an incorrect form of the plural possessive, so eliminate (C). The correct answer is (A).

24. **F** The length of the phrase changes in the answer choices, so this question tests concision. Choices (H) and (J) are the shortest options, but both choices make it sound as if the *mother,* rather than the narrator was the one who was *fidgeting.* Eliminate (H) and (J). Choice (G) makes the first part of the sentence, *I got fidgety,* an independent clause. The second part of the sentence, *she'd supply me with a new book to keep me entertained, hopefully until she had finished her business,* is also an independent clause. Two independent clauses must be separated by some type of punctuation other than a comma, so eliminate (G). In (F), the first part of the sentence, *As soon as I got fidgety,* is not an independent clause. Choice (F) also appropriately uses a comma to separate the two parts of the sentence. The correct answer is (F).

25. **A** Note the question! The question asks whether a sentence should be added to the paragraph, so it tests consistency. A sentence should be added only if it is consistent with the focus of the paragraph. The paragraph discusses how the narrator's parents used *books as pacifiers* when she was a child. The new sentence describes the books the narrator liked as a child. Although the sentence may not seem relevant to the paragraph, neither of the reasons given in (C) or (D) is accurate: the new sentence does not *contradict information given in an earlier paragraph,* and it is not *offensive.* Eliminate (C) and (D). Choice (A) accurately states that the new sentence *gives more information that is relevant to the previous comment.* The new sentence does not *explain the main idea of the paragraph,* so eliminate (B). The correct answer is (A).

26. **J** Transitions change in the answer choices, so this question tests consistency of ideas. A transition must be consistent with the relationship between the ideas it connects. The sentence before the one with the transition discusses how the narrator's mother would *supply [her] with a new book to keep [her] entertained* when they had to wait someplace. The sentence with the transition states that *now* the narrator *find[s] it nearly impossible to wait patiently unless I have reading material.* There is no contrast between these ideas so eliminate (F), (G), and (H) because they all contain contrasting transitions. Choice (J) appropriately connects the two ideas with *consequently,* which indicates that the idea in the second sentence is a result of the previous idea. The correct answer is (J).

27. **C** The length of the phrase changes in the answer choices, so this question could test concision. Sometimes, adding or removing words makes a sentence incomplete. Choice (A) is the shortest option, but it makes the sentence incomplete; eliminate (A). Choices (B) and (D) also make the

sentence incomplete, so eliminate (B) and (D) as well. Choice (C) adds a subject to the underlined portion, which makes the sentence complete. The correct answer is (C).

28. **H** Verbs change in the answer choices, so this question tests consistency of verbs. A verb must be consistent in tense and form with other verbs in the sentence. The other verbs in the sentence, *plan* and *do,* are in present tense, so the underlined verb should also be in present tense. Eliminate (G) because it is in past perfect tense. The non-underlined word *to* just before the underlined verb indicates that the sentence requires the infinitive form of the verb *to pack.* Eliminate (F) and (J) because the *-ing* form of the verb does not form the infinitive with the word *to.* Choice (H) gives the appropriate form of the verb. The correct answer is (H).

29. **B** Note the question! The question asks for the most logical sequence of sentences in the paragraph, so it tests the idea of clear. The sentences must be put in an order that makes the meaning of the paragraph clear. Look for a sequence of events or a reference to something that came before to clearly order the sentences. Sentence 4 says *if that sounds like a hassle,* so look for something that could be a *hassle* that must come before Sentence 4. Sentence 2 says *I plan to pack at least four or five [books] in my carry-on luggage,* which *sounds like a hassle,* so Sentence 4 must come directly after Sentence 2; eliminate (A) and (D). Sentence 3 also refers to something that came before: *That is an experience I never need to repeat.* Sentence 1 describes such an experience: *I've found myself reading the backs of cereal boxes or the labels on my clothes.* Sentence 3 should therefore come after Sentence 1; eliminate (C). The correct answer is (B).

30. **F** Note the question! The question asks whether a paragraph should be deleted from the essay, so it tests consistency. If the paragraph is consistent with the subject of the passage, it should be kept. The passage focuses on the reasons why the narrator always carries books with her. The final paragraph is consistent with this idea, so it should be kept; eliminate (H) and (J). The idea of returning *books to the library* does return *to the opening idea,* so keep (F). The paragraph says that the narrator will *return [her] books to the library,* not that she will *refuse to return the books,* so eliminate (G). The correct answer is (F).

Passage III

31. **B** The length of the phrase surrounding *Heinlein* changes in the answer choices, so this question tests concision. The non-underlined portion of the sentences describes Heinlein as a *writer and political commentator,* so there is no need to repeat those ideas. Eliminate (A), (C), and (D). Choice (B) is concise and makes the meaning of the sentence clear. The correct answer is (B).

32. **H** Note the question! The question asks whether a phrase should be added to the end of the sentence, so it tests the ideas of consistent and clear. A phrase should be added only if it is consistent with the focus of the sentence and makes the meaning of the sentence clearer. The sentence describes how *the Russians and the Americans were in a fierce political competition with one other,* which provided

the backdrop for the explosive race to the Moon. The new phrase repeats the idea of *competition,* so there is no need to add it. Eliminate (F) and (G). Choice (H) accurately states that *it is clear from earlier in the sentence that both groups were competing to reach the Moon.* The new phrase does not *distract the reader from the primary focus of the passage,* so eliminate (J). The correct answer is (H).

33. **A** Vocabulary changes in the answer choices, so this question tests which words give the clearest meaning. *Our world* accurately describes what is *on Earth,* and it provides a clear counterpart to *outer space* later in the sentence; keep (A). The sentence refers to *Earth* generally, not specific *places* on Earth, so eliminate (B). Both (C) and (D) are not consistent with the non-underlined phrase *on Earth* because they both refer to the inside, rather than the surface, of the planet. Eliminate (C) and (D). The correct answer is (A).

34. **H** Pronouns and apostrophes change in the answer choices, so this question tests pronoun consistency and apostrophe usage. A pronoun must be consistent in number with the noun it refers to. The underlined pronoun refers to *the International Space Station,* which is singular, so the underlined pronoun should also be singular. Eliminate (J) because *their* is always plural on the ACT. The word *its'* never occurs in English, so eliminate (G). *It's* is a contraction of *it is,* which is not necessary here, so eliminate (F). The correct answer is (H).

35. **A** Punctuation changes in the answer choices, so this question tests how to connect ideas with the appropriate punctuation. The first part of the sentence, *It can trace its lineage back to Salyut 1,* is an independent clause. The second part of the sentence, *the very first space station launched in 1971 by the Russians,* is not an independent clause. Both periods and semicolons can only be used between two independent clauses, so eliminate (C) and (D). The second part of the sentence is a descriptive phrase that is not necessary to the main meaning of the sentence, so it should be set off from the first part of the sentence by a comma. Eliminate (B). The correct answer is (A).

36. **G** Punctuation changes in the answer choices, so this question tests how to connect ideas with the appropriate punctuation. The first part of the sentence, *For example, before plummeting to Earth,* is not an independent clause. The second part of the sentence, *it orbited the planet for less than six months and was plagued by mechanical problems that ultimately resulted in the deaths of three cosmonauts,* is an independent clause. Both periods and semicolons can only be used between two independent clauses, so eliminate (H) and (J). The phrase *to Earth* is necessary to the first part of the sentence, so it should not be set off by commas; eliminate (F). The correct answer is (G).

37. **C** Note the question! The question asks whether a phrase should be added to the end of the sentence, so it tests consistency. A phrase should be added only if it is consistent with the focus of the sentence. The sentence describes the *failure* of *Salyut 1.* The new phrase states that the *cosmonauts* who were killed on *Salyut 1 were honored as heroes at their funerals.* The main focus of the sentence is the space station, not the cosmonauts, so the new phrase is not consistent and should not be added. Eliminate (A) and (B). Choice (C) accurately states that the phrase *distracts the reader from the main focus of the paragraph.* It is true that *no description of the funeral is provided,* but as *the funeral*

is not consistent with the focus of the sentence, (D) does not provide an accurate reason to not include the phrase. Eliminate (D). The correct answer is (C).

38. **F** Note the question! The question asks for the answer that *would best point out how successful Mir was,* so it tests consistency. Eliminate answers that are inconsistent with the purpose stated in the question. Choice (F) states that *Mir orbited Earth for 14 years and hosted more than two dozen long-duration crews,* which could be understood as *successes,* so keep (F). What *the name Mir...means* has nothing to do with *success,* so eliminate (G). Both the fact that *Russian cosmonauts...were unable to walk when they returned to Earth* and that *Mir fell to Earth* are negatives rather than successes, so eliminate (H) and (J). The correct answer is (F).

39. **B** The order of words changes in the answer choices, so this question tests misplaced modifiers. Eliminate answers that have an unclear word order. The sentence starts with the descriptive phrase *Hit by debris.* This phrase modifies the underlined portion, so the first noun in the underlined portion must be something that was *hit by debris. Severe damage* could not have been *hit by debris,* so eliminate (A). *Severely damaged* is another descriptive phrase that cannot be described by the opening phrase, so eliminate (C). *It* refers to *Skylab,* which could have been *hit by debris,* so keep (B) and (D). The difference between (B) and (D) is the verb tense. A verb must be consistent in tense with the rest of the sentence. The other verbs in the sentence, *was* and *repaired,* are in simple past tense, so the underlined verb should also be in simple past tense. Choice (B) is in simple past tense. There is no need for the *-ing* ending, so eliminate (D). The correct answer is (B).

40. **H** Note the question! The question asks for the best placement for the underlined portion, so it tests consistency. The underlined portion must be consistent with the word or phrase it is next to. *Mainly* is an adverb that means "for the most part." There is no indication that the *experiments* were anything other than *scientific,* so eliminate (F). Adverbs can be used to describe verbs or adjectives, but not nouns, so *mainly* cannot describe *it;* eliminate (G). It makes sense to say that the *astronauts focused* "for the most part" *on conducting scientific experiments,* so keep (H). There is no indication that the *crews* were anything other than *separate,* so eliminate (J). The correct answer is (H).

41. **A** Punctuation changes in the answer choices, so this question tests how to connect ideas with the appropriate punctuation. The first part of the sentence, *Once it was repaired, however, astronauts focused mainly on conducting scientific experiments, and three separate crews successfully docked there throughout 1973 and 1974,* is an independent clause. The second part of the sentence, *Though additional missions were planned, none were ever launched, and Skylab fell back to Earth in 1979 after about six years in orbit,* is also an independent clause. Two independent clauses must be separated by some type of punctuation other than a comma, so eliminate (B), (C), and (D). Choice (A) appropriately uses a period to separate the two independent clauses. The correct answer is (A).

42. **G** The length of the phrase surrounding *successful* changes in the answer choices, so this question tests concision. Two answer choices contain the adjective *successful,* and the other two contain the adverb *successfully. Successful* cannot be used on its own because it would describe the non-underlined verb *launched,* but an adjective cannot describe a verb; eliminate (J). *Successfully* can be used to

describe *launched,* so keep (G). There is no need to use the word *and* in the underlined portion, so eliminate (F) and (H). The correct answer is (G).

43. **D** Note the question! When a question asks which answer would be *LEAST* acceptable, eliminate answers that **are** acceptable. Vocabulary changes in the answer choices, so this question tests which words give the clearest meaning. The underlined portion refers to Russia and the United States, which can be accurately described as *countries, states,* or *lands;* eliminate (A), (B), and (C). Russia and the United States are not *cities,* so (D) is not acceptable. The correct answer is (D).

44. **J** Note the question! The question asks for the most logical sequence of sentences in the paragraph, so it tests the idea of clear. The sentences must be put in an order that makes the meaning of the sentence clear. Look for a sequence of events or a reference to something that came before to clearly order the sentences. Sentence 1 mentions *This space station,* so it must come after a reference to a space station. Sentence 3 mentions the *International Space Station,* so Sentence 1 must come after Sentence 3; eliminate (F), (G), and (H). The correct answer is (J).

45. **D** Note the question! The question asks whether the essay describes *Robert Heinlein's contributions to space exploration,* so it tests consistency. Determine whether the essay is consistent with this idea. Although the first paragraph mentions *Robert Heinlein,* the rest of the passage focuses on space stations more generally, so it is not consistent with this idea; eliminate (A) and (B). The essay is not only about *Mir,* so eliminate (C). Choice (D) accurately states that *the essay offers a broader focus on the development of space stations.* The correct answer is (D).

Passage IV

46. **G** Prepositions change in the answer choices, so this question tests idioms. The correct idiom is *made history by,* so eliminate (F), (H), and (J). The correct answer is (G).

47. **A** Prepositions change in the answer choices, so this question tests idioms. The correct idiom is *in order to,* so eliminate (C) and (D). The expression *in order to* is correctly completed with *wipe* rather than *wiping,* so eliminate (B). The correct answer is (A).

48. **H** Note the question! When a question asks which answer would *NOT* be acceptable, eliminate answers that **are** acceptable. Pronouns change in the answer choices, so this question tests consistency of pronouns. A pronoun must be consistent in gender and number with the noun it refers to. In (F), *she* refers to *Anderson.* These two words are both singular and feminine, so they are consistent; eliminate (F). In (G) and (J), *that* refers to what Anderson *thought.* These two words are both singular and non-gendered, so they are consistent; eliminate (G) and (J). The phrase *in which* is idiomatically incorrect after *thought,* so (H) is not acceptable. The correct answer is (H).

49. **D** Transitions change in the answer choices, so this question tests consistency of ideas. The previous paragraph describes how Mary Anderson *thought that there had to be a better way* of clearing snow from a trolley windshield than for the driver to stop and wipe it off. This paragraph says that she

devised a swinging arm with a rubber blade that cleaned the windshield. There is no contrast between the two sentences, so eliminate (A), (B), and (C) because they all contain contrasting transitions. The correct answer is (D).

50. **G** Apostrophes change in the answer choices, so this question tests apostrophe usage. A noun with an apostrophe shows possession. Since the *models* belong to *today,* an apostrophe is necessary; eliminate (F). *Today* is singular, so eliminate the plural possessive in (H). The difference between (G) and (J) is the comma after *models,* so the question also tests comma usage. The word *though* is not necessary to the main meaning of the sentence, so it should be set off by commas. Eliminate (J). The correct answer is (G).

51. **B** The length of the phrase surrounding *attempted* changes in the answer choices, so this question tests concision. *Tried* means the same thing as *attempted,* so there is no need to use both words. Eliminate (A), (C), and (D). Choice (B) is concise and makes the meaning of the sentence clear. The correct answer is (B).

52. **F** Commas change in the answer choices, so this question tests comma usage. The phrase *of the arm* is necessary to the main meaning of the sentence, so it should not be set off by commas; eliminate (H). The sentence contains only one complete thought, so there is no reason to break it up with a comma after *would* or after *arm;* eliminate (G) and (J). The correct answer is (F).

53. **A** Pronouns change in the answer choices, so this question tests consistency of pronouns. A pronoun must be consistent with the noun it refers to and with other pronouns in the sentence. The underlined pronoun refers to *Anderson,* and the pronoun *her* also appears in the non-underlined portion of the sentence. *Anderson* is a woman, and *her* is a feminine pronoun, so the underlined pronoun should also be feminine. Keep (A) because *her* is feminine. Eliminate (B), (C) and (D) because neither *its* nor *their* is a feminine pronoun. The correct answer is (A).

54. **J** Note the question! The question asks which answer *would best introduce the new subject of this paragraph,* so it tests consistency. Eliminate answers that are inconsistent with the purpose stated in the question. The paragraph says that *women have been responsible for many practical inventions,* and gives the example of *Josephine Cochran,* who invented the dishwasher. The paragraph does not focus on *windshield wipers,* so eliminate (F). The paragraph is also not about *Anderson* or her *invention,* so eliminate (G) and (H). Saying that *Anderson was not the only female inventor of her time* effectively introduces the idea of another inventor, so keep (J). The correct answer is (J).

55. **C** Punctuation changes in the answer choices, so this question tests how to connect ideas with the appropriate punctuation. The first part of the sentence, *At first not a huge success,* is not an independent clause. The second part of the sentence, *the machine was used only by hotels and large restaurants,* is an independent clause. Both periods and semicolons can only be used between two independent clauses, so eliminate (A) and (B). A colon can only be used after an independent clause, so eliminate (D). The correct answer is (C).

56. **G** Note the question! When a question asks which answer would be *LEAST* acceptable, eliminate answers that **are** acceptable. Vocabulary changes in the answer choices, so this question tests which words give the clearest meaning. In the sentence as written, *discouraged* means "persuaded [women] against" something. *Prevented, dissuaded,* and *stopped* all have similar meanings and are therefore all acceptable alternatives. Eliminate (F), (H), and (J). *Disturbed* could mean something similar to *discouraged,* but not in this context, so (G) is not acceptable. The correct answer is (G).

57. **B** Verbs change in the answer choices, so this question could test consistency of verbs. In this case, the verb does not have a subject—it completes the phrase *compelled many women*. The phrase must be completed with the infinitive form of the verb, *to patent,* so eliminate (A), (C), and (D). The correct answer is (B).

58. **F** The length of the phrase changes in the answer choices, so this question tests concision. The non-underlined portion of the sentence mentions *solutions,* so there is no need to repeat that idea; eliminate (G) and (H). To *fix* something is the same as coming up with a *solution,* so eliminate (J) also. Choice (F) is concise and makes the meaning of the sentence clear. The correct answer is (F).

59. **C** Verbs change in the answer choices, so this question tests consistency of verbs. A verb must be consistent in number with its subject. The subject of the verb is *each* (the phrase *of these innovations* is a prepositional phrase that modifies *each* but is not the subject of the sentence), which is singular, so the verb must also be singular. Eliminate (A), (B), and (D) because they all contain plural verbs. Choice (C) contains the singular verb *was.* The correct answer is (C).

60. **J** Note the question! The question asks whether the essay describes *key innovations in the automobile industry,* so it tests consistency. Determine whether the essay is consistent with this idea. The passage focuses on female inventors, so it is not consistent with this idea; eliminate (F) and (G). It is true that the passage *does not include information about when the windshield wipers changed from hand-activated to automatic devices,* but as *windshield wipers* are not the primary focus of the passage, (H) does not provide an accurate reason. Choice (J) accurately states that the passage *addresses only one automobile invention.* The correct answer is (J).

Passage V

61. **B** Note the question! The question asks which answer *provides the most specific support for the statement in the preceding sentence,* so it tests consistency. Eliminate answers that are inconsistent with the purpose stated in the question. The preceding sentence says that *this program was different from virtually any other throughout the world.* Choice (A) mentions *a similar program,* so eliminate (A). Choice (B) describes what *almost all other major cities* do for recycling, which is different from Chicago's program, so keep (B). Whether cities have *aggressive plan[s]* is not relevant to how Chicago's program is *different,* so eliminate (C). The *rodent problem* in Chicago is also not relevant to how its recycling program is *different,* so eliminate (D). The correct answer is (B).

62. **H** Note the question! The question asks which answer *best supports the city's logic in its choice of program, as described in this paragraph,* so it tests consistency. Eliminate answers that are inconsistent with the purpose stated in the question. The paragraph says that *many embraced the program because they felt it wouldn't inconvenience residents.* The fact that the program *was new to the city* does not have anything to do with *the city's logic in its choice of program,* so eliminate (F). Which day the recycling was picked up also has nothing to do with *the city's logic in its choice of program,* so eliminate (G). The fact that the program worked *without the hassle of driving to a recycling center* both explains *the city's logic in its choice of program* and is consistent with the idea that *it wouldn't inconvenience residents,* so keep (H). What the *old-fashioned way* is has nothing to do with the new recycling program, so eliminate (J). The correct answer is (H).

63. **D** Punctuation changes in the answer choices, so this question tests how to connect ideas with the appropriate punctuation. The first part of the sentence, *Many embraced the program because they felt it wouldn't inconvenience residents and the process would be similar to the normal garbage collection residents were used to,* is an independent clause. The second part of the sentence, *collecting all the recyclable waste into a bag, remembering the day for pickup, and then leaving the bag on the curb or in a dumpster,* is not an independent clause. A semicolon can only be used between two independent clauses, so eliminate (A). A colon is used after an independent clause and before a related list, definition, or explanation. Choice (D) appropriately uses a colon because the second part of the sentence lists the steps of *the normal garbage collection residents were used to;* keep (D). Some type of punctuation is needed between the two parts of the sentence, so eliminate (B). A comma is used to separate independent and dependent clauses, or to separate unnecessary information from the rest of the sentence. Neither of those cases applies here, so eliminate (C). The correct answer is (D).

64. **F** Punctuation changes in the answer choices, so this question tests how to connect ideas with the appropriate punctuation. The first part of the sentence, *In 2005, according to a report by city officials,* is not an independent clause. The second part of the sentence, *they had reached that goal, and many believed that Chicago was becoming a truly "green" city,* is an independent clause. Both periods and semicolons can only be used between two independent clauses, so eliminate (H) and (J). The phrase *according to a report by city officials* is not necessary to the main meaning of the sentence, so it should be set off by commas. Eliminate (G). The correct answer is (F).

65. **D** Note the question! When a question asks which answer would *NOT* be acceptable, eliminate answers that **are** acceptable. Punctuation changes in the answer choices, so this question tests how to connect ideas with the appropriate punctuation. The first part of the sentence, *According to their estimates, as little as 9% of the city's waste was being recycled and the rates of recycling among residents were still around the levels they had been in the 1980s,* is an independent clause. The second part of the sentence, *In other words, you could say that not much had changed,* is also an independent clause. A comma followed by the word *so* can be used between two independent clauses, so (A) is acceptable; eliminate (A). Both colons and semicolons can also be used between two independent clauses, so (B) and (C) are both acceptable; eliminate (B) and (C). A comma alone cannot be used to separate two independent clauses, so (D) is not acceptable. The correct answer is (D).

66. **G** Verbs change in the answer choices, so this question tests consistency of verbs. A verb must be consistent in tense with the rest of the paragraph. The paragraph is in past tense, so the underlined verb must also be in past tense. Eliminate (F) because *changes* is present tense. *Had changed* is past tense, so keep (G). *Would have* and *was to have* are conditional tenses, which are not consistent with the paragraph; eliminate (H) and (J). The correct answer is (G).

67. **C** Prepositions change in the answer choices, so this question tests idioms. The correct idiom is *wrong with;* eliminate (A), (B), and (D). The correct answer is (C).

68. **J** Note the question! When a question asks which answer would be *LEAST* acceptable, eliminate answers that **are** acceptable. Vocabulary changes in the answer choices, so this question tests which words give the clearest meaning. *Maintaining, operating,* and *sustaining* all mean something similar to *running,* as the sentence is written, so (F), (G), and (H) are all acceptable. Eliminate (F), (G), and (H). *Hiring* means "employing," which does not make the sentence clear. Choice (J) is therefore not acceptable. The correct answer is (J).

69. **D** The length of the phrase changes in the answer choices, so this question tests concision. Choice (D) is the shortest option, and it makes the meaning of the sentence clear: the subject of the verb is *financial investment,* which is singular, and *was required* is also singular. Keep (D). The phrase *such a requiring* does not make the meaning of the sentence clear, so eliminate (A). The phrase *of which* also does not make the meaning of the sentence clear, so eliminate (B). *Were* is a plural verb, which is not consistent with the singular subject, so eliminate (C). The correct answer is (D).

70. **F** The length of the phrase changes in the answer choices, so this question tests concision. Choice (F) is the shortest option, and it makes the meaning of the sentence clear; keep (F). *That* refers to *bags,* so there is no reason to add the word *they,* which would also refer to *bags;* eliminate (G). Adding *as* does not make the meaning of the sentence clearer, so eliminate (H) and (J). The correct answer is (F).

71. **B** Note the question! The question asks for the best placement for Sentence 4, so it tests consistency of ideas. The sentence must be consistent with the ideas that come both before and after it. Sentence 5 starts with the phrase *These turned out to be much more complicated,* so it must come after something plural that is *complicated.* Sentence 4 does not include such an idea, so Sentence 4 cannot be placed *where it is now;* eliminate (A). Sentence 4 describes a *problem* that could be an appropriate answer to the question posed in Sentence 1, so keep (B). Sentences 6 and 7 give an example of the complications mentioned in Sentence 5, so Sentence 4 should not interrupt that flow of ideas; eliminate (C) and (D). The correct answer is (B).

72. **G** Note the question! When a question asks which answer would *NOT* be acceptable, eliminate answers that **are** acceptable. The length of the phrase after the word *program* changes in the answer choices, so this question could test concision. Sometimes, adding a word makes part of a sentence into an independent clause. The first part of the sentence, *In May 2008, the city decided to discontinue its Blue Bag program,* is an independent clause. The second part of the sentence in (F), *and*

to replace it with a new one, is not an independent clause. No punctuation is needed between these two ideas, so (F) is acceptable. Eliminate (F). The second part of the sentence in (G), *they've replaced it with a new one,* is an independent clause. Two independent clauses must be separated by some type of punctuation other than a comma, so (G) is not acceptable. The second part of the sentence in both (H) and (J) is not an independent clause. Either a comma or no punctuation can be used to separate an independent clause from something that is not an independent clause, so (H) and (J) are both acceptable. Eliminate (H) and (J). The correct answer is (G).

73. **B** Verbs change in the answer choices, so this question tests consistency of verbs. A verb must be consistent in number with its subject. The subject of the underlined verb is *a trip,* which is singular, so the verb should also be singular. Eliminate (A) and (D) because they both contain plural verbs. A verb must also be consistent in tense with other verbs in the sentence. The other verb in the sentence, *were,* is in past tense, so the underlined verb should also be past tense. Eliminate (C) because *is* is present tense. The correct answer is (B).

74. **J** Note the question! The question asks which answer is *consistent with the writer's description of the recycling centers,* so it tests consistency. Eliminate answers that are inconsistent with the purpose stated in the question. The end of the sentence says the narrator would *have to take [his] recyclables to another center that was not so full. Lacking* is not consistent with *full,* so eliminate (F). *Undersupplied* and *neglected* are also not consistent with *full,* so eliminate (G) and (H). *Overwhelmed by* is consistent with *full.* The correct answer is (J).

75. **C** Pronouns change in the answer choices, so this question tests consistency of pronouns. A pronoun must be consistent with the noun it refers to. The underlined pronoun refers to *us,* which means the narrator and other people. The word *that* cannot be used to refer to people, so eliminate (D). A pronoun must also be consistent with its role in the sentence. The underlined pronoun is the subject of the verb *hope,* so a subject pronoun is needed. Eliminate (A) because *whose* is a possessive pronoun. Eliminate (B) because *whom* is an object pronoun. *Who* is a subject pronoun. The correct answer is (C).

Math Practice Section 1

MATHEMATICS TEST

60 Minutes—60 Questions

DIRECTIONS: Solve each problem, choose the correct answer, and then darken the corresponding oval on your answer document.

Do not linger over problems that take too much time. Solve as many as you can; then return to the others in the time you have left for this test.

You are permitted to use a calculator on this test. You may use your calculator for any problems you choose, but some of the problems may best be done without using a calculator.

Note: Unless otherwise stated, all of the following should be assumed:

1. Illustrative figures are NOT necessarily drawn to scale.
2. Geometric figures lie in a plane.
3. The word *line* indicates a straight line.
4. The word *average* indicates arithmetic mean.

---

1. A magician performing at children's birthday parties charges $120.00 total for a one-hour performance with ten goody bags for children at the party. She will provide additional goody bags for $2.50 each. For an additional $25.00, she will also present a 15-minute laser light show. The magician is always paid on the day of the show, receives no tips or other additional payments, and never varies the length of the show. If the magician performs exactly four shows one weekend, presents the light show at three of those performances, and collects $635.00 total, how many additional goody bags did she provide?

A. 26
B. 32
C. 48
D. 86
E. 254

DO YOUR FIGURING HERE.

DO YOUR FIGURING HERE.

2. In an elite marathon runner's training, total mileage consists of miles run at or faster than marathon pace and miles run slower than marathon pace. The table below shows miles run at or faster than marathon pace and total mileage for an elite marathon runner for each of 3 consecutive years.

Running at or faster than marathon pace			
Year	# Runs	Total miles	Miles/Month
2002	294	2,645	220.4
2003	179	1,614	134.5
2004	128	1,150	95.8
Total mileage			
Year	Total runs	Total miles	Miles/Month
2002	414	3,725	310.4
2003	458	4,122	343.5
2004	554	4,982	415.2

In 2004, how many miles of the runner's total mileage were miles run slower than marathon pace?

F. 1,012
G. 2,972
H. 3,368
J. 3,832
K. 3,850

3. A 24-hour day is how many times as long as 60 seconds?

A. 12
B. 30
C. 365
D. 720
E. 1,440

4. A student reads a pages per day for d days and then reads b pages per day for $2d$ days. In terms of a, b, and d, how many pages did the student read?

F. $ad + 2b$
G. $ad + 2bd$
H. $2ad + 2bd$
J. $2abd$
K. $2abd^2$

DO YOUR FIGURING HERE.

5. A trapezoidal driveway has the dimensions, in yards, given in the figure below. What is the area, in square yards, of the driveway?

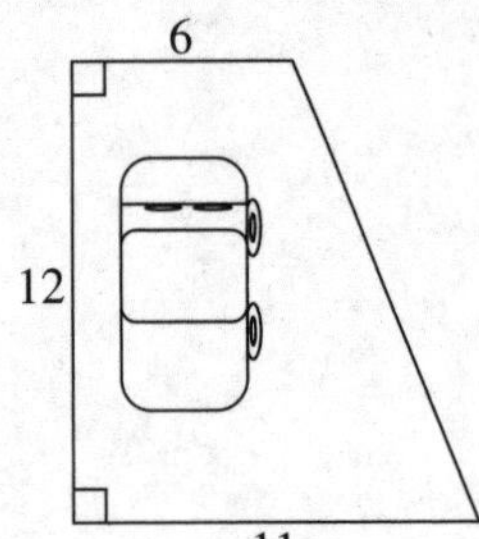

A. 42
B. 72
C. 102
D. 156
E. 204

6. The graph below shows the number of people visiting a museum during the first 5 months of the year. How many people need to visit the museum during June for the mean of the first 6 months to equal the mean of the first 5 months?

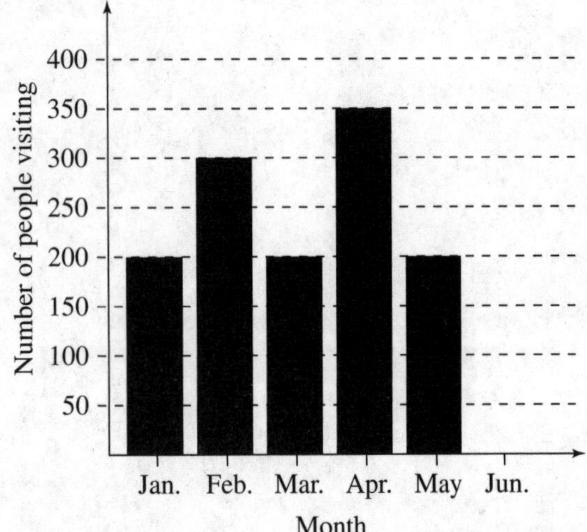

F. 0
G. 200
H. 250
J. 500
K. 1,250

7. A graduation cap is tossed upward. It is f feet above the ground s seconds after it has been thrown. The relationship between f and s is given by the equation $f = 60s - 17s^2$, where $0 \le s \le 3.5$. How many feet above the ground is the cap 3 seconds after it is thrown?

A. 27
B. 41
C. 60
D. 80
E. 163

8. The highest and lowest test scores of five students in Mr. Canyon's science class are listed below. Which student had the greatest range of scores?

DO YOUR FIGURING HERE.

	High	Low
Alicia	93	76
Brandon	91	79
Cleo	99	81
David	74	56
Emily	89	70

F. Alicia
G. Brandon
H. Cleo
J. David
K. Emily

9. Nita, Craig, and Chris catch a total of 300 fish on their trip. If Chris catches 45% of the fish and Craig catches 25 fish, what fraction of the 300 fish does Nita catch?

A. $\frac{23}{30}$
B. $\frac{41}{60}$
C. $\frac{1}{2}$
D. $\frac{7}{15}$
E. $\frac{1}{3}$

10. Given that $f(x) = 4x^2$ and $g(x) = 3 - \frac{x}{2}$, what is the value of $f(g(4))$?

F. 1
G. 4
H. 8
J. 16
K. 64

DO YOUR FIGURING HERE.

11. In the grid shown below, each small square has a side length of 1 unit. In the shaded region, each vertex lies on a vertex of a small square. What is the area, in square units, of the shaded region?

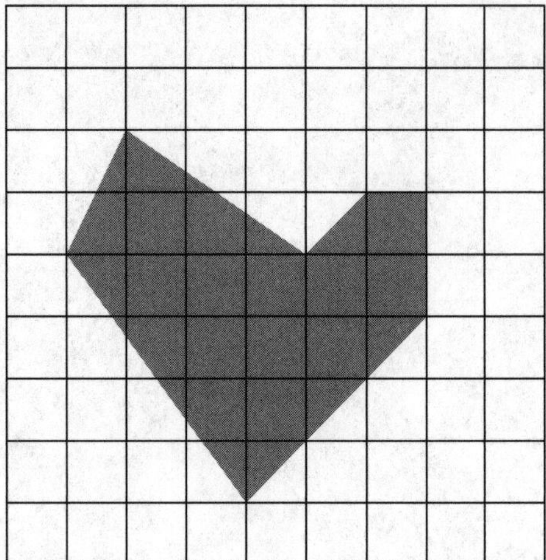

A. 35
B. 25
C. 24
D. 19
E. 13

12. A ramp rises 6 inches for each 24 inches of horizontal run. This ramp rises how many inches for 62 inches of horizontal run?

F. $15\frac{1}{2}$

G. $20\frac{2}{3}$

H. 44

J. 80

K. 248

13. What is the value of $y^x + (2x - 2y)$ when $x = 2$ and $y = -3$?

A. −10
B. 1
C. 7
D. 16
E. 19

DO YOUR FIGURING HERE.

14. In the figure below, the circle with center O is tangent to $\overline{AE}$, $\overline{BD}$, $\overline{CF}$, and $\overline{DE}$. The measure of angle $\angle BDE$ is 75° and the measure of $\angle DEA$ is 105°.

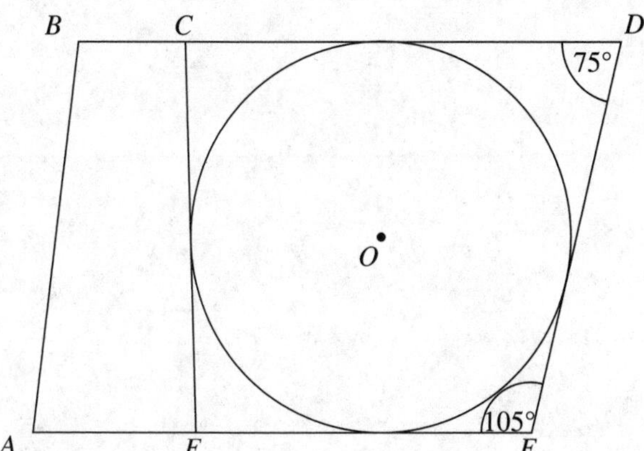

The lines in which of the following pairs of lines are necessarily parallel?

I. $\overline{AB}$ and $\overline{DE}$
II. $\overline{BD}$ and $\overline{AE}$
III. $\overline{CF}$ and $\overline{DE}$

F. I only
G. II only
H. III only
J. I and II only
K. I, II, and III

15. The day a clothing store puts out a batch of brand-name T-shirts it sells 95 shirts at \$4.10 per shirt. However, each day the shirts are on the rack, the store reduces the price of the shirts by \$0.02 and consequently sells 1 additional shirt with each price reduction. If x represents the number of \$0.02 price reductions, which of the following expressions represents the amount of money, in dollars, that the store will take in daily in sales of these brand-name T-shirts?

A. $(4.10 + 2x)(95 + x)$
B. $(4.10 - 2x)(95 + x)$
C. $(4.10 + 0.02x)(95 + x)$
D. $(4.10 - 0.02x)(95 + x)$
E. $(4.10 - 0.02x)(95 + 0.02x)$

16. The expression $x^2 - 7x + 12$ is equivalent to:

F. $(x - 12)(x + 1)$
G. $(x - 4)(x - 3)$
H. $(x - 4)(x + 3)$
J. $(x - 6)(x - 2)$
K. $(x - 6)(x + 2)$

17. When $x = 5$ and $y = 2$, the expression

$$\frac{xy}{70}+\frac{9}{5(x+y)}+\frac{1}{x+y}=?$$

A. $\frac{19}{35}$
B. $\frac{58}{105}$
C. $\frac{1}{2}$
D. $\frac{4}{7}$
E. $\frac{5}{28}$

DO YOUR FIGURING HERE.

18. The minutes and seconds on a 60-minute digital timer are represented by 3 or 4 digits. What is the *largest* product that can be obtained by multiplying the digits in one of these representations?

(Note: When the timer displays 16:15, the product of the digits is (1)(6)(1)(5) = 30.)

F. 90
G. 2,025
H. 3,481
J. 3,600
K. 6,561

19. The difference of two integers is 6. The sum of the same two integers is 42. What is the lesser of the two integers?

A. 18
B. 19
C. 21
D. 23
E. 24

20. The area of the square in the figure below is 324 square centimeters, and the two small isosceles right triangles are congruent. What is the combined area, in square centimeters, of the two small triangles?

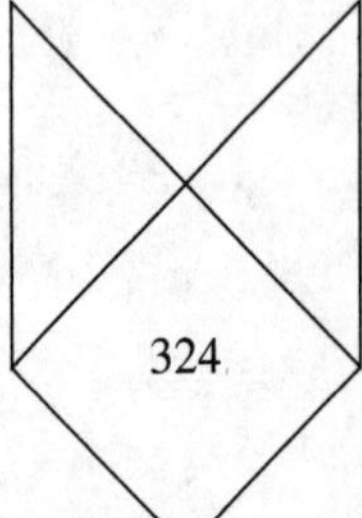

F. 108
G. 162
H. 216
J. 324
K. 648

DO YOUR FIGURING HERE.

21. Jasper wants to measure the altitude of his kite. He ties the kite string to a spike driven into the ground and measures the angle between the string and the ground. Then, he creates two similar triangles by adjusting the distance between an 8-foot pole and the spike until the angle created by a piece of string tied to the top of the pole and to the spike in the ground is the same as the angle he measured previously. The length of the string to the kite is 85 feet and the length of the string to the pole is 17 feet. Which of the following is closest to the height, in feet, that the kite is above the ground?

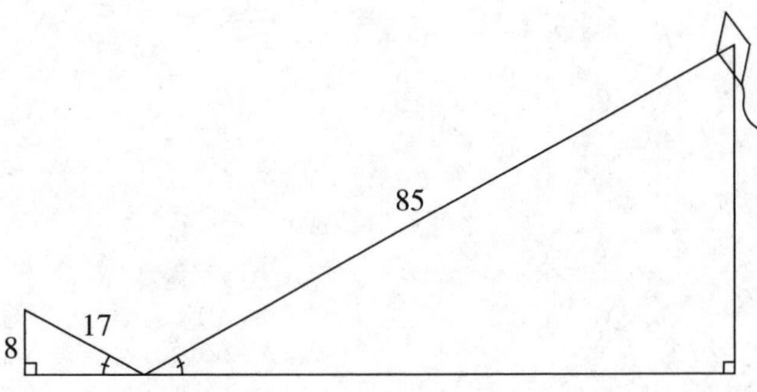

A. 25
B. 40
C. 102
D. 110
E. 181

22. For what value of x, if any, is the equation $(x - 1)^2 = (x - 7)^2$ true?

F. –4
G. –1
H. 0
J. 4
K. There is no value of x for which the equation is true.

23. ΔABC, shown below in the standard (x,y) coordinate plane, is equilateral with vertex A at $(0,w)$ and vertex B on the x-axis as shown. What are the coordinates of vertex C?

A. $(w,0)$
B. $(w,2w)$
C. $(w\sqrt{3},w)$
D. $(w\sqrt{3},2w)$
E. $(2w,w\sqrt{3})$

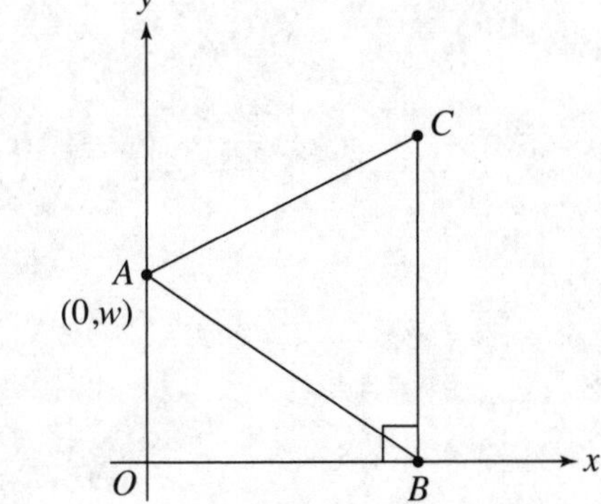

DO YOUR FIGURING HERE.

24. The diagonal of a square quilt is $4\sqrt{2}$ feet long. What is the area of the quilt in square feet?

F. $16\sqrt{2}$
G. 16
H. $4\sqrt{2}$
J. 4
K. $\sqrt{2}$

25. A painter needs to reach the top of a tall sign in the middle of a flat and level field. He uses a ladder of length x to reach a point on the sign 15 feet above the ground. The angle formed where the ladder meets the ground is noted in the figure below as θ. Which of the following relationships must be true?

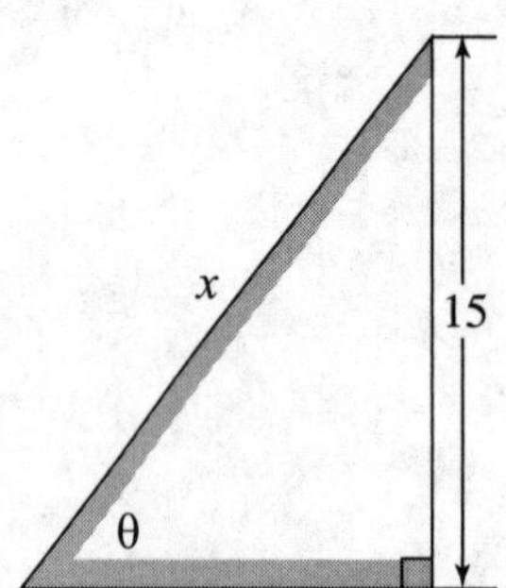

A. $\sin\theta = \frac{15}{x}$

B. $\cos\theta = \frac{15}{x}$

C. $\tan\theta = \frac{15}{x}$

D. $\theta = \frac{15}{x}$

E. $\frac{\sin\theta}{\cos\theta} = \frac{15}{x}$

26. The equation $\sqrt{45+a} + \sqrt{a} = 15$ is true for what real value of a ?

F. 9
G. 16
H. 25
J. 36
K. 64

27. In rectangle $ABCD$ below, $\overline{BC}$ is 16 inches long and $\overline{CD}$ is 12 inches long. Points E, F, and G are the midpoints of $\overline{AD}$, $\overline{AB}$, and $\overline{BC}$, respectively. What is the perimeter, in inches, of pentagon $CDEFG$?

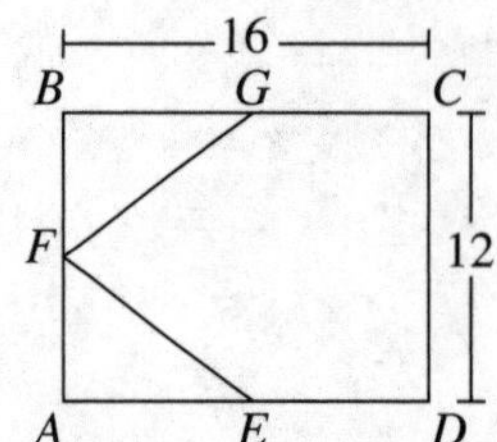

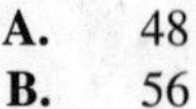

A. 48
B. 56
C. 96
D. 144
E. 192

DO YOUR FIGURING HERE.

Use the following information to answer questions 28–30.

The table below details a recent census report about the commuting habits of U.S. workers age 16 or over for the years 2004, 2005, and 2006.

U.S. workers category	2004	2005	2006
Group*			
Total	130.9	133.1	138.3
Male	70.9	72.1	74.7
Female	60.0	61.0	63.6
Commute time†			
Under 10 minutes	14.9%	14.7%	14.8%
More than 25 minutes	40.4%	41.1%	40.8%
Means of transportation†			
Car	87.8%	87.6%	86.7%
Public transportation	7.8%	7.9%	8.4%
Bicycle	1.4%	1.4%	1.6%
Walked	3.0%	3.1%	3.3%

*in millions of people, rounded to the nearest tenth of a million
†in percent, rounded to the nearest tenth of a percent
Source: U.S. Census Bureau

28. To the nearest percent, what percent of all U.S. workers age 16 or over in 2004 was female?

F. 50%
G. 48%
H. 46%
J. 44%
K. 15%

29. The circle graph (pie chart) below represents the 2006 means of transportation for U.S. workers age 16 or over for the four transportation types listed. To the nearest degree, what is the measure of the central angle for the "Public" sector?

2006 Means of Transportation

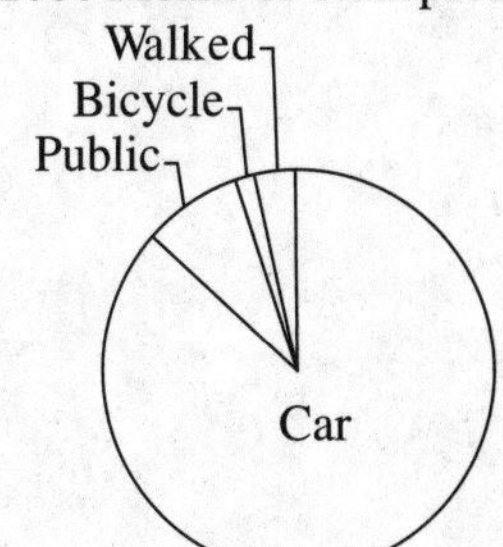

A. 8°
B. 12°
C. 20°
D. 28°
E. 30°

DO YOUR FIGURING HERE.

30. Expressed in millions of people, what was the average growth per year for female U.S. workers age 16 or over from 2004 to 2006, rounded to the nearest 0.1 million?

F. 0.5
G. 0.9
H. 1.3
J. 1.8
K. 3.6

---

31. Two hoses attached to separate water sources are available to fill a cylindrical swimming pool. If both hoses are used, the time it will take to fill the pool can be represented by the following equation: $\frac{1}{T_1}+\frac{1}{T_2}=\frac{1}{T_c}$, where T_1 and T_2 represent the time needed for hoses 1 and 2, respectively, to fill the pool on their own, and T_c represents the time needed for hoses 1 and 2 to fill the pool working together. If hose 1 alone can fill the pool in exactly 20 minutes and hose 2 alone can fill the pool in exactly 60 minutes, how many minutes will it take to fill the pool if both hoses work simultaneously?

A. 3
B. 10
C. 15
D. 18
E. 40

32. A 5-sided die, which has sides 2, 3, 4, 5, and 6, is thrown. What is the probability that the die will NOT land on a prime-numbered face?

F. $\frac{4}{5}$
G. $\frac{3}{5}$
H. $\frac{2}{5}$
J. $\frac{1}{5}$
K. 0

33. For $f(x,y) = 7x + 9y$, what is the value of $f(x,y)$ when $y = \left(\frac{5}{x}\right)^2$ and $x = 3$?

A. $\frac{68}{3}$

B. $\frac{214}{9}$

C. 36

D. 46

E. 96

DO YOUR FIGURING HERE.

34. What is the length, in coordinate units, of a diagonal of a square in the standard (x,y) coordinate plane with vertices at points (0,0), (4,0) and (4,4) ?

F. 3

G. 4

H. $4\sqrt{2}$

J. $4\sqrt{3}$

K. 8

35. What is the value of a if $\log_4 a = 3$?

A. 120

B. 64

C. 12

D. $\sqrt[4]{3}$

E. $4\sqrt{3}$

36. A certain 18-quart stockpot is filled completely with water and exposed to a heat source so that the water boils away at a constant rate. The water remaining in the stockpot can be approximated by the following equation: $y = 18 - 0.2x$, where x is the number of minutes that the pot has been heated for $0 \le x \le 90$, and y is the number of quarts remaining in the pot. According to this equation, which of the following statements is true about this stockpot?

F. After 0.2 minutes, 1 quart of water has boiled away.
G. After 1 minute, 0.2 quart of water has boiled away.
H. After 18 minutes, 0.2 quart of water has boiled away.
J. After 18 minutes, 1 quart of water has boiled away.
K. After 36 minutes, 18 quarts of water have boiled away.

37. The volume of a right circular cone with the bottom removed to create a flat base can be calculated with the following equation: $V = \frac{1}{3}\pi h(R^2 + r^2 + Rr)$, where h represents the height of the shape and R and r represent its radii, as shown in the figure below:

DO YOUR FIGURING HERE.

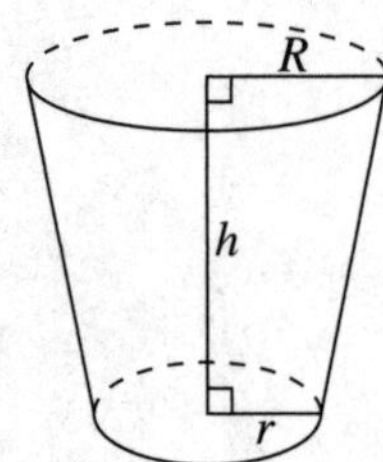

This formula can be used to determine the capacity of a large coffee mug. Approximately how many cubic inches of liquid can the cup shown below hold if it is filled to the brim and its handle holds no liquid?

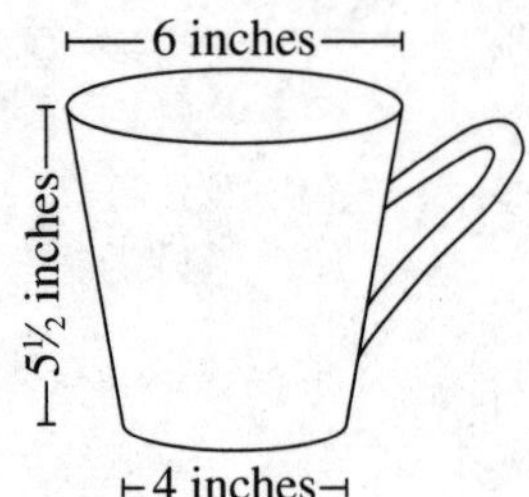

A. 19
B. 50
C. 105
D. 109
E. 438

38. Which of the following is the set of real solutions for the equation $9x + 12 = 3(3x + 4)$?

F. The set of all real numbers

G. $\{0,1\}$

H. $\{0\}$

J. $\left\{-\frac{4}{3}\right\}$

K. The empty set

39. The expression $\dfrac{\dfrac{3}{4}}{\dfrac{\frac{3}{4}-\frac{2}{3}}{\frac{3}{4}-\frac{2}{3}+\frac{1}{2}}}$ equals:

DO YOUR FIGURING HERE.

A. $\dfrac{3}{28}$

B. $\dfrac{4}{21}$

C. $\dfrac{21}{4}$

D. $\dfrac{28}{3}$

E. $\dfrac{108}{7}$

40. A thin slice is cut from a bagel, creating the cross-section represented below. The diameter of the bagel is 144 mm and the width from the inner edge of the bagel to the outer edge is uniformly 56 mm. Which of the following is closest to the area, in square millimeters, of the shaded empty space inside the cross-section of the bagel?

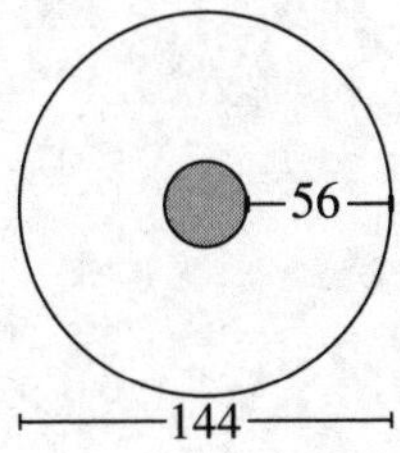

F. 100
G. 450
H. 800
J. 3,200
K. 16,000

41. For all nonzero real numbers a, b, and c, what is the value of $a^0 + b^0 + c^0$?

A. Undefined
B. $a + b + c$
C. 0
D. 1
E. 3

42. In the figure below, $ABCD$ is a rectangle, $AB = AE$, and E, F, G, and H lie on AD. Of the angles BEA, BFA, BGA, BHA, and BDA, which one has the greatest tangent?

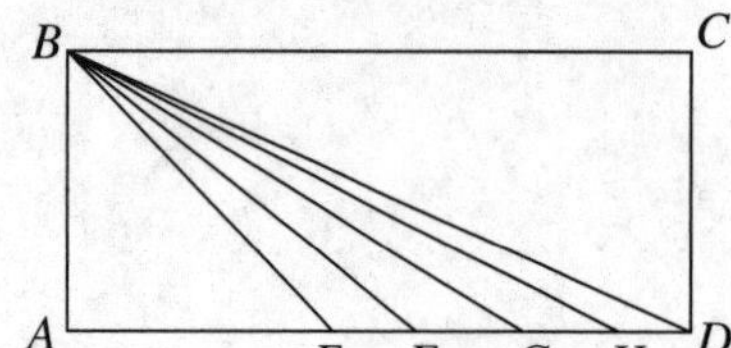

F. $\angle BEA$
G. $\angle BFA$
H. $\angle BGA$
J. $\angle BHA$
K. $\angle BDA$

DO YOUR FIGURING HERE.

Use the following information to answer questions 43–45.

The graph of $y = f(x)$ is shown in the standard (x,y) coordinate plane below with points V, W, X, Y, and Z labeled.

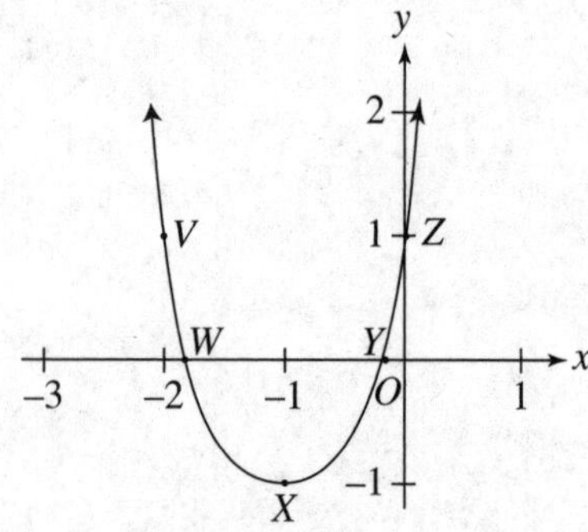

43. The y-intercept of the graph of $y = f(x)$ is located at which of the following points?

A. V
B. W
C. X
D. Y
E. Z

44. The function $y = f(x)$ can be classified as one of which of the following types of functions?

F. Trigonometric
G. Quadratic
H. Absolute value
J. Cubic
K. Linear

45. If $y = f(x)$ is to be reflected across the line $y = x$, which of the following graphs represents the result?

DO YOUR FIGURING HERE.

A.

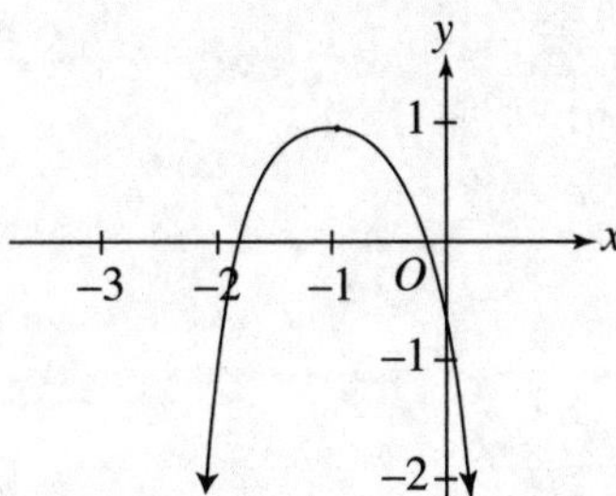

B.

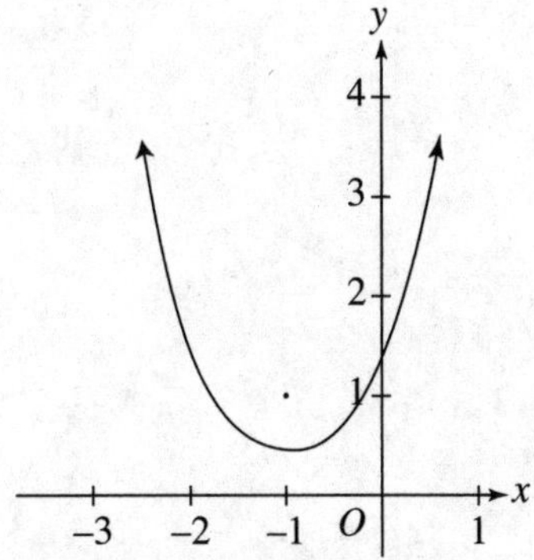

C.

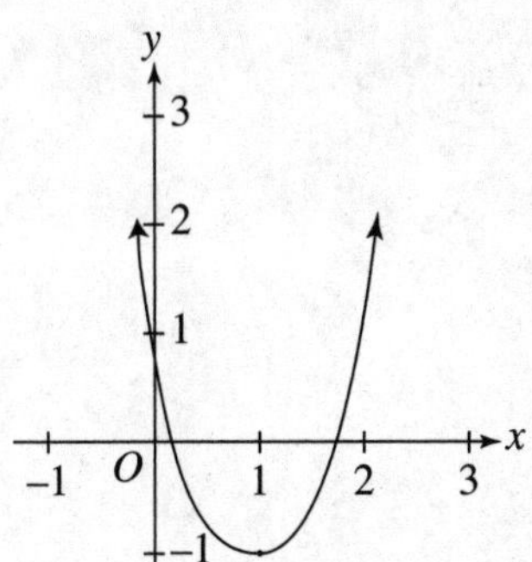

D.

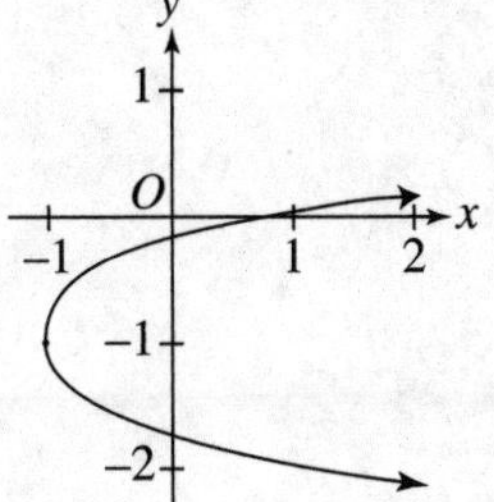

E.

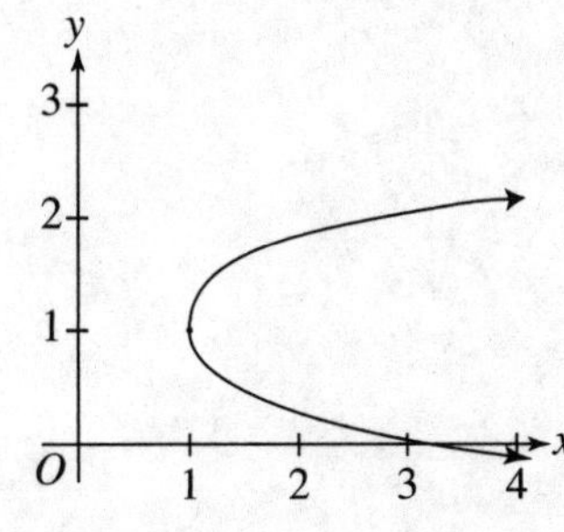

DO YOUR FIGURING HERE.

46. If a is a factor of 32 and b is a factor of 45, the product of a and b could NOT be which of the following?

F. 1,440
G. 288
H. 80
J. 54
K. 1

47. For each positive integer k, let k_o be the sum of all positive odd integers less than k. For example, $6_o = 5 + 3 + 1 = 9$ and $7_o = 5 + 3 + 1 = 9$. What is the value of $17_o \times 4_o$?

A. 16
B. 144
C. 256
D. 324
E. 816

48. If $(a,-3)$ is on the graph of the equation $x - 4y = 14$ in the standard (x,y) coordinate plane, then a = ?

F. $-\frac{17}{4}$
G. -2
H. 2
J. 17
K. 26

49. For all $t > 1$, $f(t) = \frac{t^2 - 1}{t - 1} - t$. Which of the following is true about $f(t)$?

A. It increases in proportion to t.
B. It increases in proportion to t^2.
C. It decreases in proportion to t.
D. It decreases in proportion to t^2.
E. It remains constant.

50. In the figure below, X is on $\overline{WZ}$. If the angle measures are as shown, what is the degree measure of $\angle YXZ$?

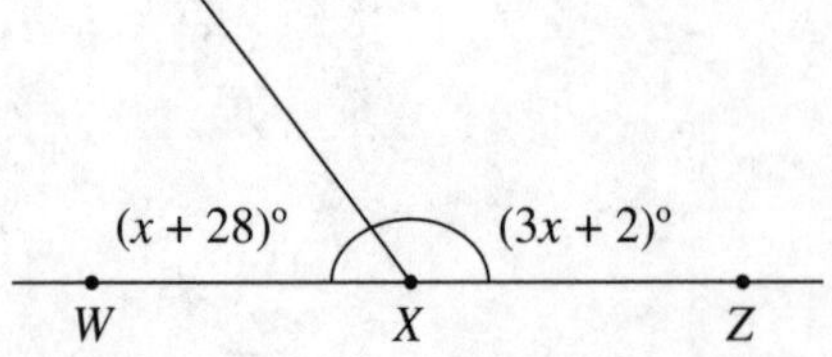

F. 25°
G. $37\frac{1}{2}°$
H. $65\frac{1}{2}°$
J. $112\frac{1}{2}°$
K. $114\frac{1}{2}°$

Y
(x + 28)°
(3x + 2)°
W
X
Z

51. Points (2,–2) and (3,10) lie on the same line in the standard (x,y) coordinate plane. What is the slope of this line?

DO YOUR FIGURING HERE.

A. 12

B. 8

C. $\frac{1}{12}$

D. –8

E. –12

52. What is the degree measure of an angle that measures $\frac{7\pi}{15}$ radians?

F. $\left(\frac{360-7\pi}{15}\right)^{\circ}$

G. $\left(180-\frac{7\pi}{15}\right)^{\circ}$

H. 252°

J. 84°

K. 12°

53. Which of the following gives the equation for the circle in the standard (x,y) coordinate plane with a center at (4,–8) and a circumference of 10π coordinate units?

A. $(x-4)^2+(y+8)^2=25$
B. $(x-4)^2+(y+8)^2=100$
C. $(x+8)^2+(y-4)^2=25$
D. $(x+8)^2-(y-4)^2=100$
E. $(x+8)^2+(y-4)^2=100$

54. For some x and y that satisfy the equation $xy=-x^2$, which of the following is FALSE?

F. $x\left(\frac{1}{y}\right)=-1$

G. $x^2\left(\frac{1}{y^2}\right)=1$

H. $x^2+y^2=-2xy$

J. $x^2=y^2$

K. $x^3-y^3=0$

DO YOUR FIGURING HERE.

55. Rectangle $ABCD$ lies in the standard (x,y) coordinate plane with corners at $A(4,2)$, $B(6,-1)$, $C(1,-4)$, and $D(-1,-1)$, and is represented by the 2×4 matrix $\begin{bmatrix} 4 & 6 & 1 & -1 \\ 2 & -1 & -4 & -1 \end{bmatrix}$. $ABCD$ is then translated, with the corners of the translated rectangle represented by the matrix $\begin{bmatrix} 1 & 3 & -2 & -4 \\ n & -3 & -6 & -3 \end{bmatrix}$. What is the value of n ?

A. 0
B. −1
C. −2
D. −3
E. −4

56. Whenever $a > 0$, which of the following real number line graphs represents the solutions for x to the inequality $|x - a| \leq 3$?

F.
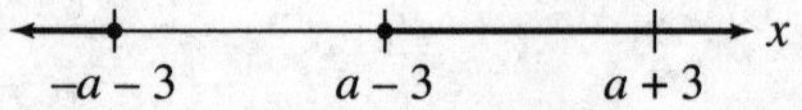

G.
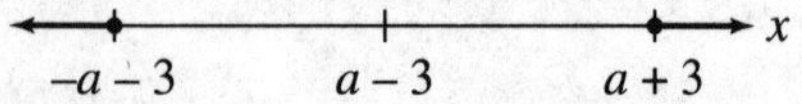

H.
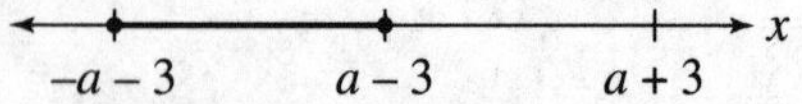

J.
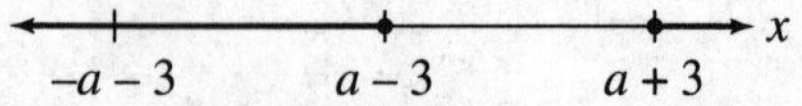

K.
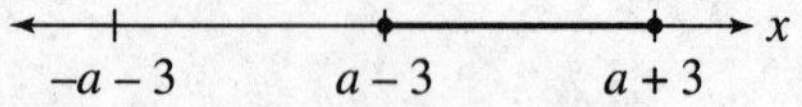

57. Three different functions are defined in the table below.

DO YOUR FIGURING HERE.

Symbol	Function	Description
→ → BOTH →	BOTH	If both inputs are 1, the output will be 1. If both inputs are 0, the output will be 0. If both inputs are different, the output will be 0.
1st → 2nd → 3rd → IF →	IF	If the first input is 1, the output will be the second input. If the first input is 0, the output will be the third input.
→ (CHANGE) →	CHANGE	If the input is 1, the output is 0. If the input is 0, the output is 1.

The diagram below uses three functions. The only values for p, q, r, s, and t are 1 and 0. Which of the following inputs (p, q, r, s, t) will produce the output 0 ?

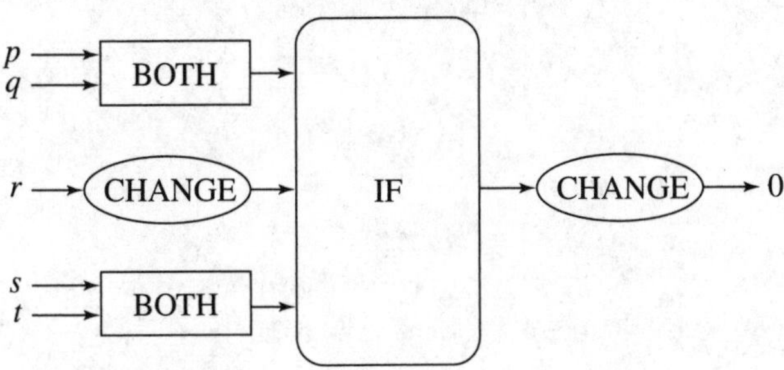

A. (0,1,1,0,1)
B. (0,1,1,1,1)
C. (0,0,1,0,1)
D. (1,0,1,0,0)
E. (1,0,1,0,1)

58. Whenever x and y are both integers, what is $(6.0 \times 10^x)(5.0 \times 10^y)$ expressed in scientific notation?

F. 30.0×100^{xy}
G. $30.0 \times 100^{x^y}$
H. 30.0×10^{xy}
J. $3.0 \times 10^{x+y+1}$
K. 3.0×10^{xy}

DO YOUR FIGURING HERE.

59. The points P, Q, R, and S lie in that order on a straight line. The midpoint of $\overline{QS}$ is R and the midpoint of $\overline{PS}$ is Q. The length of $\overline{QR}$ is x feet and the length of $\overline{PQ}$ is $4x - 16$ feet. What is the length, in feet, of $\overline{PS}$?

A. 32
B. 20
C. 16
D. 8
E. 4

60. The circle below has an area of 64π cm^2. A central angle with measure 24° intercepts minor $\overset{\frown}{CD}$. What is the length of minor $\overset{\frown}{CD}$, in centimeters?

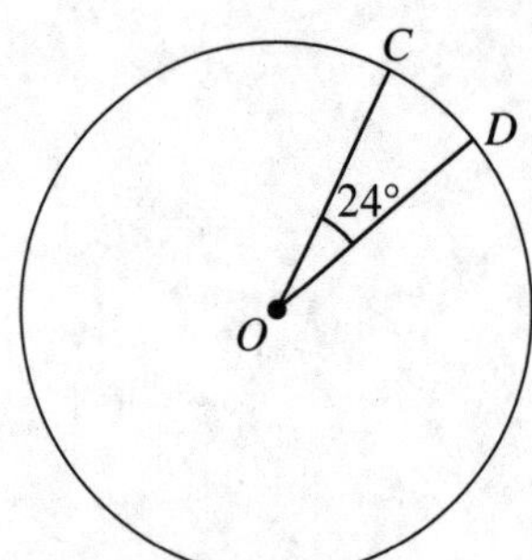

F. $\frac{1}{8}\pi$

G. $\frac{1}{4}\pi$

H. $\frac{16}{15}\pi$

J. $\frac{8}{3}\pi$

K. 192π

Math Practice Section 1 Answers and Explanations

MATH PRACTICE SECTION 1 ANSWERS

1. B
2. J
3. E
4. G
5. C
6. H
7. A
8. K
9. D
10. G
11. D
12. F
13. E
14. G
15. D
16. G
17. A
18. G
19. A
20. J
21. B
22. J
23. D
24. G
25. A
26. J
27. A
28. H
29. E
30. J
31. C
32. H
33. D
34. H
35. B
36. G
37. D
38. F
39. E
40. H
41. E
42. F
43. E
44. G
45. D
46. J
47. C
48. H
49. E
50. K
51. A
52. J
53. A
54. K
55. A
56. K
57. B
58. J
59. A
60. H

MATH PRACTICE SECTION 1 EXPLANATIONS

1. **B** The question asks for the number of additional goody bags the magician can buy. The magician receives 4($120) + 3($25) = $555 in payment for performances and light shows, leaving $635 – $555 = $80 in payment for additional goody bags. Since each costs $2.50, she provides $\frac{80}{2.5} = 32$ bags. Choice (A) calculates all 4.75 hours worked at the $120 rate. Choice (C) divides the $120 and $2.50 from the problem without answering the question, and (D) miscalculates based on three performances instead of four. Choice (E) assumes the entire $635 is for additional goody bag payments. The correct answer is (B).

2. **J** The question asks for the number of miles the runner ran slower than the marathon pace in 2004. Subtract the number of miles run at or faster than marathon pace during 2004 from the number of total miles run in 2004. This becomes 4,982 – 1,150 = 3,832. The correct answer is (J).

3. **E** The question asks how many times longer a 24-hour day is than 60 seconds. Convert the numbers into like units using conversion factors. There are 60 seconds in 1 minute, and since there are 60 minutes in 1 hour, multiply 24 hours × $\frac{60 \text{ minutes}}{1 \text{ hour}}$ to find that there are 1,440 minutes in 24 hours. The correct answer is (E).

4. **G** The question asks for the number of pages the student read. Since the student reads at two different rates in the given period, multiply each rate by the amount of days the student read at that rate and then add the rates together to find the total. This becomes $(a \times d) + (b \times 2d) = ad + 2bd$. Choice (F) omits the d in the second term, and (H) applies the 2 to both terms. Choice (J) drops the addition sign between the terms. Choice (K) multiplies the two terms instead of adding them. The correct answer is (G).

5. **C** The question asks for the area of the driveway. To find the area of the trapezoid, split it into a rectangle with dimensions of 12 and 6 and a triangle with a height of 12 and a base of 5; then add the areas of the two smaller shapes. This becomes $A = (6)(12) + \frac{1}{2}(5)(12) = 72 + 30 = 102$. Choice (B) gives the area of only the rectangular portion, and (A) gives the perimeter of the whole figure. Choice (E) doubles the area. Choice (D) finds the hypotenuse of the triangle and multiplies it by the height of the triangle. The correct answer is (C).

6. **H** The question asks for the number of visitors needed in June to keep the six-month avera[illegible] same as the five-month average. Use the graph to find the total number of visitors in [illegible] first five months; then find the average by adding the five numbers together and [illegible]

get (200 + 300 + 200 + 350 + 200) ÷ 5 = 250. For the six-month average to remain the same as this current average, the total in June must equal the current average of 250. Confirm this by testing the value in (H) and finding the new average, which is (200 + 300 + 200 + 350 + 200 + 250) ÷ 6 = 250. The correct answer is (H).

7. **A** The question asks for the height of the graduation cap after 3 seconds of flight. Use the provided equation to solve for f when $s = 3$. The equation becomes $f = 60(3) - 17(3^2) = 180 - 153 = 27$ feet. The correct answer is (A).

8. **K** The question asks which student had the greatest range in test scores. Emily's score range is 89 – 70 = 19 points. The range for Cleo's and David's scores are 18 points each, and Alicia's score range is 17 points. Choice (G) gives the *smallest* range in test scores, 91 – 79 = 12. The correct answer is (K).

9. **D** The question asks for the fractional amount of fish that Nita caught. Subtract the number of fish caught by Craig and Chris to find how many fish Nita caught. Find Chris's total by multiplying 300 by 45% to get 300 × 0.45 = 145. Since Chris caught 145 fish and Craig caught 25, Nita must have caught 300 – 145 – 25 = 140 fish. Convert this value into a fraction by putting it over the total number of fish caught and then reduce: $\frac{140}{300} = \frac{7}{15}$. The correct answer is (D).

10. **G** The question asks for the value of a compound function, so work from the inside out. Find the value of $g(4)$ and substitute it into the function given for $f(x)$. The value of $g(4) = 3 - \frac{4}{2} = 3 - 2 = 1$, and the value of $f(1) = 4(1)^2 = 4$, (G). Choice (F) stops at the value of $g(4)$ and (K) finds $f(4)$. The other choices make small math errors within each function. The correct answer is (G).

11. **D** The question asks for the area of the shaded region. Estimate by calculating the area of a 6 × 6 square surrounding the shaded figure and then counting and subtracting the unshaded squares within that 36 unit area: roughly 18 squares. Subtract 36 – 18 = 18. The closest answer to this est[illegible]). The correct answer is (D).

[illegible]sks for the total rise of the 62-inch ramp. Because the question asks about the rise [illegible]t horizontal runs, sketch one run of 24 with a ramp of 6. Sketch a second run of [illegible]. Make each a triangle by drawing a third line from the top of the ramp to the [illegible]wo triangles have three congruent angles, so they're similar. To solve, set up a [illegible] The proportion is $\frac{6}{24} = \frac{x}{62}$. Cross-multiply to get 24x = 372. Divide both [illegible] = 15.5. The correct answer is (F).

13. **E** The question asks for the value of the expression for a given x and y. Substitute the given values of x and y into the expression and simplify, using the rules of order of operations (PEMDAS). The expression becomes $(-3)^2 + [(2 \times 2) - (2 \times -3)] = 9 + [4 - (-6)] = 9 + (4 + 6) = 19$. Choice (C) drops the second negative sign in the final term, subtracting 6 from 4 instead of adding. Choice (B) subtracts 9 from 10 in the last step instead of adding. Choice (A) negates the value of $2x - 2y$. Choice (D) finds the value of xy in the first term of the expression instead of y^x. The correct answer is (E).

14. **G** The question asks which of the line pairs must be parallel based on the provided information. Because $\angle DEA$ measures 105° and $\angle BDE$ measures 75°, and the sum of these angles is 180°, $\overline{BD}$ and $\overline{AE}$ are parallel. Eliminate choices that do not include II, (F) and (H). Since there is no way to determine the measures of $\angle ABD$ or $\angle BAE$, it cannot be concluded that $\overline{AB}$ and $\overline{DE}$ are parallel. Therefore, eliminate (J) and (K). The correct answer is (G).

15. **D** The question asks for the expression that gives the total amount of money earned selling T-shirts. Multiply the price by the number of shirts sold to find the earnings for a given day. The price of the shirt would start at \$4.10 and be reduced by increments of \$0.02, which can be written as $(4.10 - 0.02x)$. Eliminate (A) and (B), which reduce the price of the shirt by increments of \$2 instead of \$0.02, and eliminate (C), which adds \$0.02 to the price instead of subtracting from it. The question states that the number of shirts sold will increase by 1 for each \$0.02 decrease in price, so eliminate (E), which increases the number of shirts sold by only 0.02. The correct answer is (D).

16. **G** The question asks for an equivalent expression. To factor $x^2 - 7x + 12$, find two numbers that multiply to +12 and add to −7. Those numbers are −4 and −3. The factored expression is $(x - 4)(x - 3)$. The correct answer is (G).

17. **A** The question asks for the value of an expression given x and y. Substitute the values given for x and y in the equation: $\frac{5(2)}{70} + \frac{9}{5(5+2)} + \frac{1}{5+2} = \frac{10}{70} + \frac{9}{35} + \frac{1}{7}$. Find a common denominator for all of the fractions by looking at the smallest multiple of 70, 35, and 7: this number is 70. The equation becomes $\frac{10}{70} + \frac{18}{70} + \frac{10}{70} = \frac{38}{70} = \frac{19}{35}$. To avoid having to simply all these fractions, another approach would be to find the decimal answer on a calculator and compare it to the decimal versions of the answers. The correct answer is (A).

18. **G** The question asks for the largest possible product of the digits displayed on a timer. To find the greatest possible product, first determine the largest number of minutes and seconds [illegible] sible, which is 59:59. After that, the timer will roll over to its maximum value [illegible] Multiply the digits together to get $(5)(9)(5)(9) = 2{,}025$. Choice (F) results from (5 [illegible] and (H) takes the product of (59)(59) instead of separating the values into di[illegible]

finds the number of seconds in an hour, and (K) assumes the largest display to be 99:99, which it cannot be because, as the problem states, this is only a 60-minute timer. The correct answer is (G).

19. **A** The question asks for the smaller of two integers with a difference of 6 and a sum of 42. The smaller number must be less than half of 42, so eliminate (C), (D), and (E). Test the remaining answers. If the smaller number is 19, the larger number would be 42 – 19 = 23. Since the difference between 23 and 19 is not 6, eliminate (B). Check (A) by following the same steps. If 18 is the smaller number, the larger number is 42 – 18 = 24. The difference between 24 and 18 is 6, so the correct answer is (A).

20. **J** The question asks for the area of the two congruent triangles. The area of the square is 324, so each side is 18. Since the two right triangles are isosceles, their respective bases and heights are congruent. For each of the triangles, $A = \frac{1}{2}bh = \frac{1}{2}(18)(18) = 162$. There are two triangles, so the total area is 162 × 2 = 324. Choice (G) gives the area of only one triangle, and (K) gives the area of the entire figure. Choice (F) assumes 324 to be the area of the entire figure and divides by three, assuming that the three smaller shapes are equal in area. Choice (H) doubles the value of (F). The correct answer is (J).

21. **B** The question asks for the vertical height of the kite. Since the triangles are similar, set up a proportion: $\frac{8}{17} = \frac{x}{85}$. Cross-multiply to get $17x = 680$; then divide both sides by 17 to find that $x = 40$. Choice (A) is 17 + 8 = 25. Choice (C) is 85 + 17 = 102. Choice (D) is 85 + 17 + 8 = 110. Choice (E) flips one side of the proportion: $\frac{8}{17} = \frac{85}{x}$. The correct answer is (B).

22. **J** The question asks for the value of x that is true for the given equation. Rewrite the equation as $(x - 1)(x - 1) = (x - 7)(x - 7)$ and multiply everything out to get $x^2 - 2x + 1 = x^2 - 14x + 49$. Subtract x^2 from each side to get $-2x + 1 = -14x + 49$. Add $14x$ to each side to get $12x + 1 = 49$. Subtr[illegible]n each side to get $12x = 48$. Divide both sides by 12 to get $x = 4$. Another approach [illegible] the answers in the equation. When $x = 4$, the equation becomes $(4 - 1)^2 = (4 - 7)^2$. [illegible] $(3)^2 = (-3)^2$ or $9 = 9$, making the equation true. The correct answer is (J).

23. **D** The question asks for the coordinates of point *C*. Draw a horizontal line at point *A* to split $\angle BAC$ in half, creating two 30°-60°-90° triangles. The *y*-value at point *A*, which is *w*, is equal to the *y*-value halfway between points *B* and *C*, so the *y*-value at point *C* is twice as big: 2*w*. Eliminate (A), (C), and (E), where the *y*-value is not 2*w*. The ratio of the sides of a 30°-60°-90° triangle is $1:\sqrt{3}:2$ from smallest to largest, so the length of the leg adjacent to the 30° angle is $\sqrt{3}$ times the length of the shorter leg, or $w\sqrt{3}$. Choice (B) neglects to multiply the *x*-value by $\sqrt{3}$. The correct answer is (D).

24. **G** The question asks for the area of a square quilt. The diagonal of a square makes two triangles with angle measures 45°, 45°, and 90°, and sides in the proportion $x{:}x{:}x\sqrt{2}$. Since the hypotenuse of one of the triangles is $4\sqrt{2}$, the legs of that triangle, which are also the sides of the square, measure 4 feet. The area of the square is side^2 = 4^2 = 16 feet^2. The correct answer is (G).

25. **A** The question asks for a true trigonometric relationship for the given triangle. Use SOHCAHTOA to remember the trigonometric relationships. Given an angle θ, the side opposite θ, and the hypotenuse, use the sine function, which is $\sin\theta = \frac{\text{opposite}}{\text{hypotenuse}}$. Here, that becomes $\sin\theta = \frac{15}{x}$, which matches (A). Choices (B) and (C) confuse cosine and tangent with sine. Choice (E) contains $\frac{\sin\theta}{\cos\theta}$, which is equal to tan θ, making (E) the same answer as (C). Choice (D) refers to the angle θ itself but does not give the trigonometric relationship between the triangle's sides. The correct answer is (A).

26. **J** The question asks which value of *a* is true for the given equation. Test the answer choices in the equation. Test (H): *a* = 25 and the equation becomes $\sqrt{45+25}+\sqrt{25} = \sqrt{70}+5$, which is approximately 13.4. Since this answer is smaller than 15, eliminate (F), (G), and (H). Test (J): the equation becomes $\sqrt{45+36}+\sqrt{36} = \sqrt{81}+6$, which simplifies to 9 + 6 and equals 15. The correct answer is (J).

27. **A** The question asks for the perimeter of the pentagon. Use the Pythagorean Theorem to find the length of $\overline{EF}$. The midpoints cut each side of the rectangle in half, so *AF* = 6 and *AE* = 8. Right triangle *AFE*, then, is a 6:8:10 triangle, and *EF* = 10. *FG* is also 10, and the perimeter of the pentagon is 10 + 10 + 8 + 12 + 8 = 48 inches. Choice (B) is the perimeter of the rectangle. Choice (C) is the area of a triangle with the same base and height as the rectangle. Choices (D) and (E) are the areas of the pentagon and rectangle, respectively. The correct answer is (A).

28. **H** The question asks for the percent of female workers in 2004. That year, there were 60 million female workers age 16 or over and there were 130.9 million total such workers. Since both units are in millions, the percent can be made with the easier-to-use numbers of 60 and 130.9. The percent of the workers who are female is found by $\frac{60}{130.9} \times 100 \approx 46\%$. The correct answer is (H).

29. **E** The question asks for the measure of the central angle for the "Public" portion of the pie chart. Since the chart shows that 8.4% of the workers took *public transportation,* the degree measure of the central angle for the "Public" sector must also be 8.4% of the 360° in a circle: $\frac{8.4}{100} \times 360 \approx 30°$. Choice (A) is the percent of workers who took public transportation in 2006. Choice (B) is the measure of the central angle for the workers in 2006 who walked in 2006. Choice (D) is the central angle that would result from using the public transportation percentage from 2004. The correct answer is (E).

30. **J** The question asks for the average yearly growth in the female workforce. In 2006, there were 63.6 million female workers. In 2004, there were 60.0 million female workers. The total growth was 3.6 million. The growth happened over a 2-year period, so the average growth per year is $3.6 \div 2 = 1.8$ million female workers per year. Choice (F) is the difference between the number of female workers in 2004 and 2005 divided by 2. Choice (G) is the result of dividing 3.6 by 4 years rather than 2 years. Choice (H) is the average growth in the number of male workers between 2005 and 2006. Choice (K) is the difference between the number of female workers in 2004 and 2006. The correct answer is (J).

31. **C** The question asks for the total time required to fill the pool using both hoses together. To solve, enter the data into the given equation and solve using a common denominator. The equation becomes $\frac{1}{20} + \frac{1}{60} = \frac{3}{60} + \frac{1}{60} = \frac{4}{60} = \frac{1}{15}$, so T_c, the combined time, is 15 minutes. Choice (A) divides the two numbers given, while (E) finds their average. Choices (B) and (D) make calculation errors. Choice (E) is also unreasonable because the combined time must be less than the time of either hose working alone. The correct answer is (C).

32. **H** The question asks for the probability that the die will NOT land on a prime-numbered face. The numbers 2, 3, and 5 are prime, while 6 and 4 are not. The probability that the die will NOT land on a prime number is 2 non-prime numbers out of 5 total numbers, or $\frac{2}{5}$. Choice (G) is the probability that the die WILL land on a prime-numbered face. The correct answer is (H).

33. **D** The question asks for the value of the function when using the provided values for x and y. Find y by substituting $x = 3$: $y = \left(\frac{5}{3}\right)^2 = \frac{25}{9}$. Now find the value of $7x + 9y$, which is $7 \times 3 + 9 \times \frac{25}{9} = 21 + 25 = 46$. The answers in (A) and (B) may result from forgetting to square the fraction or to multiply it by 9. Choice (C) comes from not squaring the $\frac{5}{3}$. Choice (E) comes from squaring only the 5 in the numerator. The correct answer is (D).

34. **H** The question asks for the length of a diagonal for the square. Start drawing the square by plotting the three provided points. Now, add in the missing fourth corner, which would logically go at (0,4). Next, draw in the diagonal from (0,0) to (4,4) or from (0,4) to (4,0). Since the diagonal of a square will divide the square into two 45-45-90 triangles, use the standard $x{:}x{:}x\sqrt{2}$ ratio of sides in a 45-45-90 triangle to find the length of the hypotenuse. Because the length of each side of the square is 4, the hypotenuse of the triangle must be $4\sqrt{2}$. Choice (G) gives the length of a side of the square, and (J) and (K) apply the side ratios of a 30-60-90 triangle instead of a 45-45-90. The correct answer is (H).

35. **B** The question asks for the value of a in the logarithm. Apply the definition of a logarithm to rewrite the equation as $4^3 = a$ and evaluate to find that $a = 64$. Choices (D) and (E) incorrectly rewrite the logarithm, and (C) multiplies 4 and 3 together instead of taking 4 to the third power. The correct answer is (B).

36. **G** The question asks which statement is true based on the given equation. An easy way to answer this question is to test each answer choice to find the pair of numbers that satisfies the equation. Choice (F) becomes $y = 18 - 0.2(0.2) = 17.96$ quarts left in the pot, so $18 - 17.96 = 0.04$ quart of water has boiled away. This isn't equal to the 1 quart in the answer, so eliminate (F). For (G), $y = 18 - 0.2(1) = 17.8$, so 0.2 quart has boiled away. This matches the information in the answer. The correct answer is (G).

37. **D** The question asks for the total amount of liquid that the cup can hold. The second figure shows that the small and large diameters of the coffee cup are 4 and 6, respectively, so the radii are 2 and 3. Plugging the numbers into the equation given results in $V = \frac{1}{3}\pi(5.5)(3^2 + 2^2 + 3\times2) = \frac{1}{3}\pi(5.5)(19) \approx 109$. Choice (A) is the portion of the equation inside the parentheses, and (C) neglects to multiply by $\frac{1}{3}\pi$. Choice (B) uses a height of $\frac{5}{2}$ instead of $5\frac{1}{2}$, or 5.5. Choice (E) plugs the diameters into the equation instead of the radii. The correct answer is (D).

38. **F** The question asks for the set of values that satisfies the given equation. Choices (F) and (K) are clues that the two sides of the equation are either always equal or never equal, and simplifying the right side of the equation to $9x + 12$ shows that the two sides are indeed the same. Since $9x + 12$ will equal itself for all real numbers, the correct answer is (F).

39. **E** The question asks for a simplified form of the compound fraction. The order of operations requires simplifying the fractions grouped in each of the three parts of the fraction as a first step, so begin with the fractions in the numerator. The denominator of that fraction, $\frac{3}{4} - \frac{2}{3}$, becomes $\frac{9}{12} - \frac{8}{12}$ and equals $\frac{1}{12}$. Since dividing by a fraction is the same as multiplying by the reciprocal, the entire numerator of the expression becomes $\frac{3}{4} \div \frac{1}{12} = \frac{3}{4} \times \frac{12}{1}$, which equals 9. Now simplify the remaining denominator: $\frac{3}{4} - \frac{2}{3} + \frac{1}{2} = \frac{9}{12} - \frac{8}{12} + \frac{6}{12} = \frac{7}{12}$. Find the final solution by dividing 9 by $\frac{7}{12}$, which becomes $9 \div \frac{7}{12} = 9 \times \frac{12}{7} = \frac{108}{7}$. The other answers to this question confuse the order of operations or represent common calculator errors. The correct answer is (E).

40. **H** The question asks for the area of the shaded circular region inside the bagel. To find the area of a circle, find the radius of the circle. Since the bagel is 144 mm across and the distance from the inner circle to the outer one is 56 mm, the diameter of the inner circle must be $144 - 56 - 56 = 32$. The radius of a circle is half of its diameter, so $r = 32 \div 2 = 16$. The area is $\pi r^2 = \pi(16^2) \approx 800$. Choice (J) uses the diameter of the inner circle instead of the radius to find the area, and (K) is the area of the total bagel. The correct answer is (H).

41. **E** The question asks for the value of the given expression. Any nonzero number raised to the 0 power = 1. So $a^0 = 1$, $b^0 = 1$, and $c^0 = 1$. Since $1 + 1 + 1 = 3$, the correct answer is (E).

42. **F** The question asks which angle has the largest tangent value. Use SOHCAHTOA to remember that $\tan\theta = \frac{\text{opposite}}{\text{adjacent}}$. For each of the angles, the opposite side is *AB*. Since *AB* is constant for each angle, the length of the adjacent side is all that matters when determining which angle has the greatest tangent value. The angle with the shortest adjacent side, $\angle BEA$, has the greatest tangent. Choice (K) gives the smallest tangent value instead of the largest one. The correct answer is (F).

43. **E** The question asks for the *y*-intercept of the function in the graph. The *y*-intercept of a graph is the point where the graph meets up with (intercepts) the vertical (*y*) axis. This graph meets up with the *y*-axis at point (0,1), which is labeled as *Z*. Choices (B) and (D) are the two *x*-intercepts of the graph. Choices (A) and (C) do not lie on either axis. The correct answer is (E).

44. **G** The question asks which type of function *f*(*x*) represents. Use Process of Elimination. The function is clearly not a straight line, so eliminate (K). The function does not repeat in a wave-like pattern, so it is not trigonometric: eliminate (F). An absolute value function forms a V pattern instead of a U-shaped one, so eliminate (H). Cubic functions are not vertically symmetrical, so eliminate (J). The correct answer is (G).

45. **D** The question asks what the function of the graph would look like if reflected along the line $y = x$. To reflect a graph over this line, switch the *x*- and *y*-coordinates of the function: point *V* at (–2,1) becomes (1,–2), point *Z* at (0,1) becomes (1,0), and point *X* at (–1,–1) stays the same. Sketch these points into a new graph and match to an answer. Choice (A) reflects the graph across the *x*-axis, and (C) reflects the graph across the *y*-axis. Choice (E) reflects the graph but moves the vertex from (–1,–1) to (1,1), and (B) simply moves the graph up two units. The correct answer is (D).

46. **J** The question asks which number could NOT be the result of multiplying together a factor from each of the two given numbers. Start by factoring the two given numbers, being careful not to forget that every real number has 1 and itself as factors. The factors of 32 are 32, 16, 8, 4, 2, and 1; the factors of 45 are 45, 15, 9, 5, 3, and 1. Now test the answers by seeing if one number taken from each list can be multiplied together to equal the answer. Choice (F) is 32×45, (G) is 32×9, (H) is 16×5, and (K) is 1×1. Since there is no factor of 32 that can be multiplied by a factor of 45 to equal 54, the correct answer is (J).

47. **C** The question asks for the sum of two numbers that have first been run through the provided function. Follow the rule given in the question to find $17_o = 15 + 13 + 11 + 9 + 7 + 5 + 3 + 1 = 64$ and $4_o = 3 + 1 = 4$. So $17_o \times 4_o = 64 \times 4 = 256$. Choice (A) is $17_o \div 4_o$. Choice (B) is 72×2, which mistakenly adds all the even values less than the two numbers instead of the odd ones. Choice (D) is 81×4, which is the result of adding all the odd numbers less than or equal to *k*. Choice (E) adds together both the odd and even values less than *k*. The correct answer is (C).

48. **H** The question asks for the value of *a*, which is the *x*-value of the equation when $y = -3$. There's no need to graph the equation or to put it into $y = mx + b$ form. Substitute *a* into the equation for *x* and –3 into the equation for *y*. The equation becomes $a - 4(-3) = 14$ or $a + 12 = 14$. Therefore, $a = 2$. Choice (F) is the result of substituting *a* for *y* and –3 for *x*. Choice (K) is the result of a sign error when substituting to get $a - 12 = 14$. The correct answer is (H).

49. **E** The question asks for a description of the function. Substitute values to see what happens as *t* grows larger. When $t = 2$, $f(t) = \dfrac{2^2 - 1}{2 - 1} - 2 = 1$. When $t = 3$, $f(t) = \dfrac{3^2 - 1}{3 - 1} - 3 = 1$. Even when $t = 1{,}000$, $f(t) = \dfrac{1{,}000^2 - 1}{1{,}000 - 1} - 1{,}000 = 1$. Choices (A), (B), (C), and (D) mirror terms from the question but do not accurately describe what happens as *t* changes. Using algebra to simplify the equation also shows that the function always equals 1: $f(t) = \dfrac{t^2 - 1}{t - 1} - t = \dfrac{(t-1)(t+1)}{(t-1)} - t = (t+1) - t = 1$. The correct answer is (E).

50. **K** The question asks for the measure of $\angle YXZ$. Since $\angle YXZ$ is clearly larger than 90°, eliminate (F), (G), and (H). Now solve for x. Since there are 180° in a straight line, the sum of the two angle measures must be equal to 180. Therefore, $(3x + 2) + (x + 28) = 180$. Simplify the equation to get $4x + 30 = 180$; then subtract 30 from both sides to get $4x = 150$. Divide both sides by 4 to find that $x = 37.5$. To find the measure of $\angle YXZ$, substitute this value of x in $3x + 2$ to get $3(37.5) + 2 = 112.5 + 2 = 114.5°$. The correct answer is (K).

51. **A** The question asks for the slope of a line containing the two given points. Use the slope formula, $m = \frac{y_2 - y_1}{x_2 - x_1}$, plugging in the provided values to get $\frac{10-(-2)}{3-2} = \frac{10+2}{1} = \frac{12}{1} = 12$. Choice (C) reverses the numerator and denominator of the slope formula, and (B), (D), and (E) confuse positive and negative signs when subtracting or dividing. The correct answer is (A).

52. **J** The question asks for the equivalent measure in degrees of an angle measure in radians. Degree measurements should not be in terms of π, so eliminate (F) and (G). Now, multiply by a conversion factor to change units. The relationship between degrees and radians is $180° = \pi$ radians. Substitute 180 for π to get an angle measure of $\frac{7(180)}{15} = \frac{1,260}{15} = 84°$. The correct answer is (J).

53. **A** The question asks for the standard equation for the circle with the given properties. The equation of a circle with center (h,k) and radius r is defined as $(x - h)^2 + (y - k)^2 = r^2$. Here, $h = 4$ and $k = -8$. Eliminate (C), (D), and (E), which all flip the values of h and k. To find the radius, use the circumference 10π given in the problem. $C = \pi d = 10\pi$, so the diameter is 10. The radius is half of that, or 5, so to complete the equation, $r^2 = 25$. Choice (B) squares the diameter instead of the radius. The correct answer is (A).

54. **K** The question asks which equation is false for values that satisfy the given equation. Choose values for x and y that make the given statement true. For example, if $x = 2$, then $2y = -(-2^2)$, which simplifies to $2y = -4$, and results in $y = -2$. Now use these values to test out the answer choices. Choice (F) becomes $2\left(\frac{1}{-2}\right) = -1$, which is true. Since the question asks about a statement that is false, eliminate (F). For (G), the equation becomes $2^2\left(\frac{1}{(-2)^2}\right) = 1$ or $\frac{4}{4} = 1$. Eliminate (G). Choice (H) becomes $(2)^2 + (-2)^2 = -2(2)(-2)$ or $4 + 4 = 8$. Eliminate (H). For (J), the equation becomes $(2)^2 = (-2)^2$ or $4 = 4$, so eliminate (J). Choice (K) must be false, and indeed the equation $(2)^3 - (-2)^3 = 0$ becomes $8 - (-8) = 0$ or $16 = 0$. The correct answer is (K).

55. **A** The question asks for the value of n in the second matrix. Compare the points of the original rectangle with the first matrix to see that the x values of A, B, C, and D run along the top row and their y-values run along the bottom row. By this logic, the value of n in the second matrix represents the y-coordinate of A after it is translated. Since translating a figure moves each corner of the figure over equal distances along the x- and y-axes, compare the y-coordinates in the first matrix to the known y-coordinates in the second matrix. Each y value is decreased by 2 ($-1 - 2 = -3$, $-4 - 2 = -6$, and $-1 - 2 = -3$) when it is translated into the second matrix, so n must be $2 - 2 = 0$. The correct answer is (A).

56. **K** The question asks for the number line graph of an absolute value inequality. First, use Process of Elimination. When an absolute value function is less than a given number, its solution is an "and": the answer would state that x is greater than one number and also less than another, and when graphed, this solution would be a single line with two defined end points. Choices (F), (G), and (J) give "or" solutions, which would work only if the given absolute value function was *greater* than a particular number: eliminate them. Now, begin solving the inequality by first considering the positive case of the absolute value, $x - a \le 3$. This simplifies to $x \le a + 3$, an endpoint which is not part of (H) but is part of (K). The correct answer is (K).

57. **B** The question asks for a possible set of inputs that yields a final output of 0. Start from the output 0. Since a CHANGE function needs to have input 1 to get output 0, the output of the IF function needs to be a 1. A 1 is the output of an IF function either if the first input is 1 and the second input is 1, or if the first input is 0 and the third input is 1. The first input could be 1 if both p and q are 1; however, no answer choices contain p and q values that are both 1. Therefore, p and q could be either 0 and 1, or 1 and 0, or 0 and 0, to yield an output of 0. This doesn't narrow any answer choices. Since the first input of the IF function is 0, the second input could be either 1 or 0, so the input of the next CHANGE function doesn't matter. However, s and t must both be 1, since the output of the BOTH function must be a 1 in order to make the third term in the IF function a 1. Choice (B) is the only answer choice that has s and t both as 1. The correct answer is (B).

58. **J** The question asks for the value of the two terms multiplied together when expressed in scientific notation. Use Process of Elimination. Since scientific notation requires the lead term be a number between 1 and 10, eliminate (F), (G), and (H). When multiplying two exponential numbers with like bases, the exponents should be added together, not multiplied, so eliminate (K). The correct answer is (J).

59. **A** The question asks for the length of $\overline{PS}$. Start by drawing a number line and filling in the provided information. If $\overline{QR}$ has a length of x feet and R is the midpoint of $\overline{QS}$, $\overline{RS}$ is the same length as $\overline{QR}$. As $\overline{QS} = \overline{QR} + \overline{RS}$, $\overline{QS} = x + x = 2x$. Since $\overline{PQ} = 4x - 16$, and Q is the midpoint of $\overline{PS}$, $\overline{PQ} = \overline{QS}$ and $2x = 4x - 16$. Simplify this equation to find that $-2x = -16$ and $x = 8$. To find the total length of $\overline{PS}$, substitute $x = 8$ into the algebraic measures of $\overline{PQ}$ and $\overline{QS}$ and add the results. When $x = 8$, $4x - 16 + 2x = 4(8) - 16 + 2(8) = 32 - 16 + 16 = 32$. The correct answer is (A).

60. **H** The question asks for the length of a minor arc on the given circle. Find the radius of the circle using the area formula: $A = \pi r^2$. For this circle, the formula becomes $64\pi = \pi r^2$ and $r = 8$. To find the length of a minor arc, first find the circumference of the circle: $C = 2\pi r = 2\pi(8) = 16\pi$. The minor arc is $\frac{24}{360} = \frac{1}{15}$ of the circumference of the circle. Therefore, the length of the minor arc is $\widehat{CD} = \left(\frac{1}{15}\right)(16\pi) = \frac{16}{15}\pi$. Choice (F) attempts to use the radius of the circle, 8, to find the fractional part of the circle. Choice (G) is similar to (F) but uses half of the radius. Choice (J) is the area divided by the central angle. Choice (K) is the radius multiplied by the central angle. The correct answer is (H).

Math Practice Section 2

MATHEMATICS TEST

60 Minutes—60 Questions

DIRECTIONS: Solve each problem, choose the correct answer, and then darken the corresponding oval on your answer document.

Do not linger over problems that take too much time. Solve as many as you can; then return to the others in the time you have left for this test.

You are permitted to use a calculator on this test. You may use your calculator for any problems you choose, but some of the problems may best be done without using a calculator.

Note: Unless otherwise stated, all of the following should be assumed:

1. Illustrative figures are NOT necessarily drawn to scale.
2. Geometric figures lie in a plane.
3. The word *line* indicates a straight line.
4. The word *average* indicates arithmetic mean.

DO YOUR FIGURING HERE.

1. What is the value of $(a-f)(j-a+f)$ for $a=3$, $f=-7$, and $j=6$?

A. −64
B. −40
C. −8
D. 16
E. 40

2. A beaker contains one ounce of Solution A and n ounces of Solution B. The salt content of each ounce of Solution A is 3.1 grams, and the salt content of each ounce of Solution B is 2.3 grams. If the beaker has a total salt content of 10 grams, which of the following models the salt content of the beaker?

F. $2.3n = 3.1n + 10$
G. $2.3n = 3.1 + 10$
H. $2.3n(3.1) = 10$
J. $2.3n + 3.1n = 10$
K. $2.3n + 3.1 = 10$

3. In ΔFGH, shown below, the measure of $\angle G$ is 76°. If $\overline{FG} \cong \overline{GH}$, what is the measure of $\angle H$?

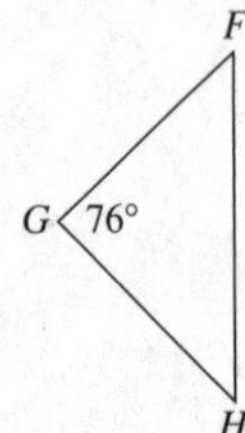

A. 52°
B. 60°
C. 76°
D. 104°
E. 128°

4. What is the perimeter, in meters, of a square with an area of 36 square meters?

DO YOUR FIGURING HERE.

F. 6
G. 12
H. 18
J. 24
K. 72

5. Victoria will randomly select 1 cookie from a jar containing exactly 16 cookies. If the jar contains 5 oatmeal raisin cookies, 4 snickerdoodle cookies, and 7 chocolate chip cookies, what is the probability that Victoria's cookie is NOT a snickerdoodle cookie?

A. $\frac{1}{16}$

B. $\frac{1}{12}$

C. $\frac{1}{3}$

D. $\frac{2}{3}$

E. $\frac{3}{4}$

6. What is the value of $-|3-24|-|-3|$?

F. −30
G. −27
H. −24
J. 24
K. 27

7. The shipping weight of a food product is the total weight of the rectangular box containing the package, the packaging elements, and the food product within. The packaging weight of a food product is the weight of the rectangular box containing the food product and all the packaging elements. The net weight of a food product is the difference between the shipping weight and the packaging weight. The shipping weight of one package of chocolate is 760 grams. The chocolate is packaged in a rectangular box weighing 225 grams. With the packaging elements as shown below, what is the net weight of the chocolate in one package?

DO YOUR FIGURING HERE.

Packaging elements	Weight in grams
Plastic inner divider	15
Wrappers for Chocolates	10
Shrink wrap on box	5
Ribbon on box	35
Nutrition facts insert	20

A. 350
B. 400
C. 450
D. 500
E. 550

8. At 10 a.m., a campaign worker has assembled 16 mailings for voters. By 2 p.m., the worker has assembled 88 mailings for voters. Which of the following is the closest to the number of mailings that this worker assembled per hour during those 4 hours?

F. 18
G. 19
H. 22
J. 26
K. 29

9. Three friends agree to share the work on a job that they know will take a total of 6 hours to complete. Jurnee works on the job by herself for $1\frac{4}{5}$ hours, then Jacob works by himself for another $2\frac{3}{5}$ hours. If Jones will complete the rest of the job by himself, how many hours will he need to work?

A. $4\frac{2}{5}$

B. $2\frac{4}{5}$

C. $1\frac{4}{5}$

D. $1\frac{3}{5}$

E. $\frac{3}{5}$

DO YOUR FIGURING HERE.

10. In the equation $\frac{3^{3n}}{9^2} = 3^2$, what is the value of n ?

F. 1
G. 2
H. 4
J. 9
K. 81

11. For $x = 2$, what is the value of $j(x) + k(x)$ when $j(x) = 4(3)^x$ and $k(x) = \frac{6}{x}$?

A. 27
B. 33
C. 39
D. 141
E. 147

DO YOUR FIGURING HERE.

12. Kunal, a pharmacist, sorted bottles of medicine in a box at the end of the day, and then he left the office for the evening. The next day, he realized he lost the piece of paper that had the quantities of the different packages in the box. He recalled that there were only 12 dose and 24 dose count bottles of medicine. He also remembered that there were 48 bottles in the box with a total of 720 doses. How many 24 dose count bottles of medicine were in the box?

F. 4
G. 12
H. 36
J. 52
K. 60

13. What is the slope of a line that has a coordinate point of (11,–2) and crosses the x-axis at (4,0) when the line is graphed in the standard (x,y) coordinate plane?

A. $-\frac{7}{2}$

B. $-\frac{2}{7}$

C. $\frac{1}{4}$

D. $\frac{4}{13}$

E. 4

14. A right triangle contains an angle with a measure of θ. If $\cos\theta = \frac{12}{13}$ and $\tan\theta = \frac{5}{12}$, what is the value of $\sin\theta$?

F. $\frac{5}{13}$

G. $\frac{13}{5}$

H. $\frac{12}{5}$

J. $\frac{12}{\sqrt{313}}$

K. $\frac{12}{\sqrt{119}}$

DO YOUR FIGURING HERE.

15. Which of the following is equivalent to $\frac{20\sqrt{32}}{5\sqrt{2}}$?

A. $4\sqrt{30}$
B. 80
C. 64
D. 20
E. 16

16. $\overline{QR}$ is intersected by $\overline{ST}$ at the point U, as shown by the figure below. If $\angle QUT$ has a measure of $(8x - 22)°$, and $\angle SUR$ has a measure of $(6x + 18)°$, what is the measure of $\angle QUS$?

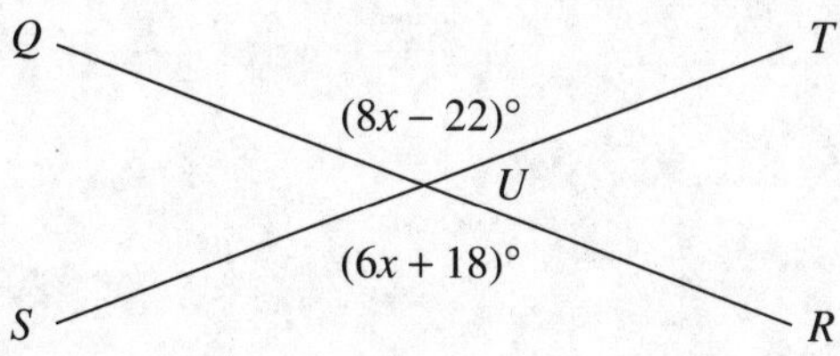

F. 24°
G. 42°
H. 96°
J. 156°
K. 160°

17. At a school picnic, 150 children scored points in a game, as shown in the table below. The lowest number of points was 2 points and the highest was 7 points. What is the probability that a child would have scored 5 points or more, rounded to the nearest hundredth?

Number of Points	Number of children
2	15
3	45
4	43
5	17
6	14
7	16

A. 0.09
B. 0.11
C. 0.20
D. 0.31
E. 0.89

DO YOUR FIGURING HERE.

18. If $y = 6$ and $y = -3$ are solutions to the equation $y^2 - 3y + p = 0$, what is the value of p ?

F. 18
G. 9
H. 3
J. −3
K. −18

19. The area of a circle is 144π square centimeters. What is the circumference of the circle in centimeters?

A. 6π
B. 24π
C. 36π
D. 144π
E. 324π

20. A college student's ID is required to contain 4 single-digit numbers alternating with 4 letters: for example, Q1P3R5S7. Only odd numbers from 1 to 9, inclusive, can be used, and none of the 5 vowels can be part of the student ID. Otherwise, each letter and each digit can be used up to 4 times. Which expression accurately represents the number of student IDs that can be generated using these requirements?

F. 21(5)(20)(5)(19)(5)(18)(5)
G. 21(5)(21)(5)(21)(5)(21)(5)
H. 21(9)(20)(8)(19)(7)(18)(6)
J. 26(9)(25)(8)(24)(7)(23)(6)
K. 26(9)(26)(9)(26)(9)(26)(9)

21. Which of the following expressions is equivalent to $4(6c - d) + 7(3c - d)$?

A. $45c - 11d$
B. $45c - 5d$
C. $45c - 2d$
D. $45c + 3d$
E. $45c + 6d$

22. A garden with an area of one square unit is divided into plots, as shown in the figure below. All plots are squares that have the same area. What is the area of the garden, in square units, that is represented by the non-shaded region?

DO YOUR FIGURING HERE.

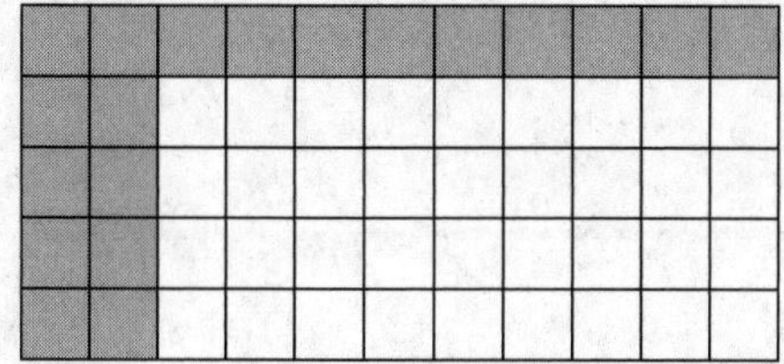

F. $\frac{1}{5} \cdot \frac{2}{11}$

G. $\frac{1}{5} \cdot \frac{9}{11}$

H. $\frac{1}{5} \cdot \frac{4}{5}$

J. $\frac{4}{5} \cdot \frac{2}{11}$

K. $\frac{4}{5} \cdot \frac{9}{11}$

23. Lucy is designing a new set of tiles. In the drawing of a single tile, $\angle NMP$ has a measure of 110°, $\angle MPO$ has a measure of 60°, $NM = MP$, and $NO = OP$. Which of the following is the measure of $\angle NOP$?

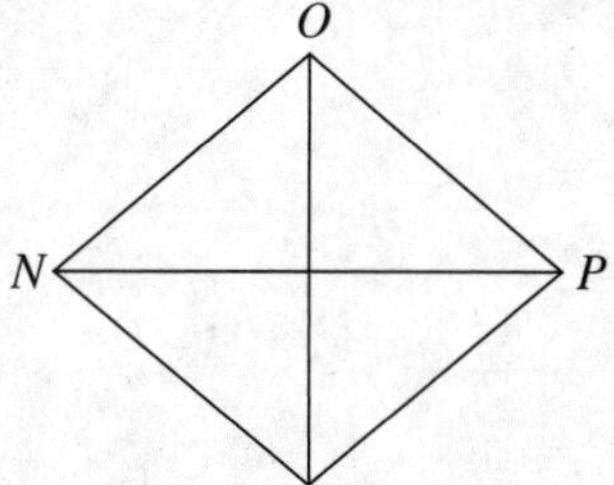

A. 25°
B. 60°
C. 85°
D. 120°
E. 130°

DO YOUR FIGURING HERE.

24. Which of the following correctly expresses the area of ΔGHI, in square centimeters, if the triangles are similar ($\Delta JKL \sim \Delta GHI$)?

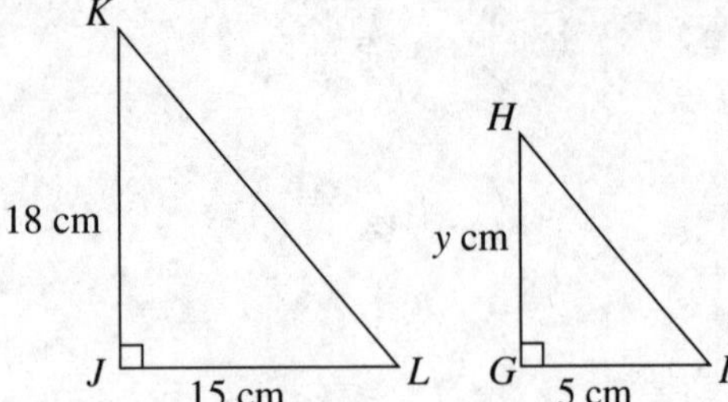

F. $\frac{1}{2}(5)(6)$

G. $\frac{1}{2}\left(\frac{18}{y}\right)(3)$

H. $\frac{1}{2}(15)(18)$

J. $\frac{1}{2}(3)(15)(18)$

K. $\frac{1}{2}(15+5)(18+y)$

25. The dimensions of the interior of a child's toy chest is 4 dm by 2 dm by 1 dm. The toy box will be filled with building blocks that have dimensions of 10 cm by 10 cm by 10 cm. If the toy chest is filled with building blocks in such a way that the chest is completely filled without overflow and the top of the toy chest can close, how many building blocks are inside the toy chest? (Note: 1 dm = 10 cm)

A. 36
B. 16
C. 10
D. 8
E. 2

DO YOUR FIGURING HERE.

Use the following information to answer questions 26–29.

Plane A is traveling from Miami to Chicago. The coordinate plane below shows the graph of velocity (v) versus time (t) for the first 30 minutes of the flight. The graph is composed of 2 line segments with endpoints at (0,0), (5,15), and (30,12). Plane A traveled 37.5 kilometers in the first 5 minutes.

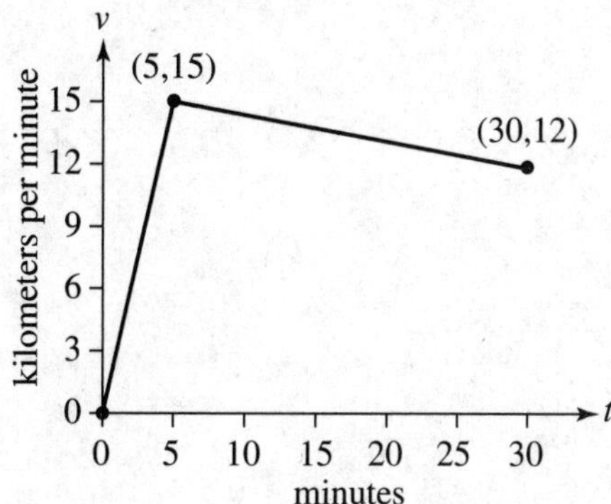

The plane speeds up when it experiences a tailwind at $t = 30$ minutes and then travels at a constant velocity for the remainder of the flight.

26. What is the velocity of Plane A at $t = 3$ minutes, in kilometers per minute?

F. 3.0
G. 7.5
H. 9.0
J. 10.5
K. 27.0

27. Over the interval from $t = 5$ minutes to $t = 30$ minutes, the acceleration, a, of Plane A is equal to the slope of the graph measured in kilometers per minute per minute. What is the value of a ?

A. $\frac{25}{3}$

B. 3

C. $\frac{3}{25}$

D. $-\frac{3}{25}$

E. $-\frac{25}{3}$

28. Plane B took off earlier than Plane A. Plane B was traveling at a constant velocity equal to $\frac{9}{10}$ of the maximum velocity of Plane A during the first 20 minutes of Plane A's flight. How far did Plane B travel during the first 20 minutes of Plane A's flight, in kilometers?

F. 60
G. 80
H. 90
J. 135
K. 270

DO YOUR FIGURING HERE.

29. Which of the graphs below best represents the portion of Plane A's flight beginning at $t = 30$ minutes?

A.
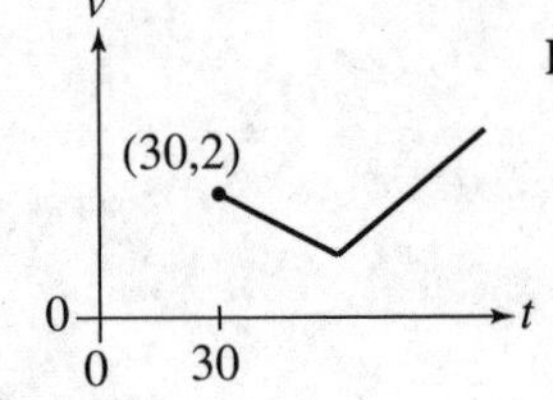

D.
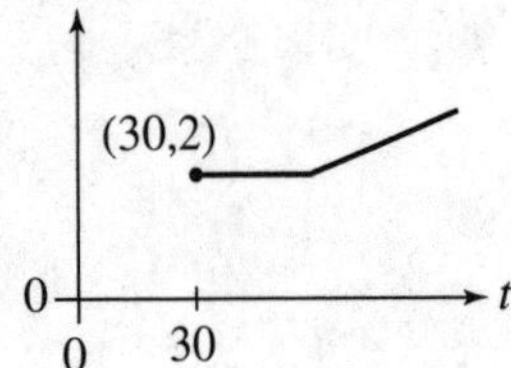

B.
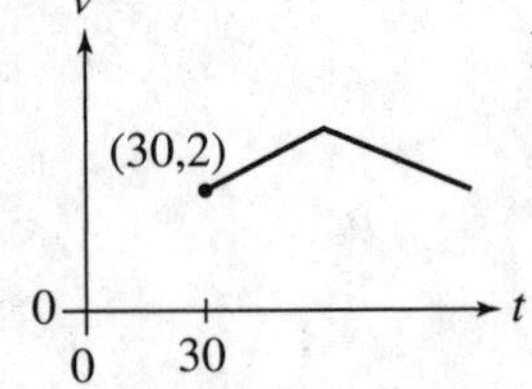

E.
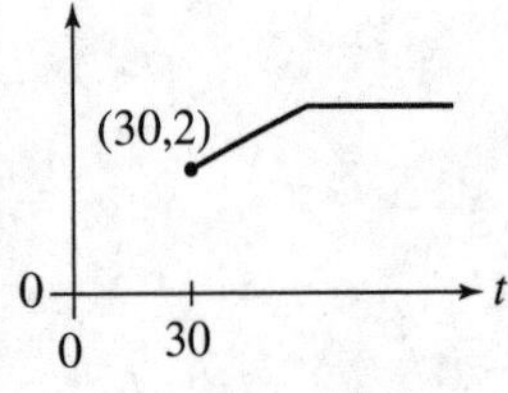

C.
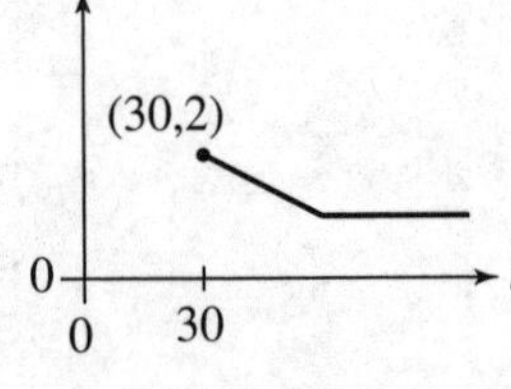

30. $-\frac{1}{2}\left(\frac{4}{50}+\frac{3}{25}\right)+\frac{7}{10}=?$

DO YOUR FIGURING HERE.

F. 1

G. $\frac{39}{50}$

H. $\frac{3}{5}$

J. $\frac{1}{25}$

K. $-\frac{1}{12}$

31. A rectangular piece of paper has 2 adjacent sides represented by $5d + 4$ inches and $d + 3$ inches. What is the area, in terms of d, of the rectangle in square inches?

A. $5d^2 + 19d + 12$
B. $5d^2 + 19d + 7$
C. $5d^2 + 9d + 12$
D. $5d^2 + 12$
E. $12d + 14$

32. Which of the inequalities below is true?

F. $6 > \sqrt{5} > 4$

G. $\frac{1}{6} > \sqrt{\frac{1}{5}} > \frac{1}{4}$

H. $\sqrt{7} > 6 > \sqrt{5}$

J. $7 > 2(\sqrt{7}) > 5$

K. $\sqrt{6} > 2(\sqrt{5}) > \sqrt{5}$

DO YOUR FIGURING HERE.

33. Two fair six-sided dice are repeatedly rolled simultaneously. What is the probability that both dice land with the number six facing up on the 48th roll?

A. $\frac{1}{4}$

B. $\frac{1}{36}$

C. $\frac{1}{48}$

D. $\frac{1}{144}$

E. $\frac{1}{192}$

34. A bowler's average score for the season is calculated based on the bowler's scores in ten games. Each game has a maximum score of 300 points. If Stacey has an average score of exactly 240 points in the first seven games of the season, how many points must she average in the last 3 games to earn an average score of 252 points exactly?

F. 253
G. 264
H. 270
J. 276
K. 280

35. When combining $\left(\frac{1}{23}\right)$ ___ 32, with each operation listed below placed in the blank, which one will produce the smallest result?

A. Multiplication
B. Averaging
C. Division
D. Addition
E. Subtraction

DO YOUR FIGURING HERE.

36. Which of the following defines a function g from R onto S given the sets below?

$$R = \{0, 1, 2, 3, 4\}$$

$$S = \{-4, 1, 6, 11, 16\}$$

F. $g(x) = x - 4$
G. $g(x) = 3x + 2$
H. $g(x) = 3x + 4$
J. $g(x) = 5x - 4$
K. $g(x) = 5x + 4$

37. What is the sequence of a, b, and c from greatest to least if

$a = \frac{5}{6} + \frac{6}{5}$, $b = \frac{3}{5} + \frac{5}{3}$, and $c = 3 - 1$?

A. $c > b > a$
B. $c > a > b$
C. $b > c > a$
D. $b > a > c$
E. $a > b > c$

38. On the isosceles triangle in the figure below, ΔEFG, $EF = 12$ centimeters, $EG = 2m$ centimeters, and $\angle EFG$ measures 122°. What is the value of m ?

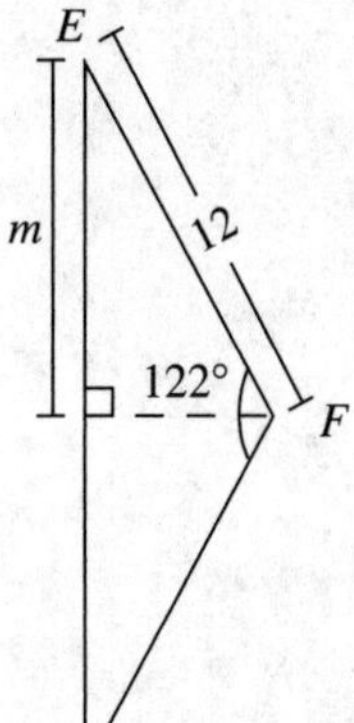

F. 12 tan 122°
G. 12 sin 122°
H. 12 csc 122°
J. 12 tan 61°
K. 12 sin 61°

39. A pair of numbers share a least common multiple (LCM) of 168. The larger number in the pair is 84. What is the greatest value the other number in the pair can have?

A. 56
B. 42
C. 21
D. 8
E. 2

DO YOUR FIGURING HERE.

40. Parabola Y with equation $y = 9x^2$ is graphed in the standard (x,y) coordinate plane. Parabola Z is the image of Parabola Y after a shift of 2 coordinate units up and 6 coordinate units to the right. Which of the following equations represents Parabola Z ?

F. $y = 9(x - 6)^2 - 2$
G. $y = 9(x - 6)^2 + 2$
H. $y = 9(x + 2)^2 - 6$
J. $y = 9(x + 6)^2 - 2$
K. $y = 9(x + 6)^2 + 2$

Use the following information to answer questions 41–43.

DO YOUR FIGURING HERE.

A study conducted in 2015 by a polling organization surveyed 811 people and asked each of them to estimate how many pairs of shoes they have at home. The data compiled in the table below summarizes the percentages for each response. To give an example, about 25% of the respondents in the survey said that they have at least 13 pairs of shoes but not more than 15 pairs of shoes in their home.

Pairs of shoes	Percent of people polled
Less than 3	4%
4 to 6	12%
7 to 9	20%
10 to 12	22%
13 to 15	25%
More than 15	15%
Did not respond	2%

41. The approximate number of people who participated in the poll and stated that they have fewer than 10 pairs of shoes at home is equal to which of the following expressions?

A. 811(0.22)
B. 811(0.36)
C. 811(22)
D. 811(36)
E. 811(58)

42. What percent of those who were polled estimated that they have at least 7 pairs of shoes at home?

F. 16%
G. 20%
H. 36%
J. 82%
K. 84%

DO YOUR FIGURING HERE.

43. The polling agency created a circle graph of the data in the table. One of the sectors of the circle graph represents the percent of people from the survey who estimated that they have more than 15 pairs of shoes in their home. The central angle of that sector of the circle chart has what measure?

A. 15°
B. 17°
C. 45°
D. 54°
E. 61°

---

44. As shown below, a paint ball is shot at the ceiling, striking it at an angle. The measure of that angle is given as x.

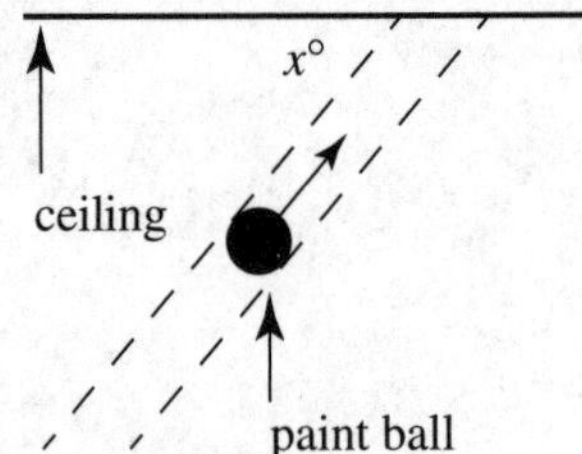

The paint from the paintball makes an oval shape on the ceiling. The maximum length and width of the oval can be measured and used to calculate angle x with the formula $\sin x = \frac{length_{max}}{width_{max}}$. The paintball stain is shown below. At approximately what angle did the paintball that made the stain strike the ceiling?

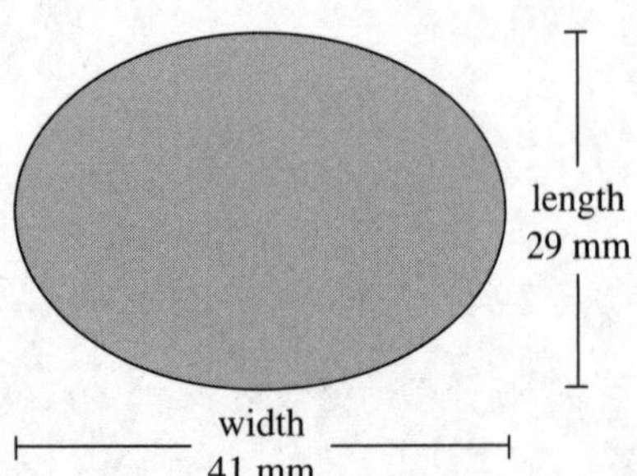

F. 0°
G. 15°
H. 30°
J. 45°
K. 120°

DO YOUR FIGURING HERE.

45. The distribution of a set of 14 integers is shown in the bar chart below. Which of the following is true about the mean, mode, and median of the numbers in the set?

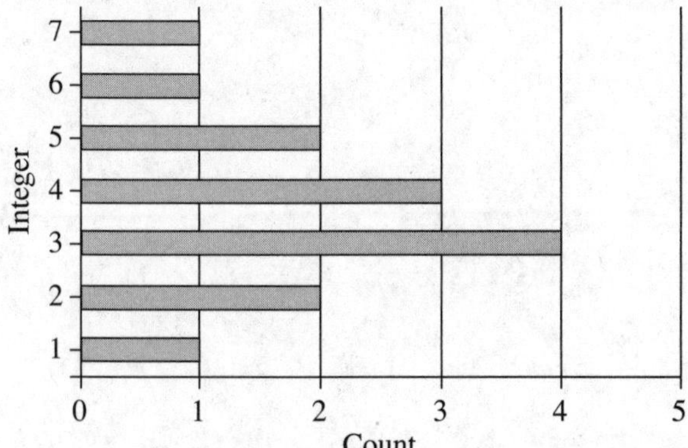

A. The mean is the greatest of the three, and the median is the least of the three.
B. The mean is the greatest of the three, and the mode and median are equal.
C. The mean is the greatest of the three, and the mode is the least of the three.
D. The mean and median are equal, and the mode is the least of the three.
E. The mean, median, and mode are all equal to each other.

46. Three dogs—an Akita, a beagle, and a collie—each have been given several chew toys by their owners. The beagle has five times as many toys as the Akita and collie have together, and the collie has three fewer toys than the Akita. If the Akita has a toys and the beagle has b toys, what is the relationship between a and b ?

F. $b = a - 3$
G. $b = a + 3$
H. $b = 5a$
J. $b = 10a - 15$
K. $b = 10a + 15$

47. Given the two points in the standard (x,y) coordinate plane $(3,2)$ and $(-1,9)$, what is the distance between them in coordinate units?

A. $\sqrt{33}$
B. $\sqrt{53}$
C. $\sqrt{65}$
D. $\sqrt{67}$
E. 11

DO YOUR FIGURING HERE.

48. A large aquarium can hold 10 cubic feet of water. How many cubic feet of water would the aquarium be able to hold if each of its three dimensions—length, width, and height—were tripled?

F. 30
G. 90
H. 270
J. 640
K. 810

49. The inequality $|a-3|>9$ is satisfied by the same set of values for a as which of the following inequalities:

A. $a<-6$ or $a>6$
B. $a<0$ or $a>12$
C. $a<-6$ or $a>12$
D. $a<-12$ or $a>6$
E. $a<-12$ or $a>12$

50. If $a^4 = 17{,}850{,}625$, which of the following is true for a ?

F. $10 < a < 100$
G. $100 < a < 1{,}000$
H. $1{,}000 < a < 10{,}000$
J. $10{,}000 < a < 100{,}000$
K. $100{,}000 < a < 10{,}000{,}000$

51. If $X = \begin{bmatrix} 1 & 0 \\ -2 & -1 \end{bmatrix}$, $Y = \begin{bmatrix} 3 & 1 & 0 \\ 1 & 2 & 6 \end{bmatrix}$, and $Z = \begin{bmatrix} 1 & 2 \\ 0 & -1 \\ 1 & 3 \end{bmatrix}$, then what is the value of $YZ + X$, if it is possible to be calculated?

A. $\begin{bmatrix} 4 & 5 \\ 5 & 17 \end{bmatrix}$

B. $\begin{bmatrix} 1 & 0 \\ -2 & -1 \end{bmatrix}$

C. $\begin{bmatrix} -5 & -4 \\ 2 & -1 \end{bmatrix}$

D. $\begin{bmatrix} 3 & 2 \\ 0 & -2 \\ 0 & 18 \end{bmatrix}$

E. $YZ + X$ cannot be calculated.

DO YOUR FIGURING HERE.

52. If it can be determined, what is the least value of the expression $\frac{a}{a+b}$ given $a \geq 10$ and $2 \leq b \leq 5$?

F. $\frac{5}{6}$

G. $\frac{2}{3}$

H. $\frac{1}{3}$

J. 0

K. Cannot be determined from the given information

53. A marathon runner records her speed in kilometers per hour while running in a marathon for 5 hours. According to the chart of the data she recorded below, what was her speed's rate of change, in kilometers per hour, between hours 1 and 3 ?

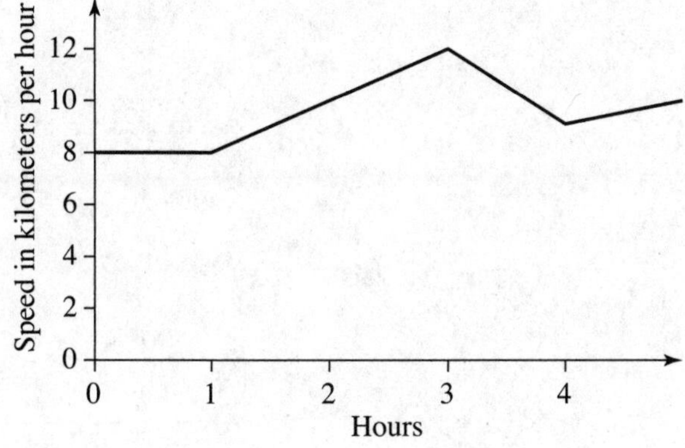

A. 1
B. 2
C. 4
D. 10
E. 12

DO YOUR FIGURING HERE.

54. A game involves rolling two dice that have an equal chance of landing on any of their sides. One of the dice has 6 sides numbered 1, 2, 3, 4, 5, and 6. The other die has 8 sides numbered 1, 2, 3, 4, 5, 6, 7, and 8. Players roll the dice and multiply the two numbers shown on the dice together. What is the probability that the product of the numbers rolled on the two dice is odd?

F. $\frac{1}{4}$

G. $\frac{3}{7}$

H. $\frac{1}{2}$

J. $\frac{4}{7}$

K. $\frac{3}{4}$

55.

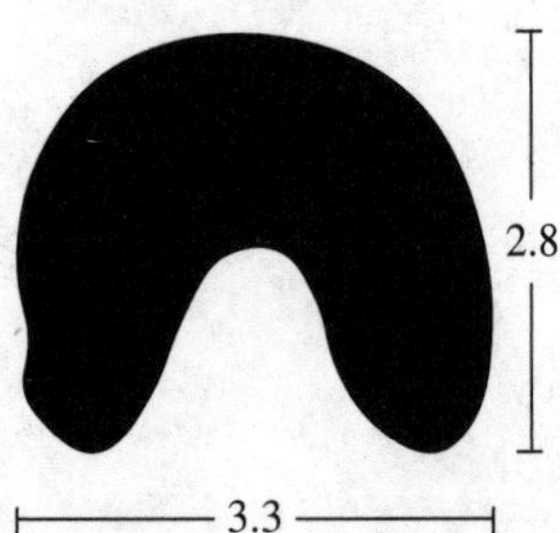

A slice of celery, as shown in the picture above, has a perimeter of 8.2 centimeters, and the top of the slice has an area of 6.4 cm^2. The celery is uniformly 0.3 centimeters thick. The lengths given in the diagram are in centimeters. What is the volume of the slice of celery, in cubic centimeters, if it can be determined?

A. 1.89
B. 1.92
C. 2.77
D. 4.38
E. Cannot be determined from the given information

56. Which of the following expressions is equivalent to the expression $[f(f-1)(f-2)\ \dots\ (1)]^g$ for all positive integer values of f and g ?

F. $(f!)^g$
G. $(g!)^f$
H. $(g^f)!$
J. $(f+g)!$
K. $[g(g-1)(g-2)\ \dots\ (1)]^f$

57. The standard (x,y) coordinate plane below shows the graph of a function with standard normal distribution ($\sigma = 1$ and $\mu = 0$). In any normal distribution, 68% of the data is within how many standard deviations of the mean?

DO YOUR FIGURING HERE.

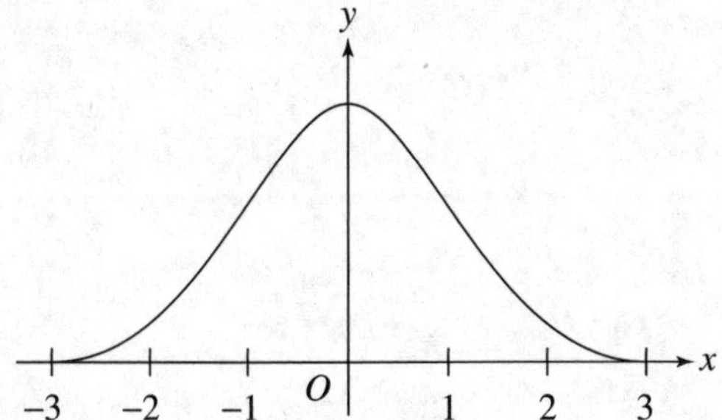

A. 0
B. 0.5
C. 1
D. 1.5
E. 2

58. The determinant of the matrix $\begin{bmatrix} 6 & x \\ 7 & 3 \end{bmatrix}$ has a value of −17.

What is the value of x ?

F. −35

G. −10

H. −5

J. 5

K. $\frac{59}{3}$

59. What values of x satisfy the equation $x^2 - 4x + 13 = 0$?

A. −1 and 5
B. $2 \pm 3i$
C. $2 \pm (\sqrt{17})i$
D. $2 \pm 6i$
E. $4 \pm 6i$

DO YOUR FIGURING HERE.

60. An artist creates a new sculpture that consists of tangent spheres. The top view, front view, and left side view are shown below, with labels to show where the top (T), front (F), and left (L) sides are in relation to each perspective. If the radius of one of the spheres is 1 m, what is the combined surface area of the spheres in the sculpture, in meters squared?

Note: the surface area of a sphere is given by the equation $4\pi r^2$.

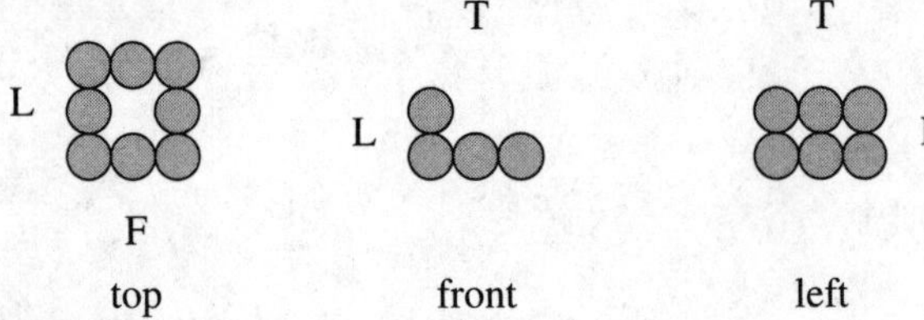

F. 24π
G. 36π
H. 44π
J. 48π
K. 72π

Math Practice Section 2 Answers and Explanations

MATH PRACTICE SECTION 2 ANSWERS

1. B
2. K
3. A
4. J
5. E
6. H
7. C
8. F
9. D
10. G
11. C
12. G
13. B
14. F
15. E
16. G
17. D
18. K
19. B
20. G
21. A
22. K
23. E
24. F
25. D
26. H
27. D
28. K
29. E
30. H
31. A
32. J
33. B
34. K
35. E
36. J
37. D
38. K
39. A
40. G
41. B
42. J
43. D
44. J
45. C
46. J
47. C
48. H
49. C
50. F
51. A
52. G
53. B
54. F
55. B
56. F
57. C
58. J
59. B
60. H

MATH PRACTICE SECTION 2 EXPLANATIONS

1. **B** The question asks for the value of an expression. Plug the given values for *a*, *f*, and *j* into the expression, being careful to put the correct value in each place. The expression becomes [3 – (–7)][6 – 3 + (–7)]. Simplify within each set of parentheses to get (3 + 7)(3 – 7), which becomes (10)(–4) = –40. The correct answer is (B).

2. **K** The question asks for an equation that models a specific situation. Translate the information into bite-sized pieces and eliminate after each piece. One piece of information says that there is *one ounce of Solution A* in the beaker. Look for other information about Solution A. The question states that *the salt content of Solution A is 3.1 grams.* The salt content provided by Solution A is 3.1 per ounce for one ounce, or just 3.1 grams. The 3.1 should not be multiplied by *n*. Eliminate (F), (H), and (J). Compare the remaining answer choices. The difference between (G) and (K) is the side of the equation that contains 3.1. The question states that the total salt content is 10 grams. This includes the 3.1 grams from Solution A plus the 2.3 grams per ounces from Solution B. The 3.1 should not be added to the 10, so eliminate (G). The correct answer is (K).

3. **A** The question asks for the value of an angle on a figure. Use the Geometry Basic Approach. Start by labeling the figure with the given information. Mark $\overline{FG}$ and $\overline{GH}$ as congruent. In a triangle with two equal sides, the angles opposite those two sides are also equal. Mark $\angle F$ and $\angle H$ as equal. There are 180° in a triangle, and $\angle G$ is given as 76°, so the sum of $\angle F$ and $\angle H$ is 180 – 76 = 104°. Divide this by 2 to find that $\angle H = \frac{104}{2} = 52°$. The correct answer is (A).

4. **J** The question asks for the perimeter of a square based on the area of the square. Use the Geometry Basic Approach. Start by drawing a square and labeling the figure with the given information. The area is *36 square meters*, and the area of a square is $A = s^2$. Plug in the value for the area to get $36 = s^2$, then take the square root of both sides to get $6 = s$. Label all 4 sides of the square as 6. The perimeter of any figure is the sum of the lengths of the sides. The perimeter of this square is 6 + 6 + 6 + 6 = 24. The correct answer is (J).

5. **E** The question asks for a probability, which is defined as $\frac{\text{number of desired outcomes}}{\text{number of total outcomes}}$. Read the question carefully to find the numbers to make the probability. There are 16 total cookies in the jar, so that is the *number of total outcomes.* Of these cookies, 5 + 7 = 12 are *NOT* snickerdoodle cookies, so that is the *number of desired outcomes.* Therefore, the probability is $\frac{12}{16}$, which reduces to $\frac{3}{4}$. The correct answer is (E).

6. **H** The question asks for the value of an expression with absolute values. When working with absolute values, do the calculations inside the absolute value symbols as if they are parentheses, then take the absolute value. The expression becomes $-|-21|-3=-21-3=-24$. The correct answer is (H).

7. **C** The question asks for *the net weight of the chocolate in one package.* Use bite-sized pieces to tackle this word problem. The question states that the *net weight* of the chocolates is the *difference between the shipping weight and the packaging weight.* The *shipping weight* of 1 package is given as 760 grams. The *packaging weight* is the weight of the box and the *packaging elements.* The question states that the box weighs 225 grams. The packaging elements are listed in the chart along with the weight of each element. Add the weight of the box and the weights in the chart to get a packaging weight of 225 + 15 + 10 + 5 + 35 + 20 = 310 grams. *Difference* means to subtract, so subtract the packaging weight from the shipping weight to get 760 – 310 = 450 grams for the net weight of the chocolates. The correct answer is (C).

8. **F** The question asks for the number of mailings *assembled per hour.* Since the question asks for a specific value and the answers contain numbers in increasing order, plug in the answers. Begin by labeling the answers as "mailings per hour" and start with (H), 22. The campaign worker started with 16 mailings. If the worker can assemble 22 more per hour for 4 hours, the total will be 16 + 22(4) = 16 + 88 = 104 mailings. The question states that the worker *has assembled 88* mailings, so this is too many. Eliminate (H). A smaller number of mailings in needed, so eliminate (J) and (K) as well. Try (F), 18, next as the result with (H) was off by quite a bit. If the worker can assemble 18 mailings per hour for 4 hours, the total will be 16 + 18(4) = 16 + 72 = 88 mailings. This matches the value given in the question, so stop here. The correct answer is (F).

9. **D** The question asks how long it will take Jones to complete the job by himself. Start by adding together the number of hours that Jurnee and Jacob worked. Add the whole numbers and the fractions separately to avoid making a mistake: $1\frac{4}{5}+2\frac{3}{5}=(1+2)+\left(\frac{4}{5}+\frac{3}{5}\right)=3+\frac{7}{5}=4\frac{2}{5}$. Now subtract $4\frac{2}{5}$ from 6 to get Jones's time as $1\frac{3}{5}$ hours. The correct answer is (D).

10. **G** The question asks for the value of the variable n in an equation with exponents. When dealing with questions about exponents, remember the MADSPM rules. The DS part of the acronym indicates that Dividing matching bases means to Subtract the exponents. In order to do this, a common base is needed. Rewrite 9 as 3^2. The equation becomes $\frac{3^{3n}}{(3^2)^2}=3^2$. The denominator now uses the PM part of the acronym, which means that to raise a base number with an exponent to another Power, Multiply the exponents. The equation now becomes $\frac{3^{3n}}{3^4}=3^2$. Now subtract the exponents to get $3^{3n-4}=3^2$. The exponents on the bases are equal, which means that $3n - 4 = 2$. Add 4 to

both sides of the equation to get $3n = 6$. Divide both sides by 3 to get $n = 2$. This question can also be solved by plugging in the answers. It may be necessary to try a few answers on a calculator, but that may be a more straightforward approach than solving. Either way, the correct answer is (G).

11. **C** The question asks for the sum of two functions for a given value of x. In function notation, the number inside the parentheses is the x-value that goes into the function, and the value that comes out of the function is the y-value. To get $j(2)$, plug $x = 2$ into the j function to get $j(2) = 4(3)^2 = 4(9) = 36$. To get $k(x)$, plug $x = 2$ into the k function to get $k(2) = \frac{6}{2} = 3$. To get $j(2) + k(2)$, add the values together to get $36 + 3 = 39$. The correct answer is (C).

12. **G** The question asks for a value in a model of a specific situation. Since the question asks for a specific value and the answers contain numbers in increasing order, plug in the answers. Begin by labeling the answers as "24 doses" and start with (H), 36. If there are 36 bottles with 24 doses in each bottle, those bottles contain 36(24) = 864 doses. There were only 720 doses altogether, so this is too many. Eliminate (H). There must be fewer of the 24-dose bottles to have a smaller total number of doses, so eliminate (J) and (K) as well. Try (G), 12. If there are 12 bottles with 24 doses in each bottle, those bottles contain 12(24) = 288 doses. There were 48 bottles, so with 12 of the 24-dose bottles, there would be 48 – 12 = 36 of the 12-dose bottles. These bottles would have 36(12) = 432 doses. Together, the two types of bottles would have 288 + 432 = 720 doses. This matches the information in the question, so stop here. The correct answer is (G).

13. **B** The question asks for the slope of a line. The slope of a line is defined as the change in y over the change in x, or $slope = \frac{y_2 - y_1}{x_2 - x_1}$. Plug in the values of the points in the question to get $m = \frac{0-(-2)}{4-11} = \frac{2}{-7} = -\frac{2}{7}$. The correct answer is (B).

14. **F** The question asks for the value of a trigonometric function. The trigonometric functions sine, cosine, and tangent have to do with right triangles, so draw a right triangle. Label one angle that is not the right angle as θ. Write out SOHCAHTOA to remember the trig definitions. The CAH part defines cosine as $\cos = \frac{\text{adjacent}}{\text{hypotenuse}}$. Since $\cos\theta = \frac{12}{13}$, label the adjacent side as 12 and the hypotenuse as 13. The TOA part defines tangent as $\tan = \frac{\text{opposite}}{\text{adjacent}}$. Since $\tan\theta = \frac{5}{12}$, label the opposite

side as 5. The question asks for the value of sin θ . The SOH part defines sine as $\sin = \frac{\text{opposite}}{\text{hypotenuse}}$, so take the side opposite the angle θ and place it over the length of the hypotenuse to get $\sin\theta = \frac{5}{13}$.

The correct answer is (F).

15. **E** The question asks for the value of an expression. Separate the expression into 2 fractions to get $\frac{20}{5} \times \frac{\sqrt{32}}{\sqrt{2}}$. Simplify the first fraction to get 4. To simplify the square root portion of the expression, put both the numerator and denominator under one square root to get $\sqrt{\frac{32}{2}} = \sqrt{16} = 4$. Next, multiply the numbers from both parts to get 4 × 4 = 16. The correct answer is (E).

16. **G** The question asks for the measure of an angle on a figure. No information is given about ∠*QUS*, so see what else can be determined. The figure has the expressions already labeled on it, so move on to the next step. Since angles opposite each other are equal, set the two expressions equal to each other to get $8x - 22 = 6x + 18$. Add 22 to both sides of the equation to get $8x = 6x + 40$. Next, subtract $6x$ from both sides of the equation to get $2x = 40$. Divide both sides of the equation by 2 to get $x = 20$. Plug $x = 20$ into one of the expressions to get the measure of the large angle: 8(20) – 22 = 160 – 22 = 138°. This is the measure of the large angles ∠*QUT* and ∠*SUR*. The question asks for the measure of the smaller angle. There are 180° in a line, so subtract 138 from 180 to get 180 – 138 = 42°. The correct answer is (G).

17. **D** The question asks for a probability, which is defined as $\frac{\text{number of desired outcomes}}{\text{number of total outcomes}}$. Read the table carefully to find the numbers to make the probability. The question asks for the probability that a child scored 5 points or more. The *number of desired outcomes* is the sum of the numbers of children who scored 5 or more points, or 17 + 14 + 16 = 47. The *number of total outcomes* is the total number of children in the table, or 150 as stated in the question. Place the numbers into the probability definition to get $\frac{47}{150} = 0.313$. The question asks for the probability *rounded to the nearest hundredth*, which is 0.31. The correct answer is (D).

18. **K** The question asks for the value of a constant in an equation given the solutions. To find the constant p, plug one of the solutions into the equation for y and solve for p. Plug $y = 6$ into the equation to get $(6)^2 - 3(6) + p = 0$. The equation becomes $36 - 18 + p = 0$. Simplify to get $18 + p = 0$. Subtract 18 from both sides of the equation to get $p = -18$. The correct answer is (K).

19. **B** The question asks for the circumference of the circle given the area of the circle. Use the Geometry Basic Approach and write out the formulas needed. The area of a circle is defined using the formula $A = \pi r^2$, where r is the radius. Plug the area of the circle into the equation to get $144\pi = \pi r^2$.

Divide both sides by π to get $144 = r^2$, then take the square root of both sides of the equation to get $12 = r$. The circumference of a circle is defined as $C = 2\pi r$. Plug the value of the radius into the formula for the circumference to get $C = 2\pi(12) = 24\pi$. The correct answer is (B).

20. **G** The question asks for the total number of possible letter/number combinations in a given scenario. The question says that the student's ID needs to alternate between 4 single digit numbers and 4 letters. The question also states that *Only odd numbers from 1 to 9, inclusive, can be used, and none of the 5 vowels can be part of the student ID*. Since there are 5 odd numbers from 1 to 9, eliminate (H), (J), and (K) because they use all 9 numbers from 1 to 9, not just the odd numbers. Because each letter and digit can be used up to four times, the number of options for each letter or number in each space should stay the same. Eliminate (F) because the number in each space where a letter would go decreases. The correct answer is (G).

21. **A** The question asks for an equivalent expression. To find the equivalent expression, first distribute to both sets of parentheses. The expression $4(6c - d) + 7(3c - d)$ becomes $24c - 4d + 21c - 7d$. Combine like terms to get $45c - 11d$. The correct answer is (A).

22. **K** The question asks for the area of the non-shaded region. The figure shows the garden divided into a grid of 11 columns and 5 rows. To find the area of the non-shaded region, use the formula $A = lw$. The length of the non-shaded region is 9 of the 11 columns, or $\frac{9}{11}$, and the width of the non-shaded region is 4 of the 5 rows, or $\frac{4}{5}$. Plug these into the formula for area to get $A = \frac{4}{5} \cdot \frac{9}{11}$. The correct answer is (K).

23. **E** The question asks for the measure of an angle. Use the Geometry Basic Approach. Since a figure is provided, label the figure with any information in the question. Label $\angle NMP$ as 110, $\angle MPO$ as 60, $NM = MP$, and $NO = OP$.

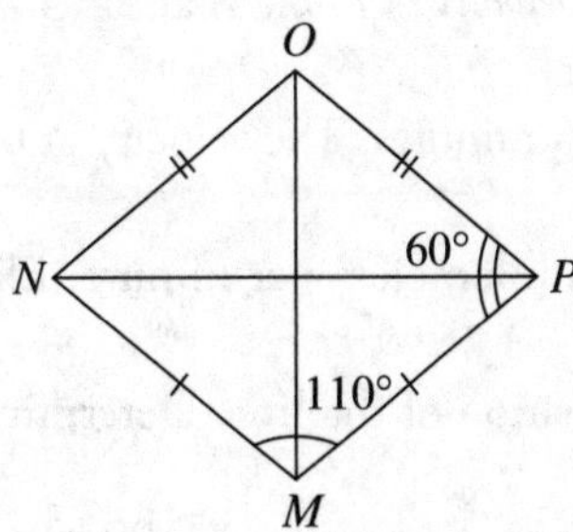

Next, if $NM = MP$, then $\angle MNP = \angle MPN$. There are 180° in a triangle, so the measure of sum of these angles is $180 - 110 = 70°$. Divide 70 by 2 to get the measure of one individual angle, which is 35°. Label this on the figure. Since $NO = OP$, this means that $\angle ONP = \angle OPN$. To find $\angle OPN$, subtract the measure of $\angle MPN$ from the measure of $\angle MPO$ to get $= 60 - 35 = 25°$. Therefore, $\angle ONP = \angle OPN = 25°$. There are 180° in ΔNOP, so $\angle NOP = 180 - 25 - 25 = 130°$. The correct answer is (E).

24. **F** The question asks for the area of ΔGHI given similar triangles. Similar triangles have congruent angles and sides that are proportional. To find the area of the smaller triangle, first find the height of the smaller triangle. The height can be found by setting up a proportion with similar sides in corresponding positions in the ratios. This becomes $\frac{GI}{JL} = \frac{GH}{JK}$. Plug in using the known side lengths to get $\frac{5}{15} = \frac{y}{18}$, then cross-multiply to get $15y = 90$. Divide both sides by 15 to get $y = 6$, which is the length of *GH*, the height of the smaller triangle. To find the area, use the formula $A = \frac{1}{2}bh$. Plugging in the values for the base and the height, the area is $A = \frac{1}{2}(5)(6)$. The correct answer is (F).

25. **D** The question asks for the number of blocks that can fit perfectly inside of a toy chest. To find the number of blocks that can fit inside without overflowing, first find the volume of the toy chest. Multiply the length by the width by the height to get $4 \times 2 \times 1 = 8$ dm^3. Before finding the volume of one building block, first change the units from centimeters to decimeters. Since there are 10 cm in 1 dm, the new dimensions of the building block are 1 dm by 1 dm by 1 dm. Find the volume of the building block by multiplying the length by the width by the height to get $1 \times 1 \times 1 = 1$ dm^3. Finally, divide the volume of the toy chest by the volume of one building block to get $\frac{8}{1} = 8$ building blocks. The correct answer is (D).

26. **H** The question asks for the *velocity of Plane A* at $t = 3$ *minutes.* Start by ballparking. A time of $t = 3$ minutes is between 0 and 5 minutes. The velocity at 0 minutes is 0 kilometers per minute, and the velocity at 5 minutes is 15 kilometers per minute. Eliminate (K), which is too large. To find the exact velocity, find the equation of the line. Determine the rate of change by calculating the slope of the interval. Use the equation $slope = \frac{y_2 - y_1}{x_2 - x_1}$. Using the points (0, 0) and (5, 15), the equation becomes $slope = \frac{15-0}{5-0} = \frac{15}{5} = 3$. The *y*-intercept of the line is 0, so the equation of the line is $v = 3t$. Plug in $t = 3$ to get $v = (3)(3) = 9$ kilometers per minute. The correct answer is (H).

27. **D** The question asks for the *acceleration* of the plane. The question says the acceleration is *equal to the slope of the graph*. Start by ballparking. From 5 minutes to 30 minutes, the speed is decreasing. The slope of this interval must be negative. Eliminate (A), (B), and (C). Now use two points and the equation $slope = \frac{y_2 - y_1}{x_2 - x_1}$ to calculate the slope of the line. For the points (5, 15) and (30, 12), the equation becomes $slope = \frac{12-15}{30-5} = -\frac{3}{25}$. The correct answer is (D).

28. **K** The question asks for the distance traveled by Plane B *during the first 20 minutes of Plane A's flight*. Translate the information in the question into bite-sized pieces. One piece of information says *Plane B was traveling at a constant velocity equal to* $\frac{9}{10}$ *of the maximum velocity of Plane A*. Look at the graph to determine the maximum velocity during Plane A's flight. The maximum point on the graph occurs at the point (5, 15), meaning the maximum velocity was 15 kilometers per minute. Plane B's velocity was $\frac{9}{10}$ of this velocity, or $\frac{9}{10}(15) = \frac{27}{2} = 13.5$ kilometers per minute. Another piece of information says that Plane B traveled at this *velocity during the first 20 minutes of Plane A's flight*. Multiply the velocity by the time to determine the total distance covered: (13.5)(20) = 270 kilometers. The correct answer is (K).

29. **E** The question asks for a graph that models a specific situation. Translate the information in the question into bite-sized pieces and eliminate after each piece. One piece of information says that *the plane speeds up when it experiences a tailwind at $t = 30$ minutes*. The velocity increases, so the graph should show a positive slope starting at $t = 30$ minutes. Eliminate (A) and (C), which show negative slopes starting at $t = 30$, and (D), which shows a slope of 0 at that time. Another piece of information says that the plane *then travels at a constant velocity for the remainder of the flight*. The graph should show a slope of 0 after the positive slope, so eliminate (B), which shows a negative slope on the right side of the graph. The correct answer is (E).

30. **H** The question asks for the solution to an expression. Follow the order of operations and add the fractions inside the parentheses first by finding the least common denominator: $-\frac{1}{2}\left(\frac{4}{50}+\frac{6}{50}\right)+\frac{7}{10} = -\frac{1}{2}\left(\frac{10}{50}\right)+\frac{7}{10}$. Reduce the fraction inside the parentheses to get $-\frac{1}{2}\left(\frac{1}{5}\right)+\frac{7}{10}$ and then multiply the first two fractions to get $-\frac{1}{10}+\frac{7}{10}$. Add the fractions to get $\frac{6}{10} = \frac{3}{5}$. The correct answer is (H).

31. **A** The question asks for the area of a rectangle. The question says the sides are *represented by* $5d + 4$ *and* $d + 3$ *inches.* The formula for the area of a rectangle is $A = lw$, so plug in the expressions given in the question to get $A = (5d + 4)(d + 3)$. Use FOIL to get $A = 5d^2 + 15d + 4d + 12$, then combine like terms to get $A = 5d^2 + 19d + 12$. The correct answer is (A).

32. **J** The question asks for a comparison of numbers with square roots. Check each answer choice, and ballpark to eliminate incorrect answers or calculate the values on a calculator. Choice (F) says $6 > \sqrt{5} > 4$. The square root of 5 is slightly greater than 2, which is not greater than 4. Eliminate (F). Choice (G) says $\frac{1}{6} > \sqrt{\frac{1}{5}} > \frac{1}{4}$. The fraction $\frac{1}{6}$ is not greater than $\frac{1}{4}$, so eliminate (G). The first part of (H) says $\sqrt{7} > 6$. The square root of 7 is between 2 and 3, so it is not greater than 6. Eliminate (H). Choice (J) says $7 > 2\left(\sqrt{7}\right) > 5$. The square root of 7 is slightly greater than 2.5, so $2\left(\sqrt{7}\right)$ is slightly greater than 5. Keep (J) because the inequality is true. There is no need to try (K), since only one answer can be true. Eliminate (K). The correct answer is (J).

33. **B** The question asks for a probability, which is defined as $\frac{\text{number of desired outcomes}}{\text{number of total outcomes}}$. The results of the first 47 rolls have no impact on the probability of the 48th roll ending up a certain way, so calculate the probability for a single roll. For each die, there is 1 side that could have *the number six, face up,* so the *number of desired outcomes* is 1, and there are 6 sides, so the *number of total outcomes* is 6. The probably of rolling a six with one die is thus $\frac{1}{6}$. To determine the chance that both will end up with the number six face up, multiply the probabilities together to get $\left(\frac{1}{6}\right)\left(\frac{1}{6}\right) = \frac{1}{36}$. The correct answer is (B).

34. **K** The question asks for the average score a bowler must earn in her last 3 games to earn a specific average for the 10-game season. The question says that *Stacey has an average score of exactly 240 points in the first seven games of the season.* The question also says Stacey must *earn an average score of 252 points exactly.* For averages, use the formula $T = AN$, in which T is the *total*, A is the *average*, and

N is the *number of things*. To determine the total number of points Stacey earned in the first seven games, the formula becomes $T = 240(7) = 1{,}680$ points. To determine the total number of points Stacey must earn in the entire 10-game season, the formula becomes $T = 252(10) = 2{,}520$ points. Subtract the 7-game total from the 10-game total to determine the total number of points Stacey must earn in the final 3 games of the season: $2{,}520 - 1{,}680 = 840$ points. Divide this total by 3 to determine the average number of points she must earn in each of the final 3 games: $\frac{840}{3} = 280$. The correct answer is (K).

35. **E** The question asks for the least value resulting from a variety of operations. Check each answer choice, and ballpark to eliminate incorrect answers. Choice (A) multiplies a small positive fraction by a positive number, which will result in a small positive number. Choice (B) averages a small positive fraction and a large positive number, which will result in a medium positive number. This is larger than a small positive number, so eliminate (B). Choice (C) divides a small positive fraction by a large positive number, which will result in a small positive number. Keep (C). Choice (D) adds a small positive fraction to a large positive number, which will result in a large positive number. Eliminate (D). Choice (E) subtracts a large positive number from a small positive fraction, which will result in a negative number. A negative number will always be less than a positive number, so now eliminate (A) and (C). The correct answer is (E).

36. **J** The question asks for the definition of a function between two data sets. The question says R *onto* S, which means the R data set is the input and the S data set is the output. There are variables in the answer choices, so plug in. Choose corresponding numbers from both data sets and test each equation. Make $x = 0$ in R, so the corresponding value of -4 in S is the target value for $g(x)$. Now plug $x = 0$ into the answer choices to see which one matches the target value. Choice (F) becomes $g(0) = (0) - 4 = -4$. This matches the target value, so keep (F), but check the remaining answer choices just in case. Choice (G) becomes $g(0) = 3(0) + 2 = 0 + 2 = 2$. Eliminate (G). Choice (H) becomes $g(0) = 3(0) + 4 = 0 + 4 = 4$. Eliminate (H). Choice (J) becomes $g(0) = 5(0) - 4 = 0 - 4 = -4$. Keep (J). Choice (K) becomes $g(0) = 5(0) + 4 = 0 + 4 = 4$. Eliminate (K). Since two answers still work, test another input and output. Make $x = 1$ in R and the target value $g(x) = 1$ in S. Choice (F) becomes $1 - 4 = -5$. Eliminate (F). Choice (J) becomes $5(1) - 4 = 5 - 4 = 1$. Keep (J). The correct answer is (J).

37. **D** The question asks for a comparison of variables representing expressions with fractions. Perform the calculation for each variable's expression, finding common denominators and using a calculator when necessary. The expression for c is the easiest to calculate, as it is simply $c = 3 - 1 = 2$. The expression for a becomes $a = \frac{5}{6} + \frac{6}{5} = \frac{25}{30} + \frac{36}{30} = \frac{61}{30}$. Use a calculator to determine that this is $2.0\overline{3}$.

Because this is larger than 2, eliminate (A), (B), and (C) which indicate that $c > a$. The expression for b becomes $b = \frac{3}{5} + \frac{5}{3} = \frac{9}{15} + \frac{25}{15} = \frac{34}{15}$. Use a calculator to determine that this is $2.2\overline{6}$. Because this is larger than $2.\overline{03}$, eliminate (E) which indicates that $a > b$. The correct answer is (D).

38. **K** The question asks for a trigonometric function representing a portion of a side of a triangle when some side lengths and angle measures are provided. The side labeled m is part of the top triangle, so focus on that. For questions about trigonometric functions in right triangles, think SOHCAH-TOA. The segment labeled m is *opposite* the known angle, and the *hypotenuse* is 12. The SOH part means that the sine is defined as the ratio of the side opposite the angle over the hypotenuse, or $\sin = \frac{\text{opposite}}{\text{hypotenuse}}$. Eliminate (F), (H), and (J), which don't include the trigonometric function *sine.* The angle in the figure represents the entire triangle *EFG*, but m only represents a side of the upper of the two right triangles. Divide the angle measure by 2 to determine the appropriate angle for m: $\frac{122}{2} = 61$. Eliminate (G). The correct answer is (K).

39. **A** The question asks for a number in a pair with a *least common multiple (LCM) of 168*. If 168 is a *multiple* of a given number, that number will be a factor of 168. Check each answer to see if it is a factor of 168. Start with (A), 56, since the question asks for the *greatest value.* The result is $\frac{168}{56} = 3$. Since 3 is a whole number, 168 is a multiple of 56. Check that 56 and 84 do not have a common multiple less than 168: the first two multiples of 84 are 84 and 168, and 84 is not a multiple of 56. Thus, 168 is the least common multiple of 84 and 56. The correct answer is (A).

40. **G** The question asks for the equation of a parabola that is shifted from another parabola. The equation of a parabola is represented as $y = a(x - h)^2 + k$ in which (h, k) is the vertex. Translate the question into bite-sized pieces. One piece of information says *Parabola Z* is *a shift of 2 coordinate units up. Up* means along the vertical axis, and k is the y-coordinator of the vertex. To shift up 2 units, the equation should have $k = 2$, so eliminate (F), (H), and (J). Another piece of information says *Parabola Z* is a shift of *6 coordinate units to the right.* Unlike transformations that move up or down, shifts to the left or the right have the opposite sign of the direction in which the graph moves. The equation should have $h = 6$, with subtraction between the x and the 6 in parentheses, so eliminate (K). If transformation of graphs gets tricky, another option is to graph $y = 9x^2$ on a graphing calculator. Then graph the equations in the answers to see which one moved in the correct way. Either way, the correct answer is (G).

41. **B** The question asks for an expression that gives *the approximate number of people who participated in the poll and stated that they have fewer than 10 pairs shoes at home.* Read the table carefully to find the correct numbers to use. The percentage of people with fewer than 10 pairs of shoes is the sum of the categories of shoes listed in the chart between 0 to 9, or 4%, 12%, and 20%, respectively, for a total of 36%. This percentage can also be written as 0.36. There are 811 people represented in the chart, so multiply 0.36 by 811 to find that the approximate number of people with fewer than 10 pairs of shoes is 811(0.36). The correct answer is (B).

42. **J** The question asks for the percent of people who *estimated that they have at least 7 pairs of shoes at home.* Read the table carefully to find the correct numbers to use. The percentage that has at least 7 pairs of shoes is the sum of all the categories with 7 or more pairs of shoes; that is 20%, 22%, 25%, and 15% respectively, for a total of 82%. Make sure not to count the people who did not respond. The correct answer is (J).

43. **D** The question asks for the central angle of a sector of a circle graph listing percentages of shoe ownership rates. The parts of a circle have a proportional relationship. In the circle graph, the proportion of the degrees of a central angle compared to the number of degrees in the whole circle is the same as the percentage of the relevant category of shoes compared to the total percentage. Set up the proportion $\frac{\text{degrees}}{360} = \frac{\text{percentage}}{100}$. The percent of people who own more than 15 pairs of shoes is 15%. Plug in the information to get $\frac{\text{degrees}}{360} = \frac{15}{100}$. Cross-multiply to get (degrees)(100) = (360)(15), or (degrees)(100) = 5,400. Divide both sides by 100 to get degrees = 54. Therefore, the central angle of the region is 54°. The correct answer is (D).

44. **J** The question asks for the measure of the angle that the paint ball strikes the ceiling, identified by $x°$. There is a formula provided, so plug in the given values. The formula is $\sin x = \frac{length_{max}}{width_{max}}$ and the relevant measurements are 29 for the length and 41 for the width. The formula becomes $\sin x = \frac{29}{41} \approx 0.707$. Take the inverse sine of both sides of the equation to get $\sin^{-1}(\sin x) = \sin^{-1}(0.707)$, which becomes $x \approx 45°$. The correct answer is (J).

45. **C** The question asks which statement about the relationship between the mean, mode, and median of a set of numbers is true. The mode of a set of numbers is the number that appears most often. Looking at the table, this is 3, which appears four times. The median of a list of numbers is the middle

number when all values are arranged in order. In lists with an even number of items, the median is the average of the middle two numbers. There are 14 integers in total in the list, so the median will be the average of the seventh and eighth numbers. The integers are already listed in order, so start counting from the least integer, which is 1. The second and third integers are 2. The fourth, fifth, sixth, and seventh integers are 3, and the eighth integer is 4. The average of the seventh and eighth integers is $\frac{3+4}{2} = \frac{7}{2} = 3.5$. This is greater than the mode, so eliminate (A), (B), and (E). To find the mean, or average, use the formula $T = AN$, in which T is the *total*, A is the *average*, and N is the *number of things*. To find the total of the integers, multiply each integer by the number of times it occurs and add the results. This becomes $(1 \times 1) + (2 \times 2) + (3 \times 4) + (4 \times 3) + (5 \times 2) + (6 \times 1) + (7 \times 1)$, which is $1 + 4 + 12 + 12 + 10 + 6 + 7 = 52$. The average formula becomes $52 = A(14)$. Divide both sides by 14 to get $3.7 \approx A$. This is greater than the median, so eliminate (D). The correct answer is (C).

46. **J** The question asks for an equation relating to the relationship between two sets of dog toys. There are variables in the answer choices, so plug in. Make $a = 5$, the number of toys the Akita has. The question states that *the collie has three fewer toys than the Akita*, so the collie has $5 - 3 = 2$ toys. The question also states that *the beagle has five times as many toys as the Akita and collie have together*. This means that $b = 5(5 + 2) = 5(7) = 35$. Now check the answer choices using $a = 5$ and $b = 35$ to see which equation is true. Choice (F) becomes $35 = 5 - 3$ or $35 = 2$. This is not true, so eliminate (F). Choice (G) becomes $35 = 5 + 3$ or $35 = 8$. Eliminate (G). Choice (H) becomes $35 = 5(5)$ or $35 = 25$. Eliminate (H). Choice (J) becomes $35 = 10(5) - 15$, which is $35 = 50 - 15$ or $35 = 35$. This is true, but check (K) just in case. Choice (K) becomes $35 = 10(5) + 15$, which is $35 = 50 + 15$ or $35 = 65$. Eliminate (K). The correct answer is (J).

47. **C** The question asks for the distance between two points. Use the distance formula: $d = \sqrt{(x_2 - x_1)^2 + (y_2 - y_1)^2}$. Plug in the points to get $d = \sqrt{(-1-3)^2 + (9-2)^2} = \sqrt{(-4)^2 + (7)^2} = \sqrt{16+49} = \sqrt{65}$. The correct answer is (C).

48. **H** The question asks how much water an aquarium would hold if all of its dimensions were tripled. Since the question asks for values in relation to each other, plug in. The equation for the volume of a rectangular solid is $V = lwh$. Select dimensions for the aquarium that would give the proper volume, which is 10 cubic feet. Let $l = 1$, $w = 1$, and $h = 10$. Triple these to get $l = 3$, $w = 3$, and $h = 30$. The new volume is then $V = (3)(3)(30) = 270$ cubic feet. The correct answer is (H).

49. **C** The question asks for the set of values satisfied by an inequality. There are variables in the answer choices, so plug in. Pick a number that is in some answer choice ranges but not others to try in the inequality. Make $a = 7$. The inequality becomes $|7 - 3| > 9$, which simplifies to $|4| > 9$ or $4 > 9$. This is not true, so 7 does not satisfy the inequality. Eliminate (A) and (D) because they include 7. Try another number that is not in all the remaining answers, such as $a = -1$. The inequality becomes $|-1 - 3| > 9$, which simplifies to $|-4| > 9$ or $4 > 9$. This is not true, so -1 does not satisfy the inequality. Eliminate (B) because it includes -1. The difference between the remaining answer choices is whether a is less than -6 or -12. Try a number between those values such as $a = -7$. The inequality becomes $|-7 - 3| > 9$, which simplifies to $|-10| > 9$ or $10 > 9$. This is true, so -7 satisfies the inequality. Eliminate (E) because it does not include this value. The correct answer is (C).

50. **F** The question asks which inequality is true for a given an equation involving a. There are variables in the answer choices, so plug in. Start in the middle of the answer choices and try 1,000 because it is between (G) and (H). Plug this into the equation to get $1{,}000^4 = 1{,}000{,}000{,}000{,}000$. This is too large, so eliminate (H), (J), and (K). Next, try 100, which is between (F) and (G). Plug this into the equation to get $100^4 = 100{,}000{,}000$. This is still too large, so eliminate (G). The correct answer is (F).

51. **A** The question asks for the value of an expression involving matrices. Start by using Process of Elimination. When doing multiplication on matrices, the resulting matrix will have the same number of rows as the first matrix and the same number of columns as the second matrix. The matrix YZ will have 2 rows and 2 columns and will retain these dimensions when matrix X is added. Eliminate (D), which does not have these dimensions. Now calculate YZ. To multiply matrices, take the products of each number in the first row of the first matrix and each number in the first column of the second matrix, then add the results to get the number in the upper left of the resulting matrix. Then continue this process with each row and column. Often it will not be necessary to completely multiply the matrices together to get the correct answer. For YZ, the number in the upper left is $3(1) + 1(0) + 0(1) = 3 + 0 + 0 = 3$. When adding matrices, just add the numbers in corresponding positions. The number in the upper left of $YZ + X$ will be $3 + 1 = 4$. Eliminate (B) and (C). Also eliminate (E) because these matrices are the correct dimensions to multiply and add, so the value of $YZ + X$ can be calculated. The correct answer is (A).

52. **G** The question asks for the least value of an expression given limits on the variables in the expression. Because all the values must be positive, the fraction will be smallest when the denominator is as large as possible. Therefore, b should be the largest value possible, which is 5. If this isn't obvious, try plugging in a few values for b to see what happens. Let $a = 10$ and $b = 2$. The expression becomes $\frac{10}{10+2} = \frac{10}{12} = \frac{5}{6}$. Now try $b = 5$. The expression becomes $\frac{10}{10+5} = \frac{10}{15} = \frac{2}{3}$. The expression has a smaller value when b is larger, so keep $b = 5$ and plug in values for a to see what happens as

a changes in value. The calculations already got $\frac{2}{3}$ as a possible answer, so eliminate (F), which is larger than $\frac{2}{3}$. Plug in a larger number for a. Let $a = 15$. The expression becomes $\frac{15}{15+5} = \frac{15}{20} = \frac{3}{4}$. This is larger than $\frac{2}{3}$. Increasing the value of a only causes the fraction to increase. Therefore, $\frac{2}{3}$ is the smallest possible value for the fraction. The correct answer is (G).

53. **B** The question asks for the rate of change of a marathon runner's speed between hours 1 and 3. *Rate of change* means slope. Use the slope formula to calculate the slope between hours 1 and 3. The equation for slope is $slope = \frac{y_2 - y_1}{x_2 - x_1}$. Read the figure carefully to find the points to use in the slope formula. The speed at 1 hour is 8, so the coordinates at hour 1 are (1, 8). The speed at 3 hours is 12, so the coordinates at hour 3 are (3, 12). Plug these into the formula to get $slope = \frac{12-8}{3-1} = \frac{4}{2} = 2$. The correct answer is (B).

54. **F** The question asks for the probability that the product of rolling two dice is odd. A product is odd when both numbers being multiplied together are odd. Find the probability that the number rolled on each die is odd. Probability is defined as $\frac{\text{number of desired outcomes}}{\text{number of total outcomes}}$. For the first die, there are 6 possible numbers, so that is the *number of total outcomes.* Of these, 3 are odd, so that is the *number of desired outcomes.* Therefore, the probability that the first die is odd is $\frac{3}{6} = \frac{1}{2}$. For the second die, there are 8 possible numbers, so that is the *number of total outcomes.* Of these, 4 are odd, so that is the *number of desired outcomes.* Therefore, the probability that the second die is odd is $\frac{4}{8} = \frac{1}{2}$. The probability that two independent events happen is the product of the probabilities of the two events happening separately. Thus, the probability that both dice are odd is $\frac{1}{2} \times \frac{1}{2} = \frac{1}{4}$. The correct answer is (F).

55. **B** The question asks for the volume, in cubic centimeters, of a piece of celery. The volume of any 3-dimensional shape that is uniform from top to bottom, no matter how weird the top and bottom are, is the area of the top times the height of the shape. Read the question carefully to find the correct numbers to use, as there is some unnecessary information there. The area of the top of the slice is 6.4 cm^2. The height or thickness of the slice is 0.3 cm. Therefore, the volume of the slice is $V = (6.4)(0.3) = 1.92$ cm^3. The correct answer is (B).

56. **F** The question asks for an equivalent form of the provided expression. There are variables in the answer choices, so plug in. Keep the numbers small due to all of the exponents and use the ! button on the calculator to do the hard work. Make $f = 3$ and $g = 2$. Plug in these numbers until the last term in the brackets is equal to 1. The given expression becomes $[3(3 - 1)(3 - 2)]^2$. This simplifies to $[3(2)(1)]^2$ or $[6]^2$, which is 36. This is the target value, circle it. Now plug $f = 3$ and $g = 2$ into the answer choices to see which one matches the target value. Choice (F) becomes $(3!)^2$, which is 6^2 or 36. This matches the target, so keep (F) but check the other answers just in case. Choice (G) becomes $(2!)^3 = 2^3 = 8$. Eliminate (G). Choice (H) becomes $(2^3)!$ or 8!, which is 40,320. Eliminate (H). Choice (J) becomes $(2 + 3)!$ or 5!, which is 120. Eliminate (J). Choice (K) becomes $[2(2 - 1)]^3$ or $[2]^3 = 8$. Eliminate (K). The correct answer is (F).

57. **C** The question asks about the number of standard deviations that represent a percent of the data. Although there are very few questions about standard deviation on the ACT, the topic does come up once in a while. For these questions, it is helpful to know the percent of the data that each standard deviation encompasses. When a data set has a normal distribution, the standard deviation function is generally broken up like this:

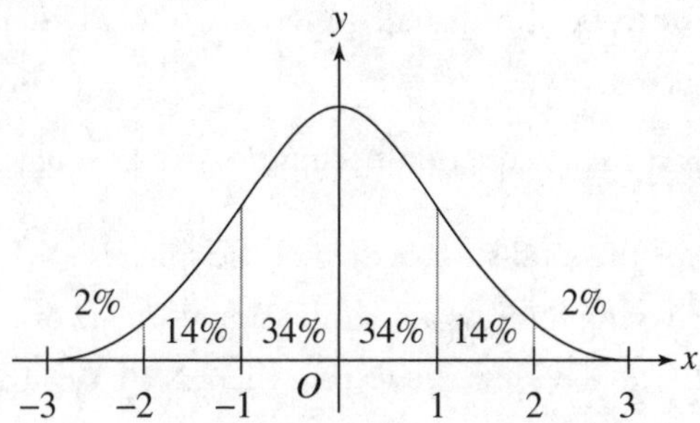

Therefore, 34% of the values are within 1 standard deviation above the mean and 34% of the values are within 1 standard deviation below the mean. The question refers to *68% of the data*, which is the sum of 34% and 34%, which means that 68% of the data is *within* 1 standard deviation of the mean. The correct answer is (C).

58. **J** The question asks for the value of x given the *determinant of the matrix*. For any matrix in the form $\begin{bmatrix} a & b \\ c & d \end{bmatrix}$, the determinant is defined as $ad - bc$. Use this definition to plug in the known values. In the given matrix, $a = 6$, $b = x$, $c = 7$, and $d = 3$. Thus, the determinant becomes $-17 = (6)(3) - (x)(7)$. This simplifies to $-17 = 18 - 7x$. Subtract 18 from both sides of the equation to get $-35 = -7x$, then divide both sides by -7 to get $5 = x$. The correct answer is (J).

59. **B** The question asks for the values of x that satisfy the equation. The fact that the answers have the $\pm$ symbol is a clue that the quadratic formula will be needed. This formula for quadratics in standard form $ax^2 + bx + c = 0$ gives the solutions as $x = \frac{-b \pm \sqrt{b^2 - 4ac}}{2a}$. For the given equation, $a = 1$, $b = -4$, and $c = 13$. Plug these into the formula to get $x = \frac{-(-4) \pm \sqrt{(-4)^2 - 4(1)(13)}}{2(1)}$. This simplifies to $x = \frac{4 \pm \sqrt{16-52}}{2} = \frac{4 \pm \sqrt{-36}}{2}$. At this point, (A) can be eliminated. It contains no i terms, and i is the result of taking the square root of a negative number. Simplify further by splitting the right side into two fractions to get $x = \frac{4}{2} \pm \frac{\sqrt{-36}}{2}$. The first fraction on the right will reduce to 2, so (E) can be eliminated. Rewrite $\sqrt{-36}$ as $\sqrt{(-1)(36)}$, which becomes $6\sqrt{-1}$. The square root of -1 is i, so the equation becomes $x = 2 \pm \frac{6i}{2}$ or $x = 2 \pm 3i$. The correct answer is (B).

60. **H** The question asks for the total surface area of the spheres in the sculpture. Use the Geometry Basic Approach. Start by trying to draw a 3-dimensional image of the sculpture to determine how many spheres it contains. The top view shows that there is a base layer of 8 spheres.

L

F

The front view shows that there must be at least one sphere in the top layer along the left side of the base, but it is not clear if it is in the front, middle, or rear position or even if there is more than one in that row. The left view shows that there are spheres in the front, middle, and back of the top layer in the row on the left. The sculpture must look like this:

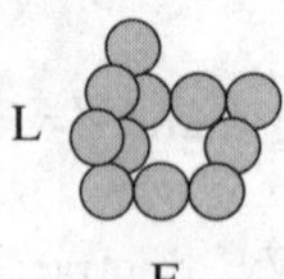

Therefore, there are 11 total spheres. Use the formula for the surface area to find the volume of 1 sphere. The radius is 1 m, so the surface area is $4\pi(1)^2 = 4\pi$. Multiply this by 11 to get the total surface area of all the spheres as $11(4\pi) = 44\pi$. The correct answer is (H).

Math Practice Section 3

MATHEMATICS TEST

60 Minutes—60 Questions

DIRECTIONS: Solve each problem, choose the correct answer, and then darken the corresponding oval on your answer document.

Do not linger over problems that take too much time. Solve as many as you can; then return to the others in the time you have left for this test.

You are permitted to use a calculator on this test. You may use your calculator for any problems you choose, but some of the problems may best be done without using a calculator.

Note: Unless otherwise stated, all of the following should be assumed:

1. Illustrative figures are NOT necessarily drawn to scale.
2. Geometric figures lie in a plane.
3. The word *line* indicates a straight line.
4. The word *average* indicates arithmetic mean.

DO YOUR FIGURING HERE.

1. For each of 3 years, the table below gives the number of different routes a runner ran, the number of runs she ran, and the total number of miles she ran.

Year	Routes	Runs	Total miles run
2005	12	395	1,255
2006	12	396	1,014
2007	11	368	1,898

To the nearest tenth of a mile, what is the average number of miles the runner ran per run in 2005 ?

A. 2.5
B. 2.6
C. 3.2
D. 4.8
E. 5.0

2. The lengths of 2 sides are not given in the polygon below. If each angle between adjacent sides measures 90°, then, in meters, what is the perimeter of the polygon?

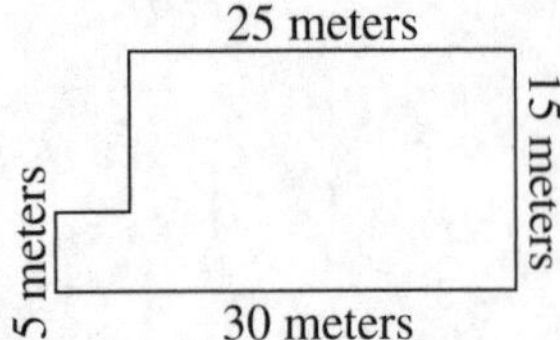

F. 75
G. 90
H. 95
J. 400
K. 450

3. Which of the following inequalities represents the graph shown below on the real number line?

DO YOUR FIGURING HERE.

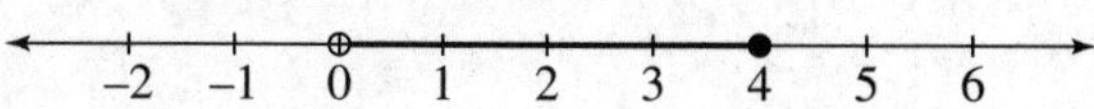

A. $0 < x < 5$
B. $0 < x \leq 4$
C. $0 \leq x < 4$
D. $1 \leq x \leq 4$
E. $-2 < x \leq 4$

4. What is the value of $4 + 3^{x-y}$ when $x = 3$ and $y = -1$?

F. 13
G. 16
H. 30
J. 85
K. 2,041

5. For integers x and y such that $xy = 14$, which of the following is NOT a possible value of x ?

A. 2
B. 1
C. −7
D. −8
E. −14

6. In cubic meters, what is the volume of a large cube whose edges each measure 6 meters in length?

F. 18
G. 36
H. 64
J. 108
K. 216

DO YOUR FIGURING HERE.

7. Pat's Pastries baked 80 apple pies and 50 loaves of apple bread to be sold at a 2-day Fall Festival. The pies were sold for $25 each and the loaves of bread were sold for $10 each. Which of the following expressions gives the total amount of money, in dollars, collected from selling all of the apple pies and b of the loaves of bread?

A. $35b$
B. $1,570b$
C. $b + 80$
D. $10b + 1,250$
E. $10b + 2,000$

8. In the figure below, W, X, and Z are collinear, the measure of $\angle WXY$ is $4a°$, and the measure of $\angle YXZ$ is $11a°$. What is the measure of $\angle WXY$?

F. 12°
G. 48°
H. 96°
J. 132°
K. 264°

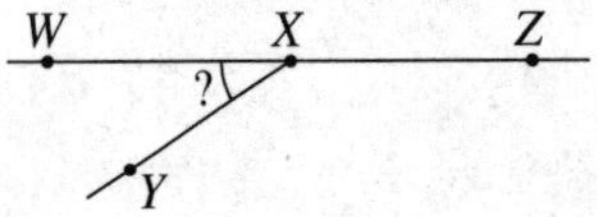

W X Z ? Y

9. Each of the following values could represent a probability EXCEPT:

A. 0.00004

B. $\frac{3}{10}$

C. 0.7

D. $\frac{51}{60}$

E. $\frac{5}{4}$

DO YOUR FIGURING HERE.

10. For the first several weeks after hiring a private tutor, Teddy's score on a standardized test increased slowly. As Teddy began to understand the concepts more clearly, though, his standardized test scores improved more rapidly. After several more weeks, Teddy stopped working with his tutor and his scores did not improve any more. Which of the following graphs could represent all of Teddy's standardized test scores as a function of time, in weeks, after he hired a private tutor?

F.

J.

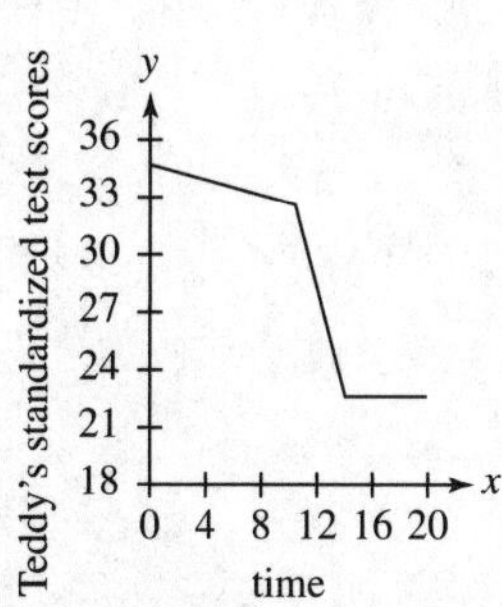

G.

K.

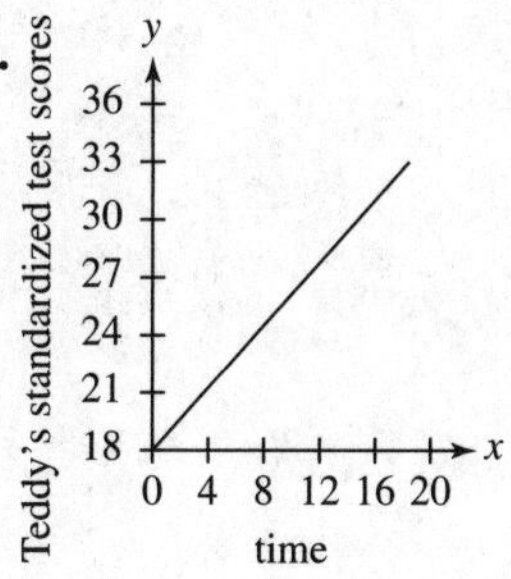

H.

11. The Northampton Volunteer Association has built a rectangular sandbox for a local elementary school and is ready to fill it with sand. The sandbox is 60 inches wide, 72 inches long, and will be filled 18 inches deep. Under the assumption that 1 bag of sand can fill 3,600 cubic inches of the sandbox, what is the minimum number of bags of sand they will need in order to fill the sandbox?

A. 1
B. 7
C. 12
D. 21
E. 22

DO YOUR FIGURING HERE.

12. Salvador is trying to scale his rectangular self-portrait down to postcard size. The painting is 9 feet wide by 16 feet long. He is using a scale of $\frac{1}{3}$ inch = 1 foot for the postcard-sized self-portrait. What will be the dimensions, in inches, of Salvador's postcard-sized self-portrait?

F. $1\frac{1}{3}$ by 4

G. 3 by $5\frac{1}{3}$

H. 3 by 4

J. 27 by 48

K. 36 by 64

13. The Crestview High School student body is made up only of freshmen, sophomores, juniors, and seniors. 25% of the students are freshmen, 35% are sophomores, and 20% are juniors. If no student can be considered to be in two classes, and there are 150 seniors, how many students make up the Crestview High School student body?

A. 230
B. 500
C. 600
D. 750
E. 1,500

14. The circumference of a car tire is 75 inches. About how many revolutions does this car tire make traveling 225 feet (2,700 inches) without slipping?

F. 3
G. 14
H. 36
J. 225
K. 432

15. $(2 - 4t + 5t^2) - (3t^2 + 2t - 7)$ is equivalent to:

A. $2t^2 - 6t + 9$
B. $2t^2 - 2t + 9$
C. $2t^4 - 2t^2 - 5$
D. $8t^2 - 6t - 5$
E. $8t^4 - 6t^2 - 5$

DO YOUR FIGURING HERE.

16. At Blackstone Café, a regular entrée costs $18.00, while an entrée off the children's menu costs less. Cliff treats his niece to dinner at the café and spends $\frac{1}{3}$ of a gift certificate on her children's entrée and a drink. Afterwards, she orders a $6.00 dessert and he pays for that as well. When Cliff has paid for all of his niece's food, he has exactly enough money left on the gift certificate to pay for his regular entrée. How much money was the gift certificate worth?

F. $34.00
G. $35.00
H. $36.00
J. $37.00
K. $38.00

17. In June, Ms. Kunkel gave her English students 15 books to read over the summer. When classes resumed in September, she asked them what percentage of the books they had finished. Which of the following is a possible percentage of books completed by one of her students?

A. 65%
B. 68%
C. 70%
D. 80%
E. 85%

18. A geometric sequence has as its first 4 terms, –0.125, 1, –8, and 64. What is the 5th term of this sequence?

F. 512
G. 73
H. –55
J. –73
K. –512

19. Which of the following is equivalent to $(a - 5b)^2$?

A. $2a - 10b$
B. $a^2 - 25b^2$
C. $a^2 - 10ab + 25b^2$
D. $a^2 - 12ab + 25b^2$
E. $a^2 - 25ab + 25b^2$

DO YOUR FIGURING HERE.

20. As shown in the figure below, Tony has determined that he must ride his skateboard down a long ramp to be able to jump a shorter ramp with enough time to complete a new trick. First, he needs to determine the dimensions of both the shorter and longer ramps. Tony is on his skateboard at point *K*, 20 feet above the ground. He then notes that the vertical height $\overline{HJ}$ of the shorter ramp is 6 feet above the ground, and the length of the shorter ramp $\overline{GJ}$ is 9 feet. Approximately how many feet long is the longer ramp?

(Note: In ΔFKG and ΔHJG, $\angle FGK$ is congruent to $\angle HGJ$.)

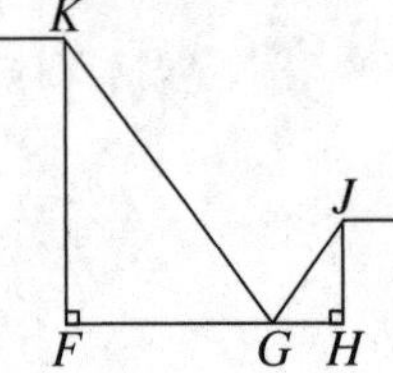

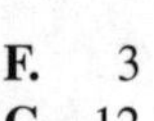

F. 3
G. 12
H. 15
J. 30
K. 35

21. What is the solution to the equation $9x - (3x - 1) = 3$?

A. -3

B. $-\frac{2}{3}$

C. $\frac{1}{3}$

D. $\frac{2}{3}$

E. 3

22. The area of ΔABC below is 54 square meters. If altitude $\overline{BD}$ is 9 meters long, how long is $\overline{AC}$, in meters?

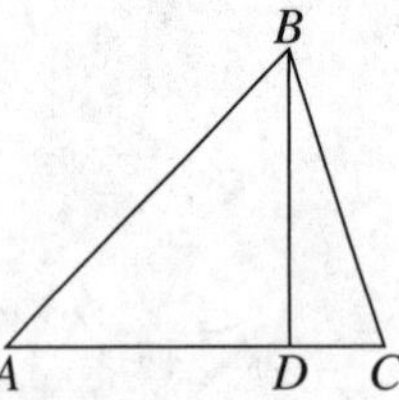

F. 3
G. 6
H. 9
J. 12
K. 15

23. Given $g(x) = 4x^2 - 8x + 2$, what is the value of $g(-5)$?

A. 442
B. 142
C. 67
D. -58
E. -138

DO YOUR FIGURING HERE.

24. A company will reimburse its employees' personal expenses on weekend business trips. It will reimburse $0.80 for every $1.00 an employee spends, up to $100.00. For the next $200 an employee spends, the company will reimburse $0.70 for every $1.00 spent. For each additional dollar spent after that, the company will reimburse $0.60. If an employee was reimbursed $400.00, approximately how many dollars must she have spent on a weekend business trip?

F. 667
G. 600
H. 500
J. 400
K. 367

25. The following table shows the ages of all the attendees of Camp Wannaboggin.

Age	9	10	11	12	13
Percent of campers	10%	24%	21%	37%	8%

What percent of the Wannaboggin campers are at least 11 years old?

A. 34%
B. 45%
C. 50%
D. 55%
E. 66%

26. What percent of $\frac{5}{8}$ is $\frac{1}{8}$?

F. 13%
G. 20%
H. 55%
J. 63%
K. 500%

27. The newspaper headline below tells about a power outage. If there are 63,000 residences in Springfield, how many residences were affected by the outage?

EXTRA! EXTRA!
Massive Local Power Outage
$\frac{2}{3}$ of Residences in Springfield Affected

A. 10,500
B. 21,000
C. 31,500
D. 42,000
E. 62,995

28. The ratio of a side of square X to the length of rectangle Z is 3:4. The ratio of a side of square X to the width of rectangle Z is 3:2. What is the ratio of the area of square X to the area of rectangle Z ?

DO YOUR FIGURING HERE.

F. 1:1
G. 2:1
H. 3:2
J. 9:4
K. 9:8

29. In her Algebra II class, Mrs. Pemdas writes the following statement on the board: "a varies inversely as the product of b^2 and c, and directly as d^3." She then asks her students to translate the statement into an equation. Which of the following equations, with k as the constant of proportionality, is a correct translation of Mrs. Pemdas's statement?

A. $a = \frac{kd^3}{b^2c}$

B. $a = \frac{kb^2c}{d^3}$

C. $a = \frac{b^2cd^3}{k}$

D. $a = \frac{b^2c}{kd^3}$

E. $a = kb^2cd^3$

30. In a certain isosceles triangle, the measure of the vertex angle is four times the measure of each of the base angles. What is the measure, in degrees, of the vertex angle?

F. 30º
G. 45º
H 60º
J. 120º
K. 150º

31. A restaurant decides on the following production model, $N = x^2 - 600x - 160{,}000$, where N is the number of ounces of flour the restaurant purchases each month, based on the number of ounces, x, the restaurant uses during the preceding month. According to this model, what is the greatest quantity of flour, in number of ounces, that the restaurant can use during a month, without having to purchase any new flour the next month?

A. 800
B. 550
C. 400
D. 350
E. 200

DO YOUR FIGURING HERE.

Use the following information to answer questions 32–34.

A poor, frustrated artist named Fresco created a plan to make money. He collected trash, repurposed it into sculptures, and then asked various celebrities to write and paint on these trash objects, which he then sold on his own as modern high art. The chart below separately shows the *cost* and *revenue* of his plan. The linear cost function, $C(x)$, represents the total money spent to make and market the art, while the linear revenue function, $R(x)$, shows the amount of money he has made in sculpture sales.

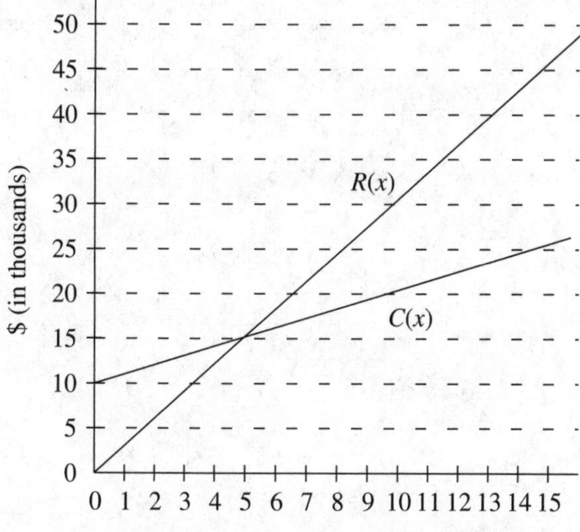

32. Fresco initially spent money promoting the project in the media. He also had to pay the celebrities to participate. After 6 months, Fresco had created and sold x number of trash sculptures and finally broke even: he hadn't made or lost any money. How many sculptures did Fresco sell in his first 6 months of the project?

F. 3
G. 5
H. 7
J. 10
K. 15

33. The cost function in the chart is determined by a constant production cost per sculpture—in this case, the amount Fresco pays each celebrity to participate—as well as a fixed cost, or the initial cost of promoting the project. What is the fixed cost of Fresco's trash sculpture project?

A. $1,000
B. $5,000
C. $10,000
D. $15,000
E. $50,000

34. The selling price of each trash sculpture is an integer number of dollars. According to the revenue function, what is the selling price of one trash sculpture?

F. $1,000
G. $1,667
H. $2,000
J. $3,000
K. Cannot be determined from the chart

DO YOUR FIGURING HERE.

---

35. Which of the following is a COMPLETE factorization of the expression $12b^2c + 6bc + 3b$?

A. $4bc + 2c + 1$
B. $3b\,(9bc + 2c + 1)$
C. $3b\,(4bc + 2c + 1)$
D. $3b\,(4bc + 2c)$
E. $6bc\,(2b + 6) + 3b$

36. Which of the following could be the equation of a line that passes through the points (–2,–7) and (2,17) in the standard (x,y) coordinate plane?

F. $3x - 2y = 8$
G. $6x - y = -5$
H. $5x - 2y = 7$
J. $9x - 2y = -16$
K. $x + y = 6$

37. A circle has a radius that is the same length as the sides of a square. If the square has a perimeter of 64 square inches, what is the area, in square inches, of the circle?

A. 16
B. 16π
C. 32π
D. 64π
E. 256π

38. What is the y-coordinate of the solution of the following system, presuming the system has a solution?

$$8x + y = 30$$
$$8x + 4y = 96$$

F. 1
G. 8
H. 19
J. 22
K. The system has no solution.

DO YOUR FIGURING HERE.

Use the following information to answer questions 39–41.

In the figure below, M is on $\overline{NL}$ and Q is on $\overline{PR}$. The measurements are given in feet. Both $NPQM$ and $MQRL$ are trapezoids. The area, A, of a trapezoid is given by $A = \frac{1}{2}h(b_1 + b_2)$, where h is the height and b_1 and b_2 are the lengths of the 2 parallel sides.

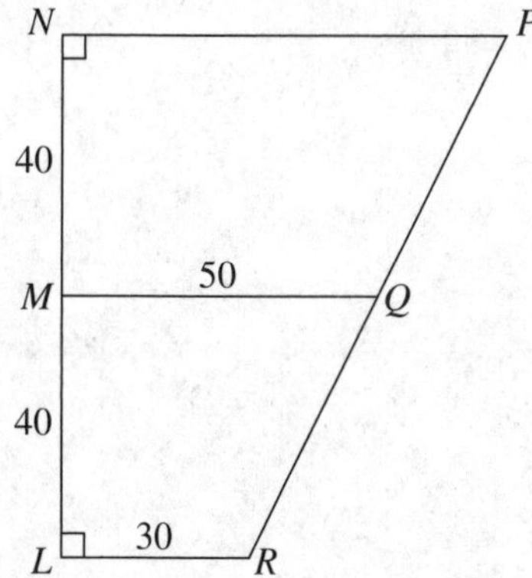

39. What is the area of $MQRL$, in square feet?

A. 3,200
B. 1,750
C. 1,600
D. 600
E. 500

40. What is the length of $\overline{QR}$, in feet?

F. $\sqrt{2{,}000}$
G. $\sqrt{1{,}640}$
H. $\sqrt{1{,}200}$
J. 50
K. 45

41. What is the diameter, in feet, of the largest circle that can be drawn inside $MNPQ$?

A. 20
B. 40
C. 50
D. 60
E. 70

42. The figure below shows a ramp for skateboarders. The base of the ramp is 25 feet long, and it rises at a 10° angle.

DO YOUR FIGURING HERE.

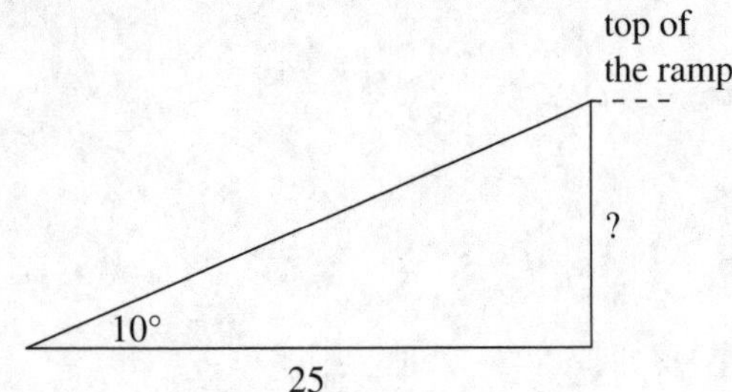

Given the trigonometric calculations in the table below, how high off the ground will a skateboarder be at the top of the ramp, rounded to the nearest 0.1 foot?

cos 10°	0.985
sin 10°	0.174
tan 10°	0.176

F. 2.3
G. 2.5
H. 4.3
J. 4.4
K. 24.6

43. The 12 numbers on a circular clock are equally spaced around the edges of the clock. Belinda chooses an integer, n, that is greater than 1. Beginning at a randomly chosen number, Belinda goes around the circle counterclockwise and paints in every nth number. She continues going around and around the clock, painting in every nth number, until all twelve numbers on the clock are painted. Which of the following could have been Belinda's integer n ?

A. 2
B. 3
C. 6
D. 7
E. 9

DO YOUR FIGURING HERE.

44. Consider the exponential equation $y = \frac{p^{(x+1)}}{K}$, where K and p are positive real constants and x is a positive real number. The value of y decreases as the value of x increases if and only if which of the following statements about p is true?

F. $0 < p < 1$
G. $1 < p < 2$
H. $p > -1$
J. $p > 0$
K. $p > 1$

45. What is the distance, in coordinate units, between the points M (1,–3) and N (–5,5) in the standard (x,y) coordinate plane?

A. $\sqrt{14}$
B. $\sqrt{20}$
C. 8
D. 10
E. 20

46. During a daily training race, Carl has to stop to tie his shoes. Melissa, whose shoes are Velcro, continues to run and gets 20 feet ahead of Carl. Melissa is running at a constant rate of 8 feet per second, and Carl starts running at a constant rate of 9.2 feet per second to catch up to Melissa. Which of the following equations, when solved for s, gives the number of seconds Carl will take to catch up to Melissa?

F. $8s + 20 = 9.2s$
G. $8s - 20 = 9.2s$
H. $\frac{20 + 9.2s}{9.2} = 8s$
J. $8s = 20$
K. $9.2s = 20$

47. Which of the following defines the solution set for the system of inequalities given below?

$$0 > 3x - 6$$
$$-4 < x$$

A. $x > -4$
B. $x < 2$
C. $-4 < x < 18$
D. $-4 < x < -2$
E. $-4 < x < 2$

DO YOUR FIGURING HERE.

48. At the company YouGroove, 35 employees work in the sales department and 50 employees work in the operations department. Of these employees, 15 work in both the sales and the operations departments. How many of the 110 employees at YouGroove do NOT work in either the sales or the operations departments?

F. 10
G. 15
H. 20
J. 35
K. 40

49. The slope of a line in the standard (x,y) coordinate plane is 4. What is the slope of a line perpendicular to that line?

A. 4

B. $\frac{1}{4}$

C. $-\frac{1}{4}$

D. -1

E. -4

50. The point (24,3) on a standard (x,y) coordinate plane is halfway between points $(z,2z + 1)$ and $(15z,z - 4)$. What is the value of z ?

F. 1
G. 1.5
H. 3
J. 7
K. 24

51. How many 4-letter orderings, where no letters are repeated, can be made using the letters of the word BADGERS ?

A. 4
B. 7
C. 256
D. 840
E. 2,401

52. As shown in the (*x*,*y*,*z*) coordinate space below, the cube with vertices *L through S* has edges that are 2 coordinate units long. The coordinates of *Q* are (0,0,0), and *S* is on the positive *x*-axis. What are the coordinates of *O* ?

DO YOUR FIGURING HERE.

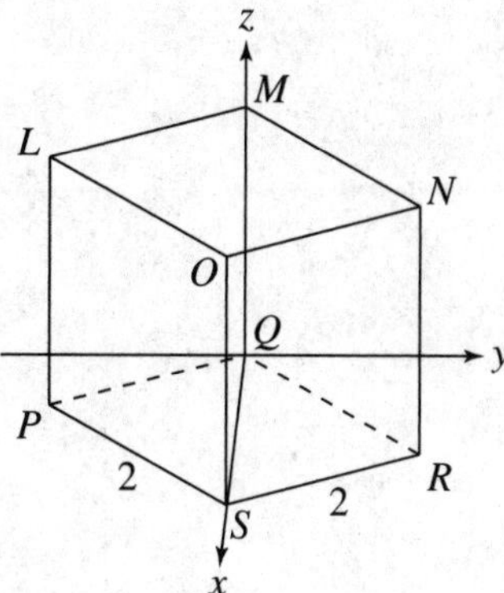

F. (2,0,2)

G. (2,2,2)

H $(2\sqrt{2},0,2)$

J. $(2\sqrt{2},0,2\sqrt{3})$

K. $(2\sqrt{2},2,0)$

53. Whenever *a*, *b*, and *c* are positive real numbers, which of the following expressions is equivalent to $\log_4 a - 2\log_8 b + \frac{1}{2}\log_4 c$?

A. $\log_4 a\sqrt{c} - \log_8 b^2$

B. $\log_4 \frac{ac}{2} - \log_8 2b$

C. $\log_4 \frac{a\sqrt{c}}{b}$

D. $\log_4(a-c) - \log_8 2b$

E. $\log_4(a-c) - \log_8 b^2$

54. If $-6 \le a \le -4$ and $3 \le b \le 7$, what is the maximum value of $|a-2b|$?

F. 10
G. 11
H. 18
J. 20
K. 42

DO YOUR FIGURING HERE.

55. The measure of the sum of the interior angles of a regular n-sided polygon is $(n - 2)180°$. A regular octagon is shown below. What is the measure of the designated angle?

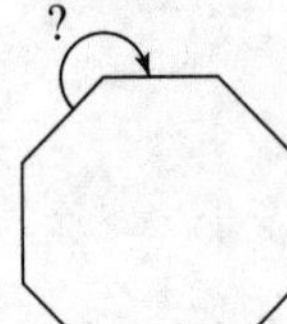

A. 135°
B. 144°
C. 200°
D. 225°
E. 315°

56. Which of the following trigonometric functions has an amplitude of 3 ?

(Note: The *amplitude* of a trigonometric function is $\frac{1}{2}$ the nonnegative difference between the maximum and minimum values of the function.)

F. $f(x) = \frac{1}{3} \sin x$
G. $f(x) = \cos 3x$
H. $f(x) = \sin(\frac{1}{3} x)$
J. $f(x) = 3 \tan x$
K. $f(x) = 3 \cos x$

57. If A, x, and y are all distinct numbers, and $A = \frac{xy - 2}{x - y}$, which of the following represents x, in terms of A and y ?

A. $\frac{Ay - 2}{A - y}$

B. $\frac{A - 2}{x - 1}$

C. $\frac{A - y}{x - y}$

D. $\frac{Ay - 2}{A + y}$

E. $\frac{2}{y - A}$

DO YOUR FIGURING HERE.

58. In the figure below, lines p and q are parallel and angle measures are as marked. If it can be determined, what is the value of a ?

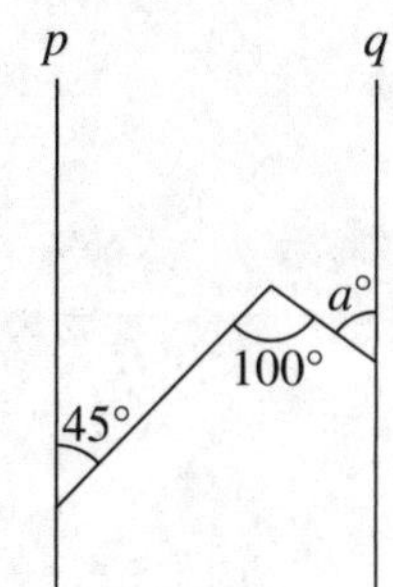

F. 35°
G. 45°
H. 55°
J. 100°
K. Cannot be determined from the information given

59. In the triangle below, the lengths of the two given sides are measured in centimeters. What is the value, in centimeters, of x ?

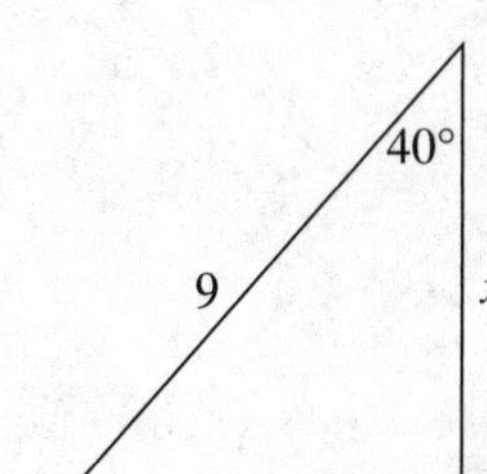

A. 9 sin 40°
B. 9 sin 50°
C. 9 cos 50°
D. 9 tan 40°
E. 9 tan 50°

60. An angle in the standard (x,y) coordinate plane has its vertex at the origin and its initial side on the positive x-axis. If the measure of an angle in standard position is (1,314°), it has the same terminal side as an angle of each of the following measures EXCEPT:

F. 594°
G. 314°
H. 234°
J. −126°
K. −486°

Math Practice Section 3 Answers and Explanations

MATH PRACTICE SECTION 3 ANSWERS

1. C
2. G
3. B
4. J
5. D
6. K
7. E
8. G
9. E
10. F
11. E
12. G
13. D
14. H
15. A
16. H
17. D
18. K
19. C
20. J
21. C
22. J
23. B
24. G
25. E
26. G
27. D
28. K
29. A
30. J
31. A
32. G
33. C
34. J
35. C
36. G
37. E
38. J
39. C
40. F
41. B
42. J
43. D
44. F
45. D
46. F
47. E
48. K
49. C
50. H
51. D
52. H
53. A
54. J
55. D
56. K
57. A
58. H
59. B
60. G

MATH PRACTICE SECTION 3 EXPLANATIONS

1. **C** The question asks for the average number of miles run in 2005. Divide the total number of miles the runner ran in 2005 by the number of runs she ran in that year to find the average number of miles per run: $\frac{1,255}{395} = 3.177$, which rounds to 3.2 miles. Be careful when finding the numbers within the table: there is more data than is required to answer the question. The correct answer is (C).

2. **G** The question asks for the perimeter of the polygon. Because the angles in the polygon are 90°, the parallel sides will be equal. Find the missing side lengths by subtracting the length of the shorter labeled side from the parallel longer side. Calculate 30 – 25 = 5, and 15 – 5 = 10, so the two missing lengths are 5 and 10. The perimeter is 30 + 15 + 25 + 10 + 5 + 5 = 90, or (G). Choice (F) adds the given values but forgets to calculate the missing sides, while (H) assumes the missing sides are equal to the given values 5 and 15. Choice (J) calculates the *area* correctly, while (K) calculates the area incorrectly (30 × 15). The correct answer is (G).

3. **B** The question asks for the inequality that describes the graph. Use Process of Elimination. Start by looking at the endpoints on the number line and match those up with the inequality signs in the answer choices. The left circle at 0 is an open circle, so this corresponds to $<$ or $>$, eliminating (C) and (D). The right circle at 4 is a closed circle, so this corresponds to $\leq$ and $\geq$, eliminating (A). Now look at the range of values covered in the line: 0 to 4—a range that does not include –2, as (E) suggests. The correct answer is (B).

4. **J** The question asks for the value of the expression for the given values of x and y. Plug in the values given into the expression, using order of operations (PEMDAS). Start with the exponent: $4 + 3^{(3-(-1))} = 4 + 3^4 = 4 + 81 = 85$. Choice (F) confuses the signs in the exponent, and (G) multiplies 3 × 4 instead of finding 3^4. Choice (H) subtracts 1 from the whole expression, instead of treating it as part of the exponent. Choice (K) adds 3 + 4 before raising it to the exponent. The correct answer is (J).

5. **D** The question asks which value of x would NOT yield an integer solution for y. Try to use each of the answer choices as values for x and find a value of y for which $xy = 14$. In (A), if $x = 2$, $y = 7$. In (B), if $x = 1$, $y = 14$. In (C), if $x = -7$, $y = -2$. In (E), if $x = -14$, $y = -1$. Only (D) does not have a complementary integer value for y. The correct answer is (D).

6. **K** The question asks for the volume of the cube. The formula for the volume of a cube is as follows: $V = s^3$. In this case, $s = 6$, so the volume is 216. Choice (F) finds $s \times 3$; (G) finds the area of a square with sides of 6; (H) makes a calculation error; and (J) finds $s^2 \times 3$. The correct answer is (K).

7. **E** The question asks for the expression that represents the total amount of money Pat's Pastries earned selling pie and bread. Add the products of 80 pies sold at \$25 each and b pies sold at \$10 each to get $(80 \times 25) + (b \times 10) = 2,000 + 10b$. Choice (D) finds the price of 50 pies instead of 80,

and (C) gives the number of baked goods sold. Choice (A) finds the price of *b* loaves of bread and *b* apple pies. Choice (B) multiplies 10*b* by the sum of all other numbers in the problem. The correct answer is (E).

8. **G** The question asks for the measure of $\angle WXY$. First, use Process of Elimination: since $\angle WXY$ is clearly smaller than 90°, eliminate (H), (J), and (K). Since the two angles together form a straight line, the sum of their measures must be 180°. Add together the provided values for each angle and set them equal to 180° to find the value of a: $4a + 11a = 180$, which simplifies to $15a = 180$ and solves to $a = 12$. Now, substitute this value for a into the equation $\angle WXY = 4a$ to find that the angle measures $4(12) = 48°$. The correct answer is (G).

9. **E** The question asks which number could NOT represent a probability. By definition, probability can be no less than 0% and no greater than 100%. As such, any probability p must be $0 \le p \le 1$. Choices (A), (B), (C), and (D) are all numbers between 0 and 1, but (E) would equal 1.25 if converted to a decimal. The correct answer is (E).

10. **F** The question asks which graph matches the description of Teddy's test scores. Use Process of Elimination. Teddy's standardized test scores do not decrease at any point, so eliminate (G) and (J). Nor do they *only* increase—at the end, his scores leveled off and neither increased nor decreased, so eliminate (K). Since these scores level off at the end, not in the middle, you can eliminate (H). Only (F) gives an accurate representation of scores that increase slowly, then increase quickly, and then remain constant. The correct answer is (F).

11. **E** The question asks for the total number of sand bags required to fill the sandbox. First, find the volume of the sandbox by substituting the provided dimensions into the formula for the volume of a rectangular prism, $V = lwh$: the equation becomes $V = (60)(72)(18)$ and solves to $V = 77{,}760$. Now, find the number of sand bags required by dividing this volume by the volume of sand in a single bag: 77,760 cubic inches ÷ 3,600 cubic inches per bag = 21.6 bags required. Since more than 21 bags would be required to fill the sandbox, round up to the nearest integer to get a final answer of 22. The correct answer is (E).

12. **G** The question asks for the dimensions of Salvador's self-portrait when shrunk to postcard size. Use proportions to convert from the original to the scaled size. Since 1 foot of original size will become $\frac{1}{3}$ inch when scaled, the new width can be found by solving $\frac{\frac{1}{3}\text{ inch}}{1\text{ foot}} = \frac{x\text{ inches}}{9\text{ feet}}$. Cross-multiply to find that $1x = 9 \times \frac{1}{3}$, so $x = 3$. Since the width is 3, eliminate (F), (J), and (K), which give incorrect widths. Repeat this process to find the height: $\frac{\frac{1}{3}\text{ inch}}{1\text{ foot}} = \frac{x\text{ inches}}{16\text{ feet}}$, which cross-multiplies to $1x = 16 \times \frac{1}{3}$ and solves to $x = 5\frac{1}{3}$. The correct answer is (G).

13. **D** The question asks for the total number of students at Crestview High School. First find what percentage of students are seniors. Since the percentage of students who are not seniors is 25 + 35 + 20 = 80, the remaining 20% of the students are seniors. Since there are 150 seniors, 150 is 20% of the total number of students. Now put the numbers into an equation: 150 = 0.20 × *total.* Divide both sides by 0.20 to find that the total is 750. Choice (C) miscalculates 150 to be 25% of the total, and (B) miscalculates it to be 30% of the total. Choice (A) adds all numbers in the problem, and (E) resembles the number of students but does not use the information given. The correct answer is (D).

14. **H** The question asks for the number of tire rotations needed to travel 225 feet or 2,700 inches. Since the circumference is given in inches, use the distance of 2,700 inches. For every single revolution, the tire will travel a horizontal distance equivalent to that tire's circumference. To find how many revolutions this tire makes, simply divide 2,700 inches ÷ 75 inches = 36 revolutions. Choice (F) incorrectly pairs units by dividing 225 *feet* by 75 *inches*, and (K) confuses the unit for 2,700 *inches* and treats that measure as if it were given in feet. The correct answer is (H).

15. **A** The question asks for an equivalent form of the given expression. Distribute the minus sign throughout the parentheses before combining like terms: $(2 - 4t + 5t^2) - (3t^2 + 2t - 7) = 2 - 4t + 5t^2 - 3t^2 - 2t + 7 = 2t^2 - 6t + 9$. The other choices all confuse signs in calculating. Choices (C) and (E) also add the exponents of the terms. The correct answer is (A).

16. **H** The question asks for the total cash value of the gift certificate. Set the total value of the certificate to x and use the information in the question to write an equation. Cliff's entrée is $18, the niece's dessert is $6, and the cost of the niece's meal can be written as $\frac{1}{3}x$, so $18 + 6 + \frac{1}{3}x = x$. Simplify to $24 + \frac{1}{3}x = x$, and then subtract $\frac{1}{3}x$ from both sides to get $24 = \frac{2}{3}x$. Multiply both sides by $\frac{3}{2}$ to get $x = 36$. The correct answer is (H).

17. **D** The question asks for a possible percentage of the 15 total books read by a student. To solve, check some possible fractions of books read (out of a possible 15): $\frac{10}{15} = 66.6666\%$; $\frac{11}{15} = 73.33333\%$; $\frac{12}{15} = 80\%$; $\frac{13}{15} = 86.6666\%$; and $\frac{14}{15} = 93.3333\%$. Only (D) gives a possible percentage. Alternately, it is possible to test each answer by setting the decimal equivalent of each listed percentage equal to $\frac{x}{15}$, such as $0.65 = \frac{x}{15}$ for (A), or $0.68 = \frac{x}{15}$ for (B), to see which answer gives a whole-number value for x. The correct answer is (D).

18. **K** The question asks for the fifth term of the geometric sequence. Even without knowing the definition of a geometric sequence, it is possible to eliminate (F) and (G) because a negative number must come next in the pattern. A geometric sequence is one that has a constant ratio be-

tween its terms. To find this constant ratio, divide the second term by the first (or the third by the second, the fourth by the third, etc.). In this case, the constant ratio between all terms is $1 \div (-0.125) = (-8) \div 1 = -8$. To find the 5th term, simply multiply the fourth term by –8: $64 \times (-8) = -512$. The correct answer is (K).

19. **C** The question asks for an equivalent form of the expression. The square refers to everything inside the parentheses, so use FOIL (<u>F</u>irst <u>O</u>uter <u>I</u>nner <u>L</u>ast). The expression becomes $(a - 5b)(a - 5b) = a^2 - 5ab - 5ab + 25b^2 = a^2 - 10ab + 25b^2$. Choices (D) and (E) miscalculate the middle term, and (B) squares each term individually. Choice (A) adds the binomials instead of multiplying them. The correct answer is (C).

20. **J** The question asks for the length of the longer ramp, which is side $\overline{GK}$. Use similar triangles. Since $\angle FGK$ is congruent to $\angle HGJ$, and angles F and H are both right angles, the remaining angles are equal as well. Because they share three congruent angles, ΔFKG and ΔHJG are similar. Since similar triangles have proportional sides, set up a proportion using the given side lengths to find the length of $\overline{GK}$: $\frac{\overline{FK}}{\overline{HJ}} = \frac{\overline{GK}}{\overline{GJ}}$, which becomes $\frac{20}{6} = \frac{\overline{GK}}{9}$. Cross-multiply to get $6\overline{GK} = 180$, and then divide both sides by 6 to get $\overline{GK} = 30$. The correct answer is (J).

21. **C** The question asks for the solution to the equation. First distribute the minus sign through the parentheses to get $9x - 3x + 1 = 3$. Combine the terms on the left and subtract 1 from both sides to get $6x = 2$. Divide both sides by 3 to find that $x = \frac{1}{3}$. Choice (B) and (D) do not distribute the parentheses, and (A) and (E) divide incorrectly. The correct answer is (C).

22. **J** The question asks for the length of $\overline{AC}$, the base of the triangle. Since the area of a triangle is $A = \frac{1}{2}bh$, substitute the known values into this equation and solve for the base. The formula becomes $54 = \frac{1}{2}b(9)$, or $54 = \frac{9}{2}b$. Multiply both sides by $\frac{2}{9}$ to find that $b = 12$. Choice (G) is the result of forgetting to include the $\frac{1}{2}$ in the area formula. The correct answer is (J).

23. **B** The question asks for the value of the function when $x = -5$. Substitute in –5 for x in the function and solve: $4(-5)^2 - 8(-5) + 2$ becomes $4(25) - (-40) + 2$. This simplifies to $100 + 40 + 2$ and ultimately equals 142. Choice (A) incorrectly applies the order of operations for $4x^2$ by multiplying first and then squaring the result. Choice (D) mistakenly gives the value of -5^2 as –25, and (E) repeats this mistake and confuses positive and negative signs for the second term. The correct answer is (B).

24. **G** The question asks for the total amount of money spent by the employee. For the first \$100.00 spent, multiply \$100.00 × \$0.80 = \$80.00 that the company will reimburse. For the next \$200.00 spent, multiply \$200.00 × \$0.70 = \$140.00. So far, for \$300.00 spent, the company will have reimbursed \$80.00 + \$140.00 = \$220.00. Subtract \$400.00 – \$220.00 = \$180.00 that the employee was reimbursed. To find the additional amount of money the employee must have spent, set up an equation with x as the additional number of dollars. The reimbursement rate on the remaining money is \$0.60 per dollar spent, so the equation is \$0.60(x) = \$180. Divide both sides by \$0.60 to find that x = \$300.00. Finally, add all of the dollars spent: \$100.00 + \$200.00 + \$300.00 = \$600.00. The correct answer is (G).

25. **E** The question asks for the percentage of campers who are at least 11 years old. The campers who are *at least 11 years old* include the 11-, 12-, and 13-year-olds. Because all the values in the chart represent percents of the same number, simply add them together to get 21 + 37 + 8 = 66%, or (E). Choice (A) counts only the 9- and 10-year-old percentages; (B) counts the percentage of everyone older than 11 (12- and 13-year olds); and (D) counts ages up to and including 11. Choice (C) incorrectly guesses 50% because 11 is the median of the 5 numbers. The correct answer is (E).

26. **G** The question asks what percent of $\frac{5}{8}$ is $\frac{1}{8}$. Translate the question into an equation and then solve: *what percent* can be rewritten as the variable x divided by 100, *of* means multiply, and *is* can be replaced with an equals sign. Therefore, the equation is $\frac{x}{100}\times\frac{5}{8}=\frac{1}{8}$ or $\frac{5x}{800}=\frac{1}{8}$. Cross-multiply to get $40x = 800$ and then divide both sides by 40 to find that x = 20%. Choice (K) solves $\frac{x}{100}\times\frac{1}{8}=\frac{5}{8}$ instead of the correct equation. The correct answer is (G).

27. **D** The question asks for the number of residences in Springfield that were affected by the power outage. Multiply the number of residences by the fraction affected by the outage to find the total number of people affected. The result is $(63{,}000)\left(\frac{2}{3}\right)=42{,}000$. Choice (B) is the number of residences not affected. Choice (C) finds $\frac{1}{2}$ of the residences. Choice (A) divides the number of residences by the product of 2 and 3, while (E) subtracts 2 and 3 from the number of residences. The correct answer is (D).

28. **K** The question asks for the ratio of areas between the two shapes. Substitute in a real value for the side length of square X to find the measure of the sides for rectangle Z, and then find the area of each shape using those values. The easiest thing to do is to use the numbers in the ratios if possible. If each side of square X measured 3 units, then the 3:4 ratio of the side of X to the length of Z gives the rectangle a length of 4. The 3:2 ratio between the side of X and the width of Z gives the rectangle a width of 2. Using these same numbers, the area of the square, s^2, is $(3)^2$ or 9; the area of the rectangle, lw, is 4 × 2 or 8. The ratio between the area of the square to the rectangle is 9:8. The correct answer is (K).

29. **A** The question asks for an equation that matches the given description. Use Process of Elimination. Inverse variation between two variables can be written in the general form of $x = \frac{1}{y}$, so *a varies inversely as the product of* b^2 *and c* means that part of the equation should be $a = \frac{1}{b^2c}$. Eliminate answers (B), (C), (D), and (E), all of which suggest that a varies *directly* with the product of b^2 and c by having $a = b^2c$ as part of the equation. The correct answer is (A).

30. **J** The question asks for the measure of the vertex angle. If the base angles, which are equal, are x, then the vertex angle can be written as $4x$. The sum of the angles in a triangle is 180°, so for this triangle, $x + x + 4x = 180$. Simplify the equation to $6x = 180$, and then divide both sides by 6 to get $x = 30$. Choice (F) gives the value of x (which also is the measure of each base angle), but the question asks for the vertex angle. This value is $4(30) = 120$. Choice (G) finds the value of x when $4x = 180$, omitting the base angles. Choice (H) gives the sum of the base angles, and (K) subtracts the value of only one base angle from 180. The correct answer is (J).

31. **A** The question asks for the greatest quantity of flour the restaurant could use in a month without needing to purchase any new flour for the next month. Since N represents the amount of flour the restaurant would need to purchase, set $N = 0$ and test the possible answer choices. The question asks for the greatest quantity that satisfies the equation, so start with (A), which is $x = 800$. Substituting this value into the equation $0 = x^2 - 600x - 160{,}000$ gives $0 = 800^2 - 600(800) - 160{,}000$, which simplifies to $0 = 640{,}000 - 480{,}000 - 160{,}000$ and ultimately yields $0 = 0$. Because 800 satisfies the equation and is the largest available value, the correct answer is (A).

32. **G** The question asks for the number of sculptures sold by Fresco in the first six months. If Fresco finally broke even, his cost should be the same as the revenue. The point where the $C(x)$ and $R(x)$ functions cross represents 5 sculptures sold, or (G). Choice (F) shows a revenue that's still less than the cost, while (H) and (J) show a profit for Fresco because the revenue is greater than the cost. Choice (K) correctly identifies where the two lines cross but gives the dollar value at that point instead of the number of sculptures made and sold. The correct answer is (G).

33. **C** The question asks for the initial cost Fresco incurred for the project. Since the initial costs would accumulate before any sculptures were made, find the value of cost function $C(x)$ when 0 sculptures have been made, which is also the y-intercept of the graph: $C(0) = \$10{,}000$. The correct answer is (C).

34. **J** The question asks for the selling price of a single trash sculpture. To determine the cost of each trash sculpture, consider a point on the revenue function line, $R(x)$, and divide the money by the number of sculptures sold $\left(\frac{y}{x}\right)$. A convenient point shows 5 sculptures sold for \$15,000, which is

\$3,000 per sculpture, or (J). Choice (F) calculates the cost per sculpture, or fee paid each celebrity (\$1,000). Choices (G) and (H) mistakenly reference points along the graph of $C(x)$ instead of $R(x)$ when performing these calculations. The correct answer is (J).

35. **C** The question asks for a complete factorization of the expression. Consider each element of the three terms and factor if possible. Look first at the coefficients: 12, 6, and 3 are all divisible by 3, so factor out a 3 to get $3(4b^2c + 2bc + b)$. Now consider the b terms: since each of the three terms contains a b, factor out a b to get $3b(4bc + 2c + 1)$. Since there is not a c in all three terms, this variable cannot be factored out. The correct answer is (C).

36. **G** The question asks for the equation of the line passing through the given points. Use the two points given to find the slope of the line: $m = \frac{y_2 - y_1}{x_2 - x_1} = \frac{17-(-7)}{2-(-2)} = \frac{24}{4} = 6$. Manipulate the answer choices to match the slope-intercept form of a line, where $y = mx + b$. For (G), add y and subtract -5 from both sides to get $6x + 5 = y$, or $y = 6x + 5$. In this equation, the slope, m, is 6, which is the correct slope. None of the other lines have this slope. Choice (H) confuses signs in calculating the slope. Choice (K) confuses the slope and y-intercept. It is also possible to solve this question by testing the answers: simply plug in the (x, y) values of the two provided points into the answers to see which equation is true for both points. The correct answer is (G).

37. **E** The question asks for the area of the circle. Start with the information provided in the question, which is the perimeter of the square. The perimeter of a square is equal to the sum of its sides. For this square, $64 = 4s$, so $s = 16$. The radius of the circle is thus also 16. To find the area of the circle, use $A = \pi r^2 = \pi\,(16)^2 = 256\pi$. Choice (A) gives the radius of the circle, and (C) gives its circumference. Choice (D) mistakes the perimeter of the square for its area, and (B) uses that calculation to find the circumference of the circle. The correct answer is (E).

38. **J** The question asks for the y-coordinate of the solution to the system. Since each equation contains an $8x$, use the elimination method to solve for y. Subtract the first equation from the second.

$$\begin{array}{r} 8x + 4y = 96 \\ \underline{-\ (8x + \ \ y = 30)} \\ 0x + 3y = 66 \end{array}$$

Divide both sides of the equation $3y = 66$ by 3 to find that $y = 22$. Choice (F) gives the value of the x-coordinate in the system. The correct answer is (J).

39. **C** The question asks for the area of trapezoid *MQRL*. Substitute the numbers in the diagram for the variables into the formula given for the area of a trapezoid: $A = \frac{1}{2}(40)(50 + 30) = 1{,}600$ ft². Choice (A) forgets to include the $\frac{1}{2}$ in the area formula. The correct answer is (C).

40. **F** The question asks for the length of $\overline{QR}$. Make a right triangle by drawing in a perpendicular line from *R* to $\overline{MQ}$. This new line will be the same height as $\overline{LM}$. Since $\overline{LR}$ is 30 feet, the base of the new triangle will be 50 – 30 = 20 feet. To find $\overline{QR}$, use the Pythagorean Theorem: $a^2 + b^2 = c^2$, where *a* and *b* are the two legs of a right triangle, and *c* is the hypotenuse. Substituting the provided values into the equation gives $20^2 + 40^2 = \overline{QR}^2$, which simplifies to $2{,}000 = (\overline{QR})^2$ and gives a solution of $\overline{QR} = \sqrt{2{,}000}$. The correct answer is (F).

41. **B** The question asks for the diameter of the largest circle that can be drawn inside *MNPQ*. For the circle to fit inside the trapezoid, it cannot have a diameter any larger than the shortest side of the trapezoid, which is $\overline{MN}$. Since $\overline{MN} = 40$, the diameter of the circle must also be 40. The correct answer is (B).

42. **J** The question asks for the height of the ramp. Start by determining which trigonometric function to use. Relative to the 10° angle, the adjacent side is known, and the question asks for the opposite side, so tangent is the correct function. Now use the formula $\tan\theta = \frac{\text{opposite}}{\text{adjacent}}$ to solve for the unknown side. Set the side opposite the angle equal to *x* and plug in the known values to get $\tan 10° = \frac{x}{25}$. Using the value of tan 10° from the table, simplify to $0.176 = \frac{x}{25}$, and then multiply both sides by 25 to find that $x \approx 4.4$. Choice (H) mistakenly uses the sine function, and (K) mistakenly uses cosine. The correct answer is (J).

43. **D** The question asks for the value of *n* that would allow Belinda to paint in all 12 numbers on the clock. Draw the circular clock and mark 12 evenly spaced points on it, and start trying out the numbers for *n* in the given problem. Choose any starting point—let's say two for this example. Starting at 2 and painting in every second number, as in (A), then in the first revolution, the numbers painted will be 4, 6, 8, 10, 12; in the second revolution, they will be 2, 4, 6, 8, 10, 12. In other words, if the integer *n* is 2, then there is no way that all of the numbers on the face of the clock will be painted. Choices (B), (C), and (E) all create the same issue. Only (D), $n = 7$, will fill in all of the numbers on successive revolutions. The correct answer is (D).

44. **F** The question asks for the possible values of *p* such that *y* will decrease as *x* increases. Since $(x + 1)$ will never be a negative exponent, increasing this exponent will always increase the value of a number greater than 1 and decrease the value of a real number between 0 and 1. The problem stipulates that *p* must be positive, so if *y* decreases as *x* increases, *p* must be a fractional constant

less than 1. If this isn't clear, pick some numbers for the variables that fit the requirements and try them in the equation to see what happens. The correct answer is (F).

45. **D** The question asks for the distance between two points. Use the distance formula, which is $D = \sqrt{(x_1 - x_2)^2 + (y_1 - y_2)^2}$. Substituting the given point coordinates results in $D = \sqrt{(1-(-5))^2 + (-3-5)^2}$, which simplifies to $\sqrt{6^2 + (-8)^2}$. This becomes $\sqrt{36+64}$ or $\sqrt{100} = 10$. The correct answer is (D).

46. **F** The question asks for the equation that correctly describes the scenario. To solve this problem, use the distance formula $d = rt$. If both runners start from the point at which Carl had to stop to tie his shoes, and both d represent the distance at which they meet, then Carl will run $d = 9.2s$ and Melissa will run $d = 8s + 20$ because she has a 20-foot head start. Because the d is the same for each equation, simply set these equations equal to each other to find $8s + 20 = 9.2s$. Choice (G) gives Carl the 20-foot head start instead of Melissa. The correct answer is (F).

47. **E** The question asks for the solution set for the system of inequalities. Manipulate the first given inequality to get x alone on one side. Subtract $3x$ from both sides to get $-3x > -6$. Then divide both sides by -3 to get $x < 2$. Don't forget to flip the inequality sign when dividing both sides by a negative number. Combine the first inequality with the second to get $-4 < x < 2$. Choice (B) gives the solution to only the first inequality, and (A) repeats the second inequality. Choices (C) and (D) make errors in manipulating the first inequality. The correct answer is (E).

48. **K** The question asks for the number of employees who do NOT work in either operations or sales. To solve this problem, use the group formula: $Total = Group_1 + Group_2 - Both + Neither$. This becomes 110 = 35 + 50 – 15 + Neither. This simplifies to 110 = 70 + Neither, so Neither = 40, (K). Choice (F) erroneously subtracts all the smaller values from the total number of employees; (G) subtracts sales employees from operations employees; (H) subtracts employees working in both departments from the number of employees in sales; and (J) subtracts employees working in both departments from the number of employees in operations. The correct answer is (K).

49. **C** The question asks for the slope of a line perpendicular to a line with a slope of 4. The slope of a perpendicular line is the negative reciprocal of the slope of the line to which it is perpendicular. The negative reciprocal of 4 is $-\frac{1}{4}$. The correct answer is (C).

50. **H** The question asks for the value of z. If (24,3) is the midpoint of the other two points, then the average of the two x-values should be 24. This becomes $\frac{z+15z}{2} = 24$ or $\frac{16z}{2}$. Multiply both sides by 2 to get $16z = 48$, so $z = 3$, or (H). Choice (G) mistakenly calculates $z + 15z = 24$ (where $z = 1.5$). The

other choices mistakenly set point values equal to each other. Choice (F) calculates $2z + 1 = 3$ (where $z = 1$); (J) calculates $z - 4 = 3$ (where $z = 7$); and (K) simply sets z equal to 24. The correct answer is (H).

51. **D** The question asks for the number of possible orderings for any four letters in the word BADGERS. First, determine how many possible options there are for each of the four positions. Since there are seven total letters in BADGERS, any of the seven letters could be the first in the new four-letter combination. Since letters cannot be repeated, there are only six possible options for the second letter in the combination, five possible options for the third, and four possible options for the fourth. To find the total number of combinations, multiply together the number of possible options for each of the four positions to get $7 \times 6 \times 5 \times 4 = 840$ orderings. The correct answer is (D).

52. **H** The question asks for the three-dimensional coordinate of point *O*. Compare point *O* to the answer choices, watching the order of the three axes. Point *O* shifts neither to the left nor right in the *y* direction, so the *y*-value will be 0, eliminating (G) and (K). The height of the cube is 2 units and side $\overline{OS}$ starts where *z* is 0, so the *z* coordinate of *O* is 2, eliminating (J). The distance along the *x*-axis from *Q* to *S* is the diagonal of square *PQRS*. The diagonal of a square is the value of its side times $\sqrt{2}$, which in this case is $2\sqrt{2}$, meaning that the *x*-value of *O* is $2\sqrt{2}$, eliminating (F). The correct answer is (H).

53. **A** The question asks for an equivalent form of the logarithmic expression. To combine logarithms (logs), the bases must be the same, so eliminate (C). Group the first and last terms together, since they have common bases, to get $\log_4 a + \frac{1}{2}\log_4 c - 2\log_8 b$. The Laws of Logarithms state that $c\log_b x = \log_b x^c$, so the expression becomes $\log_4 a + \log_4 c^{\frac{1}{2}} - \log_8 b^2$. Eliminate (B) and (D), which multiply *b* by 2 instead of squaring it. A fractional power represents a root, so $\log_4 a + \log_4 \sqrt{c} - \log_8 b^2$. Eliminate (E), which does not include $\sqrt{c}$. The Laws of Logs also state that $\log_b x + \log_b y = \log_b xy$, so the expression becomes $\log_4 a + \log_4 \sqrt{c} = \log_4 a\sqrt{c}$. The correct answer is (A).

54. **J** The question asks for the maximum value of the expression. Pair together various combinations of the smallest and largest possible values for *a* and *b*. Then test those pairs in the expression $|a - 2b|$. Using $a = -6$ and $b = 3$ gives $|-6 - 2(3)|$, which reduces to $|-12|$ and yields 12. Since this value is greater than (F) and (G), eliminate those answers. Now try $a = -6$ and $b = 7$: this gives $|-6 - 2(7)|$ and solves to $|-20| = 20$. Since 20 is greater than 18, eliminate (H). Neither of the two

remaining combinations ($a = -4$, $b = -3$ and $a = -4$, $b = 7$) gives a value for $|a - 2b|$ that is larger than 20, so the correct answer is (J).

55. **D** The question asks for the measure of the indicated angle. First, use Process of Elimination: since the angle shown is clearly larger than 180°, eliminate (A) and (B). Octagons have 8 sides, so using the formula in the question, the sum of the interior angles measures (8 – 2)180 = 1,080. The angles of regular polygons are equal, so divide by 8 to find the measure of each angle: $\frac{1{,}080}{8}$ = 135°. The designated angle in the figure is an exterior angle, and there are 360° in a circle, so subtract the interior angle from 360° to find the measure of the designated angle: 360° – 135° = 225°. The correct answer is (D).

56. **K** The question asks which of the given trigonometric functions has an amplitude of 3. First, tan x does not have an amplitude, so eliminate (J). Second, multiplying the entire function by a constant stretches the graph vertically and changes the amplitude. Both sin x and cos x alone have amplitudes of 1. Multiplying the functions sin x or cos x by a constant will make the amplitude equal to that constant. Altering the *angle,* as in (G) and (H), does not change the amplitude of the function—it changes the *period.* The correct answer is (K).

57. **A** The question asks for the value of x in terms of A and y. To solve algebraically, begin with the original equation $A = \frac{xy - 2}{x - y}$ and multiply both sides by $(x - y)$ to get $A(x - y) = xy - 2$. Distribute the A to get $Ax - Ay = xy - 2$, and then get both terms that contain an x to the same side of the equation. Adding Ay to both sides gives $Ax = xy - 2 + Ay$, and subtracting xy from both sides gives $Ax - xy = Ay - 2$. Factor the x out on the left side to get $x(A - y) = Ay - 2$, and divide both sides by $(A - y)$ to get a final solution of $x = \frac{Ay - 2}{A - y}$. It is also possible to solve this question by substituting numerical values for the three variables: for example, if x is set equal to 4 and y is set equal to 3, then $A = \frac{(4)(3) - 2}{4 - 3} = 10$. Substitute $y = 3$ and $A = 10$ into the answer choices, and only (A) equals the value that was assigned to x, which was $x = 4$. The correct answer is (A).

58. **H** The question asks for the measure of angle *a*. To complete this problem, extend the left transversal to form a triangle with *a* as one of its angles:

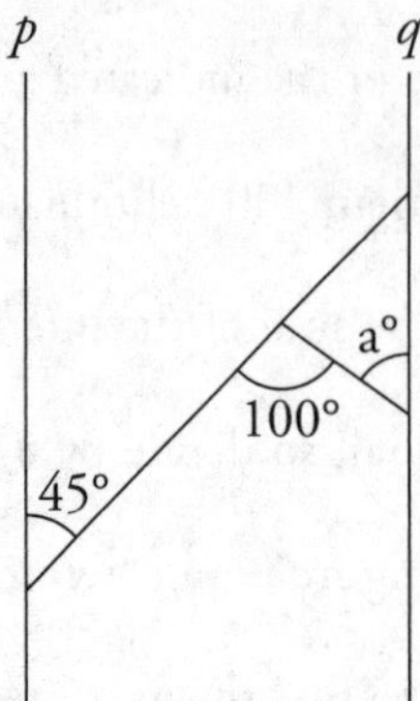

First, find that the supplement of 100° will be 80°. Note that because lines *p* and *q* are parallel, the uppermost angle of this triangle will be 45°. Now, find *a* by subtracting the two known angles from the total angle measure of the triangle: 180° – 45° – 80° = 55°. Choice (F) erroneously subtracts the 45° and 100° angles from 180°. Choice (G) cannot work because *a* does not lie along the same transversal as 45°; (J) cannot work because the 100° angle and *a* do not share any parallel lines; and (K) cannot work because the value can be determined. The correct answer is (H).

59. **B** The question asks for the value of *x*, a side on the triangle. When dealing with two sides and an angle of a right triangle, use SOHCAHTOA. The known side is the hypotenuse, and for the 40° angle, the side labelled *x* is adjacent. Use $\cos 40° = \frac{\text{adjacent}}{\text{hypotenuse}} = \frac{x}{9}$, so $x = 9 \cos 40°$. This is not a choice, so determine the measure of the other angle in the triangle. A triangle has 180°, so the other angle is 180 – 40 – 90 = 50°. For this angle, *x* is the opposite side, so now use the definition of sine. This becomes $\sin 50° = \frac{\text{opposite}}{\text{hypotenuse}} = \frac{x}{9}$, so $x = 9 \sin 50°$. The correct answer is (B).

60. **G** The question asks for the angle that does NOT have the same terminal side as 1,314°. Since terminal angles are defined as angles that are at the same rotational position on a circle, find these matching terminal angles by repeatedly subtracting full revolutions of 360° from the original angle. Begin with 1,314° – 360° = 954° and continue subtracting by 360° to get other terminal angles: 954° – 360° = 594°, eliminating (F); 594° – 360° = 234°, eliminating (H); 234° – 360° = –126°, eliminating (J); and –126° – 360° = –486°, eliminating (K). The correct answer is (G).

Reading Practice Section 1

READING TEST

35 Minutes—40 Questions

DIRECTIONS: There are four passages in this test. Each passage is followed by several questions. After reading each passage, choose the best answer to each question and blacken the corresponding oval on your answer document. You may refer to the passages as often as necessary.

Passage I

PROSE FICTION: This passage is adapted from the short story "Going Home" by Lucretia Prynne (© 2007 by Lucretia Prynne).

Summers in Alabama had always been hot. My childhood memories are filled with days spent floating in the pond, sitting on the porch swing, lying sprawled in front of any source of moving air, trying in vain to get, and stay, cool. But when I walked out of the airport, already tired from a three-hour flight that had been delayed by over half an hour, laden with suitcases and dressed for an overly air-conditioned office climate, the heat came over me like a blanket. An old, unwashed woolen blanket that had been soaked in water, allowed to dry crumpled on the floor, then resoaked and thrown at me in all of its mildewed glory. The short walk to the car-rental agency felt like a trek through the jungle; by the time I got to my rental, my shirt was soaked through in patches, my hair was limp and sticky, and my mood was foul.

During the hour-long drive home, I had plenty of time to think. About why I had left, about all the things I had chosen to leave behind, about the life I had built for myself far away from this world of heat and poverty and depression. Lost in my thoughts, I found myself driving up the gravel road leading to my childhood home before I realized where I was. The clapboard house looked the same as it had when I had left ten years earlier, save for a slight accumulation of the junk common to front yards in this part of the world. The old tire swing still hung askew from the hickory tree, half the ropes worn away from constant use. On the porch sat a rocker that had once been my grandmother's and a watering can that looked almost as old. Parking off to the side, I grabbed my bags anxiously, trying to calm my nerves, and braced myself.

No one ever used the front door to the house. I remembered that, of course, and walked instead to a side door that opened onto the kitchen. The door itself was propped open to allow for whatever breeze might meander by, the screen door shut to keep out the mosquitoes, giving me a view of the room. There was the kitchen table, covered in dents and scratches but polished to a high sheen; behind and to the right, the pantry, no doubt stocked full of the jars of preserves that my mother would have been making all summer; and straight ahead, my mother, standing at the sink. She had aged during the years of my absence. I could see it in the way she stood, slightly hunched over the sink, and in the color of her hair, pulled back as always. She had to have heard me coming—gravel roads announce visitors from miles away—but she showed no sign that she knew I was standing there in the doorway, debating whether or not to knock.

"Mother? It's me. I'm here."

Her back straightened as she replied, though she never turned or left the sink.

"Come on in, and be sure to close the screen door behind you. It's been a bad year for bugs."

I opened the door and stepped back in time. When I had announced my plan to go away for school, she had asked me how I thought I was going to pay for it. When the holidays came around, and I told her I wasn't going to be able to come home, she didn't ask why, and when I stopped calling on a regular basis, she didn't ask then either. How many nights had I spent, hating her for making those decisions so hard for me? Already I could feel the anger rising, that she could act so unconcerned at my arrival, standing at the sink shelling peas. Her only daughter, whom she hadn't seen for a decade.

As I approached the sink, ready to demand an explanation, I saw that her hands were shaking, the peas falling into the sink as much as the bowl. She looked so much older, aged even more than I had thought, in the same faded dress she'd probably worn for five years. It suddenly hit me that all that time, she hadn't called not because she didn't care, but because she did. She had never been able to leave, but I had, and she understood that I needed to strike out on my own, far from here. Now here I was, in my fancy city clothes, with my college degree and impressive job, and she didn't know what to say. I bridged the gap the only way I knew how: I rolled up my sleeves, and started to help with the peas.

1. The primary purpose of the first paragraph is to:

A. describe the narrator's transition from her everyday, working life in the city to the world of her rural childhood.
B. explain why the narrator becomes so frustrated when she arrives at her mother's house in the countryside.
C. give the reader enough background about the setting of the story to explain the events of the later parts of the passage.
D. foreshadow the narrator's feelings of abandonment as described in the last paragraphs of the passage.

2. The narrator considers the weather in Alabama during the summer to be:

F. humid and extremely hot.
G. unbearably hot and miserable.
H. cool and breezy.
J. pleasantly familiar.

3. It can reasonably be inferred from the second paragraph (lines 15–28) that the narrator's feelings upon seeing her childhood home are feelings of:

A. surprise at the dilapidated state of the building.
B. frustration and anger toward her mother.
C. joy tinged with fatigue caused by her travels.
D. familiar recognition combined with nervousness.

4. The best description of the point of view from which this passage is told is that of a:

F. daughter describing her thoughts during an event in her adult life.
G. daughter reminiscing about her distant childhood in Alabama.
H. mother remembering her daughter's visit to the family home.
J. mother who longs to visit her adult daughter but cannot.

5. As it is used in line 28, the word *braced* most nearly means:

A. fastened.
B. straightened.
C. prepared.
D. supported.

6. As revealed in the passage, the mother is best described as:

F. harsh and uncompromising.
G. uneducated yet wise.
H. altruistic and warm.
J. distant but caring.

7. The central concern presented in the passage is:

A. the anger that a daughter feels toward her distant mother and her struggles to overcome this anger.
B. the conflicting emotions experienced by the narrator upon her homecoming from her life in the city to the rural childhood of her youth.
C. the narrator's realization that her mother has aged terribly during the four years the narrator spent in college.
D. an older woman's cautious but willful acceptance of her daughter's foreign lifestyle as the older woman is forced to stay in her hometown.

8. The relationship between the narrator and her mother, as described in the last paragraph (lines 60–71) of the passage, could best be described as:

F. extremely close, built on frank emotional openness and mutual respect of one another's independent decisions.
G. based on unspoken thoughts, leading to occasional misunderstandings, but ultimately supportive and caring.
H. antagonistic, largely due to the mother's unwillingness to support her daughter's independent decision to move away.
J. a very distant relationship, largely nonexistent outside of rare visits on the part of the daughter.

9. The emotional states of the characters are primarily conveyed by the author's use of:

A. metaphorical descriptions of the setting.
B. subtle but emotionally charged dialogue.
C. visual descriptions and narrative reflections.
D. detailed psychological portraits by an objective narrator.

10. As revealed in the final paragraph, upon seeing her mother at the sink, the narrator, for the first time, realizes which of the following?

F. She wants desperately for her mother to be more expressive of her emotions.
G. Her mother has aged to such an extent that the daughter has trouble recognizing her and the house in which she lives.
H. It is difficult to leave someone and not be able to visit them every year during the holidays.
J. Her mother has been supportive of the narrator's decision to leave but has not expressed it in a way the narrator expects.

Passage II

SOCIAL SCIENCE: Passage A is adapted from the article "Some Preteens Remember Being 2" by Jennifer Welsh (© 2011 by Live Science Magazine). Passage B is adapted from the book *The Universe Within* by Morton Hunt. (Copyright © 1982 by Morton Hunt. Reprinted by permission of Georges Borchardt, Inc., on behalf of the author.)

Passage A

Most adults suffer from childhood amnesia, unable to remember infancy or toddlerhood. That's what scientists thought. But a new study indicates that even six years after the fact, a small percentage of tots as young as two can recall a unique event....

In 2011, researchers at the University of Otago in New Zealand devised a "magical" contraption to catch the attention of children in their study, called the Magic Shrinking Box. The kids put a toy in the top, cranked a lever and a mini version of the toy popped out at the bottom, with an accompaniment of sounds and lights. The researchers trained 46 of their 27-to-51-month-old participants for two days in a row, showing them how to use the machine.

On the third day the kids were asked about the box, how to use it, if they remembered it. This day-three interview was repeated six years later, when the kids were around 10 to 12. Before mentioning the words "Magic Shrinking Box" the researchers first showed the kids a medal they received after participating, asking if they remembered why they got it. Their parents were also interviewed at that time.

Only about a fifth of the children were able to recall the Magic Shrinking Box six years after playing with it, but interestingly this wasn't stratified by age, the researchers said. Even two of the youngest kids, who were under 3-years-old at the time they were engaged with the machine, were able to remember. Half of the adults remembered the game and how it worked.

The researchers then looked to see if any personality characteristics stood out amongst those kids who did remember. They looked at things like language skills and their general memory abilities. The researchers didn't find any indications that any particular personality trait impacted which kids remembered.

What they did see from the parent interviews was that kids who remembered had spent lots of time, from days to weeks, talking about the box after the researchers left. One even awaited the researchers' return with a vigil by the front door. This indicates that talking about the event shortly after it occurred may have helped to preserve it in the children's memories....

Passage B

Jean Piaget (1896–1980) was a Swiss clinical psychologist known for his original theories in the new 20th century field of child development.

The best-known aspect of Piaget's work is his stage theory—his characterization of the major levels of mental development and of the kind of thinking done in each.

From birth to about eighteen to twenty-four months infants are in the sensorimotor stage, during which they are aware of sensations and can make increasingly purposeful movements but know nothing of the world except their own perceptions; for a time, they have no mental symbols or images of things outside themselves, and even seem unaware that an object they cease to see or feel still exists. They may stare at a toy, or grasp it or suck on it, but if the toy falls out of sight or is hidden under a pillow or blanket, infants do not look for it and instantly become unaware of it, as if the object had ceased to exist. Infants, in other words, cannot think about anything but the here and now.

But by about a year to a year and a half—sooner for some, later for others—children increasingly act as if they know that things still exist even when they neither see nor are touching them; Piagetians call this the attainment of the "object concept," or "object permanence." Out of repeated encounters and developing memory, children begin to have mental images or concepts that they can use in place of sensations. Hide a toy under a pillow or roll a ball under a sofa while a child is watching, and he or she will look for it there; the child has in his or her mind the rudiments of a world that corresponds to external reality.

This is the threshold of the next stage which runs roughly from two to seven, and which Piaget called the period of preoperational thought. During this time, the child rapidly acquires images, concepts, and words that represent external objects and processes, and is increasingly able to remember things and talk about them. But his or her internal representation of the world is still primitive, lacking, at first, such organizing concepts as space, time, causality, and quantity. The child cannot perform mental operations using these ideas, which is why Piaget called this stage preoperational. Tell a three-year-old that his parents, vacationing in Europe, will be back in two weeks; no matter how you explain it, he cannot grasp it, for time, in his mind, is only "now," "before now," or "not yet." Ask a four-year-old, across the room, how objects line up from where you are looking at them; she will describe them as they look from where she is, for her thinking is still close to the infantile egocentric view of the world.

Questions 11–14 ask about Passage A.

11. In line 7, the word "magical" is most likely in quotation marks because:

A. the word is a direct quote from the researchers' study.
B. the author is skeptical regarding the magical quality of the box.
C. the children in the study were led to believe the box had magical powers.
D. the author wishes to emphasize the extraordinary power of this research tool.

12. As it is used in line 23, the word *stratified* most nearly means:

F. organized.
G. clouded.
H. layered.
J. limited.

13. The researchers most likely included sounds and lights in the function of the Magic Shrinking Box in order to:

A. distract children from the function of the machine.
B. convince children that the box had magical powers.
C. make the box more difficult to remember over time.
D. capture the children's attention by engaging multiple senses.

14. Passage A most likely refers to the child awaiting the researchers' return with a vigil by the front door in order to support the conclusion that:

F. children are more likely to remember an event if they talk about it afterwards.
G. young children are less likely to remember an event than older children.
H. parents who remember an event vividly can influence the likelihood that their children will remember the event over time.
J. children are more likely to remember an event if there is a degree of fear associated with it.

Questions 15–17 ask about Passage B.

15. According to Passage B, infants are unaware of certain objects because:

A. they are not aware of certain sensations.
B. their perceptions are interfered with by others.
C. they remember only objects that are within their immediate sight.
D. they have only recently attained object permanence.

16. With which of the following statements would Piaget most likely agree?

F. A five-year-old is more likely to remember an event than a three-year-old is.
G. A two-year-old has not yet acquired object permanence.
H. A four-year-old has no need for sensorimotor skills.
J. A seven-year-old is as egocentric as an infant.

17. The statement "sooner for some, later for others" (lines 56–57) is most nearly meant to:

A. convey the idea that object permanence takes a long time to master.
B. illustrate the range of ages by which children are able to understand external reality.
C. emphasize the importance of memory in developing mental images of external concepts.
D. suggest that object permanence is a stage different children reach at different times.

Questions 18–20 ask about both passages.

18. Passage A and Passage B differ in that Passage A:

F. asserts that a child's memory grows stronger with age, while Passage B downplays this relationship.
G. describes an experiment that supports the passage's main idea, while Passage B only describes a theory.
H. argues that adults have better recall of events than children do, while Passage B refutes that position.
J. draws a connection between memory and personality traits, while Passage B focuses on memory and age.

19. Which of the following types of evidence do both authors use to support their points?

A. Explanations from professionals
B. Descriptions of research studies
C. Hypothetical examples
D. Acknowledgement of dissenting opinions

20. Based on these two passages, which pair of phrases best compares the researchers in Passage A to Piaget and his followers as they are described in Passage B?

F. Amateurs versus experts
G. Skeptics versus believers
H. Specialists versus pioneers
J. Charlatans versus adventurers

Passage III

HUMANITIES: This passage is adapted from the memoir *Who I Was to Become* by Arnold C. Tiepolo (© 2008 by Arnold Tiepolo).

My economics professor was finally getting through to me. He was explaining the concepts of comparative advantage and opportunity cost, stating that individuals, companies, and countries choose their economic goals by comparing their ease of attaining those goals to that of their competition as well as by considering what opportunities they would be forsaking in the process. For example, if it's easier to grow bananas in New Zealand than it is in Madagascar, then New Zealand has a comparative advantage in that industry. However, if the land New Zealand would use to grow its bananas could otherwise be used to grow timber for the logging industry, then whichever commodity is sacrificed so that the other can be produced becomes the opportunity cost of that choice. As my professor continued applying these concepts to other global scenarios, I started thinking that the same thought process takes place as each of us carves out his personality and ambitions.

No choice is made in a vacuum. An incoming freshman doesn't arbitrarily major in journalism any more than a country would haphazardly make bananas one of its chief exports. The rational decision-making process we see in either case is a demonstration of self- and environmental analysis: what are my strengths, what are my priorities, and how good is my competition? As someone who teaches law school prep classes, I am often confronted by my students' quizzical looks when I tell them I am not interested in pursuing law myself. Occasionally, I find myself quite tempted to venture down that arduous but rewarding path; however, I remind myself of how much I value my free time and how much of it would be sacrificed by my becoming a lawyer. On mornings when I bike down to the beach with my guitar slung over my shoulder so that I can write songs in sandy tranquility, I am reminded of the immense trade-off between financial security and personal freedom.

In high school, my best (and practically only) friend and I would routinely pull "all-nighters": filming music videos, playing hours of table tennis, and falling asleep trying to appreciate classic movies like *The Godfather*. For the most part, our peers at school recognized us as a single unit; maybe we were opposites, one "yin" and the other "yang," but we fused together as one entity. My best friend was not viewed admirably by many, and several times I was entreated to ditch him so that I could be included in some other group. Although loyalty was a huge reason to remain his friend, I definitely weighed the opportunity costs of having one, unassailable friendship versus having a multitude of more superficial friends.

When my older brother started playing piano at age eight, I idolized him and began taking piano lessons shortly thereafter. Within a few months, my piano abilities caught up with his. He decided, rather than sharing the instrument with his brother, that he would abandon the piano in favor of the saxophone. Although his nine-year-old brain did not see it necessary to saddle me with guilt, he is quick to remind me today of how my encroachment upon his territory as the family's pianist led him to seek a new interest. My two brothers and I are extremely similar, eerily clone-like versions of each other. While any one of us could have ended up being the filmmaker, the musician, or the novelist, we seem to have purposefully avoided each other's vocations so that we could have our own distinct identities.

The need to craft a personal identity is intrinsic to anyone's life. Americans' central ethos, especially if you listen to advertisers, is the expression of individuality. We conveniently forget that, in selecting our personalities, we are almost invariably making choices that thousands of others like us are making, thereby negating any hope of true individuality. However, like economic ventures, our "gimmick" has to be unique only in our local context, whether that be our family, our circle of friends, our school, etc. Opening a barbershop is hardly treading on untouched entrepreneurial territory, but if there is no barbershop in the neighborhood, such a business could be a welcome and prosperous presence. Similarly, I don't consider myself an innovator for pursuing a career in professional music, but within the context of my family, that career choice has distinction.

While having an identifiable trait is a helpful way for people to categorize and remember you, our habitual gravitation towards labeling people according to their predominant features troubles me. When I consider every fork in the road my life has reached, I can envision any number of alternate universes in which I am studying astrophysics, already raising a family, or backpacking across the Appalachian Trail. The potential energy to realize any of these scenarios was in me, but as soon as I chose one path, all the others seemingly imploded. I am reluctant to accept any rigidity to my personality or occupation, knowing that there are untold numbers of concurrent directions my life could take. We are all that way: physicians who could be poets, dancers who could be real estate moguls, married people who could still be single. To oversimplify people by acknowledging only what we currently see them doing is to ignore the deep reservoirs of possibility that brew just under the surfaces of their choices.

21. The word *vacuum* in line 17 refers to:

A. thorough cleanliness.
B. absence of environmental context.
C. a person's subconscious.
D. a large opportunity cost.

22. Which of the following best describes how the author uses the reference to *yin* and *yang* (line 39)?

F. It provides an instance of the name-calling that the author and his best friend endured from peers who did not understand their close friendship.
G. It demonstrates the author's friend's interest in Eastern mysticism as opposed to the author's primary interest in economics.
H. It is analogous to the close bond between the narrator and his friend who are often seen as two parts that form a larger whole.
J. It is analogous to the ways people waver between choices in their lives and will at times have one profession but wish they had chosen another.

23. The passage states that one of the author's brothers is currently a:

A. novelist.
B. pianist.
C. real estate mogul.
D. physician.

24. In the passage, the author refers to having considered becoming all of the following things in his adult life EXCEPT:

F. a parent.
G. a lawyer.
H. a journalist.
J. an astrophysicist.

25. As it is used in the passage, the term *gimmick* (line 66) represents:

A. a means of defining one's individuality.
B. the way advertisers trick people into wanting unnecessary products.
C. what makes people living in the United States unique.
D. an entrepreneurial venture chosen without sufficient forethought.

26. The author would most likely agree with which of the following statements about "opportunity cost" and "comparative advantage" mentioned in the first paragraph?

F. They are the central claims of any modern economic theory and are the cornerstones of any class in the subject.
G. They were instrumental in the author's various decisions in life, particularly his decision to open a barbershop.
H. They are so useful because they can be applied without reference to any surrounding context.
J. They are ideas from economics that may also be useful in considering topics other than economics.

27. The "we" in line 86 is most likely:

A. the author and his brothers.
B. the author and other Americans.
C. the author and his best friend.
D. the author and his alternate visions of himself.

28. Based on the passage, the author most likely began playing piano when he was:

F. younger than eight years old.
G. eight years old.
H. nine years old.
J. in high school.

29. Which one of the following would the author most likely see as an example of oversimplifying others by "acknowledging only what we currently see them doing" (lines 89–90)?

A. Assuming a physician wants to be a writer or poet
B. Assuming a lawyer only pretends to like his or her job
C. Assuming a mathematician is good only at math
D. Assuming a politician no longer wants to be a politician

30. Which of the following statements about the author and his siblings is supported by the passage?

F. They would stay up all night filming and watching movies in an attempt to spend less time communicating with each other directly.
G. Every hobby one of them chose was ruined by another encroaching upon it, and they soon abandoned most things they started.
H. They drew straws to see who would pursue what career, allowing the career of each to be determined completely by chance.
J. Although very similar, they sought to differentiate themselves from each other by choosing different careers.

Passage IV

NATURAL SCIENCE: This passage is adapted from the article "Fair-Weather Warning" by Julia Mittlebury (© 2007 by Julia Mittlebury).

Could the sun be causing epidemics? Take cholera, for example, an often fatal disease caused by the bacterium *Vibrio cholerae* (*V. cholerae*). Every so often, coastal areas suffer massive outbreaks of cholera due to infected food or water. Where do these outbreaks come from?

The bacterium that causes cholera is found in areas that contain the copepod, a certain type of crustacean. The copepod depends on zooplankton for nourishment, and these zooplankton in turn depend on phytoplankton for their nourishment. Phytoplankton use photosynthesis to feed on sunlight. Although one might need to go to the bottom of the food chain, the evidence shows that an increase in sunlight might mean an increase in the potential for cholera.

Interested in this correlation, Rita Colwell and her fellow researchers at the University of Maryland are studying ways to use satellite measurements of sea temperatures, sea height, and chlorophyll concentrations in order to predict when conditions favoring a cholera outbreak are more likely. As sea temperatures rise, photosynthetic organisms such as phytoplankton become more abundant. As sea levels rise, the phytoplankton, zooplankton, copepods, and, by extension, the cholera bacterium are all brought closer to the shore. This increases the likelihood of food and water contamination.

By monitoring the cholera food chain in reverse, Colwell and her colleagues believe they can predict the emergence of cholera 4 to 6 weeks in advance. Colwell's model predicted the rate of infection during one recent cholera outbreak in Bangladesh with 95 percent accuracy. Unfortunately, because this field of study is so new and its insights are so speculative, local public health officials have not yet begun to base any preventative measures on these satellite-based forecasts.

Just up the road from Colwell and the University of Maryland, Kenneth Linthicum is leading similar efforts at the NASA Goddard Space Flight Centre in Greenbelt, Maryland. He has designed a model to analyze the spread of Rift Valley fever, a mosquito-spread virus that killed about 100,000 animals and 90,000 people back in December 1997.

Scientists observed that prior to the outbreak, the equatorial region of the Indian Ocean saw a half-degree increase in surface temperature. Although half of a degree sounds like only a slight difference, the temperature of an ocean does not change easily. Warmer ocean water in this region corresponds with strong and prolonged rains, increased cloud cover, and warmer air over equatorial parts of Africa. These characteristics favor the proliferation of mosquitoes and help keep them alive long enough for the virus to become easily transmittable.

In September 2007, Linthicum and his team became alerted to similar environmental changes. Over the next few months, they warned local health officials in Kenya, Somalia, and Tanzania that conditions were ripe for a mosquito-based outbreak. As a result, only 300 lives were lost, an almost miraculous improvement from the devastation of the 1997 outbreak. While it is impossible to know if this outbreak would have been as far-reaching as that of 1997, it seems likely that the advance warning succeeded in saving thousands, if not tens of thousands, of lives.

Similarly, a study by David Rogers at Oxford University has helped to predict outbreaks of sleeping sickness, a parasitic disease caused by West African tsetse flies. Here, Rogers first calibrated regional levels of photosynthesis to the size of a vein in the wings of the flies. The vein size is a good measure of how numerous and robust the tsetse fly population is. Today, by reading the photosynthetic levels from satellite data, even researchers outside of West Africa can predict potential epidemics in the region.

This type of research is encouraging to many in the disease prevention field, because traditional methods involve slow, costly research. The newfound ability to cull massive amounts of meteorological data from satellites and to run that data through computer models has been much more efficient.

The goal of these models is to study the relationships between disease data and climate data. However, to do so requires decades', if not centuries', worth of high quality data to identify correlating factors with accuracy. Currently, the climatic data is much more reliable than the disease data. Nevertheless, excitement about the potential usefulness of satellite-based predictions is persuading health agencies to compile and integrate their disease data more efficiently to give easier access to those trying to discover climate-disease links.

It may still take a good deal of time and energy before this technology is ready for practical application. Critics claim that the number of variables underlying the spread of disease are too numerous and varied for a climate-based approach ever to be reliable. Fluctuations in the immunity of local populations, human and animal migrations, and the resistance to drugs used to commonly treat certain diseases could confuse climate-based models. Advocates respond, though, that these non-climatic factors can similarly be incorporated into their research as long as the relevant data is collected, and the resulting models will have even better accuracy.

31. The passage mentions that all of the following are variables that could confuse climate-based models EXCEPT:

A. ocean temperature.
B. resistance to drugs.
C. animal migration.
D. fluctuations in immunity.

32. According to the sixth paragraph (lines 38–46), scientists have concluded that a half-degree increase in surface temperature in the Indian Ocean corresponds with:

F. increased cloud cover and warmer air over the ocean.
G. warmer rains at the equator.
H. strong and prolonged mosquito clouds.
J. higher populations of mosquitoes carrying the Rift Valley fever virus.

33. The correlation described in the third paragraph (lines 14–23) can be most accurately described as linking which of the following?

A. Copepods and crustaceans
B. Contamination of food and water
C. Sunlight and cholera
D. Photosynthesis and the food chain

34. According to the passage, the vein size of tsetse flies can help predict sleeping sickness outbreaks because:

F. it affects the level of photosynthesis that causes the disease.
G. the parasite that causes the disease can only live in large veins.
H. it is a good measure of how numerous and robust the fly population is.
J. satellite data can read the level of parasites in the veins.

35. Information in the ninth and tenth paragraphs (lines 66–79) regarding the relationships between disease data and climate data indicates that:

A. climate data needs to be better integrated before it can be used in conjunction with disease data.
B. studying disease data alone is faster and cheaper than studying climate data alone.
C. studying climate data alone is faster and cheaper than studying disease data alone.
D. disease data needs to be better integrated before it can be used in conjunction with climate data.

36. The passage indicates that satellite-based forecasts have not been acted upon by local health officials in:

F. Kenya.
G. Bangladesh.
H. Somalia.
J. Tanzania.

37. According to the passage, all of the following are part of a copepod's food chain EXCEPT:

A. sunlight.
B. phytoplankton.
C. chlorophyll.
D. zooplankton.

38. As it is used in line 45, the word *favor* most nearly means:

F. prefer.
G. support.
H. approve.
J. give.

39. According to the passage, the author describes satellite measurements of sea temperatures, sea height, and chlorophyll concentrations because they can be used for which of the following?

A. A survey of the food chain in coastal areas
B. An analysis of how sea temperature affects copepods
C. An estimation of how much sunlight phytoplankton need to survive
D. A prediction of when a cholera outbreak is likely

40. In the last paragraph, the author expresses the belief that the practical application of climate data to disease prevention is:

F. sure to provide better accuracy than using disease data alone.
G. likely to require significant time and energy.
H. the best course of action for epidemiologists to follow.
J. unlikely to succeed because of fluctuations in immunity.

Reading Practice Section 1 Answers and Explanations

READING PRACTICE SECTION 1 ANSWERS

1. A
2. F
3. D
4. F
5. C
6. J
7. B
8. G
9. C
10. J
11. C
12. F
13. D
14. F
15. C
16. F
17. D
18. G
19. A
20. H
21. B
22. H
23. A
24. H
25. A
26. J
27. B
28. F
29. C
30. J
31. A
32. J
33. C
34. H
35. D
36. G
37. C
38. G
39. D
40. G

READING PRACTICE SECTION 1 EXPLANATIONS

Passage I

1. **A** The question asks for the primary purpose of the first paragraph. Read the first paragraph. The paragraph describes the narrator's return to Alabama. She first recounts some of her *childhood memories.* Then she refers to herself as *dressed for an overly air-conditioned office climate* and mentions her rental car and her delayed flight, all things that relate to her life in the city. Choice (A) accurately describes the first paragraph, so keep (A). Choice (B) can be eliminated; the last sentence says *my mood was foul,* but the narrator is frustrated before arriving at her mother's house. This answer also does not address the change from the city to the country. The first paragraph does not describe the setting of the bulk of the passage; eliminate (C). Eliminate (D) because the first paragraph does not foreshadow a feeling of abandonment; the narrator's difficult relationship with her mother is in her past. The correct answer is (A).

2. **F** The question asks how the narrator describes the weather in Alabama during the summer. Look for the words *summer* and *Alabama;* these words appear in the first sentence, so read the first paragraph. The narrator compares the weather upon her arrival in Alabama to a *woolen blanket that had been soaked in water* and says that the walk to the car rental agency was like a *trek through the jungle.* In other words, the climate is described as hot and humid. Choice (F) is a match for this description; keep (F). Choice (G) also includes the word *hot,* but it is too strong; the weather is not described as unbearable, so eliminate (G). Eliminate (H) because it is the opposite of what is described. While the weather is *familiar* to the narrator, it is not pleasant, so eliminate (J). The correct answer is (F).

3. **D** The question asks about the narrator's feelings upon seeing her childhood home, as described in the second paragraph. Read the second paragraph. Lines 20–22 state that the narrator's *childhood home...looked the same as it had when [she] had left ten years earlier.* Lines 27–28 state that she had to *calm [her] nerves* and that *she grabbed [her] bags anxiously.* The word *surprise* in (A) is contradicted because she describes the house as virtually unchanged; eliminate (A). In these lines, the narrator is anxious, not angry or frustrated, so eliminate (B). The second paragraph does not mention *joy,* and *fatigue* was associated with the narrator's travels in the first paragraph; eliminate (C). Choice (D) includes both the narrator's recognition of the house and her nervousness. The correct answer is (D).

4. **F** The question asks about the point of view from which the passage is told. Because this is a general question, it should be done after all the specific questions. The narrator describes visiting her family home and seeing her mother after having moved away ten years earlier. She mentions moving away for college and having worked in an office, which matches (F). Choice (G) focuses on the narrator's childhood, which is mentioned only briefly and is not the main theme of the passage; eliminate (G). Eliminate (H) and (J) because they incorrectly identify the mother as the narrator. The correct answer is (F).

5. **C** The question asks what the word *braced* means in line 28. Go back to the text, find the word *braced* and mark it out. Carefully read the surrounding text to determine another word that would fit in the blank based on the context of the passage. Lines 27–28 say *I grabbed my bags anxiously, trying to calm my nerves, and braced myself.* The narrator is getting ready to enter her mother's house, and she is nervous, so *braced* could be replaced with "readied." *Fastened* means "attached," which does not match "readied," so eliminate (A). *Straightened* means "untwisted" or "made tidy," neither of which match "readied," so eliminate (B). *Prepared* means "readied," so keep (C). *Supported* means "helped up," which does not match "readied," so eliminate (D). The correct answer is (C).

6. **J** The question asks how the mother is best described. Look for the places in the passage where the mother is described; she is described most clearly in the final two paragraphs. Lines 57–59 say that the narrator *could feel the anger rising, that she could act so unconcerned at my arrival,* but in lines 64–66, her attitude changes: *It suddenly hit me that all that time, she hadn't called not because she didn't care, but because she did.* Choice (F) is too negative: although the narrator expresses anger at her mother, she does not describe her mother as *harsh,* and this answer misses the description of the mother as caring. Eliminate (G) because the mother's education is never discussed. Eliminate (H) because it does not adequately address the distance between the two characters. Choice (J) encompasses both the mother's seeming unconcern and her underlying caring. The correct answer is (J).

7. **B** The question asks about the central concern presented in the passage. Because this is a general question, it should be done after all the specific questions. The passage describes the narrator's experience of returning home after a long absence. The beginning of the passage focuses on her frustration and feelings of anger toward her mother, but the end of the passage finds her coming to a better understanding of her mother's motivations. Choice (A) does not reflect the narrator's final realization about and acceptance of her mother, so eliminate (A). Choice (B) captures the *conflicting emotions* of anger and acceptance, so keep (B). Eliminate (C) because it is too narrow; it focuses on one detail instead of the central concern of the passage. Eliminate (D) because it focuses on the mother's feelings instead of the narrator's. The correct answer is (B).

8. **G** The question asks about the relationship between the narrator and her mother, as described in the last paragraph. Read lines 60–71. In this paragraph, the narrator comes to an understanding about her mother that changes her perspective on their past relationship. She states that *she hadn't called not because she didn't care, but because she did...Now here I was...and she didn't know what to say.* Then, the narrator makes a connection with her mother through an action rather than with words. Eliminate (F) because it describes the relationship as *built on frank emotional openness,* which is in direct contradiction with the largely unspoken bond between the two characters. Choice (G) is supported by the last paragraph. Choice (H) is contradicted by the statement *she understood that I needed to strike out on my own,* so eliminate (H). Choice (J) is contradicted by the reconciliation recounted in the last paragraph. The correct answer is (G).

9. **C** The question asks how the author conveys the characters' emotional states. Because this is a general question, it should be done after all the specific questions. Most of the passage is told from the

point of view of the narrator, as she reflects on her journey, so her own emotions are conveyed in her thoughts: *my mood was foul; I grabbed my bags anxiously, trying to calm my nerves; I could feel the anger rising.* When she first encounters her mother, however, she notices *that her hands were shaking...She looked so much older...in the same dress she'd probably worn for five years.* From those sights, the narrator determines her mother's emotions: *she understood that I needed to strike out on my own.* The emotional states of the characters are not conveyed through the *setting*, so eliminate (A). The dialogue is limited to two lines, so eliminate (B). Choice (C) matches the ways that the narrator's and mother's emotions are conveyed. Eliminate (D) because the narrator describes her own emotional experiences and cannot be said to be *objective.* The correct answer is (C).

10. **J** The question asks what the narrator realizes for the first time when she sees her mother at the sink. The question refers to the final paragraph, so read that paragraph. It is when the narrator notices her mother's *hands...shaking, the peas falling into the sink as much as the bowl,* that the narrator writes *It suddenly hit me that all that time, she hadn't called not because she didn't care, but because she did...she understood that I needed to strike out on my own.* In the previous paragraph, the narrator expresses a wish that her mother be more expressive, so she doesn't realize this for the first time when she sees her mother at the sink; eliminate (F). Eliminate (G) because the house is described as looking the same as when the narrator left, and the narrator doesn't have *trouble recognizing* her mother. The difficulty of not being able to come home for the holidays is discussed in the previous paragraph, so this is not a new discovery; eliminate (H). Choice (J) is supported by the final paragraph. The correct answer is (J).

Passage II

11. **C** The question asks why the word *magical* is in quotation marks. The question refers to line 7, so read a window around the given line. Lines 6–10 state that the researchers *devised a "magical" contraption to catch the attention of children in their study, called the Magic Shrinking Box. The kids put a toy in the top, cranked a lever and a mini version of the toy popped out at the bottom.* This indicates that the machine was intended to appear magical to the children, and the use of quotation marks refers to the device's impression on the children. The quotation marks aren't used to indicate that the word is a direct quote, so eliminate (A). There's no indication that the scientists actually claimed the device is magical, so eliminate (B). Choice (C) refers to the device's effect on the children, so keep (C). There is no evidence that the device is particularly powerful, so eliminate (D). The correct answer is (C).

12. **F** The question asks what the word *stratified* means in line 23. Go back to the text, find the word *stratified* and mark it out. Carefully read the surrounding text to determine another word that would fit in the blank based on the context of the passage. Lines 21–23 say that only some of the children could remember the Magic Shrinking Box, but that *this wasn't stratified by age...Even two of the youngest kids, who were under 3-years-old at the time they were engaged with the machine, were*

able to remember. This indicates that *stratified* could be replaced with "grouped." *Organized* means "grouped," so keep (F). *Clouded* means "confused," so eliminate (G). *Layered* means "arranged one on top of another;" it doesn't match "grouped," so eliminate (H). *Limited* means "restricted;" it doesn't match "grouped," so eliminate (J). The correct answer is (F).

13. **D** The question asks why the researchers included sound and lights in the function of the Magic Shrinking Box. Look for the words *Magic Shrinking Box* in the passage. Lines 6–11 say that the researchers devised the box to *catch the attention of children in their study.* There is no evidence that the researchers were trying to keep the children from noticing the function of the box, so eliminate (A). There is no evidence that the researchers wanted the children to believe that the box actually *had magical powers,* so eliminate (B). There is no evidence that the researchers were trying to make the box *more difficult to remember;* eliminate (C). Choice (D) matches the stated purpose to *catch the attention of children,* and sound and lights engage the *multiple senses* of sight and hearing. The correct answer is (D).

14. **F** The question asks which conclusion the author is trying to support. Look for the phrase *awaiting the researchers' return with a vigil by the front door. Vigil* appears in line 37. Lines 34–36 state that *kids who remembered had spent lots of time...talking about the box after the researchers left.* The phrase *one even awaited the researchers'* return indicates that this is an example of how one of those children continued to think and talk about the box. Choice (F) restates the conclusion made in lines 34–36, so keep (F). There is no distinction made between *young children* and *older children* in this part of the passage, so eliminate (G). There is no discussion of how *parents* influence the memory of their *children,* so eliminate (H). There is no mention of *fear,* so eliminate (J). The correct answer is (F).

15. **C** The question asks why infants are unaware of certain objects, according to Passage B. Look for the phrase *infants are unaware of certain objects.* Lines 50–54 state that *if the toy falls out of sight... infants do not look for it and instantly become unaware of it, as if the object had ceased to exist.* The paragraph mentions *sensations,* but it doesn't say that infants are *unaware* of some of them, so eliminate (A). There is no evidence that infants' perceptions are *interfered with by others,* so eliminate (B). Choice (C) is supported by lines 50–54, so keep (C). *Object permanence* is discussed in the next paragraph; it is the ability to remember objects when they are out of sight, so eliminate (D). The correct answer is (C).

16. **F** The question asks which statement Piaget would most likely agree with. Because this is a general question, it should be done after all the specific questions for Passage B. Use words from the answer choices to locate the relevant portions of the passage. Lines 67–72 state that between the ages of *two* and *seven,* children are *increasingly able to remember things and talk about them.* Keep (F) since it is consistent with these lines. Lines 56–60 indicate that children generally gain object permanence *by about a year to a year and a half,* so eliminate (G). Lines 44–47 discuss the *sensorimotor stage,* but there is no indication that children stop needing sensorimotor skills, so eliminate (H). Lines 67–84 give the *infantile egocentric view of the world* as an example of something that changes between the ages of two and seven, so eliminate (J). The correct answer is (F).

17. **D** The question asks what the quoted statement is meant to do. Read a window in the passage around the given lines. Lines 56–59 state that *by about a year to a year and a half—sooner for some, later for others—children increasingly act as if they know that things still exist even when they neither see nor are touching them.* In context, the phrase *sooner for some, later for others* is used to imply that not all children develop this skill at exactly the same age. The phrase refers to differences among children, not the length of time it takes one child to master the skill, so eliminate (A). This part of the passage is only discussing *object permanence,* so the phrase *understand external reality* is too broad; eliminate (B). While it's true that *memory* plays a role in object permanence, this is not the purpose of the phrase in the question, so eliminate (C). Choice (D) is supported by lines 56–59. The correct answer is (D).

18. **G** The question asks about a way in which Passage A and Passage B are different. Because this is a general question, it should be done after all the specific questions on both passages. Eliminate any answer choice that misrepresents either passage. Passage A describes *a new study* that *indicates that even six years after the fact, a small percentage of tots as young as two can recall a unique event* (lines 3–5). Passage B discusses the *best-known aspect of Piaget's work* (line 41) and the introduction for Passage B states that *Piaget was known for his original theories in the new 20th century field of child development.* Passage B supports the assertion that a child's memory grows stronger with age, so eliminate (F). Keep (G), since it describes an *experiment* in Passage A and a *theory* in Passage B. Passage B does not refute the idea that adults have better recall of events than children, so eliminate (H). Passage A states that the researchers didn't find indications that any particular personality trait impacted which kids remembered, so eliminate (J). The correct answer is (G).

19. **A** The question asks which type of evidence both authors use to support their points. Eliminate any answer choice that misrepresents either passage. Because this is a general question, it should be done after all the specific questions on both passages. Passage A describes a study conducted by *researchers at the University of Otago* (line 6) and the last sentence provides the researchers' explanation for their findings: *This indicates that talking about the event shortly after it occurred may have helped to preserve it in the children's memories.* Passage B discusses the theories of Jean Piaget, who according to the introduction was *a clinical psychologist.* Keep (A) because the description *explanations from professionals* matches both of the passages. Passage A cites a *research study,* but Passage B does not, so eliminate (B). Passage B uses *hypothetical examples,* but Passage A does not, so eliminate (C). Passage A acknowledges a *dissenting opinion,* but Passage B does not, so eliminate (D). The correct answer is (A).

20. **H** The question asks which pair of phrases best compares the researchers in Passage A to Piaget and his followers as they are described in Passage B. Because this is a general question, it should be done after all the specific questions on both passages. Look for references to the researchers and to Piaget and his followers, and eliminate any answer choice that misrepresents either passage. According to the introduction for Passage B, Piaget was *a clinical psychologist,* and line 6 states that the researchers in Passage A work at *the University of Otago,* so neither passage involves *amateurs;* eliminate (F). There is no evidence that the researchers in Passage A are *skeptics,* so eliminate (G).

According to the introduction for Passage B, Piaget was *known for his original theories in the new 20th century field of child development,* so he and his followers could be described as *pioneers.* The researchers in Passage A are exploring whether young children can *recall a unique event* (lines 4–5). *Memory* is one aspect of Piaget's theories discussed in Passage B, so the researchers could be described as *specialists* within the field. Keep (H) since its descriptions of both passages are supported. The word *charlatans* means "frauds." Since the researchers are presented as reliable, eliminate (J). Alternatively, eliminate (J) because there is no indication that Piaget and his followers are *adventurers.* The correct answer is (H).

Passage III

21. **B** The question asks what the word *vacuum* refers to in line 17. Read a window in the passage around the given line. The previous paragraph states that *individuals, companies, and countries choose their economic goals by comparing their ease of attaining those goals to that of their competition* (lines 3–5), and the lines following this sentence state that *The rational decision-making process* is *a demonstration of self- and environmental analysis.* By saying *no choice is made in a vacuum,* the author is stressing the effect of outside influences on any decision, so *vacuum* refers to a lack of influences. *Cleanliness* is not related to a lack of influences, so eliminate (A). *Absence of environmental context* matches "without influences," so keep (B). The *subconscious* is not discussed, so eliminate (C). *Opportunity cost* is discussed in the previous paragraph, but it is not what *vacuum* refers to, so eliminate (D). The correct answer is (B).

22. **H** The question asks how the author uses the reference to *yin* and *yang* in line 39. Read a window in the passage around the given line. In lines 37–40, the author says that his peers viewed him and his best friend as a *single unit* and *fused together as one entity.* The passage does not mention name-calling, so eliminate (F). *Eastern mysticism* isn't related to how the author and his best friend were viewed, so eliminate (G). Choice (H) is supported by lines 37–40, so keep (H). The *yin* and *yang* metaphor is not used to discuss *people* in general nor the choice of *profession,* so eliminate (J). The correct answer is (H).

23. **A** The question asks what one of the author's brothers currently is. Look for the word *brother* in the passage. Lines 54–59 state, *My two brothers and I are extremely similar* and that *any one of us could have ended up being the filmmaker, the musician, or the novelist.* Keep (A) because it correctly names one of these professions: *a novelist.* The author's older brother decided to *abandon the piano* (line 50), so this does not answer the question about what one of the brothers is *currently;* eliminate (B). *Real estate mogul* and *physician* are hypothetical examples brought up in the final paragraph, so eliminate both of those answers. The correct answer is (A).

24. **H** The question asks which thing the author did not consider becoming in his adult life. When a question asks which answer is **not** supported, eliminate answers that **are** supported. Use words from the answer choices to locate the relevant portions of the passage. In lines 79–81, the author

says, *I can envision any number of alternate universes in which I am studying astrophysics or already raising a family,* so eliminate (F) and (J). In lines 24–27, the author indicates that he has considered *pursuing law,* so eliminate (G). When *journalism* is brought up in lines 17–19, the author is not discussing himself, so this is not something the author has considered becoming. The correct answer is (H).

25. **A** The question asks what the term *gimmick* represents as it is used in line 66. Read a window in the passage around the given line. The paragraph that begins on line 60 discusses the *need to craft a personal identity,* and the word *"gimmick"* could be replaced with the phrase *expression of individuality,* used in line 62. Choice (A) is well-supported by the surrounding context, so keep (A). *Advertisers* are mentioned in the paragraph, but the use of *gimmick* is not related to their efforts to get people to buy products, so eliminate (B). The paragraph talks about *Americans* and says that *our "gimmick" needs to be unique only in our local context,* but the passage does not say that the *gimmick* is *what makes people in the United States unique,* so eliminate (C). There is no discussion of hastily chosen opportunities, so eliminate (D). The correct answer is (A).

26. **J** The question asks which statement about opportunity cost and comparative advantage the author would most likely agree with. The question refers to the first paragraph, so read lines 1–16. Following the discussion of *opportunity cost* and *comparative advantage,* in lines 15–16 the author states, *the same thought process takes place as each of us carves out his personality and ambitions.* The statement that these ideas are the *central claims* of *any modern economic theory* is not supported, so eliminate (F). The author did not *open a barbershop,* so eliminate (G). The statement that opportunity cost and comparative advantage *can be applied without reference to any surrounding context* is contradicted in this paragraph, so eliminate (H). Choice (J) is supported by lines 15–16. The correct answer is (J).

27. **B** The question asks whom the word *we* in line 86 refers to. Read a window in the passage around the given line. The preceding paragraph states, *Americans' central ethos…is the expression of individuality. We conveniently forget that….* The author continues to use the word *we* through the end of the passage. Therefore, the *We* used in the final paragraph also refers to Americans in general. The author is not restricting this generalization to himself or to *his brothers, his friends,* or *his alternate visions of himself,* so eliminate (A), (C), and (D). Choice (B) is consistent with the context of the passage. The correct answer is (B).

28. **F** The question asks how old the author was when he began playing piano. Look for the word *piano* in the passage. Lines 46–48 state *When my older brother started playing piano at age eight, I idolized him and began taking piano lessons shortly thereafter.* Since his older brother was eight years old, the author was most likely younger than eight at that time. Choice (F) is supported by these lines, so keep (F). The *older brother* was *eight years old* when he started playing the piano, and he was *nine years old* when he stopped playing, so eliminate (G) and (H). The passage doesn't support the idea that the author was *in high school* at that time, so eliminate (J). The correct answer is (F).

29. **C** The question asks which choice the author would see as an example of oversimplifying others by *acknowledging only what we currently see them doing.* Read a window in the passage around the given lines. The last sentence of the passage states, *To oversimplify people by acknowledging only what we currently see them doing is to ignore the deep reservoirs of possibility that brew just under the surfaces of the choices,* and lines 86–88 give examples of the *untold numbers of concurrent directions* a person's *life could take: physicians who could be poets, dancers who could be real estate moguls, married people who could still be single.* Choice (A), *Assuming a physician wants to be a writer or poet,* would be the opposite of oversimplifying based on a person's current occupation, so eliminate (A). The focus in these lines is that each person *could be* something else; it is not about whether someone *likes* their job, so eliminate (B). *Assuming a mathematician is good only at math* is an example of only acknowledging someone's current profession, so keep (C). The focus in these lines is not about whether someone still *wants* their job, so eliminate (D). The correct answer is (C).

30. **J** The question asks which of the statements about the author and his siblings is supported by the passage. Look for references to the author and his siblings in the passage. The author discusses himself and his brothers in the fourth paragraph, and lines 56–59 state, *While any one of us could have ended up being the filmmaker, the musician, or the novelist, we seem to have purposefully avoided each other's vocations so that we could have our own distinct identities.* The activities in (F), *filming and watching movies,* are things the author did with his best friend, and there's no evidence that they were trying to avoid *communicating,* so eliminate (F). The passage doesn't indicate that *every hobby* the brothers chose was *ruined,* or that *most* of them were *abandoned,* so eliminate (G). The passage does not say that the author and brothers *drew straws* or determined their careers *by chance,* so eliminate (H). Choice (J) is supported by lines 56–59. The correct answer is (J).

Passage IV

31. **A** The question asks which answer choice is not a variable that could confuse climate-based models. When a question asks which answer is **not** supported, eliminate answers that **are** supported. Look for the words *climate-based* in the passage. Lines 84–87 state, *Fluctuations in the immunity of local populations, human and animal migrations, and the resistance to drugs used to commonly treat certain diseases could confuse climate-based models.* These lines include the variables given in (B), (C), and (D), so eliminate these choices. *Ocean temperature* is discussed in lines 38–46; the passage states that *Warmer ocean water…corresponds* with conditions that *favor the proliferation of mosquitoes and help keep them alive long enough for the virus to become easily transmittable* (lines 42–46). The next paragraph gives an example of a disease outbreak that was successfully predicted based on *similar environmental changes.* This is evidence that *ocean temperature* is a useful variable for prediction, and would not *confuse a climate-based model,* so keep (A). The correct answer is (A).

32. **J** The question asks what scientists think corresponds with a half-degree increase in surface temperature in the Indian Ocean. The question references the sixth paragraph, so read lines 38–46, and a few lines before or after this paragraph if needed. Lines 39–46 state that *a half-degree increase in*

surface temperature of the ocean corresponds with conditions that *favor the proliferation of mosquitoes and help keep them alive long enough for the virus to become easily transmittable.* The virus is identified in the previous paragraph as *Rift Valley fever,* a mosquito-spread virus. The passage describes *increased cloud cover...over equatorial parts of Africa,* not over *the ocean,* so eliminate (F). The passage mentions *warmer air* and *prolonged rains,* but not *warmer rains,* so eliminate (G). The passage states that *rains* are *strong and prolonged,* not that *mosquito clouds* are, so eliminate (H). Choice (J) is supported by the fifth and sixth paragraphs. The correct answer is (J).

33. **C** The question asks what two things are linked in the correlation described in the third paragraph. The question references the third paragraph, so read lines 14–23, and a few lines before or after this paragraph if needed. The reference to *this correlation* is in line 14; the word *this* indicates that the *correlation* is discussed just before this in the passage. Lines 12–13 state that *an increase in sunlight might mean an increase in the potential for cholera.* Line 7 simply states that the *copepod* is a type of *crustacean;* this is not the *correlation* the researcher is interested in, so eliminate (A). *Food and water contamination* are treated as a single variable in line 23; this is not the *correlation* the author is interested in, so eliminate (B). Keep (C) because it is supported by lines 11–13. Although there is a link between *photosynthesis* and the *food chain,* this is not the *correlation* that is discussed in line 14, so eliminate (D). The correct answer is (C).

34. **H** The question asks why the vein size of tsetse flies can help predict sleeping sickness outbreaks. Look for the words *tsetse flies* and *sleeping sickness* in the passage. Lines 57–62 state that sleeping sickness is *a parasitic disease caused by West African tsetse flies,* and that *vein size is a good measure of how numerous and robust the tsetse fly population is.* Sleeping sickness is caused by a parasite, not by *photosynthesis,* so eliminate (F). The passage does not mention the parasite's living conditions, so eliminate (G). Choice (H) is supported by lines 61–62, so keep (H). *Satellite data* is used to read *photosynthetic levels,* not *vein size,* so eliminate (J). The correct answer is (H).

35. **D** The question asks what is indicated by information regarding the relationships between disease data and climate data. The question references the ninth and tenth paragraphs, so read lines 66–79. Lines 76–79 state that health agencies are working to *integrate their disease data…to give easier access to those trying to discover climate-disease links.* Lines 74–75 state that *Currently, the climatic data is much more reliable than the disease data,* so eliminate (A). The paragraphs discuss using the two types of data together, rather than using either type *alone,* so eliminate (B) and (C). Choice (D) is supported by lines 76–79. The correct answer is (D).

36. **G** The question asks where satellite-based forecasts have not been acted upon by local health officials. Look for the words *satellite-based forecasts* and *local officials* in the passage. Lines 24–31 state that *Colwell's model predicted the rate of infection during one recent cholera outbreak in Bangladesh with 95 percent accuracy,* and it goes on to say that *local public health officials have not yet begun to base any preventative measures on these satellite-based forecasts.* Lines 47–56 describe how a satellite-based forecast of an outbreak in *Kenya, Somalia, and Tanzania* helped local health officials save *thousands, if not tens of thousands, of lives.* The countries in (F), (H), and (J) are mentioned as places where

local health officials have acted on *satellite-based forecasts,* so eliminate these choices. Choice (G) is supported by lines 24–31. The correct answer is (G).

37. **C** The question asks what is not part of a copepod's food chain. When a question asks which answer is **not** supported, eliminate answers that **are** supported. Look for the word *copepod* in the passage. Lines 6–10 describe the copepod's food chain: *The copepod depends on zooplankton for nourishment, and these zooplankton in turn depend on phytoplankton for their nourishment. Phytoplankton use photosynthesis to feed on sunlight. Sunlight, phytoplankton,* and *zooplankton* are all included in this description, so eliminate (A), (B), and (D). Keep (C) because *chlorophyll* is not included in the description. The correct answer is (C).

38. **G** The question asks what the word *favor* means in line 45. Go back to the text, find the word *favor* and mark it out. Carefully read the surrounding text to determine another word that would fit in the blank based on the context of the passage. The sentence in which the word *favor* appears states that *characteristics favor the proliferation of mosquitoes and help keep them alive.* Therefore, the word *favor* could be replaced with "encourage." *Prefer* means "like better;" it does not mean "encourage," so eliminate (F). Keep (G) because *support* is consistent with "encourage." *Approve* means "accept as satisfactory"; it does not mean "encourage," so eliminate (H). *Give* means "put into someone's possession"; it doesn't mean "encourage," so eliminate (J). The correct answer is (G).

39. **D** The question asks what potential use for satellite measurements of sea temperatures, sea height, and chlorophyll concentrations caused the author to discuss them. Look for the words *satellite measurements of sea temperatures, sea height, and chlorophyll concentrations* in the passage. Lines 14–18 state that researchers are *studying ways to use satellite measurements of sea temperatures, sea height, and chlorophyll concentrations in order to predict when conditions favoring a cholera outbreak are more likely.* Although the *food chain, copepods,* and *phytoplankton* are related to the correlation that researchers are interested in, the purpose of taking the measurements is to predict cholera outbreaks, so eliminate (A), (B), and (C). Keep (D) because it is supported by lines 14–18. The correct answer is (D).

40. **G** The question asks what belief about a practical application of climate data to disease prevention the author expresses in the last paragraph. The question references the last paragraph, so read lines 80–90. Lines 80–81 state, *It may still take a good deal of time and energy before this technology is ready for practical application.* The last sentence states that incorporating *non-climatic factors* will give climate-based models *even better accuracy,* but this is not comparing using *climate data* with using *disease data alone,* so eliminate (F). Keep (G) because it is supported by lines 80–81. Although the author feels that climate data can be useful, there is no comparison with another *course of action* in the last paragraph, so the phrase *best course of action* is not supported; eliminate (H). Although *fluctuations in immunity* are mentioned as a potential challenge in using climate data, the last sentence indicates that incorporating that kind of *non-climatic factor* with other data will lead to *even better accuracy*; the author doesn't think *the practical application of climate data to disease prevention* is *unlikely to succeed,* so eliminate (J). The correct answer is (G).

Reading Practice Section 2

READING TEST

35 Minutes—40 Questions

DIRECTIONS: There are four passages in this test. Each passage is followed by several questions. After reading each passage, choose the best answer to each question and blacken the corresponding oval on your answer document. You may refer to the passages as often as necessary.

Passage I

PROSE FICTION: This passage is adapted from the novel *A Passage to America* by Aditi C. Thakur (© 2003 by Aditi Thakur).

I'm shivering in the air conditioning. I've never gotten used to the swirl of chilled air in the apartment. I'd like to open the window, to welcome in the hot bright yellow sun, but the superintendent has painted all the building's windows shut for some unexplained reason.

Ramesh won't be home from the university for several hours, I know. The project he's working on is keeping him at the lab until later in the evenings these days. Still shivering, I mull the choices for our evening meal, scanning the vegetables, herbs, and spices I collected at the specialty food market this morning. Even after five years in the United States, I find I still seek the patterns of our life in India, including my daily morning visits to the market to do the day's food shopping.

As I pore over the curled turmeric roots and the bright orange and red mangoes—both of which appeared in the market's bins today for the first time—I remember the first time I went to an American-style supermarket. Intimidated by the unfamiliar streets and landmarks of our new city, Ramesh and I had spent the first month of our American life eating all our meals at restaurants within walking distance of the flat. Ramesh had concocted his lunches from items purchased at the university's "convenience store"; he joked that convenience was really the only desirable thing the shop offered. Once we had exhausted the menus at each of the nearby restaurants, I promised that I would brave the supermarket so we could both have a taste of the home we'd been aching for.

Naturally—or rather, unnaturally—the store was cold, and I was glad I had decided to bring along my *dupatta* to shield my otherwise bare shoulders.

At first, the enormous quantity of goods and the wildly varied colors everywhere I looked were impressive. But then I noticed that the produce section—it seemed surprisingly tucked away on the end farthest from the doors, as if the store were somehow ashamed of it—lacked items we considered favorites or even staples: no dried lentils or chickpeas, no cherimoyas or pomegranates. I wandered up and down the aisles, wondering at the slabs of meat sealed within cocoons of plastic, and at the seemingly infinite rows of boxes, each of which somehow housed "dinner for the whole family." Unable after a time to focus on the boxes' labels, I turned to a gangly, uniformed teenager who was pretending to straighten the ginger ale bottles on the bottom shelf.

"Excuse me, please, I am wondering whether you could help me find..." I began.

He glanced up at me, noting my *sari* with an eye that felt at once piercing and uncritical. "Aisle 7, on the right," he squeaked, with a wide, unexpectedly amiable grin.

My irritation at having been so easily categorized faded somewhat at discovering two shelves' worth of jars of chutneys and mixes, including one imported tandoori paste that had been one of our favorites back in India. But as I unsteadily but successfully navigated the checkout lines and paid for my few, familiar products, I observed that the supermarket's fluorescent ceiling bulbs effectively bleached out the shelves' contents. The bottles and boxes no longer seemed exotic or glamorous. It seemed to me that no matter how insistently the labels tried to draw attention to the wonders within their containers, the vividness of their colors would inevitably appear flat and lifeless under the homogenizing light.

I still go to the supermarket sometimes, but recently a colleague of Ramesh's recommended that we go to the outskirts of the city to shop at a new Indian market, where I went this morning. The old woman who manages the place moves quickly from stall to stall, urging customers to sample pieces of fruit or explaining how adding one more ingredient will perfect the planned dish. She reminds me, almost painfully, of my grandmother, who was similarly convinced that she could make others' lives better through shared food or wisdom—my grandmother, to whose image I've often come back whenever I've needed consolation or company.

I trace my finger along the beige granite countertop, as if conjuring up the rough wooden surface in my grandmother's kitchen. As a child, I'd believed the dark wood had retained every nick from every vegetable chopped, and every stain from every fruit that had yielded its sticky sweetness to my grandmother's swift, sure knife. I think of the fourteen distinct spices, each with its own grainy texture and subtle but memorable color, that she pounded into dust with her mortar and pestle. Then I recall the grayish, unfriendly curry powder I'd seen in the American supermarket, so unlike the familiar result of my grandmother's efforts. I sigh.

I don't really need to begin to prepare our dinner yet. I've learned to combine the specialty market's fresh produce with the supermarket's "quick prep" sauces and pastes, so making dinner isn't the all-day task it often was for my grandmother and even my mother. Even so, I decide to ward off the cold by shrugging on a sweatshirt embossed with the university's logo, and I set myself to work.

1. It can most reasonably be inferred from the passage that the narrator regards her grandmother as:

A. comforting.
B. frightening.
C. foolish.
D. out of touch.

2. The narrator makes clear that she shops for food in the mornings because:

F. that's when the produce arrives at the specialty market.
G. her husband works late at his job in the university lab.
H. the outdoor market is cooler during the morning hours.
J. she used to shop in the mornings when she lived in India.

3. As presented in the passage, how does the narrator's attitude toward living in the United States change from when she was a recent arrival until the present day?

A. At first, she was intimidated by unfamiliar surroundings, but she has since learned to blend Indian and American ways.
B. At first, she was excited about the prospect of learning new ways, but she has since become disillusioned by the people she meets.
C. At first, she enjoyed eating out at restaurants with her husband, but she has begun to miss him as he increasingly works late.
D. At first, she is thrilled by the supermarket displays, but she now refuses to leave her apartment.

4. The third paragraph (lines 14–26) primarily emphasizes that the narrator's visit to the supermarket is motivated by the fact that:

F. the narrator and her husband are both suffering from homesickness.
G. groceries are more inexpensive at the supermarket.
H. unlike the specialty market, the supermarket is within walking distance.
J. the narrator can't find the items she needs at the Indian specialty market.

5. When the narrator mentions the location of the produce section of the supermarket (lines 32–34), she is implying that:

A. the produce section has everything she needs to make dinner.
B. she is surprised that the produce section is not centrally located.
C. produce sections in Indian supermarkets are always out in the open.
D. she is surprised to find an imported Indian product there.

6. How can the conversation between the narrator and the supermarket clerk (lines 40–47) best be characterized?

F. The narrator is pleased that the clerk is friendly and able to tell her where to find the items she's looking for.
G. The narrator is shocked and upset by the clerk's hostility toward her.
H. The narrator is annoyed that the clerk knew what she wanted before she asked.
J. The narrator wishes the clerk had been more cooperative instead of being distracted by her clothing.

7. The narrator refers to the supermarket's "fluorescent ceiling bulbs" (line 54) in order to:

A. draw a contrast between the supermarket and the outdoor markets she remembers from India.
B. explain how her perception of the store's offerings had changed.
C. suggest one reason that the supermarket terrified her.
D. describe why she was able to see the fruits and vegetables more clearly.

8. As it is used in line 79 the word *unfriendly* most nearly suggests that:

F. the narrator thinks that the clerk doesn't want her to buy the curry powder.
G. the narrator considers this curry powder to be different from the curry powder with which she is familiar.
H. the narrator doesn't like the ingredients in the curry powder.
J. the curry powder has been imported from another country.

9. The narrator apparently believes which of the following qualities is shared by the old woman who runs the specialty market and the narrator's grandmother?

A. Frailty
B. Stinginess
C. Sociability
D. Nervousness

10. The narrator indicates that, unlike her grandmother and mother, she:

F. doesn't always spend all day preparing the evening meal.
G. doesn't wear Western-style clothing.
H. mingles easily with people she doesn't know.
J. doesn't like air conditioning.

Passage II

SOCIAL SCIENCE: This passage is excerpted from "Record Lows" by Clarence Tetley. The article comes from the book *Can Music Survive the Digital Revolution?* by Clarence Tetley and Lawrence Twinnings (© 2008 by Clarence Tetley).

Glenn Spelling's Northern Virginia record store is on the verge of closing. He has rare collectibles in 8-track, vinyl, tape, and cassette format, but the rarest commodity in his store is a customer. His landlord would not renew the store's lease on the building but allows Spelling to remain open until new tenants arrive.

"It's pretty sad to be living on borrowed time," sighs Spelling, "knowing it's only a matter of days until you run out of inventory or the landlord kicks you out."

Spelling may not be the only record store owner whose days in the business are numbered. Over 900 independent record stores have perished since the rise of digital music sales in 2003. Current estimates suggest that fewer than 2,000 remain in the United States. The ones that are hanging on are seeing their customer bases slowly erode, particularly among younger crowds. This slump in business is not isolated to the mom-and-pop independents.

Nationwide chain Tower Records was forced to declare bankruptcy in 2004.

Whereas large record store chains used to be essential ingredients in the lucrative hype machine of record labels, radio stations, and artists, record stores nowadays are not required for the recipe. Two different but simultaneous economic trends have effectively rendered record stores as obsolete as some of the bands they carry.

One giant threat to record stores is the rise of digital music downloads. Younger music consumers are increasingly willing and likely to buy their music one song at a time over the Internet and listen to it on their portable MP3 players. Since 1999, digital downloads have reduced CD sales by twenty to thirty percent. Recent technology allows thousands of songs to be held by a device the size of a pack of gum. This makes the notion of buying a physical commodity like a CD, which is harder to put in one's pocket than an MP3 player and holds less than 1 percent as much music, seem downright prehistoric.

The second factor contributing to record stores' demise is the emergence of the "Superstore," franchises such as Target and Wal-Mart, which have a range of inventory as wide as that of an entire shopping mall. As recently as ten years ago, consumers expected to go to any number of different specialized stores to buy such disparate items as groceries, clothing, and music. Superstores hold the allure of allowing a shopper to make all those purchases at the same cash register.

Because superstores expect to sell a larger volume of goods than that of a specialized store, superstores can slash their prices to razor-thin profit margins (or sometimes even sell items such as CDs at a small loss just to get customers in the door). This is an ambitious business model, developed by Sam Walton; it involves an incredible amount of initial capital to build the titanic warehouses that encase superstores and to buy the immense cornucopia of goods that will fill them. Furthermore, to attract customers, the stores need to keep prices lower than those of their competition, which means it will be years before a superstore recovers the initial money put into building it. However, once established, superstores have so much leverage in the marketplace and loyalty from their customer base that they can prosper indefinitely.

Record stores are economically powerless to match those prices. "Everyone's getting their CDs at the record label's wholesale price," explains Eric Tasker, owner of Funktown Records in Cincinnati. "If we marked up our CDs as little as [superstores] do, we wouldn't have enough revenue to pay for labor and expenses, let alone turn a profit." Tasker says that giant stores like Best Buy and Wal-Mart are able to buy in such bulk that they can often broker special deals with record labels that lower the wholesale price, further disadvantaging smaller chains and independent stores.

Some record store owners such as Spelling concede the greater affordability of superstore prices and struggle to come up with a reason why record stores deserve to stick around. "If you already know what you want, then I can see buying a CD wherever it's cheapest, but if you want to be able to talk to people about music and discover new bands, you need a record store. I guess most people don't want to do that anymore."

Some do, however, and it's about the only silver lining to the dark cloud hovering over the record store industry. Well, it's a *gray* lining actually. Older men, ages 40–60, comprise the largest segment of record store consumers, and they don't seem to be lured away by the cheaper superstore prices or the more efficient digital downloads. For these shoppers, many of their formative musical memories from childhood revolve around hanging out at their local record store, absorbing the alternative culture transmitted through posters on the wall and provocative album covers. They discovered many of their favorite bands by discussing music with the "experts" who work at record stores. Buying music is not merely shopping around for the cheapest price; it is an experience of immersion into the world of music, something that allows them to escape from their grown-up, career-driven lives and reconnect with their youthful inspirations.

11. According to the passage, which of the following is an accurate statement regarding the number of record stores?

A. Since the rise of digital music sales in 2003, over nine hundred stores have gone out of business.
B. Twenty to thirty percent of record stores that specialize in 8-track, vinyl, tape, and cassette are expected to close in the next ten years.
C. Before the rise of digital music in 2003, there were fewer than 2,000 independent stores in business.
D. Over the next ten years, another 900 stores are expected to perish.

12. Which of the following best describes the *silver lining* described in the last paragraph (line 75)?

F. Older, more technologically savvy men are relieved that innovations in downloading allow them to no longer have to travel to record stores.
G. Record stores have been forced to become cheaper and more efficient in a desperate attempt to lure superstore customers back.
H. The improved marketing of posters and album covers has been found to discourage the practice of digital downloads.
J. Older men who savor the experience of shopping at record stores remain a loyal customer base for record store owners.

13. In the context of the passage, the phrase "downright prehistoric" (line 35) is used to support the idea that:

A. older men cannot find music in 8-track, vinyl, tape, or cassette formats in most record stores.
B. downloading digital music to an MP3 player offers a size and capacity that the CD format cannot match.
C. the downloading speed of most computers is too sluggish to appeal to consumers.
D. young people would buy more CDs if the CDs were reduced in size.

14. It can reasonably be inferred from the passage that Spelling has which of the following attitudes toward consumers who have stopped using record stores?

F. They do not share any interests with the type of inquisitive shoppers who go to record stores not knowing what they want.
G. They will not find any sense of community in buying their music online since there will be no cashier to talk to while ringing up their sale.
H. They are correct in believing that record stores do not always have the best prices available for a given CD.
J. They are chiefly to blame for the hardships facing record stores, despite the fact that many people blame superstores instead.

15. In the context of the passage, the first paragraph is intended to:

A. criticize Spelling's record store for failing to keep up with the modern music market.
B. explain the lack of interest most music consumers have in collectibles.
C. demonstrate that even record stores with valuable and rare merchandise are struggling.
D. suggest that record store owners do not really understand real estate.

16. It can be reasonably inferred from the passage that before 1999, consumers purchasing their music over the Internet led to digital downloads reducing CD sales by:

F. less than 20 percent.
G. between 20 and 25 percent.
H. between 25 and 30 percent.
J. more than 30 percent.

17. According to the passage, what enables superstores to be able to sell products at small or even non-existent profit margins?

A. The significant amount of capital required to build such a superstore
B. The expectation of selling higher quantities of merchandise than smaller stores
C. The greater number they can carry due to their warehouse sizes
D. The ambitiousness of the economic planners who crafted their business models

18. According to the passage, what effect has Sam Walton had on the record store industry?

F. Record stores have based their business models on one he created.
G. He tried to change the record store industry's model of community.
H. He was one of the record store industry's most passionate critics.
J. He was involved in the evolution of the superstore, which is a competitor of record stores.

19. The passage offers all of the following as reasons modern consumers might not shop at record stores EXCEPT:

A. a higher price tag on goods available more cheaply elsewhere.
B. a fear of being unwelcome in a community of music "experts."
C. a preference for a different format of music than the CD.
D. the ability to buy music, groceries, and clothing all at once.

20. The author states that superstores will recover their initial building costs:

F. once all their capital is invested.
G. once all their goods are purchased.
H. once the store finally opens.
J. several years after the store has opened.

Passage III

HUMANITIES: Passage A is adapted from the essay "Listening" by Nicolas Lloyd (© 2003 by Nicolas Lloyd). Passage B is adapted from the essay "Music from the Heart" by Noël Kelley (© 1996 by Noël Kelley).

Passage A

I have early memories of lying in my crib, listening to the lush, powerful voices of the great Wagnerian singers that my parents played most nights after they put me to bed. The sound, building and growing in dramatic energy, would envelop me as I fell asleep, and became the soundtrack of my dreams.

I never learned to read music or play an instrument, but the primal emotions expressed in opera are part of a universal language. The forces of good and evil, love and hate, desire and revenge, emanate from the music like smells from an oven. Just as a sniff lets us know whether there is a cake or lasagna baking, a single chord can elicit a strong reaction, even to the untrained ear.

The words of Tristan and Isolde may be different from those of Mimi and Rodolfo, and Wagner's application of musical conventions distinct from Puccini's, but they come from the same place. Star-crossed lovers have existed for at least as long as the human race. While words can be used to express the combination of longing, joy, and sorrow that the lovers feel, music adds depth; it communicates those common feelings above and beyond what is possible with spoken language alone.

As Victor Hugo wrote, "Music expresses that which cannot be said and on which it is impossible to be silent."

All of the major events in my life have soundtracks, though they are not all operatic. Sometimes the music is what was playing: I met my wife for the first time at an outdoor cafe when we were in college, and some street musicians were performing "O Sole Mio" nearby. I hear that song every time I see her again after we've been separated, whether it's been an hour or a week.

Other times, my life soundtrack comes from the emotions of the event. When my mother was dying, excerpts from Mozart's *Requiem* played over and over again in my head as I sat by her bedside.

Wagner's music continues to feature prominently in my dreams. It takes me back to the beginning of consciousness. I know it is the beginning of my own consciousness, but it feels bigger than that, as if the music expresses the beginning of the world, the beginning of life.

Passage B

My parents were professional musicians. I have friends who are music teachers who enjoy having two weeks off for the winter holidays and who spend their entire summers on the beach. But holidays are busy for professional musicians. Brass players, as my parents were, are in high demand for Christmas and 4th of July concerts and summer weddings. My parents never took vacations, and we rarely had normal holiday celebrations.

When I went to college, my roommate was a music major. I rarely saw her, and she was always harried-looking when I did. She was constantly hurrying from one rehearsal to another. I quit singing in choirs, stopped practicing the piano, and declared an engineering major. I wanted to have a "regular" life, with weekends and vacations.

I had that life for a while, and then I got married and had a baby. He was chubby and bald with serious, dark eyes that studied me intently. I sang to him all day long because it made me feel more connected to him. I sang nursery rhymes while we played, old country ballads while I bathed him, hymns when we went for walks in the woods, and lullabies to soothe him to sleep. After his sister was born, I no longer wanted my "regular" life. I wanted to be with my babies, and to fill their days with song.

My parents had become musicians because it was a way of earning a living. They ran themselves ragged during the holiday season, squeezing in one more church service, one more concert, because it meant extra money that they could put towards their five children's college tuitions or the mortgage on the house that held all of us. I became a music therapist because I knew first-hand as a mother how deeply song could influence my children. It became my mission to share its healing power with others.

I have had some incredible successes. I've helped stroke victims regain the ability to speak and given children tools to manage their ADHD without medication.

But it isn't always easy. Sometimes, when I come home at the end of a long day, I'm tired and cranky, and I wonder why I do it. I have learned that I can't heal everyone, even my own children. As they've grown and become more independent, life has dealt them disappointment and heartache that doesn't go away simply by playing a silly song or dancing around the kitchen the way I did when they were little.

My parents both died before it occurred to me to ask them whether their hard work as musicians ever brought them joy. I recently came across an old picture of my mother, sitting in a rocking chair with my oldest sister who couldn't have been more than a few weeks old. There was something about the picture that was very comforting to me. It took me a while to realize why, but I finally saw it. My mother is singing in the picture. She looks happy.

Questions 21–24 ask about Passage A.

21. Lloyd mentions star-crossed lovers in order to illustrate the:

A. differences in portrayals of love in Wagner and Puccini.
B. universality of the emotions featured in operas.
C. unique ability of Wagner to express love through music.
D. possibility that animals feel emotions such as love.

22. As it is used in line 12, *untrained* most nearly means:

F. free-spirited.
G. crude.
H. coarse.
J. amateur.

23. Lloyd refers to "smells from an oven" (lines 9–10) to suggest that opera is:

A. best listened to while cooking.
B. powerful enough to evoke smells.
C. as comforting as homemade cake.
D. easily intelligible to anyone.

24. Lloyd quotes Victor Hugo to support his point that:

F. music expresses more than words can alone.
G. Wagner's music represents the beginning of conscious thought.
H. all major events in one's life should have a soundtrack.
J. unrequited love is best expressed through music.

Questions 25–27 ask about Passage B.

25. Based on Kelley's account, her family did not have normal holiday celebrations because:

A. they did not believe in celebrating in traditional ways.
B. her parents were busy working on holidays.
C. they could not afford expensive gifts for all five children.
D. they spent all their vacation time at the beach.

26. According to Kelley, her college roommate looked harried because:

F. her dreams had been overcome by Wagner's music.
G. she had a lot of different rehearsals to attend.
H. she missed having regular weekends and vacations.
J. she was worried about having enough money.

27. Kelley elaborates on how she connected with her baby by mentioning:

A. different types of songs she sang to him.
B. that different composers express the same emotion.
C. types of accomplishments she'd had as a music therapist.
D. a picture of her mother singing and rocking her older sister.

Questions 28–30 ask about both passages.

28. One way the perspectives of the authors differ is that Lloyd:

F. enjoys music for its beauty, while Kelley uses music as a tool in her job out of financial necessity.
G. is not a musician, so he lacks Kelley's deeper understanding of how music can affect a person's emotions.
H. arrived at his love for music all on his own, while Kelley learned about music from her parents who were professional musicians.
J. is a music aficionado that has always felt a strong connection to music, while Kelley is a musician that went through a period during which she distanced herself from music.

29. Which of the following do both authors use to support their ideas?

A. Specific song titles
B. Detailed explanation of performance technique
C. Recollections from childhood
D. Comparisons of different music genres

30. Based on these two passages, which of the following best relates Lloyd's relationship with music to Kelley's?

F. Impassioned amateur versus appreciative professional
G. Casual listener versus intent performer
H. Curious outsider versus jaded singer
J. Enthusiastic supporter versus disillusioned pianist

Passage IV

NATURAL SCIENCE: This passage is adapted from the entry "Migration" from *Wallace Wimpole's Bird Book* (© 1998 by Wallace Wimpole).

It has been well known among even casual observers of the natural world that many bird species make seasonal trips between cooler breeding grounds in the spring and summer, and warmer locations in the autumn and winter. Migration is a part of the annual cycle of over 50 billion individual birds worldwide. (This is not to say all birds migrate; there are many species, particularly in the tropics, that maintain a single residence year-round.) However, the biological mechanisms that prompt birds to choose a particular date to begin migration are complex and seem to be influenced by many factors.

The most obvious pressure on the timing of seasonal bird migration is the weather. As the weather cools and precipitation increases, birds living in temperate climates move in the direction of warmer weather. However, seasonal weather patterns are notoriously unpredictable. Cloud cover can obscure even reliable measures of the seasons, such as the position of the sun and the stars. Therefore, it is clear that birds must rely more heavily on an internal clock to time their seasonal movements. In fact, biologists have observed a phenomenon known as "migratory restlessness" in caged birds at the same time the wild members of their species set off on seasonal migrations.

For most migratory birds, food supply is a major factor that contributes to the need to move from one location to another. Birds must have ample nutrition to reproduce, and seasonal changes in weather affect the availability of berries, nuts, insects, rodents, and other sources of nourishment. Furthermore, birds must store a great deal of energy in the form of body fat to fuel their migration, so they have to leave while their reserves are high, before changes in weather cause the food supply to dwindle. Many species seem to anticipate changes in weather and food sources, and adjust their migration schedules to accommodate significant variations in weather and food supply that occur from year to year, causing scientists to speculate that unknown internal stimuli may have a strong effect on the timing of the migration decision.

In 1967, Russian ornithologists Viktor Dolnik and Tatiana Blyumental collected chaffinches as they migrated along the Baltic Coast. By examining the fat content and food in the gut of the carcasses of birds gathered at different stages of the waves of migration, and then comparing these findings to the number of birds out of the total population yet to migrate, the scientists determined the social influence fat, healthy birds have on the remaining population that was not as physically fit for migration. Dolnik and Blyumental found that on the first day of each wave of migration, only very fat birds flew. These birds left at sunrise, on days when weather conditions were favorable. They did not feed before beginning their migratory flight, instead relying on stored fat for energy.

On the second day, the chaffinch migration began again in the morning with fat birds. By the afternoon the migration volume peaked, as more and more lean birds began to migrate, many with the morning's food still in their stomachs. By the third day, almost all the birds that began to migrate were very lean. These birds began their migration only after feeding in the morning. Often these leaner birds began their migration despite inclement weather. Dolnik and Blyumental suggested that the social pressure exerted by the large volume of healthier birds in the flock that had already begun to migrate was an influence strong enough to override the lean birds' poor physical readiness and the adverse conditions as factors in their decision to migrate. The scientists conducted their experiment on only one species, and though chaffinches are typical of diurnal migratory land birds, they do not accurately represent sea birds, raptors, or nocturnal species. Nonetheless, Dolnik and Blyumental's work suggests that social pressure could explain why many different species of birds choose to migrate at apparently unfavorable times.

Some migratory birds travel much further than chaffinches. Most migrants spend a great deal of time storing energy to make trips that take a matter of days or weeks to complete, and travel tens to hundreds of kilometers, spending most of their lives in residence at their breeding grounds and their winter habitats. A few species, however, can spend months of each year en route between residences continents apart, and expend little more energy flying than sitting still. Wandering albatrosses spend almost all their time in the air, either migrating or foraging over oceans, moving up to 2000 kilometers on a single foraging expedition, and flying over 250,000 kilometers in a year (a distance equivalent to 4.6 times around the earth's equator.) Such sea birds rely on their specialized wing structure to hold them aloft in air currents that transport them long distances, and some travel back and forth along the same paths on schedules dictated by the prevailing winds.

31. The main purpose of the passage is to:

A. discuss the research techniques of scientists studying bird migration.
B. provide data on the distances traveled seasonally by various migratory bird species.
C. describe various factors that stimulate migratory behavior in birds.
D. prove the effects of weather on bird migration.

32. The author uses the information in parentheses in lines 6–8 primarily to:

F. prevent readers from misunderstanding the statistic cited in the previous sentence.
G. debunk claims that the biological mechanism for migration is complex.
H. imply that ornithologists disagree about whether birds choose their migration schedule.
J. prove the assertion that the migration cycle is changing due to global warming.

33. The passage mentions which of the following as a limitation to Dolnik and Blyumental's research?

A. Their focus on only one species of diurnal migratory land birds with a relatively short migration path
B. Their selection of the Baltic Coast
C. Their destruction of healthy birds for research purposes
D. Their inaccurate counts of the total number of birds in each flock, because of the constant movement of individual birds

34. The main purpose of the third paragraph (lines 22–35) is to:

F. specify the many sources of food birds use as energy to fuel their migratory movements.
G. document the weather conditions that impact birds' ability to fly.
H. present a variety of reasons why the availability of nourishment is important in the timing of bird migration.
J. summarize several scientific principles discovered by observing migratory birds.

35. As presented in the passage, the statement in lines 44–46 is best described as:

A. an assumption based on a small sample of a few captured chaffinches.
B. a characterization based on the comparison of the fat content of the bodies of many individual chaffinches.
C. an observation based on the visual appearance of chaffinches as they flew over the Baltic Coast.
D. an opinion based on the personal preferences of Dolnik and Blyumental.

36. It can reasonably be inferred that researchers have measured the longest migration periods and distances for which of the following types of migratory birds?

F. Land birds
G. Sea birds
H. Tropical birds
J. Temperate birds

37. Based on the passage, scientists observe that compared to wild birds, caged birds may be:

A. less likely to use weather conditions to time their migrations.
B. more likely to amass stores of body fat.
C. unable to differentiate between day and night.
D. just as capable of sensing the changing of the seasons.

38. Suppose that a scientist were to replicate the exact conditions of Dolnik and Blyumental's experiments as described in the passage. At which of the following times would the scientist reasonably expect to find the greatest number of birds migrating?

F. On the first day of the migration wave in the morning
G. On the second day of the migration wave in the morning
H. On the second day of the migration wave in the afternoon
J. On the third day of the migration wave in the afternoon

39. Based on the passage, how should the statement that Dolnik and Blyumental "determined the social influence healthy birds have" (lines 42–43) most likely be understood?

A. Dolnik and Blyumental found a greater number of healthy than unhealthy chaffinches in flocks that migrated.
B. During waves of migration, lean chaffinches were found to emulate the feeding behavior of fat chaffinches.
C. Dolnik and Blyumental discovered that chaffinches became less healthy as the migration continued.
D. After fatter chaffinches flew, Dolnik and Blyumental observed greater and greater numbers of leaner chaffinches begin to migrate.

40. The author most nearly characterizes the migratory pattern made by wandering albatrosses as:

F. common for coastal birds.
G. typical of temperate migrants.
H. uncommon among migratory birds.
J. unusual for long-distance migrants such as sea birds.

Reading Practice Section 2 Answers and Explanations

READING PRACTICE SECTION 2 ANSWERS

1. A
2. J
3. A
4. F
5. B
6. H
7. B
8. G
9. C
10. F
11. A
12. J
13. B
14. H
15. C
16. F
17. B
18. J
19. B
20. J
21. B
22. J
23. D
24. F
25. B
26. G
27. A
28. J
29. C
30. F
31. C
32. F
33. A
34. H
35. B
36. G
37. D
38. H
39. D
40. H

READING PRACTICE SECTION 2 EXPLANATIONS

Passage I

1. **A** The question asks how the narrator regards her grandmother. Look for the word *grandmother* in the passage. Lines 69–70 say, *my grandmother—to whose image I've often come back whenever I've needed consolation or company.* Keep (A), because these lines support the description *comforting.* The description of the grandmother is positive; it doesn't support the descriptions *frightening, foolish,* or *out of touch,* so eliminate (B), (C), and (D). The correct answer is (A).

2. **J** The question asks why the narrator shops for food in the mornings. Look for the words *shops* and *mornings* in the passage. Lines 11–13 state, *I find I still seek the patterns of our life in India, including my daily morning visits to the market to do the day's food shopping.* The passage doesn't discuss when *the produce arrives at the specialty market,* so eliminate (F). Although the narrator's husband does work late, that is not the reason the narrator shops in the morning, so eliminate (G). Although the narrator says that she's *still shivering,* she doesn't say that temperature affects her decision about when to shop, and references in lines 1–3 and 27–29 indicate that she doesn't like the cold, so eliminate (H). Choice (J) is supported by lines 11–13. The correct answer is (J).

3. **A** The question asks how the narrator's attitude toward living in the United States changed from her arrival until the present day. Since this is a general question, it should be done after all the specific questions. The narrator is initially *Intimidated by the unfamiliar streets and landmarks of our new city* (line 18), but in lines 82–88 she says that she has *learned to combine the specialty market's fresh produce with the supermarket's "quick prep" sauces,* which implies that she has become more comfortable. Keep (A), since it is supported by these references. The narrator was *intimidated* at first, not *excited,* and she is *irritated,* but not *disillusioned* by the grocery store clerk she meets in lines 43–50, so eliminate (B). The discussion of eating at restaurants in lines 18–26 doesn't indicate that the narrator *enjoyed* them, and though the first paragraph does mention that her husband works late, there is no mention of *missing* him; eliminate (C). The passage indicates that the narrator goes out shopping, so it's not true that *she now refuses to leave her apartment;* eliminate (D). The correct answer is (A).

4. **F** The question asks what motivates the narrator's visit to the supermarket. The question references the third paragraph, so read lines 14–26. Lines 25–26 state that the narrator promised her husband that she would *brave the supermarket so we could both have a taste of the home we'd been aching for.* Keep (F) because it is supported by these lines. There is no comparison of the cost of groceries at another location, so eliminate (G). The passage says that the *restaurants,* not the supermarket, are *within walking distance,* so eliminate (H). The *specialty market* is discussed in lines 60–70, and the narrator indicates that she started visiting it *recently,* after she was already shopping at the supermarket, so eliminate (J). The correct answer is (F).

5. **B** The question asks what the narrator is implying when she mentions the location of the produce section for the supermarket. Read a window in the passage around the given lines. Lines 32–35 say that the produce section *seemed surprisingly tucked away on the end farthest from the doors* and that it *lacked items we considered favorites or even staples.* This contradicts the statement that *the produce section has everything she needs,* so eliminate (A). Keep (B), since the narrator indicates that she is *surprised* by the section's location. Although the narrator seems to expect the produce section to be more centrally located, the word *always* is too strong, so eliminate (C). The narrator finds an *imported Indian product* in another part of the store (lines 48–51), so eliminate (D). The correct answer is (B).

6. **H** The question asks how the conversation between the narrator and the supermarket clerk can be characterized. Read a window in the passage around the given lines. Lines 45–51 describe the clerk's *amiable grin* and indicate that he helped the narrator find what she was looking for. However, the narrator experienced brief *irritation at having been so easily categorized.* The reference to her *irritation* indicates that the narrator is not entirely *pleased,* so eliminate (F). The clerk does not show any *hostility,* and the narrator is not *shocked,* just *irritated,* so eliminate (G). Keep (H), since it is supported by line 48. The clerk is *cooperative* and he is not *distracted* by her clothing, so eliminate (J). The correct answer is (H).

7. **B** The question asks why the narrator refers to the supermarket's *fluorescent ceiling bulbs.* Read a window in the passage around the given lines. Lines 53–59 state that the fluorescent ceiling bulbs effectively *bleached out the shelves' contents. The bottles and boxes no longer seemed exotic or glamorous,* and *the vividness of their colors would inevitably appear flat and lifeless under the homogenizing light.* The passage never mentions *outdoor markets in India,* so eliminate (A). Keep (B) because the contrast of *exotic or glamorous* with *flat and lifeless* indicates a change in the narrator's *perception of the store's offerings.* Earlier in the passage the narrator says, *I would brave the supermarket* (line 25). Though this indicates that she was initially intimidated by the prospect of going to the supermarket, the lighting is not what intimidates her, and *terrified* is too strong in any case, so eliminate (C). Lines 53–59 indicate that the lighting made the products *flat and lifeless,* not more clearly visible, and the fruits and vegetables are not discussed in this part of the passage, so eliminate (D). The correct answer is (B).

8. **G** The question asks what the word *unfriendly* suggests in line 79. Read a window in the passage around the given line. Lines 76–81 contrast the *grayish, unfriendly curry powder* in the American supermarket with the narrator's grandmother's curry, which was *familiar* and has ingredients with *subtle but memorable color.* The clerk helped the narrator find something she was looking for, so there's no reason for her to think that he *doesn't want her to buy* something; eliminate (F). Keep (G) because it is supported by the contrast with the *familiar results of my grandmother's efforts.* The passage doesn't indicate that the narrator *doesn't like the ingredients,* just that she misses the more colorful ingredients her grandmother used, so eliminate (H). There is no indication that the narrator views products *imported from another country* negatively; on the contrary, she's glad to find the *imported tandoori paste* (line 50), so eliminate (J). The correct answer is (G).

9. **C** The question asks what quality the narrator believes is shared by her grandmother and the old woman who runs the specialty market. Look for the words *old woman, specialty market,* and *grandmother* in the passage. Lines 63–66 describe how the *old woman who manages* the specialty market interacts with her customers, handing out *samples of fruit* and *explaining how adding one more ingredient will perfect the planned dish.* In lines 66–69, the narrator says that the old woman *reminds me, almost painfully, of my grandmother, who was similarly convinced that she could make others' lives better through shared food or wisdom.* There is no indication that either of the women is frail, so eliminate (A). The descriptions indicate that the women are generous and try to be helpful, so eliminate (B). Keep (C): the quality *sociability* is supported by the fact that positive interactions with other people are a key part of the descriptions of both women. There is no indication that either of the women has a quality of *nervousness,* so eliminate (D). The correct answer is (C).

10. **F** The question asks how the narrator is unlike her mother and grandmother. Look for the words *mother* and *grandmother* in the passage. In lines 82–86, the narrator explains that her use of *"quick prep" sauces and pastes* means that *making dinner isn't the all-day task it often was for my grandmother and even my mother.* Keep (F), since it is supported by these lines. Lines 86–88 say that the narrator put on a *sweatshirt,* indicating that she does *wear Western-style clothing,* so eliminate (G). Lines 66–69 suggest that the narrator's *grandmother* got along well with others, and there is no information about how the narrator's *mother* got along with others, so it's not correct to say that the narrator is *unlike* them in this respect; eliminate (H). There is no discussion about how the narrator's *grandmother* or *mother* felt about *air conditioning,* so eliminate (J). The correct answer is (F).

Passage II

11. **A** The question asks for an accurate statement regarding the number of record stores. Look for references in the passage to the number of record stores. In lines 11–14, the passage states that more than *900 independent record stores have perished since the rise of digital music sales in 2003. Current estimates suggest that fewer than 2,000 remain in the United States.* Keep (A), since lines 11–13 support this statement. *Twenty to thirty percent* is a reference from lines 30–31; it is not a percentage of record stores that are *expected to close,* so eliminate (B). *Fewer than 2,000* is the number of independent record stores that remained at the time the passage was written, not the number *in business* before 2003, so eliminate (C). *900* is the number of independent record stores that have closed since 2003, not a number that *are expected to perish,* so eliminate (D). The correct answer is (A).

12. **J** The question asks for a description of the *silver lining* mentioned in line 76. Read a window in the passage around the given line. Lines 76–79 indicate that the *silver lining* refers to *Older men* who *comprise the largest segment of record store consumers.* This paragraph also discusses the reasons they don't seem to be *lured away* by the alternatives: a trip to the record store *allows them to escape from their grown-up, career-driven lives and reconnect with their youthful inspirations.* The older men are not described as *technologically savvy,* and the paragraph indicates that they enjoy going to *record stores,* so eliminate (F). There is no discussion in this paragraph about record stores becoming

cheaper and more efficient, and lines 58–59 indicate that record stores have not been able to drop their prices enough to *lure superstore customers back,* so eliminate (G). There is no mention of *improved marketing of posters and album covers* discouraging *the practice of digital downloads,* so eliminate (H). Keep (J), since it is supported by lines 76–79. The correct answer is (J).

13. **B** The question asks what idea the phrase *downright prehistoric* is used to support. Read a window in the passage around the given line. The context of this paragraph (lines 26–35) describes *the rise of digital music downloads,* saying that *recent technology* allows *thousands of songs to be held by a device the size of a pack of gum. This makes the notion of buying a physical commodity like a CD, which is harder to put in one's pocket than an MP3 player and holds less than 1 percent as much music, seem downright prehistoric.* This paragraph does not discuss *older men* or *8-track, vinyl, tape, or cassette formats,* so eliminate (A). Keep (B) because it is supported by lines 26–35. This paragraph does not discuss the *downloading speed of computers,* so eliminate (C). Choice (D) only includes the *size* of CDs as a factor, missing the additional point that a CD holds less music than an MP3 player does; eliminate (D). The correct answer is (B).

14. **H** The question asks what attitude Spelling has toward consumers who have stopped using record stores. Look for references to *Spelling* in the passage. Lines 68–74 discuss Spelling's thoughts on consumers, stating that *Some record store owners such as Spelling concede the greater affordability of superstore prices.* Spelling also implies that people who have stopped using record stores don't want to *talk to people about music and discover new bands.* However, this does not mean that *they do not share any interests* with the people who go to record stores; this statement is too strong, so eliminate (F). Similarly, the statement that these consumers won't *find any sense of community in buying their music online* is too strong to be supported by these lines, so eliminate (G). Keep (H) since it is a valid inference based on lines 68–69. Spelling does not *blame* the consumers, but rather concedes that superstores have better prices, so eliminate (J). The correct answer is (H).

15. **C** The question asks the purpose of the first paragraph in the context of the passage. Since this is a general question, it should be done after all the specific questions. It also references the first paragraph, so read lines 1–6. The first paragraph explains that Spelling's *record store is on the verge of closing,* and that it carries *rare collectibles in 8-track, vinyl, tape, and cassette format.* The passage does not *criticize Spelling's record store,* so eliminate (A). The focus of the passage is not on *collectibles* in general, so eliminate (B). Keep (C) since it matches the first paragraph, as well as the key idea that *record stores* are *struggling.* The passage is not focused on *real estate,* so eliminate (D). The correct answer is (C).

16. **F** The question asks about the size of the decrease in CD sales before 1999 as a result of digital music downloads. Look for the words *1999* and *CD* in the passage. Lines 27–31 state that *music consumers are increasingly willing and likely to buy their music one song at a time over the Internet,* and that *since 1999, digital downloads have reduced CD sales by twenty to thirty percent.* Read the question carefully—the passage talks about the decrease in sales *since 1999,* but the question asks about the decrease in sales *before 1999.* Since consumers are *increasingly willing* to download music digitally,

it's valid to infer that the rate of decline in CD sales has also increased. Therefore, before 1999, the sales decreased by less than twenty percent. This supports (F), so keep this choice. Eliminate (G), (H), and (J), because the percentages in these answers are the same or greater than the rate of decrease after 1999. The correct answer is (F).

17. **B** The question asks what allows superstores to be able to sell products at small or even nonexistent profit margins. Look for the words *superstores* and *profit margins* in the passage. Lines 44–48 state, *Because superstores expect to sell a larger volume of goods than that of a specialized store,* superstores can afford to sell at small profit margins, or even at no profit. This paragraph also mentions the amount of *capital required to build* a superstore and the large *number* of products a superstore can carry due to its large *warehouse.* Both characteristics support a superstore's ability to sell more goods, but neither is the direct reason for their low prices, so eliminate (A) and (C). Keep (B) because it is supported by lines 44–48. The passage mentions the *ambitious business model, developed by Sam Walton,* but not *ambitiousness of economic planners,* so eliminate (D). The correct answer is (B).

18. **J** The question asks what effect Sam Walton has had on the record industry. Look for the words *Sam Walton* in the passage. Lines 48–49 state that the superstores' *business model* was *developed by Sam Walton,* and lines 36–37 identify superstores as *The second factor contributing to record stores' demise.* Lines 58–59 say that *Record stores are economically powerless to match [superstores'] prices;* this indicates that the record stores have not *based their business model* on the one that Sam Walton developed, so eliminate (F). Sam Walton developed a *business model,* not a *model of community,* so eliminate (G). There's no mention of Sam Walton being a *critic* of the *record store industry,* so eliminate (H). Keep (J) because it is supported by the discussion of *superstores* and *record stores.* The correct answer is (J).

19. **B** The question asks which is not given as a reason that modern consumers might not shop at record stores. When a question asks which answer is **not** supported, eliminate answers that **are** supported. Use words from the answer choices to locate the relevant portions of the passage. Lines 68–71 state, *Some record store owners such as Spelling concede the greater affordability of superstore prices and struggle to come up with a reason why record stores deserve to stick around;* this supports the reason given in (A), so eliminate it. Keep (B), since the *fear of being unwelcome* at a record store is never mentioned. Lines 27–35 discuss the fact that *Younger consumers are increasingly willing and likely to buy their music one song at a time over the Internet,* so eliminate (C). Lines 39–43 mention the draw of stores that allow shoppers to buy *groceries, clothing, and music* at one location, so eliminate (D). The correct answer is (B).

20. **J** The question asks when superstores will recover their initial building costs. Look for the words *recover* and *initial costs* in the passage. Lines 52–55 state, *to attract customers, the stores need to keep prices lower than those of their competition, which means it will be years before a superstore recovers the initial money put into building it.* These lines indicate that it takes *years* before the money put into building a superstore is recovered, so the costs could not be recovered as soon as the *capital is*

invested nor as soon as *the store has opened.* Eliminate (F) and (H). Lines 55–57 say that once established, *superstores…can prosper indefinitely,* so they don't have to sell *all their goods* before the initial building costs are recovered; eliminate (G). Choice (J) is supported by lines 52–55. The correct answer is (J).

Passage III

21. **B** The question asks what Lloyd is illustrating when he mentions star-crossed lovers. Look for the words *star-crossed lovers* in Passage A. Lines 7–8 state, *the primal emotions expressed in opera are part of a universal language,* and lines 13–17 state, *The words of Tristan and Isolde may be different from those of Mimi and Rodolfo…but they come from the same place. Star-crossed lovers have existed for at least as long as the human race.* The author uses the example of star-crossed lovers to emphasize the universal nature of the emotions expressed in opera. He is not emphasizing *differences,* so eliminate (A). Keep (B) because it is supported by lines 7–17. The author emphasizes how similar the operas of *Wagner* and *Puccini* are, not how Wagner is *unique,* so eliminate (C). The purpose of the phrase *at least as long as the human race* is not to suggest that *animals feel emotions such as love,* so eliminate (D). The correct answer is (B).

22. **J** The question asks what the word *untrained* means in line 12. Go back to the text, find the word *untrained* and mark it out. Carefully read the surrounding text to determine another word that would fit in the blank based on the context of the passage. Lines 7–12 make the point that *the primal emotions expressed in opera are part of a universal language;* they go on to say that *a single chord can elicit a strong reaction, even to the untrained ear.* The author is emphasizing the universal effect of the music. The word *untrained* indicates that a person does not need to have a specialized education or experience in order to feel these emotions, so *untrained* could be replaced with "non-expert." *Free-spirited* means "not constrained"; it doesn't mean "non-expert," so eliminate (F). *Crude* means "unrefined"; it doesn't mean "non-expert," so eliminate (G). *Coarse* means "rough" or "rude"; it doesn't mean "non-expert," so eliminate (H). *Amateur* matches "non-expert," so keep (J). The correct answer is (J).

23. **D** The question asks what the phrase *smells from an oven* refers to. Read a window in the passage around the given lines. Lines 7–12 state, *the primal emotions expressed in opera are part of a universal language. The forces of good and evil, love and hate, desire and revenge, emanate from the music likes smells from an oven. Just as a sniff lets us know whether there is a cake or lasagna baking, a single chord can elicit a strong reaction, even to an untrained ear.* The reference to *smells from an oven* is a comparison to the emotional experience anyone can have when listening to music. It is not a literal reference to *cooking* or *smells,* so eliminate (A) and (B). A range of emotions—*love and hate, desire and revenge*—is mentioned, so the author is not emphasizing only the *comforting* effects of music; eliminate (C). *Easily intelligible to anyone* is a paraphrase of *a universal language* and *can elicit a strong reaction, even to the untrained ear,* so keep (D). The correct answer is (D).

24. **F** The question asks what point the author is supporting with the reference to Victor Hugo. Look for the name *Victor Hugo* in Passage A. Lines 17–23 state, *While words can be used to express the combination of longing, joy, and sorrow that the lovers feel, music adds depth; it communicates those common feelings above and beyond what is possible with spoken language alone. As Victor Hugo wrote, "Music expresses that which cannot be said and on which is it impossible to be silent."* Keep (F), since it is supported by these lines. The references to *Wagner's music* and *the beginning of conscious thought* are in the last paragraph; this is not the point the author is making when he quotes Victor Hugo, so eliminate (G). The sentence after the Victor Hugo quote says, *All of the major events in my life have soundtracks,* but it does not say that life events *should* have soundtracks; this is also not the point that the Hugo quote emphasizes, so eliminate (H). The author is not making a claim about the *best* way to express *unrequited love,* so eliminate (J). The correct answer is (F).

25. **B** The question asks why Kelley's family did not have normal holiday celebrations. Look for the words *normal holiday celebrations* in Passage B. Lines 40–47 state, *My parents were professional musicians... holidays are busy for professional musicians. Brass players, as my parents were, are in high demand... My parents never took vacations, and we rarely had normal holiday celebrations.* There is no indication that the author's family *did not believe in celebrating in traditional ways,* so eliminate (A). Keep (B) because it is supported by lines 40–45. Although earning money for the *five children's college tuitions* is mentioned later (lines 66–67), there is no indication that the author's parents *could not afford* to give their children *gifts,* so eliminate (C). This paragraph states that the author's *friends* spend summers *at the beach,* but not that her family does, so eliminate (D). The correct answer is (B).

26. **G** The question asks why the author's roommate looked harried. Look for the words *roommate* and *harried* in the passage. Lines 48–51 say, *my roommate was a music major. I rarely saw her, and she was always harried-looking when I did. She was constantly hurrying from one rehearsal to another.* Passage A, not Passage B, includes the references to *Wagner* and *dreams,* so eliminate (F). Keep (G) because it is supported by lines 50–51. Lines 52–53 indicate that the author missed having *regular weekends and vacations,* but not that her roommate did, so eliminate (H). There is no indication that the roommate was *worried about having enough money,* so eliminate (J). The correct answer is (G).

27. **A** The question asks what the author mentions to elaborate on how she connected with her baby. Look for the words *baby* and *connected* in the passage. Lines 54–60 say, *and then I got married and had a baby...I sang to him all day long because it made me feel more connected to him. I sang nursery rhymes while we played, old country ballads while I bathed him, hymns when we went for walks in the woods, and lullabies to soothe him to sleep.* Keep (A) because these lines include several *different types of songs she sang him.* The discussion of *different composers* is in Passage A, not Passage B, so eliminate (B). The discussion of the author's *accomplishments* as a *music therapist* are in lines 72–74 and are not related to feeling *connected with her baby,* so eliminate (C). The picture of the author's *mother singing and rocking her older sister* is mentioned in lines 84–89 and is not related to the author feeling connected with her own baby, so eliminate (D). The correct answer is (A).

28. **J** The question asks about one way that the perspectives of the authors differ. Since this is a general question, it should be done after all the specific questions on both passages. Eliminate any answer choices that misrepresent either passage. In lines 54–71 and in lines 82–89, Kelley discusses feeling *connected* to her *baby* and her *mother* through music; it is not simply *a tool* she uses *in her job out of financial necessity,* so eliminate (F). Lloyd discusses how *a single chord can elicit a strong emotion* (line 11) and he gives examples throughout Passage A of how music has affected him personally, so eliminate (G). Lloyd says his earliest memory of music was of opera that *my parents played most nights after they put me to bed;* he did not *arrive at his love for music all on his own,* so eliminate (H). In line 24, Lloyd says, *all the major events in my life have soundtracks;* in lines 51–53, Kelley says, *I quit singing in choirs, stopped practicing the piano, and declared an engineering major.* Choice (J) reflects this difference between the two authors. The correct answer is (J).

29. **C** The question asks what both authors use to support their ideas. Eliminate any answer choices that misrepresent either passage. Since this is a general question, it should be done after all the specific questions on both passages. There are no specific *song titles* in Passage B, so eliminate (A). Neither author gives a *detailed explanation of performance technique,* so eliminate (B). Lloyd mentions *early memories of lying in my crib, listening to* music that *my parents played* (lines 1–3). Kelley says that *My parents were professional musicians…[they were] in high demand for Christmas and 4th of July concerts and summer weddings. My parents never took vacations, and we rarely had normal holiday celebrations.* Since both authors use *recollections from childhood,* keep (C). Although both authors mention *different music genres,* neither uses a *comparison* of these genres, so eliminate (D). The correct answer is (C).

30. **F** The question asks how Lloyd's relationship with music relates to Kelley's. Since this is a general question, it should be done after all the specific questions on both passages. In line 6, Lloyd states, *I never learned to read music or play an instrument,* yet the passage as a whole reflects the importance of music in his life. In lines 68–70, Kelley states, *I became a music therapist because I knew first-hand as a mother how deeply song could influence my children.* Keep (F) because it captures this relationship between Lloyd as an *impassioned amateur* and Kelley as an *appreciative professional.* Passage A doesn't support describing Lloyd's relationship to music as *casual,* and Kelley says, *I quit singing in choirs, stopped practicing the piano* (lines 51–52) and *I became a music therapist* (lines 68–69), indicating that she is not an *intent performer,* so eliminate (G). Although Kelley distanced herself from music for a time, in lines 69–71 she says, *I knew first-hand as a mother how deeply song could influence my children. It became my mission to share [music's] healing power with others.* This indicates that she is not *jaded,* nor is *outsider* an apt description for Lloyd's relationship to music, so eliminate (H). The same lines from Passage B rule out *disillusioned* as a description for Kelley, so eliminate (J). The correct answer is (F).

Passage IV

31. **C** The question asks for the main purpose of the passage. Since this is a general question, it should be done after all the specific questions. Lines 8–10 indicate the main focus of the passage: *However, the biological mechanisms that prompt birds to choose a particular date to begin migration are complex and seem to be influenced by many factors.* Although the passage does describe some *research techniques*, describing them is not the main purpose of the passage, so eliminate (A). Similarly, although the passage does provide some *data on the distances traveled* by *various migratory bird species*, this is not the passage's primary purpose, so eliminate (B). Keep (C) since this is a paraphrase of the focus outlined in lines 8–10. The passage does not *prove the effects of weather on bird migration*, so eliminate (D). The correct answer is (C).

32. **F** The question asks why the author uses the information in parentheses in lines 6–8. Read a window in the passage around the given lines. Beginning on line 4, the passage states, *Migration is a part of the annual cycle of over 50 billion individual birds worldwide. (This is not to say all birds migrate; there are many species, particularly in the tropics, that maintain a single residence year-round.)* The information in the parentheses clarifies a potential *misunderstanding* about the *statistic* given in the previous sentence, so keep (F). Lines 8–10 state that *the biological mechanisms that prompt birds to choose a particular date to begin migration are complex*, so the author is not trying to *debunk claims that the biological mechanism for migration is complex;* eliminate (G). This paragraph doesn't indicate that *ornithologists disagree*, so eliminate (H). This paragraph also doesn't discuss *the migration cycle changing due to global warming*, so eliminate (J). The correct answer is (F).

33. **A** The question asks for a limitation to Dolnik and Blyumental's research mentioned in the passage. Look for the names *Dolnik* and *Blyumental* in the passage. Lines 36–67 describe *Dolnik and Blyumental's research*. Lines 61–64 state, *The scientists conducted their experiment on only one species, and though chaffinches are typical of diurnal migratory land birds, they do not accurately represent sea birds, raptors, or nocturnal species.* Lines 68–69 state, *Some migratory birds travel much further than chaffinches.* Keep (A), since it is supported by these lines. The researchers *collected chaffinches as they migrated along the Baltic Coast* (lines 36–37). However, this was not given as a limitation of the study, so eliminate (B). The description *examining the fat content and food in the gut of the carcasses of birds* implies that the birds were killed as part of the study. However, this is not mentioned as a limitation of the study, so eliminate (C). There is no indication that there were *inaccurate counts* of birds, so eliminate (D). The correct answer is (A).

34. **H** The question asks for the main purpose of the third paragraph. Read lines 22–29. These lines state, *For most migratory birds, food supply is a major factor that contributes to the need to move from one location to another. Birds must have ample nutrition to reproduce, and seasonal changes in weather affect the availability of...sources of nourishment. Furthermore, birds must store a great deal of energy in the form of body fat to fuel their migration, so they have to leave while their reserves are high.* Lines 25–26 list several of the birds' *sources of food*, but listing them is not the main purpose of the passage, so eliminate (F). *Changes in weather* are mentioned in the paragraph, but it does not *document*

the weather conditions that impact birds' ability to fly, so eliminate (G). Keep (H), since lines 22–29 give *reasons why the availability of nourishment is important in the timing of bird migration.* The study that involved *observing migratory birds* is discussed in the fourth paragraph, not the third paragraph, so eliminate (J). The correct answer is (H).

35. **B** The question asks how to describe the statement in lines 44–46. Read a window in the passage around the given lines. The paragraph that begins on line 36 describes what researchers observed when they *collected chaffinches as they migrated along the Baltic Coast.* They examined *the fat content and food in the gut of the carcasses of birds gathered at different stages of the waves of migration* and compared *these findings to the number of birds out of the total population yet to migrate.* The statement in lines 44–46 is, *Dolnik and Blyumental found that on the first day of each wave of migration, only very fat birds flew.* This was an observation, not an *assumption,* so eliminate (A). Keep (B) because it matches the description of the study found in lines 38–42. The researchers observed *the fat content and food in the gut of the carcasses of birds;* they did not observe *the visual appearance of chaffinches as they flew over the Baltic Coast,* so eliminate (C). The researchers' *personal preferences* are never mentioned, so eliminate (D). The correct answer is (B).

36. **G** The question asks what can be inferred about which types of migratory birds researchers have measured the longest migration periods and distances for. Look for references to long migration periods and distances in the passage. Beginning on line 73, the passage states that *A few species... can spend months of each year en route between residences continents apart. Wandering albatrosses* are given as an example, and the next line states, *Such sea birds rely on their specialized wing structure to hold them aloft in air currents that transport them long distances.* These lines indicate that *sea birds* migrate farther than *land birds,* so eliminate (F). Keep (G), since *sea birds* is supported by these lines. Lines 7–8 state that *there are many species, particularly in the tropics, that maintain a single residence year-round,* so eliminate (H). There is no mention of *temperate* species migrating over the longest periods and distances, so eliminate (J). The correct answer is (G).

37. **D** The question asks what scientists observed about caged birds compared to wild birds. Look for the words *caged* and *wild* in the passage. Lines 17–21 state, *it is clear that birds must rely more heavily on an internal clock to time their seasonal movements. In fact, biologists have observed a phenomenon known as "migratory restlessness" in caged birds at the same time the wild members of their species set off on seasonal migrations.* These lines describe a similarity between *caged* and *wild birds,* whereas (A), (B), and (C) are describing differences between them. Additionally, *stores of body fat* and the ability to *differentiate between day and night* are not discussed in these lines, so eliminate (A), (B), and (C). Keep (D) because it states a similarity between *caged* and *wild birds,* which is supported by lines 17–21. The correct answer is (D).

38. **H** The question asks during which time, in an experiment replicating Dolnik and Blyumental's, the greatest number of birds would be expected to be migrating. Look for the phrase *Dolnik and Blyumental's experiments* in the passage. Lines 49–51 state that *On the second day, the chaffinch migration began again in the morning...By the afternoon the migration volume peaked.* In an experiment

that replicated this one, the greatest number of birds would also be expected on the afternoon of the second day. Since (F), (G), and (J) list different times, eliminate those choices. Keep (H), since it lists *the second day of the migration wave in the afternoon*. The correct answer is (H).

39. **D** The question asks how the statement that Dolnik and Blyumental *determined the social influence healthy birds have* should be understood. Read a window in the passage around the given lines. Lines 44–54 describe Dolnik and Blyumental's observations in their study: *on the first day of each wave of migration, only very fat birds flew...On the second day, the chaffinch migration began again in the morning with fat birds. By the afternoon, the migration volume peaked, as more and more lean birds began to migrate...By the third day, almost all the birds that began to migrate were very lean.* These lines suggest a difference in the make-up of the migration over time; they do not suggest there were *a greater number of healthy than unhealthy chaffinches* in the flocks overall; eliminate (A). These lines suggest that the lean birds emulated the migrating behavior of the fat birds, but not their *feeding behavior,* so eliminate (B). The study showed that the healthier birds began migrating sooner than the less healthy birds, but not that *the chaffinches became less healthy as the migration continued,* so eliminate (C). Keep (D), since it is supported by lines 44–54. The correct answer is (D).

40. **H** The question asks how the author characterizes the migratory pattern made by wandering albatrosses. Look for the words *wandering albatrosses* in the passage. Lines 69–80 compare the migratory behavior of different types of birds, saying *Most migrants spend a great deal of time storing energy to make trips that take a matter of days or weeks to complete, and travel tens to hundreds of kilometers...A few species, however, can spend months of each year en route between residences continents apart...Wandering albatrosses spend almost all their time in the air...moving up to 2000 kilometers on a single foraging expedition, and flying over 250,000 kilometers in a year.* This indicates that wandering albatrosses are unusual compared with most migrating birds. The descriptions *common* and *typical* are contradicted by these lines, so eliminate (F) and (G). Keep (H), since *uncommon among migratory birds* is supported by lines 69–80. In lines 80–81, just after the description of *wandering albatrosses,* the author uses the phrase *Such sea birds,* indicating a similarity between wandering albatrosses and other sea birds, so eliminate (J). The correct answer is (H).

Reading Practice Section 3

READING TEST

35 Minutes—40 Questions

DIRECTIONS: There are four passages in this test. Each passage is followed by several questions. After reading each passage, choose the best answer to each question and blacken the corresponding oval on your answer document. You may refer to the passages as often as necessary.

Passage I

PROSE FICTION: This passage is adapted from the short story "Into the Past" by Amanda C. Thomas (© 2004 by Amanda C. Thomas).

Even at eight in the morning, the thermometer was heading up towards 80 degrees when my mother put me and my brother Kiran on the southbound bus heading from our home in New York City to our aunt and uncle's place in North Carolina. Her new job on the third shift of the garment factory gave us the potential for a better life ahead, but she was wary about leaving us alone at home in the evenings and overnight. I had never been outside of New York City before, so I was nervous about moving, not to mention that I had never met my aunt and uncle before.

"Now Essie, you be on your best behavior, mind your elders and watch out for your little brother, you hear me?" Her words were admonishments, but I saw the tear in the corner of her eye and knew that she'd miss us over the next three months. She stood still, arm upraised in farewell, until her lemon-yellow dress became no more than a pinprick in the distance.

Kiran and I had promised each other that we would notice all the things that were different from New York while we were on our trip. In the bus, the heat of the road was balanced to some degree by the breeze blowing in through the windows. We pressed our noses up to the glass, peering out as the dense thicket of buildings thinned, then disappeared altogether as we hit the unfamiliar farm country in the South. We chewed the soggy pickle and butter sandwiches our mother had packed for us, sucking the juice out from between the slices of white, soft bread and watched the green fields rush by.

We were greeted at the bus station by Uncle Desmond, a quiet man whose skin shone dark from working out in the sun. He said almost nothing as he took us back to his neat, white house with its red barn that looked just like my mother's descriptions of it and the pictures in books I'd seen when I was younger. At first glance, Aunt Millie seemed the polar opposite of my mother. Where my mother was all sharp lines and tight angles, Aunt Millie was almost blurred, her hair looser and her hips more ample. Still, her kind face and shrewd glance at our city outfits showed the same deep intelligence.

"We're gonna have to see if some of your cousins' old overalls can be taken up for you. Don't want to get your nice things scuffed up. Farm life's not easy on fancy dresses and patent leather shoes and you'll both be doing your share of the chores around here, that's for sure! Now your cousin Ike'll show you where to go to get washed up for dinner."

I had never seen so much food in my life before that first meal at the farm. Collard greens, biscuits with red-eye gravy, fried chicken, macaroni and cheese—I'd eaten most of these dishes at home, but here they tasted different in a way that was hard to put a finger on at first. As though they were *from* somewhere, instead of appearing magically on our kitchen table. They tasted the way the farm smelled—of the animals and the earth. I glanced over at Kiran, and he was digging in hungrily.

The next day, Kiran and I were roused early by Aunt Millie carrying two smaller versions of what, presumably, had been Ike's old overalls. Ike and Desmond, who had both been awake hours earlier, came by carrying pails of warm milk, some of which would be put to household use while the main load was put by to be picked up by a cheese-making facility in Virginia.

Ike then taught us to gather eggs from the chickens in the henhouse. This quickly became my favorite task over that summer. I loved going out into the early dawn, the air still cool and damp and feeling my bare feet sink into grass wet with dew. I'd approach the coop with great care not to disturb the slumbering ladies, as I thought of them, making sure not to betray my presence by any quick movement or careless noise. Then, with infinite gentleness, I'd reach out, my hands rustling under the soft feathers of the hens, sensing their respiration, their warmth, feeling for the smooth white eggs and placing each one I found carefully into my basket.

At night I would take a bath and Aunt Millie would take time away from her evening chores to braid my hair. But instead of the intricate patterns my mother liked to make, Aunt Millie gave me looser plaits and even sometimes gathered them into a single tail inching down my neck. Sometimes, when Aunt Millie seemed in an especially good mood, we would condition it with egg yolk and milk, which Aunt Millie would work into my hair gently massaging each strand, working the mixture deep into the roots. Afterwards I was pleased to see how the brittle, frizzy ends softened.

My body became loose-limbed from the outdoor exercise and I noticed Kiran growing stronger and bolder as he ran through the fields with Ike. In the afternoons when it was too hot to do anything else, we'd lie in the shade of the huge oak tree, chewing on grass stems, lost in the sweet, green taste and our own thoughts.

1. The narrator's imaginative way of viewing her surroundings is best demonstrated in her description of the:

A. farmhouse.
B. hens in the chicken coop.
C. way Aunt Millie braids her hair.
D. way the earth smelled.

2. It can most reasonably be inferred from the passage that the narrator:

F. thinks New York City is superior to the farm.
G. has never visited Uncle Desmond and Aunt Millie's farm before.
H. sees the visit to the farm as the most important event in her life.
J. loves her Aunt Millie more than her mother.

3. The narrator's use of sensory details, such as the feel of the hen's feathers and the taste of the grass stems, most strongly suggests that:

A. trauma in her childhood made her unable to speak to anyone other than her brother Kiran.
B. the unfamiliarity of life outside New York makes her more aware of her physical surroundings on the farm.
C. because she is shy around her extended family, she is more perceptive than her brother Kiran is.
D. her closeness with Aunt Millie shows her how to appreciate changes in her new environment.

4. In line 35 the narrator describes Aunt Millie as "blurred," which most nearly suggests that:

F. unlike the narrator's mother, Aunt Millie doesn't have sharp features.
G. Aunt Millie is older than the narrator's mother, so she has a bad memory and forgets things.
H. Essie doesn't see well because she often reads books under her bedcovers.
J. Aunt Millie doesn't have as distinctive a personality as the narrator's mother does.

5. It can reasonably be inferred from the passage that which of the following events happened first in the narrator's life?

A. She learned to collect eggs from the henhouse.
B. She met her Aunt Millie and Uncle Desmond.
C. She visited North Carolina for the first time.
D. She lived in New York City.

6. It can reasonably be inferred from the passage that the narrator views life on the farm as:

F. requiring a great deal of hard work that is not appreciated by her aunt and uncle.
G. an escape from the difficulties of living in impoverished, restrictive conditions in New York City.
H. a place where daily chores, even those that require that the narrator wake up early, can be enjoyable and satisfying.
J. a place where the physical nature of the local recreational activities are more suited to boys than to girls.

7. As depicted in the ninth paragraph (lines 71–80), the relationship between the narrator and Aunt Millie is best described by which of the following statements?

A. Aunt Millie feels close to the narrator, as shown in the way she puts aside other tasks to braid and condition Essie's hair.
B. Aunt Millie feels emotionally cut off from the narrator because of the young girl's city manners.
C. Aunt Millie loves the narrator in spite of their different ways of seeing the world.
D. Aunt Millie is indifferent toward the narrator, seeing her as another part of her daily work.

8. Which of the following statements most nearly captures the sentiment behind the narrator's comment that the food at the farmhouse tastes like it is "*from* somewhere" (line 49)?

F. "The food tasted just like the food I had in New York."
G. "The food tasted fresh from the fields, instead of from a supermarket."
H. "The food tasted like no other food that I had ever tasted."
J. "The food tasted strongly of the rich soil that Uncle Desmond tilled."

9. Details in the second paragraph (lines 11–17) most strongly suggest that the narrator's mother:

A. hopes her children will have a good time on the farm, enjoying their summer vacation before school starts again.
B. feels saddened by the children's departure and will miss them while they're away.
C. believes that life on the farm will teach them the self-discipline they need to survive in the city.
D. is afraid for them during the long bus ride and hopes the children will not speak to strangers.

10. Which of the following statements about why the narrator and Kiran will spend the summer on the farm is supported by the passage?

F. The narrator is weak and sickly, needing the fresh air of the farm to recover her health.
G. Aunt Millie and Uncle Desmond will teach the children valuable work skills.
H. The narrator and Kiran wanted to develop a relationship with their cousins.
J. The children's mother worried about leaving them alone while she worked.

Passage II

SOCIAL SCIENCE: Passage A is adapted from "Let Me Think About It: Plants and Consciousness" by Andres C. Tejada (© 2010 by Andres Tejada). Passage B is adapted from "The Great Debate: Recent Developments in Plant Consciousness Research" by Nicole Fiori (© 2012 by Nicole Fiori).

Passage A by Andres Tejada

Sheila Jennings was making her rounds at the Boston Botanical Gardens, gently humming songs to the lilies she was watering and speaking directly to a patch of ferns into which she was scooping fertilizer. To a casual observer, she appeared to be entertaining herself during her morning routine, but Sheila's friendly behavior around the plants is actually called "social reinforcement" and is one of her job requirements. The idea that interacting with these plants will help them flourish has been common sense to gardeners for ages, but it has attained some scientific credibility mainly since the work of Clive Buckner first came to light.

Forty years ago Buckner conducted a series of experiments on his plants using "lie-detectors," polygraph galvanometer equipment. These experiments led him to conclude that plants possess a means of perception that allows them to react to human thoughts.

The scientific community was shocked. It is already hard enough to prove that higher order mammals have consciousness, despite many experiments that seem to prove the ability of non-human animals to learn and perform complex, non-instinctive behaviors. To contend that plants have some mechanism of mind-reading goes so far beyond the orthodoxy of modern scientific beliefs that anyone suggesting they might was instantly considered a heretic.

However, a steady flow of research over the next two decades would continue to revisit and replicate Clive Buckner's hypothesis. During his original experiment, Buckner noticed that his plant would produce a sharp and immediate response when he attempted to visualize the act of burning the plant's leaves. Botanists at Kansas State found they could produce a similar response by cutting the leaves of an adjacent plant. Researchers in Wyoming discovered that plants respond to the distress signals of a spider in the room. A New Jersey scientist was able to cause a plant to trigger a switch on an electric train set every time he gave himself a painful shock to the finger. One of Buckner's colleagues showed him how she was able to keep a detached leaf moist and lush for two months through daily positive encouragement while a control leaf which received no positive attention had completely withered to a dry, brittle brown.

Although these experiments seem to add fuel to the flames of Buckner's speculations about plant consciousness, he is willing to acknowledge the scientific issues involved in replicating the experiments. "Many others have failed to produce the same effects," he says. "The outcomes of the experiments seem very dependent on the experimenter's relationship to his plants." But at the same time, Buckner believes these problems actually strengthen his theories. "We are trying to demonstrate the fact that plants develop subtle yet meaningful connections with their caretakers, so the fact that the outcomes of experiments are varied is actually in *support* of our notion that plant behavior is dynamic and responsive to a given individual."

Passage B by Nicole Fiori

The world of botany has recently been buzzing with news of an unconventional experiment that produced seemingly ground-breaking results: a plant in a lead box (shut off from all electromagnetic radiation) was able to react to a human thought. Max Crusella, a plant researcher at the Marina Del Rey Plant Laboratory, is one of those who believe that this is only a small part of the mountain of evidence that plants are sensitive to their environments in ways that traditional science is not equipped to describe. "It's possible that these particular researchers have proposed overzealous explanations for their observations," Crusella said at a recent symposium on the subject, "but it is completely well-grounded to believe that there needs to be *some* kind of new scientific explanation for what are otherwise mysterious phenomena."

Sitting across the table from Crusella, both literally and figuratively, is Cornell University professor Betty Wilkinson. She points out that the lead box experiment failed to register any plant reaction when it was replicated by a different researcher. In her view, it is clear that plants are responsive to certain kinds of interaction, but she questions the reasons and means attributed to plants by other researchers. She believes the interpretations of experiments into plant consciousness are too dependent on the philosophical and metaphysical beliefs of the interpreter. "Many people without any botanical credentials are anxious to latch onto these experiments to support ideas they may have about the holistic interconnectivity of the universe," she says.

Those on Wilkinson's side are concerned that such experimenters may be merely interpreting the reactions of plants to agree with their premeditated goal of finding consciousness (scientists call this *confirmation bias*), or that they are ignoring the possibilities of alternative explanations for the sake of justifying their faulty hypotheses (scientists call this *self-deception*).

Steve Karnell, a writer for a leading scientific journal, agrees with Wilkinson. "Lacking in this so-called 'experiment' are ingredients fundamental to the scientific method like control groups and blind studies," he complains. "Work like this opens up a Pandora's box of bad science."

Questions 11–14 ask about Passage A.

11. The passage most strongly suggests that the current debate over research into plant consciousness was triggered by which of the following?

A. The invention of polygraph technology
B. An observed reaction of a plant to a spider in distress
C. Techniques introduced by the Boston Botanical Garden
D. Experiments conducted by Buckner in the late 1960s

12. According to the passage, lie-detectors are:

F. electric train trigger switches.
G. mechanisms of social reinforcement.
H. measurable distress signals.
J. polygraph galvanometer equipment.

13. The passage most strongly suggests that the social reinforcement required of Sheila Jennings at her job is designed primarily to do which of the following?

A. Condition the plants to be undisturbed by the sounds of visitors to the Botanical Gardens
B. Keep the employees alert during their monotonous work routines
C. Replicate the sounds of wildlife that the plants would hear in their natural habitats
D. Potentially lead to better plant growth than could be achieved without it

14. According to the passage, Clive Buckner believes that the potential outcome of an experiment measuring plant consciousness is:

F. highly unorthodox.
G. unfairly biased.
H. sometimes inconsistent.
J. scientifically sound.

Questions 15–17 ask about Passage B.

15. The main point of Steve Karnell's quotation in the fourth paragraph (lines 88–92) is that:

A. there are elements of how research is conducted that can make its findings less trustworthy.
B. some experimenters do not understand the function of control groups in the scientific method.
C. a blind study would have convincingly proven the existence of plant consciousness.
D. researchers working with plants are more likely to commit the error of confirmation bias.

16. According to the passage, the desire to affirm one's preconceived notions about an experimental observation is called which one of the following by scientists?

F. Control groups
G. Blind studies
H. Confirmation bias
J. Self-deception

17. The passage indicates that Max Crusella would be most likely to agree with which of the following statements?

A. The responsiveness of plants to their environments currently lacks an adequate traditional scientific explanation.
B. The results of many experiments have been tainted by self-deception on the part of the researchers.
C. There is currently some evidence to support plant consciousness but much more that contradicts it.
D. There are traditional scientific explanations that best account for the observations recorded in most of these experiments.

Questions 18–20 ask about both Passages.

18. Clive Buckner's observation of his plant as mentioned in the fourth paragraph of Passage A would most likely be described by Betty Wilkinson and Steve Karnell as which of the following?

F. Evidence that plants possess a sense of memory
G. A subtle connection between plant and caretaker
H. Something that other researchers may have trouble duplicating
J. An example of a plant's ability to perceive distress

19. Based on the information in Passage A, how would Clive Buckner most likely respond to the criticism of Betty Wilkinson as described in the second paragraph of Passage B (lines 68–80)?

A. By providing specific examples that defend his theory of plant consciousness
B. By suggesting that he does not believe that Wilkinson's criticism is a legitimate one
C. By stating his complete indifference toward Wilkinson's scientific concerns
D. By outlining how he could counsel other experimenters on how to be better caretakers of plants in order to better replicate certain results

20. Both Passage A and Passage B emphasize:

F. the importance of replicating the results of plant consciousness experiments.
G. the dramatic difference that social reinforcement makes in how well a plant grows.
H. the difficulties of interpreting the results of experiments into plant consciousness.
J. the dangers presented by confirmation bias and how to avoid them when designing an experiment.

Passage III

HUMANITIES: This passage is adapted from the entry "How Songs Make Meaning" from the volume *How to Listen to Music Like a Conductor* (© 2007 by Air Guitar Press).

I used to have to feel pain in order to write songs.

Normally, this inspiration took the form of wanting or losing a girl. My heartsickness would reach a state of such unwieldy gloom that words and melodies would coalesce and fall like raindrops to relieve the stress of carrying such a heavy cloud of misery. I think many of us mainly write songs for relief. It's unhealthy to keep swallowing unspoken words. Keep them on the tip of your tongue and they'll fester like bacteria. Stash them all in a song and you suddenly have an emotional storage unit, which un-clutters your inner world.

The first "songs" we ever write are just exaggerated expressions of our stream of consciousness. We create theme songs while jostling with action figures, concoct mocking serenades to annoy our siblings, or narrate our inner lives to a random tune. We have all been yelled at by a frustrated audience of our friends, acquaintances, and family members to cease our incessant noise making. While many learn to keep their songs to themselves as they master the rules of polite etiquette, songwriters apparently never learn. Instead, we begin to turn our songs into something people will be happy to hear.

Music somehow makes people feel unashamed about being completely expressive. In speech, someone melodramatically complaining about all the injustices of his world would probably be chastised for lacking self-control. However, in song, a proclamation of suffering is received as an almost heroic attempt to overcome adversity. Songs boldly broadcast a description of someone's inner world. Why do people want to tune into someone else's emotional episodes?

There's a balance of two opposing forces that we enjoy in music. One force soothes, the other agitates. As music plays, the actual frequencies of the individual notes are constantly lining up in different mathematical relations to each other. When they are proportional to each other, we hear chords, harmony, and unison. Songs normally end on this sort of relationship because it conveys closure, completion, resolution. Other combinations create a sense of tension, discomfort, and anticipation. Successful songs win over listeners just as successful stories do. They normally introduce a protagonist and take the listener along to experience some of his/her setbacks and triumphs. Even instrumental pieces often introduce a central melody and then explore its travels through different passages of the song's structure.

Young children often enjoy hearing soothing lullabies as a way to be distracted from anxiety or coaxed into a peaceful slumber. They take great pleasure in singing agitating songs, such as the "nenny nenny boo boo" melody that can be customized into any taunt. Similarly, adults have classical, smooth jazz, and easy listening styles of music when they want to be relaxed or distracted, and they have the more provocative extremes of punk, rap, and metal when they want to use music to express irreverence or rebellion.

We become much more selective in our musical tastes as we age. As children, we passively accept and learn to love our parents' music just like we do their cooking. It's not that a parent necessarily cooks "better" than other parents, but through sheer familiarity a child will greatly prefer her parents' cooking to that of others. Similarly, the cultural backdrop of a child's upbringing calibrates her listening tastes to a given set of rhythms, instruments, harmonic scales, and song structures. As adolescents, though, we begin to choose our own songs just as we would choose our friends. We identify with artists based on their dress, their politics, their mood, and their popularity. We look to find personal meaning in lyrics and to latch onto songs that seem to broadcast our private thoughts. Despite not being the author of our favorite songs, we wear our songs like trinkets of personal expression, telltale accessories that describe to others important parts of our psychology. When we develop a kinship with a song, we feel waves of euphoria as it plays, the feeling of our inner world radiating out.

As songwriters, we must aspire to this private release in every song we write. However, sometimes we fear that if we express ourselves too specifically, we will deny listeners the opportunity to mold our song into something they can claim as their own. We often replace specific details with general symbols, preserving for ourselves the original meaning of a lyric while infusing it with enough flexibility that someone else can derive a different significance.

The one thing we must be sure of as performers is that a song means *something* to us. Through observation of other artists, we learn to mimic expressions of joy and anguish. It becomes easy for us to write and perform songs without any genuine attachment to their emotional content. Nevertheless, just as audiences can distinguish between good and bad acting, so too will audience members feel a difference between a contrived and an authentic performance.

21. When the writer refers to "the rules of polite etiquette" in (lines 18–19), he is most likely referring to rules that:

A. diminish the role of imagination in playing with action figures or other toys.
B. are taught to children when they are enrolled in behavior modification classes.
C. are too restrictive and demanding for songwriters to abide by.
D. limit certain personal behaviors that others might find irritating or discomforting.

22. In the third paragraph (lines 11–20), the author says that a songwriter aspires to write songs people will be "happy to hear." It can reasonably be inferred that which of the following is NOT a characteristic of such songs?

F. Mimicking joy and anguish
G. Blending comfort and tension
H. Fostering a kinship with the listener
J. Allowing for different interpretations

23. It can be reasonably inferred that the primary purpose of this passage is to:

A. explain to readers that expressing pain will enable them to be good songwriters.
B. convince aspiring songwriters to stop giving in to polite etiquette and instead write catchy songs.
C. discuss ideas concerning the goals and process of songwriting as well as the relationship to age and expectations of the audience.
D. outline one author's argument that songwriters are too often limited by the cultural backdrop of their musical upbringing.

24. When the author states a songwriter must aspire to "this private release" (line 70), he is most directly referring to the idea that a songwriter must:

F. describe her experiences with very specific details.
G. outwardly project a genuine internal emotional state.
H. force listeners to develop a kinship with the song.
J. focus on the emotions of joy or anguish.

25. The author states that, unlike children, adolescents approach songs with a goal of:

A. feeling a sense of belonging and familiarity.
B. discovering new trends in fashion and politics.
C. departing from the cultural backdrop of their upbringing.
D. deriving some personal meaning from those songs.

26. The author states that our process of selecting songs can be compared to that of selecting all of the following EXCEPT:

F. our friends.
G. our parents' cooking.
H. our favorite authors.
J. personal trinkets.

27. Which of the following best describes the way the first sentence functions in relation to the passage as a whole?

A. It introduces an idea that the author later explains is not true in the real world of songwriting.
B. It is a claim that facilitates the author's anecdotal introduction to the topic of songwriting.
C. It foreshadows the essay's contention that singing about one's problems is evidence of a lack of self-control.
D. It is a vague idea that is not reinforced or clarified by the details that follow in subsequent paragraphs.

28. According to the passage, the divergent songwriting purposes of "soothes" and "agitates" (line 30) differ from one another in that:

F. soothing songs, unlike agitating ones, have a mellowing effect that is often enjoyable to adults but annoying to younger audiences.
G. soothing songs are associated with inducing sleep or reducing distress, while agitating songs can be used to convey ridicule.
H. agitating songs, unlike soothing songs, are often used by relatives to coax a child out of a state of slumber.
J. agitating songs distract us from the things that we passionately hate, while soothing songs are very gentle to our ears.

29. According to the author's analogy, acting and performing music:

A. are completely different.
B. share at least one important characteristic.
C. are more convincing expressing anguish than joy.
D. are completely identical.

30. Based on the passage, the cultural backdrop of a child's upbringing is significant to her appreciation of music because it:

F. predisposes the child to prefer the musical ingredients customary in that culture's music.
G. gives the child a model of what to avoid in order to stand out as an original songwriter.
H. instructs the child concerning the proper structure and political content of songs.
J. will later be the primary basis through which the child is able to make friends.

Passage IV

NATURAL SCIENCE: This passage is adapted from "A Comment on Comets" by Dr. Anatole C. Thierry (© 2002 by Weak Alliteration Press).

Comets are solid masses of dust and frozen gases with diameters of only a few kilometers that revolve in highly eccentric orbits around the Sun. As a comet approaches the Sun, a very small portion of the frozen matter evaporates. This creates a shroud of gas and dust, called a coma, enveloping an area up to a million kilometers around the solid nucleus of the comet. Solar winds and radiation pressure from the Sun can blow the material of the coma away from the comet's nucleus, creating a tail, which is sometimes longer than the distance from the Earth to the Sun. However, the appearance of comets is misleading; they cast no light of their own. Though the comas and tails of the brightest comets can be seen with the naked eye in cities with heavy light pollution, the nucleus of a comet cannot be detected even with the most powerful telescopes. This is not only because the solid portion of a comet is so small, but also because the highly reflective nature of the coma's material obscures the view to the nucleus.

The brightness of a comet depends primarily on two factors: its distance from the Sun and its distance from the Earth. When comets are at their closest approach to the Sun, called perihelion, evaporation of the icy material occurs at a greater rate and volume, and the solar forces that scatter the gas and dust are stronger. However, when comets are far from the Sun, they become less active and are often undetectable. Because comets come from the farthest reaches of the solar system, most take over 200 years to orbit the Sun, and most of the time they are so far away that the solar influence does not create a coma or tail, causing the comets to become invisible.

The stronger determinant of a comet's brightness is its distance to Earth, especially in relation to its perihelion. If a comet passes its nearest point to Earth after the comet's perihelion, it will be much brighter than if it reaches its closest point to Earth while it is still relatively cold and solid, before the Sun evaporates much of the comet's matter. This explains why Halley's Comet, which was very bright during its first observed pass near Earth in 1910, was so disappointing to astronomers when it returned, this time much further from the Earth, in 1986. The distance from the Earth also determines a comet's speed as observed by astronomers—the closer a comet comes to the Earth, the more quickly it moves across the sky. Typically, comets move about one or two degrees per day—much too slow to be perceived by the naked eye—and can remain visible for months. However, when comet IRAS-Araki-Alcock, the closest comet to pass the Earth in modern times, appeared in 1983, it looked both very bright and very fast. This comet moved so quickly that observers compared its motion to that of the minute hand on a clock, and it had twice the apparent diameter of the Moon.

Even dedicated sky watchers and professional astronomers are more likely to discover a comet by chance than by exacting calculations, because comets are only detectable for such a short portion of their orbits, and because it is so infrequent that the comets pass near enough to the Earth to be observed. However, astronomers' interest in comets lies in characteristics beyond the novelty of these comets. Comets are believed to be remnants of the original disc of chemical material that formed the solar system about four billion years ago. Because comets spend most of their time in the very cold areas barely within the Sun's gravitation, they are believed to have remained relatively unchanged during that time, and can thereby serve as a sort of "fossil record" of the solar system.

For this reason, planetary scientists have a great deal of interest in studying comets directly, rather than merely through telescopic observation. By studying the specific chemical composition of comets, scientists hope to learn more about the chemical origins of the solar system. Explorations of comets can provide glimpses into this past. For example, a recent collection of tiny dust particles left in the Earth's stratosphere by the passage of comet 26P/Grigg-Skjellerup has led to the discovery of a previously unknown mineral that had not been predicted by scientists to have been formed in the solar nebula. This highly unusual substance generates strong scientific interest because it, along with other new materials that may be found in comets, may cause scientists to reconsider models of how the solar system formed. Future missions are planned to retrieve material directly from comets. Some scientists, who hypothesize that water and some organic compounds may have been delivered to Earth by collisions between comets and our planet in its earliest days, hope that comet material may reveal information about the origins of life on Earth.

31. The primary purpose of the passage is to:

A. persuade readers that astronomers have not yet done adequate studies to discover the origins of the solar system.
B. encourage readers to learn to use telescopic equipment to aid in the search for new comets.
C. describe the characteristics of comets currently known by astronomers and the motivation for their research.
D. catalogue the experiments planetary scientists have done to determine the composition of comets.

32. The author would most likely agree with which of the following statements?

F. There may be minerals in the solar system yet to be discovered by astronomers.
G. Astronomers will not be able to observe comets brighter than IRAS-Araki-Alcock because their orbital periods are so long.
H. Comets are older than the Earth as indicated by their greater distance from the Sun.
J. Collections of samples directly from the surface of comets will be difficult because of comets' unpredictability.

33. According to the passage, which situation creates a comet's maximum brightness as observed from Earth?

A. Its coma is much bigger than its nucleus.
B. It is closer to the Earth and therefore moves more quickly.
C. Its perihelion occurs after it passes the Earth.
D. It is at its closest to the Earth after its perihelion.

34. Which of the following questions is NOT answered by information given in the passage?

F. What do astronomers hope to learn by studying comets?
G. What causes some comets to be trailed by such a long tail?
H. What prevents astronomers from cataloging more new comets and predicting their approach to the Earth?
J. Why do comets have such a highly eccentric orbit?

35. Information in the first paragraph indicates that "the appearance of comets" requires all of the following EXCEPT:

A. the viewer to have a powerful telescope.
B. solar winds and radiation pressure to scatter the coma.
C. a portion of the surface material to evaporate.
D. an envelope of gas and dust much larger than the nucleus.

36. The passage mentions astronomers observing all of the following about comets EXCEPT:

F. unusual minerals in the chemical composition that have not been found on Earth.
G. comets that emit bright light from their nuclei.
H. changes in apparent brightness at different times and in different environments.
J. orbits that take comets to the edges of the Sun's gravitational influence.

37. In the context of the third paragraph (lines 29–48), lines 34–38 primarily serve to emphasize the:

A. relationship a comet's apparent speed has to its other visual characteristics, such as its apparent diameter.
B. influence a comet's distance from Earth with regard to its perihelion has on a comet's apparent brightness.
C. disappointment astronomers feel when highly anticipated celestial events do not live up to their expectations.
D. difficulty in predicting when comets will be visible in the sky because of their highly eccentric orbits.

38. The passage most nearly indicates that attempts to study comets directly have been:

F. prevented by technical difficulties.
G. used to explain life on Earth.
H. unsuccessful so far.
J. promising, but incomplete.

39. As it is used in line 55, the phrase "characteristics beyond the novelty of these comets" most likely refers to:

A. the likelihood of discovering new comets.
B. the difficulty of detecting distant comets.
C. comets' chemical composition.
D. the age of comets.

40. The main purpose of the last paragraph is to:

F. describe particular experiments that have been performed on comets as they pass near the Earth.
G. convince readers that comets are responsible for the evolution of intelligent species.
H. discuss the reasons planetary scientists are interested in pursuing direct study of comet material.
J. contradict outdated information about the origin of the solar system.

Reading Practice Section 3 Answers and Explanations

READING PRACTICE SECTION 3 ANSWERS

1. B
2. G
3. B
4. F
5. D
6. H
7. A
8. G
9. B
10. J
11. D
12. J
13. D
14. H
15. A
16. H
17. A
18. H
19. B
20. H
21. D
22. F
23. C
24. G
25. D
26. H
27. B
28. G
29. B
30. F
31. C
32. F
33. D
34. J
35. A
36. G
37. B
38. J
39. C
40. H

READING PRACTICE SECTION 3 EXPLANATIONS

Passage I

1. **B** The question asks which description best demonstrates the author's *imaginative way of viewing her surroundings.* Use words from the answer choices to locate the relevant portions of the passage. In line 65, the author describes the hens as *slumbering ladies.* She describes the *farmhouse* simply as *neat* and *white;* this doesn't demonstrate an *imaginative view,* so eliminate (A). Keep (B) since the metaphorical description of the *hens* as *sleeping ladies* is imaginative. Lines 73–75 say *Aunt Millie gave me looser plaits and sometimes gathered them into a single tail inching down my neck.* This description doesn't demonstrate a particularly *imaginative* view, so eliminate (C). In lines 50–51, the author describes the farm as smelling of the earth, but she never actually describes *the way the earth smelled,* so eliminate (D). The correct answer is (B).

2. **G** The question asks what can be inferred about the narrator. Because this is a general question, it should be done after all the specific questions. The passage doesn't indicate that the narrator *thinks New York City is superior to the farm,* so eliminate (F). Line 8 says, *I had never been outside of New York City before,* and lines 30–33 say that the farmhouse *looked just like my mother's descriptions of it and the pictures in books I'd seen when I was younger,* so it is reasonable to infer that the narrator has never visited the farm before; keep (G). The narrator does not indicate that she *sees the visit to the farm as the most important event in her life,* so eliminate (H). There is no comparison made between the narrator's love for *her Aunt Millie* and *her mother,* so eliminate (J). The correct answer is (G).

3. **B** The question asks what is suggested by the *narrator's use of sensory details, such as the feel of the hen's feathers and the taste of the grass stems.* Look for the words *hen's feathers* and *grass stems* in the passage. Lines 67–68 say, *Then, with infinite gentleness, I'd reach out, my hands rustling under the soft feathers of the hens.* Lines 84–86 state, *we'd lie in the shade of the huge oak tree, chewing on grass stems, lost in the sweet, green taste and our own thoughts.* There is no mention of *trauma* or that the narrator is *unable to speak to anyone other than her brother,* so eliminate (A). Line 8 states that the narrator *had never been outside of New York City before,* and the use of sensory details does indicate that she is *aware of her physical surroundings on the farm,* so keep (B). There is no indication that the narrator is *shy around her extended family,* nor is there any comparison made between how *perceptive* she and *Kiran* are, so eliminate (C). Although the description in lines 71–80 indicates that she became close with Aunt Millie, lines 18–19 say that before they arrived at the farm, *Kiran and I promised each other that we would notice all the things that were different from New York,* and the third through eighth paragraphs mention many sensory details that the narrator noticed in her first few days on the farm. This indicates that the *closeness* with Aunt Millie wasn't what showed her *how to appreciate changes in her new environment,* so eliminate (D). The correct answer is (B).

4. **F** The question asks what is suggested by the narrator's description of *Aunt Millie* as "*blurred.*" Read a window in the passage around the given line. Lines 33–36 state, *At first glance, Aunt Millie seemed*

the polar opposite of my mother. Where my mother was all sharp lines and tight angles, Aunt Millie was almost blurred, her hair looser and her hips more ample. Keep (F), since it is supported by these lines. In lines 36–37, Aunt Millie is described as *shrewd* and having *deep intelligence,* so there is no support for the idea that she *has a bad memory and forgets things;* eliminate (G). There is no mention that Essie *often reads books under her bedcovers,* and the many visual details given throughout the passage suggest that Essie has good eyesight: the word *blurred* doesn't indicate that Essie can't see her Aunt clearly, so eliminate (H). The description *blurred* is used to refer to Aunt Millie's physical appearance, and she is described as *kind, shrewd,* and having *deep intelligence,* so there is no evidence that she *doesn't have as distinctive a personality as the narrator's mother;* eliminate (J). The correct answer is (F).

5. **D** The question asks which event occurred first in the narrator's life. Use words from the answer choices to locate the relevant portions of the passage. In lines 1–10, the narrator recounts, *when my mother put me and my brother Kiran on the southbound bus heading from our home in New York City to our aunt and uncle's place in North Carolina…I had never been outside of New York City before, so I was nervous about moving, not to mention that I had never met my aunt and uncle before.* Lines 60–61 say, *Ike then taught us to gather eggs from the chickens in the henhouse.* This occurs after the narrator arrives at the farm. These two parts of the passage establish that the narrator *lived in New York City* before she *visited North Carolina for the first time, met her Aunt Millie and Uncle Desmond,* or *learned to collect eggs from the henhouse,* so eliminate (A), (B) and (C), and keep (D). The correct answer is (D).

6. **H** The question asks what can be inferred about how *the narrator views life on the farm.* Because this is a general question, it should be done after all the specific questions. There is no evidence that the narrator's work on the farm is unappreciated by her aunt and uncle, so eliminate (F). Lines 5–6 say that the narrator's mother's *new job on the third shift of the garment factory gave us the potential for a better life ahead,* but the passage doesn't indicate that the narrator has been living in *impoverished, restrictive conditions* in New York City, so eliminate (G). In lines 60–62, the narrator states that gathering eggs *quickly became my favorite task over that summer. I loved going out into the early dawn.* This indicates that a *chore* requiring *that the narrator wake up early* was *enjoyable,* so keep (H). There is no discussion of a *recreational activity* that was *more suited to boys than to girls,* so eliminate (J). The correct answer is (H).

7. **A** The question asks which statement best describes *the relationship between the narrator and Aunt Millie.* The question references the ninth paragraph, so read lines 71–80. Lines 71–78 state, *Aunt Millie would take time away from her evening chores to braid my hair…Sometimes, when Aunt Millie seemed in an especially good mood, we would condition it with egg yolk and milk, which Aunt Millie would work into my hair gently massaging each strand.* Keep (A), since it is supported by these lines. There is no indication that *Aunt Millie feels emotionally cut off from the narrator,* or that the narrator has *city manners,* so eliminate (B). There is no discussion of these characters having *different ways of seeing the world,* so eliminate (C). These lines state that Aunt Millie *would take time away from her evening chores,* indicating that she does not see the narrator *as another part of her daily work,* so eliminate (D). The correct answer is (A).

8. **G** The question asks which statement *captures the sentiment behind the narrator's comment that the food at the farmhouse tastes like it is "from somewhere."* Read a window in the passage around the given line. Lines 46–51 state, *I'd eaten most of these dishes at home, but here they tasted different in a way that was hard to put a finger on at first. As though they were from somewhere, instead of appearing magically on our kitchen table. They tasted the way the farm smelled—of the animals and the earth.* The narrator says that *here they tasted different,* so the food does not taste *just like the food* she *had in New York;* eliminate (F). Keep (G), since it is supported by the phrases *They tasted the way the farm smelled—of the animals and the earth,* and *instead of appearing magically on our kitchen table.* Although the food tastes different to her, the narrator indicates that *I'd eaten most of these dishes at home,* so eliminate (H). The food does not literally taste like *soil,* so eliminate (J). The correct answer is (G).

9. **B** The question asks what is suggested about the *narrator's mother* by details in the second paragraph, so read lines 11–17. Lines 13–15 state, *Her words were admonishments, but I saw the tear in the corner of her eye and knew that she'd miss us over the next three months.* The previous paragraph indicates that the children are going to the farm because of their mother's *new job,* rather than for *vacation;* there is also no mention here of the mother hoping they *will have a good time,* so eliminate (A). Keep (B) since it is supported by lines 13–15. There is no mention of the children learning *the self-discipline they need to survive in the city,* so eliminate (C). The previous paragraph mentions that the mother is *wary* of leaving the children *alone at home in the evenings and overnight* (lines 6–7), but not of *the long bus ride* or talking to *strangers,* so eliminate (D). The correct answer is (B).

10. **J** The question asks *why the narrator and Kiran will spend the summer on the farm.* Look for references to reasons the children leave their home to travel to the farm. Lines 2–7 recount, *my mother put me and my brother Kiran on the southbound bus heading from our home in New York City to our aunt and uncle's place in North Carolina. Her new job on the third shift of the garment factory gave us the potential for a better life ahead, but she was wary about leaving us alone at home in the evenings and overnight.* There is no indication that *the narrator is weak and sickly,* so eliminate (F). Although the children do learn to do chores on the farm, there is no evidence that this is the reason they travel to the farm, so eliminate (G). Similarly, although the *cousins* are mentioned in the passage, there's no indication that *developing a relationship* with them is the reason the children visited the farm, so eliminate (H). Keep (J) because it is supported by lines 2–7. The correct answer is (J).

Passage II

11. **D** The question asks what triggered *the current debate over research into plant consciousness.* Use words from the answer choices to locate the relevant portions of Passage A. Lines 12–16 state that *Forty years ago Buckner conducted a series of experiments on his plants...These experiments led him to conclude that plants possess a means of perception that allows them to react to human thoughts.* Though Clive Buckner used *polygraph technology* in his research (lines 13–14), the polygraph equipment's *invention* is not discussed, so eliminate (A). In lines 25–33, the discovery that *plants respond to the*

distress signals of a spider in the room is described as part of *a steady flow of research over the next two decades* following *Clive Buckner's hypothesis;* since it happened later, this cannot be the event that triggered the debate, so eliminate (B). The *Boston Botanical Gardens* are mentioned in the first paragraph as part of an example of *social reinforcement,* but lines 10–11 state that this idea has gained *credibility mainly since the work of Clive Buckner first came to light,* so the techniques were not *introduced by the Boston Botanical Gardens,* nor were they the trigger for the debate, so eliminate (C). The introduction gives the passage's copyright date as 2010, so the *late 1960s* was approximately *forty years* before the passage was written; therefore, (D) is supported by lines 12–16. The correct answer is (D).

12. **J** The question asks what *lie-detectors* are, according to the passage. Look for the word *lie-detectors* in Passage A. Lines 12–14 state, *Buckner conducted a series of experiments on his plants using "lie-detectors," polygraph galvanometer equipment.* The reference to *train trigger switches* is part of a description of a different experiment (lines 33–36), so eliminate (F). According to the first paragraph, *social reinforcement* is *friendly behavior around* plants, while lie-detectors are described as *equipment;* eliminate (G). *Distress signals* are mentioned as part of another experiment (lines 32–33), so eliminate (H). Keep (J), since it is supported by lines 12–14. The correct answer is (J).

13. **D** The question asks what the *social reinforcement required of Sheila Jennings at her job* is primarily designed to do. Look for the words *social reinforcement* and *Sheila Jennings* in Passage A. Lines 6–9 state, *Sheila's friendly behavior around the plants is actually called "social reinforcement" and is one of her job requirements. The idea that interacting with these plants will help them flourish has been common sense to gardeners for ages.* Therefore, the *social reinforcement* is intended to *help [the plants] flourish.* There is no mention of the plants being disturbed *by the sounds of visitors to the Botanical Gardens,* so eliminate (A). Lines 4–5 say that *To a casual observer, she appeared to be entertaining herself during her morning routine,* but the next lines indicate that this is not the reason for her behavior, so eliminate (B). There is no support for the idea that the songs or speaking *replicate the sounds of wildlife,* so eliminate (C). Keep (D), since *lead to better plant growth* matches the phrase *help them flourish.* The correct answer is (D).

14. **H** The question asks what *Clive Buckner* believes about *the potential outcome of an experiment measuring plant consciousness.* Look for references to Clive Buckner in Passage A. Lines 43–47 state that Buckner *is willing to acknowledge the scientific issues involved in replicating the experiments. "Many others have failed to produce the same effects...The outcomes of the experiments seem very dependent on the experimenter's relationship to his plants."* The description *beyond the orthodoxy of modern scientific beliefs* is mentioned in lines 22–24, but it is attributed to the *scientific community,* not to Buckner, so eliminate (F). Though Buckner acknowledges *scientific issues involved in replicating the experiments,* lines 47–48 indicate that *Buckner believes these problems actually strengthen his theories.* He does not consider the results to be *unfairly biased,* so eliminate (G). Keep (H), since the phrase *the outcomes of the experiments seem very dependent on the experimenter's relationship to his plants* supports the description of the potential outcome as *sometimes inconsistent.* Since Buckner *is willing*

to acknowledge the scientific issues involved in replicating the experiments, he is not certain that the outcome is *scientifically sound,* so eliminate (J). The correct answer is (H).

15. **A** The question asks for *the main point of Steve Karnell's quotation* in the fourth paragraph, so read lines 88–92. The quotation states, "*Lacking in this so-called 'experiment' are ingredients fundamental to the scientific method like control groups and blind studies...Work like this opens up a Pandora's box of bad science.*" Keep (A), since *ingredients fundamental to the scientific method* matches *elements of how research is conducted* and *opens up a Pandora's box of bad science* matches *can make its findings less trustworthy.* The quotation states that *control groups* are *lacking,* not that *experimenters do not understand* their *function,* so eliminate (B). The quotation states that *blind studies* are one of the *ingredients fundamental to the scientific method,* but it does not indicate that a blind study alone would have *proven* a particular hypothesis, so eliminate (C). Karnell does not compare *researchers working with plants* with other researchers, so eliminate (D). The correct answer is (A).

16. **H** The question asks what scientists call *the desire to affirm one's preconceived notions about an experimental observation.* Look for a reference to affirming preconceived ideas in Passage B. Lines 81–85 state, *such experimenters may be merely interpreting the reactions of plants to agree with their premeditated goal of finding consciousness (scientists call this confirmation bias).* Lines 90–91 indicate that *control groups* and *blind studies* are *ingredients fundamental to the scientific method,* so these are seen positively. The previous paragraph indicates that scientists are *concerned* about interpreting results to affirm preconceived notions, so this is seen as a negative; eliminate (F) and (G). Keep (H) because it is supported by lines 81–85. Lines 85–87 describe *self-deception* as *ignoring the possibilities of alternative explanations for the sake of justifying their faulty hypotheses;* this problem is distinct from affirming *preconceived notions,* so eliminate (J). The correct answer is (H).

17. **A** The question asks which statement *Max Crusella* would be most likely to agree with. Look for the name *Max Crusella* in Passage B. Lines 58–67 state, *Max Crusella, a plant researcher at the Marina Del Rey Plant Laboratory, is one of those who believe that...plants are sensitive to their environments in ways that traditional science is not equipped to describe,* and they quote Crusella: "*...there needs to be some kind of new scientific explanation for what are otherwise mysterious phenomena.*" Since Crusella feels *there needs to be a new scientific explanation* for plants' sensitivity to their environments, he is likely to agree that the *responsiveness of plants to their environments currently lacks an adequate traditional scientific explanation;* keep (A). Crusella states that it is *possible* that *researchers have proposed overzealous explanations for their observations,* but this is not enough to suggest that he would agree that *many experiments have been tainted by self-deception on the part of the researchers,* so eliminate (B). Crusella doesn't discuss evidence that *contradicts* plant consciousness, so eliminate (C). Lines 58–67 contradict the statement in (D), so eliminate this choice. The correct answer is (A).

18. **H** The question asks how *Betty Wilkinson and Steve Karnell* would describe *Clive Buckner's observation of his plant.* The question references the fourth paragraph of Passage A, so read lines 25–40. Lines 27–30 describe Clive Buckner's observation: *During his original experiment, Buckner noticed that his plant would produce a sharp and immediate response when he attempted to visualize the act*

of burning the plant's leaves. Next, look for the names *Betty Wilkinson* and *Steve Karnell* in Passage B. Lines 68–72 present Betty Wilkinson's point of view: discussing an experiment similar to Buckner's, *She points out that the...experiment failed to register any plant reaction when it was replicated by a different researcher.* Lines 88–89 indicate that *Steve Karnell...agrees with Wilkinson.* Both Wilkinson and Karnell point out flaws in experiments like Buckner's, so they are not likely to draw conclusions about plants based on Buckner's observations. Choices (F), (G), and (J) each draw a conclusion about the plant, so eliminate these choices. Keep (H), since this is supported by the statement in lines 70–72. The correct answer is (H).

19. **B** The question asks how *Clive Buckner* would respond to *Betty Wilkinson*'s *criticism*. The question references the second paragraph of Passage B, so read lines 68–80. Discussing an experiment with results similar to those of Buckner's experiment, Wilkinson *points out that the...experiment failed to register any plant reaction when it was replicated by a different researcher.* Next, look for references to *Clive Buckner* in Passage A. Lines 44–53 indicate that Buckner acknowledges that other researchers have failed to replicate the results of his study and that the *outcomes of the experiments seem very dependent on the experimenter's relationship to his plants.* However, he goes on to say that *these problems actually strengthen his theories. "We are trying to demonstrate the fact that plants develop subtle yet meaningful connections with their caretakers, so the fact that the outcomes of experiments are varied is actually in support of our notion that plant behavior is dynamic and responsive to a given individual."* This indicates that Buckner would not see Wilkinson's objection as a valid criticism. Buckner is not likely to respond simply by providing *specific examples* to support his theory: Wilkinson is criticizing the validity of such an example, and additional examples would be vulnerable to the same criticism; eliminate (A). Keep (B), since it is supported by Buckner's statements in lines 47–54. Buckner responded to criticisms similar to Wilkinson's, so he would probably not state *complete indifference* to her concerns; eliminate (C). Buckner doesn't *counsel other experimenters on how to be better caretakers of plants,* so eliminate (D). The correct answer is (B).

20. **H** The question asks what is emphasized by both Passage A and Passage B. Because this is a general question, it should be done after all the specific questions on both passages. Eliminate any answer choice that misrepresents either passage. Both passages discuss experiments that seem to demonstrate plant consciousness, as well as challenges presented by these experiments' methodology. Both passages discuss *replicating results of plant consciousness experiments,* but they disagree on its importance, so eliminate (F). The effect of *social reinforcement* on *how well a plant grows* is not discussed in Passage B, so eliminate (G). Keep (H), since both passages discuss *difficulties of interpreting the results of experiments.* Passage A does not discuss *confirmation bias,* nor does either passage discuss *how to avoid* confirmation bias, so eliminate (J). The correct answer is (H).

Passage III

21. **D** The question asks which rules the writer is referring to with the phrase *"the rules of polite etiquette."* Read a window in the passage around the given lines. Lines 15–17 state, *We have all been yelled at by a frustrated audience of our friends, acquaintances, and family members to cease our incessant noise making,* and the next lines say that *many learn to keep their songs to themselves as they master the rules of polite etiquette.* The rules of polite etiquette are therefore rules that discourage people from behavior that others may find annoying. The passage doesn't say that people use less *imagination* when *playing,* so eliminate (A). There is no mention of *behavior modification classes,* so eliminate (B). Lines 19–20 indicate that songwriters never learn to keep their songs to themselves, but instead turn the *songs into something people will be happy to hear.* However, this does not imply that songwriters don't *abide by* the *rules of polite etiquette,* so eliminate (C). Keep (D), since it is supported by lines 15–19. The correct answer is (D).

22. **F** The question asks what is *NOT* a characteristic of the songs that a *songwriter aspires to write,* which people will be *happy to hear.* When a question asks which answer is **not** supported, eliminate answers that **are** supported. Use words from the answer choices to locate the relevant portions of the passage. Lines 78–85 state that songwriters *learn to mimic expressions of joy and anguish* and *to write and perform songs without any genuine attachment to their emotional content.* However, the author says that audiences *can feel a difference between a contrived and an authentic performance.* This implies that *mimicking joy and anguish* is not something that songwriters should aspire to, so keep (F). Lines 29–31 explain that *There's a balance of two opposing forces that we enjoy in music. One force soothes, the other agitates.* This indicates that *people will be happy to hear* songs that blend *comfort and tension,* so eliminate (G). Lines 67–69 state, *When we develop a kinship with a song, we feel waves of euphoria as it plays.* This indicates that *people are happy to hear* songs that foster *a kinship with the listener,* so eliminate (H). Lines 70–77 state that songwriters don't want to *deny listeners the opportunity to mold our song into something they can claim as their own,* so the songwriters make efforts to give a song *enough flexibility that someone else can derive a different significance.* This indicates that songwriters aspire to write songs that allow *for different interpretations,* so eliminate (J). The correct answer is (F).

23. **C** The question asks for the primary purpose of the passage. Because this is a general question, it should be done after all the specific questions. The author discusses music from the perspective of both the listener and the songwriter, including what songwriters try to accomplish when they write a song and the ways that people's taste in music develops as they age. Lines 37–39 suggest that *Successful songs...include both setbacks and triumphs,* and lines 63–77 explain that good songs allow the listener to *develop a kinship with a song,* and don't just include the songwriter's *private release.* Therefore, the author's purpose is not to *explain to readers that expressing pain will enable them to be good songwriters,* so eliminate (A). There is no mention of *catchy songs* in the passage, and the author does not try to *convince aspiring songwriters to stop giving in to polite etiquette,* so eliminate (B). Keep (C) because it captures the passage's focus on the *goals and process of songwriting* and on

the audience's developing *expectations*. Lines 57–59 state that *the cultural backdrop of a child's upbringing calibrates her listening taste to a given set of rhythms, instruments, harmonic scales, and song structures,* but the author doesn't argue that *songwriters are too often limited by* this cultural backdrop, so eliminate (D). The correct answer is (C).

24. **G** The question asks what the author is referring to with the statement that a *songwriter must aspire to "this private release."* Read a window in the passage around the given line. Lines 67–71 state, *When we develop a kinship with a song, we feel waves of euphoria as it plays, the feeling of our inner world radiating out. As songwriters, we must aspire to this private release in every song we write.* Lines 71–74 explain that songwriters *often replace specific details with general symbols* in order to allow *listeners the opportunity to mold our song into something they can claim as their own,* so eliminate (F). Keep (G) since it conveys the idea of *the inner world radiating out.* The author doesn't advocate that songwriters *force listeners to develop a kinship* with their songs, so eliminate (H). *Joy* and *anguish* are mentioned as two expressions that songwriters can *learn to mimic* (lines 79–80); they are not emotions the author says songwriters must *focus on,* so eliminate (J). The correct answer is (G).

25. **D** The question asks for a goal with which *adolescents approach songs* that differs from that of children. Look for the words *children* and *adolescents* in the passage. Lines 52–59 discuss how children approach music, and lines 60–69 discuss how adolescents differ in their approach, saying, *We look to find personal meaning in lyrics and to latch onto songs that seem to broadcast our private thoughts.* The passage emphasizes *familiarity* as a quality that children prefer, so eliminate (A). The passage says that adolescents *identify with artists based on their dress, their politics,* but it does not say that adolescents are trying to discover *new trends,* so eliminate (B). The passage indicates that *the cultural backdrop of a child's upbringing calibrates her listening tastes,* and that an adolescent's preferences are influenced by other things. However, it does not say that adolescents have a *goal* of *departing from* their *cultural backdrop,* so eliminate (C). Keep (D) because it is supported by lines 63–64. The correct answer is (D).

26. **H** The question asks what selection process cannot be compared to our *process of selecting songs.* When a question asks which answer is **not** supported, eliminate answers that **are** supported. Look for references to selecting songs in the passage. Lines 52–69 discuss the ways we select songs as children and adolescents. Lines 60–61 say, *we begin to choose our own songs just as we would choose our friends,* so eliminate (F). Lines 53–54 say, *we passively accept and learn to love our parents' music just like we do their cooking,* so eliminate (G). The word *author* appears in line 65, but the phrase says, *Despite not being the author of our favorite songs;* this is not a comparison with choosing *our favorite authors,* so keep (H). Lines 65–66 say, *we wear our songs like trinkets of personal expression, telltale accessories that describe to others important parts of our psychology,* so eliminate (J). The correct answer is (H).

27. **B** The question asks how the *first sentence functions in relation to the passage as a whole.* Because this is a general question, it should be done after all the specific questions. The passage as a whole discusses songwriting, and the first two paragraphs relate the author's personal experience as a songwriter. The first sentence states, *I used to have to feel pain in order to write songs.* This is an introduction to

the author's personal story. In lines 80–82, the author says, *It becomes easy for us to write and perform songs without any genuine attachment to their emotional content.* This indicates that the requirement given in the first sentence changed for the author over time, but not that it is *not true in the real world of songwriting,* so eliminate (A). Keep (B) because it is supported by surrounding context of the passage. The passage does not contend that *singing about one's problems is evidence of a lack of self-control,* so eliminate (C). The second paragraph elaborates on the first sentence, so eliminate (D). The correct answer is (B).

28. **G** The question asks how the *divergent songwriting purposes of "soothes" and "agitates" differ from one another.* Read a window in the passage around the given line. Lines 43–47 state, *Young children often enjoy hearing soothing lullabies as a way to be distracted from anxiety or coaxed into a peaceful slumber. They take great pleasure in singing agitating songs, such as the "nenny nenny boo boo" melody that can be customized into any taunt.* There is no indication that soothing songs are *annoying to younger audiences,* so eliminate (F). Keep (G) because it is supported by lines 43–47. *Agitating songs* are not related to *slumber* in the passage, so eliminate (H). The passage says that *soothing* songs can distract children from anxiety; it does not say that *agitating songs distract us from the things that we passionately hate,* so eliminate (J). The correct answer is (G).

29. **B** The question asks what the author's analogy conveys about *acting and performing music.* Look for the words *acting* and *performing* in the passage. Lines 83–85 state that *just as audiences can distinguish between good and bad acting, so too will audience members feel a difference between a contrived and an authentic performance.* The author is highlighting a similarity between acting and performing, so eliminate (A) and keep (B). There is no contrast made between *expressing anguish* and *joy;* both are listed as expressions that performers *learn to mimic,* so eliminate (C). The author only mentions one shared aspect of acting and performing; there is not support for the statement that they are *completely identical,* so eliminate (D). The correct answer is (B).

30. **F** The question asks why *the cultural backdrop of a child's upbringing is significant to her appreciation of music.* Look for the words *cultural backdrop of a child's upbringing* in the passage. Lines 57–59 state that *the cultural backdrop of a child's upbringing calibrates her listening tastes to a given set of rhythms, instruments, harmonic scales, and song structures.* Keep (F) because it is a paraphrase of lines 57–59. This paragraph is not discussing *what to avoid in order to stand out as an original songwriter,* so eliminate (G). *Political content* is not mentioned in relationship to cultural backdrop, and there is no discussion of what is *proper,* only what is familiar; eliminate (H). The passage does not state that a child's cultural backdrop is a *basis through which the child is able to make friends,* so eliminate (J). The correct answer is (F).

Passage IV

31. **C** The question asks for the primary purpose of the passage. Because this is a general question, it should be done after all the specific questions. The first three paragraphs of the passage discuss some of the characteristics of comets, including what factors affect *the brightness of a comet,* and the last two paragraphs discuss the reasons for *astronomers' interest in comets.* The last paragraph says that discoveries about comets *may cause scientists to reconsider models of how the solar system formed* (lines 73–74). However, this is discussed in only one paragraph, so it is not the primary purpose of the passage; eliminate (A). The author does not *encourage readers to learn to use telescopic equipment,* so eliminate (B). Keep (C) since it includes both *the characteristics of comets currently known by researchers* and the *motivation for their research.* The passage mentions only one study that has already been done (lines 67–71), so the passage's purpose is not to *catalogue the experiments planetary scientists have done;* eliminate (D). The correct answer is (C).

32. **F** The question asks which statement the author would most likely agree with. Use words from the answer choices to locate the relevant portions of the passage. Lines 67–74 state that *a recent collection of tiny dust particles left in the Earth's stratosphere by* a passing comet *led to the discovery of a previously unknown mineral* and that…*it, along with other new materials that may be found in comets, may cause scientists to reconsider models of how the solar system formed.* Keep (F), since it is supported by these lines. Lines 43–45 state that *IRAS-Araki-Alcock* was the *closest comet to pass the Earth in modern times* and that it looked *very bright,* but there is no indication that *astronomers will not be able to observe comets brighter than* this one. In addition, lines 17–20 state, *The brightness of a comet depends primarily on two factors: its distance from the Sun and its distance from the Earth,* rather than the *length of its orbital period.* For these reasons, eliminate (G). The passage indicates that comets travel in orbits: although they *spend most of their time in the very cold areas barely within the Sun's gravitation* (lines 58–59), at their *perihelion,* they are closer to the Sun (line 20–21). The passage also doesn't state that *distance from the Sun* is indicative of age. For these reasons, eliminate (H). Lines 75–76 state, *Future missions are planned to retrieve material directly from comets,* and there is no mention of this being *difficult because of comets' unpredictability,* so eliminate (J). The correct answer is (F).

33. **D** The question asks which *situation creates a comet's maximum brightness as observed from Earth.* Look for the words *brightness* and *Earth* in the passage. Lines 29–34 state, *The stronger determinant of a comet's brightness is its distance to Earth, especially in relation to its perihelion. If a comet passes its nearest point to Earth after the comet's perihelion, it will be much brighter than if it reaches its closest point to Earth while it is still relatively cold and solid, before the Sun evaporates much of the comet's matter.* The sizes of the *coma* and the *nucleus* are discussed in the first paragraph, and there is no indication that this affects *brightness,* so eliminate (A). Lines 41–43 state that *comets move about one or two degrees per day—much too slow to be perceived by the naked eye—and can remain visible for months.* In other words, the comet is visible despite moving slowly; it is the motion that is imperceptible; therefore, speed does not affect brightness, so eliminate (B). The passage indicates that a comet will be *brighter* if it *passes its nearest point to Earth after the comet's perihelion;* eliminate (C) because it says the opposite. Keep (D) because it matches these lines. The correct answer is (D).

34. **J** The question asks which question is *NOT* answered by information given in the passage. When a question asks which answer is **not** supported, eliminate answers that **are** supported. Use words from the answer choices to locate the relevant portions of the passage. The last paragraph states, *By studying the specific chemical composition of comets, scientists hope to learn more about the chemical origins of the solar system* (lines 64–66) and that *scientists...hope that comet material may reveal information about the origins of life on Earth* (lines 76–80), so eliminate (F). Lines 7–10 state, *Solar winds and radiation pressure from the Sun can blow the material of the coma away from the comet's nucleus, creating a tail, which is sometimes longer than the distance from the Earth to the Sun,* so eliminate (G). Lines 49–54 state that *Even...professional astronomers are more likely to discover a comet by chance than by exacting calculations, because comets are only detectable for such a short portion of their orbits, and because it is so infrequent that the comets pass near enough to the Earth to be observed,* so eliminate (H). Lines 1–3 state that comets *revolve in highly eccentric orbits,* but there is no explanation of why this is true, so keep (J). The correct answer is (J).

35. **A** The question asks what is not required for "*the appearance of comets.*" When a question asks which answer is **not** supported, eliminate answers that **are** supported. The question references the first paragraph, so read lines 1–17. The paragraph says that *the comas and tails of the brightest comets can be seen with the naked eye* and that *the nucleus of a comet cannot be detected even with the most powerful telescopes;* therefore, *a powerful telescope* is not required, so keep (A). It states that the *tail* is created when *Solar winds and radiation pressure from the Sun...blow the material of the coma away from the comet's nucleus,* so eliminate (B). It states that the *coma* is created when *a very small portion of the frozen matter evaporates,* so eliminate (C). The *coma* is described as *a shroud of gas and dust... enveloping an area up to a million kilometers around the solid nucleus of the comet,* and the *nucleus* is described as *small,* so eliminate (D). The correct answer is (A).

36. **G** The question asks what is not mentioned as something that *astronomers* observe *about comets.* When a question asks which answer is **not** supported, eliminate answers that **are** supported. Use words from the answer choices to locate the relevant portions of the passage. Lines 67–71 describe the *discovery of a previously unknown mineral* in *dust particles left...by the passage of* a *comet,* so eliminate (F). Lines 14–15 state that *the nucleus of a comet cannot be detected even with the most powerful telescopes,* so astronomers have not observed *comets that emit bright light from their nuclei;* keep (G). Lines 34–38 contrast the brightness of Halley's comet on two occasions, saying it *was very bright during its first observed pass near Earth in 1910,* but *so disappointing to astronomers when it returned, this time much further from the Earth, in 1986;* eliminate (H). Lines 1–3 state that comets *revolve in highly eccentric orbits,* and lines 58–59 state that *comets spend most of their time in...areas barely within the Sun's gravitation,* so eliminate (J). The correct answer is (G).

37. **B** The question asks what lines 34–38 emphasize *in the context of the third paragraph,* so read lines 29–48. Lines 34–38 give an example about *Halley's comet,* beginning with the phrase *This explains why.* The word *this* indicates that the explanation is given just prior to the example, and lines 30–34 state, *If a comet passes its nearest point to Earth after the comet's perihelion, it will be much brighter than if it reaches its closest point to Earth while it is still relatively cold and solid, before the Sun*

evaporates much of the comet's matter. These lines do not mention *a comet's apparent speed* or *apparent diameter,* so eliminate (A). Keep (B) because it matches lines 30–34. Although the passage says that the Halley's comet was *disappointing to astronomers when it returned,* the surrounding context does not focus on this, so eliminate (C). The paragraph also doesn't discuss *difficulty in predicting when comets will be visible* or *highly eccentric orbits,* so eliminate (D). The correct answer is (B).

38. **J** The question asks what the passage indicates about *attempts to study comets directly.* Look for the words *study comets directly* in the passage. Lines 62–80 discuss scientists' *interest in studying comets directly.* The paragraph gives an example of *a recent collection of tiny dust particles that has led to the discovery of a previously unknown mineral,* and also discusses topics that *scientists hope to learn more about.* There is no mention of *technical difficulties* that have *prevented* study, so eliminate (F). The paragraph states that scientists *hope that comet material may reveal information about the origins of life on Earth;* the word *hope* indicates that the information has not already been *used* for this purpose, so eliminate (G). The *discovery of a previously unknown material* was a success, so eliminate (H). Keep (J), since the word *promising* reflects the successful discovery and scientists' *hope* for future discoveries, and the word *incomplete* reflects the fact that these discoveries have not been made yet. The correct answer is (J).

39. **C** The question asks what the phrase *characteristics beyond the novelty of these comets* most likely refers to in line 55. Read a window in the passage around the given line. Lines 54–58 state, *astronomers' interest in comets lies in characteristics beyond the novelty of these comets. Comets are believed to be remnants of the original disc of chemical material that formed the solar system about four billion years ago.* These lines don't refer to *discovering new comets,* so eliminate (A). The paragraph starts with a discussion of the difficulty and rarity of detecting or observing a comet, but the sentence in question begins with the word *However,* and states that the interest lies *beyond the novelty of these comets,* so the interest is not in the *difficulty of detecting distant comets;* eliminate (B). Keep (C) because *comets' chemical composition* is supported by the reference to the *original disc of chemical material that formed the solar system.* Although the comets' *age* is part of what makes them a *possible "fossil record" of the solar system,* their age is not the characteristic that interests the scientists, so eliminate (D). The correct answer is (C).

40. **H** The question asks for the main purpose of the last paragraph, so read lines 62–80. This paragraph discusses scientists' *interest in studying comets directly* and the topics that *scientists hope to learn more about.* The paragraph gives only one example of an experiment that has been performed, so eliminate (F). The scientists hope that *comet material may reveal information about the origins of life on Earth,* but the author does not try to *convince readers that comets are responsible for the evolution of intelligent species,* so eliminate (G). Keep (H), since it is supported by the discussion of scientists' *hope to learn more about the chemical origins of the solar system* and *information about the origins of life on Earth.* The passage states that discoveries made in studying comets directly *may cause scientists to reconsider models of how the solar system formed,* but the purpose of the paragraph is not to *contradict outdated information,* so eliminate (J). The correct answer is (H).

Science Practice Section 1

SCIENCE TEST

35 Minutes—40 Questions

DIRECTIONS: There are six passages in the following section. Each passage is followed by several questions. After reading a passage, choose the best answer to each question and blacken the corresponding oval on your answer document. You may refer to the passages as often as necessary.

You are NOT permitted to use a calculator on this test.

Passage I

A study was conducted regarding the fossil shells of a particular species of turtle that lives off the coast of the Opulasian Peninsula. Scientists discovered a continuous record of fossilized shells in the seabed off the coast dating back 120,000 years. In addition to examining the fossilized turtle shells, the scientists also examined the shells of living turtles.

From each layer of seabed, the scientists randomly selected 100 complete, unbroken fossilized shells. Each shell was carefully prepared, measured, and photographed. A bit of each shell was then clipped off and sent to a laboratory for radiocarbon dating to determine the precise age of each shell.

Table 1

	% shells with the following scute pattern:		
Age of shells (years)	M-m-M-M-m	M-M-m-m-M	M-m-M-m-M
120,000	46	44	10
90,000	42	54	4
87,000	30	67	3
85,000	21	72	7
80,000	20	66	14
50,000	76	21	3
27,000	100	0	0
15,000	100	0	0
8,000	100	0	0
4,000	100	0	0
1,000	68	28	4
300	74	20	6
0	86	2	12

Study 1

All of the living turtles had a distinct band of hexagonal *scutes* (bony plates) running the length of their shells, from head to tail. The fossilized shells' scutes were not visible to the naked eye; however, upon application of a particular dye, a similar band of scutes from head to tail was observed in every shell.

Scutes extending greater than $\frac{1}{8}$ of the length of the shell were labeled *major* (M), where scutes extending less than or equal to $\frac{1}{8}$ of the length of the shell were labeled *minor* (m). The pattern of scutes was recorded for each fossil. For each time period, the percent of fossils exhibiting each pattern is given in Table 1.

Study 2

For each shell, the surface area of the shell and the height of the shell's *bridge* (the part of the shell linking the upper and lower plates) were recorded (see Figure 1).

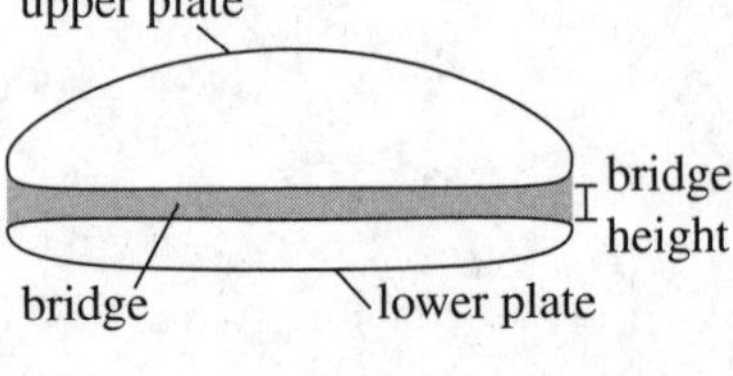

Figure 1

For the shells of each age, the average of each measurement was calculated. The results are presented in Figure 2.

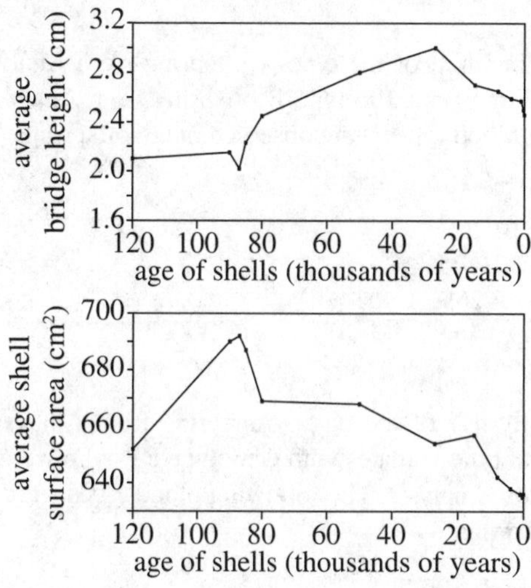

Figure 2

1. In a layer of seabed determined to be 250,000 years old, the scientists found fragments of twelve turtle shells, but no complete, intact shells. Which of the following is the most likely reason this layer of seabed was not included in the studies?

   A. 250,000 years is too old to obtain an accurate radiocarbon date.
   B. Shells that were 250,000 years old would have been irrelevant to the studies.
   C. Accurate measurements of the dimensions of the shells could have been impossible to obtain.
   D. The scientists would not have been able to accurately determine the color of the shells.

2. With regard to the descriptions given in Study 1, the shells with the M-M-m-m-M band of scutes probably most closely resembled which of the following?

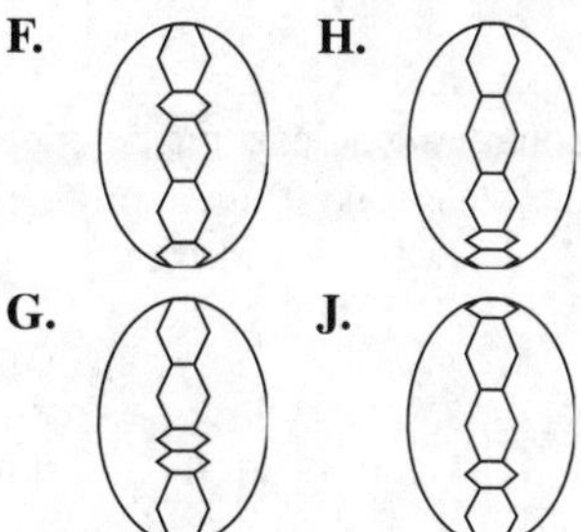

3. In Study 2, the average shell surface area of fossilized turtle shells that were 80,000 years old was closest to:

   A. 670 cm²
   B. 680 cm²
   C. 690 cm²
   D. 700 cm²

4. Suppose, in Study 1, the scientists had found another seabed layer with fossilized shells that were radiocarbon dated and found to be 86,000 years old. Based on the results of Study 1, the scute pattern percents for the group of shells would most likely have been closest to which of the following?

	M-m-M-M-m	M-M-m-m-M	M-m-M-m-M
F.	100%	0%	0%
G.	50%	25%	25%
H.	36%	61%	4%
J.	26%	69%	5%

5. According to the results of Study 2, how do the average shell surface area and the average bridge height of living turtles of the Opulasian Peninsula compare to those of the turtles of the Opulasian Peninsula from 120,000 years ago? For the living turtles:

   A. both the average shell surface area and the average bridge height are larger.
   B. both the average shell surface area and the average bridge height are smaller.
   C. the average shell surface area is larger, and the average bridge height is smaller.
   D. the average shell surface area is smaller, and the average bridge height is larger.

6. Which of the following statements best describes how Study 1 differed from Study 2 ?

   F. In Study 1, the scientists examined 2 characteristics regarding the shape and size of turtle shells; but in Study 2, the scientists examined the frequency of occurrence of different patterns of scutes on turtle shells.
   G. In Study 1, the scientists examined the frequency of occurrence of different patterns of scutes on turtle shells; but in Study 2, the scientists examined the environment in which turtles live.
   H. In Study 1, the scientists examined the frequency of occurrence of different patterns of scutes on turtle shells; but in Study 2, the scientists examined 2 characteristics regarding the shape and size of turtle shells.
   J. In Study 1, the scientists examined 2 characteristics regarding the shape and size of turtle shells; but in Study 2, the scientists examined the environment in which turtles live.

7. From 100,000 years ago to 80,000 years ago, the average shell surface area:

   A. increased only.
   B. increased, then decreased.
   C. remained constant, then decreased.
   D. varied with no general trend.

Passage II

The 4 different blood types in sheep are A, B, AB, and O. The blood type of an offspring is determined by the blood types of its parents. Each parent contributes one version of a gene, or an *allele*, to its offspring. The *genotype* of an offspring refers to the combination of the offspring's two alleles, each of which came from one parent. The *phenotype* refers to the observable characteristics of a trait.

There are three possible alleles of this gene: the type-A blood allele (I^A), the type-B blood allele (I^B), and the type-O blood allele (I^O). Both I^A and I^B are *dominant* to I^O, and I^O is *recessive* to I^A and I^B. This means that an individual with one I^A and one I^O will have type-A blood, and an individual with one I^B and one I^O will have type-B blood. When an individual has one I^A and one I^B allele, this individual will have type-AB blood, due to the *codominance* of the I^A and I^B alleles.

Table 1

Blood Type	Possible Genotypes
A	I^AI^A or I^AI^O
B	I^BI^B or I^BI^O
AB	I^AI^B
O	I^OI^O

To explore the inheritance patterns of blood types in sheep, researchers conducted 4 analyses. In each analysis, male and female sheep of differing blood types were mated and the resultant blood types of their offspring recorded.

Analysis 1

One thousand males with type-O blood were mated with 1,000 females with type-AB blood. The following blood types were observed in the offspring:

Type A: 50%
Type B: 50%

Analysis 2

Two hundred of the type-A offspring from Analysis 1 were mated with 200 type-O mates from no previous experiment. The following blood types were observed in the offspring:

Type A: 50%
Type O: 50%

Analysis 3

One hundred of the type-A offspring from Analysis 1 parented children with 100 type-B offspring from Analysis 1. The following blood types were observed in the offspring:

Type A: 25%
Type B: 25%
Type AB: 25%
Type O: 25%

Analysis 4

Twenty-five of the type-A offspring from Analysis 3 were mated with type-B mates with Genotype I^BI^B who were not from any previous analysis. The following blood types were observed in the offspring:

Type AB: 50%
Type B: 50%

8. Which of the following is true of the offspring produced in Analysis 4 ?

F. Some of the offspring have both the same genotype and phenotype as one of their parents.
G. Some of the offspring have the same genotype as one of their parents, but no offspring have the same phenotype as a parent.
H. Some of the offspring have the same phenotype as one of their parents, but no offspring have the same genotype as a parent.
J. None of the offspring have the same phenotype or genotype as one of their parents.

9. The ratio of blood types containing at least one I^A allele to the blood types containing at least one I^B allele produced in Analysis 3 was:

A. 1:0.
B. 1:1.
C. 2:1.
D. 3:1.

10. An offspring whose blood type exhibits codominance has which of the following genotypes?

F. I^BI^B
G. I^BI^O
H. I^AI^B
J. I^AI^O

11. To produce only offspring with AB blood, one would mate two sheep with which of the following sets of genotypes?

A. $I^AI^B \times I^AI^B$
B. $I^AI^B \times I^OI^O$
C. $I^AI^A \times I^BI^B$
D. $I^BI^B \times I^AI^O$

12. In Analysis 3, the offspring used from Analysis 1 most likely had which of the following genotypes?

F. I^AI^O and I^BI^B
G. I^AI^O and I^BI^O
H. I^AI^A and I^BI^B
J. I^AI^A and I^BI^O

13. Some or all of the offspring had 1 allele for type-O blood in Analyses:

A. 1 and 2 only.
B. 2 and 3 only.
C. 1, 2, and 4 only.
D. 1, 2, 3, and 4.

14. Suppose that 300 offspring were produced in Analysis 3. Based on the results, the number of offspring with type-B blood produced in Analysis 3 would most likely have been closest to:

F. 25.
G. 50.
H. 75.
J. 100.

Passage III

Vasoconstriction involves a narrowing of blood vessels that could lead to poor blood flow in the body if it persists over a long time. *Ergotamine* is a substance that can cause vasoconstriction. When ergotamine is injected into a normal blood vessel, vasoconstriction occurs quickly at the site of the injection (see Figure 1).

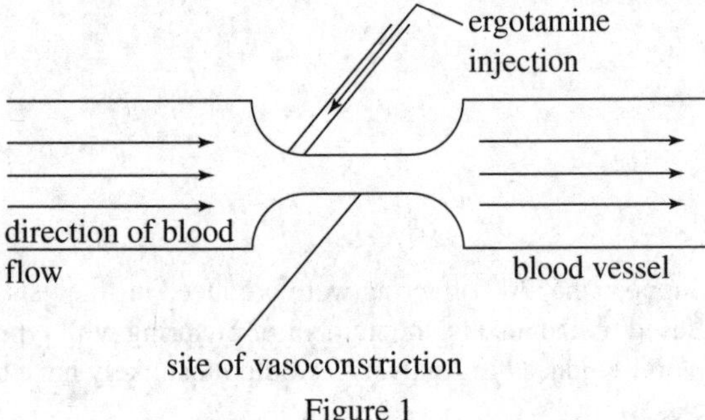

Figure 1

The diameter of the blood vessel at the site of vasoconstriction is less than the diameter of the normal blood vessel, so blood flow has a higher velocity through this narrow site. As a result, the blood pressure in the site of vasoconstriction is less than the blood pressure in the normal blood vessel. Moreover, the higher the velocity of the blood flow through the site of vasoconstriction, the lower the blood pressure at that site.

The percent change in blood pressure ($\%\Delta BP$) can be defined as:

$$\%\Delta BP = 100 \times \frac{\text{(normal blood pressure} - \text{pressure at site of vasoconstriction)}}{\text{normal blood pressure}}$$

Blood vessel sections of similar diameters were isolated from laboratory rats and $\%\Delta BP$ was measured over three experiments. When the researchers needed to create a site of vasoconstriction for some of the experimental trials, they would inject ergotamine to induce vasoconstriction within the blood vessel section.

Experiment 1

An artificial heart, which mimics a human's heartbeat, is used to move a constant volume of 500 mL of blood with each beat through four blood vessel sections. These four blood vessel sections were injected with the same amount of ergotamine, leading to sites of vasoconstriction of the same diameter. The rate at which the blood is pumped was varied for the four different blood vessel sections, and the $\%\Delta BP$ values that resulted were measured.

Table 1

Rate of artificial heart beat (beats per minute)	$\%\Delta BP$
60	1.2
90	9.3
120	22.3
150	45.1

Experiment 2

The artificial heart used in Experiment 1 was then used to pump a constant volume of 500 mL of blood with each beat at a constant rate of 90 beats per minute through five other blood vessel sections. These blood vessel sections were injected with different amounts of ergotamine, resulting in sites of vasoconstriction with different diameters. The $\%\Delta BP$ values were then measured.

Table 2

Diameter of site of vasoconstriction (cm)	$\%\Delta BP$
0.4	40.3
0.6	18.6
0.8	9.3
1.0	4.6
1.2	2.5

Experiment 3

The artificial heart used in Experiment 1 was used to pump different volumes of blood at a constant rate of 90 beats per minute through five blood vessel sections with the same diameter at the site of vasoconstriction. The $\%\Delta BP$ values were then measured.

Table 3

Volume of blood pumped (mL)	$\%\Delta BP$
400	8.4
450	8.8
500	9.3
550	9.7
600	10.2

15. Under the conditions described for Experiment 3, a $\%\Delta BP$ of 9.0 would most likely be obtained if the entering volume of blood was approximately:

A. 350 mL.
B. 475 mL.
C. 550 mL.
D. 650 mL.

16. Based on the results of Experiment 1, if the rate of the artificial heartbeat had been less than 60 beats per minute, then the *%ΔBP* would most likely have been:

F. less than 1.2.
G. between 1.2 and 9.3.
H. between 9.3 and 22.3.
J. greater than 22.3.

17. Which of the following is the most likely explanation for the results of Experiment 1? As the rate of the artificial heartbeat increases, *%ΔBP*:

A. increases, because the velocity of blood through the site of vasoconstriction increases.
B. increases, because the velocity of blood through the site of vasoconstriction decreases.
C. decreases, because the velocity of blood flow through the site of vasoconstriction increases.
D. decreases, because the velocity of blood flow through the site of vasoconstriction decreases.

18. Consider blood flow through three regions of the same blood vessel, each of which has a different diameter. The velocity of blood flow is measured in milliliters per minute (mL/min) and the blood pressure is measured in millimeters of mercury (mmHg), and their values for each of the blood vessel regions are shown in the following table:

Location	Velocity of blood flow (mL/min)	Blood pressure (mmHg)
A	500	31
B	1,000	29
C	900	30

Based on the information in the passage about blood flow, which of the following diagrams best represents the relative diameters of the three blood vessel regions?

F.
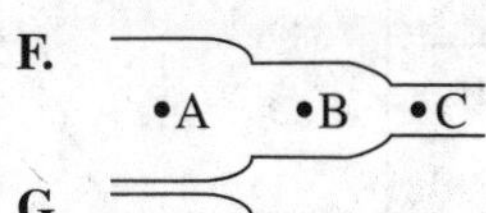

H.
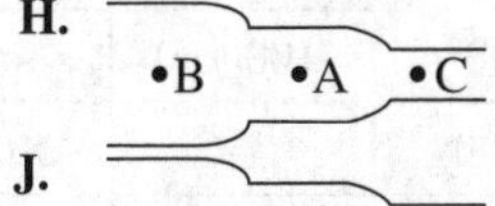

G. •C •B •A

J. •A •C •B

19. Based on the results of Experiments 1 and 2, what was the diameter of the site of vasoconstriction in the blood vessel section used in Experiment 3 ?

A. 0.4 cm
B. 0.6 cm
C. 0.8 cm
D. 1.0 cm

20. For the blood vessel sections used in Experiment 2 that had sites of vasoconstriction with diameters of 0.4, 0.8, and 1.2 cm, which of the following graphs best displays the comparison between blood pressure at each site of vasoconstriction and blood pressure in the normal region of the blood vessel leading to the site of vasoconstriction?

■ Normal blood pressure
□ Blood pressure at the site of vasoconstriction

F.
pressure (mmHg)
0.4 0.8 1.2
diameter of site of vasoconstriction (cm)

G.
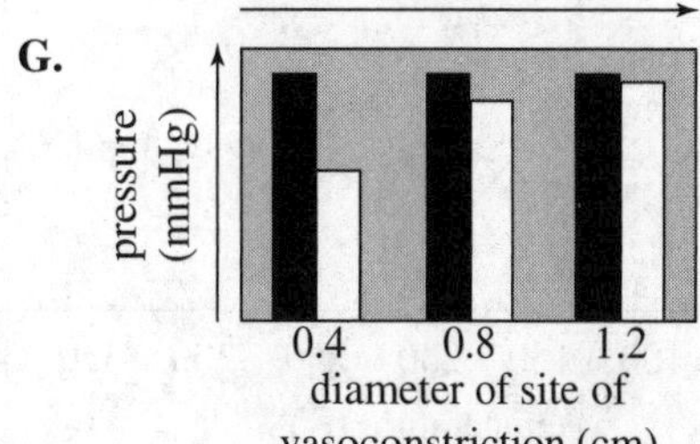

H.
pressure (mmHg)
0.4 0.8 1.2
diameter of site of vasoconstriction (cm)

J.
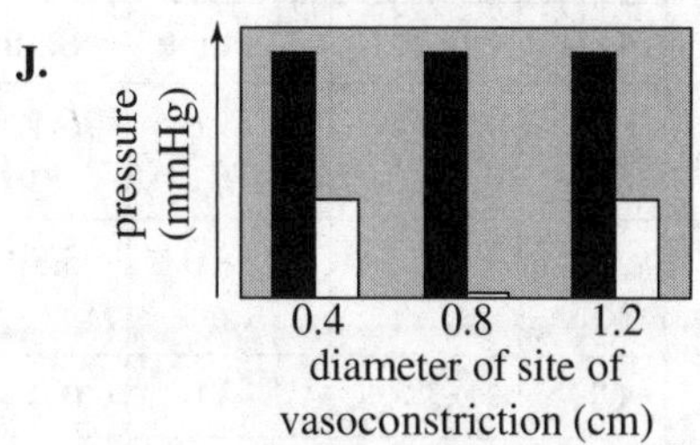

21. Suppose the normal blood pressure (without vasoconstriction) for the artificial heart at a constant volume of 500 mL and a rate of 90 beats per minute is 31 mmHg. Based on Table 2, which of the following, in mmHg, is closest to the blood pressure measured at a diameter of 0.8 cm at the site of vasoconstriction in Experiment 2 ?

A. 22
B. 28
C. 34
D. 40

Passage IV

There are four planets in our solar system called gas giants: Jupiter, Saturn, Uranus, and Neptune. They are so named because they are composed largely of gases rather than solids. Figure 1 shows how temperatures of the atmospheres of Jupiter, Neptune, and Saturn vary with altitude in relation to the cloud tops. Table 1 gives the composition of the planets in both relative abundance of gases and the altitude at which those gases are most abundant. Table 2 gives what the temperature at the cloud tops would be without greenhouse warming.

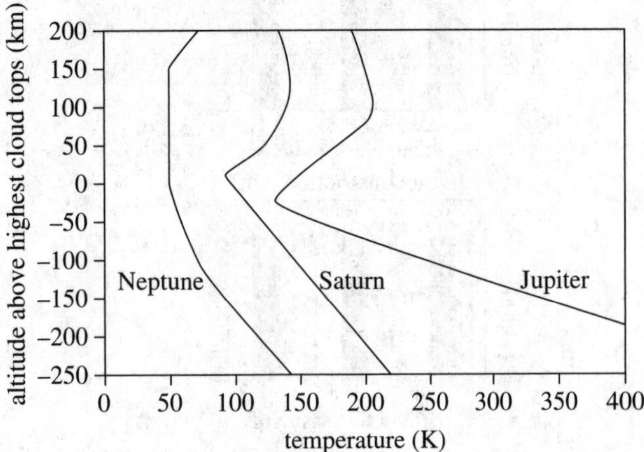

Figure 1

Table 2

Planet	Temperature at cloud tops without greenhouse warming (K)
Jupiter	100
Neptune	50
Saturn	25

Table 1

	Relative abundance (%)			Altitude above cloud tops where most abundant (km)		
Gas	Jupiter	Neptune	Saturn	Jupiter	Neptune	Saturn
H	86.1	79.0	96.1	–1,000 to –70,000	–10,000 to –23,000	–1,000 to –60,000
He	13.6	18.0	3.3	–500 to –1,000	–500 to –10,000	–500 to –900
CH_3	0.2	3.0	0.4	0 to 300	–100 to 0	0 to 200
NH_3	0.0045	0	0.0035	0 to –100	–	–50 to –200
H_2O vapor	0.0055	0	0.0065	–50 to –100	–	–200 to –300

22. According to Figure 1, the temperature of Neptune remains the same as altitude above the highest cloud tops increases from:

F. –250 km to –200 km.
G. –150 km to –50 km.
H. 0 km to 100 km.
J. 150 km to 200 km.

23. According to Figure 1, the temperature of Jupiter changes the most between:

A. –150 km and –50 km.
B. –50 km and 50 km.
C. 50 km and 100 km.
D. 100 km and 200 km.

24. Considering only the gases listed in Table 1, which gas is more abundant in the atmosphere of Jupiter than in the atmosphere of either Neptune or Saturn?

F. H
G. CH_3
H. NH_3
J. He

25. Based on Table 2, the average temperature at Saturn's cloud tops *without* greenhouse warming is how many degrees cooler than the temperature given in Figure 1 ?

A. 5 K
B. 25 K
C. 75 K
D. 150 K

26. Which of the following statements about H and He in the atmospheres of the 3 planets is supported by the data in Table 1 ?

F. Both Saturn and Neptune have a higher relative abundance of He than of H.
G. Both Saturn and Jupiter have a higher relative abundance of He than of H.
H. Both Jupiter and Neptune have an equivalent relative abundance of He and H.
J. Both Saturn and Neptune have a lower relative abundance of He than of H.

27. A researcher states that Neptune, Saturn, and Jupiter all exhibit greenhouse warming at the cloud tops. Does the information in the passage support this statement?

A. Yes; all three planets are between 25 K and 100 K warmer at the cloud tops than they would be without greenhouse warming.
B. Yes; all three planets are between 25 K and 100 K cooler at the cloud tops than they would be without greenhouse warming.
C. No; Neptune is 50 K warmer at the cloud tops than it would be without greenhouse warming.
D. No; Neptune is the same temperature at the cloud tops as it would be without greenhouse warming.

Passage V

Nuclear fission occurs when the *nucleus* (central core) of an atom splits into multiple parts. This splitting is accompanied by the release of a large amount of energy, as in nuclear weapons and nuclear power plants.

A chemical element that is prone to fission is said to be *radioactive*. Fission is often the result of the nucleus of a radioactive atom absorbing a *free neutron* (an uncharged nuclear particle). When a *fission event* occurs, the nucleus often splits into two new nuclei and produces free neutrons. This process generates the possibility of a chain reaction. If, on average, a fission event produces one neutron and that neutron causes another nucleus to fission, the reaction is said to be *critical*; that is, it will sustain itself, but not increase in magnitude. If one fission event releases more free neutrons than are required to initiate another fission event, the reaction is said to be *supercritical*; that is, it will sustain and increase in magnitude. If more neutrons are required to initiate a fission event than are released in fission, the reaction is said to be *subcritical*: the reaction will not sustain itself.

Many factors affect how many neutrons from each fission event will trigger another fission event. The most important factor is the mass (m) of the substance. The criticality of a substance also depends on the substance's purity, shape, density, temperature, and whether or not it is surrounded by a material that reflects neutrons.

In a nuclear weapon, a radioactive substance is made highly supercritical. One of the primary challenges in building a nuclear weapon is keeping the radioactive material subcritical prior to detonation, then upon detonation, keeping it supercritical for a long enough period of time for all of the material to fission before it is blown apart by the energy of the blast. A *fizzle* occurs when a nuclear weapon achieves supercriticality but is blown apart before all of the radioactive material fissions.

The first nuclear weapons were made of enriched uranium, or U-235. The density (ρ) of U-235 under normal conditions is 19.1 g/cm^3. For U-235 to attain a supercritical state, the product of its mass and density must exceed 10^6 g^2/cm^3. If it is assembled over too long a time (t), it will achieve slight supercriticality and then fizzle. Therefore, the speed of assembly (measured as t divided by ρ), must be less than 10^{-5} sec $\times$ cm^3/g (*Michelson's Criterion*).

Two schemes for the assembly of a supercritical amount of U-235 that avoid fizzle are discussed below.

Gun-Type Weapon

At one end of a tube, similar to a gun barrel, is a hollow, subcritical cylinder of U-235 with a mass of 48 kg; on the other end is a subcritical pellet of U-235 with a mass of 12 kg. The pellet is propelled by a small explosion down the tube and into the cylinder of U-235. The combined mass of the two pieces of U-235 is great enough to induce a supercritical state. Since the combined cylinder of U-235 is at or near normal density, the assembly process must be completed in less than 2×10^{-4} sec to meet Michelson's Criterion.

Implosion-Type Weapon

A 15-kg sphere of U-235 is surrounded by explosives. When the explosives are simultaneously detonated, the U-235 is compressed in order to achieve supercriticality. The explosives are designed to compress the U-235 to a density of approximately 70 g/cm^3 in less than 10^{-7} sec.

28. Scientists are trying to build a bomb using only 8 kg of U-235. Presently they can achieve a ρ of 150 g/cm^3 with $t = 10^{-2}$ sec. Which of the following changes would be the most likely to get the weapon to meet Michelson's Criterion?

F. Decrease both t and ρ
G. Decrease t and leave ρ the same
H. Increase t and decrease ρ
J. Increase t and leave ρ the same

29. For both types of weapon, avoiding fizzle is difficult because:

A. the mass of U-235 must be large.
B. 2 separate pieces of U-235 must be brought together.
C. U-235 is highly unstable.
D. of the speed with which the U-235 must be assembled.

30. Comparing the mass of uranium used in the two types of weapons reveals that:

F. the mass of U-235 used in the implosion-type weapon is less than the mass of U-235 used in the gun-type weapon.
G. the mass of U-235 used in the implosion-type weapon is greater than the mass of U-235 used in the gun-type weapon.
H. the mass of U-235 used in the implosion-type weapon is greater in some cases and less in some cases than the mass used in the gun-type weapon.
J. the mass of U-235 used in both weapons is approximately the same.

31. Both types of weapons use explosives in order to:

A. increase the heat of the U-235.
B. release the nuclear energy of the weapon from the confinement of the bomb's casing.
C. achieve supercriticality of U-235.
D. generate neutrons to start the chain reaction.

32. For an implosion-type weapon, when U-235 has reached supercriticality, to which of the following is the value of ρ closest?

F. 10^{-3} g/cm^3
G. 0.1 g/cm^3
H. 100 g/cm^3
J. 10^6 g/cm^3

33. In the implosion-type weapon, the explosives are used to:

A. trigger the first fission events.
B. heat the U-235 so it will become supercritical.
C. increase the density of U-235.
D. produce additional damage.

34. In order to achieve a supercritical state just before detonation, both methods:

F. increase the product of the mass and density of the U-235.
G. decrease the product of the mass and density of the U-235.
H. increase the amount of U-235 in the weapon.
J. decrease the time necessary for all the U-235 to fission.

Passage VI

A scientist studying hemoglobin investigated the impact of temperature and carbon dioxide (CO_2) partial pressures on the binding capacity of oxygen (O_2). The scientist observed the binding of oxygen to hemoglobin molecules as the partial pressure of oxygen was increased. The temperature and CO_2 were varied to identify their direct impact on the binding capacity of O_2.

Figure 1 displays the impact of changes in temperature on the binding (percent of hemoglobin saturated) of oxygen when the partial pressure of carbon dioxide is held constant. Figure 2 displays the impact of varying carbon dioxide partial pressures on oxygen binding when the temperature is held constant. Under normal conditions, the core body temperature is 37°C, and the carbon dioxide and oxygen partial pressures are 40 mmHg and 100 mmHg, respectively.

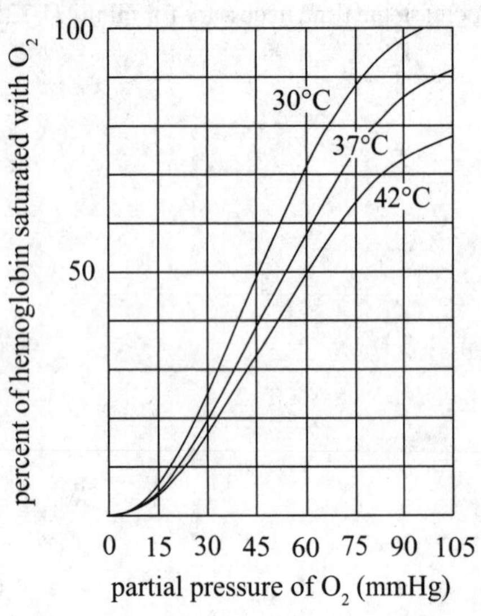

Figure 1

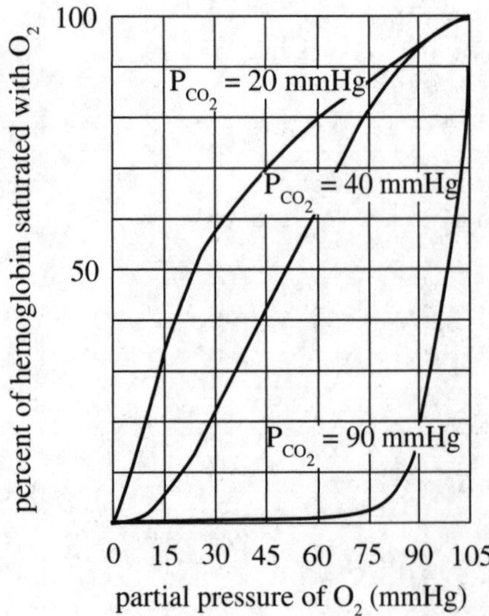

Figure 2

35. Assume the data in Figure 2 was collected at a constant temperature of 37° C. Based on the information in Figures 1 and 2, the data in Figure 1 was most likely collected when the P_{CO_2} was:

A. less than 20 mmHg.
B. between 20 and 40 mmHg.
C. between 40 and 90 mmHg.
D. greater than 90 mmHg.

36. According to Figure 1, if the temperature is 42°C, which of the following changes in partial pressure of oxygen will cause the least increase in the percent of hemoglobin saturated with O_2?

F. 0–15 mmHg
G. 15–30 mmHg
H. 30–45 mmHg
J. 45–60 mmHg

37. According to Figure 1, which of the following sets of temperature and partial pressure of oxygen results in the lowest hemoglobin saturation with oxygen?

	Temperature (°C)	Partial Pressure of Oxygen (mmHg)
A.	37	45
B.	37	60
C.	42	45
D.	42	60

38. According to Figure 1, if the partial pressure of oxygen is 100 mmHg and 65% of hemoglobin molecules are saturated with oxygen, then the core body temperature is most likely within which of the following ranges?

F. Less than 30°C
G. 30°C–37°C
H. 37°C–42°C
J. Greater than 42°C

39. Based on Figure 2, if an individual has 70% of his hemoglobin molecules saturated at a partial pressure of 75 mmHg of oxygen, then the individual's carbon dioxide partial pressure is most likely closest to which of the following?

A. 30 mmHg
B. 50 mmHg
C. 70 mmHg
D. 90 mmHg

40. According to Figure 2, at a CO_2 partial pressure of 90 mmHg, as the partial pressure of O_2 is increased from 45 mmHg to 90 mmHg, the percent of hemoglobin saturated with oxygen:

F. increases slowly, then increases more rapidly.
G. increases rapidly, then remains constant.
H. increases slowly, then decreases slowly.
J. decreases slowly, then increases rapidly.

Science Practice Section 1

Answers and Explanations

SCIENCE PRACTICE SECTION 1 ANSWERS

1. C
2. G
3. A
4. J
5. D
6. H
7. B
8. H
9. B
10. H
11. C
12. G
13. D
14. H
15. B
16. F
17. A
18. J
19. C
20. G
21. B
22. H
23. A
24. H
25. C
26. J
27. D
28. G
29. D
30. F
31. C
32. H
33. C
34. F
35. C
36. F
37. C
38. J
39. B
40. F

SCIENCE PRACTICE SECTION 1 EXPLANATIONS

Passage I

1. **C** The question asks why the 250,000-year-old layer of seabed was not included in the studies. To determine why a *layer of seabed* was included, look for those key words in the passage. Paragraph 2 states that *from each layer of seabed, the scientists randomly selected 100 complete, unbroken fossilized shells.* Nothing is mentioned in the passage about how far back radiocarbon dating is accurate, so (A) is incorrect. There is nothing to suggest that the scientists are interested only in a certain time period, so (B) can be eliminated. Choice (C) states that *accurate measurements could have been impossible to obtain* and one reason is that only *fragments of twelve turtle shells but no complete, intact shells were found,* so keep it. The scientists are not trying to *determine the color of the shells,* so eliminate (D). The correct answer is (C).

2. **G** The question asks which picture most accurately depicts *the shells with the M-M-m-m-M band of scutes,* according to the descriptions in Study 1. Look at the description of Study 1. It states that *all of the living turtles had a distinct band of hexagonal scutes (boney plates) running the length of their shells* and that *scutes extending greater than ⅛ of the length of the shell were labeled major (M), where the scutes extending less than or equal to ⅛ of the length of the shell were labeled minor (m).* This means that the uppercase *M* represents the large hexagonal scutes and the lowercase *m* represents the small hexagonal scutes. Look for the answer that shows two large hexagons, followed by two small hexagons, followed by one large hexagon, as described by the pattern given in the question stem. Eliminate (F), (H), and (J). The correct answer is (G).

3. **A** The question asks what *the average shell surface area* was for *turtle shells that were 80,000 years old,* according to Study 2. Look at the third graph in Figure 2 of Study 2. The *age of shells* is located on the *x*-axis. Find 80,000 years old and draw a line up to the graph line. Next, draw a horizontal line to the *y*-axis. The average shell surface area is about 670 cm^2. The correct answer is (A).

4. **J** The question asks what *the scute pattern percents* would be for each group of shells if in Study 1 *scientists had found another seabed layer with fossilized shells that were radiocarbon dated and found to be 86,000 years old.* Look at Table 1 in Study 1 which shows *the percents of shells* with each of the three different *scute patterns.* Look at the left-most column and draw a line straight across the graph where the data for the 86,000-year-old shells would belong, between 85,000- and 87,000-year-old shells. Notice that the line falls between 21 and 30 percent of shells with the M-m-M-M-m pattern. Eliminate (F), (G), and (H) because the percent with that pattern is greater than 30. Keep (J) because the percentage is 26, which is in range. Since there is no distinct trend in that first column, check to make sure that the percentages from the other columns are also appropriate. In the column M-M-m-m-M, 69% falls between 67% and 72%; in the column M-m-M-m-M, 5% falls between 3% and 7%. The correct answer is (J).

5. **D** The question asks to compare the *average shell surface area* and the *average bridge height* from *currently living* turtles to turtles who *lived 120,000 years ago.* Since the question asks about Study 2, refer to Figure 2 to find the answer. Start with the average shell surface area in the bottom graph. At the point for 120,000 years ago, the average shell surface area was about 650 cm^2. Currently, at 0 years ago, the average shell surface area is closer to 640 cm^2. Therefore, average shell surface area has *decreased.* Use this information to eliminate (A) and (C). Now examine average bridge height in the upper graph. At the point for 120,000 years ago, the average bridge height was about 2.1 cm. Currently, at 0 years ago, the average bridge height is about 2.5 cm. Therefore, average bridge height has *increased.* Eliminate (B). The correct answer is (D).

6. **H** The question asks about the differences between Study 1 and Study 2. Read through the answers and look for false statements to help eliminate incorrect choices. Choices (G) and (J) claim that *the environment in which turtles live* was examined in Study 2. This is false, as environments were not examined in either of the studies. Eliminate (G) and (J). Notice that the remaining choices are opposites and that one of them must therefore be correct. Refer back to the tables and figures for each study to help find the answer. Study 1 examined the *different patterns of scutes on turtle shells,* while Study 2 examined *2 characteristics regarding the shape and size of turtle shells.* The only answer choice that matches this information is (H). The correct answer is (H).

7. **B** The question asks about *average shell surface area,* so refer to the bottom graph of Figure 2. For this question, compare the trend in average shell surface area between 100,000 years ago and 80,000 years ago. At 100,000 years ago, the average shell surface area was approximately 675 cm^2. From this point, it continues to increase sharply until about 90,000 years ago when it abruptly begins to decrease. By 80,000 years ago, the average shell surface area was approximately 670 cm^2. Since average shell surface area first *increased* and then *decreased,* the correct answer is (B).

Passage II

8. **H** The question asks about the offspring produced in Analysis 4. The passage states that *phenotype refers to the observable characteristics of a trait,* which is the blood type in this case. In Analysis 4, the phenotypes of the parents were type-A and type-B. Meanwhile, the phenotypes of the offspring were type-AB and type-B. Since some of the offspring have the same phenotype as a parent (type-B), eliminate (G) and (J), which contradict this information. Since the remaining choices ask for a comparison between the genotypes of the parents and their offspring, it is important to figure out genotypes for both parents and their offspring. The study states that the type-B parent is I^BI^B, but the choices in Table 1 indicate that the type-B offspring can either be I^BI^B or I^BI^O. All of the offspring must have inherited one I^B allele from their type-B parent. However, since the other parent is type-A, the only alleles these offspring could have inherited from their type-A parent are I^A or I^O. Accordingly, all of the offspring are either I^AI^B (type-AB) or I^BI^O (type-B). Since the two different types of offspring all have different genotypes as both of their parents, eliminate (F). The correct answer is (H).

9. **B** The question asks for the *ratio of blood types containing at least one I^A allele to the blood types containing at least one I^B allele produced in Analysis 3*. Look at Analysis 3. There are two types that contain I^A: type-A (25%) and type-AB (25%). Together, they make up 50% of the offspring. There are two types that contain I^B, type-B (25%) and type-AB (25%). Together, they make up 50% of the offspring. Because they each represent 50% of the offspring, it is a 1:1 ratio. The correct answer is (B).

10. **H** The question asks which genotypes would exhibit *codominance*. Since there is no information about *codominance* in the table, look for the key word *codominance* in the text of the passage. The second paragraph says, *when an individual has one I^A and one I^B allele, this individual will have type-AB blood, due to the codominance of the I^A and I^B alleles*. Choice (H) contains I^AI^B, which is type-AB blood. The correct answer is (H).

11. **C** The question asks which genotypes are needed *to produce only offspring with AB blood*. Since there is no information about *offspring* in Table 1, look for the key word *offspring* in the text. Paragraph 1 states that *the blood type of an offspring is determined by the blood types of its parents* and that *each parent contributes a single allele to its offspring*. Therefore, the offspring would need to inherit an I^A allele from one parent and an I^B allele from the other. Eliminate (A) because it is possible for the offspring to inherit an I^A allele from each parent, making its blood type-A. Eliminate both (B) and (D) because they each contain the I^O allele. Choice (C) contains a parent with only I^A alleles and a parent with only I^B alleles, so its offspring would inherit one I^A and one I^B, making its blood type-AB. The correct answer is (C).

12. **G** The question asks about the genotypes of *the offspring...from Analysis 1* that were used in Analysis 3. Look at Analysis 1. The explanation says that *one thousand males with type-O blood were mated with 1,000 females with type-AB blood*. Look at Table 1 to find possible genotypes for these blood types. The males with type-O blood must have had I^OI^O genotype. The females with type-AB blood must have had I^AI^B genotype. As offspring receive one gene from each parent, mating would produce offspring with I^AI^O and I^BI^O genotypes. The correct answer is (G).

13. **D** The question asks which analyses produced offspring that *had 1 allele for type-O blood*. Look at Table 1. Table 1 shows which alleles are present in each blood type. Type-O blood has a genotype of I^OI^O, so all offspring from a type-O parent will receive an allele for type-O blood. Analysis 1 and Analysis 2 both involve a type-O parent, so eliminate (B). Since the parents in Analysis 3 came from Analysis 1, the genotypes of the parents both had to include a type-O allele: I^AI^O and I^BI^O. Since there is only one parental type-A allele and one parental type-B allele, the type-A and type-B offspring in Analysis 3 must also be I^AI^O and I^BI^O, respectively. Eliminate both (A) and (C) because they do not include Analysis 3. The correct answer is (D).

14. **H** The question asks about *the number of offspring with type-B blood* that would have been produced in Analysis 3 had there been a total of 300 offspring. Look at the percentages of offspring produced in Analysis 3. According to the data, 25% of the offspring would be type-B. 25% of 300 is 75. The correct answer is (H).

Passage III

15. **B** The question asks which volume of blood would lead to a %ΔBP value of 9.0 in Experiment 3. Look at the results of Experiment 3. Table 3 shows the volume of blood pumped and the measured values of %ΔBP. As the volume of blood pumped increases, %ΔBP also increases. Find where 9.0 would be located, between 8.8 and 9.3. The volume of blood pumped would be between 450 and 500 at this point. Only (B) is between 450 and 500. Eliminate (A), (C) and (D). The correct answer is (B).

16. **F** The question asks what the %ΔBP would most likely be if the rate of the artificial heartbeat used in Experiment 1 had been less than 60 beats per minute. Look at the results of Experiment 1. The data in Table 1 shows the rate of the artificial heartbeat and the resulting %ΔBP. As the rate increases, the %ΔBP also increases. At 60 beats per minute, the %ΔBP was 1.2. If the beats per minute had been less than 60, the %ΔBP would be less than 1.2. The correct answer is (F).

17. **A** The question asks how the increased rate of the artificial heartbeat affects the %ΔBP, according to Experiment 1. Look at the results of Experiment 1. Table 1 shows that as rate of artificial heartbeat increases, the %ΔBP also increases. Eliminate both (C) and (D) because they state that %ΔBP decreases. Both (A) and (B) compare the *velocity of blood through the site of vasoconstriction*. There is no information about *velocity* in Table 1, so look for the key word *velocity* in the passage. According to the second paragraph, *the higher the velocity of the blood flow through the site of vasoconstriction, the lower the blood pressure at that site.* Since %ΔBP is calculated by subtracting the pressure at the site of vasoconstriction from the normal blood pressure, %ΔBP increases with a lower pressure at the site of vasoconstriction. Thus, an increase in velocity causes an increase in %ΔBP. Eliminate (B) because it states that the velocity decreases. The correct answer is (A).

18. **J** The question asks about the relative *diameters* of three hypothetical *regions of the same blood vessel*, according to *information in the passage about blood flow*. Look for the key words *blood flow* and *diameter* in the passage. According to paragraph 2, *the diameter of the blood vessel at the site of vasoconstriction is less than the diameter of the normal blood vessel, so blood flow has a higher velocity through this narrow site.* As a result, the region with the highest velocity must have the smallest diameter. Look at the table presented in the question. The region with the highest velocity is location B, so location B must have the smallest diameter. The only graphic which accurately places location B in the region with the smallest diameter is (J). The correct answer is (J).

19. **C** The question asks for the *diameter of the site of vasoconstriction in the blood vessel section used in Experiment 3*, according to the results of Experiments 1 and 2. Look at the description of Experiment 3 and notice that *a constant rate of 90 beats per minute* was used. Look at the results of Experiment 1. According to Table 1, the %ΔBP of the blood pumped at 90 beats per minute is 9.3. Now look at the results of Experiment 2, which shows the diameter relative to the %ΔBP. According to Table 2, when the %ΔBP is 9.3, the diameter is 0.8. The correct answer is (C).

20. **G** The question asks which graph most accurately displays the relationship between blood pressure at three different sites of vasoconstriction, with three different diameters, and the blood pressure within a normal region of blood vessel, according to Experiment 2. Look at Table 2. As the *diameter of site of vasoconstriction* increases, %Δ*BP* decreases. According to the %Δ*BP* formula, as blood pressure increases, %Δ*BP* decreases. Therefore, as the *diameter of site of vasoconstriction* increases, blood pressure also increases. Look at the graphs in each answer choice. The *diameter of site of vasoconstriction,* located along the *x*-axis increases from left to right. Choice (F) shows pressure decreasing as diameter increases. This is the opposite relationship; eliminate (F). Choice (G) shows pressure increasing as diameter increases; keep it. Eliminate (H) because as diameter increases, pressure stays constant. Also, eliminate (J) because it shows that as the diameter increases, pressure decreases and then increases. The correct answer is (G).

21. **B** The question asks about the blood pressure of the artificial heart used in Experiment 2. The question states that under the conditions used in Experiment 2, the heart has a *normal blood pressure (without vasoconstriction) of 31 mmHg.* The question asks what the blood pressure measured at a site of vasoconstriction with a diameter of 0.8 cm must have been. According to the passage, *the blood pressure in the site of vasoconstriction is less than the blood pressure in the normal blood vessel.* Using this information, eliminate (C) and (D). To determine how much the blood pressure would decrease by, look at Table 2. A vasoconstriction of 0.8 cm would result in a %Δ*BP* of 9.3. This means that the blood pressure will decrease by approximately 10%. Since 10% of 31 mmHg is about 3 mmHg, the resulting blood pressure would be about 28 mmHg. The correct answer is (B).

Passage IV

22. **H** The question asks at which range of *altitude above the highest cloud tops* Neptune's temperature remains the same, according to Figure 1. Look at Figure 1. The temperature is located on the *x*-axis and the altitude above the highest cloud tops is located on the *y*-axis. Look at the curve representing Neptune and locate the range of each answer choice. From –250 km to –200 km, temperature decreases, so eliminate (F). From –150 km to –50 km, temperature decreases, so eliminate (G). From 0 km to 100 km, temperature remains constant at 50 K; keep (H). From 150 km to 200 km, temperature increases, so eliminate (J). The correct answer is (H).

23. **A** The question asks which range of altitudes has the largest temperature change on Jupiter, according to Figure 1. Look at Figure 1 and use the values in the answer choices to determine the temperature change within each range of altitudes. Choice (A) shows a range of –150 km to –50 km. Between those altitudes, the temperature on Jupiter ranges from about 150 K to 300 K, a difference of 150 K. Choice (B) shows a range of –50 km to 50 km. Between those altitudes, the temperature on Jupiter ranges from about 150 K to 200 K, a difference of 50 K. This temperature change is smaller than that of (A), so eliminate (B). Choice (C) shows a range of 50 km to 100 km. Between

those altitudes, the temperature on Jupiter ranges from about 200 K to 210 K, a difference of 10 K, which is smaller than that of (A), so eliminate (C). Choice (D) shows a range of 100 km to 200 km. Between those altitudes, the temperature on Jupiter ranges from about 190 K to 200 K, a difference of 10 K, so eliminate (D). The largest temperature change occurred in the range of altitudes in (A). The correct answer is (A).

24. **H** The question asks *which gas is more abundant in the atmosphere of Jupiter than in the atmospheres of either Neptune or Saturn,* according to Table 1. Look at Table 1. Use the answer choices to find the *relative abundance* of each gas on Jupiter and compare the value to that found on the other two planets. The amount of H is greater on Saturn than on Jupiter, so eliminate (F). The amount of CH_3 is greater on both Neptune and Saturn than on Jupiter, so eliminate (G). The amount of NH_3 is greatest on Jupiter, so keep (H). The amount of He is greatest on Neptune, so eliminate (J). The correct answer is (H).

25. **C** The question asks for the difference between *the average temperature at Saturn's cloud tops without greenhouse warming,* given in Table 2, and *the temperature given in Figure 1.* Look at Table 2. The *temperature at cloud tops* on Saturn is 25 K. Look at Figure 1. Find the curve that represents the temperature on Saturn. Altitude is located on the *y*-axis; find 0 km above cloud tops. Draw a line to meet Saturn's curve, and then draw a line down to the *x*-axis to determine the temperature at the cloud tops, which is 100 K. The difference between 25 K and 100 K is 75 K, (C). The correct answer is (C).

26. **J** The question asks which statement about H and He is supported by the data in Table 1. Look at Table 1 and eliminate any answers that contradict the given data. Choice (F) states that *both Saturn and Neptune have a higher relative abundance of He than of H.* The relative abundance of He on Saturn is 3.3%, and the relative abundance of H on Saturn is 96.1%. The relative abundance of He is not higher than that of H, so eliminate (F). Choice (G) also states that Saturn has *a higher relative abundance of He than of H,* so eliminate (G). Choice (H) states that *both Jupiter and Neptune have an equivalent relative abundance of He and H.* The relative abundance of He on Jupiter is 13.6% and on Neptune it is 18%. They are not equivalent, so eliminate (H). Choice (J) is consistent with the data in Table 1. The correct answer is (J).

27. **D** The question asks if the passage supports the statement that *Neptune, Saturn, and Jupiter all exhibit greenhouse warming at the cloud tops.* The cloud top temperatures for the 3 planets without greenhouse warming are 100 K for Jupiter, 50 K for Neptune, and 25 K for Saturn. Now look at Figure 1 to find the actual temperatures for the 3 planets at the cloud tops. Draw a horizontal line across the 0 km point on the graph. Find the points of intersection for each planet. The cloud top temperatures for the 3 planets are 50 K for Neptune, 100 K for Saturn, and 150 K for Jupiter. Notice that the temperature on Neptune is the same in both Figure 1 and Table 2. Therefore, the statement in the question is *not* supported by the passage. Eliminate (A) and (B). The reason the statement is false is because Neptune's observed temperature remains the same as that without greenhouse warming. The correct answer is (D).

Passage V

28. **G** The question asks which change in t and ρ would be *most likely to get the weapon to meet Michelson's Criterion.* Look for the key words *Michelson's Criterion* in the passage. According to paragraph 5, *the speed of assembly (measured as t divided by* ρ*), must be less than* 10^{-5} *sec ×* cm^3/g *(Michelson's Criterion).* In order to make $\frac{t}{\rho}$ less than a particular number, t would have to decrease or ρ would have to increase. Eliminate (H) and (J) because they both state *increase t.* Eliminate (F) because it states *decrease both t and* ρ. The correct answer is (G).

29. **D** The question asks why *avoiding fizzle is difficult.* Look for the key word *fizzle* in the passage. According to paragraph 4, *a fizzle occurs when a nuclear weapon achieves supercriticality but is blown apart before all of the radioactive material fissions.* This explains what a fizzle is but it does not mention why avoiding it may be difficult. According to paragraph 5, *if [the weapon] is assembled over too long a time (t), it will achieve slight supercriticality and then fizzle.* Accordingly, if the assembly process takes too long, it may fizzle. Eliminate (A), (B), and (C) because time and speed are not mentioned. The correct answer is (D).

30. **F** The question asks how the mass of uranium used in the two types of weapons differs. Look for the key word *mass* in both weapon types. According to paragraph 7, 48 kg and 12 kg of uranium is used for the *gun-type weapon.* According to paragraph 8, 15 kg of uranium is used for the *implosion-type weapon.* The mass of uranium used in the *gun-type weapon* is greater than that used in the *implosion-type weapon.* Choice (F) is consistent with this, so keep it. Eliminate (G) because it states that the mass *used in the implosion-type weapon is greater than the mass...used in the gun-type weapon,* which is the opposite of what the text indicates. Eliminate (H) because it suggests that the relative mass of uranium used in each weapon changes, which is not stated. Eliminate (J) because it states that the mass of uranium used in each weapon is approximately equal. The correct answer is (F).

31. **C** The question asks why both *weapons use explosives.* Look for the key word *explosive* under each weapon type. According to paragraph 7, an explosion propels a pellet of uranium down a tube in order to combine it with the cylinder of uranium *to induce a supercritical state.* According to paragraph 8, *when the explosives are simultaneously detonated, the U-235 is compressed in order to achieve supercriticality.* Therefore, both weapons use explosives in order to achieve supercriticality. Eliminate (A), (B), and (D) because none of them mentions *supercriticality.* The correct answer is (C).

32. **H** The question asks which value is closest to ρ *when U-235 has reached supercriticality for an implosion-type weapon.* Look for ρ in the text. It does not appear in the *implosion-type weapon,* so look in the introduction. Paragraph 5 indicates that ρ is *density.* Now look for *density* under the *implosion-type weapon.* According to paragraph 8, *in order to achieve supercriticality,* U-235 is compressed *to a density of approximately 70* g/cm^3. Eliminate (F) and (G) because they are too small. Keep (H) because the value is close to 70. Eliminate (J) because the value is too large. The correct answer is (H).

33. **C** The question asks what *the explosives are used* for *in the implosion-type weapon.* Look for the key word *explosives* in the text, under the *implosion-type weapon.* According to the text, *the explosives are designed to compress the U-235 to a density of approximately 70 g/cm³.* Eliminate (A) because the text does not state that the explosives are used as a trigger. Eliminate (B) because the text does not mention heating the U-235. Keep (C) because compression increases density. Eliminate (D) because the text does not mention producing *additional damage.* The correct answer is (C).

34. **F** The question asks how both methods of creating a nuclear weapon *achieve a supercritical state just before detonation.* Look for the key words *supercritical state* in the passage. According to paragraph 5, *for U-235 to attain a supercritical state, the product of its mass and density must exceed 10^6 g²/cm³.* To increase the product of mass and density, either mass or density must be increased. Look for evidence of this under each weapon method's subheading. According to paragraph 7, *the combined mass of the two pieces of U-235 is great enough to induce a supercritical state,* which means the mass is increased and therefore the product of the mass and density will also increase, which causes supercriticality. According to paragraph 8, *the explosives are designed to compress the U-235 to a density of approximately 70 g/cm³.* If something is compressed, its density increases and this will increase the product of its mass and density, causing a supercritical state. Keep (F) because it is consistent with the descriptions of both weapons. Eliminate (G) because it presents the opposite. Eliminate (H) because increasing the *amount* of U-235 will not cause supercriticality. Eliminate (J) because decreasing the *time* will not cause supercriticality. The correct answer is (F).

Passage VI

35. **C** The question asks about the P_{CO_2} of Figure 1, given that the values in Figure 2 were obtained at a temperature of 37°C. To answer this, start by examining the curve for 37°C in Figure 1. Notice that at its highest point (when the partial pressure of O_2 is at 105 mmHg), the percentage of hemoglobin saturated with O_2 is slightly greater than 90%. Also notice that at an O_2 partial pressure of 60 mmHg, the percentage of hemoglobin saturated with O_2 is slightly less than 60%. Compare this curve and these points to the curves in Figure 2. While the 37°C curve in Figure 1 most closely resembles the 40 mmHg P_{CO_2} curve in Figure 2, the values noted in the 37°C curve are slightly less. This indicates that the P_{CO_2} at 37°C must be somewhere between 40 mmHg and 90 mmHg. The correct answer is (C).

36. **F** The question asks which change *in the partial pressure of oxygen will cause the least increase in the percent of hemoglobin saturated with O_2* at 42°C, according to Figure 1. Look at Figure 1. The *partial pressure of O_2* is on the *x*-axis and the *percent of hemoglobin saturated with O_2* is on the *y*-axis. The lowest curve represents conditions at 42°C. Look up each range of partial pressure in the answer choices to find *the percent of hemoglobin saturated with O_2*. In order to evaluate (F), find 0–15 mmHg on the *x*-axis; the 42°C curve increases from 0 percent to about 5 *percent of hemoglobin saturated with O_2*. This is an increase of 5%. To evaluate (G), find 15–30 mmHg on the *x*-axis; the 42°C curve increases from 5 percent to about 15 *percent of hemoglobin saturated with O_2*. This is

an increase of 10%. Eliminate (G) because the increase is greater than that in (F). To evaluate (H), find 30–45 mmHg on the *x*-axis; the 42°C curve increases from 15 percent to about 32 *percent of hemoglobin saturated with* O_2. This is an increase of 17%. Eliminate (H) because the increase is greater than that in (F). To evaluate (J), find 45–60 mmHg on the *x*-axis; the 42°C curve increases from 32 percent to about 50 *percent of hemoglobin saturated with* O_2. This is an increase of 18%. Eliminate (J) because the increase is greater than that in (F). The correct answer is (F).

37. **C** The question asks which conditions would result in the *lowest hemoglobin saturation with oxygen,* according to Figure 1. First, look at Figure 1 to determine the relationship between hemoglobin saturation and temperature. At any given partial pressure, greater than zero, the *percent of hemoglobin saturated with* O_2 decreases as temperature increases. Eliminate (A) and (B) because a temperature of 37° always has a higher percent of hemoglobin saturated with O_2 than a temperature of 42° does. Next, look at Figure 1 to determine the relationship between the partial pressure of oxygen and *hemoglobin saturation with* O_2. At 45 mmHg, the *percent of hemoglobin saturated with* O_2 is lower for all temperatures than at 60 mmHg. Eliminate (D). The correct answer is (C).

38. **J** The question asks what the core body temperature would most likely be if the *partial pressure of oxygen is 100 mmHg and 65% of hemoglobin molecules are saturated with oxygen,* according to Figure 1. Look at Figure 1. Find 100 mmHg on the *x*-axis and draw a vertical line to the top of the graph. Find 65 percent on the *y*-axis and draw a horizontal line across the graph at this value. Circle the intersection of these two lines. This point is below the 42°C curve. Compare the 30°C, 37°C, and 42°C curves. As the temperature increases, the curve location gets lower, so the temperature at this point on the graph would be higher than 42°C. The correct answer is (J).

39. **B** The question asks what the carbon dioxide partial pressure would be closest to if 70% of *hemoglobin molecules are saturated at a partial pressure of 75 mmHg of oxygen,* according to Figure 2. Look at Figure 2. Find 70% on the *y*-axis and draw a horizontal line to the other side of the graph. Find 75 mmHg on the *x*-axis and draw a vertical line to the top of the graph. Circle the intersection of this point. The carbon dioxide partial pressure increases from the left-hand line to the right-hand line. The intersecting point is slightly to the right of the 40 mmHg curve and so therefore must be slightly larger than 40. Eliminate (A) because it is smaller than 40. Keep (B) because it is slightly larger than 40. Eliminate (C) and (D) because they are too large. The correct answer is (B).

40. **F** The question asks how the percentage of hemoglobin saturated with O_2 changes as the partial pressure of oxygen increases from 45 mmHg to 90 mmHg for the P_{CO_2} = 90 mmHg in Figure 2. Go to Figure 2 and locate the curve for P_{CO_2} = 90 mmHg. Follow the curve and notice that the curve first increases very slowly until a partial pressure of about 75 mmHg of O_2, at which the curve begins to increase more rapidly. This trend is best described in (F). The correct answer is (F).

Science Practice Section 2

SCIENCE TEST

35 Minutes—40 Questions

DIRECTIONS: There are six passages in the following section. Each passage is followed by several questions. After reading a passage, choose the best answer to each question and blacken the corresponding oval on your answer document. You may refer to the passages as often as necessary.

You are NOT permitted to use a calculator on this test.

Passage I

In agriculture, soils can be classified based on *mineral content* (the amount of various metals present in the soil), and *organic content* (the percent of soil volume occupied by material made by living organisms). Ideal concentrations of various minerals are given in parts per million (*ppm*) in Table 1. If the concentrations of different minerals, relative to their ideal concentrations, are all similar to each other, the soil is said to be *well defined.* If the concentrations of different minerals in a soil vary widely relative to each other, the soil is said to be *poorly defined.*

Table 1

Mineral	Ideal concentration (ppm)
Nitrogen	22
Phosphorus	14
Potassium	129
Chloride	12
Sulfur	88
Iron	6.9
Manganese	2.7

Study 1

Soil was taken from 5 different farms to a laboratory. The soils were *desiccated* (all water was removed), and a 1 L sample of each soil was prepared. In order to make sure that no minerals were trapped within the organic matter of a soil, the organic matter of each soil was burned by heating the soil to 500°C for 20 minutes. The ash of the organic matter was removed and the remaining soil analyzed for the concentration of various minerals. The results are shown, as percent of ideal concentration, in Table 2.

Table 2

Mineral	Concentration of minerals (% of ideal concentration)				
	Farm 1	Farm 2	Farm 3	Farm 4	Farm 5
Nitrogen	89	112	160	78	210
Phosphorus	76	19	212	94	34
Chloride	124	106	64	87	65
Sulfur	290	97	189	102	112
Iron	57	26	73	91	165
Manganese	86	45	89	97	109

Study 2

To determine the percentage of the mass of each soil composed of organic matter, the above procedure was repeated, with the soil weighed before being heated to 500°C and after having the ash removed. The number of live cells (bacteria, fungi, etc.) in a cubic millimeter of each soil was determined by microscopic analysis. The results are presented in Table 3.

Table 3

Farm	% organic matter	# living cells per mm^3
1	7.1	2,964
2	8.9	3,920
3	4.8	1,642
4	6.6	2,672
5	18.9	9,467

1. Based on Table 1 and Table 2, the concentration, in ppm, of sulfur measured in the soil of Farm 1 was closest to:

   A. 88 ppm.
   B. 170 ppm.
   C. 255 ppm.
   D. 290 ppm.

2. Soils with more living cells per mm^3 generally consume more oxygen than soils with fewer living cells. Based on this information, the soil of which farm would be expected to consume the most oxygen?

   F. Farm 1
   G. Farm 2
   H. Farm 3
   J. Farm 5

3. If, in Study 2, before and after heating a soil sample to 500ºC for 20 minutes and removing the ash, the mass of the sample was approximately the same, which of the following is the most reasonable conclusion?

   A. There was little or no water in the soil.
   B. There was a large quantity of water in the soil.
   C. There was little or no organic matter in the soil.
   D. There was little or no mineral content in the soil.

4. In Study 2, before heating the sample to 500ºC, it was necessary for the scientists to desiccate the soil in order to ensure that:

   F. the water was not mistaken for a mineral.
   G. the water was not consumed by the living cells.
   H. it was possible to count live cells by making sure the soil didn't stick together.
   J. the mass of the water was not mistaken for organic matter.

5. Based on Study 2, if the scientists took a soil sample from another farm, and the number of living cells per mm^3 was determined to be 2,100, the % organic matter in that soil would most likely be:

   A. less than 4.8.
   B. between 4.8 and 6.6.
   C. between 6.6 and 7.1.
   D. greater than 7.1.

6. Beans grow fastest in soils with high nitrogen and iron levels. If all other growth factors were equal, then based on the results of Study 1, which of the farms would be expected to produce the fastest-growing beans?

   F. Farm 2
   G. Farm 3
   H. Farm 4
   J. Farm 5

7. The soil of which of the farms would likely be considered the most well defined, based on the information in Study 1 ?

   A. Farm 1
   B. Farm 2
   C. Farm 3
   D. Farm 4

Passage II

Rock candy was made by putting a mixture of 180°F water and an amount of sugar (S1) into an apparatus shown in Figure 1, inserting a string through the top, and allowing the mixture to stand and cool. The internal container was made of glass, and the external container was made of plastic.

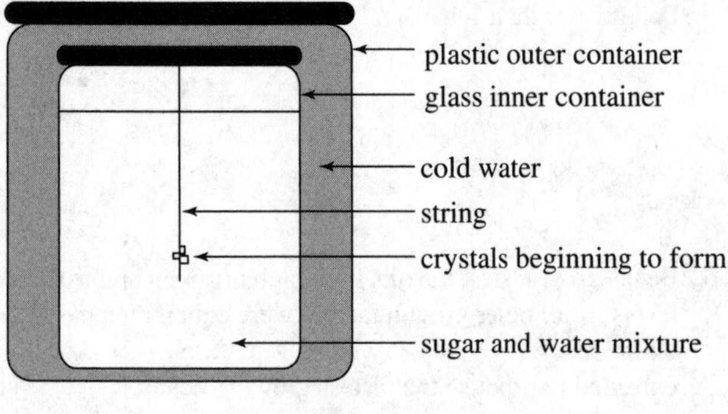

Figure 1

Figure 2 shows how the temperature of S1 and the temperature of the cold water in the plastic outer container varied with time as the mixture was allowed to stand.

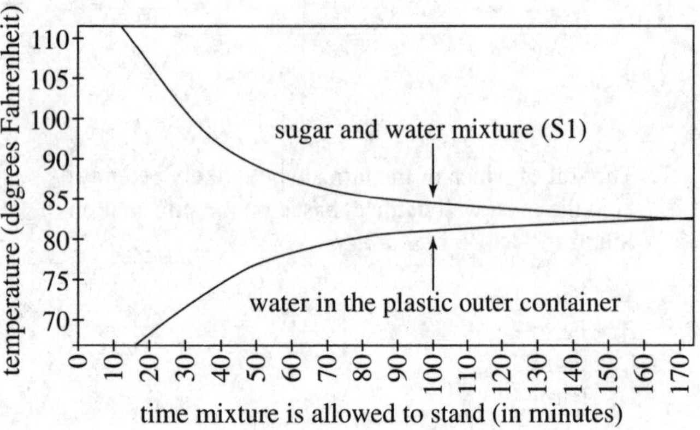

Figure 2

According to the *Second Law of Thermodynamics*, as the temperature of S1 *decreases*, the orderliness of the atoms in the solution must *increase*. This is why crystals form on the string, creating rock candy. Because of the Second Law of Thermodynamics, temperature of the sugar and water mixture can be monitored to measure orderliness of the atoms in the mixture. Two other sugar and water mixtures (S2 and S3) were monitored under standing conditions the same as those used for S1.

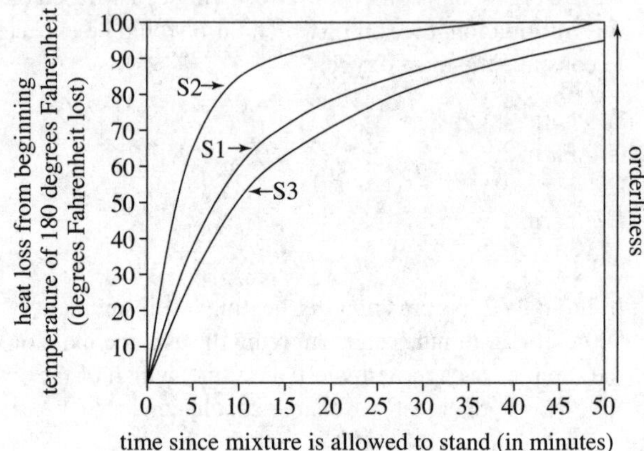

Figure 3

8. According to Figure 3, for S3, the heat lost from the beginning temperature of 180°F after being allowed to stand for 30 minutes is *closest* to which of the following?

   F. 10° Fahrenheit
   G. 50° Fahrenheit
   H. 80° Fahrenheit
   J. 100° Fahrenheit

9. According to Figures 2 and 3, as the temperature of the water in the plastic outer container increased, the heat loss from the beginning temperature of 180°F for S1:

A. decreased only.
B. increased only.
C. decreased, and then increased.
D. increased, and then decreased.

10. An additional sugar and water mixture (S4) was monitored under conditions identical to those used to gather the data in Figure 3. The heat lost after being allowed to stand 5 minutes was 50°F. At 5 minutes of standing time, how does the orderliness of the atoms in S4 compare with the orderliness of the atoms in mixtures S1, S2, and S3 ?

F. The orderliness of S4 was greater than the orderliness of S1, S2, and S3.
G. The orderliness of S4 was less than the orderliness of S1, S2, and S3.
H. The orderliness of S4 was greater than the orderliness of S2 and S3, but less than the orderliness of S1.
J. The orderliness of S4 was greater than the orderliness of S1 and S3, but less than the orderliness of S2.

11. Based on Figure 1, which of the following best explains the trends shown in Figure 2? In sum, as the time the mixture was allowed to stand increased, the heat was conducted by the:

A. glass inner container from the sugar and water mixture to the water in the plastic outer container.
B. glass inner container from the water in the plastic outer container to the sugar and water mixture.
C. plastic outer container from the sugar and water mixture to the string.
D. plastic outer container from the string to the sugar and water mixture.

12. Rock candy begins to form when the temperature of the sugar and water mixture has lost 100°F from its beginning temperature. Based on Figure 3, which mixture, if any, would begin to form rock candy first?

F. S1
G. S2
H. S3
J. All mixtures would begin to form rock candy at the same time.

13. *Thermal conductivity* is a measure of the rate at which a material transfers heat. Adding solutes such as sugar or salt increases the thermal conductivity of an aqueous solution. Which of the following solutions likely has the *lowest* concentration of sugar?

A. S1
B. S2
C. S3
D. All three solutions have the same concentration of sugar.

Passage III

The *Citric cycle* is an essential process used to transform carbohydrates, lipids, and proteins into energy in aerobic organisms. If yeast is unable to produce *succinate*, it cannot survive. The Citric cycle steps leading to the creation of succinate in yeast are shown in Figure 1. Each step in this cycle is catalyzed by an enzyme, which is essential to overcome the energy barrier between reactant and product. In the first step, Enzyme 1 is the enzyme, citrate is the reactant, and isocitrate is the product.

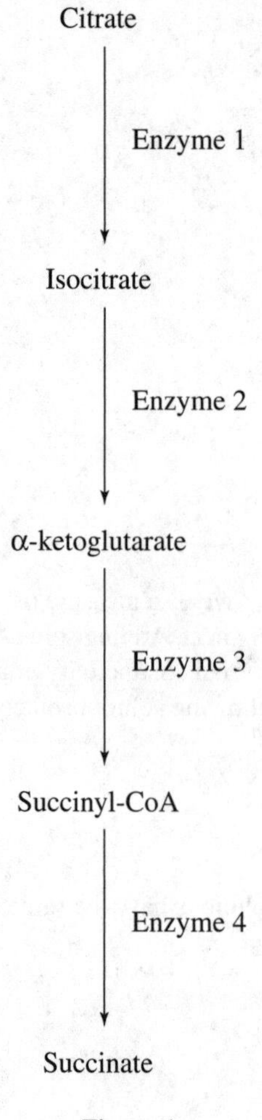

Figure 1

Experiment

A scientist grew four strains of yeast on several different growth media. Each strain was unable to produce succinate because it lacked one of the enzymes required for the reaction pathway shown in Figure 1. Table 1 shows the results of the scientist's experiment: "Yes" indicates that the strain was able to grow in the basic nutrition solution (BNS) + the particular chemical. An undamaged strain of yeast would be able to grow in the basic nutrition solution without any additional chemical. If a strain was able to grow in a given growth medium, then it was able to produce succinate from the additional chemical added to the basic nutrition solution.

Table 1

Growth medium	Yeast strain			
	W	X	Y	Z
BNS				
BNS + Isocitrate	Yes			
BNS + α- ketoglutarate	Yes	Yes		
BNS + Succinyl-CoA	Yes	Yes	Yes	
BNS + Succinate	Yes	Yes	Yes	Yes

If certain genes are damaged, the essential enzymes cannot be produced, which means that the reactions that the enzyme catalyzes cannot occur. Table 2 lists the genes responsible for the enzymes in the steps of the Citric cycle leading to succinate production in yeast. If an enzyme cannot be produced, then the product of the reaction that enzyme catalyzes cannot be synthesized and the reactant in that reaction will become highly concentrated. If a gene is damaged, then it is notated with a superscript negative sign, as in Cat3^{-}; if a gene is not damaged, it is notated with a superscript positive sign, as in Cat3^{+}.

Table 2

Gene	Enzyme
Cat1	Enzyme 1
Cat2	Enzyme 2
Cat3	Enzyme 3
Cat4	Enzyme 4

14. Based on the information in the passage, which of the following is the correct notation for yeast Strain Y ?

F. Cat1^{-} Cat2^{+} Cat3^{-} Cat4^{+}
G. Cat1^{-} Cat2^{-} Cat3^{+} Cat4^{+}
H. Cat1^{+} Cat2^{+} Cat3^{-} Cat4^{-}
J. Cat1^{+} Cat2^{+} Cat3^{-} Cat4^{+}

15. Based on the information presented, the highest concentration of isocitrate would most likely be found in which of the following yeasts?

A. Yeast that cannot produce Enzyme 1
B. Yeast that cannot produce Enzyme 2
C. Yeast that cannot produce Enzyme 3
D. Yeast that cannot produce Enzyme 4

16. According to the information in the passage and Table 2, a strain of yeast that is Cat1$^+$ Cat2$^-$ Cat3$^-$ Cat4$^+$ *cannot* produce:

F. Enzyme 1 and Enzyme 2.
G. Enzyme 1 and Enzyme 4.
H. Enzyme 2 and Enzyme 3.
J. Enzyme 3 and Enzyme 4.

17. Which of the following statements best describes the relationships between citrate, isocitrate, and α-ketoglutarate as shown in Figure 1 ?

A. Isocitrate is a product of a reaction of α-ketoglutarate, and α-ketoglutarate is a product of a reaction of citrate.
B. α-ketoglutarate is a product of a reaction of isocitrate, and isocitrate is a product of a reaction of citrate.
C. α-ketoglutarate is a product of a reaction of citrate, and citrate is a product of a reaction of isocitrate.
D. Citrate is a product of a reaction of isocitrate, and isocitrate is a product of a reaction of α-ketoglutarate.

18. Strain X yeast was most likely unable to synthesize:

F. isocitrate from citrate.
G. α-ketoglutarate from isocitrate.
H. succinyl-CoA from α-ketoglutarate.
J. succinate from succinyl-CoA.

19. One of the growth media shown in Table 1 was a control that the scientist used to demonstrate that all four strains of yeast had genetic damage that prevented the reactions shown in Figure 1, the reactions which are responsible for the synthesis of succinate. Which growth media was used as a control?

A. BNS
B. BNS + succinate
C. BNS + isocitrate
D. BNS + succinyl-CoA

20. For each of the four strains of yeast, W–Z, shown in Table 1, if a given strain was able to grow in BNS + succinyl-CoA, then it was also able to grow in:

F. BNS.
G. BNS + isocitrate.
H. BNS + α-ketoglutarate.
J. BNS + succinate.

Passage IV

Many viruses are known to persist more prevalently during certain times of the year. A study of four relatively unknown viruses was conducted to examine their annual rate of prevalence and mortality in a host population. A large survey was conducted of a local population for the presence of antigen markers indicative of viral exposures to the four virus types. Measurements were acquired monthly beginning in January of 2000 and concluding two years later. All monthly measurements were averaged for comparison.

Figure 1 shows the incidence (cases per 1,000 individuals studied) of viral infections attributed to each viral type over the duration of the study. Figure 2 shows the number of deaths (per 1,000 individuals studied) attributed to virus A and D infections.

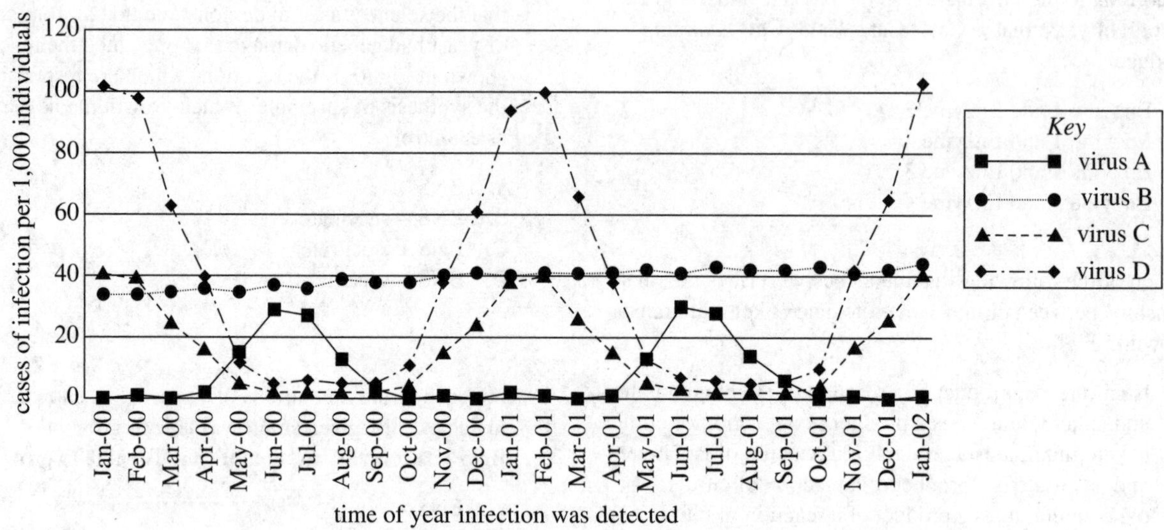

Figure 1

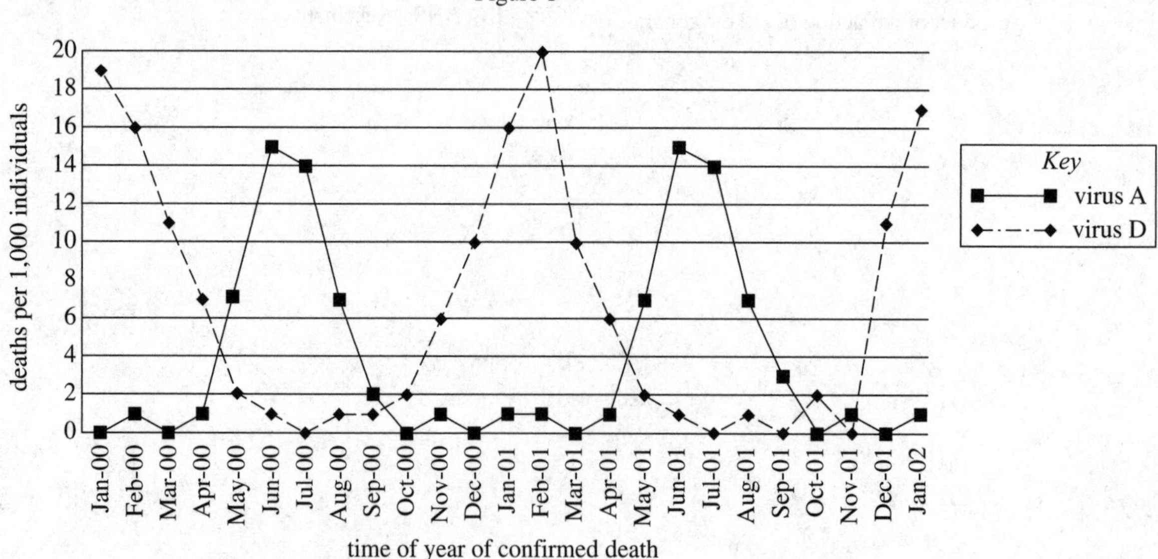

Figure 2

21. According to Figure 1, the incidence of virus A is *greatest* during which season of the year?

A. Spring (Mar–May)
B. Summer (Jun–Aug)
C. Fall (Sep–Nov)
D. Winter (Dec–Feb)

22. A study shows that many seasonal flu viruses thrive in the winter because they are more stable in cold temperatures and the lower humidity allows the particles to remain airborne longer. Changes in temperature and humidity likely have the *least* effect on which of the following viruses?

F. Virus A
G. Virus B
H. Virus C
J. Virus D

23. In a previous study, a virologist claimed that the incidence of virus B has always exceeded the incidence of virus C. As shown in Figure 1, the data for which of the following months is *inconsistent* with the virologist's claims?

A. January 2000
B. February 2001
C. August 2001
D. December 2001

24. If approximately 800 cases of virus B were recorded in the surveyed population in November 2000, which of the following is closest to the total population surveyed?

F. 320
G. 2,000
H. 20,000
J. 32,000

25. During both years of the survey, in one month every year, 7 out of 1,000 individuals died as a result of infection with virus A and 2 out of 1,000 individuals died as a result of infection with virus D. According to Figure 2, these data most likely were obtained during which of the following months?

A. January
B. March
C. May
D. October

26. The *case fatality rate* of a virus is the percentage of infected individuals that die from the illness. Based on the information in Figures 1 and 2, compared to virus A, the case fatality rate of virus D is:

F. Higher; there are more total deaths from virus D than from virus A.
G. Lower; approximately half of the cases of infection from virus A lead to death.
H. Higher; approximately half of the cases of infection from virus A lead to death.
J. Lower; there are more total deaths from virus D than from virus A.

Passage V

The pH at which a protein is uncharged is called its *isoelectric point (pI)*. As the surrounding pH decreases, proteins gain an increasing positive charge. As the surrounding pH increases, proteins gain an increasingly negative charge. In *gel electrophoresis*, a mixture of proteins can be separated based on their relative charge. The proteins are first dissolved in a solvent and then placed at the starting point of an agarose gel. A current is applied to the gel and the proteins migrate different distances according to their charge (see Figure 1).

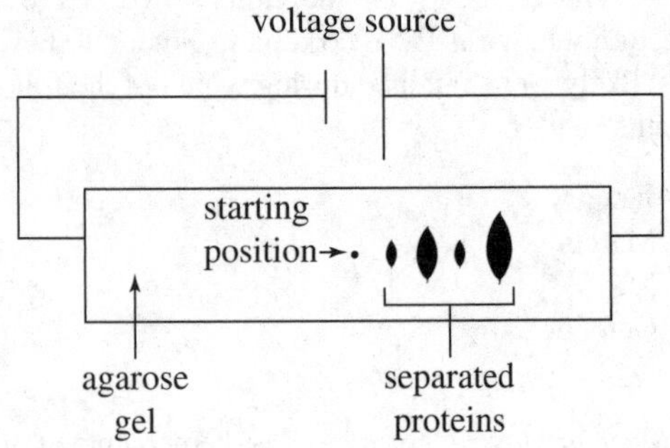

Figure 1

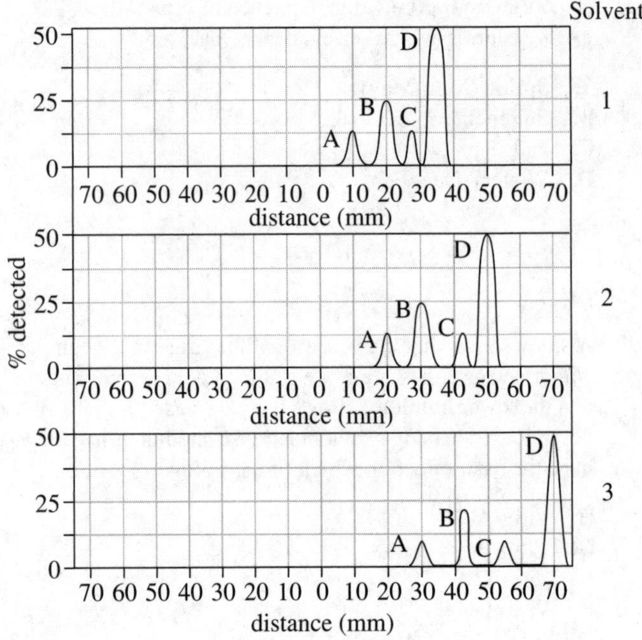

Figure 2

The following experiments were done to determine how varying the pH of a solvent affects the separation of proteins with gel electrophoresis. Table 1 shows the isoelectric points of the proteins and the pH values of the solvents used. The pH scale is logarithmic. Solutions with a pH less than 7.0 are acidic, while those with a pH more than 7.0 are basic.

Table 1

Protein	*pI*
A	8.2
B	7.4
C	6.8
D	5.9
Solvent	**pH**
1	8.9
2	9.6
3	10.2

Experiment 1

A special paper 150 mm long is treated with an agarose gel. Electrodes were attached on each end and wired to a 100-volt source. A 150 μg mixture of proteins A–D was added to Solvent 1 to make a 200 μL solution. The solution was placed at the starting point of the gel and allowed to separate for 60 minutes. The density of the separated proteins was plotted as a percentage over their distance traveled. The procedure was repeated for Solvents 2 and 3 and the results presented in Figure 2.

Experiment 2

The procedures of Experiment 1 were repeated after reversing the electrode attachments on the voltage source. Results are shown in Figure 3.

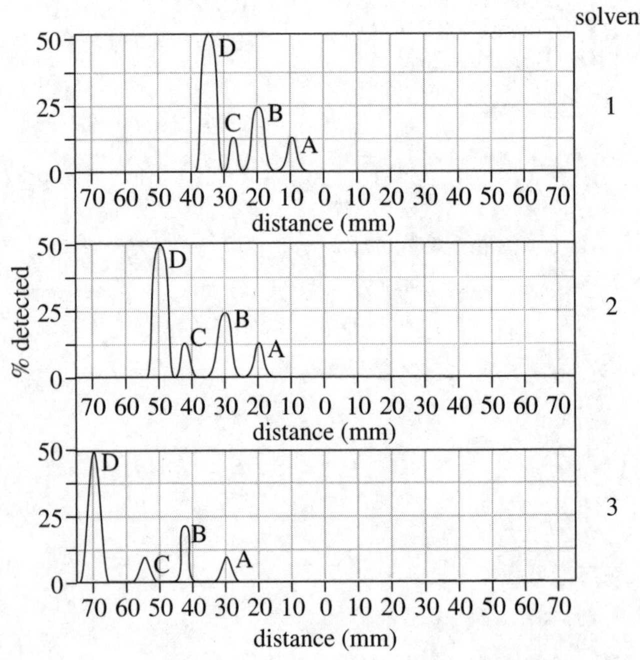

Figure 3

27. A fifth protein, Protein E, has a *pI* of 9.1. If Protein E was placed in Solvent 1 in Experiment 1, it would migrate:

A. in the opposite direction as Proteins A–D because Protein E would have a negative charge.
B. in the same direction as Proteins A–D because Protein E would have a negative charge.
C. in the opposite direction as Proteins A–D because Protein E would have a positive charge.
D. in the same direction as Proteins A–D because Protein E would have a negative charge.

28. In Experiment 2, when Solvent 2 was used, the majority of Protein D migrated a distance from the starting point closest to:

F. 15 mm.
G. 35 mm.
H. 50 mm.
J. 65 mm.

29. Suppose that Experiment 1 were repeated using a solvent with a pH of 8.4. The migration distance of Protein A would most likely peak at:

A. less than 10 mm.
B. between 10 mm and 20 mm.
C. between 20 mm and 30 mm.
D. greater than 30 mm.

30. Protein L has an isoelectric point (*pI*) of 6.6. The results of Experiments 1 and 2 would be most similar to the plots shown in Figures 1 and 2 if, in each trial, Protein L were added to the protein mixture after removing:

F. Protein A.
G. Protein B.
H. Protein C.
J. Protein D.

31. The *resolution* of gel electrophoresis decreases as the overall distance between the peaks on the density plot decreases. Based on the results of Experiments 1 and 2, which of the following sets of conditions had the lowest resolution for the separation?

	Experiment 1	Experiment 2
A.	Solvent 1	Solvent 1
B.	Solvent 3	Solvent 3
C.	Solvent 2	Solvent 3
D.	Solvent 3	Solvent 1

32. Suppose that Experiment 1 will be repeated using Solvent 2, but Protein Y (*pI* = 7.1) is added to the overall mixture. Which of the following best predicts the order of migration distances of the 5 proteins, from shortest to longest?

F. D, C, Y, B, A
G. D, Y, C, B, A
H. A, B, Y, C, D
J. A, Y, B, C, D

33. In Experiment 2, for Solvent 2, at the migration distance where Protein B returned to its 0% migration detection, the percent of Protein A that migrated using Solvent 3 was closest to:

A. 0%.
B. 25%.
C. 50%.
D. 75%.

Passage VI

Students studying gravity and motion were given the following information:

- *Gravity* is an attractive force between two bodies that is directly related to their *mass* and indirectly related to the square of the *distance* between their centers.
- *Acceleration due to gravity* is the acceleration of an object that results from the *force* of gravity.
- *Weight* is the *force* on an object that results from *gravity*, and is not the same as *mass*.
- *Drag* is a force directly related to the *velocity* of a moving object and which results from air resistance and acts to *slow* an object down.
- When the *drag* on a free-falling object is equivalent to the *weight* of that object, the object maintains a constant velocity called *terminal velocity*.

The students' teacher then described the following experiment:

The experimenter dropped a ball from a known height and recorded the time it took to hit the ground. In a second location, a second ball was dropped from the same height and the experimenter observed that it took a longer time to fall to the ground.

Providing no additional information, the teacher asked her three students to provide an explanation of the experimental conditions that would account for the different times it took the two balls to fall.

Student 1

Both trials were conducted in air with the same atmospheric properties. The balls had the same mass and weight, but the second ball had a larger radius and *surface area*. Therefore, the second ball was subjected to more drag and reached a lower terminal velocity than the first. This resulted in an increased fall time.

Student 2

Each ball had identical dimensions, but the first ball was made of a denser material giving it both greater mass and weight. Each ball was dropped through air with the same atmospheric properties. Since the second ball was subjected to less gravitational force and weighed less, it reached a lower terminal velocity compared to the first. Therefore, the second ball took more time to hit the ground.

Student 3

Both balls had the same dimensions and mass. The first ball was dropped above the Earth, while the second ball was dropped above the Moon. The first ball reached terminal velocity in the Earth's atmosphere. The second ball was not subjected to any atmosphere or air resistance. However, there was substantially less gravitational force on the second ball and subsequently it weighed less than the first ball. The overall net result was that the second ball fell more slowly and took longer to hit the ground.

34. Based on Student 1's explanation, the velocity of the first ball as it landed most likely equaled:

F. the product of acceleration of gravity and the time it took to fall.
G. the product of one-half the acceleration of gravity and the time it took to fall squared.
H. the velocity of the ball directly before it landed.
J. zero.

35. The teacher added another question to the students' assignment: Suppose the experimenter repeated the experiment by dropping two balls at the same time from the same height in a single *vacuum*, where no air resistance was present. The balls have different dimensions but identical weights, and they hit the ground at the same time. This new result is consistent with the explanations of which student(s)?

A. Student 1 only
B. Student 2 only
C. Students 1 and 2 only
D. Students 1, 2, and 3

36. According to Student 1, which of the following graphs demonstrates the velocity of the two balls as time increases?

F.

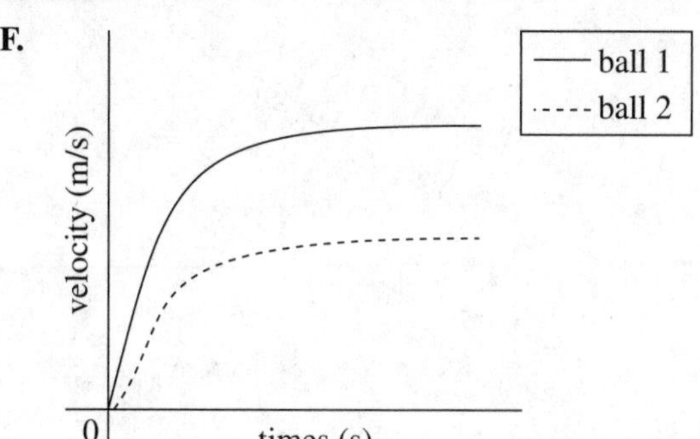

G.

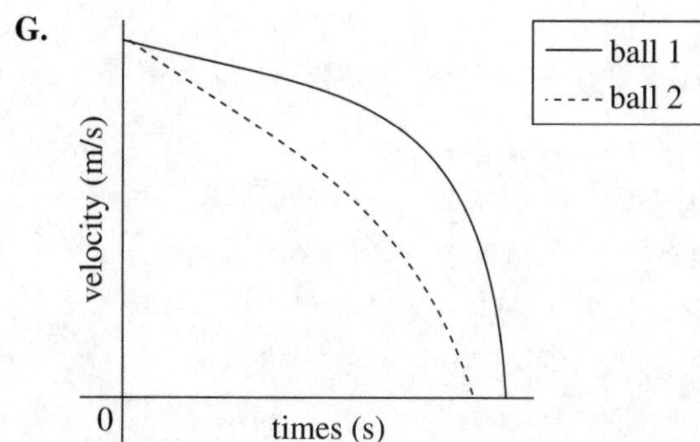

H.

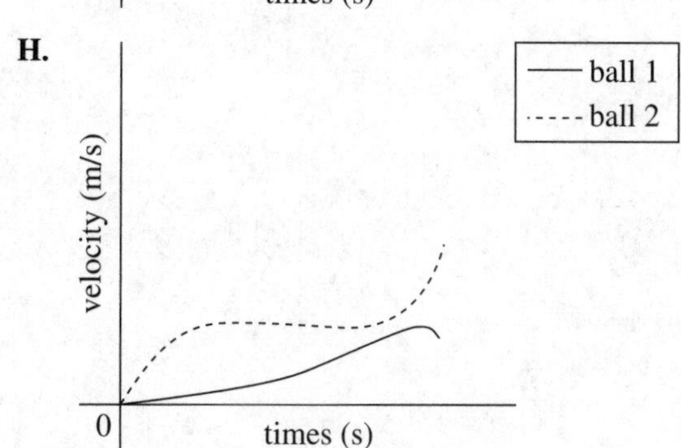

J.

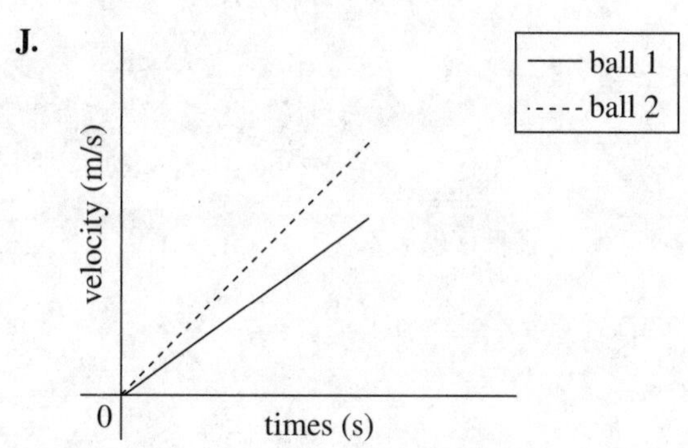

37. According to Student 1, did the surface area of the second ball have an effect on its terminal velocity?

A. Yes; as the surface area of a ball decreases, its terminal velocity decreases only.
B. Yes; as the surface area of a ball increases, its terminal velocity decreases only.
C. No; as the surface area of a ball increases, its terminal velocity decreases, then increases.
D. No; as the surface area of a ball increases, its terminal velocity is not affected.

38. Assuming that Student 3's explanation is correct, once the second ball starts falling, does it reach terminal velocity?

F. Yes, because the weight of the ball was constant and drag force increased.
G. Yes, because the weight of the ball decreased and no drag force was present.
H. No, because the weight of the ball decreased and drag force was constant.
J. No, because the weight of the ball was constant and no drag force was present.

39. The 3 explanations of the motion of the balls are similar to each other in that all 3 explanations suggest that:

A. differences in the gravitational force are responsible for the change in falling times.
B. increases in velocity result from gravity.
C. drag plays only a small part in determining how long it takes an object to fall.
D. a lead ball would have fallen faster.

40. Based on the explanations of the 3 students, what did all 3 students assume about the first ball?

F. The velocity did not change.
G. The velocity increased only.
H. The velocity decreased only.
J. The velocity increased for a time, and then reached terminal velocity.

Science Practice Section 2 Answers and Explanations

SCIENCE PRACTICE SECTION 2 ANSWERS

1. C
2. J
3. C
4. J
5. B
6. J
7. D
8. H
9. B
10. J
11. A
12. G
13. C
14. J
15. B
16. H
17. B
18. G
19. A
20. J
21. B
22. G
23. A
24. H
25. C
26. G
27. C
28. H
29. A
30. H
31. A
32. H
33. A
34. H
35. D
36. F
37. B
38. J
39. B
40. J

SCIENCE PRACTICE SECTION 2 EXPLANATIONS

Passage I

1. **C** The question asks for the concentration of sulfur in ppm in the soil on Farm 1. Refer to Table 2, which shows the concentration of minerals in each farm, *expressed as a percentage of the ideal concentration*. The concentration of sulfur in the soil on Farm 1 is 290% of the ideal concentration. To find the ideal concentration, refer to Table 1. According to Table 1, the ideal concentration of sulfur is 88 ppm. Since the concentration of sulfur in the soil on Farm 1 is almost 300% of this ideal concentration, the concentration of sulfur will be about *three times* the ideal concentration. Since 88 ppm × 3 is approximately 260 ppm, the best answer is 255 ppm. The correct answer is (C).

2. **J** The question asks *which farm would be expected to produce the most oxygen* based on the fact that *soils with more living cells per mm³ generally consume more oxygen than soils with fewer living cells.* Look at Table 3, which shows the number of *living cells per mm³* of the soil collected at the five different farms. The largest number under the heading *# living cells per mm³* is 9,467, which was collected at Farm 5. The correct answer is (J).

3 **C** The question asks which conclusion would be the most reasonable if *the mass of the [soil] sample was approximately the same before and after heating a soil sample to 500°C for 20 minutes and removing the ash,* based on Study 2. Look for the key word *mass* in the description of the study to find out how this process affects the soil and its mass. It says that *to determine the percentage of the mass of each soil composed of organic matter,* the samples were *weighed before being heated to 500°C and after having the ash removed.* Choices (A) and (B) mention *water* but not *organic matter,* so eliminate them. Choice (C) mentions *organic matter,* so keep it. Choice (D) mentions *mineral content* but not *organic matter;* eliminate (D). The correct answer is (C).

4. **J** The question asks why the scientists desiccated the soil in Study 2. Look for the key word *desiccate* in the description of Study 2. There is no mention of it; however, it does say that *the above procedure was repeated to determine the percentage of the mass of each soil composed of organic matter,* so look for the key word *desiccate* in the description of Study 1. It says that *the soils were desiccated,* which means *all water was removed.* Eliminate (F) because it refers to *minerals* and not *organic matter.* The text makes no mention of water being *consumed,* so eliminate (G). Eliminate (H) because the text never states anything about the soil sticking together. Choice (J) is consistent with the purpose of the study, to measure the organic matter. The correct answer is (J).

5. **B** The question asks what the *% organic matter* in a soil sample with 2,100 *living cells per mm³* would be, according to Study 2. Look at the results of Study 2 found in Table 2. Look for numbers of *living cells per mm³* closest to 2,100. Farm 3 had 1,642 and farm 4 had 2,672. So, *% organic matter* for this new soil sample should fall within the range of the *% organic matter* found on Farms 3 and 4, between 4.8 and 6.6. The correct answer is (B).

6. **J** The question asks which farm would produce the fastest-growing beans given the information that *beans grow fastest in soils with high nitrogen and iron growth factors.* Refer to Table 2, which gives detailed information about the concentrations of each mineral on all of the farms. Look across the row for nitrogen and notice that Farm 5 has the highest concentration (210% ideal concentration). Do the same for iron and notice again that Farm 5 has the highest concentration (165% ideal concentration). Therefore, the beans will grow the fastest on Farm 5. The correct answer is (J).

7. **D** The question asks which of the farms would likely be considered *the most well defined,* according to Study 1. Since there is no mention of *well defined* in the description of Study 1, look for those key words in the introduction. Paragraph 1 states that *if the concentrations of different minerals, relative to their ideal concentrations, are all similar to each other, the soil is said to be well defined.* Look for the farm that has mineral percentages most similar to each other in Table 2. The smallest range of mineral concentration is present in Farm 4. The correct answer is (D).

Passage II

8. **H** The question asks about the amount of *heat loss from the beginning temperature of 180°F* for S3 after 30 minutes, according to Figure 3. Look at Figure 3 and locate 30 minutes on the *x*-axis. Then draw a line straight up and stop at the curve marked S3. From this point, draw a line to the *y*-axis to find the *heat loss from the beginning temperature of 180°F,* 80. The correct answer is (H).

9. **B** The question asks how *the temperature of the water in the plastic outer container* is related to *the heat loss from the beginning temperature of 180°F* of S1, according to Figures 2 and 3. First look at Figure 2. As time increases, so does *the temperature of the water in the plastic outer container.* Next look at Figure 3. As time increases, so does *the heat loss from the beginning temperature of 180°F.* Eliminate (A), (C), and (D) because neither relationship had a *decrease.* The correct answer is (B).

10. **J** The question asks about the initial orderliness of the atoms in a new mixture, S4. According to the information in the question, *the heat lost after being allowed to stand for 5 minutes was 50°F.* To examine the orderliness of the mixtures, refer to Figure 3. Draw a point at the intersection between the 5-minute mark and 50°F. This point falls between the curves for the S2 and S1 mixtures. Since orderliness increases according to the right *y*-axis, the S4 mixture is more orderly than S1 and S3, but less orderly than S2. This data matches the information in (J). The correct answer is (J).

11. **A** The question asks for an explanation of the trends in Figure 2, based on the diagram of the experiment in Figure 1. According to Figure 1, a glass of *sugar and water mixture* was submerged in a plastic container of *cold water.* Figure 2 shows that as the temperature of the *sugar and water mixture* decreased, the temperature of *water in the plastic outer container* increased. The explanation in (A) is consistent with this, so keep it. Eliminate (B) as it is the opposite relationship. Eliminate both (C) and (D) because there is no data about the string. The correct answer is (A).

12. **G** The question asks which mixture would first *begin to form rock candy,* which happens *when the temperature of the sugar and water mixture* loses *100°F from its beginning temperature,* according to Figure 3. Look at Figure 3. All three solutions lose *100°F.* S2 achieves this after 37 minutes, before S1 and S3. The correct answer is (G).

13. **C** The question asks which solution has the lowest concentration of sugar. According to the question, adding solutes *increases the thermal conductivity of an aqueous solution.* Since thermal conductivity is defined as the *rate at which a material transfers heat,* a solution with a high concentration of solutes will have a high rate of heat transfer. This question is asking for the solution with the *lowest* concentration of solute and it will therefore have the *lowest* rate of heat transfer. According to Figure 3, the S3 mixture loses the lowest amount of heat over time and must therefore have the lowest concentration of sugar. The correct answer is (C).

Passage III

14. **J** The question asks for the correct notation of yeast Strain Y. In the second paragraph of the passage, it says that *each strain was unable to produce succinate because it lacked one of the enzymes required for the reaction pathway.* According to the information preceding Table 2, a damaged gene that does not produce an enzyme is denoted with a negative superscript. Therefore, the correct answer should have only one negative superscript since the passage states that each strain is missing only *one* enzyme. Eliminate (F), (G), and (H). The only answer that shows only one damaged gene is (J). Choice (J) indicates that Cat3 is damaged. If Enzyme 3 is not produced, then a yeast is unable to produce succinyl-CoA and would therefore grow only if it were provided with succinyl-CoA or the final product, succinate. This matches the information in Table 1 for Yeast Y. The correct answer is (J).

15. **B** The question asks which yeast would most likely contain *the highest concentration of isocitrate.* Since there is no information about *highest concentration* in any of the figures, look for these key words in the description of the experiment. Paragraph 3 says that a *reactant becomes highly concentrated if an enzyme cannot be produced* and *the product of the reaction that the enzyme catalyzes cannot be synthesized.* According to Figure 1, isocitrate is a reactant in the second step and it will become *highly concentrated* if Enzyme 2 cannot be produced. Choice (B) is consistent with this information. The correct answer is (B).

16. **H** The question asks which enzymes cannot be produced by a strain of yeast that is $Cat1^{+}$ $Cat2^{-}$ $Cat3^{-}$ $Cat4^{+}$, according to the passage and Table 2. Look for the key words *cannot produce* in the passage text above Table 2. Paragraph 3 says, *if certain genes are damaged, the essential enzymes cannot be produced.* It goes on to say that *if a gene is damaged, then it is notated with a superscript negative sign, as in* $Cat3^{-}$; *if a gene is not damaged, it is notated with a superscript positive sign, as in* $Cat3^{+}$. This means that $Cat2^{-}$ and $Cat3^{-}$ are both damaged and cannot produce their essential enzymes. Look at Table 2. The essential enzymes associated with $Cat2^{-}$ and $Cat3^{-}$ are Enzymes 2 and 3. The correct answer is (H).

17. **B** The question asks about the relationship between citrate, isocitrate, and α-ketoglutarate, as shown in Figure 1. The first paragraph states that *in the first step, Enzyme 1 is the enzyme, citrate is the reactant, and isocitrate is the product.* So, isocitrate is the product of the reactant citrate, and α-ketoglutarate is a product of the reactant isocitrate. Eliminate (A) because isocitrate is not the *product of the reactant* α-ketoglutarate. Keep (B) because it is consistent with the data shown in Figure 1. Eliminate (C) because α-ketoglutarate is not *a product of the reactant citrate,* and eliminate (D) because citrate is not *a product of the reactant isocitrate.* The correct answer is (B).

18. **G** The question asks what *Strain X yeast was most likely unable to synthesize.* The yeast strains are shown in Table 1. Circle the column labeled Strain X. According to the explanation of the experiment above, *"Yes" indicates that the strain was able to grow in the basic nutrition solution (BNS) + the particular chemical.* Strain X was unable to grow in the BNS until α-ketoglutarate was added. This indicates that α-ketoglutarate could not be made naturally by Strain X. The only choice consistent with the data is (G). The correct answer is (G).

19. **A** The question asks *which growth media, shown in Table 1, was used as a control.* A control is an unaltered factor in an experiment that can be used as a standard of comparison against the groups in which another variable is altered. Look at Table 1. Each of the growth mediums contains BNS, and in four of the five media, something else was added to BNS. Because BNS is present in all of the media, the medium with only BNS must be the control. The correct answer is (A).

20. **J** The question asks which growth medium a strain of yeast would also be able to grow in if it had been able to grow in BNS + Succinyl-CoA, according to Table 1. Strains W, X, and Y were all able to grow in BNS + Succinyl-CoA, and every strain was able to grow in BNS + Succinate. The correct answer is (J).

Passage IV

21. **B** The question asks during which season of the year is the incidence of virus A the greatest. Refer to Figure 1 as directed. Virus A is indicated by the square data points. The highest incidences are indicated by the peaks in the curve. These peaks are at June and July of both 2000 and 2001. Since these months represent the summer, the correct answer is (B).

22. **G** The question asks which virus would be the least affected by temperature and humidity. According to the question, temperature and humidity vary by season, but by looking at Figure 1, the number of infected cases from virus B (circle data points) remain unchanged throughout the year, independent of the season. Therefore, the correct answer is (G).

23. **A** The question asks which data is inconsistent with the virologist's claim that *the incidence of virus B has always exceeded the incidence of virus C.* Examine Figure 1, and look for time points when the incidence of virus C (triangle data points) was actually *higher* than the incidence of virus B (circle data points). Use the answer choices to help. Start with (A), which points to January of 2000. Since

the triangle data point is *higher* than the circle data point, the incidence of virus C is actually *higher* than the incidence of virus B. Since this time point is inconsistent with the virologist's claim, the correct answer is (A).

24. **H** The question asks what value is the closest to the total population surveyed in November of 2000 given that 800 cases of virus B were recorded during this month. According to the data in Figure 1, 40 cases of infection of virus B were recorded for every 1,000 individuals surveyed in November of 2000. Set up a proportion to find the total population surveyed: $\frac{40}{1,000} = \frac{800}{x}$. Cross-multiply to get $40x = 800,000$. Divide both sides by 40 to find that $x = 20,000$. The correct answer is (H).

25. **C** The question asks during which months the data in Figure 2 shows that 7 of 1,000 individuals died as a result of infection with virus A and 2 out of 1,000 individuals died as a result of infection with virus D. Refer to Figure 2 and find which months show 7 individuals died from virus A (square data points). In both May and August of both years, 7 individuals died from virus A. Since August is not an answer choice, the correct answer must be (C). Double-check by confirming that 2 individuals died from virus D (diamond data points) in May of both years. The correct answer is (C).

26. **G** The question asks about the *case fatality rate* of viruses A and D and defines case fatality rate as *the percentage of infected individuals who die from the illness.* Start by examining virus A in both graphs. In Figure 1, the largest incidence of infection for virus A occurred during June and July, with approximately 30 cases per 1,000 individuals. Now look at virus A in Figure 2. During June and July, there were approximately 15 deaths from infection with virus A. This means that the case fatality rate of virus A was about 50%. Now compare this to virus D. In Figure 1, the largest incidence of infection for virus D occurred during January of 2001, with approximately 100 cases per 1,000 individuals. Now look at virus D in Figure 2. During January of 2001, there were approximately 20 deaths from infection with virus D. This means that the case fatality rate of virus D was about 20%. Therefore, the case fatality rate of virus D is *lower* than that of virus A. Eliminate (F) and (H). Since (G) gives the correct explanation that approximately half of the cases of infection from virus A lead to death, the correct answer is (G).

Passage V

27. **C** The question asks about the migration of a fifth protein, Protein E, which has a *pI* of 9.1. Look to the answers for clues that may help to eliminate choices and notice that the charge of Protein E needs to be determined. In Experiment 1, the pH of Solvent 1 is 8.9. According to Paragraph 1 of the passage, the isoelectric point (*pI*) is the pH at which the protein is uncharged, but *as the surrounding pH decreases, proteins gain an increasing positive charge.* Since the pH of the solvent is *less* than the *pI* of the protein, Protein E will be positively charged. Eliminate (A) and (B). Now, notice that all four proteins shown in Table 1 have a *pI* less than 8.9, so they would all be negatively

charged. Since Protein E has a different charge than that of the other proteins, (C) is a more likely answer, but to confirm, examine the differences between Figure 2 and Figure 3. In Figure 2, the proteins all migrated to the right, but in Figure 3, the proteins all migrated to the left. Since the only difference between Experiment 1 and Experiment 2 is the placement of the positive and negative electrodes, it can be concluded that the charge affects the direction of protein migration. The correct answer is (C).

28. **H** The question asks *what distance from the starting point Protein D migrated* to *when Solvent 2 was used,* according to Experiment 2. Look at the results of Experiment 2 and locate the graph that corresponds to Solvent 2. The *distance* of Protein D is 50 mm. The correct answer is (H).

29. **A** The question asks at which value *the migration distance of Protein A would most likely peak* if *Experiment 1 were repeated using a solvent with a pH of 8.4.* First, look at Table 1, which shows pH. The pH of this new solvent is slightly less than the pH of Solvent 1. Next, look at the results of Experiment 1. As the pH of each solvent increases, the distance Protein A travels also increases. Therefore, *the migration distance of Protein A would most likely peak* at a shorter distance than it did in Solvent 1, which was 10 mm. Eliminate (B), (C), and (D) because they contain values that are greater than 10 mm. The correct answer is (A).

30. **H** The question asks which protein could be replaced by Protein L, which has an isoelectric point (*pI*) of 6.6, while keeping the results of Experiments 1 and 2 similar to the plots shown in Figures 2 and 3. Look at Table 1, which shows *pI.* The isoelectric point of Protein L is most similar to that of Protein C, so if it were replaced by Protein L, the results would be similar as well. The correct answer is (H).

31. **A** The question asks which solvents displayed the *lowest resolution,* according to the results of Experiments 1 and 2. The question specifies that resolution *decreases as the overall distance between the peaks on the density plot decreases.* The *overall distance between the peaks* in Solvent 1 is 25 mm in both figures. The *overall distance between the peaks* in Solvent 2 is 30 mm in both figures. The *overall distance between the peaks* in Solvent 3 is 40 mm in both figures. Therefore, the *lowest resolution* occurs in Solvent 1. The correct answer is (A).

32. **H** The question asks for a list of proteins, from shortest migration to longest, when Protein Y with a *pI* of 7.1 is added to Solvent 2 in Experiment 1. Look at Table 1. The *pI* of Protein Y falls between Proteins B and C. Look at the results of Experiment 1. For each solvent, the migration path from shortest to longest is A, B, C, D. As a result, the new order should be A, B, Y, C, D. The correct answer is (H).

33. **A** The question asks for *the percent of Protein A that migrated using Solvent 3, at the migration distance where Protein B returned to its 0% migration detection* in Solvent 2, in Experiment 2. Look at the results of Experiment 2 when Solvent 2 was used. Protein B returns to 0% migration detected at 35 mm. Now locate 35 mm on the graph of data from when Solvent 3 was used. At 35 mm, the *percent of Protein A that migrated* was 0. The correct answer is (A).

Passage VI

34. **H** The question asks for information regarding *the velocity of the first ball as it landed,* according to Student 1's explanation. Look for the key word *velocity* in Student 1's explanation. It states that *the second ball...reached a lower terminal velocity than the first,* which implies that the first reached terminal velocity. Look for the term *terminal velocity* in the passage. The fifth bullet point defines *terminal velocity* as *a constant velocity* that is reached *when the drag on a free-falling object is equivalent to the weight of that object.* Therefore, before the first ball lands, it is falling at a constant velocity, and its velocity a split second before landing would be the same as when it lands, which is consistent with (H). Eliminate (F) and (G) because there is no information given about formulas to calculate velocity. A velocity of zero would mean that the ball was not moving, in which case it would not have collided with Earth, so eliminate (J). The correct answer is (H).

35. **D** The question asks which students' explanations would be consistent with the results of a new trial, in which two balls were dropped *at the same time from the same height in a single vacuum, where no air resistance is present* and with balls that *have different dimensions but identical weights.* By placing two balls in a vacuum, where no air resistance is present, the experimenter would have eliminated the effects of drag. This suggests that air resistance had an effect on the results, which supports Student 1. Eliminate (B) because it does not include Student 1. The new experiment uses balls with identical weights, which suggests that weight can affect the results, which supports Student 2. Eliminate (A) because it does not include Student 2. This experiment also placed both balls in the same location with the same force of gravity. This suggests that gravitational force can play a role, which supports the views of Student 3. Eliminate (C) because it does not include Student 3. The correct answer is (D).

36. **F** The question asks which graph *demonstrates the velocity of the two balls as time increases,* according to Student 1. Look for the key word *velocity* in the explanation provided by Student 1. It states that *the second ball...reached a lower terminal velocity than the first,* which implies that both balls reached terminal velocity. Look for the term *terminal velocity* in the passage. The fifth bullet point defines *terminal velocity* as *a constant velocity* that is reached *when the drag on a free-falling object is equivalent to the weight of that object.* The only graph that shows velocity reaching a terminal level and holding constant is in (F). The correct answer is (F).

37. **B** The question asks whether *the surface area of the second ball [had] an effect on its terminal velocity,* according to Student 1. Look for the key words *surface area* in Student 1's explanation. It states *the second ball had a larger radius and surface area...therefore, the second ball...reached a lower terminal velocity than the first. Therefore,* Student 1 believes that as surface area increases, terminal velocity decreases. Eliminate (C) and (D) because they state that surface area had no effect on terminal velocity. Choice (A) states the opposite relationship, so eliminate (A). The correct answer is (B).

38. **J** The question asks whether the second ball reaches terminal velocity, according to Student 3's explanation. Look for the key words *second ball* in the explanation provided by Student 3. It states that *the second ball was not subjected to any atmosphere or air resistance.* According to the introduction of the passage, drag force results from air resistance. Therefore, there is no drag force; eliminate (F) and (H). Student 3 states that the second ball *weighed less than the first ball* but does not say that *the weight decreased;* eliminate (G). Choice (J) is consistent with Student 3's explanation. The correct answer is (J).

39. **B** The question asks in what way *the 3 explanations of the motion of the balls are similar to each other.* Eliminate (A) because only Student 3 discusses *differences in the gravitational force.* Keep (B) because all 3 students imply that the balls accelerate until they reach terminal velocity. Eliminate (C) because *drag* is the primary cause of the slower falling time for Student 1. Eliminate (D) because only Student 2 discusses different *material.* The correct answer is (B).

40. **J** The question asks what all three students assumed about the first ball, based on the explanations of all three students. All three students believe that the first ball reached *terminal velocity.* Look for the term *terminal velocity* in the passage. The fifth bullet point defines *terminal velocity* as *a constant velocity* that is reached *when the drag on a free-falling object is equivalent to the weight of that object.* Velocity would need to increase in order to reach a *terminal velocity,* so eliminate (F) and (H). Eliminate (G) because it does not match the definition of *terminal velocity* in the passage. The correct answer is (J).

Science Practice Section 3

SCIENCE TEST

35 Minutes—40 Questions

DIRECTIONS: There are six passages in the following section. Each passage is followed by several questions. After reading a passage, choose the best answer to each question and blacken the corresponding oval on your answer document. You may refer to the passages as often as necessary.

You are NOT permitted to use a calculator on this test.

Passage I

Sylvatic, or jungle, Yellow Fever is caused by a virus transmitted by mosquitoes from monkeys to humans. Figure 1 shows the life cycle of the mosquitoes who carry this disease. These mosquitoes' eggs do not hatch unless there is enough water for the next two stages of their life cycles. Yellow Fever is passed when an adult of these mosquitoes first bites a monkey that is infected with the virus and then bites a human. Two studies were done on the incidence of Yellow Fever in a particular jungle.

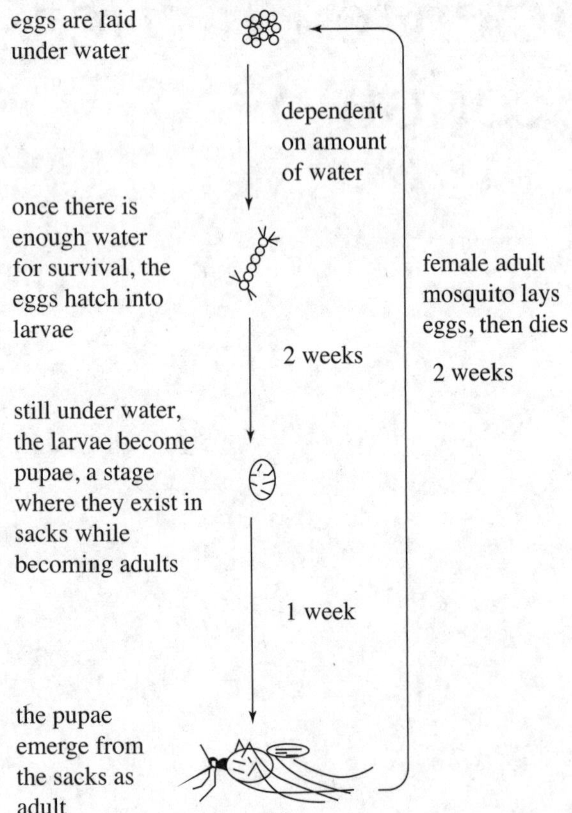

Figure 1

Study 1

For one year, researchers collected data on the monthly rainfall and the number of new cases of Yellow Fever that occurred in a village in the jungle. The results are shown in Figure 2.

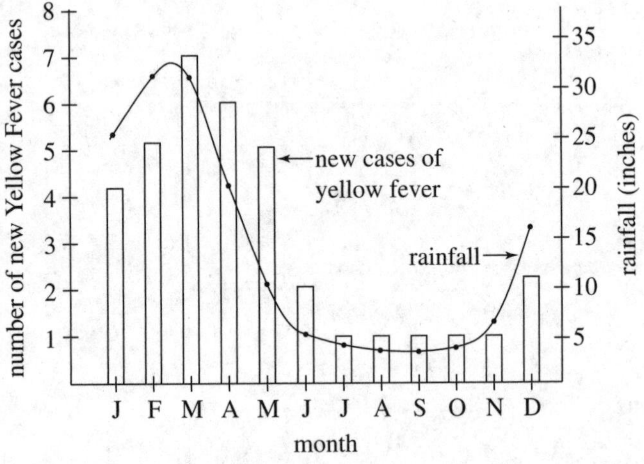

Figure 2

Study 2

Five ecologists conducted a study in five separate villages in the same jungle. Each ecologist moved into the village for one year to collect data. Table 1 shows the population of each village, the number of water sources within 2 miles of the center of the village, the average number of monkeys seen by the ecologist each month, the number of mosquito bites received by the ecologist over the course of the year, and the percentage of the village that was infected with Yellow Fever at some point over the year.

Table 1

Village	Population	Number of water sources	Average number of monkeys seen	Number of mosquito bites	Percent of village infected with Yellow Fever
A	910	2	36	100	10%
B	1,012	4	20	156	18%
C	1,109	7	43	210	29%
D	811	11	38	220	38%
E	913	15	58	338	52%

1. Based on Figure 1, what is essential in maintaining the mosquito population?

A. Jungle
B. Water
C. Monkeys
D. Humans

2. Based on Table 1, the average percent of villagers affected by the yellow fever virus was closest to:

F. 20%.
G. 30%.
H. 60%.
J. 80%.

3. Suppose additional data had been gathered in Study 2 about the number of mosquito bites per month. Based on Figure 2 and Table 1, in which of the following months would you expect to have the largest total of mosquito bites per month?

A. April
B. June
C. August
D. November

4. According to Figure 2, the amount of rainfall was different for each of the following pairs of months EXCEPT:

F. May and December.
G. February and March.
H. January and October.
J. April and May.

5. Based on Table 1, as the number of water sources increased, the number of monkeys seen:

A. increased only.
B. decreased only.
C. increased, then decreased.
D. varied with no consistency.

6. A nearby village with 8 water sources within 2 miles has a population of 1,200. Based on the information in Table 1, the number of people in the village that the ecologists would expect to be infected with Yellow Fever over the course of the study is most likely closest to:

F. 300.
G. 400.
H. 500.
J. 800.

7. An extended drought in the jungle leads to a 3-month period with no mosquito bites or new Yellow Fever cases in the surrounding jungle towns. Based on Figure 1, what is most likely the *minimum* amount of time that the ecologists would expect to pass between the first rainfall and the first recurrences of mosquito bites?

A. Less than 1 week
B. Between 1 and 2 weeks
C. Between 2 and 3 weeks
D. At least 3 weeks

Passage II

Ethanolamines are compounds that contain both alcohol (–OH or HO–) and amine ($-NH_3$, $-RNH_2$, $-R_2NH$, or $-R_3N$) subgroups. They remove weakly acidic gases from the atmosphere of enclosed spaces such as on a submarine. An example is the use of *monoethanolamine* (MEA) to remove CO_2 from the atmosphere as shown in Figure 1.

$$2\text{ MEA (liquid)} + CO_2\text{(gas)} \xrightarrow{H_2O} \text{(MEA)COO}^-\text{(aqueous)} + \text{(MEA) H}^+\text{(aqueous)} + \text{heat}$$

Figure 1

If the temperature rises sufficiently, ethanolamines will release any absorbed acidic gases back into the environment, creating a potential hazard.

Scientists studied the absorption properties of 2 ethanolamines (MEA and DEA).

Experiment 1

At 0°C and 1 atmosphere (atm) pressure, 1 mole (6.02×10^{23} molecules) of MEA was spread at the base of a reaction vessel containing CO_2 gas at a concentration of 1,000 parts per million (ppm). As the CO_2 was absorbed, its ambient concentration decreased. The *scrub time* (time for CO_2 concentration to drop to at least 10 ppm) was measured. Longer scrub times indicate a slower rate of absorption. The experimental procedure was repeated at varying temperatures and for DEA, with results recorded in Table 1.

Table 1

Temperature (°C)	Scrub time (msec)	
	MEA	DEA
0	11,400	8,600
5	11,150	8,410
10	11,025	8,315
15	10,925	8,240
20	10,850	8,190
25	10,790	8,145
30	10,740	8,105
35	10,700	8,075

Experiment 2

The scrub times of MEA for different acidic gases were measured using the procedures of Experiment 1 at 26°C (see Table 2). Each of the gases listed is toxic and poses a significant safety hazard if its concentration becomes elevated within an enclosed space.

Table 2

Gas	Formula	Scrub time (msec)
Hydrogen chloride*	HCl	8,500
Hydrogen cyanide	HCN	14,400
Hydrogen sulfide	H_2S	12,200
Sulfur dioxide	SO_2	8,930
Sulfur trioxide	SO_3	9,120

*Hydrogen chloride forms gaseous hydrochloric acid upon contact with atmospheric humidity.

8. In which of the following ways was the procedure of Experiment 2 different from that of Experiment 1? In Experiment 2:

F. temperature was varied; in Experiment 1, the temperature was held constant.
G. temperature was held constant; in Experiment 1, the temperature was varied.
H. only MEA was used; in Experiment 1, only DEA was used.
J. only DEA was used; in Experiment 1, only MEA was used.

9. In Experiment 1, during the DEA trial at 20°C, as the time progressed from 0 to 8,190 msec, the concentration of CO_2 in the vessel:

A. increased from 10 ppm to 1,000 ppm.
B. increased from 1,000 ppm to 10 ppm.
C. decreased from 10 ppm to 1,000 ppm.
D. decreased from 1,000 ppm to 10 ppm.

10. If, in Experiment 1, an additional trial were done at 12°C, the scrub times (in msec) for MEA and DEA would most likely be closest to which of the following?

	MEA	DEA
F.	10,805	8,370
G.	10,985	8,285
H.	11,000	8,365
J.	11,025	8,315

11. Based on the information in the passage, which of the following is a possible chemical formula for an ethanolamine?

A. $HO—(CH_2)_2—NH_3$
B. $HO—(CH_2CF_2)_2—CH_3$
C. $H^3C—(CH_2)_4—NH_3$
D. $H_3N—(CH_2CHCl)_2—NH_3$

12. A scientist claims that under the same conditions, DEA will always absorb CO_2 at a faster rate than will MEA. Do the results of Experiment 1 support this claim?

F. No; at all temperatures tested, the scrub time for DEA was more than that for MEA.
G. No; at all temperatures tested, the scrub time for MEA was more than that for DEA.
H. Yes; at all temperatures tested, the scrub time for DEA was more than that for MEA.
J. Yes; at all temperatures tested, the scrub time for MEA was more than that for DEA.

13. Based on the results of Experiment 2, which acidic gas had the slowest absorption by MEA at 26°C ?

A. HCl
B. HCN
C. H_2S
D. SO_2

14. Which of the following correctly identifies a reactant and a product for a reaction that occurred in Experiment 1 ?

	Reactant	Product
F.	MEA	CO_2
G.	DEA	Heat
H.	CO_2	H_2O
J.	DEA	H_2O

Passage III

Taraxicum, the common dandelion, can reproduce both through spreading seeds and through vegetative reproduction. To spread its seeds, the dandelion grows seed pods shaped like globes, in which the seeds are loosely attached to a central ball; each seed grows a parachute-like tuft that lets it travel long distances on the wind (or when blown upon by humans). In vegetative reproduction, a new dandelion stalk and leaves can grow up from an existing root system. Two students discuss the spread of dandelion populations.

Student 1

In *Taraxicum*, vegetative reproduction and seed distribution make up the only means of growing new plants. Each accounts for 50% of the growth of new dandelions.

Taraxicum grows throughout North America. In many places there is very little wind. Therefore, *Taraxicum* must have a non-wind-based means of spreading itself. While blowing dandelion seeds is a common pastime among humans, this human influence is very recent in evolutionary terms; it is very unlikely that *Taraxicum* evolved to rely on humans to distribute its seeds.

The way *Taraxicum* grows in a typical field shows that both vegetative reproduction and seed distribution are at work. While seeds scatter over the whole field, the dandelions tend to grow together in clumps. This suggests that individual seeds sprout the first new dandelions, which then grow several more through vegetative reproduction.

Student 2

Seed distribution is the main way *Taraxicum* spreads itself. Without seed distribution, there are very few new dandelions. *Taraxicum* does use vegetative reproduction, sending new stalks from existing roots, but this is mainly to replace the above-ground plant if it has been cut or eaten. This allows the plant to survive threats in the environment but does not allow for the growth of new plants.

Plant studies show that plants which rely on vegetative reproduction to spread themselves tend to have large, complex root networks or underground root clusters. *Taraxicum* plants, however, each have a single large, deep taproot. This makes them very difficult to uproot, but it also means that their roots do not spread out underground, so any new plants growing from the roots would compete with each other for sunlight. Even a slight breeze or the brush of a passing animal is enough to spread dandelion seeds to a new area. Additionally, all known types of *Taraxicum* produce seed globes. If half the new dandelions grew from vegetative reproduction, then a seedless dandelion should not be at a competitive disadvantage and should be commonly observed in the wild.

Experiment

The students proposed 3 trials using an introduced *Taraxicum* population in three fields in a windy area where *Taraxicum* can naturally thrive (see Table 1).

Table 1

Trial	Procedure
1	Several *Taraxicum* plants are planted in the soil of a field with no other *Taraxicum* plants. They are allowed to grow and spread normally.
2	*Taraxicum* specimens are planted in the soil of a similar field with no other *Taraxicum* plants. Their flowers are covered with plastic bags once they have grown seeds.
3	*Taraxicum* specimens are planted in large glass jars, which are then buried in a third similar field. Seeds are allowed to blow normally, but the plant roots cannot grow out of the glass jars.

15. Suppose an experiment were performed in which several new *Taraxicum* plants were planted in a field with their roots in glass jars and with plastic bags over the flowers. Assuming that Student 1's hypothesis is correct, the number of new dandelions in the field would most likely be what percent of the number in a control field?

A. 0%
B. 25%
C. 50%
D. 100%

16. Which of the following trials most likely provided the control group in the students' experiment?

F. Trial 1, in which *Taraxicum* specimens are planted in the soil of a field with no other *Taraxicum* plants
G. Trial 1, in which *Taraxicum* specimens are planted in large glass jars, which are then buried in the soil of a field with no other *Taraxicum* plants
H. Trial 2, in which *Taraxicum* specimens are planted in the soil of a field similar to that of Trial 1
J. Trial 3, in which specimens are planted in large glass jars in a field similar to that of Trial 1

17. Student 1 states that dandelions growing in clumps "suggests that individual seeds sprout the first new dandelions, which then grow several more through vegetative reproduction." Which of the following indicates why Student 2 believes this cannot be true? Student 2 says:

A. *Taraxicum* tends to grow from a root network, while vegetative reproducers grow from single roots.
B. *Taraxicum* tends to grow from a single root, while vegetative reproducers grow from root networks.
C. *Taraxicum* has seeds that are attached loosely to the stem, a fact that suggests they are not important to *Taraxicum*'s reproductive strategy.
D. *Taraxicum* has seeds that are attached loosely to the stem, but vegetative reproducers tend not to have seeds at all.

18. Student 2 would most likely agree with the statement that *Taraxicum:*

F. uses vegetative reproduction to compensate for windless environments.
G. improves its ability to survive by using vegetative reproduction to regenerate.
H. has evolved a dependency on humans to distribute its seeds.
J. tends to grow in clumps in fields to which it has spread itself.

19. With regard to the experiment described in the table, Students 1 and 2 would most likely agree that the increase in the *Taraxicum* population would be greatest in a field where:

A. neither plastic bags nor glass jars were used.
B. plastic bags were used, but not glass jars.
C. glass jars were used, but not plastic bags.
D. both plastic bags and glass jars were used.

20. Suppose Trial 3 of the experiment was performed as described. Based on Student 1's hypothesis, the resulting population would be closest to what percentage of a control population?

F. 0%
G. 25%
H. 50%
J. 100%

21. Suppose the 3 trials were performed as described. Student 2's hypothesis about the way *Taraxicum* reproduces would be best supported if the number of new dandelions fit which of the following patterns?

A. The field in Trial 3 had roughly the same number of dandelions as the field in Trial 1, both of which had fewer dandelions than the field in Trial 2.
B. The field in Trial 1 had more dandelions than the field in either Trial 2 or Trial 3, while the fields in Trials 2 and 3 had roughly equal numbers of dandelions.
C. The field in Trial 2 had fewer dandelions than the field in Trial 3, which had more dandelions than the field in Trial 1.
D. The field in Trial 3 had slightly fewer dandelions than the field in Trial 1, both of which had many more dandelions than the field in Trial 2.

Passage IV

Metals differ in their relative abilities to conduct electricity. *Resistance* is a measurement in ohms (Ω) of how much a metal opposes electric current at a particular voltage.

A scientist performed 3 experiments using the circuit shown in Figure 1.

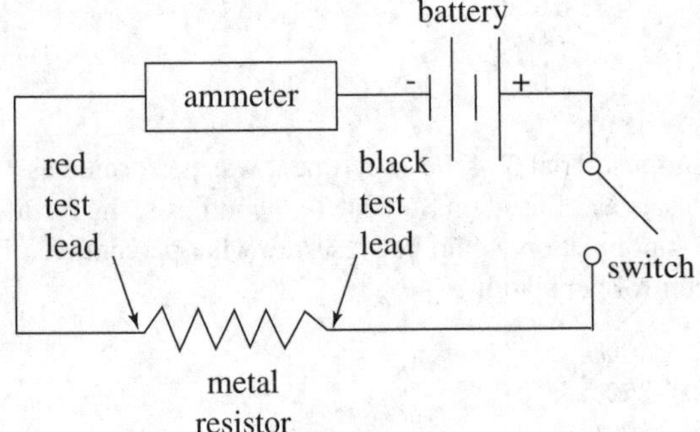

Figure 1

The *metal resistor* consisted of a coil of metallic wire with a known cross-sectional area and length (see Figure 2).

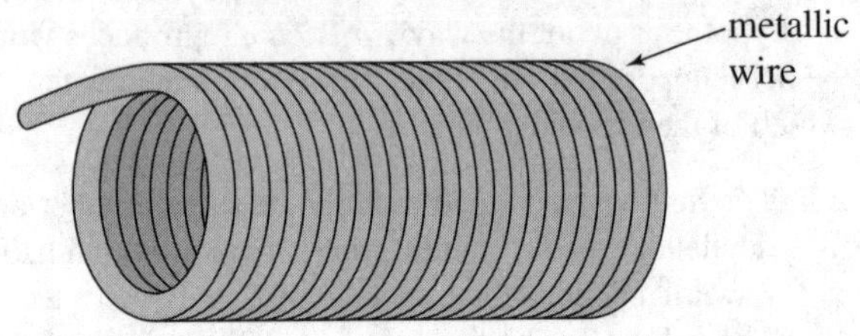

Figure 2

At the outset, the switch was open and no current flowed through the circuit. A 9-volt battery was used, and the black and red test leads of the circuit were attached to a metal resistor. When the switch was closed, electrons (negatively charged) flowed away from the negative battery terminal, through the circuit, and back to the positive battery terminal. The magnitude of current (charge per unit time) from this electron flow was measured by an *ammeter*, and was 1.0×10^{-3} coulombs/second for the first trial of each experiment. The resistance (R) of the metal resistor was calculated in ohms (Ω) from the resulting values for voltage (V) and current (I).

Experiment 1

Three nickel resistor coils, each with a cross-sectional area of 7.61×10^{-10} m^2 but with different lengths, were attached separately to the circuit. Results were recorded in Table 1.

Table 1

Resistor length (m)	I (coulombs/second)	R (Ω)
100	1.0×10^{-3}	9,000
50	2.0×10^{-3}	4,500
25	4.0×10^{-3}	2,250

Experiment 2

Three gold resistor coils of varying cross-sectional areas were tested. Each resistor coil had a measured length of 100 m. The results were recorded in Table 2.

Table 2

Resistor cross-sectional area (m^2)	I (coulombs/second)	R (Ω)
2.7×10^{-10}	1.0×10^{-3}	9,000
8.0×10^{-10}	3.0×10^{-3}	3,000
2.4×10^{-9}	9.0×10^{-3}	1,000

Experiment 3

Three coils made of different metals were tested. Each resistor had a cross-sectional area of 2.67×10^{-10} m^2 and a length of 100 m. The value ρ is related to each metal's inherent *resistivity* to current flow. Results were recorded in Table 3.

Table 3

Metal	ρ	I (coulombs/second)	R (Ω)
Gold	2.4×10^{-8}	1.0×10^{-3}	9,000
Nickel	6.9×10^{-8}	4.4×10^{-4}	25,690
Tin	1.1×10^{-7}	3.4×10^{-4}	41,250

22. If Experiment 1 had been conducted with gold resistors, at each resistor length:

F. the resistance would be lower than shown in Table 1, and the current would be higher.
G. the resistance would be higher than shown in Table 1, and the current would be lower.
H. the resistance would be lower than shown in Table 1, and the current would remain the same.
J. the resistance would be the same as shown in Table 1, and the current would be lower.

23. In Experiment 2, the scientist varied which of the following aspects of the metal resistor?

A. Identity of the metal coil
B. Cross-sectional area of the coil
C. Length of the coil
D. Value ρ of the metal composing the coil

24. Assume that as ρ increases, a metal's ability to conduct current decreases. Based on the results of Experiment 3, which of the following correctly lists gold, nickel, and tin in order of increasing ability to conduct electrons when shaped as a wire coil?

F. Gold, nickel, tin
G. Gold, tin, nickel
H. Tin, nickel, gold
J. Tin, gold, nickel

25. In the first trial of Experiments 1–3, once the resistor was attached and the switch closed, what charge returned to the positive battery terminal each second?

A. -1.0×10^{-3} coulombs
B. -2.0×10^{-3} coulombs
C. -3.0×10^{-3} coulombs
D. -4.0×10^{-3} coulombs

26. Based on the results of the 3 experiments, the resistor with which of the following values of length, cross-sectional area, and metal type will have the highest current at a given voltage?

	Length (m)	Cross-sectional area (m²)	Metal
F.	100	2.00×10^{-10}	nickel
G.	50	2.00×10^{-10}	tin
H.	50	4.00×10^{-10}	gold
J.	50	2.00×10^{-10}	gold

27. In Experiment 1, the current across the circuit increased and the resistance of the resistor decreased as the:

A. value ρ of the metal resistor increased.
B. cross-sectional area of the metal resistor decreased.
C. length of the metal resistor increased.
D. length of the metal resistor decreased.

28. When the switch is closed in the circuit described in the passage, the battery caused electrons to flow in the direction(s) shown by which of the following diagrams?

F.

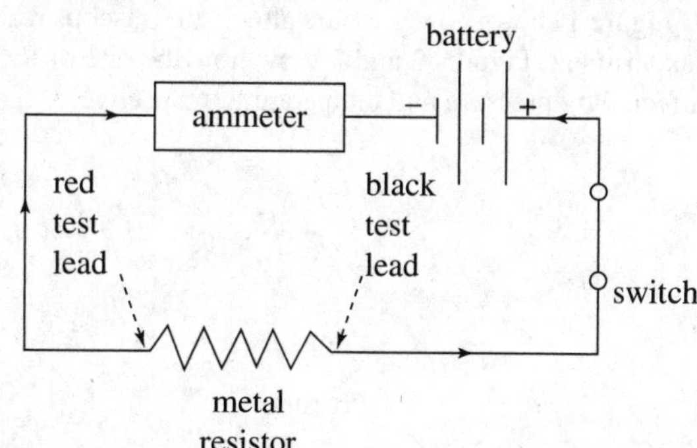

G.

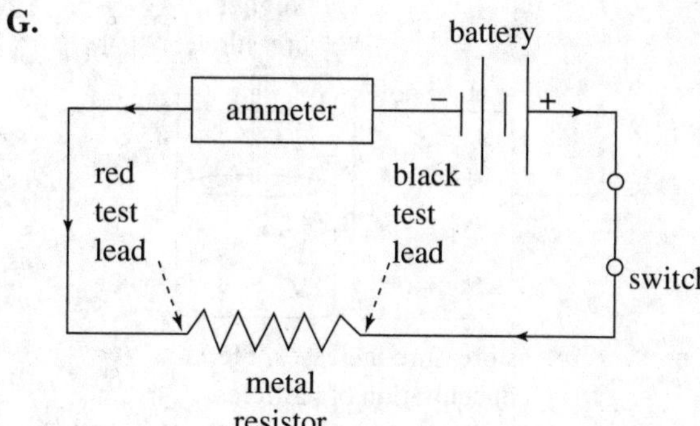

H.

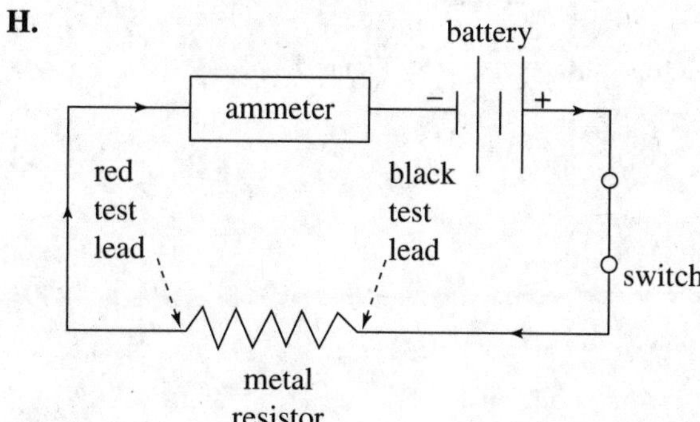

J.

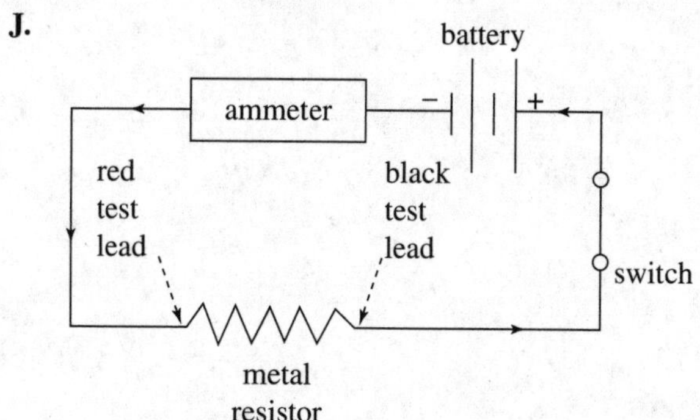

Passage V

Pressure, temperature, volume, and amount of reactant are four variables that affect the rate at which a reaction in the gas phase occurs. A change in any of these variables changes the likelihood of particles running into each other and reacting.

Pressure is measured in atmospheres, atm, where 1 atm is the sea level pressure of Earth's atmosphere. Volume is measured in liters, L. The amount of reactant is measured in moles, where 1 mole is 6.02×10^{23} molecules.

Figure 1 shows how pressure affects the gaseous reactants in an experiment. Figures 2 and 3 show how the rate of Reaction A is affected by pressure and temperature, respectively.

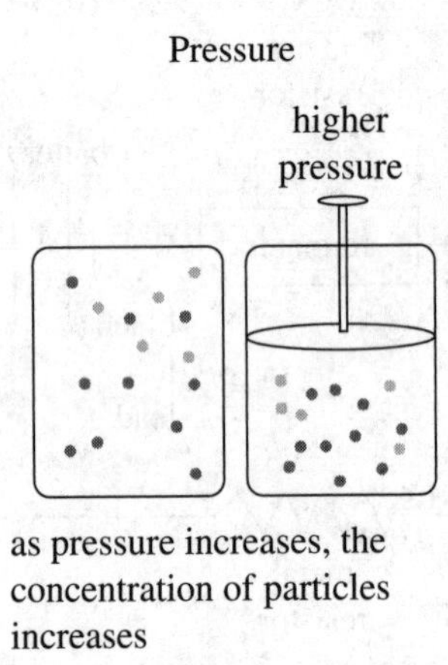

Figure 1

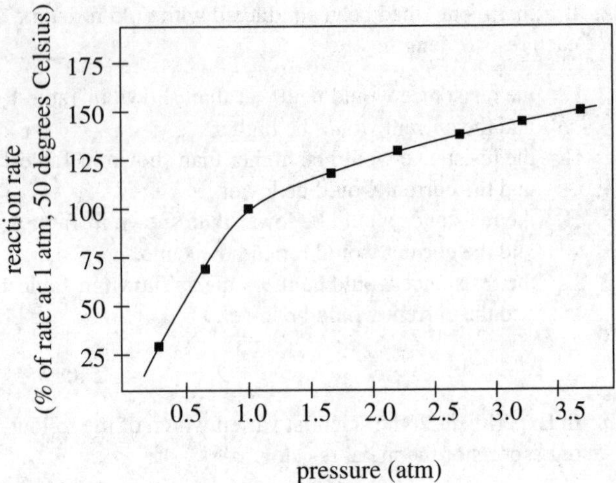

Figure 2

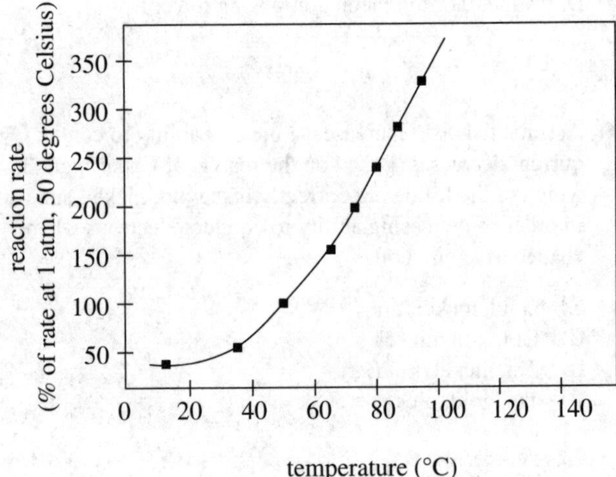

Figure 3

29. A scientist claimed that increasing temperature increases the rate at which Reaction A occurs and increasing pressure increases the rate at which Reaction A occurs. Is the scientist's claim supported by the data in Figures 2 and 3 ?

A. Yes; the rate at which Reaction A occurred increased as temperature increased and increased as pressure increased.
B. Yes; the rate at which Reaction A occurred increased as pressure decreased.
C. No; the rate at which Reaction A occurred increased as temperature increased, but decreased as pressure increased.
D. No; the rate at which Reaction A occurred decreased as pressure increased.

30. According to Figures 2 and 3, the reactions occur at the same rate at what pressure and temperature?

F. 20°C and 2.0 atm
G. 40°C and 1.5 atm
H. 50°C and 1.0 atm
J. 70°C and 1.5 atm

31. The amounts of reactants in Reaction A are 1 mole/L of Compound Y and 2 mole/L of Compound Z. According to the passage, the number of molecules of Compound Y is:

A. one-quarter of the number of molecules of Compound Z in the reactants.
B. one-half the number of molecules of Compound Z in the reactants.
C. equal to the number of molecules of Compound Z in the reactants.
D. twice the number of molecules of Compound Z in the reactants.

32. A scientist tests a new Reaction B. This reaction is conducted with the same gas phase reactants, volume, and temperature as Reaction A, but the amounts (moles) of reactants are doubled. Based only on the information in the passage and Figures 1–3, how will the rate of Reaction B compare with the rate of Reaction A ?

F. Reaction B will be slower than Reaction A because temperature will be lower.
G. Reaction B will be faster than Reaction A because temperature will be lower.
H. Reaction B will be faster than Reaction A because the concentration of reactants is greater, so the likelihood of reactant molecules colliding and reacting is greater.
J. Reaction B will be slower than Reaction A because the concentration of reactants is greater, so the likelihood of reactant molecules colliding and reacting is greater.

33. Based on the data in Figures 2 and 3, which of the following changes would lead to the greatest increase in the reaction rate of Reaction A ?

A. Decreasing the pressure from 1 atm to 0.5 atm
B. Increasing the pressure from 1 atm to 3 atm
C. Decreasing the temperature from 50°C to 20°C
D. Increasing the temperature from 50°C to 100°C

34. Which of the following is true of the volume of the gas in Figure 2 as the pressure increases from 1.0 atm to 2.0 atm ?

F. It increases by 50% because pressure and volume are inversely proportional.
G. It decreases by 50% because pressure and volume are inversely proportional.
H. It increases by 50% because pressure and volume are directly proportional.
J. It decreases by 50% because pressure and volume are directly proportional.

Passage VI

An experiment is set up to look at the physics of bouncing a ball, as shown in Figure 1.

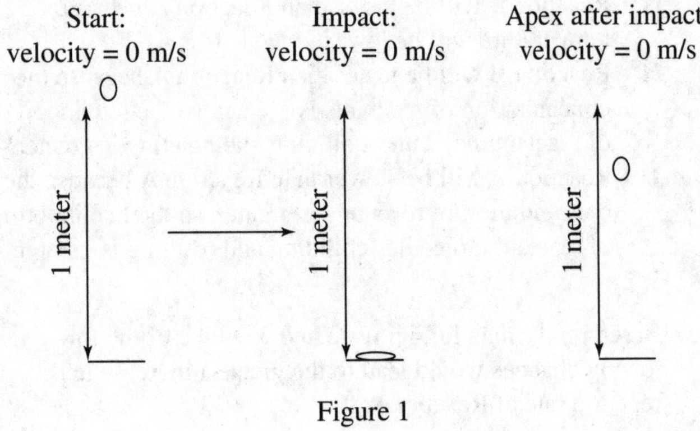

Figure 1

When the ball is dropped, its initial velocity is 0 m/s. Velocity will increase until impact with the ground, at which point the ball's velocity immediately drops to 0 m/s again. After impact, velocity almost immediately increases to maximum post-impact velocity, and then begins to fall again as gravity works against it, slowing it down. The ball's velocity returns to 0 m/s when the ball is at its *apex*, or highest vertical point, post impact.

When a ball bounces, it deforms and becomes flatter. This is called *elasticity*. The more elasticity a material has, the better it is able to act like a spring and absorb force by being compressed, then use this force to "spring" back into the air. Post-impact velocity and the amount of time between velocity of 0 m/s at impact and velocity of 0 m/s at post-impact apex are affected by elasticity. Figure 2 shows the velocity of a ball versus time for balls with various elasticities and weights dropped from 1 meter height. Because gravity causes all objects to fall at the same speed regardless of weight, pre-impact velocities are identical for all balls.

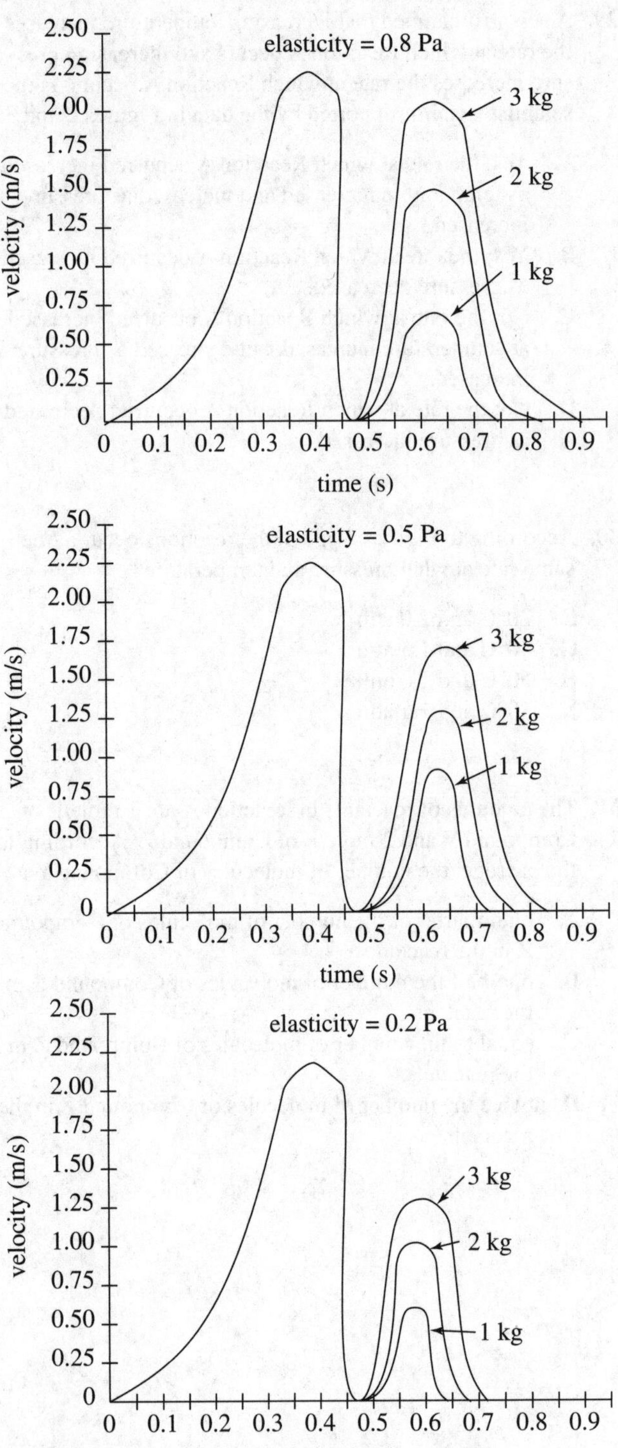

Figure 2

35. The ball with an elasticity of 0.8 Pa and a weight of 3 kg is dropped from a height of 1.5 meters. Based on the information in the passage and Figure 2, the maximum velocity of the ball after impact would be:

A. greater than 2 m/s.
B. approximately equal to 2 m/s.
C. between 1.5 and 2 m/s.
D. less than 1.5 m/s.

36. Based on the data in Figure 2, the maximum post-impact velocity of a ball will be smallest if the elasticity of the ball is:

F. greater than 1.5 Pa.
G. between 1 and 1.5 Pa.
H. between 0.5 and 1 Pa.
J. less than 0.5 Pa.

37. Based on the information in Figure 2, a ball being dropped from 1 meter height with an elasticity of 0.2 Pa and a weight of 0.5 kg would have a maximum post-impact velocity of:

A. less than 0.50 m/s.
B. 0.75 m/s.
C. 1.0 m/s.
D. greater than 1.25 m/s.

38. Consider a ball as it completes one bounce, from drop to post-impact apex. If this ball has a weight of 2 kg and an elasticity of 0.50 Pa, based on the data in Figure 2, how many times does the ball have a velocity of 1.00 m/s ?

F. One time
G. Two times
H. Three times
J. Four times

39. Based on the data in Figure 2, how does the velocity of a ball change as it goes from drop to apex?

	Drop to Impact	Impact to Apex
A.	Increases only	Increases only
B.	Decreases only	Increases then decreases
C.	Increases then decreases	Increases then decreases
D.	Decreases then increases	Increases only

40. A ball will deform permanently and not spring back off the ground if the velocity with which it hits the ground exceeds the ball's *elastic limit.* Based on the data in Figure 2, if a ball is dropped from one meter and has a weight of 3 kg, an elasticity of 0.8 Pa, and an elastic limit of 2.75 m/s, will the ball deform permanently?

F. Yes, because the velocity with which the ball hits the ground is less than its elastic limit.
G. Yes, because the velocity with which the ball hits the ground is greater than its elastic limit.
H. No, because the velocity with which the ball hits the ground is less than its elastic limit.
J. No, because the velocity with which the ball hits the ground is greater than its elastic limit.

Science Practice Section 3 Answers and Explanations

SCIENCE PRACTICE SECTION 3 ANSWERS

1. B
2. G
3. A
4. G
5. D
6. G
7. D
8. G
9. D
10. G
11. A
12. J
13. B
14. G
15. A
16. F
17. B
18. G
19. A
20. H
21. D
22. F
23. B
24. H
25. A
26. H
27. D
28. J
29. A
30. H
31. B
32. H
33. D
34. G
35. A
36. J
37. A
38. J
39. C
40. H

SCIENCE PRACTICE SECTION 3 EXPLANATIONS

Passage I

1. **B** The question asks what is essential in maintaining the mosquito population, according to Figure 1. Figure 1 shows the life cycle of mosquitoes. The first step indicates that the eggs are laid underwater and that egg-hatching is *dependent* on sufficient water for survival. The *jungle, monkeys,* and *humans* are not mentioned in Figure 1. Eliminate (A), (C), and (D). The correct answer is (B).

2. **G** The question asks for the approximate average percent of villagers affected by Yellow Fever, based on Table 1. Refer to Table 1 and examine the percentages of villagers affected for each village. To help find the average, round each value. Village A has about 10% affected. Village B has about 20% affected, and Village C has about 30% affected. Village D has about 40% affected. Village E has about 50% affected. Eliminate (H) and (J) because these are both higher than any of the values in the table. Look at the remaining answers. The averages of three of the towns are all well above 20%, and only village A is well below 20%. The average has to be higher than this, so eliminate (F). The correct answer is (G).

3. **A** The question asks which month would be expected to have the *largest total of mosquito bites per month,* given the data in Study 2 and Figure 2. Since number of mosquito bites per village was measured in Study 2, look here first. As the number of mosquito bites increases, the percentage of the group affected by Yellow Fever increases. Therefore, the greatest number of mosquito bites would be expected in months with the greatest number of Yellow Fever cases. Refer to Figure 2 and find the month with the greatest number of new Yellow Fever cases. In April there were 6 new Yellow Fever cases, and in June there were 2 new Yellow Fever cases. Eliminate (B). In both August and November there was only 1 new Yellow Fever case. Eliminate (C) and (D). The correct answer is (A).

4. **G** The question asks for which pair of months was the amount of rainfall NOT different. The question states that each of the pairs of months have different amounts of rainfall except for one. The correct answer will be the pair with the same amount of rainfall. Use Figure 2 and work through the answer choices. Start with (F). In May the rainfall was 10″, and in December the rainfall was 16″. Since these are different, eliminate (F). For (G), both February and March had about 32″ of rainfall. These are the same, so keep (G). Since January and October had different rainfalls (25″ versus 4″), eliminate (H). Since April and May also had different rainfalls (20″ versus 10″), eliminate (J). The correct answer is (G).

5. **D** The question asks about the relationship between the number of water sources and the number of monkeys seen. Refer to Table 1, which shows that the number of water sources increases from Village A to Village E. Meanwhile, the number of monkeys neither consistently increases nor decreases. Since there is no distinct pattern, the correct answer is (D).

6. **G** The question asks about the predicted number of people who will be infected with Yellow Fever in a hypothetical village. According to the question, this village has 8 water sources within 2 miles and a population of 1,200. In Table 1, the number of water sources is directly proportional to the percentage of the village affected by Yellow Fever. Since the village described in the question has 8 water sources, it is most closely represented by Village C, which had 29% of the village affected by yellow fever. In this hypothetical village, the predicted number of people infected would be approximately 30% of 1,200, which is about 400 people. The best answer is (G).

7. **D** The question asks about the minimum amount of time expected to pass between the first rainfall and the first reoccurrence of mosquito bites after an extended drought, according to Figure 1. The figure indicates that mosquito eggs will not hatch unless there is sufficient water; this would represent the first rainfall after a drought. At this point, it takes 2 weeks for the hatched eggs to progress from larvae to pupae. It then takes an additional week for pupae to emerge from their sacks and become adult mosquitos. At this point the mosquitos will begin biting and infecting people. Therefore, after an extended drought, it would take a minimum of 3 weeks before the first reoccurrence of mosquito bites. The correct answer is (D).

Passage II

8. **G** The question asks in what way the procedure of Experiment 2 differed from that of Experiment 1. Both (F) and (G) mention temperature. Look for the word *temperature* in the descriptions of Experiments 1 and 2. According to the description of Experiment 1, *the experimental procedure was repeated at varying temperatures,* and according to the description of Experiment 2, the same procedures were repeated but this time at *26°C.* Eliminate (F) because it states that *temperature was varied* in Experiment 2 and *in Experiment 1, the temperature was held constant,* which is incorrect. Choice (G) accurately represents the data. Eliminate (H) and (J) because both *MEA* and *DEA* were used in Experiment 1. The correct answer is (G).

9. **D** The question asks how *the concentration of* CO_2 changed *as the time progressed from 0 to 8,190 msec during the DEA trial at 20°C,* according to the data in Experiment 1. Since there is no mention of *the concentration of* CO_2 in Table 1, look for CO_2 in the explanation of Experiment 1. *The scrub time,* or *time for* CO_2 *concentration to drop at least 10 ppm was measured* in this experiment. Eliminate (A) and (B) because they both state that *the concentration of* CO_2 increased. Eliminate (C) because although it uses the word *decreased,* the numbers show an increase. The only answer choice that states that *the concentration of* CO_2 *decreased* and shows a drop in values is (D). The correct answer is (D).

10. **G** The question asks for the *scrub times (in msec) for both MEA and DEA* if *an additional trial were done at 12°C* in Experiment 1. Look at the results of Experiment 1 in Table 1. As temperature increases, the scrub times for both MEA and DEA decrease. Draw a horizontal line across the table where 12°C would fall, in between 10°C and 15°C. The scrub time for MEA would fall between 10,925 and 11,025 msec. Eliminate (F) because the scrub time listed for MEA is out of range. Keep

(G) and (H) because the scrub times listed for MEA are within range. Eliminate (J) because the scrub time listed for MEA is equivalent to that of a trial done at 10°C. According to Table 2, the scrub time for DEA at 10°C is 8,315 and at 15°C it is 8,240, so the scrub time for DEA at 12°C must be between those values. Eliminate (H) because the time listed is out of range. The correct answer is (G).

11. **A** The question asks for *a possible chemical formula for an ethanolamine,* based on the information in the passage. Paragraph 1 states that *ethanolamines are compounds that contain both alcohol (–OH* or *HO–) and amine (–NH_3, –RNH_2, –R_2NH,* or *–R_3N) subgroups.* Both (A) and (B) contain HO– so keep them. Eliminate (C) and (D) because neither contains *–OH* or *HO–*. Eliminate (B) because it does not contain *–NH_3, –RNH_2, –R_2NH,* or *–R_3N.* The correct answer is (A).

12. **J** The question asks whether the results of Experiment 1 support the following claim: *DEA will always absorb CO_2 at a faster rate than will MEA.* Look at the results of Experiment 1 as listed in Table 1. *CO_2* is not present in Table 1, so look for *CO_2* in the description of Experiment 1. The passage defines *scrub time* as the *time for CO_2 concentration to drop at least 10 ppm.* Table 1 shows that the scrub time of MEA is always more than that of DEA. The passage states that *longer scrub times indicate a slower rate of absorption.* Therefore, the claim is supported; *DEA will always absorb CO_2 at a faster rate than will MEA.* Eliminate (F) and (G) because they say *no.* Although (H) states that the claim is supported, its explanation is opposite. Only (J) states that the claim is supported and that *the scrub time for MEA was more than that for DEA.* The correct answer is (J).

13. **B** The question asks *which acidic gas had the slowest absorption by MEA at 26°C,* according to Experiment 2. Look for the word *absorption* in the passage. The description of Experiment 1 states that *longer scrub times indicate a slower rate of absorption.* Look at Table 2. The formula with the longest scrub time is HCN. The correct answer is (B).

14. **G** The question asks for a reactant and a product from the reaction in Experiment 1. Experiment 1 studies either MEA or DEA, and, according to the formula in Figure 1, is mixed with gaseous CO_2. Since all of the answer choices list MEA, DEA, or CO_2 as potential reactants, this doesn't help eliminate any answers. However, refer to Figure 1 for the possible products of Experiment 1. None of the listed products is water (H_2O), so eliminate (H) and (J). Additionally, CO_2 is not a product—it's a reactant, so eliminate (F) as well. The only correct product shown in Figure 1 is heat. Therefore, the correct answer is (G).

Passage III

15. **A** The question asks what percent of the number of dandelions in a control field would the number of new dandelions be if another experiment were conducted, *in which several new Taraxicum plants were planted in a field with their roots in glass jars and with plastic bags over the flowers,* assuming that Student 1's hypothesis is correct. Look at Student 1's explanation. The first paragraph of Student 1's explanation states that *in Taraxicum, vegetative reproduction and seed distribution make up the only means of growing new plants. Vegetative reproduction* is described in the introduction as a

process in which *a new dandelion stalk and leaves can grow up from an existing root system.* The new experiment described would prevent vegetative reproduction with the glass jars. It would also prevent seed distribution with the plastic bags, so no new plants would ever grow. The correct answer is (A).

16. **F** The question asks which trial *provided the control group in the students' experiment.* A control group is one that is left alone, with no variables. According to Table 1, Trial 1 was performed *in the soil of a field with no other Taraxicum plants,* and the new *Taraxicum* plants *are allowed to spread normally.* Trial 1 is the control, so eliminate (H) and (J). Eliminate (G) because it mentions glass jars, which were not used in Trial 1. The correct answer is (F).

17. **B** The question asks why Student 2 does not believe Student 1's statement *that dandelions growing in clumps "suggests that individual seeds sprout the first new dandelions, which then grow through vegetative reproduction."* Look for words from the answer choices in Student 2's explanation. Eliminate (A) because the second paragraph of Student 2's explanation states that the roots of *Taraxicum* plants *do not spread out underground.* Keep (B) because the second paragraph of Student 2's explanation states that *Taraxicum...each have a single large, deep taproot* and that *plants which rely on vegetative reproduction...tend to have large, complex root networks.* Eliminate (C) because, according to Student 2, *seed distribution is the main way Taraxicum spreads itself* and so seeds **are** important to *Taraxicum's reproductive strategy.* Eliminate (D) because Student 2 states in paragraph 6 that *all known types of Taraxicum produce seed globes.* The correct answer is (B).

18. **G** The question asks which statement Student 2 would most likely agree with. Look for words from the answer choices in Student 2's explanation. Eliminate (F) because this is Student 1's position. Keep (G) because Student 2 states that *Taraxicum does use vegetative reproduction...mainly to replace the above-ground plant if it has been cut or eaten,* which would *improve its ability to survive.* Eliminate (H) because Student 2 states that *even a slight breeze or brush of a passing animal is enough to spread dandelion seeds to a new area,* but there is no mention of *humans.* Eliminate (J) because Student 1 states that *the dandelions tend to grow together in clumps,* but Student 2 does not discuss this idea. The correct answer is (G).

19. **A** The question asks under which conditions of the experiment the *Taraxicum* plants would be greatest in number, according to Students 1 and 2. Student 1 believes *vegetative reproduction and seed distribution make up the only means of growing new plants.* Student 2 believes *seed distribution is the main way Taraxicum spreads itself,* but that *Taraxicum does use vegetative reproduction.* They would both agree that plastic bags would prevent *seed distribution*, so eliminate (B) and (D). *Vegetative reproduction* is described in the introduction as a process in which *a new dandelion stalk and leaves can grow up from an existing root system.* Both students would therefore agree that glass jars would limit *vegetative reproduction;* eliminate (C). Choice (A) is the only option that uses neither. The correct answer is (A).

20. **H** The question asks what percentage of a control population the resulting population of Trial 3 would be, according to Student 1. In paragraph 2, Student 1 states that *vegetative reproduction* and *seed*

distribution...each accounts for 50% of the growth of new dandelions. Vegetative reproduction is described in the introduction as a process in which *a new dandelion stalk and leaves can grow up from an existing root system.* Look at Table 1. Trial 3 prevented *vegetative reproduction* by placing the roots in a glass jar. Therefore, the plants would be half as likely to reproduce. The correct answer is (H).

21. **D** The question asks which pattern would support *Student 2's hypothesis about the way Taraxicum reproduces.* Student 2's explanation states that *seed distribution is the main way Taraxicum spreads itself* even though it *does use vegetative reproduction.* Eliminate (A) and (B) because Trial 2 would prevent *seed distribution* so, according to Student 2, it would have fewer plants than Trials 1 and 3. Eliminate (C) because the seeds were not covered in Trial 3, so according to Student 2, it should have the same number of dandelions as Trial 1. Keep (D) because Student 2 believes that the glass jar would prevent a few dandelions from growing in Trial 3, and Student 2 also believes that the plastic bags in Trial 2 covering the seeds would prevent *many more dandelions* from growing. The correct answer is (D).

Passage IV

22. **F** The question asks what would happen if Experiment 1 were conducted with gold resistors. Experiment 1 was initially conducted with nickel resistors. For information about resistors made of different metals, refer to Table 3. According to Table 3, resistors made of gold will have much lower resistances than those made of nickel (25,690 Ωs compared to 9,000 Ωs). This means if Experiment 1 were repeated with gold resistors, the resistance would be lower. Use this information to eliminate (G) and (J). Table 3 also indicates that current (I) would also be lower with gold resistors. The correct answer is (F).

23. **B** The question asks which *aspects of the metal resistor* varied in Experiment 2. Look at the results of Experiment 2 in Table 2. The only variable from the answer choices that appears in the table is *cross-sectional area.* Since none of the variables in (A), (C), or (D) appears in the table, they must have been held constant in the experiment. Eliminate (A), (C), and (D). The correct answer is (B).

24. **H** The question asks for a list of the metals used in Experiment 3, *in order of increasing ability to conduct electrons,* assuming *that as ρ increases, a metal's ability to conduct current decreases.* Look at the results of Experiment 3, found in Table 3. The metal with the highest *ability to conduct electrons* is the one with the lowest *ρ*. *Tin* has the highest *ρ*, so eliminate (F) and (G). The metal with the next highest *ability to conduct electrons* is *nickel,* so eliminate (J). The correct answer is (H).

25. **A** The question asks for the value of the *charge* that *returned to the positive battery terminal each second...in the first trial of Experiments 1–3, once the resistor was attached and the switch closed.* Look for the word *switch* in the passage. According to the introduction, *when the switch was closed, electrons (negatively charged) flowed away from the negative battery terminal and back to the positive battery terminal.* The passage goes on to say that *the magnitude of current (charge per unit time) from this electron flow was...*1.0×10^{-3} *coulombs/second for the first trial of each experiment.* The correct answer is (A).

26. **H** The question asks which resistor *will have the highest current at a given voltage,* based on the results of the three experiments. The introduction states that *current* is referred to as *I.* Look at the results of Experiment 1, which tested *different lengths,* found in Table 1. As lengths decrease, current increases. A shorter resistor will have a higher current; eliminate (F) because it has the longest length. Experiment 2 tested *varying cross-sectional areas.* Look at Table 2. As the *resistor cross-sectional area* increases, the current also increases. Eliminate both (G) and (J) because they have a lower *cross-sectional area* than that of (H). The correct answer is (H).

27. **D** The question asks what happens when the *current across the circuit increased and the resistance of the resistor decreased* in Experiment 1. Look at the results of Experiment 1 in Table 1, which shows that as the *current,* I, increased, *the resistance of the resistor,* R, decreased, and the *resistor length* decreased. Eliminate (A) because Table 1 does not include *r.* Eliminate (B) because Table 1 does not include *cross-sectional area.* Eliminate (C) because the *length of the metal resistor decreased.* The correct answer is (D).

28. **J** The question asks which diagram shows the electrons flowing in the right direction *when the switch is closed,* according to the description in the passage. Look for the word *switch* in the passage. According to the passage, *when the switch was closed, electrons (negatively charged) flowed away from the negative battery terminal, through the circuit, and back to the positive battery terminal.* The diagrams in each answer choice have arrows running along the circuit. Look at the negative side of the battery. In order to be consistent with the passage, the arrows should point away from the negative terminal of the battery and continue in the same direction toward the positive terminal of the battery. Eliminate (F) and (G) because the arrows do not continue in the same direction around the current. Eliminate (H) because the arrows are pointing in the opposite direction, away from the positive terminal and toward the negative terminal. Choice (J) is consistent with the description in the passage. The correct answer is (J).

Passage V

29. **A** The question asks whether a scientist's claim that *increasing temperature increases the rate at which Reaction A occurs and increasing pressure increases the rate at which Reaction A occurs* is consistent with Figures 2 and 3. Figure 2 shows that as pressure increases, reaction rate also increases. Figure 3 shows that as temperature increases, reaction rate also increases. The scientist's claim is true, so eliminate both (C) and (D). Eliminate (B) because it inaccurately states that *the rate at which Reaction A occurred increased as pressure decreased.* The correct answer is (A).

30. **H** The question asks, *according to Figures 2 and 3,* at *what pressure and temperature* do the reactions occur *at the same rate.* Look at Figure 2. According to the label on the *y*-axis, the temperature is constant at 50°C in this figure. Eliminate (F), (G), and (J), because the only possible temperature in Figure 2 is 50°C. Therefore, the only point in common between the two figures occurs at 50°C and 1.0 atm, where the reaction rate is 100%. The correct answer is (H).

31. **B** The question asks how *the number of molecules* in 1 mole/L *of Compound Y* compares to *the number of molecules* in 2 mole/L *of Compound Z,* according to the passage. Look for the words *molecule* and *mole* in the passage. Paragraph 2 states that *1 mole is* 6.02×10^{23} *molecules.* Since Compound Y contains 1 mole, it has 6.02×10^{23} molecules. Compound Z has 2 moles, so it has 12.04×10^{23} molecules. Compound Y has half as many molecules as Compound Z. The correct answer is (B).

32. **H** The question asks how the rate of Reaction B compares to that of Reaction A, when Reaction B *is conducted with the same gas phase reactants, volume, and temperature as Reaction A, but the amounts (moles) of reactants are doubled,* based on the information in the passage and Figures 1–3. Eliminate (F) and (G) because the question says that temperature does not change. Look for information in the passage about *reactants.* The first paragraph states that *pressure, temperature, volume, and amount of reactant are four variables that affect the rate at which a reaction in the gas phase occurs* and that *a change in any one of these variables changes the likelihood of particles running into each other and reacting.* Reaction B will be faster than Reaction A because it has more reactants. Eliminate (J) because it states the opposite. The correct answer is (H).

33. **D** The question asks which change would lead to the greatest increase in the reaction rate of Reaction A, based on the data in Figures 2 and 3. According to Figure 2, reaction rate increases with increasing pressure, so eliminate (A). According to Figure 3, reaction rate also increases with increasing temperature, so eliminate (C). In Figure 2, increasing the pressure from 1.0 atm to 3.0 atm as suggested in (B) causes only modest increases in reaction rate (from 100% to about 140%). Meanwhile, increasing the temperature from 50°C to 100°C would cause the reaction rate to increase drastically (from 100% to about 325%). Therefore, this is the change that would lead to the greatest increase in the reaction rate of Reaction A. The correct answer is (D).

34. **G** The question asks about the volume of the gas in Figure 2 as the pressure increases from 1.0 atm to 2.0 atm. Figure 1 shows that as pressure increases, the concentration of particles increases and the volume decreases. Therefore, as the pressure increases from 1.0 atm to 2.0 atm, the volume will decrease. Eliminate (F) and (H). This relationship is inversely proportional (one value increases as the other decreases), so eliminate (J). The correct answer is (G).

Passage VI

35. **A** The question asks about the maximum velocity after impact for a ball with an elasticity of 0.8 Pa and a weight of 3 kg dropped from a height of 1.5 meters. The top graph of Figure 2 shows a ball with this elasticity and weight dropped from 1 meter. According to Figure 2, the maximum velocity after impact for the 3 kg ball is approximately 2.0 m/s. A ball dropped from a height of 1.5 meters instead of 1 meter would have a faster velocity prior to impact, and therefore, would have a faster post-impact velocity than the one shown in Figure 2. The correct answer is (A).

36. **J** The question asks which elasticity would cause a ball to have the smallest *maximum post-impact velocity,* according to Figure 2. Look at Figure 2. The graphs display the velocity of a ball over time

after it has been dropped. The curve begins at 0 seconds and 0 m/s, just before the ball is dropped. Each ball increases in velocity until it hits the ground at around 0.45 seconds. The *maximum post-impact velocity* is shown in each graph as the second peak. The *maximum post-impact velocity* of the 3 kg ball in the first graph with *elasticity = 0.8 Pa* is about 2.05. The *maximum post-impact velocity* of the 3 kg ball in the second graph with *elasticity = 0.5 Pa* is about 1.75. The *maximum post-impact velocity* of the 3 kg ball in the third graph with *elasticity = 0.2 Pa* is about 1.30, which is the smallest. Therefore, the lower the elasticity, the smaller the *maximum post-impact velocity.* Choice (J) has the lowest value for elasticity. The correct answer is (J).

37. **A** The question asks for the *maximum post-impact velocity* of *a ball being dropped from 1 meter height with an elasticity of 0.2 Pa and a weight of 0.5 kg,* based on the information in Figure 2. Look for similar conditions in Figure 2. The third graph displays information regarding a ball with 0.2 elasticity. Look at the curve representing a 1 kg ball. Its *maximum post-impact velocity* is 0.50. As weight decreases, so does *maximum post-impact velocity,* so the *maximum post-impact velocity* of a ball that weighs 0.5 kg should be less than that of the 1 kg ball. Eliminate (B), (C), and (D) because they are greater than 0.5 kg. The correct answer is (A).

38. **J** The question asks how many times a ball, with a weight of 2 kg and an elasticity of 0.50 Pa, had a velocity of 1.00 m/s, according to the data in Figure 2. Look for similar conditions in Figure 2. The second graph shows data regarding a ball with an elasticity of 0.50. Locate 1.00 m/s on the *y*-axis and draw a straight line to the other side of the graph. The curve representing the velocity of the 2 kg ball intersects the line drawn four times, which means the 2 kg ball had a velocity of 1.00 m/s four times. The correct answer is (J).

39. **C** The question asks *how the velocity of a ball change[s] as it goes from drop to apex,* according to Figure 2. Look at Figure 2. The curve representing the velocity of the ball begins at 0 m/s, when the ball is at rest, just before it is dropped. The ball then increases in velocity until just before it hits the ground. There is a rapid decrease to 0 m/s at the moment when the ball hits the ground. Eliminate (A) because it says the velocity increases only from drop to impact. Eliminate (B) because it says the velocity decreases only from drop to impact. Keep (C) because it correctly states that, from drop to impact, the velocity increases and then decreases. Eliminate (D) because it states the opposite. The correct answer is (C).

40. **H** The question asks whether, according to Figure 2, a ball will deform permanently if it has *a weight of 3 kg, an elasticity of 0.8 Pa, and an elastic limit of 2.75 m/s,* given that *a ball will deform permanently...if the velocity with which it hits the ground exceeds the ball's elastic limit.* Look for similar conditions in Figure 2. The first graph displays data regarding a ball with an elasticity of 0.8 Pa. The ball begins at rest and increases in velocity until it impacts the ground at just before 0.45 seconds; the velocity just before it hits the ground is 2.25 m/s. This is less than the *elastic limit of 2.75 m/s,* so the ball will not *deform permanently.* Eliminate (F) and (G) because they state that it will deform permanently. Keep (H) and eliminate (J) because *the velocity with which the ball hits the ground is less than its elastic limit.* The correct answer is (H).

Writing Practice
Section 1

Directions

This is a test of your writing skills. You will have forty (40) minutes to read the prompt, plan your response, and write an essay in English. Before you begin working, read all material in this test booklet carefully to understand exactly what you are being asked to do.

You will write your answer on the lined pages in the answer document provided. Your writing on those pages will be scored. You may use the unlined pages in this test booklet to plan your essay. Your work on these pages will not be scored.

Your essay will be evaluated based on the evidence it provides of your ability to:

- clearly state your own perspective on a complex issue and analyze the relationship between your perspective and at least one other perspective
- develop and support your ideas with reasoning and examples
- organize your ideas clearly and logically
- communicate your ideas effectively in standard written English

Lay your pencil down immediately when time is called.

DO NOT OPEN THIS BOOK UNTIL YOU ARE TOLD TO DO SO.

Composition paper for the essay can be found beginning on page 562.

The Banishment of Cigarettes

Over the last several decades, society has become increasingly aware of the detrimental effects of tobacco products. A person is far more likely to see an anti-smoking advertisement on television that illustrates the harmful effects of the product than to see one that is in favor of it, and print ads are accompanied by large warnings from the surgeon general. Some argue that even though they increase awareness of tobacco's harmful side effects, these advertisements are still advocating for the purchase of the product. Due to the findings, some maintain that cigarettes and other tobacco products should be banned.

Read and carefully consider these perspectives. Each suggests a particular way of thinking about the conflict over whether cigarettes should be banned.

Perspective One

Dangerous drugs are already banned by the federal government. While marijuana is illegal in many parts of the United States, many argue that cigarettes are worse than marijuana for a variety of reasons. Cigarettes have a negative effect on individuals and society as a whole and should be banned.

Perspective Two

The government cannot ban everything that carries a risk. Unhealthy foods have led to diseases such as diabetes and obesity, yet people are still free to enjoy the plethora of options available to them. A ban on cigarettes is unnecessary and infringes on an individual's right to control his or her own life.

Perspective Three

In history, Prohibition was largely unsuccessful and led to social uprising. Certain historians argue that due to this failure, the ban would be largely unsuccessful and potentially dangerous.

Essay Task

Write a unified, coherent essay in which you evaluate the multiple perspectives on the banishment of cigarettes. In your essay, be sure to:

- clearly state your own perspective on the issue and analyze the relationship between your perspective and at least one other perspective
- develop and support your ideas with reasoning and examples
- organize your ideas clearly and logically
- communicate your ideas effectively in standard written English

Your perspective may be in full agreement with any of the others, in partial agreement, or wholly different. Whatever the case, support your ideas with logical reasoning and detailed, persuasive examples.

The Princeton Review
Diagnostic ACT Form

ESSAY

Begin your essay on this side. If necessary, continue on the opposite side.

Continue on the opposite side if necessary.

The Princeton Review
Diagnostic ACT Form

Continued from previous page.

PLEASE PRINT YOUR INITIALS

First	Middle	Last

The Princeton Review
Diagnostic ACT Form

Continued from previous page.

PLEASE PRINT YOUR INITIALS

First	Middle	Last

The Princeton Review
Diagnostic ACT Form

Continued from previous page.

PLEASE PRINT YOUR INITIALS

First	Middle	Last

Writing Practice Section 2

Directions

This is a test of your writing skills. You will have forty (40) minutes to read the prompt, plan your response, and write an essay in English. Before you begin working, read all material in this test booklet carefully to understand exactly what you are being asked to do.

You will write your answer on the lined pages in the answer document provided. Your writing on those pages will be scored. You may use the unlined pages in this test booklet to plan your essay. Your work on these pages will not be scored.

Your essay will be evaluated based on the evidence it provides of your ability to:

- clearly state your own perspective on a complex issue and analyze the relationship between your perspective and at least one other perspective
- develop and support your ideas with reasoning and examples
- organize your ideas clearly and logically
- communicate your ideas effectively in standard written English

Lay your pencil down immediately when time is called.

DO NOT OPEN THIS BOOK UNTIL YOU ARE TOLD TO DO SO.

Composition paper for the essay can be found beginning on page 570.

Dress Codes in Schools

Some parents have advocated for the enforcement of strict dress codes in schools. Student organizations and groups have argued against this, citing that such an act stifles individuality and denies freedom of expression. Private Institutions have rules about what students may or may not wear, with a number of those institutions requiring uniforms. When public schools have tried to implement and recommend reform, they have been met with resistance from the student body.

Read and carefully consider these perspectives. Each suggests a particular way of thinking about the conflict over whether dress codes should be implemented by schools.

Perspective One

The unconstitutionality of the dress code is the reason that it cannot be put into effect. This would violate the individualistic right to expression. Though some articles of clothing may be controversial, many individuals like to express their views and feelings through the clothing they wear.

Perspective Two

While the ability to express oneself is an inalienable right, it does carry some limits. Schools have the authority to ban articles of clothing that are hindering the learning process. A dress code is the surest way to maintain the primary focus of learning.

Perspective Three

Dress codes have the potential to be sexist, especially if they affect some students more than others. Many students have called for gender-equal dress codes to allow for fairness and to not just restrict the rights of one group.

Essay Task

Write a unified, coherent essay in which you evaluate multiple perspectives on dress codes in schools. In your essay, be sure to:

- clearly state your own perspective on the issue and analyze the relationship between your perspective and at least one other perspective
- develop and support your ideas with reasoning and examples
- organize your ideas clearly and logically
- communicate your ideas effectively in standard written English

Your perspective may be in full agreement with any of the others, in partial agreement, or wholly different. Whatever the case, support your ideas with logical reasoning and detailed, persuasive examples.

The Princeton Review
Diagnostic ACT Form

ESSAY

Begin your essay on this side. If necessary, continue on the opposite side.

Continue on the opposite side if necessary.

The Princeton Review
Diagnostic ACT Form

Continued from previous page.

PLEASE PRINT YOUR INITIALS

First	Middle	Last

The Princeton Review
Diagnostic ACT Form

Continued from previous page.

PLEASE PRINT YOUR INITIALS

First	Middle	Last

The Princeton Review
Diagnostic ACT Form

Continued from previous page.

PLEASE PRINT YOUR INITIALS

First	Middle	Last

Writing Practice Section 3

Directions

This is a test of your writing skills. You will have forty (40) minutes to read the prompt, plan your response, and write an essay in English. Before you begin working, read all material in this test booklet carefully to understand exactly what you are being asked to do.

You will write your answer on the lined pages in the answer document provided. Your writing on those pages will be scored. You may use the unlined pages in this test booklet to plan your essay. Your work on these pages will not be scored.

Your essay will be evaluated based on the evidence it provides of your ability to:

- clearly state your own perspective on a complex issue and analyze the relationship between your perspective and at least one other perspective
- develop and support your ideas with reasoning and examples
- organize your ideas clearly and logically
- communicate your ideas effectively in standard written English

Lay your pencil down immediately when time is called.

DO NOT OPEN THIS BOOK UNTIL YOU ARE TOLD TO DO SO.

Composition paper for the essay can be found beginning on page 578.

Increase the Driving Age

Due to the rising incidence of accidents among teenage drivers, many have sought to increase the legal driving age. With the increased dependence on technology, there are many proposing this ramification. An influential auto safety group in Chicago is calling on states to raise the age for getting a driver's license to 17 or even 18. Some have even commissioned reports calling for a 12-month learner permit that requires at least 120 hours of practice.

Read and carefully consider these perspectives. Each suggests a particular way of thinking about the conflict over whether the driving age should be raised.

Perspective One

Operating a vehicle requires a maturity that is simply not acquired by an individual at the tender age of 16. To join the armed services and to vote, the legal age is 18. To be able to rent a car, an individual must be 25 years old. At 16 years of age, a person is not prepared to operate a vehicle.

Perspective Two

Increasing the driving age will not reduce the number of traffic accidents. Instead, by making it more difficult to get experience driving, it will just make it harder for those who are "of age" to get behind the wheel. This, in turn, will increase the number of accidents among older drivers.

Perspective Three

A driving curfew could be an effective deterrent. This act would distribute 120 practice hours: 100 during the day and 20 at night, all under the supervision of a licensed driver for at least three years. This would see the roads clear of newly qualified drivers between 10 P.M. and 5 A.M.

Essay Task

Write a unified, coherent essay in which you evaluate multiple perspectives on the issue of increasing the legal driving age. In your essay, be sure to:

- clearly state your own perspective on the issue and analyze the relationship between your perspective and at least one other perspective
- develop and support your ideas with reasoning and examples
- organize your ideas clearly and logically
- communicate your ideas effectively in standard written English

Your perspective may be in full agreement with any of the others, in partial agreement, or wholly different. Whatever the case, support your ideas with logical reasoning and detailed, persuasive examples.

The Princeton Review
Diagnostic ACT Form

ESSAY

Begin your essay on this side. If necessary, continue on the opposite side.

Continue on the opposite side if necessary.

The Princeton Review
Diagnostic ACT Form

Continued from previous page.

PLEASE PRINT YOUR INITIALS

First	Middle	Last

The Princeton Review
Diagnostic ACT Form

Continued from previous page.

PLEASE PRINT YOUR INITIALS

First	Middle	Last

The Princeton Review
Diagnostic ACT Form

Continued from previous page.

PLEASE PRINT YOUR INITIALS

First	Middle	Last

WRITING TEST

Essay Checklist

1. The Introduction
   Did you
   o start with a topic sentence that paraphrases or restates the prompt?
   o clearly state your position on the issue?

2. Body Paragraph 1
   Did you
   o start with a transition/topic sentence that discusses the opposing side of the argument?
   o give an example of a reason that one might agree with the opposing side of the argument?
   o clearly state that the opposing side of the argument is wrong or flawed?
   o show what is wrong with the opposing side's example or position?

3. Body Paragraphs 2 and 3
   Did you
   o start with a transition/topic sentence that discusses your position on the prompt?
   o give one example or reason to support your position?
   o show the grader how your example supports your position?
   o end the paragraph by restating your thesis?

4. Conclusion
   Did you
   o restate your position on the issue?
   o end with a flourish?

5. Overall
   Did you
   o write neatly?
   o avoid multiple spelling and grammar mistakes?
   o try to vary your sentence structure?
   o use a few impressive-sounding words?

Test 2

Please turn to page 641 to find the bubble sheet for this test.

ENGLISH TEST

45 Minutes—70 Questions

DIRECTIONS: In the five passages that follow, certain words and phrases are underlined and numbered. In the right-hand column, you will find alternatives for each underlined part. In most cases, you are to choose the one that best expresses the idea, makes the statement appropriate for standard written English, or is worded most consistently with the style and tone of the passage as a whole. If you think the original version is best, choose "NO CHANGE." In some cases, you will find in the right-hand column a question about the underlined part. You are to choose the best answer to the question.

You will also find questions about a section of the passage or the passage as a whole. These questions do not refer to an underlined portion of the passage but rather are identified by a number or numbers in a box.

For each question, choose the alternative you consider best and blacken the corresponding oval on your answer document. Read each passage through once before you begin to answer the questions that accompany it. For many of the questions, you must read several sentences beyond the question to determine the answer. Be sure that you have read far enough ahead each time you choose an alternative.

Passage I

The following paragraphs may or may not be in the most logical order. Each paragraph is numbered in brackets, and question 14 will ask you to choose where Paragraph 5 should most logically be placed.

A Window into History

[1]

One very long summer during high school, my mom volunteered me to help Grandpa research our family tree. Great, I thought, imagining hours spent pawing through dusty, rotting boxes and listening to boring stories about people I didn't know. [1] "You'll be surprised," my mom promised. "Family histories can be very interesting."

[2]

In truth, Grandpa didn't want to limit my work to just research. Hoping [2] to also preserve our family memories. He'd discovered a computer program that helps digitally scan old pictures, and letters [3] to preserve their contents before they

1. Given that all the choices are true, which one best conveys the author's initial expectations and effectively leads into her mother's comments?
   - A. NO CHANGE
   - B. bonding with the grandfather I barely knew.
   - C. remembering fun times I had with relatives.
   - D. trying to operate an unfamiliar machine.

2. F. NO CHANGE
   - G. research. Hope
   - H. research, that hope
   - J. research, hoping

3. A. NO CHANGE
   - B. pictures, and, letters
   - C. pictures and letters,
   - D. pictures and letters

GO ON TO THE NEXT PAGE.

crumble from old age. Grandpa wanted me to help him connect the scanner and set up the computer program. He could type documents and send <u>e-mails, but he had</u> [4] never used a scanner.

4. Which of the following choices is NOT an acceptable substitute for the underlined portion?
   - **F.** e-mails but having
   - **G.** e-mails, yet he had
   - **H.** e-mails; however, he had
   - **J.** e-mails but had

[3]

[1] Instead of sorting through dusty boxes as I had imagined, we spent a lot of time in my grandpa's bright, tidy computer room. [2] The scanner hummed happily, turning my <u>relatives precious memories</u> [5] into permanent digital images. [3] A scanner is a device which makes electronic copies of actual items. [4] I worked happily while Grandpa shared stories that turned out not to be boring at all. [6]

5. **A.** NO CHANGE
   - **B.** relatives precious memory's
   - **C.** relatives' precious memories
   - **D.** relatives' precious memory's

6. Which of the following sentences in this paragraph is LEAST relevant to the progression of the narrative and therefore could be deleted?
   - **F.** Sentence 1
   - **G.** Sentence 2
   - **H.** Sentence 3
   - **J.** Sentence 4

[4]

Perusing through <u>her</u> [7] belongings, I felt I was opening a window into the world of my relatives, a world long since gone.

7. **A.** NO CHANGE
   - **B.** their
   - **C.** one's
   - **D.** there

Grandpa showed me a bundle of yellowed letters he <u>had send</u> [8] to Grandma from the front lines of World War II, and I could almost smell the gunpowder. I turned the brittle pages of my great-grandmother's recipe book and could envision her sitting in her immaculate <u>kitchen penning</u> [9] meticulously every entry. All of the people who had been merely names to me now had faces to match and lives lived.

8. **F.** NO CHANGE
   - **G.** send
   - **H.** has sent
   - **J.** had sent

9. **A.** NO CHANGE
   - **B.** kitchen, penning
   - **C.** kitchen, which penned
   - **D.** kitchen that penned

[5]

[10] I asked Grandpa to tell the story behind every picture

10. Which of the following true statements, if added here, would most successfully introduce readers to the information relayed in the paragraph?
    - **F.** My family has been around for generations, so there were a lot of names to remember.
    - **G.** My grandfather inundated me with items to catalogue on the computer.
    - **H.** As I learned more about some relatives, I forgot about others.
    - **J.** As the summer progressed, I became fascinated with my relatives' lives.

GO ON TO THE NEXT PAGE.

and letter we scanned. Besides, the [11] stories helped me not only understand but also relate to my relatives. Like me, they had celebrated achievements, overcome failures, pulled silly pranks, played sports, and, [12] attended concerts. I became so hungry for more information that Grandpa needed additional props to keep me satisfied. He showed me a chest filled with family artifacts, all covered in dust.

11. A. NO CHANGE
    B. Because the
    C. Therefore, the
    D. The

12. F. NO CHANGE
    G. sports, and
    H. sports and,
    J. sports and

[6]

As the new school year approached, Grandpa admitted, "I probably could have done this project myself. I just wanted someone to share it with." I can't thank him enough for sharing the experience and making me appreciate the family members who have made me the person I am. I will cherish family memories and mementoes and hope that someday, I will be able to pass them down to my own grandchildren. [13]

13. Which of the following provides the best conclusion to the paragraph and the essay as a whole?
    A. NO CHANGE
    B. My grandpa will teach me something new next summer.
    C. I never have to tell my mother she was right that family history isn't tedious and boring.
    D. I can figure out other ways to use my computer.

Questions 14 and 15 ask about the preceding passage as a whole.

14. Where should the author place Paragraph 5 in order to have a logical, coherent essay?
    F. Where it is now
    G. Before Paragraph 2
    H. Before Paragraph 3
    J. Before Paragraph 4

15. Suppose the writer's purpose had been to write an essay about some of the benefits of genealogical research. Does this essay succeed in achieving that purpose?
    A. Yes, because it describes the technological skills gained in the process of researching one's relatives.
    B. Yes, because it provides an example of how one person gained personal insights from her family history.
    C. No, because it provides only one person's research, which is susceptible to bias and cannot be reliable.
    D. No, because genealogical research requires statistics in order to prove there were benefits.

GO ON TO THE NEXT PAGE.

Passage II

Moving to a New Life

I stand on the corner of Elm Avenue and Main Street by me, watching [16] my parents walk away and feeling nothing but apprehension about adjusting to this new town. I try not to show the passersby just how scared I really am, but it's not possible. My tears start to flow, and I quickly run to my new, cold, [17] bedroom.

I know I am making a complete spectacle of [18] myself, but I can't help it. I am an only child whom has [19] never been more than 30 minutes away from her parents, yet here I am, on the other side of the country, moving in to my new college dorm. We all want to take responsibility for one's own lives. [20] I just never realized that in order to do so, I would have to leave my family. No longer will I wake up to Mom's Sunday breakfast of non-pasteurized milk, and fresh orange juice, fluffy [21] scrambled eggs and crisp bacon. I'll have to tackle the daily crossword puzzle on my own, without Dad's carefully veiled hints. Everything is gone. [22] Can anyone understand what I'm going through?

16. F. NO CHANGE
    G. me watching
    H. myself, watching
    J. myself. Watching

17. A. NO CHANGE
    B. new, cold
    C. new cold
    D. new cold,

18. F. NO CHANGE
    G. completely spectacle about
    H. completely spectacle of
    J. complete spectacle about

19. A. NO CHANGE
    B. whom have
    C. who has
    D. who have

20. F. NO CHANGE
    G. their own life.
    H. our own lives.
    J. your own life.

21. A. NO CHANGE
    B. milk, and fresh orange juice, fluffy,
    C. milk and fresh orange juice fluffy
    D. milk and fresh orange juice, fluffy

22. The writer is considering revising the sentence "Everything is gone" in the preceding sentence to read:

    It feels like everything I have ever loved is being ripped away from me.

    Should the writer make this change, or keep the sentence as it is?

    F. Make the revision, because it conveys more vividly the type of emotions felt by the writer.
    G. Make the revision, because it describes the stages of emotion the writer faces as she mourns.
    H. Keep the sentence as it is, because it is already specific and does not need to be changed.
    J. Keep the sentence as it is, because it's short and more concise than the proposed revision.

GO ON TO THE NEXT PAGE.

As I lie crying into my pillow, hearing [23] the door to the dorm suite open. It must be one of my two roommates. I quickly stop crying—I couldn't stand the embarrassment if she knew her new roommate was an emotional wreck! [24] Being full of surprise, [25] I hear *her* crying as she runs to her room. Curiosity overwhelming me and I [26] tiptoe through the common room to her still-open door.

I stand in the doorway for merely a second before she reacts. Slowly, [27] her face jolts up, and her sudden shock at my appearance is clearly written on her face. "Are you okay?" I quietly ask. "I'm sorry," she stammers. [28] "I thought I was alone. I know this must seem very childish to you. I'm just very close to my younger sister, and saying goodbye to her just now…." Her sentence trails off as she turns her face away from me. "I remember when she was born." [29]

"I completely understand," I say, and I really do. "Maybe we can help each other get used to this new college life."

23. **A.** NO CHANGE
B. I was hearing
C. I hear
D. having heard

24. If the writer were to delete the phrase "—I couldn't stand the embarrassment if she knew her new roommate was an emotional wreck!" from the preceding sentence, the passage would primarily lose:

F. a description of the uneasy relationship between the roommates.
G. an insight into the reason the writer stopped crying.
H. a justification for her dissatisfaction with college.
J. nothing at all, since the writer has already expressed her sadness.

25. **A.** NO CHANGE
B. Since I was surprised,
C. Being surprised,
D. Much to my surprise,

26. **F.** NO CHANGE
G. me, and I
H. me, I
J. me. I

27. Given that all the choices are true, which one provides the best transition by illustrating how quickly the roommate responded to the writer's presence?

A. NO CHANGE
B. Abruptly,
C. After several moments,
D. Sluggishly,

28. **F.** NO CHANGE
G. asserts.
H. quotes.
J. screams.

29. Given that all the choices are true, which conclusion to this paragraph is most consistent with the writer's subsequent response?

A. NO CHANGE
B. "My sister has always been so fun to live with."
C. "I wish that they had left sooner."
D. "It's going to be hard to adjust, that's all."

GO ON TO THE NEXT PAGE.

Question 30 asks about the preceding passage as a whole.

30. Suppose the writer's goal was to describe personal hardships first-time college students may experience. Does this essay successfully accomplish that goal?
   F. Yes, because it gives an anecdotal account of separation anxiety experienced by the writer and her roommate.
   G. Yes, because it focuses on the initial awkwardness between roommates who don't know each other.
   H. No, because it focuses on the emotions of only one person instead of the experiences of many students.
   J. No, because it fails to provide enough background information on the narrator's mental state before college.

Passage III

The following paragraphs may or may not be in the most logical order. Each paragraph is numbered in brackets, and question 45 will ask you to choose where Paragraph 2 should most logically be placed.

Thrill Seekers Wanted

[1]

Like Indiana Jones, the staid college professor who undertakes daring adventures in his spare time, my father is a businessman by day and a thrill-seeking adrenaline fanatic by night. [31] His enthusiasm rubbed off on me, and I have been lucky to be his sidekick on many an adventure. We started out small by conquering America's fastest, most twisted rollercoasters. After that, a whitewater rafting excursion through

31. The writer is considering deleting the phrase "Like Indiana Jones, the staid college professor who undertakes daring adventures in his spare time," from the preceding sentence (and capitalizing the word *my*). Should the phrase be kept or deleted?
   A. Kept, because it clarifies that the writer's father is also named Indiana.
   B. Kept, because it adds a descriptive detail that heightens the thrill of the adventures described later in the passage.
   C. Deleted, because it draws attention from the paragraph's focus on the father and places it on movies.
   D. Deleted, because the information fails to specify if the writer's father is interested in archaeology.

GO ON TO THE NEXT PAGE.

the Grand Canyon on the majestic, if murky Colorado River [32] jumpstarted our search for other extreme thrills across the globe.

[2]

Anyone who loves a challenging thrill should try canyoning. [33] Our adventure began with a 90-foot rappel down a canyon wall into a rushing, ice-cold river, and [34] without wetsuits we surely would have become popsicles! Intrepidly, we traversed the bone-chilling water toward the mouth of the river, our final destination, where the reward for the journey would be a panoramic view of the natural wonder [35] of the lush Interlaken basin.

[3]

Spectacular thrills awaited us at every corner of the world. A remarkable activity in its own right, like skydiving was [36] especially momentous when performed from a helicopter over the breathtaking Swiss Alps. We have gone spelunking in damp and ominous Peruvian caves. [37] We have traveled to New Zealand for *Zorb*, a strange activity in which participants enter a giant, inflatable ball and roll down steep, grassy hills. Most recently, in Interlaken, Switzerland, we attempted "canyoning,"

32. **F.** NO CHANGE
 G. majestic if murky
 H. majestic; if murky,
 J. majestic, if murky,

33. The writer is considering deleting the phrase "who loves a challenging thrill" from the preceding sentence. Should the phrase be kept or deleted?
 A. Kept, because it clarifies the term *anyone* and contributes to the logic of the paragraph.
 B. Kept, because it indicates the paragraph's focus on people who love challenges.
 C. Deleted, because the term *anyone* describes all people and does not need clarification.
 D. Deleted, because the phrase is too long and confuses the focus of the sentence.

34. **F.** NO CHANGE
 G. river,
 H. river
 J. river and

35. **A.** NO CHANGE
 B. view naturally of the wonder
 C. viewing of the wonderful nature
 D. view

36. **F.** NO CHANGE
 G. skydiving was
 H. skydiving,
 J. like skydiving

37. At this point, the writer is considering adding the following true statement:

 We have bungee jumped from the world's highest platform, Bloukrans Bridge in South Africa.

 Should the writer make this addition here?
 A. Yes, because it is an additional detail consistent with the main point of this paragraph.
 B. Yes, because it helps establish the main idea that Africa has the most exciting thrills in the world.
 C. No, because its focus is on a location and activity different than those in the rest of the paragraph.
 D. No, because the other activities in this paragraph do not involve the use of a bungee cord.

GO ON TO THE NEXT PAGE.

because of which was our most exhilarating adventure yet!
38

[4]

We had to navigate both the flowing river and the canyon walls we became amphibious, moving seamlessly between land and water. We slid over slick rocks at one moment,
39

leapt and descended from waterfalls and swam through underwater tunnels the next. Back and forth we alternated, scaling rope ladders before zooming down zip lines back into the fresh mountain water. Certainly, danger from possible miscalculations were lurking in each of these activities, but that very danger provided the rush. Canyoning was indeed one thrill after another, from beginning to end.
40 41 42

[5]

While canyoning is possible only in certain locales, thrills and adventure can be found anywhere. Our humble beginnings in the United States showed us just that. We continue to seek the big thrills, but in doing so, we have learned to seek lesser forms of excitement in daily life as well. After all, we can't go canyoning every day, and small thrills are better than none for us thrill seekers.
43 44

38. F. NO CHANGE
G. and which
H. which
J. in which

39. A. NO CHANGE
B. walls,
C. walls so
D. walls, so

40. F. NO CHANGE
G. leapt
H. leapt in the air and descended down
J. leapt to descend

41. A. NO CHANGE
B. miscalculations will be
C. miscalculations was
D. miscalculations

42. Given that all the choices are true, which one best clarifies the distinction between the two types of activities mentioned in this paragraph?
F. NO CHANGE
G. both on rocky surfaces and in the chilly water.
H. adventure after adventure.
J. long after the waterfalls.

43. A. NO CHANGE
B. and
C. moreover,
D. furthermore,

44. Given that all the choices are true, which one concludes the paragraph with a phrase that relates to the main topic of the essay?
F. NO CHANGE
G. and that's a shame.
H. because we don't live near any canyons.
J. but it's the last thrill I'll ever need!

Question 45 asks about the preceding passage as a whole.

45. For the sake of the logic and coherence of this essay, the best placement for Paragraph 2 would be:
A. where it is now.
B. before Paragraph 1.
C. before Paragraph 4.
D. before Paragraph 5.

GO ON TO THE NEXT PAGE.

Passage IV

Enriching the American Tradition

The Mexican-American War, with its many conflicts and compromises, represent [46] a largely overlooked part of the history of the United States, but its importance in the current shape and culture of the United States cannot be overstated. Certainly, it is difficult to imagine the present-day United States without the list of former Mexican territories, which includes [47] Texas, Arizona, California, and others, but it is equally difficult to imagine America's vibrant multicultural society without the influence of Mexican-Americans.

But despite the obvious richness that Mexican-Americans have brought to American culture, one aspect of their contributions, to American arts [48] is often overlooked: literature. Although the names of many famous Mexican-Americans are identifiable in film and music, many Americans are at a loss to name even a single Mexican-American author. Carlos Santana, a musician born and raised in Mexico, has achieved widespread popularity in the United States. [49]

A major landmark in early Mexican-American literature came in 1885, when author, María Amparo Ruiz de Burton, [50] published her second novel, *The Squatter and the Don*. In addition to being the first major novel written in English by an author of Mexican descent, *The Squatter and the Don* was also noteworthy for its revolutionary perspective. [51] María

46. F. NO CHANGE
G. represents
H. have represented
J. representing

47. A. NO CHANGE
B. includes:
C. included,
D. included:

48. F. NO CHANGE
G. contributions, to American arts,
H. contributions to American arts,
J. contributions to American arts

49. A. NO CHANGE
B. A musician who has achieved popularity in the United States is Carlos Santana, who was born and raised in Mexico.
C. However, many Americans can easily identify Carlos Santana, a popular musician born and raised in Mexico.
D. DELETE the underlined portion.

50. F. NO CHANGE
G. author María Amparo Ruiz de Burton
H. author, María Amparo Ruiz de Burton
J. author María Amparo Ruiz de Burton,

51. If the writer were to delete the phrase "In addition to being the first major novel written in English by an author of Mexican descent," from the preceding sentence, the essay would primarily lose:

A. an indication of Ruiz de Burton's command of the English language.
B. a fact that reveals that the novel was the first by a Mexican author to be read in the United States.
C. information that helps to strengthen the sense of the novel's historical importance.
D. a suggestion that María Amparo Ruiz de Burton considered writing the novel in her native Spanish.

GO ON TO THE NEXT PAGE.

Amparo Ruiz de Burton helped to <u>acquaint American readers with and introduce them to</u> [52] an as yet unfamiliar genre through her fictional family, the Alamars. A family of landed gentry living in San Diego, <u>nearly all is lost to the Alamars</u> [53] after the American annexation of California <u>during</u> [54] the Mexican-American War. As a result of the lopsided Treaty of Guadalupe Hidalgo, Mexico lost nearly forty percent of its previous territories and many, like Ruiz de Burton and her creations the Alamars, were uprooted from their previous comfort and made citizens of a new nation. Ruiz de Burton's wish <u>that</u> [55] her works would speak for the many Mexican-Americans who felt the same concerns. [56] *The Squatter and the Don* marked an early and important exploration of many themes that Mexican-American authors continue to <u>explore</u>, [57] including themes of personal integrity, identity, and the relationships between individuals and collective history.

[1] Poet Ana Castillo has been publishing well-received novels and volumes of poetry prolifically since 1977, and

52. **F.** NO CHANGE
G. give American readers a glimpse at
H. introduce American readers unacquainted with Mexican-American literature to
J. introduce American readers to

53. **A.** NO CHANGE
B. the Alamars lose nearly all that they own
C. losing all that they own
D. Ruiz de Burton describes a family that loses all that they own

54. **F.** NO CHANGE
G. within
H. throughout
J. through

55. **A.** NO CHANGE
B. being that
C. was that
D. being

56. At this point, the writer is considering adding the following true statement:

> After the Louisiana Purchase in 1803, many people of French descent living in the United States felt displaced as well.

Should the writer make the addition here?

F. Yes, because it provides historical information about another group that deepens the reader's understanding of the difficulties faced by Mexican-Americans.
G. Yes, because it links those with French descent with the characters in *The Squatter and the Don.*
H. No, because it does not provide a direct connection between the work of María Amparo Ruiz de Burton and the work of later Mexican-American authors.
J. No, because it is clear from the essay that the Louisiana Purchase had no importance to the Mexican-American authors discussed.

57. Which of the following alternatives to the underlined portion would be LEAST acceptable?

A. investigate
B. examine
C. look into
D. solve

GO ON TO THE NEXT PAGE.

her work has been essential in bringing issues of Mexican-American women, particularly those living in urban places such as Castillo's hometown of Chicago, to a larger audience. [2] Sandra Cisneros is the author of *The House on Mango Street*, which has sold over two million copies since its original publication in 1984, and her work, including the novel *Caramelo*, published in 2002, has helped give voice to the often difficult position of living between two cultures that Mexican-Americans face. [3] Ruiz de Burton's writings and <u>that of</u> (58) other authors remain important parts of American literature today.

[4] Along with many others, <u>these authors</u> (59) continue to expand the boundaries of American literature, just as Mexican-Americans all over the country continue to enrich and challenge accepted notions of what we call "American culture." [60]

58. **F.** NO CHANGE
G. by
H. those of
J. with

59. **A.** NO CHANGE
B. the writers Ana Castillo and Sandra Cisneros and many other Mexican-American authors
C. the Mexican-American authors being published today
D. the many Mexican-American authors whose work as a whole represents them

60. For the sake of the logic and coherence of this paragraph, Sentence 3 should be placed:
F. where it is now.
G. before Sentence 1.
H. before Sentence 2.
J. after Sentence 4.

Passage V

A Simple but Complex Modern Vision

Ludwig Mies van der Rohe, typically cited alongside Walter Gropius and Le Corbusier as a pioneer of modern <u>architecture. Was</u> (61) integral to the founding and proliferation of the "modern style" in architecture. Van der Rohe felt the design of a building should be reflective of its age, as the Gothic and Classical masterpieces surely were. Van der Rohe, called Mies by friends and students, found many architects' attitudes toward architectural design problematic, particularly these architects' reliance on older, outdated architectural styles.

61. **A.** NO CHANGE
B. architecture. Being
C. architecture, being
D. architecture, was

GO ON TO THE NEXT PAGE.

Van der Rohe, instead, sought to express through his buildings what he feels to be the core tenets of modern existence. The buildings based on van der Rohe's designs, were primarily constructed with industrial steel and plate glass—that is, only the materials of modern, twentieth-century life and industry. By using only the bare minimum materials produced from American and German factories, Mies sought to cast off what he found to be one of the main problems with contemporary architecture, and overly decorative and ornamental structures with no "function" were wasteful uses of space and material. Through steel and plate glass, van der Rohe felt that he could better practice the idea of "efficiency" that he had pulled from his earlier readings of Russian Constructivism, and using these materials as he did to create simple, planar, rectilinear designs, Mies invested his buildings with a strange intensity that conveyed at once the simplicity of design and many of the buildings have been named National Historic Landmarks.

62. **F.** NO CHANGE
G. is feeling
H. felt
J. who felt

63. **A.** NO CHANGE
B. buildings based on van der Rohe's designs
C. buildings, based on van der Rohe's designs
D. buildings based on van der Rohe's designs;

64. Which of the following alternatives to the underlined portion would NOT be acceptable?

F. from
G. using
H. out of
J. into

65. **A.** NO CHANGE
B. that is
C. this is,
D. this is

66. **F.** NO CHANGE
G. architecture that
H. architecture, which
J. architecture: that

67. Given that all the choices are true, which one would add the most effective detail to the description of the visual appeal of the buildings mentioned in the first part of the sentence?

A. NO CHANGE
B. the structure that had taken months, even years, to build.
C. the complex beauty of the free-flowing structures inside.
D. the buildings on display in many American and European cities.

GO ON TO THE NEXT PAGE.

Van der Rohe's architectural education was unique, and many describe the architect as largely self-taught. From 1908 to 1912, under teacher Peter Behrens's guidance, [68] Mies became a proponent of many modern and avant-garde ideas in architecture in Germany. From Behrens, van der Rohe began to see the potential of developing an architecture of ideas, and indeed, he was a "self-taught" expert in many ancient and modern philosophical concepts. This [69] helped him to understand the character of the modern world, and with his maturing ideas of this character, van der Rohe set out to create a style truly of the twentieth century. While [70] van der Rohe was committed to creating a philosophical, theoretical basis for his works, he helped to create a new vocabulary for the creation and study of architecture.

68. F. NO CHANGE
    G. teacher, Peter Behrens's guidance,
    H. teacher Peter Behrens's guidance;
    J. teacher, Peter Behrens's guidance

69. A. NO CHANGE
    B. Studying philosophy
    C. Something
    D. This thing

70. F. NO CHANGE
    G. Even though
    H. Moreover
    J. Because

[1] In order to escape the oppressive Nazi regime, van der Rohe who left [71] Germany for the United States in 1937. [2] Mies was originally invited to become head of the school and to contribute designs for the school's growing campus (which, as the Illinois Institute of Technology, continues to grow today). [3] He had two commissions waiting for him there—one in Wyoming and another [72] at the Armour Institute of Technology in Chicago. [4] Pupils learning [73] his new method and architectural vocabulary, van der Rohe worked tirelessly as an educator, with only limited success. [5] While many students were initially

71. A. NO CHANGE
    B. left
    C. leaves
    D. leaving

72. Which of the following alternatives to the underlined portion would NOT be acceptable?
    F. the other
    G. one
    H. this one
    J. the other one

73. A. NO CHANGE
    B. While pupils learn
    C. To teach pupils
    D. Pupils being taught

GO ON TO THE NEXT PAGE.

enthusiastic, Mies van der Rohe's influence was eventually [74] eclipsed by the rise of Postmodern Architecture in the early 1980s. [75]

There can be no doubt, though, that van der Rohe has left a huge mark on the look of the North American city. Not only do his buildings help to create the skylines of Chicago, New York, and Toronto, but van der Rohe also gave architects from all over the world a new vocabulary and set of materials with which to create spaces for living and working, and he helped to make architecture one of the great arts of the twentieth century.

74. **F.** NO CHANGE
G. enthusiastic and extremely excited,
H. enthusiastic, overwhelmed with excitement,
J. enthusiastic, thrilled,

75. For the sake of the logic and coherence of this paragraph, Sentence 3 should be placed:
A. where it is now.
B. after Sentence 1.
C. after Sentence 4.
D. after Sentence 5.

END OF TEST 1
STOP! DO NOT TURN THE PAGE UNTIL TOLD TO DO SO.

MATHEMATICS TEST

60 Minutes—60 Questions

DIRECTIONS: Solve each problem, choose the correct answer, and then darken the corresponding oval on your answer sheet.

Do not linger over problems that take too much time. Solve as many as you can; then return to the others in the time you have left for this test.

You are permitted to use a calculator on this test. You may use your calculator for any problems you choose, but some of the problems may best be done without using a calculator.

Note: Unless otherwise stated, all of the following should be assumed:

1. Illustrative figures are NOT necessarily drawn to scale.
2. Geometric figures lie in a plane.
3. The word *line* indicates a straight line.
4. The word *average* indicates arithmetic mean.

DO YOUR FIGURING HERE.

1. Violet is baking a mixed berry pie that contains blueberries, cherries, blackberries, and raspberries. She uses three times as many blackberries as cherries, twice as many blueberries as raspberries, and the same number of blackberries and raspberries. If Violet has 10 cherries, how many of each of the other berries must she use?

	Raspberries	Blueberries	Blackberries
A.	3	2	3
B.	30	2	3
C.	30	2	30
D.	30	60	10
E.	30	60	30

2. The expression $(3x - 5)(x + 2)$ is equivalent to:

F. $3x^2 - 10$
G. $3x^2 + x + 10$
H. $3x^2 + x - 10$
J. $3x^2 + 11x - 10$
K. $3x^2 - 11x - 10$

3. A function f is defined by $f(x,y) = x - (xy - y)$. What is the value of $f(8,6)$?

A. −46
B. −34
C. 46
D. 50
E. 62

4. What is $\frac{1}{7}$ of 28% of 8,000 ?

F. 32
G. 320
H. 1,568
J. 3,200
K. 15,680

GO ON TO THE NEXT PAGE.

5. If $6x + 3 = 12 + 3x$, then $x = ?$

DO YOUR FIGURING HERE.

A. 6

B. 5

C. 3

D. $\frac{5}{3}$

E. 1

6. The second term of an arithmetic sequence is –2, and the third term is 8. What is the first term?

(Note: An arithmetic sequence has a common difference between consecutive terms.)

F. –12

G. –10

H. $\frac{1}{2}$

J. 3

K. 10

7. Stacie has a bag of solid colored jellybeans. Each jellybean is orange, purple, or pink. If she randomly selects a jellybean from the bag, the probability that the jellybean is orange is $\frac{2}{9}$, and the probability that it is purple is $\frac{1}{3}$. If there are 72 jellybeans in the bag, how many pink jellybeans are in the bag?

A. 16
B. 24
C. 32
D. 40
E. 48

8. A cellular phone company unveiled a new plan for new customers. It will charge a flat rate of \$100 for initial connection and service for the first two months, and \$60 for service each subsequent month. If Bob subscribes to this plan for one year, how much does he pay in total for the year?

F. \$600
G. \$700
H. \$720
J. \$800
K. \$820

GO ON TO THE NEXT PAGE.

9. A square and a regular pentagon (a 5-sided polygon with congruent sides and interior angles) have the same perimeter. One side of the pentagon measures 20 inches. How many inches long is one side of the square?

DO YOUR FIGURING HERE.

A. 4
B. 16
C. 25
D. 36
E. 100

10. Two contractors bid on a job to build a brick wall in a yard. Contractor A charges a flat fee of $1,600 plus $2 per brick. Contractor B charges a flat fee of $400 plus $8 per brick. If x represents the number of bricks in the wall, which of the following equations could be solved to determine the number of bricks which would make B's charge to build the wall equal to A's charge?

F. $1{,}600 + 2x = 400 + 8x$
G. $1{,}600 + 8x = 400 + 2x$
H. $2x + 8x = x$
J. $2x + 8x = 1{,}600$
K. $2x + 8x = 400$

11. Given that $E = ABCD$, which of the following is an expression of B, in terms of E, A, C, and D ?

A. $\frac{ACD}{E}$

B. $E + ACD$

C. $E - ACD$

D. $\frac{E}{ACD}$

E. $EACD$

GO ON TO THE NEXT PAGE.

DO YOUR FIGURING HERE.

12. Lines $\overline{XV}$ and $\overline{YV}$ intersect at point V on line $\overline{WZ}$, as shown in the figure below. The measures of 2 angles are given in terms of a, in degrees. What is the measure of $\angle XVZ$ in degrees?

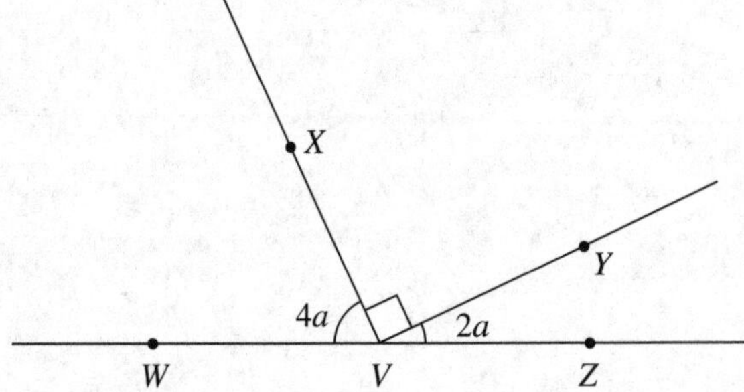

F. 30
G. 90
H. 120
J. 150
K. 180

13. An outdoor thermometer in Hanover, NH reads 70°F. The temperature in Hanover is 25°F cooler than in New Orleans, LA. What is the temperature, C, in degrees Celsius, in New Orleans?

(Note: $F = \frac{9}{5}C + 32$)

A. 21°C
B. 35°C
C. 68°C
D. 95°C
E. 113°C

14. If $3x + 2y = 5$, what is the value of the expression $6x + 4y - 7$?

F. –2
G. 3
H. 8
J. 10
K. 19

GO ON TO THE NEXT PAGE.

DO YOUR FIGURING HERE.

15. Mike sold $3\frac{2}{7}$ pounds of beef at his deli on Wednesday and $2\frac{1}{3}$ pounds of beef on Saturday. Which of the following ranges includes the total amount of beef, in pounds, Mike sold during these two days?

A. At least 5 and less than $5\frac{1}{2}$

B. At least $5\frac{1}{2}$ and less than $5\frac{2}{3}$

C. At least $5\frac{2}{3}$ and less than 6

D. At least 6 and less than $6\frac{1}{2}$

E. At least $6\frac{1}{2}$ and less than $6\frac{2}{3}$

16. Dave leaves his house and bikes directly east for 3 miles. He then turns and bikes directly south for 4 miles. How many miles is Dave from his house?

F. 3
G. 4
H. 5
J. 6
K. 7

17. A sensor records a piece of data every 0.0000000038 seconds. The sensor will record 100,000,000,000 pieces of data in how many seconds?

A. 3,800
B. 380
C. 38
D. 3.8
E. 0.0038

18. Alan has a rectangular photograph that is 20 centimeters wide by 30 centimeters long. Alan wants to reduce the area of the photograph by 264 square centimeters by decreasing the width and length by the same amount. What will be the new dimensions (width by length), in centimeters?

F. 11 by 24
G. 12 by 22
H. 12 by 28
J. 14 by 24
K. 16 by 21

GO ON TO THE NEXT PAGE.

19. A quadrilateral has a perimeter of 36 inches. If the lengths of the sides are 4 consecutive, even integers, what is the length, in inches, of the shortest side?

A. 2
B. 4
C. 6
D. 7
E. 8

DO YOUR FIGURING HERE.

20. In the standard (x,y) coordinate plane, what is the slope of the line with equation $7y - 3x = 21$?

F. $-\frac{3}{7}$

G. $\frac{3}{7}$

H. $\frac{7}{3}$

J. 3

K. 7

21. In the figure shown below, points A, B, C, and D are collinear, and distances marked are in feet. Rectangle $ADEG$ has an area of 48 square feet. What is the area, in square feet, of the trapezoid $BCEF$?

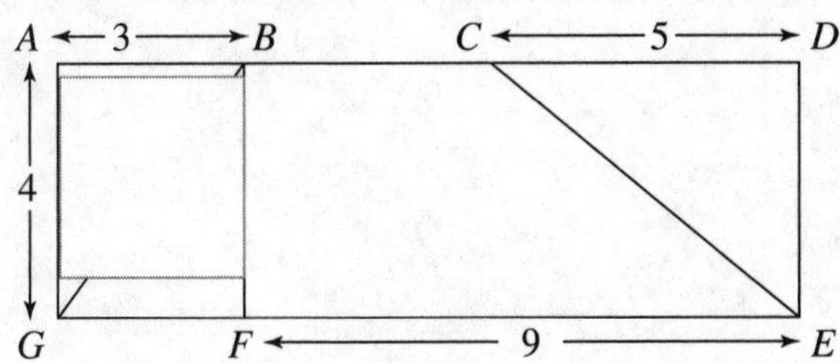

A. 16
B. 20
C. 26
D. 36
E. 58

GO ON TO THE NEXT PAGE.

DO YOUR FIGURING HERE.

Use the following information to answer questions 22–24.

Quadrilateral *FGHJ* is shown below in the standard (*x*,*y*) coordinate plane. For this quadrilateral, $\overline{FG} = 10$, $\overline{FJ} = 6$, $\overline{HJ} = \sqrt{136}$, and $\overline{GH} = 12$.

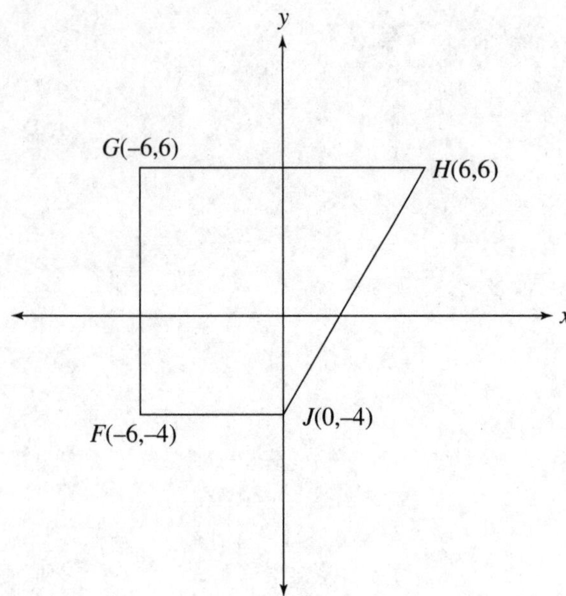

22. Which of the following is closest to the perimeter of quadrilateral *FGHJ*, in coordinate units?

F. 28.0
G. 39.7
H. 60.0
J. 108.0
K. 120.0

23. What is the length of $\overline{GJ}$, in coordinate units?

A. 4
B. 8
C. 16
D. $\sqrt{108}$
E. $\sqrt{136}$

GO ON TO THE NEXT PAGE.

DO YOUR FIGURING HERE.

24. Which of the following are the coordinates of the image of *J* under a 90° clockwise rotation about the origin?

F. (–4, 0)
G. (0, –4)
H. (0, 0)
J. (0, 4)
K. (4, 0)

---

25. Which of the following geometric figures has at least 1 rotational symmetry and at least 1 reflectional symmetry?

(Note: The angle of rotation for the rotational symmetry must be less than 360°.)

A.

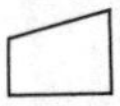

B.

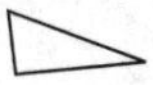

C.

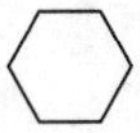

D.

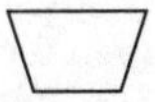

E.

26. What is the coefficient of x^8 in the product of the polynomials below?

$$(-x^4 + 3x^3 - 5x^2 + x - 5)(5x^4 - 2x^3 + x^2 - 5x + 2)$$

F. 0
G. 5
H. 4
J. –2
K. –5

GO ON TO THE NEXT PAGE.

DO YOUR FIGURING HERE.

Use the following information to answer questions 27–28.

The stem-and-leaf plot below shows the scores for each golfer in a recent tournament at the Lehigh Valley Golf Club. There were 13 golfers participating in the tournament.

Stem	Leaf
6	6, 7
7	1, 2, 2, 3, 5, 7, 9
8	2, 3, 3, 7

(Note: For example, a score of 72 would have a stem value of 7 and a leaf value of 2.)

27. Which of the following is closest to the mean score of all the golfers in the tournament?

A. 72.0
B. 74.4
C. 75.0
D. 75.9
E. 83.0

28. If a score represented in the stem-and-leaf plot is selected randomly, what is the probability that the score selected is exactly 83 ?

F. $\frac{2}{13}$

G. $\frac{4}{13}$

H. $\frac{83}{87}$

J. $\frac{83}{987}$

K. $\frac{166}{987}$

---

29. What is the least common multiple of 8, 2, 3*a*, 6*b*, and 4*ab* ?

A. $16ab$
B. $24ab$
C. $24a^2b$
D. $54ab$
E. $60a^2b$

GO ON TO THE NEXT PAGE.

DO YOUR FIGURING HERE.

30. Aleksandra began collecting model airplanes in May of 2008. The number of model airplanes that she owns in each month can be modeled by the function $A(m) = 2m + 2$, where $m = 0$ corresponds to May. Using this model, how many model airplanes would you expect Aleksandra to own in December of 2008 ?

F. 2
G. 12
H. 14
J. 16
K. 18

31. In the standard (x,y) coordinate plane, line segment $\overline{CD}$ has end points $C(-3,5)$ and $D(11,-7)$. What is the midpoint of $\overline{CD}$?

A. (14, –12)
B. (8, 2)
C. (7, 1)
D. (7, –6)
E. (4, –1)

32. Given $x \neq \pm 4$, which of the following is equivalent to the expression $\frac{x^2 - 8x + 16}{x^2 - 16}$?

F. $\frac{1}{2}x - 1$

G. $-8x$

H. $\frac{x-2}{2}$

J. $\frac{1}{x+4}$

K. $\frac{x-4}{x+4}$

33. Evan purchased 6 boxes of sugar cookies, each box containing 10 snack bags and each bag containing 12 cookies. Evan could have purchased the same amount of cookies by buying how many family-sized packs of 30 cookies each?

A. 12
B. 24
C. 48
D. 72
E. 180

GO ON TO THE NEXT PAGE.

34. When $\frac{r}{s} = -\frac{1}{2}$, $16r^4 - s^4 = ?$

DO YOUR FIGURING HERE.

F. −32
G. −16
H. 0
J. 16
K. 32

35. Emilia is going to bake cookies. She rolls out a square of dough that is 12 inches wide by 12 inches long and cuts 9 identical circular cookies from the dough, as shown in the figure below. Each circular cut-out is tangent to the circular cut-outs next to it and tangent to the edge or edges of the square piece of dough it touches. Approximately, what is the area, in square inches, of the remaining dough, as shown in the figure?

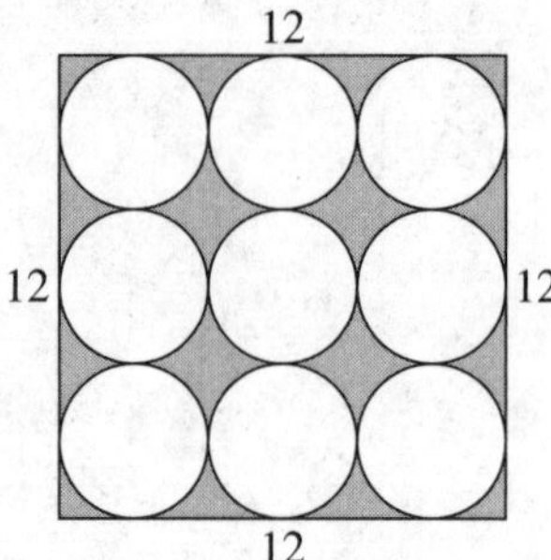

A. 30.9
B. 42.3
C. 50.24
D. 87.5
E. 113.04

36. Which of the following lists contains only prime numbers?

F. 63, 73, and 97
G. 71, 87, and 91
H. 73, 89, and 91
J. 79, 89, and 97
K. 81, 87, and 97

GO ON TO THE NEXT PAGE.

37. The costs of tutoring packages of different lengths, given in quarter hours, are shown in the table below.

DO YOUR FIGURING HERE.

Number of quarter hours	8	10	12	20
Cost	\$200	\$230	\$260	\$380

Each cost consists of a fixed charge and a charge per quarter hour. What is the fixed charge?

A. \$15
B. \$23
C. \$80
D. \$120
E. \$380

38. At 3 P.M., the afternoon sun shines over a building and its rays hit the ground at a 34° angle. The building is 100 meters tall and is perpendicular to the ground. How long, to the nearest meter, is the building's shadow that is cast by the sun?

(Note: $\sin 34° \approx 0.56$, $\cos 34° \approx 0.83$, $\tan 34° \approx 0.67$)

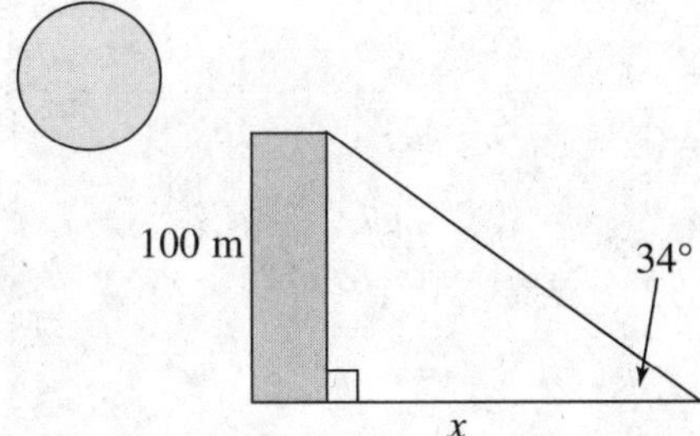

F. 56
G. 67
H. 83
J. 120
K. 148

39. In the standard (x,y) coordinate system, circle O has its center at $(4,-3)$ and a radius of 12 units. Which of the following is an equation of the circle?

A. $(x-4)^2 + (y+3)^2 = 12$
B. $(x+4)^2 + (y+3)^2 = 12$
C. $(x+4)^2 - (y+3)^2 = 12$
D. $(x-4)^2 + (y-3)^2 = 144$
E. $(x-4)^2 + (y+3)^2 = 144$

GO ON TO THE NEXT PAGE.

40. What is the least integer value of x that makes the inequality $\frac{14}{21} < \frac{x}{12}$ true?

F. 7
G. 8
H. 9
J. 10
K. 11

DO YOUR FIGURING HERE.

41. When $f(a) = a^2 + 2a + 5$, what is the value of $f(a + b)$?

A. $a^2 + b^2 + 2ab + 5$
B. $a^2 + b^2 + 2a + 2b + 10$
C. $a^2 + b^2 + 2a + 2b + 5$
D. $(a + b)^2 + a + b + 5$
E. $(a + b)^2 + 2a + 2b + 5$

42. In the figure below, M is on $\overline{LN}$ and O is on $\overline{NP}$. $\overline{LP}$ and $\overline{MO}$ are parallel. The dimensions given are in feet. What is the length, in feet, of $\overline{NO}$?

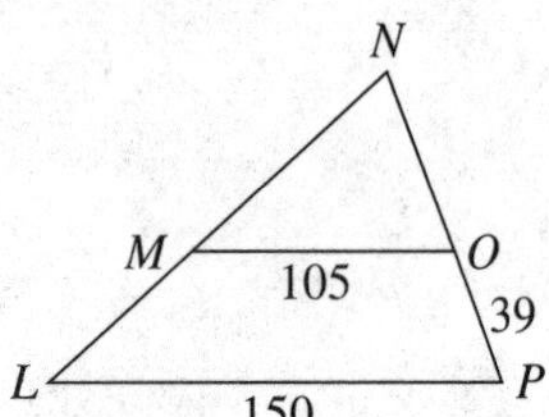

F. 39
G. 91
H. 105
J. 273
K. 294

43. Gina watched as a plane took off from the runway and climbed to 30,000 feet. She calculated the plane's height, h feet, t seconds after takeoff to be given by $h = 1{,}200 + 32t$. To the nearest second, how many seconds did it take the plane to climb to a height of 2 miles? (Note: 1 mile = 5,280 feet)

A. 37
B. 128
C. 293
D. 900
E. 1,264

GO ON TO THE NEXT PAGE.

DO YOUR FIGURING HERE.

44. In ΔABC, the measures of $\angle A$, $\angle B$, and $\angle C$ are $2x°$, $3x°$, and $5x°$, respectively. What is the measure of $\angle C$?

F. 18°
G. 36°
H. 54°
J. 90°
K. 180°

45. A basketball player has attempted 30 free throws and made 12 of them. Starting now, if he makes every free throw attempted, what is the *least* number of additional free throws he must attempt to raise his free-throw percentage to at least 55% ?

(Note: Free-throw percentage = $\frac{\textit{number of free throws made}}{\textit{number of free throws attempted}} \times 100$)

A. 5
B. 10
C. 16
D. 17
E. 29

46. If y is a negative integer, which of the following has the least value?

F. $\sqrt[3]{y^2}$

G. 100^y

H. $\frac{\pi}{y}$

J. $\frac{1}{y^2}$

K. $\frac{1}{y^3}$

47. Jonathan, Ellery, and 3 other groomsmen are rehearsing for a wedding by walking down an aisle one at a time, one groomsman in front of the other. Each time all 5 walk down the aisle, the groom tells them to walk in a different order from first to last. What is the greatest number of times the groomsmen can walk down the aisle without walking in the same order twice?

A. 3,125
B. 720
C. 120
D. 100
E. 25

GO ON TO THE NEXT PAGE.

48. In the circle below, O is the center and measures 5 inches from chord $\overline{MN}$. The area of the circle is 169π square inches. What is the length of $\overline{MN}$, in inches?

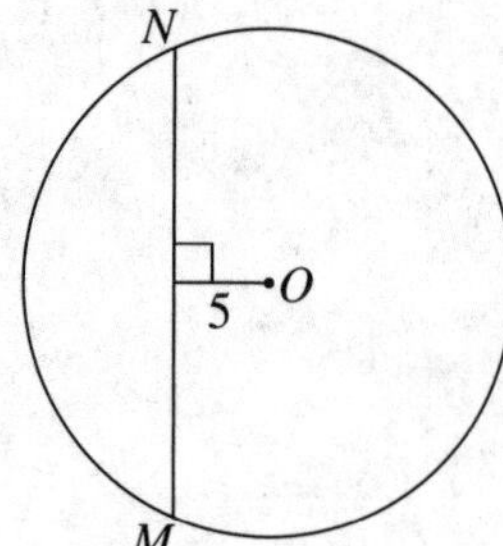

F. 12
G. 13
H. 18
J. 24
K. 26

DO YOUR FIGURING HERE.

49. What is the x–intercept of the line that passes through points (–3,7) and (6,4) in the standard (x,y) coordinate plane?

A. (18,0)

B. $(0, \frac{1}{3})$

C. (0, 6)

D. (0,18)

E. $(\frac{1}{3}, 0)$

50. Which of the following equations represents a graph that intersects the x-axis at $x = 7$?

F. $y = (x + 7)^2$
G. $y = (x - 7)^2$
H. $y = (-x - 7)^2$
J. $y - 7 = x^2$
K. $y + 7 = x^2$

GO ON TO THE NEXT PAGE.

DO YOUR FIGURING HERE.

51. If $0° < \theta < 90°$ and $\tan\theta = \frac{2}{9}$, what is $\sin\theta + \cos\theta$?

A. $\frac{11}{\sqrt{85}}$

B. $\frac{-7}{\sqrt{170}}$

C. $\frac{11}{\sqrt{170}}$

D. $\frac{9}{\sqrt{85}}$

E. $\frac{2}{\sqrt{85}}$

52. In the figure below, $\overline{OA} = \overline{AB}$, and $\overline{OB}$ is a radius of the circle, having a length of 8 inches. What is the area of ΔOAB, in square inches?

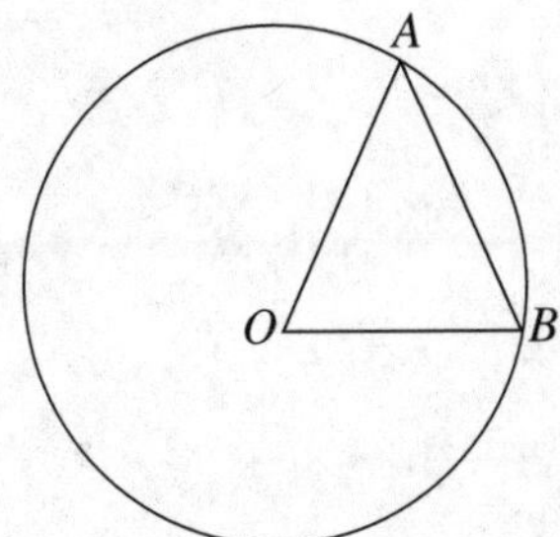

F. $8\sqrt{3}$

G. $16\sqrt{3}$

H. 32

J. $32\sqrt{3}$

K. 64

GO ON TO THE NEXT PAGE.

53. In ΔXYZ, shown below, $\overline{YZ} = 30$. Which of the following represents the length of $\overline{XY}$?

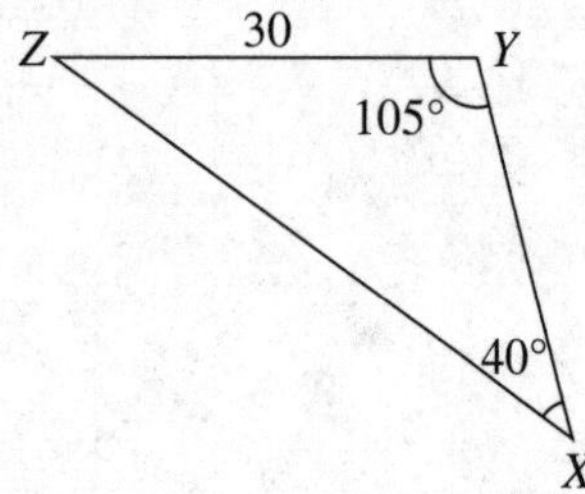

(Note: For a triangle with sides of lengths x, y, and z, and respective opposite angles measuring X, Y, and Z, it will be true that: $\frac{\sin X}{x} = \frac{\sin Y}{y} = \frac{\sin Z}{z}$, according to the Law of Sines.)

A. $\frac{30 \sin 105°}{\sin 35°}$

B. $\frac{30 \sin 105°}{\sin 40°}$

C. $\frac{30 \sin 35°}{\sin 40°}$

D. $\frac{30 \sin 40°}{\sin 105°}$

E. $\frac{30 \sin 35°}{\sin 105°}$

DO YOUR FIGURING HERE.

54. Points P and Q lie on circle O with radius of 9 feet. The measure of $\angle POQ$ is 120°. What is the length, in feet, of minor arc $\overset{\frown}{PQ}$?

F. 3π
G. 6π
H. 9π
J. 18π
K. 27π

GO ON TO THE NEXT PAGE.

DO YOUR FIGURING HERE.

55. $\begin{bmatrix} w & x \\ y & z \end{bmatrix} - \begin{bmatrix} x & y \\ z & w \end{bmatrix} - \begin{bmatrix} \frac{1}{w+x} & \frac{1}{x+y} \\ \frac{1}{y+z} & \frac{1}{z+w} \end{bmatrix} = ?$

A. $\begin{bmatrix} 1 & 1 \\ 1 & 1 \end{bmatrix}$

B. $\begin{bmatrix} \frac{w-x}{w+x} & \frac{x-y}{x+y} \\ \frac{y-z}{y+z} & \frac{d-a}{d+a} \end{bmatrix}$

C. $\begin{bmatrix} w-x-\frac{1}{w+x} & x-y-\frac{1}{x+y} \\ y-z-\frac{1}{y+z} & z-w-\frac{1}{z+w} \end{bmatrix}$

D. $\begin{bmatrix} \frac{wx}{w+x} & \frac{xy}{x+y} \\ \frac{yz}{y+z} & \frac{zw}{z+w} \end{bmatrix}$

E. $\begin{bmatrix} \frac{1}{2w-2x} & \frac{1}{2x-2y} \\ \frac{1}{2y-2z} & \frac{1}{2z-2w} \end{bmatrix}$

56. If function f is defined by $f(x) = -2x^3$, then what is the value of $f(f(1))$?

F. –16
G. –8
H. 4
J. 8
K. 16

GO ON TO THE NEXT PAGE.

57. The function y varies directly as x for all real numbers in the (x,y) coordinate plane. Which of the following could be the graph of y ?

DO YOUR FIGURING HERE.

A.

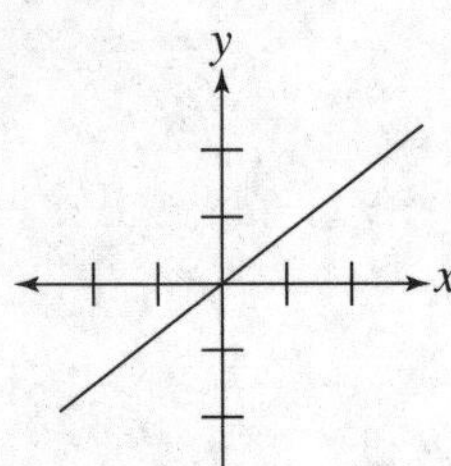

D.

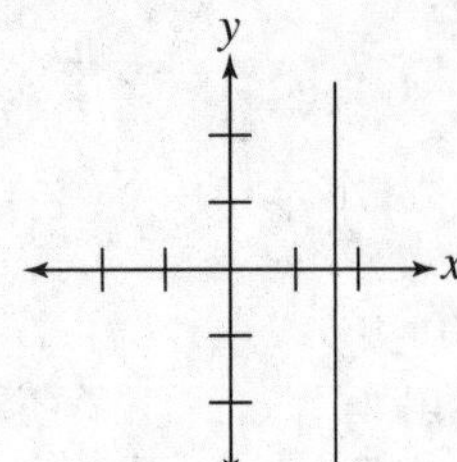

B.

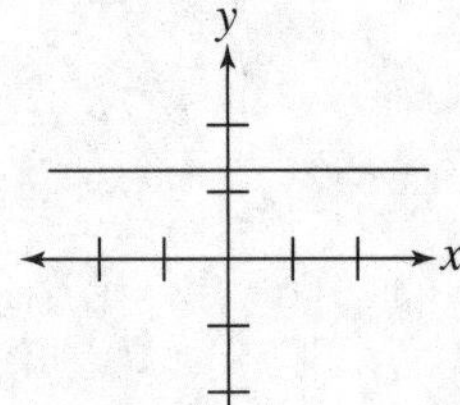

E.

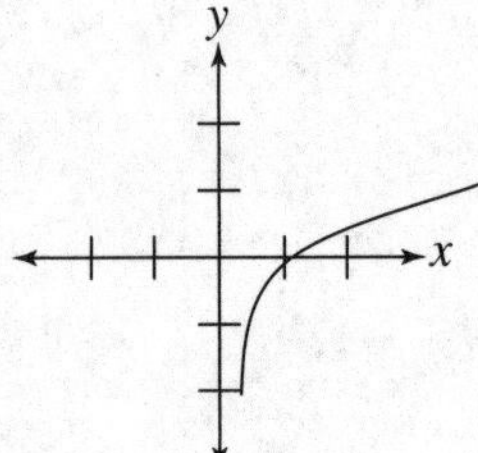

C.

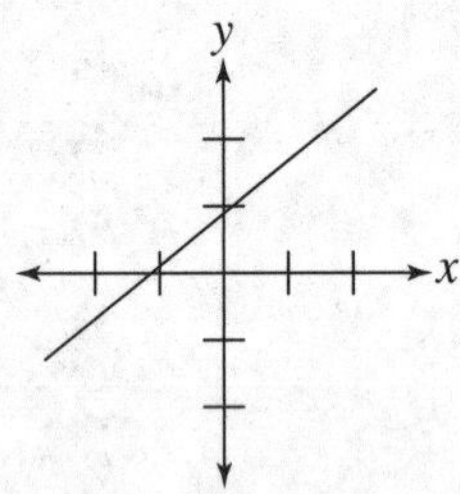

58. Gopi took 5 quizzes for which the scores are integer values ranging from 0 to 10. The median of her scores is 9. The mean of her scores is 8. The only mode of her scores is 10. Which of the following *must* be true about her quiz scores?

F. Her lowest score is 4.
G. Her lowest score is 5.
H. The median of the 3 lowest scores is 6.
J. The sum of the 5 scores is 50.
K. The sum of the 2 lowest scores is 11.

59. To make a cardboard table for her dollhouse, Ouisie uses a rectangular piece of cardboard measuring 40 inches wide and 60 inches long. She cuts out four equal-sized squares from each corner and folds down the sides at a 90° angle. If the top of the table measures 800 square inches, how tall, in inches, is the table?

A. 40
B. 30
C. 25
D. 20
E. 10

GO ON TO THE NEXT PAGE.

60. Which of the following expressions gives the area, in square feet, of $\angle ABC$ shown below with the given side lengths in feet?

DO YOUR FIGURING HERE.

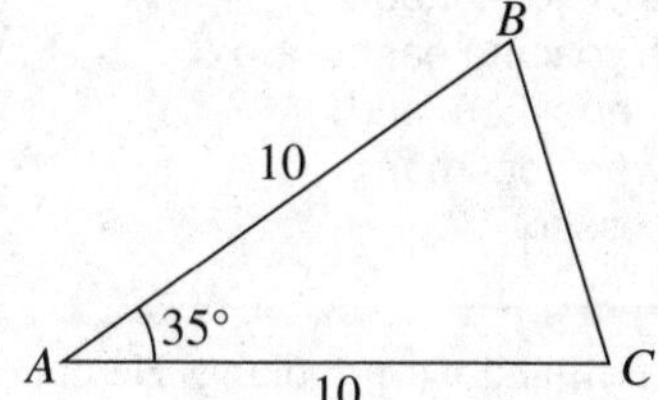

F. 50 tan 35°
G. 50 cos 35°
H. 50 sin 35°
J. 100 cos 35°
K. 100 sin 35°

END OF TEST 2
STOP! DO NOT TURN THE PAGE UNTIL TOLD TO DO SO.
DO NOT RETURN TO THE PREVIOUS TEST.

READING TEST

35 Minutes—40 Questions

DIRECTIONS: There are four passages in this test. Each passage is followed by several questions. After reading each passage, choose the best answer to each question and blacken the corresponding oval on your answer document. You may refer to the passages as often as necessary.

Passage I

PROSE FICTION: This passage is adapted from the novel *Shipwreck* by Adam C. Thomas (© 2005 by Adam Thomas).

"Let the dead bury their dead."

The words rang in the boy's ears as he trudged through the inhospitable jungle, vines snarling around his ankles. Over and over again, he heard the captain shout, "Full speed ahead, let the dead bury their dead."

Now the captain was gone and the boy felt alone despite his companions, now leading him through the alien jungle. He wondered what the words meant. How can the dead do anything? How can the dead have dead of their own?

These thoughts circled the boy's head, intermingled with the events of the last days. Again he heard the roar of the storm, felt the ship bucking and braying beneath his feet. The typhoon had come out of nowhere, it had seemed; even the captain, who surely knew everything, was taken aback by its sudden appearance.

"Avast and hold the mainsail!" he shouted to the crew. "Stay fast and let the dead bury their dead!"

The boy had held fast, even as the ship had come apart. Even as the lightning lit up the sky like the fireworks the boy had heard about, but never seen. Even as the thunder filled the air, shaking the very timbers of the ship with its bellowing ferocity. The walls of water rose up, crashing over the deck, then receded for an instant of calm before rising up as a dark mountain to once again besiege the small ship.

These memories would come to the boy in a split-second, filling his brain before he had a chance to consciously remember what had happened. Then they would recede, just as the storm had eventually receded, and the jungle would return, the monotonous trudging, day after day amid the vines and trees that were nothing like his second home on the ocean.

Sometimes, the boy would think back to before the storm, and even before the ship, to his life on land—the stultifying life on the farm where he felt landlocked before he even understood what that word signified. He thought of his mother and father, frail and worn-looking. He believed his parents did all they could to create a home for him, but his mother's sad, creased face and his father's cracked hands crowded out all other childhood memories. They filled the boy's sky, just as the thunder had, and were just as devastating, in their own way, as the storm.

For the boy, his birthplace's rocky ground yielded only a life he could not live and a place he could not love. But the sea was softer, a malleable place in which an enterprising lad could reinvent himself. So the boy had run off to sea. He vowed to leave the land forever to live atop the ocean. Now he had learned the hardness of the sea, he thought, as he jerked his mind back to the jungle.

Soon, his thoughts drifted back to his blissful days upon the ship. Although he had come aboard as a stowaway, the captain took him in and gave him daily lessons in reading the stars and plotting the ship's course. "Ignorance is dangerous, not only aboard ship but also in life," the captain warned. The eager boy soon grew familiar with the night's sky and knew the maps in the captain's quarters as well as he knew his own reflection. He had felt so secure in the captain's knowledge and in his own growing understanding.

But if the captain could be caught unawares, how could the boy ever feel safe again? How could he trust that everything the captain had said wouldn't lead to the same disastrous end?

"Let the dead bury their dead." Well, he had seen the dead after the storm. As the remaining crew members had urged him away from the wreckage, finally having to pull him by his arms to force his legs to move, the words "Let the dead bury their dead" appeared unbidden in his mind. But what did those words mean? Searching his memory, the boy was shocked to find that after the shipwreck, his mind's eye could no longer distinguish the captain from any other man—the cook, the lowest deckhand, or even the boy's father. Was that what the captain meant by "their dead"—that all the dead belonged to one another?

He walked mechanically, pace after pace, leading him away from the remains of his home and the only man he had ever loved. Toward what? He had no knowledge of what lay ahead. But still his legs moved, seemingly of their own

GO ON TO THE NEXT PAGE.

accord, his heart continued to beat, his lungs continued to fill with air. His mind continued to retrace his life, and with the beating of his heart and the filling of his lungs, still he walked.

1. As it is used in line 32, the word *stultifying* most nearly means:

A. stifling.
B. strengthening.
C. welcoming.
D. productive.

2. The first seven paragraphs (lines 1–30) establish all of the following about the boy EXCEPT that he:

F. had companions on the walk through the jungle.
G. had often watched fireworks light up the sky.
H. respected the captain.
J. often had his thoughts filled with memories of the storm.

3. The passage states that the boy saw himself as:

A. contented with life in the jungle.
B. afraid of his mother.
C. toughened by farm labor.
D. at home on the sea.

4. The time sequence of the passage indicates that the shipwreck takes place:

F. after the boy leaves the farm.
G. after the boy walks through the jungle.
H. before the boy meets the captain.
J. before his mother tries to protect him.

5. How does the twelfth paragraph (lines 60–70) offer one way to interpret the phrase "let the dead bury their dead," as implied by the passage?

A. The boy remembers the captain's explanation of this phrase.
B. The dead cannot do anything, so one should trust only the living.
C. Death erases the distinctions that make the living unique individuals.
D. Without his experiences, the boy cannot expect to lead a better life.

6. Compared to the captain's ideas, the boy's are:

F. opposing; the captain is uncertain about the meaning of the phrase, "let the dead bury their dead."
G. opposing; the captain understood why the boy's father was worn down.
H. similar; the captain disliked the harsh life of the sea.
J. similar; the captain valued learning and knowledge.

7. It is most reasonable to infer from the passage that the ship's remaining crewmates accompanying the boy on his walk through the jungle would agree with which of the following statements about the boy?

A. The boy's grief over the captain's death made him unwilling to leave the scene of the shipwreck.
B. The boy's grief over the captain's death made him run away from his companions.
C. The boy was constantly startled by loud noises.
D. The boy hated his life on land and had escaped to the sea to find freedom.

8. Which of the following statements best describes the actions taken by the captain on finding the boy stowed away on the ship?

F. He scolds the boy because he did not pay the fare for passage on the ship.
G. He teaches the boy the meaning of the phrase "let the dead bury their dead."
H. He teaches the boy how to navigate using maps and the stars.
J. He ignores the boy, leaving him to fend for himself.

9. According to the passage, the storm features all of the following EXCEPT:

A. loud thunder.
B. huge walls of water.
C. bright lightning.
D. ferocious hail.

10. Which of the following statements about the storm is supported by the passage?

F. It blew up without warning, taking the captain by surprise.
G. It happened in the middle of the night.
H. It was the most violent storm any of the crew had ever seen.
J. It was the storm the boy's father had warned him about.

GO ON TO THE NEXT PAGE.

Passage II

SOCIAL SCIENCE: This passage is adapted from the article "Slang: Why It's Totally Sweet" by Patrick Tyrrell (© 2008 by Patrick Tyrrell).

Tony Thorne's email inbox is bloated with messages from teenagers and college students around the world explicating the meaning behind local terms such as "toop," "tonk," and "chung." Why would the Director of the Language Center at King's College of London concern himself with seemingly nonsensical linguistic inventions?

Thorne is busy compiling a current dictionary of slang from around the English-speaking world. Although *neologisms*, new adaptations or inventions of words, are normally born out of a specific geographic and cultural context, the ease of worldwide communication ushered in by the technological age has made slang an instantly exportable commodity. College students in Iowa are just as likely to use British slang like "bum" (one's posterior) as British homemakers are to employ American slang like "dust bunny," since both groups are exposed to each other's movies, TV, music, and other media.

In the world of linguistics, slang is often viewed condescendingly as an affliction of vulgar speech, its users condemned for their intellectual laziness. Early 20th century linguist Oliver Wendell Holmes described slang as "at once a sign and a cause of mental atrophy." Meanwhile, Thorne points out, some legendary authors such as Walt Whitman elevated the status of slang, referring to it as "an attempt by common humanity to escape from bald literalism, and express itself illimitably."

What are the origins of most slang words? Many philologists, those who attempt to study and determine the meaning of historical texts, believe that slang is created as a response to the status quo, that its usage represents a defiant opposition of authority. For example, many Americans use the phrase *a cup of joe* to refer to a cup of coffee; however, few know that it originated from one Admiral Joe Daniels who in 1914 denied his sailors wine. As a result, they decided their strict leader was a fitting namesake for the terribly acidic black coffee they were forced to drink instead.

Thorne, however, would point out that most slang is derived for much more innocent purposes. For example, terms like "ankle-biters" (infants), "ramping up" (on the job training), and "Googling" (searching on the Internet) do not involve opposition to authority. Usually, slang evolves out of very insular groups with specific needs for informative or vibrant expressions that normal language does not encapsulate. It is the marriage of jargon, nuance, and effective imagery. While traditional hotbeds of slang have been the military, industrial factories, and street markets, most modern slang comes from such arenas as corporate offices, college campuses, and users/designers of computers.

In determining the sources of slang terms, Thorne and his contemporaries repeatedly refine their definition of "slang" as distinctive from "idioms," "euphemisms," "hyperbole," and other instances of conventional figurative language. Many linguists consider slang the polar opposite of formal speech, with other figurative language devices falling somewhere in between. Whereas a "colloquialism" still indicates a measure of respect owed to the expression's regional usefulness, "slang" brands a word as having fallen into a state of overused emptiness.

How do we know when a word has become overused or empty? Much slang is attached to some sense of style or fad and therefore risks being as short-lived in nature as the trend upon which it is based. However, some terms such as "punk" and "cool" have been in common use for a century or more and have completely assimilated into the acceptable mainstream dialect. Clearly, then, some words fall into a gray area between slang and proper language. Although lexicologists like Thorne attempt to define and apply standard principles in their classification of slang, there is definitely some subjectivity involved in determining whether a term deserves the maligning moniker.

Furthermore, intellectuals who would categorically denounce slang struggle with the fact that slang, when first conceived, involves as much inherent creativity and word play as the figurative language revered in poetry. It is ultimately how the word survives, or rather who continues to use it, that determines its stature as artful rhetoric or the dreaded slang. If "respectable" people continue to use an expression for its conceptual vivacity, then the word was a clever invention worth enriching a nation's lexicon. If the "common man" uses a term and uses it too liberally, the word is deemed slang, and an eloquent speaker will have the tastefulness to avoid it.

Whatever slang's level of social esteem, Thorne believes that it is an essential project to compile accurate modern dictionaries of its usage. When one considers the large amount of written artifacts our present world creates on a daily basis, it is reasonable to also consider providing future generations (or civilizations) of humans with an effective way of decoding our meaning, which could easily be confused by our prevalent use of slang. Imagine how much less debate there would be over the meaning of some Shakespearean verses if we had a detailed description of his contemporary slang. Because of this need to inform future scholars, Thorne's dictionary of slang attempts to not only define each term but also to explain its origins, connotations, and typical conversational uses.

GO ON TO THE NEXT PAGE.

11. Based on the passage, Thorne most likely describes some slang as *innocent* (line 37) to indicate his belief that not all slang is created to be:

A. rebellious.
B. informative.
C. nuanced.
D. accusatory.

12. The author includes the information in the last paragraph primarily to:

F. criticize Thorne for being too subjective with which words he chooses to include in his dictionary.
G. illustrate how a future scholar might be able to use Thorne's dictionary as a resource.
H. identify the ways Thorne uses Shakespearean slang to describe modern terms.
J. argue that Thorne's dictionary should be the primary focus of modern linguistics.

13. All of the following groups are mentioned in the passage as related to the academic study of slang EXCEPT:

A. philologists.
B. college professors.
C. linguists.
D. lexicologists.

14. The quotation marks around the phrase "common man" in line 78 primarily serve to:

F. emphasize the subjective and somewhat derogatory process of categorizing people and the words they use.
G. reveal the author's suspicion that the man in question is not common at all.
H. introduce a demeaning term the author believes is appropriate to describe users of slang.
J. show how an inventive term may enjoy popularity briefly but ultimately does not have the proper usage to survive.

15. As it is used in line 18, the word *vulgar* most nearly means:

A. sickening.
B. malicious.
C. unsophisticated.
D. profane.

16. The passage indicates that the efforts to compile current dictionaries of slang are viewed by some as essential because these dictionaries:

F. could possibly provide future scholars with a way of deciphering the meaning of today's writings.
G. are the only way that speakers of other languages can decode the subtle meaning of English texts.
H. currently do not exist except for those chronicling Shakespeare's era.
J. will provide modern English speakers with the correct conversational uses of each slang term.

17. According to the passage, Walt Whitman seems to view the use of slang as an attempt to:

A. show civility.
B. conform to traditions.
C. broaden expression.
D. defy authority.

18. The main purpose of the first paragraph in relation to the passage is to:

F. acquaint the reader with some examples of slang.
G. establish that British scholars are the leaders in slang research.
H. introduce slang as a possibly surprising topic of academic study.
J. outline Tony Thorne's problems with managing his email inbox.

19. The author's reference to groups like the military as being *hotbeds of slang* (line 44) most nearly means that such groups are:

A. prophetic.
B. old-fashioned.
C. innovative.
D. strict.

20. The passage suggests that of the following, which one encapsulates the greatest obstacle for intellectuals who would categorically denounce slang?

F. Their own invention of some slang terms
G. Disagreement on how certain slang terms are used
H. Respect for Thorne's academic interest and tireless determination.
J. Appreciation for the creativity involved in the origination of slang

GO ON TO THE NEXT PAGE.

Passage III

HUMANITIES: Passage A is adapted from the article, "A hand-written note from Harper Lee is the politest rejection." (Used with permission of The Associated Press Copyright © 2016. All rights reserved.) Passage B is adapted from the article, "Marja Mills addresses Harper Lee controversy at literary event" by Courtney Crowder. (From Chicago Tribune. © 2014 Chicago Tribune. All rights reserved. Used under license.)

Passage A

It was, without a doubt, the nicest rejection of my journalistic career.... The author of "To Kill a Mockingbird" hadn't granted an interview in about four decades, but I figured it was worth a shot. So I crafted a letter and sent it off to Monroeville, Alabama, care of attorney Alice F. Lee—the author's older sister and chief gatekeeper.... I didn't really expect a reply.

Nine days later, a letter arrived.... The note was brief. "Dear Mr. Breed: Thank you for your kind letter and its enclosures. You show much talent as a non-fiction writer!" she wrote in a clear script that sloped somewhat down to the right. "I simply don't give interviews—I gave all my publisher and the movie people asked me to give long ago (before you were born), and that was it. However, if I ever decide to give another, you will be near the top of the waiting list!" There was a brief postscript on the backside of the page. "My eyesight is failing, and I must look sideways to write," it read, "so please forgive the slant!" ....

In an age when people feel compelled to update their Facebook statuses constantly, Lee kept her thoughts to herself. Not a post, nor a tweet. With the 2014 publication of *The Mockingbird Next Door: Life with Harper Lee*, it appeared that Lee's resolve had softened. Then in February 2015, publisher Harper announced the pending release of her *Go Set a Watchman*, even including a rare statement from Lee: "I am humbled and amazed that this will now be published after all these years."

No, she did not talk with me. Yes, I would have gladly trumpeted an exclusive interview. But part of me was hoping that she'd stick to her guns and let the singular accomplishment of *Mockingbird* speak for itself. We have this notion that our heroes—movie stars, athletes or authors—owe us more than just the fruits of their talents; that being public figures means they are public property. Lee was able to keep her own counsel and, along with friends and relatives, protect her privacy. I like a scoop as much as the next reporter, but the idea of prying into Lee's life always felt a bit like killing a mockingbird—the bird you leave alone because all it does is sing....

Passage B

Less than a week after the publication of Marja Mills' memoir, *The Mockingbird Next Door*, her story of befriending the famously reclusive 88-year-old author Harper Lee, the book remains embroiled in controversy. On July 14, the day before the book's publication date, Lee, author of the American classic *To Kill a Mockingbird*, issued a statement refuting the memoir's main narrative: that Mills was allowed unique access to the author and her sister, Alice Lee, 102, and that the sisters told her stories with the knowledge that Mills was going to use them in a book. "Rest assured, as long as I am alive any book purporting to be with my cooperation is a falsehood," Lee's statement said.

On Monday at a sold-out Tribune-sponsored book discussion at Tribune Tower, Mills, a former Tribune reporter, addressed the dispute: Lee "had always been encouraging and also quite specific about stories that she was sharing for the book and those that were to remain private, and I did respect those...I can only speak the truth, that Nelle Harper Lee and Alice F. Lee were aware I was writing this book and my friendship with both of them continued during and after my time in Monroeville."...

Mills' journey to the center of Lee's social circle began in 2001, when the Tribune assigned her to capture the spirit of Monroeville, Ala., Lee's hometown, when the Chicago Public Library selected *To Kill a Mockingbird* as the first pick for the One Book, One Chicago program. After the exhaustive and meticulously researched Tribune article was published in 2002, Mills remained friends with the sisters, although Harper Lee, characteristically, had declined to comment for the article. In 2004, Mills moved into the house next door to them with their blessing, according to the book jacket. For the next 18 months, from fall 2004 to spring 2006, Mills accompanied the sisters as they ate, explored and even did their laundry....

Mills described her book as focusing on "the last chapter of life as (the Lees) knew it." In 2007, Harper Lee had a serious stroke and had to move into an assisted-living facility. Soon after, Alice Lee also moved out of the house they had both lived in for nearly all their lives. "So much that has been said about (the Lees) has been secondhand or speculated," Mills said. "I just wanted to get out of the way. I wanted to show them sitting at the kitchen table, listening to Nelle tell stories, or being in the car with them as they talked about the Monroeville of 1930 versus now."

GO ON TO THE NEXT PAGE.

Questions 21–23 ask about Passage A.

21. It can most reasonably be inferred from Passage A that after Breed received Harper Lee's letter, he:

A. had difficulty reading her writing and posted her letter on social media.
B. felt angry that she had agreed to another reporter's request but approved of her decision.
C. appreciated her compliment of his writing style but regretted losing the exclusive interview.
D. felt glad that she maintained her privacy and appreciated receiving the reply.

22. Which of the following is a detail from Passage A that best supports the idea that Lee kept herself out of the public eye?

F. Lee was worried that she might not live up to people's high expectations.
G. Lee did not reply to interview requests.
H. Lee announced the release of a new publication in 2014.
J. Lee had not granted an interview for forty years.

23. Regarding the publication of *The Mockingbird Next Door*, Passage A makes clear that its appearance:

A. seemed to show that Lee was opening up to public scrutiny after all.
B. proved that Lee had softened her resolve.
C. led Lee to express humility and amazement.
D. amounted to another author prying into Lee's life.

Questions 24–27 ask about Passage B.

24. Based on Passage B, Harper Lee's reaction to Mills's book was:

F. angry but also accepting that the public wanted to know more about her life.
G. dismissive; she claimed that she had not authorized its publication.
H. negative but also proud because people took interest in her writing.
J. encouraging; she was pleased to give a first-hand account of her life.

25. According to Crowder, Mills's article can best be described as:

A. controversial but exhausting.
B. encouraging and specific.
C. thorough and well-researched.
D. speculative and second-hand.

26. It can most reasonably be inferred from Passage B that Mills published her book in part because she:

F. wanted to publicize the exclusive interviews she was able to hold with the Lees.
G. aspired to capture the spirit of Monroeville, Alabama, both in the past and in the present.
H. felt compelled to reveal the truth about her friendship with the Lees.
J. hoped she could provide first-hand information on the Lees' daily lives and conversations.

27. Lines 53–56 most nearly mean that Mills:

A. acted in accordance with all of Lee's wishes regarding the book.
B. earned the Lees' respect by sharing meals and household chores with them.
C. censored several of Lee's stories in the final version of the book.
D. did not include some of Lee's stories in the book.

Questions 28–30 ask about both passages.

28. Which statement most accurately compares the content of the two passages?

F. Both describe first-hand accounts of contact with Lee that had different outcomes.
G. Both analyze Lee's readers but draw different conclusions about their motivations.
H. Both present the same anecdotes about Lee to explain her change of heart late in life.
J. Both explore the psychological motivations for Lee's self-identification with a bird.

29. Based on the passages, it's most likely that Breed and Crowder would agree that Harper Lee's privacy was:

A. secondary; her central concern was always for the reception of her novel.
B. significant; Lee had avoided publicity since the publication of her novel.
C. misplaced; famous people must be accountable to the public.
D. misconstrued; reports about her concerns were mostly second-hand.

GO ON TO THE NEXT PAGE.

30. It can most reasonably be inferred from the passages that the author of the text referred to in lines 20–22 is:

F. Alice F. Lee.
G. Marja Mills.
H. Courtney Crowder.
J. Allan G. Breed.

Passage IV

NATURAL SCIENCE: This passage is excerpted from the article "Frank Drake and Project Ozma" by Arnold C. Topton (© 2004 by Crackpot Press).

On a cool April night in 1960, in Green Bank, West Virginia, Frank Drake became a scientific pioneer. Careful research had given him reason to believe that, if he tuned his radio to the correct frequency and aimed it at the correct stars, he might pick up interstellar transmissions from another planet. Hoping for a breakthrough, he tuned the radio and began to listen.

So began Project Ozma, widely considered the first organized attempt to detect alien life by way of radio. Although it was ultimately unsuccessful in its goal of finding other intelligent life in the universe, Project Ozma was hugely influential, inspiring the creation of many similar programs. The following fifty years would see a steady increase in both the sophistication and the scope of similar programs, ranging from a wide-ranging but short-term program funded by NASA to the meticulously orchestrated Project Phoenix, designed to monitor carefully selected regions of space over a period of ten years. Today, many such programs are ongoing, in locations as august as the University of California at Berkeley and the University of Western Sydney, both of which have reputations that draw respected scientists from around the world.

The scientists involved in the Search for Extraterrestrial Intelligence, or SETI, are far from the wide-eyed dreamers that many people associate with the field. The SETI scientists are, in fact, esteemed academics, typically specializing in the areas of physics, astronomy, and engineering. Indeed, they have to be able to complete such complex tasks as calculating where to position the radios so as to achieve the best effect, deciding what messages are most likely to be understood by an alien culture, and determining which stars to monitor.

Although these scientists' understanding of the origins of life on Earth is still imperfect, those involved in SETI do have some idea of what combinations of size, location, and chemical composition make a planet more likely to harbor intelligent life. The general understanding is that there are two main factors that determine whether or not a planet is habitable (able to sustain life): temperature and mass. There are other factors that are often considered, such as the presence of certain chemicals, the proximity of other planets, and planetary age, but temperature and mass are the initial, and most crucial, tests.

Liquid water is widely believed to be critical to the development of life, and this belief has led scientists to hypothesize that, in order to support life, a planet must experience temperatures that fall within a range that allows for the presence of liquid water. This, in turn, suggests that hospitable planets must be located within a certain distance of their respective suns. If a planet is too far from the Sun, its temperatures will fall below that range, as in the case of Saturn. If a planet is too close to the Sun, as in the case of Venus, its temperatures will be too high. Planets that fall within the range of appropriate temperatures are often called "Goldilocks Planets," since they are neither too hot nor too cold but instead "just right" to provide environments hospitable to life. However, even when a planet is found that is within this range, there is still no guarantee that all of the related factors will be suitable. It is also necessary that the planet have an orbit that allows the planet to rotate at a speed and angle that prevents either side from freezing or boiling, ruling out most binary systems due to their unstable orbits.

The other key to habitability is the mass of a planet. In order to sustain life, a planet must have sufficient mass to hold a gravitational field, while not having so much as to create an excessively heavy atmosphere. Truly massive planets also tend to retain hydrogen gases and become "gas giants" with no solid surface. How large a planet can be, while retaining the ability to host living organisms, depends in part on that planet's distance from the Sun. Larger planets have heavier atmospheres, so they also tend to retain more heat, creating a greenhouse effect, wherein atmospheric gases absorb radiation, causing an increase in temperature. Therefore, a planet on the outer edge of the Goldilocks zone might be able to sustain life if its mass were great enough to hold in enough heat to bring the temperature back into the habitable zone, while a smaller planet might be able to do the same on the inner edge.

The search for extraterrestrial life, and perhaps intelligence, that started in West Virginia back in 1960 continues today. The more knowledge scientists are able to gather about our own galaxy, the better equipped they will be when it comes to seeking out similar planets outside our solar system. Perhaps someday Frank Drake's dream of a message from outer space will come true—once we know where to look for it.

GO ON TO THE NEXT PAGE.

31. According to the passage, Frank Drake:

A. was one of the first scientists to use radio technology to look for alien life.
B. successfully found signs of extraterrestrial life.
C. ran Project Phoenix from his radio telescope in West Virginia.
D. is a highly esteemed astronomer and physicist.

32. Which of the following would be the most appropriate characterization of Project Ozma, as portrayed by the author of the passage?

F. Its unexpected success took the scientific community by surprise, altering the face of the field.
G. Although it was a failure in one sense, it helped usher in a new era of interstellar research.
H. Drake's goals were unrealistic, given his limited knowledge and resources.
J. Without the financial support of institutions such as NASA, the Project was doomed to failure.

33. As it is used in line 19, the word *august* most nearly means:

A. summery.
B. elusive.
C. esteemed.
D. antique.

34. As conveyed in the passage, the author's attitude toward the search for life on other planets is:

F. ironic yet sympathetic.
G. scornful and angry.
H. hopeful yet pragmatic.
J. uncertain and fearful.

35. According to the passage, scientists involved in the search for life on other planets are likely to be:

A. trained in scientific disciplines such as physics, astronomy, and engineering.
B. wide-eyed dreamers prone to unrealistic expectations about space.
C. employed at institutions such as universities or NASA.
D. skilled radio mechanics, due to their work with radio telescopes.

36. The primary point of the fourth paragraph (lines 31–41) is that:

F. even today scientists do not understand why life developed on our planet.
G. liquid water is crucial to the evolution of intelligent life on any planet.
H. only planets within a "Goldilocks Zone" are able to sustain life.
J. there appear to be two crucial components in determining whether a planet may be habitable.

37. It can reasonably be inferred that, as it is used in line 46, the term *hospitable planets* is intended to mean:

A. planets with cultures that are similar to those found on our planet.
B. locations outside of our solar system that are in close proximity to the Sun.
C. binary planets with generally stable orbits and moderate temperatures.
D. places with temperatures and masses that fall within the range able to support life.

38. Based on the information in the passage, Saturn is most likely unable to sustain life because:

F. its close proximity to the Sun causes a greenhouse effect.
G. the atmosphere is too heavy to allow for liquid water to exist.
H. its distance from the Sun is too great for it to contain liquid water.
J. it is an unstable gas giant, due to the chemical combinations present.

39. The passage indicates that any new planet discovered in a location that is comparable to Venus's location, relative to the sun, would most likely be:

A. an overheated gas giant, due to its heavy atmosphere.
B. incapable of supporting life due to its lack of a gravitational field.
C. prone to the development of an unstable orbit.
D. unable to sustain life unless it were small enough not to retain too much heat.

40. According to the passage, Goldilocks Planets are characterized by:

F. temperatures that are moderate enough to allow for the existence of liquid water.
G. heavy atmospheres that retain hydrogen gases, creating a greenhouse effect.
H. either extremely hot or extremely cold temperatures, depending on proximity to the sun.
J. the presence of both liquid water and a high concentration of hydrogen gases.

END OF TEST 3
STOP! DO NOT TURN THE PAGE UNTIL TOLD TO DO SO.
DO NOT RETURN TO A PREVIOUS TEST.

SCIENCE TEST

35 Minutes—40 Questions

DIRECTIONS: There are six passages in the following section. Each passage is followed by several questions. After reading a passage, choose the best answer to each question and blacken the corresponding oval on your answer document. You may refer to the passages as often as necessary.

You are NOT permitted to use a calculator on this test.

Passage I

In recent years, the technology of magnetic levitation ("maglev") has been investigated to provide an alternative rapid transportation option. Using repulsion of magnetic fields, maglev trains can be pushed forward at speeds of up to 300 miles per hour. One specific type of magnetic levitation currently being investigated is electrodynamic suspension (EDS).

In EDS, magnetic rods are located at the bottom of the maglev train and within the track underneath the train. An electric current can induce a magnetic field in the magnets of the track. If this magnetic field can be induced to repel constantly the magnet in the maglev train, then the train will maintain a distance above the track known as an "air gap" and move forward. Theoretically, the maglev train in EDS should travel at least 4 inches above the track, so there would be virtually no energy lost to friction. If the system does lose energy, it will be in the form of thermal energy.

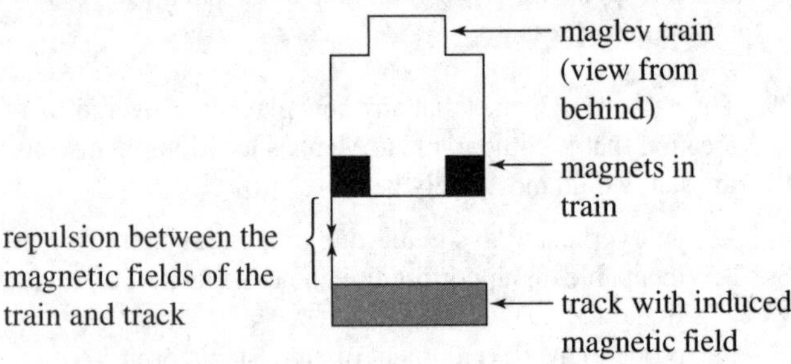

Figure 1

Under controlled conditions, scientists conducted tests on an experimental maglev track oriented in an east-to-west direction.

Study 1

A maglev train with magnetic rods of fixed length was moved along the experimental track from east to west at various velocities v. The current I in the track required to induce these velocities was measured in amperes (A).

Table 1

Trial	v (m/s)	I (A)
1	40	50
2	80	100
3	120	150
4	160	200
5	200	250

Study 2

The maglev train was run in five trials with varying lengths, L, of the magnetic rods, and run at a constant velocity of 40 m/s. The current I in the track required to induce this velocity given the different lengths of the rods was recorded.

Table 2

Trial	L (m)	I (A)
6	0.6	50
7	0.8	67
8	1.0	84
9	1.2	100
10	1.4	116

Study 3

The magnetic field, B, measured in tesla (T), was varied in the maglev track. The current running through the maglev track was then measured in five new trials. Throughout these trials, the lengths of the magnetic rods and the maglev train velocities were kept constant.

GO ON TO THE NEXT PAGE.

Table 3		
Trial	*B* (T)	*I* (A)
11	5.90×10^{-4}	300
12	7.87×10^{-4}	400
13	9.84×10^{-4}	500
14	1.05×10^{-3}	600
15	1.20×10^{-3}	700

Study 4

The maglev train with magnetic rods of fixed length was moved along the experimental track from west to east at various velocities, and the current in the track required to induce these velocities was measured. The magnetic field was kept constant for each of these trials.

Table 4		
Trial	*v* (m/s)	*I* (A)
16	40	−50
17	80	−100
18	120	−150
19	160	−200
20	200	−250

1. In Study 1, *I* would most likely have equaled 500 A if *v* had been:

A. 40 m/s.
B. 125 m/s.
C. 200 m/s.
D. 400 m/s.

2. In Study 2, as the length of the magnetic rods in the maglev train increased, the amount of the current required to induce the train's velocity:

F. increased only.
G. decreased only.
H. remained constant.
J. varied, but with no consistent trend.

3. In Study 3, *I* would most likely have equaled 570 A if *B* had equaled which of the following?

A. 6.00×10^{-4} T
B. 8.00×10^{-4} T
C. 1.00×10^{-3} T
D. 1.50×10^{-3} T

4. During each trial, an electrical current moves through the magnetic track because a nonzero voltage was produced in the track. During which of the following trials in Study 3 was the voltage greatest?

F. Trial 11
G. Trial 12
H. Trial 13
J. Trial 14

5. In which of the studies, if any, did the electrical current flow in the opposite direction as compared with the other studies?

A. Study 1 only
B. Study 4 only
C. Studies 1 and 3 only
D. None of these studies

6. The results of Study 3 are best represented by which of the following graphs?

F.

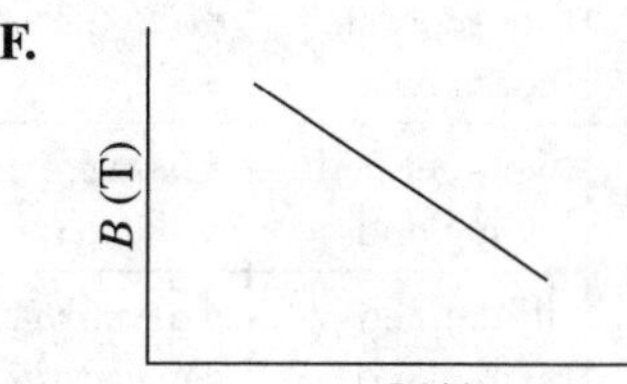

G.

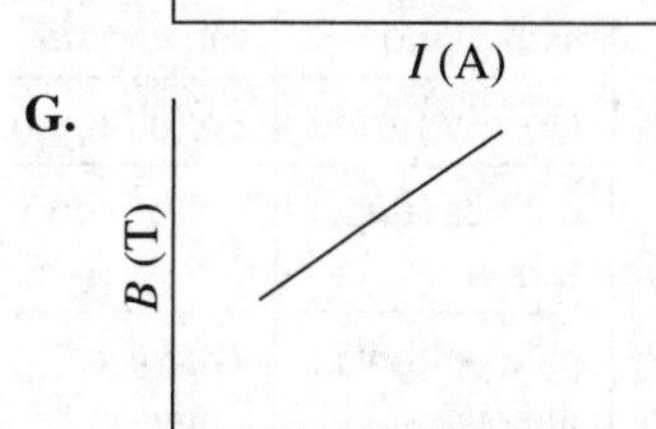

H.

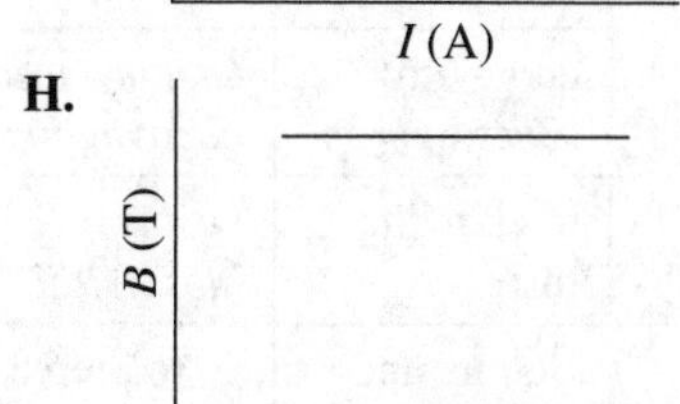

J.

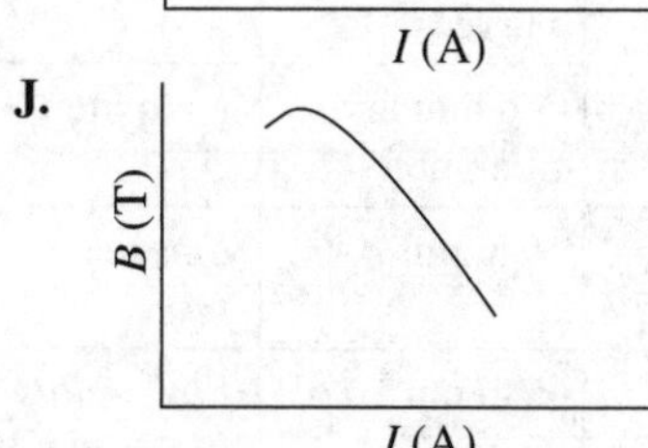

7. Based on the results of Studies 1 and 2, the length of the maglev trains used in Study 1 was most likely:

A. 0.6 m.
B. 0.8 m.
C. 1.0 m.
D. 1.2 m.

GO ON TO THE NEXT PAGE.

Passage II

Bats of the family *Vespertilionidae* (Vesper bats) are commonly found in North America. A guide for identifying Vesper bats found in Utah is presented in Table 1.

Table 1

Step	Trait	Appearance	Result
1	If the ears are	longer than 25 mm	go to Step 2
		shorter than 25 mm	go to Step 5
2	If the dorsum (back) has	3 white spots	*Euderma maculotum*
		no spots	go to Step 3
3	If the ears are	separated at the base	*Antrozous pallidus*
		not separated at the base	go to Step 4
4	If the muzzle has	well-defined skin glands	*Idionycteris phyllotis*
		ill-defined skin glands	*Corynorhinus townsendii*
5	If the uropatagium* is	heavily furred	go to Step 6
		not heavily furred	go to Step 7
6	If the fur color is	pale yellow at the base	*Lasiurus cinereus*
		dark with silver tips	*Lasionycteris noctivagans*
		brick red to rust	*Lasiurus blossevillii*
7	If the tragus** is	< 6 mm and curved	go to Step 8
		> 6 mm and straight	go to Step 9
8	If the forearm length is	> 40 mm	*Eptesicus fuscus*
		< 40 mm	*Pipistrellus hesperus*
9	If there is an obvious fringe of fur	on the edge of the uropatagium	*Myotis thysanodes*
		between the elbows and knees	*Myotis volans*

*Wing-like tissue between hind legs
**Cartilage structure in the ear

Students observed Vesper bats in a Utah nature reserve and recorded descriptions of them in Table 2.

Table 2

Bat	I	II	III	IV
Ears	20 mm long, separate at base	18 mm long	30 mm long, joined at base	15 mm long
Dorsum	no spots	no spots	no spots	no spots
Muzzle	ill-defined skin glands	ill-defined skin glands	well-defined skin glands	ill-defined skin glands
Uropatagium	not heavily furred	not heavily furred; only an obvious fringe of fur on its edge	not heavily furred	heavily furred
Fur	brown	brown	olive	black with silver tips
Tragus	4 mm, curved	7 mm, straight	9 mm, curved	4 mm, curved
Forearm	50 mm long	25 mm long	30 mm long	20 mm long

8. Based on the information in Tables 1 and 2, *Idionycteris phyllotis* most likely has an average forearm length that is:

- **F.** greater than 40 mm; Bat I has a forearm length greater than 40 mm.
- **G.** greater than 40 mm; Bat III has a forearm length less than 40 mm.
- **H.** less than 40 mm; Bat I has a forearm length greater than 40 mm.
- **J.** less than 40 mm; Bat III has a forearm length less than 40 mm.

9. Based on the given information, which of the following characteristics distinguishes Bat IV from a *Pipistrellus hesperus*?

- **A.** 4 mm and curved tragus
- **B.** 15 mm long ears
- **C.** 20 mm long forearm
- **D.** Heavily furred uropatagium

GO ON TO THE NEXT PAGE.

10. Based on Table 1, Bats I and II share the same results through Step:

F. 1.
G. 5.
H. 7.
J. 9.

11. Which of the following best describes the family *Vespertilionidae*?

A. Mammals
B. Protists
C. Lampreys
D. Birds

12. According to Table 1, *Lasiurus cinereus* and *Lasiurus blossevillii* could have all of the following traits in common EXCEPT:

F. ears not separated at the base.
G. 35 mm long ears.
H. a heavily furred uropatagium.
J. 20 mm long ears.

13. Based on Table 1, which of the following is likely to be most genetically similar to Bat II ?

A. *Lasiurus blossevillii*
B. *Idionycteris phyllotis*
C. *Lasionyceris noctivagans*
D. *Myotis volans*

GO ON TO THE NEXT PAGE.

Passage III

Pepsin is an enzyme in humans that catalyzes the digestion of proteins, like the milk protein *casein*, into smaller subunits called peptides. Pepsin is active only in acidic solutions.

The researchers prepared a solution of casein, a solution of *anserine* (a small peptide), a solution of pepsin, and various *buffer solutions* (solutions maintaining a constant pH). The following experiments were conducted using these solutions.

Experiment 1

Seven solutions were prepared in test tubes using a 5 mL solution buffered to pH 3.0. Different amounts of casein, anserine, and pepsin solutions were added to each tube, and then diluted to 10 mL with the buffer solution, so that the final pH in each test tube would be 3.0. Each tube was incubated at a constant temperature for 15 minutes, and then was monitored to determine whether there was any activity by pepsin (see Table 1).

Table 1

Trial	Casein (mL)	Anserine (mL)	Pepsin (mL)	Temperature (°C)	Pepsin Activity
1	1	1	1	30	No
2	1	1	1	35	Low
3	1	1	1	40	High
4	1	0	1	40	High
5	0	1	1	40	No
6	0	0	1	40	No
7	1	1	1	45	No

Experiment 2

Seven solutions were prepared in test tubes according to the same procedure as in Trial 3 of Experiment 1, and each test tube was diluted with different buffer solutions of varying pH (see Table 2).

Table 2

Trial	pH	Pepsin activity
8	2.5	high activity
9	3.0	high activity
10	3.5	high activity
11	4.0	low activity
12	4.5	low activity
13	5.0	low activity
14	5.5	no activity

14. Suppose Trial 10 were repeated, but the researcher forgot to add the anserine. Would the solution show any pepsin activity?

F. Yes, because Trial 4 shows high pepsin activity.
G. Yes, because Trial 6 shows no pepsin activity.
H. No, because Trial 4 shows high pepsin activity.
J. No, because Trial 6 shows no pepsin activity.

GO ON TO THE NEXT PAGE.

15. Pepsin is most likely to be found in which of the following organs?

A. Kidney
B. Heart
C. Stomach
D. Spinal cord

16. Suppose another trial had been performed in Experiment 2, and the results showed a high level of pepsin activity. Which of the following would be the most likely pH of the buffer solution used in this new trial?

F. 2.0
G. 4.0
H. 6.0
J. 8.0

17. Which of the following is the most likely reason that Trials 3 and 4 show high levels of pepsin activity, while Trial 5 shows no pepsin activity?

A. Pepsin activity is dependent on both casein and anserine.
B. Pepsin activity is blocked by anserine.
C. Pepsin is able to digest casein, but not anserine.
D. Pepsin is able to digest anserine, but not casein.

18. According to the results from Experiment 1, which of the following trials are most likely to contain undigested casein?

F. Trials 1, 3, 4, and 7 only
G. Trials 1, 5, 6, and 7 only
H. Trials 1 and 7 only
J. Trials 5, 6, and 7 only

19. The experimental conditions for Trial 3 are most similar to those for which of the following trials?

A. Trial 9
B. Trial 11
C. Trial 13
D. Trial 14

20. According to the results from Experiments 1 and 2, which of the following best explains the relationship between pepsin activity, pH, and temperature?

F. Pepsin digests proteins at a fast rate when the pH is greater than 4.0 and the temperature is about 40ºC.
G. Pepsin digests proteins at a fast rate when the pH is less than 4.0 and the temperature is about 40ºC.
H. Pepsin digests proteins at a fast rate when the pH is greater than 3.0 and the temperature is about 30ºC.
J. Pepsin digests proteins at a fast rate when the pH is less than 3.0 and the temperature is about 30ºC.

GO ON TO THE NEXT PAGE.

Passage IV

Chemical researchers studied the *viscosity* (a fluid's resistance to flow) for several liquids. Highly viscous fluids take more time to flow through a vessel than do fluids with lower viscosities. They measured the viscosity in *centipoise* (cP) (.01 grams per centimeter per second). Some solutions were treated with chemical additives before the fluids were heated. The results are shown in Figures 1–3.

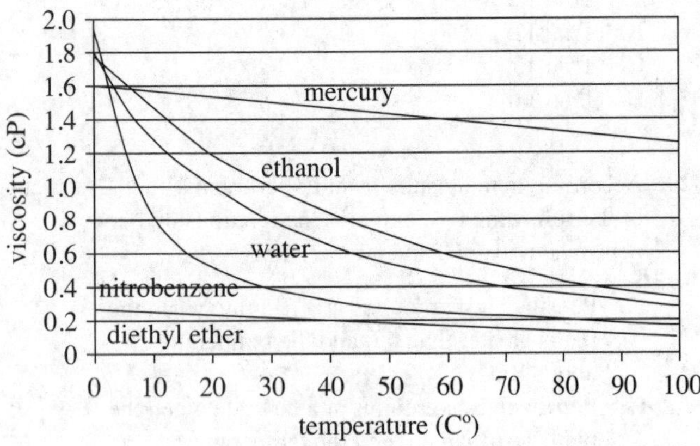

Figure 1

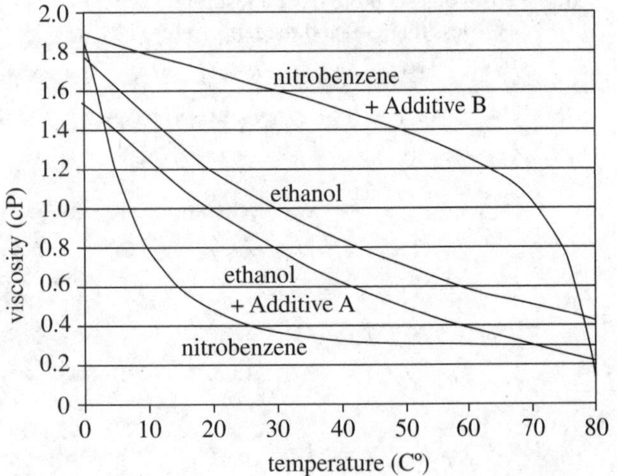

Figure 2

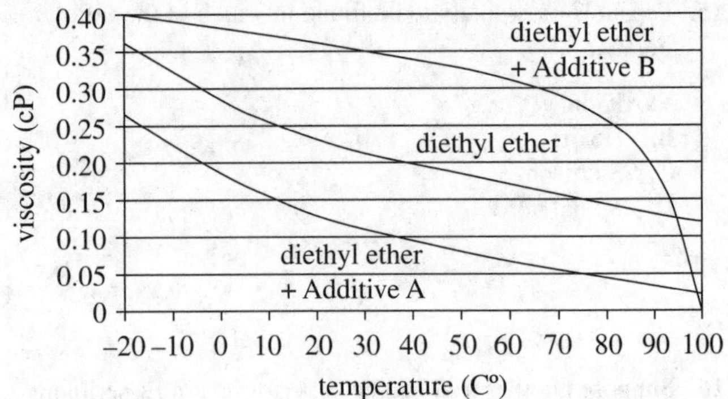

Figure 3

21. For which of the 3 figures did at least one sample fluid have a viscosity greater than 1.0 cP at a temperature of 0°C ?

A. Figure 1 only
B. Figure 3 only
C. Figures 1 and 2 only
D. Figures 1, 2, and 3

GO ON TO THE NEXT PAGE.

22. According to Figure 2, for the sample that contained nitrobenzene without Additive B, the greatest decrease in fluid viscosity occurred over which of the following intervals of temperature change?

F. From 0°C to 10°C
G. From 10°C to 20°C
H. From 30°C to 40°C
J. From 40°C to 50°C

23. According to Figure 1, after water was heated to reach a temperature of 70°C, the viscosity was closest to which of the following?

A. 1.0 cP
B. 0.7 cP
C. 0.4 cP
D. 0.2 cP

24. Based on the information given, which of the following best describes and explains the experimental results presented in Figure 2? As the temperature increased, the time required for the sample fluids to flow out of their containers:

F. decreased, because heating the fluids increased each fluid's viscosity.
G. decreased, because heating the fluids decreased each fluid's viscosity.
H. increased, because heating the fluids increased each fluid's viscosity.
J. increased, because heating the fluids decreased each fluid's viscosity.

25. A researcher hypothesized that a solution of nitrobenzene treated with Additive A would have a lower viscosity at 60°C than would untreated diethyl ether at that same temperature. Do the results in the figures confirm this hypothesis?

A. Yes; according to Figure 2, at 60°C, nitrobenzene had a higher viscosity than did nitrobenzene treated with Additive B.
B. Yes; according to Figure 3, at 60°C, diethyl ether had a higher viscosity than did diethyl ether treated with Additive A.
C. No; according to Figure 2, at 60°C, nitrobenzene had a higher viscosity than did nitrobenzene treated with Additive B.
D. No; according to Figures 1–3, samples of nitrobenzene treated with Additive A were not tested for viscosity.

26. Researchers conducted a study in which they suspended a capped funnel with 100 mL of solution over a beaker, as shown in Figure 4.

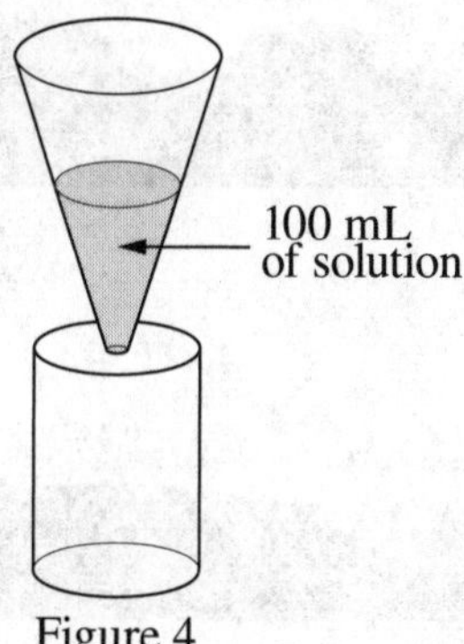

Figure 4

After removing the funnel cap, they recorded the amount of time elapsed until the solution in the beaker reached 50 mL. If this process was repeated for each solution shown in Figures 1–3, which of the following solutions, at 10°C, would reach 50 mL in the shortest amount of time?

F. Diethyl ether
G. Nitrobenzene
H. Diethyl ether + Additive A
J. Nitrobenzene + Additive B

GO ON TO THE NEXT PAGE.

Passage V

Earthquakes disrupt the infrastructure of buildings and dwellings by displacing the ground beneath them as a result of surface waves. The origin of an earthquake is known as the *epicenter*. Surface waves propagate from the epicenter outward and are directly affected by the density of the ground through which they propagate. As seen in Figure 1, the strength of the wave may be characterized into three distinct types: strong, moderate, and weak.

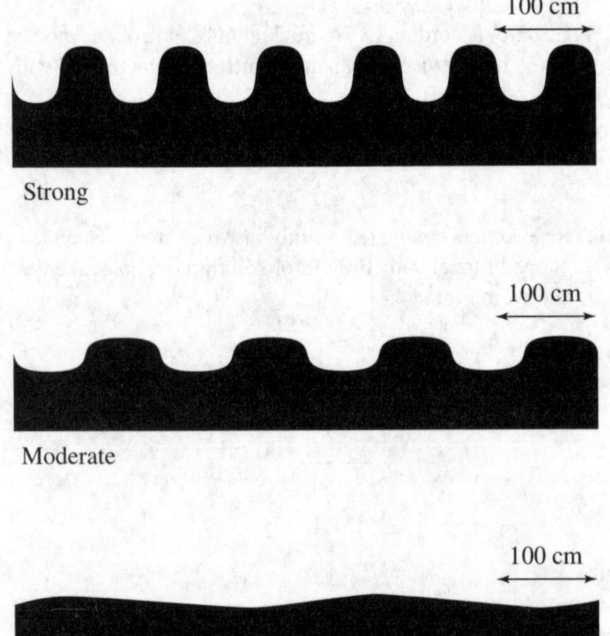

Figure 1

In order to study the effect of ground density on wave propagation, a seismologist has assembled circular small-scale models with varying densities. Propagation duration was held constant in the experiment. In each study, the procedure was repeated at various densities of earth and clay from 1,000 to 2,000 kg/m³. Seismometers were positioned to detect the type of waves propagating at specific locations. A large speaker was placed 2 m below the surface of the epicenter to mimic an earthquake and each study was conducted over a period of 2 min with a fixed frequency of 10 Hz.

Study 1

The sound source was adjusted to 60 dB to mimic the impact of a magnitude 5 earthquake. The resulting *waveform plot* (exhibits wave type as a result of varying densities and distances from the epicenter) is shown in Figure 2.

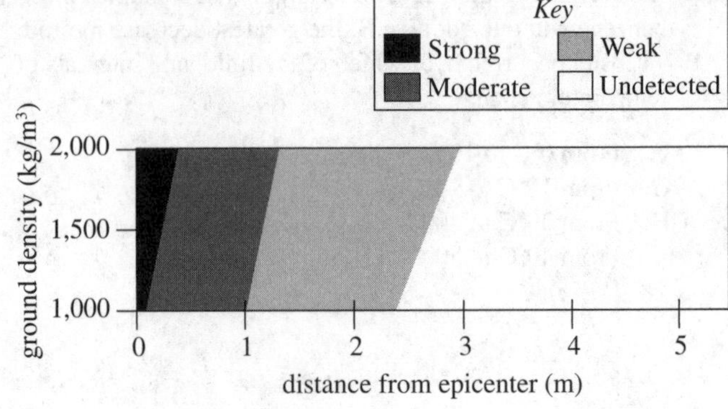

Figure 2

Study 2

Study 1 was repeated with the sound source adjusted to 80 dB to mimic the impact of a magnitude 7 earthquake. The resulting waveform plot is shown in Figure 3.

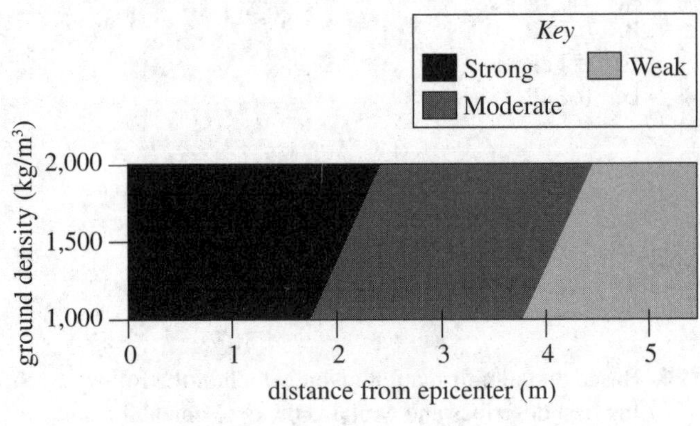

Figure 3

Study 3

The study was repeated with the sound source adjusted to 100 dB to mimic the impact of a magnitude 9 earthquake. The resulting waveform plot is shown in Figure 4.

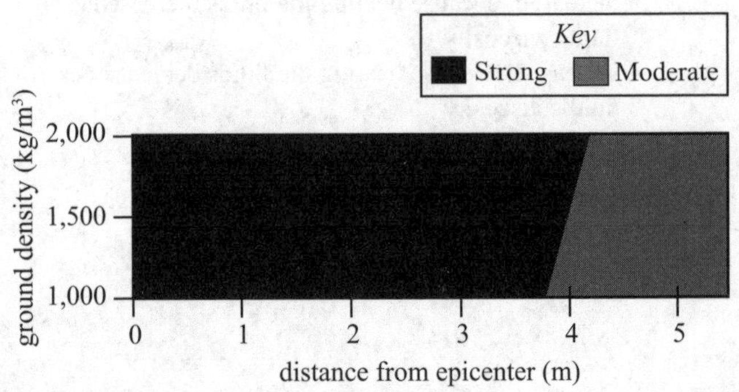

Figure 4

GO ON TO THE NEXT PAGE.

27. What was the independent (manipulated) variable across the 3 studies, and what was the independent variable within each study?

	across the studies	within each study
A.	distance from epicenter	wave type
B.	sound intensity	ground density
C.	ground density	distance from epicenter
D.	sound intensity	wave type

28. According to the results of Study 2, for all ground densities between 1,000 and 2,000 kg/m^3, as the distance from the epicenter increases from 0 to 3 m, the type of wave observed:

F. remained strong.
G. changed from strong to moderate.
H. changed from moderate to strong.
J. remained moderate.

29. According to the results of Studies 2 and 3, which of the following statements comparing the maximum distance from the epicenter for strong wave propagation and maximum distance for moderate wave propagation is true?

A. At all ground densities studied, the maximum distance from the epicenter at which strong waves may propagate was greater than the corresponding maximum distance from the epicenter at which moderate waves propagated.
B. At all ground densities studied, the maximum distance from the epicenter at which strong waves may propagate was less than the corresponding maximum distance from the epicenter at which moderate waves propagated.
C. For some of the ground densities studied, the maximum distance from the epicenter at which strong waves may propagate was greater than the corresponding maximum distance from the epicenter at which moderate waves propagated.
D. For some of the ground densities studied, the maximum distance from the epicenter at which strong waves may propagate was less than the corresponding maximum distance from the epicenter at which moderate waves propagated.

30. Which of the following factors in the seismologist's studies was NOT directly controlled?

F. Sound intensity (in dB)
G. Ground density
H. Propagation duration
J. Wave type

31. Consider the relative wavelengths of a moderate wave and a weak wave, as shown in Figure 1. Which, if either, is less than 100 cm ?

A. The wavelength of a moderate wave only
B. The wavelength of a weak wave only
C. Both the wavelength of the moderate wave and the wavelength of the weak wave
D. Neither the wavelength of the moderate wave nor the wavelength of the weak wave

32. Suppose Study 1 were repeated using a sound intensity of 70 dB. The resulting waveform plot would include which of the wave types referred to in the passage?

F. Strong waves only
G. Strong and weak waves only
H. Strong and moderate waves only
J. Strong, moderate, and weak waves

33. A study was conducted using a sound intensity between 75 dB and 85 dB. The minimum ground density where strong waves began propagating ranged from 1,000 kg/m^3 to 2,000 kg/m^3. Based on the information presented, the distance from the epicenter was most likely:

A. less than 2.5 m.
B. between 2.5 and 3.5 m.
C. between 3.5 and 4.5 m.
D. greater than 4.5 m.

GO ON TO THE NEXT PAGE.

Passage VI

A *solution* results from dissolving a *solute* into a *solvent.* The van 't Hoff factor (*i*) is the number of moles (1 mole = 6.02 × 10^{23} entities such as molecules, ions, or atoms) of particles produced in solution for every 1 mole of solute dissolved.

The temperature at which a solution changes state from liquid to solid is the *freezing point.* Two scientists observed that the freezing point of H_2O decreased after adding KCl to it. To explore this further, they conducted an experiment and each scientist provided separate explanations of the results.

Experiment

One mole each of fructose, KCl, and $MgCl_2$ were separately dissolved in 1 kg of pure water. The concentration of each solution was thus 1.0 mole/kg. In addition, 1 kg of pure water only was placed in a fourth container. The containers were placed in a cooling device. The temperature was gradually decreased and the freezing point of each solution was recorded. The results are shown in Table 1.

Table 1

Solution	Solute	*i*	Solution properties	Freezing point
1	—	—	Pure water only	0°C
2	fructose	1	1 dissolved neutral particle	–1.9°C
3	KCl	2	2 dissolved charged particles (K^+ and Cl^-)	–3.8°C
4	$MgCl_2$	3	3 dissolved charged particles (Mg^{2+} and 2 Cl^-)	–5.7°C

Scientist 1

For a solvent to freeze, its molecules must arrange in an orderly fashion relative to each other. When a solute is added, the dissolved solute molecules are attracted to the solvent molecules by the intermolecular force of charge. The attraction of the solute particles to the solvent particles interferes with the orderly arrangement of solvent molecules, and the net effect is that the freezing point is lowered. This decrease in freezing point is related only to the charge of the solute particles and occurs with solutes that form charged particles in solution.

Scientist 2

The freezing point of a solvent is the temperature at which the liquid and solid states of that solvent have equivalent energetic potentials. Below the freezing point, the solvent has a lower energetic potential in the solid state. When a solute is dissolved in a solvent, the energetic potential of the liquid phase is decreased more than the energetic potential of the solid phase. Because of the different energetic potentials, it takes a larger drop in temperature for the liquid to freeze. Thus, the size of the decrease in freezing point is in direct proportion with the van 't Hoff factor. This decrease in freezing point is related only to the concentration of particles, not to the identity or properties of each individual particle.

34. Based on the results in Table 1, how did the concentration of dissolved particles in Solution 4 compare with the concentration of dissolved particles in Solution 2? Solution 4 contained:

F. fewer particles in solution than did Solution 2, resulting in a lower freezing point.
G. more particles in solution than did Solution 2, resulting in a lower freezing point.
H. fewer particles in solution than did Solution 2, resulting in a higher freezing point.
J. more particles in solution than did Solution 2, resulting in a higher freezing point.

GO ON TO THE NEXT PAGE.

35. The freezing point of benzene is lowered with the addition of the solute naphthalene ($C_{10}H_8$), which has no charge. According to the information in the passage, this observation *disagrees* with the explanation provided by:

A. Scientist 1, who argued that only charged particles can have an effect on the freezing point of a solution.
B. Scientist 1, who argued that any solute is capable of increasing the stability of the liquid phase of a solvent.
C. Scientist 2, who argued that only charged particles can have an effect on the freezing point of a solution.
D. Scientist 2, who argued that any solute is capable of increasing the stability of the liquid phase of a solvent.

36. With which of the following statements about solutes would both scientists agree? Adding to a liquid a substance that has:

F. a positive or negative charge will decrease the liquid's freezing point.
G. a positive or negative charge will increase the liquid's freezing point.
H. no charge will decrease the liquid's freezing point.
J. no charge will increase the liquid's freezing point.

37. Suppose an experiment showed that adding the positively charged solute $NaClO_4$ to the solvent H_2O but holding the concentration of the solution constant, the freezing point was significantly lower than an equally concentrated uncharged solution of $NaClO_4$ in pure H_2O. This finding would support the explanation(s) of which of the scientists, if either?

A. Scientist 1 only
B. Scientist 2 only
C. Both Scientists 1 and 2
D. Neither Scientist

38. Of the following diagrams, which best illustrates how Scientist 1 would describe the results after a charged solute (•) has been added to H_2O (×) ?

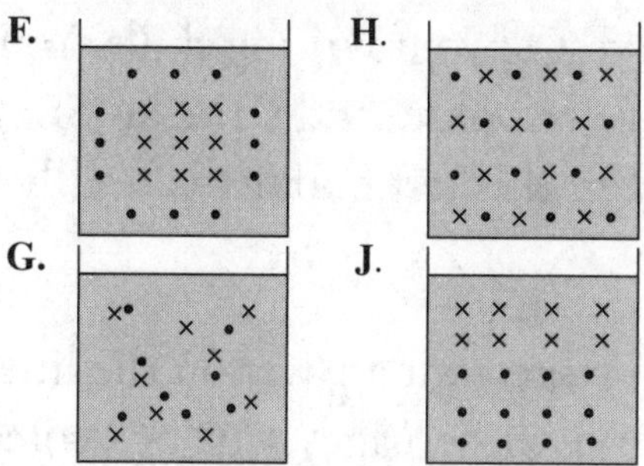

39. Do the scientists offer different explanations for the impact of a solute's physical properties, such as solute charge, on the decrease in freezing point of a solution?

A. Yes; Scientist 1 states that solute physical properties have an impact, but Scientist 2 states they do not.
B. Yes; Scientist 2 states that solute physical properties have an impact, but Scientist 1 states they do not.
C. No; both scientists state that solute physical properties have an impact on solution freezing point.
D. No; neither Scientist discusses the impact of solute physical properties on solution freezing point.

40. Assume the following for the addition of a substance to a pure liquid: k is a constant, ΔT is the decrease in freezing point, and i is the van 't Hoff factor. Which of the following equations is most consistent with Scientist 2's explanation?

F. $\Delta T = k/i$
G. $\Delta T = ki^2$
H. $\Delta T = k/i^2$
J. $\Delta T = ki$

END OF TEST 4
STOP! DO NOT RETURN TO ANY OTHER TEST.

Directions

This is a test of your writing skills. You will have forty (40) minutes to read the prompt, plan your response, and write an essay in English. Before you begin working, read all material in this test booklet carefully to understand exactly what you are being asked to do.

You will write your answer on the lined pages in the answer document provided. Your writing on those pages will be scored. You may use the unlined pages in this test booklet to plan your essay. Your work on these pages will not be scored.

Your essay will be evaluated based on the evidence it provides of your ability to:

- clearly state your own perspective on a complex issue and analyze the relationship between your perspective and at least one other perspective
- develop and support your ideas with reasoning and examples
- organize your ideas clearly and logically
- communicate your ideas effectively in standard written English

Lay your pencil down immediately when time is called.

DO NOT OPEN THIS BOOK UNTIL YOU ARE TOLD TO DO SO.

Composition paper for the essay can be found beginning on page 645.

More Food Is Better

Foods that have had their DNA altered are known as genetically modified foods. This technology is used to make crops disease- and pest-resistant, produce more food with fewer chemicals, and increase the nutritional value of foods. Advocates of this approach maintain that it allows more people to be fed, food to be grown in various climates, and many other benefits. Opponents voice their concerns about environmental issues and safety to human consumption.

Read and carefully consider these perspectives. Each suggests a particular way of thinking about the conflict over genetically modified foods.

Perspective One	Perspective Two	Perspective Three
Genetically modified foods are unnecessary. The problem of world hunger is real and must be solved, but it is the result of an unequal distribution of food, not a lack of it.	Genetically modified foods are better for the environment. Because these foods have already been engineered to be pest resistant, there is no need to treat them with dangerous chemical pesticides.	Genetically modified foods can make people sick. When the natural components of a crop are restructured, this can cause someone who ingests something not originally contained in the food to have an allergic reaction.

Essay Task

Write a unified, coherent essay in which you evaluate multiple perspectives on the use of genetically modified foods. In your essay, be sure to:

- clearly state your own perspective on the issue and analyze the relationship between your perspective and at least one other perspective
- develop and support your ideas with reasoning and examples
- organize your ideas clearly and logically
- communicate your ideas effectively in standard written English

Your perspective may be in full agreement with any of the others, in partial agreement, or wholly different. Whatever the case, support your ideas with logical reasoning and detailed, persuasive examples.

ACT Diagnostic Test Form

USE A SOFT LEAD NO. 2 PENCIL ONLY.
(Do NOT use a mechanical pencil, ink, ballpoint, correction fluid, or felt-tip pen.)

E-MAIL: ____________________

PHONE NO.: ____________________
(Print)

SCHOOL: ____________________

CLASS OF: ____________________

IMPORTANT: Please fill in these boxes exactly as shown on the back cover of your tests book.

2. TEST FORM

3. TEST CODE

0 0 0 0
1 1 1 1
2 2 2 2
3 3 3 3
4 4 4 4
5 5 5 5
6 6 6 6
7 7 7 7
8 8 8 8
9 9 9 9

ALL examinees must complete Blocks A, B, C, and D – please print.

A NAME, MAILING ADDRESS, AND TELEPHONE
(Please print.)

Last Name | First Name | MI (Middle Initial)

House Number & Street (Apt. No.); or PO Box & No.; or RR & No.

City | State/Province | ZIP/Postal Code

Area Code / Number | Country

B MATCH NAME
(First 5 letters of last name)

A B C D E F G H I J K L M N O P Q R S T U V W X Y Z

C MATCH NUMBER

1 2 3 4 5 6 7 8 9 0

D DATE OF BIRTH

Month | Day | Year

January
February
March
April
May
June
July
August
September
October
November
December

BOOKLET NUMBER

1 2 3 4 5 6 7 8 9 0

FORM

Print your 3-character **Test Form** in the boxes above and fill in the corresponding oval at the right.

BE SURE TO FILL IN THE CORRECT FORM OVAL.

PRE

Marking Directions: Mark only **one** oval for each question. Fill in response completely. Erase errors cleanly without smudging.

Correct mark:

Do NOT use these *incorrect* or *bad* marks.

Incorrect marks:
Overlapping mark:
Cross-out mark:
Smudged erasure:
Mark is too light:

THIS PAGE INTENTIONALLY LEFT BLANK

The Princeton Review Diagnostic ACT Form

USE A SOFT LEAD NO. 2 PENCIL ONLY.
(Do NOT use a mechanical pencil, ink, ballpoint, correction fluid, or felt-tip pen.)

TEST 1: ENGLISH

1 A B C D	14 F G H J	27 A B C D	40 F G H J	53 A B C D	66 F G H J
2 F G H J	15 A B C D	28 F G H J	41 A B C D	54 F G H J	67 A B C D
3 A B C D	16 F G H J	29 A B C D	42 F G H J	55 A B C D	68 F G H J
4 F G H J	17 A B C D	30 F G H J	43 A B C D	56 F G H J	69 A B C D
5 A B C D	18 F G H J	31 A B C D	44 F G H J	57 A B C D	70 F G H J
6 F G H J	19 A B C D	32 F G H J	45 A B C D	58 F G H J	71 A B C D
7 A B C D	20 F G H J	33 A B C D	46 F G H J	59 A B C D	72 F G H J
8 F G H J	21 A B C D	34 F G H J	47 A B C D	60 F G H J	73 A B C D
9 A B C D	22 F G H J	35 A B C D	48 F G H J	61 A B C D	74 F G H J
10 F G H J	23 A B C D	36 F G H J	49 A B C D	62 F G H J	75 A B C D
11 A B C D	24 F G H J	37 A B C D	50 F G H J	63 A B C D	
12 F G H J	25 A B C D	38 F G H J	51 A B C D	64 F G H J	
13 A B C D	26 F G H J	39 A B C D	52 F G H J	65 A B C D	

TEST 2: MATHEMATICS

1 A B C D E	11 A B C D E	21 A B C D E	31 A B C D E	41 A B C D E	51 A B C D E
2 F G H J K	12 F G H J K	22 F G H J K	32 F G H J K	42 F G H J K	52 F G H J K
3 A B C D E	13 A B C D E	23 A B C D E	33 A B C D E	43 A B C D E	53 A B C D E
4 F G H J K	14 F G H J K	24 F G H J K	34 F G H J K	44 F G H J K	54 F G H J K
5 A B C D E	15 A B C D E	25 A B C D E	35 A B C D E	45 A B C D E	55 A B C D E
6 F G H J K	16 F G H J K	26 F G H J K	36 F G H J K	46 F G H J K	56 F G H J K
7 A B C D E	17 A B C D E	27 A B C D E	37 A B C D E	47 A B C D E	57 A B C D E
8 F G H J K	18 F G H J K	28 F G H J K	38 F G H J K	48 F G H J K	58 F G H J K
9 A B C D E	19 A B C D E	29 A B C D E	39 A B C D E	49 A B C D E	59 A B C D E
10 F G H J K	20 F G H J K	30 F G H J K	40 F G H J K	50 F G H J K	60 F G H J K

The Princeton Review Diagnostic ACT Form

USE A SOFT LEAD NO. 2 PENCIL ONLY. (Do NOT use a mechanical pencil, ink, ballpoint, correction fluid, or felt-tip pen.)

TEST 3: READING

1 Ⓐ Ⓑ Ⓒ Ⓓ	8 Ⓕ Ⓖ Ⓗ Ⓙ	15 Ⓐ Ⓑ Ⓒ Ⓓ	22 Ⓕ Ⓖ Ⓗ Ⓙ	29 Ⓐ Ⓑ Ⓒ Ⓓ	36 Ⓕ Ⓖ Ⓗ Ⓙ
2 Ⓕ Ⓖ Ⓗ Ⓙ	9 Ⓐ Ⓑ Ⓒ Ⓓ	16 Ⓕ Ⓖ Ⓗ Ⓙ	23 Ⓐ Ⓑ Ⓒ Ⓓ	30 Ⓕ Ⓖ Ⓗ Ⓙ	37 Ⓐ Ⓑ Ⓒ Ⓓ
3 Ⓐ Ⓑ Ⓒ Ⓓ	10 Ⓕ Ⓖ Ⓗ Ⓙ	17 Ⓐ Ⓑ Ⓒ Ⓓ	24 Ⓕ Ⓖ Ⓗ Ⓙ	31 Ⓐ Ⓑ Ⓒ Ⓓ	38 Ⓕ Ⓖ Ⓗ Ⓙ
4 Ⓕ Ⓖ Ⓗ Ⓙ	11 Ⓐ Ⓑ Ⓒ Ⓓ	18 Ⓕ Ⓖ Ⓗ Ⓙ	25 Ⓐ Ⓑ Ⓒ Ⓓ	32 Ⓕ Ⓖ Ⓗ Ⓙ	39 Ⓐ Ⓑ Ⓒ Ⓓ
5 Ⓐ Ⓑ Ⓒ Ⓓ	12 Ⓕ Ⓖ Ⓗ Ⓙ	19 Ⓐ Ⓑ Ⓒ Ⓓ	26 Ⓕ Ⓖ Ⓗ Ⓙ	33 Ⓐ Ⓑ Ⓒ Ⓓ	40 Ⓕ Ⓖ Ⓗ Ⓙ
6 Ⓕ Ⓖ Ⓗ Ⓙ	13 Ⓐ Ⓑ Ⓒ Ⓓ	20 Ⓕ Ⓖ Ⓗ Ⓙ	27 Ⓐ Ⓑ Ⓒ Ⓓ	34 Ⓕ Ⓖ Ⓗ Ⓙ	
7 Ⓐ Ⓑ Ⓒ Ⓓ	14 Ⓕ Ⓖ Ⓗ Ⓙ	21 Ⓐ Ⓑ Ⓒ Ⓓ	28 Ⓕ Ⓖ Ⓗ Ⓙ	35 Ⓐ Ⓑ Ⓒ Ⓓ	

TEST 4: SCIENCE

1 Ⓐ Ⓑ Ⓒ Ⓓ	8 Ⓕ Ⓖ Ⓗ Ⓙ	15 Ⓐ Ⓑ Ⓒ Ⓓ	22 Ⓕ Ⓖ Ⓗ Ⓙ	29 Ⓐ Ⓑ Ⓒ Ⓓ	36 Ⓕ Ⓖ Ⓗ Ⓙ
2 Ⓕ Ⓖ Ⓗ Ⓙ	9 Ⓐ Ⓑ Ⓒ Ⓓ	16 Ⓕ Ⓖ Ⓗ Ⓙ	23 Ⓐ Ⓑ Ⓒ Ⓓ	30 Ⓕ Ⓖ Ⓗ Ⓙ	37 Ⓐ Ⓑ Ⓒ Ⓓ
3 Ⓐ Ⓑ Ⓒ Ⓓ	10 Ⓕ Ⓖ Ⓗ Ⓙ	17 Ⓐ Ⓑ Ⓒ Ⓓ	24 Ⓕ Ⓖ Ⓗ Ⓙ	31 Ⓐ Ⓑ Ⓒ Ⓓ	38 Ⓕ Ⓖ Ⓗ Ⓙ
4 Ⓕ Ⓖ Ⓗ Ⓙ	11 Ⓐ Ⓑ Ⓒ Ⓓ	18 Ⓕ Ⓖ Ⓗ Ⓙ	25 Ⓐ Ⓑ Ⓒ Ⓓ	32 Ⓕ Ⓖ Ⓗ Ⓙ	39 Ⓐ Ⓑ Ⓒ Ⓓ
5 Ⓐ Ⓑ Ⓒ Ⓓ	12 Ⓕ Ⓖ Ⓗ Ⓙ	19 Ⓐ Ⓑ Ⓒ Ⓓ	26 Ⓕ Ⓖ Ⓗ Ⓙ	33 Ⓐ Ⓑ Ⓒ Ⓓ	40 Ⓕ Ⓖ Ⓗ Ⓙ
6 Ⓕ Ⓖ Ⓗ Ⓙ	13 Ⓐ Ⓑ Ⓒ Ⓓ	20 Ⓕ Ⓖ Ⓗ Ⓙ	27 Ⓐ Ⓑ Ⓒ Ⓓ	34 Ⓕ Ⓖ Ⓗ Ⓙ	
7 Ⓐ Ⓑ Ⓒ Ⓓ	14 Ⓕ Ⓖ Ⓗ Ⓙ	21 Ⓐ Ⓑ Ⓒ Ⓓ	28 Ⓕ Ⓖ Ⓗ Ⓙ	35 Ⓐ Ⓑ Ⓒ Ⓓ	

I hereby certify that I have truthfully identified myself on this form. I accept the consequences of falsifying my identity.

____
Your signature

____
Today's date

The Princeton Review
Diagnostic ACT Form

ESSAY

Begin your essay on this side. If necessary, continue on the opposite side.

Continue on the opposite side if necessary.

The Princeton Review
Diagnostic ACT Form

Continued from previous page.

PLEASE PRINT YOUR INITIALS

First	Middle	Last

The Princeton Review
Diagnostic ACT Form

Continued from previous page.

PLEASE PRINT YOUR INITIALS

First	Middle	Last

The Princeton Review
Diagnostic ACT Form

Continued from previous page.

PLEASE PRINT YOUR INITIALS

First	Middle	Last

Test 2
Answers and Explanations

TEST 2 ENGLISH ANSWERS

1. A
2. J
3. D
4. F
5. C
6. H
7. B
8. J
9. B
10. J
11. D
12. G
13. A
14. J
15. B
16. H
17. B
18. F
19. C
20. H
21. D
22. F
23. C
24. G
25. D
26. H
27. B
28. F
29. D
30. F
31. B
32. J
33. A
34. F
35. D
36. G
37. A
38. H
39. D
40. G
41. C
42. G
43. A
44. F
45. C
46. G
47. A
48. J
49. D
50. G
51. C
52. J
53. B
54. F
55. C
56. H
57. D
58. H
59. A
60. G
61. D
62. H
63. B
64. J
65. A
66. J
67. C
68. F
69. B
70. J
71. B
72. H
73. C
74. F
75. B

TEST 2 MATH ANSWERS

1. E
2. H
3. B
4. G
5. C
6. F
7. C
8. G
9. C
10. F
11. D
12. H
13. B
14. G
15. B
16. H
17. B
18. J
19. C
20. G
21. C
22. G
23. E
24. F
25. C
26. K
27. D
28. F
29. B
30. J
31. E
32. K
33. B
34. H
35. A
36. J
37. C
38. K
39. E
40. H
41. E
42. G
43. C
44. J
45. B
46. H
47. C
48. J
49. A
50. G
51. A
52. G
53. C
54. G
55. C
56. K
57. A
58. K
59. E
60. H

TEST 2 READING ANSWERS

1. A
2. G
3. D
4. F
5. C
6. J
7. A
8. H
9. D
10. F
11. A
12. G
13. B
14. F
15. C
16. F
17. C
18. H
19. C
20. J
21. D
22. J
23. A
24. G
25. C
26. J
27. D
28. F
29. B
30. G
31. A
32. G
33. C
34. H
35. A
36. J
37. D
38. H
39. D
40. F

TEST 2 SCIENCE ANSWERS

1. D
2. F
3. C
4. J
5. B
6. G
7. A
8. J
9. D
10. G
11. A
12. G
13. D
14. F
15. C
16. F
17. C
18. H
19. A
20. G
21. C
22. F
23. C
24. G
25. D
26. H
27. B
28. G
29. B
30. J
31. D
32. J
33. A
34. G
35. A
36. F
37. A
38. G
39. A
40. J

SCORING YOUR PRACTICE EXAM

Step A

Count the number of correct answers for each section and record the number in the space provided for your raw score on the Score Conversion Worksheet below.

Step B

Using the Score Conversion Chart on the next page, convert your raw scores on each section to scaled scores. Then compute your composite ACT score by averaging the four subject scores. Add them up and divide by four. Don't worry about the essay score; it is not included in your composite score.

Score Conversion Worksheet		
Section	**Raw Score**	**Scaled Score**
1	______/75	________
2	______/60	________
3	______/40	________
4	______/40	________

Scale Score	English	Math	Reading	Science	Scale Score
36	75	60	40	40	**36**
35	73–74	59	39	39	**35**
34	72	58	38	38	**34**
33	71	57	37	37	**33**
32	70	56	36	—	**32**
31	69	54–55	34–35	36	**31**
30	68	53	33	35	**30**
29	67	51–52	32	34	**29**
28	65–66	49–50	30–31	33	**28**
27	64	46–48	29	32	**27**
26	62–63	44–45	28	30–31	**26**
25	60–61	41–43	27	28–29	**25**
24	58–59	39–40	26	27	**24**
23	55–57	37–38	24–25	25–26	**23**
22	53–54	35–36	23	23–24	**22**
21	50–52	33–34	22	21–22	**21**
20	47–49	31–32	21	19–20	**20**
19	44–46	28–30	19–20	17–18	**19**
18	42–43	25–27	18	15–16	**18**
17	40–41	22–24	17	14	**17**
16	37–39	18–21	16	13	**16**
15	34–36	15–17	15	12	**15**
14	31–33	11–14	13–14	11	**14**
13	29–30	9–10	12	10	**13**
12	27–28	7–8	10–11	9	**12**
11	25–26	6	8-9	8	**11**
10	23–24	5	7	7	**10**
9	21–22	4	6	6	**9**
8	18–20	3	5	5	**8**
7	15–17	—	—	4	7
6	12–14	2	4	3	**6**
5	9–11	—	3	2	**5**
4	7–8	1	2	—	**4**
3	5–6	—	—	1	**3**
2	3–4	—	1	—	**2**
1	0–2	0	0	0	**1**

TEST 2 ENGLISH ANSWERS AND EXPLANATIONS

Passage I

1. **A** Note the question! The question asks for the answer that *best conveys the author's initial expectations and effectively leads into her mother's comments,* so it tests consistency. Eliminate answers that are inconsistent with the purpose stated in the question. The phrase *boring stories* in (A) is consistent with the negative tone of *dusty, rotting boxes,* and *boring stories about people I didn't know* effectively leads into *Family histories* in the next sentence, so keep (A). The word *bonding* is too positive to be consistent with *the author's initial expectations,* so eliminate (B). *Fun times* is also inconsistent with the negative tone in the first part of the sentence, so eliminate (C). There is no mention in this paragraph of *an unfamiliar machine,* so eliminate (D). The correct answer is (A).

2. **J** Punctuation changes in the answer choices, so this question tests how to connect ideas with the appropriate punctuation. The first part of the sentence, *In truth, Grandpa didn't want to limit my work to just research,* is an independent clause. The second part, *hoping to also preserve our family memories,* is not an independent clause. A period can only be used between two independent clauses, so eliminate (F). Changing *hoping* to *hope* does not make the second part of the sentence an independent clause, and it also contains a period, so eliminate (G). Adding the word *that* makes the sentence sound as if *research* is the subject of the verb *hope,* which is both inconsistent (*research* is singular, but *hope* is a plural verb) and makes the sentence unclear; eliminate (H). Choice (J) appropriately uses a comma to separate the two parts of the sentence. The correct answer is (J).

3. **D** Commas change in the answer choices, so this question tests comma usage. *Pictures* and *letters* form a list of two items in the sentence. No comma is needed before the word *and* when a list contains only two items, so eliminate (A) and (B). There is no need to break up the phrase *scan old pictures and letters to preserve their contents* with a comma, so eliminate (C). The correct answer is (D).

4. **F** Note the question! When a question asks which answer would *NOT* be acceptable, eliminate answers that **are** acceptable. Punctuation and transition words change in the answer choices, so this question tests how to connect ideas with the appropriate punctuation. The first part of the sentence, *He could type documents and send e-mails,* is an independent clause. The second part (after the transition), *he had never used a scanner,* is also an independent clause. Choice (F) changes the beginning of the second part of the sentence in a way that makes the entire sentence incomplete. Choice (F) is therefore not acceptable. A comma followed by the coordinating conjunction *yet* can be used between two independent clauses, so (G) is acceptable. Eliminate (G). A semicolon can be used to separate two independent clauses, and although (H) adds the word *however* to the second part of the sentence, it is still an independent clause. Choice (H) is therefore acceptable; eliminate (H). The word *he* is taken out of the second part of the sentence in (J), which means it is no longer an independent clause, so it is acceptable to not have any punctuation in the sentence. Eliminate (J). The correct answer is (F).

5. **C** Apostrophes change in the answer choices, so this question tests apostrophe usage. A noun with an apostrophe shows possession. The *precious memories* belong to the *relatives,* so the word *relatives* needs an apostrophe; eliminate (A) and (B). Nothing belongs to *memories,* so no apostrophe is necessary there; eliminate (D). The correct answer is (C).

6. **H** Note the question! The question asks for the sentence that is *LEAST* relevant to the passage, so it tests consistency. Eliminate the answer choices that **are** relevant to the passage. The paragraph describes the writer's experience *in my grandpa's bright, tidy computer room.* Sentence 1 connects to the writer's initial idea from the first paragraph (*Instead of sorting through dusty boxes as I had imagined*) and also provides the setting for this paragraph, so eliminate (F). Sentence 2 refers to *my relatives' precious memories,* which is consistent with the focus of the passage as a whole, so eliminate (G). Although a *scanner* is mentioned, the paragraph is focused more on the narrator's experience than on the device itself; Sentence 3 is therefore not relevant. Sentence 4 gives more details about the writer's experience, so eliminate (J). The correct answer is (H).

7. **B** Pronouns change in the answer choices, so this question tests consistency of pronouns. A pronoun must be consistent in number with the noun it refers to. The underlined pronoun refers to *my relatives,* which is plural, so the underlined pronoun should also be plural. Eliminate (A) and (C) because *her* and *one's* are both singular. Choice (B) appropriately uses the plural possessive pronoun *their.* The word *there* is not a pronoun; it indicates location. *There* is not appropriate in this context, so eliminate (D). The correct answer is (B).

8. **J** Verbs change in the answer choices, so this question tests consistency of verbs. A verb must be consistent in number with its subject and consistent in tense with the rest of the sentence. The subject of the underlined verb is *Grandpa,* which is singular, so the underlined verb should also be singular. *Send* is a plural verb, so eliminate (G). *Had send* is an incorrect form of the past perfect tense, so eliminate (F). The difference between (H) and (J) is present perfect versus past perfect tense. Present perfect tense is used to describe an action that started in the past and continues to the present, while past perfect is used to describe an action that started in the past and then stopped. Because the verb refers to something that the grandpa did during *World War II,* it ended in the past. Eliminate (H) because *has sent* is present perfect tense. The correct answer is (J).

9. **B** The length of the phrase changes in the answer choices, so this question tests concision. There is no need to include either of the relative pronouns *which* or *that,* because they both make it sound as if the *kitchen* was what *penned…every entry* instead of the grandma; eliminate (C) and (D). The difference between (A) and (B) is a comma, so this question also tests comma usage. The phrase *penning meticulously every entry* is a descriptive phrase that is not necessary to the main meaning of the sentence, so it should be set off by a comma. Eliminate (A) because it doesn't contain a comma. The correct answer is (B).

10. **J** Note the question! The question asks for the answer that *would most successfully introduce readers to the information relayed in the paragraph,* so it tests consistency. Eliminate answers that are inconsistent with the purpose stated in the question. The paragraph says that the writer *asked Grandpa*

to tell the story behind every picture and letter we scanned. The stories helped me not only understand but also relate to my relatives. There is no mention of any of the family *names,* so eliminate (F). The paragraph does not focus on the number of *items to catalogue,* so eliminate (G). There is no mention of anyone whom the writer *forgot about,* so eliminate (H). The paragraph does focus on how the writer *became fascinated with my relatives' lives,* so (J) is consistent. The correct answer is (J).

11. **D** Transitions change in the answer choices, so this question tests consistency of ideas. A transition must be consistent with the relationship between the ideas it connects. The sentence before the transition says that the writer *asked Grandpa to tell the story behind every picture and letter we scanned.* The sentence that starts with the transition states that *the stories helped me not only understand but also relate to my relatives.* There is no contrast between the two sentences, so eliminate (A) because it contains a contrasting transition. Adding the word *Because* to the beginning of the sentence makes it incomplete, so eliminate (B). The second sentence is not a conclusion of the idea in the first sentence, so eliminate (C). No transition is necessary. The correct answer is (D).

12. **G** Commas change in the answer choices, so this question tests comma usage. The underlined word *sports* is part of a list: *celebrated achievements, overcome failures, pulled silly pranks, and played sports.* Commas are used in a list of three or more items to separate the items, so a comma is necessary after *sports;* eliminate (H) and (J). The word *and* is not one of the items in the list, so there is no reason to put a comma after it; eliminate (F). The correct answer is (G).

13. **A** Note the question! The question asks for the answer that *provides the best conclusion to the paragraph and the essay as a whole,* so it tests consistency. Eliminate answers that are inconsistent with the purpose stated in the question. The paragraph focuses on how grateful the writer was to her grandpa for *sharing the experience and making me appreciate the family members who have made me the person I am.* The idea of the writer being *able to pass [family memories and mementoes] down to my own grandchildren* is consistent with the paragraph's focus on the appreciation of family, so keep (A). Although the writer's grandpa did *teach [her] something new,* the focus of both this paragraph and the passage is on family rather than on learning, so eliminate (B). Similarly, (C) can be eliminated because, although the writer's mother was *right that family history isn't tedious and boring,* that is not the main focus of either this paragraph or the passage. Choice (D) also mentions a small detail from the passage, the writer *using [her] computer,* but that is not its main focus. Eliminate (D). The correct answer is (A).

14. **J** Note the question! The question asks for the best placement for Paragraph 5, so it tests consistency of ideas. Paragraph 5 must be consistent in focus with the paragraphs before and after it. Paragraph 5 starts by saying that the writer *asked Grandpa to tell the story behind every picture and letter we scanned.* The paragraph ends by describing a *chest filled with family artifacts.* Paragraph 3 mentions the *scanner.* The opening of Paragraph 5 therefore logically follows after Paragraph 3. Paragraph 4 describes the *belongings* of the writer's relatives, so it is consistent with the end of Paragraph 5. Paragraph 5 should therefore be placed between Paragraphs 3 and 4. The correct answer is (J).

15. **B** Note the question! The question asks whether the essay describes *some of the benefits of genealogical research,* so it tests consistency. Determine whether the essay is consistent with this idea. The passage focuses on how much the writer learned from and enjoyed going through family history with her grandpa, so it is consistent with this idea. Eliminate (C) and (D). The passage does mention using a scanner, but its main focus is not the *technological skills gained in the process of researching one's relatives,* so eliminate (A). Choice (B) accurately describes the passage. The correct answer is (B).

Passage II

16. **H** Pronouns change in the answer choices, so this question tests consistency of pronouns. All the pronouns are first-person singular, so choose the one that has the appropriate case. The idiomatically correct expression is *by myself,* not *by me;* eliminate (F) and (G). Punctuation also changes in the answer choices, so this question also tests how to connect ideas with the appropriate punctuation. The first part of the sentence, *I stand on the corner of Elm Avenue and Main Street by myself,* is an independent clause. The second part of the sentence, *watching my parents walk away and feeling nothing but apprehension about adjusting to this new town,* is not an independent clause. A period can only be used between two independent clauses; eliminate (J). Choice (H) appropriately uses a comma to separate the two parts of the sentence. The correct answer is (H).

17. **B** Commas change in the answer choices, so this question tests comma usage. The word *cold* is necessary to the sentence, so it should not be set off by commas; eliminate (A). *Cold* directly describes *bedroom,* so there is no need for a comma between those two words; eliminate (D). When two adjectives both describe the same noun, they can be separated by a comma. In this sentence, *new* and *cold* both describe *bedroom,* so there should be a comma after *new.* Eliminate (C). The correct answer is (B).

18. **F** Prepositions change in the answer choices, so the question tests idioms. The correct idiom is *making a…spectacle of,* not *making a…spectacle about,* so eliminate (G) and (J). The difference between (F) and (H) is the adjective *complete* versus the adverb *completely.* The word is used to describe the noun *spectacle.* An adverb cannot be used to describe a noun, so eliminate (H). Choice (F) correctly uses an adjective to describe a noun. The correct answer is (F).

19. **C** Verbs and pronouns change in the answer choices, so this question tests consistency of verbs and pronouns. A verb must be consistent in number with its subject. The subject of the underlined verb is *child,* which is singular, so the underlined verb should also be singular. Eliminate (B) and (D) because *have* is plural. A pronoun must be consistent with the noun it refers to. The underlined pronoun refers to *child,* which is singular. Both *who* and *whom* are singular, so choose the one that has the appropriate case. The underlined pronoun is the subject of the verb *has never been,* so a subject pronoun is needed. Eliminate (A) because *whom* is an object pronoun. Choice (C) correctly uses the subject pronoun *who.* The correct answer is (C).

20. **H** Pronouns change in the answer choices, so this question tests consistency of pronouns. A pronoun must be consistent with the noun it refers to and with other pronouns in the sentence. The sentence contains the first-person plural pronoun *we,* so the underlined pronoun should also be first person and plural. Eliminate (F) because *one's* is singular. Eliminate (G) because *their* is third person. Choice (H) appropriately uses the first-person plural pronoun *our.* Eliminate (J) because *your* is second person. The correct answer is (H).

21. **D** Commas change in the answer choices, so this question tests comma usage. The phrase *and fresh orange juice* is necessary to the sentence and is not, on its own, an item in a list; eliminate (A) and (B). The sentence contains a list of two items, each of which is a longer phrase: the breakfast drinks *(milk and fresh orange juice)* and the breakfast foods *(fluffy scrambled eggs and crisp bacon).* Because there is no conjunction between these two phrases, they must be separated by a comma. Eliminate (C). The correct answer is (D).

22. **F** Note the question! The question asks whether a sentence should be revised, so it tests the idea of clear. The sentence should be revised only if it makes the meaning of the paragraph clearer. The sentence comes after a list of things that the narrator will miss about being at home with her parents. The revised version of the sentence adds more detail: instead of *everything,* the revision specifies *everything I have ever loved,* and instead of *is gone,* the revision specifies that it *feels like* things are *being ripped away from me.* The revision makes the meaning of the sentence and the paragraph clearer, so it should be made; eliminate (H) and (J). Choice (F) accurately states that the revision *conveys more vividly the type of emotions felt by the writer.* The revision does not *describe the stages of emotion,* so eliminate (G). The correct answer is (F).

23. **C** Verbs change in the answer choices, so this question tests consistency of verbs. Verbs must be consistent in tense with other verbs in the sentence. The other verb in the sentence, *lie,* is in present tense, so the underlined verb should also be in present tense. Eliminate (B) and (D) because they are both past tense. Eliminate (A) because it makes the sentence incomplete. Choice (C) makes the sentence complete by including the subject *I* along with the present-tense verb *hear.* The correct answer is (C).

24. **G** Note the question! The question asks what would be lost if a phrase were deleted, so it tests consistency. Eliminate answer choices that are not consistent with the role of the phrase. The phrase gives a reason for the action in the first part of the sentence. The phrase does not describe the *relationship between the roommates,* so eliminate (F). It does give a *reason the writer stopped crying,* so keep (G). The phrase does not discuss the writer's *dissatisfaction with college,* so eliminate (H). The phrase does add to the meaning of the sentence, so eliminate (J). The correct answer is (G).

25. **D** The length of the phrase changes in the answer choices, so this question could test concision. Choice (C) is the shortest option, but it does not make the meaning of the sentence clear: it makes it sound as if the reason the writer *heard her [roommate] crying* is that the writer was *surprised.* Eliminate (C). Choices (A) and (B) make the meaning of the sentence unclear in similar ways; eliminate (A) and (B). Choice (D) makes the meaning of the sentence clear. The correct answer is (D).

26. **H** Punctuation changes in the answer choices, so this question tests how to connect ideas with the appropriate punctuation. The first part of the sentence, *Curiosity overwhelming me,* is not an independent clause. The second part of the sentence, *I tiptoe through the common room to her still-open door,* is an independent clause. A period can only be used between two independent clauses, so eliminate (J). The first part of the sentence is a descriptive phrase that modifies *I,* so there is no need to use the word *and* between the two parts of the sentence. Eliminate (F) and (G). Choice (H) appropriately uses a comma to separate the descriptive phrase from the main part of the sentence. The correct answer is (H).

27. **B** Note the question! The question asks for the answer that illustrates *how quickly the roommate responded to the writer's presence,* so it tests consistency. Eliminate answers that are inconsistent with the purpose stated in the question. Eliminate (A) because *Slowly* is not consistent with the idea of *quickly. Abruptly* does indicate *quickly,* so keep (B). Both *After several moments* and *Sluggishly* are inconsistent with the idea of *quickly,* so eliminate (C) and (D). The correct answer is (B).

28. **F** Vocabulary changes in the answer choices, so this question tests which words gives the clearest meaning. The sentence describes the roommate's reaction to being caught in an emotional moment when she *thought [she] was alone. Stammers* indicates that she was surprised and unsure, which is consistent with the passage; keep (F). *Asserts* would indicate confidence, so eliminate (G). *Quotes* would indicate she is referring to something someone else said, which is not the case; eliminate (H). *Screams* would indicate anger, which is not consistent with the passage; eliminate (J). The correct answer is (F).

29. **D** Note the question! The question asks for the answer that *is most consistent with the writer's subsequent response,* so it tests consistency. Eliminate answers that are inconsistent with the purpose stated in the question. In the following paragraph, the writer says, *"Maybe we can help each other get used to this new college life."* The memories of when her sister *was born* are not consistent with the writer's response, so eliminate (A). Whether the roommate's sister is *fun to live with* is also not relevant, so eliminate (B). Wishing that her family *had left sooner* contradicts the roommate's sadness at their absence, so eliminate (C). The idea that *It's going to be hard to adjust* is consistent with getting *used to this new college life,* so keep (D). The correct answer is (D).

30. **F** Note the question! The question asks whether the essay describes *personal hardships first-time college students may experience,* so it tests consistency. Determine whether the essay is consistent with this idea. The passage focuses on the writer and her roommate both being upset when their families leave them at college, which is consistent with the idea of *personal hardships;* eliminate (H) and (J). Choice (F) accurately describes the passage. The passage was not focused on *the initial awkwardness between roommates,* so eliminate (G). The correct answer is (F).

Passage III

31. **B** Note the question! The question asks whether a phrase should be deleted from the essay, so it tests the ideas of consistent and clear. If the phrase is consistent with the subject of the paragraph and makes the meaning clearer, it should be kept. The phrase gives a simile that helps describe the writer's father, so it should not be deleted; eliminate (C) and (D). There is no indication that *the writer's father is also named Indiana,* so eliminate (A). Choice (B) accurately describes the phrase. The correct answer is (B).

32. **J** Punctuation changes in the answer choices, so this question tests how to connect ideas with the appropriate punctuation. The first part of the sentence, *After that, a whitewater rafting excursion through the Grand Canyon on the majestic,* is not an independent clause. The second part of the sentence, *if murky Colorado River jumpstarted our search for other extreme thrills across the globe,* is also not an independent clause. A semicolon can only be used between two independent clauses, so eliminate (H). The phrase *if murky* is not necessary to the main meaning of the sentence, so it should be set off by commas. Eliminate (F) because it lacks a comma after *murky.* Eliminate (G) because it doesn't use any commas. Choice (J) appropriately places commas before and after the phrase *if murky.* The correct answer is (J).

33. **A** Note the question! The question asks whether a phrase should be deleted from the essay, so it tests the ideas of consistent and clear. If the phrase is consistent with the subject of the paragraph and makes the meaning clearer, it should be kept. The phrase makes the sentence more specific, as it narrows down the idea of *anyone* to just those *who love a challenging thrill,* so it should not be deleted. Eliminate (C) and (D). Choice (A) accurately describes the phrase. Eliminate (B) because the focus of the paragraph is not *people who love challenges.* The correct answer is (A).

34. **F** Commas and the word *and* change in the answer choices, so this question tests how to connect ideas with the appropriate punctuation. The first part of the sentence, *Our adventure began with a 90-foot rappel down a canyon wall into a rushing, ice-cold river,* is an independent clause. The second part of the sentence, *without wetsuits we surely would have become popsicles,* is also an independent clause. Two independent clauses must be separated by some kind of punctuation other than a comma alone; eliminate (G), (H), and (J). Choice (F) appropriately uses a comma followed by the coordinating conjunction *and* to connect the two independent clauses. The correct answer is (F).

35. **D** The length of the phrase surrounding the word *view* changes in the answer choices, so this question tests concision. The non-underlined portion of the sentence indicates that the view was *of the lush Interlaken basin.* It is clear from the context that the basin is a *wonder,* so there is no need to repeat that idea. Eliminate (A), (B), and (C). Choice (D) is concise and makes the meaning of the sentence clear. The correct answer is (D).

36. **G** The length of the phrase surrounding the word *skydiving* changes in the answer choices, so this question could test concision. Choice (H) is the shortest option, but the sentence is incomplete because it lacks a verb. Eliminate (H). Eliminate (J) as well because it also doesn't contain a verb.

Choice (G) adds the verb *was,* which makes the sentence complete. *Skydiving* is the main subject of the sentence, not an example, so there is no need to include the word *like;* eliminate (F). The correct answer is (G).

37. **A** Note the question! The question asks whether a sentence should be added to the paragraph, so it tests consistency. A sentence should be added only if it is consistent with the focus of the paragraph. The new sentence gives an example of one of the thrills the writer and her father have experienced. The paragraph includes other examples of their adventures, so the new sentence is consistent and should be added; eliminate (C) and (D). Choice (A) accurately describes the new sentence. The main idea of the paragraph is not *that Africa has the most exciting thrills in the world,* so eliminate (B). The correct answer is (A).

38. **H** The length of the phrase surrounding the word *which* changes in the answer choices, so this question tests concision. Choice (H) is the shortest option, and it makes the meaning of the sentence clear, so keep (H). There is no cause/effect relationship between the beginning and end of the sentence, as *because* would indicate, so eliminate (F). The second part of the sentence is a description of the first part, not an additional point, so there is no need to use the word *and;* eliminate (G). The first part of the sentence already uses the word *in* to establish location, so there is no need to repeat that word; eliminate (J). The correct answer is (H).

39. **D** Commas and the word *so* change in the answer choices, so this question tests how to connect ideas with the appropriate punctuation. The first part of the sentence, *We had to navigate both the flowing river and the canyon walls,* is an independent clause. The second part of the sentence, *we became amphibious, moving seamlessly between land and water,* is also an independent clause. Two independent clauses must be separated by some kind of punctuation other than a comma alone; eliminate (A), (B) and (C). Choice (D) appropriately uses a comma followed by the coordinating conjunction *so* to connect the two independent clauses. The correct answer is (D).

40. **G** The length of the phrase surrounding the word *leapt* changes in the answer choices, so this question tests concision. The non-underlined portion indicates that the writer and her father *leapt from waterfalls,* which indicates that they were jumping down, so there is no need to repeat the idea that they *descended.* Eliminate (F), (H), and (J). Choice (G) is concise and makes the meaning of the sentence clear. The correct answer is (G).

41. **C** Verbs change in the answer choices, so this question tests consistency of verbs. A verb must be consistent in number with its subject and consistent in tense with other verbs in the sentence. The subject of the verb is *danger* (the phrase *from possible miscalculations* is a prepositional phrase that describes *danger* and cannot be the subject of the sentence), which is singular, so the underlined verb should also be singular. Eliminate (A) because *were* is plural. The other verb in the sentence, *provided,* is in past tense, so the underlined verb should also be in past tense. Eliminate (B) because *will be* is future tense. Choice (C) correctly uses the singular, past tense verb *was.* Choice (D) makes the sentence incomplete, so eliminate (D). The correct answer is (C).

42. **G** Note the question! The question asks for the answer that *best clarifies the distinction between the two types of activities mentioned in this paragraph,* so it tests consistency. Eliminate answers that are inconsistent with the purpose stated in the question. The paragraph states that the writer and her father *had to navigate both the flowing river and the canyon walls,* and that they moved *seamlessly between land and water. From beginning to end* does not specify *two types of activities,* so eliminate (F). Choice (G) mentions *rocky surfaces and...chilly water,* which is consistent with the activities presented in the paragraph; keep (G). Neither (H) nor (J) describes *two types of activities,* so eliminate them both. The correct answer is (G).

43. **A** Transitions change in the answer choices, so this question tests consistency of ideas. A transition must be consistent with the relationship between the ideas it connects. The first part of the sentence says that the writer and her father *continue to seek the big thrills,* and the second part says that they *have learned to seek lesser forms of excitement in daily life as well.* There is a contrast between these ideas. Choice (A) appropriately uses the contrasting transition *but;* keep (A). Eliminate (B), (C), and (D) because they all contain transitions that indicate agreement between ideas. The correct answer is (A).

44. **F** Note the question! The question asks for the answer that *concludes the paragraph with a phrase that relates to the main topic of the essay,* so it tests consistency. Eliminate answers that are inconsistent with the purpose stated in the question. The main topic of the passage is the different types of thrills the writer and her father have experienced. The phrase *us thrill seekers* in (F) is consistent with this idea, so keep (F). Eliminate (G) and (H) because neither one mentions anything about *thrills.* There is no indication that the writer is no longer interested in thrills, so eliminate (J). The correct answer is (F).

45. **C** Note the question! The question asks for the best placement for Paragraph 2, so it tests consistency of ideas. Paragraph 2 must be consistent in focus with the paragraphs before and after it. Paragraph 2 introduces the idea of *canyoning.* Neither Paragraph 1 nor Paragraph 3 discusses *canyoning,* so eliminate (A) and (B). Paragraph 4 describes *canyoning* in more detail. Since Paragraph 2 introduces *canyoning,* it should come before Paragraph 4. The correct answer is (C).

Passage IV

46. **G** Verbs change in the answer choices, so this question tests consistency of verbs. A verb must be consistent in number with its subject. The subject of the underlined verb is *the Mexican-American War,* which is singular, so the underlined verb should also be singular. Eliminate (F) and (H) because they both contain plural verbs. The *-ing* form of the verb makes the sentence incomplete, so eliminate (J). The correct answer is (G).

47. **A** Verbs change in the answer choices, so this question tests consistency of verbs. A verb must be consistent in tense with other verbs in the sentence. The other verb in the sentence, *is,* is in present tense, so the underlined verb should also be present tense. Eliminate (C) and (D) because *included*

is past tense. Punctuation also changes in the answer choices, so this question also tests how to connect ideas with the appropriate punctuation. The first part of the sentence, *Certainly, it is difficult to imagine the present-day United States without the list of former Mexican territories, which includes,* is not an independent clause. A colon can only be used after an independent clause, so eliminate (B). The correct answer is (A).

48. **J** Commas change in the answer choices, so this question tests comma usage. The phrase *to American arts* is necessary to the sentence, so it should not be set off by commas; eliminate (G). There is no need to break up the clause *one aspect of their contributions to American arts is often overlooked* with a comma, so eliminate (F) and (H). The correct answer is (J).

49. **D** The length of the sentence about *Carlos Santana* changes in the answer choices, so this question tests concision. There is also the option to DELETE; consider this choice carefully as it's often the correct answer. The paragraph focuses on Mexican-American *literature,* so the information about a *musician* is not relevant, and the sentence should be deleted. The correct answer is (D).

50. **G** Commas change in the answer choices, so this question tests comma usage. The name *María Amparo Ruiz de Burton* is necessary to the sentence, so it should not be set off by commas; eliminate (F). There is no need to break up the phrase *when author María Amparo Ruiz de Burton published her novel* with commas, so eliminate (H) and (J). The correct answer is (G).

51. **C** Note the question! The question asks what would be lost if a phrase were deleted, so it tests consistency. Eliminate answer choices that are not consistent with the role of the phrase. The phrase describes something *noteworthy* about *The Squatter and the Don.* Although the phrase mentions *English,* it does not describe *Ruiz de Burton's command of the English language,* so eliminate (A). The phrase says nothing about whether the book was *the first by a Mexican author to be read in the United States,* so eliminate (B). The phrase does *strengthen the sense of the novel's historical importance,* so keep (C). There is no discussion of whether Ruiz de Burton *considered writing the novel in...Spanish,* so eliminate (D). The correct answer is (C).

52. **J** The length of the phrase around *American readers* changes in the answer choices, so this question could test concision. *Acquaint* and *introduce* mean the same thing in this context, so there is no need to use both terms; eliminate (F). It is logical that someone who is *unacquainted* with something would need to be *introduced* to it, so there is no need to include both those terms. Eliminate (H). *A glimpse* means "see briefly," which does not make sense in this context; eliminate (G). Choice (J) is concise and makes the meaning of the sentence clear. The correct answer is (J).

53. **B** The length of the phrase changes in the answer choices, so this question could test concision. Choice (C) is the shortest option, but it makes the sentence incomplete; eliminate (C). It is clear from the context that the *family* in this sentence was described by Ruiz de Burton, so eliminate (D). The difference between (A) and (B) is the order of the words, so the question also tests misplaced modifiers. Eliminate answers that have an unclear word order. The first part of the sentence, *A family of landed gentry living in San Diego,* is a descriptive phrase that refers to *the Alamars.* Choice (A)

makes the meaning of the sentence unclear by making it sound as though *nearly all* is the *family of landed gentry;* eliminate (A). Choice (B) makes the meaning of the sentence clear. The correct answer is (B).

54. **F** Prepositions change in the answer choices, so the question tests idioms. *The American annexation of California* was not a continuous event, as *throughout* would imply, so eliminate (H). The annexation was something that took place "at the time of" *the Mexican-American War,* so *during* is the correct choice. Keep (F). Neither *within* nor *through* makes the meaning of the sentence clear, so eliminate (G) and (J). The correct answer is (F).

55. **C** Verbs change in the answer choices, so this question tests consistency of verbs. Verbs must be consistent in tense with other verbs in the sentence. The other verb in the sentence, *felt,* is in past tense, so the underlined verb should also be in past tense. Eliminate (B) and (D) because *being* is present tense. Choice (A) lacks a verb and makes the sentence incomplete; eliminate (A). The correct answer is (C).

56. **H** Note the question! The question asks whether a sentence should be added to the paragraph, so it tests consistency. A sentence should be added only if it is consistent with the focus of the paragraph. The paragraph focuses on Ruiz de Burton's book *The Squatter and the Don;* the book was *an early and important exploration of many themes that Mexican-American authors continue to explore.* The new sentence discusses *the Louisiana Purchase,* and *people of French descent living in the United States,* which is not consistent with the paragraph. The sentence should therefore not be added; eliminate (F) and (G). Choice (H) accurately states that the sentence *does not provide a direct connection between the work of María Amparo Ruiz de Burton and the work of later Mexican-American authors.* The passage does not discuss *the Louisiana Purchase,* so eliminate (J). The correct answer is (H).

57. **D** Note the question! When a question asks which answer would be *LEAST* acceptable, eliminate answers that **are** acceptable. Vocabulary changes in the answer choices, so this question tests which words give the clearest meaning. The words *investigate, examine,* and *look into* all mean something similar to *explore* in this context, so they are all acceptable. Eliminate (A), (B), and (C). *Solve* means "find a solution," which does not work in this context. Choice (D) is therefore not acceptable. The correct answer is (D).

58. **H** Prepositions and pronouns change in the answer choices, so this question tests the idea of clear. Choices (G) and (J) do not include pronouns, and neither choice makes the meaning of the sentence clear; eliminate (G) and (J). The difference between (F) and (H) is the pronouns *that* versus *those.* A pronoun must be consistent with the noun it refers to. The underlined pronoun refers to *writings,* which is plural, so the underlined pronoun should also be plural. Eliminate (F) because *that* is singular. The correct answer is (H).

59. **A** The length of the phrase changes in the answer choices, so this question tests concision. Choice (A) is the shortest option, and it clearly refers back to *Ana Castillo* and *Sandra Cisneros,* who are both mentioned earlier in the paragraph. There is no need to repeat the names, so eliminate (B). This

paragraph is about two writers in particular, not about all *Mexican-American authors,* so eliminate (C) and (D). The correct answer is (A).

60. **G** Note the question! The question asks for the best placement for Sentence 3, so it tests consistency of ideas. The sentence must be consistent with the ideas that come both before and after it. Sentence 3 mentions *Ruiz de Burton,* who is discussed earlier in the passage, but not anyplace else in this paragraph. Sentence 3 also introduces the idea of *other authors*. Sentences 1 and 2 introduce two *other authors,* so Sentence 3 provides a logical transition from the previous paragraph, which is about *Ruiz de Burton,* to this one. Sentence 3 should be placed before Sentence 1. The correct answer is (G).

Passage V

61. **D** Punctuation changes in the answer choices, so this question tests how to connect ideas with the appropriate punctuation. The first part of the sentence, *Ludwig Mies van der Rohe, typically cited alongside Walter Gropius and Le Corbusier as a pioneer of modern architecture,* is not an independent clause. The second part of the sentence, *was integral to the founding and proliferation of the "modern style" in architecture,* is also not an independent clause. A period can only be used between two independent clauses, so eliminate (A) and (B). Changing the word *was* to *being* makes the sentence as a whole incomplete, so eliminate (C). Choice (D) appropriately uses commas to set off the phrase *typically cited alongside Walter Gropius and Le Corbusier as a pioneer of modern architecture* from the rest of the sentence. The correct answer is (D).

62. **H** Verbs change in the answer choices, so this question tests consistency of verbs. A verb must be consistent in tense with other verbs in the sentence. The other verb in the sentence, *sought,* is in past tense, so the underlined verb should also be in past tense. Eliminate (F) and (G) because they are both present tense. Adding the word *who* to the underlined portion makes the sentence incomplete, so eliminate (J). The correct answer is (H).

63. **B** Punctuation changes in the answer choices, so this question tests how to connect ideas with the appropriate punctuation. The first part of the sentence, *The buildings based on van der Rohe's designs,* is not an independent clause. The second part of the sentence, *were primarily constructed with industrial steel and plate glass—that is, only the materials of modern, twentieth-century life and industry,* is also not an independent clause. A semicolon can only be used between two independent clauses, so eliminate (D). There is no reason to break up the clause *the buildings based on van der Rohe's designs were primarily constructed with industrial steel and plate glass,* so eliminate (A) and (C). The correct answer is (B).

64. **J** Note the question! When a question asks which answer would *NOT* be acceptable, eliminate answers that **are** acceptable. Vocabulary changes in the answer choices, so this question tests which words give the clearest meaning. *From, using,* and *out of* all make clear that *industrial steel and plate*

glass were the materials used in construction, so (F), (G), and (H) are all acceptable and can all be eliminated. *Into* would mean that the *buildings* "became" *industrial steel and plate glass,* which does make sense in this context. Choice (J) is therefore not acceptable. The correct answer is (J).

65. **A** Vocabulary changes in the answer choices, so this question tests which word gives the clearest meaning. The phrase *that is* is an introductory phrase that introduces a restatement of a previous idea. The part of the sentence after the dash gives a restatement of the idea before the dash, so *that is* is appropriate in this context. *This* is a pronoun that does not clearly refer to anything in this sentence; eliminate (C) and (D). The difference between (A) and (B) is a comma, so this question also tests comma usage. The phrase *that is* is not necessary to the main meaning of the sentence, so it should be set off with a comma. Eliminate (B) because it lacks a comma after that phrase. The correct answer is (A).

66. **J** Transitions change in the answer choices, so this question tests consistency of ideas. A transition must be consistent with the relationship between the ideas it connects. The first part of the sentence mentions *one of the main problems with contemporary architecture,* and the second part of the sentence specifies what that problem was. The word *and* is not appropriate in this context because it would indicate that the second part is an additional point, rather than an explanation of the first part. Eliminate (F). The word *which* makes the meaning of the sentence unclear, so eliminate (H). *That* appropriately refers back to *one of the main problems.* The difference between (G) and (J) is the colon, so this question also tests how to connect ideas with the appropriate punctuation. The first part of the sentence, *By using only the bare minimum materials produced from American and German factories, Mies sought to cast off what he found to be one of the main problems with contemporary architecture,* is an independent clause. Some type of punctuation is needed to separate the two parts of the sentence, so eliminate (G). Choice (J) appropriately uses a colon after an independent clause and before a related explanation. The correct answer is (J).

67. **C** Note the question! The question asks for the answer that *would add the most effective detail to the description of the visual appeal of the buildings mentioned in the first part of the sentence,* so it tests consistency. Eliminate answers that are inconsistent with the purpose stated in the question. Eliminate (A) and (B) because neither mentions anything about the *visual appeal* of any buildings. Choice (C) discusses *the complex beauty* of the buildings, which is consistent with the idea of *visual appeal.* Eliminate (D) because, although it mentions *buildings on display,* it does not provide any *details* about *visual appeal.* The correct answer is (C).

68. **F** Punctuation changes in the answer choices, so this question tests how to connect ideas with the appropriate punctuation. The first part of the sentence, *From 1908 to 1912, under teacher Peter Behrens's guidance,* is not an independent clause. The second part of the sentence, *Mies became a proponent of many modern and avant-garde ideas in architecture in Germany,* is an independent clause. A semicolon can only be used between two independent clauses, so eliminate (H). There is no reason to break up the phrase *under teacher Peter Behrens's guidance* with a comma, so eliminate (G) and (J). Choice (F) appropriately uses commas to set off the phrase *under teacher Peter Behrens's guidance* from the rest of the sentence. The correct answer is (F).

69. **B** Pronouns and nouns change in the answer choices, so this question tests the idea of clear. A pronoun can only be used if it is clear what it refers to. The word *this* does not clearly refer to only one thing, so it cannot be used in this context; eliminate (A). Keep choice (B) because it makes the meaning of the sentence clear. Neither *something* nor *this thing* clearly refers to only one noun, so eliminate (C) and (D). The correct answer is (B).

70. **J** Transitions change in the answer choices, so this question tests consistency of ideas. A transition must be consistent with the relationship between the ideas it connects. The first part of the sentence states that *van der Rohe was committed to creating a philosophical, theoretical basis for his works,* and the second part says that *he helped to create a new vocabulary for the creation and study of architecture.* There is no contrast between these two ideas, so eliminate (F) and (G), which both contain contrasting transitions. The word *moreover* is used to connect two ideas in different sentences, but the underlined transition must connect the two ideas in the same sentence; eliminate (H). The word *because* effectively indicates that the second part of the sentence was an effect of the idea in the first part. The correct answer is (J).

71. **B** Verbs change in the answer choices, so this question tests consistency of verbs. A verb must be consistent in tense with the rest of the paragraph. The paragraph is in past tense, so the underlined verb should also be in past tense. Eliminate (C) and (D) because they are both present tense. The word *who* makes the sentence incomplete, so eliminate (A). The correct answer is (B).

72. **H** Note the question! When a question asks which answer would *NOT* be acceptable, eliminate answers that **are** acceptable. The length of the phrase changes in the answer choices, so this question could test concision. The shortest option is (G); the word *one* is consistent with the phrase *one in Wyoming* in the non-underlined portion of the sentence, so (G) is acceptable. Eliminate (G). *The other* is also consistent with the non-underlined phrase *one in Wyoming,* so (F) is also acceptable. Eliminate (F). The word *this* in (H) does not clearly refer to anything, so (H) is not acceptable. Choice (J) is consistent with the non-underlined portion, so eliminate (J). The correct answer is (H).

73. **C** Verbs change in the answer choices, so this question tests consistency of verbs. A verb must be consistent in tense with other verbs in the sentence. The other verb in the sentence, *worked,* is in past tense. Eliminate (A) and (B) because both *learning* and *learn* are present tense (learning is, specifically, present progressive because the action is taking place now). The main subject of the sentence is also *van der Rohe,* not *pupils,* so some form of the verb *teach* makes the meaning of the sentence clearer than the verb *learn* does. Choice (C) contains the infinitive form of the verb *to teach,* which does not have a tense. The infinitive appropriately provides a reason in the first part of the sentence *(To teach pupils his new method and architectural vocabulary)* for the action in the second part of the sentence *(van der Rohe worked tirelessly as an educator).* Eliminate (D) because *being taught* is in present tense, and it does not make the meaning of the sentence clear. The correct answer is (C).

74. **F** The length of the phrase surrounding the word *enthusiastic* changes in the answer choices, so this question tests concision. *Excited* and *thrilled* mean the same thing as *enthusiastic* in this context, so there is no need to use both words. Eliminate (G), (H), and (J). Choice (F) is concise and makes the meaning of the sentence clear. The correct answer is (F).

75. **B** Note the question! The question asks for the best placement for Sentence 3, so it tests consistency of ideas. The sentence must be consistent with the ideas that come both before and after it. Sentence 3 says that van der Rohe *had two commissions waiting for him there,* so it must come after a mention of a specific place. Sentence 1 says that van der Rohe *left Germany for the United States.* Sentence 2 says that he was *invited to become head of the school;* Sentence 3 introduces a school, *the Armour Institute of Technology.* Sentence 3 therefore belongs between Sentences 1 and 2. The correct answer is (B).

TEST 2 MATH ANSWERS AND EXPLANATIONS

1. **E** The question asks for the number of raspberries, blueberries, and blackberries that Violet uses. Figure out the number of one kind of berry at a time and use Process of Elimination. Since Violet has 10 cherries, she uses *three times* 10 = 30 blackberries, eliminating (A), (B), and (D). Thus, she also uses 30 raspberries and *twice* 30 = 60 blueberries. Choice (C) lists 2 rather than 2 × 30 for the number of blueberries, eliminating (C). The correct answer is (E).

2. **H** The question asks for an equivalent form of the expression. Expand the equation with FOIL (First, Outer, Inner, Last) to get $(3x)(x) + (3x)(2) + (-5)(x) + (-5)(2) = 3x^2 + 6x + (-5x) + (-10)$. Combine the middle terms to get the simplified expression $3x^2 + x - 10$. Choices (G), (J), and (K) are the results of confusing the signs. Choice (F) multiplies only the first terms and the last terms, which is not the correct way to multiply binomials. The correct answer is (H).

3. **B** The question asks for the value of the function for the provided values of x and y. Substitute 8 and 6 for x and y, respectively, into the equation $f(x,y)$, to get $f(8,6) = 8 - [(8 \times 6) - 6] = 8 - 42 = -34$. Choices (A), (C), (D), and (E) are wrong because they do not distribute the negative correctly. The correct answer is (B).

4. **G** The question asks for a fractional portion of a percentage of 8,000. Use the words in the problem to create an equation: *percent* means "divide by 100," *of* means "multiply," *is* means "equals," and *what* means "use a variable." The equation is $x = \frac{1}{7} \times \frac{28}{100} \times 8{,}000$. Therefore, $x = 320$. Choice (H) is $7 \times \frac{28}{100} \times 8{,}000$, a common fraction mistake. The correct answer is (G).

5. **C** The question asks for the value of x in the equation. Begin by subtracting 3 from both sides of the original equation to get $6x = 9 + 3x$; then subtract $3x$ from both sides to get $3x = 9$. Solve by dividing both sides by 3 to find that $x = 3$. It is also possible to answer the question by testing the answer choices in the original equation. For example, checking (C) by substituting in 3 for x gives $6(3) + 3 = 12 + 3(3)$, which simplifies to $21 = 21$, which is true. The correct answer is (C).

6. **F** The question asks for the first term of the arithmetic sequence. First, calculate the difference of the third and second terms: $8 - (-2) = 10$. The first term, therefore, is the second term minus the difference: $(-2) - 10 = -12$. Choices (G) and (K) are variations of the actual common difference, rather than the value of the first term. Choice (H) calculates the first term in a geometric, rather than arithmetic, sequence. Choice (J) incorrectly uses -2 as the first term and calculates what would then be the second. The correct answer is (F).

7. **C** The question asks for the number of pink jellybeans in the bag. When dealing with probabilities, the total of all possible outcomes must equal either 100% or 1, so use the provided probabilities to find the chance of selecting a pink one. The probability of pink, $1 - \frac{2}{9} - \frac{1}{3}$, can be rewritten with

common denominators as $\frac{9}{9} - \frac{2}{9} - \frac{3}{9}$, so the probability of picking a pink jellybean must be $\frac{4}{9}$. Since probability is defined as $\frac{\text{number of desired outcomes}}{\text{number of total outcomes}}$, find the number of pink jellybeans by setting the probability of $\frac{4}{9}$ equal to $\frac{x}{72}$ and solving. Given $\frac{4}{9} = \frac{x}{72}$, cross-multiply to get $9x = 288$, which solves to $x = 32$. The correct answer is (C).

8. **G** The question asks for the total cost of Bob's cell phone plan over a single year. Because the flat rate of \$100 includes the first two months, Bob will be billed \$60/month for only 10 months out of the year. The total cost is \$100 + \$60 (10) = \$700, so (G) is correct. Choice (F) is the result of mistakenly charging \$100 for every two-month period. The flat rate applies only for the first two months. Choice (H) calculates the total without the flat rate. Choice (J) incorrectly charges the flat rate twice for the first two months. Choice (K) adds 12, rather than 10, months of service charges to the flat rate. The correct answer is (G).

9. **C** The question asks for the length of a side of the square. If one side of the pentagon measures 20 inches, the perimeter of the pentagon is 100 inches (20 × 5). Because the pentagon and the square have the same perimeter, the square also has a perimeter of 100 inches. Each side of the square is then 25 inches (100 ÷ 4). Choice (E) is wrong because it is equal to the perimeter of both the square and the pentagon, which is not what the question asks for. Choices (A), (B), and (D) give a perimeter that is not equal to the target of 100 inches. The correct answer is (C).

10. **F** The question asks for the equation that finds the number of bricks for which the two companies would charge the same price. Translate the words into an equation, making x the number of bricks. Contractor A charges \$1,600 *plus* \$2 *times* the number of bricks, which can be written as $1{,}600 + 2x$. Contractor B charges \$400 plus \$8 times the number of bricks, $400 + 8x$. Set the expressions equal to each other to get $1{,}600 + 2x = 400 + 8x$. Choice (G) sets each contractor's flat rate plus the other contractor's per brick charge equal. Choice (H) sets the sum of each contractor's per brick charges and the number of bricks equal. Choices (J) and (K) set the per brick charges equal to Contractor A's and B's flat rates, respectively. The correct answer is (F).

11. **D** The question asks for the expression in terms of B. Solve for B. Divide both sides of the equation by ACD to get $B = \frac{E}{ACD}$. The correct answer is (D).

12. **H** The question asks for the measure of $\angle XVZ$. Start by using Process of Elimination: since $\angle XVZ$ is clearly larger than 90°, eliminate (F) and (G). Since the three angles together form a straight line, they must add up to 180°. Find a by solving $4a + 90° + 2a = 180°$, which simplifies to $6a + 90° = 180°$. Subtract 90 from both sides and divide both sides by 6 to get $a = 15°$. Now, find the measure of $\angle XVZ$ by adding together the measures of $\angle XVY$ and $\angle YVZ$: substituting $a = 15$ gives $90° + 2(15)°$, which equals 120°. The correct answer is (H).

13. **B** The question asks for the temperature in degrees Celsius in New Orleans. First, find the temperature in New Orleans in °F by adding 25°F to 70°F to get 95°. Now, substitute F = 95° into the provided equation to find the equivalent temperature in °C: $95 = \frac{9}{5}C + 32$, which simplifies to $63 = \frac{9}{5}C$. Multiply both sides of the equation by $\frac{5}{9}$ to get a temperature of C = 35°. The correct answer is (B).

14. **G** The question asks for the value of the expression. Look at the given expression and try to find a way to make it match the requested expression. Since $3x + 2y = 5$, find the value of $6x + 4y$ by multiplying the entire equation by 2, which gives $6x + 4y = 10$. Substitute this value into the expression to find that $10 - 7 = 3$. The correct answer is (G).

15. **B** The question asks for the range that includes the amount of beef Mike sold over two days. The total amount of beef in pounds is $3\frac{2}{7}+2\frac{1}{3}$. To add fractions without the same denominator, get a common denominator or find the decimal equivalent on a calculator. The common denominator here is 21, so change the numbers to $3\frac{6}{21}+2\frac{7}{21}=5\frac{13}{21}$. It may be difficult to compare this to the ranges in the answers. To simplify the process, use a calculator to convert $5\frac{13}{21}$ into its decimal equivalent of ≈ 5.619. This eliminates (A), (D), and (E). The decimal equivalent of $5\frac{2}{3}=5.\overline{66}$, so the pounds of meat are slightly less than that. The correct answer is (B).

16. **H** The question asks for the distance Dave is from his house. Draw a picture. Since Dave went directly east and then directly south, the distance to his house can be found using a right triangle. The distance is $d=\sqrt{3^2+4^2}=5$. Be careful not to select (K), which is the sum of the two legs of the triangle! The correct answer is (H).

17. **B** The question asks for the length of time in which the sensor will record 100 billion pieces of data. The rate at which the sensor records—1 piece of data every 0.0000000038 seconds, or $\frac{1}{0.0000000038}$—is constant, and therefore the ratio of pieces of data recorded per second will be equal for any given number of pieces of data or seconds. Set $\frac{1}{0.0000000038}$ equal to the ratio 100,000,000,000 pieces of data every x seconds: $\frac{1}{0.0000000038}=\frac{100{,}000{,}000{,}000}{x}$. Cross-multiply to get $x \times 1 = 100{,}000{,}000{,}000 \times 0.0000000038$, so $x = 380$. The correct answer is (B).

18. **J** The question asks for the new dimensions of the photograph. Use Process of Elimination. The area of a rectangle can be found by using the formula $A = lw$, so the area of the original photograph is $20 \times 30 = 600$. Reducing this area by 264 square centimeters would give a new area of 336. Eliminate (F) and (G), which do not give this area. Now, test the remaining answers to determine which one correctly reduces the length and width by the same amount. Choice (H) reduces the width by $20 - 12 = 8$ but reduces the length by $30 - 28 = 2$, and (K) reduces the width by $20 - 16 = 4$ but reduces the length by $30 - 21 = 9$, so both can be eliminated. The correct answer is (J).

19. **C** The question asks for the length of the *shortest* side of the quadrilateral. First, since all four sides must have lengths that are even integers, eliminate (D). Now test the remaining answer choices, starting with the middle value. For (C), if the shortest side is 6, the other three sides would be 8, 10, and 12. The perimeter of the resulting quadrilateral would be $6 + 8 + 10 + 12 = 36$. Since this perimeter matches the description in the question, the correct answer is (C).

20. **G** The question asks for the slope of the line. Since the equation is written in standard form, $Ax + By = C$, the slope of the line is equal to $\frac{-A}{B}$. In the given equation, $A = 7$ and $B = -3$, so the slope is $\frac{-(-3)}{7}$ or simply $\frac{3}{7}$. It is also possible to find the slope by converting the equation into slope-intercept form, $y = mx + b$, where m is the slope. To do this, start with the original equation and add $3x$ to both sides to get $7y = 3x + 21$, then divide both sides by 7 to get $y = \frac{3}{7}x + 3$. The correct answer is (G).

21. **C** The question asks for the area of trapezoid *BCEF*. To find the area of the trapezoid *BCEF*, subtract the area of triangle *CDE* from the area of rectangle *BDEF*. The area of a rectangle is $A = lw$, so the area of *BDEF* is $(9)(4) = 36$ square feet. The area of a triangle is $A = \frac{1}{2}bh$, so the area of triangle *CDE* is $\frac{1}{2}(5)(4) = 10$ square feet. The area of trapezoid *BCEF* is $36 - 10 = 26$ square feet. Choice (A) is incorrect because it finds the area of the square with sides *BC* and *BF*. Choice (D) is incorrect because it is solving only for the area of the rectangle *BDEF*. The correct answer is (C).

22. **G** The question asks for the perimeter of the quadrilateral. Add together the four side lengths provided above the diagram: $10 + 6 + \sqrt{136} + 12$ becomes $28 + \sqrt{136}$. Since $\sqrt{136} \approx 11.7$, the final sum is about $28 + 11.7 = 39.7$. Choice (F) forgets to add in $\sqrt{136}$, and (J) gives the area instead of the perimeter. The correct answer is (G).

23. **E** The question asks for the length of $\overline{GJ}$. Since $\overline{FG}$ and $\overline{FJ}$ form a 90° angle, drawing in $\overline{GJ}$ would create a right triangle with $\overline{GJ}$ as the hypotenuse. As with any right triangle, use the Pythagorean Theorem, $a^2 + b^2 = c^2$, to find the length of the unknown side: substituting the provided side

lengths gives $(10)^2 + (6)^2 = c^2$, which simplifies first to $100 + 36 = c^2$ and then to $c^2 = 136$. Taking the square root of both sides gives a final solution of $GJ = \sqrt{136}$. The correct answer is (E).

24. **F** The question asks for the new coordinates of point J after the quadrilateral is rotated. Since the graph is rotating clockwise, the point will be moving 90° and will have a new point on the x-axis. Any point on the x-axis must have a y-coordinate of 0, so eliminate (G) and (J) immediately. Choice (K) rotates the point *counterclockwise* instead of clockwise. Rotating the figure clockwise will give a negative value for the x-coordinate. The correct answer is (F).

25. **C** The question asks for the shape that has both reflectional and rotational symmetry. A geometric figure has rotational symmetry if it looks the same after a certain amount of rotation. A geometric figure has reflectional symmetry when one half is the reflection of the other half. The shapes in (C), (D), and (E) all have reflectional symmetry if cut vertically in half, but (C) is the only figure that has rotational and reflectional symmetry. The correct answer is (C).

26. **K** The question asks for the coefficient of the x^8 term in expanded expression. Since the question does not ask about any other terms, only multiply the terms that will have x^8. When multiplying numbers with the same base and different exponents, add the exponents. Multiplying the first term in each set of parentheses results in $(-x^4)(5x^4) = -5x^8$. No other combination of terms will result in a product with x^8, so the coefficient on x^8 is –5. Choice (G) confuses the sign of the coefficient, (H) incorrectly adds the coefficients, and (J) multiplies the wrong terms. The correct answer is (K).

27. **D** The question asks for the mean of the data set. To find the mean, add all the scores: 66 + 67 + 71 + 72 + 72 + 73 + 75 + 77 + 79 + 82 + 83 + 83 + 87 = 987. Divide this number by the total number of scores, 13, to find $\frac{987}{13} \approx 75.9$. Choice (C) gives the median instead of the mean, and (B) takes the mean of the stems and leaves as separate elements instead of in their combined integer form. The correct answer is (D).

28. **F** The question asks for the probability that a randomly selected score is 83. Since probability is defined as $\frac{\text{number of desired outcomes}}{\text{number of total outcomes}}$, find both the number of scores that equal 83 and the total number of scores on the list. There are 2 scores of 83 and 13 total golfers, so the probability is $\frac{2}{13}$. Choices (J) and (K) mistakenly consider the value of scores instead of the count of the scores. The correct answer is (F).

29. **B** The question asks for the least common multiple of the given numbers. First, factor each number. In this problem, the given numbers are all products of 2, 3, *a*, and *b*. To find the lowest common multiple of the given values, figure out the maximum number of times each component (2, 3, *a*, and *b*) appears in any one of the given values. $8 = 2 \times 2 \times 2$, so the lowest common multiple must have $2 \times 2 \times 2$ as a factor. No value has more than one factor of 3, so the number is required to have only one factor of 3. Finally, the least common multiple must have one *a* and one *b*. Multiply the mandatory factors together, $2 \times 2 \times 2 \times 3 \times a \times b$, to get $24ab$. The correct answer is (B).

30. **J** The question asks for the number of model airplanes that Aleksandra would own by December 2008. To solve for the function, determine the value of *m* in December. Since December is 7 months after May and $m = 0$ in May, $m = 7$ in December. Substitute 7 for *m* in the function to get $A(7) = 2(7) + 2$, so Aleksandra will have 16 model airplanes. Choice (F) is the number of airplanes she had in May. Choices (G), (H), and (K) all substitute incorrect values for *m* in the equation when solving. The correct answer is (J).

31. **E** The question asks for the midpoint of $\overline{CD}$. The midpoint of a line is $\left(\frac{x_1 + x_2}{2}\right), \left(\frac{y_1 + y_2}{2}\right)$. Thus, the *x*-coordinate of the midpoint is $\frac{-3+11}{2} = 4$, eliminating (A), (B), (C), and (D). The only remaining choice is (E), which also has the correct *y*-coordinate of $\frac{5-7}{2} = -1$. Be careful not to subtract x_2 from x_1, which would give an *x*-coordinate of 7. Choices (A) and (B) merely add or subtract the *x*- and *y*-coordinates, rather than finding their averages. The correct answer is (E).

32. **K** The question asks for an equivalent form of the expression. Factor the numerator and denominator separately: $\frac{(x-4)(x-4)}{(x+4)(x-4)}$. The factor $(x – 4)$ on both the top and the bottom of the fraction cancel each other out, so $\frac{(x-4)}{(x+4)}$ is all that remains. Choices (F), (G), and (H) are all the result of incorrectly canceling out terms without factoring. Choice (J) cancels both factors from the numerator, which is not possible with only one $(x – 4)$ in the denominator. The correct answer is (K).

33. **B** The question asks for the amount of family-sized packs of cookies that would have given Evan the same number of cookies as his original purchase. If Evan purchased 6 boxes, with 10 bags in each box, and 12 cookies in each bag, he will have purchased $6 \times 10 \times 12 = 720$ cookies. Dividing 720 by 30 will give the number of family packs with 30 cookies that he could have purchased instead: $720 \div 30 = 24$. Choices (A), (B), (C), and (E) are wrong because they do not result in the target amount of total cookies. The correct answer is (B).

34. **H** The question asks for the value of the expression. If $\frac{r}{s} = -\frac{1}{2}$, then $s = -2r$ by cross-multiplication. Substitute $-2r$ for s in the given expression: $16r^4 - (-2r)^4 = 16r^4 - 16r^4 = 0$. Choice (K) is the result of making a sign error when computing. The correct answer is (H).

35. **A** The question asks for the area of cookie dough remaining after the cookies have been cut out. Because the nine circles fit into the square "as shown," quickly estimate the area that remains to eliminate any answer choices that couldn't possibly be correct. Roughly, it appears that $\frac{1}{4}$ of the square remains. Since the total area of the square is 144 square inches, and $144 \div 4 = 36$, (C), (D), and (E) are out because they are too big. Choice (A) is slightly closer to the estimate than (B), but it is possible to solve the question mathematically to confirm this estimate. Since the circles are identical and are tangent to all adjacent circles and to the edges, the diameter of any circle must be $\frac{1}{3}$ of a 12-inch side, or 4 inches, and the radius of any circle must be 2. The area of each circle is πr^2, or 3.14×4, or 12.56. Multiply 12.56 square inches by 9 cookie cut-outs to get 113.04 square inches cut out, and 30.96 square inches remaining. The correct answer is (A).

36. **J** The question asks for the list that contains only prime numbers. A prime number has only two distinct factors—1 and itself. Go through the answers one at a time and eliminate any that contain numbers that have more than 2 distinct factors. Choice (F) contains 63, which is divisible by 3, 7, 9, and 21, so eliminate (F). Choice (G) contains 91, which is divisible by 7 and 13. This eliminates (G) and (H), which also contains 91. Choice (K) contains 81, which is divisible by 3, 9, and 27, so eliminate (K). The correct answer is (J).

37. **C** The question asks for the fixed charge for the tutoring packages shown in the table. First, determine the cost per quarter hour using the rate formula: $\text{rate} = \frac{\text{change in cost}}{\text{change in quarter-hours}}$. Pick two different packages to set up the equation $\frac{\$230 - \$200}{10 - 8} = \frac{\$30}{2}$ to find the rate that is \$15 per quarter-hour. Now use the 8 quarter-hour package to set up the equation fixed cost + $\$15 \times 8$ = \$200 to find that the fixed cost is \$80. Choice (B) finds the rate for the 10-quarter-hour package without a fixed cost. Choice (D) is a partial answer. The correct answer is (C).

38. **K** The question asks for the length of the building's shadow, which is the base of the triangle. Relative to the 34° angle, the side opposite is provided and the side adjacent is the unknown, so by the rules of SOHCAHTOA, tangent is the correct function to use. Plug in the provided values into the formula $\tan\theta = \frac{\text{opposite}}{\text{adjacent}}$ to get $\tan 34° = \frac{100}{x}$. Use the provided value of tan 34° to get $0.67 = \frac{100}{x}$. Now, solve by multiplying both sides by x to get $0.67x = 100$; then divide both sides by 0.67 to get $x \approx 148$. Choices (F), (H), and (J) use the wrong trigonometric function when solving, and (G) reverses the order of the opposite and adjacent sides when evaluating for the tangent. The correct answer is (K).

39. **E** The question asks for the equation of the circle. The general equation for a circle with center (h,k) and radius r, is $(x-h)^2 + (y-k)^2 = r^2$. Because $h = 4$, $k = -3$, and $r = 12$, the equation for this circle is $(x-4)^2 + (y+3)^2 = 144$. Choices (A), (B), and (C) are incorrect because they do not square r. Choice (D) is incorrect because it does not distribute the negative in the $(y-k)^2$ term. The correct answer is (E).

40. **H** The question asks for the smallest integer value for x that satisfies the inequality. Use a calculator to make the comparisons easier: $\frac{14}{21} = 0.\overline{66}$. Because the question asks for the least value, test the answers, starting WITH the least. Choice (F) is $\frac{7}{12} = 0.58\overline{3}$, which is less than $0.\overline{66}$, and (G) is $\frac{8}{12} = 0.\overline{66}$, which makes the two fractions equal. Choice (H) is $\frac{9}{12} = 0.75$, which makes the inequality true. Choices (J) and (K) also make the inequality true but neither is the *least* integer that makes the inequality true. The correct answer is (H).

41. **E** The question asks for the value of the function. Substitute $(a + b)$ into the function for a to get $f(a + b) = (a + b)^2 + 2(a + b) + 5$. Distribute the 2 to get $f(a + b) = (a + b)^2 + 2a + 2b + 5$. The correct answer is (E).

42. **G** The question asks for the length of $\overline{NO}$. It is possible to solve by estimating: since $\overline{NO}$ appears to be about the same length as $\overline{MO}$ in the figure, (G) or (H) would be the only reasonable answers. To find the correct one, use the information given. Since lines $\overline{MO}$ and $\overline{LP}$ are parallel, $\angle NMO \cong \angle NLP$ and $\angle NOM \cong \angle NPL$. Thus, ΔMNO and ΔLNP are similar triangles with congruent angles and proportional sides. To find the length of $\overline{NO}$, set up a proportion: $\frac{\overline{MO}}{\overline{LP}} = \frac{\overline{NO}}{\overline{NP}}$.

Using x for $\overline{NO}$, solve for x: $\frac{105}{150}=\frac{x}{x+39}$. Cross-multiply to get $150x = 105x + 4{,}095$; then subtract $105x$ from both sides to get $45x = 4{,}095$. Therefore, $\overline{NO} = 91$ feet. Choice (F) gives the length of $\overline{OP}$. Choice (K) is the sum of the three side lengths. The correct answer is (G).

43. **C** The question asks for the number of seconds needed for the plane to climb 2 miles. First, convert 2 miles to feet, $2 \text{ miles} \times \frac{5{,}280 \text{ feet}}{1 \text{ mile}} = 10{,}560$ feet because height, h, is given in feet in the equation. Now, substitute the answer choices for the value of t to see which choice equals 10,560 feet. Start in the middle—if that answer provides a value that is too large or too small, more than one answer can be eliminated. Choice (C) becomes $1{,}200 + 32(293) = 10{,}576$. The precise answer is 292.5 seconds, but the question asked for the nearest second. The correct answer is (C).

44. **J** The question asks for the measure of $\angle C$. The sum of the three angles of a triangle will always equal 180°, so $2x + 3x + 5x = 180$. Therefore, $10x = 180$, and $x = 18°$, the measure of $\angle C$ is $5x = 180 \div 2 = 90°$. Choices (F) and (K) are partial answers. Choices (G) and (H) give the measures for the wrong angles. The correct answer is (J).

45. **B** The question asks for the least number of additional free throws the basketball player must make to raise his average to 55%. If the basketball player made 12 out of his 30 shots, he currently has a free-throw percentage of 40%. Use the answers to calculate the least number of additional free throws he must make. Make sure to add the number to both the numerator and denominator, since any additional free throws are both attempted and made. Choice (B) gives $\frac{12+10}{30+10} \times 100 = 55\%$. Choice (A) is the result of adding 5 only to the numerator. Choices (C) and (D) approximate 55% to 56% of 30 free throws. Choice (E) incorrectly raises the percentage *by* 55% rather than *to* 55%. The correct answer is (B).

46. **H** The question asks which expression would have the least value for negative integer values of y. Pick a negative value for y such as $y = -2$ and try out the answers. Choice (F) becomes $\sqrt[3]{(-2)^2} = \sqrt[3]{4} \approx 1.587$. Choice (G) becomes $100^{-2} = \frac{1}{100^2} = 0.0001$, which is smaller than (F),

so eliminate (F). Choice (H) becomes $\frac{\pi}{-2} \approx -1.57$, which is smaller than (G), so eliminate (G). Choice (J) becomes $\frac{1}{(-2)^2} = \frac{1}{4}$. This is greater than (H), so eliminate (J). Choice (K) becomes $\frac{1}{(-2)^3} = -\frac{1}{8} = -0.125$. This is greater than (H), so eliminate (K). The correct answer is (H).

47. **C** The question asks for the number of possible orders in which the five groomsmen could walk down the aisle. Figure out how many different groomsmen can go in each position. For the first position, any of the 5 groomsmen can go. For the second position, there are only 4 groomsmen remaining. For the third position, there are 3, for the fourth position, there are 2, and for the fifth position, there is only one. To get the total possible combinations, multiply these values together to get $5 \times 4 \times 3 \times 2 \times 1 = 120$ possible orders. The correct answer is (C).

48. **J** The question asks for the length of $\overline{MN}$. As with all circle problems, it is helpful to first calculate and draw the radius. Given the area of the circle is 169π square inches, use the area formula: $A = 169\pi = \pi r^2$, so $r = 13$. Radii $\overline{MO}$ and $\overline{NO}$ form two right triangles with chord $\overline{MN}$, so use the Pythagorean Theorem to find the length of the two missing legs: $5^2 + b^2 = 13^2$, so $b = 12$. The length of the chord is $2 \times 12 = 24$ inches. Choice (F) gives only half the length of the chord. Choices (G) and (K) give the radius and diameter of the circle, rather than the chord. Choice (H) is the sum of 5 and 13, which is not the correct operation to calculate lengths of a right triangle. The correct answer is (J).

49. **A** The question asks for the x-intercept of the line that passes through the two given points. The x-intercept occurs where $y = 0$, eliminating (B), (C), and (D). Next, find the slope of the line: $\frac{y_2 - y_1}{x_2 - x_1} = \frac{4-7}{6+3} = -\frac{3}{9}$, or $-\frac{1}{3}$. The line to the x-intercept must have the same slope. The slope between (A) and (–3,7) is $\frac{7-0}{-3-18} = -\frac{1}{3}$. Be careful not to select (E), which is the y-intercept. The correct answer is (A).

50. **G** The question asks for the equation that intersects the x-axis at $x = 7$. Intercepting the x-axis at $x = 7$ means the equation must satisfy the coordinate (7,0). The only equation that does this is (G). Choices (F) and (H) incorrectly give x-intercepts at (–7,0). Choice (J) gives the y-intercept at $y = 7$, and (K) gives the y-intercept at (0,–7). The correct answer is (G).

51. **A** The question asks for the value of sin θ + cos θ. Use SOHCAHTOA. Since the definition of tangent is $\tan\theta = \frac{\text{opposite}}{\text{adjacent}}$ and $\tan\theta = \frac{2}{9}$, then the side opposite θ is 2 and the side adjacent to θ is 9. Sine and cosine are defined in terms of the hypotenuse of the triangle, so use Pythagorean Theorem ($a^2 + b^2 = c^2$) to get $2^2 + 9^2 = h^2$. This becomes $85 = h^2$, so $h = \sqrt{85}$. The definition of sine is $\sin\theta = \frac{\text{opposite}}{\text{hypotenuse}}$, so $\sin\theta = \frac{2}{\sqrt{85}}$. The definition of cosine is $\cos\theta = \frac{\text{adjacent}}{\text{hypotenuse}}$, so $\cos\theta = \frac{9}{\sqrt{85}}$. The value of sin θ + cos θ is $\frac{2}{\sqrt{85}} + \frac{9}{\sqrt{85}} = \frac{11}{\sqrt{85}}$. The correct answer is (A).

52. **G** The question asks for the area of the triangle. Triangle *OAB* is equilateral since *OA* and *OB* are both radii of the circle and *OA* = *AB*. The formula for the area of a triangle is $A = \frac{1}{2}bh$. The base of ΔOAB is 8. To find the height of ΔOAB, draw a line from *A* that is perpendicular to *OB*, creating two 30°-60°-90° triangles. Using the relationship $a : a\sqrt{3} : 2a$, the height of ΔOAB is $4\sqrt{3}$. For this triangle, $A = \frac{1}{2}(8)\left(4\sqrt{3}\right) = 16\sqrt{3}$. Choice (J) forgets to include the $\frac{1}{2}$ in the area formula. Choice (F) uses 4 for the base. Choice (H) uses 8 for both the base and the height of the triangle. The correct answer is (G).

53. **C** The question asks for the expression that gives the length of $\overline{XY}$. Use the formula given and replace variables with values from the diagram. Since the question asks for the length of the side opposite angle *Z*, find the measure of angle *Z* as the first step. Given that there are 180° in a triangle, subtract 105° and 40° from 180° to get 35° for angle *Z*. Now plug in all of the information into the equation: $\frac{\sin 40°}{30} = \frac{\sin 35°}{z}$. Solve for *z* by multiplying both sides by *z* and by 30 to get *z* sin 40° = 30 sin 35°. Divide both sides by sin 40° to get $z = \frac{30 \sin 35°}{\sin 40°}$. The correct answer is (C).

54. **G** The question asks for the length of minor arc *PQ*. To find arc length, use a ratio of $\frac{\text{sector}}{\text{circle}}$: $\frac{\text{central angle}}{360°} = \frac{\text{arc length}}{\text{circumference}}$. Since the radius is 9 feet, the circumference is $C = 2\pi r = C = 2\pi(9) = 18\pi$. Now, fill known values into the ratio: $\frac{120°}{360°} = \frac{\text{arc } PQ}{18\pi}$. Reduce the left side to $\frac{1}{3}$ and then cross-multiply to get $18\pi = 3(\text{arc } PQ)$. Solve to find the length of the arc is 6π. Choice (J) is a partial answer that gives the circumference rather than arc length. Choice (K) is the sector's area, rather than arc length. The correct answer is (G).

55. **C** The question asks for the solution to a matrix subtraction expression. In order to subtract these matrices, combine the corresponding elements from each matrix. That is, subtract the first row, first column numbers in the second and third matrices from the first row, first column number in the first matrix. Thus, the matrix is $\begin{bmatrix} w-x-\frac{1}{w+x} & x-y-\frac{1}{x+y} \\ y-z-\frac{1}{y+z} & z-w-\frac{1}{z+w} \end{bmatrix}$. Choices (A), (B), and (E) all improperly subtract fractions and integers. Choice (D) uses multiplication rather than subtraction. The correct answer is (C).

56. **K** The question asks for the value of a compound function. To deal with compound functions, the trick is to work inside out. First, determine the value of the inside $f(1) = -2(1)^3 = -2$. The value of $f(1)$ becomes the new x-value for the outside f function, so determine $f(-2) = -2(-2)^3 = -2(-8) = 16$. A negative number raised to an odd integer stays negative; (F) and (G) are wrong because they confuse the signs. Choice (H) is the value of $-x^3$, rather than $-2x^3$. Choice (J) is the result of multiplying $f(x)$ by $f(x)$, which is not the same operation as compound functions. The correct answer is (K).

57. **A** The question asks for the graph of a function in which y varies directly as x for all real numbers. If a function y varies directly with x, this means that as x increases, y increases proportionally, eliminating (B) and (D). This proportionality means that the function must be a straight line with the equation $y = kx$, where k is a constant, eliminating (E). This line must then pass through the origin, because if $x = 0$, then $y = 0$. Choice (C) is incorrect because it does not pass through the origin. The correct answer is (A).

58. **K** The question asks for the statement that *must* be true for Gopi's quiz scores. If the quiz scores are listed from lowest to highest, the middle score, the median, is 9. The two highest scores are both 10. Since the only mode of the quiz scores is 10, the remaining two scores must be distinct integers. The mean of the 5 scores is 8, so the sum of the five scores is 8 × 5 = 40. The sum of the two lowest scores must be 40 – (9 + 10 + 10) = 11. Choices (F), (G) and (H) *could* be true because the quiz scores could be (3, 8, 9, 10, 10), (4, 7, 9, 10, 10), or (5, 6, 9, 10, 10). Choice (J) is the number of scores multiplied by the mode. The correct answer is (K).

59. **E** The question asks for the height of the table. Set the height of the table equal to x; then draw a diagram for the question.

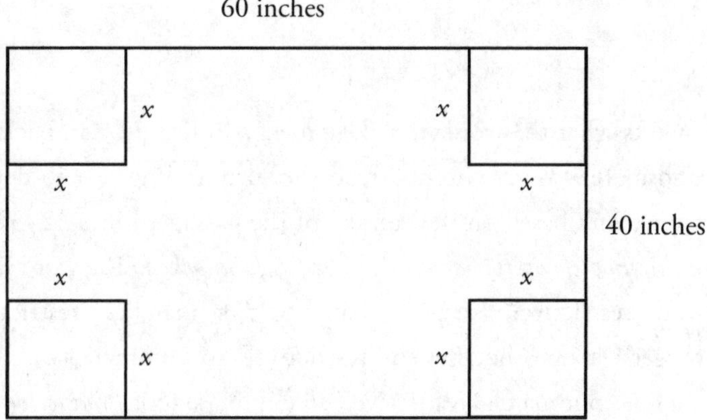

As the diagram shows, height x cannot be greater than half of the length or width of the total rectangle, so eliminate (A), (B), (C), and (D). The correct answer is (E).

60. **H** The question asks for the area of ΔABC. To find the area of a triangle, use the formula $A=\frac{1}{2}bh$. The base of 10 is given, so draw in a height from point B that is perpendicular to line $\overline{AC}$ and then find its length. Now that there is a right triangle, it is possible to use the trigonometric proportions of SOHCAHTOA. Relative to the 35° angle, the height is opposite and $\overline{AB}$ is the hypotenuse. Set up the sine function, $\frac{\text{opposite}}{\text{hypotenuse}}$, to get $\sin 35° = \frac{h}{\overline{AB}}$. The length of $\overline{AB}$ is 10, so multiply both sides by 10 to get h = 10 sin 35°. The area of the triangle is $A=\frac{1}{2}(10)(10\sin 35°)=50\sin 35°$. Choices (F), (G), and (J) use the wrong trigonometric functions. Choice (K) does not take $\frac{1}{2}$ the product of bh. The correct answer is (H).

TEST 2 READING ANSWERS AND EXPLANATIONS

Passage I

1. **A** The question asks what the word *stultifying* means in line 32. Go back to the text, find the word *stultifying*, and mark it out. Carefully read the surrounding text to determine another word that would fit in the blank based on the context of the passage. Lines 32–33 are about the boy's *life on land—the stultifying life on the farm where he felt landlocked*. The word *stultifying* could be replaced with the word "restrictive." Keep (A), since *stifling* matches "restrictive." *Strengthening* means "making stronger"; it does not match "restrictive," so eliminate (B). *Welcoming* means "greeting hospitably"; it does not match "restrictive," so eliminate (C). *Productive* means "yielding results"; it does not match stultifying, so eliminate (D). The correct answer is (A).

2. **G** The question asks what is not established about the boy in the first seven paragraphs. When a question asks which answer is **not** supported, eliminate answers that **are** supported. Use words from the answer choices to locate the relevant portions of lines 1–30. Lines 6–7 say that *the boy felt alone despite his companions, now leading him through the alien jungle,* so eliminate (F). Lines 19–20 say, *Even as the lightning lit up the sky like the fireworks the boy had heard about, but never seen*. Since these lines establish that he has not seen *fireworks,* keep (G). Line 14 mentions *the captain, who surely knew everything*. This indicates that the boy *respected the captain*, so eliminate (H). Lines 10–24 describe the boy's memories of the storm, and line 25 continues, *These memories would come to the boy in a split-second, filling his brain before he had a chance to consciously remember what had happened*. These lines indicate that the *memories of the storm* come to the boy *often*, so eliminate (J). The correct answer is (G).

3. **D** The question asks how *the boy saw himself*. Because this is a general question, it should be done after all the specific questions. Use words from the answer choices to locate the relevant portions of the passage. Lines 2–3 describe the boy *as he trudged through the inhospitable jungle, vines snarling around his ankles*. The boy does not feel *contented with life in the jungle,* so eliminate (A). Lines 34–40 describe the boy's mother as *frail and worn-looking,* with a *sad, creased face* and say that *his parents did all they could to create a home for him*. The boy is not *afraid of his mother,* so eliminate (B). Lines 32–33 describe the boy's *stultifying life on the farm,* and lines 41–42 say, *his birthplace's rocky ground yielded only a life he could not live and a place he could not love*. The boy does not see himself as *toughened by farm labor,* so eliminate (C). Lines 48–56 describe the boy's *blissful days upon the ship,* using the words *familiar* and *secure;* the boy felt *at home on the sea,* so keep (D). The correct answer is (D).

4. **F** The question asks what the time sequence indicates about when *the shipwreck takes place*. Use words from the answer choices to locate the relevant portions of the passage. Lines 31–33 say, *Sometimes, the boy would think back to before the storm, and even before the ship, to his life on land—the stultifying life on the farm*. Then, line 44 indicates that the boy left the farm and *had run off to sea*. Keep

(F), since the shipwreck must take place *after the boy leaves the farm.* In lines 1–30, the boy is remembering the shipwreck, and the passage states, *The words rang in the boy's ear as he trudged through the inhospitable jungle* (lines 2–3). Therefore, the boy *walks through the jungle* after the shipwreck, so eliminate (G). Lines 49–51 describe the boy's time on the ship, saying *Although he had come aboard as a stowaway, the captain took him in and gave him daily lessons.* This indicates that the boy *meets the captain* before the shipwreck, so eliminate (H). There is no description of the boy's *mother* trying to *protect him,* and the only mention of her is in lines 31–40, when he is describing his memories of the time *before the storm, and even before the ship,* so eliminate (J). The correct answer is (F).

5. **C** The question asks what interpretation is suggested for the phrase *let the dead bury their dead.* The question references the 12th paragraph, so read lines 60–70. This paragraph recounts the boy's memories of having *seen the dead after the storm* and recalling the captain's words, *"Let the dead bury their dead."* Lines 64–68 read, *But what did those words mean? Searching his memory, the boy was shocked to find that after the shipwreck, his mind's eye could no longer distinguish the captain from any other man—the cook, the lowest deckhand, or even the boy's father.* The *captain* does not give an *explanation of this phrase,* so eliminate (A). The paragraph does not discuss *trust* for *the living* or the fact that *the dead cannot do anything,* so eliminate (B). Keep (C) because it is supported by the boy's statement that he could *no longer distinguish the captain from any other man.* This paragraph doesn't discuss whether the boy can *expect to lead a better life,* so eliminate (D). The correct answer is (C).

6. **J** The question asks how the boy's ideas compare with the captain's. Look for references to the boy and the captain in the passage. Lines 49–52 state that the captain gave the boy *lessons* and told him, *"Ignorance is dangerous, not only aboard ship but also in life."* The second part of this paragraph indicates that the boy *soon grew familiar* with what the captain was teaching him, and *felt so secure in the captain's knowledge and in his own growing understanding.* This paragraph indicates that the boy's ideas are similar to the captain's, not *opposing.* Furthermore, there is no indication that the captain is *uncertain about the meaning of the phrase, "let the dead bury their dead,"* nor that the captain *understood why the boy's father was worn down;* eliminate (F) and (G). There is no indication that the captain *disliked the harsh life of the sea,* so eliminate (H). Keep (J) because it is supported by the discussion of *knowledge* in lines 49–56. The correct answer is (J).

7. **A** The question asks for a statement about the boy that *the ship's remaining crewmates accompanying the boy on his walk through the jungle* would agree with. Look for the references to the remaining crewmates in the passage. Lines 60–63 indicate that the boy *had seen the dead after the storm* and that *the remaining crew members had urged him away from the wreckage, finally having to pull him by his arms to force his legs to move.* The second half of this paragraph indicates that *the captain* was among the dead, and lines 72–73 refer to the captain as *the only man* the boy *had ever loved.* Keep (A), since it is supported by lines 60–73. There is no indication that the boy had *run away from his companions,* so eliminate (B). There is no indication that the boy is *startled by loud noises,* so eliminate (C). Lines 31–47 do support the statement about the boy in (D); however, the question asks what the *ship's remaining crewmates* would agree with, and there is no evidence that the crewmates

know about the boy's life from before he arrived on the ship, so eliminate (D). The correct answer is (A).

8. **H** The question asks for a description of the captain's actions *on finding the boy stowed away on the ship.* Look for the words *stowed away* in the passage. Lines 49–51 state, *Although he had come aboard as a stowaway, the captain took him in and gave him daily lessons in reading the stars and plotting the ship's course.* There is no indication that the captain *scolds the boy,* so eliminate (F). The captain uses the phrase, *Let the dead bury their dead,* but does not teach the boy *the meaning of the phrase,* so eliminate (G). Keep (H) because it is supported by lines 49–51. The captain does not ignore the boy or leave him to *fend for himself,* so eliminate (J). The correct answer is (H).

9. **D** The question asks what *the storm* does not feature. When a question asks which answer is **not** supported, eliminate answers that **are** supported. Look for descriptions of the storm in the passage. Lines 18–24 describe the storm and mention that *lightning lit up the sky like fireworks, thunder filled the air, shaking the very timbers of the ship, and walls of water arose up as a dark mountain.* Based on these descriptions, eliminate (A), (B), and (C). Keep (D), since there is no mention of *hail.* The correct answer is (D).

10. **F** The question asks which statement about *the storm* is supported. Look for references to the storm in the passage. Lines 13–15 state, *The typhoon had come out of nowhere, it had seemed; even the captain…was taken aback by its sudden appearance.* Keep (F), since it is supported by these lines. There is no evidence that the storm *happened in the middle of the night,* so eliminate (G). The storm is described as violent, but there's no comparison with other storms, so the passage doesn't support the statement that it *was the most violent storm* the *crew had ever seen;* eliminate (H). There is no mention of *the boy's father* warning him about a storm, so eliminate (J). The correct answer is (F).

Passage II

11. **A** The question asks, based on the description of slang as *innocent,* what Thorne believes that not all slang is created to be. Read a window in the passage around the given line. Lines 26–35 discuss the belief that *slang is created as a response to the status quo, that its usage represents a defiant opposition of authority.* Lines 36–40 state, *Thorne, however, would point out that most slang is derived for much more innocent purposes,* and give examples of slang phrases that *do not involve opposition to authority.* Note that the question asks what Thorne believes that slang is *not* intended to be. Keep (A), since *rebellious* matches *involve opposition to authority.* Lines 40–42 indicate that slang often comes from *specific needs for informative or vibrant expressions,* so eliminate (B). Lines 42–43 state that slang is *a marriage of jargon, nuance, and effective imagery,* so eliminate (C). These lines are not focused on whether or not slang is *accusatory,* so eliminate (D). The correct answer is (A).

12. **G** The question asks why the author includes the information in the last paragraph, so read lines 81–94. This paragraph states *Thorne believes that it is an essential project to compile accurate modern dictionaries of [slang's] usage,* in order to provide *future generations (or civilizations) of humans with*

an effective way of decoding our meaning. Specifically, the paragraph mentions the *need to inform future scholars.* There is no criticism of Thorne or any indication that he is *subjective with which words he chooses to include in his dictionary,* so eliminate (F). Keep (G) because it is consistent with the discussion of *the need to inform future scholars.* The reference to *Shakespearean verses* is an analogy illustrating why a slang dictionary might be useful for future scholars; there's no mention of Thorne using *Shakespearean slang to describe modern terms,* so eliminate (H). The author doesn't make an argument about what the *primary focus of modern linguistics* should be, so eliminate (J). The correct answer is (G).

13. **B** The question asks which group is not mentioned in the passage *as related to the academic study of slang.* When a question asks which answer is **not** supported, eliminate answers that **are** supported. Use words from the answer choices to locate the relevant portions of the passage. Lines 26–30 discuss the beliefs of *philologists* about slang, so eliminate (A). Keep (B), since there is no mention of college professors in the passage. Lines 17–18 state that *In the world of linguistics, slang is often viewed condescendingly as an affliction of vulgar speech,* so eliminate (C). Lines 65–67 discuss how *lexicologists* try to *define and apply standard principles in their classifications of slang,* so eliminate (D). The correct answer is (B).

14. **F** The question asks for the primary purpose of the quotation marks around the phrase *common man.* Read a window in the passage around the given line. Lines 67–69 make the point that *there is definitely some subjectivity involved in determining whether a term deserves the maligning moniker [slang].* In the next paragraph, the author states that *intellectuals who would categorically denounce slang struggle with the fact that slang…involves as much inherent creativity and word play as the figurative language revered in poetry.* Despite this similarity, the author notes that *it is who continues to use [a term] that determines its stature as artful rhetoric or the dreaded slang.* Therefore, the author is arguing against categorizing words and the people who use them; he puts the terms *"respectable people"* and the *"common man"* in quotation marks to indicate that these categories are subjective. Keep (F) because it is supported by the discussion in these lines. The phrase *common man* does not refer to one particular man, so eliminate (G). The author is opposed to using *a demeaning term to describe users of slang,* so eliminate (H). The passage discusses the people who continue to use a term, so the author does not believe that slang terms do *not have the proper usage to survive;* eliminate (J). The correct answer is (F).

15. **C** The question asks what the word *vulgar* means in line 18. Go back to the text, find the word *vulgar* and mark it out. Carefully read the surrounding text to determine another word that would fit in the blank based on the context of the passage. Lines 17–19 state, *In the world of linguistics, slang is often viewed condescendingly as an affliction of vulgar speech, its users condemned for their intellectual laziness.* The word *vulgar* could be replaced with the word "unrefined." *Sickening* means "repulsive"; it doesn't match "unrefined," so eliminate (A). *Malicious* means "intentionally harmful"; it doesn't match "unrefined," so eliminate (B). Keep (C) because *unsophisticated* matches "unrefined." *Profane* means "sacrilegious" or "secular"; it doesn't match "unrefined," so eliminate (D). The correct answer is (C).

16. **F** The question asks why some view the *efforts to compile current dictionaries of slang* as *essential.* Look for the words *compile current dictionaries* in the passage. The last paragraph, beginning on line 81, states, *Thorne believes that it is an essential project to compile accurate modern dictionaries of [slang's] usage* to provide *future generations (or civilizations) of humans with an effective way of decoding our meaning, which could easily be confused by our prevalent use of slang.* Later, the paragraph mentions the *need to inform future scholars.* Keep (F), since it is supported by these lines. The paragraph discusses how the dictionaries could be used by *future generations,* not by *speakers of other languages,* so eliminate (G). The reference to *Shakespeare* in the paragraph is an analogy to illustrate how *future scholars* might use a dictionary of current slang; the passage does not indicate that dictionaries *currently do not exist except for those chronicling Shakespeare's era,* so eliminate (H). The paragraph discusses how the dictionaries could be used by *future generations,* not by *modern English speakers,* so eliminate (J). The correct answer is (F).

17. **C** The question asks what *Walt Whitman views slang as an attempt* to do. Look for the name *Walt Whitman* in the passage. Lines 22–25 state that *Walt Whitman elevated the status of slang* and quote him as saying that slang is *"an attempt by common humanity to escape from bald literalism, and express itself illimitably."* These lines do not discuss an attempt to *show civility,* so eliminate (A). These lines also do not refer to an attempt to *conform to traditions,* so eliminate (B). Keep (C), since the phrase *broaden expression* is supported by the phrase *express itself illimitably.* The attempt to *defy authority* is discussed in the next paragraph and is not Walt Whitman's view, so eliminate (D). The correct answer is (C).

18. **H** The question asks for the main purpose of the first paragraph in relation to the passage. Because this is a general question, it should be done after all the specific questions. The passage as a whole discusses slang, in particular, a linguist's efforts to compile *a current dictionary of slang* (line 7). The question references the first paragraph, so read lines 1–6. These lines say that Tony Thorne receives many emails *explicating the meaning behind local terms,* and asks, *Why would the Director of the Language Center at King's College of London concern himself with seemingly nonsensical linguistic inventions?* This paragraph gives a few *examples of slang,* but the question at the end suggests that the paragraph's main purpose is not simply introducing the examples, so eliminate (F). Although the paragraph indicates that Thorne is from London, the author does not try to *establish that British scholars are the leaders in slang research,* so eliminate (G). Keep (H), since the phrase *a possibly surprising topic of academic study* is supported by the question about *why* Thorne would *concern himself* with the slang terms. Although the passage describes Thorne's email inbox as *bloated,* the author never discusses Thorne *struggling to manage his email inbox,* so eliminate (J). The correct answer is (H).

19. **C** The question asks what the author indicates about *groups like the military* by referring to them as *hotbeds* of slang. Read a window in the passage around the given line. Lines 40–42 say, *Usually, slang evolves out of...groups with specific needs for informative or vibrant expressions that normal language does not encapsulate.* There is no indication that the author sees these groups as *prophetic,* so eliminate (A). The word *traditional* indicates that these groups were the ones that previously created

most of our slang, in contrast with the arenas where *most modern slang comes from;* it doesn't indicate that the groups are *old-fashioned,* so eliminate (B). Keep (C), since the description *innovative* is supported by the phrase *vibrant expressions that normal language does not encapsulate.* Although the military may be *strict,* that is not what is indicated by the word *hotbeds,* so eliminate (D). The correct answer is (C).

20. **J** The question asks for the *greatest obstacle for intellectuals who would categorically denounce slang.* Look for the words *intellectuals who would categorically denounce slang* in the passage. Lines 70–73 state that *intellectuals who would categorically denounce slang struggle with the fact that slang, when first conceived, involves as much inherent creativity and word play as the figurative language revered in poetry.* There is no indication that the intellectuals invent *their own* slang terms, so eliminate (F). There is no mention of *disagreement* about how *slang terms are used,* so eliminate (G). There is no mention of intellectuals' *respect for Thorne's academic interest* and *determination,* so eliminate (H). Keep (J) because it is supported by lines 70–73. The correct answer is (J).

Passage III

21. **D** The question asks what can be inferred about Breed's reaction to receiving Harper Lee's letter. Because this is a general question, it should be done after all the specific questions about Passage A. Harper's letter to Breed was a rejection of Breed's request for an interview with her. Lines 1–2 state, *It was, without a doubt, the nicest rejection of my journalistic career.* In lines 28–29, Breed says, *part of me was hoping that she'd stick to her guns,* and lines 33–35 state, *Lee was able to keep her own counsel…and protect her privacy.* These lines indicate that Breed appreciated Lee's reply and respected her desire for privacy. Line 10 describes Lee's handwriting as *clear script,* and the only reference to social media, in lines 18–20, states that Lee did not *post* or *tweet;* there's no indication that Breed posted Lee's letter publicly, so eliminate (A). There is no indication that Breed is *angry,* so eliminate (B). Although Breed describes Harper's reply as the *nicest rejection* of his career, he doesn't indicate that it was her *compliment of his writing style* that he appreciated. Additionally, in line 6 he indicates that he *didn't really expect a reply* to his request, indicating that he didn't regret *losing the exclusive interview,* so eliminate (C). Keep (D), since it is supported by the lines cited above. The correct answer is (D).

22. **J** The question asks for a detail that *supports the idea that Lee kept herself out of the public eye.* Use words from the answers choices to locate the relevant portions of Passage A. There is no indication that *Lee was worried that she might not live up to people's high expectations,* so eliminate (F). Lines 8–17 quote from Lee's *reply* to the author's *interview request;* eliminate (G) because it is contradicted by the passage. The passage says that Lee published a book *in 2014,* but *announced the pending release* of a publication in 2015. Moreover, making such an announcement put her more in the public eye; this is the opposite of what the question asks for, so eliminate (H). Keep (J) because lines 2–3 indicate that Lee *hadn't granted an interview in about four decades.* The correct answer is (J).

23. **A** The question asks what is made clear in Passage A about the publication of *The Mockingbird Next Door.* Look for the words *The Mockingbird Next Door* in Passage A. Lines 19–22 state that *Lee kept her thoughts to herself...With the 2014 publication of The Mockingbird Next Door: Life with Harper Lee, it appeared that Lee's resolve had softened.* In other words, publishing the book seemed to indicate that Lee would no longer keep her thoughts private. Keep (A) because it is supported by these lines. The passage says only that *it appeared* that Lee had softened her resolve; the word *proved* is not supported by the passage, so eliminate (B). Lee's statement *"I am humbled and amazed that this will now be published"* (line 25) referred to different book, *Go Set a Watchman,* so eliminate (C). Although Passage B discusses the possibility that the author of *The Mockingbird Next Door* was *prying into Lee's life,* this is not made clear in Passage A, so eliminate (D). The correct answer is (A).

24. **G** The question asks for *Harper Lee's reaction to Mills's book,* based on Passage B. Look for references to Lee's reaction in Passage B. Lines 43–50 indicate that Lee *issued a statement refuting* the claim that Mills's book was written with Lee's cooperation. There is no indication that Lee was *accepting that the public wanted to know more about her life,* so eliminate (F). Keep (G) because it is supported by lines 43–50. There is no indication that Lee felt *proud* in reaction to the book, so eliminate (H). The information in lines 43–50 contradicts the idea that Lee was *encouraging* or that she was *pleased to give a first-hand account of her life,* so eliminate (J). The correct answer is (G).

25. **C** The question asks how *Mills's article* can be described, according to Crowder. According to the introduction, Crowder is the author of Passage B; look for the word *article* in the passage. In lines 64–65, the author describes the article as *exhaustive and meticulously researched.* Mills's book is described as controversial, but there's no evidence that her *article* was controversial; additionally, the word used to describe the article is *exhaustive,* not *exhausting,* so eliminate (A). There is no mention of the article being *encouraging,* so eliminate (B). Keep (C) since it is a paraphrase of the description in lines 64–65. The description *meticulously researched* contradicts the idea that the article was *speculative,* so eliminate (D). The correct answer is (C).

26. **J** The question asks what can be inferred from Passage B about why *Mills published her book.* Look for references in the passage to Mills's motivation for writing the book. Lines 76–81 quote Mills, *"So much that has been said about (the Lees) has been secondhand or speculated...I wanted to show them sitting at the kitchen table, listening to Nelle tell stories, or being in the car with them as they talked about the Monroeville of 1930 versus now."* The passage indicates that Mills *remained friends with the sisters,* and even *moved into the house next door to (the Lees).* This description indicates that the information Mills gained did not come from *interviews,* but from having an ongoing relationship with the Lees; the mention of an *exclusive interview* comes from Passage A, so eliminate (F). Although Mills's article was about Monroeville, and she mentions the Lees talking about *the Monroeville of 1930 versus now,* Mills indicates that it was the Lees she wanted to focus on in her book, so eliminate (G). There is no indication that Mills hid her friendship with the Lees, so eliminate (H). Keep (J) because it is supported by Mills's quote. The correct answer is (J).

27. **D** The question asks what lines 53–56 indicate about Mills. Read a window in the passage around the given lines. These lines include a quote by Mills saying that Lee was *"quite specific about stories that she was sharing for the book and those that were to remain private, and I did respect those."* This indicates that Mills left some of the stories that Lee told out of the book, according to Lee's wishes. This statement is only about which stories Lee wanted included in the book; there is not enough information to support the statement that Mills *acted in accordance with all of Lee's wishes regarding the book,* so eliminate (A). The reference to *respect* is that Mills respected Lee's wishes, not that Lee respected Mills. Additionally, the reference to *meals* and *chores* comes from another part of the passage (lines 70–71); eliminate (B). The phrase *censored several of Lee's stories* would suggest that Mills left out parts of some stories; however, the passage states that Mills left some stories out of the book altogether, so eliminate (C). Keep (D), since it is a better match for the statements in lines 53–56. The correct answer is (D).

28. **F** The question asks which statement most accurately compares the content of the two passages. Eliminate any answer choice that misrepresents either passage. Both passages discuss journalists' personal interactions with the very private author Harper Lee. The author of Passage 1, although he did not get the interview he sought, writes of his respect for Lee's choice to maintain her privacy. Passage 2 recounts the controversy around Marja Mills's memoir *The Mockingbird Next Door;* namely, how Mills and Lee came to be at odds over the book's publication. Keep (F), since it reflects the *first-hand accounts of contact with Lee* as well as the *different outcomes* of the two encounters. There is not an analysis of *Lee's readers* in either passage, so eliminate (G). The two passages discuss different events, so eliminate (H). Although others compare her with a *mockingbird,* there is no mention in either passage to Lee's *self-identification with a bird,* so eliminate (J). The correct answer is (F).

29. **B** The question asks for a statement about *Lee's privacy* that Breed and Crowder would agree with. Eliminate any answer choice that misrepresents either passage. In Passage A, Breed says, *In an age when people feel compelled to update their Facebook statuses constantly, Lee kept her thoughts to herself* (lines 18–20) and *Lee was able to keep her own counsel and...protect her privacy* (lines 33–35). In Passage B, Crowder refers to Lee as the famously reclusive 88-year-old author; in regard to the idea that Lee granted Mills *unique access* to her life, Lee is quoted as saying, *"Rest assured...any book purporting to be with my cooperation is a falsehood."* Based on these references, both authors consider Lee's sense of privacy *significant,* so eliminate (A) and keep (B). Neither author argues that famous people must be accountable to the public, so eliminate (C). Both authors quote Lee first-hand, in instances when she was taking pains to protect her privacy, so eliminate (D). The correct answer is (B).

30. **G** The question asks who the author of the text referred to in lines 20–22 is, based on the passages. Read a window in Passage A around the given lines. Lines 20–22 discuss the publication of *The Mockingbird Next Door: Life with Harper Lee.* Next, look for a reference to the author of this text in Passage B. Lines 39–40 refer to the publication of Marja Mills's memoir, *The Mockingbird Next Door.* Therefore, it is reasonable to assume that Marja Mills is the author of the text. Eliminate (F), (H), and (J) because they identify other people, and keep (G). The correct answer is (G).

Passage IV

31. **A** The question asks for a true statement about *Frank Drake.* Look for the name *Frank Drake* in the passage. Lines 2–7 state that *Frank Drake became a scientific pioneer* when *he tuned the radio and began to listen,* believing he *might pick up interstellar transmissions from another planet.* Keep (A) because it is supported by these lines. Lines 10–11 state that the project *was ultimately unsuccessful in its goal of finding other intelligent life in the universe,* so eliminate (B). Lines 8–16 indicate that Frank Drake was associated with *Project Ozma,* and that Project Ozma inspired *the creation of many similar programs,* including *Project Phoenix,* so eliminate (C). The passage doesn't indicate what Drake's fields of study were, so eliminate (D). The correct answer is (A).

32. **G** The question asks for the *most appropriate characterization of Project Ozma.* Look for the words *Project Ozma* in the passage. Lines 9–12 state, *Although it was ultimately unsuccessful in its goal of finding other intelligent life in the universe, Project Ozma was hugely influential, inspiring the creation of many similar programs.* The project was not successful in its goal of finding intelligent life, so eliminate (F). Keep (G) because it is supported by lines 9–12. There is no indication that Drake had *limited knowledge and resources,* so eliminate (H). There is no indication that the project was *doomed to failure* because of a lack of *financial support,* so eliminate (J). The correct answer is (G).

33. **C** The question asks what the word *august* means in line 19. Go back to the text, find the word *august* and mark it out. Carefully read the surrounding text to determine another word that would fit in the blank based on the context of the passage. Lines 18–21 reference *locations as august as the University of California at Berkeley and the University of Western Sydney, both of which have reputations that draw respected scientists from around the world.* The word *august* could be replaced with the words "highly respected." *Summery* means "like or appropriate for summer"; it doesn't match "highly respected," so eliminate (A). *Elusive* means "hard to catch"; it doesn't match "highly respected," so eliminate (B). Keep (C) because *esteemed* matches "highly respected." *Antique* means "belonging to earlier times"; it doesn't match "highly respected," so eliminate (D). The correct answer is (C).

34. **H** The question asks for the *author's attitude toward the search for life on other planets.* Because this is a general question, it should be done after all the specific questions. In lines 79–84 the author says, *The more knowledge scientists are able to gather about our own galaxy, the better equipped they will be when it comes to seeking out similar planets outside our own solar system. Perhaps someday Frank Drake's dream of a message from outer space will come true—once we know where to look for it.* There's no evidence that the author finds the search for extraterrestrial life *ironic,* so eliminate (F). There is no evidence that the author is *scornful* or *angry,* so eliminate (G). Keep (H), because the author expresses hope that *perhaps someday* the *dream of a message from outer space will come true,* but also advocates a practical or *pragmatic* approach of gathering more information. There is no evidence that the author is *fearful,* so eliminate (J). The correct answer is (H).

35. **A** The question asks what is likely to be true of *scientists involved in the search for life on other planets.* Look for references in the passage to scientists involved in the search for life on other planets. Lines 22–26 describe *The scientists involved in the Search for Extraterrestrial Intelligence, or SETI,* saying that they are *esteemed academics, typically specializing in the areas of physics, astronomy, and engineering.* Keep (A), since it is supported by these lines. Lines 22–24 say that these scientists are *far from the wide-eyed dreamers that many people associate with the field,* so eliminate (B). The passage does mention studies at universities and funded by NASA (lines 15–21), but the passage does not specify that most of the scientists in the field are *employed at* these institutions, so eliminate (C). The passage does not state that the scientists are *radio mechanics,* so eliminate (D). The correct answer is (A).

36. **J** The question asks for the primary point of the fourth paragraph, so read lines 31–41. This paragraph discusses which characteristics *make a planet more likely to harbor intelligent life,* and says, *The general understanding is that there are two main factors that determine whether or not a planet is habitable…temperature and mass.* The paragraph begins with the phrase, *Although these scientists' understanding of the origins of life on Earth is still imperfect,* but the word *although* and the information given in the rest of the paragraph indicate that this is not the paragraph's *primary point,* so eliminate (F). *Liquid water* is not discussed in this paragraph, so eliminate (G). The *"Goldilocks Zone"* is also not mentioned in this paragraph, so eliminate (H). Keep (J) since it is supported by lines 35–37. The correct answer is (J).

37. **D** The question asks what the term *hospitable planets* is intended to mean as it is used in line 46. Read a window in the passage around the given line. Lines 42–46 discuss the hypothesis that *in order to support life, a planet must experience temperatures that fall within a range that allows for the presence of liquid water.* Line 61 states, *The other key to habitability is the mass of a planet.* There is no mention of *cultures* in the passage, so eliminate (A). Lines 46–48 state that *hospitable planets must be located within a certain distance of their respective suns;* however, it does not say that they must be *in close proximity to the Sun,* so eliminate (B). Lines 59–60 indicate that *most binary systems* are ruled out, so eliminate (C). Keep (D) because the lines cited above support the criteria *temperatures* and *masses* in the range able to *support life.* The correct answer is (D).

38. **H** The question asks why *Saturn is most likely unable to support life,* based on information in the passage. Look for the word *Saturn* in the passage. Beginning on line 44, the passage explains, *in order to support life, a planet must experience temperatures that fall within a range that allows for the presence of liquid water.* It goes on to say that *If a planet is too far from the sun, its temperatures will fall below that range, as in the case of Saturn.* The passage indicates that Saturn is *too far from the sun* to support life, so eliminate (F). Although the next paragraph discusses the effects of a *heavy atmosphere,* it is not clear from the information in the passage whether this applies to Saturn, and the passage does not state that having a heavy atmosphere is related to the presence of *liquid water,* so eliminate (G). Keep (H) because it matches lines 42–49. The next paragraph discusses *gas giants,* but it isn't clear whether this applies to Saturn, so eliminate (J). The correct answer is (H).

39. **D** The question asks what would most likely be true of *any new planet discovered in a location comparable to Venus's location, relative to the sun.* Look for the word *Venus* in the passage. Lines 46–51 state that *hospitable planets must be located within a certain distance of the respective suns,* and that if *a planet is too close to the Sun, as in the case of Venus, its temperatures will be too high.* The passage calls this optimal zone the *Goldilocks zone.* However, the next paragraph states that the *other key to habitability is the mass of a planet,* because *larger planets have heavier atmospheres [and] tend to retain more heat, creating a greenhouse effect.* Lines 75–76 indicate that *a smaller planet might be able to* sustain life if it was *on the inner edge* of the Goldilocks zone. Lines 64–65 indicate that *gas giants* are *massive planets;* there is no indication that this is true of Venus, so eliminate (A). There is also no indication that Venus lacks *a gravitational field,* so eliminate (B). Lines 59–60 say that *unstable orbits* are a property of *most binary systems,* and there is no indication that this is true of Venus, so eliminate (C). Keep (D) because this is a valid inference based on the information in lines 46–76. The correct answer is (D).

40. **F** The question asks for a characteristic of *Goldilocks Planets.* Look for the term *Goldilocks Planets* in the passage. Lines 44–54 explain, *in order to support life, a planet must experience temperatures that fall within a range that allows for the presence of liquid water. This, in turn, suggests that hospitable planets must be located within a certain distance of their respective suns. If a planet is too far from the Sun, its temperatures will fall below that range…If a planet is too close to the Sun…its temperatures will be too high. Planets that fall within the range of appropriate temperatures are often called "Goldilocks Planets," since they are neither too hot nor too cold but instead "just right" to provide environments hospitable to life.* Keep (F) because it is supported by these lines. *Heavy atmosphere* is not a quality associated with the term *Goldilocks Planet;* furthermore, the passage does not state that *hydrogen gases* create *a greenhouse effect,* so eliminate (G). The passage states that Goldilocks Planets *are neither too hot nor too cold;* eliminate (H) because it is contradicted. The passage indicates that the presence of liquid water is possible on Goldilocks Planets, but it does not state that liquid water is actually present on these planets; furthermore, *a high concentration of hydrogen gases* is not a characteristic associated with Goldilocks Planets, so eliminate (J). The correct answer is (F).

TEST 2 SCIENCE ANSWERS AND EXPLANATIONS

Passage I

1. **D** The question asks what the value of v would have been if I had equaled 500 A, according to Study 1. Look at the results of Study 1, found in Table 1. As v increases, so does the value of I. If I is greater than 250 A, then v must be greater than 200 m/s. Eliminate (A) and (B) because they are less than 200 m/s. Eliminate (C) because it is equal to 200 m/s. Keep (D) because it is the only value greater than 200 m/s. The correct answer is (D).

2. **F** The question asks how *the amount of current required to induce the train's velocity* changed *as the length of the magnetic rods in the maglev train increased,* according to Study 2. Look at the results of Study 2, found in Table 2. As the value for L, *the length of the magnetic rods,* increases, I, *the amount of current required to induce the train's velocity,* also increases. The correct answer is (F).

3. **C** The question asks for the value of B at which I would *most likely have equaled 570 A,* according to Study 3. Look at the results of Study 3, found in Table 3. Locate where $I = 570$ A would be located, between $I = 500$ A and $I = 600$ A. As I increases, B also increases. When $I = 500$ A, $B = 9.84 \times 10^{-4}$ T, and when $I = 600$ A, $B = 1.05 \times 10^{-3}$ T, so the value of B when $I = 570$ A must be in between those values. Eliminate (A) and (B) because they are too small. Keep (C) because it is within range. Eliminate (D) because it is too big. The correct answer is (C).

4. **J** The question asks for the trial in Study 3 with the greatest voltage, given that *during each trial, an electrical current moves through the magnetic track because a nonzero voltage was produced in the track.* This suggests that the *electrical current* is directly related to the *voltage,* and Study 1 proves this relationship. Look at the results of Study 3, found in Table 3. Choose the answer choice with the electrical current, which is Trial 14. The correct answer is (J).

5. **B** The question asks for the studies in which *the electrical current flowed in the opposite direction as compared with the other studies.* Look at the values listed for the *electrical current (I)* in the results of each study. Tables 1, 2, and 3 show all positive values while Table 4 shows negative values. The *electrical current* must have flowed in the opposite direction in Study 4. The correct answer is (B).

6. **G** The question asks which graph accurately represents the data found in the results of Study 3. Look at Table 3. As B increases, I also increases. The only graph that reflects this relationship is the one found in (G). The correct answer is (G).

7. **A** The question asks about the length of the maglev trains used in Study 1, based on the results of Studies 1 and 2. Study 1 used maglev trains of fixed length and measured current with varying velocities. No current is given in Table 2, but the passage states that in Study 2 the maglev trains were run at a *constant velocity of 40 m/s.* This matches up with Trial 1 in Table 1, which found that at a velocity of 40 m/s, the current measured was 50 A. In Study 2, the trial that produced a current of 50 A was Trial 6, which was performed with a maglev train with a length of 0.6 m. Therefore, the maglev trains in Study 1 must have been 0.6 m. The correct answer is (A).

Passage II

8. **J** The question asks for the average forearm length of *Idionycteris phyllotis* based on Tables 1 and 2. Find *Idionycteris phyllotis* in Table 1 and circle it. *Idionycteris phyllotis* appears in Step 4, with the option of *well-defined skin glands.* In Table 2, only Bat III has *well-defined skin glands,* so look at the information about the forearm given for Bat III. Since Bat III has a forearm length that is 30 mm long, eliminate (F) and (G). The data about Bat I is not relevant to *Idionycteris phyllotis,* so eliminate (H). The correct answer is (J).

9. **D** The question asks which characteristic *distinguishes Bat IV from a Pipistrellus hesperus.* Check each answer choice against the information given about Bat IV and *Pipistrellus hesperus.* Bat IV is listed in in Table 2, and has all the characteristics given in the answer choices. *Pipistrellus hesperus* is located in Step 8 of Table 1. Step 8 indicates *forearm length,* and *Pipistrellus hesperus* has a *forearm length* of *<40 mm,* which is consistent with (C). Eliminate (C) since this does not indicate a difference between the two bats. Step 7 indicates *tragus.* A measurement of *<6 mm and curved* gives the option of going to Step 8 where *Pipistrellus hesperus* is located. This is consistent with (A), so eliminate (A). The *uropatagium* is in Step 5. A *heavily furred uropatagium* leads to Step 6, which does not include *Pipistrellus hesperus,* so (D) describes a difference between the two bats. The *ears* are in Step 1; ears *shorter than 25 mm* lead to Step 5. From Step 5 it is possible to get to Step 7, and then Step 8, and to *Pipistrellus hesperus,* which is consistent with (B). Eliminate (B). The correct answer is (D).

10. **G** The question asks for the step number through which Bats I and II share the same results, according to Table 1. Check each answer choice against the information in the table. Step 1 indicates ear length. Bat I has ears that are 20 mm long and Bat II has ears that are 18 mm long. These are both *shorter than 25 mm,* so both bats share the same results. Next, look at Step 5, which indicates the *uropatagium.* Both Bats I and II share the trait of a *not heavily furred uropatagium,* so they share the same results through Step 5. For this reason, eliminate (F). Next, look at Step 7, which indicates the *tragus.* Bat I has a 4 mm curved *tragus* and Bat II has a 7 mm straight *tragus.* This difference leads to different results, so eliminate (H) and (J). The correct answer is (G).

11. **A** The question asks for the best description of the family *Vespertilionidae.* The word *Vespertilionidae* appears in the introduction, which indicates that it is a family of *Vesper bats.* The passage does not give any further information about the family, so this is an outside knowledge question. Bats are not *protists, lampreys,* or *birds,* so eliminate (B), (C), and (D). Bats are *mammals.* The correct answer is (A).

12. **G** The question asks which trait *Lasiurus cinereus* and *Lasiurus blossevillii* do not have in common, according to Table 1. Since the question asks for the trait that is **not** shared, eliminate traits that **are** shared. Both *Lasiurus cinereus* and *Lasiurus blossevillii* appear in Step 6 of Table 1. To get to Step 6, the choice in Step 1 must be ears *shorter than 25 mm.* Therefore, both of these bats could have *20 mm long ears;* eliminate (J). Neither bat could have *35 mm long ears,* because it is not possible to get from the *longer than 25 mm* choice in Step 1 to Step 6. Keep (G) because *Lasiurus cinereus* and *Lasiurus blossevillii* do not have this trait in common. Ear separation is listed in Step 3, but no decision on this trait is required for the identification of either *Lasiurus cinereus* or *Lasiurus blossevillii,* so they could both have *ears not separated at the base;* eliminate (F). To get to Step 6, the

choice in Step 5 must be a *heavily furred* uropatagium, so both bats must have that characteristic; eliminate (H). The correct answer is (G).

13. **D** The question asks for the bat that is *most genetically similar to Bat II,* according to Table 1. In Table 1, circle the names of the bats in the answer choices, and check their characteristics against those given for Bat II in Table 2. *Idionycteris phyllotis* appears in Step 4, as a result of choosing *well-defined skin glands.* Since Bat II has *ill-defined skin glands,* eliminate (B). Both *Lasionycteris noctivagans* and *Lasiurus blossevillii* appear in Step 6 of Table 2. All characteristics of those two bats up to Step 6 must be the same, and neither of those bats has the same *fur color* as Bat II, which means that neither of those bats could be *more genetically similar* to Bat II than the other; eliminate (A) and (C). *Myotis volans* appears in Step 9 of Table 1. To get to Step 9, a bat must have ears *shorter than 25 mm* from Step 1, a *not heavily furred uropatagium* from Step 5, and a *>6 mm and straight* tragus from Step 8. Bat II has all these characteristics, so it is *genetically similar* to *Myotis volans.* The correct answer is (D).

Passage III

14. **F** The question asks whether there would be any pepsin activity if Trial 10 were repeated without anserine. Trial 10 has high pepsin activity, but Table 2 does not give any information about *anserine.* The passage indicates that all trials in Table 2 were prepared *according to the same procedure as Trial 3,* so look at Trial 3. In Trial 3, equal amounts of casein and anserine were used, the temperature was 40°C, and the pepsin activity was high. Look at the trials listed in the answer choices to help answer this question. In Trial 4, anserine was eliminated from the reaction while the temperature remained constant, and the pepsin activity remained high. This indicates that at 40°C, the activity of pepsin is unaffected by the addition of anserine; eliminate (H) and (J). Trial 6 is not relevant to this question, because it removes casein as well as anserine, which is not what the question specifies; eliminate (G). The correct answer is (F).

15. **C** The question asks in which organ *pepsin is most likely to be found.* Look for the key word *pepsin* in the passage. Paragraph 1 states that *pepsin is an enzyme in humans that catalyzes the digestion.* Eliminate (A), (B), and (D) because those organs are not found in the digestive system. The correct answer is (C).

16. **F** The question asks what the pH of a *buffer solution* would most likely be if *another trial had been performed in Experiment 2, and the results showed a high level of pepsin activity.* Look at the results of Experiment 2, found in Table 2, which show that lower pH values coincide with a *high level of pepsin activity.* A pH value of 4.0 or higher is associated with *low activity;* eliminate (G), (H), and (J). The correct answer is (F).

17. **C** The question asks for the reason that *Trial 5 shows no pepsin activity,* while *Trials 3 and 4 show high levels of pepsin activity.* Look at Trials 3–5 in Table 1. Because the answer choices are based on *casein* and *anserine,* look at those columns in Table 1. *Casein* is present in Trials 3 and 4 but not

in Trial 5, so its absence could explain the lack of pepsin activity in Trial 5. Use this knowledge to eliminate (D). *Anserine* is present in Trials 3 and 5 but not in Trial 4, so its presence could not provide the explanation for why Trial 3 and Trial 4 have high levels of pepsin activity. Use this knowledge to eliminate (A) and (B). The correct answer is (C).

18. **H** The question asks which *trials are most likely to contain undigested casein,* according to the results of Experiment 1. Look at the results of Experiment 1, found in Table 1. Only Trials 1–4 and 7 used solutions that contained *casein,* so eliminate (G) and (J) because the solutions of Trials 5 and 6 did not contain *casein.* Paragraph 1 states that *pepsin is an enzyme in humans that catalyzes the digestion of proteins, like the milk protein casein.* Look at Table 1. In Trials 1 and 7 there was *no pepsin activity,* which means the *casein* did not get digested. In Trials 3 and 4, there was a *high* level of *pepsin activity,* which means *casein* did get digested; eliminate (F). The correct answer is (H).

19. **A** The question asks which trial's experimental conditions were most similar to those of Trial 3. Look at Table 1. The *pepsin activity* for Trial 3 is *high.* All of the trials listed in the answers are in Table 2, so look at Table 2. Only Trials 8–10 had *high pepsin activity.* Eliminate (B), (C), and (D) because they had either *low activity* or *no activity* at all. The correct answer is (A).

20. **G** The question asks for an explanation of *the relationship between pepsin activity, pH, and temperature,* according to the results of Experiments 1 and 2. Check the answer choices against the results found in Tables 1 and 2. Since each answer choice compares pH to the rate of pepsin digestion, examine Table 2. As pH increases, pepsin activity decreases. Therefore, pepsin digests at the fastest rate at low pHs. Eliminate (F) and (H). Refer to Table 1 to examine the relationship between pepsin activity and temperature. Choice (J) indicates that pepsin rate would be the fastest at 30°C; however, there was no pepsin activity in Trial 1. Eliminate (J). The correct answer is (G).

Passage IV

21. **C** The question asks for the figures in which at *least one sample fluid had a viscosity greater than 1.0 cP at a temperature of 0°C.* Look at Figure 1. At 0°C, four *sample fluid[s] have a viscosity greater than 1.0 cP.* Eliminate (B) because it doesn't include Figure 1. Look at Figure 2. At 0°C, all four *sample fluid[s] have a viscosity greater than 1.0 cP.* Eliminate (A) because it doesn't include Figure 2. Look at Figure 3. At 0°C, no *sample fluid[s] have a viscosity greater than 1.0 cP;* eliminate (D) because it includes this sample. The correct answer is (C).

22. **F** The question asks for the interval of *temperature change* that had *the greatest decrease in fluid viscosity* for *the sample that contained nitrobenzene without Additive B,* according to Figure 2. Look at Figure 2 and locate the curve that represents the data regarding *nitrobenzene without Additive B.* From 0°C–10°C, there is a slightly more than 1.0 cP change in *viscosity.* From 10°C–20°C, there is about a 0.2 cP change in *viscosity;* eliminate (G) because this is less than the change in (F). From 30°C–40°C, there is a less than 0.1 cP change in *viscosity;* eliminate (H) because this is less than the change in (F). From 40°C–50°C, there is almost no change in *viscosity;* eliminate (J). The correct answer is (F).

23. **C** The question asks for the *viscosity* of water after it *was heated to reach a temperature of 70°C,* according to Figure 1. Look at Figure 1 and locate the curve that represents the data regarding water. At 70°C, the water had a *viscosity* of 0.4 cP. The correct answer is (C).

24. **G** The question asks for an explanation of the relationship between *temperature* and *the time required for the sample fluids to flow out of their containers,* according to Figure 2. Look at Figure 2. As *temperature* increases, *viscosity* decreases. Since Figure 2 does not show *time,* look for the word *time* in the passage. The passage says that *highly viscous fluids take more time to flow through a vessel than do low viscous fluids.* So, as *viscosity* increases, *the time required for the sample fluids to flow out of their containers* also increases. Therefore, as *temperature* increases, *the time required for the sample fluids to flow out of their containers* decreases. Eliminate (H) and (J) because they state that the time increased, which is the opposite relationship. Eliminate (F) because it erroneously states that as *temperature* increases, *viscosity* also increases. The correct answer is (G).

25. **D** The question asks whether *a solution of nitrobenzene treated with Additive A would have a lower viscosity at 60°C than would untreated diethyl ether at that same temperature,* according to the results in the figures. Look for *nitrobenzene treated with Additive A* in Figures 1–3. Since it has not been tested, the results of the figures cannot confirm the hypothesis put forth in the question stem. Eliminate (A) and (B) because they both state that the hypothesis is confirmed. Eliminate (C) because the hypothesis was not about *nitrobenzene treated with Additive B.* The correct answer is (D).

26. **H** The question asks which of the solutions listed would fill the beaker in Figure 4 to 50 mL in the shortest amount of time at a temperature of 10°C. The figures do not give any data about time, so look for the word *time* in the passage. According to the passage, fluids with a higher viscosity *take more time to flow through a vessel than do fluids with lower viscosities.* Therefore, the fluid with the lowest viscosity at 10°C will fill the beaker in the shortest amount of time. Choice (F), diethyl ether, is shown in Figure 1 and has a viscosity of about 0.3 cP at 10°C. Choice (G), nitrobenzene, is also shown in Figure 1 and has a viscosity of about 0.8 cP at 10°C. Eliminate (G) because it has a higher viscosity than (F) does. Choice (H), diethyl ether + Additive A, is shown in Figure 3 and has a viscosity of about 0.15 cP at 10°C. This is lower than diethyl ether alone, so eliminate (F). Choice (J), nitrobenzene + Additive B, is shown in Figure 2 and has a viscosity of about 1.8 cP at 10°C. This is higher than diethyl ether + Additive A so eliminate (J). The correct answer is (H).

Passage V

27. **B** The question asks for the *independent (manipulated) variable* across all 3 studies and within each individual study. Read the descriptions of each study to determine what was changed, or manipulated, *across all 3 studies.* Study 1 used a sound source of 60 dB, Study 2 used a sound source of 80 dB, and Study 3 used a sound source of 100 dB. Therefore, *sound intensity* was varied across all 3 studies; eliminate (A) and (C). *Within each study,* the type of wave that was produced was measured by the experimental conditions. This is the result of the experiment and not a manipulated variable, so

eliminate (D). Each study varied the density of the ground from 1,000–2,000 g/km^3, so this is the independent variable within each study. The correct answer is (B).

28. **G** The question asks what happens to *the type of wave observed* as the *distance from the epicenter increases from 0 to 3 m* in Study 2. The *y*-axis in Figure 3 shows ground densities between 1,000 to 2,000 kg/m^3, so look at the entire graph. As the distance from the epicenter increases from 0 m to 3 m, the wave type changes from strong (black) to moderate (dark grey). The correct answer is (G).

29. **B** The question asks which statement is true regarding *the maximum distance from the epicenter for strong wave propagation and maximum distance for moderate wave propagation,* according to the results of Studies 2 and 3. Check each answer choice against the information found in Figures 3 and 4. Eliminate (A), (C), and (D) because *the maximum distance from the epicenter for strong wave propagation* is always less than the *maximum distance for moderate wave propagation.* Keep (B) because it states this relationship. The correct answer is (B).

30. **J** The question asks which *factors in the seismologist's studies* were *NOT directly controlled.* Since the question asks for the factors that were *NOT* controlled, eliminate factors that **were** controlled. Because there is no information in the figures about which factors were controlled, look for the word *controlled* in the text. Paragraph 2 states that *propagation duration was held constant in the experiment;* eliminate (H). Additionally, the paragraph states that *the procedure was repeated at various densities of earth and clay,* which means that the seismologist controlled the density within each trial. Eliminate (G). It also states that *seismometers were positioned to detect the type of waves,* which means *wave type* was not being controlled; keep (J). Paragraph 3 states that *the sound source was adjusted to 60 dB,* meaning the seismologist was controlling the sound intensity; eliminate (F). The correct answer is (J).

31. **D** The question asks whether *the relative wavelengths of a moderate wave and a weak wave would be less than 100 cm,* according to Figure 1. Look at Figure 1. A wavelength is the distance from the crest of one wave to the crest of the next. The *relative wavelength* of the moderate wave is about 150 cm and that of the weak wave is even longer. So, neither type of wave has a wavelength of less than 100 cm. Eliminate (A), (B), and (C). The correct answer is (D).

32. **J** The question asks which wave types would be included in the *waveform plot* if Study 1 *were repeated using a sound intensity of 70 dB,* according to the passage. There is no information about *dB* in the figures, so look for *dB* in the text of the passage. The description of each study indicates the dB level at which each was performed. Study 1 was done at *60 dB,* and Study 2 was done at *80 dB.* Since all three wave types were present in both Study 1 and Study 2, all three would also be present at 70 dB, which falls between the levels in those studies. The correct answer is (J).

33. **A** The question asks for the likely distance from the epicenter when *a study was conducted using a sound intensity between 75 dB and 85 dB,* based on information in the passage. There is no information about *dB* in the figures, so look for *dB* in the text of the passage. The description of each study indicates the dB level at which each was performed. Study 2 was done at *80 dB,* so look at Figure 3 and

use the data as a comparison. Strong waves begin between 1.8 and 2.3 m from the epicenter depending upon the ground density, so the distance should be less than 2.5 cm. The correct answer is (A).

Passage VI

34. **G** The question asks how *the concentration of dissolved particles in Solution 4 compares with the concentration of dissolved particles in Solution 2,* based on the results of Table 1. Look at Table 1. Solution 4 has 3 *dissolved charged particles,* while Solution 2 has only 1 *dissolved neutral particle.* Eliminate (F) and (H) because they state the opposite of this. Now compare the respective freezing point of each solution. The freezing point of Solution 2 was –1.9°C, while the freezing point for Solution 4 was lower at –5.7°C; eliminate (J). The correct answer is (G).

35. **A** The question asks which scientist's explanation is in disagreement with the following observation: *the freezing point of benzene is lowered with the addition of the solute naphthalene* ($C_{10}H_8$)*, which has no charge.* Look at Scientist 1's explanation in paragraph 4. It states that a *decrease in freezing point is related only to the charge of the solute particles.* This disagrees with the observation in the question stem, so eliminate (C) and (D). Eliminate (B) because it erroneously states that Scientist 1 believes that ***any*** *solute is capable of increasing the stability of the liquid phase of a solvent.* The correct answer is (A).

36. **F** The question asks which statements both Scientists 1 and 2 would agree with. Check each answer choice against the information in the passage. Look at Scientist 1's explanation in paragraph 4. It states that a *decrease in freezing point is related only to the charge of the solute particles;* eliminate (H) because it states that *no charge will decrease the liquid's freezing point.* Eliminate (G) and (J) because they mention *increase* in a liquid's freezing point and neither scientist discussed this. The correct answer is (F).

37. **A** The question asks which scientist's position would be supported by the following finding: *an experiment showed that adding the positively charged solute* $NaClO_4$ *to the solvent* H_2O *but holding the concentration of the solvent constant, the freezing point was significantly lower than an equally concentrated uncharged solution of* $NaClO_4$ *in pure* H_2O*.* Look at Scientist 1's explanation in paragraph 4. It states that a *decrease in freezing point is related only to the charge of the solute particles.* This is consistent with the finding in the question stem, so eliminate (B) and (D) because they do not include Scientist 1. Look at Scientist 2's explanation in paragraph 5. It states that a *decrease in freezing point is related only to the concentration of particles.* The experiment in the question stem holds the concentration of the particles constant, so eliminate (C). The correct answer is (A).

38. **G** The question asks which diagram *best illustrates how Scientist 1 would describe the results after a charged solute has been added to* H_2O*.* Look at Scientist 1's explanation in paragraph 4, which states, *when a solute is added the...charge...interferes with the orderly arrangement of solvent molecules.* Eliminate (F), (H), and (J) because they all show *orderly arrangements of the solvent molecules.* Choice (G) has no order to the arrangement of molecules. The correct answer is (G).

39. **A** The question asks whether *the scientists offer different explanations for the impact of a solute's physical properties, such as solute charge, on the decrease in freezing point of a solution.* Look at Scientist 1's explanation in paragraph 4. It states that a *decrease in freezing point is related only to the charge of the solute particles,* so Scientist 1 does discuss the *impact of...charge on the decrease in freezing point.* Eliminate (B) and (D) because they say that Scientist 1 does not say such properties have an impact. Look at Scientist 2's explanation in paragraph 5. It states that a *decrease in freezing point is related only to the concentration of particles, not to the identity or properties of each individual particle.* Since Scientist 2 disagrees that physical properties play a role in decreasing freezing point, eliminate (C). The correct answer is (A).

40. **J** The question asks which equation *is most consistent with Scientist 2's explanation,* assuming that *k is a constant, ΔT is the decrease in freezing point, and i is the van 't Hoff factor.* Look for the key words *van 't Hoff factor* in Scientist 2's explanation. Scientist 2 states that *the size of the decrease in freezing point is in direct proportion with the van 't Hoff factor.* Eliminate (F) and (H) because they both show inverse proportions. Eliminate (G) because it shows a direct proportion with the square of the van 't Hoff factor. Choice (J) shows a direct proportion between the decrease in freezing point and the van 't Hoff factor. The correct answer is (J).

WRITING TEST

Essay Checklist

- ❒ Clearly state your own perspective.
- ❒ Reference the ideas of all 3 perspectives.
- ❒ Use examples to explain your point of view.
- ❒ Have 2–3 body paragraphs with 5–7 sentences each.
- ❒ Have an introduction and a conclusion paragraph.
- ❒ Write neatly.
- ❒ Use a formal tone and a mature level of vocabulary.
- ❒ Avoid spelling and grammar errors.

Test 3

Please turn to page 759 to find the bubble sheet for this test.

ENGLISH TEST

45 Minutes—75 Questions

DIRECTIONS: In the five passages that follow, certain words and phrases are underlined and numbered. In the right-hand column, you will find alternatives for each underlined part. In most cases, you are to choose the one that best expresses the idea, makes the statement appropriate for standard written English, or is worded most consistently with the style and tone of the passage as a whole. If you think the original version is best, choose "NO CHANGE." In some cases, you will find in the right-hand column a question about the underlined part. You are to choose the best answer to the question.

You will also find questions about a section of the passage or the passage as a whole. These questions do not refer to an underlined portion of the passage but rather are identified by a number or numbers in a box.

For each question, choose the alternative you consider best and blacken the corresponding oval on your answer document. Read each passage through once before you begin to answer the questions that accompany it. For many of the questions, you must read several sentences beyond the question to determine the answer. Be sure that you have read far enough ahead each time you choose an alternative.

Passage I

Roast Done Right

Just like being the artist[1] sculpting the *Venus de Milo* or painting the Sistine Chapel, preparing a delicious meal is an art. Even the seemingly mundane pot roast can be a true masterpiece. Nothing can be more rewarding to a cook than the sign[2] of a roast done right.

Cooking a delicious roast with vegetables require[3] three things: the freshest ingredients, a slow-cooker, and good timing. My friend Eric goes to the butcher shop just after[4] its 5 A.M. delivery to snatch up the best cuts of meat, then heads to the local farmer's market. He fills his canvas shopping bag with ripe red tomatoes, crisp yellow onions, and thick russet potatoes. The tastiest vegetables are the results of natural sunshine and of a farmer's[5] careful tending.

1. A. NO CHANGE
   B. the artist
   C. one
   D. DELETE the underlined portion.

2. The writer would like to convey the distinct scent of a properly cooked roast. Given that all the choices are true, which best accomplishes the writer's goal?
   F. NO CHANGE
   G. the swirling rush of robust aromas
   H. the fine textures of vegetables and meats
   J. the diners' eager expectation

3. A. NO CHANGE
   B. has the requirements of
   C. requiring
   D. requires

4. Which of the following would be the LEAST acceptable alternative for the underlined portion?
   F. out to the butcher shop right before
   G. into the butcher shop just around
   H. at the butcher shop right after
   J. to the butcher shop close to

5. A. NO CHANGE
   B. sunshine, of which a farmer is
   C. sunshine, and a farmer is
   D. sunshine, which is a farmer's

GO ON TO THE NEXT PAGE.

With supplies in tote, Eric heads to the kitchen. While the beef marinates in garlic and spices, he chops the colorful array of fresh vegetables. Eric slowly places the vegetables (6) around the meat in the slow-cooker's pot, he alternates (7) rings of bright orange carrots and chunks of red potatoes. He sprinkles in sliced onions and herbs until the ingredients nearly spill over the top. Like many others, (8) Eric has a secret, final ingredient: a splash of red wine for flavor.

At this point, (9) it's time to cram the lid onto the heaping potful of ingredients and turn on the cooker. The temperature inside the pot rises slowly as the contents stew (10) in their natural juices. The roast will take six to eight hours to cook, but after an hour or two, the first spicy scents start wafting through the kitchen. (11) A few hours later, the rich, juicy smell of beef begins to escape. Every half hour, using a long, meat thermometer (12) Eric reads the temperature of the roast and carefully examines the stewing contents. He doesn't want it overcooked or undercooked, but

6. The writer wishes to emphasize Eric's attention to detail in making his pot roast. Given that all the choices are true, which one best accomplishes the writer's goal?
   - **F.** NO CHANGE
   - **G.** is very careful when pouring the vegetables
   - **H.** meticulously layers the finely cut vegetables
   - **J.** arranges the vegetables in a kind of order

7. **A.** NO CHANGE
   - **B.** he has alternated
   - **C.** alternates
   - **D.** alternating

8. **F.** NO CHANGE
   - **G.** Like many cooks,
   - **H.** Similar to others,
   - **J.** Just like those others,

9. Which of the following alternatives to the underlined portion would be LEAST acceptable?
   - **A.** Next,
   - **B.** After that,
   - **C.** Now,
   - **D.** At least,

10. Given that all the choices are true, which one provides the most specific sensory detail and maintains the style and tone of the essay?
    - **F.** NO CHANGE
    - **G.** rises slowly but surely, stewing
    - **H.** rises slowly to a lazy, bubbling boil, stewing the savory contents
    - **J.** increases to about 200 degrees Fahrenheit to stew the contents

11. **A.** NO CHANGE
    - **B.** drifting through the air to make the whole kitchen smell.
    - **C.** wafting and floating through the whole kitchen.
    - **D.** wafting through the air of the kitchen.

12. **F.** NO CHANGE
    - **G.** half hour, using a long meat thermometer,
    - **H.** half hour using a long meat thermometer
    - **J.** half hour, using a long meat thermometer;

GO ON TO THE NEXT PAGE.

"just right." [13]

13. The writer is considering deleting the preceding sentence. Should it be kept or deleted?

A. Kept, because it provides a reason for Eric's diligent attention to the temperature.
B. Kept, because it reinforces that roasts are typically done cooking after 8 hours.
C. Deleted, because it puts the focus on Eric and his cooking, rather than the roast.
D. Deleted, because it doesn't provide enough information about temperature's effects on the roast.

Lift[14] the finished roast out of the pot to serve, the tender meat plops juicily onto our plates in generous servings. He tops it off with zesty, steaming vegetables. Eric is obviously proud to share his work of art, and his friends are more than willing to eat it, this masterpiece of his.[15]

14. F. NO CHANGE
G. As he lifts
H. When you lift
J. Lifting

15. A. NO CHANGE
B. ready for us to eat.
C. a masterpiece.
D. DELETE the underlined portion, replacing the comma with a period after "it."

Passage II

Growing Up On a Farm

Back in middle school, I went to live with my mother for two years on her farm. Whenever people hear that I lived on a farm, they immediately conjure up an image visualized in their minds[16] of dairy cows, tractors, hay, and overalls. Nothing could be further from the truth.

16. F. NO CHANGE
G. assuming that they know what it was like
H. of my life on the farm that consists
J. DELETE the underlined portion.

To start,[17] I wasn't on the kind of farm everyone imagines. I didn't feed cows or pigs;[18] I didn't grow corn or wheat. I helped my mother breed llamas.

17. Which of the following alternatives to the underlined portion would NOT be acceptable?

A. First of all,
B. To begin,
C. For start,
D. Firstly,

18. F. NO CHANGE
G. or, pigs
H. or pigs,
J. or pigs

[1] It is odd that such non-traditional livestock should be raised on a long-established farm such as ours, which has been

GO ON TO THE NEXT PAGE.

in the family for generations. [19] [2] Our family did indeed grow field crops, harvest orchards, and raise traditional livestock for many decades. [3] He must of learned that wool from llamas (20) was more profitable than wool from sheep. [4] The llama wool business turned out to be so successful in fact, that (21) my great-grandfather converted the family business to a full-fledged llama farm. [22]

Before I began to live (23) on the farm, I had held naive illusions of rural life. What could possibly be easier than feeding and grooming some animals? After I (24) had settled into my new home, however, I realized that farm work was much more

19. The writer is considering deleting the phrase "which has been in the family for generations" (and ending the sentence with a period) from the preceding sentence. If the writer were to make this change, the essay would primarily lose:

A. evidence of a broken relationship between the narrator and his mother.
B. a transition into the discussion of traditional farm practices.
C. a detail that reinforces the longevity of the family farm.
D. an indication of what will eventually happen to the narrator.

20. **F.** NO CHANGE
G. of learned of
H. have learned that
J. have learned about

21. **A.** NO CHANGE
B. successful, in fact, that
C. successful, in fact that
D. successful in fact that

22. Upon reviewing this paragraph and realizing that some information has been left out, the writer composes the following sentence:

> Then, fifty years ago, my great-grandfather decided to buy a llama.

This sentence should most logically be placed after Sentence:

F. 1.
G. 2.
H. 3.
J. 4.

23. Which of the following alternatives to the underlined portion would NOT be acceptable?

A. started to live
B. began living
C. went to live
D. begun to live

24. Which of the following alternatives to the underlined portion would NOT be acceptable?

F. As soon as I
G. When I
H. Once I
J. I

GO ON TO THE NEXT PAGE.

involved than I <u>had expected.</u> [25] Collecting manure, for example, doesn't seem so bad when someone else does it on TV, but I had to get up before dawn every day to finish that chore before catching the bus to school.

<u>School in the country was also not what I had expected.</u> [26] The school I attended had twenty students total: that's from first to twelfth grade, and I was the only student in my grade.

We had one teacher who would occasionally <u>educate us on a specific academic study and methods of learning,</u> [27] but most of my learning came from <u>studying textbooks on my own.</u> [28]

I don't mean to say that my life on the farm was a bad experience. I learned a lot about myself: for example, I'm not a morning person. I also learned about <u>llama's habits,</u> [29] such as spitting when they are unhappy. Most importantly, my mother and I got to spend a lot of time together during those years, for which I'm so grateful. Although I doubt I'll pursue a <u>career as</u> [30] farming, I look forward to returning to the family farm for short visits.

25. **A.** NO CHANGE
B. would expect.
C. would be expecting.
D. have expected.

26. Given that all the choices are true, which one most effectively introduces the information that follows in this paragraph?

F. NO CHANGE
G. Farming is a full-time job, taking up your entire day.
H. Llamas can grow to be six feet tall.
J. Life on the farm was tough but worthwhile.

27. **A.** NO CHANGE
B. verbally acknowledge how well the class was working for us,
C. tell us how to learn about a specific academic study,
D. lecture about a specific topic,

28. Which choice provides the most specific and precise information?

F. NO CHANGE
G. studying.
H. other things.
J. reading by myself.

29. **A.** NO CHANGE
B. llamas' habits,
C. llamas habits
D. llamas habits,

30. **F.** NO CHANGE
G. career of
H. career in
J. careers of

GO ON TO THE NEXT PAGE.

Passage III

The following paragraphs may or may not be in the most logical order. Each paragraph is numbered in brackets, and question 45 will ask you to choose where Paragraph 2 should most logically be placed.

Conjuring a Prophetic Literary Career

[1]

Born in Ohio in 1858, Charles W. Chesnutt was an author and essayist whom,^31 during the Reconstruction era, spent much of his youth in North Carolina. Though his parents were free African-Americans, Chesnutt felt intensely the struggles of African-Americans in the United States in the period directly after the Civil War. [32] Amid all the turmoil of the South of his boyhood, Chesnutt took solace in literature, and he^33 had already decided, in his teens, that he would become a writer.

[2]

Although Chesnutt continues^34 to write until his death in 1932, it had become as clear as day^35 that the work he completed after *The House Behind the Cedars* and *The Marrow of Tradition* (1901) had become too inflammatory to a society ever uneasy about the topic of race relations in the United States, particularly when authors had brought these problems as close to the surface as Chesnutt had. In recent years, however, Chesnutt's reputation has been restored and he has been treated as the pioneer that he most certainly was. Today, as much as in the late nineteenth century, Chesnutt's works provide us with a

31. A. NO CHANGE
B. who,
C. which,
D. DELETE the underlined portion.

32. If the writer were to delete the last part of the preceding sentence (ending the sentence with a period after the word *States*), the paragraph would primarily lose:
F. a direct link to the following paragraph.
G. an unnecessary digression into historical details.
H. an important detail about the period of Chesnutt's youth.
J. a fact suggesting the extent of Chesnutt's historical writing.

33. Which of the following alternatives to the underlined portion would NOT be acceptable?
A. literature; he
B. literature, and he consequently
C. literature, he
D. literature. He

34. F. NO CHANGE
G. has continued
H. still continues
J. continued

35. A. NO CHANGE
B. so extremely clear
C. clear
D. clear to an incredible degree

GO ON TO THE NEXT PAGE.

number of literary masterpieces and a powerful and prophetic vision of race relations in the United States.

[3]

"The Goophered Grapevine," published in 1887 in *The Atlantic*, was Chesnutt's first major literary success, and this success encouraged Chesnutt to publish additional tales, which were eventually collected in *The Conjure Woman* (1899). *The Conjure Woman* was written in the tradition of earlier folklorists <u>from a previous era</u> [36] Joel Chandler Harris and Thomas Nelson <u>Page. However,</u> [37] it presented a much more frank treatment of race relations in the South during slavery and Reconstruction. [38] *The Conjure Woman* and <u>it's</u> [39] narrator, Uncle Julius McAdoo, were clearly written in response to the immensely popular Uncle Remus of Harris's tales, but the similarities between the two authors' works ended

36. F. NO CHANGE
 G. from a previous time
 H. from the years before
 J. DELETE the underlined portion.

37. A. NO CHANGE
 B. Page, however,
 C. Page. Consequently,
 D. Page, consequently,

38. At this point, the writer is considering adding the following true statement:

 The slaves were freed with the Emancipation Proclamation in 1862, but many conditions like those under slavery resurfaced after the collapse of Reconstruction efforts in 1877.

 Should the writer add the sentence here?

 F. Yes, because it shows how many of the gains made by ex-slaves were later taken away.
 G. Yes, because it is necessary to understand Chestnutt's motivation.
 H. No, because it provides information that is detailed later in this essay.
 J. No, because it would distract readers from the essay's main focus.

39. A. NO CHANGE
 B. their
 C. its
 D. its'

GO ON TO THE NEXT PAGE.

there. While Harris's tales used mostly animals and not voodoo, conjure, and the injustices of slavery, which *The Conjure Woman* did, also incorporating human characters instead of Brer Rabbit and animals. 40

[4]

Chesnutt's true masterpiece, however, is *The House Behind the Cedars*. The novel details the lives of an African-American familys 41 children who have chosen to "pass" as white, making *The House Behind the Cedars* one of the first novels to talk about racial passing. 42 Chesnutt uses his characters' divided status to travel back and forth between the black and white worlds of the South, and in the process, Chesnutt manages to show both the shocking disparity between the two worlds and the insurmountable difficulties his characters, and those who "pass" in real life, face. From the moment it was published in 1900, 43 the novel was a sensation in American letters, garnering the respect and admiration of such prominent white literary critics as William Dean Howells and black intellectuals such as W.E.B. Dubois.

40. Which choice provides the most logical arrangement of the parts of this sentence?

F. NO CHANGE
G. Humans were used as characters by *The Conjure Woman* and participated in tales relating to conjure, and the injustice of slavery and voodoo, which was different from Brer Rabbit and the animals from Harris's tales.
H. Conjure, voodoo, and the injustices of slavery and others were used by *The Conjure Woman*, along with real human characters instead of animals and Brer Rabbit from Harris's tales.
J. In the place of Brer Rabbit and the animals from Harris's tales, *The Conjure Woman* used human characters in stories that incorporated conjure, voodoo, and the injustices of slavery.

41. A. NO CHANGE
B. families
C. family's
D. families's

42. F. NO CHANGE
G. it.
H. them.
J. its topics.

43. Which of the following alternatives to the underlined portion would NOT be acceptable?

A. From the moment of its publication in 1900,
B. Having been first published in 1900,
C. Publishing it first in 1900,
D. In 1900, the year of its initial publication,

GO ON TO THE NEXT PAGE.

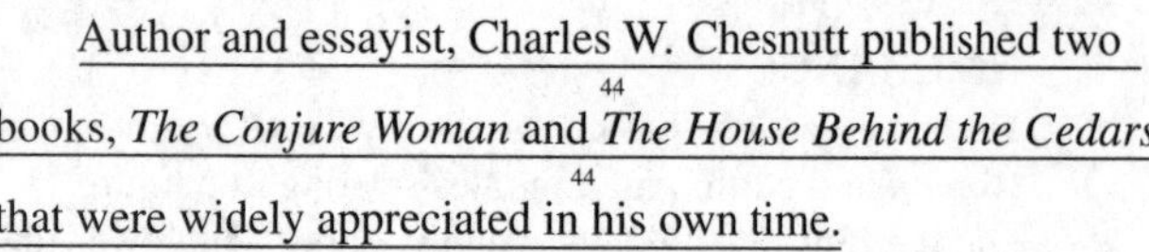

[5]

Author and essayist, Charles W. Chesnutt published two books, *The Conjure Woman* and *The House Behind the Cedars*, that were widely appreciated in his own time.

44. Given that all the choices are true, which one most effectively concludes and summarizes this essay?
F. NO CHANGE
G. Both author and essayist, Charles W. Chesnutt was a pioneer in African-American literature whose novels and tales are as meaningful today as they were when first published.
H. Author of *The House Behind the Cedars*, Charles W. Chesnutt already knew he wanted to be a writer in his teens during the era of Reconstruction in the history of the United States.
J. Author of *The Conjure Woman*, Charles W. Chesnutt succeeded where earlier writers Joel Chandler Harris and Thomas Nelson Page had failed in representing the characters in their stories as people.

Question 45 asks about the preceding passage as a whole.

45. For the sake of the logic and coherence of this essay, Paragraph 2 should be placed:
A. where it is now.
B. before Paragraph 1.
C. after Paragraph 3.
D. after Paragraph 4.

Passage IV

Jackie Robinson: More Than a Ballplayer

When baseball resumes in America every spring, one April day is always reserved to honor Jackie Robinson, the man who broke the color barrier of America's national pastime. While his accomplishments on the baseball field was numerous and impressive, his civil rights activism was according to his widow Rachel Robinson, equally important and often overlooked without being noticed.

46. F. NO CHANGE
G. is
H. will be
J. were

47. A. NO CHANGE
B. was, according,
C. was, according
D. was—according

48. F. NO CHANGE
G. while not being noticed.
H. as no one notices.
J. DELETE the underlined portion and end the sentence with a period.

GO ON TO THE NEXT PAGE.

The tenacious and spirited way for the Brooklyn Dodgers [49] Jackie Robinson played baseball was a reflection of his focus on civil rights. From the outset of the "Great Experiment" of having African-Americans in baseball; he knew that his [50] performance on the field would be a determining factor in sports segregation. Robinson gradually converted jeers and harassment into cheers and acceptance because white spectators [51] could see his immense talent from any seat in the stadium. Robinson became a highly respected figure by continually succeeding on and off the field, all the while displaying stoic restraint in the face of initial prejudice. [52]

49. The best placement for the underlined portion would be:
A. where it is now.
B. after the word *baseball.*
C. after the word *focus.*
D. after the word *rights.*

50. F. NO CHANGE
G. baseball, and he
H. baseball. He
J. baseball, he

51. Which choice fits most specifically with the information at the end of this sentence?
A. NO CHANGE
B. people
C. popcorn vendors
D. pitchers

52. If the writer were to delete this paragraph from the essay, which of the following would be lost?
F. A scientific explanation of the "Great Experiment"
G. A description of the way Robinson influenced society's outlook on segregation in baseball
H. A passionate plea to end prejudice around the world
J. A comment on why the Brooklyn Dodgers were the best team in baseball

[1] The vast amount of energy Robinson expended avoiding a myriad of potential pitfalls could have caused an ordinary man to wilt; for example, [53] Robinson instinctively and relentlessly increased his efforts for positive civil rights changes, both in his sport and in the African-American community at large.

[2] While many athletes today use their [54] status to garner endorsements and live as celebrities, Robinson constantly utilized his

53. A. NO CHANGE
B. as a result,
C. rather,
D. therefore,

54. F. NO CHANGE
G. his
H. its
J. theirs

GO ON TO THE NEXT PAGE.

status to stimulate civil rights advancements. [55] [3] He often used his baseball travels as opportunities to speak publicly to blacks in U.S. cities about ending segregation and vigilantly defending their rights. [4] Post-baseball, Robinson became an entrepreneur, but his focus did not stray as he found time to write impassioned letters and telegrams to various U.S. presidents during the civil rights movement. [5] He had the status to demand that they too remain firmly focused on civil rights measures. [57]

Though Jackie Robinson's baseball exploits may be most widely known than his tireless efforts in the civil rights movement his astonishing courage on the baseball field was itself a resounding stance against segregation and inequality. His numerous detractors consistently found that not only was Robinson undeterred, but he was excelling in his efforts. As a result, the spark of positive change was ignited. Robinson turned that spark for civil rights into a torch and carried it his entire life.

55. The writer is considering deleting the preceding sentence. Should this sentence be kept or deleted?

- **A.** Kept, because it describes important information about Jackie Robinson's endorsement deals.
- **B.** Kept, because it helps the reader understand how Jackie Robinson sacrificed personal advancement in favor of civil rights work.
- **C.** Deleted, because it doesn't provide exact details about the civil rights laws that Jackie Robinson enacted.
- **D.** Deleted, because it draws focus toward other athletes and away from Jackie Robinson.

56.
- **F.** NO CHANGE
- **G.** entrepreneur,
- **H.** entrepreneur
- **J.** entrepreneur; and

57. If the writer were to divide the preceding paragraph into two shorter paragraphs in order to differentiate between Robinson's civil rights activism during and after his baseball career, the new paragraph should begin with Sentence:

- **A.** 2.
- **B.** 3.
- **C.** 4.
- **D.** 5.

58.
- **F.** NO CHANGE
- **G.** very widely
- **H.** more widely
- **J.** widelier

59.
- **A.** NO CHANGE
- **B.** movement. His
- **C.** movement; his
- **D.** movement, his

60. Which of the following alternatives to the underlined portion would be LEAST acceptable?

- **F.** Consequently,
- **G.** Instead,
- **H.** Thus,
- **J.** Therefore,

GO ON TO THE NEXT PAGE.

Passage V

Antarctica's Adaptable Survivors

Many inhabit sporadic green patches of moss; fertilized by excrement from migrating birds and sheltered by the rocky mountainsides. Some hibernate in the winter, frozen in ice under rocks and stones, becoming active again when the climate warms and the ice is melting. Extreme cold and wind are all good to go for survival; indeed, some species are able to endure temperatures as low as –30 degrees Celsius. These adaptable invertebrates classified as arthropods; are able to survive on a continent once thought to arctic, to windy, and to icy, to maintain any permanent land animals. The coldest place on Earth, Antarctica is home to great quantities of life that don't simply tolerate the lower temperatures; they flourish in them.

Microscopic mites, springtails, and wingless midges accompanied lice and ticks as the most prevalent permanent land fauna on Antarctica. The tiny midges and mites tolerate the cold due to the antifreeze liquid they carry in their bodies. Parasitic lice and ticks seek shelter from the harsh climate in the

61. A. NO CHANGE
B. patches, of moss
C. patches, of moss,
D. patches of moss

62. Which of the following options to the underlined portion would NOT be acceptable?
F. stones, only to become active
G. stones. Becoming active
H. stones. Then they become active
J. stones, and then become active

63. A. NO CHANGE
B. melting.
C. melts.
D. to melt.

64. F. NO CHANGE
G. cool
H. all right
J. suitable

65. A. NO CHANGE
B. invertebrates, classified as arthropods
C. invertebrates, classified as arthropods,
D. invertebrates classified as arthropods,

66. F. NO CHANGE
G. to arctic, to windy, and to icy
H. too arctic, too windy, and too icy
J. too, arctic, too windy, and too icy,

67. Which of the following options to the underlined portion would NOT be acceptable?
A. temperatures they
B. temperatures; in fact, they
C. temperatures. They
D. temperatures—they

68. F. NO CHANGE
G. accompany
H. had accompanied
J. were accompanying

GO ON TO THE NEXT PAGE.

warm fur of seals, the waters of Antarctica teeming with marine life,[69] and the feathers of sea birds and penguins.

In the Dry Valleys located on the western coast of McMurdo Sound in Antarctica, nematode worms feed on bacteria, algae, and tiny organisms known as rotifers and tardigrades. [70] Here, ice-covered land is not as abundant.[71] Beneath the moss-covered polar rock, nematodes thrive, coping ingeniously by dehydrating themselves in the winter with the low temperatures[72] and coming back to life with the summer and increasing moisture.

69. A. NO CHANGE
B. seals, who return to land to breed,
C. seals, six different types in all,
D. seals

70. The writer is considering deleting the following phrase from the previous sentence (and adjusting the capitalization accordingly):

In the Dry Valleys located on the western coast of McMurdo Sound in Antarctica,

Should this phrase be kept or deleted?

F. Deleted, because this fact is presented later in this paragraph.
G. Deleted, because it negates the preceding paragraph, which makes it clear that only insects live in Antarctica.
H. Kept, because it clarifies that nematodes live both in Antarctica and McMurdo Sound.
J. Kept, because it gives specific details about the "Here" mentioned in the subsequent sentence.

71. Given that all the choices are true, which one most explicitly and vividly describes the terrain of McMurdo Sound?

A. NO CHANGE
B. rocky land is colored vibrantly by green, yellow, and orange lichen, algae, and moss.
C. there are signs that this is a place with extremely low humidity and no snow cover.
D. the effects of low humidity are apparent in the presence of flora and orange lichen.

72. The best place for the underlined portion would be:

F. where it is now.
G. after the word *thrive*.
H. after the word *coping*.
J. after the word *moisture*.

GO ON TO THE NEXT PAGE.

Algae are another resilient life form of the Dry Valleys of Antarctica.[73] In an effort to adjust to the strong winds and icy temperatures, some algae live inside the rocks as opposed to on top of them. Phytoplankton, the most common of Antarctica's algae, is an important food resource within Antarctica's ecosystem. These tiny free-floating plants are preyed upon by copepods and krill, which then provide food for fish, seals, whales, and penguins. [74]

73. Given that all the choices are true, which one would LEAST effectively introduce the subject of this paragraph?
   - **A.** NO CHANGE
   - **B.** Algae lack the various structures that characterize land plants, such as the moss and lichen that inhabit Antarctica, which is why algae are most prominent in bodies of water.
   - **C.** Algae are typically autotrophic organisms whose adaptive qualities enable them to live successfully in the Dry McMurdo Valleys.
   - **D.** Although most often found in water, algae also inhabit terrestrial environments such as the Dry Valleys of Antarctica.

74. The writer is considering deleting the following phrase from the preceding sentence:

   which then provide food for fish, seals, whales, and penguins.

   Should this clause be kept or deleted?
   - **F.** Kept, because it clarifies how phytoplankton support Antarctica's ecosystem.
   - **G.** Kept, because it addresses the most important life forms in Antarctica's waters: seals, penguins, and whales.
   - **H.** Deleted, because it is irrelevant to the passage as a whole, which addresses the smaller life forms living on Antarctica.
   - **J.** Deleted, because it misleads the reader into thinking that penguins, seals, and whales are among the permanent land dwelling life forms of Antarctica.

Excluding its aquatic life, Antarctica has a lower species diversity than any other place on Earth. Nevertheless,[75] Antarctica is a haven for 67 documented species of insects and 350 species of flora, proof that life persists in the most dramatic of conditions.

75.
   - **A.** NO CHANGE
   - **B.** Indeed,
   - **C.** Consequently,
   - **D.** Therefore,

END OF TEST 1

STOP! DO NOT TURN THE PAGE UNTIL TOLD TO DO SO.

MATHEMATICS TEST

60 Minutes—60 Questions

DIRECTIONS: Solve each problem, choose the correct answer, and then darken the corresponding oval on your answer document.

Do not linger over problems that take too much time. Solve as many as you can; then return to the others in the time you have left for this test.

You are permitted to use a calculator on this test. You may use your calculator for any problems you choose, but some of the problems may best be done without using a calculator.

Note: Unless otherwise stated, all of the following should be assumed:

1. Illustrative figures are NOT necessarily drawn to scale.
2. Geometric figures lie in a plane.
3. The word *line* indicates a straight line.
4. The word *average* indicates arithmetic mean.

DO YOUR FIGURING HERE.

1. $|8-5|-|5-8|=$?

A. -6
B. -5
C. -3
D. 0
E. 6

2. A science tutor charges $60 an hour to help students with biology homework. She also charges a flat fee of $40 to cover her transportation costs. How many hours of tutoring are included in a session that costs $220 ?

F. $2\frac{1}{5}$
G. 3
H. $3\frac{2}{3}$
J. 4
K. $5\frac{1}{2}$

3. Train A averages 16 miles per hour, and Train B averages 24 miles per hour. At these rates, how many more hours does it take Train A than Train B to go 1,152 miles?

A. 20
B. 24
C. 40
D. 48
E. 72

4. $33r^2-24r+75-41r^2+r$ is equivalent to:

F. $44r^2$
G. $44r^6$
H. $-8r^2-24r+75$
J. $-8r^4-23r^2+75$
K. $-8r^2-23r+75$

GO ON TO THE NEXT PAGE.

DO YOUR FIGURING HERE.

5. Six equilateral triangles form the figure below. If the perimeter of each individual triangle is 15 inches, what is the perimeter of *ABCDEF*, in inches?

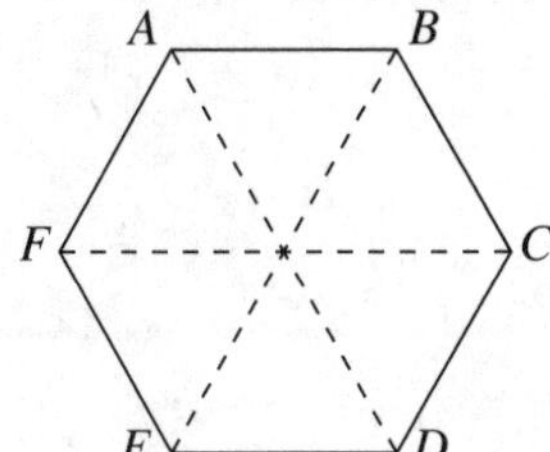

A. 18
B. 30
C. 60
D. $54\sqrt{3}$
E. 90

6. The expression $(5x + 2)(x - 3)$ is equivalent to:

F. $5x^2 + 13x - 6$
G. $5x^2 - 13x - 6$
H. $5x^2 - 4x + 5$
J. $5x^2 - 6$
K. $5x^2 - 5$

7. If 35% of a given number is 14, then what is 20% of the given number?

A. 2.8
B. 4.9
C. 7.0
D. 7.7
E. 8.0

8. The 7 consecutive integers below add up to 511,
$x - 2, x - 1, x, x + 1, x + 2, x + 3,$ and $x + 4$.
What is the value of x ?

F. 71
G. 72
H. 73
J. 74
K. 75

9. In the standard (x,y) coordinate plane, point B with coordinates of (5,6) is the midpoint of line $\overline{AC}$, and point A has coordinates at (9,4). What are the coordinates of C ?

A. (13, 2)
B. (7, 5)
C. (1, 8)
D. (14,10)
E. (–1,–8)

GO ON TO THE NEXT PAGE.

DO YOUR FIGURING HERE.

10. Isosceles trapezoid *ABCD*, with equal sides $\overline{AB}$ and $\overline{CD}$, has vertices *A* (3,0), *B* (6,6), and *D* (15,0). These vertices are graphed below in the standard (*x*,*y*) coordinate plane. What are the coordinates of one possible vertex *C* ?

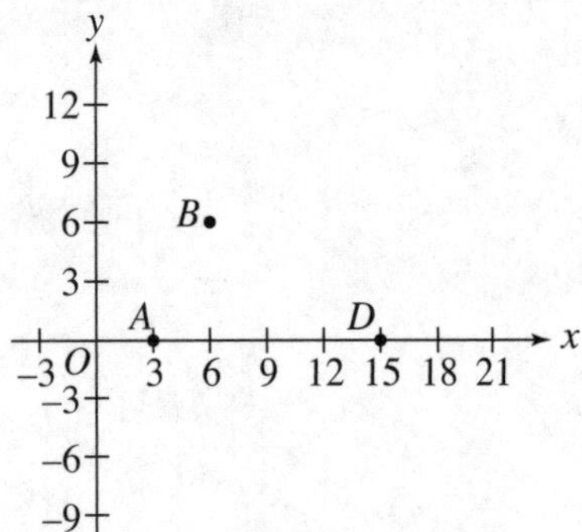

F. (11,7)
G. (13,6)
H. (12,6)
J. (13,5)
K. (12,7)

11. The town of Ashville has three bus stations (A, B, and C) that offer round-trip fares to its business district at both peak and off-peak rates. The matrices below show the average weekly sales for each station at each rate and the costs for both rates. In an average week, what are the combined peak and off-peak sales for Ashville's three bus stations?

	Peak	Off-peak
A	180	60
B	200	120
C	150	70

	Cost
Peak	\$3
Off-peak	\$2

A. \$ 780
B. \$1,590
C. \$1,950
D. \$2,090
E. \$2,340

GO ON TO THE NEXT PAGE.

12. The triangle shown below has exterior angles *a*, *b*, and *c*. What is the sum of those angles?

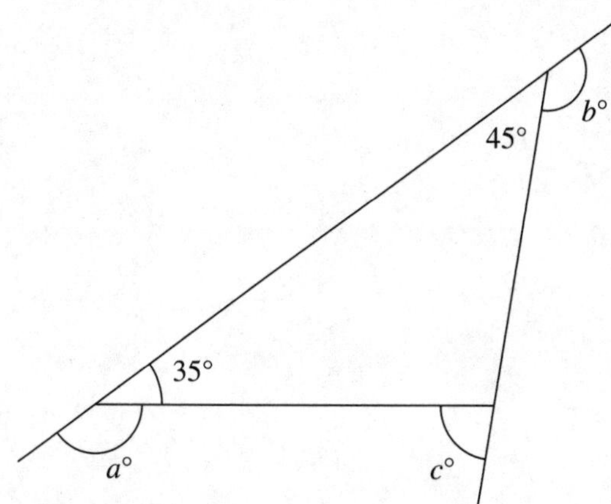

F. 360°
G. 315°
H. 225°
J. 180°
K. Cannot be determined from the information given

Use the following information to answer questions 13–15.

A sample of 300 jellybeans was removed from a barrel of jellybeans. All of the jellybeans in the barrel are one of four colors: red, orange, green, and purple. For the sample, the number of jellybeans of each color is shown in the table below.

Color	Number of jellybeans
red	75
orange	120
green	60
purple	45

13. What percent of the jellybeans in the sample are green?

A. 15%
B. 20%
C. 25%
D. 40%
E. 60%

GO ON TO THE NEXT PAGE.

DO YOUR FIGURING HERE.

14. The sample of jellybeans was removed from a barrel containing 25,000 jellybeans. If the sample is indicative of the color distribution in the barrel, which of the following is the best estimate of the number of red jellybeans in the barrel?

F. 3,750
G. 5,000
H. 6,250
J. 10,000
K. 18,750

15. If the information in the table were converted into a circle graph (pie chart), then the central angle of the sector for orange jellybeans would measure how many degrees?

A. 54°
B. 72°
C. 90°
D. 120°
E. 144°

---

16. In rectangle *ABCD* shown below, *E* is the midpoint of $\overline{BC}$, and *F* is the midpoint of $\overline{AD}$. Which of the following is the ratio of the area of quadrilateral *AECF* to the area of the entire rectangle?

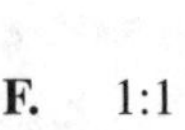

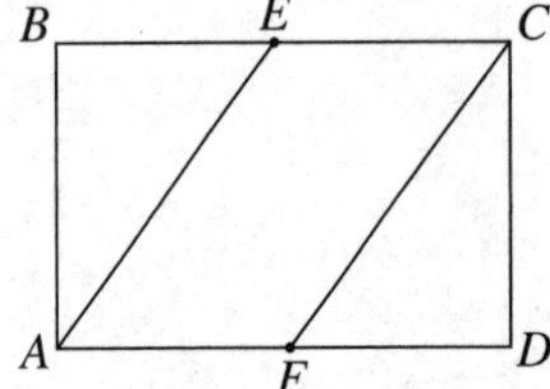

F. 1:1
G. 1:2
H. 1:3
J. 1:4
K. 2:5

17. In the standard (*x*,*y*) coordinate plane, what is the slope of the line parallel to the line $y = \frac{1}{2}x - 3$?

A. -3

B. -2

C. $-\frac{1}{2}$

D. $\frac{1}{2}$

E. 2

GO ON TO THE NEXT PAGE.

DO YOUR FIGURING HERE.

18. Aru watches a movie that is 120 minutes long in 2 sittings. The ratio of the 2 sitting times is 3:5. What is the length, in minutes, of the longer sitting?

F. 8
G. 15
H. 45
J. 60
K. 75

19. Which of the following could be a value of x if $11 < x < 12$?

A. $\sqrt{23}$
B. $\sqrt{121}$
C. $\sqrt{140}$
D. $\sqrt{145}$
E. $\sqrt{529}$

20. Susan is planning the layout of her garden. She wants to plant tomatoes in 3 plots, each 10 feet by 16 feet. Within the total area, she will leave a 4-foot-by-6-foot rectangular plot for beans, and a $2\frac{1}{2}$-foot-by-5-foot rectangular plot for lettuce. If each packet of tomato seeds will cover between 150 and 200 square feet of soil, which of the following is the minimum number of packets of seeds Susan needs to buy to plant tomatoes?

F. 5
G. 4
H. 3
J. 2
K. 1

21. What values of x are solutions in the equation $x^2 + 4x = 12$?

A. 8 and 12
B. 0 and 4
C. –2 and 6
D. –4 and 0
E. –6 and 2

GO ON TO THE NEXT PAGE.

DO YOUR FIGURING HERE.

22. For all $xy \neq 0$, and when both x and y are greater than 1, the expression $\frac{x^4y^2}{x^2y^4}$ equals which of the following?

F. $-\frac{x^2}{y^2}$

G. $-\frac{y^2}{x^2}$

H. 1

J. $\frac{x^2}{y^2}$

K. $\frac{y^2}{x^2}$

23. If point A has a nonzero x-coordinate and a nonzero y-coordinate and at least one of these coordinate values is positive, then point A MUST be located in which of the 4 quadrants labeled below?

Quadrants of the standard (x,y) coordinate plane

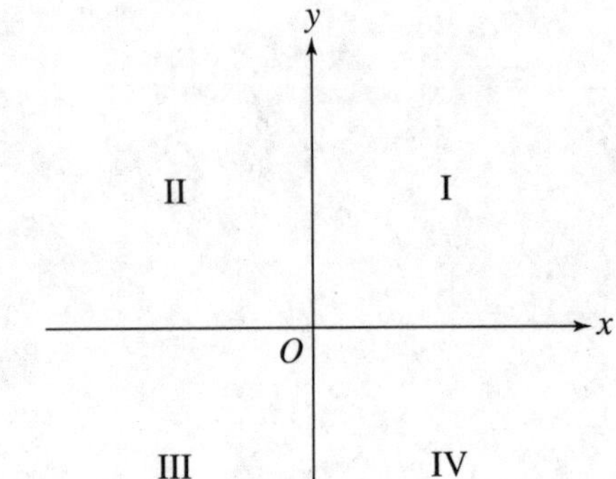

A. I only
B. I or II only
C. II or IV only
D. II, III, or IV only
E. I, II, or IV only

24. The variable cost to produce a box of paper is $4.75. The fixed cost for the paper production machinery is $1,600.00 each day. Which of the following expressions correctly models the cost of producing b boxes of paper each day?

F. $1{,}600b + 4.75$
G. $1{,}600b - 4.75$
H. $1{,}600 + 4.75b$
J. $4.75b - 1600$
K. $1{,}600b$

GO ON TO THE NEXT PAGE.

DO YOUR FIGURING HERE.

25. In the figure below, where $\Delta ABC \sim \Delta XYZ$, lengths are given in inches and the perimeter of ΔABC is 576 inches. What is the length, in inches, of $\overline{AC}$?

(Note: The symbol ~ means "is similar to.")

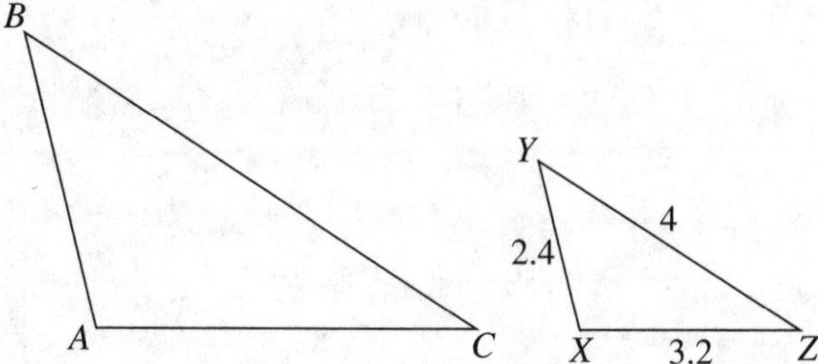

A. $126\frac{2}{5}$

B. 144

C. $168\frac{1}{5}$

D. 192

E. 240

26. Given that $\frac{\sqrt{11}}{x} \times \frac{6}{\sqrt{11}} = \frac{3\sqrt{11}}{11}$, what is the value of x ?

F. $\sqrt{11}$

G. 6

H. $2\sqrt{11}$

J. 11

K. 121

27. Natalie starts at the finish line of a straight 1,300-foot track and runs to the left toward the starting line at a constant rate of 12 feet per second. Jonathon starts 150 feet to the right of the starting line and runs to the right toward the finish line at a constant rate of 9 feet per second. To the nearest tenth of a second, after how many seconds will Natalie and Jonathon be at the same point on the track?

A. 483.3
B. 383.3
C. 63.7
D. 54.8
E. 10.9

GO ON TO THE NEXT PAGE.

28. Steve is going to buy an ice cream sundae. He first must choose 1 of 3 possible ice cream flavors. Next, he must choose 1 of 2 types of syrup. Finally, he must choose 1 of 6 kinds of candy toppings. Given these conditions, how many different kinds of sundaes could Steve possibly order?

F. 162
G. 36
H. 18
J. 9
K. 6

DO YOUR FIGURING HERE.

29. The width of a rectangular cardboard box is half its length and twice its height. If the box is 12 cm long, what is the volume of the box in cubic centimeters?

A. 72
B. 216
C. 252
D. 1,296
E. 1,728

30. At the end of each month, a credit card company uses the formula $D = B(1 + r) + 10m^2$ to calculate debt owed, where D is the cardholder's total debt; B is the amount charged to the card; r is the rate of interest; and m is the number of payments the cardholder has previously missed. If Daniel has charged $2,155 to his credit card with a 13% interest rate and has missed 2 payments, which value is closest to Daniel's total credit card debt?

F. $2,195
G. $2,435
H. $2,455
J. $2,475
K. $2,495

31. In the figure below, a cone is shown, with dimensions given in centimeters. What is the total surface area of this cone, in square centimeters? (Note: The total surface area of a cone is given by the expression $\pi r^2 + \pi rs$, where r is the radius and s is the slant height.)

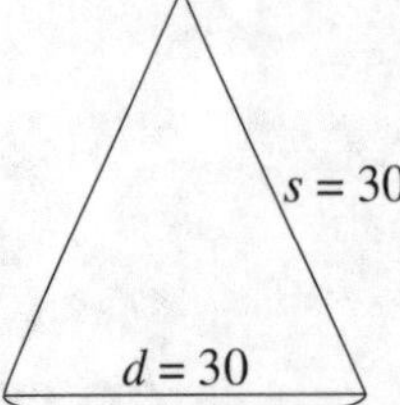

A. 225π
B. 450π
C. 465π
D. 675π
E. 18,000π

GO ON TO THE NEXT PAGE.

DO YOUR FIGURING HERE.

32. Given the functions f and g are defined as $f(a) = 3a - 4$ and $g(a) = 2a^2 + 1$, what is the value of $f(g(a))$?

F. $6a^2 - 1$
G. $6a^2 - 3$
H. $2a^2 + 3a - 3$
J. $-2a^2 + 3a + 3$
K. $18a^2 - 48a + 33$

33. The table below shows the results of a recent poll in which 262 high school students were asked to rank a recent movie on a scale from 1 to 5 stars. To the nearest hundredth, what was the average star-rating given to this movie?

Stars given	Number of students who gave this rating
1	51
2	18
3	82
4	49
5	62

A. 0.31
B. 2.02
C. 3.06
D. 3.20
E. 18.8

34. Lines p, q, r, and s are shown in the figure below and the set of all angles that are supplementary to $\angle x$ is $\{1,3,8,11\}$. Which of the following is the set of all lines that *MUST* be parallel?

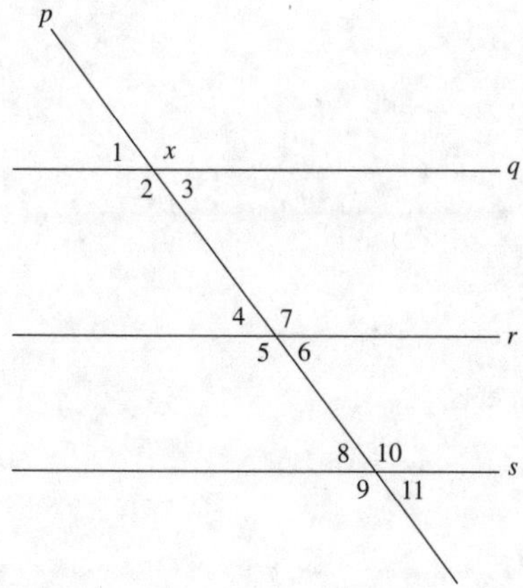

F. $\{q,r\}$
G. $\{q,s\}$
H. $\{r,s\}$
J. $\{p,q\}$
K. $\{q,r,s\}$

GO ON TO THE NEXT PAGE.

DO YOUR FIGURING HERE.

35. $(4x^4y^4)^4$ is equivalent to:

A. xy
B. $16x^8y^8$
C. $16x^{16}y^{16}$
D. $256x^8y^8$
E. $256x^{16}y^{16}$

36. Which of the following expressions is equivalent to the inequality $6x - 8 > 8x + 14$?

F. $x < -11$
G. $x > -11$
H. $x < -3$
J. $x > -3$
K. $x < 11$

37. As shown in the standard (x,y) coordinate plane below, A (2,4) lies on the circle with center L (10,–2) and radius 10 coordinate units. What are the coordinates of the image of A after the circle is rotated 90° counterclockwise (↺) about the center of the circle?

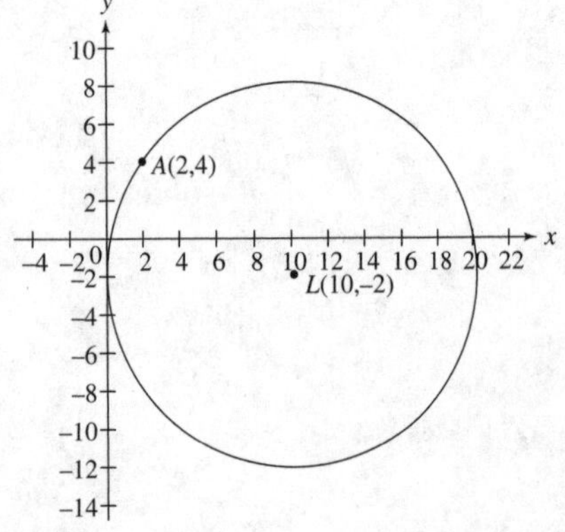

A. (10, 2)
B. (–2, 10)
C. (2, –8)
D. (0, –2)
E. (4,–10)

GO ON TO THE NEXT PAGE.

38. The length of the hypotenuse of the right triangle figured below is 16, and the length of one of its legs is 12. What is the cosine of angle θ ?

DO YOUR FIGURING HERE.

F. $\frac{\sqrt{112}}{16}$

G. $\frac{16}{\sqrt{112}}$

H. $\frac{\sqrt{112}}{12}$

J. $\frac{12}{16}$

K. $\frac{16}{12}$

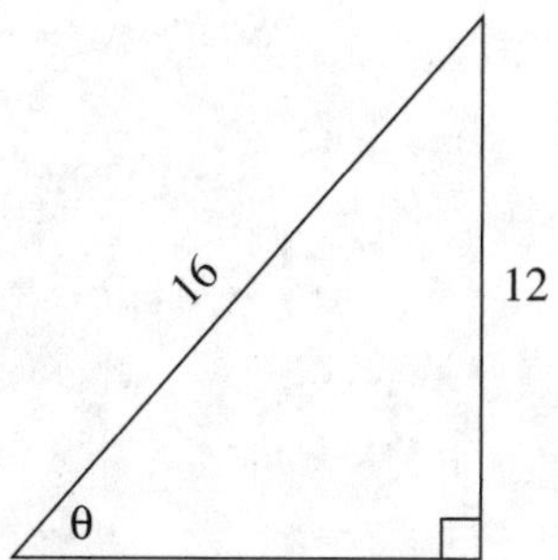

39. In the figure shown below, $\overline{CA}$ bisects $\angle BAD$, and $\overline{DA}$ bisects $\angle CAE$. What is the measure of $\angle CAD$?

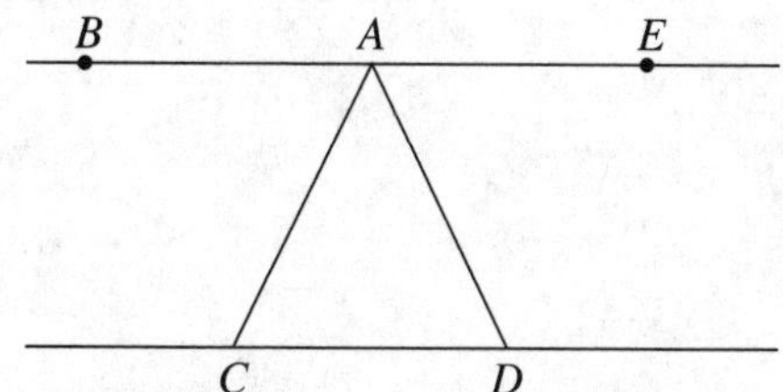

A. 30°
B. 45°
C. 60°
D. 90°
E. Cannot be determined from the given information

40. If the average number of carbon dioxide molecules per cubic inch in a container is 3×10^4 and there are 6×10^8 molecules of carbon dioxide in the container, what is the volume of the container in cubic inches?

F. 5×10^{-5}
G. 2×10^2
H. 2×10^4
J. 18×10^{12}
K. 18×10^{32}

GO ON TO THE NEXT PAGE.

DO YOUR FIGURING HERE.

41. The figure below shows the screen of an automobile navigation map. Point A represents the car's starting point, point B represents the driver's intended destination, and point C, the center of the circle, is the car's current position. Currently, point A is 15 miles from point C and 250° clockwise from due north, and point B is 20 miles from point C and 30° clockwise from due north. Which of the following represents the shortest distance (a straight line) between the car's starting point and the driver's desired destination?

(Note: For any ΔABC in which side a is opposite $\angle A$, side b is opposite $\angle B$, and side c is opposite $\angle C$, the Law of Cosines applies: $c^2 = a^2 + b^2 - 2ab\cos\angle C$.)

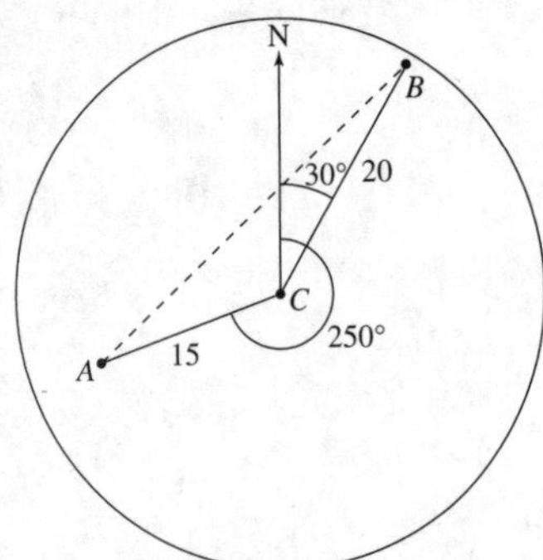

A. $\sqrt{15^2 + 20^2 - 2(15)(20)\cos 30°}$

B. $\sqrt{15^2 + 20^2 - 2(15)(20)\cos 140°}$

C. $\sqrt{15^2 + 20^2 - 2(15)(20)\cos 220°}$

D. $\sqrt{15^2 + 20^2 - 2(15)(20)\cos 250°}$

E. $\sqrt{15^2 + 20^2 - 2(15)(20)\cos 280°}$

42. What real number is halfway between $\frac{1}{4}$ and $\frac{1}{6}$?

F. $\frac{1}{6}$

G. $\frac{1}{5}$

H. $\frac{1}{2}$

J. $\frac{5}{24}$

K. $\frac{7}{24}$

GO ON TO THE NEXT PAGE.

DO YOUR FIGURING HERE.

43. In isosceles triangle ΔACE, shown below, B and D are the midpoints of congruent sides $\overline{AC}$ and $\overline{CE}$, respectively. $\angle ABE$ measures 95°, and $\angle DAE$ measures 35°. What is the measure of $\angle DEB$?

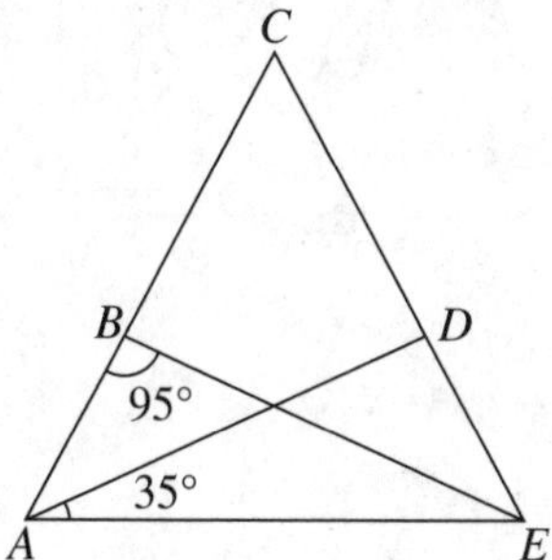

A. 50°
B. 30°
C. 25°
D. 15°
E. 10°

44. A small square table and an L-shaped table fit together with no space between them to create a large square table. The area of the large square table is 108 square feet and is nine times the area of the small square. What is x, the edge of the L-shaped table labeled in the figure below in square feet?

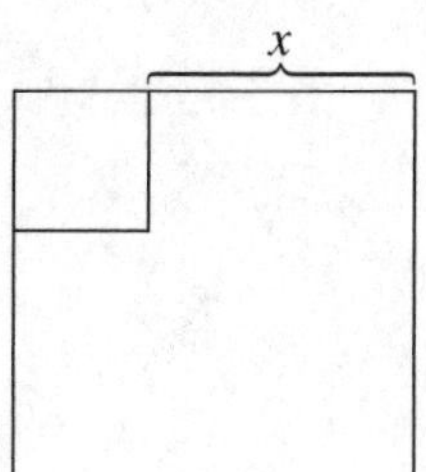

F. $2\sqrt{3}$
G. 4
H. $4\sqrt{3}$
J. $4\sqrt{6}$
K. 12

45. Which of the following is NOT an irrational number?

A. $\sqrt{\pi}$

B. $\sqrt{5}$

C. $\sqrt{8}$

D. $\sqrt{\dfrac{7}{49}}$

E. $\sqrt{\dfrac{81}{25}}$

GO ON TO THE NEXT PAGE.

DO YOUR FIGURING HERE.

46. If $x < 0$ and $y < 0$, then $|x + y|$ is equivalent to which of the following?

F. $x + y$

G. $-(x + y)$

H. $x - y$

J. $|x - y|$

K. $\sqrt{x^2 + y^2}$

47. Jane wants to bring her bowling average up to an 85 with her performance on her next game. So far she has bowled 5 out of 7 equally weighted games, and she has an average score of 83. What must her score on her next game be in order to reach her goal?

A. 83
B. 85
C. 90
D. 93
E. 95

48. In a complex plane, the vertical axis is the *imaginary axis* and the horizontal axis is the *real axis*. Within the complex plane, a complex number $a + bi$ is comparable to the point (a,b) in the standard (x,y) coordinate plane. $\sqrt{a^2 + b^2}$ is the modulus of the complex point $a + bi$. Which of the complex numbers F, G, H, J, and K below has the smallest modulus?

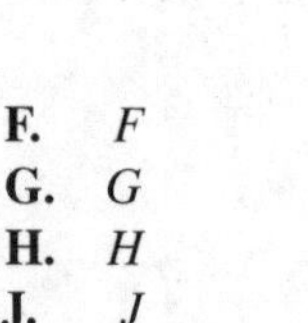

F. F
G. G
H. H
J. J
K. K

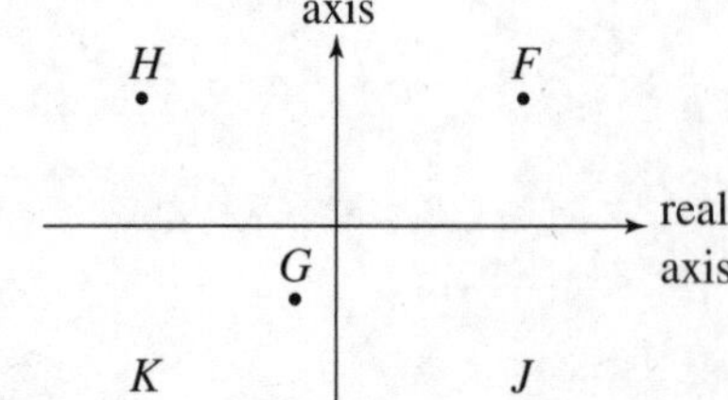

GO ON TO THE NEXT PAGE.

DO YOUR FIGURING HERE.

49. In the real numbers, what is the solution of the equation $9^{x-4} = 27^{3x+2}$?

A. $-\frac{6}{7}$
B. –2
C. –3
D. $-\frac{7}{2}$
E. –4

50. The graph of the trigonometric function $f(x) = 2\sin\frac{1}{2}x$ is represented below. Which of the following is true of this function?

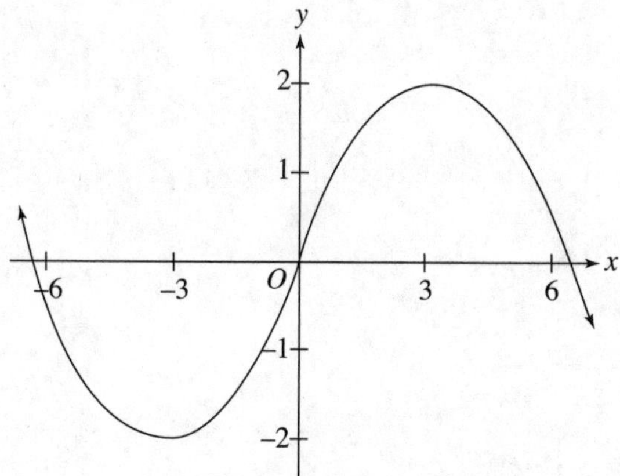

F. $f(x)$ is a 1:1 function (that is, x is unique for all $f(x)$ and $f(x)$ is unique for all x).
G. $f(x)$ is undefined at $x = 0$.
H. $f(x)$ is even (that is, $f(x) = f(-x)$ for all x).
J. $f(x)$ is odd (that is, $f(-x) = -f(x)$ for all x).
K. $f(x)$ falls entirely within the domain $-6 \le x \le 6$.

51. An integer from 299 through 1,000, inclusive, will be chosen randomly. What is the probability that the number chosen will have 1 as at least 1 of its digits?

A. $\frac{234}{1{,}000}$
B. $\frac{134}{702}$
C. $\frac{70}{702}$
D. $\frac{63}{702}$
E. $\frac{17}{702}$

GO ON TO THE NEXT PAGE.

DO YOUR FIGURING HERE.

52. In the figure below, side $\overline{MN}$ of isosceles triangle ΔNLM lies on the line $y+\frac{2}{3}x=2$ in the standard (x,y) coordinate plane, and side $\overline{NL}$ is parallel to the x-axis. What is the slope of $\overline{LM}$?

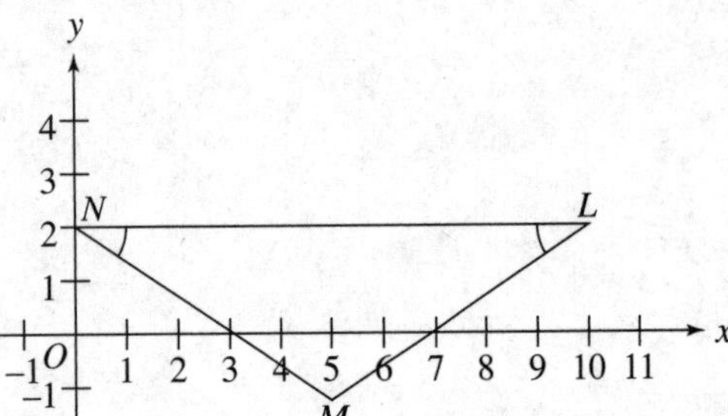

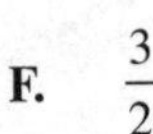

F. $\frac{3}{2}$

G. $\frac{2}{3}$

H. $\frac{1}{3}$

J. $-\frac{2}{3}$

K. $-\frac{3}{2}$

53. In the figure below, $0 < y < x$. One of the angle measures in the triangle is $\sin^{-1}\left(\frac{x}{\sqrt{x^2+y^2}}\right)$. What is $\tan\left[\sin^{-1}\left(\frac{x}{\sqrt{x^2+y^2}}\right)\right]$?

A. $\frac{x}{y}$

B. $\frac{y}{x}$

C. $\frac{x}{\sqrt{x^2+y^2}}$

D. $\frac{y}{\sqrt{x^2+y^2}}$

E. $\frac{\sqrt{x^2+y^2}}{x}$

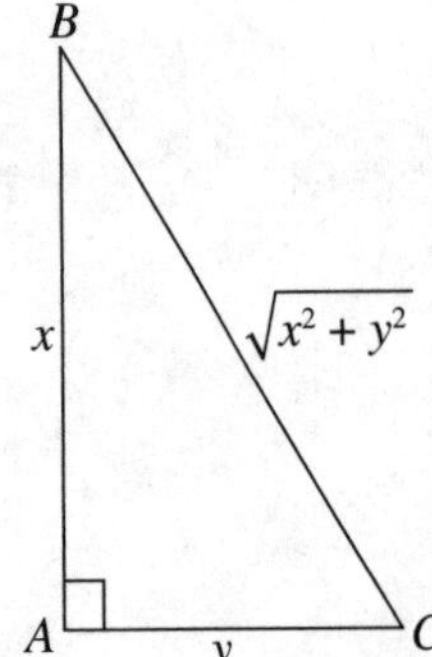

GO ON TO THE NEXT PAGE.

Use the following information to answer questions 54–56.

DO YOUR FIGURING HERE.

Melissa attaches her dog's leash to a metal anchor in the grass so that the dog can roam only within a radius of 12 feet in any direction from the anchor. A map of the area accessible to the dog is shown below in the standard (x,y) coordinate plane, with the anchor at the origin and 1 coordinate unit representing 1 foot.

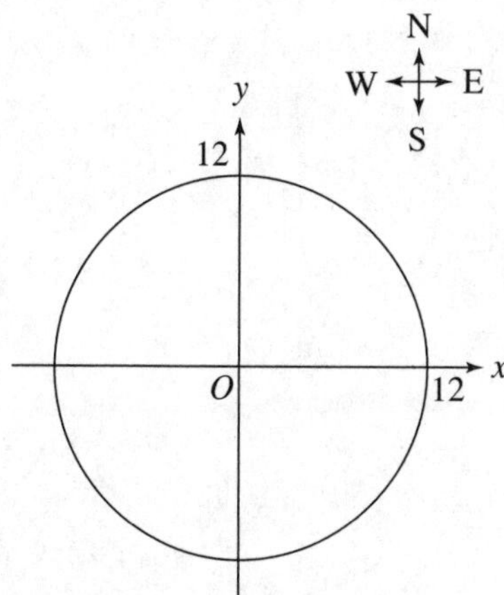

54. Which of the following is closest to the area, in square feet, the dog can roam?

F. 75
G. 144
H. 452
J. 904
K. 1,420

55. Which of the following is an equation of the circle shown on the map?

A. $(x - y)^2 = 12$
B. $(x + y)^2 = 12$
C. $(x + y)^2 = 12^2$
D. $x^2 + y^2 = 12$
E. $x^2 + y^2 = 12^2$

56. Joy takes her dog to the same park and anchors her dog 30 feet away from Melissa's anchor along a walking trail. Joy's dog can roam only within a radius of 20 feet in all directions from its anchor. For how many feet along the walking trail can BOTH dogs roam?

(Note: Assume the leashes can't stretch.)

F. 2
G. 8
H. 10
J. 18
K. 42

GO ON TO THE NEXT PAGE.

DO YOUR FIGURING HERE.

57. The graphs of the equations $y = -(x) + 1$ and $y = -(x+1)^2 + 4$ are shown in the standard (x,y) coordinate plane below. What real values of x, if any, satisfy the following inequality: $-(x + 1)^2 + 4 > -(x) + 1$?

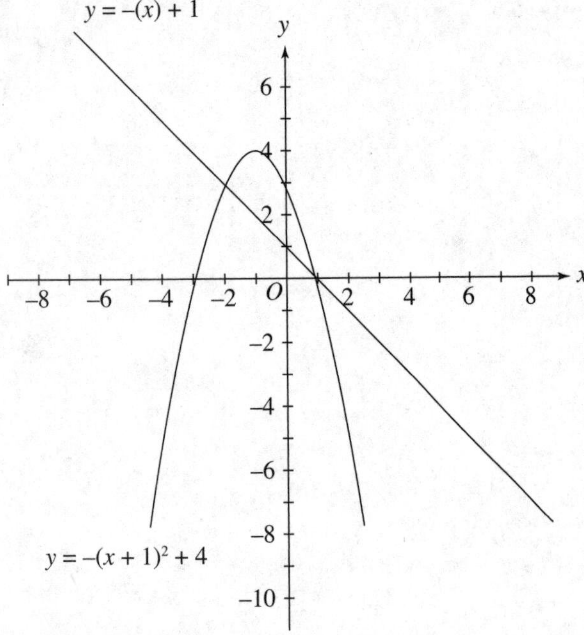

A. $x < -3$ and $x > 1$
B. $x < -2$ and $x > 1$
C. $-3 < x < 1$
D. $-2 < x < 1$
E. No real values

58. For any positive two-digit integer x with tens digit t, units digit u, and $t \neq u$, y is the two-digit integer formed when the digits of x are reversed. What is the greatest possible value of $(y - x)$ when t is less than u ?

F. $u - t$
G. $ut - tu$
H. $t^2 - 10tu + u^2$
J. $9|u - t|$
K. Cannot be determined from the given information

GO ON TO THE NEXT PAGE.

59. In the figure below, the vertices of parallelogram $ABCD$ are A (2,–4), B (8,–4), C (10,–2), and D (4,–2). What is the area of the parallelogram?

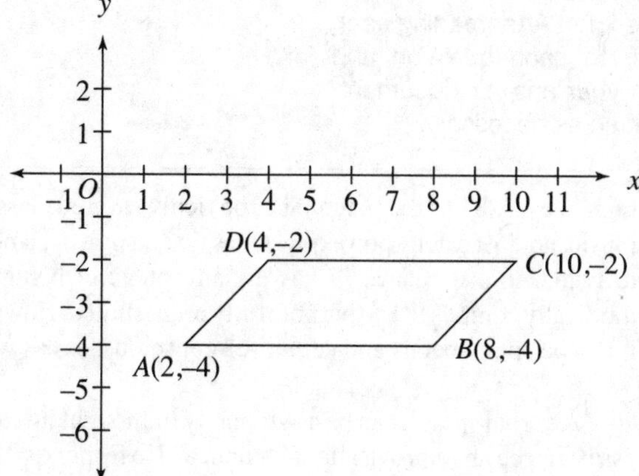

A. 6
B. $6\sqrt{2}$
C. 12
D. $12\sqrt{2}$
E. 16

60. The sum, S, of an arithmetic sequence with the first term x_1 is given by $S = n\left(\frac{x_1 + x_n}{2}\right)$, where n is the number of terms in the sequence. The sum of 5 consecutive terms in a given arithmetic sequence is 145, and x_5 is 48. What is the sixth term of this sequence?

F. 49
G. 57.5
H. 77
J. 154.5
K. 174

END OF TEST 2
STOP! DO NOT TURN THE PAGE UNTIL TOLD TO DO SO.
DO NOT RETURN TO THE PREVIOUS TEST.

READING TEST

35 Minutes—40 Questions

DIRECTIONS: There are four passages in this test. Each passage is followed by several questions. After reading each passage, choose the best answer to each question and blacken the corresponding oval on your answer document. You may refer to the passages as often as necessary.

Passage I

PROSE FICTION: This passage is adapted from the short story "A Prisoner in His Castle" by Curtis Longweather (© 2008 by Curtis Longweather).

Since he returned from the hospital, he has been unable to reclaim his speaking voice. That is not to say that he can't make sounds, but that he often can't make his thoughts into sounds like words and sentences. Something is polluting the chemistry that distills mental language into vocal output. His mind lights up with ideas just like mine does, but his ideas cannot escape. His thoughts are dispatched like knights to battle only to find they are unable to cross the moat that surrounds their castle. They are held prisoner in their own home, quarantined in frustrated isolation from the outside world.

"I fear that I will eventually choke on my own thoughts," he worries aloud to me in one of his desperate letters.

"Then expel them all on to the page," I remind him. He is a volcano with no air vents to relieve the pressure of the heat churning in his belly. His insides roil with fire, occasionally bubbling to the surface. His core vibrates with tightly coiled anticipation, the roof of his head eventually shedding off all shingles as a prelude to its propelling explosively into the atmosphere.

I tell him that his speaking voice may be like the oceanic cloud of dust and debris that the volcano spews into the air, but his writing can flow like omni-directional lava, indiscriminately absorbing everything in its path. Eventually, the continents that form as this lava cools will be fertile grounds for his readers. Each of his letters stands proudly as an island within the sloshing seas of his mind, and his clarity of prose allows us explorers to navigate him.

"There is plenty of solace in writing," he acknowledges, but maintains, "never explain to someone who can't run that at least he can drive a car."

He will always hear his thoughts as an echo, either reverberating within his own skull or as a crude imitation when transferred by pen.

I concede that the Page's shortcoming is a lack of dynamic human ears, but I optimistically point to the fact that written language has the potential to be seen by *countless* human eyes. It has the potential to be richly revered classical music, not just catchy pop expressions that inspire bystanders to twitch in accordance. It has the advantage of being methodically composed and purposefully orchestrated. However, it can be spontaneous and stream-of-consciousness as well.

"A verbal speech can be a symphony of thought just as an essay can be an improvisational blunder." He responds. "You are wrongly contrasting two styles of music when the more appropriate comparison is two very different instruments."

His distinction is a valid one, but I continue to stubbornly assert the superiority of literary communication. When we *speak* to convey meaning, I argue, we can too easily get away with lazy word choice by using context, body language, tone, and other non-verbal devices to supplement our stated words. In a piece of writing, the words exist in isolation from their author. They belong only to each other, like pirates who share a common destiny but no longer pledge allegiance to any sovereign entity. Judge them by your own standards if you wish to be confused, but realize that the only telling diagnosis rests in the internal consistency of their ways. Do the various tensions created by the professed actions, ideas, and feelings of the writing allow the reader to vicariously behold the mental state of the author? If so, then the reader has the satisfying experience of being simultaneously in the audience and backstage as well.

He enjoys coming to watch me during my trials. Sometimes I look over at him while I am delivering my closing arguments to a jury, and I see the mix of pride and pain in his eyes as he listens to me express myself more lucidly than he may ever be able to again. If my profession would allow it, I would gladly yield my voice to him and become a mere puppet for his ideas, just so he could again experience the instant gratification of vocal persuasion. (I frequently wonder if my friendship with him will ultimately venture into the territory of Cyrano de Bergerac, who so wished to woo the heart of a woman that he enlisted the help of a friend to speak his thoughts aloud to her.)

It is not the organization of thought that he treasures in listening to my courtroom orations. It is the expressiveness that a human voice can add to the meaning of words that he deeply misses. He will occasionally have me rehearse my

GO ON TO THE NEXT PAGE.

speeches to him and never permits me to begin reciting my words too mechanically. The moment I begin *reading* and not *speaking*, he will clap his hands and signal me to return back to the beginning of the idea.

In this way, just as I continue to remind him of the unspeakable value of written language, he continues to remind me of the irreplaceable value of the human voice.

1. As it relates to his friend's fear as described in the third paragraph, the narrator's description of a volcano (lines 13–19) most serves to:

A. elaborate the friend's inner torment.
B. speculate that his friend's thoughts will be unleashed.
C. explain why the friend is unable to speak.
D. imply the friend needs to be more patient.

2. Which of the following best describes the structure of the passage?

F. A detailed character study of two close friends by means of describing one extended argument between them
G. A debate about a topic during which the two main characters take equal turns discussing their positions and reasons
H. An exploration of the author's experience of his friend's speech impairment using their verbal and written exchanges as a primary source
J. The depiction of a unique friendship that allows the narrator to explain his successes and struggles as a lawyer

3. The erupting volcano simile refers to a dust cloud and a lava flow to portray:

A. intuition and logic.
B. simplicity and complexity.
C. instinct and deliberation.
D. vocal and non-vocal expression.

4. Based on the passage, which of the following statements most clearly portrays the respective attitudes of the narrator and his friend?

F. The friend is argumentative and cynical; the narrator is jaded and indifferent.
G. The friend is scornful and depressed; the narrator is apologetic and idealistic.
H. The friend is anxious and despondent; the narrator is sympathetic and encouraging.
J. The friend is shy and reclusive; the narrator is outgoing and nonchalant.

5. In the passage, the narrator most nearly describes Cyrano de Bergerac as:

A. someone who was afraid of losing the love of his life.
B. unable to produce any sound of his own due to a physical condition.
C. someone who had reason to communicate indirectly with a woman.
D. too caught up in the emotions of love to be able to describe them.

6. Which of the following statements about pirates is best supported by the narrator's characterization of them?

F. They have no rules of conduct that they must follow.
G. They succeed by means of confusing their enemies.
H. They are not accountable to anyone other than themselves.
J. They recognize the superior value of written language.

7. It can be most strongly inferred from the passage that the friend values which of the following in vocal speech?

A. Meaningful expression
B. Proper mechanics
C. Rich vocabulary
D. Clever humor

8. According to the passage, the friend is worried he may:

F. say something embarrassing if he speaks.
G. grow exasperated from his inability to vocalize thoughts.
H. be damaging the narrator's chances of courtroom success.
J. not be clever enough to compose a symphony of thought.

9. As it is used in (line 68), the word *puppet* most nearly means:

A. entertainer.
B. conversationalist.
C. toy.
D. mouthpiece.

10. Based on the narrator's account, the friend's reaction to watching the narrator during legal proceedings is:

F. appreciative and yearning.
G. confused and hopeless.
H. awestruck and overbearing.
J. bitter and resentful.

GO ON TO THE NEXT PAGE.

Passage II

SOCIAL SCIENCE: This passage is adapted from the entry "Larsen B" in *Down Off the Shelf: Recent Antarctic Natural Disasters* (© 2009 Subzero Publications).

Most people associate Antarctica with frigid temperatures, glaciers, and massive sheets of ice; however, recent geological events highlight not the cold, but issues of warming. Further, such events emphasize the ways in which human behavior influences climactic and geological changes. Though scientists may disagree as to the extent of human influence, there is no doubt that our behavior does have significant and lasting outcomes. One of the most dramatic environmental events in recent years is the loss of ice shelves that float around much of Antarctica; in particular, the collapse of the Larsen B ice shelf. This long, fringing mass was assumed to be the latest in a long line of victims of Antarctic summer heat waves linked to global warming; new research, however, calls this assumption into question.

In 2002, the northern section of the Larsen B ice shelf (a thick floating sheet of freshwater ice fed by glaciers) shattered and separated from the continent in the largest single event in a 30-year series of ice-shelf retreats in the peninsula. The Larsen B was about 220 meters thick and is thought to have existed for at least 400 years prior to its collapse. The shattered ice from Larsen B set thousands of icebergs adrift in the Weddell Sea, east of the Antarctic Peninsula. A total of about 1,250 square miles of shelf area disintegrated in a 35-day period beginning on January 31 of 2002. The collapse was perhaps foreshadowed when standing water appeared on the ice. (Scientists theorize that once melt-water appears on the surface of an ice shelf, the rate of ice disintegration increases; pooling water puts weight on the ice, filling small cracks that expand, eventually causing breakage.) The appearance of standing water on ice shelves is generally attributed to global warming; thus, the collapse of the Larsen B ice shelf seemed to be one of the most obvious and stunning signs of worldwide climate change.

In support of this postulation, the *Journal of Climate* published a 2006 study by Dr. Gareth Marshall of the British Antarctic Survey, providing the first direct evidence linking human activity to the collapse of Antarctic ice shelves. Scientists revealed that stronger westerly winds in the northern Antarctic Peninsula, driven principally by human-induced climate change, are responsible for the significant increase in summer temperatures that led to the retreat and collapse of the Larsen B. They argue that global warming and the ozone hole have changed Antarctic weather patterns such that strengthened westerly winds force warm air eastward over the natural barrier created by the Antarctic Peninsula's mountain chain. Elevated temperatures in the summer warm the area by approximately five degrees Celsius, creating the conditions that allowed melt-water to drain into crevasses on the Larsen ice shelf, a key process that led to its 2002 break-up. Dr. Marshall asserts that this is the first time anyone has demonstrated a process directly linking the collapse to human activity, and that climate change does not impact our planet evenly, as evidenced by the significant increase in temperatures in certain geographical areas, particularly the western Antarctic Peninsula. According to his research, this icy region has shown the largest increase in temperatures observed anywhere on Earth over the past half-century.

Marshall's breakthrough research was followed, two years later, by new and somewhat contradictory information. In a paper published in the *Journal of Glaciology*, Professor Neil Glasser and Dr. Ted Scambos assert that despite the dramatic nature of the break-up in 2002, observations by glaciologists and computer modeling by scientists at NASA pointed to an ice shelf in distress for decades. Glasser and Scambos contend that the shelf was already teetering on the brink of collapse before the final summer, and though they acknowledge that global warming had a major role in the collapse, they emphasize that it is only one of a number of atmospheric, oceanic and glaciological factors. The amount of melt-water on the Larsen B shelf just before the collapse caused many to assume that air temperature increases were primarily to blame, but Scambos and Glasser's research shows that ice-shelf breakup is not controlled simply by climate, citing, for example, that the location and spacing of crevasses and rifts on the ice do much to determine its strength. Scientists in the field consider this study imperative, as the collapse of ice shelves contributes (albeit indirectly) to global sea-level rise.

Scientists agree that the break-up of Larsen B alone will not change sea level, but other glaciers previously restricted by the ice shelf have surged forward, lowering their surfaces. Since lower elevations have warmer temperatures, these glaciers melt more quickly, causing more ice to flow into the sea, and levels to rise. If more and more ice shelves are lost in subsequent years, the concern is that the rise in sea levels could affect ecosystems worldwide, generating such problems as widespread flooding, loss of coastal cities and island countries, decreased crop yields, and the possible extinction of millions of species. Determining the cause of ice shelf collapse, and the ways in which humans can contribute to both the problem and the solution, may help to prevent such catastrophes in the future; it becomes clear, then, why researchers are compelled to continue their studies of ice shelves in the Antarctic.

GO ON TO THE NEXT PAGE.

11. The author most nearly characterizes the role of human activity in regard to the collapse of ice shelves as:

A. a significant though previously unproven contributing factor.
B. insignificant in comparison to glaciological influences.
C. less of a contributor than initial evidence predicted.
D. the primary and irreversible cause of all detrimental effects.

12. The author lists all of the following as possible effects of sea level rise EXCEPT:

F. loss of island countries.
G. extinction of millions of species.
H. decreased crop yields.
J. surging glaciers.

13. The author indicates that the common factor in Dr. Marshall's study (lines 34–57) and that of Doctors Scambos and Glasser (lines 58–77) is that both studies:

A. cite global warming as a reason for the Larsen B ice-shelf collapse
B. discredit climate change as a reason for the Larsen B ice-shelf collapse.
C. found little compelling evidence to explain the Larsen B ice-shelf collapse.
D. agree that structural weaknesses caused the Larsen B ice-shelf collapse.

14. In his statement in lines 50–55, the author most nearly means that human activity:

F. is inconsequential compared to other factors influencing climate change.
G. could eventually affect weather patterns worldwide, doing great harm.
H. makes certain areas of the world much warmer than they would otherwise be.
J. will cause the sea level to rise, wiping out entire countries and species of animals.

15. The author calls which of the following a stunning sign of worldwide climate change?

A. Worldwide sea-level rise
B. Melt-water on the Larsen B ice shelf prior to its collapse
C. The collapse of the Larsen B ice shelf
D. Increased temperatures in the western Antarctic Peninsula

16. The author includes the findings in lines 64–75 primarily in order to:

F. support the prevailing theory that global warming causes glacier break-up.
G. encourage people to make environmentally-friendly choices in their daily lives.
H. imply that ice shelf break-up is simpler than scientists originally thought.
J. highlight the interaction between factors in a major environmental event.

17. The main idea of the third paragraph is that the Larsen B ice-shelf collapse:

A. was not caused by global warming.
B. was foreshadowed for years prior to the event.
C. was caused by the uneven impact of climate change on the Earth.
D. was caused in part by direct human activity.

18. Which of the following is NOT listed in the passage as a cause of ice-shelf collapse?

F. Global warming
G. Human activity
H. Spacing and location of crevasses and rifts
J. Deep ocean currents

19. The author calls the increased westerly winds in the northern Antarctic Peninsula:

A. irrelevant to the problem of ice-shelf collapse.
B. responsible for an increase in summer temperatures.
C. a common weather pattern in certain times of year.
D. an unmistakable warning of sea-level rise.

20. The author uses the remark "largest increase in temperatures observed anywhere on Earth" (lines 56–57) to:

F. demonstrate how scientists are prone to exaggeration when talking about ice shelves.
G. give a strong incentive for people to change their behavior.
H. explain that global warming doesn't occur at the same rate in all regions.
J. clarify a common misconception about weather patterns in cold areas.

GO ON TO THE NEXT PAGE.

Passage III

HUMANITIES: Passage A is adapted from the article "What makes a good book-to-film adaptation?" by Scott Tobias (Reprinted with permission of The Onion. Copyright © 2016, by Onion, Inc. www.theonion.com; www.avclub.com.). Passage B is adapted from the article "Infidelity, Grandly Staged," a review of the 2012 film version of *Anna Karenina,* by A. O. Scott. (From *The New York Times*. © 2012, The New York Times Company. All rights reserved. Used under license.)

Passage A

The degree of faithfulness—or the impetus to be faithful—should not be part of the book-to-film equation at all. With something like *The Hunger Games* (or *Harry Potter*, or *Twilight*, or any other franchise based on a bestselling property), I'm sure there's an enormous amount of pressure from fans and from the studio simply to deliver on the material as straightforwardly as possible. Otherwise, devotees will revolt, perhaps the author will distance herself from it publicly, and the wave of ill feeling will crash over the casual viewers who have no stake in the fight, but are now wary about seeing the movie at all. There's also the fact that filmmakers rarely have an antagonistic relationship to the book they're adapting; ... most want to do right by something they loved.

Yet doing right by a great book and being faithful to it are, to my mind, two separate issues. Skillful as it is, *The Hunger Games* suffers from all the pitfalls of faithfulness that I noted in my review and Linda Holmes addressed: It hits all the expected plot points from a novel that offers a straightforward cinematic blueprint, but it feels thinned-out as a result, because it can only deal glancingly with key relationships from the book, like Katniss's relationship with Rue. When co-writer/director Gary Ross actually pauses long enough to set up a sequence carefully and let the drama breathe a little, you get "The Reaping," by far the film's most affecting and artful minutes. But once Katniss gets swept into the Games, there's no time allotted to build complex relationships or evoke this world more vividly; in order to stay faithful, Ross just ticks off the boxes. As I said, "stenography in light."

What I want is not faithfulness, but an active engagement with the material, which doesn't have to preclude faithfulness. The question filmmakers should ask is not, "How can I bring this story to the screen without losing anything?," but "What in this book do I want to emphasize?" If you're reading a book, I think it's natural to home in on themes, characters, and scenes that are most meaningful to you. Granted, the big problem with something like *The Hunger Games* is having to make something coherent out of the narrative's many moving parts, but a good adaptation has to make choices about what's truly important. And it also has to exist independently from the novel: Films content with merely illustrating books are more concerned with problem-solving and translation than artistic expression. As Holmes says about *The Hunger Games*, "it's faithful to the point of not adding anything you haven't seen in your head when you read the book." If that's the case, what's the point of making it? Selling Katniss Barbie dolls?

Passage B

Bad literary adaptations are all alike, but every successful literary adaptation succeeds in its own way. The bad ones—or let's just say the average ones, to spare the feelings of hard-working wig makers and dialect coaches—are undone by humility, by anxious fidelity to the cultural prestige of literature. The good ones succeed through hubris, through the arrogant assumption that a great novel is not a sacred artifact but rather a lump of interesting material to be shaped according to the filmmaker's will.

The British director Joe Wright has seemed to me—up to now—to belong to the dreary party of humility. His screen versions of Jane Austen's *Pride and Prejudice* and Ian McEwan's *Atonement* are not terrible, just cautious and responsible. For all their technical polish and the admirable discipline of their casts, those films remain trapped in literariness. Instead of strong, risky interpretations, they offer crib notes and the pale flattery of imitation. The proof of their mediocrity is that admirers of Austen or Mr. McEwan will find no reason for complaint.

Mr. Wright's *Anna Karenina* is different. It is risky and ambitious enough to count as an act of artistic hubris, and confident enough to triumph on its own slightly—wonderfully—crazy terms. Pious Tolstoyans may knit their brows about the stylistic liberties Mr. Wright and the screenwriter, Tom Stoppard, have taken, but surely Tolstoy can withstand (and may indeed benefit from) their playful, passionate rendering of his masterpiece.

The challenge of *Anna Karenina* is that Tolstoy's loose and baggy monster of a novel is more than large, bigger than great: it is comprehensive. As it glides among its many characters, reading their thoughts and dissecting their desires, the book becomes a vivid panorama of an entire society, you might even say a whole species. *Anna Karenina* does not take place, as movie-trailer voice-overs might say, "in a world" of such and such exotic customs. The book lives in the world, in the busy, contingent present tense of mid-19th-century Imperial Russia, which contained everything Tolstoy knew. To try to reproduce that world according to the canons of 21st-century movie realism would be to diminish and falsify his narrative, which ascends through cultural and social detail into a realm of universal emotion. Mr. Wright's brilliant gamble is to arrive at this level of emotional authenticity by way of self-conscious artifice....

GO ON TO THE NEXT PAGE.

Questions 21–24 ask about Passage A.

21. The main purpose of the second paragraph of Passage A (lines 14–28) is to:

A. suggest that remaining faithful to the plot of the book does not necessarily make a good film.
B. praise the film version of *The Hunger Games* for hitting all of the expected plot points.
C. indicate Gary Ross's frustration at his inability to portray the complex relationships in the book.
D. argue that stenography in light is the most important consideration of a film adaptation.

22. Tobias refers to "selling Katniss Barbie dolls" (line 45) in order to suggest that:

F. some films meant for older audiences inappropriately target young children.
G. selling toys is the primary purpose for a film like *The Hunger Games*.
H. there is little point in making a film that merely illustrates the book it's based on.
J. the marketing of film-related merchandise hampers the artistic vision of the filmmaker.

23. According to Passage A, Tobias believes the film version of *The Hunger Games* suffers from:

A. excessive faithfulness to the plot of the novel.
B. over-emphasizing Katniss's relationship with Rue.
C. adding more than you see in your head when you read the book.
D. spending too much time on "The Reaping" scene.

24. According to Passage A, Tobias believes that a good adaptation should:

F. offer a straightforward cinematic blueprint.
G. exist independently from the novel.
H. become a box office hit.
J. have an antagonistic relationship to the book.

Questions 25–27 ask about Passage B.

25. According to Passage B, Joe Wright's literary adaptations of *Pride and Prejudice* and *Atonement* were:

A. full of strong, risky interpretations.
B. terrible recreations of their literary sources.
C. overly reliant on the filmmaker's hubris.
D. cautious, responsible, and mediocre films.

26. Based on Passage B, the film version of *Anna Karenina* is successful because:

F. Wright's disciplined cast had elaborate costumes and appropriate accents.
G. Wright fashioned a technically polished film version of a sacred novel.
H. Wright focused on the emotional truths of the novel rather than on the details of its setting.
J. Wright ignored the cultural prestige of literature in favor of 21st-century movie realism.

27. Which of the following statements best expresses the opinion the author of Passage B seems to have about the film *Anna Karenina*?

A. It is interesting because it does not reproduce the novel too closely.
B. It is similar to the film versions of *Pride and Prejudice* and *Atonement*.
C. It was a box office success.
D. It is better than the novel it is based on.

Questions 28–30 ask about both passages.

28. Based on the passages, both authors believe that a film adaptation of a novel should:

F. focus on the hubris of the filmmaker and not worry about upsetting the book's fans.
G. communicate the broad themes of the book, while also expressing the filmmaker's vision.
H. actively engage with the literary source to provide a faithful rendition.
J. ascend through cultural and social details to dissect the universal desires of the characters.

29. Based on the passages, it can most reasonably be inferred that both authors believe a book's fans:

A. are usually the harshest critics of a poorly made film adaptation.
B. will never go to see a film unless it adheres exactly to the plot of the book.
C. find no reason to complain about a film that includes elaborate period costumes.
D. are unlikely to be upset by an adaptation that follows the book closely.

GO ON TO THE NEXT PAGE.

30. Another author wrote the following about book-to-film adaptations:

A filmmaker is unlikely to devote time and energy to a film version of a book she does not love; ironically, this very love for the book often spells failure for a film.

Which passage most closely echoes the view presented in this quotation?

F. Passage A, because it addresses the filmmaker's relationship to the book.
G. Passage A, because it criticizes films that merely illustrate the major plot points of a book.
H. Passage B, because it stresses that literary adaptations are not always box-office successes.
J. Passage B, because it explains why some of Wright's films are better than others.

Passage IV

NATURAL SCIENCE: This passage is excerpted from the article "Alternative Medicines: A New Perspective" by Audrey C. Tristan (© 2004 by Audrey Tristan).

The view of health as a holistic and integrative state of physical, spiritual, and emotional well-being is deeply rooted in mind-body philosophies that have survived thousands of years. Traditional *mindful movement* therapies found in *yoga, tai chi,* and *qigong,* for example, couple aerobic and anaerobic exercise with mental focus. These practices, which originated in Eastern medicine, guide participants through a series of specialized movements synchronized to the breath and mental images. Involving more than cardiovascular activity, these exercise routines are said to improve overall health by bringing deeper awareness to the body and promoting strength, flexibility, and balance.

Modern Western biomedicine, on the other hand, has advanced largely by splitting the mind and body to allow for the objective study of health and disease mechanisms, and thus has been slow to embrace the implications of mind-body health. However, as alternative and traditional therapies have become increasingly more popular and available in the West, researchers have begun to delve deeper into mind-body therapy efficacy, that is, the ability to consistently produce a desired, therapeutic effect.

There is particularly solid research to support the use of mind-body therapy to counteract the debilitating effects of stress. Certain mind-body therapies may alter the way we experience pain and manage stress through the use of conscious strategies to avert automatic responses. Stress, as defined in biomedical terms, is the physiological response to a perceived threat. It is not to be confused with the common usage of the term, which generally equates stress with those activities that provoke a stress response (these are deemed *stressors*). When the central nervous system perceives a threat, the sympathetic division of the autonomic nervous system is engaged, signaling the release of stress hormones such as epinephrine and cortisol into the bloodstream that in turn activate particular physiological responses: heart and respiratory rate acceleration, muscle tension, perspiration, indigestion, and pupil dilation.

This "fight-or-flight" response alludes to the conditions of ancestral humans and the presumed adaptive function of such a response in evolutionary history. The response, however, does not occur only in reaction to isolated incidences. Indeed, most stressors today, related to work, family, school, and interpersonal relationships, are prolonged, and the fight-or-flight responses are thus sustained. This continual state of arousal results in deleterious effects on health over time, such as high blood pressure, cardiovascular disease, diabetes, digestive disorders, and suppressed immune response.

Mind-body therapies, such as guided imagery and meditation, essentially work by altering responses to stressors. The simple act of breathing deeply and focusing on the breath will, in contrast to a stress response, engage the parasympathetic division of the autonomic nervous system, which lowers blood pressure, heart, and respiratory rates, and decreases muscle tension, thus counteracting the negative consequences of fight-or-flight response.

Other mind-body therapies alter the experience of pain itself. Pain is a multidimensional experience that traverses four physiological pathways. *Transduction* occurs first, as sensory neurons, the *nociceptors*, detect potentially damaging stimuli and transmit signals from affected tissue to neural activity. The next step is *transmission*, in which the pain messages are exchanged between the nociceptors and the spinal cord. *Central representation* follows as the information is relayed from the spinal cord through the thalamus to the limbic and cortical structures of the brain, which identify the sensations relayed. *Modulation,* the last step, is a descending pathway in which the brain sends signals back to the spinal cord to moderate the sensation of pain, basically "numbing" the pain. Since the limbic system is also the brain center for emotion, memory, and autonomic nervous system integration, the experience of pain is ultimately mediated by emotions, an individual's own past experiences, and present external environment.

In clinical hypnosis, or *hypnotic analgesia,* patients are taught alternative skills to alter the experience of pain. Hypnotic analgesia produces psychophysiological effects as patients are taught to consciously re-evaluate and manage a painful stimulus, using visual imagery and positive emotional reinforcement. A recent review of controlled studies of hypnotic analgesia suggests that the treatment can reduce pain in chronic conditions resulting from osteoarthritis, cancer,

GO ON TO THE NEXT PAGE.

fibromyalgia, and disability. The authors cautioned, however, that a number of questions remain unanswered.

Mind-body research has provided important insights into both the efficacy of such therapies and our understanding of the cognitive and physiological perception of pain. More investigation is needed, however, to ascertain if outcome expectations influence the success of particular therapies, if response rates differ as a result of pain type or pain diagnosis, and to what degree variation in individual response, and if research design should preclude broader inferences.

31. The studies reviewed in the seventh paragraph (lines 73–82) have shown that hypnotic analgesia may be effective in:

A. restructuring the brain non-invasively.
B. fighting cancer and fibromyalgia.
C. decreasing depression in patients.
D. altering the experience of pain.

32. According to the sixth paragraph, (lines 56–72), when a door slams on a person's hand, the detection of pain results from:

F. the transmission of nerve signals from damaged tissue to the spinal cord and sympathetic nervous system.
G. the transmission of nerve signals from damaged tissue to the spinal cord and brain.
H. the sympathetic nervous system releasing chemical hormones, which reach the heart via the bloodstream.
J. the sympathetic nervous system releasing chemical hormones, which reach the brain via the spinal cord.

33. According to the passage, overall health may be improved in part through any of the following EXCEPT:

A. exercise combined with mental focus.
B. cardiovascular activity combined with nutritious diet.
C. awareness of the body.
D. movement synchronized with breath and mental imagery.

34. As it is used in line 33, the word *engaged* most nearly means:

F. stimulated.
G. taken.
H. obligated.
J. destined.

35. According to the passage, the limbic system would be directly involved in all of the following EXCEPT:

A. pain modulation.
B. stress management.
C. muscle movement.
D. memory.

36. Information in the second paragraph indicates that mind-body therapies in Western medicine have been:

F. increasingly used in place of biomedicine.
G. rejected because there have not been enough clinical studies.
H. an emerging field of scientific investigation.
J. successful in curing many conditions and diseases.

37. The mind-body therapies mentioned in the fifth paragraph (lines 48–55) function by:

A. preventing stress hormones from activating negative physiological responses.
B. engaging the sympathetic nervous system to reduce stress responses.
C. effectively eliminating emotional stressors.
D. counterbalancing the effects of flight or fight responses.

38. According to the passage, stress responses with adaptive functions, as would have evolved in ancestral conditions, can be expected to:

F. increase cortisol levels in the blood.
G. suppress immune activity.
H. perceive threats.
J. decrease muscle tension.

39. In the last paragraph, the author expresses the belief that mind-body therapy should be further investigated because results from research are:

A. carefully controlled to yield results consistent with expectations.
B. valid only when analyzing Western-originating therapies.
C. susceptible to external variables, the effects of which are yet to be determined.
D. proof of the effectiveness in fighting stress and eliminating pain.

40. According to the passage, healthy mind-body therapies would have been deemed ineffective if which of the following effects occurred after patients engaged in positive meditation to manage work-related stress?

F. Nociceptive signals were transmitted.
G. The parasympathetic nervous system was engaged.
H. The fight-or-flight response was prolonged.
J. Spinal cord activity diminished.

END OF TEST 3
STOP! DO NOT TURN THE PAGE UNTIL TOLD TO DO SO.
DO NOT RETURN TO A PREVIOUS TEST.

SCIENCE TEST

35 Minutes—40 Questions

DIRECTIONS: There are six passages in the following section. Each passage is followed by several questions. After reading a passage, choose the best answer to each question and blacken the corresponding oval on your answer document. You may refer to the passages as often as necessary.

You are NOT permitted to use a calculator on this test.

Passage I

In the solar system, solid planets and moons are made up of different layers, which have different compositions. The Earth's moon is surrounded by an outer crust, which is visible to observers on Earth. Beneath this crust is a solid *lithosphere*. Beneath the lithosphere is another layer called the *asthenosphere*. This layer is thought to have high temperatures, so the structure of this layer is said to be *plastic*, or easily changed. The innermost region of the Moon is called the *core*, and it is thought to contain iron.

A solar eclipse occurs when the Moon travels directly between the Earth and the Sun, temporarily blocking the transmission of sunlight to the Earth and creating a shadow. Most solar eclipses are partial, because the Moon does not always travel entirely within the path of the sunlight. However, complete solar eclipses are possible because the Moon and the Sun have approximately the same diameter from the perspective of a viewer on the Earth. An observer on the Earth would view the sky as occupying 180 degrees. Of this entire distance, the Moon takes up 0.54 degrees, while the Sun takes up 0.52 degrees. Since the Sun appears to take up a smaller section of the sky, the Sun's rays can be blocked from traveling to the Earth during a complete solar eclipse (see Figure 1).

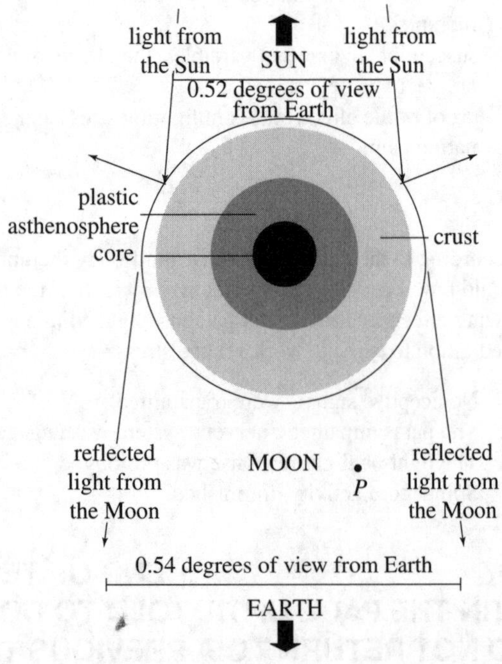

light from the Sun
SUN
light from the Sun
0.52 degrees of view from Earth
plastic asthenosphere
core
crust
reflected light from the Moon
MOON
P
reflected light from the Moon
0.54 degrees of view from Earth
EARTH

Figure 1

The gravitational force exerted on the Earth by the Moon, and by the Sun to a lesser extent, results in water *tides*, which are the changes in the level of the Earth's ocean surface. Figure 2 shows data collected by a tidal station on the western coast of the United States, showing the change in the ocean water level over a 72-hour period. This tidal station experiences a "mixed" tidal cycle in which there are two high tides of unequal height per cycle known as *higher high tide* and *lower high tide.* During this period, the highest water level was 6 feet above mean sea level, while the lowest water level was approximately half of a foot below mean sea level (between "0" and "–1" feet).

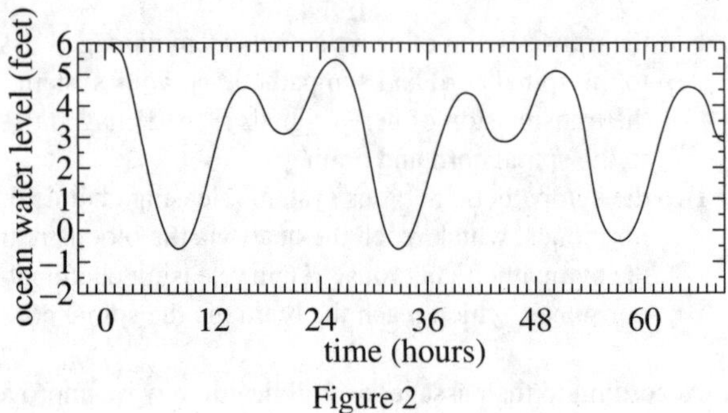

Figure 2

The highest and lowest ocean surface levels change over the course of a year. Figure 3 shows the change in the highest and lowest water levels measured by the same tidal station over a year.

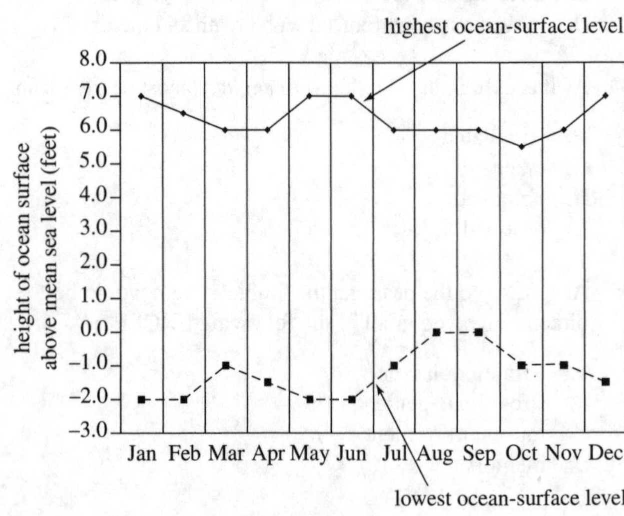

Figure 3

GO ON TO THE NEXT PAGE.

1. Figure 1 shows that a lunar orbiter at point *P* would be able to view which of the following?

   A. The Moon only
   B. The Sun only
   C. The Moon and the Earth only
   D. The Moon, the Sun, and the Earth

2. According to Figure 1, when the Sun's rays encounter the surface of the Moon during a solar eclipse, the rays most likely:

   F. stop transmitting forward and do not continue to the Earth's surface.
   G. enter the plastic asthenosphere and are absorbed.
   H. reflect off the surface of the Moon, and then continue to the Earth.
   J. transmit unobstructed to the Earth's surface.

3. The time elapsed between two successive higher high tides is closest to:

   A. 12 hours.
   B. 24 hours.
   C. 48 hours.
   D. 60 hours.

4. Based on the information provided in Figure 3, the data in Figure 2 could NOT have been collected during which of the following months?

   F. March
   G. July
   H. August
   J. November

5. According to Figure 2, which of the following statements best describes the ocean surface level between $t = 0$ hours and $t = 12$ hours?

   A. The ocean surface level rises continuously during that entire time.
   B. The ocean surface level falls continuously during that entire time.
   C. The ocean surface level rises and then falls during that time.
   D. The ocean surface level falls and then rises during that time.

6. During each 28-day lunar cycle, there are 2 *spring* tides and 2 *neap* tides. Spring tides, which coincide with full and new moons, have the largest difference between the highest and lowest water levels. Neap tides, which coincide with quarter moons (half-illumination), have the least difference between the highest and lowest water levels. Which of the following diagrams could represent the moon phases for the 72-hour period shown in Figure 2 ?

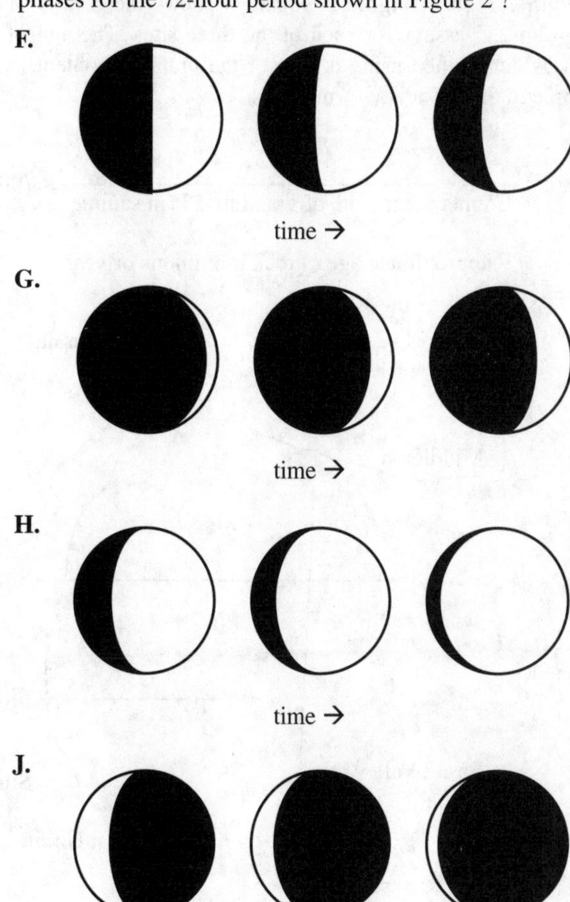

GO ON TO THE NEXT PAGE.

Passage II

Approximately 45,000 to 35,000 years ago, Lake Brussia straddled the boundary between modern Smith and Union counties. As seen in Figure 1, the cities of Middleton, West Union, and Basalt Valley rest over the sediment of the ancient lake. The lake was believed to have been formed as a result of seismic activity in the region. In order to test this hypothesis, a study examining the strata of the region was conducted using radioactive dating. Inconsistencies in the age of the rock layers indicate the presence of a fault in the region.

Radioactive dating is a technique that utilizes the amount of radiation exhibited by a distinct isotope within a sample to approximate its age. Uranium-235 is an isotope commonly found in varying types of strata with a half-life of approximately 700 million years. The half-life of an isotope is the time it takes for half of the isotope to decompose. Researchers acquired core samples from the surface to a depth of 850 m below sea level for each of three sites between the modern cities of Middleton and West Union, as seen in Figure 2. Figure 3 shows the results of the uranium-235 assays for each of the three sites. The age of the rock is determined using a ratio of the uranium content in the sample to that of newly formed rock.

Note: $\frac{64}{\text{Counts per minute of uranium-235 in sample}} \times 700 =$ approximate age of rock in millions of years

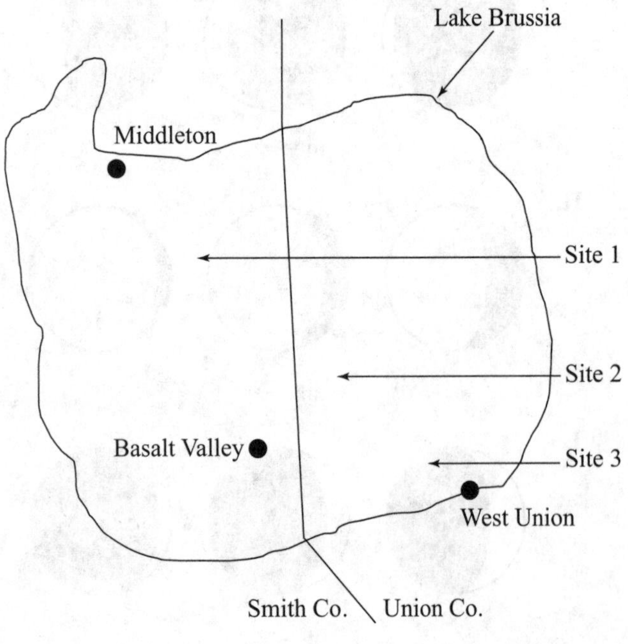

Figure 1

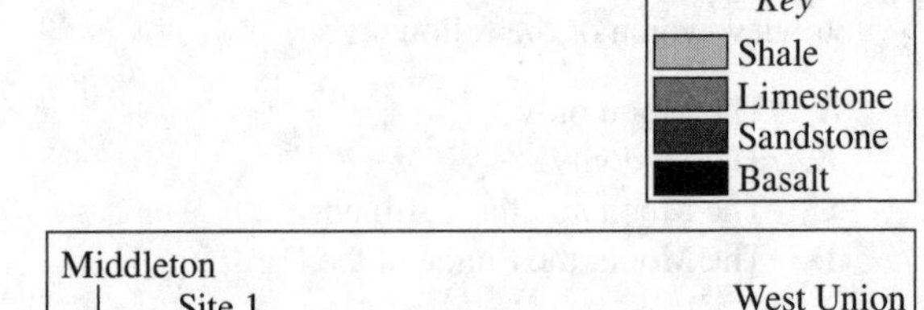

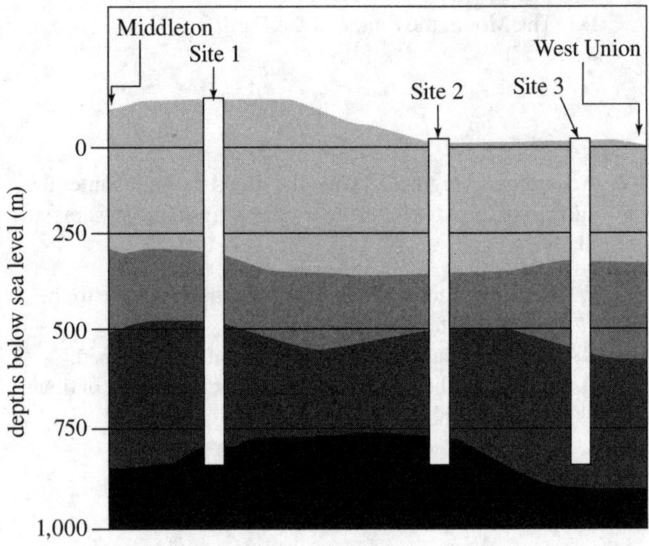

Figure 2

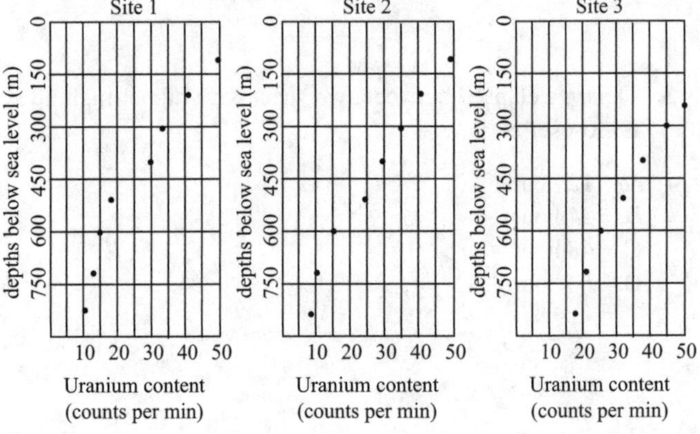

Figure 3

7. A scientist states that at every depth below sea level, the rock at Site 2 is older than the rock at Site 1. Is this statement supported by the information in Figure 3 ?

A. Yes; at every depth, the uranium counts are higher at Site 2 than at Site 1.
B. Yes; at every depth, the uranium counts are lower at Site 2 than at Site 1.
C. No; at approximately 500 m below sea level, the uranium count is higher at Site 2 than at Site 1.
D. No; at approximately 700 m below sea level, the uranium count is lower at Site 2 than at Site 1.

GO ON TO THE NEXT PAGE.

8. According to Figure 2, the shale layer was thickest at which of the following cities or sites?

F. Middleton
G. Site 1
H. Site 3
J. West Union

9. According to Figure 2, as the thickness of shale decreases between Sites 2 and 3, the thickness of limestone residing below:

A. increases.
B. decreases.
C. first decreases then increases.
D. remains constant.

10. According to Figures 2 and 3, the uranium content of the limestone layer of Site 1 ranges from approximately:

F. 11 to 49 counts per minute.
G. 18 to 33 counts per minute.
H. 24 to 35 counts per minute.
J. 33 to 49 counts per minute.

11. According to Figure 3, at Sites 1, 2, and 3 the highest number of counts of uranium-235 detected were recorded at a depth of:

A. less than 300 m below sea level.
B. between 300 and 450 m below sea level.
C. between 450 and 600 m below sea level.
D. greater than 600 m below sea level.

12. The uranium recorded in Sites 1, 2, and 3 is reduced by ½ roughly every 0.7 billion years. Based on Figure 3, and assuming no alteration of this uranium decay, the age of the rock with the greatest depth surveyed at Site 2 is closest to:

F. 2.8 billion years old.
G. 5.6 billion years old.
H. 280 million years old.
J. 560 million years old.

GO ON TO THE NEXT PAGE.

Passage III

For a science fair, a middle school student tested the hypothesis that bubbles in liquids would affect how far a water gun could shoot. To do this, she set up a holding device so that the water gun would always shoot at the same angle (the angle of inclination) and from the same place. She then measured the horizontal distance from the holding device to the furthest observable trace of liquid (see Figure 1).

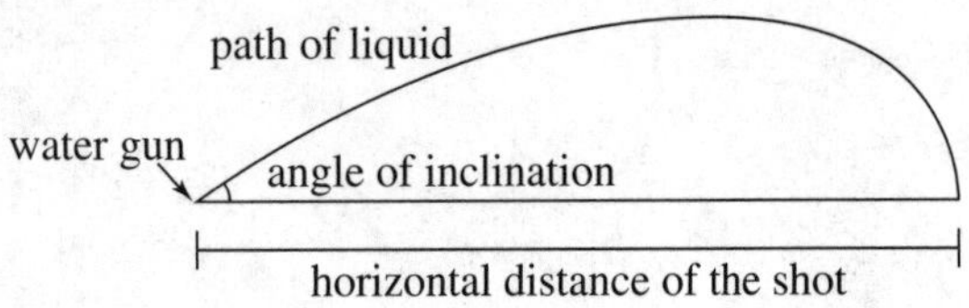

Figure 1

The angle of inclination was 30° in all experiments. The same metal water gun was used in Experiments 1 and 2.

Experiment 1

The student filled the metallic water canister of a water gun to 80% of its capacity with water from her tap (water with no bubbles in it) and measured how far from the holding device the water gun shot. Then, she again filled the canister to 80% of its capacity with tap water, shook the water gun, and immediately measured how far it shot. She repeated these tests with water mixed with laundry detergent, which contained many bubbles, and a flat-tasting cola beverage that showed no visible bubbles. Table 1 shows the results of these trials.

Table 1

Trial	Liquid	Distance shot	
		before shaking (meters)	after shaking (meters)
1	water	6.42	6.42
2	water with detergent	5.36	4.79
3	flat-tasting cola	6.23	5.49

Experiment 2

Next, the student filled the water gun canister to 80% of its capacity with the flat-tasting cola, shook it to create bubbles and then let it sit, undisturbed. When 10 minutes had elapsed, she tested how far the water gun shot the cola, before and after shaking it (Trial 4). She then let it sit undisturbed for an hour before again testing how far it shot before and after shaking it (Trial 5). Table 2 shows the results of these trials.

Table 2

Trial	Distance shot	
	before shaking (meters)	after shaking (meters)
4	5.98	5.49
5	6.23	5.61

Experiment 3

For the third experiment, the student used an old-fashioned, plastic water gun, with transparent walls and the water container in the handle of the water gun. The student added the flat-tasting cola to fill the water container to 80% of its capacity, shot the water gun, and observed that no bubbles formed upon shooting. She then shook the water gun, which caused bubbles to form. After 10 minutes, there were still some visible bubbles in the cola; however, after an hour had passed, there were no visible bubbles.

13. In Experiment 3, what is the most likely reason the student chose to use an old-fashioned plastic water gun rather than a metal water gun? Compared to the metal water gun, the plastic water gun:

A. exhibited different effects of bubbles on shooting distance.
B. did not shoot as far as the metal gun.
C. allowed the student to view the bubbles in the liquid.
D. was easier to fit into the holding device.

GO ON TO THE NEXT PAGE.

14. Based on the results of Experiments 1 and 2, in which of the following two trials, before shaking the water gun, were the distances shot the same?

F. Trials 1 and 4
G. Trials 2 and 3
H. Trials 3 and 4
J. Trials 3 and 5

15. In Experiment 2, a result of shaking the water gun containing the flat-tasting cola was that the:

A. density of the liquid increased.
B. bubbles in the liquid disappeared.
C. distance the liquid was shot increased.
D. distance the liquid was shot decreased.

16. In Trial 5, is it likely that bubbles were present in large numbers in the cola immediately before the canister was shaken?

F. Yes; based on the results of Experiment 1, the bubbles generated in Trial 4 probably lasted for less than 10 minutes.
G. Yes; based on the results of Experiment 1, the bubbles generated in Trial 4 probably lasted for more than 1 hour.
H. No; based on the results of Experiment 3, the bubbles generated in Trial 4 probably lasted for less than 1 hour.
J. No; based on the results of Experiment 3, the bubbles generated in Trial 4 probably lasted for more than 2 hours.

17. Suppose that in Experiment 2, the student had decided to measure the distance the water gun shot the cola one hour after finishing Trial 5 without shaking the water gun again. Based on the observations made in Trials 4 and 5, the horizontal distance the cola was shot would most likely have been:

A. less than 5.49 meters.
B. between 5.49 and 5.51 meters.
C. between 5.52 and 5.98 meters.
D. greater than 5.98 meters.

18. Based on the results of Trials 3–5, if the student filled the metal water gun to 80% of its capacity with the flat-tasting cola and shook it, the time it would take for the bubbles in the cola to disappear to the point that they would have no effect on the distance of the shot would most likely have been:

F. greater than 1 hour.
G. between 10 minutes and 1 hour.
H. between 3 minutes and 9 minutes.
J. less than 3 minutes.

19. In Experiment 2, which of the following best explains the difference between the distances the cola traveled *after shaking* in Trial 4 and in Trial 5 ?

A. The cola traveled further in Trial 4 because there were more bubbles after shaking in Trial 4 than in Trial 5.
B. The cola traveled further in Trial 5 because there were more bubbles after shaking in Trial 4 than in Trial 5.
C. The cola traveled further in Trial 4 because there were more bubbles after shaking in Trial 5 than in Trial 4.
D. The cola traveled further in Trial 5 because there were more bubbles after shaking in Trial 5 than in Trial 4.

GO ON TO THE NEXT PAGE.

Passage IV

Oceanographers conducted a series of experiments with water to explore the relationship between temperature, salinity (% salt by mass), and density (mass per unit volume).

Experiment 1

In a beaker, 35 g of NaCl and 965 g of distilled H_2O were mixed, and the solution was brought to a specific temperature. A graduated cylinder was then used to measure 150 mL of the solution. The mass of this 150-mL sample was measured with an electronic balance and the density (g/mL) was calculated. This procedure was repeated for 5 different temperatures with the results recorded in Table 1.

Table 1

Sample	Solution mass (g)	Temperature (°C)	Density (g/mL)
I	154.2	0	1.028
II	154.1	10	1.027
III	153.9	15	1.026
IV	153.8	20	1.025
V	153.3	30	1.022

Experiment 2

A graduated cylinder was placed on an electronic balance and a certain mass of NaCl was added. Distilled water at 10°C was added to make a 150 mL solution, and the total mass of this was noted. The density (g/mL) and salinity (%) of the solution were calculated. This procedure was repeated for 5 different quantities of NaCl with the results recorded in Table 2.

Table 2

Sample	Solution mass (g)	Salinity (%)	Density (g/mL)
VI	153.0	2.60	1.020
VII	152.7	2.35	1.018
VIII	152.4	2.10	1.016
IX	152.1	1.83	1.014
X	151.8	1.58	1.012

Experiment 3

Water samples from Experiments 1 and 2 were used individually to fill a test pool. For each sample, multiple prototypes of a newly designed instrument were placed in the pool. If a prototype stayed afloat, it was marked with a (+). If a prototype sank, it was marked with a (–). These data were then collected and recorded in Table 3.

Table 3

Water sample	Prototype					
	R5	R6	U3	U4	X1	X2
I	+	+	+	+	+	+
II	+	+	+	+	+	+
III	–	+	+	+	+	+
IV	–	+	+	+	+	+
V	–	–	+	+	+	+
VI	–	–	–	+	+	+
VII	–	–	–	–	+	+
VIII	–	–	–	–	–	+
IX	–	–	–	–	–	–
X	–	–	–	–	–	–

20. In Experiment 1, if an additional sample were brought to 40°C and a density of 1.018 g/mL, what would its expected mass be in the graduated cylinder?

F. 150.9 g
G. 151.8 g
H. 152.7 g
J. 153.6 g

GO ON TO THE NEXT PAGE.

21. Based on Table 2, what is the most likely density of water at 10°C and 2.50% salinity?

A. 1.019
B. 1.017
C. 1.013
D. 1.010

22. An engineer states that prototype U3 is better suited than X2 for water surface data collection in a 10°C and 2.35% salinity environment. Do the results of the experiments support this claim?

F. Yes, because prototype U3 will sink and X2 will float in these water conditions.
G. Yes, because prototype U3 will float and X2 will sink in these water conditions.
H. No, because prototype U3 will sink and X2 will float in these water conditions.
J. No, because prototype U3 will float and X2 will sink in these water conditions.

23. A new prototype is tested in water samples IV through VII in a manner similar to Experiment 3. Which of the following results would NOT be possible?

	Water sample			
	IV	V	VI	VII
A.	–	–	–	–
B.	+	+	+	+
C.	+	+	–	–
D.	–	–	+	+

24. In Experiment 1, samples were transferred to a graduated cylinder to obtain a more accurate and precise measurement of the:

F. mass of the NaCl added to the H_2O.
G. salinity after it reached the designated temperature.
H. volume used to calculate the density.
J. temperature used to determine the final salinity.

25. In a later analysis, the density of prototype U3 is manually determined. Which of the following values would be consistent with the results of Experiments 1 through 3 ?

A. 1.021 g/mL
B. 1.023 g/mL
C. 1.026 g/mL
D. 1.028 g/mL

26. Based on the information in Experiments 1 and 2, the salinity of all of the samples in Experiment 1 was:

F. greater than 3.00%.
G. between 2.00% and 3.00%.
H. between 1.50% and 2.00%.
J. less than 1.50%.

GO ON TO THE NEXT PAGE.

Passage V

Haloarchaea are single-celled microorganisms that can use light to generate energy, through a unique form of *photosynthesis*. To compare haloarchaeal photosynthesis with plant photosynthesis and bacterial fermentation, researchers performed two experiments in which they exposed plant haloarchaeal and bacterial cells to either red or green light. The researchers measured the growth of these cells by measuring how much acid and CO_2 were produced; production of either of these indicates growth.

Experiment 1

Water containing salt and sucrose was added to eight large test tubes. Next, *phenolphthalein* (a pH indicator that is colorless in the presence of acid and has a pink color in its absence) was added to each large test tube. A smaller test tube was then added, inverted, into each large test tube to collect CO_2; if CO_2 had been produced, a gas bubble would appear in this smaller tube (see Figure 1).

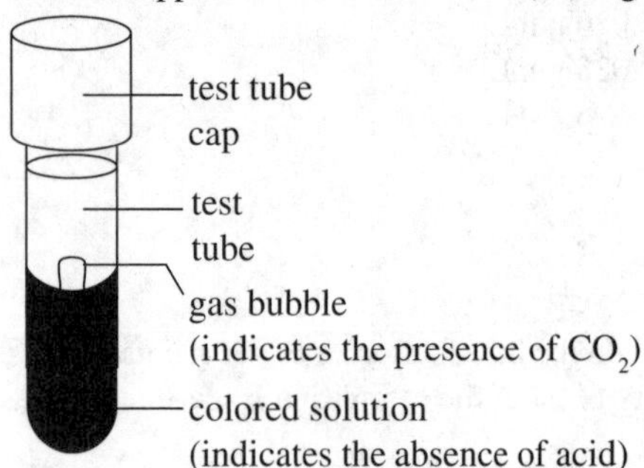

Figure 1

The large test tubes were capped, heated until the solutions were sterile, and then cooled. Nothing was added to the first test tube (T1). Cells of the plant *Rosa carolina* were added to the second test tube (T2), cells of the haloarchaea *NRC-1* were added to the third test tube (T3), and cells of the bacterium *Bacillus anthracis* were added to the fourth test tube (T4). These four test tubes were exposed to red light, and incubated at 37°C for 48 hr. Then, the procedure was repeated with exposure to green light, using the four remaining test tubes: T5 (no cells), T6 (plant cells), T7 (haloarchaeal cells), and T8 (bacterial cells). In Table 1, + means presence and – means absence.

Table 1

Red light			Green light		
	Acid	CO_2		Acid	CO_2
T1: Control	–	–	T5: Control	–	–
T2: Plant	–	+	T6: Plant	–	–
T3: Haloarchaea	–	–	T7: Haloarchaea	+	–
T4: Bacterium	+	+	T8: Bacterium	+	+

Experiment 2

Some of the cells tested in Experiment 1 are thought to contain pigments that help them absorb light. To determine whether these cells absorbed light to generate energy, cells of the same species are exposed to red and green light in new test tubes. The researchers measure the *transmittance*, or the amount of light that transmits through the test tube. If the transmittance is low, then the cells in the test tube are assumed to contain pigments that absorb most of the light to generate energy. If the transmittance is high, then the cells are assumed to contain no pigment that could absorb light and generate energy. Instead, most of the light passes through the test tube.

Table 2

Red light		Green light	
	Transmittance		Transmittance
T9: Plant	Low	T12: Plant	High
T10: Haloarchaea	High	T13: Haloarchaea	Low
T11: Bacterium	High	T14: Bacterium	High

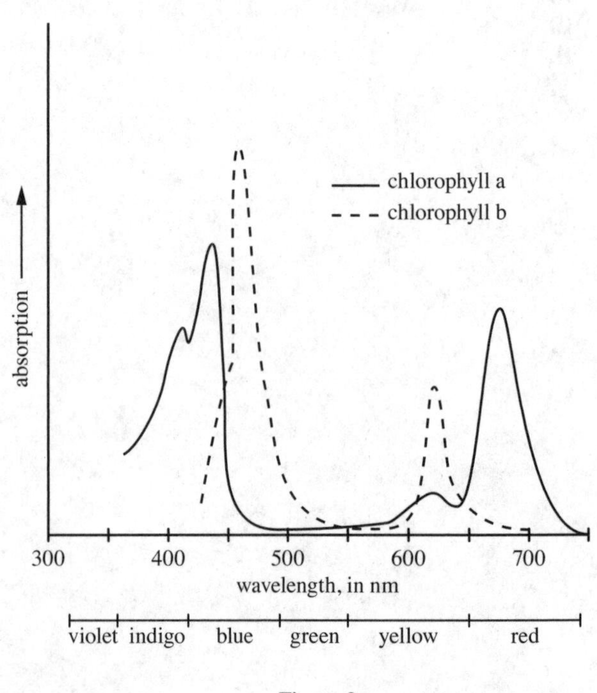

Figure 2

GO ON TO THE NEXT PAGE.

27. Figure 2 shows the absorption of light by two different forms of chlorophyll at various wavelengths. Which of the strains of chlorophyll is most likely responsible for photosynthesis in *Rosa carolina*?

A. Chlorophyll *a*; the absorption of chlorophyll *a* is higher than that of chlorophyll *b* in green light.
B. Chlorophyll *b*; the absorption of chlorophyll *b* is higher than that of chlorophyll *a* in green light.
C. Chlorophyll *a*; the absorption of chlorophyll *a* is higher than that of chlorophyll *b* in red light.
D. Chlorophyll *b*; the absorption of chlorophyll *b* is higher than that of chlorophyll *a* in red light.

28. In Experiment 1, which cell types grew in the presence of green light?

F. Plant cells only
G. Plant and bacterial cells only
H. Plant and haloarchaeal cells only
J. Haloarchaeal and bacterial cells only

29. Suppose that plant cells and haloarchaeal cells that are situated close to each other do not interfere with each other's absorption of light and generation of energy. If a new test tube containing both plant and haloarchaeal cells were prepared, what would be the most likely results for Experiments 1 and 2 ?

	Red light			Green light		
	Acid	CO_2	Transmittance	Acid	CO_2	Transmittance
A.	–	–	High	–	–	High
B.	–	+	Low	+	–	Low
C.	+	–	Low	–	+	High
D.	+	+	High	+	+	Low

30. Suppose that a scientist isolates a cell type that is one of the four cell types used in Experiment 1. She finds that this cell type produces CO_2 in the presence of red light. She then tests the cell type in the presence of green light and finds that neither CO_2 nor acid is produced. Based on the results of Experiment 1, the cell type is most likely the:

F. control with nothing added.
G. plant *Rosa carolina*.
H. haloarchea *NRC-1*.
J. bacterium *Bacillus anthracis*.

31. What is the evidence from Experiments 1 and 2 that haloarchaea can generate energy when exposed to green light?

A. In the presence of green light, haloarchaea show low transmittance and produce no acid.
B. In the presence of green light, haloarchaea show high transmittance and produce acid.
C. In the presence of green light, haloarchaea show low transmittance and produce acid.
D. In the presence of green light, haloarchaea show high transmittance and produce no acid.

32. Which of the following best illustrates the results of Experiment 1 for the plant *Rosa carolina* in red light?

F.
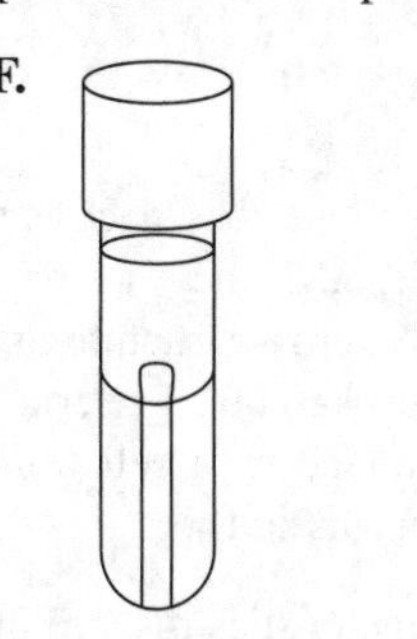

H.
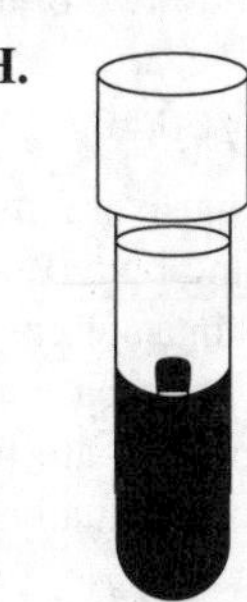

G.
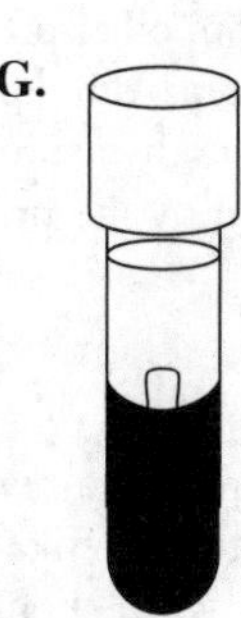

J.
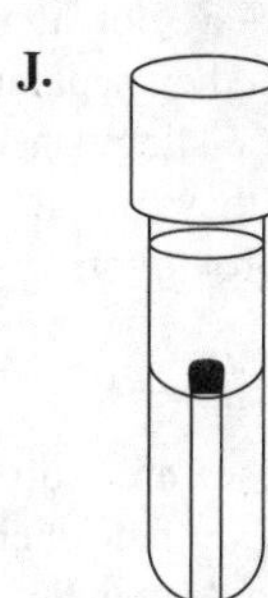

33. Do the results of Experiment 1 support the hypothesis that haloarchaea and bacteria use similar processes to generate energy?

A. Yes, because both haloarchaea and bacteria produce CO_2 in the presence of green light.
B. Yes, because both haloarchaea and bacteria produce CO_2 in the presence of red light.
C. No, because haloarchaea produce only acid in the presence of green light, while bacteria produce acid and CO_2 in both red and green light.
D. No, because neither haloarchaea nor bacteria produce CO_2 in the presence of either red or green light.

GO ON TO THE NEXT PAGE.

Passage VI

For most of the 20th century, scientists recognized two basic domains of living organisms, *prokaryotes* and *eukaryotes*. The presence of nuclei and other membrane-bound organelles within the cell primarily distinguished eukaryotes from prokaryotes. The possibility of revising this dichotomy resulted from the discovery of the *Archaea*, organisms with unique cell membrane and *ribosomal RNA (rRNA)* structure. Cell membranes are composed of *phospholipids* that have both water-insoluble and water-soluble subunits. *Ribosomes* are made of protein and rRNA and build new proteins within the cell.

Two scientists in the 1990s debate whether organisms should be classified into two or three domains.

2-Domain Hypothesis

The Archaea are prokaryotes because they lack intracellular membrane-bound organelles. Although they are found in extreme and unusual environments, the gross structure and life cycle of the Archaea are similar to prokaryotic bacteria. Like bacteria, their cells are usually surrounded by a cell wall, and they reproduce asexually through binary fission.

The structural and metabolic characteristics that are unique to the Archaea are not significantly different from other prokaryotes to warrant their separation into a third domain. Although the Archaea were distinguished very early on in the diversification of life, today they remain appropriately defined by the original definition of prokaryote.

3-Domain Hypothesis

The Archaea are a distinct form of life requiring a revision of the previously held dichotomy of prokaryote and eukaryote. Eukaryota should remain the same, but prokaryotes should be split into Archaea and Bacteria because of significant differences in genetics, structure, and metabolism.

Archaea as a domain is justified by detailed analysis. The genetic sequence of rRNA in the Archaea is so distinct from prokaryotes and eukaryotes that these groups of organisms likely diverged over 3 billion years ago. Archaea cell membranes contain more rigid *ether linkages* instead of the *ester linkages* found in eukaryotes and bacteria. This contributes to their survival in harsh environments. Finally, the Archaea are capable of exploiting a wider range of energy sources compared to eukaryotes and bacteria.

34. Which of the following statements is most consistent with the *3-Domain Hypothesis*? The time, in millions of years ago, when two groups of organisms diverge on the evolutionary tree increases as the:

F. similarities between rRNA gene sequences increase.
G. differences between rRNA gene sequences increase.
H. number of ester linkages in the cell membrane increases.
J. number of ether linkages in the cell membrane decreases.

35. By referring to the observation that the newly discovered organisms do not have membrane-bound organelles, the scientist supporting the 2-Domain Hypothesis implies that these new organisms do not have which of the following structures?

A. Phospholipids
B. Ribosomes
C. rRNA
D. Nuclei

36. According to the passage, a similarity between eukaryotes and prokaryotes is that both groups of organisms:

F. have ester linkages in their membranes.
G. contain membrane-bound organelles.
H. reproduce sexually.
J. are composed of cells.

37. According to the scientist who supports the 2-Domain Hypothesis, which of the following is the strongest argument AGAINST using a 3-Domain classification?

A. rRNA does not exist in prokaryotes.
B. Ether linkages are found in the cell membranes of the Archaea.
C. The Archaea meet the primary definition of prokaryotic.
D. The Archaea synthesize proteins in the cell cytoplasm.

GO ON TO THE NEXT PAGE.

38. It is shown that the Archaea have protein synthesis structures and mechanisms more like eukaryotes than prokaryotes. This observation contradicts arguments stated in which hypothesis?

F. The 2-Domain Hypothesis, because the discovery would show that the new organisms and bacteria fundamentally differ in cellular metabolism.
G. The 2-Domain Hypothesis, because the discovery would show that the new organisms and eukaryotes fundamentally differ in cellular metabolism.
H. The 3-Domain Hypothesis, because the discovery would show that the new organisms and bacteria fundamentally differ in cellular metabolism.
J. The 3-Domain Hypothesis, because the discovery would show that the new organisms and eukaryotes fundamentally differ in cellular metabolism.

39. The scientist who supports the 3-Domain Hypothesis implies that the 2-Domain Hypothesis is WEAKENED by which observation?

A. The Archaea have membrane-bound organelles.
B. Microscopes cannot accurately describe organisms.
C. The Archaea lack ester linkages in their cell membranes.
D. Eukaryotes are not related to the Archaea.

40. Which of the following illustrations of a portion of a phospholipid cell membrane is consistent with the description in the passage?

Key
○ — water soluble
|| — water insoluble

F.
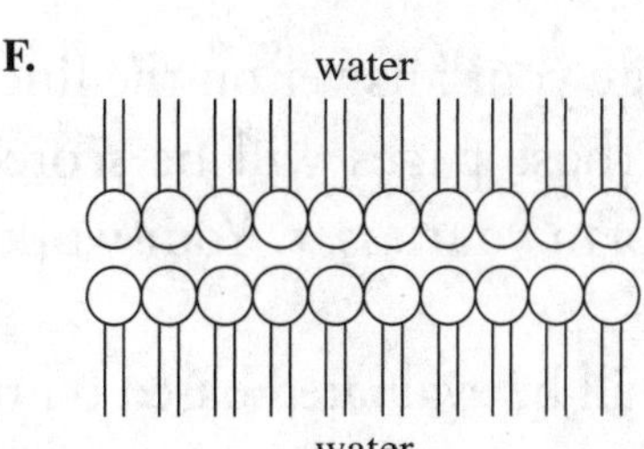

G.
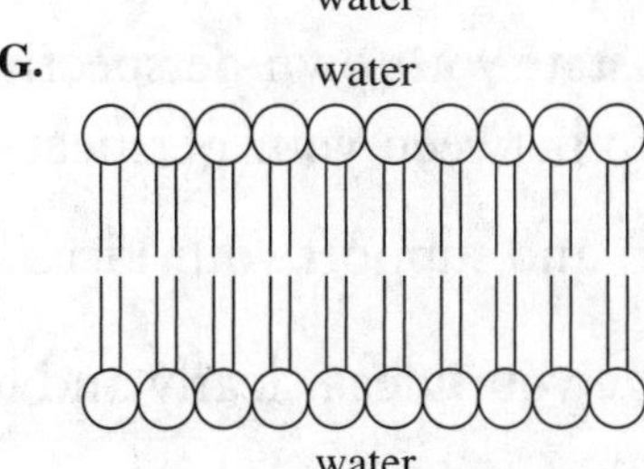

H.
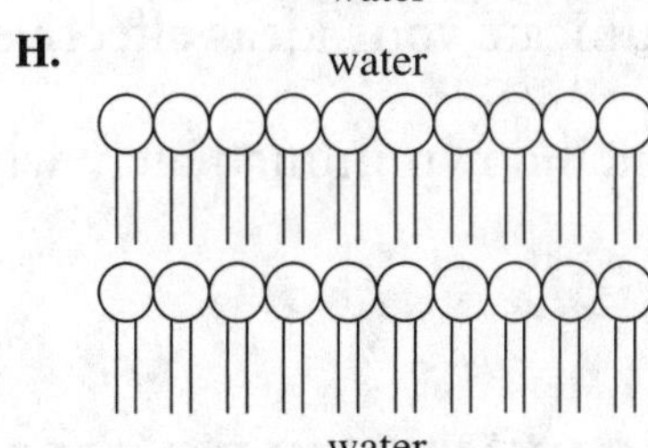

J.
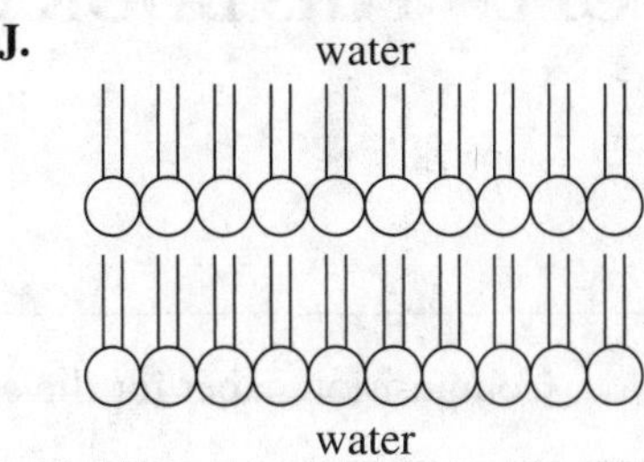

END OF TEST 4
STOP! DO NOT RETURN TO ANY OTHER TEST.

Directions

This is a test of your writing skills. You will have forty (40) minutes to read the prompt, plan your response, and write an essay in English. Before you begin working, read all material in this test booklet carefully to understand exactly what you are being asked to do.

You will write your answer on the lined pages in the answer document provided. Your writing on those pages will be scored. You may use the unlined pages in this test booklet to plan your essay. Your work on these pages will not be scored.

Your essay will be evaluated based on the evidence it provides of your ability to:

- clearly state your own perspective on a complex issue and analyze the relationship between your perspective and at least one other perspective
- develop and support your ideas with reasoning and examples
- organize your ideas clearly and logically
- communicate your ideas effectively in standard written English

Lay your pencil down immediately when time is called.

DO NOT OPEN THIS BOOK UNTIL YOU ARE TOLD TO DO SO.

Composition paper for the essay can be found beginning on page 763.

Social Media Bridging the Generation Gap

As the various forms of social media continue to proliferate and distract in today's society, it is rare to encounter an individual who doesn't have an account on a popular social networking site. According to a 2015 poll, one such site has around 1,490,000,000 active users with approximately 25% aged 16-24, 29% aged 25-34, 22% aged 35-44, and 24% aged 45 and older. Families are able to keep up to date on events without directly communicating. Products are more likely to be sold thanks to targeted advertisements. Employers are able to reach a larger number of potential employees with job postings.

Read and carefully consider these perspectives. Each suggests a particular way of thinking about the conflict over how social media affects each generation.

Perspective One

It's shocking that people over a certain age still use social media. As social media outlets continue to grow, they are aimed primarily at the youth market, not the older market. Since more than half of the users are at or younger than 34 years old, social media outlets should focus on prospective younger users than older users.

Perspective Two

Since parents can access their children's social profiles, many teenagers have been forced to create secondary accounts to keep their privacy intact. Emotional conflicts arise when children block parents from accessing their profiles, which can drive wedges into familial and generational relationships.

Perspective Three

Social media is what drives communication throughout the world. Currently, younger members can interact with the world around them, and older members can interact with acquaintances with whom they have lost touch. The increase in exposure to different voices and perspectives helps bring awareness to issues that can lead to greater understanding between individuals of different generations.

Essay Task

Write a unified, coherent essay in which you evaluate multiple perspectives on the issue of social media bridging the gap among generations. In your essay, be sure to:

- clearly state your own perspective on the issue and analyze the relationship between your perspective and at least one other perspective
- develop and support your ideas with reasoning and examples
- organize your ideas clearly and logically
- communicate your ideas effectively in standard written English

Your perspective may be in full agreement with any of the others, in partial agreement, or wholly different. Whatever the case, support your ideas with logical reasoning and detailed, persuasive examples.

ACT Diagnostic Test Form

USE A SOFT LEAD NO. 2 PENCIL ONLY. (Do NOT use a mechanical pencil, ink, ballpoint, correction fluid, or felt-tip pen.)

E-MAIL: ____________________

PHONE NO.: ____________________
(Print)

SCHOOL: ____________________

CLASS OF: ____________________

IMPORTANT: Please fill in these boxes exactly as shown on the back cover of your tests book.

2. TEST FORM

3. TEST CODE

⓪ ⓪ ⓪ ⓪
① ① ① ①
② ② ② ②
③ ③ ③ ③
④ ④ ④ ④
⑤ ⑤ ⑤ ⑤
⑥ ⑥ ⑥ ⑥
⑦ ⑦ ⑦ ⑦
⑧ ⑧ ⑧ ⑧
⑨ ⑨ ⑨ ⑨

ALL examinees must complete Blocks A, B, C, and D – please print.

A NAME, MAILING ADDRESS, AND TELEPHONE (Please print.)

Last Name | First Name | MI (Middle Initial)

House Number & Street (Apt. No.); or PO Box & No.; or RR & No.

City | State/Province | ZIP/Postal Code

Area Code / Number | Country

B MATCH NAME (First 5 letters of last name)

A B C D E F G H I J K L M N O P Q R S T U V W X Y Z

C MATCH NUMBER

1 2 3 4 5 6 7 8 9 0

D DATE OF BIRTH

Month | Day | Year

January
February
March
April
May
June
July
August
September
October
November
December

BOOKLET NUMBER

1 2 3 4 5 6 7 8 9 0

FORM

Print your 3-character **Test Form** in the boxes above and fill in the corresponding oval at the right.

BE SURE TO FILL IN THE CORRECT FORM OVAL.

PRE ◯

Marking Directions: Mark only **one** oval for each question. Fill in response completely. Erase errors cleanly without smudging.

Correct mark:

Do NOT use these *incorrect* or *bad* marks.

Incorrect marks:
Overlapping mark:
Cross-out mark:
Smudged erasure:
Mark is too light:

THIS PAGE INTENTIONALLY LEFT BLANK

The Princeton Review Diagnostic ACT Form

USE A SOFT LEAD NO. 2 PENCIL ONLY. (Do NOT use a mechanical pencil, ink, ballpoint, correction fluid, or felt-tip pen.)

TEST 1: ENGLISH

1 Ⓐ Ⓑ Ⓒ Ⓓ	14 Ⓕ Ⓖ Ⓗ Ⓙ	27 Ⓐ Ⓑ Ⓒ Ⓓ	40 Ⓕ Ⓖ Ⓗ Ⓙ	53 Ⓐ Ⓑ Ⓒ Ⓓ	66 Ⓕ Ⓖ Ⓗ Ⓙ
2 Ⓕ Ⓖ Ⓗ Ⓙ	15 Ⓐ Ⓑ Ⓒ Ⓓ	28 Ⓕ Ⓖ Ⓗ Ⓙ	41 Ⓐ Ⓑ Ⓒ Ⓓ	54 Ⓕ Ⓖ Ⓗ Ⓙ	67 Ⓐ Ⓑ Ⓒ Ⓓ
3 Ⓐ Ⓑ Ⓒ Ⓓ	16 Ⓕ Ⓖ Ⓗ Ⓙ	29 Ⓐ Ⓑ Ⓒ Ⓓ	42 Ⓕ Ⓖ Ⓗ Ⓙ	55 Ⓐ Ⓑ Ⓒ Ⓓ	68 Ⓕ Ⓖ Ⓗ Ⓙ
4 Ⓕ Ⓖ Ⓗ Ⓙ	17 Ⓐ Ⓑ Ⓒ Ⓓ	30 Ⓕ Ⓖ Ⓗ Ⓙ	43 Ⓐ Ⓑ Ⓒ Ⓓ	56 Ⓕ Ⓖ Ⓗ Ⓙ	69 Ⓐ Ⓑ Ⓒ Ⓓ
5 Ⓐ Ⓑ Ⓒ Ⓓ	18 Ⓕ Ⓖ Ⓗ Ⓙ	31 Ⓐ Ⓑ Ⓒ Ⓓ	44 Ⓕ Ⓖ Ⓗ Ⓙ	57 Ⓐ Ⓑ Ⓒ Ⓓ	70 Ⓕ Ⓖ Ⓗ Ⓙ
6 Ⓕ Ⓖ Ⓗ Ⓙ	19 Ⓐ Ⓑ Ⓒ Ⓓ	32 Ⓕ Ⓖ Ⓗ Ⓙ	45 Ⓐ Ⓑ Ⓒ Ⓓ	58 Ⓕ Ⓖ Ⓗ Ⓙ	71 Ⓐ Ⓑ Ⓒ Ⓓ
7 Ⓐ Ⓑ Ⓒ Ⓓ	20 Ⓕ Ⓖ Ⓗ Ⓙ	33 Ⓐ Ⓑ Ⓒ Ⓓ	46 Ⓕ Ⓖ Ⓗ Ⓙ	59 Ⓐ Ⓑ Ⓒ Ⓓ	72 Ⓕ Ⓖ Ⓗ Ⓙ
8 Ⓕ Ⓖ Ⓗ Ⓙ	21 Ⓐ Ⓑ Ⓒ Ⓓ	34 Ⓕ Ⓖ Ⓗ Ⓙ	47 Ⓐ Ⓑ Ⓒ Ⓓ	60 Ⓕ Ⓖ Ⓗ Ⓙ	73 Ⓐ Ⓑ Ⓒ Ⓓ
9 Ⓐ Ⓑ Ⓒ Ⓓ	22 Ⓕ Ⓖ Ⓗ Ⓙ	35 Ⓐ Ⓑ Ⓒ Ⓓ	48 Ⓕ Ⓖ Ⓗ Ⓙ	61 Ⓐ Ⓑ Ⓒ Ⓓ	74 Ⓕ Ⓖ Ⓗ Ⓙ
10 Ⓕ Ⓖ Ⓗ Ⓙ	23 Ⓐ Ⓑ Ⓒ Ⓓ	36 Ⓕ Ⓖ Ⓗ Ⓙ	49 Ⓐ Ⓑ Ⓒ Ⓓ	62 Ⓕ Ⓖ Ⓗ Ⓙ	75 Ⓐ Ⓑ Ⓒ Ⓓ
11 Ⓐ Ⓑ Ⓒ Ⓓ	24 Ⓕ Ⓖ Ⓗ Ⓙ	37 Ⓐ Ⓑ Ⓒ Ⓓ	50 Ⓕ Ⓖ Ⓗ Ⓙ	63 Ⓐ Ⓑ Ⓒ Ⓓ	
12 Ⓕ Ⓖ Ⓗ Ⓙ	25 Ⓐ Ⓑ Ⓒ Ⓓ	38 Ⓕ Ⓖ Ⓗ Ⓙ	51 Ⓐ Ⓑ Ⓒ Ⓓ	64 Ⓕ Ⓖ Ⓗ Ⓙ	
13 Ⓐ Ⓑ Ⓒ Ⓓ	26 Ⓕ Ⓖ Ⓗ Ⓙ	39 Ⓐ Ⓑ Ⓒ Ⓓ	52 Ⓕ Ⓖ Ⓗ Ⓙ	65 Ⓐ Ⓑ Ⓒ Ⓓ	

TEST 2: MATHEMATICS

1 Ⓐ Ⓑ Ⓒ Ⓓ Ⓔ	11 Ⓐ Ⓑ Ⓒ Ⓓ Ⓔ	21 Ⓐ Ⓑ Ⓒ Ⓓ Ⓔ	31 Ⓐ Ⓑ Ⓒ Ⓓ Ⓔ	41 Ⓐ Ⓑ Ⓒ Ⓓ Ⓔ	51 Ⓐ Ⓑ Ⓒ Ⓓ Ⓔ
2 Ⓕ Ⓖ Ⓗ Ⓙ Ⓚ	12 Ⓕ Ⓖ Ⓗ Ⓙ Ⓚ	22 Ⓕ Ⓖ Ⓗ Ⓙ Ⓚ	32 Ⓕ Ⓖ Ⓗ Ⓙ Ⓚ	42 Ⓕ Ⓖ Ⓗ Ⓙ Ⓚ	52 Ⓕ Ⓖ Ⓗ Ⓙ Ⓚ
3 Ⓐ Ⓑ Ⓒ Ⓓ Ⓔ	13 Ⓐ Ⓑ Ⓒ Ⓓ Ⓔ	23 Ⓐ Ⓑ Ⓒ Ⓓ Ⓔ	33 Ⓐ Ⓑ Ⓒ Ⓓ Ⓔ	43 Ⓐ Ⓑ Ⓒ Ⓓ Ⓔ	53 Ⓐ Ⓑ Ⓒ Ⓓ Ⓔ
4 Ⓕ Ⓖ Ⓗ Ⓙ Ⓚ	14 Ⓕ Ⓖ Ⓗ Ⓙ Ⓚ	24 Ⓕ Ⓖ Ⓗ Ⓙ Ⓚ	34 Ⓕ Ⓖ Ⓗ Ⓙ Ⓚ	44 Ⓕ Ⓖ Ⓗ Ⓙ Ⓚ	54 Ⓕ Ⓖ Ⓗ Ⓙ Ⓚ
5 Ⓐ Ⓑ Ⓒ Ⓓ Ⓔ	15 Ⓐ Ⓑ Ⓒ Ⓓ Ⓔ	25 Ⓐ Ⓑ Ⓒ Ⓓ Ⓔ	35 Ⓐ Ⓑ Ⓒ Ⓓ Ⓔ	45 Ⓐ Ⓑ Ⓒ Ⓓ Ⓔ	55 Ⓐ Ⓑ Ⓒ Ⓓ Ⓔ
6 Ⓕ Ⓖ Ⓗ Ⓙ Ⓚ	16 Ⓕ Ⓖ Ⓗ Ⓙ Ⓚ	26 Ⓕ Ⓖ Ⓗ Ⓙ Ⓚ	36 Ⓕ Ⓖ Ⓗ Ⓙ Ⓚ	46 Ⓕ Ⓖ Ⓗ Ⓙ Ⓚ	56 Ⓕ Ⓖ Ⓗ Ⓙ Ⓚ
7 Ⓐ Ⓑ Ⓒ Ⓓ Ⓔ	17 Ⓐ Ⓑ Ⓒ Ⓓ Ⓔ	27 Ⓐ Ⓑ Ⓒ Ⓓ Ⓔ	37 Ⓐ Ⓑ Ⓒ Ⓓ Ⓔ	47 Ⓐ Ⓑ Ⓒ Ⓓ Ⓔ	57 Ⓐ Ⓑ Ⓒ Ⓓ Ⓔ
8 Ⓕ Ⓖ Ⓗ Ⓙ Ⓚ	18 Ⓕ Ⓖ Ⓗ Ⓙ Ⓚ	28 Ⓕ Ⓖ Ⓗ Ⓙ Ⓚ	38 Ⓕ Ⓖ Ⓗ Ⓙ Ⓚ	48 Ⓕ Ⓖ Ⓗ Ⓙ Ⓚ	58 Ⓕ Ⓖ Ⓗ Ⓙ Ⓚ
9 Ⓐ Ⓑ Ⓒ Ⓓ Ⓔ	19 Ⓐ Ⓑ Ⓒ Ⓓ Ⓔ	29 Ⓐ Ⓑ Ⓒ Ⓓ Ⓔ	39 Ⓐ Ⓑ Ⓒ Ⓓ Ⓔ	49 Ⓐ Ⓑ Ⓒ Ⓓ Ⓔ	59 Ⓐ Ⓑ Ⓒ Ⓓ Ⓔ
10 Ⓕ Ⓖ Ⓗ Ⓙ Ⓚ	20 Ⓕ Ⓖ Ⓗ Ⓙ Ⓚ	30 Ⓕ Ⓖ Ⓗ Ⓙ Ⓚ	40 Ⓕ Ⓖ Ⓗ Ⓙ Ⓚ	50 Ⓕ Ⓖ Ⓗ Ⓙ Ⓚ	60 Ⓕ Ⓖ Ⓗ Ⓙ Ⓚ

The Princeton Review Diagnostic ACT Form

USE A SOFT LEAD NO. 2 PENCIL ONLY.
(Do NOT use a mechanical pencil, ink, ballpoint, correction fluid, or felt-tip pen.)

TEST 3: READING

1 Ⓐ Ⓑ Ⓒ Ⓓ	8 Ⓕ Ⓖ Ⓗ Ⓙ	15 Ⓐ Ⓑ Ⓒ Ⓓ	22 Ⓕ Ⓖ Ⓗ Ⓙ	29 Ⓐ Ⓑ Ⓒ Ⓓ	36 Ⓕ Ⓖ Ⓗ Ⓙ
2 Ⓕ Ⓖ Ⓗ Ⓙ	9 Ⓐ Ⓑ Ⓒ Ⓓ	16 Ⓕ Ⓖ Ⓗ Ⓙ	23 Ⓐ Ⓑ Ⓒ Ⓓ	30 Ⓕ Ⓖ Ⓗ Ⓙ	37 Ⓐ Ⓑ Ⓒ Ⓓ
3 Ⓐ Ⓑ Ⓒ Ⓓ	10 Ⓕ Ⓖ Ⓗ Ⓙ	17 Ⓐ Ⓑ Ⓒ Ⓓ	24 Ⓕ Ⓖ Ⓗ Ⓙ	31 Ⓐ Ⓑ Ⓒ Ⓓ	38 Ⓕ Ⓖ Ⓗ Ⓙ
4 Ⓕ Ⓖ Ⓗ Ⓙ	11 Ⓐ Ⓑ Ⓒ Ⓓ	18 Ⓕ Ⓖ Ⓗ Ⓙ	25 Ⓐ Ⓑ Ⓒ Ⓓ	32 Ⓕ Ⓖ Ⓗ Ⓙ	39 Ⓐ Ⓑ Ⓒ Ⓓ
5 Ⓐ Ⓑ Ⓒ Ⓓ	12 Ⓕ Ⓖ Ⓗ Ⓙ	19 Ⓐ Ⓑ Ⓒ Ⓓ	26 Ⓕ Ⓖ Ⓗ Ⓙ	33 Ⓐ Ⓑ Ⓒ Ⓓ	40 Ⓕ Ⓖ Ⓗ Ⓙ
6 Ⓕ Ⓖ Ⓗ Ⓙ	13 Ⓐ Ⓑ Ⓒ Ⓓ	20 Ⓕ Ⓖ Ⓗ Ⓙ	27 Ⓐ Ⓑ Ⓒ Ⓓ	34 Ⓕ Ⓖ Ⓗ Ⓙ	
7 Ⓐ Ⓑ Ⓒ Ⓓ	14 Ⓕ Ⓖ Ⓗ Ⓙ	21 Ⓐ Ⓑ Ⓒ Ⓓ	28 Ⓕ Ⓖ Ⓗ Ⓙ	35 Ⓐ Ⓑ Ⓒ Ⓓ	

TEST 4: SCIENCE

1 Ⓐ Ⓑ Ⓒ Ⓓ	8 Ⓕ Ⓖ Ⓗ Ⓙ	15 Ⓐ Ⓑ Ⓒ Ⓓ	22 Ⓕ Ⓖ Ⓗ Ⓙ	29 Ⓐ Ⓑ Ⓒ Ⓓ	36 Ⓕ Ⓖ Ⓗ Ⓙ
2 Ⓕ Ⓖ Ⓗ Ⓙ	9 Ⓐ Ⓑ Ⓒ Ⓓ	16 Ⓕ Ⓖ Ⓗ Ⓙ	23 Ⓐ Ⓑ Ⓒ Ⓓ	30 Ⓕ Ⓖ Ⓗ Ⓙ	37 Ⓐ Ⓑ Ⓒ Ⓓ
3 Ⓐ Ⓑ Ⓒ Ⓓ	10 Ⓕ Ⓖ Ⓗ Ⓙ	17 Ⓐ Ⓑ Ⓒ Ⓓ	24 Ⓕ Ⓖ Ⓗ Ⓙ	31 Ⓐ Ⓑ Ⓒ Ⓓ	38 Ⓕ Ⓖ Ⓗ Ⓙ
4 Ⓕ Ⓖ Ⓗ Ⓙ	11 Ⓐ Ⓑ Ⓒ Ⓓ	18 Ⓕ Ⓖ Ⓗ Ⓙ	25 Ⓐ Ⓑ Ⓒ Ⓓ	32 Ⓕ Ⓖ Ⓗ Ⓙ	39 Ⓐ Ⓑ Ⓒ Ⓓ
5 Ⓐ Ⓑ Ⓒ Ⓓ	12 Ⓕ Ⓖ Ⓗ Ⓙ	19 Ⓐ Ⓑ Ⓒ Ⓓ	26 Ⓕ Ⓖ Ⓗ Ⓙ	33 Ⓐ Ⓑ Ⓒ Ⓓ	40 Ⓕ Ⓖ Ⓗ Ⓙ
6 Ⓕ Ⓖ Ⓗ Ⓙ	13 Ⓐ Ⓑ Ⓒ Ⓓ	20 Ⓕ Ⓖ Ⓗ Ⓙ	27 Ⓐ Ⓑ Ⓒ Ⓓ	34 Ⓕ Ⓖ Ⓗ Ⓙ	
7 Ⓐ Ⓑ Ⓒ Ⓓ	14 Ⓕ Ⓖ Ⓗ Ⓙ	21 Ⓐ Ⓑ Ⓒ Ⓓ	28 Ⓕ Ⓖ Ⓗ Ⓙ	35 Ⓐ Ⓑ Ⓒ Ⓓ	

I hereby certify that I have truthfully identified myself on this form. I accept the consequences of falsifying my identity.

____
Your signature

____
Today's date

The Princeton Review
Diagnostic ACT Form

ESSAY

Begin your essay on this side. If necessary, continue on the opposite side.

Continue on the opposite side if necessary.

The Princeton Review
Diagnostic ACT Form

Continued from previous page.

PLEASE PRINT YOUR INITIALS

First	Middle	Last

The Princeton Review Diagnostic ACT Form

Continued from previous page.

PLEASE PRINT YOUR INITIALS

First	Middle	Last

The Princeton Review
Diagnostic ACT Form

Continued from previous page.

PLEASE PRINT YOUR INITIALS

First	Middle	Last

Test 3
Answers and Explanations

TEST 3 ENGLISH ANSWERS

1. D
2. G
3. D
4. H
5. A
6. H
7. D
8. G
9. D
10. H
11. A
12. G
13. A
14. G
15. D
16. J
17. C
18. F
19. C
20. H
21. B
22. G
23. D
24. J
25. A
26. F
27. D
28. F
29. B
30. H
31. B
32. H
33. C
34. J
35. C
36. J
37. A
38. J
39. C
40. J
41. C
42. F
43. C
44. G
45. D
46. J
47. C
48. J
49. B
50. J
51. A
52. G
53. C
54. F
55. B
56. F
57. C
58. H
59. D
60. G
61. D
62. G
63. C
64. J
65. C
66. H
67. A
68. G
69. D
70. J
71. B
72. H
73. B
74. F
75. A

TEST 3 MATH ANSWERS

1. D
2. G
3. B
4. K
5. B
6. G
7. E
8. G
9. C
10. H
11. D
12. F
13. B
14. H
15. E
16. G
17. D
18. K
19. C
20. H
21. E
22. J
23. E
24. H
25. D
26. H
27. D
28. G
29. B
30. J
31. D
32. F
33. D
34. G
35. E
36. F
37. E
38. F
39. C
40. H
41. B
42. J
43. D
44. H
45. E
46. G
47. E
48. G
49. B
50. J
51. B
52. G
53. A
54. H
55. E
56. F
57. D
58. J
59. C
60. G

TEST 3 READING ANSWERS

1. A
2. H
3. D
4. H
5. C
6. H
7. A
8. G
9. D
10. F
11. A
12. J
13. A
14. H
15. C
16. J
17. D
18. J
19. B
20. H
21. A
22. H
23. A
24. G
25. D
26. H
27. A
28. G
29. D
30. F
31. D
32. G
33. B
34. F
35. C
36. H
37. D
38. F
39. C
40. H

TEST 3 SCIENCE ANSWERS

1. C
2. F
3. B
4. H
5. D
6. G
7. C
8. G
9. A
10. G
11. A
12. G
13. C
14. J
15. D
16. H
17. D
18. G
19. B
20. H
21. A
22. H
23. D
24. H
25. A
26. F
27. C
28. J
29. B
30. G
31. C
32. G
33. C
34. G
35. D
36. J
37. C
38. F
39. C
40. G

SCORING YOUR PRACTICE EXAM

Step A

Count the number of correct answers for each section and record the number in the space provided for your raw score on the Score Conversion Worksheet below.

Step B

Using the Score Conversion Chart on the next page, convert your raw scores on each section to scaled scores. Then compute your composite ACT score by averaging the four subject scores. Add them up and divide by four. Don't worry about the essay score; it is not included in your composite score.

Score Conversion Worksheet		
Section	**Raw Score**	**Scaled Score**
1	______/75	________
2	______/60	________
3	______/40	________
4	______/40	________

Scale Score	English	Math	Reading	Science	Scale Score
36	75	60	40	40	**36**
35	73–74	59	39	39	**35**
34	72	58	38	38	**34**
33	71	57	37	37	**33**
32	70	56	36	—	**32**
31	69	54–55	34–35	36	**31**
30	68	53	33	35	**30**
29	67	51–52	32	34	**29**
28	65–66	49–50	30–31	33	**28**
27	64	46–48	29	32	**27**
26	62–63	44–45	28	30–31	**26**
25	60–61	41–43	27	28–29	**25**
24	58–59	39–40	26	27	**24**
23	55–57	37–38	24–25	25–26	**23**
22	53–54	35–36	23	23–24	**22**
21	50–52	33–34	22	21–22	**21**
20	47–49	31–32	21	19–20	**20**
19	44–46	28–30	19–20	17–18	**19**
18	42–43	25–27	18	15–16	**18**
17	40–41	22–24	17	14	**17**
16	37–39	18–21	16	13	**16**
15	34–36	15–17	15	12	**15**
14	31–33	11–14	13–14	11	**14**
13	29–30	9–10	12	10	**13**
12	27–28	7–8	10–11	9	**12**
11	25–26	6	8-9	8	**11**
10	23–24	5	7	7	**10**
9	21–22	4	6	6	**9**
8	18–20	3	5	5	**8**
7	15–17	—	—	4	**7**
6	12–14	2	4	3	**6**
5	9–11	—	3	2	**5**
4	7–8	1	2	—	**4**
3	5–6	—	—	1	**3**
2	3–4	—	1	—	**2**
1	0–2	0	0	0	**1**

TEST 3 ENGLISH ANSWERS AND EXPLANATIONS

Passage I

1. **D** The length of the phrase changes in the answer choices, so this question tests concision. There is also the option to DELETE; consider this choice carefully as it's often the correct answer. The sentence makes a comparison between *sculpting the Venus de Milo or painting the Sistine Chapel* on the one hand, versus *preparing a delicious meal* on the other hand. The second, non-underlined part of the comparison, *preparing a delicious meal,* is an action, so the first part should also be an action to make the comparison consistent. Adding *the artist* or *one* makes the first part of the comparison about a person rather than an action, so eliminate (A), (B), and (C). The correct answer is (D).

2. **G** Note the question! The question asks for the answer that would *convey the distinct scent of a properly cooked roast,* so it tests consistency. Eliminate answers that are inconsistent with the purpose stated in the question. *The sign* does not include any reference to *scent,* so eliminate (F). Choice (G) mentions *aroma*, which is consistent with *scent,* so keep (G). Neither the *textures of vegetables and meats* nor *the diners' eager expectation* addresses the idea of *scent,* so eliminate (H) and (J). The correct answer is (G).

3. **D** Verbs change in the answer choices, so this question tests consistency of verbs. A verb must be consistent in number with its subject. The subject of the underlined verb is *cooking* (the phrase *a delicious roast with vegetables* describes what is *cooking,* but it is not the subject of the verb), which is singular, so the underlined verb should also be singular. Eliminate (A) because *require* is a plural verb. Eliminate (C) because *requiring* makes the sentence incomplete. Choices (B) and (D) both express the same idea, but (D) is more concise; eliminate (B). The correct answer is (D).

4. **H** Note the question! When a question asks which answer would be *LEAST* acceptable, eliminate answers that **are** acceptable. Prepositions change in the answer choices, so this question tests idioms. *Goes out to the butcher shop* is idiomatically correct, so eliminate (F). *Goes into the butcher shop* is also idiomatically correct, so eliminate (G). *Goes at the butcher shop* is not correct, so keep (H). *Goes to the butcher shop* is idiomatically correct, so eliminate (J). The correct answer is (H).

5. **A** Transitions change in the answer choices, so this question tests consistency of ideas. A transition must be consistent with the relationship between the ideas it connects. The sentence contains a list of two items that produce *the tastiest vegetables*: *natural sunshine* and *a farmer's careful tending.* The two items in the list should be connected with the word *and*, so eliminate (B) and (D). The two items in the list should also be consistent with each other; since the non-underlined *natural sunshine* is a noun, the second item should also be a noun. The phrase *a farmer's careful tending* is a noun, so keep (A). The phrase *a farmer is careful tending* is both incorrect (the word *careful* cannot describe the verb *is tending*) and is a noun-verb combination, which is not consistent with the first item in the list. Eliminate (C). The correct answer is (A).

6. **H** Note the question! The question asks for the answer that would *emphasize Eric's attention to detail in making his pot roast,* so it tests consistency. Eliminate answers that are inconsistent with the purpose stated in the question. The word *slowly* could be consistent with *attention to detail,* but there could be other reasons for slowness; eliminate (F). The idea that Eric *is very careful* could be consistent with *attention to detail,* but the word *meticulously* and the phrase *finely cut vegetables* in (H) more clearly convey *attention to detail.* Eliminate (G) and keep (H). The phrase *a kind of order* does not clearly convey *attention to detail,* so eliminate (J). The correct answer is (H).

7. **D** Verbs and the presence of a subject change in the answer choices, so this question tests how to connect ideas in a sentence. The first part of the sentence, *Eric meticulously layers the finely cut vegetables,* is an independent clause. As written, the second part of the sentence, *he alternates rings of bright orange carrots and chunks of red potatoes,* is also an independent clause. A comma on its own cannot be used between two independent clauses, so eliminate (A). Eliminate (B) both because the verb is inconsistent in tense with the sentence, and because it makes the same mistake with two independent clauses that (A) does. Both (C) and (D) remove the subject *he* from the second part of the sentence so that it is no longer an independent clause. The word *alternating* makes the meaning of the sentence clearer because it makes the second part of the sentence a description of the action in the first part. Eliminate (C). The correct answer is (D).

8. **G** Pronouns and nouns change in the answer choices, so this question tests the idea of clear. A pronoun can be used only if it is clear what it refers to. It is not clear what the pronoun *others* refers to, so eliminate (F), (H), and (J). Choice (G) makes the meaning of the sentence clear. The correct answer is (G).

9. **D** Note the question! When a question asks which answer would be *LEAST* acceptable, eliminate answers that **are** acceptable. Transitions change in the answer choices, so this question tests consistency of ideas. A transition must be consistent with the relationship between the ideas it connects. The previous paragraph describes the ingredients that Eric puts in the slow cooker, and this paragraph describes the actual cooking of the roast. There is a sequence of events, so the time transitions *next, after that,* and *now,* are all acceptable alternatives. Eliminate (A), (B), and (C). There is no contrast between the paragraphs, so the contrasting transition *at least* is not acceptable in this context. The correct answer is (D).

10. **H** Note the question! The question asks for the answer that would provide *the most specific sensory detail,* so it tests consistency. Eliminate answers that are inconsistent with the purpose stated in the question. Neither (F) nor (G) gives a *sensory detail,* so eliminate them both. Choice (H) describes the *lazy, bubbling boil,* which evokes a visual sense of the pot, and the word *savory* evokes a smell. Keep (H). Choice (J) does not include any *sensory detail,* so eliminate (J). The correct answer is (H).

11. **A** The length of the phrase changes in the answer choices, so this question tests concision. The non-underlined portion of the sentence mentions *scents,* so there is no need to use the word *smell;* eliminate (B). *Wafting* and *floating* mean the same thing in this context, so there is no need to use both words; eliminate (C). Choices (A) and (D) both express the same idea, but (A) is more concise. Eliminate (D). The correct answer is (A).

12. **G** Punctuation changes in the answer choices, so this question tests how to connect ideas with the appropriate punctuation. The first part of the sentence, *Every half hour, using a long meat thermometer,* is not an independent clause. The second part, *Eric reads the temperature of the roast and carefully examines the stewing contents,* is an independent clause. A semicolon can only be used between two independent clauses, so eliminate (J). The phrase *using a long meat thermometer* is not necessary to the main meaning of the sentence, so it should be set off by commas. Eliminate (H) because it lacks commas. Choice (F) places an extra comma in the middle of the unnecessary phrase; eliminate (F). The correct answer is (G).

13. **A** Note the question! The question asks whether a sentence should be deleted from the essay, so it tests the ideas of consistent and clear. If the sentence is consistent with the subject of the paragraph and makes the meaning clearer, it should be kept. The paragraph focuses on cooking the pot roast, and the sentence in question gives a reason that *Eric reads the temperature,* as described in the previous sentence. The sentence in question is therefore consistent with the paragraph and should not be deleted; eliminate (C) and (D). Choice (A) accurately describes the sentence. The sentence does not *reinforce that roasts are typically done cooking after 8 hours,* so eliminate (B). The correct answer is (A).

14. **G** The length of the phrase changes in the answer choices, so this question could test concision. Choices (F) and (J) are the shortest options; they contain different forms of the verb. In (F), the first part of the sentence, *Lift the finished roast out of the pot to serve,* is an independent clause. The second part of the sentence, *the tender meat plops juicily onto our plates in generous servings,* is also an independent clause. A comma on its own cannot be used between two independent clauses, so eliminate (F). Changing the verb to *lifting* means that the first part of the sentence is no longer an independent clause, but it is now a descriptive phrase that does not appropriately describe the noun that comes immediately after it, *the tender meat;* eliminate (J). Choices (G) and (H) have different pronouns. A pronoun must be consistent with the noun it refers to. The pronoun refers to *Eric,* who is male, so the underlined pronoun must be masculine. Eliminate (H) because *you* is not gendered. The correct answer is (G).

15. **D** The length of the phrase changes in the answer choices, so this question tests concision. There is also the option to DELETE; consider this choice carefully as it's often the correct answer. The underlined phrase gives a description of *it,* but *it* clearly refers to *his work of art* earlier in the sentence. Therefore, there is no reason to include the underlined portion. The correct answer is (D).

Passage II

16. **J** The topic of the underlined portion changes in the answer choices, so this question tests the ideas of consistent and clear. There is also the option to DELETE; consider this choice carefully as it's often the correct answer. The focus of the underlined portion must be consistent with the sentence and make the meaning of the sentence clearer. The non-underlined portion of the sentence says that people would *immediately conjure up an image,* which means the same thing in this context as *visualized in their minds,* so there is no reason to use both phrases; eliminate (F). The last sentence

of the paragraph, *Nothing could be farther from the truth,* indicates that people's idea of farm life was wrong. If someone can *conjure up an image* of something, it would mean that *they know what it was like,* so it is not necessary to include both ideas. Eliminate (G). The non-underlined portion introduces the idea *that I lived on a farm,* so there is no need to repeat it; eliminate (H). Choice (J) is concise and makes the meaning of the sentence clear. The correct answer is (J).

17. **C** Note the question! When a question asks which answer would *NOT* be acceptable, eliminate answers that **are** acceptable. Transitions change in the answer choices, so this question could test consistency of ideas. All of the answer choices express the same idea, that the sentence that starts with the transition gives the first of several reasons for the idea in the previous sentence. Choice (C), *For start,* is idiomatically incorrect, so it is not an acceptable alternative. Choices (A), (B), and (D) are all acceptable alternatives, so eliminate (A), (B), and (D). The correct answer is (C).

18. **F** Punctuation changes in the answer choices, so this question tests how to connect ideas with the appropriate punctuation. The first part of the sentence, *I didn't feed cows or pigs,* is an independent clause. The second part of the sentence, *I didn't grow corn or wheat,* is also an independent clause. Two independent clauses must be separated by some kind of punctuation other than a comma; eliminate (G), (H), and (J). Choice (F) appropriately uses a semicolon to separate the two independent clauses. The correct answer is (F).

19. **C** Note the question! The question asks what would be lost if a phrase were deleted, so it tests consistency. Eliminate answer choices that are not consistent with the role of the phrase. The phrase establishes how long the family has had the farm. There is nothing about *a broken relationship between the narrator and his mother* in the phrase, so eliminate (A). The phrase does not provide *a transition into the discussion of traditional farm practices,* so eliminate (B). Choice (C) accurately describes the phrase. The phrase talks about the past, not about *what will eventually happen to the narrator,* so eliminate (D). The correct answer is (C).

20. **H** The words *of* and *have* change in the answer choices, so this question tests frequently confused words. The phrase *must of* is an incorrect spelling of the contraction *must've,* which is short for *must have;* eliminate (F) and (G). The rest of the sentence contains a fact *that* someone learned *(wool from llamas was more profitable than wool from sheep),* rather than a thing that someone learned *about.* The word *about* does not make sense in this context, so eliminate (J). The correct answer is (H).

21. **B** Commas change in the answer choices, so this question tests comma usage. The phrase *in fact* is not necessary to the main meaning of the sentence, so it should be set off by commas. Eliminate (A) because it lacks a comma before *in fact.* Choice (B) appropriately places commas both before and after *in fact.* Eliminate (C) because it lacks a comma after *in fact,* and eliminate (D) because it doesn't have any commas. The correct answer is (B).

22. **G** Note the question! The question asks for the best placement for the new sentence, so it tests consistency of ideas. The sentence must be consistent with the ideas that come both before and after it.

The new sentence says, *fifty years ago, my grandfather decided to buy a llama.* Sentence 3 contains the pronoun *he,* which does not clearly refer to anything in Sentence 2. The new sentence introduces *my grandfather,* which *he* could refer to, so the new sentence must go after Sentence 2. The correct answer is (G).

23. **D** Note the question! When a question asks which answer would *NOT* be acceptable, eliminate answers that **are** acceptable. Vocabulary changes in the answer choices, so this question tests which words give the clearest meaning. *Started, began,* and *went to* all indicate that the narrator commenced an activity, so they are all acceptable; eliminate (A), (B), and (C). *Begun* is the past participle of the verb *to begin* and can be used only with a helping verb such as *have* or *had.* Since there is no helping verb in the sentence, (D) is not acceptable. The correct answer is (D).

24. **J** Note the question! When a question asks which answer would *NOT* be acceptable, eliminate answers that **are** acceptable. Transition words change in the answer choices. Since there is the option to remove a conjunction, this question tests how to connect ideas in a sentence. In (J), the first part of the sentence, *I had settled into my new home,* is an independent clause. The second part of the sentence, *however, I realized that farm work was much more involved than I had expected,* is also an independent clause. A comma on its own cannot be used between two independent clauses, so (J) is not acceptable. Adding a conjunction to the first part of the sentence means that it is no longer an independent clause. Choices (F), (G), and (H) are therefore all acceptable. Eliminate (F), (G), and (H). The correct answer is (J).

25. **A** Verbs change in the answer choices, so this question tests consistency of verbs. A verb must be consistent in tense and form with the rest of the paragraph. The other verbs in the sentence are in past tense, so the underlined verb should also be in past tense. Eliminate (B) and (C) because they are both conditional tense. The difference between (A) and (D) is present perfect versus past perfect tense. Present perfect tense is used to describe an action that started in the past and continues to the present, while past perfect is used to describe an action that started in the past and then stopped. The narrator stopped expecting once he moved to the farm, so the action ended in the past. Eliminate (D) because *have expected* is present perfect. The correct answer is (A).

26. **F** Note the question! The question asks for the answer that would *most effectively introduce the information that follows in this paragraph,* so it tests consistency. Eliminate answers that are inconsistent with the purpose stated in the question. This paragraph describes the narrator's *school.* Choice (F) introduces the idea of *school,* so it is consistent; keep (F). The fact that *farming is a full-time job* is not relevant to *school,* so eliminate (G). How tall *llamas* can get is also not relevant to *school,* so eliminate (H). The quality of *life on the farm* is also not relevant to *school,* so eliminate (J). The correct answer is (F).

27. **D** The length of the phrase changes in the answer choices, so this question tests concision. Eliminate (B) because the idea of *how well the class was working* is not relevant to this paragraph. Choices (A), (C), and (D) all express the same idea, but (D) is most concise. Eliminate (A) and (C). The correct answer is (D).

28. **F** Note the question! The question asks for the answer that *provides the most specific and precise information,* so it tests consistency. Eliminate answers that are inconsistent with the purpose stated in the question. Choices (F) and (G) both begin with *studying,* but (G) does not elaborate on that idea. Choice (F) is more precise than (G) is, so eliminate (G). Eliminate (H) because *other things* is not *specific* or *precise.* Choice (J) expresses an idea similar to that in (F), but the word *textbooks* makes (F) more precise; eliminate (J). The correct answer is (F).

29. **B** Apostrophes change in the answer choices, so this question tests apostrophe usage. A noun with an apostrophe shows possession. The *habits* belong to the *llamas,* so an apostrophe is necessary; eliminate (C) and (D). The difference between (A) and (B) is the singular versus plural possessive. Since there is no article (*a* or *the*) indicating that the sentence is referring to only one llama, and *habits* is plural, *llamas* should also be plural. Eliminate (A) because *llama's* is singular. Choice (B) appropriately uses the plural possessive. The correct answer is (B).

30. **H** Prepositions change in the answer choices, so this question tests idioms. The correct idiom is *a career in,* so eliminate (F), (G), and (J). The correct answer is (H).

Passage III

31. **B** Pronouns change in the answer choices, so this question tests consistency of pronouns. There is also the option to DELETE; consider this choice carefully as it's often the correct answer. Deleting the underlined portion makes the sentence incomplete, so eliminate (D). A pronoun must be consistent with the noun it refers to. The underlined pronoun refers to *Charles W. Chesnutt;* the word *which* cannot be used to refer to a person, so eliminate (C). Both (A) and (B) can be used to refer to a person, so choose the one that has the appropriate case. The underlined pronoun is the subject of the non-underlined verb *spent,* so a subject pronoun is required. Eliminate (A) because *whom* is an object pronoun. Choice (B) appropriately uses the subject pronoun *who.* The correct answer is (B).

32. **H** Note the question! The question asks what would be lost if a phrase were deleted, so it tests consistency. Eliminate answer choices that are not consistent with the role of the phrase. The phrase specifies a time period. It does not contain *a direct link to the following paragraph,* so eliminate (F). It is not an *unnecessary digression* as it is relevant to the paragraph's focus on Chesnutt, so eliminate (G). It does give *the period of Chesnutt's youth,* so keep (H). The phrase does not say anything about *the extent of Chesnutt's historical writing,* so eliminate (J). The correct answer is (H).

33. **C** Note the question! When a question asks which answer would *NOT* be acceptable, eliminate answers that **are** acceptable. Punctuation changes in the answer choices, so this question tests how to connect ideas with the appropriate punctuation. The first part of the sentence, *Amid all the turmoil of the South of his boyhood, Chesnutt took solace in literature,* is an independent clause. The second part of the sentence, *he had already decided, in his teens, that he would become a writer,* is also an independent clause. Both semicolons and periods can be used between two independent clauses, so (A) and (D) are both acceptable. Eliminate (A) and (D). The addition of the word *consequently*

in (B) does not impact the second part of the sentence—it is still an independent clause. A comma followed by the coordinating conjunction *and* can be used between two independent clauses, so (B) is acceptable; eliminate (B). A comma by itself cannot be used between two independent clauses, so (C) is not acceptable. The correct answer is (C).

34. **J** Verbs change in the answer choices, so this question tests consistency of verbs. A verb must be consistent in tense and form with other verbs in the sentence. The other verbs in the sentence are in past tense, so the underlined verb should also be in past tense. Eliminate (F) and (H) because they are both present tense. Choice (G) is present perfect tense, which is used to describe an action that started in the past but continues in the present. The sentence indicates that Chesnutt died in 1932, so he cannot still be writing; eliminate (G). The correct answer is (J).

35. **C** The length of the phrase around the word *clear* changes in the answer choices, so this question tests concision. None of the extra words in (A), (B), or (D) makes the meaning of the sentence clearer, so eliminate those three answers. Choice (C) is concise and makes the meaning of the sentence clear. The correct answer is (C).

36. **J** Vocabulary changes in the answer choices, so this question tests which words give the clearest meaning. There is also the option to DELETE; consider this choice carefully as it's often the correct answer. The non-underlined portion of the sentence has the phrase *earlier folklorists.* The phrase *from a previous era* means the same thing as *earlier,* so there is no need to repeat the idea; eliminate (F). Choices (G) and (H) also express the same idea as *earlier,* so eliminate (G) and (H) as well. The underlined portion is not necessary to make the meaning of the sentence clear. The correct answer is (J).

37. **A** Punctuation and transitions change in the answer choices, so this question tests how to connect ideas with the appropriate punctuation. The first part of the sentence, *The Conjure Woman was written in the tradition of earlier folklorists Joel Chandler Harris and Thomas Nelson Page,* is an independent clause. The second part of the sentence, *However, it presented a much more frank treatment of race relations in the South during slavery and Reconstruction,* is also an independent clause. Two independent clauses must be separated by some type of punctuation other than a comma, so eliminate (B). Changing *however* to *consequently* does not affect the second part of the sentence; it is still an independent clause, so eliminate (D) also. A transition must be consistent with the relationship between the ideas it connects. The first sentence mentions the *tradition* that *The Conjure Woman* followed, while the second sentence says that it *presented a much more frank treatment of race relations.* There is a contrast between these ideas, so eliminate (C) because *Consequently* indicates that ideas agree. *However* is a contrasting transition. The correct answer is (A).

38. **J** Note the question! The question asks whether a sentence should be added to the paragraph, so it tests consistency. A sentence should be added only if it is consistent with the focus of the paragraph. The paragraph focuses on some of Chesnutt's writings. The new sentence is about the end of slavery, which is not consistent with the paragraph, so it should not be added. Eliminate (F) and (G). The

information in the new sentence is not *detailed later in this essay,* so eliminate (H). Choice (J) accurately states that the new sentence *would distract readers from the essay's main focus.* The correct answer is (J).

39. **C** Pronouns and apostrophes change in the answer choices, so this question tests pronoun consistency and apostrophe usage. A pronoun must be consistent in number with the noun it refers to. The underlined pronoun refers to the book *The Conjure Woman,* which is singular, so the underlined pronoun should also be singular. Eliminate (B) because *their* is always plural on the ACT. The word *its'* never occurs in English, so eliminate (D). *It's* is a contraction of *it is,* which is not necessary here, so eliminate (A). The correct answer is (C).

40. **J** Note the question! The question asks for the answer that would *provide the most logical arrangement of the parts of this sentence,* so it tests consistency. Eliminate answers that are inconsistent with the purpose stated in the question. The *most logical arrangement* of the sentence is the one that will give the clearest meaning. Choice (F) is an incomplete sentence, so eliminate (F). Choice (G) contains the comparative phrase *different from.* The two things being contrasted in the sentence must be consistent with each other. The first part of the sentence describes actions (*Humans were used* and *participated*), while the second part describes nouns (*Brer Rabbit and the animals*), so the two things are not consistent. Eliminate (G). In (J), the phrase *stories that incorporated conjure, voodoo, and the injustices of slavery* makes the meaning of the sentence clearer than the beginning of (H), which says that *Conjure, voodoo, and the injustices of slavery and others were used by The Conjure Woman,* but does not mention anything about *stories.* Eliminate (H). Choice (J) makes the meaning of the sentence clear. The correct answer is (J).

41. **C** Apostrophes change in the answer choices, so this question tests apostrophe usage. A noun with an apostrophe shows possession. Since the *children* belong to the *family,* an apostrophe is necessary; eliminate (A) and (B). Choice (D) is an incorrect version of the plural possessive *families',* so eliminate (D). Since the underlined portion is preceded by the singular article *an,* the singular possessive *family's* is appropriate. The correct answer is (C).

42. **F** Pronouns and nouns change in the answer choices, so this question tests the idea of clear. A pronoun can be used only if it is clear what it refers to. Choice (F) makes the meaning of the sentence clear, so keep (F). The word *it* could refer to several singular nouns in the sentence, so it is not clear; eliminate (G). The word *them* could refer to either *lives* or *children,* so it is not clear; eliminate (H). In (J), it is not clear what the *topics* of the book are, so eliminate (J). The correct answer is (F).

43. **C** Note the question! When a question asks which answer would *NOT* be acceptable, eliminate answers that **are** acceptable. The order of words changes in the answer choices, so this question tests misplaced modifiers. The underlined portion is an introductory phrase to the main part of the sentence, the subject of which is *the novel.* Choices (A), (B), and (D) all clearly describe *the novel,* so they are all acceptable. Eliminate (A), (B), and (D). Because (C) contains the verb *publishing,* it cannot refer to *the novel* (because a novel can *be published,* but it cannot *publish*). Choice (C) is therefore unacceptable. The correct answer is (C).

44. **G** Note the question! The question asks for the answer that *most effectively concludes and summarizes this essay,* so it tests consistency. Eliminate answers that are inconsistent with the purpose stated in the question. Choice (F) mentions only two of Chestnutt's works and fails to mention his reputation *today,* which is the focus of Paragraph 2. Eliminate (F). Choice (G) provides an effective summary of the passage, so keep (G). Choice (H) restates a minor detail from the end of the first paragraph but does not provide an effective summary of the passage, so eliminate (H). The passage focuses primarily on Chesnutt, not on *Joel Chandler Harris and Thomas Nelson Page,* so eliminate (J). The correct answer is (G).

45. **D** Note the question! The question asks for the best placement for Paragraph 2, so it tests consistency of ideas. Paragraph 2 must be consistent in focus with the paragraphs before and after it. Paragraph 2 mentions Chesnutt's *death in 1932,* and how his writings are received *today.* Paragraph 1 begins with Chesnutt's birth in 1858, and Paragraph 3 begins with *Chesnutt's first major literary success.* Paragraph 2 does not fit into the chronology of these paragraphs, so eliminate (A) and (B). Paragraph 4 continues the chronology begun in the first two paragraphs, so eliminate (C) also. Paragraph 2 fits best with the chronology of the passage if it is placed after Paragraph 4. The correct answer is (D).

Passage IV

46. **J** Verbs change in the answer choices, so this question tests consistency of verbs. A verb must be consistent in number with its subject and consistent in tense with other verbs in the sentence. The subject of the underlined verb is *accomplishments* (the phrase *on the baseball field* is a prepositional phrase that describes *accomplishments* but cannot be the subject of the verb), which is plural, so the underlined verb should also be plural. Eliminate (F) and (G) because they are both singular. The sentence is in past tense, so the underlined verb should also be in past tense. Eliminate (H) because *will be* is future tense. The correct answer is (J).

47. **C** Commas change in the answer choices, so this question tests comma usage. The phrase *according to his widow Rachel Robinson* is not necessary to the main meaning of the sentence, so it should be set off by commas both before and after it. Eliminate (A) because there is no comma before *according.* Eliminate (B) because there is no reason to break up that phrase with a comma after *according.* Choice (C) appropriately places commas both before and after the unnecessary phrase. Although dashes can be used to set off an unnecessary phrase, the non-underlined punctuation after the phrase is a comma, not a dash, so a dash cannot be used at the beginning of the phrase; eliminate (D). The correct answer is (C).

48. **J** The length of the phrase around the word *noticed* changes in the answer choices, so this question tests concision. There is also the option to DELETE; consider this choice carefully as it's often the correct answer. The non-underlined portion of the sentence says that Robinson's *activism was... often overlooked,* which means the same thing as not *being noticed,* so there is no reason to use both

phrases. Eliminate (F), (G), and (H). Choice (J) is concise and makes the meaning of the sentence clear. The correct answer is (J).

49. **B** Note the question! The question asks for the best placement for the underlined portion, so it tests consistency. The underlined portion must be consistent with the word or phrase it is next to. The underlined portion mentions *the Brooklyn Dodgers,* so it must come next to something that has to do with baseball. Where it is now, the underlined portion breaks up the phrase *The tenacious and spirited way Jackie Robinson played baseball* in an unclear way; eliminate (A). The underlined portion logically describes the *way Jackie Robinson played baseball,* so it makes sense to put it after that phrase; keep (B). The underlined portion does not belong in the phrase *his focus on civil rights,* as that is not related to baseball; eliminate (C) and (D). The correct answer is (B).

50. **J** Punctuation changes in the answer choices, so this question tests how to connect ideas with the appropriate punctuation. The first part of the sentence, *From the outset of the "Great Experiment" of having African-Americans in baseball,* is not an independent clause. The second part of the sentence, *he knew that his performance on the field would be a determining factor in sports segregation,* is an independent clause. Semicolons and periods can only be used between two independent clauses, so eliminate (F) and (H). A comma followed by the coordinating conjunction *and* can also only be used between two independent clauses, so eliminate (G). Choice (J) appropriately uses a comma between the two parts of the sentence. The correct answer is (J).

51. **A** Note the question! The question asks for the answer that *fits most specifically with the information at the end of this sentence,* so it tests consistency. Eliminate answers that are inconsistent with the purpose stated in the question. The sentence says that the people mentioned in the underlined portion *could see his immense talent from any seat in the stadium. Spectators* are people who sit in the seats of a stadium, so keep (A). While *people* could sit in the seats of a stadium, (B) is less specific than (A) is, so eliminate (B). Neither *popcorn vendors* nor *pitchers* would sit in the seats of a stadium, so eliminate (C) and (D). The correct answer is (A).

52. **G** Note the question! The question asks what would be lost if a paragraph were deleted, so it tests consistency. Eliminate answer choices that are not consistent with the role of the paragraph. The paragraph states that the way Robinson played *was a reflection of his focus on civil rights,* and that *he knew his performance on the field would be a determining factor in sports segregation.* There is no *scientific explanation of the "Great Experiment"* in the paragraph, so eliminate (F). Choice (G) accurately describes the paragraph, so keep (G). Although the word *prejudice* appears in the paragraph, there is no *passionate plea,* so eliminate (H). The paragraph does not discuss whether *the Brooklyn Dodgers were the best team in baseball,* so eliminate (J). The correct answer is (G).

53. **C** Transitions change in the answer choices, so this question tests consistency of ideas. A transition must be consistent with the relationship between the ideas it connects. The first part of the sentence says that *the vast amount of energy Robinson expended...could have caused an ordinary man to wilt.* The second part says that *Robinson instinctively and relentlessly increased his efforts.* There is a

contrast between these two ideas, so eliminate (A), (B), and (D), which all contain transitions that indicate agreement between ideas. Choice (C) appropriately uses a contrasting transition. The correct answer is (C).

54. **F** Pronouns change in the answer choices, so this question tests consistency of pronouns. A pronoun must be consistent in number with the noun it refers to. The underlined pronoun refers to *athletes,* which is plural, so the underlined pronoun should also be plural. Eliminate (G) and (H) because they both use singular pronouns. The word *theirs* is used in place of a noun, while the word *their* is used to describe a noun. The underlined word is followed by the noun *status,* so *their* is the appropriate choice. Eliminate (J). The correct answer is (F).

55. **B** Note the question! The question asks whether a sentence should be deleted from the essay, so it tests the ideas of consistent and clear. If the sentence is consistent with the subject of the paragraph and makes the meaning clearer, it should be kept. The paragraph focuses on Jackie Robinson's work on civil rights, and the sentence gives an example of how he helped *stimulate civil rights advancements.* It is therefore consistent with the paragraph and should be kept; eliminate (C) and (D). The sentence does not *describe important information about Jackie Robinson's endorsement deals,* so eliminate (A). Choice (B) accurately describes the sentence. The correct answer is (B).

56. **F** Punctuation changes in the answer choices, so this question tests how to connect ideas with the appropriate punctuation. The first part of the sentence, *Post-baseball, Robinson became an entrepreneur,* is an independent clause. The second part of the sentence, *his focus did not stray as he found time to write impassioned letters and telegrams to various U.S. presidents during the civil rights movement,* is also an independent clause. Two independent clauses must be separated by some kind of punctuation other than a comma alone, so eliminate (G) and (H). A comma followed by the coordinating conjunction *but* can be used between two independent clauses, and the word *but* appropriately connects the contrasting ideas in the sentence. Keep (F). Eliminate (J) because the word *and* would indicate that the two parts of the sentence agree. The correct answer is (F).

57. **C** Note the question! The question asks where the paragraph should be divided *to differentiate between Robinson's civil rights activism during and after his baseball career,* so it tests consistency. Eliminate answers that divide the paragraph at a point where the focus does not change. Sentence 2 says that *Robinson...utilized his status to stimulate civil rights advancements,* which refers to a period of time *during his baseball career,* so Sentence 2 should not begin the new paragraph; eliminate (A). Sentence 3 discusses what he did during *his baseball travels,* which again is *during his baseball career,* so Sentence 3 should not begin the new paragraph; eliminate (B). Sentence 4 starts with the phrase *post-baseball,* which means it introduces the new idea of *after his baseball career,* so keep (C). Sentence 5 also discusses the period of time *after his baseball career,* but it is not where that idea is introduced, so eliminate (D). The correct answer is (C).

58. **H** The comparison words are changing in the answer choices, so this question tests idioms. *Widelier* is not a word, so eliminate (J). The correct idiom is *more...than,* so eliminate (F) and (G). The correct answer is (H).

59. **D** Punctuation changes in the answer choices, so this question tests how to connect ideas with the appropriate punctuation. The first part of the sentence, *Though Jackie Robinson's baseball exploits may be more widely known than his tireless efforts in the civil rights movement,* is not an independent clause. The second part of the sentence, *his astonishing courage on the baseball field was itself a resounding stance against segregation and inequality,* is an independent clause. Both periods and semicolons can only be used between two independent clauses, so eliminate (B) and (C). The first part of the sentence expresses a different idea than the second part does, so the two parts of the sentence need to be separated with a comma. Eliminate (A) because it lacks a comma. The correct answer is (D).

60. **G** Note the question! When a question asks which answer would be *LEAST* acceptable, eliminate answers that **are** acceptable. Transitions change in the answer choices, so this question tests consistency of ideas. A transition must be consistent with the relationship between the ideas it connects. The sentence before the transition says that Robinson *was excelling in his efforts* to reduce segregation and inequality. The sentence that begins with the transitions says that *the spark of positive change was ignited.* These two statements agree with each other, so (F), (H), and (J), which all contain transitions that indicate agreement, are all acceptable. Eliminate (F), (H), and (J). Choice (G) uses a contrasting transition, so it is not acceptable. The correct answer is (G).

Passage V

61. **D** Punctuation changes in the answer choices, so this question tests how to connect ideas with the appropriate punctuation. The first part of the sentence, *Many inhabit sporadic green patches of moss,* is an independent clause. The second part of the sentence, *fertilized by excrement from migrating birds and sheltered by the rocky mountainsides,* is not an independent clause. A semicolon can only be used between two independent clauses, so eliminate (A). The phrase *of moss* is necessary to the main meaning of the sentence, so it should not be set off by commas; eliminate (C). There is no reason to break up the phrase *patches of moss* with a comma, so eliminate (B). No punctuation is necessary. The correct answer is (D).

62. **G** Note the question! When a question asks which answer would *NOT* be acceptable, eliminate answers that **are** acceptable. Punctuation changes in the answer choices, so this question tests how to connect ideas with the appropriate punctuation. The first part of the sentence, *Some hibernate in the winter, frozen in ice under rocks and stones,* is an independent clause. The second part of the sentence in (F), *only to become active again when the climate warms and the ice melts* is not an independent clause. Choice (F) appropriately uses a comma to separate the two parts of the sentence, so eliminate (F). In (G), the second part of the sentence, *Becoming active again when the climate warms and the ice melts,* is not an independent clause. A period can only be used between two independent clauses, so (G) is not acceptable. The second part of the sentence in (H), *Then they become active again when the climate warms and the ice melts,* is an independent clause. Choice (H) appropriately uses a period between two independent clauses; eliminate (H). With (J), the ideas compose a single sentence. Notice that there is a comma before the phrase *frozen in ice under rocks*

and stones, so there must be another comma after that phrase, as (J) does correctly. Choice (J) also properly connects the ideas with the word *and* to state, *Some hibernate... and then become active...*, which is consistent. Choice (J), therefore, is acceptable, so eliminate (J). The correct answer is (G).

63. **C** Verbs change in the answer choices, so this question tests consistency of verbs. A verb must be consistent in tense and form with other verbs in the sentence. The other verbs in the sentence are in present tense, so the underlined verb should also be in present tense. Eliminate (A) and (B) because none of the other verbs in the sentence have *-ing* endings. Keep (C) because it appropriately uses present tense. Eliminate (D) because the infinitive form of the verb *to melt* is not consistent with the other verbs in the sentence. The correct answer is (C).

64. **J** Vocabulary changes in the answer choices, so this question could test which words give the clearest meaning. All four answer choices have similar meanings, but some have a more informal tone. The best answer should be consistent in tone with the rest of the passage. Choice (F), (G), and (H) are all informal and not consistent with the passage, so eliminate all three. Choice (J) is consistent in tone with the passage. The correct answer is (J).

65. **C** Punctuation changes in the answer choices, so this question tests how to connect ideas with the appropriate punctuation. The first part of the sentence, *These adaptable invertebrates classified as arthropods,* is not an independent clause. The second part of the sentence, *are able to survive on a continent once thought too arctic, too windy, and too icy to maintain any permanent land animals,* is also not an independent clause. A semicolon can only be used between two independent clauses, so eliminate (A). The phrase *classified as arthropods* is not necessary to the main meaning of the sentence, so it should be set off by commas both before and after it. Eliminate (B) and (D) because each has only one of the necessary commas. The correct answer is (C).

66. **H** The words *to* and *too* change in the answer choices, so this question tests frequently confused words. *To* is a preposition that indicates direction, which is not appropriate in this context; eliminate (F) and (G). *Too* means "excessively," which is the correct word in this context. Commas also change in the answer choices, so this question also tests comma usage. The sentence contains a list of three items, which should be separated by commas. *Too arctic* is one item in the list, so there is no need to put a comma after *too;* eliminate (J). The correct answer is (H).

67. **A** Note the question! When a question asks which answer would *NOT* be acceptable, eliminate answers that **are** acceptable. Punctuation changes in the answer choices, so this question tests how to connect ideas with the appropriate punctuation. The first part of the sentence, *The coldest place on Earth, Antarctica is home to great quantities of life that don't simply tolerate the lower temperatures,* is an independent clause. The second part of the sentence, *they flourish in them,* is also an independent clause. Punctuation is necessary between two independent clauses, so (A) is not acceptable. Periods and semicolons can both be used between two independent clauses, so (B) and (C) are both acceptable (the addition of the phrase *in fact* in (B) does not affect the second part of the sentence, so it is still an independent clause). Eliminate (B) and (C). A single long dash in a sentence can also be used between two independent clauses, so eliminate (D). The correct answer is (A).

68. **G** Verbs change in the answer choices, so this question tests consistency of verbs. A verb must be consistent in tense with other verbs in the paragraph. The paragraph is in present tense, so the underlined verb should also be in present tense. Eliminate (F), (H), and (J) because they are all past tense. Choice (G) is present tense. The correct answer is (G).

69. **D** The length of the phrase after the word *seals* changes in the answer choices, so this question tests concision. The paragraph discusses *land fauna on Antarctica,* not *the waters of Antarctica,* so eliminate (A). Where the seals *breed* is not relevant to the sentence, so eliminate (B). The number of *different types* of seals is also not relevant to the sentence, so eliminate (C). Choice (D) is concise and makes the meaning of the sentence clear. The correct answer is (D).

70. **J** Note the question! The question asks whether a phrase should be deleted from the essay, so it tests the ideas of consistent and clear. If the phrase is consistent with the subject of the paragraph and makes the meaning clearer, it should be kept. The paragraph discusses *nematode worms* in Antarctica, including a description of the terrain where they live, and the phrase in question identifies the location where the nematode worms are found. The phrase is consistent with the paragraph, so it should not be deleted; eliminate (F) and (G). The phrase indicates that *McMurdo Sound* is part of *Antarctica,* not a separate place as (H) implies; eliminate (H). Choice (J) accurately states that the phrase *gives specific details about the "Here" mentioned in the subsequent sentence.* The correct answer is (J).

71. **B** Note the question! The question asks for the answer that *most explicitly and vividly describes the terrain of McMurdo Sound* so it tests consistency. Eliminate answers that are inconsistent with the purpose stated in the question. Whether the land is *abundant* does not *describe the terrain,* so eliminate (A). Choice (B) gives a vivid description of the land, so keep (B). The *humidity* does not describe the land, so eliminate (C) and (D). The correct answer is (B).

72. **H** Note the question! The question asks for the best placement for the underlined portion, so it tests consistency. The underlined portion must be consistent with the word or phrase it is next to. The underlined portion contains the preposition *with,* so it must create an idiomatically correct phrase with the word it comes after. Although *winter* could be modified by the phrase *with low temperatures,* where the underlined portion is now actually modifies the verb *dehydrating themselves,* which cannot be correctly modified by *with the low temperatures;* eliminate (F). It is idiomatically incorrect to say that *nematodes thrive with the low temperatures* (the correct idiom would be *thrive in*), so eliminate (G). It is correct to say *coping with the low temperatures,* so keep (H). The phrase *increasing moisture* is a characteristic of *summer,* which cannot be modified by *with the low temperatures,* so eliminate (J). The correct answer is (H).

73. **B** Note the question! When a question asks which answer would be *LEAST* acceptable, eliminate answers that **are** acceptable. The question asks for the least effective introduction to the paragraph, so it tests consistency. Eliminate answer choices that **are** consistent with the paragraph. The paragraph focuses on *Antarctica's algae,* which have not been previously discussed in the passage. Choice (A) effectively introduces the idea of *algae,* so eliminate (A). Choice (B) contrasts the structure of algae with that of other plants, which is not relevant to the paragraph; keep (B). Choices (C) and (D) both effectively introduce the idea of *algae,* so eliminate (C) and (D). The correct answer is (B).

74. **F** Note the question! The question asks whether a phrase should be deleted from the essay, so it tests the ideas of consistent and clear. If the phrase is consistent with the subject of the paragraph and makes the meaning clearer, it should be kept. The paragraph discusses *phytoplankton,* and says that it is *an important food resource within Antarctica's ecosystem.* The phrase in question gives more details about phytoplankton's role in the food chain, so it is consistent with the paragraph and should not be deleted. Eliminate (H) and (J). Choice (F) accurately describes the phrase, so keep (F). The phrase does not *address the most important life forms in Antarctica's waters,* so eliminate (G). The correct answer is (F).

75. **A** Transitions change in the answer choices, so this question tests consistency of ideas. A transition must be consistent with the relationship between the ideas it connects. The sentence before the transition says that *Antarctica has a lower species diversity than any other place on Earth.* The sentence that starts with the transition says that *Antarctica is a haven for 67 documented species of insects and 350 species of flora.* The ideas in the two sentences contrast with each other; keep (A), which has a contrasting transition. Eliminate (B), (C), and (D), which all use transitions that indicate that ideas agree with each other. The correct answer is (A).

TEST 3 MATH ANSWERS AND EXPLANATIONS

1. **D** The question asks for the difference between two absolute value expressions. Treat absolute value bars like parentheses and evaluate what's inside the absolute value bars first: $|8-5|-|5-8|=|3|-|-3|=3-3=0$. Remember that absolute value is a measure of distance, so the result is always nonnegative. Choice (E) is 3 – (–3) = 6. The correct answer is (D).

2. **G** The question asks for the number of hours of tutoring that come with a session costing $220. First, subtract the flat fee from the total cost to determine how much the tutor charged exclusively for tutoring: $220 – $40 = $180. Divide this amount by the cost per hour, $60, to get $180 ÷ $60 = 3 hours of tutoring. Choice (F) incorrectly uses $40 + $60 = $100 as the hourly rate. Choices (H) and (K) divide $220 by $60 and $40, respectively, without subtracting the flat fee. Choice (J) calculates the session with a $60 flat fee and $40 hourly rate. The correct answer is (G).

3. **B** The question asks for a comparison between the times it takes the two trains to travel 1,152 miles. The time it takes Train A can be found by dividing the number of miles it goes by the speed, $\frac{1,152}{16}=72$. Follow the same steps for Train B to find that it takes $\frac{1,152}{24}=48$ hours. To find out how many more hours it takes Train A to travel than Train B, subtract the two values: 72 – 48 = 24 hours. Choice (A) is the result of averaging the miles per hour values, and (C) is the result of adding them. Choices (D) and (E) are the hours that each train takes, not the difference. The correct answer is (B).

4. **K** The question asks for the expression that is equivalent to the given one. Simplify the expression by combining like terms. Just combine one term at a time and then eliminate. The r^2 terms are $33r^2$ and $-41r^2$, so combining them results in $-8r^2$. Eliminate (F) and (G), which combine all coefficients between unlike terms. Also eliminate (J), which incorrectly multiplies variables rather than just adding the coefficients. The r terms are $-24r$ and r, so combining them results in $-23r$. Eliminate (H). The correct answer is (K).

5. **B** The question asks for the perimeter of the figure. Use the information given about the triangles to get the sides of the hexagon. Since the triangles are equilateral and each one's perimeter is 15, each side is 5. Figure *ABCDEF* has six sides, so its perimeter is 6(5) = 30. Choice (D) finds the area of the figure rather than its perimeter. Choice (E) treats the sides of each triangle, rather than the perimeter of each triangle, as 15. Choice (A) miscalculates the side of the triangle as 3 inches, and (C) includes the dotted interior lines in calculating the perimeter. The correct answer is (B).

6. **G** The question asks for the expression that is equivalent to the given one. Because there are two binomials being multiplied in the question, use the FOIL method (First, Outer, Inner, Last). Multiply and combine like terms to get $(5x+2)(x-3)=5x^2-15x+2x-6=5x^2-13x-6$. The correct answer is (G).

7. **E** The question asks for the value of 20% of the given number. Use the words in the problem to create an equation: *percent* means "divide by 100," *of* means "multiply," *is* means "equals," and *what* means "use a variable." The first equation is $\frac{35}{100}x = 14$ and x = 40. The second equation is $y = \frac{20}{100}(40) = 8$. Choice (A) is 20% of 14. Choice (B) is 35% of 14. Choice (D) is (20% + 35%) of 14. The correct answer is (E).

8. **G** The question asks for the value of x in the given situation. The list of integers adds up to $7x + 7$. This sum is equal to 511, so $7x + 7 = 511$. Subtract 7 from both sides to get $7x = 504$; then divide both sides by 7 to get $x = 72$. Choice (H) divides 511 by 7 without first subtracting 7, and (J) mistakenly adds 7 to the sum. Choices (F) and (K) are both incorrect estimates. The correct answer is (G).

9. **C** The question asks for the coordinates of point *C*. The given points are all over the (x,y) coordinate plane, so a sketch can help with ballparking the point's location. Draw the coordinate plane, and then plot and label the points given. Point *B* is the midpoint of $\overline{AC}$, so point *C* must be near $x = 0$ and above $y = 6$. The only choice near (0,6) is (C). To check if this produces the correct midpoint, use the midpoint formula, $\left(\frac{x_1 + x_2}{2}, \frac{y_1 + y_2}{2}\right)$. This becomes $\left(\frac{1+9}{2}, \frac{8+4}{2}\right) = (5,6)$, which is the correct midpoint. Choice (A) incorrectly takes *C* as the midpoint. The other answers do not use the midpoint formula correctly. The correct answer is (C).

10. **H** The question asks for the coordinates of a possible vertex *C*. Because the trapezoid is isosceles, its two vertical halves are mirror images of each other. To get from *A* to *B* requires adding 3 to the x-value, and 6 to the y-value of *A*, so to get from *D* to *C*, instead subtract 3 from the x-value and add 6 to the y-value of *D*. The correct answer is (H).

11. **D** The question asks for the combined peak and off-peak sales for the three bus stations in Asheville. To find the total average sales at each bus station, multiply the values of each column of the first matrix by the relevant row in the second matrix. This becomes 180(3) + 200(3) + 150(3) + 60(2) + 120(2) + 70(2) = 2,090. Choice (A) finds the number of tickets sold, and (C) multiplies that total by $2.50, the average of the two fare rates. Choice (B) gives only the peak fare sales. Choice (E) finds the total if all of the fares were bought at the peak $3 price. The correct answer is (D).

12. **F** The question asks for the sum of the measurements of the angles labeled *a*, *b*, and *c*. These angles are opposite the interior angles of the triangle, so use the fact that there are 180° in a line. Since $a° + 35° = 180°$, $a = 145$. Since $b° + 45° = 180°$, $b = 135$. To find the measure of *c*, get the third angle of the triangle. There are 180° in a triangle, so the third angle is 180° – 35° – 45° = 100°. Therefore, c = 180° – 100°, which equals 80°, and the sum of *a*, *b*, and *c* is 145 + 135 + 80 = 360°. The correct answer is (F).

13. **B** The question asks for the percent of the jellybeans that are green. Use the words in the problem to create an equation: *percent* means "divide by 100," *of* means "multiply," and *what* means "use a variable." The equation is $\frac{x}{100} \times 300 = 60$, so x = 20%. Choice (A) is the percent of purple jellybeans. Choice (C) is the percent of red jellybeans. Choice (D) is the percent of orange jellybeans. Choice (E) confuses the number of green jellybeans and the percent of the sample consisting of green jellybeans. The correct answer is (B).

14. **H** The question asks for the best estimate of the jellybeans in the barrel that are red. Set up a proportion: $\frac{75 \text{ red}}{300 \text{ total}} = \frac{x}{25{,}000 \text{ total}}$. Cross-multiply to get $300x$ = 1,875,000; then divide both sides by 300 to get x = 6,250. Choice (F) is the estimate for the number of purple jellybeans in the barrel. Choice (G) is the estimate for the number of green jellybeans. Choice (J) is the estimate for the number of orange jellybeans. Choice (K) assumes that the 75 red jellybeans in the sample is the same as the percentage of red jellybeans and finds 75% of 25,000. The correct answer is (H).

15. **E** The question asks for the number of degrees in the central angle for orange jellybeans. To find the central angle, first find what fraction of the sample is composed of orange jellybeans: $\frac{120}{300} = \frac{2}{5}$. The central angle is part of the total number of degrees, so it must be some fraction of 360°. The central angle for the orange sector is $\frac{2}{5} \times 360° = 144°$. Choice (A) is the central angle for the purple sector. Choice (B) is the central angle for the green sector. Choice (C) is the central angle for the red sector. Choice (D) confuses the number of orange jellybeans with the degree measure of the central angle. The correct answer is (E).

16. **G** The question asks for the ratio of part of the figure to the area of the entire rectangle. Because E and F are both midpoints, draw a line between them and divide the rectangle into 4 equal parts. Quadrilateral $AECF$ contains 2 of these 4 parts, and this ratio can be reduced to 1:2. Choice (J) shows the ratio using ΔABE instead of quadrilateral $AECF$, while (F) shows the ratio of the quadrilateral to the other half of the rectangle. Choice (H) assumes the 3 parts in the original diagram are equal. Choice (K) divides the rectangle into 5 parts. The correct answer is (G).

17. **D** The question asks for the slope of a line parallel to the given line. Parallel lines have the same slope. In the slope-intercept form, $y = mx + b$, the slope of the line is $m = \frac{1}{2}$. Choice (B) is the slope of

the line perpendicular to the given line. Choice (A) is the y-intercept. Choices (C) and (E) are the opposite and reciprocal, respectively, of the correct slope. The correct answer is (D).

18. **K** The question asks for the length of time, in minutes, that the longer sitting lasted. Try using the answer choices, starting with (H) to help eliminate answers if it is too big or too small. If the longer sitting was 45 minutes, the shorter one was 120 – 45 = 75 minutes. This doesn't make any sense, so eliminate (F), (G), and (H). A much longer time is needed, so try (K). If the longer sitting was 75 minutes, the shorter one was 120 – 75 = 45 minutes. The ratio of 45:75 can be reduced by a factor of 15 to 3:5. This matches the question. Choice (H), though already eliminated, is the shorter sitting time, and (G) is the factor by which the ratio can be reduced. The correct answer is (K).

19. **C** The question asks for a possible value of x in the given inequality. Use a calculator to find the exact values of the square roots given in the answers, starting with the middle choice. In (C), $\sqrt{140} \approx 11.83$. This satisfies the inequality in the question. Choice (B) is 11 exactly; the question asks for something greater. The value of (D) is a little more than 12, so it is too big. Choice (A) adds the numbers from the problem without answering what is asked for, and (E) = 23, the sum of the numbers in the problem. The correct answer is (C).

20. **H** The question asks for the minimum number of seed packets Susan needs based on the size of her garden. The area of the entire space of the garden is 10 × 16 × 3 = 480 ft². The rectangular plot for beans is 4 × 6 = 24 ft², and the rectangular plot for lettuce is $2\frac{1}{2} \times 5 = 12.5$ ft². Subtract the spaces for beans and lettuce from the total space for tomatoes. The result is 480 – 24 – 12.5 = 443.5 ft². Since the maximum number of square feet that can be covered by a packet is 200, estimate $\frac{443.5 \text{ ft}^2}{200 \text{ ft}^2 \text{ per packet}} > 2$ packets. Susan will need to buy a minimum of 3 packets. The correct answer is (H).

21. **E** The question asks for the solutions for x in the given equation. First, bring the 12 to the left side of the equation, so the whole equation is equal to 0 (i.e., $x^2 + 4x - 12 = 0$). Factor the equation by thinking of what two numbers when multiplied together = –12 and when added together = 4: 6 and –2 satisfy those conditions. Make the equation $(x + 6)(x - 2) = 0$, and then set $(x + 6) = 0$ and $(x - 2) = 0$ and solve for x in both cases. x is either –6 or 2. Another approach would be to try the numbers from the answer choices and see which ones satisfy the equation. The correct answer is (E).

22. **J** The question asks for the expression that is equivalent to the given one. When dividing variables with exponents, subtract the exponents of common terms. To visualize what's happening, write out the expression as $\frac{x \cdot x \cdot x \cdot x \cdot y \cdot y}{x \cdot x \cdot y \cdot y \cdot y \cdot y}$. Cancel like terms in the numerator and denominator to get

$\frac{x \cdot x}{y \cdot y}$, or $\frac{x^2}{y^2}$. Choices (F) and (G) negate the value of the entire expression, and (K) flips the numerator and denominator. Choice (H) incorrectly assumes $x^2 = y^2$. The correct answer is (J).

23. **E** The question asks for the possible quadrant locations of point *A*. If point *A* must have at least one positive coordinate value, it could be located in any quadrant except for III. Points in Quadrant III have negative *x*-coordinates and negative *y*-coordinates. Choice (C) incorrectly assumes the point has exactly 1 positive coordinate. Choice (A) assumes the point has exactly 2 positive coordinates, while (D) assumes it cannot have 2 positive coordinates. The correct answer is (E).

24. **H** The question asks for the expression that best represents the given situation. Translate the information in the question into an algebraic expression. The fixed cost each day of the company is $1,600 and the variable cost is the additional cost each day of producing each box. The equation then would be the fixed cost plus the variable cost, which is 1,600 + 4.75*b*, or (H). Choices (F) and (K) switch the fixed and variable costs. Choices (G) and (J) find the difference between the variable costs and the fixed cost instead of adding them to form the total cost. The correct answer is (H).

25. **D** The question asks for the length of $\overline{AC}$, the base of the larger of two similar triangles. The sides of similar triangles are proportional in length. To find how many times larger the larger triangle's perimeter is than the smaller triangle's perimeter (which is 2.4 + 4 + 3.2 = 9.6), divide the two known perimeters to get $\frac{576"}{9.6"} = 60$ times larger. $\overline{AC}$ will also be 60 times larger than $\overline{XZ}$, so $\overline{AC} = 3.2" \times 60" = 192"$. The correct answer is (D).

26. **H** The question asks for the value of *x* in the given equation. Multiply the fractions on the left so that $\frac{6\sqrt{11}}{x\sqrt{11}} = \frac{3\sqrt{11}}{11}$. Cross-multiply to get $66\sqrt{11} = 33x$, which simplifies to $x = 2\sqrt{11}$. Another approach would be to substitute the answer choices in for *x* to see which works in the equation. Choice (F) is half the value needed, and (J) is its square. Choice (K) is 11^2. Choice (G) is a number from the problem that does not answer the given question. The correct answer is (H).

27. **D** The question asks for the number of seconds it will take for Natalie and Jonathan to be at the same point on the track. Set up an equation for each runner, with the number of seconds to get to the crossing point, as well as the number of feet from point "0 feet" being equal for both runners. Jonathan starts 150 feet in from what can be called "0 feet" on the track, or at the 150 ft point. He runs at a speed of 9 ft/second for *x* seconds, covering *y* feet. Therefore, Jonathan's equation is

150 ft + 9 ft/second × (x seconds) = y feet. Natalie starts at 1,300 feet and runs in the opposite direction at 12 ft/second for x seconds, covering y feet. Therefore, Natalie's equation is 1,300 ft – 12 ft/second × (x seconds) = y feet. Since both equations = y, set them equal to each other and solve for x seconds. The equation becomes $150 + 9x = 1{,}300 - 12x$. Add $12x$ to both sides to get $150 + 21x = 1{,}300$; then subtract 150 from both sides to get $21x = 1{,}150$. Dividing both sides by 21 results in $x \approx 54.8$ seconds. All that can be a little tricky to set up, so another approach could be to use the answer choices as the values for the number of seconds and work backward from there. Using that time to find how far each runner is along the track won't get an exact answer, but it can help eliminate some. The correct answer is (D).

28. **G** The question asks for the number of different kinds of sundaes that Steve could order. For each of the 3 possible ice cream flavors, there are 2 possible types of syrup, so multiply 3 × 2. For each of those 6 possible orders, there are 6 possible kinds of candy toppings, so multiply 6 × 6 = 36 total possibilities. The correct answer is (G).

29. **B** The question asks for the volume of the box. The formula for the volume of a rectangular solid is $V = lwh$, so find those dimensions. The width of the box is half its length, so if its length is 12 cm, its width is 6 cm. The width is also twice the box's height, so the height is 3 cm. To find the volume, multiply all three dimensions to get $V = 12(6)(3) = 216$. Choice (D) incorrectly calculates the sides as 6, 12, and 24, and (E) incorrectly calculates the sides as 12, 24, and 48. Choice (A) neglects to multiply by the depth. Choice (C) finds the surface area of the box. The correct answer is (B).

30. **J** The question asks for the total value of Daniel's credit card debt. Based on the question, B = \$2,155, r = 13 percent, or 0.13, and $m = 2$. Substitute these values into the equation to get $D = 2{,}155(1 + 0.13) + 10(2)^2$. This becomes $D = 2{,}155(1.13) + 40 = 2{,}435.15 + 40 = \$2{,}475.15$. Choice (F) forgets to calculate the interest rate. Choice (G) forgets to add the $10(2)^2$, while (H) adds only 20. Choice (K) incorrectly calculates the interest rate at 14%. The correct answer is (J).

31. **D** The question asks for the total surface area of the cone. The equation for surface area is given as the expression $\pi r^2 + \pi rs$, where r is the radius and s is the slant height. The radius in the figure is half of the diameter, which is given as 30, so $r = 15$. The slant height is 30. Plug these values into the equation to get $(15)^2\pi + (15)(30)\pi$, which equals $225\pi + 450\pi = 675\pi$. Choice (C) is the result of forgetting to square the radius. Choice (E) uses the diameter instead of the radius in the equation. Choices (A) and (B) each result from evaluating only half of the expression. The correct answer is (D).

32. **F** The question asks for the value of $f(g(a))$ for the given functions f and g. To solve a composite function, work inside out starting with the value of $g(a)$, and then take the function f of $g(a)$. $g(a)$ is given as $2a^2 + 1$, so $f(g(a)) = f(2a^2 + 1)$. Substitute $2a^2 + 1$ for a in the $f(a)$ equation to get $f(2a^2 + 1) = 3(2a^2 + 1) - 4$. Distribute the 3 within the parentheses to get $6a^2 + 3 - 4$, which simplifies to $6a^2 - 1$. The correct answer is (F).

33. **D** The question asks for the average star-rating given to the movie based on the table. The average of a list of numbers is the total divided by the number of things, which in this case is the total number of stars divided by the number of students surveyed. This becomes $\frac{1(51) + 2(18) + 3(82) + 4(49) + 5(62)}{262} \approx 3.20$. If time is running low at this point in the test, cross out answer choices that are too large or too small to be the average and take a reasonable guess. Choice (A) is much too small, and (E) is much too large. Choice (A) flips the numerator and the denominator. Choice (E) divides 262 by the sum of the column on the left and its answer is rounded to only the nearest tenth. Choices (B) and (C) each drop one of the components of the numerator when calculating. The correct answer is (D).

34. **G** The question asks for the set of all lines on the figure that must be parallel given information about supplementary angles. Two angles are supplementary if the sum of their degrees measures is 180°. To create supplementary angles when two lines are intersected by a third line, the two lines must be parallel. Since $\angle x$ is supplementary to angles 8 and 11, lines q and s must be parallel. Since angles 4 and 6 are not necessarily supplementary to $\angle x$, lines q and r need not be parallel, eliminating (F) and (K). Since angles 7 and 5 are not necessarily supplementary to angles 8 and 11, lines r and s need not be parallel, eliminating (H). Lines p and q intersect so they cannot be parallel, eliminating (J). The correct answer is (G).

35. **E** The question asks for the expression that is equivalent to the given one. When an expression in parentheses is raised to a power, that exponent is applied to each term inside the parentheses. The numeral inside the parentheses (4) gets *raised to the power* of 4, and then the exponents inside the parentheses are *multiplied by* 4. Choices (B) and (C) incorrectly multiply the numeral by 4, and (D) incorrectly adds 4 to the variables' exponents. Choice (A) divides all the numbers by 4. Choice (E) correctly takes 4^4 to get 256 and $(x^4y^4)^4$ to get $x^{16}y^{16}$. The correct answer is (E).

36. **F** The question asks for the simplified inequality that is equivalent to the given one. To do this, isolate x by first subtracting $6x$ from both sides of the inequality to get $-8 > 2x + 14$. Subtract 14 from both sides to get $-22 > 2x$, and then divide both sides by 2. The inequality becomes $-11 > x$ or $x < -11$. The correct answer is (F).

37. **E** The question asks for the coordinates of point A after the circle is rotated. Since the circle is rotated counterclockwise, the point should be in Quadrant IV with a positive x-value and negative y-value, eliminating (A) and (B). With a 90° rotation, the line formed by the new point A and center L will be perpendicular to the existing $\overline{AL}$. Find the slope of $\overline{AL}$ by counting the rise over the run from A to $L = \frac{6}{-8}$. The perpendicular slope will be the negative reciprocal $\frac{8}{6}$, so move 8

units down and 6 units left from the center of the circle: (10 – 6, –2 – 8) = (4, –10). The correct answer is (E).

38. **F** The question asks for the cosine of the angle labeled as θ on the triangle. According to SOHCAH-TOA, $\cos\theta = \frac{\text{adjacent}}{\text{hypotenuse}}$. For angle θ, the *adjacent* is not given, but the *hypotenuse* is 16. Since the denominator of the cosine proportion is the *hypotenuse,* and must be 16, eliminate (G), (H), and (K). Of the two remaining answers, (F) is more likely to be correct, since it does not use the *opposite* side of 12. To find the actual length of the side *adjacent* to θ, use the Pythagorean Theorem ($a^2 + b^2 = c^2$) to see that it is $\sqrt{112}$. The correct answer is (F).

39. **C** The question asks for the measure of ∠*CAD* on the figure. Since $\overline{CA}$ bisects ∠*BAD*, ∠*BAC* and ∠*CAD* are equal, and since $\overline{DA}$ bisects ∠*CAE*, ∠*DAE* and ∠*CAD* are equal. Since ∠*BAC* and ∠*DAE* are both equal to ∠*CAD*, ∠*BAD* = ∠*DAE* = ∠*CAD*. Given that there are 180° in a straight line, and ∠*BAC*, ∠*DAE*, and ∠*CAD* are all adjacent, ∠*CAD* = $\frac{1}{3}$(180°) = 60°. The correct answer is (C).

40. **H** The question asks for the volume of the container based on the number of molecules inside. To find the volume of the container, set up the equation $\frac{6\times10^8 \text{ molecules}}{x \text{ cubic inches}} = \frac{3\times10^4 \text{ molecules}}{\text{cubic inch}}$. Multiply both sides by x, and then divide both sides by 3×10^4 to get $x = \frac{6\times10^8}{3\times10^4}$. Remember to subtract the exponents when dividing quantities with like bases, so $x = 2 \times 10^4$. Choice (F) is $\frac{3\times10^4}{6\times10^8}$. Choice (G) is the result of dividing the exponents. Choice (J) is the result of multiplying the numbers in the problem. Choice (K) is $(3 \times 6) \times (10^{4\times8})$. The correct answer is (H).

41. **B** The question asks for the shortest distance between the starting point of the car and the driver's desired destination. According to the question, this is the distance from point *A* to point *B*. To use the Law of Cosines, the measure of ∠*ACB* must be determined to find the length of *AB*. There are 360° in a circle, so ∠*ACN* = 360 – 250 = 110. ∠*ACB* = ∠*ACN* + ∠*BCN* = 110 + 30 = 140°. The only difference in the answer choices is the angle used, so there is no need to worry about how to set up the rest of the Law of Cosines. The correct answer is (B).

42. **J** The question asks for the real number that is halfway between $\frac{1}{4}$ and $\frac{1}{6}$. The number halfway between $\frac{1}{4}$ and $\frac{1}{6}$ can be found by averaging the two numbers. This results in $\frac{\frac{1}{4}+\frac{1}{6}}{2}=\frac{5}{24}$, which is a real number. The other answer choices are real numbers but are not even between or exactly halfway between the two values. Choice (G) is between the two values, but it is not halfway. The correct answer is (J).

43. **D** The question asks for the measure of $\angle DEB$ on the figure. Use the information given to try to find the angles in ΔADE. ΔADE and ΔEBA are congruent because they have congruent sides: both triangles share $\overline{AE}$; $\overline{BA}$ and $\overline{DE}$ are each half the length of congruent sides; and diagonals $\overline{DA}$ and $\overline{BE}$ are equal. Therefore, $\angle EBA = \angle EDA = 95°$, and $\angle DAE = \angle BEA = 35°$. There are 180° in a triangle, so $\angle AED = 180 - 35 - 95 = 50°$. $\angle AED$ also equals $\angle AEB + \angle DEB$, so $50 = 35 + \angle DEB$, and $\angle DEB = 15°$. The correct answer is (D).

44. **H** The question asks for the value of x on the diagram. The measure of x is the side of the large square table minus the side of the small square table. Since $A = s^2$, $\sqrt{A} = s$. The side of the large square table is $\sqrt{108} = \sqrt{36 \times 3} = 6\sqrt{3}$. The area of the small square table is $\frac{108}{9} = 12$, so its side is $\sqrt{12} = \sqrt{4 \times 3} = 2\sqrt{3}$. Therefore, $x = 6\sqrt{3} - 2\sqrt{3} = 4\sqrt{3}$. Choice (F) gives the side of the small square table instead of x, and (K) gives the area of the small square table. Choice (G) subtracts terms with a common radical incorrectly. Choice (J) subtracts the two areas and then takes the square root of the result, instead of first taking the square root of each area and then subtracting the results. The correct answer is (H).

45. **E** The question asks for the number that is NOT irrational. A rational number is one which can be expressed as a fraction. Only (E) can be reduced to integer values in the numerator and denominator: $\sqrt{\frac{81}{25}} = \frac{\sqrt{81}}{\sqrt{25}} = \frac{9}{5}$. The correct answer is (E).

46. **G** The question asks for the expression that is equivalent to the given inequality. Pick a value for both x and y. If $x = -5$ and $y = -3$, the absolute value expression becomes $|-5+(-3)| = |-8| = 8$. Check the answer choices to see which one also equals 8 for these values of x and y. Choice (F) is $-5 - 3 = -8$, and (G) is $-(-5 - 3) = -(-8) = 8$. Eliminate (F) and keep (G), but check the rest of the

answers just in case. Choice (H) is –5 – (–3) = –5 + 3 = –2, (J) is $|-5-(-3)| = |-5+3| = |-2| = 2$, and (K) is $\sqrt{(-5)^2+(-3)^2} = \sqrt{25+9} = \sqrt{34}$. The correct answer is (G).

47. E The question asks for the score Jane must get on her next game to reach her goal average. To determine this, figure out how many total points she will need and how many she has already earned. To find the total points she needs on the six games, multiply her desired average by the number of games: 85 × 6 = 510. To find the number of points she has already gotten, multiply her average on the first 5 games by the number of games, which is 5 × 83 = 415. The difference between these numbers is the score she must get in order to get an average of 85 on the 6 games. This means that the score she needs is 510 – 415 = 95, which is (E). Choice (C) is the score she would have to get in the next two games for an average of 85. Choices (A) and (B) can be eliminated—Jane wants her average to go up, so she needs a higher score on the next game. The correct answer is (E).

48. **G** The question asks for the complex number that has the smallest modulus. Since the modulus is $\sqrt{a^2+b^2}$, then the quadrant that the point is found in is negligible since all points are squared. Thus, the point with the greatest distance from the origin will have the greatest modulus, and the point with the shortest distance from the origin will have the smallest. It is possible to make up sample points to see how this is true. On the diagram, point *G* the closest to the origin, and thus has the smallest modulus. The correct answer is (G).

49. **B** The question asks for the solution to the given equation. Since 9 = 3^2 and 27 = 3^3, make $9^{x-4} = 27^{3x+2}$ into $3^{2(x-4)} = 3^{3(3x+2)}$. The equation now reads: "3 to some power = 3 to some power." Therefore, the exponents are equal: $2(x - 4) = 3(3x + 2)$. Distribute the 2 and the 3 to get $2x - 8 = 9x + 6$. Subtract $9x$ and add 8 to each side of the equation to get $-7x = 14$. Divide both sides by –7 to get $x = -2$. The correct answer is (B).

50. **J** The question asks for a true statement about the given sine function based on the graph. Go through the answers and use Process of Elimination. To test (F), see if any horizontal lines (at any *y*-values) can be drawn that hit the sine wave more than once. If *y* is between –1 and 1, the horizontal lines will intersect the graph at multiple *x*-values. This means that *x* is not unique for all *f*(*x*), and (F) is false. Choice (G) says that the function is undefined at $x = 0$, but the graph clearly goes through the origin. Therefore, (G) is false. To test (H), try some values from the function, which appears to contain the points (3,2) and (–3, –2). The value of *f*(*x*) is the *y*-coordinate of the point, so these points reveal that $f(3) \neq f(-3)$. Eliminate (H). These same points do show, however, that $f(-3) = -f(3) = -2$. This means that the function is odd. Choice (K) is incorrect because the arrows at the ends of the sine wave indicate that it continues past the domain $-6 \leq x \leq 6$ shown here. The correct answer is (J).

51. **B** The question asks for the probability that a randomly selected number will have 1 as at least one of its digits. Probability is defined as the number of outcomes that fit the requirements divided by

the total number of outcomes. Start by finding the total number of outcomes. It is tempting to just subtract, but that does not include the numbers at both ends of the spectrum. To get *299 through 1,000, inclusive,* find the difference and then add 1. The total outcomes = 1,000 – 299 + 1 = 702. Choice (A) mistakenly uses 1,000 for the denominator, so eliminate it. Now find the number of integers that have at least one 1, listing them out at first to make sure none are skipped. From 299 to 399, the list is 301, 310, 311, 312, 313, 314, 315, 316, 317, 318, 319, 321, 331, 341, 351, 361, 371, 381, and 391. There are 19 numbers on the list, and there will be another 19 for 400–499, 500–599, 600–699, 700–799, 800–899, and 900–999. This means there is a total of 7 sets of 19 numbers, or 133 numbers. The final one that works is 1,000, so the probability is $\frac{134}{702}$. The correct answer is (B).

52. **G** The question asks for the slope of $\overline{LM}$ on the figure. This line has a positive slope, so eliminate (J) and (K) right away. Because $\overline{NL}$ is parallel to the *x*-axis and ΔNLM is isosceles, the slope of $\overline{LM}$ is the negative of the slope of $\overline{MN}$. Find the slope of $\overline{MN}$ by rewriting the equation $y+\frac{2}{3}x=2$ as $y = -\frac{2}{3}x + 2$, where the slope *m* is $-\frac{2}{3}$. The slope of $\overline{LM}$, therefore, is $\frac{2}{3}$. The correct answer is (G).

53. **A** The question asks for the tangent of $\sin^{-1}$ of $\frac{x}{\sqrt{x^2+y^2}}$ based on the figure. The notation $\sin^{-1}\left(\frac{x}{\sqrt{x^2+y^2}}\right)$ means find the angle that has a sine value of $\frac{x}{\sqrt{x^2+y^2}}$. Recall that the sine of an angle is $\frac{\text{opposite}}{\text{hypotenuse}}$. The side marked *x* is opposite $\angle ACB$ so that's the angle in question. Now, use SOHCAHTOA to find that $\tan(\angle ACB)=\frac{\text{opposite}}{\text{adjacent}}=\frac{x}{y}$. The correct answer is (A).

54. **H** The question asks for the area of the circle in which the dog can roam. The area of a circle is πr^2, which in this case is $\pi\,(12)^2$, or approximately 452. Choice (F) incorrectly calculates the circumference ($2\pi r$). Choice (G) creates a square by forgetting to multiply by π. Choice (J) calculates $2\pi r^2$, while (K) shows $\pi^2 r^2$. The correct answer is (H).

55. **E** The question asks for the equation of the circle drawn on the map. The standard equation of a circle is $(x - h)^2 + (y - k)^2 = r^2$, where (h,k) is the center and r is the radius. In this circle, $r = 12$, so the equation must be equal to 12^2. Eliminate (A), (B), and (D). When the center is at the origin, the equation becomes $(x - 0)^2 + (y - 0)^2 = r^2$ or just $x^2 + y^2 = r^2$. The correct answer is (E).

56. **F** The question asks for the number of feet along the trail that both dogs can roam. If the 2 anchors are 30 feet apart, and Joy's dog is on a 20-foot leash, it can get within 10 feet of Melissa's anchor (30 – 20 = 10). Melissa's dog can run 12 feet from its anchor, so there is an overlap of 2 feet. If necessary, draw a sketch of the situation to see why this is true. Choice (G) is the difference of the two dog leashes. Choices (H) and (J) subtract each dog leash length from 30. Choice (K) is the sum of the two leashes. The correct answer is (F).

57. **D** The question asks for the values of x, if any exist, that satisfy the given inequality. Look at the graph of the two equations. Find the x-values where the y-value of the equation $y = -(x + 1)^2 + 4$ is greater than the y-value of the equation $y = (-x + 1)$. According to the figure, the parabola has a higher y-value than the line between the x-values –2 and 1. The correct answer is (D).

58. **J** The question asks for the greatest possible value of an expression under certain conditions. Test numbers to answer this question. To make the value of $y - x$ as large as possible, make y a larger two-digit number and x a small two-digit number. If $t = 1$ and $u = 9$, then $x = 19$ and $y = 91$. Therefore, $y - x = 91 - 19 = 72$. That is the largest possible value given the restrictions, so these values of t and u can be used to test out the answers. The value of (F) is 9 – 1 = 8, which is not 72. Eliminate (F). Choice (G) is (9)(1) – (1)(9) = 9 – 9 = 0. Eliminate (G). Choice (H) is $1^2 - 10(1)(9) + 9^2 = 1 - 90 + 81 = -8$, so (H) can be eliminated. Choice (J) is $9|9-1| = 9|8| = 72$. Choice (K) can be eliminated as well since (J) matches the maximum value. The correct answer is (J).

59. **C** The question asks for the area of the parallelogram in the (x,y) coordinate plane. Use the formula for the area of a parallelogram: *Area* = *base* × *height*. Find the length of the base by calculating the length of $\overline{AB}$: 8 – 2 = 6. Find the height by dropping an altitude perpendicular to the base from point D to point (4, –4), which has a length of 2. *Area* = 6 × 2 = 12. Choice (D) incorrectly uses side $\overline{AD}$ with length $2\sqrt{2}$ for the height. Choice (A) gives the value of the base, (B) gives the base times the square root of the height, and (E) gives 2 times the base + 2 times the height. The correct answer is (C).

60. **G** The question asks for the sixth term in an arithmetic sequence. To determine the sixth term, first find the common difference between consecutive terms in the sequence. Use the given formula to solve for x_1: $145 = 5\left(\frac{x_1 + 48}{2}\right)$, so $x_1 = 10$. The common difference in an arithmetic sequence is basically the slope of a straight line: $difference = \frac{x_n - x_1}{n - 1} = \frac{48 - 10}{5 - 1} = 9.5$. The sixth term, therefore, is 48 + 9.5 = 57.5. Choice (F) calculates $n + 1$, rather than x_{n+1}. Choices (H) and (K) use averages, rather than a common difference. Choice (J) incorrectly adds the difference to the sum, rather than x_5. The correct answer is (G).

TEST 3 READING ANSWERS AND EXPLANATIONS

Passage I

1. **A** The question asks what purpose the narrator's *description of a volcano* serves, as it relates to his friend's fear. The question references the third paragraph, so read lines 13–19, and a few lines before and after if needed. The first paragraph describes the experience of the narrator's friend, who *has been unable to reclaim his speaking voice,* although...*his mind lights up with ideas.* The friend's fear is expressed in lines 11–12: *"I fear that I will eventually choke on my own thoughts."* In lines 13–19, the narrator compares the friend to *a volcano with no air vents to relieve the pressure of the heat churning in his belly.* The narrator uses the metaphor of the volcano to illustrate the friend's difficult experience. Keep (A), since the volcano is an illustration of *the friend's inner torment.* The narrator is not speculating about what will happen, so eliminate (B). The explanation of *why the friend is unable to speak* is in the first paragraph; that is not the purpose of the description of the volcano, so eliminate (C). The author does not *imply the friend needs to be more patient,* so eliminate (D). The correct answer is (A).

2. **H** The question asks for a description of the structure of the passage. Because this is a general question, it should be done after all the specific questions. The passage focuses on the narrator's experience with a friend who loses his ability to speak, recounting some of their conversations and letters in which they compare spoken and written communication. The passage is not a character study, since it focuses on ideas about communication rather than on the personalities of the two friends; additionally, their exchanges are not best described as an *argument,* so eliminate (F). The passage is mostly written from one perspective; there are brief excerpts from a letter from the author's friend, but they don't *take equal turns discussing their positions,* so eliminate (G). Keep (H) because it captures the main topic as well as *the verbal and written exchanges* included in the passage. The author's successes and struggles as a lawyer are not discussed, so eliminate (J). The correct answer is (H).

3. **D** The question asks what the *dust cloud* and *lava flow* portray in the *erupting volcano simile.* Look for the words *dust cloud* and *lava flow* in the passage. Lines 20–23 state *I tell him that his speaking voice may be like the oceanic cloud of dust and debris that the volcano spews into the air, but his writing can flow like omni-directional lava, indiscriminately absorbing everything in its path.* There is no comparison of *intuition and logic* in these lines, so eliminate (A). There is also no discussion of *simplicity and complexity,* so eliminate (B). In lines 39–45, the author and the friend discuss *methodically composed* and *spontaneous* communication, but the dust cloud and lava flow don't portray *instinct and deliberation,* so eliminate (C). Keep (D) because the phrase *vocal and non-vocal expression* is supported by *his speaking voice* and *his writing.* The correct answer is (D).

4. **H** The question asks which statement most clearly portrays the respective attitudes of the narrator and his friend. Because this is a general question, it should be done after all the specific questions. At the beginning of the passage, the friend shows anxiety in his statement, *"I fear that I will eventually choke on my own thoughts,"* (line 11) and later the passage refers to a *mix of pride and pain in*

his eyes (lines 64–65) and says that he *deeply misses* the *expressiveness that a human voice can add to the meaning of words* (lines 75–77). The narrator is sympathetic to his friend's experience, as indicated by statements such as, *"If my profession would allow it, I would gladly yield my voice to him* (lines 66–67). The narrator is also encouraging, as in lines 35–37: *I optimistically point to the fact that written language has the potential to be seen by countless human eyes.* Though the author and the friend debate, the friend *acknowledges* that *There is plenty of solace in writing* (line 28) and helps the narrator with his speeches (lines 77–81). Therefore, he is not *argumentative* or *cynical.* Based on the references above, the narrator is not *jaded* or *indifferent;* eliminate (F). The friend is not *scornful* or *depressed,* and there's no indication that the narrator is *apologetic,* so eliminate (G). Keep (H) because it is supported by the lines cited above. The friend doesn't speak because he has lost his voice, not because he is *shy,* and he comes to the narrator's trials (line 62), so he is not *reclusive.* In the passage, the narrator only speaks to his friend and in court, so there is no evidence that he is *outgoing,* and the effort he puts into the debate with his friend indicates that he is not *nonchalant;* eliminate (J). The correct answer is (H).

5. **C** The question asks how the narrator describes *Cyrano de Bergerac.* Look for the name *Cyrano de Bergerac* in the passage. Lines 71–73 describe *Cyrano de Bergerac, who so wished to woo the heart of a woman that he enlisted the help of a friend to speak his thoughts aloud to her.* There is no indication that he is *afraid of losing* the woman, nor that she is *the love of his life,* so eliminate (A). There is no mention that Cyrano de Bergerac has a *physical condition* that prevents him from speaking, so eliminate (B). Keep (C) because it is supported by lines 71–73. The passage doesn't indicate that he was not *able to describe* the *emotions of love,* so eliminate (D). The correct answer is (C).

6. **H** The question asks which statement about *pirates* is best supported by the narrator's characterization of them. Look for the word *pirates* in the passage. In lines 52–54, the author compares written words to pirates, saying the words *belong only to each other, like pirates who share a common destiny but no longer pledge allegiance to any sovereign entity.* There is not support for the statement that pirates have *no rules of conduct,* so eliminate (F). The author uses the phrase *if you wish to be confused* in relation to his argument about words (line 55); it is not a reference to *pirates,* so eliminate (G). Keep (H) because it is supported by lines 52–54. The author makes a comparison between pirates and written words; he doesn't indicate what the *pirates* think of *written language,* so eliminate (J). The correct answer is (H).

7. **A** The question asks what the friend values in *vocal speech.* Look for references to something that the friend *values* in the passage. Lines 74–77 state, *It is not the organization of thought that he treasures in listening to my courtroom orations. It is the expressiveness that a human voice can add to the meaning of words that he deeply misses.* Keep (A) because it is supported by these lines. There is no mention of *proper mechanics, rich vocabulary,* or *clever humor,* so eliminate (B), (C), and (D). The correct answer is (A).

8. **G** The question asks what the friend is worried about. Look for references to the friend's worry in the passage. In lines 9–12, the author says that his friend's words *are held prisoner in their own home,*

quarantined in frustrated isolation from the outside world. "I fear that I will eventually choke on my own thoughts," he worries aloud to me in one of his desperate letters. Therefore, the friend worries that he will be overwhelmed by his frustration at not being able to speak. The friend is not able to speak, and there is no mention of saying *something embarrassing,* so eliminate (F). Keep (G) because it is supported by lines 9–12. Lines 74–81 describe how the friend helps the narrator with his speeches for court; there is no indication that the friend might be *damaging the narrator's chances of courtroom success;* eliminate (H). The reference to *a symphony of thought* is in line 42; the friend is describing the potential of vocal speech; he isn't discussing a fear that he will *not be clever enough to compose a symphony of thought,* so eliminate (J). The correct answer is (G).

9. **D** The question asks what the word *puppet* means in line 68. Go back to the text, find the word *puppet,* and mark it out. Carefully read the surrounding text to determine another word that would fit in the blank based on the context of the passage. In lines 66–69, the narrator says *If my profession would allow it, I would gladly yield my voice to him and become a mere puppet for his ideas, just so he could again experience the instant gratification of vocal persuasion.* The phrase *become a mere puppet for his ideas* refers to *yield my voice to him,* so *puppet* could be replaced with the phrase "one who speaks another's words." An *entertainer* is a person who "performs for others' amusement"; it doesn't match "one who speaks another's words," so eliminate (A). A *conversationalist* is a person who "converses often or well"; it doesn't match "one who speaks another's words," so eliminate (B). A *toy* is a "plaything"; it doesn't match "one who speaks another's words," so eliminate (C). A *mouthpiece* is a "one who expresses another's views"; this matches "one who speaks another's words," so keep (D). The correct answer is (D).

10. **F** The question asks for a description of *the friend's reaction to watching the narrator during legal proceedings.* Look for a reference in the passage to the friend watching the narrator during legal proceedings. Lines 62–66 describe, *He enjoys coming to watch me during my trials. Sometimes I look over at him while I am delivering my closing arguments to a jury, and I see the mix of pride and pain in his eyes as he listens to me express myself more lucidly than he may ever be able to again.* Keep (F), since the phrase *appreciative and yearning* is supported by this description. There is no mention of the friend being *confused,* and although there is *pain in his eyes,* he is not *hopeless,* so eliminate (G). There is no indication that the friend is either *awestruck* or *overbearing,* so eliminate (H). Though the friend experiences pain as he watches the narrator, the passage doesn't indicate that the friend is *bitter* or *resentful,* so eliminate (J). The correct answer is (F).

Passage II

11. **A** The question asks how the author characterizes *the role of human activity in regard to the collapse of ice shelves.* Because this is a general question, it should be done after all the specific questions. Lines 34–37 cite a study *providing the first direct evidence linking human activity to the collapse of Antarctic ice shelves.* The passage goes on to say that *stronger westerly winds in the northern Antarctic*

Peninsula, driven principally by human-induced climate change, are responsible for the significant increases in summer temperatures that led to the retreat and collapse of the Larsen B. Keep (A) since it is supported by this reference. The scientists discussed in lines 58–77 do say that global warming is *only one of a number of atmospheric, oceanic and glaciological factors*. However, they *acknowledge that global warming had a major role in the collapse,* so the author does not characterize *the role of human activity* as *insignificant in comparison to glaciological influences,* so eliminate (B). This study indicates that human activity was *less of a contributor* to the collapse of the Larsen B ice shelf than the earlier study indicated, but this is not quite a match for (C). Choice (C) says that human activity is *less of a contributor* to the *collapse of ice shelves* in general than *initial evidence predicted.* Since the study discussed in lines 58–77 is only about the Larsen B ice shelf, its conclusion cannot be said to apply to all ice shelves, and the *Journal of Climate* study was the first *direct* evidence that linked human activity to Antarctic ice shelf collapse, but it is not the *initial evidence* that *predicted* a link between human activity and ice shelf collapse; eliminate (C). The passage does not support the statement that human activity is the *primary* cause of ice shelf collapse, nor that the damage is *irreversible,* so eliminate (D). The correct answer is (A).

12. **J** The question asks which of the answers is not listed as a *possible effect of sea level rise*. When a question asks which answer is **not** supported, eliminate answers that **are** supported. Look for the words *sea level rise* in the passage. Lines 84–88 state that *the concern is that the rise in sea levels could affect ecosystems worldwide, generating such problems as widespread flooding, loss of coastal cities and island countries, decreased crop yields, and the possible extinction of millions of species.* The effects listed in (F), (G), and (H) are all included in these lines, so eliminate these choices. Lines 79–83 say that glaciers that have *surged forward* are a cause of sea level rise, not an effect, so keep (J). The correct answer is (J).

13. **A** The question asks for *the common factor in Dr. Marshall's study* and that of *Doctors Scambos and Glasser*. Read a window in the passage around the given lines. Lines 42–50 trace the chain of events cited in Dr. Marshall's study, beginning with *global warming and the ozone hole* and ultimately resulting in the *break-up* of the *Larsen ice shelf.* Lines 64–67 indicate that *Glasser and Scambos acknowledge that global warming had a major role in the collapse* of the Larsen B ice shelf. Therefore, the author indicates that both sets of scientists *cite global warming as a reason for the Larsen B ice-shelf collapse,* so keep (A) and eliminate (B). These lines indicate that both sets of scientists did find *compelling evidence to explain the Larsen B ice-shelf collapse,* so eliminate (C). The author says that, according to Glasser and Scambos, *the location and spacing of crevasses and rifts on the ice do much to determine its strength;* however, there is no mention of *structural weaknesses* in the discussion of Dr. Marshall's findings, so eliminate (D). The correct answer is (A).

14. **H** The question asks what the author's statement in lines 51–54 most nearly means about *human activity.* Read a window in the passage around the given lines. This statement is a discussion of Dr. Marshall's findings, which *demonstrated a process directly linking the collapse to human activity, and that climate change does not impact our planet evenly, as evidenced by the significant increase in temperatures in certain geographical areas.* There is no mention of *other factors influencing climate change,*

so eliminate (F). These lines don't include enough evidence to support *worldwide* or *do great harm,* so eliminate (G). Keep (H) because it is supported by the reference to *the significant increase in temperatures in certain geographical areas.* This statement doesn't include enough evidence to support the prediction that sea level rise due to human activity will destroy *entire countries and species of animals,* so eliminate (J). The correct answer is (H).

15. **C** The question asks what the author calls *a stunning sign of worldwide climate change.* Look for the words *stunning sign of worldwide climate change* in the passage. Lines 31–33 state that *the collapse of the Larsen B ice shelf seemed to be one of the most obvious and stunning signs of worldwide climate change.* Lines 84–85 state that the *rise in sea levels could affect ecosystems worldwide;* this indicates that sea level rise significant enough to have worldwide effect has not occurred yet, so eliminate (A). Lines 69–73 state *The amount of melt-water on the Larsen B shelf just before the collapse caused many to assume that air temperature increases were primarily to blame, but Scambos and Glasser's research shows that ice-shelf breakup is not controlled simply by climate,* so eliminate (B). Keep (C), because it is the choice that is most closely related to the statement in lines 31–33. Lines 53–55 discuss *the significant increase in temperatures...in the western Antarctic Peninsula,* but this is not referred to as *a stunning sign of worldwide climate change,* so eliminate (D). The correct answer is (C).

16. **J** The question asks why the author includes the findings in lines 64–75. Read a window in the passage around the given lines. These lines discuss the fact that *global warming* is *only one of a number of atmospheric, oceanic and glaciological factors* that contributed to the collapse of the Larsen B ice shelf. These lines give several causes in addition to *global warming,* so eliminate (F). There is no mention of the *choices* that people make *in their daily lives,* so eliminate (G). The previous paragraphs discuss an earlier belief that the Larsen B ice shelf collapse could be attributed to *worldwide climate change,* while lines 64–75 indicate that there are actually several contributing factors. This implies that ice shelf break-up is more complex than previously thought, not *simpler,* so eliminate (H). Keep (J) because it is supported by lines 64–75. The correct answer is (J).

17. **D** The question asks for the main idea of the third paragraph, so read lines 34–57. These lines discuss a study that provided *the first direct evidence linking human activity to the collapse of Antarctic ice shelves.* Specifically, the scientists argued that *global warming and the ozone hole* created conditions that led to the *break-up* of the *Larsen B* ice shelf. These lines contradict (A), so eliminate it. There is no indication within this paragraph that the collapse was *foreshadowed for years,* so eliminate (B). Although lines 52–53 state that *climate change does not impact our planet evenly,* the main idea is not that the uneven impact caused the collapse, so eliminate (C). Keep (D) because it is supported by the paragraph. The correct answer is (D).

18. **J** The question asks what is *NOT* listed in the passage as *a cause of ice-shelf collapse.* When a question asks which answer is **not** supported, eliminate answers that **are** supported. Use words from the answer choices to locate the relevant portions of the passage. Global warming is cited as a cause of ice-shelf collapse in lines 37–50 and in lines 66–67; eliminate (F). *Human activity* is cited as a cause of ice-shelf collapse in lines 36–37, so eliminate (G). The *location and spacing of crevasses and*

rifts on the ice is mentioned as a cause of ice-shelf collapse in lines 72–75, so eliminate (H). Keep (J), because *deep ocean currents* are never discussed in the passage. The correct answer is (J).

19. **B** The question asks how the author describes the *increased westerly winds in the northern Antarctic Peninsula*. Look for the words *westerly winds* and *northern Antarctic Peninsula* in the passage. Lines 37–42 state that *Scientists revealed that stronger westerly winds in the northern Antarctic Peninsula, driven principally by human-induced climate change, are responsible for the significant increase in summer temperatures that led to the retreat and collapse of the Larsen B [ice shelf].* These lines contradict (A), which says that the winds are *irrelevant* to ice-shelf collapse, so eliminate (A). Keep (B) because it is supported by these lines. The fact that these winds are *driven principally by human-induced climate change* indicates that they are not *a common weather pattern,* so eliminate (C). The passage later suggests that continuing ice-shelf collapse could lead to a *rise in sea-level,* but this does not support the statement that the winds are an *unmistakable warning of sea-level rise,* so eliminate (D). The correct answer is (B).

20. **H** The question asks why the author uses the remark "*largest increase in temperatures observed anywhere on Earth.*" Read a window in the passage around the given lines. Lines 52–57 state that *climate change does not impact our planet evenly, as evidenced by the significant increase in temperatures in certain geographical areas, particularly the western Antarctic Peninsula,* which *has shown the largest increase in temperatures observed anywhere on Earth over the past half-century.* There is no indication that this statement is an *exaggeration,* so eliminate (F). The author does not discuss the need *for people to change their behavior,* so eliminate (G). Keep (H) because it is supported by the statement *climate change does not impact our planet evenly.* There is no mention of *a common misconception,* so eliminate (J). The correct answer is (H).

Passage III

21. **A** The question asks for the main purpose of the second paragraph of Passage A, so read lines 14–28. This paragraph begins with the author saying that *doing right by a great book and being faithful to it are, to my mind, two separate issues.* Then, the author illustrates this point with the example of the film adaptation of *The Hunger Games,* saying it *suffers from the pitfalls of faithfulness.* Keep (A), since it is supported by the paragraph. The author is not praising *The Hunger Games,* so eliminate (B). The paragraph doesn't indicate that *Gary Ross* was frustrated about an *inability to portray the complex relationships in the book;* it says that *there's no time allotted to build complex relationships* throughout most of the film, so eliminate (C). The phrase *stenography in light* is used critically, just after the author says that *Ross just ticks off the boxes,* so eliminate (D). The correct answer is (A).

22. **H** The question asks what Tobias suggests when he refers to *selling Katniss Barbie dolls.* The introduction indicates that *Tobias* is the author of passage A, so read a window in Passage A around the given line. Lines 40–45 state that *Films content with merely illustrating books are more concerned with problem-solving and translation than artistic expression...if that's the case, what's the point of making*

it? Selling Katniss Barbie dolls? The author asks this question to emphasize that there is no point in making a film that simply tries to recreate a book. The author does not discuss *older audiences* or *young children,* so eliminate (F). He does not actually believe that *selling toys is the primary purpose for such films,* so eliminate (G). Keep (H) because it is supported by lines 40–45. The author's point is not about *film-related merchandise,* so eliminate (J). The correct answer is (H).

23. **A** The question asks what *The Hunger Games* suffers from, according to Tobias. Tobias is the author of Passage A, so look for the words *The Hunger Games* in Passage A. Lines 15–21 state that *Skillful as it is, The Hunger Games suffers from all the pitfalls of faithfulness that I noted in my review…It hits all the expected plot points from a novel…but it feels thinned-out as a result, because it can only deal glancingly with key relationships from the book.* Keep (A) because it is supported by these lines. Line 21 references *Katniss's relationship with Rue* as an example of the key relationships that the film *can only deal glancingly with;* this contradicts (B), so eliminate this choice. In lines 43–44, Tobias quotes another review of the film: *"it's faithful to the point of not adding anything you haven't seen in your head when you read the book."* This contradicts (C), so eliminate this choice. Lines 21–25 refer to *"The Reaping"* as *by far the film's most affecting and artful minutes,* because the director *actually pauses long enough to set up a sequence carefully and let the drama breathe a little.* These lines contradict (D), so eliminate this choice. The correct answer is (A).

24. **G** The question asks what Tobias believes *a good adaptation* should do. Tobias is the author of Passage A, so look for the words *good adaptation* in Passage A. Lines 38–40 state, *a good adaptation has to…exist independently from the novel.* Lines 18–19 use the phrase *offers a straightforward cinematic blueprint* to describe a film that *suffers from all the pitfalls of faithfulness.* This is not something the author thinks a *good adaptation* should do, so eliminate (F). Keep (G) because it is supported by lines 38–40. There is no discussion of a film becoming *a box office hit,* so eliminate (H). Lines 11–15 say that *filmmakers rarely have an antagonistic relationship to the book they're adapting...they want to do right by something they loved. Yet doing right by a great book and being faithful to it are, to my mind, two separate issues.* The author does not think that a *good adaptation* needs to *have an antagonistic relationship to the book;* he simply thinks that *being faithful* to the book isn't necessary to *do right by* it. Therefore, eliminate (J). The correct answer is (G).

25. **D** The question asks how Passage B describes *Joe Wright's literary adaptations of Pride and Prejudice and Atonement.* Look for the words *Joe Wright, Pride and Prejudice,* and *Atonement* in Passage B. Lines 55–58 refer to *British Director Joe Wright* and his *screen versions of Jane Austen's Pride and Prejudice and Ian McEwan's Atonement,* describing the films as *not terrible, just cautious and responsible.* Line 62 refers to the *proof of their mediocrity.* Choice (A) is contradicted by lines 61–62, which say, *Instead of strong, risky interpretations, they offer crib notes and the pale flattery of imitation;* eliminate (A). The passage says the films are *not terrible,* so eliminate (B). Choice (C) is contradicted by lines 48–51, which state that *average [literary adaptations]…are undone by humility,* while *the good ones succeed through hubris;* eliminate (C). Keep (D) because it is supported by lines 55–62. The correct answer is (D).

26. **H** The question asks why *the film version of Anna Karenina is successful,* based on Passage B. Look for the words *Anna Karenina* in Passage B. The last paragraph begins with a description of the *comprehensive* world of the novel *Anna Karenina.* Lines 83–88 suggest that the film version did not reproduce the novel's setting in detail, but instead was true to the novel's emotional realm: *To try to reproduce that world according to the canon of 21st-century movie realism would be to diminish and falsify his narrative, which ascends through cultural and social detail into a realm of universal emotion. Mr. Wright's brilliant gamble is to arrive at this level of emotional authenticity by way of self-conscious artifice.* There is no mention of *elaborate costumes* or *appropriate accents* in the passage. The discussion of Wright's other films refers to the casts' *admirable discipline* (line 59) but this is not said about *Anna Karenina,* so eliminate (F). *Technical polish* (line 59) is also a reference to Wright's other films, so eliminate (G). Keep (H) because it is supported by the discussion in the last paragraph. This paragraph indicates that Wright did not attempt *21st-century movie realism* in *Anna Karenina,* so eliminate (J). The correct answer is (H).

27. **A** The question asks which statement best expresses the opinion of the author of Passage B about the film *Anna Karenina.* Because this is a general question about Passage B, it should be done after all the specific questions about Passage B. The passage begins by discussing what makes for a good literary adaptation, saying the *average ones* suffer from *anxious fidelity* while the *good ones succeed* because they treat *great novels* as *a lump of interesting material to be shaped according to the filmmaker's will.* After discussing some examples of *average* film adaptations, the author states, *Mr. Wright's Anna Karenina is different. It is risky and ambitious.* He says the director and screenwriter took *stylistic liberties* with the novel that the film is based on, and this resulted in a *playful, passionate rendering of* the novel. Keep (A) because it is supported by these references from the passage. *Pride and Prejudice* and *Atonement* are films the author contrasts with *Anna Karenina,* so eliminate (B). There is no mention of *box office success,* so eliminate (C). The author says, *surely Tolstoy can withstand (and may even benefit from) their playful, passionate rendering of his masterpiece.* However, the final paragraph describes the novel with phrases such as *bigger than great,* and *a vivid panorama of an entire society.* This indicates that the author respects the novel; he is not arguing that the film is *better than the novel,* so eliminate (D). The correct answer is (A).

28. **G** The question asks what both authors believe *a film adaptation of a novel* should do. Because this is a general question, it should be done after all the specific questions on both passages. Eliminate any answer choices that misrepresent either passage. In lines 29–33, the author of Passage A states, *What I want is not faithfulness, but an active engagement with the material...The question filmmakers should ask is not, "How can I bring this story to the screen without losing anything?," but "What in this book do I want to emphasize?"* In lines 51–54, the author of Passage B states that *good [literary adaptations] succeed...through the...assumption that a great novel is not a sacred artifact but rather a lump of interesting material to be shaped according to the filmmaker's will.* Later, discussing the film adaptation of *Anna Karenina,* the author emphasizes that the director successfully captured the novel's *level of emotional authenticity.* Therefore, both authors believe that a film adaption should emphasize important aspects of the novel it is based on and also be shaped by the filmmaker's

vision. Passage B says that a good film adaptation *succeeds through hubris,* not that it should *focus on* the hubris; eliminate (F). Keep (G) because it includes both the *themes of the book* and the *filmmaker's vision.* Both authors criticize film adaptations that aim for strict faithfulness to a book, so eliminate (H). In lines 85–86, the phrase *ascends through cultural and social detail into a realm of universal emotion* refers to a novel, not a film adaptation, so eliminate (J). The correct answer is (G).

29. **D** The question asks what both authors believe about *a book's fans.* Eliminate any answer choices that misrepresent either passage. In lines 5–7, the author of Passage A says that, when creating a film adaption of a book, *I'm sure there's an enormous amount of pressure from fans...simply to deliver on the material as straightforwardly as possible.* In lines 55–64, the author of Passage B describes two film adaptations that faithfully recreate the novels they are based on and says, *admirers of [the novel's authors] will find no reason for complaint.* Therefore, both authors think that when a book is adapted into a film, the book's fans want the film to closely follow the book. Book fans are not compared with other critics, and the authors don't agree with the fans about what makes an adaptation good or poor, so there is no basis to say that the book fans are the *harshest critics of a poorly-made film adaptation.* The words *never* and *exactly* in (B) are too strong; this choice is not supported by the passages, so eliminate (B). There is no discussion about how fans feel about *elaborate period costumes,* so eliminate (C). Keep (D) because it is supported by lines 5–7 and 55–64. The correct answer is (D).

30. **F** The question asks which passage most closely echoes the view of another author about book-to-film adaptations. The new quotation states, *A filmmaker is unlikely to devote time and energy to a film version of a book she does not love; ironically, this very love for the book often spells failure for a film.* Look for references in either passage to filmmakers making adaptations of books they love. In lines 11–13, the author of Passage A states, *filmmakers rarely have an antagonistic relationship to the book they're adapting;...most want to do right by something they loved.* Earlier in this paragraph, the author indicates that these filmmakers feel pressure to *deliver on the material [of the book] as straightforwardly as possible,* and the rest of the passage discusses the *pitfalls of faithfulness.* Passage B never mentions filmmakers loving the books they adapt. Therefore, Passage A most closely echoes the view in the quotation; eliminate (H) and (J). As mentioned, only Passage A discusses *the filmmaker's relationship to the book,* so keep (F). Both passages *criticize* book-to-film adaptations that are overly focused on faithfulness, so this is not what makes Passage A a closer match for the quotation; eliminate (G). The correct answer is (F).

Passage IV

31. **D** The question asks what the studies reviewed in the seventh paragraph have shown that *hypnotic analgesia may be effective in.* The question references the seventh paragraph, so read lines 73–82. These lines indicate that in *hypnotic analgesia, patients are taught alternative skills to alter the experience of pain,* and that a *recent review of controlled studies of hypnotic analgesia suggests that the treatment can reduce pain in chronic conditions resulting from osteoarthritis, cancer, fibromyalgia, and*

disability. There is no discussion of *restructuring the brain,* so eliminate (A). The passage states hypnotic analgesia can *reduce pain...resulting from...cancer* and *fibromyalgia,* but not that it treats these conditions themselves, so eliminate (B). There is no discussion of *depression,* so eliminate (C). Keep (D) because it is supported by the seventh paragraph. The correct answer is (D).

32. **G** The question asks what the detection of pain results from *when a door slams on a person's hand.* The question references the sixth paragraph, so read lines 56–72. These lines describe the process that occurs as pain *traverses four physiological pathways.* First, the *sensory neurons, the nociceptors...detect potentially damaging stimuli.* Next, *the pain messages are exchanged between the nociceptors and the spinal cord.* Then, *the information is relayed from the spinal cord through the thalamus to the limbic and cortical structures of the brain.* The *sympathetic division of the autonomic nervous system* and *stress hormones* are mentioned in lines 22–37 as part of the body's response to *stress,* not *pain,* so eliminate (F), (H), and (J). Keep (G) because it is supported by the sixth paragraph. The correct answer is (G).

33. **B** The question asks what does not improve *overall health.* When a question asks which answer is **not** supported, eliminate answers that **are** supported. Look for the words *improve overall health* in the passage. Lines 4–12 discuss *mindful movement therapies* that are said to *improve overall health.* Lines 5–6 state that the therapies *couple aerobic and anaerobic exercise with mental focus,* so eliminate (A). There is no mention of *diet,* so keep (B). Lines 10–11 state that the therapies *improve overall health by bringing deeper awareness to the body,* so eliminate (C). Lines 6–9 state that *These practices...guide participants through a series of specialized movements synchronized to the breath and mental images,* so eliminate (D). The correct answer is (B).

34. **F** The question asks what the word *engaged* means in line 33. Go back to the text, find the word *engaged,* and mark it out. Carefully read the surrounding text to determine another word that would fit in the blank based on the context of the passage. Lines 31–35 state that *When the central nervous system perceives a threat, the sympathetic division of the autonomic nervous system is engaged, signaling the release of stress hormones...that in turn activate particular physiological responses.* The word *engaged* could be replaced with the word "activated." Keep (F) because *stimulated* matches "activated." *Taken* means "transferred into someone's possession"; it doesn't match "activated," so eliminate (G). *Obligated* means "required"; it doesn't match "activated," so eliminate (H). *Destined* means "predetermined"; it doesn't match "activated," so eliminate (J). The correct answer is (F).

35. **C** The question asks what the *limbic system* would not be directly involved with. When a question asks which answer is **not** supported, eliminate answers that **are** supported. Look for the words *limbic system* in the passage. The *limbic system* is mentioned in line 64 in a discussion of the pathways involved in the experience of pain; one of the pathways is *modulation,* so eliminate (A). Lines 69–70 identify the limbic system as the *brain center for autonomic nervous system integration,* and the *autonomic nervous system* is identified as part of the *stress* response in lines 32–33. Therefore, the limbic system would be involved in *stress management,* so eliminate (B). There is no mention of *muscle movement* in connection with the limbic system, so keep (C). Line 69 states that *the limbic system is also the brain center for...memory,* so eliminate (D). The correct answer is (C).

36. **H** The question asks what information in the second paragraph indicates about *mind-body therapies in Western medicine.* The question references the second paragraph, so read lines 13–21. Lines 17–21 say that *as alternative and traditional therapies have become increasingly more popular and available in the West, researchers have begun to delve deeper into mind-body therapy efficacy.* The passage doesn't state that mind-body therapies are being used *in place of biomedicine* in the West, so eliminate (F). The passage states that more research is being done and that *alternative and traditional therapies have become increasingly more popular,* so eliminate (G). Keep (H) because it is supported by lines 17–21. There is no discussion in this paragraph about whether mind-body therapies are *successful in curing* disease, so eliminate (J). The correct answer is (H).

37. **D** The question asks how the *mind-body therapies* mentioned in the fifth paragraph function. The question references the fifth paragraph, so read lines 48–55. These lines state that *Mind-body therapies...essentially work by altering responses to stressors...thus counteracting the negative consequences of fight-or-flight response.* There is no indication that these therapies *prevent stress hormones from activating negative* responses; the passage simply says that the therapies counteract these responses, so eliminate (A). Lines 51–52 say the therapies *engage the parasympathetic,* not the sympathetic, nervous system; eliminate (B). The passage doesn't indicate that the therapies *eliminate* the stressors; it says they work by *altering responses* to them; eliminate (C). Keep (D) because it is supported by the lines 54–55. The correct answer is (D).

38. **F** The question asks what *stress responses with adaptive functions, as would have evolved in ancestral conditions,* can be expected to do. Look for the words *adaptive functions* and *ancestral* in the passage. Lines 38–40 state that *This "fight-or-flight" response alludes to the conditions of ancestral humans and the presumed adaptive function of such a response in evolutionary history.* The word *this* indicates that the fight-or-flight response is discussed just before this line, so read the previous paragraph. Beginning on line 26, the passage explains that *Stress...is the physiological response to a perceived threat...When the central nervous system perceives a threat, the sympathetic division of the autonomic nervous system is engaged, signaling the release of stress hormones such as epinephrine and cortisol into the bloodstream.* Keep (F) since *increase cortisol levels in the blood* is supported by these lines. *Suppressed immune response* is mentioned in line 47 as a result of modern-day stressors, not *ancestral conditions,* so eliminate (G). The passage indicates that the stress response is a *response to a perceived threat;* perceiving threats is not something the stress response would *do,* so eliminate (H). Lines 35–36 indicate that a stress response will *activate...muscle tension,* not *decrease* it, so eliminate (J). The correct answer is (F).

39. **C** The question asks for the characteristic of research results that causes the author to believe that *mind-body therapy should be further investigated.* The last paragraph is referenced, so read lines 83–90. Lines 85–90 state, *More investigation is needed...to ascertain if outcome expectations influence the success of particular therapies, if response rates differ as a result of pain type or pain diagnosis, and to what degree variation in individual response, and if research design should preclude broader inferences.* These lines indicate that research results may be affected by factors that haven't been accounted for in the studies and that, for this reason, the author believes more investigation is needed. The author

indicates that *outcome expectations* might influence results but doesn't say that the *research results are carefully controlled to yield results consistent with expectations,* so eliminate (A). There is no indication that the author believes research results are *valid only when analyzing Western-originating therapies,* so eliminate (B). Keep (C) because it is supported by lines 85–90. The author says, *Mind-body research has provided important insights into…the efficacy of such therapies* but advocates *further investigation* to confirm the results. Therefore, the author doesn't believe the results are *proof of the effectiveness,* so eliminate (D). The correct answer is (C).

40. **H** The question asks which effect, if it had *occurred after patients engaged in positive meditation to manage work-related stress,* would have caused *healthy mind-body therapies to be deemed ineffective.* Look in the passage for references to effects caused by work-related stress. Lines 42–44 state that *most stressors today, related to work, family, school, and interpersonal relationships, are prolonged, and the fight-or-flight responses are thus sustained.* This indicates that if a therapy intended to manage work-related stress was ineffective, fight-or-flight responses would continue. *Nociceptors signals* are mentioned in lines 59–60 as part of the pain response; they are not related to stress, so eliminate (F). Lines 48–55 explain that mind-body therapies counteract stress by engaging *the parasympathetic division of the autonomic nervous system.* If the *parasympathetic nervous system was engaged,* it would be a sign that the meditation was effective, not ineffective, so eliminate (G). Keep (H) because it is consistent with the explanation in lines 42–44. The passage doesn't give details about how *spinal cord activity* is related to stress, so eliminate (J). The correct answer is (H).

TEST 3 SCIENCE ANSWERS AND EXPLANATIONS

Passage I

1. **C** The question asks what *a lunar orbiter at point P would be able to view.* Look at Figure 1 and find point *P*. Draw a line from Point *P* toward the word *Sun* on the figure. The Moon is in between Point *P* and the Sun, so the Sun would not be visible from a lunar orbiter at Point *P*. The figure doesn't indicate that there's anything between Point *P* and Earth, so the Earth would be visible from Point *P*. Eliminate (B) and (D) because these choices include the *Sun.* Eliminate (A) because this choice does not include the Earth. The correct answer is (C).

2. **F** The question asks what the Sun's rays most likely do when they *encounter the surface of the Moon during a solar eclipse,* according to Figure 1. The end of the second paragraph indicates that Figure 1 shows a solar eclipse. Look at Figure 1 and find the Sun's rays and the Moon. Figure 1 shows that during a solar eclipse, the Moon does not allow the transmission of the Sun's rays to the Earth. Therefore, the Sun's rays stop transmitting forward and do not continue to the Earth's surface. Choice (F) is consistent with Figure 1. Eliminate (G) because Figure 1 shows that the *light from the Sun* does not reach the *plastic asthenosphere.* Eliminate (H) because, although Figure 1 shows *reflected light from the Moon* continuing from the *Moon,* it does not indicate that this light continues to the *Earth.* The second paragraph also states that *the Sun's rays can be blocked from traveling to the Earth during a complete solar eclipse.* Eliminate (J) because Figure 1 shows the *Moon* obstructing the path of the *light from the Sun* toward *Earth.* The correct answer is (F).

3. **B** The question asks for the *time elapsed between two successive higher high tides,* based on Figure 2. Look for information about high tides in Figure 2. The ocean water level is measured on the vertical axis, which shows that for each pair of consecutive peaks in water level, one peak is higher and one is slightly lower. For example, at about 15 hours, there is a peak of about 4.5 feet, and at about 26 hours, there is a peak of about 5.5 feet. The higher of these two peaks is the measurement for the *higher high tide* referenced in the question. Therefore, the peak at about 26 hours and the peak at about 50 hours show *two successive higher high tides.* A period of 24 hours elapses between these measurements. Eliminate (A), (C), and (D). The correct answer is (B).

4. **H** The question asks when *the data in Figure 2 could NOT have been collected,* based on the information in Figure 3. When a question asks which answer is **not** supported, eliminate answers that **are** supported. Look at Figures 2 and 3. Both figures show changes in ocean water level compared with *mean sea level,* so compare water level measurements for the two figures. In Figure 2, the lowest ocean water level is at approximately –0.5 feet on the graph, which is 0.5 feet below mean sea level. In Figure 3, the lowest ocean surface height for March, July, and November is at approximately –1 foot on the graph, or 1 foot below sea level. These measurements are consistent with the data in Figure 2, since there may have been a lower measurement during the month than the one taken during the 72-hour period shown in Figure 2. Eliminate (F), (G), and (J). In August, the lowest ocean surface height is at 0 feet on the graph, which is at mean sea level. This minimum water level is not consistent with the

data in Figure 2, since the minimum water level in Figure 2 is below mean sea height. So, the data in Figure 2 could not have been collected in August. The correct answer is (H).

5. **D** The question asks which statement *best describes the ocean surface level between t = 0 hours and t = 12 hours,* according to Figure 2. Look at Figure 2. At t = 0 hours, Figure 2 indicates an ocean water level of 6 feet. The ocean surface level then falls until about t = 8 hours, and then rises again, reaching a level between 2 and 3 feet at t = 12 hours. Eliminate (A) and (B) because the ocean surface level neither rises nor falls continuously during the entire time. The ocean surface level first falls and then rises during that time, so eliminate (C), which says that it *rises and then falls.* Choice (D) is consistent with Figure 2. The correct answer is (D).

6. **G** The question asks which diagram *could represent the moon phases for the 72-hour period shown in Figure 2.* Look at Figure 2 and compare it with the information given in the question. The question states that *spring tides, which coincide with full and new moons, have the largest difference between the highest and lowest water levels. Neap tides, which coincide with quarter moons (half-illumination), have the least difference between the highest and lowest water levels.* In Figure 2, the highest and lowest ocean water levels represent high and low tides, respectively. Between 0 and 12 hours, the difference between the highest and lowest tide is about 6.5 feet. Between 12 and 36 hours, the difference between the highest and lowest tides is about 6 feet. Between 36 and 60 hours, the difference between the highest and lowest tides is about 5 feet. Since the difference between the high and low tides is decreasing, the Moon phases must be approaching a quarter moon, moving away from either a new moon or full moon. The diagram in (F) shows a progression from quarter moon toward full moon; eliminate (F). The diagram in (G) shows a progression from just after the new moon moving toward quarter moon; keep (G). The diagram in (H) shows a progression that occurs just before the full moon; eliminate (H). The diagram in (J) shows a progression that occurs just before the new moon; eliminate (J). The correct answer is (G).

Passage II

7. **C** The question asks whether the information in Figure 3 supports the statement that *at every depth below sea level, the rock at Site 2 is older than the rock at Site 1.* Look at Figure 3 and compare the uranium content at the various depths for Site 1 and Site 2. At a depth of approximately 500 meters, the uranium content at Site 2 is higher than the uranium content at Site 1. Eliminate (B). At a depth of approximately 700 meters, the uranium content at Site 2 is lower than the uranium content at Site 1. Eliminate (A). Next, look for information in the passage about the age of the rock. Use the equation that is given below the second paragraph to compare the ages of the rock at Sites 1 and 2. Given this equation, a higher value for uranium content will result in a lower value for age. Since the uranium content is higher at Site 2 than at Site 1 at a depth of 500 meters, the rock at Site 2 is younger than the rock at Site 1 at that depth. Choice (C) is consistent with this information. Eliminate (D) because a lower uranium count at Site 2 indicates that the rock at Site 2 is older than the rock at Site 1. The correct answer is (C).

8. **G** The question asks where *the shale layer was thickest,* according to Figure 2. Look at Figure 2. According to the key, the shale layer is the lightest grey layer in the figure. This layer is thicker at Site 1 than at Site 2, Site 3, or either of the cities. Eliminate (F), (H), and (J). The correct answer is (G).

9. **A** The question asks what happens to the *thickness of limestone residing below* Sites 2 and 3 as the *thickness of shale decreases* between these sites, according to Figure 2. Look at Figure 2. Moving from Site 2 to Site 3 on the figure, the thickness of the shale decreases, and the thickness of the limestone increases. Eliminate (B), (C), and (D). The correct answer is (A).

10. **G** The question asks for the range of *the uranium content of the limestone layer of Site 1,* according to Figures 2 and 3. Look at Figures 2 and 3. According to Figure 2, the limestone layer at Site 1 extends from approximately 300 to 500 meters below sea level. Look at the information about Site 1 in Figure 3. Between 300 and 500 meters below sea level, the uranium count ranges from approximately 33 to 18 counts per minute. Eliminate (F), (H), and (J). The correct answer is (G).

11. **A** The question asks at what depth *the highest number of counts of uranium-235 detected were recorded* at Sites 1, 2, and 3, according to Figure 3. Look at Figure 3. Figure 3 shows uranium content and depth for three different sites. At each site, the highest uranium content recorded is about 50 counts per minute. At Site 1, the highest uranium content was recorded at a depth between 0 and 150 m below sea level. At Site 2, the highest uranium content was recorded at a depth between 0 and 150 m below sea level. At Site 3, the highest uranium content was recorded at a depth between 150 and 300 m below sea level. Therefore, the highest number of counts of uranium-235 was recorded at depths less than 300 m below sea level at all three sites. Eliminate (B), (C), and (D). The correct answer is (A).

12. **G** The question asks for *the age of the rock with the greatest depth surveyed at Site 2.* Look at Figure 3. Information about Site 2 is given by the middle graph. Depth is recorded on the vertical axis, and the greatest depth is at the bottom of the graph. Therefore, the rock with the greatest depth surveyed at Site 2 was at a depth more than 750 m below sea level, and it had a uranium content of about 8 counts per minute. The equation given after the second paragraph gives the approximate age of rock in millions of years. Using the value 8 for the *Counts per minute of Uranium-235 in Sample,* the equation gives $\frac{64}{8} \times 700 = 5{,}600$. The figure of 5,600 is the approximate age of the rock in *millions* of years, which is equivalent to 5.6 billion years. Note that (J) is *560 million years old* instead of *5,600 million years old.* Eliminate (F), (H), and (J). The correct answer is (G).

Passage III

13. **C** The question asks for the *most likely reason the student chose to use an old-fashioned plastic water gun rather than a metal water gun* in Experiment 3. Read the description of Experiment 3. According to the description, *the student used an old-fashioned, plastic water gun, with transparent walls.* The description also states that the student *observed no bubbles formed upon shooting* and later that there *were still some visible bubbles in the cola.* This indicates that the student needed to be able to see the liquid inside the water gun. There are no measurements of *shooting distance* in Experiment 3, so eliminate (A) and (B). Choice (C) is consistent with the description of the experiment. There is no mention of how difficult or easy it was for the water gun *to fit into the holding device,* so eliminate (D). The correct answer is (C).

14. **J** The question asks for two trials in which the distances shot *before shaking the water gun* were *the same,* based on the results of Experiments 1 and 2. Look at Table 1 and Table 2 for information about the *distance shot before shaking.* The values recorded for distance shot before shaking for Trial 3 and Trial 5 are each 6.23 meters, while none of the values for the other trials are the same. Eliminate (F), (G), and (H). The correct answer is (J).

15. **D** The question asks for *a result of shaking the water gun containing the flat-tasting cola* in Experiment 2. Look for the key words *flat-tasting cola* in the description of Experiment 2. The information given states that Trials 4 and 5 were conducted using *flat-tasting cola,* so look at the information for these trials in Table 2. There is no mention of the *density of the liquid* or of *bubbles in the liquid,* so eliminate (A) and (B). In Trial 4, the distance shot before shaking was 5.98 meters, and the distance shot after shaking was 5.49 meters. In Trial 5, the distance shot before shaking was 6.23 meters, and the distance shot after shaking was 5.61 meters. Since the distances recorded after shaking are less than the distances recorded before shaking, shaking the water gun caused *the distance the liquid was shot* to decrease; eliminate (C). The correct answer is (D).

16. **H** The question asks whether it is *likely that bubbles were present in large numbers in the cola immediately before the canister was shaken* in Trial 5. Trial 5 is listed in Table 2, so look at the description of Experiment 2. The description indicates that the student shook the water gun containing the canister before Trial 4, and *then let it sit undisturbed for an hour* before Trial 5. Notice that the answer choices for this question include references to Experiments 1 and 3. According to the description given, Experiment 1 was conducted with *tap water,* not cola, so information from this experiment is not relevant to the question; eliminate (F) and (G). The description of Experiment 3 states that the student shook a water gun filled with cola, *which caused bubbles to form…however, after an hour had passed, there were no visible bubbles.* This indicates that the bubbles generated in Trial 4 probably lasted for less than 1 hour, so eliminate (J). The correct answer is (H).

17. **D** The question asks what *the horizontal distance the cola was shot would most likely have been* if *the student had decided to measure the distance the water gun shot the cola one hour after finishing Trial 5 without shaking the water gun again.* Look for information about trials 4 and 5 in the description of

Experiment 2. The description indicates that before Trial 4, the student shook the water gun *to create bubbles and then let it sit undisturbed* for *10 minutes,* and then *tested how far the water gun shot the cola.* Then the student shook the gun again and immediately shot the gun and measured the distance. The distance shot before shaking (after waiting 10 minutes) in Trial 4 was 5.98 meters. After Trial 4, the student let the water gun *sit undisturbed for an hour before testing how far it shot* in Trial 5. The distance shot before shaking (after waiting an hour) in Trial 5 was 6.23 meters. The results of these two trials show that letting the water gun sit undisturbed for a longer period of time before testing it increased the distance the cola was shot. Therefore, if the student measured the distance the water gun shot the cola one hour after finishing Trial 5 without shaking the water gun again, the cola would likely have been shot a distance greater than 5.98 meters. Eliminate (A), (B), and (C). The correct answer is (D).

18. **G** The question asks *how much time it would take for the bubbles in the cola to disappear to the point that they would have no effect on the distance of the shot* if *the student filled the metal water gun to 80% of its capacity with the flat-tasting cola and shook it.* The question references Trials 3–5; first look for information about Trial 3 in Experiment 1. The description of Experiment 1 indicates that in Trial 3, the student *filled the metallic water canister of a water gun to 80% of its capacity* with *a flat-tasting cola beverage that showed no visible bubbles,* and measured *how far from the holding device the water gun shot,* both before and after shaking the water gun. According to Table 1, in Trial 3 the distance shot before shaking was 6.23 meters. Look for information about Trials 4 and 5 in Experiment 2. According to the description of Experiment 2, in Trial 4 *the student filled the water gun canister to 80% of its capacity with the flat-tasting cola, shook it to create bubbles and then let it sit undisturbed* for *10 minutes* before testing the distance shot. Then the student shook the gun again and immediately shot the gun and measured the distance. The distance shot before shaking in Trial 4 (after waiting 10 minutes) was 5.98 meters. In Trial 5, the student let the water gun *sit undisturbed for an hour before again testing how far it shot.* The distance shot before shaking in Trial 5 (after waiting an hour) was 6.23 meters. This is the same distance recorded in Trial 3, when the gun had not been shaken. This indicates that after an hour, the bubbles had no effect on the shot distance; however, after just 10 minutes, the bubbles still had an effect on the shot distance. Therefore, the time it would take for the bubbles in the cola to disappear to the point that they would have no effect on the distance of the shot would most likely be between 10 minutes and 1 hour. Eliminate (F), (H), and (J). The correct answer is (G).

19. **B** The question asks for an explanation for *the difference between the distances the cola traveled after shaking in Trial 4 and in Trial 5* in Experiment 2. Look for information about Trial 4 and Trial 5 in Experiment 2. According to Table 2, the cola traveled further after shaking in Trial 5 than in Trial 4. Eliminate (A) and (C). According to the description of Experiment 2, the student shook the water gun containing the cola *to create bubbles and then let it sit undisturbed* for *10 minutes* before taking the measurements recorded for Trial 4. After Trial 4, the student let the water gun *sit undisturbed for an hour* before taking the measurements recorded for Trial 5. In Experiment 3, the

student *shook the water gun, which caused bubbles to form. After 10 minutes, there were still some visible bubbles in the cola; however, after an hour had passed, there were no visible bubbles.* These results indicate that there were likely more bubbles after shaking in Trial 4 than in Trial 5. Eliminate (D). The correct answer is (B).

Passage IV

20. **H** The question asks for the *expected mass* of an additional sample in Experiment 1 if it *were brought to 40°C and a density of 1.018 g/mL.* Look at Table 1 and find where 40°C and 1.018 g/mL would fit in with the existing data. As temperature increases and density decreases in Table 1, the solution mass decreases. 40°C would be greater than 30°C, and 1.018 g/mL would be less than 1.022 g/mL, so the corresponding solution mass would be less than 153.3 g. Eliminate (J). To choose between (F), (G), and (H), estimate: the change in mass from sample to sample is not consistent, but it never decreases by more than 0.5 g, making (H) the only reasonable estimate. Eliminate (F) and (G). The correct answer is (H).

21. **A** The question asks for *the most likely density of water at 10°C and 2.50% salinity,* based on Table 2. Look at Table 2 and find where 10°C and 2.50% salinity would fit with the existing data. The description of Experiment 2 indicates that *distilled water at 10°C was added to make* the solution, so 10°C was a constant in the experiment. As salinity decreases in Table 2, density also decreases. 2.50% would fit between 2.60% and 2.35%, so the density at a salinity of 2.50% would fall between 1.020 g/mL and 1.018 g/mL. Eliminate (B), (C), and (D). The correct answer is (A).

22. **H** The question asks whether *the results of the experiments support* the claim that *prototype U3 is better suited than X2 for water surface data collection in a 10°C and 2.35% salinity environment.* U3 and X2 are included in Table 3, so look at Table 3. According to the description of Experiment 3, U3 and X2 are *prototypes of a newly designed instrument* and they *were placed in a pool. If a prototype stayed afloat, it was marked with a (+). If a prototype sank, it was marked with a (–).* Table 2 includes salinity, and the description for Experiment 2 indicates that a temperature of 10°C was a constant. According to Table 2, Sample VII had a salinity of 2.35%. Look for Sample VII in Table 3. For Sample VII, there is a (–) for U3 and a (+) for X2. This indicates that in these water conditions, prototype U3 sank and prototype X2 floated. Eliminate (G) and (J). Since U3 sank and X2 floated, U3 would not be better suited to collecting data at the water's surface; eliminate (F). The correct answer is (H).

23. **D** The question asks which *results would NOT be possible* for *a new prototype* that is *tested in water samples IV through VII in a manner similar to Experiment 3.* When a question asks which answer is **not** possible, eliminate answers that **are** possible. Look for Samples IV through VII in Table 3. For Prototype R5, there is a (–) listed for all Samples IV through VII, so (A) is possible; eliminate (A). For Prototypes XI and X2, there is a (+) listed for all Samples IV through VII, so (B) is possible; eliminate (B). For Prototype U3, there is a (+) listed for Samples IV and V and a (–) listed

for Samples VI and VII, so (C) is possible; eliminate (C). None of the prototypes include a (–) for Samples IV and V and a (+) for Samples VI and VII, so (D) is not a possible result. The correct answer is (D).

24. **H** The question asks what *accurate and precise measurement* was the goal when the *samples were transferred to a graduated cylinder* in Experiment 1. Look for the key words *graduated cylinder* in the description of Experiment 1. The description states, *A graduated cylinder was then used to measure 150 mL of the solution.* 150 mL is a measure of volume, and the description goes on to say the *mass of this 150 mL sample was measured...and the density (g/mL) was calculated.* Therefore, the graduated cylinder was used to measure volume, which in turn was used to calculate the density. There is no information given about how the *35 g of NaCl* was measured, so eliminate (F). There is no mention of *salinity* in Experiment 1, so eliminate (G) and (J). Choice (H) is consistent with the description. The correct answer is (H).

25. **A** The question asks for a value for *the density of prototype U3* that *would be consistent with the results of Experiments 1 through 3.* Prototype U3 is in Table 3, so look at Table 3. According to the description of (+) and (–) symbols in the description of Experiment 3, prototype U3 floated in water sample V, but sank in water sample VI. If the density of an object is less than that of the surrounding liquid, the object will float. If the density of the object is greater than that of the surrounding liquid, the object will sink. This indicates that U3 is less dense than Sample V but denser than Sample VI. Look for the densities of Samples V and VI in Tables 1 and 2. According to Table 1, Sample V had a density of 1.022 g/mL. According to Table 2, Sample VI had a density of 1.020 g/mL. The density for prototype U3 should be between 1.020 g/mL and 1.022 g/mL. Eliminate (B), (C), and (D). The correct answer is (A).

26. **F** The question asks for *the salinity of all of the samples in Experiment 1, based on the information in Experiments 1 and 2.* Look at Table 2. As solution mass decreases by 0.3 g and density decreases by 0.002 g/mL in Table 2, the salinity decreases by 0.25%. The lowest value for solution mass in Table 1 is greater than the highest value for solution mass in Table 2. Similarly, the lowest value for density in Table 1 is greater than the highest value for density in Table 2. Since both mass and density values are greater in Experiment 1 than in Experiment 2, the salinity values in Experiment 1 would be greater than the salinity values in Experiment 2. The highest salinity in Experiment 2 was 2.60%, so the lowest salinity value in Experiment 1 would be greater than 2.60%. Eliminate (H) and (J). Furthermore, the samples in Experiment 2 were all created using *distilled water at 10°C,* which is the same temperature as sample II in Table 1. Continue the trend in Table 2 to see that the salinity of Sample II is about 3.50%. Each sample in Experiment 1 came from the same solution, so they have the same salinity. Eliminate (G). The correct answer is (F).

Passage V

27. **C** The question asks *which of the strains of chlorophyll is most likely responsible for photosynthesis in Rosa Carolina,* given the information in Figure 2. Look at Figure 2. The absorption of chlorophyll *a* is higher than the absorption of chlorophyll *b* in red light. Eliminate (D). Neither chlorophyll *a* nor chlorophyll *b* consistently has higher absorption in green light; eliminate (A) and (B). The correct answer is (C).

28. **J** The question asks *which cell types grew in the presence of green light* in Experiment 1. Look for *green light* in Table 1. According to the description of Experiment 1, *in Table 1, + means presence and – means absence.* For Green light in Table 1, there are – signs in both columns for T6: Plant. According to the description of the experiment, this indicates that plant cells did not grow in the presence of green light; eliminate (F), (G), and (H). There are + signs in one or both columns for T7: Haloarchaea and T8: Bacterium, indicating that both of these cell types grew in the presence of green light; this is consistent with (J). The correct answer is (J).

29. **B** The question asks *what would be the most likely results for Experiments 1 and 2* if *a new test tube containing both plant and haloarchaeal cells were prepared.* Look at Table 1. According to the passage, in Experiment 1, *researchers exposed plant, haloarchaeal, and bacterial cells to either red or green light. The researchers measured the growth of these cells by measuring how much acid and CO_2 were produced; production of either of these indicates growth.* According to the description of Experiment 1, *in Table 1, + means presence and – means absence.* The results recorded in Table 1 indicate that the plant cells grew in the red light, producing CO_2, while the haloarchaeal cells did not grow in the red light. If both plant and haloarchaeal cells were tested together under red light, the plant cells would still grow and produce CO_2, so there would be a + for CO_2 and – for acid. These results are consistent with (B), and inconsistent with (A), (C), and (D). The results for the plant and haloarchaeal cells under green light are also consistent with (B) and inconsistent with (A), (C), and (D). To confirm the results for transmittance, look at Experiment 2. According to the description of Experiment 2, *cells of the same species are exposed to red and green light...If the transmittance is low, then the cells in the test tube are assumed to contain pigments that absorb most of the light to generate energy. If the transmittance is high, then the cells are assumed to contain no pigment that could absorb light.* Therefore, if transmittance is low for either plant or haloarchaeal cells when they are tested separately, the most likely result would be low transmittance when both are tested together. In Table 2, the plant cells had low transmittance in red light and the haloarchaeal cells had low transmittance in green light, so the expected results for both types of cells together would be low transmittance in both red and green light. These results are consistent with (B). The correct answer is (B).

30. **G** The question asks which cell type would most likely produce *CO_2 in the presence of red light* and *neither CO_2 nor acid* in *green light,* based on the results of Experiment 1. Look at Table 1. According to the passage, in Experiment 1, *researchers exposed plant, haloarchaeal, and bacterial cells to either red or green light. The researchers measured the growth of these cells by measuring how much acid*

and CO_2 were produced. According to the description of Experiment 1, *in Table 1, + means presence and – means absence.* The results for plant cells in Table 1 show a + for CO_2 in red light and a – for both CO_2 and acid in green light. These results are consistent with the results described in the question. The results for the control group, the haloarchaeal cells, and the bacterial cells do not match these, so eliminate (F), (H), and (J). The correct answer is (G).

31. **C** The question asks for *the evidence from Experiments 1 and 2 that haloarchaea can generate energy when exposed to green light.* Look at Table 1 and Table 2. Table 2 shows low transmittance for haloarchaea in the presence of green light; eliminate (B) and (D). According to the description of Experiment 1, *in Table 1, + means presence and – means absence.* Table 1 shows that the haloarchaeal cells produced acid in the presence of green light; eliminate (A). The correct answer is (C).

32. **G** The question asks which figure *best illustrates the results of Experiment 1 for the plant Rosa Carolina in red light.* Look at Figure 1 and Table 1. The description of Figure 1 states that a colored solution *indicates the absence of acid* and a gas bubble *indicates the presence of CO_2*. According to the description of Experiment 1, *in Table 1, + means presence and – means absence.* The results for the plant in red light in Table 1 indicate the absence of acid and the presence of CO_2. Choice (G) shows a colored solution and a gas bubble, which is consistent with these results. Choices (F) and (J) show no colored solution, so eliminate (F) and (J). Choice (H) does not show a gas bubble, so eliminate (H). The correct answer is (G).

33. **C** The question asks whether *the results of Experiment 1 support the hypothesis that haloarchaea and bacteria use similar processes to generate energy.* Look at Table 1. According to the description of Experiment 1, *in Table 1, + means presence and – means absence.* Table 1 indicates that for haloarchaeal cells, CO_2 is absent in both red and green light; eliminate (A) and (B). The results in (C) are consistent with Table 1. For bacterial cells, CO_2 is present in both red and green light; eliminate (D). The correct answer is (C).

Passage VI

34. **G** The question asks which statement *is most consistent with the 3-Domain Hypothesis.* Look at the 3-Domain Hypothesis. The 3-Domain Hypothesis states that *the genetic sequence of rRNA in the Archaea is so distinct from prokaryotes and eukaryotes that these groups of organisms likely diverged over 3 billion years ago.* In other words, significant *differences* between organisms' rRNA gene sequences indicate that they diverged a long time ago; eliminate (F) and keep (G). The hypothesis does not discuss a relationship between time of divergence and the *number of ester linkages in the cell membrane,* so eliminate (H) and (J). The correct answer is (G).

35. **D** The question asks what is implied in the 2-Domain Hypothesis by *the observation that the newly discovered organisms do not have membrane-bound organelles.* Look for the key words *membrane-bound organelles* in the 2-Domain Hypothesis and in the introduction. The 2-Domain Hypothesis

says that the newly-discovered organisms *are prokaryotes because they lack intracellular membrane-bound organelles.* The introduction states that the *presence of nuclei and other membrane-bound organelles within the cell primarily distinguished eukaryotes from prokaryotes.* Therefore, *nuclei* are intracellular membrane-bound organelles. The passage does not indicate that phospholipids, ribosomes, or rRNA are membrane-bound organelles, so eliminate (A), (B), and (C). Choice (D) is consistent with the passage. The correct answer is (D).

36. **J** The question asks for *a similarity between eukaryotes and prokaryotes.* Look for key words in the answer choices to locate relevant parts of the passage. The last paragraph of the 3-Domain hypothesis states that *Archaea cell membranes contain...ether linkages instead of the ester linkages found in eukaryotes and bacteria.* Bacteria are prokaryotes, so having ester linkages is a point of similarity between eukaryotes and some prokaryotes, but Archaea do not have ester linkages, so eliminate (F). The introduction states that *the presence of...membrane-bound organelles within the cell primarily distinguished eukaryotes from prokaryotes,* so eliminate (G). The second paragraph of the 2-Domain Hypothesis indicates that *Archaea are similar to prokaryotic bacteria* in that *they reproduce asexually;* eliminate (H). Keep (J) because the passage discusses properties of the cells of both prokaryotes and eukaryotes, so both groups of organisms *are composed of cells.* The correct answer is (J).

37. **C** The question asks for *the strongest argument against using a 3-Domain classification*, according to the *scientist who supports the 2-Domain Hypothesis.* Look at the 2-Domain Hypothesis. The first sentence of the 2-Domain Hypothesis states, *The Archaea are prokaryotes because they lack intracellular membrane-bound organelles.* According to the introduction, the *presence of...membrane-bound organelles within the cell primarily distinguished eukaryotes from prokaryotes.* Eliminate (A) because the 2-Domain Hypothesis does not argue that *rRNA does not exist in prokaryotes. Ether linkages* are discussed as support for the 3-Domain Hypothesis, not the 2-Domain Hypothesis, so eliminate (B). Keep (C) because it is consistent with the passage. The 2-Domain Hypothesis does not discuss whether the *Archaea synthesize proteins in the cell cytoplasm,* so eliminate (D). The correct answer is (C).

38. **F** The question asks which hypothesis is contradicted by the observation that the Archaea have protein synthesis structures and mechanisms more like eukaryotes than prokaryotes. Look at one hypothesis at a time, and use Process of Elimination. The 2-Domain Hypothesis states, *The structural and metabolic characteristics that are unique to the Archaea are not significantly different from other prokaryotes to warrant their separation into a third domain.* The 3-Domain Hypothesis states that *prokaryotes should be split into Archaea and Bacteria because of significant differences in genetics, structure, and metabolism.* If the Archaea had structures and mechanisms more like eukaryotes than prokaryotes, this would contradict the 2-Domain Hypothesis and be consistent with the 3-Domain Hypothesis; eliminate (H) and (J). The observation shows that the Archaea are *more like* eukaryotes than prokaryotes, so eliminate (G). The correct answer is (F).

39. **C** The question asks which observation weakens the 2-Domain Hypothesis, according to the *scientist who supports the 3-Domain Hypothesis.* Look at the 3-Domain Hypothesis. The 3-Domain Hypothesis states, *Archaea cell membranes contain more rigid ether linkages instead of the ester linkages found in eukaryotes and bacteria.* The 3-Domain Hypothesis does not state that the *Archaea have membrane-bound organelles;* eliminate (A). It also doesn't state that *microscopes cannot accurately describe organisms;* eliminate (B). The observation that *eukaryotes are not related to the Archaea* would not weaken the 2-Domain Hypothesis, since that hypothesis states that Archaea are prokaryotes rather than eukaryotes; eliminate (D). The correct answer is (C).

40. **G** The question asks which illustration *of a portion of a phospholipid cell membrane is consistent with the description in the passage.* Look for the key words *phospholipid cell membrane* in the passage. The introduction states, *Cell membranes are composed of phospholipids that have both water-insoluble and water-soluble subunits.* The key in question 40 indicates that the circles are water soluble and the lines are water insoluble. Cell membranes allow some fluid to pass into and out of the cell, so the water-soluble subunits must be on the outside of the membrane, next to the water. This is consistent with (G) and inconsistent with (F), (H), and (J). Though this question calls for outside knowledge, some Process of Elimination is possible. The illustrations in (H) and (J) are very similar; they place both soluble and insoluble subunits next to the water. Since these choices are so similar to one another, it's unlikely that either would be correct; eliminate (H) and (J). The correct answer is (G).

WRITING TEST

Essay Checklist

- ❐ Clearly state your own perspective.
- ❐ Reference the ideas of all 3 perspectives.
- ❐ Use examples to explain your point of view.
- ❐ Have 2–3 body paragraphs with 5–7 sentences each.
- ❐ Have an introduction and a conclusion paragraph.
- ❐ Write neatly.
- ❐ Use a formal tone and a mature level of vocabulary.
- ❐ Avoid spelling and grammar errors.